K... ... ... Thai

T... ...

W

- Both **Thai–E...** ...act...ze

- Revolutionary ... ...eakers:

  - **E...** ... and
    a... ...).

  - **T...** ... by
    it...

  - **T...**

Becker, Benjawan
Poomsan.
  Thai-English,
English-Thai compact
dictionary

- **Use...** ... ...nd
  for a short while or living there permanently, you will
  find most of the vocabulary used in everyday life,
  including basic medical, cultural, political and scientific
  terms. More than 28,000 entries (36,000+ definitions).

- **Completely Updated:** More entries and much more
  detail for each entry; includes modern terms like 'blog'.

- Comfortable **large print size** is easy on the eyes.

- Our signature **Paiboon⁺ pronunciation system** gives
  you the **tones** and everything else you need to speak
  and understand Thai words; extensive intro included.
  Perfect fit with our other books like *Thai for Beginners*.

- Lists **classifiers** for 1A,000+ nouns; key to effective Thai.

- Includes **writing guide** to help you read and write Thai
  script, including handy **font chart** for reading Thai signs.

Also Available: Desktop Edition

For those wanting a more in-depth desktop reference for home use and study, Paiboon Publishing has a Desktop Edition Thai–English, English–Thai dictionary with:

- **Thousands more words**, including medical, cultural, political and scientific terms.

- **More meanings, definitions and classifiers** for each word, along with more detailed usage information.

- Same **Paiboon⁺ pronunciation system** that makes it easy for English speakers to master the Thai language.

Available Late 2009

Thai–English
English–Thai
COMPACT DICTIONARY

With Classifiers and Tones
For English Speakers

By

Benjawan Poomsan Becker
Chris Pirazzi

PAIBOON
PUBLISHING

Thai–English, English–Thai Compact Dictionary

ISBN 978-1-887A21-32-1

Copyright ©2009 Benjawan Poomsan Becker and Chris Pirazzi

All rights reserved สงวนลิขสิทธิ์

Printed in Thailand

สำนักพิมพ์ไพบูลย์ภูมิแสน

A82 ถนนนวมินทร์ 90

บึงกุ่ม กรุงเทพฯ 10230

Thailand

Tel +66-2-A09-8632

(02-A09-8632 in Thailand)

Fax +66-2-A19-A437

(02-A19-A437 in Thailand)

Paiboon Publishing

PMB 2A6, 1442A Walnut Street

Berkeley, California 94709

USA

Tel +1-800-837-2979

Tel +1-A10-848-7086

Fax +1-866-800-1840

Fax +1-A10-666-8862

orders@paiboonpublishing.com

www.paiboonpublishing.com

Cover design: Douglas Morton, 72 Studio, Chiang Mai

Paiboon Publishing Dictionary Production Team: Nicholas Terlecky, Kanokrat Kanokyurapan, Panjagarn Wannathong, Naruemon Rorick, Nuanrudee Kaewtha, Jacob Carver.

Table of Contents

How to Use this Dictionary 1
  Three-Way Means Three Sections........................1
  How to Read Entries...2
Speaking and Understanding Thai 3
  The Paiboon⁺ Pronunciation System......................3
  Consonant Sounds 4
  Basic Vowel Sounds...6
  Long and Short Vowels...7
  Vowels 8
  Tones..10
  Similar Sounds...11
  Syllables and Stress...12
  Other Irregular Sounds 13
  Finding Words by Sound 14
  Parts of Speech 1A
  Classifiers..18
  Word Register (Formality)....................................20
Reading and Writing Thai 21
  Consonants...21
  Consonant Alphabetical Order 27
  Vowels and Syllables..28
  Other Symbols..3A
  What Determines the Tone 3A
  Irregular Spellings 39
  Dictionary Order...40

Section One: English 43

Section Two: Thai Script A87

Section Three: Thai Sound 89A

Appendices 96A

    Common Classifiers 96A

    Colors 968

    Numbers 969

    Mathematical Symbols 970

    Days of the Week 972

    Buddhist Holidays 972

    Months 973

    The Twelve-Year Cycle 974

    The 76 Provinces of Thailand 97A

Quick Reference 982

How to Use this Dictionary
Three-Way Means Three Sections

This dictionary has three sections instead of the usual two.

The **English** section lets you look up English words to find the Thai translations. All Thai words are shown in both Thai script and in our Paiboon⁺ pronunciation system:

> **easy** *adj.* ง่าย ngâai, หมู mǔu ●
> **friendly** *adj.* เป็นมิตร bpen-mít

The **Thai Script** section lets you, or your Thai friend, look up Thai words using Thai script (the Thai alphabet) to find the English meaning. Again, we always give pronunciation:

> หน้า **nâa** *adv.* ahead, in front
> หน้า **nâa** *n.* face, page (e.g. book), season [หน้า nâa]

The unique **Thai Sound** section lets you look up a Thai word by its sound, without needing to know the Thai alphabet! To help keep the dictionary small and allow us to give you more words and detail in the other sections, each entry in the Thai Sound gives you the page number(s) of that word in the Thai Script section:

> **nâa**......................712, 8A6
> **nâa-rák**.........................714

See p. 14 for some tips on using this section.

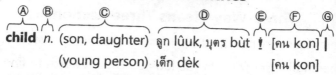

Ⓐ Ⓑ Ⓒ Ⓓ Ⓔ Ⓕ Ⓖ

child *n.* (son, daughter) ลูก lûuk, บุตร bùt ❗ [คน kon] |

(young person) เด็ก dèk   [คน kon]

ⒶⒹ For each English word or phrase Ⓐ, we give you a list of interchangeable Thai translations Ⓓ. See p. 3 for pronunciation details, and p. 21 for Thai script details.

Ⓑ Part of speech for both Thai and English (see p. 1A).

Ⓒ Some English words have multiple meanings that translate differently in Thai; we clarify each meaning in parentheses. If you do not see Ⓒ, then the Thai words provided cover all common meanings of the English word. If Ⓒ begins with "e.g.," then we've given you some sample meanings, but there are others also. If Ⓒ is "act" for a noun like "cut," it means "act of cutting."

Ⓔ Small symbols like ❗ (formal) and ☒ (vulgar) give you extra info about the one Thai word immediately preceding them. See p. 20 for the complete list.

Ⓕ For many nouns, we list classifiers in square brackets. Classifiers are a critical part of Thai grammar for even basic usage. See p. 18 for details.

Ⓖ We use a heavy bar | to separate different meanings and/or sets of Thai words with different classifiers.

Speaking and Understanding Thai
The Paiboon⁺ Pronunciation System

All Thai words in this dictionary are written in both Thai script (the Thai alphabet, e.g. น้ำตาล) and an English-like pronunciation system (e.g. nám-dtaan) called Paiboon⁺. This is the same system used in all Paiboon Publishing books, such as *Thai for Beginners, Thai for Lovers, and Thai for Advanced Readers*, with a few small enhancements. Technically, it is a "phonemic transcription system with some phonetic elements" but it is sometimes also called "transliteration" or "romanization."

Paiboon⁺ gives you exactly the information you need to pronounce and understand Thai words without any of the challenges of Thai spelling; you can learn it in a few minutes by reading this section.

What to Expect: Beginning Thai learners sometimes hope to be able to "intuitively" read a pronunciation guide as if it were English and get the real Thai sound. Unfortunately, that's not possible for any system, not only because of huge dialect differences in English (think about how a UK and a US English speaker might try to pronounce "gaw" or "pornthep"), but also because Thai has tones and certain other sounds that English spelling cannot express at all. Just read this and you'll be on your way to effective Thai.

Consonant Sounds

Here's a guide to Thai consonants based on English words. Visit **http://slice-of-thai.com/language** to hear them all.

b	บ	<u>b</u>oy	Thai words can start with the bp sound (in English it only usually occurs after s). The bp sound is an abrupt pop that doesn't have the breathy, windy, sigh-like sound (**aspiration**) of <u>p</u>et, nor does it have the initial **voiced** sound buildup before you open your mouth, like <u>b</u>oy. bp is the sound in French "le pain."
p	พ	<u>p</u>et	
bp	ป	s<u>p</u>ot	
d	ด	<u>d</u>og	d/t/dt parallels b/p/bp: The dt sound is an abrupt tick that doesn't have the aspiration of <u>t</u>ime, and is not voiced like <u>d</u>og.
t	ท	<u>t</u>ime	
dt	ต	s<u>t</u>op	
g	ก	s<u>k</u>y	The g sound does not have aspiration; the k sound does. Neither is voiced. The g sound is more like s<u>k</u>y than <u>g</u>o.
k	ค	<u>k</u>iss	
j	จ	glass <u>j</u>ar	The j sound does not have aspiration; the ch sound does. Neither is voiced. The Thai j and ch sound very dainty; the tongue barely taps the roof of the mouth.
ch	ช	<u>ch</u>arm	

f	ฟ	<u>f</u>og	As in English.
h	ฮ	<u>h</u>ave	Soft, aspirated h like <u>h</u>ave, not like <u>h</u>erb.
l	ล	<u>l</u>ove	In "proper" Thai speech, r is rolled as in Spanish bu<u>rr</u>o, and l is like English. In reality, especially in the North-East of Thailand, all r's and l's get mushed together into an l-like sound. So expect to be called "fà~làng" instead of "fà~ràng" sometimes! Also, many Thais drop r and l at the end of clusters, so bplaa (fish) becomes bpaa, and bprà~dtuu (door) becomes bpà~dtuu.
r	ร	bu<u>rr</u>o (rolled)	
m	ม	<u>m</u>an	As in English.
n	น	<u>n</u>ation	As in English.
ng	ง	thi<u>ng</u>	Thai words can start with ng, unlike English. Practice saying "thingy-yup, ingy-yup, ngy-yup" (not "ni-yup") and you've got เงียบ ngîiap, meaning "quiet."
s	ซ	<u>s</u>ex	As in English.
w	ว	<u>w</u>alk	Officially a "w," but you might hear "v."
y	ย	<u>y</u>es	As in English.

Basic Vowel Sounds

All vowels in Thai are built from the following basic sounds.
Use our sample words to practice with a Thai, or visit
http://slice-of-thai.com/language to hear all the sounds.

a	The classic Boston accent sound: "**p<u>a</u>rk the c<u>a</u>r in H<u>a</u>rvard Y<u>a</u>rd**." In US and UK English, this sound is in the first half of l<u>ie</u>, h<u>ow</u>, and h<u>ouse</u> but never appears by itself (outside Boston!). For most English speakers, it's not quite the same as f<u>a</u>ther. In Spanish it's <u>a</u>migo. มา maa (come), กะทะ gà~tá (wok), บ้าน bâan (house)
e	The sound in **p<u>a</u>le/m<u>ai</u>l**. When this sound appears in a short syllable with a final consonant, some Thais will change it to the sound in **g<u>e</u>t/p<u>e</u>n** (US English). เป้ bpêe (backpack), เผ็ด pèt (spicy), เมฆ mêek (cloud)
ɛ	The sound in **c<u>a</u>t**. แม่ mɛ̂ɛ (mother), และ lɛ́ (and), แฟน fɛɛn (girlfriend)
ə	The sound from **sof<u>a</u>**, **<u>a</u>bout** and often "**d<u>uuuuuh</u>!**" เบอร์ bəə (number), เลอะเทอะ lə́-tə́ (messy)
i	The sound in **b<u>ee</u>t/fl<u>ea</u>**. When this sound appears in a short syllable with a final consonant, some Thais will change it to the sound in **b<u>i</u>t/t<u>i</u>n** (US English). มี mii (have), ปิด bpìt (close), มีด mîit (knife)
o	The sound from US or Irish English **n<u>o</u>te/g<u>o</u>**. This sound is not common in other dialects of English. โมโห moo-hǒo (angry), โต๊ะ dtó (table), สด sòt (fresh)

ɔ	The sound from **US** English **law/bought**. Closer to the **UK lot/pot** than the deeper UK bo<u>ugh</u>t/b<u>a</u>ll. For most English speakers, it's not the same as f<u>a</u>ther. หล่อ lɔ̀ɔ (handsome), เกาะ gɔ̀ (island), กอด gɔ̀ɔt (hug)
u	The sound from US and UK English **boot**. ดู duu (look), ทุก túk (every), ถุง tǔng (bag)
ʉ	The famous Thai vowel sound that does not appear in any dialect of English! To make this sound, say b<u>oo</u>t, but instead of puckering your lips as with a normal u, spread your lips as far left and right as you can, into a wide smile as you might do when saying b<u>ee</u>t (but keep your teeth and tongue as you do when saying b<u>oo</u>t). Think of the bar on the ʉ as a little toothpick that holds the edges of your lips apart. The ʉ sound is very different from the French u and the German ü. Ask a Thai person to help you. มือ mʉʉ (hand), ลึก lʉ́k (deep), มืด mʉ̂ʉt (dark)

Long and Short Vowels

Most Thai vowels have a long and short version: it's the same basic sound, with a long (drawn out) or short (clipped, cut off) duration. You must say the right one or you'll be saying a different word! In the Paiboon⁺ system, all long vowels begin with a double letter (e.g. aa, iia, ʉʉai), and all short vowels begin with a single letter (e.g. a, ia, ui).

Vowels

The basic vowel sounds combine to make the Thai vowels. Visit **http://slice-of-thai.com/language** to hear them, or practice with a Thai using the words below.

Long				**Short**			
aa	ป่า	bpàa	jungle	**a**	ปะ	bpà	mend
	จาน	jaan	plate		จันทร์	jan	moon
aai	สาย	sǎai	late	**ai**	ใส	sǎi	clear
	นาย	naai	Mr.		ใน	nai	in
aao	ข้าว	kâao	rice	**ao**	เข้า	kâo	enter
	ราว	raao	handrail		เรา	rao	we
ee	เป้	bpêe	backpack	**e**	เป๊ะ	bpé	exactly
	เพศ	pêet	gender		เผ็ด	pèt	spicy
eeo	เอว	eeo	waist	**eo**	เร็ว	reo	fast
ɛɛ	แช่	chɛ̂ɛ	soak	**ɛ**	แฉะ	chɛ̀	wet
	แพทย์	pɛ̂ɛt	doctor		แผ่น	pɛ̀n	sheet
ɛɛɔ	แก้ว	gɛ̂ɛɔ	glass	**ɛɔ**	แจ๋ว	jɛ̌ɔ	clear
əə	เดิน	dəən	walk	**ə**	เงิน	ngən	money
əəi	เนย	nəəi	butter	**əi**	เฮ่ย	hə̂i	hey!
ii	ตี	dtii	hit	**i**	ติ	dtì	criticize
	ขีด	kìit	draw		คิด	kít	think
				iu	หิว	hǐu	hungry
iia	เสีย	sǐia	broken	**ia**	เดี๊ยะ	día	exactly
	เหรียญ	rǐian	coin				
iiao	เดี๋ยว	dǐiao	just a sec				

oo	โต	dtoo	big	**o**	โต๊ะ	dtó	table
	โสด	sòot	unmarried		สด	sòt	fresh
ooi	โดย	dooi	by				
ɔɔ	ก่อ	gɔ̀ɔ	build	**ɔ**	เกาะ	gɔ̀	island
	หลอก	lɔ̀ɔk	deceive		ล็อก	lɔ́k	lock
ɔɔi	ดอย	dɔɔi	hill	**ɔi**	บ่อย	bɔ̀i	often
	น้อย	nɔ́ɔi	few, small				
uu	ดู	duu	look	**u**	ดุ	dù	fierce
	คูณ	kuun	multiply		คุณ	kun	you
uui	อุ๊ย	úui	whoa!	**ui**	คุย	kui	chat
uua	หัว	hǔua	head	**ua**	ผัวะ	pùa	clap!
	สวน	sǔuan	garden				
uuai	สวย	sǔuai	beautiful	**uai**	ส่วย	sùai	tribute
	ช่วย	chûuai	help		หน่วย	nùai	unit
ɨɨ	ชื่อ	chɨ̂ɨ	name	**ɨ**	อื	ɨ̀	poop
	ตื่น	dtɨ̀ɨn	wake up		ดึก	dtɨ̀k	building
ɨɨa	เนื้อ	nɨ́ɨa	meat				
	เมือง	mɨɨang	city				
ɨɨai	เหนื่อย	nɨ̀ɨai	tired				

You can use the words above to practice pairs of long and short vowels, or similar-sounding vowels like u/ɨ, ə/ɔ, etc. There are more practice words on p. 11.

Tones

In English, tone—the pitch of your voice—changes the meaning of a whole sentence ("He's cold?" "He's cold!"). In Thai, tone changes the meaning of individual words! Thai has five different tones. A syllable with the same vowel and consonants could have five different meanings, depending on its tone, so it's crucial to use the right one. The Paiboon⁺ system uses marks over the vowel for tone:

(none)	The **mid tone** simply stays at your normal, comfortable speaking pitch. ไมล์ mai (mile), คน kon (person), ครู kruu (teacher)
`	The **low tone** starts and ends lower than normal. ใหม่ mài (new), หนึ่ง nùng (one), บาท bàat (Baht)
^	The **falling tone** starts higher than normal, and slides down to lower than normal. ไม่ mâi (not), ห้า hâa (five), บ้าน bâan (house)
´	The **high tone** starts higher than normal, and slides up even higher. If you feel like a chipmunk when you're doing it, you got it right! ไม้ máai (wood), รัก rák (love), น้ำ náam (water)
ˇ	The **rising tone** starts lower than normal, and slides up to higher than normal (similar to asking a question in English). It's critical to start very low to distinguish this tone from the high tone. ไหม mǎi (silk), สูง sǔung (tall), เขา kǎo (mountain)

Visit **http://slice-of-thai.com/language** to hear each tone, or practice with a Thai using the words we provide.

Similar Sounds

Practice your tones, vowel length, and consonants:

มา maa (come), ม้า máa (horse), หมา mǎa (dog)
เสื่อ sùua (floor mat), เสื้อ sûua (shirt), เสือ sǔua (tiger)
ซี sii (letter C), สี่ sìi (four), สี sǐi (color)

เคา kao (not a word)	คาว kaao (fishy)
เข่า kào (knee)	ข่าว kàao (news)
เข้า kâo (enter)	ข้าว kâao (rice)
เค้า káo (he, she)	ค้าว káao (not a word)
เขา kǎo (hill)	ขาว kǎao (white)

ดี dii (good)	ตี dtii (hit)	ที tii (turn)
เดา dao (guess)	เตา dtao (stove)	เทา tao (gray)
ใบ bai (leaf)	ไป bpai (go)	ภัย pai (danger)
เบ็ด bèt (fishhook)	เป็ด bpèt (duck)	เผ็ด pèt (spicy)

นา naa (rice field)	งา ngaa (sesame)
ถุง tǔng (bag)	ถึง tǔng (arrive)
กลัว gluua (scared)	เกลือ gluua (salt)
เครื่อง krûuang (machine)	ครึ่ง krûng (half)

Syllables and Stress

Now you know how to say and hear a Paiboon⁺ syllable.
Syllables combine into words using - and ~:

แสดง	sà~dɛɛng	show
สะใจ	sà-jai	satisfied
มหาวิทยาลัย	má~hǎa-wít-tá~yaa-lai	university
หนังสือ	nǎng~sǔu	book

A syllable that's followed by - is **stressed** and Thais usually
pronounce it just as shown (the last syllable of a word is
always stressed). A syllable that's followed by ~ is
unstressed, which means that in full-speed, fluent speech,
Thais often slur the syllable in one or more of these ways:

- the tone becomes mid instead of the "real" tone:
  e.g. nǎng~sǔu → nang~sǔu
- the vowel slurs towards ə instead of the "real" vowel:
  e.g. English "A-mer-i-ca" → "A-mer-ə-ca"
  e.g. má~hǎa-wít-tá~yaa-lai → mə~hǎa-wít-tə~yaa-lai
- short vowels at the end of a syllable flow right into the
  next (e.g. English "a dang," แสดง sà~dɛɛng), as opposed
  to first cutting off the flow of air at the throat (e.g.
  English "uh oh", สะใจ sà-jai; known as a "glottal stop").

Knowing which Thai syllables are unstressed can help you
understand Thais better because you will expect this kind
of slurring. For speaking, you're usually better off trying to
say the tones and vowels clearly rather than slurring them.

Other Irregular Sounds

There's a few other common cases where the real sounds Thais make won't match what you would expect:

- Certain extremely common words with rising tones shorten to high tones; our dictionary includes these irregular pronunciations, marked as spoken (❀).
  ดิฉัน dì~chǎn (I, for female speaker) → ดิชั้น dì~chán ❀
  เขา kǎo (he, she) → เค้า káo ❀
  ไหม mǎi (yes/no question word) → มั้ย mái ❀

- Certain words shorten in compounds, as our Paiboon⁺ indicates: e.g. น้ำ <u>náam</u> (water), but น้ำแข็ง <u>nám</u>-kěng (ice)

- Many words borrowed from English and other languages have multiple pronunciations in Thai. "Celsius" might be seo-sîiat, sen-sîiat, or seo-sîias! We usually list only one or two possibilities. In general, you get variation when syllables end with ch, f, l, r, or s; Thai syllables cannot end this way, but many modern Thais are learning how to make these final sounds.

- As with any language, any vowel or consonant can get slurred in sloppy speech. When Thais get up for work before dawn and order rice porridge (ข้าวต้ม kâao-dtôm), you're much more likely to hear them say (kɔ-dtôm). This magic phrase might help you with such speech:
  ช่วย พูด ช้าๆ หน่อย chûuai pûut cháa-cháa nɔ̀i
  (please speak more slowly).

14
Finding Words by Sound

To find a Paiboon⁺ word in our Thai Sound section:

- Start in the tab for the first sound you hear (you can see the tabs along the edge of each page of the section). Note that bp, ch, dt, and ng each have their own tab.
- Search within a tab using this alphabetical order: a b c d e ɛ ə f g h i j k l m n o ɔ p r s t u ʉ w y
- Words differing only by tone will be adjacent.
- The page numbers listed have the full entries. "2x623" means to look for 2 different Thai spellings on page 623.

If you hear a word and are having trouble finding it in our Thai Sound section, here are some tips:

- Try a similar-sounding first letter. Commonly mistaken groups include: b/p/bp, d/t/dt, g/k, j/ch, n/ng (see p. 4)
- Try the other vowel length, e.g. a/aa, eo/eeo
- Try similar-sounding vowels, especially u/ʉ and e/ɛ/a/ə
- If you're hearing l, it's possible that your Thai friend's r and l sound the same. Try looking under r.
- Your Thai friend may have dropped an l or r that is the second sound of a cluster: for example, if you hear bpaa, look under bplaa and bpraa, too.
- Try to get another word with the phrase ไม่ เข้าใจ คำ ว่า __ mâi kâo-jai kam wâa __ (don't understand the word __).

Parts of Speech

n.	**Noun:** รถ rót (car), วัน wan (day) In Thai, you use the same noun for both singular and plural. Whenever you want to count a noun ("two cars") or say "that car," "first car," etc., you must use a special word called a classifier, which we provide for you (see p. 18).
pron.	**Pronoun:** ผม pǒm ดิฉัน dì~chǎn (I), คุณ kun (you) In Thai you must carefully pick your pronoun (even "I" or "you") depending on the situation; our pronoun entries give you advice.
art.	**Article:** a, an, the Thai doesn't use articles. Just skip them!
numb.	**Number:** หนึ่ง nɯ̀ng (one), สิบห้า sìp-hâa (fifteen) Use classifiers to count nouns (see p. 18).
adj.	**Adjective:** เร็ว reo (quick), สนุก sà~nùk (fun) Thai adjectives appear after the noun. In English we say "red car," but in Thai it's "car red" (รถ แดง rót dɛɛng). Thai does not use the verb "to be" with adjectives. "She is cute" would be "she cute" (เขา น่ารัก kǎo nâa-rák).
adv.	**Adverb:** เร็ว reo (quickly), ตอนนี้ dtɔɔn-níi (now) Unlike English, most Thai adjectives can also serve as adverbs. Two for one! In these cases, we generally list only the adjective.

	Verbs and Verb Phrases are marked as:
vi.	*vi.* if you **cannot** add a noun object (**intransitive**): ตาย dtaai (die), กินข้าว gin-kâao (dine) (you can't "die something;" you just "die")
vt.	*vt.* if you **must** add a noun object (**transitive**): แจก jÈÈk (hand out), เอา_มา ao-_-maa (bring) (you can't "bring;" you must "bring something")
v.	*v.* if you can choose to do **either one**: กิน gin (eat), อธิบาย à-tí-baai (explain) (you can "eat" or "eat something")

Often a verb has a *vi.* usage ("I drown") and a *vt.* usage ("I drown him") that translate differently into Thai; *vi./vt.* tells you which you're getting.

Add the object after the verb, unless you see "_" (as in "bring" above), which tells you where to put the object: เอา รถ มา ao-rót-maa ("bring the car").

We choose *vi./vt.* based on the most restrictive language. You can "dine someone" in English, but กินข้าว gin-kâao (dine) is *vi.* because you cannot add an object in Thai. แจก jÈÈk (hand out) is *vt.* because you must have an object in English.

In Thai, you can drop the object of a *v./vt.* verb if it's known from context: "That's his car. I like it!" can be just "I like!" in Thai. Actually, Thais even drop the subject if it's known from context: "like!"

aux.	**Auxiliary Verb:** จะ jà (will), อาจจะ àat-jà (might) Thai verbs do not change with **tense** (e.g. "go," "went"). To say "I went" or "I have gone," add in extra words like "I go already" or "I go yesterday." For "I will go," use the auxiliary จะ jà (will). For "I do go" and "I am going," just use "I go."
prep.	**Preposition:** จาก jàak (from), ใน nai (in)
conj.	**Conjunction:** และ lé (and), หรือ rǔu (or)
idm.	**Idiom:** ไม่เป็นไร mâi-bpen-rai (no problem)
interj.	**Interjection:** ออกไป ɔ̀ɔk-bpai (go away!)
let.	**Letter of the Alphabet:** ก. ไก่ gɔɔ-gài (first letter)
pref.	**Prefix:** ปฏิ bpà~dtì- (anti-) These are meant to be glued to other words.
part.	**Particle:** ครับ kráp ค่ะ kâ (polite), สิ sì (emphatic) Thais add particles to the end of sentences in order to add politeness, emphasis, or other meanings. You should use ครับ kráp (male speaker) or ค่ะ kâ (female speaker) to be polite.
clf.	**Classifier:** เล่ม lêm, คัน kan, อัน an, แผ่น pèn Very important in Thai grammar: see p. 18

Questions: To ask what/where/why/how in Thai, don't use "do;" plug the question word right in, like: "I eat what?" "You go where?" "I pay how much?" For yes/no questions, add ไหม mǎi to the end; if the answer starts with ไม่ mâi or เปล่า bplàao, the answer is no, otherwise the answer is yes.

Classifiers

Whenever you want to count a noun (e.g. "two cars," "two bottles of beer"), or use a noun in phrases like "this car" or "the first car," you **must** use a special Thai word called a classifier. English also has classifiers ("two <u>pairs</u> of pants," "two <u>head</u> of cattle," "two <u>cups</u> of sugar") but in Thai, classifiers are required for counting or measuring anything. We list classifiers for nouns in [square brackets], like this:

car n. รถ rót [คัน kan]
beer n. เบียร์ biia [ขวด kùuat (bottle), แก้ว gɛ̂ɛo (glass)]

So the classifier for "รถ rót" is "คัน kan," and two classifiers for "เบียร์ biia" are "ขวด kùuat" and "แก้ว gɛ̂ɛo." Some nouns can have many classifiers, so we list a few useful ones. To count or measure with a classifier, use this pattern (our example uses the number two, สอง sɔ̌ɔng: see p. 969):

Noun	+ Number	+ Classifier	
รถ rót	สอง sɔ̌ɔng	คัน kan	Two cars
เบียร์ biia	สอง sɔ̌ɔng	ขวด kùuat	Two bottles of beer
เบียร์ biia	สอง sɔ̌ɔng	แก้ว gɛ̂ɛo	Two glasses of beer

If the noun is already known from context, you can skip it, but you still need the classifier. If asked "Do you want more beer?" you can say "เอา สอง ขวด ao sɔ̌ɔng kùuat," meaning "want two bottles."

Any adjectives, like เย็น yen (cold), go after the noun, as in บีียร์ เย็น สอง ขวด biia yen sɔ̌ɔng kùuat: "two bottles of cold beer."

Certain nouns like "คน kon (person)" are their own classifier, so you can skip the noun (สอง คน sɔ̌ɔng kon: "two people") unless there's an adjective, as in คน ไทย สอง คน kon tai sɔ̌ɔng kon: "two Thai people."

Other fun things you can do with classifiers include:

Noun	**+ Classifier +**	**ที่ tîi +**	**Number**
รถ rót	คัน kan	ที่ tîi	สอง sɔ̌ɔng The **second** car

Noun	**+ Classifier +**	
รถ rót	คัน kan	นี้ níi	**This** car
รถ rót	คัน kan	นั้น nán	**That** car
รถ rót	คัน kan	โน้น nóon	The car **over there**
รถ rót	คัน kan	แรก rɛ̂ɛk	The **first** car
รถ rót	คัน kan	สุดท้าย sùt-táai	The **last** car

There are a few classifiers that can be used for nearly any noun (e.g. อย่าง yàang (kind) as in "two kinds of beer"), so we don't list these in individual noun entries.

For a list of these and other common classifiers, see p. 965.

Word Register (Formality)

In English, you might ask your friend to "eat," ask the guests at a formal ball to "dine," or read a scientific report about how to "consume sustenance." All these words just mean "eat," but they have different **registers**, meaning that they are appropriate in different social contexts. Thai words very often fall into different registers. When needed, we mark Thai words with the following symbols:

⚜	only used by monks or about monks
♔	only used by royalty or about royalty
🕸	obsolete word not used any more at all
✍	poetic, literary; used only for art, or when you want to sound eloquent
✗	technical; unusually precise; used by scientists and experts
!	used in settings where those of higher social rank are present; formal, respectful, deferential
(none)	no special connotation of formality or informality
🗣	spoken, slang, informal, colloquial (use among friends or in informal settings)
💣	impolite (use among friends) but still not vulgar
☠	obscene; taboo and forbidden; we warned you!

Reading and Writing Thai
Consonants

Here we list Ⓐ each of the 46 Thai consonants in order, ⒹⒺⒻ each consonant's standardized and universal name (useful for spelling words out verbally), Ⓒ its consonant class (**L**ow, **M**id or **H**igh: more on this later), samples of that consonant in ten common Thai fonts, and the Paiboon⁺ sound (see p. 3) that the consonant makes at the beginning Ⓑ or end Ⓖ of a syllable.

Ⓐ	Ⓑ	Ⓒ	Ⓓ	Ⓔ	Ⓕ	Ⓖ
ก	g	**M**	กอ ไก่	gɔɔ-gài	chicken	k
		ก ก ∩ ∩ ∩ ∩ ∩ ∩ ฦ				
ข	k	**H**	ขอ ไข่	kɔ̌ɔ-kài	egg	k
		ข ข ∪ ∪ ∪ ∪ ∪ V ∦				
ฃ	k	**H**	ฃอ ขวด	kɔ̌ɔ-kùuat	bottle (**obsolete**)	k
		ฃ ฃ ∪ ∪ ∪ ∪ ∦ ∦ ∦				
ค	k	**L**	คอ ควาย	kɔɔ-kwaai	water buffalo	k
		ค ค ∩ ∩ ∩ ∩ ∩ ∩ ค				
ฅ	k	**L**	ฅอ คน	kɔɔ-kon	person (**obsolete**)	k
		ฅ ฅ ∩ ฅ ฅ ฅ ฅ ฅ ฅ				

ฆ	k	**L** ฆอ ระฆัง	kɔɔ-rá~kang	bell	k
		ฆ ฆ **ฆ ฆ** ฌ **ฌ** ฆ ฆ			
ง	ng	**L** งอ งู	ngɔɔ-nguu	snake	ng
		ง ง **ง ง** ง ง ง ง			
จ	j	**M** จอ จาน	jɔɔ-jaan	plate	t
		จ จ **จ** จ จ จ จ จ			
ฉ	ch	**H** ฉอ ฉิ่ง	chɔ̌ɔ-chìng	chime	t
		ฉ ฉ **ฉ ฉ** ฉ ฉ ฉ ฉ			
ช	ch	**L** ชอ ช้าง	chɔɔ-cháang	elephant	t
		ช ช **ช ช** ช ช ช ช			
ซ	s	**L** ซอ โซ่	rɔɔ-sôo	chain	t
		ซ ซ **ซ ซ** ซ ซ ซ ซ			
ฌ	ch	**L** ฌอ เฌอ	chɔɔ-chəə	tree, bush	t
		ฌ ฌ **ฌ ฌ** ฌ ฌ ฌ ฌ			
ญ	y	**L** ญอ หญิง	yɔɔ-yǐng	woman	n
		ญ ญ **ญ ญ** ญ ญ ญ ญ			
ฎ	d	**M** ฎอ ชฎา	dɔɔ-chá~daa	traditional hat	t
		ฎ ฎ **ฎ ฎ** ฎ ฎ ฎ ฎ			

ฏ	dt	**M** ฏอ ปฏัก	dtɔɔ-bpà~dtàk	spear		t
		ฏ ฏ ฏ ฏ ฏ ฏ ฏ ฏ ฏ				
ฐ	t	**H** ฐอ ฐาน	tʃɔɔ-tǎan	base		t
		ฐ ฐ ฐ ฐ ฐ ฐ ฐ ฐ ฐ				
ฑ	t	**L** ฑอ มณโฑ	tɔɔ-mon-too	mythical lady		t
		ฑ ฑ ฑ ฑ ฑ ฑ ฑ ฑ ฑ				
ฒ	t	**L** ฒอ ผู้เฒ่า	tɔɔ-pûu-tâo	old man		t
		ฒ ฒ ฒ ฒ ฒ ฒ ฒ ฒ ฒ				
ณ	n	**L** ณอ เณร	nɔɔ-neen	novice monk		n
		ณ ณ ณ ณ ณ ณ ณ ณ ณ				
ด	d	**M** ดอ เด็ก	dɔɔ-dèk	child		t
		ด ด ด ด ด ด ด ด ด				
ต	dt	**M** ตอ เต่า	dtɔɔ-dtào	turtle		t
		ต ต ต ต ต ต ต ต ต				
ถ	t	**H** ถอ ถุง	tʃɔɔ-tǔng	bag		t
		ถ ถ ถ ถ ถ ถ ถ ถ ถ				
ท	t	**L** ทอ ทหาร	tɔɔ-tá~hǎan	soldier		t
		ท ท ท ท ท ท ท ท ท				

ธ	t	**L** ธอ ธง	tɔɔ-tong	flag		t
		ธ ธ **ร** ฉ ธ ธ ฮ δ ธ				
น	n	**L** นอ หนู	nɔɔ-nǔu	mouse, rat		n
		น น **น** ฒ น น น ห น				
บ	b	**M** บอ ใบไม้	bɔɔ-bai-máai	leaf		p
		บ บ **บ บ** U บ ช U บ				
ป	bp	**M** ปอ ปลา	bpɔɔ-bplaa	fish		p
		ป ป **ป ป** U ป ช U ป				
ผ	p	**H** ผอ ผึ้ง	pɔɔ-pûng	bee		p
		ผ ผ **ผ น** ฒ ผ ฝ ฝ ฬ				
ฝ	f	**H** ฝอ ฝา	fɔɔ-fǎa	lid		p
		ฝ ฝ **ฝ ฝ** ฒ ฝ ฝ ฝ ฬ				
พ	p	**L** พอ พาน	pɔɔ-paan	offering tray		p
		พ พ **พ พ** ฒ พ ฬ พ ฬ				
ฟ	f	**L** ฟอ ฟัน	fɔɔ-fan	tooth		p
		ฟ ฟ **ฟ พ** ฒ ฟ ฬ พ ฬ				
ภ	p	**L** ภอ สำเภา	pɔɔ-sǎm-pao	Asian boat		p
		ภ ภ **ภ ภ** ภ ภ ภ ภ ภ				

ม	m	L	มอ ม้า	mɔɔ-máa	horse									m
		ม	ม	**ม**	**ม**	ม	**ม**	ม	ม	ม				m
ย	y	L	ยอ ยักษ์	yɔɔ-yák	demon, giant									i
		ย	ย	**ย**	**ย**	ย	**ย**	ย	ย	ย				
ร	r	L	รอ เรือ	rɔɔ-rɯɯa	boat									n
		ร	ร	**ร**	**ร**	ร	**ร**	ร	ร	ร				
ฤ	r	L	ฤ	rɯ́	(none)									
		ฤ	ฤ	**ฤ**	**ฤ**	ก	**ฤ**	ฤ	ฤ	ฤ				
ล	l	L	ลอ ลิง	lɔɔ-ling	monkey									n
		ล	ล	**ล**	**ล**	ล	**ล**	ล	ล	ล				
ฦ	l	L	ฦ	lɯ́	(**obsolete**)									
		ฦ	ฦ	**ฦ**	**ฦ**	ก	**ฦ**	ฦ	ฦ	ฦ				
ว	w	L	วอ แหวน	wɔɔ-wɛ̌ɛn	ring									o
		ว	ว	**ว**	**ว**	ว	**ว**	ว	ว	ว				
ศ	s	H	ศอ ศาลา	sɔ̌ɔ-sǎa-laa	gazebo									t
		ศ	ศ	**ศ**	**ศ**	ศ	**ศ**	ศ	ศ	ศ				
ษ	s	H	ษอ ฤๅษี	sɔ̌ɔ-rɯɯ-sǐi	hermit									t
		ษ	ษ	**ษ**	**ษ**	ษ	**ษ**	ษ	ษ	ษ				

ส	s	**H** สอ เสือ	รว้ว-sǔua	tiger		t
		ส ส **ส** ส ส ส ส่ ส ๙				
ห	h	**H** หอ หีบ	hǐiu-hìip	trunk, chest		
		ห ห **ห** ห ห ห ห ห ห				
ฬ	l	**L** ฬอ จุฬา	lɔɔ-jù-laa	a kind of kite		n
		ฬ ฬ **ฬ** ฬ ฬ ฬ ฬ ฬ ฬ				
อ		**M** ออ อ่าง	ɔɔ-àang	basin, tub		
		อ อ **อ** อ อ อ อ อ อ				
ฮ	h	**L** ฮอ นกฮูก	hɔɔ-nók-hûuk	owl		
		ฮ ฮ **ฮ** ฮ ฮ ฮ ฮ ฮ ฮ				

At the beginning of a syllable, the 46 consonants make the 20 **initial** consonant sounds that you learned on p. 4, shown in column Ⓑ. At the end of a syllable (column Ⓖ), only 8 **final** consonant sounds are possible in Thai:

- **k, t, p:** the **stop finals** (the ones that you can't sing)
- **ng, n, m, i, o:** the **sonorant finals** (which you can sing)

There are 9 mid consonants, 11 high consonants, and 26 low consonants. ฅ and ฃ are obsolete. ฦ lɯ́ is virtually obsolete. The bizarre, fairly rare consonant-vowel ฤ rɯ́ may sound like rəə, rɯ, ri or (as ฤๅ) rɯɯ depending on the word.

Some Thai words begin with a **cluster** of two consonants ending in **r** or **l** (e.g. พระ prá (monk), เพลง pleeng (music)). A few words have irregular cluster sounds that you have to memorize (e.g. จริง jing (true), สระ sà (pool), ศรี sǐi (fortune), ทราย saai (sand)). Some words have clusters with silent ห or อ (see p. 38). Any vowel or tone marks always go over the second letter, e.g. กล้า glâa (brave). Finally, a single consonant may be shared between two syllables, as in ผลไม้ pǒn-lá~máai (fruit) where ล is both final **n** and initial **l**.

Consonant Alphabetical Order

Amazingly, the first 33 Thai consonants are sorted by the place in your mouth where you make the sound, then by class. This can help you look up a word more quickly:

Place in Mouth	Paiboon⁺ Sound	MID	HIGH	LOW Paired	LOW Unpaired
	g,k,ng	ก	ข ฃ	ค ฅ ฆ	ง
	j,ch,s,y	จ	ฉ	ช ซ ฌ	ญ
	d,dt,t,n	ฎ ฏ	ฐ	ฑ ฒ	ณ
		ด ต	ถ	ท ธ	น
	b,bp,p,m	บ ป	ผ ฝ	พ ฟ ภ	ม

The remaining 13 consonants are ย ร ฤ ล ฦ ว (**y,r,l,w**), then ศ ษ ส (the three high **s** consonants), and then ห ฬ อ ฮ (**h,l**).

Vowels and Syllables

Every Thai syllable has an initial consonant, a vowel, and an optional final consonant (e.g. ก g + า aa + น n = กาน gaan). Various Thai vowels are written to the right of the initial consonant (กา gaa), to the left of it (เก gee), above it (กี gii), below it (กู guu), or even some combination of these (เกือ guua), but in every case you say the initial consonant first. When a syllable begins with a vowel, write the silent initial consonant ออ-àang อ (e.g. อา aa, เอ ee, อี ii, อู uu), which serves as a placeholder around which to write the vowel.

In our vowel examples, we use a dash – to mark the place where the initial consonant goes (e.g. –า for กา, เ– for เก). The final consonant, if any, always goes at the end of the syllable (e.g. กา gaa + น n = กาน gaan). Some vowels, such as those for **a** and **e**, change form when there is a final consonant (e.g. กะ gà + น n = กัน gan); for these vowels, we show both forms, and the form with the final consonant has a second dash (e.g. –ะ for กะ, –ั– for กัน).

For each Thai vowel Ⓑ, we show samples of that vowel in ten common Thai fonts, Ⓐ the Paiboon⁺ sound that it makes (see p. 8), Ⓒ whether it's **LONG** or **SHORT** (see p. 7), Ⓓ whether it's **LIVE** or **DEAD** (more on this later), and Ⓔ some sample words that use it. The vowels appear in the same order as p. 8 (for alphabetical order, see p. 40).

Ⓐ	Ⓑ	Ⓒ	Ⓓ	Ⓔ
aa	–า	LONG	LIVE	มา maa (come), มาก mâak (very)
		–า	-า	**-า**	-า	–า	–า	**–า**	-า	–า
a	–ะ	SHORT	DEAD	จะ jà (will)
		-ะ	-ะ	**-ะ**	-ะ	-ะ	-ะ	-ะ	-ะ	-ะ
	–ั	SHORT		จับ jàp (touch)
		-ั	-ั	**-ั**	-ั	-ั	-ั	-ั	-ั
ai	ใ–	SHORT	LIVE	ใบ bai (leaf)
		ใ-	ใ-	**ใ-**	ใ-	ใ-	ใ-	ใ-	ใ-
ai	ไ–	SHORT	LIVE	ไป bpai (go)
		ไ-	ไ-	**ไ-**	ไ-	ไ-	ไ-	ไ-	ไ-
ao	เ–า	SHORT	LIVE	เดา dao (guess)
		เ-า	เ-า	**เ-า**	เ-า	เ-า	เ-า	เ-า	เ-า
ee	เ–	LONG	LIVE	เท tee (pour), เทพ têep (angel)
		เ-	เ-	**เ-**	เ-	เ-	เ-	เ-	เ-
e	เ–ะ	SHORT	DEAD	เละ lé (mushy)
		เ-ะ	เ-ะ	**เ-ะ**	เ-ะ	เ-ะ	เ-ะ	เ-ะ	เ-ะ
	เ–็	SHORT		เล็ก lék (small)
		เ-็	เ-็	**เ-็**	เ-็	เ-็	เ-็	เ-็	เ-็

εε	แ–	**LONG** **LIVE** แพ pεε (raft), แลก lε̂εk (exchange
		แ–	แ–	**แ–**	แ–	แ–	แ–	แ–	แ–	แ–
ε	แ–ะ	**SHORT** **DEAD** และ lέ (and)
		แ–ะ	แ–ะ	**แ–ะ**	แ–ะ	แ–ะ	แ–ะ	แ–ะ	แ–ะ	แ–ะ
	แ̆––	**SHORT**	แข็ง kε̆ng (stiff)
		แ̆––	แ̆––	**แ̆––**	แ̆––	แ̆––	แ̆––	แ̆––	แ̆––	แ̆––
əə	เ–อ	**LONG** **LIVE** เธอ təə (you), เทอม təəm (term)
		เ–อ	เ–อ	**เ–อ**	เ–อ	เ–อ	เ–อ	เ–อ	เ–อ	เ–อ
	เ̂––	**LONG**	เดิน dəən (walk)
		เ̂––	เ̂––	**เ̂––**	เ̂––	เ̂––	เ̂––	เ̂––	เ̂––	เ̂––
ə	เ–อะ	**SHORT** **DEAD** เยอะ yə́ (lots)
		เ–อะ	เ–อะ	**เ–อะ**	เ–อะ	เ–อะ	เ–อะ	เ–อะ	เ–อะ	เ–อะ
əəi	เ–ย	**LONG** **LIVE** เนย nəəi (butter)
		เ–ย	เ–ย	**เ–ย**	เ–ย	เ–ย	เ–ย	เ–ย	เ–ย	เ–ย
ii	–ี	**LONG** **LIVE** ปี bpii (year), ปีน bpiin (climb)
		–ี	–ี	–ี	–ี	–ี	–ี	–ี	–ี	–ี
i	–ิ	**SHORT** **DEAD** ติ dtì (criticize), ติด dtìt (attach)
		–ิ	–ิ	–ิ	–ิ	–ิ	–ิ	–ิ	–ิ	–ิ
iu	–ิว	**SHORT** **LIVE** ผิว pǐu (skin)
		–ิว	–ิว	–ิว	–ิว	–ิว	–ิว	–ิว	–ิว	–ิว

iia	เ–ีย	LONG	LIVE	เสีย sĭia (spoil), เสียง sĭiang (tone)
		เ–ีย	เ–ีย	**เ–ีย**	เ–ีย	เ–ีย	**เ–ีย**	เ–ีย	เ–ีย	เ–ีย

ia	เ–ียะ	SHORT	DEAD	เดี๊ยะ día (exactly): rare
		เ–ียะ	เ–ียะ	**เ–ียะ**	เ–ยะ	เ–ียะ	**เ–ียะ**	เ–ียะ	เ–ียะ	เ–ียะ

oo	โ–	LONG	LIVE	โต dtoo (big), โกน goon (shave)
		โ–	โ–	**โ–**	ใ–	โ–	โ–	โ–	โ–	โ–

	โ–ะ	SHORT	DEAD	โต๊ะ dtó (table)
o		โ–ะ	โ–ะ	**โ–ะ**	ใ–ะ	โ–ะ	โ–ะ	โ–ะ	โ–ะ	โ–ะ
	––	SHORT		ตก dtòk (fall)
		––	––	**––**	––	––	––	––	––	––

ɔɔ	–อ	LONG	LIVE	ขอ kɔ̆ɔ (ask), ขอบ kɔ̀ɔp (edge)
		–อ	–อ	**–อ**	–อ	–อ	**–อ**	–อ	–อ	–อ

	เ–าะ	SHORT	DEAD	เกาะ gɔ̀ (island)
ɔ		เ–าะ	เ–าะ	**เ–าะ**	เ–าะ	เ–าะ	**เ–าะ**	เ–าะ	เ–าะ	เ–าะ
	–็อ–	SHORT		ล็อก lɔ́k (lock)
		–็อ–	–็อ–	**–็อ–**	–็อ–	–็อ–	–็อ–	–็อ–	–็อ–	–็อ–

uu	–ู	LONG	LIVE	ดู duu (look), ดูด dùut (suck)
		–ู	–ู	**–ู**	–ู	–ู	–ู	–ู	–ู	–ู

u	–ุ	SHORT	DEAD	ดุ dù (fierce), จุด jùt (place)
		–ุ	–ุ	**–ุ**	–ุ	–ุ	–ุ	–ุ	–ุ	–ุ

uua	◌ัว	**LONG**	**LIVE**	หัว hǔua (head)							
		◌ัว	◌ัว	**◌ัว**	◌ั◌	◌ัว	◌ัง	◌ัว	◌ัว	◌	
	−ว−	**LONG**		หวง hǔuang (possessive, jealous							
		−ว−	−ว−	**−ว−**	−◌−	−ว−	−ง−	−ว−	−ว−	−◌	
ua	◌ัวะ	**SHORT**	**DEAD**	ผัวะ pùa (clap!): rare							
		◌ัวะ	◌ัวะ	**◌ัวะ**	◌ั◌ะ	◌ัวะ	◌ังะ	◌ัวะ	◌ัวะ	◌	
ɯɯ	◌ือ	**LONG**	**LIVE**	มือ mɯɯ (hand)							
		◌ือ	◌ือ	**◌ือ**	◌ื◌	◌ือ	◌ือ	◌ือ	◌ือ	◌	
	◌ื	**LONG**		มืด mɯ̂ɯt (dark)							
		◌ื	◌ื	**◌ื**	◌ื	◌ื	◌ื	◌ื	◌ื	◌	
ɯ	◌ึ	**SHORT**	**DEAD**	อึ ɯ̀ (poop), ดึก dɯ̀k (latenight)							
		◌ึ	◌ึ	**◌ึ**	◌ึ	◌ึ	◌ึ	◌ึ	◌ึ	◌	
ɯɯa	เ◌ือ	**LONG**	**LIVE**	เรือ rɯɯa (boat), เดือน dɯɯan (month)							
		เ◌ือ	เ◌ือ	**เ◌ือ**	เ◌ื◌	เ◌ือ	เ◌ือ	เ◌ือ	เ◌ือ	◌	

Notice how some of the vowels include อ, ย and ว, which
can also be consonants: try not to confuse the two uses.
Above, we've shown all the basic written vowel forms. By
adding ย (yɔɔ-yák) as a final consonant, you can add an **i**
sound to get a new vowel (e.g. กา gaa + ย i = กาย gaai).
By adding ว (wɔɔ-wɛ̌ɛn) as a final consonant, you can add
an **o** sound (e.g. กา gaa + ว o = กาว gaao). With these two
tricks, you can build all the vowel sounds from p. 8:

	Long			Short	
aa	—า	—า—	a	—ะ	—ั
aai	—าย		ai	ไ—	ไ—— ใ— —ัย ไ—ย
aao	—าว	—าว—	ao	เ—า	
ee	เ—	เ——	e	เ—ะ	เ—็—
eeo	เ—ว		eo	เ—็ว	
ɛɛ	แ—	แ——	ɛ	แ—ะ	แ—็—
ɛɛo	แ—ว		ɛo	แ—็ว	
əə	เ—อ	เ—ิ—	เ—อ—	ə	เ—อะ	
əəi	เ—ย		əi	เ—ย	(see p. 39)
ii	—ี	—ี—	i	—ิ	—ิ—
			iu	—ิว	
iia	เ—ีย	เ—ีย—	ia	เ—ียะ	
iiao	เ—ียว				
oo	โ—	โ——	o	โ—ะ	——
ooi	โ—ย				
ɔɔ	—อ	—อ—	ɔ	เ—าะ	—็อ—
ɔɔi	—อย		ɔi	—็อย	
uu	—ู	—ู—	u	—ุ	—ุ—
uui	—ูย		ui	—ุย	
uua	—ัว	—ว—	ua	—ัวะ	
uuai	—วย		uai	—วย	(see p. 39)
ʉʉ	—ือ	—ื—	ʉ	—ึ	—ึ—
ʉʉa	เ—ือ	เ—ือ—			
ʉʉai	เ—ือย				

The table above includes all the written vowels commonly found in Thai without (–า) and with (–า–) final consonants.

- Another symbol you'll often see is –ำ **am**, which includes the vowel **a** plus a built-in final consonant **m**. It's usually SHORT (นำ nam (to lead)) but sometimes LONG in irregular words (น้ำ náam (water)). It is LIVE.

- The short **o** vowel –– is **implicit**, meaning that it has no vowel markings at all (e.g. กด gòt (push)). If the final consonant is ร, the sound changes to ɔɔ (ศร sɔ̌ɔn (arrow)). Some Thai words also have an implicit **a** with no final consonant (e.g. ตลาด dtà~làat (market), instead of ตะลาด); you just have to memorize these.

- The word ก็, meaning "also," is pronounced gɔ̂ɔ.

- Many Thai words have an irregular vowel length that won't match this table. For example, เงิน (money) should be ngəən according to the table, but is actually pronounced ngən. See p. 39 for more.

- Certain vowels in the table, such as เ–อ– əə, are mostly used to "import" foreign words (e.g. เทอม təəm (term)).

- If you see รร followed by a final consonant, รร sounds like **a** (กรรม gam (karma)). รร without a final consonant sounds like **an** (กรรไกร gan-grai (scissors)).

Other Symbols

Here are some other symbols you may encounter:

ๆ	ไม้ยมก mái-yá~mók means that you **repeat** the word or phrase before it, e.g. ดีๆ dii-dii (really good), สบายๆ sà~baai-sà~baai (chilled out).
์	การันต์ gaa-ran over a letter means that letter is **silent**, e.g. ฟาร์ม faam (farm), อาทิตย์ aa-tít (week). Very common in "imported" foreign words containing sounds that are "illegal" in Thai.
ฯ	ไปยาลน้อย bpai-yaan-nɔ́ɔi means that the word before it is **abbreviated**. กรุงเทพฯ grung-têep is thankfully the common name for Bangkok, whose full Thai name is more than 60 syllables long!
ฯลฯ	ไปยาลใหญ่ bpai-yaan-yài is similar to **etc.** in English.

What Determines the Tone

On p. 10, you learned how to say the five Thai tone sounds (เสียง sǐiang (sound)), which were: **mid** (เสียงสามัญ sǐiang-sǎa-man), **low** (เสียงเอก sǐiang-èek), **falling** (เสียงโท sǐiang-too), **high** (เสียงตรี sǐiang-dtrii), and **rising** (เสียงจัตวา sǐiang-jàt-dtà~waa). Here are the rules that determine the tone of a written Thai syllable (if it's a regular syllable):

If there is a tone mark: If the Thai syllable has one of the four Thai tone marks $-\grave{}\ -\acute{}\ -\tilde{}\ -\overset{+}{}$, then the tone is determined by the mark and the class (p. 21) of its initial consonant:

Mark	**M**id Class	**H**igh Class	**L**ow Class
$-\grave{}$ ไม้เอก mái-èek	**LOW TONE** ป่า bpàa (jungle)	**LOW TONE** ข่า kàa (galanga)	**FALLING TONE** ค่า kâa (price)
$-\acute{}$ ไม้โท mái-too	**FALLING TONE** ป้า bpâa (aunt)	**FALLING TONE** ข้า kâa (servant)	**HIGH TONE** ค้า káa (trade)
$-\tilde{}$ ไม้ตรี mái-dtrii	**HIGH TONE** โป๊ bpóo (naked)	(not used)	(not used)
$-\overset{+}{}$ ไม้จัตวา mái-jàt-dtà~waa	**RISING TONE** ป๋า bpǎa (sugar daddy)	(not used)	(not used)

Notice how the same tone mark (ไม้ mái (mark)) can make different tone sounds (เสียง sĭiang (sound)) depending on the initial consonant class. The table above shows each tone mark in ten common Thai fonts, as well as a sample word for each mark and initial consonant class.

f there is no tone mark then you must ask yourself:

- A. Does the syllable end in a **LIVE** vowel (see p. 28) or a sonorant final consonant (see p. 26: these are the consonants you can sing: **ng, n, m, i, o**)? The tone is:

Mid Class	High Class	Low Class
MID TONE	**RISING TONE**	**MID TONE**
ตา dtaa	ขา kǎa	มา maa
(eye)	(leg)	(come)

- B. Otherwise (the syllable ends in a **DEAD** vowel or a stop final consonant) the tone is:

Mid Class	High Class	Low Class
LOW TONE	**LOW TONE**	Is the vowel **SHORT?**
เด็ก dèk	หีบ hìip	**HIGH TONE**
(child)	(trunk, chest)	นก nók
		(bird)
		Is the vowel **LONG?**
		FALLING TONE
		ฮูก hûuk
		(owl)

The names of these three Thai consonants are a handy memory aid for rule A and B; they demonstrate all cases:

	Mid Class		High Class		Low Class	
A	ด	ดอ dɔɔ	ห	หอ hɔ̌ɔ	ฮ	ฮอ hɔɔ
B		เด็ก dèk		หีบ hìip		นก nók
						ฮูก hûuk

Sample **M**id, **H**igh, and **L**ow class words showing the rules:

ด่าน dàan (border) ผ่าน pàan (pass) ม่าน mâan (curtain)
ด้าน dâan (face) ข้าง kâang (side) ค้าง káang (pending)
เป๊ะ bpé (exactly)
เดี๋ยว dǐiao (just a sec)

จีน jiin (Chinese) แขน kěɛn (arm) แคน kɛɛn (Thai organ)
จีบ jìip (flirt) แฉะ chè (humid) และ lé (and)
แลก lɛ̂ɛk (exchange)

กัน gan (prevent) เฉย chǒəi (calm) คำ kam (word)
กับ gàp (with) สด sòt (fresh) เยอะ yá (lots)
เงียบ ngîiap (quiet)

ไป bpai (go) ผิว pǐu (skin) ภัย pai (danger)
อีก ìik (another) ขาด kàat (torn) เคาะ kɔ́ (knock)
มีด mîit (knife)

If the syllable starts with a consonant cluster (see p. 27), the tone is determined by the class of the first consonant in the cluster. For example, ผลัก plàk (push) has a low tone because high-class ผ is first in the initial consonant cluster ผล. You will find many words with consonant clusters beginning with a silent ห (and four words with อ), whose sole purpose is to change the tone of that word:

ห + วาน waan (ask) = หวาน wǎan (sweet)
อ + ยาก yâak (hard) = อยาก yàak (want)

Silent ห or อ occur with the **Unpaired** consonants from p. 27.

Irregular Spellings

Thai is fairly phonetic, but here are some cases where the real Thai sound (which we show in our entries) doesn't match the Thai spelling. You just have to memorize these:

- **Vowel Length:** A lot of Thai words with long vowels and final consonants are actually pronounced short—many words with the ◌่ or ◌้ tone mark and sonorant finals (e.g. เล่น lên (play), ส้อม sɔ̂m (fork), but sometimes others too (e.g. เงิน ngən (money), เพชร pét (diamond)). A few words are irregularly long (e.g. เก้า gâao (nine)); some re-shorten in compounds (น้ำ náam (water), but น้ำแข็ง nám-kěng (ice); ได้ dâai (able to) but ได้ยิน dâi-yin (hear)).

- **Tone:** There are hundreds of common words where a syllable ending in **a** or **am** "forces" its consonant class onto the next syllable for tone rule purposes, such as ถนน tà~nǒn (road), ตำรวจ dtam-rùuat (policeman), and สนาม sà~nǎam (field). This nearly always happens when the first syllable has a **M**id or **H**igh initial consonant and the second syllable begins with a sonorant initial consonant (see p. 26), but not always (e.g. สมาชิก sà~maa-chík (member), not sà~mǎa-chík).

- **Junk Letters:** Quite a few (mostly formal) Thai words have silent, historical junk letters left in them (not always marked with ◌์ การันต์ gaa-ran), as in สามารถ sǎa-mâat (able to), พุทธ pút (Buddha), ชาติ châat (race).

- **Western Words:** All rules go out the window. Don't expect any tone to make sense, e.g. เบคอน bee-kôn (bacon), ไกด์ gái (guide), แอปเปิล ép-bpân (apple).

Some Thai words have **multiple pronunciations** (e.g. มกรา mók-gà~raa, má~gà~raa (January)) and some have **multiple spellings** (e.g. มนต์, มนตร์ mon (magic spell)). We show all possibilities in our Thai Sound and Thai Script section, but just one in our English section.

Dictionary Order

Thai dictionary order is based only on individual written symbols: it's oblivious to syllables, complex vowels, silent consonants, and whether symbols like ย serve as a consonant (e.g. ยา) or part of a vowel (e.g. เ–ย).

Simple Method: The Thai Script section has 46 tabs (ก–ฮ), seen on the edge of each page. To find your word, go to the tab for its first consonant (e.g. ก for ไก่, ห for หนาว). If your word begins with two consonants (e.g. กด, หนาว), find the second consonant near the beginning of the tab, otherwise look later in the tab for your word's first vowel symbol in this order: –ะ –ั –า –ำ –ิ –ี –ึ –ื –ุ –ู เ– แ– โ– ใ– ไ–
At this point you can often find the word on the page. If not, apply the rules above to the next consonant or vowel symbol. Ignore the marks –่ –้ –๊ –๋ –็ completely.

Real Method: The simple method works for finding most words, but is incomplete. The master order of symbols is:

ก ข ฃ ค ฅ ฆ ง จ ฉ ช ซ ฌ ญ ฎ ฏ ฐ ฑ ฒ ณ ด ต ถ ท ธ น บ ป ผ ฝ พ ฟ ภ ม ย ร ฤ ล ฦ ว ศ ษ ส ห ฬ อ ฮ	base symbols
–ะ –ั –า –ำ	after-symbols
–่ –้ –๊ –๋	above-symbols
–ุ –ู	below-symbols
เ– แ– โ– ใ– ไ–	before-symbols
ๆ	"repeat" symbol

See p. 27 for some tips on the order of base symbols.

To compare two words, ignore the marks –่ –้ –๊ –๋ –ั –็ and split up the remaining symbols of each word (e.g. กา → ก า, ผลัด → ผ ล –ั ด, ผิว → ผ –ิ ว, ตู้ → ต –ู). Now, compare the symbols of each word, side by side. If the two words have the same symbol, move on to the next symbol in each word. A word "wins" (sorts first) if it ends first, or its symbol comes first in the master order above:

กะ	กด	
ก	ก	same
–ะ	**ด**	กด wins!

ต้อง	ต่อ	
ต	ต	same
อ	อ	same
ง		ต่อ wins!

ผิว	ผลัด	
ผ	ผ	same
–ิ	**ล**	ผลัด wins!

But there's a trick: if a word has a before-symbol (e.g. เก),
compare the one symbol to the right of it first (ก then เ).
This is necessary to prevent all the เ– แ– โ– ใ– ไ– words from
clumping together in the dictionary:

ไก่	แห่	
ก	ห	ไก่ wins!

เกรง	เกย	
ก	ก	same
เ	เ	same
ร	ย	เกย wins!

เด็ก	เดช	
ด	ด	same
เ	เ	same
ก	ช	เด็ก wins!

If two words match exactly except for marks, break the tie
by comparing each position, left to right, with the ordering:
– (lack of a mark sorts first) ่ ้ ๊ ๋ ็ ์.

So, you can find your word by going to the tab for its first
consonant (e.g. ก for ไก่, ห for หนาว) then comparing your
word with dictionary words using the method above.

Unlike some dictionaries, we follow strict alphabetical
order and do not try to group "related" subwords (e.g.
น้ำแข็ง under น้ำ).

Some Thai dictionary guides present an alphabetical list of
Thai complex vowels (e.g. เ– เ–ย เ–ีย เ–ียะ). Such a list is
misleading because Thai is not really ordered that way. For
example, the three words เกม เกย เกรง appear in that order
even though เกย uses เ–ย and เกม/เกรง use เ–. In reality, it's
all based on individual symbols, not complex vowels.

Section One: English

See p. 2 for a guide on using this section.

A

a *art.* (one) เดียว diiao, หนึ่ง nÙng

abacus *n.* ลูกคิด lûuk-kít [ราง raang, ลูก lûuk]

abandon *v.* (desert) ทอดทิ้ง tɔ̂ɔt-tíng

abbot *n.* เจ้าอาวาส jâo-aa-wâat [รูป rûup]

abbreviate *vt.* ย่อ yɔ̂ɔ

abbreviation *n.* (letter) ตัวย่อ dtuua-yɔ̂ɔ [ตัว dtuua]

abdomen *n.* ท้อง tɔ́ɔng

abduct *vt.* ลักพาตัว lák-paa-dtuua

abet *v.* ช่วยเหลือ chûuai-lŮua

ability *n.* ความสามารถ kwaam-sǎa-mâat

able *adj.* (good at) เก่ง gèng

able to *vt.* ได้ dâai, สามารถ sǎa-mâat ⚡

abnormal *adj.* ผิดปกติ pìt-bpà-gà~dtì

aboard *adv.* (e.g. plane, boat, vehicle) บน bon

abolish *vt.* ล้มเลิก lóm-lə̂ək

abort *vt.* (cancel) ยกเลิก yók-lə̂ək

abortion *n.* การทำแท้ง gaan-tam-téng

about *adv.* (approx.) ประมาณ bprà~maan, ราวๆ raao-raao

about *prep.* (relating to) เกี่ยวกับ gìiao-gàp

above *prep.* (more than) มากกว่า mâak-gwàa | (over) เหนือ nŮua

abrasive *adj.* (material) กัดเซาะ gàt-sɔ́

abridge *v.* ย่อ yɔ̂ɔ

abroad *adv.* ต่างประเทศ dtàang-bprà~têet

abrupt *adj.* (sudden) ทันที tan-tii

absent *adj.* ขาด kàat, ไม่อยู่ mâi-yùu

absent-minded *adj.* ใจลอย jai-lɔɔi

absolute *adj.* (e.g. power, ruler) เด็ดขาด dèt-kàat

absolutely *adv.* อย่างแน่นอน yàang-nɛ̂ɛ-nɔɔn

absorb *vt.* ดูดซึม dùut-sʉm ⚡

abstain from *vt.* งดเว้น ngót-wén, อด òt ✶

abstract *adj.* (theoretical)

ทางทฤษฎี taang-trút-sà~dii

abstract n. (summary) บทคัดย่อ bòt-kát-yɔ̂ɔ [บท bòt]

abundant adj. มากมาย mâak-maai, อุดมสมบูรณ์ ù-dom-sǒm-buun

abuse vt. (bully, mistreat) ข่มเหง kòm-hěeng | (misuse) ใช้_ในทางที่ผิด chái-_-nai-taang-tîi-pìt

academic adj. ด้านวิชาการ dâan-wí-chaa-gaan

academy n. (academic institution) สถาบันการศึกษา sà~tǎa-ban-gaan-sùk-sǎa [แห่ง hèng]

accelerate vi. (speed up) เร่ง rêng

accelerator n. (gas pedal) คันเร่ง kan-rêng [อัน an]

accent n. (dialect, pronunciation) สำเนียง sǎm-niiang [สำเนียง sǎm-niiang]

accept v. ยอมรับ yɔɔm-ráp

acceptable adj. ยอมรับได้ yɔɔm-ráp-dâai

access vt. เข้าถึง kâo-tǔng

accessible adj. (easy to

approach) เข้าถึงได้ง่าย kâo-tǔng-dâi-ngâai

accessory n. (jewelry) เครื่องประดับ krûuang-bprà~dàp [ชิ้น chín (piece), ชุด chút (set)] | (part) อุปกรณ์ ùp-bpà~gɔɔn [ชิ้น chín (piece), ชุด chút (set)]

accident n. (e.g. car) อุบัติเหตุ ù-bàt-dtì~hèet [ครั้ง kráng]

accidental adj. บังเอิญ bang-əən

acclimate vi. (to weather) ปรับตัวให้ชินกับอากาศ bpràp-dtuua-hâi-chin-gàp-aa-gàat

accommodation n. (lodging) ที่พัก tîi-pák [แห่ง hèng]

accompany v. (go with) ไปด้วย bpai-dûuai

accomplice n. ผู้สมรู้ร่วมคิด pûu-sǒm-rúu-rûuam-kít ⚡ [คน kon]

accomplish vt. ทำ_สำเร็จ tam-_-sǎm-rèt

accomplishment n. ความสำเร็จ kwaam-sǎm-rèt

accordingly *adv.* ตามนั้น dtaam-nán

according to *prep.* ตามที่ dtaam-tîi

accordion *n.* หีบเพลง hìip-pleeng [เครื่อง krûuang]

account *n.* บัญชี ban-chii [เล่ม lêm]

accountant *n.* นักบัญชี nák-ban-chii [คน kon]

accounting *n.* การบัญชี gaan-ban-chii

accumulate *vt.* สะสม sà-sŏm

accurate *adj.* (correct) ถูกต้อง tùuk-dtôɔng | (precise) แม่นยำ mên-yam

accusation *n.* (charge) ข้อหา kɔ̂ɔ-hǎa [ข้อ kɔ̂ɔ]

accuse *vt.* (charge) กล่าวหา glàao-hǎa

accustomed to *adj.* ชิน chin, ชินกับ chin-gàp

ace *n.* (in playing cards) เอซ èet [ใบ bai]

ache *vi.* ปวด bpùuat

achieve *vi.* สำเร็จ sǎm-rèt

achieve *vt.* ทำ_สำเร็จ tam-_-sǎm-rèt

acid *n.* กรด gròt [ตัว dtuua]

acidity *n.* (hyperacidity) ความมีกรดมาก kwaam-mii-gròt-mâak | (sourness, tartness) ความเปรี้ยว kwaam-bprîiao

acknowledge *vt.* (admit the existence of) ยอมรับ yɔɔm-ráp | (recognize) รับรอง ráp-rɔɔng

acme *n.* จุดสูงสุด jùt-sǔung-sùt [จุด jùt]

acne *n.* สิว sǐu [เม็ด mét, หัว hǔua ✲]

acorn *n.* ผลต้นโอ๊ก pǒn-dtôn-óok [ลูก lûuk]

acquaintance *n.* คนรู้จัก kon-rúu-jàk [คน kon]

acquire *vt.* (something) ได้_มา dâi-_-maa

acquit *vt.* (e.g. of crime, debt) ปล่อย bplɔ̀i

acre *n.* เอเคอร์ ee-kêə

acrobat *n.* นักกายกรรม nák-gaai-yá~gam [คน kon]

acronym *n.* คำย่อจาก อักษรต้น kam-yɔ̂ɔ-jàak-àk-sɔ̌ɔn-dtôn [คำ kam]

across *adv.* (on the other side) ตรงข้าม dtrong-kâam

across *prep.* ตรงข้ามกับ dtrong-kâam-gàp

act *n.* (of a play) ฉาก chàak [ฉาก chàak]

act *vi.* (behave) ทำตัว tam-dtuua | (e.g. on TV) แสดง sà~dɛɛng | (take action) ลงมือทำ long-mɯɯ-tam

acting *adj.* (substitute) รักษาการแทน rák-sǎa-gaan-tɛɛn

action *n.* การกระทำ gaan-grà~tam

activate *vt.* (turn on) ให้_เริ่มทำงาน hâi-_-rôəm-tam-ngaan

active *adj.* (energetic) กระฉับกระเฉง grà~chàp-grà~chěeng | (fast, agile) คล่องแคล่ว klông-klɛ̂o

activity *n.* กิจกรรม gìt-jà~gam [ครั้ง kráng]

actor *n.* (male) ดาราชาย daa-raa-chaai [คน kon]

actress *n.* (female) ดาราหญิง daa-raa-yǐng [คน kon]

actual *adj.* จริง jing | (current) มีอยู่ในเวลานี้ mii-yùu-nai-wee-laa-níi

actually *adv.* จริงๆแล้ว jing-jing-lɛ́ɛo ✦

acupuncture *n.* การฝังเข็ม gaan-fǎng-kěm

acute *adj.* (e.g. injury) สาหัส sǎa-hàt | (e.g. storm) ฉับพลัน chàp-plan

A.D. *n.* คริสตศักราช krít-dtà~sàk-gà~ràat [ปี bpii]

adage *n.* สุภาษิต sù-paa-sìt [บท bòt]

adapt *vi.* (oneself) ปรับตัว bpràp-dtuua

adapt *vt.* (modify) ดัดแปลง dàt-bplɛɛng

adapter *n.* เครื่องแปลง krɯ̂ɯang-bplɛɛng [เครื่อง krɯ̂ɯang]

add *vt.* (fill up, increase) เติม dtəəm, เพิ่ม pôəm | (mix in) รวม ruuam | (numbers) บวก bùuak

addendum *n.* (appendix) ภาคผนวก pâak-pà~nùuak [ส่วน sùuan, ภาค pâak]

addict *n.* (drug) คนติดยา kon-dtìt-yaa, ขี้ยา kîi-yaa

✱ [คน kon]

addicted *adj*. (to drug)
ติดยา dtìt-yaa

additive *n*. สิ่งที่เพิ่มเข้าไป
sìng-tîi-pâ̂əm-kâo-bpai
[สิ่ง sìng, อัน an]

address *n*. (for mailing)
ที่อยู่ tîi-yùu [แห่ง hɛ̀ng] |
(greeting) คำทักทาย
kam-ták-taai

addressee *n*. ผู้รับ pûu-
ráp [คน kon]

adequate *adj*. พอเพียง
pɔɔ-piiang

adhesive *adj*. ติดแน่น
dtìt-nɛ̂n

adhesive tape *n*. เทปกาว
téep-gaao [ชนิด chá~nít]

adjective *n*. คำคุณศัพท์
kam-kun-ná~sàp [คำ
kam]

adjust *vt*. ปรับ bpràp

adjustable *adj*. ปรับได้
bpràp-dâai

administer *vt*. (manage)
บริหาร bɔɔ-rí~hǎan

administration *n*.
การบริหาร gaan-bɔɔ-rí~
hǎan

admire *vt*. ชื่นชม chû̂un-
chom

admission *n*. (confession)
คำสารภาพ kam-sǎa-rá~
pâap

admission fee *n*.
ค่าผ่านประตู kâa-pàan-
bprà~dtuu

admit *vt*. (accept) ยอมรับ
yɔɔm-ráp | (confess)
รับสารภาพ ráp-sǎa-rá~
pâap

admonish *vt*. (caution,
remind) ตักเตือน dtàk-
dtʉʉan

adolescent *n*. (teenager)
วัยรุ่น wai-rûn [คน kon]

adopt *vt*. (child,
informally) เลี้ยง_เป็นลูก
líiang-_-bpen-lûuk |
(child, legally)
รับ_เป็นบุตรบุญธรรม ráp-
_-bpen-bùt-bun-tam

adorable *adj*. น่าชื่นชม
nâa-chʉ̂ʉn-chom

adult *adj*. (for mature
audiences) สำหรับผู้ใหญ่
sǎm-ràp-pûu-yài

adult *n*. ผู้ใหญ่ pûu-yài
[คน kon]

adulterer *n*. (lover) ชู้
chúu [คน kon]

adulteress see adulterer

adultery n. การคบชู้ gaan-kóp-chúu

advance n. (money) เงินล่วงหน้า ngэn-lûuang-nâa [จำนวน jam-nuuan]

advance vi. (get promoted) เลื่อนขึ้น lûuan-kûn | (improve) ก้าวหน้า gâao-nâa

advanced adj. (high-level) ระดับสูง rá~dàp-sǔung | (improved) ก้าวหน้า gâao-nâa

advantage n. (favor) ความได้เปรียบ kwaam-dâi-bprìiap | (good point) ข้อดี kɔ̂ɔ-dii [ข้อ kɔ̂ɔ]

adventure n. การผจญภัย gaan-pà~jon-pai

adventurous adj. ชอบผจญภัย chɔ̂ɔp-pà~jon-pai

advertise v. โฆษณา koo-sà~naa

advertisement n. การโฆษณา gaan-koo-sà~naa

advice n. คำแนะนำ kam-né-nam [อัน an]

advise vt. (give advice to) แนะนำ né-nam

adviser n. ที่ปรึกษา tîi-bprùk-sǎa [ท่าน tân ❢, คน kon]

aerobic adj. แอโรบิก ɛɛ-roo-bìk

aerosol n. (liquid substance) ของเหลวอัดกระป๋อง kɔ̌ɔng-lěeo-àt-grà~bpɔ̌ng

affair n. (anything requiring action) งาน ngaan [งาน ngaan] | (errands, business) ธุระ tú-rá [เรื่อง rûuang, อัน an ✎] | (matter) เรื่อง rûuang [เรื่อง rûuang] | (romantic) เรื่องชู้สาว rûuang-chúu-sǎao

affect vt. มีผลกระทบต่อ mii-pǒn-grà~tóp-dtɔ̀ɔ

affection n. (fondness) ความเสน่หา kwaam-sà~nèe-hǎa

affectionate adj. รักใคร่ rák-krâi

affidavit n. คำให้การเป็น ลายลักษณ์อักษร kam-hâi-gaan-bpen-laai-lák-àk-sɔ̌ɔn

affirm vt. (e.g. statement)
ยืนยัน yʉʉn-yan

affix vt. (join, attach) ติด
dtìt

afford vt. (be able to buy)
ซื้อ_ได้ sʉʉ-_-dâai

affordable adj. พอซื้อได้
pɔɔ-sʉʉ-dâai

afraid adj. กลัว gluua

Africa n. อาฟริกา áa-frí-
gaa [ทวีป tá~wîip]

aft adv. (of a ship)
ข้างท้ายเรือ kâang-táai-
ruua

after adv. ภายหลัง paai-
lăng, หลัง lăng, หลังจาก
lăng-jàak

afternoon n. ตอนบ่าย
dtɔɔn-bàai, บ่าย bàai
[ตอน dtɔɔn]

afterward adv. (at a later
time) ภายหลัง paai-lăng |
(subsequently) จากนั้น
jàak-nán

afterwards see afterward

again adv. อีก ìik, ใหม่ mài
🔊

against prep. (e.g. wind,
institution) ต่อต้าน dtɔ̀ɔ-
dtâan | (in contact with)
ติดกับ dtìt-gàp | (on
opposite side)

อยู่ฝ่ายตรงข้าม yùu-fàai-
dtrong-kâam

age n. (e.g. young age,
middle age, old age) วัย
wai [วัย wai] | (era) ยุค
yúk [ยุค yúk] | (number
of years old) อายุ aa-yú

age vi. แก่ gὲὲ

aged adj. (of the age of,
having lived long) มีอายุ
mii-aa-yú

agency n. (representative)
ตัวแทน dtuua-tɛɛn [คน
kon (person), แห่ง hὲng
(place)]

agent n. (representative)
ตัวแทน dtuua-tɛɛn,
เอเย่นต์ ee-yên [คน kon
(person), แห่ง hὲng
(place)] | (spy) สายลับ
săai-láp [คน kon]

aggravate vt. (irritate)
ยั่วยุ yûua-yú | (worsen)
ทำให้_เลวลง tam-hâi-_-
leeo-long

aggression n. การบุกรุก
gaan-bùk-rúk

aggressive adj. ก้าวร้าว
gâao-ráao

agile adj. คล่องแคล่ว
klɔ̂ng-klɛ̂o

aging *adj.* แก่ตัวลง gÈɛ-dtuua-long

agitate *vt.* (mind) ทำให้_ร้อนใจ tam-hâi-_-rɔ́ɔn-jai

ago *adv.* ก่อน gɔ̀ɔn, มาแล้ว maa-lɛ́ɛo

agony *n.* (pain) ความเจ็บปวด kwaam-jèp-bpùuat

agree *v.* (with someone) เห็นด้วย hěn-dûuai

agree *vi.* (accept, promise) ตกลง dtòk-long

agreement *n.* สัญญา sǎn-yaa [ข้อ kɔ̂ɔ (clause), ฉบับ chà~bàp (whole)]

agriculture *n.* (livestock and crops) เกษตรกรรม gà~sèet-dtà~gam ! | (planting) กสิกรรม gà~sì~gam

ahead *adv.* (in front) ก่อน gɔ̀ɔn, หน้า nâa

ahead of *prep.* ข้างหน้า kâang-nâa

aid *n.* ความช่วยเหลือ kwaam-chûuai-lǔua

aid *vt.* ช่วยเหลือ chûuai-lǔua

AIDS *n.* โรคเอดส์ rôok-èet [โรค rôok]

ailing *adj.* (very sick) ป่วย bpùai

ailment *n.* โรคภัยไข้เจ็บ rôok-pai-kâi-jèp

aim *n.* (goal) เป้าหมาย bpâo-mǎai [อัน an]

aim *vt.* (e.g. gun) เล็ง leng

aimless *adj.* (without goal) ไร้จุดหมาย rái-jùt-mǎai

air *n.* (in tires) ลม lom | (outside air) อากาศ aa-gàat

air *v.* (broadcast) ออกอากาศ ɔ̀ɔk-aa-gàat

air bag *n.* ถุงลม tǔng lom [ใบ bai]

airborne *adj.* ทางอากาศ taang-aa-gàat

air-conditioned *adj.* ปรับอากาศ bpràp-aa-gàat

air conditioner *n.* เครื่องปรับอากาศ krûuang-bpràp-aa-gàat, แอร์ ɛɛ • [เครื่อง krûuang]

airfare *n.* ค่าเครื่องบิน kâa-krûuang-bin

air force *n.* กองทัพอากาศ gɔɔng-táp-aa-gàat [กอง gɔɔng]

airline *n.* สายการบิน sǎai-gaan-bin [สาย săai]

airmail *n.* ไปรษณีย์อากาศ bprai-sà~nii-aa-gàat

airplane *n.* เครื่องบิน krûuang-bin [ลำ lam, เครื่อง krûuang]

airport *n.* สนามบิน sà~năam-bin [แห่ง hèng]

aisle *n.* ทางเดินระหว่างที่นั่ง taang-dəən-rá~wàang-tîi-nâng [ทาง taang]

a.k.a. *adv.* เรียกอีกอย่างหนึ่งว่า rîiak-ìik-yàang-nùng-wâa

Akha *n.* (hilltribe) อาข่า aa-kàa [เผ่า pào]

a la carte *adj.* อาหารเป็นจานๆ aa-hăan-bpen-jaan-jaan

alarm *n.* สัญญาณ săn-yaan [สัญญาณ săn-yaan, เสียง sĭiang]

alarm *vt.* (distress) ทำให้_กลัว tam-hâi-_-gluua

alarm clock *n.* นาฬิกาปลุก naa-lí~gaa-bplùk [เรือน ruuan]

album *n.* อัลบั้ม aa-lá~bâm [เล่ม lêm]

alcohol *n.* (chemical) แอลกอฮอล์ ɛn-gɔɔ-hɔɔ | (liquor) เหล้า lâo [ขวด kùuat (bottle), แก้ว gɛ̂ɛo (glass)]

alcoholic *adj.* (containing alcohol) มีแอลกอฮอล์ mii-ɛn-gɔɔ-hɔɔ

alcoholic *n.* (addict) คนติดเหล้า kon-dtìt-lâo [คน kon]

ale *n.* เหล้าที่ทำจากข้าวมอลต์ lâo-tîi-tam-jàak-kâao-mɔɔ

alert *adj.* ตื่นตัว dtùun-dtuua

algae *n.* สาหร่าย săa-ràai [ชนิด chá~nít]

algebra *n.* พีชคณิต pii-chá-ká~nít [วิชา wí-chaa]

alias *n.* นามแฝง naam-fɛ̌ɛng [นาม naam]

alibi *n.* การอ้างฐานที่อยู่เป็นข้อแก้ตัว gaan-âang-tăan-tîi-yùu-bpen-kɔ̂ɔ-gɛ̂ɛ-dtuua

alien *n.* (immigrant) ชาวต่างด้าว chaao-dtàang-dâao [ชาว chaao]

alike *adv.* เหมือนกัน

mǔuan-gan

alimony *n.* ค่าเลี้ยงดูภรรยา kâa-líiang-duu-pan-rá~ yaa [จำนวน jam-nuuan]

a little bit *adv.* นิดหน่อย nít-nòi

alive *adj.* (living) เป็น bpen, มีชีวิต mii-chii-wít

alkali *n.* ด่าง dàang

all *adj.* (every) ทุก túk

all *adv.* (entirely) ทั้งหมด táng-mòt

all *pron.* (everyone) ทุกคน túk-kon

all-around *adj.* (broadly) รอบด้าน rɔ̂ɔp-dâan

allegation *n.* (charge) ข้อหา kɔ̂ɔ-hǎa [ข้อ kɔ̂ɔ]

allege *vt.* (charge) กล่าวหา glàao-hǎa, ฟ้องร้อง fɔ́ɔng-rɔ́ɔng

allegory *n.* การเปรียบเทียบ gaan-bpriiap-tîiap

allergic *adj.* (to something) แพ้ pɛ́ɛ

allergy *n.* โรคภูมิแพ้ rôok-puum-pɛ́ɛ [โรค rôok]

alleviate *vt.* บรรเทา ban-tao

alley *n.* (lane) ซอย sɔɔi [ซอย sɔɔi]

alliance *n.* พันธมิตร pan-tá~mít [กลุ่ม glùm]

alligator *n.* จระเข้ jɔɔ-rá~ kêe [ตัว dtuua]

all night *adv.* ทั้งคืน táng-kuun

allot *vt.* (distribute) แจกจ่าย jɛ̀ɛk-jàai

all over *adv.* (throughout) ตลอด dtà~lɔ̀ɔt

all over *prep.* (throughout) ทั่ว tûua

allow *vt.* (permit) อนุญาตให้ à-nú-yâat-hâi

allowance *n.* (money) เงินใช้สอย ngən-chái-sɔ̌ɔi [จำนวน jam-nuuan]

alloy *n.* โลหะผสม loo-hà-pà~sǒm

all right *adj.* (feeling well) สบายดี sà~baai-dii | (safe) ปลอดภัย bplɔ̀ɔt-pai

all right *idm.* (yes) ใช่ châi

all-round see all-around

all the time *adv.* ตลอดเวลา dtà~lɔ̀ɔt-wee-laa

all the way *adv.* ตลอดทาง dtà~lɔ̀ɔt-taang

all-time adj. (greatest)
ยิ่งใหญ่ที่สุด yîng-yài-tîi-
sùt | (never surpassed)
ไม่เป็นรองใคร mâi-bpen-
rɔɔng-krai

ally n. ฝ่ายพันธมิตร fàai-
pan-tá~mít [ฝ่าย fàai]

almost adv. เกือบ gùuap

alms n. (for monks)
สังฆทาน sǎng-ká~taan
[ชุด chút]

aloe n. หางจระเข้ hǎang-
jɔɔ-rá~kêe [ต้น dtôn]

alone adj. (one person)
คนเดียว kon-diiao |
(oneself) เอง eeng |
(without friends)
ไม่มีเพื่อน mâi-mii-pûuan

alone adv. (by oneself)
ลำพัง lam-pang

along prep. (e.g. road)
ตาม dtaam

along with prep.
ด้วยกันกับ dûuai-gan-gàp

a lot adv. มาก mâak

a lot of adj. มาก mâak

aloud adv. อย่างดัง
yàang-dang

alphabet n. ชุดตัวอักษร
chút-dtuua-àk-sɔ̌ɔn ✘
[ชุด chút]

alphabetical adj.
เรียงตามอักษร riiang-
dtaam-àk-sɔ̌ɔn

already adv. แล้ว lέεo

also adv. ก็ gɔ̂ɔ, ด้วย
dûuai, และ lέ, เหมือนกัน
mǔuan-gan

alter v. (modify) เปลี่ยน
bplìian

alternate vi. สลับกัน sà~
làp-gan

alternative n. ทางเลือก
taang-lûuak [ทาง taang]

although conj. ถึงแม้ว่า
tǔng-mέε-wâa, ทั้งที่
táng-tîi ✦

altitude n. (elevation)
ความสูงเหนือระดับน้ำทะเล
kwaam-sǔung-nǔua-
rá~dàp-nám-tá~lee

altogether adj. (total)
รวมทั้งหมด ruuam-
táng-mòt

aluminum n. อลูมิเนียม
à~luu-mí~niiam

alumni n. ศิษย์เก่า sìt-gào
[คน kon]

always adv. ตลอดเวลา
dtà~lɔɔt-wee-laa, เสมอ
sà~mɔ̌ɔ

Alzheimer's disease n.

โรคความจำเสื่อม rôok-kwaam-jam-sùuam [โรค rôok]

a.m. *adv.* ก่อนเที่ยง gɔ̀ɔn-tîiang

am see be

amateur *n.* มือสมัครเล่น muu-sà~màk-lên [คน kon]

amazed *adj.* ประหลาดใจ bprà~làat-jai

amazing *adj.* น่าทึ่ง nâa-tûng, น่าประหลาดใจ nâa-bprà~làat-jai

ambassador *n.* เอกอัครราชทูต èek-àk-ká~râat-chá~tûut [ท่าน tân ⚑, คน kon]

amber *n.* (fossil resin) อำพัน am-pan [ก้อน gɔ̂ɔn]

ambidextrous *adj.* ถนัดทั้งสองมือ tà~nàt-táng-sɔ̌ɔng-muu

ambiguous *adj.* กำกวม gam-guuam

ambitious *adj.* ทะเยอทะยาน tá~yəə-tá~yaan

ambulance *n.* รถพยาบาล rót-pá~yaa-baan [คัน kan]

ambush *vt.* ซุ่มโจมตี sûm-joom-dtii, ลอบทำร้าย lɔ̂ɔp-tam-ráai

amen! *interj.* สาธุ sǎa-tú, อาเมน aa-men

amend *vt.* (correct) แก้ไข gɛ̂ɛ-kǎi | (improve) ปรับปรุง bpràp-bprung

America *n.* อเมริกา à~mee-rí~gaa, สหรัฐอเมริกา sà~hà-rát-à~mee-rí~gaa ⚑ [ประเทศ bprà~têet]

amethyst *n.* เขี้ยวหนุมาน kîiao-hà~nú~maan

amino acid *n.* กรดอะมิโน gròt-à~mí~noo

ammunition *n.* (dynamite) ดินระเบิด din-rá~bèət [ก้อน gɔ̂ɔn]

amnesia *n.* อาการหลงลืม aa-gaan-lǒng-luum

amnesty *n.* การอภัยโทษ gaan-à~pai-yá~tôot

among *prep.* (in the midst of) ระหว่าง rá~wàang | (surrounded by) ท่ามกลาง tâam-glaang

amongst see among

amount *n.* จำนวน jam-nuuan [จำนวน jam-nuuan]

amp see ampere

ampere *n.* แอมป์ ɛm

amphetamine *n.*
แอมเฟตามีน ɛm-fét-
dtaa-miin ✕ | ยาบ้า yaa-
bâa ❀ [เม็ด mét]

amphibian *n.* (animal)
สัตว์ครึ่งบกครึ่งน้ำ sàt-
krûng-bòk-krûng-náam
[ตัว dtuua, ชนิด chá~nít
(kind)]

amplifier *n.*
เครื่องขยายเสียง
krûuang-kà~yǎai-sǐiang
[เครื่อง krûuang]

amplify *vt.* (increase)
ขยาย kà~yǎai

amputate *vt.* ตัด_ออก
dtàt-_-ɔ̀ɔk

amputated *adj.* ด้วน
dûuan

amulet *n.* เครื่องราง
krûuang-raang [ชิ้น chín,
อัน an]

amuse *vt.* (entertain)
ทำให้_สนุก tam-hâi-_-
sà~nùk | (make laugh)
ทำให้_หัวเราะ tam-hâi-_-
hǔua-rɔ́

amused *adj.* (by
performance) เพลิดเพลิน
plə̂ət-pləən | (pleased)

ชอบใจ chɔ̂ɔp-jai

amusement *n.* (anything
that amuses)
สิ่งที่ทำให้สนุกสนาน sìng-
tîi-tam-hâi-sà~nùk-sà~
nǎan

amusement park *n.*
สวนสนุก sǔuan-sà~nùk
[แห่ง hèng]

amusing *adj.*
(entertaining) สนุก sà~
nùk, สนุกสนาน sà~nùk-
sà~nǎan | (funny)
น่าหัวเราะ nâa-hǔua-rɔ́

an see a

anal *adj.* ทางทวาร taang-
tá~waan, ทางตูด taang-
dtùut ☆

analog *adj.* อะนาลอก à~
naa-lɔ̂ɔk

analogy *n.*
การเปรียบเทียบ gaan-
bpriiap-tîiap

analysis *n.* การวิเคราะห์
gaan-wí-krɔ́

analyst *n.* นักวิเคราะห์
nák-wí-krɔ́ [คน kon]

analyze *vt.* วิเคราะห์ wí-krɔ́

anatomy *n.* กายวิภาค
ศาสตร์ gaai-yá~wí-pâak-
sàat [วิชา wí-chaa]

ancestor *n.* บรรพบุรุษ

ban-pá-bù~rùt

anchor *n.* สมอเรือ sà~mɔ̌ɔ-ruua [ตัว dtuua]

ancient *adj.* (antiquated) โบราณ boo-raan | (old) เก่า gào

and *conj.* กับ gàp, และ lɛ́, กะ gà ✸

and/or *prep.* และหรือ lɛ́-rǔu

anecdote *n.* เกร็ด grèt [อัน an]

anemia *n.* โรคโลหิตจาง rôok-loo-hìt-jaang ! [โรค rôok]

anesthetic *n.* ยาชา yaa-chaa

anesthetist *n.* หมอวางยาสลบ mɔ̌ɔ-waang-yaa-sà~lòp [คน kon]

angel *n.* (female) นางฟ้า naang-fáa [องค์ ong] | (male) เทวดา tee-wá~daa [องค์ ong]

anger *n.* ความโกรธ kwaam-gròot

angle *n.* มุม mum [มุม mum]

angry *adj.* โกรธ gròot, โมโห moo-hǒo

anguish *n.* (agony)

ความเจ็บปวด kwaam-jèp-bpùuat | (grief) ความโศกเศร้า kwaam-sòok-sâo

animal *n.* สัตว์ sàt [ตัว dtuua, ชนิด chá~nít (kind)]

animation *n.* (cartoon) การ์ตูนที่เคลื่อนไหวได้ gaa-dtuun-tîi-klʉ̂uan-wǎi-dâai [ภาพ pâap, ตัว dtuua]

aniseed *n.* ยี่หร่า yîi-ràa [ต้น dtôn (plant), ใบ bai (leave)]

ankle *n.* ข้อเท้า kɔ̂ɔ-táao [ข้อ kɔ̂ɔ]

anklebone *n.* ตาตุ่ม dtaa-dtùm [ข้าง kâang (of one leg), คู่ kûu (of both legs)]

anklet *n.* กำไลเท้า gam-lai-táao [วง wong]

annex *n.* (building) โรงเรือนต่อกับตึกใหญ่ roong-ruuan-dtɔ̀ɔ-gàp-dtʉ̀k-yài [หลัง lǎng]

anniversary *n.* วันครบรอบปี wan-króp-rɔ̂ɔp-bpii [วัน wan]

announce *vi.* ประกาศ bprà~gàat

B
C
D
E
F
G
H
I
J
K
L
M
N
O
P
Q
R
S
T
U
V
W
X
Y
Z

announce *vt.* แจ้ง jɛ̂ɛng

announcement *n.* การประกาศ gaan-bprà~gàat [ครั้ง kráng]

announcer *n.* โฆษก koo-sòk, ผู้ประกาศ pûu-bprà~gàat [คน kon]

annoy *vt.* ทำให้_รำคาญ tam-hâi-_-ram-kaan, รบกวน róp-guuan

annoyed *adj.* เคือง kɯɯang, รำคาญ ram-kaan

annoying *adj.* น่ารำคาญ nâa-ram-kaan

annual *adj.* ทุกปี túk-bpii, ประจำปี bprà~jam-bpii

annually *adv.* ประจำปี bprà~jam-bpii

annul *vt.* ยกเลิก yók-lə̂ək

anonymous *adj.* นิรนาม ní-rá~naam

another *adj.* อีก ìik, อื่น ɯ̀ɯn

answer *n.* คำตอบ kam-dtɔ̀ɔp [ข้อ kɔ̂ɔ]

answer *v.* ตอบ dtɔ̀ɔp | (phone) รับ ráp

answering machine *n.* เครื่องรับฝากข้อความ krɯ̂ɯang-ráp-fàak-kɔ̂ɔ-kwaam [เครื่อง krɯ̂ɯang]

ant *n.* มด mót [ตัว dtuua]

antacid *n.* ยาลดกรด yaa-lót-gròt [ขวด kùuat (bottle)]

Antarctica *n.* แอนตาร์คติกา ɛɛn-dtáak-dtì~gâa [ทวีป tá~wîip]

antenna *n.* (transmission) เสาอากาศ sǎo-aa-gàat [ต้น dtôn]

anthem *n.* (national) เพลงชาติ pleeng-châat [เพลง pleeng]

anthropology *n.* มานุษยวิทยา maa-nút-sà~yá-wít-tá~yaa [วิชา wí-chaa]

anti- *pref.* ปฏิ bpà~dtì- !

antibiotic *adj.* ปฏิชีวนะ bpà~dtì-chii-wá~ná

anticipate *vt.* (look forward to) คาดหวัง kâat-wǎng

anticlockwise see counterclockwise

antidiarrheal *n.* ยาแก้ท้องเสีย yaa-gɛ̂ɛ-tɔ́ɔng-sǐia

antidote *n.* ยาแก้พิษ yaa-gɛ̂ɛ-pít

antihistamine *n.* ยาแก้แพ้

yaa-gêe-péε

anti-inflammatory n.
ยาแก้อักเสบ yaa-gêe-àk-
sèep

antioxidant n.
สารต้านอนุมูลอิสระ săan-
dtâan-à-nú-muun-ìt-sà~
rà [ตัว dtuua]

antique adj. โบราณ boo-
raan

antique n. ของเก่า
kŏng-gào, โบราณวัตถุ
boo-raan-ná~wát-tù ‼
[ตัว dtuua (furniture), ชิ้น
chín (piece)]

anus n. ทวารหนัก tá~
waan-nàk, ตูด dtùut ✦,
ดาก dàak ⚥

anxiety n. ความกังวล
kwaam-gang-won

anxious adj. (eager)
ร้อนใจ rón-jai | (worried)
กังวล gang-won, หนักใจ
nàk-jai

any adj. (some) บาง
baang | (whatsoever) ใด
dai ‼

any adv. (to some extent)
บ้าง bâang

anybody pron. ใครก็ได้
krai-gɔ̂ɔ-dâai, ใครๆ krai-

krai ✦ | (in question) ใคร
krai

anyhow adv. อย่างไรก็ตาม
yàang-rai-gɔ̂ɔ-dtaam,
ยังไงก็ตาม yang-ngai-
gɔ̂ɔ-dtaam ✦

anymore adv. อีกต่อไป
ìik-dtɔ̀ɔ-bpai

anyone see anybody

anything pron. อะไรก็ได้
à~rai-gɔ̂ɔ-dâai,
อะไรก็ตาม à~rai-gɔ̂ɔ-
dtaam ‼ | (in question)
อะไร à~rai

anytime adv. ทุกเวลา
túk-wee-laa, เมื่อไหร่ก็ได้
mûɑ-rài-gɔ̂ɔ-dâai ✦

anyway adv. อย่างไรก็ตาม
yàang-rai-gɔ̂ɔ-dtaam,
ยังไงก็ตาม yang-ngai-
gɔ̂ɔ-dtaam ✦

anyways adv. ยังไงก็ตาม
yang-ngai-gɔ̂ɔ-dtaam ✦

anywhere adv. ที่ไหนก็ได้
tîi-năi-gɔ̂ɔ-dâai

apart adv. (separated)
ห่างกัน hàang-gan

apart from adv. นอกจาก
nɔ̂ɔk-jàak

apartment n.
อาพาร์ตเมนท์ aa-páat-

mén [ห้อง hɔ̂ng]

ape n. ลิง ling [ตัว dtuua]

apologize vi. ขอโทษ kɔ̌ɔ-tôot, ขออภัย kɔ̌ɔ-à~pai !

apparatus n. (appliance) อุปกรณ์ ùp-bpà~gɔɔn [ชิ้น chín (piece), ชุด chút (set)] | (tool) เครื่องมือ krûuang-mɯɯ [ชิ้น chín (piece), ชุด chút (set)]

apparel n. (attire) เครื่องแต่งกาย krûuang-dtɛ̀ng-gaai [ชุด chút (set), ตัว dtuua (piece)]

apparent adj. (obvious) เด่นชัด dèn-chát

appeal vi. (request new hearing) อุทธรณ์ ùt-tɔɔn

appeal to vt. (attract) ดึงดูดใจ dɯng-dùut-jai | (beg) อ้อนวอน ɔ̂ɔn-wɔɔn

appear vi. (be in sight) ปรากฏ bpraa-gòt | (present oneself) ปรากฏตัว bpraa-gòt-dtuua

appearance n. (look) ลักษณะ lák-sà~nà | (look) ท่าทาง tâa-taang [ท่า tâa] | (presentation

of oneself) การปรากฏตัว gaan-bpraa-gòt-dtuua [ครั้ง kráng]

appear in court vi. ขึ้นศาล kɯ̂n-sǎan

appease vt. (pacify) ระงับ rá~ngáp | (satisfy, please) เอาใจ ao-jai

appendicitis n. ไส้ติ่งอักเสบ sâi-dtìng-àk-sèep [ก้อน gɔ̂ɔn]

appendix n. (addendum) ภาคผนวก pâak-pà~nùuak [ส่วน sùuan, ภาค pâak] | (body part) ไส้ติ่ง sâi-dtìng [ก้อน gɔ̂ɔn, อัน an]

appetite n. ความเจริญอาหาร kwaam-jà~rəən-aa-hǎan

appetizer n. อาหารเรียกน้ำย่อย aa-hǎan-rîiak-nám-yɔ̂i [จาน jaan]

applaud vi. (clap) ปรบมือ bpròp-mɯɯ

applause n. (clapping sound) เสียงปรบมือ sǐiang-bpròp-mɯɯ [เสียง sǐiang]

apple n. แอปเปิล ép-bpə̂n

[ลูก lûuk (fruit)]

appliance *n.* (device) เครื่องใช้ krûuang-chái [ชิ้น chín (piece), ชุด chút (set)]

applicant *n.* (one who applies) ผู้สมัคร pûu-sà~màk [คน kon]

application *n.* (act of applying) การสมัคร gaan-sà~màk | (computer program) แอปพลิเคชั่น ép-plí~kee-chân

application form *n.* ใบสมัคร bai-sà~màk [ใบ bai]

applied *adj.* ประยุกต์ bprà~yúk

apply *vt.* (e.g. cream or medicine) ทา taa

apply for *vt.* (e.g. a job) สมัคร sà~màk

appoint *vt.* (to a position) แต่งตั้ง dtɛ̀ng-dtâng

appointment *n.* (e.g. doctor) การนัดหมาย gaan-nát-mǎai [ครั้ง kráng] | (e.g. friend) นัด nát [ครั้ง kráng]

appraisal *n.* การประเมิน gaan-bprà~məən

appraise *vt.* (estimate the price of) ตีราคา dtii-raa-kaa | (evaluate) ประเมิน bprà~məən

appreciate *vt.* (be grateful for) รู้คุณค่าของ rúu-kun-kâa-kɔ̌ɔng | (cherish) ชื่นชม chûun-chom

appreciation *n.* (thankfulness) ความขอบคุณ kwaam-kɔ̀ɔp-kun

apprehend *vt.* (arrest) จับ jàp

apprehensive *adj.* (fearful) กลัว gluua

approach *n.* (means, method) วิธีการ wí-tii-gaan [วิธี wí-tii]

approach *v.* (come near) เข้าใกล้ kâo-glâi

approach *vt.* (go see) เข้าหา kâo-hǎa

appropriate *adj.* (proper) สมควร sǒm-kuuan | (suitable) เหมาะสม mɔ̀-sǒm

approval *n.* (consent) การยินยอม gaan-yin-yɔɔm

approve vi. (agree)
ยินยอม yin-yɔɔm

approve vt. (formally, e.g.
budget) อนุมัติ à-nú-mát

approximate adj. (near)
ใกล้เคียง glâi-kiiang

approximate v.
(estimate) ประมาณ
bprà~maan

approximately adv.
(around) ประมาณ
bprà~maan, ราวๆ raao-
raao

apricot n. แอพปริคอท ɛ́p-
bprì~kɔ́t [ลูก lûuk (fruit)]

April n. เมษายน mee-
sǎa-yon [เดือน dɯɯan]

apron n. ผ้ากันเปื้อน pâa-
gan-bpûɯan [ผืน pɯ̌ɯn]

aptitude n. (ability)
ความถนัด kwaam-tà~nàt

aquarium n. (fish bowl)
ตู้ปลา dtûu-bplaa [ตู้
dtûu] | (museum)
พิพิธภัณฑ์สัตว์น้ำ pí-pít-
tá~pan-sàt-náam [แห่ง
hɛ̀ng]

Aquarius n. ราศีกุมภ์ raa-
sǐi-gum [ราศี raa-sǐi]

Arab n. ชาวอาหรับ chaao-
aa-ràp [คน kon]

Arabic adj. อาราบิค aa-rá~
bìk

Arabic numeral n.
เลขอาราบิค lêek-aa-rá~bìk
[ตัว dtuua]

arbitrator n. คนกลาง
kon-glaang [คน kon]

arc n. (curve) ส่วนโค้ง
sùuan-kóong [ส่วน
sùuan]

arcade n. (shopping)
ย่านขายของ yâan-kǎai-
kɔ̌ɔng [แห่ง hɛ̀ng] |
(video) แหล่งเล่นเกม
lɛ̀ng-lên-geem [แห่ง
hɛ̀ng, ที่ tîi]

arch n. (doorway)
ประตูโค้ง bprà~dtuu-
kóong [บาน baan]

archaeology n. โบราณคดี
boo-raan-ná~ká~dii
[วิชา wí-chaa]

archer n. นักยิงธนู nák-
ying-tá~nuu [คน kon]

archipelago n. หมู่เกาะ
mùu-gò [แห่ง hɛ̀ng]

architect n. (building)
สถาปนิก sà~tǎa-bpà~ník
[คน kon]

architecture n.
สถาปัตยกรรม sà~tǎa-

bpàt-dtà~yá~gam [วิชา wí-chaa]

are see be

area n. (district, e.g. election) เขต kèet [แห่ง hɛ̀ng] | (surface area) พื้นที่ púun-tîi [แห่ง hɛ̀ng] | (vicinity, zone) บริเวณ bɔɔ-rí~ween, แถว tɛ̌ɛo ☙ [แห่ง hɛ̀ng]

area code n. รหัสโทรศัพท์ rá~hàt-too-rá~sàp [ตัว dtuua]

arena n. สนามกีฬา sà~năam-gii-laa [แห่ง hɛ̀ng]

argue vi. (talk back, dispute) เถียงกัน tǐiang-gan

argument n. (dispute) การโต้เถียง gaan-dtôo-tǐiang

Aries n. ราศีเมษ raa-sǐi-mêet [ราศี raa-sǐi]

arise vi. (happen) เกิดขึ้น gɤ̀ɤt-kɤ̂n

arithmetic n. เลขคณิต lêek-ká~nít [วิชา wí-chaa]

arm n. (body part) แขน kɛ̌ɛn [ข้าง kâang] | (weapon) อาวุธ aa-wút [ชิ้น chín]

arm vt. (give weapons to) ติดอาวุธให้ dtìt-aa-wút-hâi

armed adj. มีอาวุธ mii-aa-wút

armor n. เกราะ grɔ̀ [ชุด chút (suit)]

armpit n. รักแร้ rák-rɛ́ɛ [ข้าง kâang]

army n. (military forces) กองทัพบก gɔɔng-táp-bòk [กอง gɔɔng]

aroma n. กลิ่นหอม glìn-hɔ̌ɔm

around prep. (approximately) ประมาณ bprà~maan | (in circle, around edge) รอบ rɔ̂ɔp | (in same area) ใกล้ glâi, ใกล้ๆ glâi-glâi

arouse vt. กระตุ้น grà~dtûn | (sexually) ปลุก bplùk

arrange vt. (manage, prepare) จัด jàt, จัดการ jàt-gaan

arrest vt. (e.g. police) จับ jàp

arrest warrant n. หมายจับ mǎai-jàp [ใบ bai, ฉบับ chà~bàp ☝]

arrival n. การมาถึง gaanmaa-tǔng

arrive *vi.* ถึง tǔng

arrive at *vt.* ถึง tǔng

arrogant *adj.* หยิ่ง yìng

arrow *n.* (symbol) ลูกศร lûuk-rǒɔn [ตัว dtuua] | (weapon) ศร rɔ̌ɔn ➤ | (weapon) ลูกธนู lûuk-tá~nuu [ดอก dɔ̀ɔk]

arsenal *n.* คลังอาวุธ klang-aa-wút

arson *n.* การลอบวางเพลิง gaɛn-lɔ̂ɔp-waang-pləəng [ครั้ง kráng]

art *n.* ศิลปะ sǐn-lá~bpà

artery *n.* (blood vessel) เส้นเลือดแดง sên-lɯ̂at-dɛɛng [เส้น sên]

art gallery *n.* ที่แสดงงานศิลปะ tîi-sà~dɛɛng-ngaan-sǐn-lá~bpà [แห่ง hɛ̀ng]

arthritis *n.* โรคข้ออักเสบ rôok-kɔ̂ɔ-àk-sèep [โรค rôok]

article *n.* (e.g. newspaper) บทความ bòt-kwaam [เรื่อง rɯ̂ang] | (object, thing) สิ่งของ sìng-kɔ̌ɔng [อัน an, ชิ้น chín] | (part

of speech) คำนำหน้านาม kam-nam-nâa-naam [คำ kam]

articulate *vi.* พูดชัดเจน pûut-chát-jeen

artificial *adj.* (fake) เทียม tiiam | (synthetic) สังเคราะห์ sǎng-krɔ́ | (unnatural) ไม่ธรรมชาติ mâi-tam-má~châat

artificial insemination *n.* การผสมเทียม gaan-pà~sǒm-tiiam

artisan *n.* ช่างฝีมือ châng-fǐi-mɯɯ [คน kon]

artist *n.* ศิลปิน sǐn-lá~bpin [คน kon]

as *adv.* (in the same manner, equally) เหมือนกับ mɯ̌an-gàp

as *conj.* (while) ตอนที่ dtɔɔn-tîi

as *prep.* (that, which) ที่ tîi

as before *adv.* ตามเดิม dtaam-dəəm

as far as *adv.* (just, only) แค่ kɛ̂ɛ, เพียง piiang

as far as *prep.* เท่าที่ tâo-tîi

ash *n.* (fire residue) ขี้เถ้า kîi-tâo [ผง pǒng] | (from cremation) อัฐิ àt-tì [ผง

pǒng (dust), ชิ้น chín (piece)]

ashamed *adj.* (at losing face) ขายหน้า kǎai-nâa | (embarrassed at mistake) อาย aai | (guilty about transgression) รู้สึกผิด rúu-sùk-pìt, ละอายใจ lá~aai-jai

ashore *adv.* เทียบฝั่ง tîiap-fàng

ashtray *n.* ที่เขี่ยบุหรี่ tîi-kìia-bù~rìi [อัน an]

Asia *n.* เอเชีย ee-chiia [ทวีป tá~wîip]

Asian *n.* คนเอเชีย kon-ee-chiia [คน kon]

aside *adv.* (to the side) ข้างๆ kâang-kâang, ไปทางข้าง bpai-taang-kâang

aside from *prep.* นอกจาก nɔ̂ɔk-jàak

as if *conj.* ราวกับว่า raao-gàp-wâa

ask *v.* (question) ถาม tǎam

ask for *vt.* ขอ kɔ̌ɔ

asleep *adj.* นอนหลับ nɔɔn-làp, หลับ làp

as long as *conj.* จนกว่า

jon-gwàa, เท่าที่ tâo-tîi

asparagus *n.* หน่อไม้ฝรั่ง nɔ̀ɔ-máai-fà~ràng [ต้น dtôn]

aspect *n.* (appearance) ลักษณะ lák-sà~nà [อย่าง yàang] | (point of view) แง่มุม ngɛ̂ɛ-mum [มุม mum]

aspirin *n.* แอสไพริน ɛ̀ɛs-pai-rin [เม็ด mét]

ass *n.* (bottom) ก้น gôn, ตูด dtùut 💣 | (donkey) ลา laa [ตัว dtuua]

assassinate *vt.* ลอบฆ่า lɔ̂ɔp-kâa

assassination *n.* การลอบสังหาร gaan-lɔ̂ɔp-sǎng-hǎan ⚡

assault *vt.* (raid) โจมตี joom-dtii

assemble *vi.* (people) รวมตัวกัน ruuam-dtuua-gan

assemble *vt.* (put things together) ประกอบ bprà~gɔ̀ɔp

assert *vt.* (insist) ยืนยัน yʉʉn-yan

assessment *n.* การประเมิน gaan-bprà~məən

asset *n.* (property)

ทรัพย์สิน sáp-sǐn ! [ชิ้น chín]

asshole *n.* ทวารหนัก tá~waan-nàk, รูก้น ruu-gôn !

assign *vt.* (designate) มอบหมาย mɔ̂ɔp-mǎai

assignment *n.* (duty) หน้าที่ nâa-tii [หน้าที่ nâa-tii] | (homework) การบ้าน gaan-bâan [อย่าง yàang]

assist *v.* (help) ช่วย chûai

assistance *n.* การช่วยเหลือ gaan-chûai-lǔ̌a

assistant *n.* ผู้ช่วย pûu-chûai [คน kon]

associate with *vt.* (interact with socially) คบหา kóp-hǎa

association *n.* (society) สมาคม sà~maa-kom [แห่ง hɛ̀ng]

as soon as *conj.* ทันทีที่ tan-tii-tîi, พอ pɔɔ !

assorted *adj.* คละกัน klá-gan

assume *v.* (presume) สันนิษฐาน sǎn-nít-tǎan | (suppose) สมมุติ sǒm-mút

assumption *n.* (presumption)

การสันนิษฐาน gaan-sǎn-ní-tǎan

assure *vt.* (guarantee, insure) ประกัน bprà~gan | (reassure) ยืนยันกับ yʉʉn-yan-gàp

asthma *n.* โรคหอบหืด rôok-hɔ̀ɔp-hʉ̀ʉt

as though *conj.* ราวกับ raao-gàp

astonish *vt.* (amaze) ทำให้_ประหลาดใจ tam-hâi-_-bprà~làat-jai

astringent *adj.* (taste, e.g. underripe fruit) ฝาด fàat

astringent *n.* (medicine) ยาสมาน yaa-sà~mǎan

astrology *n.* โหราศาสตร์ hǒo-raa-sàat [วิชา wí-chaa]

astronaut *n.* นักบินอวกาศ nák-bin-à~wà~gàat [คน kon]

astronomy *n.* ดาราศาสตร์ daa-raa-sàat [วิชา wí-chaa]

as usual *adv.* เช่นเคย chên-kəəi

as well *adv.* ด้วย dûai, เหมือนกัน mǔ̌an-gan

as well as *conj.* เช่นเดียวกับ chên-diiao-gàp

asylum *n.* (mental hospital)
โรงพยาบาลคนบ้า roong-pá~yaa-baan-kon-bâa [แห่ง hèng] | (sanctuary)
สถานที่ลี้ภัย sà~tǎan-tîi-líi-pai [แห่ง hèng]

at *prep.* (place) ที่ tîi, ใน nai | (time) ตอน dtɔɔn

at all *adv.* เลย ləəi

at first *adv.* แต่แรก dtɛ̀ɛ-rɛ̂ɛk

athlete *n.* นักกีฬา nák-gii-laa [คน kon]

athlete's foot *n.*
โรคน้ำกัดเท้า rôok-nám-gàt-táao [โรค rôok]

athletic *adj.* (fit) ล่ำสัน lâm-sǎn | (strong)
มีร่างกายแข็งแรง mii-râang-gaai-kɛ̌ng-rɛɛng

atlas *n.* (map book)
สมุดแผนที่ sà~mùt-pɛ̌ɛn-tîi [เล่ม lêm]

at last *adv.* ในที่สุด nai-tîi-sùt

ATM machine *n.*
ตู้เอทีเอ็ม dtûu-ee-tii-em [เครื่อง krɨ̂ɨang]

atmosphere *n.* บรรยากาศ ban-yaa-gàat

atom *n.* อะตอม à~dtɔm [อะตอม à~dtɔm]

atomic bomb *n.*
ระเบิดปรมาณู rá~bə̀ət-bpà~rá~maa-nuu [ลูก lûuk]

attach *v.* (affix, adhere) ติด dtìt

attach *vt.* (e.g. document) แนบ nɛ̂ɛp

attachment *n.* (feeling that binds)
ความรู้สึกผูกพัน kwaam-rúu-sùk-pùuk-pan | (something that attaches) สิ่งที่แนบมา sìng-tîi-nɛ̂ɛp-maa [อัน an, ชิ้น chín]

attack *v.* (physically) โจมตี joom-dtii | (verbally)
วิจารณ์ wí-jaan

attain *vt.* (achieve) บรรลุ ban-lú !

attempt *vt.* (try) พยายาม pá~yaa-yaam

attend *v.* (participate in) เข้าร่วม kâo-rûuam

attend *vi.* (school) เข้าเรียน kâo-riian

attendance *n.* (to school)

การเข้าเรียน gaan-kâo-riian | (to work)
การเข้าทำงาน gaan-kâo-tam-ngaan

attendant n. (e.g. parking, gas station) ผู้ให้บริการ pûu-hâi-bɔɔ-rí~gaan [คน kon]

attention n. (heed) การเอาใจใส่ gaan-ao-jai-sài

attic n. ห้องใต้หลังคา hɔ̂ng-dtâai-lǎng-kaa [ห้อง hɔ̂ng]

attire n. (clothes) เครื่องแต่งกาย krûuang-dtɛ̀ng-gaai ! [ชุด chút (set), ตัว dtuua (piece)]

attitude n. (of mind or feeling) ทัศนคติ tát-sà~ná-ká~dtì [อัน an] | (viewpoint) ความคิดเห็น kwaam-kít-hěn [อัน an]

attorney n. ทนายความ tá~naai-kwaam, ทนาย tá~naai ✲ [คน kon]

attract vt. ดึงดูด dʉng-dùut

attractive adj. (beautiful) สวย sǔuai | (charming) มีเสน่ห์ mii-sà~nèe

auction n. การประมูล gaan-bprà~muun [ครั้ง kráng]

audible adj. ฟังได้ยิน fang-dâi-yin

audience n. (listener) ผู้ฟัง pûu-fang [คน kon] | (reader) ผู้อ่าน pûu-àan [คน kon] | (viewer) ผู้ชม pûu-chom [คน kon]

audio adj. (pertaining to sound) เกี่ยวกับเสียง gìiao-gàp-sǐiang

audit vt. (check accounts of) ตรวจสอบบัญชีของ dtrùuat-sɔ̀ɔp-ban-chii-kɔ̌ɔng

audition n. (trial performance) การทดลองแสดง gaan-tót-lɔɔng-sà~dɛɛng

auditor n. (accounting) ผู้ตรวจบัญชี pûu-dtrùuat-ban-chii [คน kon]

auditorium n. (convention hall) หอประชุม hɔ̌ɔ-bprà~chum [แห่ง hɛ̀ng]

August n. สิงหาคม sǐng-hǎa-kom [เดือน dʉʉan]

aunt n. (father or

mother's older sister) ป้า bpâa [คน kon] | (father's younger sister) อา aa [คน kon] | (mother's younger sister) น้า náa [คน kon]

auspicious *adj.* เป็นมงคล bpen-mong-kon

Australia *n.* ออสเตรเลีย ɔ̀t-sà~dtree-liia [ประเทศ bprà~têet]

Austria *n.* ออสเตรีย ɔ̀ɔt-sà~dtriia [ประเทศ bprà~têet]

authentic *adj.* จริง jing, แท้ tɛ́ɛ

author *n.* (writer) นักเขียน nák-kĭian, ผู้แต่ง pûu-dtèng [คน kon]

authority *n.* (official) เจ้าหน้าที่ jâo-nâa-tîi [คน kon] | (power) อำนาจ am-nâat

authorize *vt.* (assign authority to) มอบอำนาจให้ mɔ̂ɔp-am-nâat-hâi

autism *n.* ออติสซึ่ม ɔɔ-dtít-sʉ̂m

autograph *n.* ลายเซ็น laai-sen [อัน an]

automatic *adj.* อัตโนมัติ àt-dtà~noo-mát

automobile *n.* รถ rót, รถยนต์ rót-yon [คัน kan]

autopsy *n.* การชันสูตรศพ gaan-chan-ná~sùut-sòp [ครั้ง kráng]

autumn *n.* ฤดูใบไม้ร่วง rʉ́-duu-bai-máai-rûuang [ฤดู rʉ́-duu]

availability *n.* ความพร้อมในการใช้งาน kwaam-prɔ́ɔm-nai-gaan-chái-ngaan

available *adj.* (not occupied) ว่าง wâang | (not run out yet) มีอยู่ mii-yùu | (obtainable) หาได้ hăa-dâai

avant-garde *n.* กองหน้า gɔɔng-nâa [กอง gɔɔng]

avenue *n.* ถนน tà~nǒn [เส้น sên, สาย săai]

average *adj.* (ordinary) ธรรมดา tam-má~daa

average *n.* (mathematical) ค่าเฉลี่ย kâa-chà~lìia [ค่า kâa]

avian flu *n.* ไข้หวัดนก kâi-wàt-nók

aviation *n.* (operation of aircraft) การบิน gaan-bin

avid *adj.* (desirous)
คลั่งไคล้ klâng-klái

avocado *n.* อะโวคาโด้ à~
woo-kaa-dôo [ลูก lûuk]

avoid *vt.* หลีกเลี่ยง lìik-
lîiang

awake *adj.* (gain
consciousness) รู้สึกตัว
rúu-sɨ̀k-dtuua | (not
sleeping) ตื่น dtɨ̀ɨn

award *n.* รางวัล raang-
wan [รางวัล raang-wan]

aware *adj.* (conscious)
รู้ตัว rúu-dtuua

away *adv.* ไป bpai, ไปจาก
bpai-jàak

awesome *adj.* (wonderful)
เลิศ lə̂ət

awesome! *interj.* สุดยอด
sùt-yɔ̂ɔt, เจ๋ง jěng ✿

awful *adj.* (terrible)
แย่มาก yɛ̂ɛ-mâak

awhile *adv.* ชั่วครู่ chûua-
krûu

awkward *adj.* (clumsy)
งุ่มง่าม ngûm-ngâam

awning *n.* (shade) ผ้าใบ
pâa-bai [ผืน pɨ̌ɨn, แผ่น
pèn]

ax *n.* ขวาน kwǎan [เล่ม
lêm]

axe see ax

axis *n.* (e.g. earth, graph)
แกน gɛɛn [แกน gɛɛn]

axle *n.* (of wheel) แกนล้อ
gɛɛn-lɔ́ɔ [แกน gɛɛn] |
(shaft of machine) เพลา
plao [เพลา plao]

B

babble *vi.* พูดเรื่อยเปื่อย
pûut-rɨ̂uai-bpɨ̀uai

baby *n.* เด็กเล็ก dèk-lék,
เด็กอ่อน dèk-ɔ̀ɔn, ทารก
taa-rók [คน kon]

baby bud see cotton
swab

baby carriage *n.*
รถเข็นเด็ก rót-kěn-dèk
[คัน kan]

babysitter *n.* คนช่วย
เลี้ยงเด็ก kon-chûuai-
líiang-dèk [คน kon]

bachelor *n.* (graduate)
ผู้จบชั้นปริญญาตรี pûu-
jòp-chán-bpa~rin-yaa-
dtrii [คน kon] | (single
man) ชายโสด chaai-sòot
[คน kon]

bachelor's degree *n.*
ปริญญาตรี bpà~rin-yaa-
dtrii [ปริญญา bpà~rin-

yaa (degree), ใบ bai
(certificate)]

back *adj.* หลัง lăng

back *n.* (body part) หลัง
lăng

back *vt.* (support)
สนับสนุน sà~nàp-sà~
nŭn, หนุนหลัง nŭn-lăng

background *n.* (history)
ความเป็นมา kwaam-
bpen-maa, ภูมิหลัง
puum-lăng

back order *n.* สินค้าค้างส่ง
sĭn-káa-káang-sòng
[จำนวน jam-nuuan
(number), ปริมาณ bpà~
rí~maan (quantity)]

back out *vi.* กลับคำ glàp-
kam

backpack *n.* เป้ bpêe [ใบ
bai]

backpacker *n.* (budget
traveler) แบ็คแพ็คเกอร์
bék-pék-gə̀ə [คน kon]

backtrack *vi.* กลับทางเดิม
glàp-taang-dəəm

back up *v.* (data) แบ็กอัพ
bék-àp

back up *vi.* (vehicle,
oneself) ถอยหลัง tŏoi-lăng

backup *adj.* (reserve or
substitute) สำรอง săm-

rɔɔng

backward *adj.* (behind in
progress or
development) ล้าหลัง láa-
lăng

backward *adv.* (moving)
ข้างหลัง kâang-lăng |
(wrong way around)
กลับหลัง glàp-lăng

backyard *n.* สนามหลังบ้าน
sà~năam-lăng-bâan
[สนาม sà~năam]

bacon *n.* เบคอน bee-kɔ̂n
[ชิ้น chín]

bacteria *n.* เชื้อโรค
chúua-rôok [ชนิด chá~
nít]

bad *adj.* ไม่ดี mâi-dii, เลว
leeo

badge *n.* (e.g. police)
เครื่องหมาย krûuang-
măai [อัน an]

badminton *n.* แบดมินตัน
bὲt-min-dtân

bag *n.* (e.g. paper or
plastic) ถุง tŭng [ใบ bai] |
(hand luggage) กระเป๋า
grà~bpăo [ใบ bai]

baggage *n.*
กระเป๋าเดินทาง grà~
bpăo-dəən-taang [ใบ bai]

baht *n.* เงินบาท ngən-bàat, บาท bàat [บาท bàat]

bail *n.* (money amount) เงินประกัน ngən-bprà~gan

bail *vt.* (legal) ประกันตัว bprà~gan-dtuua

bailiff *n.* (in courtroom) จ่าศาล jàa-sǎan [คน kon]

bailsman *n.* นายประกัน naai-bprà~gan [คน kon]

bait *n.* (e.g. fish) เหยื่อ yùua [อัน an] | (tempting item) สิ่งล่อใจ sìng-lɔ̂ɔ-jai [สิ่ง sìng]

bake *vt.* อบ òp

baker *n.* คนทำขนมปัง kon-tam-kà~nǒm-bpang [คน kon]

bakery *n.* ร้านขนมปัง ráan-kà~nǒm-bpang [ร้าน ráan]

balance *n.* (accounting) ดุล dun | (equilibrium) ความสมดุล kwaam-sǒm-dun, สมดุล sǒm-dun

balanced *adj.* สมดุล sǒm-dun

balance sheet *n.* บัญชีงบดุล ban-chii-ngóp-dun [บัญชี ban-chii]

balcony *n.* ระเบียง rá~biiang [แห่ง hɛ̀ng]

bald *adj.* ล้าน láan, หัวล้าน hǔua-láan

ball *n.* (sports) ลูกบอล lûuk-bɔn [ลูก lûuk]

ballet *n.* การเต้นบัลเลต์ gaan-dtên-ban-lêe, บัลเลต์ ban-lêe

balloon *n.* (toy, decoration) ลูกโป่ง lûuk-bpòong [ใบ bai]

ballot *n.* บัตรเลือกตั้ง bàt-lûuak-dtâng [ใบ bai]

ballpoint pen *n.* ปากกาลูกลื่น bpàak-gaa-lûuk-lʉ̂ʉn [ด้าม dâam]

ballroom dance *n.* ลีลาศ lii-lâat

balm *n.* ยาหม่อง yaa-mɔ̀ng [ตลับ dtà~làp (tin)]

bamboo *n.* (material) ไผ่ pài [มัด mát (bundle), เส้น sên (piece)] | (tree) ต้นไผ่ dtôn-pài, ไม้ไผ่ mái-pài [ลำ lam (piece), ต้น dtôn (tree), กอ gɔɔ (group)]

bamboo rocket *n.* บั้งไฟ

bâng-fai [บั้ง bâng, ลูก lûuk]

bamboo shoot *n.* หน่อไม้ nɔ̀ɔ-máai [หน่อ nɔ̀ɔ]

ban *vt.* ห้าม hâam

banana *n.* กล้วย glûuai [ลูก lûuk (one), หวี wǐi (bunch)]

band *n.* (fastener) สายรัด sǎai-rát [เส้น sên] | (music) วงดนตรี wong-don-dtrii [วง wong]

bandage *n.* ผ้าพันแผล pâa-pan-plɛ̌ɛ [ม้วน múuan (roll), ชิ้น chín (piece)]

bang *n.* (hair) ผมหน้าม้า pǒm-nâa-máa [ทรง song] | (loud noise) เสียงดัง sǐiang-dang

Bangkok *n.* กรุงเทพ grung-têep [เมือง mʉʉang]

bank *n.* (money institution) ธนาคาร tá~naa-kaan [แห่ง hɛ̀ng] | (shore) ฝั่ง fàng [แห่ง hɛ̀ng, ฝั่ง fàng]

bank account *n.* บัญชีเงินฝาก ban-chii-

ngən-fàak [บัญชี ban-chii]

banker *n.* นายธนาคาร naai-tá~naa-kaan [คน kon]

banknote *n.* ธนบัตร tá~ná~bàt [ใบ bai]

bankrupt *adj.* ล้มละลาย lóm-lá~laai

banner *n.* (flag) ธง tong [ผืน pʉ̌ʉn] | (sign) ป้าย bpâai [ป้าย bpâai, แผ่น pɛ̀n]

banquet *n.* งานเลี้ยง ngaan-líiang [งาน ngaan]

baptism *n.* พิธีล้างบาป pí-tii-láang-bàap [พิธี pí-tii]

bar *n.* (e.g. on phone for signal strength) ขีด kìit [ขีด kìit] | (e.g. soap) ก้อน gɔ̂ɔn [ก้อน gɔ̂ɔn] | (metal or wood pole) ราว raao [ราว raao] | (where drinks are served) บาร์ baa [แห่ง hɛ̀ng, ร้าน ráan]

bar *vt.* (block) กั้น gân, ขวาง kwǎang

barb *n.* หนาม nǎam [อัน an]

barbarous *adj.* ป่าเถื่อน bpàa-tʉ̀ʉan

barbecue see barbeque

barbed wire n. ลวดหนาม lûuat-năam [เส้น sên (strand), ม้วน múuan (roll)]

barbeque vt. บาร์บีคิว baa-bii-kiu, ย่าง yâang

barber n. ช่างตัดผม châng-dtàt-pǒm [คน kon]

barbershop n. ร้านตัดผม ráan-dtàt-pǒm [ร้าน ráan]

bar code n. บาร์โคด baa-kóot [อัน an]

bare adj. (e.g. cupboard) ไม่มีอะไร mâi-mii-à~rai | (e.g. hands, walls) เปล่า bplàao | (naked) เปลือย bpluuai

barefoot adv. เท้าเปล่า táao-bplàao

bargain n. (good buy) สินค้าราคาถูก sǐn-káa-raa-kaa-tùuk [ชิ้น chín]

bargain vi. (haggle) ต่อราคา dtɔ̀ɔ-raa-kaa

barge n. เรือบรรทุก ruua-ban-túk [ลำ lam]

bar girl n. ผู้หญิงบาร์ pûu-yǐng-baa [คน kon]

bark n. (of a tree)

เปลือกไม้ bpluuak-máai [ชิ้น chín]

bark vi. เห่า hào

barn n. ฉาง chăang, ยุ้งข้าว yúng-kâao [หลัง lăng]

barren adj. (dry) แห้งแล้ง hɛ̂ɛng-lɛ́ɛng | (sterile) เป็นหมัน bpen-măn

bartender n. บาร์เทนเดอร์ baa-ten-də̂ə [คน kon]

barter vi. แลกเปลี่ยนสินค้า lɛ̂ɛk-bpliian-sǐn-káa

base n. (foundation) ฐาน tăan [ฐาน tăan] | (military) ฐานทัพ tăan-táp [แห่ง hɛ̀ng]

baseball n. (sport) เบสบอล bées-bɔɔn

basement n. ห้องใต้ดิน hɔ̂ng-dtâai-din [ห้อง hɔ̂ng]

basic adj. พื้นฐาน púun-tăan

basil n. (holy) กะเพรา gà~prao [ต้น dtôn (plant), ใบ bai (leaf)] | (sweet) โหระพา hǒo-rá~paa [ต้น dtôn (plant), ใบ bai (leaf)]

basin *n.* (e.g. river basin) ที่ราบลุ่ม tîi-râap-lûm [แห่ง hɛ̀ng] | (sink) อ่าง àang [ใบ bai]

basis *n.* (fundamental element) มูลฐาน muun-tǎan

basket *n.* (deep) ตะกร้า dtà~grâa [ใบ bai]

basketball *n.* (sport) บาสเก็ตบอล báas-gét-bɔn

bass *adj.* (sound) เสียงต่ำ sǐiang-dtàm

bass *n.* (fish) ปลากะพง bplaa-gà~pong [ตัว dtuua]

bastard! *interj.* (bad person) ไอ้ชั่ว âi-chûua ☞

bat *n.* (animal) ค้างคาว káang-kaao [ตัว dtuua]

batch *n.* (group) ชุด chút [ชุด chút]

bathe *vi.* อาบ àap, อาบน้ำ àap-náam

bathing suit *n.* ชุดว่ายน้ำ chút-wâai-náam [ชุด chút]

bathroom *n.* (toilet, restroom) ห้องน้ำ hɔ̂ng-náam [ห้อง hɔ̂ng]

bathtub *n.* อ่างอาบน้ำ àang-àap-náam [อ่าง àang]

baton *n.* (club) กระบอง grà~bɔɔng [อัน an]

batter *n.* (flour mix) แป้งผสม bpɛ̂ɛng-pà~sǒm [กล่อง glɔ̀ng (box)]

battery *n.* (e.g. camera) ถ่าน tàan [ก้อน gɔ̂ɔn] | (e.g. for car) แบตเตอรี่ bɛ̀t-dtəə-rîi [ใบ bai]

battle *n.* (armed fight) การรบ gaan-róp [ครั้ง kráng]

battle *vt.* (fight) ต่อสู้กับ dtɔ̀ɔ-sûu-gàp

battlefield *n.* สนามรบ sà~nǎam-róp [แห่ง hɛ̀ng]

bay *n.* อ่าว àao [อ่าว àao]

B.C. *adv.* ก่อนคริสต์ศักราช gɔ̀ɔn-krít-sàk-gà~ràat

be *v.* (as follows) คือ k̶u̶u̶ | (something) เป็น bpen | (somewhere) อยู่ yùu

beach *n.* ชายหาด chaai-hàat [แห่ง hɛ̀ng]

bead *n.* (small, round object) ลูกปัด lûuk-bpàt [ลูก lûuk (seed), เม็ด mét (seed)]

beak *n.* ปากนก bpàak-nók [ปาก bpàak]

beam *n.* (light) ลำแสง lam-sɛ̌ɛng [ลำ lam] | (long piece of wood) คาน kaan [อัน an]

bean *n.* ถั่ว tùua [เม็ด mét]

bean curd *n.* เต้าหู้ dtâo-hûu [ชนิด chá~nít]

bean sprout *n.* ถั่วงอก tùua-ngɔ̂ɔk [เส้น sên (sprout)]

bear *n.* หมี mǐi [ตัว dtuua]

bear *vt.* (carry) หาม hǎam | (child) คลอด klɔ̂ɔt

bearable *adj.* (tolerable) รับไหว ráp-wǎi

beard *n.* เครา krao [กระจุก grà~jùk (tuft)]

bear fruit *vi.* ออกผล ɔ̀ɔk-pǒn

bear with *vt.* อดทนกับ ɔ̀t-ton-gàp

beast *n.* (nonhuman) สัตว์เดรัจฉาน sàt-dee-rát-chǎan [ตัว dtuua, ชนิด chá~nít (kind)]

beat *n.* (rhythm) จังหวะ jang-wà [จังหวะ jang-wà]

beat *vi.* (e.g. heart) เต้น dtên

beat *vt.* (defeat) ชนะ chá~ná | (hit, mix) ตี dtii

beaten *adj.* (defeated) แพ้ pɛ́ɛ

beat up *vt.* (person) ตี_จนบาดเจ็บ dtii-_-jon-bàat-jèp

beautiful *adj.* สวย sǔuai, สวยงาม sǔuai-ngaam *!*, งดงาม ngót-ngaam *~*, งาม ngaam *~* | (for music) เพราะ prɔ́, ไพเราะ pai-rɔ́ *!*

beautify *vt.* (decorate) แต่ง dtɛ̀ng

beauty *n.* (beautiful woman) หญิงงาม yǐng-ngaam [คน kon] | (quality) ความงาม kwaam-ngaam

beauty parlor *n.* ร้านเสริมสวย ráan-sɵ̌ɵm-sǔuai [ร้าน ráan]

beauty queen *n.* นางงาม naang-ngaam [คน kon] | เทพี tee-pii *!* [คน kon]

beaver *n.* บีเวอร์ bíip-wɵ̂ɵ [ตัว dtuua]

be careful! *interj.* ระวัง rá~wang

because *conj.* เพราะ prɔ́,

เพราะว่า prɔ́-wâa
because of *prep.* (due to) เนื่องจาก nʉ̂ʉang-jàak
become *vt.* กลายเป็น glaai-bpen
bed *n.* (furniture) เตียง dtiiang [เตียง dtiiang]
bed and breakfast *n.* ที่พักพร้อมบริการอาหารเช้า tîi-pák-prɔ́ɔm-bɔɔ-rí~gaan-aa-hǎan-cháao [แห่ง hɛ̀ng]
bedbug *n.* ไร rai [ตัว dtuua]
bedroom *n.* ห้องนอน hɔ̂ng-nɔɔn [ห้อง hɔ̂ng]
bedtime *n.* เวลานอน wee-laa-nɔɔn [เวลา wee-laa]
bee *n.* (animal) ผึ้ง pʉ̂ng [ตัว dtuua (each one), ฝูง fǔung (swarm)]
beef *n.* เนื้อวัว nʉ́ʉa-wuua [ชิ้น chín]
beefsteak *n.* สเต็กเนื้อ sà~dtéek-nʉ́ʉa [ชิ้น chín]
beehive *n.* รังผึ้ง rang-pʉ̂ng [รัง rang]
been see be
beep *n.* (beeping sound) เสียงบี๊ปๆ sǐiang-bíip-bíip | (vehicle horn) เสียงแตร sǐiang-dtrɛɛ [เสียง sǐiang]
beep *vi.* ส่งเสียงเตือนบี๊ปๆ sòng-sǐiang-dtʉʉan-bíip-bíip
beer *n.* เบียร์ biia [กระป๋อง grà~bpɔ̌ng (can), ขวด kùuat (bottle), แก้ว gɛ̂ɛo (glass)]
beeswax *n.* ขี้ผึ้ง kîi-pʉ̂ng [ชนิด chá~nít (type), หลอด lɔ̀ɔt (tube), ตลับ dtà~làp (tin)]
beet *n.* หัวผักกาดแดง hǔua-pàk-gàat-dɛɛng [ต้น dtôn]
beetle *n.* แมลงปีกแข็ง má~lɛɛng-bpìik-kɛ̌ng [ตัว dtuua]
before *adv.* ก่อน gɔ̀ɔn
before *prep.* ก่อน gɔ̀ɔn
beforehand *adv.* ล่วงหน้า lûuang-nâa
beg *v.* ขอ kɔ̌ɔ
beggar *n.* ขอทาน kɔ̌ɔ-taan [คน kon]
begin *v.* เริ่ม rə̂əm
beginner *n.* ผู้เริ่มเรียน pûu-rə̂əm-riian [คน kon]

beginning *adj.* ต้น dtôn

beginning *n.* (start, origin) จุดเริ่มต้น jùt-rôฺam-dtôn [จุด jùt]

behave *vi.* ประพฤติ bprà~prút ⚠, ทำตัว tam-dtuua ⚫

behavior *n.* (action) ความประพฤติ kwaam-bprà~prút

behind *prep.* (toward the rear) ข้างหลัง kâang-lăng

behold *vt.* ดู duu

being *n.* (living thing) สิ่งมีชีวิต sìng-mii-chii-wít [ตัว dtuua (animal), คน kon (human)]

Belgium *n.* เบลเยี่ยม ben-yîiam [ประเทศ bprà~têet]

belief *n.* (opinion) ความเชื่อ kwaam-chûฺua [อัน an]

believable *adj.* น่าเชื่อ nâa-chûฺua

believe *v.* (in something) เชื่อ chûฺua

believe *vt.* (in a religion) นับถือ náp-tŭฺu

bell *n.* (cast metal) ระฆัง rá~kang [ใบ bai, ลูก lûuk]

| (doorbell, buzzer) กริ่ง grìng [อัน an]

bellboy *n.* พนักงานยกกระเป๋า pá~nák-ngaan-yók-grà~bpăo, บ๋อย bŏ̌i ⚫ [คน kon]

bell pepper *n.* พริกหยวก prík-yùuak [เม็ด mét]

belly *n.* ท้อง tว́ɔng | พุง pung ⚫ [พุง pung]

belly button *n.* สะดือ sà~duu

belong *vi.* (be in proper place) เหมาะ mว̀

belongings *n.* สิ่งของ sìng-kว̌ɔng [อัน an, ชิ้น chín]

belong to *vt.* (someone) เป็นของ bpen-kว̌ɔng

beloved *adj.* เป็นที่รัก bpen-tîi-rák

below *prep.* (less than) น้อยกว่า nว́ɔi-gwàa | (physically) ข้างล่าง kâang-lâang | (under) ต่ำกว่า dtàm-gwàa, ใต้ dtâai

belt *n.* เข็มขัด kĕm-kàt [เส้น sên]

bench *n.* (seat) ม้านั่ง

máa-nâng [ตัว dtuua]

bend *v.* งอ ngɔɔ

bend *vt.* ดัด dàt

bend over *vi.* (bow) ก้ม
gôm

beneath see below

beneficiary *n.*
ผู้รับผลประโยชน์ pûu-
ráp-pǒn-bprà~yòot [คน
kon]

benefit *n.* (advantage)
ประโยชน์ bprà~yòot
[อย่าง yàang] | (charity
event) งานกุศล ngaan-
gù-~sǒn [งาน ngaan] |
(reward) ผลประโยชน์
pǒn-bprà~yòot

benign *adj.* (not
dangerous) ไม่อันตราย
mâi-an-dtà~raai

bent *adj.* งอ ngɔɔ

beside *prep.* ข้าง kâang,
อยู่ข้าง yùu-kâang

besides *prep.* นอกจาก
nɔ̂ɔk-jàak

besiege *vt.* ล้อม lɔ́ɔm

best *adj.* ดีที่สุด dii-tîi-sùt

best man *n.* เพื่อนเจ้าบ่าว
pûuan-jâo-bàao [คน kon]

best-selling *adj.* ขายดี
kǎai-dii

bet *n.* (wager) เดิมพัน
dəəm-pan [ครั้ง kráng]

bet *v.* (wager) พนัน pá~
nan

betel nut *n.* หมาก màak
[ลูก lûuk (fruit), ต้น dtôn
(tree)]

betray *vt.* (be disloyal to)
ทรยศ tɔɔ-rá~yót

better *adj.* (than before)
ดีขึ้น dii-kûn | (than
something) ดีกว่า dii-
gwàa

between *prep.* ระหว่าง
rá~wàang

beverage *n.* เครื่องดื่ม
krûuang-dùum [ชนิด
chá~nít]

beware *v.* ระวัง rá~wang

bewildered *adj.* งุนงง
ngun-ngong

beyond *prep.* (besides)
นอกจาก nɔ̂ɔk-jàak |
(further away than) เลย
ləəi | (more than)
มากกว่า mâak-gwàa

bias *n.* (prejudice) อคติ à-
ká~dtì

biased *adj.* ลำเอียง lam-
iiang

bib *n.* (child)

ผ้ากันเปื้อนเด็ก pâa-gan-
bpʉʉan-dèk [ผืน pʉ̌ʉn]

Bible *n.* คัมภีร์ไบเบิ้ล
kam-pii-bai-bên [เล่ม
lêm]

bicycle *n.* จักรยาน jàk-
grà~yaan [คัน kan]

bid *n.* การประมูล gaan-
bprà~muun [ครั้ง kráng]

bid *vi.* ประมูล bprà~muun

big *adj.* โต dtoo, ใหญ่ yài

big deal *n.* เรื่องใหญ่
rûuang-yài ✦ [เรื่อง
rûuang]

bike *n.* (bicycle) จักรยาน
jàk-grà~yaan [คัน kan] |
(motorcycle) มอเตอร์ไซค์
mɔɔ-dtəə-sai [คัน kan]

bikini *n.* บิกินี bì~gì~nii
[ตัว dtuua]

bilingual *adj.* ได้สองภาษา
dâi-sɔ̌ɔng-paa-sǎa

bill *n.* (check) บิล bin [ใบ
bai] | (legislative act)
พระราชบัญญัติ prá~râat-
chá~ban-yàt [ฉบับ chà~
bàp (version), มาตรา
mâat-dtraa (section)] |
(money note) ธนบัตร

tá~ná~bàt [ใบ bai]

billboard *n.* ป้าย bpâai
[ป้าย bpâai, แผ่น pɛ̀n]

billiard *n.* บิลเลียด bin-lîiat

billion *numb.* (thousand
million) หนึ่งพันล้าน
nùng-pan-láan

bin see trash can

bind *vt.* (tie) ผูก pùuk, มัด
mát

binding *n.* (book)
การเข้าเล่ม gaan-kâo-lêm

binoculars *n.*
กล้องส่องทางไกล glɔ̂ng-
sɔ̀ng-taang-glai [ตัว
dtuua]

biography *n.* ชีวประวัติ
chii-wá-bprà~wàt [เรื่อง
rûuang]

biology *n.* ชีววิทยา chii-
wá-wít-tá~yaa [วิชา wí-
chaa]

biopsy *n.* การตัดเนื้อเยื่อไป
ตรวจ gaan-dtàt-nʉ́ʉa-
yʉ̂ʉa-bpai-dtrùuat

bird *n.* นก nók [ตัว dtuua]

bird flu see avian flu

birdwatch *vi.* ส่องนก
sɔ̀ng-nók

birth *n.* (act) การเกิด
gaan-gə̀ət | (origin)

ต้นกำเนิด dtôn-gam-nə̀ət
[แห่ง hɛ̀ng]

birth certificate *n.* ใบเกิด
bai-gə̀ət [ใบ bai] | สูติบัตร
sǔu-dtì-bàt ‼ [ฉบับ chà~
bàp]

birth control *n.*
การคุมกำเนิด gaan-kum-
gam-nə̀ət

birthday *n.* วันเกิด wan-
gə̀ət [วัน wan]

birth mark *n.* ปาน bpaan
[แห่ง hɛ̀ng ‼, ที่ tîi]

birth place *n.* สถานที่เกิด
sà~tǎan-tîi-gə̀ət ‼ [ที่ tîi]

biscuit *n.* ขนมปังกรอบ
kà~nǒm-bpang-grɔ̀ɔp
[ชิ้น chín]

bisexual *adj.* (orientation)
ไบ bai

bishop *n.* (in chess)
ตัวบิชอป dtuua-bít-chɔ̀p
[ตัว dtuua]

bit *adv.* (somewhat)
นิดหน่อย nít-nɔ̀i, หน่อย
nɔ̀i

bit *n.* (small piece) เศษ
sèet [ชิ้น chín]

bitch *n.* (bad woman)
หญิงเลว yǐng-leeo [คน

kon] | (female dog)
หมาตัวเมีย mǎa-dtuua-
miia [ตัว dtuua]

bitch *vi.* (nag) บ่นจู้จี้ bòn-
jûu-jîi

bite *n.* (of food) คำ kam
[คำ kam]

bite *v.* กัด gàt

bitter *adj.* (taste) ขม kǒm

bitter melon *n.* มะระ
má~rá [ลูก lûuk]

bizarre *adj.* (strange)
ประหลาด bprà~làat

black *adj.* ดำ dam, สีดำ
sǐi-dam

black *n.* สีดำ sǐi-dam [สี sǐi]

blackberry *n.* แบลคเบอร์รี่
blɛ́k-bəə-rîi [ลูก lûuk]

blackboard *n.* กระดานดำ
grà~daan-dam [แผ่น pɛ̀n]

blackhead *n.* สิวหัวดำ
sǐu-hǔua-dam [เม็ด mét,
หัว hǔua ●]

blacklist *n.* บัญชีดำ ban-
chii-dam [เล่ม lêm]

blackmail *v.* ขู่เอาเงิน
kùu-ao-ngən

black market *n.* ตลาดมืด
dtà~làat-mûut [แห่ง
hɛ̀ng]

black out *vi.* (pass out)

สลบ sà~lòp

blackout *n.* (power failure) ไฟดับ fai-dàp

black sheep *n.* แกะดำ gὲ-dam [ตัว dtuua (animal), คน kon (human)]

blacksmith *n.* ช่างเหล็ก châng-lèk [คน kon]

bladder *n.* กระเพาะปัสสาวะ grà~pɔ́-bpàt-sǎa~wá

blade *n.* ใบมีด bai-mîit [ใบ bai]

blame *vt.* (condemn) กล่าวโทษ glàao-tôot | (criticize) ติเตียน dtì-dtiian

bland *adj.* (tasteless) จืดชืด jùut-chûut

blank *adj.* (empty) ว่างเปล่า wâang-bplàao ⚡

blank *n.* (e.g. on form) ช่องว่าง chɔ̂ng-wâang [ช่อง chɔ̂ng]

blanket *n.* ผ้าห่ม pâa-hòm [ผืน pʉ̌ʉn]

blast *vi.* (explode) ระเบิด rá~bə̀ət

blast *vt.* (shoot) ยิง ying

blaze *n.* เปลวไฟ bpleeo-fai [อัน an]

bleach *n.* (agent) น้ำยาฟอกขาว nám-yaa-fɔ̂ɔk-kǎao

bleed *vi.* เลือดไหล lʉ̂ʉat-lǎi, เลือดออก lʉ̂ʉat-ɔ̀ɔk

blemish *n.* (e.g. on face) ริ้วรอย ríu-rɔɔi [แห่ง hὲng]

blend *vt.* ผสม pà~sǒm

bless *vt.* ให้พร hâi-pɔɔn

blessing *n.* (something blessed) พร pɔɔn [ข้อ kɔ̂ɔ, ประการ bprà~gaan ⚡]

blind *adj.* (ตาบอด dtaa-bɔ̀ɔt, บอด bɔ̀ɔt

blind *n.* (window shade) ม่านบังตา mâan-bang-dtaa [ผืน pʉ̌ʉn]

blindfold *vt.* เอาผ้าปิดตา ao-pâa-bpìt-dtaa

blind spot *n.* จุดบอด jùt-bɔ̀ɔt [จุด jùt]

blink *vi.* (eyes) กะพริบตา gà~príp-dtaa | (light) กะพริบ gà~príp

blister *n.* แผลพุพอง plɛ̌ɛ-pú-pɔɔng [แห่ง hὲng]

blizzard *n.* พายุหิมะ paa-yú-hì~má

bloated *adj.* ป่อง bpòng

block *n.* (piece of wood)

ท่อนไม้ tôn-máai [ท่อน tôn]

block *vt.* (shut off) กั้น gân

blog *n.* (on the web) บล็อก blɔ́k [อัน an]

blond *adj.* สีบลอนด์ sǐi-blɔɔn, สีเหลืองอ่อน sǐi-lǔuang-ɔ̀ɔn

blood *n.* เลือด lɯ̂uat, โลหิต loo-hìt !

blood pressure *n.* ความดันเลือด kwaam-dan-lɯ̂uat

blood test *n.* การตรวจเลือด gaan-dtrùuat-lɯ̂uat

blood type *n.* กลุ่มเลือด glùm-lɯ̂uat [กลุ่ม glùm]

blood vessel *n.* เส้นเลือด sên-lɯ̂uat [เส้น sên]

bloody *adj.* (bad) เลว leeo | (with blood) มีเลือดออก mii-lɯ̂uat-ɔ̀ɔk

bloom *vi.* บาน baan

blossom *vi.* บาน baan

blot *n.* (stain) รอยเปื้อน rɔɔi-bpɯ̂uan [จุด jùt]

blouse *n.* (for women) เสื้อผู้หญิง sɯ̂ua-pûu-yǐng [ตัว dtuua]

blow *vi.* (e.g. wind, fan)

พัด pát | (with lungs) เป่า bpào

blow-dry *vi.* เป่าผม bpào-pǒm

blow job *n.* การทำออรัลให้ผู้ชาย gaan-tam-ɔɔ-rɔ̂n-hâi-pûu-chaai

blow out *vt.* (e.g. candle) ดับ dàp

blow up *vi.* (explode) ระเบิด rá~bèət

blue *adj.* (navy blue) น้ำเงิน nám-ngən, สีน้ำเงิน sǐi-nám-ngən | (sky blue) สีฟ้า sǐi-fáa

bluff *v.* ตบตา dtòp-dtaa

blunt *adj.* (not sharp) ทื่อ tɯ̂ɯ | (obtuse) ป้าน bpâan

blurry *adj.* มัว muua

blush *vi.* (in face) หน้าแดง nâa-dɛɛng

boa *n.* (snake) งูเหลือม nguu-lǔuam [ตัว dtuua]

boar *n.* (wild boar) หมูป่า mǔu-bpàa [ตัว dtuua]

board *n.* (committee) คณะกรรมการ ká~ná~gam-má~gaan [คณะ ká~ná] | (plank of wood) กระดาน grà~daan,

ไม้กระดาน mái-grà~daan [แผ่น pɛ̀n]

board *vi.* (vehicle) ขึ้นรถ kʉ̂n-rót

boarding pass *n.* บัตรขึ้นเครื่อง bàt-kʉ̂n-krʉ̂ʉang [ใบ bai]

boarding school *n.* โรงเรียนกินนอน roong-riian-gin-nɔɔn [แห่ง hɛ̀ng ❢]

boast *vi.* คุยโม้ kui-móo, อวด ùuat

boastful *adj.* ขี้โม้ kîi-móo, ขี้อวด kîi-ùuat

boat *n.* เรือ rʉʉa [ลำ lam]

bobby pin *n.* กิ๊บ gíp [ตัว dtuua]

body *n.* สรีระ sà~rii-rá ⚒ | ตัว dtuua, ร่างกาย râang-gaai ❢ [ตัว dtuua]

bodyguard *n.* คนคุ้มกัน kon-kúm-gan [คน kon]

body lotion *n.* โลชั่นทาตัว loo-chân-taa-dtuua [ขวด kùuat]

body shop *n.* (for autos) อู่ซ่อมรถ ùu-sɔ̂m-rót [อู่ ùu]

bog *n.* (marsh) บึง bʉng, หนอง nɔ̌ɔng [แห่ง hɛ̀ng]

boil *vi.* เดือด dʉ̀ʉat

boil *vt.* ต้ม dtôm | (rice) หุง hǔng

bold *adj.* (brave) กล้า glâa, ใจกล้า jai-glâa | (typography) หนา nǎa

bolt *n.* (deadbolt) กลอน glɔɔn [ตัว dtuua] | (threaded fastener) สกรูน็อต sà~gruu-nɔ́t [ตัว dtuua]

bomb *n.* ระเบิด rá~bə̀ət, ลูกระเบิด lûuk-rá~bə̀ət [ลูก lûuk]

bomb *v.* ระเบิด rá~bə̀ət

bond *n.* (bail money) เงินประกันตัว ngən-bprà~gan-dtuua [จำนวน jam-nuuan]

bone *n.* (fish) ก้าง gâang [ชิ้น chín] | (of person, animal, but not fish) กระดูก grà~dùuk [ซี่ sîi, ชิ้น chín]

bonnet see hood

bonus *n.* (money) เงินโบนัส ngən-boo-nát [จำนวน jam-nuuan]

bon voyage! *interj.* ขอให้

เดินทางโดยสวัสดิภาพ
kˇɔɔ-hâi-dəən-taang-
dooi-sà~wàt-dì~pâap ‼

bony *adj.* (skinny)
ผอมเหลือแต่กระดูก pˇɔɔm-
lˇɯa-dtɛ̀ɛ-grà~dùuk

booger *n.* (dried mucus)
ขี้มูกแห้ง kîi-mûuk-hˆɛɛng

book *n.* หนังสือ nˇang~sˇɯɯ
[เล่ม lêm]

book *v.* (reserve) จอง
jɔɔng

bookkeeper *n.* คนทำบัญชี
kon-tam-ban-chii [คน
kon]

booklet *n.* หนังสือเล่มเล็ก
nˇang~sˇɯɯ-lêm-lék [เล่ม
lêm]

bookmark *n.* ที่คั่นหนังสือ
tîi-kân-nˇang~sˇɯɯ [อัน an
☙, แผ่น pèn]

bookshelf *n.* ชั้นหนังสือ
chán-nˇang~sˇɯɯ [ชั้น
chán]

bookstore *n.* ร้านหนังสือ
ráan-nˇang~sˇɯɯ [ร้าน
ráan]

boom *n.* (noise)
เสียงสนั่นหวั่นไหว sˇiiang-
sà~nàn-wàn-wˇai

boom *vi.* (grow quickly)

เติบโตอย่างรวดเร็ว
dtə̀əp-dtoo-yàang-
rûuat-reo

boomerang *n.* บูมเมอแรง
buum-məə-rɛɛng [อัน an]

boost *vt.* (encourage,
promote) ส่งเสริม sòng-
sˇəəm | (raise) ยก_ขึ้น
yók-_-kˆɯn

boot *n.* (shoe) รองเท้าบูท
rɔɔng-táao-búut [ข้าง
kâang (one), คู่ kûu (pair)]
| (trunk of a car)
กระโปรงหลังรถ grà-
proong-lˇang-rót [ที่ tîi]

boot *v.* (computer) สตาร์ท
sà~dtáat, บูท búut ☙

booth *n.* (for selling
merchandise) แผง pˇɛɛng
[แผง pˇɛɛng]

bootleg *adj.* เถื่อน tˆɯan

border *n.* (e.g. country)
ชายแดน chaai-dɛɛn [แห่ง
hˆɛng]

bored *adj.* เบื่อ bɯ̀a

boring *adj.* น่าเบื่อ nˆaa-
bɯ̀a | (e.g. party) กร่อย
grɔ̀i

born *adj.* เกิด gə̀ət, กำเนิด
gam-nə̀ət ‼

born-again adj. (reborn)
เกิดใหม่ gə̀ət-mài

borrow vt. (item) ขอยืม
kɔ̌ɔ-yɯɯm, ยืม yɯɯm |
(money at interest) กู้ gûu

bosom n. (breast, chest)
อก òk

boss n. เจ้านาย jâo-naai,
หัวหน้า hǔua-nâa [คน
kon] | (who pays you)
นายจ้าง naai-jâang [คน
kon]

bossy adj. เจ้าบงการ jâo-
bong-gaan

botany n. พฤกษศาสตร์
prúk-sà~sàat [วิชา wí-
chaa]

both adj. ทั้งคู่ táng-kûu

both pron. ทั้งสอง táng-
sɔ̌ɔng

bother vi. (take the
trouble) ใส่ใจ sài-jai

bother vt. (disturb)
รบกวน róp-guuan

bottle n. ขวด kùuat [ขวด
kùuat]

bottom adj. (lowest part)
ล่างสุด lâang-sùt

bottom n. (body part) ตูด
dtùut 💧 | (lowest part)
ก้น gôn [ก้น gôn]

bottom line n. (crucial
factor) ส่วนสำคัญ sùuan-
sǎm-kan

boulevard n. ถนนใหญ่
tà~nǒn-yài [เส้น sên, สาย
sǎai]

bounce vi. (e.g. ball,
check) เด้ง dêng

bound adj. (obliged,
compelled) มีข้อผูกมัด
mii-kɔ̂ɔ-pùuk-mát

bound vi. (leap) กระโดด
grà~dòot

boundary n. (territory)
อาณาเขต aa-naa-kèet 💧
[แห่ง hèng] | (territory)
เขตแดน kèet-dɛɛn [เขต
kèet]

bouquet n. ช่อดอกไม้
chɔ̂ɔ-dɔ̀ɔk-máai [ช่อ chɔ̂ɔ]

bow n. (for arrows) คันธนู
kan-tá~nuu [คัน kan] |
(ribbon) หูกระต่าย hǔu-
grà~dtàai [อัน an]

bow vi. (bend down) โค้ง
kóong

bowel n. ลำไส้ lam-sâi
[ท่อน tɔ̂n (strip), ขด kòt
(coil)]

bowl n. (food) ถ้วย tûuai
[ใบ bai] | (water) ขัน kǎn

[ใบ bai]

bowl *vi.* (play bowling) โยนโบว์ลิ่ง yoon-boo-lîng

bowling *n.* (game) โบว์ลิ่ง boo-lîng

box *n.* (e.g. cardboard) กล่อง glòng [ใบ bai]

box *vi.* (fight) ชก chók, ต่อย dtòi, ชกต่อย chók-dtòi ⚡, ชกมวย chók-muuai ⚡

boxer *n.* (dog) สุนัขพันธุ์บอกเซอร์ sù~nák-pan-bɔ́k-sə̂ə ⚡ [ตัว dtuua] | (fighter) นักมวย nák-muuai [คน kon]

boxing glove *n.* นวม nuuam [คู่ kûu (pair), ข้าง kâang (one)]

boy *n.* เด็กชาย dèk-chaai [คน kon]

boycott *vt.* คว่ำบาตร kwâm-bàat

boyfriend *n.* (just a friend) เพื่อนชาย pûuan-chaai ⚡ [คน kon] | (non-exclusive partner) กิ๊ก gík ⚡ [คน kon] | (romantic partner) แฟน fɛɛn, แฟนชาย fɛɛn-chaai [คน

kon]

boy scout *n.* ลูกเสือ lûuk-sǔua [คน kon]

bra *n.* เสื้อชั้นใน sûua-chán-nai, ยกทรง yók-song ⚡ [ตัว dtuua]

brace *vt.* (hold up, support) ค้ำ kám | (strengthen) ดาม daam

bracelet *n.* กำไล gam-lai [วง wong]

bracket *n.* (parentheses) วงเล็บ wong-lép [ตัว dtuua (one), คู่ kûu (pair)]

brag *vi.* คุยโต kui-dtoo, โอ้อวด ôo-ùuat

Brahmin *n.* พราหมณ์ praam [คน kon]

braid *n.* (hair) ผมเปีย pǒm-bpiia [เส้น sên]

Braille *n.* อักษรเบรล àk-sǒɔn-breeo [ตัว dtuua]

brain *n.* สมอง sà~mǒɔng [ก้อน gɔ̂ɔn]

brainwash *vt.* ล้างสมอง láang-sà~mǒɔng

brake *n.* (e.g. car) เบรค brèek [ตัว dtuua]

brake *v.* (stop) หยุด yùt

bran *n.* รำข้าว ram-kâao

branch *n.* (e.g. bank or restaurant) สาขา săa-kăa [สาขา săa-kăa] | (of a tree) กิ่ง gìng [กิ่ง gìng]

brand *n.* (trademark) ตรา dtraa [ตรา dtraa] | (trademark) ยี่ห้อ yîi-hɔ̂ɔ [ยี่ห้อ yîi-hɔ̂ɔ]

brand *vt.* (stigmatize) ตราหน้า dtraa-nâa

brand new *adj.* ใหม่เอี่ยม mài-ìiam

brandy *n.* บรั่นดี bà~ràn-dii [ขวด kùuat (bottle), แก้ว gɛ̂ɛo (glass)]

brass *n.* ทองเหลือง tɔɔng-lŭɯang

brassiere see bra

brat *n.* เด็กสารเลว dèk-săa-rá~leeo [คน kon]

brave *adj.* กล้า glâa, ใจกล้า jai-glâa, กล้าหาญ glâa-hăan ̣

bravo! *interj.* ไชโย chai-yoo

Brazil *n.* บราซิล braa-sin [ประเทศ bprà~têet]

bread *n.* ขนมปัง kà~nŏm-bpang [แถว tɛ̌ɛo (loaf), ก้อน gɔ̂ɔn (round),

แผ่น pèn (piece)]

break *vi.* (stop or rest) หยุดพัก yùt-pák

break *vt.* (bend and break) หัก hàk | (smash, shatter) ทำแตก tam-dtɛ̀ɛk

breakable *adj.* (fragile) แตกง่าย dtɛ̀ɛk-ngâai

break a record *v.* ทำลายสถิติ tam-laai-sà-tì~dtì

break down *vi.* (cease to function) หยุดทำงาน yùt-tam-ngaan

breakfast *n.* ข้าวเช้า kâao-cháao, อาหารเช้า aa-hăan-cháao ̣ [มื้อ mɯ́ɯ]

break in *vi.* (burgle) งัดแงะ ngát-ngɛ́ | (interrupt) ขัดจังหวะ kàt-jang-wà

break off *vt.* (piece) หักออก hàk-ɔ̀ɔk

break out *vi.* (escape) หนี nĭi | (having acne) เป็นสิว bpen-sĭu

break through *vt.* (penetrate) ทะลุ tá~lú

break up *vi.* (into many pieces) ทำให้_แตกละเอียด tam-

hâi-_-dtɛ̀ɛk-lá~ìiat |
(relationship) เลิกกัน
lə̂ək-gan

breast *n.* (chest) หน้าอก
nâa-òk, อก òk |
(woman's) นม nom,
เต้านม dtâo-nom ⚠, อึ๋
ม ǔm ✿ [เต้า dtâo]

breastfeed *vi.* ให้กินนมแม่
hâi-gin-nom-mɛ̂ɛ

breath *n.* (air) ลมหายใจ
lom-hǎai-jai

breathe *v.* หายใจ hǎai-jai

breed *n.* พันธุ์ pan [พันธุ์
pan]

breed *vi.* (procreate)
แพร่พันธุ์ prɛ̂ɛ-pan

breed *vt.* (raise, e.g.
horses) เลี้ยง líiang

breeze *n.* (gentle wind)
ลมโชย lom-chooi

brevity *n.* (concise
expression) ความกะทัดรัด
ในใจความ kwaam-gà~
tát-rát-nai-jai-kwaam |
(duration) ระยะเวลาสั้น
rá~yá-wee-laa-sân [ระยะ
rá~yá]

brew *vi.* (alcohol) ต้มเหล้า
dtôm-lâo | (beer)

หมักเบียร์ màk-biia

brewery *n.* โรงกลั่นเบียร์
roong-glàn-biia [แห่ง
hɛ̀ng]

bribe *n.* สินบน sǐn-bon
[อัน an]

bribe *vt.* ติดสินบน dtìt-
sǐn-bon, ให้สินบน hâi-
sǐn-bon

brick *n.* (clay) อิฐ ìt [ก้อน
gɔ̂ɔn (block)]

bride *n.* เจ้าสาว jâo-sǎao
[คน kon]

bride and groom *n.*
คู่บ่าวสาว kûu-bàao-sǎao
[คู่ kûu]

bridegroom *n.* เจ้าบ่าว
jâo-bàao [คน kon]

bridesmaid *n.*
เพื่อนเจ้าสาว pɯ̂an-jâo-
sǎao [คน kon]

bridge *n.* (for crossing)
สะพาน sà~paan [แห่ง
hɛ̀ng]

brief *adj.* (short) สั้น sân,
โดยย่อ dooi-yɔ̂ɔ ⚠ |
(succinct) กะทัดรัด gà~
tát-rát, รวบรัด rûuap-rát

brief *vt.* (summarize for)
สรุปให้ sà~rùp-hâi

briefcase *n.*
กระเป๋าเอกสาร grà~
bpǎo-èek-gà~sǎan [ใบ
bai]

briefly *adv.* ชั่วครู่ chûa-
krûu, ในเวลาสั้นๆ nai-
wee-laa-sân-sân

bright *adj.* (annoyingly)
จ้า jâa | (color) สดใส sòt-
sǎi | (explicit, clear)
แจ่มแจ้ง jὲm-jɛ̂ɛng ǃ |
(intelligent) ฉลาด chà~
làat | (light intensity)
สว่าง sà~wàang

brighten *vt.* ทำให้_สว่าง
tam-hâi-_-sà~wàang

brilliant *adj.* (intelligent)
ฉลาด chà~làat | (very
intense light) สว่าง sà~
wàang, สุกใส sùk-sǎi

bring *vt.* (⌐ (someone)
from here (to)) พา_ไป
paa-_-bpai | (⌐
(someone) here (to))
พา_มา paa-_-maa | (⌐
(something, some
vehicle) from here (to))
เอา_ไป ao-_-bpai | (⌐
(something, some
vehicle) here (to)) เอา_มา
ao-_-maa

bring about *vt.* (cause)

ทำให้เกิด tam-hâi-gὲɘt

bring back *vt.*
(something) เอา_กลับคืน
ao-_-glàp-kɯɯn

bring in *vt.* (submit) ส่ง
sòng

bring up *vt.* (mention)
พูดถึง pûut-tǔng | (raise
a child) เลี้ยงดู líiang-duu

brisk *adj.* (cool) เย็น yen |
(fast) ปราดเปรียว
bpràat-bpriiao

brittle *adj.* (fragile) เปราะ
bprɔ̀, หักง่าย hàk-ngâai

broad *adj.* กว้าง gwâang

broadcast *v.* (transmit)
ถ่ายทอด tàai-tɔ̂ɔt

broadcast *vt.* (make
known) เผยแพร่ pǎɘi-prɛ̂ɛ

broaden *vt.* ทำให้_กว้าง
tam-hâi-_-gwâang

broad-minded *adj.*
ใจกว้าง jai-gwâang

broccoli *n.* (Chinese kale,
kai lan) คะน้า ká~náa [ต้น
dtôn (plant), ใบ bai
(leaf)] | (Western)
บร็อคโคลี่ brɔ́k-koo-lîi
[ต้น dtôn (plant)]

brochure *n.* โบรชัวร์
broo-chuua [ฉบับ chà~

bàp]

broil *vt.* (grill) ปิ้ง bpîng, ย่าง yâang

broke *adj.* (penniless) หมดตัว mòt-dtuua, ถังแตก tǎng-dtɛ̀ɛk ✱

broken *adj.* (not functioning) เสีย sǐia | (shattered, e.g. glass) แตก dtɛ̀ɛk | (split, e.g. wood) หัก hàk | (torn) ขาด kàat

broken-down *adj.* (not working) ไม่ทำงาน mâi-tam-ngaan

broken-hearted *adj.* อกหัก òk-hàk

broker *n.* นายหน้า naai-nâa [คน kon]

bronze *adj.* (color) สีทองแดง sǐi-tɔɔng-dɛɛng

bronze *n.* (metal) ทองเหลือง tɔɔng-lǔuang

brooch *n.* (pin) เข็มกลัด kěm-glàt [ตัว dtuua]

brook *n.* ลำธาร lam-taan [สาย sǎai]

broom *n.* ไม้กวาด mái-gwàat [อัน an]

broth *n.* น้ำแกง nám-gɛɛng [ถ้วย tûuai]

brothel *n.* ซ่อง sɔ̂ng [แห่ง hɛ̀ng]

brother *n.* (older) พี่ชาย pîi-chaai [คน kon] | (younger) น้องชาย nɔ́ɔng-chaai [คน kon]

brother-in-law *n.* (older) พี่เขย pîi-kěəi [คน kon] | (younger) น้องเขย nɔ́ɔng-kěəi [คน kon]

brow *n.* (forehead) หน้าผาก nâa-pàak

brown *adj.* น้ำตาล nám-dtaan, สีน้ำตาล sǐi-nám-dtaan

brown *n.* สีน้ำตาล sǐi-nám-dtaan [สี sǐi]

brown rice *n.* ข้าวซ้อมมือ kâao-sɔ́ɔm-mɯɯ [เม็ด mét]

browse *vt.* (look around) มองไปรอบๆ mɔɔng-bpai-rɔ̂ɔp-rɔ̂ɔp

bruise *n.* (contusion) รอยช้ำ rɔɔi-chám [รอย rɔɔi]

Brunei *n.* บรูไน bruu-nai [ประเทศ bprà~têet]

brush *n.* แปรง bprɛɛng [อัน an]

brush *vt.* (touch with brush) แปรง bprɛɛng

brush the teeth *vi.* แปรงฟัน bprɛɛng-fan

brush up *vi.* (improve skills) ปรับปรุงทักษะ bpràp-bprung-ták-sà

brutal *adj.* โหดร้าย hòot-ráai

B.S. *n.* (degree) ปริญญาตรี bpà~rin-yaa-dtrii [ปริญญา bpà~rin-yaa (degree), ใบ bai (certificate)]

B.S.! see bullshit!

bubble *n.* ฟอง fɔɔng [ฟอง fɔɔng]

buck *n.* (male deer) กวางตัวผู้ gwaang-dtuua-pûu [ตัว dtuua] | (one dollar) หนึ่งดอลล่าร์ nɯ̀ng-dɔɔn-lâa

bucket *n.* ถัง tǎng [ใบ bai]

buckle *n.* (belt) หัวเข็มขัด hǔua-kěm-kàt [อัน an]

buckle *vt.* (fasten) รัด rát

bud *n.* (offshoot) หน่อ nɔ̀ɔ [หน่อ nɔ̀ɔ] | (undeveloped flower) ดอกตูม dɔ̀ɔk-dtuum [ดอก dɔ̀ɔk]

bud *vi.* (produce buds) แตกหน่อ dtɛ̀ɛk-nɔ̀ɔ | (sprout) งอก ngɔ̂ɔk, ผลิ plì

Buddha *n.* พระพุทธเจ้า prá~pút-tá~jâao [องค์ ong, พระองค์ prá-ong]

Buddha image *n.* พระพุทธรูป prá-pút-tá~rûup [องค์ ong]

Buddhism *n.* ศาสนาพุทธ sàat-sà~nǎa-pút [ศาสนา sàat-sà~nǎa]

Buddhist *adj.* พุทธ pút

Buddhist *n.* ชาวพุทธ chaao-pút [คน kon]

Buddhist Era *n.* พ.ศ. pɔɔ-sɔ̌ɔ, พุทธศักราช pút-tá~sàk-gà~ràat ! [ปี bpii]

Buddhist monk *n.* พระสงฆ์ prá-sǒng [รูป rûup]

buddy *n.* เพื่อนสนิท pɯ̂uan-sà~nìt [คน kon]

budget *n.* งบประมาณ ngóp-bprà~maan [จำนวน jam-nuuan]

buffalo *n.* ควาย kwaai [ตัว dtuua]

buffer *n.* (floor) เครื่องขัดเงา krûuang-kàt-ngao [เครื่อง krûuang]

buffet *n.* บุฟเฟต์ búp-fêe
[มื้อ múu]

bug *n.* (defect)
ความบกพร่อง kwaam-
bòk-prông | (insect)
แมลง má~lɛɛng [ตัว
dtuua] | (wire tap)
เครื่องดักฟัง krûuang-
dàk-fang [เครื่อง krûuang]

bug *vt.* (bother) รบกวน
róp-guuan

build *vt.* (construct)
ก่อสร้าง gɔ̀ɔ-sâang ! |
(create) สร้าง sâang |
(originate) ก่อ gɔ̀ɔ

builder *n.* (construction
worker) ช่างก่อสร้าง
châng-gɔ̀ɔ-sâang [คน
kon]

building *n.* ตึก dtʉk,
อาคาร aa-kaan [หลัง lǎng]

build up *v.* (increase) เพิ่ม
pɤ̂ɤm

built-in *adj.* (included
with device) มากับเครื่อง
maa-gàp-krûuang

bulb *n.* (light bulb)
หลอดไฟ lɔ̀ɔt-fai [หลอด
lɔ̀ɔt] | (plant) หัว hǔua
[หัว hǔua]

bulk *n.* (greater part)

ขนาดใหญ่ kà~nàat-yài

bulky *adj.* เทอะทะ tɤ́-tá

bull *n.* (male cattle or ox)
วัวตัวผู้ wuua-dtuua-pûu
[ตัว dtuua]

bulldozer *n.* รถแทรกเตอร์
rót-trék-dtɤ̂ɤ ● [คัน kan]

bullet *n.* ลูกปืน lûuk-
bpʉʉn [ลูก lûuk, นัด nát]

bulletin *n.* (brief report)
รายงานข่าว raai-ngaan-
kàao [ฉบับ chà~bàp]

bulletin board *n.*
กระดานข่าว grà~daan-
kàao [แผ่น pɛ̀n]

bullfrog *n.* อึ่งอ่าง ʉ̀ng-
àang [ตัว dtuua]

bullring *n.* สนามวัวกระทิง
sà~nǎam-wuua-grà~ting
[แห่ง hɛ̀ng]

bullshit! *interj.* ตอแหล
dtɔɔ-lɛ̌ɛ ●

bully *n.* (ruffian, hooligan)
นักเลง nák-leeng [คน
kon]

bully *vt.* (molest) รังแก
rang-gɛɛ

bump *n.* (something
protruding) โหนก nòok
[อัน an]

bump *vt.* (bang, slam)

กระแทก grà~tɛ̂ɛk
bumper *n.* (e.g. car)
เครื่องกันชน krûuang-
gan-chon, กันชน gan-
chon ✿ [อัน an]
bumper sticker *n.*
สติ๊กเกอร์ติดท้ายรถ sà~
dtík-gɤ̂ɤ-dtìt-táai-rót
[แผ่น pɛ̀n]
bumpy *adj.* ขรุขระ krù-krà
bun *n.* (bread roll)
ขนมปังนุ่มรสหวาน kà~
nǒm-bpang-nûm-rót-
wǎan [แถว tɛ̌ɛo (loaf),
ก้อน gɔ̂ɔn (piece), แผ่น
pɛ̀n (piece)] | (of the
hair) มวยผม muuai-pǒm
[มวย muuai, ลูก lûuk]
bunch *n.* (bananas) หวี wǐi
[หวี wǐi] | (e.g. grapes)
พวง puuang [พวง
puuang] | (flowers) ช่อ
chɔ̂ɔ [ช่อ chɔ̂ɔ] |
(vegetables) กำ gam [กำ
gam]
bundle *n.* (handful) กำ
gam [กำ gam] |
(package) ห่อ hɔ̀ɔ [ห่อ
hɔ̀ɔ]
bundle *vt.* (tie) มัด mát |
(wrap) ห่อ hɔ̀ɔ

bungalow *n.* บังกะโล
bang-gà~loo [หลัง lǎng]
bunion *n.* ตาปลา dtaa-
bplaa [อัน an, ที่ tîi]
buoy *n.* (float) ชูชีพ chuu-
chîip [อัน an]
burden *n.* (responsibility,
duty) ภาระ paa-rá [อัน an]
burden *vt.*
(inconvenience)
เป็นภาระกับ bpen-paa-
rá-gàp
bureau *n.* (institute,
agency) สำนัก sǎm-nák
[สำนัก sǎm-nák]
bureaucrat *n.* ข้าราชการ
kâa-râat-chá~gaan [คน
kon]
bureaucratic *adj.*
มีพิธีรีตองมาก mii-pí-tii-
rii-dtɔɔng-mâak
burglar *n.* ขโมย kà~mooi
[คน kon]
burglar alarm *n.*
สัญญาณกันขโมย sǎn-
yaan-gan-kà~mooi
[เครื่อง krûuang]
burial *n.* (ceremony)
พิธีฝังศพ pí-tii-fǎng-sòp
[พิธี pí-tii]
Burma *n.* พม่า pá~mâa

[ประเทศ bprà~têet]

burn n. (area that is burned) บริเวณที่ไหม้ bɔɔ-rí~ween-tîi-mâi [บริเวณ bɔɔ-rí~ween]

burn vi. ไหม้ mâi

burn vt. เผา pǎo

burned out adj. (tired) เหนื่อยล้า nὺuai-láa

burn off vt. (remove by burning) เผาทำลาย pǎo-tam-laai

burp vi. เรอ rəə

burst vi. (explode) ระเบิด rá~bèət

bury vt. ฝัง fǎng

bus n. รถบัส rót-bás [คัน kan] | (aircon) รถเมล์ติดแอร์ rót-mee-dtìt-ɛɛ [คัน kan] | (ordinary) รถเมล์ไม่ติดแอร์ rót-mee-mâi-dtìt-ɛɛ [คัน kan]

busboy n. คนเก็บจานในร้านอาหาร kon-gèp-jaan-nai-ráan-aa-hǎan [คน kon]

bush n. พุ่ม pûm, พุ่มไม้ pûm-máai [พุ่ม pûm]

business n. (commerce) การค้า gaan-káa, ธุรกิจ tú-rá~gìt | (errand, personal affairs) ธุระ tú-rá [เรื่อง rûuang, อัน an ✦]

business card n. นามบัตร naam-bàt [ใบ bai]

business owner n. เจ้าของธุรกิจ jâo-kɔ̌ɔng-tú-rá-gìt [คน kon] | (male) เถ้าแก่ tâo-gɛ̀ɛ ✦ [คน kon]

businessperson n. นักธุรกิจ nák-tú-rá-gìt [คน kon]

bus station n. สถานีรถเมล์ sà~tǎa-nii-rót-mee, ขนส่ง kǒn-sòng ✦ [สถานี sà~tǎa-nii]

bus stop n. ป้ายรถเมล์ bpâai-rót-mee [ป้าย bpâai]

bust n. (chest) หน้าอก nâa-òk | (sculpture) รูปปั้นท่อนบน rûup-bpân-tɔ̂n-bon

bus terminal n. สถานีรถโดยสาร sà~tǎa-nii-rót-dooi-sǎan [สถานี sà~tǎa-nii]

busy adj. (crowded, congested) พลุกพล่าน plúk-plâan | (having work or errand) มีธุระ mii-tú-rá | (occupied) ยุ่ง yûng

but conj. แต่ dtɛ̀ɛ, แต่ว่า dtɛ̀ɛ-wâa

but prep. (except) นอกจาก nɔ̂ɔk-jàak, เว้นแต่ wén-dtɛ̀ɛ

butch n. (lesbian) หญิงที่แต่งตัวเป็นชาย yǐng-tîi-dtɛ̀ng-dtuua-bpen-chaai [คน kon]

butt n. (cigarette, body part) ก้น gôn [ก้น gôn]

butter n. เนย nəəi [กล่อง glɔ̀ng (box)]

butter vt. ทาเนย taa-nəəi

butterfly n. (animal) ผีเสื้อ pǐi-sûua [ตัว dtuua] | (flirt) คนเจ้าชู้ kon-jâo-chúu [คน kon]

butt in vi. (interrupt conversation) พูดขัดจังหวะ pûut-kàt-jang-wà | (meddle) ยุ่ง yûng, เสือก sùuak 💣

buttocks n. ก้น gôn, ตูด dtùut 💣

button n. (e.g. phone) ปุ่ม bpùm [ปุ่ม bpùm] | (e.g. shirt, blouse) กระดุม grà~dum [เม็ด mét (piece)]

buy v. (purchase) ซื้อ sɯ́ɯ

buyer n. คนซื้อ kon-sɯ́ɯ, ผู้ซื้อ pûu-sɯ́ɯ ‼ [คน kon]

buzz n. เสียงพึมพำ sǐiang-pɯm-pam

buzz vi. (make sound) ร้องหึ่งๆ rɔ́ɔng-hɯ̀ng-hɯ̀ng

buzzer n. กริ่ง grìng [อัน an]

by prep. (created by) โดย dooi | (next to) ข้าง kâang | (route, e.g. ground, air) ทาง taang | (using, e.g. fork, hand) ด้วย dûuai | (vehicle, e.g. car, plane) โดย dooi

by air adv. ทางอากาศ taang-aa-gàat

by airmail adv. ทางไปรษณีย์อากาศ taang-bprai-sà~nii-aa-gàat

by chance adv. บังเอิญ bang-əən

bye! see bye-bye!

bye-bye! interj. บ๊ายบาย báai-baai, ลาก่อน laa-gɔ̀ɔn

by land *adv.* ทางบก taang-bòk

by mail *adv.* ทางไปรษณีย์ taang-bprai-sà~nii

by means of *prep.* โดย dooi

by oneself *adv.* ด้วยตัวเอง dûuai-dtuua-eeng, โดยลำพัง dooi-lam-pang !

bypass *n.* (around city) ถนนรอบเมือง tà~nǒn-rɔ̂ɔp-mɯɯang [เส้น sên, สาย sǎai] | (detour) ทางอ้อม taang-ɔ̂ɔm [ทาง taang]

by-product *n.* ของที่เหลือ kɔ̌ɔng-tîi-lɯ̌a [ชิ้น chín]

by sea *adv.* ทางทะเล taang-tá~lee

bystander *n.* (who witnesses event) ผู้เห็นเหตุการณ์ pûu-hěn-hèet-gaan [คน kon]

by way of *prep.* โดย dooi

C

cab *n.* รถแท็กซี่ rót-ték-sîi [คัน kan]

cabaret *n.* การแสดงคาบาเร่ต์ gaan-sà~dɛɛng-kaa-baa-rêe

cabbage *n.* กะหล่ำปลี gà~làm-bplii [หัว hǔua]

cabin *n.* (cottage) กระท่อม grà~tɔ̂m [หลัง lǎng] | (small room) ห้องเล็ก hɔ̂ng-lék [ห้อง hɔ̂ng]

cabinet *n.* (cupboard) ตู้ dtûu [ใบ bai]

cable *n.* สายเคเบิล sǎai-kee-bân [สาย sǎai]

cactus *n.* ตะบองเพชร dtà~bɔɔng-pét [ต้น dtôn]

caddie *n.* เด็กแบกถุงกอล์ฟ dèk-bɛ̀ɛk-tǔng-gɔ́ɔp [คน kon]

cadet *n.* นักเรียนทหาร nák-riian-tá~hǎan [คน kon]

cafe *n.* ร้านกาแฟ ráan-gaa-fɛɛ [ร้าน ráan]

cafeteria *n.* โรงอาหาร roong-aa-hǎan [แห่ง hèng]

caffeine *n.* คาเฟอีน kaa-fee-iin

cage *n.* (e.g. bird) กรง grong [ใบ bai]

cake *n.* ขนมเค้ก kà~nǒm-kéek [ชิ้น chín

(piece), ก้อน gɔ̂ɔn (whole)]

calamity *n.* หายนะ hǎa-yá~ná

calcium *n.* แคลเซี่ยม kɛn-sîiam

calculate *v.* คำนวณ kam-nuuan

calculator *n.* เครื่องคิดเลข krûuang-kít-lêek [เครื่อง krûuang]

calculus *n.* (math) แคลคูลัส kɛo-kuu-lás [วิชา wí-chaa]

calendar *n.* ปฏิทิน bpà~dtì-tin [แผ่น pèn (wall)]

calf *n.* (baby cow) ลูกวัว lûuk-wuua [ตัว dtuua] | (body part) น่อง nɔ̂ng [ข้าง kâang, อัน an (for animal)]

caliber *n.* (e.g. gun) ขนาดลำกล้องปืน kà~nàat-lam-glɔ̂ng-bpʉʉn

call *n.* (phone) การโทรศัพท์ gaan-too-rá~sàp

call *v.* เรียก rîiak

call *vt.* (phone) โทรศัพท์หา too-rá~sàp-hǎa

call back *vi.* โทรกลับ too-

glàp

called *adj.* (named) เรียกว่า rîiak-wâa

caller *n.* (phone) ผู้โทรศัพท์ pûu-too-rá~sàp [คน kon]

call in witnesses *v.* เบิกพยาน bə̀ək-pá~yaan

calm *adj.* (mind) ใจเย็น jai-yen | (quiet) สงบ sà~ngòp | (still) เฉย chə̌əi

calm down! *interj.* ใจเย็นๆ jai-yen-yen

calorie *n.* แคลอรี่ kɛɛ-lɔɔ-rîi ✗ [แคลอรี่ kɛɛ-lɔɔ-rîi]

Cambodia *n.* เขมร kà~měen, กัมพูชา gam-puu-chaa ! [ประเทศ bprà~têet]

Cambodian *adj.* เขมร kà~měen

Cambodian *n.* (people) ชาวเขมร chaao-kà~měen [คน kon]

camel *n.* อูฐ ùut [ตัว dtuua]

camera *n.* กล้อง glɔ̂ng [กล้อง glɔ̂ng]

camera man *n.* ช่างภาพ châng-pâap, ตากล้อง dtaa-glɔ̂ng ✎ [คน kon]

camp *n.* ค่าย kâai [ค่าย

kâai]

camp *vi.* (with tent)
ตั้งแคมป์ dtâng-kém

campaign *n.* การรณรงค์
gaan-ron-ná~rong [ครั้ง
kráng]

camper *n.* (e.g. scout,
summer) ผู้เข้าค่าย pûu-
kâo-kâai [คน kon]

campervan see motor
home

campus *n.* (university
ground)
บริเวณมหาวิทยาลัย bɔɔ-
rí~ween-má~hǎa-wít-
tá~yaa-lai

can *aux.* (able to) ได้ dâai,
สามารถ sǎa-mâat ǃ

can *n.* กระป๋อง grà~bpɔ̌ng
[ใบ bai]

Canada *n.* ประเทศแคนาดา
bprà~têet-kɛɛ-naa-daa
[ประเทศ bprà~têet]

canal *n.* คลอง klɔɔng
[คลอง klɔɔng, สาย sǎai]

canary *n.* (bird) นกคีรีบูน
nók-kii-rii-buun [ตัว
dtuua]

cancel *v.* (call off) ยกเลิก
yók-lə̂ək, ล้มเลิก lóm-
lə̂ək | (discontinue, stop)
งด ngót

cancellation *n.* การยกเลิก
gaan-yók-lə̂ək

Cancer *n.* (astrological
sign) ราศีกรกฎ raa-sǐi-
gɔɔ-rá~gòt [ราศี raa-sǐi]

cancer *n.* มะเร็ง má~reng

candid *adj.* (honest)
จริงใจ jing-jai

candidate *n.* ผู้สมัคร pûu-
sà~màk [คน kon]

candle *n.* เทียน tiian [เล่ม
lêm]

candlestick *n.* เชิงเทียน
chəəng-tiian [อัน an]

candlewick *n.* ไส้เทียน
sâi-tiian [เส้น sên]

candy *n.* (sweets)
ของหวาน kɔ̌ɔng-wǎan
[อัน an (piece), ชิ้น chín
(piece), ถ้วย tûuai (bowl)]
| (toffee) ลูกอม lûuk-om
[เม็ด mét]

cane *n.* (flogging rod)
ไม้เรียว mái-riiao [อัน an]
| (for walking) ไม้เท้า
mái-táao [อัน an]

canine *adj.* เกี่ยวกับสุนัข
gìiao-gàp-sù~nák

canker *n.* ปากเปื่อย
bpàak-bpɯ̀ɯai

canker sore *n.* แผลในปาก plɛ̌ɛ-nai-bpàak [ที่ tîi]

cannabis see marijuana

cannibal *n.* (man eater) มนุษย์กินคน má~nút-gin-kon [คน kon]

cannon *n.* ปืนใหญ่ bpʉʉn-yài [กระบอก grà~bɔ̀ɔk]

cannot *aux.* ไม่ได้ mâi-dâai, ไม่สามารถ mâi-sǎa-mâat ⚑, ไม่ไหว mâi-wǎi ✿

canoe *n.* เรือแคนู rʉʉa-kɛɛ-nuu [ลำ lam]

can opener *n.* ที่เปิดกระป๋อง tîi-bpòət-grà~bpɔ̌ng [อัน an, เครื่อง krʉ̂uang (device)]

canopy *n.* โจม joom [หลัง lǎng]

can't see cannot

cantaloupe *n.* แคนตาลูป kɛɛn-dtaa-lúup [ลูก lûuk]

canteen *n.* (cafeteria) โรงอาหาร roong-aa-hǎan [แห่ง hɛ̀ng] | (water container) กระติก grà~dtìk [ใบ bai]

canvas *n.* ผ้าใบ pâa-bai

[ผืน pʉ̌ʉn, แผ่น pèn]

canyon *n.* หุบเขาลึก hùp-kǎo-lʉ́k [แห่ง hɛ̀ng]

cap *n.* (cover, lid) ฝา fǎa [ฝา fǎa, ชิ้น chín] | (hat) หมวก mùuak [ใบ bai]

capability *n.* (ability) ความสามารถ kwaam-sǎa-mâat

capable *adj.* (able) มีความสามารถ mii-kwaam-sǎa-mâat

capacity *n.* (ability) ความสามารถ kwaam-sǎa-mâat | (volume) ปริมาณความจุ bpà~rí~maan-kwaam-jù

cape *n.* (peninsula) แหลม lɛ̌ɛm [แห่ง hɛ̀ng]

capital *n.* (city) เมืองหลวง mʉʉang-lǔuang [แห่ง hɛ̀ng] | (investment) ทุน tun [ก้อน gɔ̂ɔn]

capitalism *n.* ทุนนิยม tun-ní-yom

capitalist *n.* (advocate of capitalism) นักทุนนิยม nák-tun-ní-yom [คน kon] | (one with capital) นายทุน naai-tun [คน kon]

capitalize *vt.* (make

upper case) เขียนด้วยตัว
อักษรใหญ่ kǐian-dûuai-
dtuua-àk-sǔuan-yài

capital letter n.
ตัวพิมพ์ใหญ่ dtuua-pim-
yài [ตัว dtuua]

capital punishment n.
โทษประหาร tôot-bprà~
hǎan [ครั้ง kráng]

capitol n. (building)
อาคารรัฐสภา aa-kaan-
rát-tà~sà~paa [หลัง lǎng
(building)]

Capricorn n. ราศีมังกร
raa-sǐi-mang-gɔɔn [ราศี
raa-sǐi]

capsule n. แคปซูล kép-
suun [เม็ด mét]

captain n. กัปตัน gàp-
dtan, หัวหน้าทีม hǔua-
nâa-tiim [คน kon]

caption n. (e.g. video)
คำบรรยายภาพ kam-ban-
yaai-pâap [คำ kam]

captive adj. (confined)
ถูกจับกุม tùuk-jàp-gum

captive n. เชลย chá~ləəi,
นักโทษ nák-tôot [คน kon]

capture vt. จับ jàp

car n. (automobile) รถ rót,
รถยนต์ rót-yon [คัน kan]

| (sedan) รถเก๋ง rót-gěng
[คัน kan]

caramel n. กะละแม gà~
lá~mɛɛ [อัน an, ชิ้น chín]

carat n. กะรัต gà~ràt
[กะรัต gà~ràt]

caravan n.
ขบวนนักเดินทาง kà~
buuan-nák-dəən-taang
[ขบวน kà~buuan
(procession), กอง gɔɔng
(group)]

caravan see motor home

carbohydrate n.
คาร์โบไฮเดรต kaa-boo-
hai-drèet

carbon n. คาร์บอน kaa-
bɔn [กลุ่ม glùm]

carbonated adj. มีก๊าซ
mii-gáat ✦

carbon dioxide n.
คาร์บอนไดออกไซด์ kaa-
bɔn-dai-ɔ̀k-saai

card n. (e.g. credit, I.D.)
บัตร bàt [ใบ bai] |
(playing) ไพ่ pâi [ใบ bai
(card), สำรับ sǎm-ráp
(deck)]

cardboard n. กระดาษแข็ง
grà~dàat-kěng [แผ่น pèn]

cardiac arrest n.

ภาวะหัวใจหยุดเต้น paa-wá-hǔua-jai-yùt-dtên

cardigan *n.* เสื้อกันหนาว sûua-gan-nǎao [ตัว dtuua]

cardinal number *n.* เลขจำนวนนับ lêek-jam-nuuan-náp [จำนวน jam-nuuan]

cardiology *n.* (study) การศึกษาเกี่ยวกับหัวใจ gaan-sùk-sǎa-giiao-gàp-hǔua-jai

care *n.* (treatment) การรักษา gaan-rák-sǎa

care about *vt.* (be interested in) สนใจ sǒn-jai

career *n.* (profession) อาชีพ aa-chîip [อาชีพ aa-chîip]

care for *vt.* (be fond of) รักใคร่ rák-krâi | (take care of) ดูแล duu-lɛɛ

carefree *adj.* ไร้กังวล rái-gang-won

careful *adj.* รอบคอบ rɔ̂ɔp-kɔ̂ɔp | (cautious) ระมัดระวัง rá~mát-rá~wang

careless *adj.* ประมาท bprà~màat

caress *vt.* เล้าโลม láo-loom ✍

carjacking *n.* การจี้รถ gaan-jîi-rót

carnation *n.* ดอกคาร์เนชั่น dɔ̀ɔk-kaa-nee-chân [ดอก dɔ̀ɔk]

carnival *n.* เทศกาล têet-sà~gaan [งาน ngaan]

carnivorous *adj.* ที่กินเนื้อสัตว์ tîi-gin-núua-sàt

carousel *n.* (merry-go-round) ม้าหมุน máa-mǔn [ตัว dtuua] | (revolving belt) สายพาน sǎai-paan [เส้น sên]

carp *n.* ปลาตะเพียน bplaa-dtà~piian [ตัว dtuua]

car park see parking lot

carpenter *n.* ช่างไม้ châng-máai [คน kon]

carpet *n.* พรม prom [ผืน pǔun]

car pool *n.* การใช้รถร่วมกัน gaan-chái-rót-rûuam-gan

carriage *n.* (horse-drawn vehicle) รถม้า rót-máa [คัน kan]

carrier n. (cargo airplane) เครื่องบินขนส่ง krûuang-bin-kǒn-sòng [ลำ lam, เครื่อง krûuang] | (disease) พาหะนำโรค paa-hà-nam-rôok [ตัว dtuua] | (e.g. mobile phone) ผู้ให้บริการ pûu-hâi-bɔɔ-rí~gaan [ราย raai ‼, เจ้า jâao]

carrot n. แครอท kɛɛ-rɔ̀t [หัว hǔua (whole), ชิ้น chín (piece)]

carry vt. (cradle in arms) อุ้ม ûm | (hold) ถือ tʉ̌ʉ | (in arithmetic) ทด tót | (on the shoulder) สะพาย sà~paai

carry on v. (do more) ทำ_ต่อ tam-_-dtɔ̀ɔ

carry-on n. กระเป๋าที่นำขึ้นเครื่องได้ grà~bpǎo-tîi-nam-kʉ̂n-krûuang-dâai [ใบ bai]

car seat n. ที่นั่งของเด็กบนรถ tîi-nâng-kɔ̌ɔng-dèk-bon-rót [อัน an, ตัว dtuua]

carsick adj. เมารถ mao-rót

cart n. (drawn by animals)

เกวียน gwiian [เล่ม lêm] | (e.g. shopping) รถเข็น rót-kěn [คัน kan]

carton n. กล่องกระดาษ glɔ̀ng-grà~dàat [ใบ bai]

cartoon n. การ์ตูน gaa-dtuun [เรื่อง rʉ̂ʉang (story)]

cartridge n. (e.g. gun) กระสุนปืน grà~sǔn-bpʉʉn [นัด nát, ลูก lûuk]

carve v. (sculpture) แกะสลัก gɛ̀-sà~làk

Casanova n. ขุนแผน kǔn-pɛ̌ɛn [คน kon]

case n. (law) คดี ká~dii [คดี ká~dii] | (law or medicine) กรณี gɔɔ-rá~nii [กรณี gɔɔ-rá~nii ‼, อย่าง yàang] | (matter) เรื่อง rʉ̂ʉang [เรื่อง rʉ̂ʉang] | (pouch) ซอง sɔɔng [ซอง sɔɔng, อัน an ‼]

cash n. เงินสด ngən-sòt [แบงค์ béng (bill), เหรียญ rǐian (coin)]

cash vt. (e.g. check, chips) เอา_ไปขึ้นเงิน ao-_-bpai-kʉ̂n-ngən

cashew *n.* มะม่วงหิมพานต์ má~mûuang-hǐm-má~paan [ลูก lûuk]

cashew nut *n.* เม็ดมะม่วงหิมพานต์ mét-má~mûuang-hǐm-má~paan [เม็ด mét]

cashier *n.* คนเก็บเงิน kon-gèp-ngən [คน kon]

cashier's check *n.* เช็คที่สั่งจ่ายโดยธนาคาร chék-tîi-sàng-jàai-dooi-tá~naa-kaan ! [ใบ bai]

cash machine see ATM machine

cash register *n.* เครื่องคิดเงิน krûuang-kít-ngən [เครื่อง krûuang]

casino *n.* คาสิโน kaa-sì~noo [แห่ง hèng] | บ่อน bɔ̀n [บ่อน bɔ̀n, แห่ง hèng]

casket *n.* (coffin) หีบศพ hìip-sòp [หีบ hìip]

cassette *n.* ตลับเทป dtà~làp-téep [ตลับ dtà~làp]

cast *n.* (actors) นักแสดง nák-sà~dɛɛng [ชุด chút] | (medical) เฝือก fùuak [อัน an]

cast *vt.* (in a mold) หล่อ lɔ̀ɔ

cast a ballot *vi.* ลงคะแนน long-ká~nɛɛn

caste *n.* (class) ชนชั้น chon-chán [กลุ่ม glùm (group)] | (in India) วรรณะ wan-ná [ชั้น chán]

castle *n.* ปราสาท bpraa-sàat [หลัง lǎng (building)]

castrate *vt.* ตอน dtɔɔn

casual *adj.* (informal) ไม่มีพิธีรีตรอง mâi-mii-pí-tii-rii-dtrɔɔng

casualty *n.* (people or property) การสูญเสีย gaan-sǔun-sǐia

cat *n.* แมว mɛɛo [ตัว dtuua]

catalog *n.* แคตตาลอก két-dtaa-lɔ́k [เล่ม lêm]

cataract *n.* (eye) ต้อกระจก dtɔ̂ɔ-grà~jòk [อัน an (piece)]

catastrophe *n.* ความหายนะ kwaam-hǎa-yá~ná

catch *vt.* (capture, seize) จับ jàp | (disease) ติด dtit | (e.g. bus) ไปทัน bpai-tan

catch up with *vt.* ตามทัน dtaam-tan

categorize *vt.* แยกประเภท yêɛk-bprà~pêet

category n. (class, kind) ประเภท bprà~pêet [ประเภท bprà~pêet] | (group, section) หมวดหมู่ mùuat-mùu [หมวด mùuat]

cater vi. (food) จัดอาหาร jàt-aa-hǎan

caterpillar n. (hairless variety) บุ้ง bûng [ตัว dtuua] | (wormlike larva) หนอน nɔ̌ɔn [ตัว dtuua]

cater to vt. (appeal to) ดึงดูด dʉng-dùut

catfish n. ปลาดุก bplaa-dùk [ตัว dtuua]

cathedral n. โบสถ์ใหญ่ bòot-yài [หลัง lǎng (building)]

Catholic adj. เกี่ยวกับคาธอลิก gìiao-gàp-kaa-tɔɔ-lík

CAT scan n. การถ่ายเอ็กซ เรย์ด้วยคอมพิวเตอร์ gaan-tàai-éek-sà~ree-dûuai-kɔm-píu-dtɤ̂ə

cattle n. วัวควาย wuua-kwaai [ฝูง fǔung (herd)]

catwalk n. (walkway) ทางเดินยาวและแคบ taang-dəən-yaao-lé-kɛ̂ɛp [ทาง taang]

Caucasian n. (Westerner) ฝรั่ง fà~ràng ✦ [คน kon] | (white-skinned person) คนผิวขาว kon-pǐu-kǎao [คน kon]

cauliflower n. กะหล่ำดอก gà~làm-dɔ̀ɔk [หัว hǔua]

caulk n. วัสดุอุดรอยรั่ว wát-sà~dù-ùt-rɔɔi-rûua [หลอด lɔ̀ɔt (tube)]

cause n. กรณี gɔɔ-rá~nii [กรณี gɔɔ-rá~nii ⚡, อย่าง yàang] | สาเหตุ sǎa-hèet [ข้อ kɔ̂ɔ]

cause vt. เป็นเหตุให้ bpen-hèet-hâi

caution n. (warning) คำเตือน kam-dtʉʉan

cautious adj. ระมัดระวัง rá~mát-rá~wang

cave n. ถ้ำ tâm [แห่ง hɛ̀ng, ถ้ำ tâm]

cavern see cave

cavity n. (dental) ฟันผุ fan-pù [ซี่ sîi] | (hole) โพรง proong [โพรง proong, อัน an] | (in earth) หลุม lǔm [รู ruu, หลุม lǔm]

CD n. แผ่นซีดี pèn-sii-dii, แผ่นดิสก์ pèn-dít [แผ่น pèn]

CD burner n. เครื่องเบิร์นซีดี krûuang-bəən-sii-dii [เครื่อง krûuang]

CD player n. เครื่องเล่นซีดี krûuang-lên-sii-dii [เครื่อง krûuang]

CD-ROM n. ซีดีรอม sii-dii-rɔɔm [แผ่น pèn (disc)]

cease v. (stop) หยุด yùt

cease-fire n. การหยุดยิง gaan-yùt-ying

cedar n. ต้นสนซีดาร์ dtôn-sǒn-sii-dâa [ต้น dtôn]

ceiling n. เพดาน pee-daan [แผ่น pèn]

celebrate v. ฉลอง chà~lɔ̌ɔng

celebration n. (festival) งานฉลอง ngaan-chà~lɔ̌ɔng [งาน ngaan]

celebrity n. คนมีชื่อเสียง kon-mii-chûu-sǐiang [คน kon]

celery n. ขึ้นฉ่าย kɨ̂n-chàai [ต้น dtôn (plant)]

celibacy n. (sexual abstention) การละเว้นจากการร่วมเพศ gaan-lá-wéen-jàak-gaan-rûuam-pêet

cell n. (in the body) เซลล์ seo [เซลล์ seo]

cellar n. ห้องใต้ดิน hɔ̂ng-dtâai-din [ห้อง hɔ̂ng]

cello n. เชลโล cheen-loo [เครื่อง krûuang]

cellophane noodles n. (glass noodles, bean threads) วุ้นเส้น wún-sên [เส้น sên (strand), ห่อ hɔ̀ɔ (pack)]

cellphone n. โทรศัพท์มือถือ too-rá~sàp-mɨɨ-tɨ̌ɨ, มือถือ mɨɨ-tɨ̌ɨ ● [เครื่อง krûuang]

Celsius n. เซลเซียส seo-sîiat [องศา ong-sǎa]

cement n. ปูนซีเมนต์ bpuun-sii-men [กระสอบ grà~sɔ̀ɔp (sack)]

cemetery n. ป่าช้า bpàa-cháa, สุสาน sù-sǎan ! [แห่ง hɛ̀ng]

censor v. เซ็นเซอร์ sen-sə̂ə

census n. สำมะโนครัว

săm-má~noo-kruua [ครั้ง kráng]

cent *n.* เซ็นต์ sen [เซ็นต์ sen]

center *n.* ศูนย์กลาง sŭun-glaang [ศูนย์ sŭun]

centimeter *n.* เซนติเมตร sen-dtì~méet

centipede *n.* ตะขาบ dtà~kàap [ตัว dtuua]

central *adj.* กลาง glaang

century *n.* ศตวรรษ sàt~dtà~wát [ศตวรรษ sàt~dtà~wát]

ceramic *adj.* เซรามิก see-raa-mìk

cereal *n.* (e.g. breakfast) ซีเรียล sii-riiao [ชนิด chá~nít]

ceremony *n.* พิธี pí-tii [พิธี pí-tii]

certain *adj.* (definite, inevitable) แน่นอน nɛ̂ɛ-nɔɔn | (some) บางอย่าง baang-yàang | (sure) แน่ใจ nɛ̂ɛ-jai

certainly *adv.* อย่างแน่นอน yàang-nɛ̂ɛ-nɔɔn

certainly *idm.* (that's right) ใช่ châi

certificate *n.* ใบประกาศ bai-bprà~gàat ◆ [ใบ bai, แผ่น pèn] | ใบรับรอง bai-ráp-rɔɔng [ใบ bai, แผ่น pèn]

certificate of marriage *n.* ทะเบียนสมรส tá~biian-sŏm-rót [ใบ bai]

certification *n.* การรับรอง gaan-ráp-rɔɔng

certified check *n.* เช็คที่ธนาคารรับรอง chék-tîi-tá~naa-kaan-ráp-rɔɔng [ใบ bai]

certified public accountant *n.* ผู้ตรวจบัญชี pûu-dtrùuat-ban-chii [คน kon]

certify *vt.* รับรอง ráp-rɔɔng

cervix *n.* ปากมดลูก bpàak-mót-lûuk

Cesarean section *n.* การคลอดโดยการผ่าตัด gaan-klɔ̂ɔt-dooi-gaan-pàa-dtàt

chaff *n.* (of rice) แกลบ glɛ̀ɛp

chain *n.* (metal) โซ่ sôo [เส้น sên, สาย săai]

chain *vt.* (tether, restrain) ล่ามโซ่ lâam-sôo

chain letter *n.*

จดหมายลูกโซ่ jòt-măai-lûuk-sôo [ฉบับ chà~bàp]

chainsaw n. เลื่อยไฟฟ้า lûuai-fai-fáa [เครื่อง krûuang]

chain smoker n. คนสูบบุหรี่มวนต่อมวน kon-sùup-bù~rìi-muuan-dtɔ̀ɔ-muuan [คน kon]

chair n. (president) ประธาน bprà~taan [ท่าน tân ⸙, คน kon] | (to sit on) เก้าอี้ gâo-îi [ตัว dtuua]

chairman n. ประธาน bprà~taan [ท่าน tân ⸙, คน kon]

chalk n. ชอล์ก chɔ́k [แท่ง têng]

challenge v. ท้าทาย táa-taai

challenger n. ผู้ท้าชิง pûu-táa-ching [คน kon]

challenging adj. ท้าทาย táa-taai

chamber n. ห้อง hɔ̂ng [ห้อง hɔ̂ng]

chamber of commerce n. หอการค้า hɔ̌ɔ-gaan-káa [แห่ง hèng]

chameleon n. กิ้งก่าเปลี่ยนสี gîng-gàa-bpliian-sǐi [ตัว dtuua]

champagne n. แชมเปญ chɛm-bpeen [ขวด kùuat (bottle)]

champion n. ผู้ชนะเลิศ pûu-chá~ná-lə̂ət ⸙ [คน kon]

chance n. (opportunity) โอกาส oo-gàat [ครั้ง kráng]

change n. (money returned) เงินทอน ngən-tɔɔn [จำนวน jam-nuuan]

change v. เปลี่ยน bpliian

change hands vi. เปลี่ยนมือ bpliian-muu

change money vi. แลกเงิน lɛ̂ɛk-ngən

channel n. (e.g. TV) ช่อง chɔ̂ng [ช่อง chɔ̂ng]

chant v. (pray) สวด sùuat | (sing) ร้องเพลง rɔ́ɔng-pleeng

chaos n. ความวุ่นวาย kwaam-wûn-waai

chaotic adj. ยุ่งเหยิง yûng-yə̌əng

chapel n. (small church) โบสถ์เล็ก bòot-lék [แห่ง

hèng (location), หลัง lǎng (building)]

chaperon *n.* ผู้ควบคุม pûu-kûuap-kum [คน kon]

chapter *n.* (part) ตอน dtɔɔn [ตอน dtɔɔn] | (section) บท bòt [บท bòt]

character *n.* (appearance) ลักษณะ lák-sà~nà [ลักษณะ lák-sà~nà] | (in a play) ตัวละคร dtuua-lá~kɔɔn [คน kon, ตัว dtuua] | (nature, habit) นิสัย ní-sǎi | (of the alphabet) ตัวอักษร dtuua-àk-sɔ̌ɔn [ตัว dtuua]

characteristic *n.* (nature, habit) ลักษณะนิสัย lák-sà~nà-ní-sǎi, บุคลิกภาพ bùk-ká~lík-gà~pâap ⚠

charcoal *n.* ถ่าน tàan [ก้อน gɔ̂ɔn]

charge *n.* (admission) ค่าผ่านประตู kâa-pàan-bprà~dtuu | (legal) คดี ká~dii [คดี ká~dii] | (legal) ข้อหา kɔ̂ɔ-hǎa [กระทง grà~tong]

charge *v.* (electricity) ชาร์จ cháat ✱ | (legal) ฟ้องร้อง fɔ́ɔng-rɔ́ɔng |

(money, e.g. in restaurant) เก็บเงิน gèp-ngən | (price) คิดราคา kít-raa-kaa

charger *n.* ที่ชาร์จ tîi-cháat ✱ [อัน an]

charisma *n.* (of a leader) ความเป็นผู้นำ kwaam-bpen-pûu-nam

charitable *adj.* ใจบุญ jai-bun

charity *n.* การกุศล gaan-gù~sǒn

charm *n.* (e.g. for luck) เครื่องราง krûuang-raang [ชิ้น chín, อัน an] | (magic spell) มนต์เสน่ห์ mon-sà~nèe, เวทย์มนต์ wêet-mon

charming *adj.* มีเสน่ห์ mii-sà~nèe

chart *n.* (graph) แผนภาพ pɛ̌ɛn-pâap [แผ่น pɛ̀n]

chase *n.* การติดตาม gaan-dtìt-dtaam

chase *vt.* (pursue rapidly) ไล่ lâi

chastity *n.* (virtue) ความดีงาม kwaam-dii-ngaam

chat *vi.* คุย kui, พูดคุย

pûut-kui ⚡

chauffeur n. คนขับรถ
kon-kàp-rót, โชว์เฟอร์
choo-fə̂ə ❀ [คน kon]

cheap adj. (e.g. women)
ใจง่าย jai-ngâai | (price)
ถูก tùuk | (stingy)
ขี้เหนียว kîi-nĭiao

cheat vi. (e.g. on test) โกง
goong | (on one's lover)
นอกใจ nɔ̂ɔk-jai

cheat vt. (deceive)
หลอกลวง lɔ̀ɔk-luuang

cheating adj. โกง goong,
ขี้โกง kîi-goong ❀

check n. (bank draft) เช็ค
chék [ใบ bai (piece), ฉบับ
chà~bàp ⚡ (piece)] |
(food bill) บิล bin [ใบ bai]

check v. (verify) ตรวจ
dtrùuat, เช็ค chék ❀

check vt. (review)
ตรวจสอบ dtrùuat-sɔ̀ɔp

check in vi. (e.g. hotel)
เช็คอิน chék-in | (for
work) ลงเวลาทำงาน
long-wee-laa-tam-ngaan

check out vi. (e.g. hotel)
เช็คเอาท์ chék-áo

check out vt. (look at) ดู
duu

check please! interj.
เช็คบิล chék-bin ❀

checkup n. การตรวจเช็ค
gaan-dtrùuat-chék

cheek n. แก้ม gɛ̂ɛm [ข้าง
kâang]

cheer vi. (make sound)
เชียร์ chiia ❀

cheer vt. (encourage)
ให้กำลังใจ hâi-gam-lang-
jai

cheerful adj. ร่าเริง râa-
rəəng

cheerleader n.
เชียร์ลีดเดอร์ chiia-lìit-də̂ə
[คน kon]

cheers! interj. ไชโย chai-
yoo

cheese n. เนยแข็ง nəəi-
kɛ̌ŋ [ชิ้น chín (piece)]

cheetah n. เสือชีตาร์
sʉ̌ua-chii-dtâa [ตัว dtuua]

chef n. เชฟ chép ❀ [คน
kon] | (head) หัวหน้า
พ่อครัว hŭua-nâa-pɔ̂ɔ-
kruua ⚡ [คน kon]

chemical adj. ทางเคมี
taang-kee-mii

chemical solution n.
น้ำยาเคมี nám-yaa-kee-
mii [ชนิด chá~nít, ตัว

dtuua ❧]
chemical substance n.
สารเคมี sǎan-kee-mii
[ชนิด chá~nít]
chemist n. (pharmacist)
เภสัชกร pee-sàt-chá~
gɔɔn [คน kon] |
(scientist) นักเคมี nák-
kee-mii [คน kon]
chemistry n. เคมี kee-mii
[วิชา wí-chaa]
chemotherapy n.
เคมีบำบัด kee-mii-bam-
bàt
cheque n. เช็ค chék [ใบ
bai (piece), ฉบับ chà~bàp
❢ (piece)]
cherish vt. (care for)
ทะนุถนอม tá~nú-tà~
nǔɔm
cherry n. เชอรี่ chəə-rîi
[ลูก lûuk]
chess n. หมากรุก màak-
rúk [กระดาน grà~daan
(board), ตัว dtuua
(piece), ชุด chút (set)]
chest n. (breast) หน้าอก
nâa-òk | (cabinet) ตู้ dtûu
[ใบ bai] | (cabinet) หีบ
hìip [ใบ bai]
chestnut n. เกาลัด gao-lát

[ลูก lûuk, เม็ด mét]
chest of drawers n.
ตู้มีลิ้นชัก dtûu-mii-lín-
chák [ใบ bai]
chew v. เคี้ยว kíiao
chew on v. (gnaw, e.g.
bone) แทะ té
chick n. (baby chicken)
ลูกไก่ lûuk-gài [ตัว dtuua]
| (young woman)
สาวน้อย sǎao-nɔ́ɔi ❧ [คน
kon]
chicken n. ไก่ gài [ตัว
dtuua]
chicken pox n. อีสุกอีใส ii-
sùk-ii-sǎi
chief adj. หลัก làk
chief n. (boss) หัวหน้า
hǔua-nâa [คน kon]
child n. (son or daughter)
ลูก lûuk [คน kon] |
(young person) เด็ก dèk
[คน kon]
childhood n. วัยเด็ก wai-
dèk
childish adj. (childlike)
เหมือนเด็ก mǔuan-dèk |
(innocent) ไร้เดียงสา rái-
diiang-sǎa | (silly) งี่เง่า
ngîi-ngâo

children n. เด็กๆ dèk-dèk [คน kon]

child support n. เงินเลี้ยงดูบุตร ngən-líiang-duu-bùt [จำนวน jam-nuuan]

chili see chilli

chill vi. (shiver) หนาวสั่น năao-sàn

chill vt. (e.g. food) ทำให้_เย็น tam-hâi-_-yen

chilled out adj. สบายๆ sà~baai-sà~baai

chilli n. พริก prík [เม็ด mét (seed), ต้น dtôn (plant)]

chilly adj. (weather) หนาว năao

chime n. (harmonious sound) เสียงกังวาน sĭiang-gang-waan

chimney n. ปล่องไฟ bplòng-fai [ปล่อง bplòng]

chimpanzee n. ชิมแพนซี chim-pɛɛn-sii [ตัว dtuua]

chin n. คาง kaang [คาง kaang]

China n. จีน jiin [ประเทศ bprà~têet]

china n. (porcelain) เครื่องดินเผา krûuang-din-păo [ชิ้น chín]

Chinese adj. จีน jiin

Chinese n. (language) ภาษาจีน paa-săa-jiin [ภาษา paa-săa] | (person) คนจีน kon-jiin [คน kon]

Chinese celery n. ขึ้นฉ่าย kûn-chàai [ต้น dtôn (plant), ใบ bai (leaf)]

chip n. (French fry) มันฝรั่งทอด man-fà~ràng-tɔ̂ɔt [ชิ้น chín] | (e.g. computer) ชิพ chíp [ชิ้น chín] | (gambling) เบี้ย bîia [อัน an] | (potato chip) มันฝรั่งแผ่นทอดกรอบ man-fà~ràng-pɛ̀n-tɔ̂ɔt-grɔ̀ɔp [ชิ้น chín (piece), ห่อ hɔ̀ɔ (pack), กล่อง glɔ̀ng (box)] | (small piece) เศษ sèet [ชิ้น chín]

chiropractor n. หมอนวดจับเส้น mɔ̌ɔ-nûuat-jàp-sên [คน kon]

chirp vi. (e.g. bird sound) ร้องจิ๊บๆ rɔ́ɔng-jíp-jíp

chisel n. สิ่ว sìu [อัน an, ปาก bpàak]

chives n. หอมเล็ก hɔ̌ɔm-lék [หัว hǔua]

chlorine n. คลอรีน klɔɔ-riin

chocolate n. (candy) ช็อคโกแลต chɔ́k-goo-lét [ชิ้น chín] | (cocoa) โกโก้ goo-gôo [แก้ว gɛ̂ɛo (glass)]

choice n. (of actions or destinations) ทางเลือก taang-lɯ̂ɯak [ทาง taang] | (of people or things) ตัวเลือก dtuua-lɯ̂ɯak [ตัว dtuua]

choir n. คณะประสานเสียง ká~ná-bprà~sǎan-sǐiang [คณะ ká~ná, กลุ่ม glùm ❋]

choke n. (vehicle) โช้ค chóok [อัน an]

choke vi. (e.g. on water, food) สำลัก sǎm-lák

choke vt. (strangle) บีบคอ bìip-kɔɔ

cholera n. อหิวาต์ à~hì-waa

cholesterol n. คอเลสเตอรอล kɔɔ-lées-dtəə-rɔ̂n

choose v. (select) คัด kát, เลือก lɯ̂ɯak

chop n. (meat)

เนื้อติดกระดูก nɯ́ɯa-dtìt-grà~dùuk [ชิ้น chín]

chop v. (cut) ตัด dtàt | (e.g. piece of wood) ฟัน fan

chopsticks n. ตะเกียบ dtà~gìiap [ข้าง kâang (piece), คู่ kûu (pair)]

chord n. (musical) สายเครื่องดนตรี sǎai-krɯ̂ɯang-don-dtrii [สาย sǎai, เส้น sên]

chore n. (house) งานบ้าน ngaan-bâan [งาน ngaan]

chorus n. คณะนักร้องประสานเสียง ká~ná~nák-rɔ́ɔng-bprà~sǎan-sǐiang ❢ [คณะ ká~ná]

Christ n. พระเยซู prá-yee-suu [องค์ ong]

Christianity n. ศาสนาคริสต์ sàat-sà~nǎa-krít [ศาสนา sàat-sà~nǎa]

Christmas n. วันคริสต์มาส wan-krít-sà~mât [วัน wan]

Christmas Eve n. คืนก่อนวันคริสต์มาส kɯɯn-gɔ̀ɔn-wan-krít-sà~mât [คืน kʉʉn]

chromosome n. โครโมโซม kroo-moo-soom [อัน an, คู่ kûu (pair)]

chronic adj. เรื้อรัง rʉ́ʉa-rang

chronological adj. ตามลำดับเหตุการณ์ dtaam-lam-dàp-hèet-gaan

chuckle vi. หัวเราะหึๆ hǔua-rɔ́-hʉ̀-hʉ̀

chunk n. (long bar) แท่ง têng [แท่ง têng] | (lump) ก้อน gɔ̂ɔn [ก้อน gɔ̂ɔn]

church n. โบสถ์ bòot [แห่ง hèng (location), หลัง lǎng (building)]

cicada n. จักจั่น jàk-gà~jàn [ตัว dtuua]

cider n. น้ำแอปเปิ้ล nám-ɛ́p-bpên

cigar n. ซิการ์ sí-gâa [มวน muuan]

cigarette n. บุหรี่ bù~rìi [ซอง sɔɔng (pack), มวน muuan (each)]

cilantro n. ผักชี pàk-chii [ใบ bai (leave), ต้น dtôn (plant)]

cinder n. (ash) ขี้เถ้า kîi-tâo

cinema n. (movie theater) โรงหนัง roong-nǎng ✦ [แห่ง hèng]

cinnamon n. อบเชย òp-chəəi

circle n. (ring, round object, etc.) วงกลม wong-glom [วง wong]

circuit n. (cyclical journey) รอบ rɔ̂ɔp [รอบ rɔ̂ɔp] | (electrical) วงจรไฟฟ้า wong-jɔɔn-fai-fáa [วงจร wong-jɔɔn]

circuit breaker n. เครื่องตัดกระแสไฟฟ้า krʉ̂ʉang-dtàt-grà~sɛ̌ɛ-fai-fáa [เครื่อง krʉ̂ʉang]

circular adj. (shape) กลม glom, เป็นวงกลม bpen-wong-glom

circular n. หนังสือเวียน nǎng~sʉ̌ʉ-wiian [ฉบับ chà~bàp !, แผ่น pèn]

circulate vi. (e.g. air, person, handout) หมุนเวียน mǔn-wiian

circulation n. (air or fluid) การหมุนเวียน gaan-mǔn-wiian

circumcision *n.* การขลิบ
gaan-klìp

circumference *n.*
เส้นรอบวง sên-rôop-
wong [เส้น sên]

circumstance *n.*
(condition) สภาพแวดล้อม
sà~pâap-wɛ̂ɛt-lɔ́ɔm

circumstances *n.*
(situation) เหตุการณ์
hèet-gaan

circus *n.* ละครสัตว์ lá~
kɔɔn-sàt [คณะ ká~ná]

citation *n.* (e.g. traffic)
ใบสั่ง bai-sàng [ใบ bai]

cite *vt.* (quote) อ้างถึง
âang-tǔng | (ticket for
violation) ให้ใบสั่ง hâi-
bai-sàng

citizen *n.* พลเมือง pon-
lá~mɯɯang, ราษฎร râat-
sà~dɔɔn ‼ [คน kon]

citizenship *n.* สัญชาติ
sǎn-châat [สัญชาติ sǎn-
châat]

city *n.* เมือง mɯɯang
[เมือง mɯɯang]

city hall *n.* ศาลากลาง sǎa-
laa-glaang [หลัง lǎng
(building), แห่ง hɛ̀ng
(location)]

city limit *n.* เขตเทศบาล
kèet-têet-sà~baan [เขต
kèet]

civic *adj.* เกี่ยวกับเมือง
gìiao-gàp-mɯɯang

civil *adj.* (legal,
concerning individuals)
เกี่ยวกับคดีแพ่ง gìiao-
gàp-ká~dii-pêng |
(relating to citizens)
เกี่ยวกับพลเรือน gìiao-
gàp-pon-lá~rɯɯan

civil case *n.* คดีแพ่ง ká~
dii-pêng [คดี ká~dii]

civil engineer *n.*
วิศวกรโยธา wít-sà~wá~
gɔɔn-yoo-taa [คน kon]

civilian *n.* พลเรือน pon-
lá~rɯɯan [คน kon]

civilization *n.* อารยธรรม
aa-rá~yá-tam,
ความศิวิไลซ์ kwaam-sì~
wí~lai ✦

civilized *adj.* เจริญ jà~rəən

civil law *n.* กฎหมายแพ่ง
gòt-mǎai-pêng

civil servant *n.* ข้าราชการ
kâa-râat-chá~gaan [คน
kon]

civil war *n.*
สงครามกลางเมือง sǒng-
kraam-glaang-mɯɯang

[ครั้ง kráng]

claim v. (demand, request) เรียกร้อง rîiak-rว́วng

claim vt. (assert) อ้าง âang

claim damages vi. เรียกร้องค่าเสียหาย rîiak-rว́วng-kâa-sǐia-hǎai

clairvoyant adj. ตาทิพย์ dtaa-típ

clam n. หอยกาบ hǒoi-gàap [ตัว dtuua]

clamp n. (tool) เหล็กบีบยึด lèk-bìip-yút [ตัว dtuua]

clamp vt. (with teeth or beak) คาบ kâap

clan n. (lineage) วงศ์ตระกูล wong-dtrà~guun [วงศ์ wong]

clap n. (sound of slapping) ผัวะ pùa

clap vi. (hands) ตบมือ dtòp-muu

clarify vt. (make clear) ทำให้_ชัดเจน tam-hâi-_-chát-jeen

clarity n. ความชัดเจน kwaam-chát-jeen

clash n. (conflict) ความขัดแย้ง kwaam-kàt-yɛ́ɛng

clash vi. (argue)

ทะเลาะกัน tá~lɔ́-gan | (colors) ตัดกัน dtàt-gan

clasp n. (fastening, such as a hook or buckle) ตัวเชื่อมต่อ dtuua-chûuam-dtɔ̀ɔ [ตัว dtuua, คู่ kûu (pair)]

class n. (category) ประเภท bprà~pêet [ประเภท bprà~pêet] | (rank) ระดับ rá~dàp [ระดับ rá~dàp] | (social, school) ชั้น chán [ชั้น chán] | (students in class) นักเรียน nák-riian [คน kon]

classic adj. คลาสสิก klâat-sìk

classifier n. (Thai part of speech) ลักษณนาม lák-sà~nà-naam [ประเภท bprà~pêet (category), คำ kam (word)]

classify vt. แบ่งประเภท bɛ̀ng-bprà~pêet

classmate n. เพื่อนร่วมชั้น pûuan-rûuam-chán [คน kon]

classroom n. ห้องเรียน hɔ̂ng-riian [ห้อง hɔ̂ng]

clause n. (contract) ข้อ

kôo [ข้อ kôo]

claw n. (of animals with toes) อุ้งเล็บ ûng-lép [ข้าง kâang]

clay n. (soil) ดินเหนียว din-nĭiao [ก้อน gôon (chunk)]

clean adj. สะอาด sà~àat

clean v. ทำความสะอาด tam-kwaam-sà~àat | (with liquid) ล้าง láang

cleaner n. (liquid) น้ำยาทำความสะอาด nám-yaa-tam-kwaam-sà~àat [ชนิด chá~nít (type), ขวด kùuat (bottle)] | (person) คนทำความสะอาด kon-tam-kwaam-sà~àat [คน kon]

cleanse vt. ชำระ cham-rá ǃ

cleanser n. (for face) ครีมล้างหน้า kriim-láang-nâa [ชนิด chá~nít (type), ขวด kùuat (bottle)]

clean up vi. (put things away) เก็บของ gèp-kŏong

clear adj. (easily seen) ชัด chát | (free from clouds, dust, etc.) ใส săi | (obvious) ชัดเจน chát-jeen, ชัดแจ้ง chát-jêeng ǃ,

แจ้ง jêeng ✍ | (transparent) แจ๋ว jěo

clear vt. (remove) ย้าย_ออก yáai-_-òok

cleared adj. (clearcut) โล่งเตียน lôong-dtiian ǃ

clearly adv. อย่างชัดเจน yàang-chát-jeen

cleaver n. อีโต้ ii-dtôo [เล่ม lêm]

clemency n. (leniency) ความเมตตา kwaam-mêet-dtaa

clerk n. (in an office) เสมียน sà~mĭian [คน kon]

clever adj. เก่ง gèng, ฉลาด chà~làat

click n. (sound) เสียงดังคลิก sĭiang-dang-klík

click v. (computing) คลิก klík

client n. (customer) ลูกค้า lûuk-káa [คน kon] | (of a lawyer) ลูกความ lûuk-kwaam [คน kon]

cliff n. ผา păa [แห่ง hèng]

climate n. (in geography) ภูมิอากาศ puu-mí-aa-gàat | (weather) อากาศ aa-gàat

climax n. (story, orgasm)

จุดสุดยอด jùt-sùt-yôɔt
[จุด jùt]

climax *vi.* (orgasm)
ถึงจุดสุดยอด tʉ̌ng-jùt-
sùt-yôɔt

climb *v.* (tree, mountain)
ปีน bpiin

climb *vi.* (increase, e.g.
price) ขึ้น kʉ̂n

climb *vt.* (e.g. stairs) ขึ้น
kʉ̂n

cling to *vt.* (grab, hold)
เกาะ gɔ̀, ยึด yʉ́t

clinic *n.* คลินิก klí-ník,
สถานพยาบาล sà~tǎan-
pá~yaa-baan ! [แห่ง
hèng]

clip *n.* (clasp) ที่หนีบ tîi-
nìip [อัน an] | (video
excerpt) คลิปวีดีโอ klíp-
wii-dii-oo, ภาพยนตร์สั้น
pâap-pá~yon-sân [เรื่อง
rʉ̂ʉang (story), ตอน
dtɔɔn (part)]

clip *vt.* (cut off) ตัด_ออก
dtàt-_-ɔ̀ɔk

clitoris *n.* แตด dtɛ̀ɛt ♀ |
ปุ่มกระสัน bpùm-grà~
sǎn, คลิตอริส klí-dtɔɔ-rít
✖ [ปุ่ม bpùm, จุด jùt]

cloak *n.* เสื้อคลุม sʉ̂ʉa-
klum [ตัว dtuua]

clock *n.* นาฬิกา naa-lí~
gaa [เรือน rʉʉan]

clockwise *adv.*
ตามเข็มนาฬิกา dtaam-
kěm-naa-lí~gaa

clog *v.* (e.g. pores, pipes)
อุดตัน ùt-dtan

clone *vt.* โคลน kloon

close *adj.* (e.g. friend)
สนิท sà~nìt | (near) ใกล้
glâi | (next to) ชิด chít |
(similar) คล้าย kláai

close *v.* ปิด bpìt

closed *adj.* (not open) ปิด
bpìt

close one's eyes *vi.*
หลับตา làp-dtaa

closeout *adj.* ลดราคา lót-
raa-kaa

closet *n.* (for clothes)
ตู้เสื้อผ้า dtûu-sʉ̂ʉa-pâa
[ใบ bai]

clot *n.* (small pieces)
ก้อนเล็กๆ gɔ̂ɔn-lék-lék
[ก้อน gɔ̂ɔn]

clot *vi.* เกาะกันเป็นก้อน
gɔ̀-gan-bpen-gɔ̂ɔn

cloth *n.* ผ้า pâa [ชิ้น chín,

ผืน pǔɨn]

clothe vt. (dress)
ใส่เสื้อผ้าให้ sài-sɨ̂ɨa-
pâa-hâi

clothes n. เครื่องแต่งกาย
krɨ̂ɨang-dtɛ̀ng-gaai,
เสื้อผ้า sɨ̂ɨa-pâa,
เครื่องนุ่งห่ม krɨ̂ɨang-
nûng-hòm ! [ชุด chút
(set), ตัว dtuua (piece)]

clothing see clothes

cloud n. เมฆ mêek [กลุ่ม
glùm (cluster), ก้อน gɔ̂ɔn
(mass)]

cloudy adj. (e.g. mirror)
ฝ้า fâa | (e.g. water) ขุ่น
kùn | (overcast) มีเมฆ
mii-mêek

clove n. (of garlic)
กลีบกระเทียม glìip-grà~
tiiam [กลีบ glìip]

clown n. ตัวตลก dtuua-
dtà~lòk [คน kon, ตัว
dtuua]

club n. (association) ชมรม
chom-rom [ชมรม chom-
rom] | (card suit) ดอกจิก
dɔ̀ɔk-jìk

clue n. เงื่อน ngɨ̂ɨan, ปม
bpom, ร่องรอย rɔ̂ng-rɔɔi

[อัน an]

clumsy adj. ซุ่มซ่าม sûm-
sâam ☜

cluster n. กระจุก grà~jùk
[อัน an]

clutch n. (vehicle) คลัตช์
klát [แผ่น pɛ̀n, ชุด chút
(set)]

clutch vt. (clench) กำ gam

clutter vt.
ทำให้_ไม่เรียบร้อย tam-
hâi-_-mâi-rîiap-rɔɔi

coach n. (class in a plane
or train)
ชั้นโดยสารราคาถูก chán-
dooi-sǎan-raa-kaa-tùuk |
(trainer) ครูฝึก kruu-fɨ̀k
[คน kon]

coal n. ถ่านหิน tàan-hǐn !
[ก้อน gɔ̂ɔn]

coarse adj. (lacking in
fineness) หยาบ yàap

coast n. ชายฝั่ง chaai-
fàng, ฝั่งทะเล fàng-tá~
lee [แห่ง hɛ̀ng, ฝั่ง fàng] |
(e.g. West Coast) ฝั่ง fàng
[แห่ง hɛ̀ng, ฝั่ง fàng]

coast vi. ไหล lǎi

coaster n. (e.g. for cups)
ที่รองแก้ว tîi-rɔɔng-gɛ̂ɛo

[อัน an]

coast guard n.

หน่วยลาดตระเวนชายฝั่ง nùai-lâat-dtrà~ween-chaai-fàng [คน kon]

coat n. เสื้อโค้ท sûua-kóot ✽ [ตัว dtuua]

coat vt. เคลือบ klûuap

cobra n. งูเห่า nguu-hào [ตัว dtuua]

cobweb n. หยากไย่ yàak-yâi [ใย yai]

cocaine n. โคเคน koo-keen

Cochin n. (chicken) ไก่ตะเภา gài-dtà~pao, นิโคลัส ní-koo-lát [ตัว dtuua]

cock n. (penis) องคชาติ ong-ká~châat ⚡, นกเขา nók-kǎo ✽, ควย kuuai ⚥ [อัน an] | (rooster) ไก่ตัวผู้ gài-dtuua-pûu [ตัว dtuua]

cockfight n. ชนไก่ chon-gài

cockpit n. (airplane) ห้องคนขับเครื่องบิน hông-kon-kàp-krûuang-bin [ห้อง hông]

cockroach n. แมลงสาบ má~lɛɛng-sàap [ตัว dtuua]

cocktail n. ค้อกเทล kɔ́k-teeo [แก้ว gɛ̂ɛo (glass), ชนิด chá~nít (type)]

cocoa n. โกโก้ goo-gôo [แก้ว gɛ̂ɛo (glass)]

coconut n. มะพร้าว má~práao [ลูก lûuk]

coconut cream n. กะทิ gà~tí [กล่อง glòng (box)]

coconut juice n. น้ำมะพร้าว nám-má~práao [แก้ว gɛ̂ɛo (glass)]

coconut milk see coconut cream

cocoon n. (larvae) ดักแด้ dàk-dɛ̂ɛ [ตัว dtuua]

cod n. ปลาคอด bplaa-kɔ́ɔt [ตัว dtuua]

code n. รหัส rá~hàt [ตัว dtuua]

co-ed adj. สหศึกษา sà~hà-sɯ̀k-sǎa

coerce vt. (force) บังคับ bang-káp

coffee n. กาแฟ gaa-fɛɛ [ถ้วย tûuai (cup)]

coffee pot n. หม้อกาแฟ mɔ̂ɔ-gaa-fɛɛ [ใบ bai]

coffee shop n. ร้านกาแฟ

ráan-gaa-fɛɛ [ร้าน ráan]

coffin *n.* โลงศพ loong-sòp [โลง loong, ใบ bai]

coil *n.* ขด kòt [ขด kòt]

coil *v.* (self up) เกลียว gliiao, ขด kòt | (something up) ม้วน múuan

coiled *adj.* เกลียว gliiao

coin *n.* เหรียญ rǐian [เหรียญ rǐian, อัน an]

coincide *vi.* (happen at same time) ประจวบเหมาะกัน bprà~jùuap-mɔ̀-gan

coincidence *n.* ความบังเอิญ kwaam-bang-əən

cold *adj.* (cool, chilly) เย็น yen | (emotion) เย็นชา yen-chaa | (weather or personal sensation) หนาว nǎao

cold *n.* (disease) ไข้หวัด kâi-wàt

cold-blooded *adj.* เลือดเย็น lɨ̂uat-yen

coldness *n.* ความเย็น kwaam-yen

cold season *n.* หน้าหนาว nâa-nǎao ✿ [หน้า nâa]

cold sore *n.* ปากเป็นแผล bpàak-bpen-plɛ̌ɛ

cold war *n.* สงครามเย็น sǒng-kraam-yen [ครั้ง kráng]

collapse *vi.* (faint) ล้มลง lóm-long | (structure or institution) พัง pang

collar *n.* (animal wears around its neck) ปลอกคอ bplɔ̀ɔk-kɔɔ [อัน an] | (e.g. shirt, coat) คอเสื้อ kɔɔ-sɨ̂ua [คอ kɔɔ]

collard *n.* คะน้า ká~náa [ต้น dtôn (plant), ใบ bai (leaf)]

colleague *n.* เพื่อนร่วมงาน pɨ̂uan-rûuam-ngaan [คน kon]

collect *vt.* สะสม sà-sǒm

collect call *n.* โทรเก็บเงินปลายทาง too-gèp-ngən-bplaai-taang

collection *n.* (act) การสะสม gaan-sà-sǒm

collector *n.* (hobbyist) นักสะสม nák-sà-sǒm [คน kon]

college *n.* (for education) วิทยาลัย wít-tá~yaa-lai [แห่ง hɛ̀ng]

college student *n.*
นักศึกษา nák-sèuk-sǎa,
นิสิต ní-sìt [คน kon]

collide *vi.* (hit) ชนกัน
chon-gan, ปะทะกัน bpà~
tá-gan

colloquial *adj.* ภาษาพูด
paa-sǎa-pûut

cologne *n.* โคโลญจ์ koo-
loon [ชนิด chá~nít (type),
ขวด kùuat (bottle)]

colon *n.* (large intestine)
ลำไส้ใหญ่ lam-sâi-yài
[ท่อน tɔ̂n (strip), ขด kòt
(coil)] | (punctuation
mark) เครื่องหมายโคลอน
krûuang-mǎai-koo-lɔɔn
[ตัว dtuua]

colonel *n.* (in the
marines) พันเอก pan-èek
[นาย naai ✝, คน kon]

colonial *adj.*
ที่เป็นอาณานิคม tîi-bpen-
aa-naa-ní-kom

colonize *vt.* (subjugate a
place) ทำให้_เป็นเมืองขึ้น
tam-hâi-_-bpen-
mʉʉang-kʉ̂n

colony *n.* เมืองขึ้น
mʉʉang-kʉ̂n [เมือง
mʉʉang] | (e.g. ant) ฝูง

fǔung [ฝูง fǔung]

color *adj.* (e.g. TV) สี sǐi

color *n.* สี sǐi [สี sǐi]

color *v.* (paint) ระบาย rá~
baai

colorblind *adj.* ตาบอดสี
dtaa-bɔ̀ɔt-sǐi

colorful *adj.* สีสดใส sǐi-
sòt-sǎi, มีสีสัน mii-sǐi-sǎn
✽

column *n.* (article) คอลัมน์
kɔɔ-lâm [คอลัมน์ kɔɔ-
lâm] | (typography) แถว
tɛ̌ɛo [แถว tɛ̌ɛo]

columnist *n.*
นักเขียนคอลัมน์ nák-
kǐian-kɔɔ-lâm [คน kon]

coma *n.* (symptom)
อาการโคม่า aa-gaan-
koo-mâa

comb *n.* (hair) หวี wǐi [เล่ม
lêm]

comb *vt.* (hair) หวี wǐi

combat *n.* (fight) การต่อสู้
gaan-dtɔ̀ɔ-sûu [ครั้ง
kráng]

combat *vt.* สู้รบกับ sûu-
róp-gàp

combination *n.*
การผสมกัน gaan-pà~
sǒm-gan

combine *vi.* (come together) รวมตัวกัน ruuam-dtuua-gan

combine *vt.* (put together) เอา_มารวมกัน ao-_-maa-ruuam-gan

combustion *n.* (burning) การเผาไหม้ gaan-pǎo-mâi

come *vi.* (have an orgasm) เสร็จ sèt ♦ | (reach, arrive) มา maa

come across *vt.* (encounter) พบ_โดยบังเอิญ póp-_-dooi-bang-əən

come around *vi.* (change opinion) เปลี่ยนความคิด bpliian-kwaam-kít | (regain consciousness) ฟื้นคืนสติ fúun-kuun-sà~dtì !

come back *vi.* (return) กลับมา glàp-maa, หวนกลับ hǔuan-glàp ⚘

come by *v.* (drop by) มาเยี่ยม maa-yîiam, แวะมา wé-maa ♦

come by *vt.* (obtain) ได้_มา dâi-_-maa

comedian *n.* (performer) นักแสดงตลก nák-sà~ dɛɛng-dtà~lòk [คน kon]

comedy *n.* (humor) ความขบขัน kwaam-kòp-kǎn | (humorous play) ละครตลก lá~kɔɔn-dtà~ lòk [เรื่อง rûuang (story), ตอน dtɔɔn (episode)]

come from *vt.* มาจาก maa-jàak

come in *v.* เข้ามา kâo-maa

come on *vi.* (e.g. disease) เริ่ม rôəm

come on! *interj.* (do it!) มาเถอะ maa-tè

come out *vi.* (result as, e.g. photo, vote) ออกมา ɔ̀ɔk maa | (reveal one's sexuality) เปิดตัว bpəət-dtuua

come over *vi.* (visit) มาหา maa-hǎa

come round see come around

comet *n.* ดาวหาง daao-hǎang [ดวง duuang]

come to *vi.* (regain consciousness) ฟื้น fúun

come to visit *v.* มาเยี่ยม maa-yîiam

comfort *n.* การปลอบโยน gaan-bplɔ̀ɔp-yoon

comfort *vt.* (relieve) ทำให้_สบาย tam-hâi-_-

sà~baai | (soothe, console) ปลอบโยน bplɔɔp-yoon

comfortable *adj.* สบาย sà~baai, สะดวกสบาย sà~dùuak-sà~baai ⚡

comforter *n.* (quilt) ผ้านวม pâa-nuuam [ผืน pʉʉn]

comic *adj.* ตลก dtà~lòk

comical *adj.* น่าขัน nâa-kǎn ⚡

comic book *n.* หนังสือการ์ตูน nǎng~sʉʉ-gaa-dtuun [เล่ม lêm]

comma *n.* จุลภาค jun-lá~pâak ✗ [ตัว dtuua]

command *n.* (order) คำสั่ง kam-sàng [เรื่อง rʉ̂uang, อัน an ⚡]

command *v.* (order) สั่ง sàng

commander *n.* (in military) ผู้บัญชาการ pûu-ban-chaa-gaan [คน kon, ท่าน tân ⚡]

commemorate *vt.* ฉลอง chà~lɔ̌ɔng

commence *v.* เริ่ม rə̂əm

comment *n.* (opinion) ข้อคิดเห็น kɔ̂ɔ-kít-hěn

[ประเด็น bprà~den ⚡, ข้อ kɔ̂ɔ]

comment *vi.* แสดงความคิดเห็น sà~dɛɛng-kwaam-kít-hěn

commerce *n.* การค้า gaan-káa, การพาณิชย์ gaan-paa-nít ✗

commercial *adj.* ทางการค้า taang-gaan-káa

commercial *n.* (on radio or TV) โฆษณา koo-sà~naa [ชิ้น chín]

commission *n.* (fee or percentage) ค่านายหน้า kâa-naai-nâa

commissioner *n.* (authorized person) กรรมาธิการ gam-maa-tí-gaan [คน kon (person), คณะ ká~ná (group)]

commit *vi.* (in relationship) ผูกมัด pùuk-mát

commit *vt.* (do) ทำ tam

commit a crime *vi.* ทำผิดกฎหมาย tam-pìt-gòt-mǎai

commit adultery *vi.* ผิดประเวณี pìt-bprà~wee-nii ⚡, มีชู้ mii-chúu ⚡

commitment n.
(dedication)
ความตั้งใจมั่น kwaam-dtâng-jai-mân | (duty, responsibility) หน้าที่ nâa-tîi [หน้าที่ nâa-tîi]

commit suicide vi.
ฆ่าตัวตาย kâa-dtuua-dtaai

committee n.
คณะกรรมการ ká~ná~gam-má~gaan [คณะ ká~ná]

commodity n. สินค้า sǐn-káa [ชนิด chá~nít (kind), ชิ้น chín (piece), กล่อง glòng (box), ห่อ hòo (wrap)]

common adj. (normal)
ธรรมดา tam-má~daa

common cold n. ไข้หวัด kâi-wàt

commoner n. สามัญชน sǎa-man-chon [คน kon]

commonly adv. (usually)
มักจะ mák-jà

common sense n.
สามัญสำนึก sǎa-man-sǎm-nɯ́k

commotion n.
ความวุ่นวาย kwaam-wûn-waai

communicate v. ติดต่อ
สื่อสาร dtìt-dtɔ̀ɔ-sɯ̀ɯ-sǎan, สื่อสาร sɯ̀ɯ-sǎan

communication n.
การติดต่อ gaan-dtìt-dtɔ̀ɔ, คมนาคม kom-má~naa-kom

communist n. คอมมิวนิสต์ kɔm-miu-nít [คน kon]

community n. (of people)
ชุมชน chum-chon [ชุมชน chum-chon]

community property n.
ทรัพย์สินส่วนรวม sáp-sǐn-sùuan-ruuam [ชิ้น chín]

commute vi. (travel back and forth)
เดินทางไปๆมาๆ dəən-taang-bpai-bpai-maa-maa

compact adj. (packable)
กะทัดรัด gà~tát-rát

compact vt. อัด_ให้แน่น àt-_-hâi-nɛ̂n

companion n. (friend)
เพื่อน pɯ̂ɯan [คน kon] | (one who travels with)
เพื่อนร่วมทาง pɯ̂ɯan-rûuam-taang [คน kon]

company n. (firm) บริษัท

bɔɔ-rí~sàt [แห่ง hɛ̀ng] |
(group of persons) คณะ
ká~ná [คณะ ká~ná]

compare vt. เปรียบเทียบ
bpriiap-tiiap

comparison n.
การเปรียบเทียบ gaan-
bpriiap-tiiap

compartment n. (room)
ห้อง hɔ̂ng [ห้อง hɔ̂ng] |
(slot, small space) ช่อง
chɔ̂ng [ช่อง chɔ̂ng]

compass n. (device)
เข็มทิศ kěm-tít [อัน an]

compassion n.
(understanding one's
feeling) ความเห็นใจ
kwaam-hěn-jai

compatible adj.
(harmonious) กลมกลืน
glom-gluun, เข้ากันได้ดี
kâo-gan-dâi-dii

compel vt. บังคับ bang-
káp

compensate v. ชดเชย
chót-chəəi

compensation n. (money
given) ค่าชดเชย kâa-
chót-chəəi

compete vi. แข่งขัน
kèng-kǎn

competence n. (ability)
ความสามารถ kwaam-
sǎa-mâat

competent adj. (capable)
มีความสามารถ mii-
kwaam-sǎa-mâat

competition n.
การแข่งขัน gaan-kèng-
kǎn

competitor n. (one who
competes with another)
คู่แข่ง kûu-kèng [คน kon]

compile vt. (put together)
รวบรวม rûuap-ruuam

complain vi. (make a
complaint) ร้องทุกข์
rɔ́ɔng-túk | (whine) บ่น
bòn

complaint n. (formal
accusation) การร้องทุกข์
gaan-rɔ́ɔng-túk

complete adj. (done,
finished) เสร็จ sèt |
(having all parts) ครบ
króp, ครบถ้วน króp-
tûuan, สมบูรณ์ sǒm-buun

complete vi. เสร็จ sèt

complete vt. ทำ_ให้เสร็จ
tam-_-hâi-sèt

completion n.
การทำให้สมบูรณ์ gaan-
tam-hâi-sǒm-buun

complex adj. ซับซ้อน

sáp-rûuak

complexion *n.* (skin color) สีผิว sǐi-pǐu

complexity *n.* ความซับซ้อน kwaam-sáp-rûuak

complicate *vt.* (make complicated) ทำให้_ซับซ้อน tam-hâi-_-sáp-rûuak

complicated *adj.* ซับซ้อน sáp-rûuak

complication *n.* (medicine) โรคแทรกซ้อน rôok-sɛ̂ɛk-rúuak [โรค rôok]

complicity *n.* การสมรู้ร่วมคิด gaan-sǒm-rúu-rûuam-kít

compliment *n.* คำชมเชย kam-chom-chəəi [คำ kam]

compliment *vt.* ชมเชย chom-chəəi ‼

complimentary *adj.* (given free) อภินันทนาการ à~pí-nan-tá~naa-gaan

comply *vi.* (do as told) ทำตาม tam-dtaam

component *n.* ส่วนประกอบ sùuan-bprà~gɔ̀ɔp [ส่วน sùuan,

ชิ้น chín]

compose *vt.* (e.g. music) แต่ง dtɛ̀ng

composed of *adj.* ประกอบด้วย bprà~gɔ̀ɔp-dûuai

composer *n.* นักแต่งเพลง nák-dtɛ̀ng-pleeng [คน kon]

composition *n.* (literary, musical) บทประพันธ์ bòt-bprà~pan [เรื่อง rûuang]

compound *adj.* (combined) ผสม pà~sǒm

comprehend *v.* (understand) เข้าใจ kâo-jai

compress *vt.* (pressurize) อัด àt | (squeeze, e.g. computer file, herb) บีบ bìip

compromise *vi.* (conciliate, reconcile) ประนีประนอม bprà~nii-bprà~nɔɔm | (settle legal case) ยอมความ yɔɔm-kwaam

compulsory *adj.* บังคับ bang-káp

compute *v.* คำนวณ kam-nuuan

computer *n.* คอมพิวเตอร์ kɔm-píu-dtə̂ə [เครื่อง krûuang]

comrade *n.* สหาย sà~hǎai [คน kon]

con *n.* (disadvantage) ข้อเสีย kɔ̂ɔ-sǐia [ข้อ kɔ̂ɔ]

concave *adj.* (e.g. lens) เว้า wáo

conceal *vt.* (hide) ซ่อน sɔ̂n, ปกปิด bpòk-bpìt

concede *vi.* (stop trying to win) ยอมแพ้ yɔɔm-pɛ́ɛ | (yield) ยินยอม yin-yɔɔm

conceited *adj.* (arrogant) หยิ่ง yìng | (haughty) ถือตัว tǔu-dtuua

conceive *vi.* (become pregnant) ตั้งท้อง dtâng-tɔ́ɔng

concentrate *vi.* (direct efforts to one goal) ตั้งใจ dtâng-jai | (focus the mind, be composed) มีสมาธิ mii-sà~maa-tí

concentrate *vt.* (e.g. food) ทำให้_เข้มข้น tam-hâi-_-kêm-kôn

concentrated *adj.* (rich) เข้ม kêm | (thick) ข้น kôn

concentration *n.*

(density) ความเข้มข้น kwaam-kêm-kôn | (mental focus) สมาธิ sà~maa-tí | (paying attention) ความเอาใจใส่ kwaam-ao-jai-sài

concept *n.* ความคิดรวบยอด kwaam-kít-rûuap-yɔ̂ɔt ❗

concern *n.* (worry) ความกังวล kwaam-gang-won

concern *vt.* (affect) ส่งผลกระทบต่อ sòng-pǒn-grà~tóp-dtɔ̀ɔ | (be relevant to) เกี่ยวข้องกับ gìiao-kɔ̂ɔng-gàp | (worry) ทำให้_เป็นกังวล tam-hâi-_-bpen-gang-won

concert *n.* การแสดงดนตรี gaan-sà~dɛɛng-don-dtrii, คอนเสิร์ต kɔn-sə̀ət [ครั้ง kráng (event), วง wong (band)]

conch *n.* สังข์ sǎng [ขอน kɔ̌ɔn]

concierge *n.* (hotel staff) คนบริการแขกของโรงแรม kon-bɔɔ-rí~gaan-kɛ̀ɛk-kɔ̌ɔng-roong-rɛɛm [คน kon]

concise *adj.* (brief and

clear) กะทัดรัด gà~tát-rát

conclude v. (summarize) สรุป sà~rùp

conclude vt. (finish) ทำ_ให้เสร็จ tam-_-hâi-sèt

conclusion n. (in writing) บทสรุป bòt-sà~rùp [บท bòt]

concord n. (harmony) ความสอดคล้องกัน kwaam-sòɔt-klɔ́ɔng-gan

concrete adj. (not abstract) ที่เป็นรูปธรรม tîi-bpen-rûup-bpà~tam

concrete n. (cement) คอนกรีต kɔn-grìit

concubine n. (harlot) นางบำเรอ naang-bam-rəə [คน kon]

concur vi. (agree) เห็นด้วย hěn-dûuai

concussion n. (strong collision) การกระแทกอย่างแรง gaan-grà~têɛk-yàang-rɛɛng

condemn vt. (reproach) ประณาม bprà~naam

condense vt. (make concise) ย่อ yɔ̂ɔ

condensed milk n. นมข้น nom-kôn [กระป๋อง grà~

bpɔ̌ng (can)]

condiment n. เครื่องปรุงรส krûuang-bprung-rót [ชนิด chá~nít]

condition n. (existing circumstances) สภาพ sà~pâap [สภาพ sà~pâap] | (stipulation) เงื่อนไข ngûuan-kǎi [ข้อ kɔ̂ɔ]

conditional adj. มีข้อแม้ mii-kɔ̂ɔ-méɛ

conditioner n. (for hair) ครีมนวดผม kriim-nûuat-pǒm [ชนิด chá~nít (type), ขวด kùuat (bottle)]

condo n. คอนโด kɔɔn-doo [หลัง lǎng (building), ห้อง hɔ̂ng (room)]

condolence n. การปลอบโยน gaan-bplɔɔp-yoon

condom n. คอนดอม kɔn-dɔm, ถุงยาง tǔng-yaang [อัน an, ชิ้น chín]

condominium n. คอนโดมิเนียม kɔɔn-doo-mí-niiam [หลัง lǎng (building), ห้อง hɔ̂ng (room)]

condone vt. ไม่เอาโทษ

mâi-ao-tôot

conduct n. (behavior) ความประพฤติ kwaam-bprà~prút

conduct vt. (lead) นำ nam

conductor n. (electrical) ตัวนำไฟฟ้า dtuua-nam-fai-fáa [ชนิด chá~nít, ตัว dtuua ●] | (orchestra) ผู้นำวงดนตรี pûu-nam-wong-don-dtrii [คน kon]

cone n. (shape) กรวย gruuai [อัน an, กรวย gruuai]

confederate n. พันธมิตร pan-tá~mít [กลุ่ม glùm]

confederation n. สมาพันธ์ sà~maa-pan [กลุ่ม glùm]

confer vi. (discuss) ปรึกษากัน bprùk-sǎa-gan

conference n. การประชุม gaan-bprà~chum

confess v. สารภาพ sǎa-rá~pâap

confession n. การสารภาพ gaan-sǎa-rá~pâap

confidant n. คนที่เชื่อใจได้ kon-tîi-chûua-jai-dâai [คน kon]

confide in vt. (tell a secret to) บอกความลับกับ bɔ̀ɔk-kwaam-láp-gàp

confidence n. ความมั่นใจ kwaam-mân-jai

confident adj. มั่นใจ mân-jai

confidential adj. เป็นความลับ bpen-kwaam-láp, ลับ láp

confine vt. (people, animals) กักขัง gàk-kǎng

confirm vt. (affirm) ยืนยัน yʉʉn-yan | (guarantee) รับรอง ráp-rɔɔng

confirmation n. การรับรอง gaan-ráp-rɔɔng

confiscate vt. ยึด yʉ́t, ริบ ríp

conflict n. การขัดแย้ง gaan-kàt-yɛ́ɛng

conflict vi. (disagree) ขัดแย้งกัน kàt-yɛ́ɛng-gan

conform vi. (comply) ทำตาม tam-dtaam

confront vt. เผชิญหน้ากับ pà~chəən-nâa-gàp

confuse vt. ทำให้_สับสน tam-hâi-_-sàp-sǒn

confused adj. สับสน sàp-sǒn

confusing adj. วุ่นวาย wûn-waai, สับสน sàp-sǒn

confusion n. ความสับสน

kwaam-sàp-sŏn

congested *adj.* (packed or crowded) แออัด ɛɛ-àt

congestion *n.* (crowding) ความแออัด kwaam-ɛɛ-àt

congratulate *vt.* แสดงความยินดีกับ sà~ dɛɛng-kwaam-yin-dii-gàp

congratulations! *interj.* ยินดีด้วย yin-dii-dûuai, ขอแสดงความยินดี kɔ̌ɔ- sà~dɛɛng-kwaam-yin-dii ❗

congregation *n.* การชุมนุม gaan-chum- num [กลุ่ม glùm]

congress *n.* สภานิติบัญญัติ sà~paa-ní-dtì-ban-yàt [สภา sà~paa]

conjugation *n.* (linguistics) การผันกริยา gaan-pǎn-grì-yaa

conjunction *n.* (part of speech) คำสันธาน kam- sǎn-taan [คำ kam]

con man *n.* นักต้มตุ๋น nák-dtôm-dtǔn [คน kon]

connect *vi.* (e.g. over phone, network) ติด dtìt | (join) เชื่อมต่อกัน chûuam-dtɔ̀ɔ-gan

connect *vt.* (join) ต่อ dtɔ̀ɔ

connection *n.* ความเกี่ยวพัน kwaam- gìiao-pan | (e.g. flight, train) เส้นทางเชื่อมต่อ sên-taang-chûuam-dtɔ̀ɔ [ทาง taang]

connect to *vt.* (e.g. over phone, network) ต่อ dtɔ̀ɔ

connoisseur *n.* (expert) ผู้เชี่ยวชาญ pûu-chîiao- chaan [คน kon]

connote *v.* มีความหมายแฝง mii- kwaam-mǎai-fɛ̌ɛng

conquer *vt.* ชนะ chá~ná

conscience *n.* (awareness) สติ sà~dtì

conscious *adj.* (awake) มีสติ mii-sà~dtì, รู้สึกตัว rúu-sùk-dtuua

consciousness *n.* ความมีสติ kwaam-mii- sà~dtì

consent *vi.* ยินยอม yin- yɔɔm

consequence *n.* ผลลัพธ์ pǒn-láp

conservative *adj.* หัวโบราณ hǔua-boo-raan ❀ | (old-fashioned) หัวเก่า hǔua-gào

conservative *n.* (person)

นักอนุรักษ์นิยม nák-à~
nú~rák-ní-yom [คน kon]
conserve v. เก็บรักษา
gèp-rák-sǎa | (e.g.
natural resources)
อนุรักษ์ à-nú~rák
consider v. (think over)
พิจารณา pí-jaa-rá~naa
consider vt. (count as,
reckon as) นับว่า náp-wâa
considerate adj.
(sympathetic)
เห็นใจคนอื่น hěn-jai-
kon-ùun
consignment n.
(shipment to seller with
payment on resale)
การฝากขาย gaan-fàak-
kǎai
consistent adj. (not
changing) ไม่เปลี่ยนแปลง
mâi-bplìian-bplɛɛng
consist of vt. (comprise)
ประกอบด้วย bprà~gɔ̀ɔp-
dûuai
consolation n.
การปลอบใจ gaan-bplɔ̀ɔp-
jai
console vt. ปลอบ bplɔ̀ɔp
consolidate vt. (combine)
รวม_เข้าด้วยกัน ruuam-
_-kâo-dûuai-gan

consonant n. พยัญชนะ
pá~yan-chá~ná [ตัว
dtuua]
conspicuous adj. โดดเด่น
dòot-dèn
conspiracy n.
การสมรู้ร่วมคิด gaan-
sǒm-rúu-rûuam-kít
constant adj. คงที่ kong-tîi
constellation n. หมู่ดาว
mùu-daao [กลุ่ม glùm]
constipation n.
อาการท้องผูก aa-gaan-
tɔ́ɔng-pùuk
constituent n.
(component) องค์ประกอบ
ong-bprà~gɔ̀ɔp [ส่วน
sùuan, ชิ้น chín] | (voter)
ผู้มีสิทธิ์เลือกตั้ง pûu-mii-
sìt-lûuak-dtâng [คน kon]
constitute vt. (consist of)
ประกอบด้วย bprà~gɔ̀ɔp-
dûuai | (establish) ก่อตั้ง
gɔ̀ɔ-dtâng
constitution n.
รัฐธรรมนูญ rát-tà~tam-
má~nuun [ฉบับ chà~bàp]
construct vt. สร้าง sâang,
ก่อสร้าง gɔ̀ɔ-sâang ‼
construction n.

การก่อสร้าง gaan-gòo-
sâang

consul *n.* กงสุล gong-sǔn
[คน kon, ท่าน tân ⚡]

consulate *n.* สถานกงสุล
sà~tǎan-gong-sǔn [แห่ง
hèng]

consul general *n.*
กงสุลใหญ่ gong-sǔn-yài
[คน kon, ท่าน tân ⚡]

consultant *n.* ที่ปรึกษา
tîi-bprùk-sǎa [ท่าน tân ⚡,
คน kon]

consult with *vt.* ปรึกษา
bprùk-sǎa

consume *v.* (eat, spend)
บริโภค bɔɔ-rí~pôok ✗ |
(spend) อุปโภค ùp-bpà~
pôok ✗

consumer *n.* ผู้บริโภค
pûu-bɔɔ-rí~pôok ✗ [คน
kon]

contact *n.*
(communication)
การติดต่อสื่อสาร gaan-
dtìt-dtòo-sùu-sǎan |
(person) คนรู้จัก kon-rúu-
jàk [คน kon]

contact *vt.* (communicate
with) ติดต่อ dtìt-dtòo |
(touch) สัมผัส sǎm-pàt

contact lens *n.* คอนแทค
kɔɔn-tɛ̂ɛk ✿ [คู่ kûu]

contagious *adj.* (easy to
transmit)
แพร่กระจายได้ง่าย prêɛ-
grà~jaai-dâi-ngâai

contagious disease *n.*
โรคติดต่อ rôok-dtìt-dtòo
[โรค rôok]

contain *vt.* บรรจุ ban-jù |
(include) ประกอบด้วย
bprà~gòop-dûuai

container *n.* ภาชนะ paa-
chá~ná [ใบ bai, ชิ้น chín]

contaminate *vt.* (make
impure) ทำให้_ไม่บริสุทธิ์
tam-hâi-_-mâi-bɔɔ-rí~sùt

contemporary *adj.* (same
age, time) ร่วมสมัย
rûuam-sà~mǎi

contempt *n.* การดูหมิ่น
gaan-duu-mìn

content *adj.* พอใจ pɔɔ-jai

content *n.* (e.g. of book,
article) เนื้อหา nʉ́ʉa-hǎa

contented *adj.* (be
joyous) สบายใจ sà~baai-
jai

contentment *n.*
ความพึงพอใจ kwaam-
pʉng-pɔɔ-jai

contents n. (table of contents) สารบัญ săa-rá~ban [สารบัญ săa-rá~ban]

contest n. (competition) การประกวด gaan-bprà~gùuat

contest vi. (compete) แข่งขัน kɛ̀ng-kǎn

contest vt. (disagree with) โต้แย้ง dtôo-yɛ́ɛng

contestant n. (e.g. beauty contest) ผู้เข้าประกวด pûu-kâo-bprà~gùuat [คน kon] | (e.g. car race) ผู้เข้าแข่งขัน pûu-kâo-kɛ̀ng-kǎn [คน kon]

context n. (linguistics) บริบท bɔɔ-rí~bòt

continent n. ทวีป tá~wîip [ทวีป tá~wîip]

continual adj. (continuous) ต่อเนื่อง dtɔ̀ɔ-nʉ̂ʉang

continue vt. ทำ_ต่อไป tam-_-dtɔ̀ɔ-bpai

continuous adj. ต่อเนื่อง dtɔ̀ɔ-nʉ̂ʉang, ติดต่อกัน dtìt-dtɔ̀ɔ-gan

contour n. (outline of a figure) เค้าโครง káo-

contents n. (table of contents) kroong [แบบ bɛ̀ɛp]

contraception n. การคุมกำเนิด gaan-kum-gam-nə̀ət

contraceptive n. ยาคุมกำเนิด yaa-kum-gam-nə̀ət [เม็ด mét (pill), แผง pʰɛ̌ɛng (mat)]

contract n. (legal agreement) สัญญา săn-yaa [ข้อ kɔ̂ɔ (clause), ฉบับ chà~bàp (whole)]

contract vi. (shrink) หด hòt

contract vt. (disease) ติดต่อ dtìt-dtɔ̀ɔ

contraction n. (shrinking) การหดตัว gaan-hòt-dtuua

contractor n. (e.g. construction) ผู้รับเหมา pûu-ráp-mǎo [คน kon]

contradict v. คัดค้าน kát-káan, แย้ง yɛ́ɛng

contrary adj. (obstinate) ขัดแย้ง kàt-yɛ́ɛng

contribute v. (donate) บริจาค bɔɔ-rí~jàak

contribution n. การสนับสนุน gaan-sà~nàp-sà~nǔn

control vt. ควบคุม kûuap-kum

controversial *adj.* โต้แย้ง dtôo-yɛ́ɛng

controversy *n.* การโต้แย้ง gaan-dtôo-yɛ́ɛng

convene *vi.* (meet) ประชุม bprà~chum

convenience *n.* ความสะดวก kwaam-sà~ dùuak

convenient *adj.* สะดวก sà~dùuak

convention *n.* (meeting, gathering) การชุมนุม gaan-chum-num

conventional *adj.* (traditional) เป็นธรรมเนียม bpen- tam-niiam

conversation *n.* การพูดคุย gaan-pûut-kui | บทสนทนา bòt-sǒn-tá~ naa [บท bòt]

converse *vi.* พูดคุยกัน pûut-kui-gan, สนทนากัน sǒn-tá~naa-gan !

convert *n.* (religious) ผู้เปลี่ยนศาสนา pûu- bplìian-sàat-sà~nǎa [คน kon]

convert *vt.* (change) เปลี่ยน bplìian

converter *n.* (electrical)

เครื่องแปลงไฟ krûuang- bplɛɛng-fai [เครื่อง krûuang]

convertible *adj.* ที่เปลี่ยนแปลงได้ tîi- bplìian-bplɛɛng-dâai

convertible *n.* (car) รถเปิดประทุน rót-bpəət- bprà~tun [คัน kan]

convex *adj.* นูน nuun

convey *vt.* (e.g. ideas, feelings) ถ่ายทอด tàai- tɔ̀ɔt | (transport) ลำเลียง lam-liiang

conveyor belt *n.* สายพาน sǎai-paan [เส้น sên]

convict *n.* นักโทษ nák- tôot [คน kon]

convict *vt.* (pronounce guilty) เห็นว่า_ผิด hěn- wâa-_-pìt

conviction *n.* (laws) การลงโทษ gaan-long- tôot

convince *vt.* (persuade) ทำให้_เชื่อ tam-hâi-_- chûua

convincing *adj.* น่าเชื่อ nâa-chûua

convulsion *n.* (body contortion)

การหดเกร็งของกล้ามเนื้อ gaan-hòt-greng-kɔ̌ɔng-glâam-núua

coo *vi.* (e.g. doves) ขัน kǎn

cook *n.* (female) แม่ครัว mɛ̂ɛ-kruua [คน kon] | (male) พ่อครัว pɔ̂ɔ-kruua, กุ๊ก gúk ● [คน kon]

cook *vi.* (make food) ทำอาหาร tam-aa-hǎan

cook *vt.* (bake) อบ òp | (boil) ต้ม dtôm | (deep fry) ทอด tɔ̂ɔt | (steam) นึ่ง nûng | (stir fry) ผัด pàt

cookie *n.* คุกกี้ kúk-gîi [ชิ้น chín, อัน an ●]

cool *adj.* (chilly) เย็น yen, หนาว nǎao | (good) จ๊าบ jáap ● | (indifferent) เย็นชา yen-chaa

cooler *n.* (air conditioner) เครื่องทำความเย็น krûuang-tam-kwaam-yen [เครื่อง krûuang] | (ice container) ถังน้ำแข็ง tǎng-nám-kɛ̌ng [ถัง tǎng]

co-op *n.* สหกรณ์ sà~hà~gɔɔn [แห่ง hὲng]

coop *n.* (poultry) สุ่ม sùm [ใบ bai]

cooperate *vi.* ร่วมมือ rûuam-muu

cooperative *n.* สหกรณ์ sà~hà~gɔɔn [แห่ง hὲng]

coordinate *vi.* (organize) ประสานงาน bprà~sǎan-ngaan, ร่วมกัน rûuam-gan

coordination *n.* (working together) การประสานงาน gaan-bprà~sǎan-ngaan

coordinator *n.* ผู้ประสานงาน pûu-bprà~sǎan-ngaan [คน kon]

cop *n.* (police officer) ตำรวจ dtam-rùuat [นาย naai ⚡, คน kon]

cope *vi.* รับมือได้ ráp-muu-dâai

copier *n.* (copy machine) เครื่องถ่ายสำเนา krûuang-tàai-sǎm-nao, เครื่องถ่ายเอกสาร krûuang-tàai-èek-gà~sǎan [เครื่อง krûuang]

co-pilot *n.* ผู้ช่วยกัปตัน pûu-chûuai-gàp-dtan [คน kon]

copper *n.* ทองแดง tɔɔng-dɛɛng

copy *n.* (duplicate) สำเนา

săm-nao [แผ่น pèn (piece), ฉบับ chà~bàp (whole)]

copy *vt.* (imitate, bootleg) เลียนแบบ liian-bὲὲp | (photocopy) ถ่ายเอกสาร tàai-èek-gà~săan

copyright *n.* ลิขสิทธิ์ lí-kà~sìt [ฉบับ chà~bàp]

coral *n.* ปะการัง bpà~gaa-rang [ต้น dtôn (plant), กิ่ง gìng (piece)]

cord *n.* สาย săai [เส้น sên, สาย săai] | (electrical) สายไฟ săai-fai [เส้น sên] | (string) เส้น sên [เส้น sên]

core *n.* (central part) แกน gɛɛn [แกน gɛɛn] | (fruit) ไส้ sâi

cork *n.* (e.g. bottle) จุกไม้ก๊อก jùk-mái-gɔ́k [จุก jùk]

corkscrew *n.* สว่านเปิดจุกขวด sà~ wàan-bpə̀ət-jùk-kùuat [อัน an]

corn *n.* (plant) ข้าวโพด kâao-pôot [ต้น dtôn (plant), ฝัก fàk (cob)]

cornea *n.* กระจกตา grà~ jòk-dtaa

corner *n.* มุม mum [มุม mum]

corner *vt.* (drive into a corner) ต้อน_เข้ามุม dtɔ̂ɔn-_-kâo-mum

cornflakes *n.* ข้าวโพดกรอบ kâao-pôot-grɔ̀ɔp

coronation *n.* ราชาภิเษก raa-chaa-pí-sèek

coroner *n.* เจ้าหน้าที่ชันสูตรศพ jâo-nâa-tîi-chan-ná~sùut-sòp [คน kon]

corporal *n.* (in the marines) สิบโท sìp-too [คน kon]

corporation *n.* (company) บริษัท bɔɔ-rí~sàt [แห่ง hὲng]

corps *n.* (combat unit) หน่วยทหาร nùai-tá~hăan [หน่วย nùai] | (group of workers) กลุ่มคนทำงานร่วมกัน glùm-kon-tam-ngaan-rûuam-gan [กลุ่ม glùm]

corpse *n.* (dead body) ศพ sòp [ศพ sòp]

correct *adj.* ถูก tùuk, ถูกต้อง tùuk-dtɔ̂ng

correct *vt.* แก้ gɛ̂ɛ, แก้ไข

gêε-kǎi

correction n.
(punishment) การลงโทษ
gaan-long-tôot

correspond vi. (relate)
สอดคล้องกัน sɔ̀ɔt-
klɔ́ɔng-gan | (write
letters)
ติดต่อกันทางจดหมาย
dtìt-dtɔ̀ɔ-gan-taang-
jòt-mǎai

corridor n. ระเบียง rá~
biiang [แห่ง hèng]

corrosive adj. กัดกร่อน
gàt-grɔ̀n

corrupt adj. โกง goong,
ทุจริต tút-jà~rìt

corruption n. การทุจริต
gaan-tút-jà~rìt

cosign vi. ร่วมลงนาม
rûuam-long-naam ⚑

cosmetics n. เครื่องสำอาง
krûuang-sǎm-aang [ชนิด
chá~nít (type), ยี่ห้อ yîi-
hɔ̂ɔ (brand)]

cost n. (expense) ค่าใช้จ่าย
kâa-chái-jàai [จำนวน
jam-nuuan] | (price) ราคา
raa-kaa

cost vt. มีราคา mii-raa-kaa

costly adj. (expensive)

ราคาแพง raa-kaa-pɛɛng

cost of living n.
ค่าครองชีพ kâa-krɔɔng-
chîip

costume n. เครื่องแต่งกาย
krûuang-dtὲng-gaai [ชุด
chút (set), ตัว dtuua
(piece)] | ชุด chút ✿ [ชุด
chút] | (in a play)
ชุดแสดงละคร chút-sà~
dɛɛng-lá~kɔɔn [ชุด chút]

cot n. (baby bed) เตียงเด็ก
dtiiang-dèk [เตียง
dtiiang]

cottage n. กระท่อม grà~
tɔ̂m [หลัง lǎng]

cotton n. (plant) ฝ้าย fâai
[ต้น dtôn] | (wool) สำลี
sǎm-lii [ก้อน gɔ̂ɔn
(piece), แผ่น pὲn (sheet)]

cotton swab n. สำลีแท่ง
sǎm-lii-têng [ก้าน gâan,
อัน an]

couch n. (sofa) เก้าอี้โซฟา
gâo-îi-soo-faa [ตัว dtuua]

cough vi. ไอ ai

cough drop n. ลูกอมแก้ไอ
lûuk-om-gêε-ai [เม็ด mét]

cough medicine n.
ยาแก้ไอ yaa-gêε-ai [ขวด

kùuat (bottle)]

council *n.* (board) สภา
sà~paa [แห่ง hèng, สภา
sà~paa]

councilor *n.* สมาชิกสภา
sà~maa-chík-sà~paa
[คน kon]

counsel *n.* (lawyer)
ทนายความ tá~naai-
kwaam [คน kon]

counsel *vt.* ให้คำปรึกษากับ
hâi-kam-bprùk-sǎa-gàp

counselor *n.* (advisor)
ที่ปรึกษา tîi-bprùk-sǎa
[ท่าน tân ♣, คน kon]

count *n.* (in an
indictment) ข้อหา kɔ̂ɔ-
hǎa [ข้อหา kɔ̂ɔ-hǎa]

count *v.* นับ náp

countdown *n.*
การนับถอยหลัง gaan-
náp-tɔ̌ɔi-lǎng

counter *n.* (table)
เคาน์เตอร์ káo-dtəə
[เคาน์เตอร์ káo-dtəə]

counterbalance *vt.*
คานอำนาจ kaan-am-nâat

counterclockwise *adj.*
ทวนเข็มนาฬิกา tuuan-
kěm-naa-lí~gaa

counterfeit *adj.* ปลอม
bplɔɔm

count on *vt.* ไว้วางใจ
wái-waang-jai

country *n.* (nation)
ประเทศ bprà~têet
[ประเทศ bprà~têet]

countryman *n.* ชาวชนบท
chaao-chon-ná~bòt [คน
kon]

countryside *n.* ชนบท
chon-ná~bòt, บ้านนอก
bâan-nɔ̂ɔk ♣ [แห่ง hèng]

countrywoman see
countryman

county *n.* (district) แขวง
kwěeng [แขวง kwěeng]

coup *n.* รัฐประหาร rát-
tà~bprà~hǎan

coup d'état see coup

couple *n.* (husband and
wife) สามีภรรยา sǎa-mii-
pan-rá~yaa [คู่ kûu] |
(pair) คู่ kûu [คู่ kûu]

coupon *n.* คูปอง kuu-
bpɔɔng [ใบ bai]

courier *n.* ผู้ส่งสาร pûu-
sòng-sǎan [คน kon]

course *n.* (path) เส้นทาง
sên-taang [สาย sǎai, เส้น
sên] | (syllabus) หลักสูตร
làk-sùut [หลักสูตร làk-
sùut]

court n. (e.g. basketball) สนาม sà~nǎam [แห่ง hɛ̀ng] | (of law) ศาล sǎan [ศาล sǎan]

court v. (woo) จีบ jìip

court appearance n. การปรากฏตัวในศาล gaan-bpraa-gòt-dtuua-nai-sǎan

courtesy adj. (free) โดยไม่คิดค่าบริการ dooi-mâi-kít-kâa-bɔɔ-rí~gaan

courtesy n. (decency) มารยาท maa-rá~yâat

court house n. ศาล sǎan [ศาล sǎan]

court reporter n. ผู้บันทึกรายงานศาล pûu-ban-túk-raai-ngaan-sǎan [คน kon]

court room n. ห้องพิจารณาคดี hông-pí-jaa-rá~naa-ká~dii [ห้อง hông]

courtyard n. ลาน laan [ลาน laan, แห่ง hɛ̀ng]

cousin n. ลูกพี่ลูกน้อง lûuk-pîi-lûuk-nɔ́ɔng [คน kon]

cover n. (e.g. book) ปก bpòk [ใบ bai, แผ่น pɛ̀n] | (e.g. jar) ฝา fǎa [ฝา fǎa,

ชิ้น chín]

cover vt. (close off) ปิด bpìt | (wrap) คลุม klum, ปกปิด bpòk-bpìt

coverage n. (insurance) เงินคุ้มครอง ngən-kúm-krɔɔng | (news) การรายงานข่าว gaan-raai-ngaan-kàao

cow n. วัว wuua [ตัว dtuua] | (female) วัวตัวเมีย wuua-dtuua-miia [ตัว dtuua]

cowboy n. คาวบอย kaao-bɔɔi [คน kon]

CPA see certified public accountant

Crab n. (astrological sign) ราศีกรกฏ raa-sǐi-gɔɔ-rá~gòt [ราศี raa-sǐi]

crab n. ปู bpuu [ตัว dtuua]

crack n. (split line) รอยร้าว rɔɔi-ráao [รอย rɔɔi]

crack vi. (split) ร้าว ráao

crack vt. (split) ทำให้_ร้าว tam-hâi-_-ráao

cracked adj. ร้าว ráao

cracker n. ขนมปังกรอบ kà~nǒm-bpang-grɔ̀ɔp [ชิ้น chín]

cradle n. (for baby) อู่ ùu

[อยู่ ùu] | (for baby)
เปลเด็ก bplee-dèk [เปล
bplee]

craft *n.* (art work)
งานศิลปะที่ทำด้วยมือ
ngaan-sǐn-lá~bpà~tîi-
tam-dûai-muu

craftsman *n.* (artisan)
ช่างฝีมือ châng-fǐi-muu
[คน kon]

cramp *n.* (muscular)
ตะคริว dtà~kriu

cramped *adj.* (e.g.
muscle) เป็นตะคริว
bpen-dtà~kriu | (limited
in space) คับแคบ káp-
kɛ̂ɛp

cranberry *n.* แครนเบอรี่
krɛɛn-bəə-rîi [ลูก lûuk, ช่อ
chɔ̂ɔ (bunch)]

crane *n.* (machine) ปั้นจั่น
bpân-jàn [ตัว dtuua]

cranky *adj.* (peevish)
อารมณ์เสีย aa-rom-sǐia

crap *adj.* (nonsense)
ไร้สาระ rái-sǎa-rá

crap *n.* (feces) ขี้ kîi ☙
[กอง gɔɔng, ก้อน gɔ̂ɔn]

crap! *interj.* เฮงซวย
heng-suuai

crash *n.* (collision)

การชนกัน gaan-chon-
gan | (loud noise)
เสียงดัง sǐiang-dang

crash *vi.* (e.g. car) ชนกัน
chon-gan | (e.g.
computer) พัง pang |
(e.g. plane, stock market)
ตก dtòk

crate *n.* (shipping) ลังไม้
lang-máai [ใบ bai]

crave *vt.* (desire) กระหาย
grà~hǎai

crawl *vi.* (e.g. babies)
คลาน klaan

crayon *n.* ดินสอสี din-sɔ̌ɔ-
sǐi [แท่ง tɛ̂ng]

craze *n.* ความนิยมชั่วคราว
kwaam-ní-yom-chûua-
kraao

crazy *adj.* บ้า bâa, บ้าๆบอๆ
bâa-bâa-bɔɔ-bɔɔ ☙

crazy about *adj.* คลั่งไคล้
klâng-klái, บ้า bâa,
หลงใหล lǒng-lǎi

creak *n.* เสียงดังเอี๊ยด
sǐiang-dang-íiat

cream *adj.* (color)
เป็นสีนวล bpen-sǐi-nuuan

cream *n.* ครีม kriim

crease *n.* (e.g. face)
รอยย่น rɔɔi-yôn [รอย rɔɔi,

ที่ tîi] | (e.g. paper, clothes) รอยพับ rɔɔi-páp [รอย rɔɔi]

create vt. (build) ก่อ gɔ̀ɔ, สร้าง sâang

creative adj. ที่สร้างสรรค์ tîi-sâang-sǎn

creator n. (producer) ผู้สร้างสรรค์ pûu-sâang-sǎn [คน kon]

creature n. (animal) สัตว์ sàt [ตัว dtuua, ชนิด chá~nít (kind)]

credible adj. เชื่อถือได้ chûua-tǔu-dâai | (reliable) น่าเชื่อถือ nâa-chûua-tǔu

credit n. (e.g. college) หน่วยกิต nùai-gìt [หน่วย nùai] | (trust) ความไว้วางใจ kwaam-wái-waang-jai | (trustworthiness) เครดิต kree-dìt [เครดิต kree-dìt]

credit vt. (acknowledge) ให้เครดิต hâi-kree-dìt

credit card n. บัตรเครดิต bàt-kree-dìt [ใบ bai]

creditor n. เจ้าหนี้ jâo-nîi [คน kon, ราย raai ⚠]

credulous adj. เชื่อคนง่าย chûua-kon-ngâai

creed n. (system of belief) ลัทธิ lát-tí [ลัทธิ lát-tí]

creek n. ลำธาร lam-taan [สาย sǎai]

creep vi. ไต่ dtài | (e.g. plants) เลื้อย lúuai

cremate a body v. เผาศพ pǎo-sòp

crematorium n. เมรุ meen [แห่ง hèng]

crescent moon n. พระจันทร์ครึ่งเสี้ยว prá~jan-krûng-sîiao

crest n. (e.g. bird) หงอน ngɔ̌ɔn [หงอน ngɔ̌ɔn] | (mountain) ยอดเขา yɔ̂ɔt-kǎo [ยอด yɔ̂ɔt]

crew n. (aircraft) เจ้าหน้าที่ประจำเครื่องบิน jâo-nâa-tîi-bprà~jam-krûuang-bin [คน kon]

crib n. (for babies) เตียงนอนเด็ก dtiiang-nɔɔn-dèk [เตียง dtiiang]

cricket n. (insect) จิ้งหรีด jîng-rìit [ตัว dtuua]

crime n. อาชญากรรม àat-chá~yaa-gam

criminal adj. ทางอาญา

taang-aa-yaa

criminal *n.* อาชญากร àat-chá~yaa-gɔɔn [คน kon]

criminal case *n.* คดีอาญา ká~dii-aa-yaa [คดี ká~dii]

criminal law *n.* กฎหมายอาญา gòt-mǎai-aa-yaa

cripple *n.* คนพิการ kon-pí-gaan, คนง่อย kon-ngɔ̂i ✿ [คน kon]

crippled *adj.* พิการ pí-gaan | (for hands) ง่อย ngɔ̂i | (lame) เป๋ bpě ✿

crisis *n.* วิกฤตการณ์ wí-grìt-dtà~gaan ⚡

crisp *n.* (potato chip) มันฝรั่งแผ่นทอดกรอบ man-fà~ràng-pèn-tɔ̂ɔt-grɔ̀ɔp [ชิ้น chín (piece), ห่อ hɔ̀ɔ (pack), กล่อง glɔ̀ng (box)]

crispy *adj.* กรอบ grɔ̀ɔp

criterion *n.* (rule) เกณฑ์ geen [หลัก làk]

critic *n.* นักวิจารณ์ nák-wí-jaan [คน kon]

critical *adj.* (emergency) วิกฤต wí-grìt | (important) สำคัญ sǎm-kan

criticism *n.* (act of criticizing) การวิจารณ์ gaan-wí-jaan

criticize *v.* วิจารณ์ wí-jaan

crocodile *n.* จระเข้ jɔɔ-rá~kêe [ตัว dtuua]

croissant *n.* ครัวซอง kruua-sɔɔng [ชิ้น chín]

crooked *adj.* (bent) งอ ngɔɔ | (dishonest) โกง goong

crop *n.* (plant) พืชผล pɯ̂ɯt-pǒn [ชนิด chá~nít (type), ต้น dtôn (plant)]

cross *n.* (X mark) กากบาท gaa-gà~bàat [ตัว dtuua] | (in Christianity) ไม้กางเขน mái-gaang-kěen [อัน an]

cross *v.* (e.g. street) ข้าม kâam

cross-examine *v.* ถามค้าน tǎam-káan

cross-eyed *adj.* ตาเข dtaa-kěe

crossroads *n.* ทางแยก taang-yɛ̂ɛk [แห่ง hɛ̀ng]

crosswalk *n.* ทางม้าลาย taang-máa-laai [แห่ง hɛ̀ng]

crossword puzzle *n.*

ปริศนาอักษรไขว้ bprìt-sà~nǎa-àk-sɔ̌ɔn-kwâi [ชุด chút]

crotch n. (between the legs) หว่างขา wàang-kǎa

crouch v. หมอบ mɔ̀ɔp

crow n. กา gaa [ตัว dtuua]

crow vi. (e.g. rooster) ขัน kǎn

crowbar n. ชะแลง chá~lɛɛng [อัน an]

crowd n. (people) ฝูงชน fǔung-chon [กลุ่ม glùm]

crowd vi. (jam-pack) เบียดเสียดกัน bìiat-sìiat-gan

crowd around v. มุง mung, รุม rum, รายล้อม raai-lɔ́ɔm ⚡

crowded adj. แออัด ɛɛ-àt

crown n. (headgear) มงกุฎ mong-gùt [องค์ ong ♚ (for king), มงกุฎ mong-gùt] | (tooth) ครอบฟัน krɔ̂ɔp-fan [ซี่ sîi]

crow's-feet n. ตีนกา dtiin-gaa [รอย rɔɔi]

crucial adj. (important) สำคัญ sǎm-kan

crucify vt. (on cross) ตรึง_บนไม้กางเขน

dtrɯng-_-bon-mái-gaang-kěen ⚡

crude adj. (obscene) หยาบโลน yàap-loon | (roughly put together) หยาบ yàap

crude oil n. น้ำมันดิบ nám-man-dìp [ลิตร lít]

cruel adj. ใจร้าย jai-ráai, โหดร้าย hòot-ráai

cruise n. (pleasure ship) เรือสำราญ rɯɯa-sǎm-raan [ลำ lam]

cruise vi. (in ship) แล่นเรือ lɛ̂n-rɯɯa

crumb n. (remnant) เศษ sèet [ชิ้น chín]

crumble vi. แตกละเอียด dtɛ̀ɛk-lá~ìiat

crumble vt. ทำให้_เป็นเศษเล็กๆ tam-hâi-_-bpen-sèet-lék-lék

crumple vt. (e.g. paper) ขยำ kà~yǎm, ขยี้ kà~yîi

crumpled adj. (wrinkled) ยู่ยี่ yûu-yîi ✿

crunch n. (crisis) ภาวะวิกฤติ paa-wá-wí-grìt [ภาวะ paa-wá]

crunch v. (chew loudly) เคี้ยว_เสียงดัง kíiao-_-

sĭiang-dang

crush n. (infatuation) อาการตกหลุมรัก aa-gaan-dtòk-lǔm-rák

crush vt. (pound, grind) บด bòt

crushed adj. ละเอียด lá~ìiat, แหลก lɛ̀ɛk

crust n. (bread) ขอบขนมปัง kɔ̀ɔp-kà~nǒm-bpang [ชิ้น chín] | (rind, pod, husk) เปลือก bplùuak [ชิ้น chín]

crutch n. ไม้ยันรักแร้ mái-yan-rák-rɛ́ɛ [อัน an]

cry vi. ร้อง rɔ́ɔng, ร้องไห้ rɔ́ɔng-hâi

cry out vi. (make a loud noise) ร้องเสียงดัง rɔ́ɔng-sĭiang-dang

crystal n. (clear glass) แก้วคริสตัล gɛ̂ɛo-krís-dtân [ใบ bai]

c-section see Cesarean section

cub n. (baby tiger) ลูกเสือ lûuk-sǔua [ตัว dtuua] | (young animal) ลูกสัตว์ lûuk-sàt [ตัว dtuua]

cube n. ลูกบาศก์ lûuk-bàat [ลูก lûuk]

cuckold n. ผู้ชายที่ภรรยามีชู้ pûu-chaai-tîi-pan-rá~yaa-mii-chúu [คน kon]

cucumber n. แตงกวา dtɛɛng-gwaa [ลูก lûuk]

cuddle vt. กก gòk, โอบกอด òop-gɔ̀ɔt

cue n. (billiards) ไม้บิลเลียด mái-bin-lîiat [อัน an]

cuff n. (end of sleeve, leg) ข้อมือเสื้อ kɔ̂ɔ-mɯɯ-sɯ̂ɯa [ข้าง kâang]

cuisine n. อาหาร aa-hǎan [อย่าง yàang (dish), ประเภท bprà~pêet (kind)]

culprit n. (responsible person) ตัวการ dtuua-gaan [ตัว dtuua, คน kon]

cult n. (religious followers) ผู้เลื่อมใสศรัทธา pûu-lɯ̂am-sǎi-sàt-taa [คน kon]

cultivate vt. (plant) ปลูก bplùuk

cultural adj. (relating to culture) ทางวัฒนธรรม taang-wát-tá~ná~tam

culture n. (customs)

วัฒนธรรม wát-tá~ná~tam [อัน an]

cunning *adj.* (tricky) เจ้าเล่ห์ jâo-lêe

cunt *n.* หี hǐi ☻

cup *n.* (container) ถ้วย tûuai [ใบ bai] | (of bra) คัพ káp

cupboard *n.* ตู้ dtûu [ใบ bai]

cupid *n.* กามเทพ gaam-má~têep [ตน dton]

curb *n.* (along the edge of a street) ขอบถนน kòop-tà~nǒn [ที่ tîi]

cure *vt.* (remedy) แก้ gɛ̂ɛ | (treat) รักษา rák-sǎa

curfew *n.* การห้าม ออกนอกบ้านยามวิกาล gaan-hâam-ɔ̀ɔk-nɔ̂ɔk-bâan-yaam-wí-gaan

curious *adj.* (nosy) อยากรู้อยากเห็น yàak-rúu-yàak-hěn

curl *n.* (hair) ผมหยิก pǒm-yìk [ลอน lɔɔn]

curl *vt.* ม้วน múuan

curled *adj.* หยิก yìk

curler *n.* ที่ม้วนผม tîi-múuan-pǒm [อัน an]

curly *adj.* (hair) หยักศก yàk-sòk

currency *n.* (money) เงินตรา ngən-dtraa

current *adj.* (present) ปัจจุบัน bpàt-jù-ban

current *n.* (electrical) กระแสไฟ grà~sɛ̌ɛ-fai [แอมป์ ɛm] | (water) กระแสน้ำ grà~sɛ̌ɛ-náam [กระแส grà~sɛ̌ɛ]

curriculum *n.* หลักสูตร làk-sùut [หลักสูตร làk-sùut]

curriculum vitae *n.* ประวัติย่อ bprà~wàt-yɔ̂ɔ

curry *n.* (dish) แกงกะหรี่ gɛɛng-gà~rìi [ชนิด chá~nít (type), ถ้วย tûuai (bowl)] | (dish) แกง gɛɛng [ถ้วย tûuai (bowl)]

curse *v.* ด่า dàa, สาปแช่ง sàap-chêng

curtain *n.* ม่าน mâan [ผืน pʉʉn]

curve *n.* (line) เส้นโค้ง sên-kóong [เส้น sên] | (road) ทางโค้ง taang-kóong [แห่ง hɛ̀ng, ที่ tîi]

curved *adj.* (e.g. line) โค้ง

kóong, งอ ngɔɔ

cushion n. (mat) เบาะ bɔ̀
[ใบ bai, ลูก lûuk]

custard n. คัสตาร์ด kát-
sà~dtàat, สังขยา sǎng-
kà~yǎa

custody n. (of child)
การได้สิทธิในตัวลูก gaan-
dâi-sìt-nai-dtuua-lûuk |
(of prisoner) การถูกจับกุม
gaan-tùuk-jàp-gum

custom n. (tradition)
ประเพณี bprà~pee-nii
[แบบ bɛ̀ɛp, อย่าง yàang]

customer n. ลูกค้า lûuk-
káa [คน kon]

customer service n.
แผนกบริการลูกค้า pà~
nɛ̀ɛk-bɔɔ-rí~gaan-lûuk-
káa [แผนก pà~nɛ̀ɛk]

customs n. ศุลกากร sǔn-
lá~gaa-gɔɔn [แผนก pà~
nɛ̀ɛk]

customs house n.
ด่านศุลกากร dàan-sǔn-
lá~gaa-gɔɔn [ด่าน dàan]

cut n. (wound) บาดแผล
bàat-plɛ̌ɛ [แห่ง hɛ̀ng, ที่ tîi]

cut v. ตัด dtàt | (chop) หั่น
hàn

cute adj. (lovely) น่ารัก

nâa-rák

cuticle n. กำพร้า gam-
práa [ชั้น chán]

cut off vt. (slice off)
ตัด_ออก dtàt-_-ɔ̀ɔk

cutting board n. เขียง
kǐiang [อัน an, เขียง
kǐiang]

cuttlefish n. ปลาหมึก
bplaa-mʉ̀k [ตัว dtuua]

C.V. see curriculum vitae

cycle n. (e.g. life) วงจร
wong-jɔɔn [วงจร wong-
jɔɔn] | (rotation,
anniversary) รอบ rɔ̂ɔp
[รอบ rɔ̂ɔp]

cycle vi. (ride a bicycle)
ขี่จักรยาน kìi-jàk-grà~
yaan

cyclone n. ไซโคลน sai-
kloon | พายุหมุน paa-
yú-mǔn [ลูก lûuk]

cylinder n. กระบอก grà~
bɔ̀ɔk [กระบอก grà~bɔ̀ɔk]

cymbal n. (large) ฉาบ
chàap [ข้าง kâang
(piece), คู่ kûu (pair)] |
(small) ฉิ่ง chìng [ข้าง
kâang (piece), คู่ kûu
(pair)]

cynical adj. เยาะเย้ย yɔ́-

yée̯i

D

D.A n. อัยการ ai-yá~gaan
[คน kon]

dab v. ป้าย bpâai

dad n. พ่อ pɔ̂ɔ [คน kon]

daily adv. ทุกวัน túk-wan,
ประจำวัน bprà~jam-wan

dairy adj. (product)
ผลิตภัณฑ์นม pà~lìt-
dtà~pan-nom

daisy n. ดอกเดซี่ dɔ̀ɔk-
dee-sîi [ดอก dɔ̀ɔk]

dam n. เขื่อน kùuan [เขื่อน
kùuan, แห่ง hɛ̀ng]

damage n. ความเสียหาย
kwaam-sǐia-hǎai

damage vt. ทำให้_เสียหาย
tam-hâi-_-sǐia-hǎai

damaged adj. เสีย sǐia,
ชำรุด cham-rút

damages n. (legal)
ค่าชดใช้ kâa-chót-chái

damned adj. (accursed)
จัญไร jan-rai

damp adj. ชื้น chúun

dance n. (ballroom) ลีลาศ
lii-lâat | (party) งานเต้นรำ
ngaan-dtên-ram [งาน
ngaan]

dance vi. (ballroom)
เต้นรำ dtên-ram | (disco,
no step) ดิ้น dîn |
(modern) เต้น dtên |
(traditional) ฟ้อน fɔ́ɔn, รำ
ram

dancer n. นักเต้นรำ nák-
dtên-ram [คน kon] | (in a
band) หางเครื่อง hǎang-
krûuang [คน kon]

dandruff n. รังแค rang-kɛɛ

danger n. อันตราย an-
dtà~raai, ภัย pai

dangerous adj. อันตราย
an-dtà~raai

dangle vt. (hang) แขวน
kwɛ̌ɛn | (swing) แกว่ง
gwɛ̀ng

dare v. กล้า glâa

dark adj. (color) แก่ gɛ̀ɛ |
(gloomy) กลุ้ม glûm |
(light level) มืด mûut

dark horse n. ม้ามืด
máa-mûut [คน kon
(person), ตัว dtuua
(animal)]

darkroom n. ห้องมืด
hɔ̂ng-mûut [ห้อง hɔ̂ng]

darling n. ที่รัก tîi-rák [คน
kon]

dart *n.* ลูกดอก lûuk-dɔ̀ɔk [ลูก lûuk]

dash *n.* (punctuation mark) เครื่องหมายขีดยาว krûuang-mǎai-kìit-yaao [ตัว dtuua]

dashboard *n.* (of a car) แผงหน้าปัดรถยนต์ pɛ̌ɛng-nâa-bpàt-rót-yon [ที่ tîi]

data *n.* ข้อมูล kɔ̂ɔ-muun [ชนิด chá~nít (type), ชุด chút (set)]

database *n.* เดต้าเบส dee-dtâa-bèet, ฐานข้อมูล tǎan-kɔ̂ɔ-muun ✘ [ชุด chút]

date *n.* (appointment) การนัด gaan-nát [ครั้ง kráng] | (calendar day) วันที่ wan-tîi [วัน wan] | (companion) คู่เดท kûu-dèet [คน kon] | (fruit) อินทผลัม in-tá~pà~lam [ลูก lûuk]

date *v.* (romantic) เดท dèet ✱

date *vt.* (write the date on) ลงวันที่ใน long-wan-tîi-nai

dateline *n.* เส้นแบ่งวันที่ sên-bɛ̀ng-wan-tîi [เส้น sên]

dating *n.* (romantic) การนัดหมาย gaan-nát-mǎai [ครั้ง kráng]

daughter *n.* ลูกสาว lûuk-sǎao [คน kon]

daughter-in-law *n.* ลูกสะใภ้ lûuk-sà~pái [คน kon]

dawn *n.* เช้ามืด cháao-mʉ̂ʉt, รุ่งเช้า rûng-cháao ✱

day *n.* วัน wan [วัน wan]

day after tomorrow *n.* เมื่อรืนนี้ mʉ̂ʉa-rʉʉn-níi [วัน wan]

day before yesterday *n.* วันก่อน wan-gɔ̀ɔn [วัน wan]

daybreak see dawn

day by day *adj.* (each day) แต่ละวัน dtɛ̀ɛ-lá~wan

day care *n.* (center) สถานรับเลี้ยงเด็ก sà~tǎan-ráp-líiang-dèk [แห่ง hɛ̀ng]

daydream *n.* ฝันกลางวัน fǎn-glaang-wan

daylight *n.* (sunlight)

แสงแดด sɛ̌ɛng-dɛ̀ɛt

daylight saving time *n.* เวลาที่เปลี่ยนเพื่อประหยัดพลังงาน wee-laa-tîi-bpliian-pûua-bprà~yàt-pá~lang-ngaan

daytime *n.* เวลากลางวัน wee-laa-glaang-wan

dazed *adj.* (stunned) มึน mʉn

dead *adj.* (not alive) ตาย dtaai | (not working) หยุดทำงาน yùt-tam-ngaan

deadbolt *n.* กลอนประตู glɔɔn-bprà~dtuu [อัน an]

dead end *n.* ทางตัน taang-dtan [ทาง taang]

deadline *n.* กำหนดเวลา gam-nòt-wee-laa, เส้นตาย sên-dtaai ☻ [ครั้ง kráng]

deadly *adj.* (lethal) ถึงตายได้ tʉ̌ng-dtaai-dâai

deaf *adj.* หูหนวก hǔu-nùuak

deal *n.* (business) การติดต่อธุรกิจ gaan-dtìt-dtɔ̀ɔ-tú-rá~gìt [ครั้ง kráng]

deal *vi.* (cards) แจกไพ่ jɛ̀ɛk-pâi

dealer *n.* (card) คนแจกไพ่ kon-jɛ̀ɛk-pâi [คน kon] | (merchant) พ่อค้า pɔ̂ɔ-káa [คน kon]

deal with *vt.* (do business with) ติดต่อธุรกิจ dtìt-dtɔ̀ɔ-tú-rá~gìt | (handle) จัดการ jàt-gaan

dean *n.* (e.g. in college) คณบดี ká~ná-bɔɔ-dii [คน kon]

dear *adj.* (expensive) แพง pɛɛng

dear *n.* (loved one) ที่รัก tîi-rák [คน kon]

death *n.* การเสียชีวิต gaan-sǐia-chii-wít, ความตาย kwaam-dtaai

death penalty *n.* โทษประหารชีวิต tôot-bprà~hǎan-chii-wít [ครั้ง kráng]

debate *v.* (argue about) โต้เถียง dtôo-tǐiang | (formally) โต้วาที dtôo-waa-tii

debit *vt.* (from account) หักบัญชี hàk-ban-chii

debris *n.* (rubble) เศษขยะ sèet-kà~yà

debt *n.* หนี้สิน nîi-sǐn

[จำนวน jam-nuuan]

debtor *n.* ลูกหนี้ lûuk-nîi
[ราย raai ⚡, คน kon]

debug *vt.*
แก้ข้อผิดพลาดของ gɛ̂ɛ-
kɔ̂ɔ-pìt-plâat-kɔ̌ɔng

decade *n.* ทศวรรษ tót-
sà~wát [ทศวรรษ tót-
sà~wát]

decaf *n.*
กาแฟที่ไม่มีคาเฟอีน gaa-
fɛɛ-tîi-mâi-mii-kaa-fee-iin

decay *vi.* (fall into ruin,
decline) เสื่อม sùuam |
(rot) เน่าเปื่อย nâo-bpùuai

deceased *adj.* ตาย dtaai

deceased *n.* ผู้ตาย pûu-
dtaai [คน kon]

deceive *v.* (fool) โกง
goong, หลอก lɔ̀ɔk,
หลอกลวง lɔ̀ɔk-luuang

December *n.* ธันวาคม
tan-waa-kom [เดือน
duuan]

decent *adj.* (adequate)
พอสมควร pɔɔ-sǒm-
kuuan | (respectable)
น่านับถือ nâa-náp-tǔu

deception *n.*
การหลอกลวง gaan-lɔ̀ɔk-
luuang

decide *v.* (determine)
ตัดสินใจ dtàt-sǐn-jai |
(rule legally) ตัดสิน dtàt-
sǐn

decimal *adj.*
เกี่ยวกับทศนิยม gìiao-
gàp-tót-sà~ní-yom

decimal point *n.*
จุดทศนิยม jùt-tót-sà~
ní~yom [จุด jùt]

decision *n.*
(determination)
การตัดสินใจ gaan-dtàt-
sǐn-jai

decisive *adj.* (crucial,
conclusive) ที่ชี้ขาด tîi-
chíi-kàat | (unwavering)
แน่วแน่ nɛ̂o-nɛ̂ɛ

deck *n.* (e.g. ship) ดาดฟ้า
dàat-fáa [แห่ง hèng,
ดาดฟ้า dàat-fáa] | (of
cards) ชุดไพ่ chút-pâi
[สำหรับ sǎm-ráp]

declare *vt.* (at customs)
สำแดง sǎm-dɛɛng |
(proclaim) ประกาศ
bprà~gàat

decline *v.* (deny, refuse)
ปฏิเสธ bpà~dtì-sèet

decline *vi.* (go down)
ลดต่ำลง lót-dtàm-long

decode v. ถอดรหัส tɔ̀ɔt-rá~hàt

decompose vi. (disintegrate) ย่อยสลาย yɔ̂i-sà~lǎai

decontaminate vt. ขจัดพิษออกจาก kà~jàt-pít-ɔ̀ɔk-jàak

decorate v. ตกแต่ง dtòk-dtɛ̀ng, ประดับ bprà~dàp

decoration n. (act) การตกแต่ง gaan-dtòk-dtɛ̀ng

decoy n. (object) เป้าหลอก bpâo-lɔ̀ɔk [เป้า bpâo] | (person) นกต่อ nók-dtɔ̀ɔ ✱ [คน kon]

decrease vi. ลดลง lót-long

decree n. (order) คำสั่ง kam-sàng [เรื่อง rûuang, อัน an ✱]

dedicate vt. อุทิศ ù-tít

deduce vt. (infer) อนุมาน à~nú-maan ✗

deduct v. (subtract) หัก hàk

deductible adj. หักออกได้ hàk-ɔ̀ɔk-dâai

deductible n. (insurance) ส่วนที่ต้องจ่ายเอง sùuan-tîi-dtɔ̂ng-jàai-eeng

deduction n. (subtraction) การหักออก gaan-hàk-ɔ̀ɔk

deed n. (action) การกระทำ gaan-grà~tam | (e.g. land) โฉนด chà~nòot [ฉบับ chà~bàp]

deem vt. (consider) ถือว่า tǔu-wâa, นับว่า náp-wâa

deep adj. ลึก lʉ́k

deep-fried adj. ทอด tɔ̂ɔt

deer n. (animal) กวาง gwaang [ตัว dtuua]

deface vt. (make ugly) ทำให้_เสียโฉม tam-hâi-_-sǐia-chǒom

defame vt. (destroy name of) ทำลายชื่อเสียงของ tam-laai-chʉ̂ʉ-sǐiang-kɔ̌ɔng

default vi. (on contract) ไม่ทำตามสัญญา mâi-tam-dtaam-sǎn-yaa

defeat n. (failure) ความล้มเหลว kwaam-lóm-lěeo

defeat v. (conquer, win over) เอาชนะ ao-chá~ná

defeated adj. แพ้ pɛ́ɛ, ปราชัย bpraa-chai ⁉

defecate v. อึ ʉ̀, ขับถ่าย

kàp-tàai ⚠, ขี้ kîi 💥

defect *n.* (scar, flaw) ตำหนิ
dtam-nìi [ที่ tîi]

defective *adj.* (damaged)
ชำรุด cham-rút ⚠ |
(having a fault) มีข้อเสีย
mii-kɔ̂ɔ-sǐia

defend *vt.* (be a lawyer
for) เป็นทนายให้ bpen-
tá~naai-hâi | (physically)
ป้องกัน bpɔ̂ng-gan |
(verbally) แก้ต่าง gɛ̂ɛ-
dtàang

defendant *n.* (in court)
จำเลย jam-ləəi [คน kon]

defense *n.* (argument in
court) คำแก้ต่าง kam-
gɛ̂ɛ-dtàang | (in sports)
ฝ่ายรับ fàai-ráp [ฝ่าย fàai]
| (protection) การป้องกัน
gaan-bpɔ̂ng-gan

defer *v.* (postpone)
ยืดเวลา yʉ̂ʉt-wee-laa

defer *vi.* (yield) อนุโลม à-
nú-loom

defiant *adj.* (resisting)
ไม่ยอมทำตาม mâi-yɔɔm-
tam-dtaam

deficiency *n.*
(inadequacy)
ความบกพร่อง kwaam-

bòk-prɔ̂ng

deficient *adj.* (missing,
lacking) ขาดแคลน kàat-
klɛɛn | (not enough)
ไม่พอ mâi-pɔɔ

deficit *n.* (business loss)
การขาดดุล gaan-kàat-dun

define *vt.* (fix, specify)
กำหนด gam-nòt | (give
meaning of)
ให้คำจำกัดความของ hâi-
kam-jam-gàt-kwaam-
kɔ̌ɔng ✗

definite *adj.* (certain)
แน่นอน nɛ̂ɛ-nɔɔn

definitely *adv.*
อย่างแน่นอน yàang-nɛ̂ɛ-
nɔɔn

definition *n.* (meaning)
คำจำกัดความ kam-jam-
gàt-kwaam [คำ kam]

deflated *adj.* แบน bɛɛn

deform *vt.* (bend shape
or disfigure)
ทำให้_ผิดรูปร่าง tam-hâi-
_-pìt-rûup-râang

deformed *adj.*
(disfigured) ผิดรูปร่าง pìt-
rûup-râang

defrost *vi.* ละลายน้ำแข็ง
lá~laai-nám-kɛ̌ng

defunct *adj.* (e.g. person,

organization) ตาย dtaai **|**
(e.g. species) สูญพันธุ์
sǔun-pan

defy vi. (challenge) ท้าทาย
táa-taai **|** (resist) ต่อต้าน
dtɔ̀ɔ-dtâan

degrade vi. (erode or
corrode) สึกกร่อน sùk-
grɔ̀n

degrade vt. (disgrace)
ทำให้_อับอาย tam-hâi-_-
àp-aai

degree n. (e.g. B.A., M.A.)
ปริญญา bpà~rin-yaa [ใบ
bai] **|** (stage, level) ระดับ
rá~dàp [ระดับ rá~dàp] **|**
(temperature) องศา ong-
sǎa [องศา ong-sǎa]

dehydrate vi. (lose water
or fluids) สูญเสียน้ำ
sǔun-sǐia-náam

dehydrated adj. (all water
removed) แห้ง hêng **|**
(lacking sufficient water)
ขาดน้ำ kàat-náam

deja vu n. สิ่งที่เหมือน
กับเคยเห็น sìng-tîi-
mǔuan-gàp-kəəi-hěn
[สิ่ง sìng]

delay vt. (make late,
postpone) ทำให้_ล่าช้า

tam-hâi-_-lâa-cháa

delayed adj. ล่าช้า lâa-cháa

delegate n. ตัวแทน
dtuua-tɛɛn [คน kon]

delete vt. ลบ_ออก lóp-_-
ɔ̀ɔk

deli see delicatessen

deliberate adj.
(intentional) เจตนา jèet-
dtà~naa

deliberate vi. (jury)
ปรึกษากันก่อนตัดสิน
bprɨk-sǎa-gan-gɔ̀ɔn-
dtàt-sǐn **|** (think carefully)
คิดอย่างรอบคอบ kít-
yàang-rɔ̂ɔp-kɔ̂ɔp

delicate adj. (finely
crafted) ประณีต bprà~
nîit **|** (fragile) แตกง่าย
dtɛ̀ɛk-ngâai

delicatessen n. ร้านอาหาร
สำเร็จรูป ráan-aa-hǎan-
sǎm-rèt-rûup [ร้าน ráan]

delicious adj. อร่อย à~rɔ̀i,
แซ่บ sɛ̂p ✿

delighted adj. ยินดี yin-dii

delinquent adj.
(neglectful) ละเลย lá-ləəi

delirious adj. คลุ้มคลั่ง
klúm-klâng, เพ้อเจ้อ pə́ə-
jə̂ə

deliver v. (baby) คลอด

klɔ̂ɔt | (e.g. mail) ส่ง sòng

delivery *n.* (childbirth) การคลอดลูก gaan-klɔ̂ɔt-lûuk | (products) การส่งสินค้า gaan-sòng-sǐn-káa

delivery room *n.* (baby) ห้องคลอด hɔ̂ng-klɔ̂ɔt [ห้อง hɔ̂ng]

delta *n.* (river) ปากแม่น้ำ bpàak-mɛ̂ɛ-náam [แห่ง hɛ̀ng]

delude *vt.* (deceive) หลอกลวง lɔ̀ɔk-luuang

deluxe *adj.* หรูหรา rǔu-rǎa

demand *n.* (requirement) ข้อเรียกร้อง kɔ̂ɔ-rîiak-rɔ́ɔng [ข้อ kɔ̂ɔ, ประการ bprà~gaan ‼]

demand *v.* (require) เรียกร้อง rîiak-rɔ́ɔng

demanding *adj.* ต้องการมาก dtɔ̂ng-gaan-mâak

democracy *n.* ประชาธิปไตย bprà~chaa-típ-bpà~dtai

democratic *adj.* เป็นประชาธิปไตย bpen-bprà~chaa-típ-bpà~dtai

Democratic Party *n.* พรรคประชาธิปัตย์ pák-

bprà~chaa-tí-bpàt | (U.S.) พรรคเดโมแครต pák-dee-moo-krèt

demolish *vi.* (tear down) รื้อถอน rʉ́ʉ-tɔ̌ɔn

demon *n.* (devil) ปีศาจ bpii-sàat [ตัว dtuua]

demonstrate *vi.* (by example) สาธิต sǎa-tít | (protest) ประท้วง bprà~túuang

demonstrator *n.* (protester) ผู้ประท้วง pûu-bprà~túuang [คน kon]

demote *vt.* (reduce level or class) ลดชั้น lót-chán

den *n.* (animal) ถ้ำ tâm [แห่ง hɛ̀ng, ถ้ำ tâm]

dengue fever *n.* ไข้เลือดออก kâi-lʉ̂ʉat-ɔ̀ɔk

Denmark *n.* เดนมาร์ก den-màak [ประเทศ bprà~têet]

denomination *n.* (bank note) ธนบัตร tá~ná~bàt [ใบ bai] | (religious group) นิกาย ní-gaai [นิกาย ní-gaai]

dense *adj.* (e.g. jungle) ทึบ túp | (small and

heavy) หนาแน่น nǎა-nɛ̂n

dent *n.* (on a surface) รอย
rɔɔi [รอย rɔɔi]

dental *adj.* เกี่ยวกับฟัน
giiao-gàp-fan

dental floss *n.* ไหมขัดฟัน
mǎi-kàt-fan [เส้น sên]

dented *adj.* (dimpled) บุ๋ม
bǔm

dentist *n.* หมอฟัน mɔ̌ɔ-
fan [คน kon]

denture *n.* ฟันปลอม fan-
bplɔɔm [ซี่ sîi (each one),
ชุด chút (set)]

deny *vt.* (refuse) ปฏิเสธ
bpà~dtì-sèet

deodorant *n.* (room)
ยาดับกลิ่น yaa-dàp-glìn
[ขวด kùuat] | (underarm)
ลูกกลิ้ง lûuk-glîng [ขวด
kùuat]

depart *vi.* ออกเดินทาง
ɔ̀ɔk-dəən-taang

depart *vt.* ออกจาก ɔ̀ɔk-
jàak

department *n.* แผนก
pà~nɛ̀ɛk [แผนก pà~nɛ̀ɛk]

department store *n.* ห้าง
hâang, ห้างสรรพสินค้า
hâang-sàp-pá~sǐn-káa !
[ห้าง hâang]

departure *n.* (taking a
trip, taking off)
การออกเดินทาง gaan-
ɔ̀ɔk-dəən-taang

dependable *adj.* วางใจได้
waang-jai-dâai

dependent *adj.* (on
others) ต้องพึ่งพาคนอื่น
dtɔ̂ng-pûng-paa-kon-
ùùn

depend on *vt.* (be
contingent on) แล้วแต่
lέεo-dtɛ̀ɛ | (rely on for
support) พึ่งพา pûng-paa
| (trust) ไว้ใจ wái-jai

depict *vt.* บรรยาย ban-
yaai

deport *vt.* (send back to
one's own country)
ส่ง_กลับประเทศ sòng-_-
glàp-bprà~têet

deposit *n.* (down
payment, security)
เงินมัดจำ ngən-mát-jam
[จำนวน jam-nuuan]

deposit *v.* (money) ฝาก
fàak

deposition *n.* (legal
evidence) การให้การ
เป็นพยาน gaan-hâi-
gaan-bpen-pá~yaan

depot *n.* (for supplies)

คลังพัสดุ klang-pát-sà~
dù [แห่ง hὲng]

depressed *adj.* (sad) กลุ้ม
glûm, หดหู่ hòt-hùu

depression *n.* (economic)
ภาวะเศรษฐกิจตกต่ำ paa-
wá-sèet-tà~gìt-dtòk-
dtàm | (sadness)
ความเศร้าสลด kwaam-
sâo-sà~lòt | (weather)
ความกดอากาศต่ำ
kwaam-gòt-aa-gàat-
dtàm

deprive *vt.* (take _ away
from _) พราก_จาก_
prâak-_-jàak-_

depth *n.* ความลึก kwaam-
lúk

deputy *adj.* (second in
command) รอง rɔɔng |
(substitute, stand-in)
รักษาการ rák-sǎa-gaan

derby *n.* (horse race)
การแข่งม้าครั้งสำคัญ
ประจำปี gaan-kὲng-máa-
kráng-sǎm-kan-bprà~
jam-bpii [ครั้ง kráng]

dermatologist *n.*
หมอโรคผิวหนัง mɔ̌ɔ-
rôok-pǐu-nǎng [คน kon]

descend *v.* (go down) ลง
long

descendant *n.* ทายาท
taa-yâat [คน kon]

describe *vt.* (list
characteristics) อธิบาย à-
tí-baai, บรรยาย ban-yaai

description *n.*
(explanation) การอธิบาย
gaan-à~tí-baai

desert *n.* ทะเลทราย tá~
lee-saai [แห่ง hὲng]

desert *vt.* (leave a person,
place, etc.) ละทิ้ง lá~tíng

deserted *adj.*
(abandoned) ร้าง ráang

deserve *vt.* สมควรได้รับ
sǒm-kuuan-dâi-ráp

design *n.* (plan or sketch)
แบบ bὲεp [แบบ bὲεp
(whole), แผ่น pὲn (piece)]
| (style) ลาย laai [ลาย laai]

design *v.* ออกแบบ ɔ̀ɔk-
bὲεp

designate *vt.* (appoint _
as _) แต่งตั้ง_เป็น_
dtὲng-dtâng-_-bpen-_

designated driver *n.*
คนขับที่ไม่ดื่ม kon-kàp-
tîi-mâi-dὐum [คน kon]

designer *n.* นักออกแบบ
nák-ɔ̀ɔk-bὲεp, ดีไซน์เนอร์

dii-saai-nêə ● [คน kon]

desirable *adj.* (pleasing)
ถูกใจ tùuk-jai

desire *vt.* (want) อยากได้
yàak-dâai

desk *n.* โต๊ะ dtó [ตัว dtuua]

desktop *n.* (computer)
คอมพิวเตอร์ที่ติดตั้งบนโต๊ะ
kɔm-píu-dtêə-tîi-dtìt-
dtâng-bon-dtó [เครื่อง
krûuang]

despair *n.* (hopelessness)
ความสิ้นหวัง kwaam-sîn-
wăng

desperate *adj.* (having
lost all hope) หมดหวัง
mòt-wăng

despicable *adj.* ชั่วร้าย
chûua-ráai

despise *vt.* (hate)
เหยียดหยาม yìiat-yăam

despite *prep.* (in spite of)
โดยไม่คำนึงถึง dooi-mâi-
kam-nɯng-tɯ̆ng

dessert *n.* ของหวาน
kɔ̆ɔng-wăan [อัน an
(piece), ชิ้น chín (piece),
ถ้วย tûuai (bowl)]

destination *n.* (place)
ปลายทาง bplaai-taang [ที่
tîi]

destiny *n.* (fate)
พรหมลิขิต prom-lí-kìt |
(fortune told) ชะตา
chá~dtaa, โชคชะตา
chôok-chá~dtaa |
(karma) เคราะห์กรรม
krɔ́-gam

destroy *vt.* (ruin) ทำลาย
tam-laai

destruction *n.* (act of
destroying) การทำลาย
gaan-tam-laai |
(annihilation) วิบัติ wí-
bàt, พินาศ pí-nâat ●

detach *vt.* (unfasten) ปลด
bplòt

detail *n.* รายละเอียด raai-
lá~iiat [อัน an]

detailed *adj.* ละเอียด lá~
iiat

detain *vt.* (delay or
retard) ยับยั้ง yáp-yáng |
(keep in custody) กักขัง
gàk-kăng

detect *vt.* (find) ตรวจพบ
dtrùuat-póp | (search)
สืบหา sɯ̀ɯp-hăa

detective *n.* (spy) นักสืบ
nák-sɯ̀ɯp [คน kon]

detention *n.* (at school)
การลงโทษนักเรียนให้อยู่
หลังเลิกเรียน gaan-long-

tôot-nák-riian-hâi-yùu-
lǎng-lêǝk-riian

detergent n. ผงซักฟอก
pǒng-sák-fɔ̂ɔk [ถุง tǔng
(bag), กล่อง glòng (box),
ห่อ hɔ̀ɔ (pack)]

deteriorate vi. (grow
worse) เลวลง leeo-long |
(weaken or disintegrate)
เสื่อม sùuam

determination n.
(firmness, perseverance)
ความแน่วแน่ kwaam-
nɛ̂o-nɛ̂ɛ

determine vt. (constrain,
fix boundaries of) กำหนด
gam-nòt | (decide)
ตัดสินใจ dtàt-sǐn-jai

detour n. ทางเลี่ยง taang-
lîiang [ทาง taang]

Deutsche mark n.
เงินมาร์ค ngən-máak

devalue v. (devaluate)
ลดค่า lót-kâa

devastate vt. (ravage)
ล้างผลาญ láang-plǎan

develop v. (improve)
พัฒนา pát-tá~naa

development n.
(improvement) การพัฒนา
gaan-pát-tá~naa

develop pictures vi.

ล้างรูป láang-rûup

deviate vi. (swerve,
change course) หันเห
hǎn-hěe

deviation n. การเบี่ยงเบน
gaan-bìiang-been,
การหันเห gaan-hǎn-hěe

device n. (appliance)
เครื่องใช้ krûuang-chái
[ชิ้น chín (piece), ชุด chút
(set)] | (machinery)
เครื่องกลไก krûuang-
gon-gai [เครื่อง krûuang]

devil n. (demon) ปีศาจ
bpii-sàat [ตัว dtuua]

devil-may-care adj.
(reckless) ไม่ระวัง mâi-
rá~wang

devil's advocate n. (who
argues other view)
ผู้สนับสนุนการคัดค้าน
pûu-sà~nàp-sà~nǔn-
gaan-kát-káan

devious adj. (shifty,
crooked) ทุจริต tút-jà~rìt

devote vt. (time, money)
อุทิศ ù-tít

devour vt. (eat up
greedily) กิน_อย่างตะกละ
gin-_-yàang-dtà~glà

dew n. (water droplets)

น้ำค้าง nám-káang [หยด yòt]

dexterity n. (in movement) ความคล่องแคล่ว kwaam-klôɲ-klɛ̂ɛo

Dharma n. ธรรม tam, ธรรมะ tam-má [ข้อ kɔ̂ɔ]

diabetes n. เบาหวาน bao-wǎan [โรค rôok]

diagnose vt. (make a diagnosis of) วินิจฉัย wí-nít-chǎi

diagonal adj. ทแยงมุม tá~yɛɛŋ-mum

diagram n. (chart, graph) แผนภาพ pɛ̌ɛn-pâap [แผ่น pèn]

dial n. (face of a clock) หน้าปัด nâa-bpàt [อัน an]

dial vt. (touch-tone phone) กด gòt

dialect n. ภาษาถิ่น paa-sǎa-tìn [ภาษา paa-sǎa]

dialogue n. (conversation) บทสนทนา bòt-sǒn-tá~naa [บท bòt] | (exchange of ideas) การสนทนา gaan-sǒn-tá~naa

dial tone n. สัญญาณโทรศัพท์ sǎn-yaan-too-rá~sàp [เสียง sǐiang]

diameter n. เส้นผ่าศูนย์กลาง sên-pàa-sǔun-glaang [เส้น sên]

diamond n. (mineral) เพชร pét [เม็ด mét (stone), กะรัต gà~ràt (carat)] | (shape) ข้าวหลามตัด kâao-lǎam-dtàt [รูป rûup] | (suit) ข้าวหลามตัด kâao-lǎam-dtàt [ใบ bai]

diaper n. ผ้าอ้อม pâa-ɔ̂ɔm [ผืน pǔɯn]

diaphragm n. (body part) กะบังลม gà~bang-lom | (contraceptive device) แผ่นยางคุมกำเนิด pèn-yaang-kum-gam-nə̀ət [แผ่น pèn, อัน an]

diarrhea n. ท้องเสีย tɔ́ɔŋ-sǐia [อาการ aa-gaan]

diary n. สมุดบันทึก sà~mùt-ban-túk [เล่ม lêm]

dice n. ลูกเต๋า lûuk-dtǎo [ลูก lûuk]

dictate vi. (give orders) สั่งการ sàŋ-gaan | (read to transcriber)

ให้เขียนตามคำบอก hâi-kǐian-dtaam-kam-bɔ̀ɔk

dictator *n.* เผด็จการ pà~dèt-gaan [คน kon]

dictionary *n.* พจนานุกรม pót-jà~naa-nú-grom, ดิคดิ๊ก ✿ [เล่ม lêm]

did *see* do

didn't *aux.* ไม่ได้ mâi-dâai

die *vi.* ตาย dtaai, ถึงแก่กรรม tʉ̌ng-gɛ̀ɛ-gam !, เสียชีวิต sǐia-chii-wít !, มรณภาพ mɔɔ-rá~ná-pâap ✿

die for *v.* ยอมตายเพื่อ yɔɔm-dtaai-pʉ̂ʉa

diesel *n.* (gasoline) ดีเซล dii-seo

diet *n.* (food or drink) โภชนา poo-chá~naa ✖

diet *v.* (control weight) ควบคุมอาหาร kûuap-kum-aa-hǎan

dietetics *n.* โภชนาการ poo-chá~naa-gaan

differ *vi.* (be unlike) แตกต่าง dtɛ̀ɛk-dtàang

different *adj.* (not same) ต่าง dtàang, ต่างกัน dtàang-gan, แตกต่าง dtɛ̀ɛk-dtàang ! |

(unusual) ผิดปกติ pìt-bpà-gà~dtì

different from *adj.* ต่างกับ dtàang-gàp

differentiate between *vt.* แยกแยะ_ออกจาก_ yɛ̂ɛk-yɛ́-_-ɔ̀ɔk-jàak-_

difficult *adj.* (causing hardship) ลำบาก lam-bàak | (not easy) ยาก yâak

difficulty *n.* (hardship) ความยากลำบาก kwaam-yâak-lam-bàak

diffused *adj.* (to be expanded) รุ่งเรือง rûng-rʉʉang

dig *v.* (with tool) ขุด kùt

digest *vi.* (food) ย่อยอาหาร yɔ̂i-aa-hǎan

digit *n.* (numeral, 0-9) ตัวเลข dtuua-lêek [ตัว dtuua] | (place, e.g. 1s, 10s, 100s) หลัก làk [หลัก làk]

digital *adj.* (electronics, computers) ดิจิตอล dí-jì~dtɔn

dignified *adj.* (graceful) สง่า sà~ngàa

dignity *n.* (honor) เกียรติ giiat

digress *vi.* ออกนอกเรื่อง

ɔɔk-nɔɔk-rûɐang

dike *n.* (embankment) ทำนบ tam-nóp [แห่ง hèng]

dilate *v.* (enlarge) ขยาย kà~yǎai

dildo *n.* ของเทียม kɔɔng-tiiam ♣ [อัน an]

dilemma *n.* (difficult situation) สถานการณ์ลำบาก sà~tǎa-ná~gaan-lam-bàak

diligence *n.* (steady effort) ความขยัน kwaam-kà~yǎn

diligent *adj.* ขยัน kà~yǎn

dill *n.* ผักชีลาว pàk-chii-laao [ต้น dtôn]

dilute *vt.* ทำให้_จาง tam-hâi-_-jaang

dim *adj.* (faintly outlined) เลือน lɐɐan | (not bright) มัว muua

dimension *n.* มิติ mí-dtì [มิติ mí-dtì]

diminish *vi.* ลดลง lót-long

dimple *n.* (on cheek) ลักยิ้ม lák-yím [แห่ง hèng]

dine *v.* (have a meal) รับประทานอาหาร ráp-bprà~taan-aa-hǎan ⚠, กินข้าว gin-kâao ♣

dine out *vi.* กินข้าวข้างนอก gin-kâao-kâang-nɔ̂ɔk

dining room *n.* ห้องกินข้าว hɔ̂ng-gin-kâao, ห้องรับประทานอาหาร hɔ̂ng-ráp-bprà~taan-aa-hǎan ⚠ [ห้อง hɔ̂ng]

dinner *n.* ข้าวเย็น kâao-yen, อาหารเย็น aa-hǎan-yen ⚠ [มื้อ mɯ́ɯ]

dinosaur *n.* ไดโนเสาร์ dai-noo-sǎo [ตัว dtuua]

dip *n.* (creamy sauce) น้ำจิ้ม nám-jîm

dip *vt.* (into liquid) จุ่ม jùm, ชุบ chúp

diphtheria *n.* คอตีบ kɔɔ-dtìip [โรค rôok]

diploma *n.* (for graduation) ประกาศนียบัตร bprà~gàat-sà~nii-yá~bàt [ใบ bai]

diplomat *n.* นักการทูต nák-gaan-tûut [คน kon]

direct *adj.* (straight) ตรง dtrong

direct *v.* (advise) แนะ né

direct *vt.* (e.g. movie)

กำกับ gam-gàp
direction *n.* (e.g. north)
ทิศ tít [ทิศ tít] |
(instructions) คำอธิบาย
kam-à~tí-baai [คำ kam
(word)] | (way) ทิศทาง
tít-taang [ทิศ tít]
directly *adv.* โดยตรง
dooi-dtrong
director *n.* (e.g. manager
at work, movie director)
ผู้กำกับ pûu-gam-gàp
[คน kon] | (executive,
e.g. headmaster, C.E.O.)
ผู้อำนวยการ pûu-am-
nuuai-gaan [คน kon]
dirt *n.* (dust) ฝุ่น fùn |
(soil) ดิน din [กอง gɔɔng,
ก้อน gɔ̂ɔn]
dirty *adj.* (obscene) ลามก
laa-mók | (soiled) สกปรก
sòk-gà~bpròk
disability *n.* (handicap)
ความพิการ kwaam-pí-
gaan
disable *v.* (make
unusable)
ทำให้_ใช้การไม่ได้ tam-
hâi-_-chái-gaan-mâi-dâai
disadvantage *n.* (bad
point) ข้อเสีย kɔ̂ɔ-sǐia [ข้อ
kɔ̂ɔ] | (unfavorable

position) ความเสียเปรียบ
kwaam-sǐia-bpriiap
disagree *vi.* ไม่เห็นด้วย
mâi-hěn-dûuai
disagreement *n.* (lack of
agreement)
ความไม่เห็นด้วย
kwaam-mâi-hěn-dûuai |
(quarrel) การโต้แย้ง
gaan-dtôo-yéeng
disappear *vi.* (vanish from
sight) หายตัว hǎai-dtuua,
หายไป hǎai-bpai
disappoint *vt.*
ทำให้_ผิดหวัง tam-hâi-_-
pìt-wǎng
disappointed *adj.* ผิดหวัง
pìt-wǎng
disapprove *vi.* (disagree)
ไม่เห็นด้วย mâi-hěn-
dûuai | (refuse
permission) ไม่อนุมัติ
mâi-à~nú-mát
disarm *vi.* ปลดอาวุธ
bplòt-aa-wút
disaster *n.* หายนะ hǎa-
yá~ná
disc see disk
discard *vt.* (throw away)
ทิ้ง tíng
discharge *vt.* (release, let
go) ปล่อย bplòi

disciple n. (in religion) สาวก săa-wók [องค์ ong ❀, คน kon]

discipline n. (self control, rule) วินัย wí-nai [ข้อ kɔ̂ɔ]

disc jockey n. ดีเจ dii-jee [คน kon]

disclaim vt. (deny) ปฏิเสธ bpà~dtì-sèet

disclose vt. เปิดเผย bpə̀ət-pə̌əi

discomfort n. (inconvenience) ความไม่สะดวกสบาย kwaam-mâi-sà~dùuak-sà~baai

disconnect vi. (hang up phone) วางสาย waang-săai

disconnect vt. (cut off phone) ตัดสาย dtàt-săai | (e.g. cable) ดึง_ออก dɯng-_-ɔ̀ɔk

discontent adj. ไม่พอใจ mâi-pɔɔ-jai

discontinue vt. (cancel) ยกเลิก yók-lə̂ək | (stop) หยุด yùt

discotheque n. ดิสโก้เท็ค dís-gôo-tèk, เท็ก tèk ❀ [แห่ง hɛ̀ng]

discount n. ส่วนลด sùuan-lót [จำนวน jam-nuuan (amount)]

discount v. (reduce price of) ลดราคา lót-raa-kaa

discourage vt. ทำให้_เสียกำลังใจ tam-hâi-_-sǐia-gam-lang-jai

discouraged adj. หมดกำลังใจ mòt-gam-lang-jai

discover vt. ค้นพบ kón-póp

discovery n. (act of discovering something) การค้นพบ gaan-kón-póp [ครั้ง kráng]

discreet adj. (prudent) ระมัดระวัง rá~mát-rá~wang

discrepancy n. ความขัดแย้งกัน kwaam-kàt-yέεng-gan

discriminate vi. (play favorites) เลือกที่รักมักที่ชัง lɯ̂ak-tîi-rák-mák-tîi-chang

discrimination n. (e.g. class, race) การปฏิบัติที่ไม่เป็นธรรม gaan-bpà~dtì-bàt-tîi-mâi-bpen-tam

discus n. (used in

throwing competitions)
จักร jàk [อัน an]

discuss vt. (argue about)
โต้เถียงเรื่อง dtôo-tĭiang-rûuang | (converse about) เจรจาเรื่อง jee-rá~jaa-rûuang

disdain n.
การดูถูกเหยียดหยาม gaan-duu-tùuk-yìiat-yǎam

disease n. โรค rôok [โรค rôok] | (ailment) ความเจ็บป่วย kwaam-jèp-bpùai

disembark vi. (go ashore from a ship) ขึ้นฝั่ง kûn-fàng | (leave a vehicle or aircraft) ลงจากเครื่อง long-jàak-krûuang

disfigure vt. (deform) ทำให้_ผิดรูปร่าง tam-hâi-_-pìt-rûup-râang

disfigured adj. เสียโฉม sĭia-chŏom

disgrace n. (loss of honor, respect) ความเสื่อมเสีย kwaam-sùuam-sĭia

disgraceful adj. เสื่อมเสีย sùuam-sĭia

disguise n. (costume)

ชุดที่ใช้ปลอมตัว chút-tîi-chái-bplɔɔm-dtuua [ชุด chút]

disguise vt. (conceal)
ซ่อนเร้น sɔ̂n-rén

disgusted adj. ขยะแขยง kà~yà-kà~yɛ̌ɛng

disgusting adj. (obscene) ทุเรศ tú-rêet | (yucky, revolting) น่ารังเกียจ nâa-rang-gìiat

dish n. (food to eat with rice) กับข้าว gàp-kâao [อย่าง yàang (kind), จาน jaan (plate)] | (plate) จาน jaan [ใบ bai, ลูก lûuk]

dishonest adj. (crooked) ไม่ซื่อสัตย์ mâi-sûu-sàt | (insincere) ไม่จริงใจ mâi-jing-jai

dishwasher n. (machine) เครื่องล้างจาน krûuang-láang-jaan [เครื่อง krûuang]

disinfect vt. ฆ่าเชื้อใน kâa-chúua-nai

disk n. (audio) แผ่นเสียง pèn-sĭiang [แผ่น pèn] | (data) แผ่นดิสก์ pèn-dít [แผ่น pèn] | (flat, circular object) แผ่นกลม pɛ̀n-glom [แผ่น pɛ̀n]

disk jockey *n.* ดีเจ dii-jee [คน kon]

dislike *vt.* ไม่ชอบ mâi-chɔ̂ɔp

dislocated joint *n.* ข้อเคล็ด kɔ̂ɔ-klét

dismiss *vt.* (legal case) ยกฟ้อง yók-fɔ́ɔng | (permit to leave) อนุญาตให้_ไปได้ à-nú-yâat-hâi-_-bpai-dâai

disobedient *adj.* ไม่เชื่อฟัง mâi-chûua-fang

disobey *vt.* ไม่เชื่อฟัง mâi-chûua-fang

disordered *adj.* (chaotic) ระส่ำระสาย rá~sàm-rá~sǎai | (messy) ไม่เป็นระเบียบ mâi-bpen-rá~bìiap

disorganized *adj.* (lacking order) ไม่เป็นระเบียบ mâi-bpen-rá~bìiap

disoriented *adj.* (lost) หลงทาง lǒng-taang

disown *vt.* (as family) ตัดญาติกับ dtàt-yâat-gàp

disparage *vt.* เหยียดหยาม yìiat-yǎam

dispatch *vt.* (send, transmit) ส่ง sòng

dispenser *n.* (soap) เครื่องจ่ายสบู่ krûuang-jàai-sà~bùu [อัน an] | (tissue) กล่องใส่กระดาษทิชชู glòng-sài-grà~dàat-tít-chûu [ใบ bai]

disperse *vi.* กระจาย grà~jaai

disperse *vt.* (drive off, e.g. crowd) ไล่_ไป lâi-_-bpai

displace *vt.* (supplant, take place of) แทนที่ tɛɛn-tîi

displaced person *n.* คนพลัดถิ่น kon-plát-tìn [คน kon]

display *vt.* แสดง sà~dɛɛng, โชว์ choo ✶

displeased *adj.* ไม่พอใจ mâi-pɔɔ-jai

disposable *adj.* (single-use) ใช้ครั้งเดียวทิ้ง chái-kráng-diiao-tíng

dispose of *vt.* (throw away) เอาทิ้ง ao-tíng

disposition *n.* (mood or attitude) นิสัยใจคอ ní-sǎi-jai-kɔɔ

dispute *vt.* (angrily)
โต้เถียง dtôo-tǐiang, วิวาท
wí-wâat 🐾 | (politely)
ค้าน káan

disqualified *adj.*
ถูกตัดสิทธิ์ tùuk-dtàt-sìt

disrespect *vt.* (show a
lack of respect for)
ไม่เคารพ mâi-kao-róp

disrobe *vi.* (from
monkhood) สึก sùk ✿

dissatisfied *adj.*
(discontented) ไม่พอใจ
mâi-pɔɔ-jai

dissertation *n.* (Ph.D.)
ดุษฎีนิพนธ์ dùt-sà~dii-
ní-pon [เล่ม lêm (book),
เรื่อง rûuang (topic)]

dissolve *vi.* (e.g. salt)
ละลาย lá~laai

dissolve *vt.* (e.g. salt)
ทำให้_ละลาย tam-hâi-_-
lá~laai

dissolve parliament *vi.*
ยุบสภา yúp-sà~paa

distance *n.* ระยะทาง rá~
yá-taang [กิโลเมตร gì~
loo-méet (kilo), เมตร
méet (meter), ไมล์ maai
(mile)]

distant *adj.* ห่างไกล
hàang-glai ❢

distill *vt.* กลั่น glàn

distilled water *n.* น้ำกลั่น
nám-glàn [ขวด kùuat
(bottle), แก้ว gɛ̂ɛo (glass)]

distinct *adj.* (clear) ชัดเจน
chát-jeen | (different,
separate) แตกต่าง dtɛ̀ɛk-
dtàang

distinction *n.* (standing
out) ความโดดเด่น
kwaam-dòot-dèn

distinctive *adj.*
(prominent, eminent)
เด่น dèn

distinguish *vt.*
แยกแยะ_จาก_ yɛ̂ɛk-yɛ́-_-
jàak-_

distort *vt.* (bend shape
of) ทำให้_บิดเบี้ยว tam-
hâi-_-bìt-bîiao

distorted *adj.* บิดเบือน
bìt-buuan

distract *v.* (attention)
เบนความสนใจ been-
kwaam-sǒn-jai | (break
concentration)
ทำให้_เสียสมาธิ tam-hâi-
_-sǐia-sà~maa-tí

distracted *adj.* (losing
attention) วอกแวก
wɔ̂ɔk-wɛ̂ɛk

distraction *n.* (obstacle to attention) สิ่งล่อใจ sìng-lòo-jai [อย่าง yàang]

distress *n.* (peril) อันตราย an-dtà~raai

distribute *vt.* (pass out) จำหน่าย jam-nàai ⚑ | (scatter) กระจาย grà~jaai

distribution *n.* (marketing and supplying goods) การแจกจ่าย gaan-jɛ̀ɛk-jàai

distributor *n.* (wholesaler) ผู้แทนจำหน่าย pûu-tɛɛn-jam-nàai [คน kon]

district *n.* (outside Bangkok) อำเภอ am-pəə [อำเภอ am-pəə] | (within Bangkok) เขต kèet [แห่ง hɛ̀ng]

district attorney *n.* อัยการ ai-yá~gaan [คน kon]

district office *n.* อำเภอ am-pəə [อำเภอ am-pəə]

disturb *vt.* (bother) กวน guuan, รบกวน róp-guuan

ditch *n.* (trench, moat) คู kuu [คู kuu]

dive *vi.* ดำน้ำ dam-náam

diver *n.* นักดำน้ำ nák-dam-náam [คน kon]

diverse *adj.* (various) ต่างๆ dtàang-dtàang

diversion *n.* (detour) ทางเลี่ยง taang-lîiang [ทาง taang]

diversity *n.* (variety) ความหลากหลาย kwaam-làak-lǎai

divide *v.* (math) หาร hǎan

divide *vt.* (separate into parts) แบ่ง bɛ̀ng

dividend *n.* เงินปันผล ngən-bpan-pǒn

divine *adj.* (of or being a deity) เกี่ยวกับพระเจ้า gìiao-gàp-prá~jâao | (sacred) ศักดิ์สิทธิ์ sàk-sìt

divine being *n.* เทพพระเจ้า têep-prá~jâao ⚑ [องค์ ong]

divisible *adj.* (mathematics) หารได้ลงตัว hǎan-dâai-long-dtuua

division *n.* (department) แผนก pà~nɛ̀ɛk [แผนก pà~nɛ̀ɛk] | (government) กรม grom [กรม grom] | (math) การหาร gaan-hǎan

divorce *n.* การหย่าร้าง gaan-yàa-ráang

divorce v. หย่า yàa

divorce certificate n.
ใบหย่า bai-yàa [ใบ bai]

divorced adj. หย่าร้าง yàa-
ráang

dizzy adj. วิงเวียน wing-
wiian

do vt. ทำ tam, กระทำ
grà~tam ǃ, ปฏิบัติ bpà~
dtì-bàt ǃ

docile adj. (tame) เชื่อง
chûuang

dock n. (harbor) ท่าเรือ
tâa-ruua [แห่ง hèng] |
(shipyard) อู่เรือ ùu-ruua
[อู่ ùu]

docket n. (in a court)
ทะเบียนคดี tá··biian-ká~
dii [ทะเบียน tá~biian]

doctor n. หมอ mɔ̌ɔ, แพทย์
pɛ̂ɛt ǃ [คน kon]

doctorate degree n.
ปริญญาเอก bpà~rin-yaa-
èek [ปริญญา bpà~rin-yaa
(degree), ใบ bai
(certificate)]

doctrine n. (principle)
หลักการ làk-gaan
[หลักการ làk-gaan] |
(religion) ลัทธิ lát-tí [ลัทธิ
lát-tí]

document n. เอกสาร
èek-gà~sǎan [ฉบับ chà~
bàp]

documentary n. สารคดี
sǎa-rá-ká~dii [เรื่อง
rûuang]

doe n. กวางตัวเมีย
gwaang-dtuua-miia [ตัว
dtuua]

does see do

doesn't aux. ไม่ mâi

dog n. หมา mǎa, สุนัข
sù~nák ǃ [ตัว dtuua]

dog collar n. (for dog)
ปลอกคอสุนัข bplɔ̀ɔk-kɔɔ-
sù~nák [อัน an]

dog-ear a page vi.
พับมุมหน้าหนังสือ páp-
mum-nâa-nǎng~sǔu

doggie style adj. ท่าหมา
tâa-mǎa

doggy bag n. (for
leftovers)
ถุงอาหารที่ถือกลับบ้าน
tǔng-aa-hǎan-tîi-tǔu-
glàp-bâan [ใบ bai]

do-it-yourself adj.
ทำได้ด้วยตัวเอง tam-dâi-
dûuai-dtuua-eeng

doll n. ตุ๊กตา dtúk-gà~
dtaa [ตัว dtuua]

dollar *n.* (bill) ดอลล่าร์ dɔn-lâa [ใบ bai]

dolly *n.* รถเข็น rót-kěn [คัน kan]

dolphin *n.* ปลาโลมา bplaa-loo-maa [ตัว dtuua]

domain *n.* (territory) อาณาเขต aa-naa-kèet ! [แห่ง hèng]

dome *n.* (roof) หลังคารูปทรงกลม lǎng-kaa-rûup-song-glom [อัน an]

domestic *adj.* (household) ในบ้าน nai-bâan | (within the country) ในประเทศ nai-bprà~têet

domestic violence *n.* การใช้ความรุนแรงใน ครัวเรือน gaan-chái-kwaam-run-rɛɛng-nai-kruua-ruuan

dominate *vt.* (have power over) มีอำนาจเหนือ mii-am-nâat-nʉ̌ʉa

donate *v.* บริจาค bɔɔ-rí~jàak

donation *n.* (act of giving) การบริจาค gaan-bɔɔ-rí~jàak | (gift or grant) ของบริจาค kɔ̌ɔng-bɔɔ-rí~jàak

done *adj.* (cooked, well done) สุก sùk | (finished) เสร็จแล้ว sèt-lɛ́ɛo

donkey *n.* ลา laa [ตัว dtuua]

donor *n.* ผู้บริจาค pûu-bɔɔ-rí~jàak [คน kon]

do not *aux.* (forbiddance) อย่า yàa | (negation) ไม่ mâi

don't see do not

donut *n.* โดนัท doo-nát [ชิ้น chín, ก้อน gɔ̂ɔn]

doom *n.* (tragic fate) เคราะห์ร้าย krɔ́-ráai

door *n.* ประตู bprà~dtuu [ประตู bprà~dtuu]

doorbell *n.* กระดิ่ง grà~dìng, กริ่ง grìng [อัน an]

doorknob *n.* ลูกบิดประตู lûuk-bìt-bprà~dtuu [ลูก lûuk, อัน an]

doorman *n.* คนเฝ้าประตู kon-fâo-bprà~dtuu [คน kon]

dope *n.* (narcotic) สารมึนเมา sǎan-mʉn-mao

dork *n.* (stupid person)

คนงี่เง่า kon-ngîi-ngâo
[คน kon]

dorky adj.
(unfashionable) เชย
chəəi ☙

dorm n. หอพัก hɔ̌ɔ-pák
[หลัง lăng (building)]

dormitory see dorm

dosage see dose

dose n. (of medicine)
ปริมาณยาต่อครั้ง bpà~
rí~maan-yaa-dtɔ̀ɔ-kráng

dot n. จุด jùt [จุด jùt]

double adj. (two times
more) สองเท่า sɔ̌ɔng-tâo

double vi. ทวีคูณ tá~wii-
kuun

double vt.
เพิ่ม_เป็นสองเท่า pə̂əm_
_bpen-sɔ̌ɔng-tâo

double bed n.
เตียงเดี่ยวสำหรับสองคน
dtiiang-dìiao-săm-ràp-
sɔ̌ɔng-kon [เตียง dtiiang]

double boil vt. ตุ๋น dtŭn

double-check n.
การตรวจอีกครั้ง gaan-
dtrùuat-ìik-kráng

double-cross vt. ทรยศ
tɔɔ-rá~yót

doubled adj. (twice as

great) เป็นสองเท่า bpen-
sɔ̌ɔng-tâo

double-dealing adj.
(treacherous, deceitful)
ไม่ซื่อ mâi-sûu

double-dealing n.
(duplicity, deception)
การหลอกลวง gaan-lɔ̀ɔk-
luuang

double occupancy adj.
(two in one room) สำหรับ
สองคนในห้องเดียวกัน
săm-ràp-sɔ̌ɔng-kon-nai-
hɔ̂ɔng-diiao-gan

double talk n.
(ambiguous language)
การพูดกำกวม gaan-
pûut-gam-guuam

doubt n. (uncertainty)
ข้อสงสัย kɔ̂ɔ-sŏng-săi

doubt vt. (not believe)
ไม่เชื่อ mâi-chûua |
(suspect: object is
expected outcome) สงสัย
sŏng-săi

doubtful adj. (causing
doubt) น่าสงสัย nâa-
sŏng-săi

dough n. (for bread)
แป้งนวด bpɛ̂ɛng-nûuat

doughnut see donut

dove n. นกพิราบ nók-pí-râap [ตัว dtuua]

down *adv.* ข้างล่าง kâang-
lâang

down *n.* (bird feathers)
ขนนก kǒn-nók [เส้น sên]
| (duck feathers) ขนเป็ด
kǒn-bpèt [เส้น sên]

downgrade *n.*
(descending slope)
ทางลาด taang-lâat [ทาง
taang]

downgrade *vt.* (lower in
salary) ลดเงินเดือน lót-
ngən-dɯɯan | (lower in
status) ลดฐานะ lót-tǎa-ná

downhill *adv.* (down a
hill) ลงเขา long-kǎo

download *v.* ดาวน์โหลด
daao-lòot

down payment *n.*
เงินดาวน์ ngən-daao
[จำนวน jam-nuuan]

downpour *n.* ฝนตกหนัก
fǒn-dtòk-nàk

downshift *vi.* (vehicle)
เปลี่ยนเป็นเกียร์ต่ำ
bpliian-bpen-giia-dtàm

downstairs *adj.* ชั้นล่าง
chán-lâang

downstairs *n.* ชั้นล่าง
chán-lâang [ชั้น chán]

down-to-earth *idm.* (not
pretentious) ติดดิน dtìt-
din ✦ | (realistic)
ไม่เพ้อฝัน mâi-pə́ə-fǎn

downtown *n.* ใจกลางเมือง
jai-glaang-mɯɯang,
ดาวน์ทาว daao-taao ✦
[แห่ง hɛ̀ng]

downward *adv.* ลงต่ำ
long-dtàm

dowry *n.* สินสอด sǐn-sɔ̀ɔt
[จำนวน jam-nuuan
(amount), ชิ้น chín
(piece)]

doze *vi.* (nap) งีบหลับ
ngîip-làp | (nod off)
สัปหงก sàp-bpà~ngòk

dozen *adj.* (twelve) สิบสอง
sìp-sɔ̌ɔng

dozen *n.* โหล lǒo

draft *n.* (of written work)
ฉบับร่าง chà~bàp-râang
[ฉบับ chà~bàp]

draft *vt.* (e.g. letter) ร่าง
râang | (soldier) เกณฑ์
geen

drag *vt.* (haul, tow) ลาก
lâak

drag on *v.* (e.g. meeting)
ยืดออกไปอีก yɯ̂ɯt-ɔ̀ɔk-
bpai-iik

dragon n. มังกร mang-gɔɔn [ตัว dtuua]

dragonfly n. แมลงปอ má~lɛɛng-bpɔɔ [ตัว dtuua]

drain n. (fixture) หัวท่อระบายน้ำ hǔua-tɔ̂ɔ-rá~baai-náam [หัว hǔua, อัน an]

drain vi. (liquid) ระบาย rá~baai

drain vt. (liquid) ถ่าย_ออก tàai-_-ɔ̀ɔk

drain pipe n. ท่อระบาย tɔ̂ɔ-rá~baai [ท่อ tɔ̂ɔ]

drama n. (play, life turbulence) ละคร lá~kɔɔn [ตอน dtɔɔn (episode), ฉาก chàak (scene), เรื่อง rûuang (story)]

dramatic adj. เร้าใจ ráo-jai

drape n. ม่าน mâan [ผืน pʉ̌ʉn]

draw n. (tie) การเสมอกัน gaan-sà~mə̌ə-gan

draw v. (line figure) ขีด kìit | (picture) วาด wâat

drawer n. (of furniture) ลิ้นชัก lín-chák [ลิ้นชัก lín-chák]

draw in vt. (attract, e.g. customers) ดึงดูด dʉng-dùut | (lure, e.g. victims) ล่อหลอก lɔ̂ɔ-lɔ̀ɔk

drawing n. (picture) ภาพวาด pâap-wâat [ภาพ pâap] | (plan, design) แบบแปลน bɛ̀ɛp-bplɛɛn [แบบ bɛ̀ɛp (whole), แผ่น pɛ̀n (piece)]

draw out vt. (lengthen) ทำให้_ยืดออกไป tam-hâi-_-yʉ̂ʉt-ɔ̀ɔk-bpai

dreadful adj. (extremely bad) เลวร้ายมาก leeo-ráai-mâak | (fearful) น่าสะพรึงกลัว nâa-sà~pʉng-gluua

dream n. ความฝัน kwaam-fǎn [อัน an]

dream v. ฝัน fǎn

dreamer n. คนช่างฝัน kon-châng-fǎn [คน kon]

dream of vt. ฝันถึง fǎn-tʉ̌ng

dress n. (one-piece women's garment) ชุด chút [ชุด chút]

dress vi. (put on clothes) แต่งตัว dtɛ̀ng-dtuua

dress vt. (decorate) แต่ง dtɛ̀ng

dresser n. (furniture)
โต๊ะเครื่องแป้ง dtó-
krûuang-bpɛ̂ɛng [ตัว
dtuua]

dressing n. (sauce) น้ำซอส
nám-sɔ́ɔt

dressmaker n. ช่างตัดเสื้อ
châng-dtàt-sûua [คน
kon]

dress up vi. (wear fancy
clothes) แต่งตัวให้ดูดี
dtɛ̀ng-dtuua-hâi-duu-dii

dried adj. แห้ง hɛ̂ng

drift vi. (be carried along
current) เลื่อนลอย lûuan-
lɔɔi

drill n. (tool) สว่าน sà~
wàan [ตัว dtuua] |
(training) การฝึกฝน
gaan-fʉ̀k-fǒn

drill v. (cut a hole) เจาะ jɔ̀

drill vi. (train) ซ้อม sɔ́ɔm

drink n. เครื่องดื่ม
krûuang-dʉ̀ʉm [ชนิด
chá~nít]

drink v. ดื่ม dʉ̀ʉm

drinkable adj. (potable)
ดื่มได้ dʉ̀ʉm-dâai

drip vi. (fall in drops) หยด
yòt

drip infusion n.
การให้น้ำเกลือ gaan-hâi-
nám-glʉʉa

drive n. (motivation)
แรงกระตุ้น rɛɛng-grà~
dtûn

drive v. ขับ kàp

driver n. คนขับรถ kon-
kàp-rót [คน kon]

driver's license n. ใบขับขี่
bai-kàp-kìi [ใบ bai]

driveway n. (into home)
ทางเข้าบ้าน taang-kâo-
bâan [ทาง taang]

drizzle vi. (rain lightly)
ฝนตกปรอยๆ fǒn-dtòk-
bprɔɔi-bprɔɔi

drool vi. (let saliva run)
น้ำลายไหล nám-laai-lǎi

droop v. (sag, be
weakened) เหนื่อยอ่อน
nʉ̀uai-ɔ̀ɔn

drop n. (e.g. water) หยด
yòt [หยด yòt]

drop vi. (fall) ตกลง dtòk-
long

drop vt. ทำ_ตก tam-_-
dtòk

drop a course vi.
ถอนวิชาเรียน tɔ̌ɔn-wí-
chaa-riian

drop in vi. (visit

informally) มาเยี่ยม maa-
yîiam

drop off *vt.* (deliver) ไปส่ง
bpai-sòng

drought *n.* ความแห้งแล้ง
kwaam-hêng-léeng

drown *vi.* จมน้ำตาย jom-
náam-dtaai

drown *vt.* กดคอ_จมน้ำตาย
gòt-kɔɔ-_-jom-náam-
dtaai

drowsy *adj.* (sleepy) ง่วง
ngûuang, สัปหงก sàp-
bpà~ngòk

drug *n.* (medicine) ยา yaa
[ชนิด chá~nít (kind), เม็ด
mét (pill), ขวด kùuat
(bottle), ซอง sɔɔng
(pack), แผง pɛ̌ɛng (set),
หลอด lɔ̀ɔt (tube)] |
(narcotic) ยาเสพติด yaa-
sèep-dtìt [ชนิด chá~nít]

drug *vt.* (against one's
will) วางยา waang-yaa

drug addict *n.* (person)
คนติดยา kon-dtìt-yaa,
ขี้ยา kîi-yaa ❀ [คน kon]

drugstore *n.* ร้านขายยา
ráan-kǎai-yaa [ร้าน ráan]

drum *n.* (musical) กลอง
glɔɔng [ใบ bai]

drum *vi.* ตีกลอง dtii-
glɔɔng

drumstick *n.* (chicken)
ขาไก่ kǎa-gài [ขา kǎa] |
(musical) ไม้ตีกลอง mái-
dtii-glɔɔng [อัน an]

drunk *adj.* เมา mao,
เมาเหล้า mao-lâo

drunkard *n.* คนขี้เมา kon-
kîi-mao [คน kon]

dry *adj.* แห้ง hɛ̂ɛng

dry *vt.* ทำให้_แห้ง tam-
hâi-_-hɛ̂ɛng

dry-clean *vt.* ซักแห้ง sák-
hɛ̂ɛng

dryer *n.* (e.g. hair, heat
gun) เครื่องเป่า krûuang-
bpào [เครื่อง krûuang]

dry run *n.* (practice)
การฝึกซ้อม gaan-fùk-
sɔ́ɔm

dry season *n.* หน้าแล้ง
nâa-léeng [หน้า nâa]

dual *adj.* (paired) คู่ kûu

dub *vt.* (record over)
บันทึกทับ ban-túk-táp

duck *n.* เป็ด bpèt [ตัว
dtuua]

duck *vi.* (avoid collision)
หลบ lòp | (e.g. under low
door) มุด mút

duckling *n.* ลูกเป็ด lûuk-bpèt [ตัว dtuua]

duckweed *n.* แหน nɛ̌ɛ

due *adj.* (owed as a debt) ที่ค้างชำระ tîi-káang-cham-rá | (reached deadline) ครบกำหนด króp-gam-nòt

duel *n.* การดวลกัน gaan-duuan-gan

duet *n.* (two singers) นักร้องคู่ nák-rɔ́ɔng-kûu [คน kon]

due to *conj.* เนื่องจาก nûuang-jàak, เพราะว่า prɔ́-wâa

DUI *n.* การขับรถขณะมึนเมา gaan-kàp-rót-kà~nà~mʉn-mao

dull *adj.* (bored, boring) เซ็ง seng ✹ | (not sharp) ที่อ tûʉ | (stupid) โง่ ngôo

dumb *adj.* เป็นใบ้ bpen-bâi | (stupid) โง่ ngôo

dummy *n.* (human figure) หุ่นจำลอง hùn-jam-lɔɔng [ตัว dtuua] | (in bridge) ดัมมี่ dam-mîi [คน kon] | (stupid person) คนโง่ kon-ngôo [คน kon]

dump *n.* (where trash is dumped) ที่ทิ้งขยะ tîi-tíng-kà~yà [ที่ tîi]

dump *vt.* (empty out) ทิ้ง tíng

dung *n.* (feces) ขี้ kîi ✹ [กอง gɔɔng, ก้อน gɔ̂ɔn]

duo *n.* คู่ kûu [คู่ kûu]

duplicate *n.* (copy) สำเนา sǎm-nao [แผ่น pèn (piece), ฉบับ chà~bàp (whole)]

durable *adj.* (withstands wear and tear) ทนทาน ton-taan

durian *n.* (fruit) ทุเรียน tú-riian [ลูก lûuk]

during *prep.* (at one moment in a period) ขณะ kà~nà, ในระหว่าง nai-rá~wàang, ระหว่าง rá~wàang

dusk *n.* (evening) เวลาเย็นก่อนค่ำ wee-laa-yen-gɔ̀ɔn-kâm

dust *n.* (dry particles) ผง pǒng, ฝุ่น fùn

dust *vi.* (wipe) ปัดฝุ่น bpàt-fùn

dustpan *n.* ที่โกยผง tîigooi-pŏng [อัน an]

dusty *adj.* (having lots of dust) มีฝุ่นมาก mii-fùn-mâak

duty *n.* (responsibility) ภาระ paa-rá | (responsibility) หน้าที่ nâa-tîi [หน้าที่ nâa-tîi] | (tax) ภาษี paa-sĭi

duty-free *adj.* ปลอดภาษี bplòot-paa-sĭi

DVD player *n.* เครื่องเล่นดีวีดี krûuang-lên-dii-wii-dii [เครื่อง krûuang]

dwarf *n.* คนแคระ kon-krɛ́ [คน kon]

dwarf *vt.* ทำให้_ดูเล็กลง tam-hâi-_-duu-lék-long, ทำให้_แคระเกร็น tam-hâi-_-krɛ́-gren ⚡

dwell *vi.* (reside) อยู่ yùu, อาศัย aa-sǎi ⚡

dwelling *n.* ที่อยู่ tîi-yùu [แห่ง hɛ̀ng]

dwell on *vt.* (spend a lot of time on) ใช้เวลามากกับ chái-wee-laa-mâak-gàp

dwell upon see dwell on

dye *n.* สีย้อม sĭi-yɔ́ɔm [สี sĭi, ชนิด chá~nít (kind)]

dye *v.* ย้อม yɔ́ɔm

dynamic *adj.* (active) คล่องแคล่ว klɔ̂ng-klɛ̂o | (lively) มีชีวิตชีวา mii-chii-wít-chii-waa

dynamite *n.* ดินระเบิด din-rá~bə̀ət [ลูก lûuk]

dynamo *n.* (generator) เครื่องกำเนิดไฟฟ้า krûuang-gam-nə̀ət-fai-fáa, ไดนาโม dai-naa-moo [เครื่อง krûuang]

dynasty *n.* ราชวงศ์ râat-chá~wong [ราชวงศ์ râat-chá~wong]

E

each *adj.* แต่ละ dtɛ̀ɛ-lá

each *adv.* (per item) ต่ออัน dtɔ̀ɔ-an

each other *pron.* กัน gan, กันและกัน gan-lɛ́-gan

each time *prep.* คราวละ kraao-lá, แต่ละครั้ง dtɛ̀ɛ-lá~kráng

eager *adj.* (desiring intensely) กระหาย grà~hǎai | (enthusiastic) กระตือรือร้น grà~dtuu-ruu-rón

eagle *n.* นกอินทรี nók-in-sii [ตัว dtuua]

eagle-eyed *adj.* ตาไว dtaa-wai

ear *n.* (e.g. rice, corn) รวง ruuang [รวง ruuang] | (organ) หู hǔu [หู hǔu, ข้าง kâang]

earache *n.* ปวดหู bpùuat-hǔu

ear drop *n.* ยาหยอดหู yaa-yɔ̀ɔt-hǔu

eardrum *n.* แก้วหู gɛ̂ɛo-hǔu [ชิ้น chín]

ear infection *n.* หูติดเชื้อ hǔu-dtìt-chúua [ข้าง kâang]

earlier *adj.* (previous) ที่มาก่อน tîi-maa-gɔ̀ɔn

earlier *adv.* (previously) ก่อน gɔ̀ɔn

earlobe *n.* ติ่งหู dtìng-hǔu

early *adj.* (in the morning) แต่เช้า dtɛ̀ɛ-cháao | (sooner than usual) ที่มาเร็ว tîi-maa-reo

early *adv.* (ahead of time) แต่วัน dtɛ̀ɛ-wan ✱

earmuff *n.* ที่ปิดหูกันหนาว tîi-bpìt-hǔu-gan-nǎao [คู่ kûu]

earn *vt.* (deserve) สมควรได้รับ sǒm-kuuan-dâi-ráp | (get as profit) ได้กำไร dâi-gam-rai

earn a living *vi.* หาเลี้ยงชีพ hǎa-líiang-chîip

earning *n.* (profit) ผลกำไร pǒn-gam-rai | (revenue) รายได้ raai-dâai | (wages, salary) เงินเดือน ngən-duuan [จำนวน jam-nuuan]

earphone *n.* หูฟัง hǔu-fang [อัน an (piece), คู่ kûu (pair)]

earplug *n.* ที่อุดหู tîi-ùt-hǔu [อัน an (one)]

earring *n.* ตุ้มหู dtûm-hǔu [คู่ kûu (pair)]

earth *n.* (electrical) สายดิน sǎai-din [สาย sǎai (wire)] | (globe, world) โลก lôok [ใบ bai] | (ground, soil) ดิน din

earthquake *n.* แผ่นดินไหว pɛ̀n-din-wǎi [ครั้ง kráng]

earthworm *n.* ไส้เดือน sâi-duuan [ตัว dtuua]

earwax *n.* ขี้หู kîi-hǔu [ก้อน gɔ̂ɔn]

ease *vt.* (alleviate) บรรเทา ban-tao

easel *n.* ขาตั้งภาพ kǎa-dtâng-pâap [อัน an]

easily *adv.* (with ease) อย่างง่ายดาย yàang-ngâai-daai

east *n.* ตะวันออก dtà~wan-ɔ̀ɔk, ทิศตะวันออก tít-dtà~wan-ɔ̀ɔk [ทิศ tít]

eastern *adj.* ตะวันออก dtà~wan-ɔ̀ɔk, ทางทิศตะวันออก taang-tít-dtà~wan-ɔ̀ɔk

easy *adj.* ง่าย ngâai, หมู mǔu ✿

easygoing *adj.* (relaxed) สบายๆ sà~baai-sà~baai | (unhurried) ไม่รีบเร่ง mâi-rîip-rêng

eat *v.* ทาน taan, รับประทาน ráp-bprà~taan ⚑, ฉัน chǎn ✿, กิน gin ✿, กินข้าว gin-kâao ✿, แดก dɛ̀ɛk ☙

eaves *n.* ชายคา chaai-kaa

eavesdrop *v.* (listen in) แอบฟัง ɛ̀ɛp-fang

ebb *n.* (tide) น้ำลด náam-

lót

ebony *n.* (tree) ตะโก dtà~goo [ต้น dtôn]

eccentric *adj.* (odd) ประหลาด bprà~làat

echo *n.* (sound) เสียงก้อง sǐiang-gɔ̂ng, เสียงสะท้อน sǐiang-sà~tɔ́ɔn

eclipse *n.* (moon) จันทรุปราคา jan-tá~rú-bprà~raa-kaa [ครั้ง kráng] | (sun) สุริยุปราคา sù~rí~yúp-bprà~raa-kaa [ครั้ง kráng]

ecology *n.* นิเวศน์วิทยา ní-wêet-wít-tá~yaa

economic *adj.* เกี่ยวกับเศรษฐศาสตร์ gìiao-gàp-sèet-tà~sàat

economical *adj.* (thrifty) ประหยัด bprà~yàt

economics *n.* เศรษฐศาสตร์ sèet-tà~sàat [วิชา wí-chaa]

economist *n.* นักเศรษฐศาสตร์ nák-sèet-tà~sàat [คน kon]

economy *n.* เศรษฐกิจ sèet-tà~gìt

ecstasy *n.* (drug) ยาอี yaa-ii, ยาหลอนประสาท yaa-

โว้ย-bprà~sàat ✗

edge *n.* (margin, rim) ขอบ kɔ̀ɔp, ริม rim

edible *adj.* กินได้ gin-dâai

edit *vt.* (revise or correct) แก้ไข gɛ̂ɛ-kǎi

edition *n.* (publication) ฉบับพิมพ์ chà~bàp-pim [ฉบับ chà~bàp]

editor *n.* บรรณาธิการ ban-naa-tí-gaan [คน kon]

educate *v.* (teach) สั่งสอน sàng-sɔ̌ɔn

education *n.* การศึกษา gaan-sùk-sǎa

eel *n.* ปลาไหล bplaa-lǎi [ตัว dtuua]

effect *n.* (influence) ผลกระทบ pǒn-grà~tóp

effective *adj.* มีประสิทธิภาพ mii-bprà~ sìt-tí~pâap

efficiency *n.* ประสิทธิภาพ bprà~sìt-tí~pâap

effort *n.* ความพยายาม kwaam-pá~yaa-yaam

e.g. *idm.* เช่น chên, ตัวอย่าง dtuua-yàang

egg *n.* ไข่ kài [ฟอง fɔɔng]

egg noodle *n.* บะหมี่ bà~mìi [ซาม chaam

(bowl), ถ้วย tûuai (bowl), เส้น sên (strand)]

eggplant *n.* มะเขือ má~ kʉ̌ʉa [ลูก lûuk]

egg roll *n.* ไข่ม้วน kài-múuan [แผ่น pèn]

egg white *n.* ไข่ขาว kài-kǎao

egg yolk *n.* ไข่แดง kài-dɛɛng

ego *n.* (self-esteem) ความถือตัวเองเป็นสำคัญ kwaam-tʉ̌ʉ-dtuua-eeng-bpen-sǎm-kan

egoistic *adj.* (self-centered) เห็นแก่ตัว hěn-gɛ̀ɛ-dtuua

eight *numb.* แปด bpɛɛt

eighteen *numb.* สิบแปด sìp-bpɛɛt

eighth *adj.* (one-eighth) หนึ่งในแปด nʉ̀ng-nai-bpɛɛt | (ordinal) ที่แปด tîi-bpɛɛt

either *adj.* (one or the other) อันใดอันหนึ่ง an-dai-an-nʉ̀ng

either *pron.* (each) อันใดอันหนึ่ง an-dai-an-nʉ̀ng

either...or *conj.* ไม่_ก็_

mâi-_-gɔ̂ɔ-_, หรือ rǔ̌ɯ

ejaculate vi. (eject semen)
หลั่งอสุจิ làng-à~sù-jì

eject vt. (e.g. CD) เอา_ออก
ao-_-ɔ̀ɔk

elaborate adj. ประณีต
bprà~nîit

elaborate vi. (explain
more) อธิบายเพิ่มเติม à-
tí-baai-pə̂əm-dtəəm

elastic adj. (springy)
ยืดหดได้ yʉ̂ʉt-hòt-dâai

elastic band n. ยางยืด
yaang-yʉ̂ʉt [เส้น sên] |
(rubber band) ยางรัด
yaang-rát [เส้น sên]

elbow n. ศอก sɔ̀ɔk [ข้อ
kɔ̂ɔ, ข้าง kâang]

elder adj. (older) แก่กว่า
gɛ̀ɛ-gwàa

elder n. (senior) ผู้อาวุโส
pûu-aa-wú-sǒo [คน kon]

elder brother n. พี่ชาย
pîi-chaai [คน kon]

elderly adj. อาวุโส aa-wú-
sǒo, สูงอายุ sǔung-aa-yú
❗

elder sister n. พี่สาว pîi-
sǎao [คน kon]

eldest adj. อายุมากที่สุด

aa-yú-mâak-tîi-sùt

eldest n. คนโต kon-dtoo
[คน kon]

elect vt. เลือก lʉ̂ʉak

election n. การเลือกตั้ง
gaan-lʉ̂ʉak-dtâng [ครั้ง
kráng]

elective n. (class) วิชาเลือก
wí-chaa-lʉ̂ʉak [วิชา wí-
chaa]

electric adj. ไฟฟ้า fai-fáa

electrical see electric

electric blanket n.
ผ้าห่มไฟฟ้า pâa-hòm-fai-
fáa [ผืน pʉ̌ʉn]

electric chair n. เก้าอี้ไฟฟ้า
gâo-îi-fai-fáa [ตัว dtuua]

electric current n.
กระแสไฟฟ้า grà~sɛ̌ɛ-fai-
fáa [แอมป์ ɛm]

electric fan n. พัดลมไฟฟ้า
pát-lom-fai-fáa [ตัว
dtuua, เครื่อง krʉ̂ʉang]

electrician n. ช่างไฟฟ้า
châng-fai-fáa [คน kon]

electricity n. ไฟฟ้า fai-fáa

electric train n. รถไฟฟ้า
rót-fai-fáa [ขบวน kà~
buuan, คัน kan]

electrocardiogram n.

คลื่นไฟฟ้าหัวใจ klûun-fai-
fáa-hǔua-jai

electrocute v. (shock)
ช็อต chɔ́t

electronic adj.
อิเล็กทรอนิกส์ ì~lék-trɔɔ-
nìk

electronics n.
อิเล็กทรอนิกส์ ì~lék-trɔɔ-
nìk

elegant adj. (graceful)
สง่างาม sà~ngàa-ngaam

element n. (component)
ส่วนประกอบ sùuan-
bprà~gɔ̀ɔp | (substance)
ธาตุ tâat [ชนิด chá~nít,
ตัว dtuua ✦]

elementary adj. (primary)
เบื้องต้น bûuang-dtôn

elementary school n.
โรงเรียนประถม roong-
riian-bprà~tǒm [แห่ง
hɛ̀ng]

elephant n. ช้าง cháang
[ตัว dtuua (wild), เชือก
chûuak (tamed)]

elevation n. (above sea
level)
ความสูงเหนือระดับน้ำทะเล
kwaam-sǔung-nǔua-
rá~dàp-nám-tá~lee

elevator n. ลิฟต์ líp [ตัว
dtuua]

eleven numb. สิบเอ็ด sìp-èt

elf n. (fairy) เทพยดา
têep-pá~yá~daa [ตน
dton]

eligible adj. (have a right)
มีสิทธิ์ mii-sìt

eliminate vt. (get rid of)
กำจัด gam-jàt | (select
out) คัด_ออก kát-_-ɔ̀ɔk

elite n. (best of anything)
หัวกะทิ hǔua-gà~tí ✦
[คน kon] | (high class)
ผู้ดีชั้นสูง pûu-dii-chán-
sǔung [คน kon]

elope vi. (run away with a
lover) หนีตาม nǐi-dtaam

eloquent adj. คารมดี kaa-
rom-dii

else adj. (more, e.g. want
anything else?) อีก ìik |
(other, e.g. ask someone
else) อื่น ùun

else adv. (other, e.g. how
else?) อื่น ùun

elsewhere adv. ที่อื่น tîi-
ùun

email n. อีเมล ii-meo ✦
[ฉบับ chà~bàp]

embankment n. (levee)

ทำนบ tam-nóp [แห่ง
hɛ̀ng]

embarrass vt. (cause
shame to) ทำให้_อาย
tam-hâi-_-aai

embarrassed adj.
(ashamed) อับอาย àp-aai

embarrassing adj. น่าอาย
nâa-aai

embassy n. สถานทูต sà~
tăan-tûut [แห่ง hɛ̀ng]

embezzle vt. ยักยอก yák-
yɔ̂ɔk

emblem n. (mark)
เครื่องหมาย krɨ̂uang-
măai [อัน an]

embrace v. (hug) กอด gɔ̀ɔt

embroidery n.
การเย็บปักถักร้อย gaan-
yép-bpàk-tàk-rɔ́ɔi

embryo n. (animal or
human) ตัวอ่อน dtuua-
ɔ̀ɔn [ตัว dtuua]

emerald n. มรกต mɔɔ-
rá~gòt [เม็ด mét, ก้อน
gɔ̂ɔn (not cut)]

emerge vi. (come out)
โผล่ plòo

emergency n. เหตุการณ์
ฉุกเฉิน hèet-gaan-chùk-
chə̌ən [ครั้ง kráng]

emergency room n.
ห้องฉุกเฉิน hɔ̂ng-chùk-
chə̌ən [ห้อง hɔ̂ng]

emigrant n. ผู้อพยพ pûu-
òp-pá~yóp [คน kon]

emigrate vi. อพยพ òp-
pá~yóp

emit vt. (sound, light)
เปล่ง bplèng

emotion n. ความรู้สึก
kwaam-rúu-sɨ̀k, อารมณ์
aa-rom

emperor n. จักรพรรดิ jàk-
grà~pát [พระองค์ prá-
ong]

emphasize vt. เน้น néen

empire n. อาณาจักร aa-
naa-jàk [แห่ง hɛ̀ng]

employ vt. (hire) จ้าง jâang

employee n. พนักงาน
pá~nák-ngaan, ลูกจ้าง
lûuk-jâang [คน kon]

employer n. นายจ้าง naai-
jâang [คน kon]

employment n. (hire)
การว่าจ้าง gaan-wâa-
jâang

empress n. จักรพรรดินี
jàk-grà~pát-dì-nii
[พระองค์ prá-ong]

empty adj. (containing

nothing) เปล่า bplàao | (unoccupied) ว่าง wâang
empty *vt.* (make empty) ทำให้_ว่างเปล่า tam-hâi-_-wâang-bplàao | (pour off) เททิ้ง tee-tíng
empty-handed *adj.* มือเปล่า mʉʉ-bplàao
emu *n.* นกอีมู nók-ii-muu [ตัว dtuua]
enable *vt.* (activate) ทำให้_เริ่มใช้งานได้ tam-hâi-_-rə̂əm-chái-ngaan-dâai | (make possible) ทำให้_เป็นไปได้ tam-hâi-_-bpen-bpai-dâai
enact *vt.* (law) บัญญัติ ban-yàt
enamel *n.* (coating) สิ่งที่ใช้เคลือบ sìng-tîi-chái-klʉ̂ʉap
enchant *vt.* (attract) ทำให้_ลุ่มหลง tam-hâi-_-lûm-lǒng
enchanted *adj.* (bewitched) ต้องมนตร์ dtɔ̂ng-mon
enchantment *n.* (magical spell) เสน่ห์ sà~nèe
encircle *vt.* (enclose) ล้อมรอบ lɔ́ɔm-rɔ̂ɔp
enclose *vt.* (printed materials) แนบ_ไว้ใน nɛ̂ɛp-_-wái-nai | (put into) ใส่ sài | (surround, e.g. fence) ล้อม lɔ́ɔm
enclosure *n.* (case, e.g. hard drive) ที่หุ้ม tîi-hûm [อัน an] | (printed materials) สิ่งที่แนบมา sìng-tîi-nɛ̂ɛp-maa
encore *n.* การแสดงซ้ำตามคำเรียกร้อง gaan-sà~dɛɛng-sám-dtaam-kam-rîiak-rɔ́ɔng
encounter *vt.* (find or meet unexpectedly) พบ póp, เจอ jəə 🗣
encourage *vt.* (support) สนับสนุน sà~nàp-sà~nǔn, ให้กำลังใจ hâi-gam-lang-jai
encouragement *n.* การให้กำลังใจ gaan-hâi-gam-lang-jai
encyclopedia *n.* สารานุกรม sǎa-raa-nú-grom [เล่ม lêm]
end *n.* (edge, point) ปลาย bplaai | (rear) ท้าย táai
end *vi.* จบ jòp
end *vt.* ทำให้_สิ้นสุดลง

tam-hâi-_-sîn-sùt-long

endanger *vt.*
ทำให้_อยู่ในอันตราย tam-hâi-_-yùu-nai-an-dtà~raai

endeavor *n.* ความพยายาม kwaam-pá~yaa-yaam

ending *n.* (last part, e.g. movie) ตอนจบ dtɔɔn-jòp

endless *adj.* (having no end) ไม่จบสิ้น mâi-jòp-sîn

endorse *vt.* (sign name on) ลงนามรับรอง long-naam-ráp-rɔɔng ⚠

end up at *vi.* ลงเอยที่ long-ǝǝi-tîi ✦

end up doing *vi.* ลงเอยด้วยการ long-ǝǝi-dûuai-gaan ✦

endurance *n.* (patience) ความอดกลั้น kwaam-òt-glân | (perseverance) ความพากเพียร kwaam-pâak-piian

endure *vi.* (persevere) อดทน òt-ton

endure *vt.* (for person) อดทนต่อ òt-ton-dtɔ̀ɔ | (for thing) ทน ton

enduring *adj.* (durable) คงทน kong-ton

enemy *n.* ข้าศึก kâa-sʉ̀k,

ศัตรู sàt-dtruu [คน kon (person), พวก pûuak (group)]

energetic *adj.* (full of energy) กระฉับกระเฉง grà~chàp-grà~chěeng, มีกำลัง mii-gam-lang

energy *n.* (e.g. electrical) พลังงาน pá~lang-ngaan | (power, strength) กำลัง gam-lang, พลัง pá~lang

enforce *vt.* (compel) บังคับใช้ bang-káp-chái

enforcement *n.* การบังคับใช้ตามกฎหมาย gaan-bang-káp-chái-dtaam-gòt-mǎai

engage *vt.* (activate) ทำให้_เริ่มใช้งานได้ tam-hâi-_-rɤ̂ɤm-chái-ngaan-dâai | (for marriage) หมั้นกับ mân-gàp

engaged *adj.* (engrossed) ติดพัน dtìt-pan | (for marriage) มีคู่หมั้นแล้ว mii-kûu-mân-lɛ́ɛo | (telephone) สายไม่ว่าง sǎai-mâi-wâang

engagement ring *n.* แหวนหมั้น wɛ̌ɛn-mân [วง wong]

engine *n.* เครื่อง krûuang,
เครื่องยนต์ krûuang-yon
[เครื่อง krûuang]

engineer *n.* วิศวกร wít-
sà~wá~gɔɔn [คน kon]

engineering *n.* วิศวกรรม
wít-sà~wá~gam

England *n.* อังกฤษ ang-
grìt [ประเทศ bprà~têet]

English *adj.* อังกฤษ ang-
grìt

English *n.* (language)
ภาษาอังกฤษ paa-sǎa-
ang-grìt [ภาษา paa-sǎa] |
(person) ชาวอังกฤษ
chaao-ang-grìt [คน kon]

engrave *v.* สลัก sà~làk

engraving *n.* (act)
การแกะสลักจารึก gaan-
gɛ̀-sà~làk-jaa-rúk

enhance *vt.* ทำให้_ดีขึ้น
tam-hâi-_-dii-kûn

enjoy *vt.* สนุกกับ sà~nùk-
gàp

enlarge *v.* (expand) ขยาย
kà~yǎai

enlighten *vt.* (impart
knowledge to)
ให้ความกระจ่างกับ hâi-
kwaam-grà~jàang-gàp

enlightened *adj.* (e.g.

Lord Buddha) ตรัสรู้
dtràt-sà~rúu

enlightenment *n.*
การรู้แจ้งเห็นจริง gaan-
rúu-jɛ̂ɛng-hěn-jing

enlist *vi.* (for military
service) สมัครเป็นทหาร
sà~màk-bpen-tá~hǎan

enormous *adj.* มหึมา má-
hù-maa

enough *adj.* พอ pɔɔ,
เพียงพอ piiang-pɔɔ

enough already! *interj.*
พอแล้ว pɔɔ-lɛ́ɛo

enroll *v.* (register)
ลงทะเบียน long-tá~biian

ensure *vt.* (make certain)
รับประกัน ráp-bprà~gan

entangled *adj.* ยุ่งเหยิง
yûng-yěong

enter *v.* เข้า kâo

enterprise *n.* (venture)
วิสาหกิจ wí-sǎa-hà~git

entertain *vi.* (host guests)
รับรองแขก ráp-rɔɔng-kɛ̀ɛk

entertain *vt.* (provide
entertainment)
ทำให้_สนุกสนาน tam-
hâi-_-sà~nùk-sà~nǎan

entertainer *n.* (actor,
performer) ผู้แสดง pûu-
sà~dɛɛng [คน kon]

entertaining *adj.* สนุก
sà~nùk

entertainment *n.*
การบันเทิง gaan-ban-
təəng

enthusiastic *adj.*
กระตือรือร้น grà~dtɯɯ-
rɯɯ-rón, ไฟแรง fai-rɛɛng
💠

entice *vt.* ล่อลวง lɔ̂ɔ-
luuang

entire *adj.* ทั้ง táng,
ทั้งหมด táng-mòt, ทุก túk

entirely *adv.* (altogether)
ทั้งหมด táng-mòt, ทั้งสิ้น
táng-sîn 💠

entity *n.* เอกลักษณ์ èek-
gà~lák

entrails *n.* เครื่องใน
krɯ̂uang-nai [ชิ้น chín]

entrance *n.* ทางเข้า
taang-kâo [ทาง taang]

entrepreneur *n.*
ผู้บริหารกิจการ pûu-bɔɔ-
rí~hǎan-gìt-jà~gaan [คน
kon]

entrust *vt.* (someone with
something)
ไว้วางใจ_เรื่อง_ wái-
waang-jai-_-rɯ̂uang-_

envelope *n.* ซอง sɔɔng

[ซอง rɔɔng]

envious *adj.* อิจฉา ìt-chǎa
| (between lovers) หึง
hɯ̌ng

environment *n.*
สิ่งแวดล้อม sìng-wɛ̂ɛt-
lɔ́ɔm

environmental *adj.*
ด้านสิ่งแวดล้อม dâan-
sìng-wɛ̂ɛt-lɔ́ɔm

envy *vt.* อิจฉา ìt-chǎa

enzyme *n.* เอนไซม์ en-
saai [ชนิด chá~nít]

ephedrine *n.* ยาอี yaa-ii

epic *n.* มหากาพย์ má~
hǎa-gàap [เรื่อง rɯ̂uang]

epidemic *n.* (disease)
โรคระบาด rôok-rá~bàat
[โรค rôok]

epidermis *n.* หนังกำพร้า
nǎng-gam-práa [ชั้น
chán]

epilepsy *n.* ลมบ้าหมู lom-
bâa-mǔu [โรค rôok]

episode *n.* (e.g. in a
show) ตอน dtɔɔn [ตอน
dtɔɔn]

epoch *n.* ยุค yúk [ยุค yúk]

equal *adj.* เท่ากัน tâo-gan

equal *vt.* เท่ากับ tâo-gàp

equality n.
ความเท่าเทียมกัน
kwaam-tâo-tiiam-gan

equation n. (in math)
สมการ sà~má~gaan
[สมการ sà~má~gaan]

equator n. เส้นศูนย์สูตร
sên-sǔun-sùut [เส้น sên]

equilibrium n.
สมดุลยภาพ sǒm-dun-
lá~yá~pâap

equip vt. (prepare _ for _)
จัดเตรียม_ให้_ jàt-
dtriiam-_-hâi-_

equipment n. อุปกรณ์
ùp-bpà~gɔɔn [ชิ้น chín
(piece), ชุด chút (set)]

equivalent adj. เท่ากัน
tâo-gan, เท่ากับ tâo-gàp

era n. (age, period) สมัย
sà~mǎi [สมัย sà~mǎi] |
(age, period) ยุค yúk [ยุค
yúk]

erase vt. ลบ_ออก lóp-_-
ɔ̀ɔk

eraser n. (rubber) ยางลบ
yaang-lóp [อัน an]

erect adj. (upright) ตั้งตรง
dtâng-dtrong

erect vi. (get hard) แข็งตัว
kěng-dtuua

erect vt. (build) สร้าง
sâang

erection n. (e.g. male
sexual erection)
การแข็งตัว gaan-kěng-
dtuua | (structure)
การตั้งตรง gaan-dtâng-
dtrong

erode vi. (wear away)
สึกกร่อน sùk-grɔ̀n

erotic adj.
ที่กระตุ้นความรู้สึกทางเพศ
tîi-grà~dtûn-kwaam-
rúu-sùk-taang-pêet

err vi. (make a mistake)
ทำผิดพลาด tam-pìt-plâat

errand n. ธุระ tú-rá [เรื่อง
rûuang, อัน an ✹]

error n. ความผิดพลาด
kwaam-pìt-plâat

erupt vi. ระเบิด rá~bə̀ət

escalator n. บันไดเลื่อน
ban-dai-lûuan [ตัว dtuua]

escape n. การหลบหนี
gaan-lòp-nǐi

escape v. หลบหนี lòp-nǐi

escort n. (guide or friend)
ผู้ที่ไปเป็นเพื่อน pûu-tîi-
bpai-bpen-pûuan [คน
kon] | (hired companion)
เอสคอร์ท és-kɔ̀ɔt ✹ [คน

kon]

escrow *n.* ทรัพย์สินที่
เตรียมไว้โอน sáp-sĭn-tîi-
dtriiam-wái-oon, เอสโคร
ét-sà~kroo ✖

esophagus *n.* หลอดอาหาร
lɔ̀ɔt-aa-hăan [หลอด lɔ̀ɔt]

especially *adv.*
โดยเฉพาะอย่างยิ่ง dooi-
chà~pɔ́-yàang-yîng,
เฉพาะ chà~pɔ́ ☙

espionage *n.* จารกรรม
jaa-rá~gam [ครั้ง kráng]

essay *n.* เรียงความ riiang-
kwaam [เรื่อง rûueang]

essence *n.* (content,
meaning) ใจความ jai-
kwaam [อัน an] |
(important element)
จุดสำคัญ jùt-săm-kan [จุด
jùt]

essential *adj.* (important)
สำคัญ săm-kan |
(necessary) จำเป็น jam-
bpen

establish *vt.* ก่อตั้ง gɔ̀ɔ-
dtâng

estate *n.* (property)
ทรัพย์สิน sáp-sĭn ! [ชิ้น
chín] | (property at

death) มรดก mɔɔ-rá~
dòk [กอง gɔɔng, ชิ้น chín]

esteemed *adj.* (worthy of
respect) น่านับถือ nâa-
náp-tŭu

estimate *n.* (price quote)
การตีราคา gaan-dtii-raa-
kaa

estimate *v.* (calculate
approximately) ประมาณ
bprà~maan | (speculate)
กะ gà ☙

estranged *adj.* บาดหมาง
bàat-măang

etc. see et cetera

et cetera *idm.* เป็นต้น
bpen-dtôn, และอื่นๆ อีก
lɛ́-ùun-ùun-ìik

etching *n.* การสลัก gaan-
sà~làk

eternal *adj.* (endless)
ไม่มีที่สิ้นสุด mâi-mii-tîi-
sîn-sùt

eternity *n.* (forever,
infinite time) นิรันดร ní-
ran-dɔɔn ☙

ethical *adj.* (ethically
correct) ถูกต้องตาม
จริยธรรม tùuk-dtɔ̂ng-
dtaam-jà-rí-yá-tam

ethics *n.* (system of moral
principles) จริยธรรม jà~

rí-yá-tam
ethnic adj.
เกี่ยวกับชาติพันธุ์ gìiao-
gàp-châat-pan
etiquette n. (manner)
มารยาท maa-rá~yâat
eulogy n. (for deceased)
คำกล่าวถึงผู้ตาย kam-
glàao-tǔng-pûu-dtaai
[คำ kam]
eunuch n. ขันที kǎn-tii
[คน kon]
Euro n. เงินยูโร ngən-yuu-
roo [จำนวน jam-nuuan]
Europe n. ยุโรป yú-ròop
[ทวีป tá~wîip]
European n. ชาวยุโรป
chaao-yú-ròop [คน kon]
evacuate vi. อพยพ òp-
pá~yóp
evade v. หลบเลี่ยง lòp-
lîiang
evaluate vt. ประเมิน
bprà~məən
evaporate vi. (vaporize)
ระเหย rá~hǒi
evasive adj. หลบหลีก lòp-
lìik
eve n. เวลาเย็น wee-laa-
yen
even adj. (equal) เสมอ

sà~mǎə | (flat) เรียบ rîiap
even adv. แม้แต่ mέε-dtὲε
even if conj. แม้ mέε,
แม้ว่า mέε-wâa
evening n. ตอนเย็น
dtɔɔn-yen, เย็น yen
even number n. เลขคู่
lêek-kûu [ตัว dtuua]
event n. (situation,
circumstance) เหตุการณ์
hèet-gaan
even though conj.
ถึงแม้ว่า tǔng-mέε-wâa,
ทั้งๆ ที่ táng-táng-tîi
eventually adv. ในที่สุด
nai-tîi-sùt
ever adv. (always)
ตลอดไป dtà~lɔ̀ɔt-bpai |
(at some time) เคย kəəi
every adj. (all) ทุก túk,
ทุกๆ túk-túk
everybody pron. ทุกคน
túk-kon
every day adv. ทุกวัน
túk-wan
everyday adj. (ordinary)
ธรรมดา tam-má~daa
every month adv.
ทุกเดือน túk-duuan
everyone see everybody
everything pron. ทุกอย่าง

túk-yàang

every time *adv.* ทุกครั้ง
túk-kráng, ทุกที túk-tii

every week *adv.*
ทุกอาทิตย์ túk-aa-tít,
ทุกสัปดาห์ túk-sàp-daa ‼

everywhere *adv.* ทุกที่
túk-tîi, ทุกแห่ง túk-hèng

evict *vt.* (expel) ขับไล่ kàp-
lâi

evidence *n.* หลักฐาน làk-
tǎan [ชิ้น chín]

evident *adj.* (apparent)
แจ่มแจ้ง jὲm-jɛ̂ɛng

evil *adj.* (sinful) เป็นบาป
bpen-bàap | (wicked)
ร้าย ráai

evil *n.* สิ่งชั่วร้าย sìng-
chûua-ráai

evoke *vt.* (bring
memories of)
ทำให้_ระลึกความหลัง
tam-hâi-_-rá~lɯ́k-
kwaam-lǎng

evolution *n.* (in nature)
วิวัฒนาการ wí-wát-tá~
naa-gaan

ewe *n.* แกะตัวเมีย gὲ-
dtuua-miia [ตัว dtuua]

exact *adj.* ตรง dtrong |

(accurate) แม่นยำ mên-
yam | (e.g. date, figure)
แน่นอน nɛ̂ɛ-nɔɔn

exactly *adv.* (accurately)
อย่างแน่นอน yàang-nɛ̂ɛ-
nɔɔn | (precisely) เป๊ะ
bpé ✦

exaggerate *vi.* (overstate)
พูดเกินความจริง pûut-
gəən-kwaam-jing

examination *n.* (e.g.
physical) การตรวจสอบ
gaan-dtrùuat-sɔ̀ɔp |
(test) การทดสอบ gaan-
tót-sɔ̀ɔp, การสอบ gaan-
sɔ̀ɔp

examine *vt.* (check,
review) ตรวจ dtrùuat |
(inspect) พิจารณา pí-jaa-
rá~naa

example *n.* ตัวอย่าง
dtuua-yàang [อัน an ✦,
ตัวอย่าง dtuua-yàang]

excavate *v.* ขุดค้น kùt-kón

exceed *vt.* (surpass) เกิน
gəən, เกินกว่า gəən-gwàa

excel *vi.* (do extremely
well) ทำได้ยอดเยี่ยม
tam-dâi-yɔ̂ɔt-yîiam

excellent *adj.* ยอดเยี่ยม
yɔ̂ɔt-yîiam

excellent! *interj.* เยี่ยม

yîiam, สุดยอด sùt-yɔ̂ɔt ✎

except *prep.* นอกจาก
nɔ̂ɔk-jàak, ยกเว้น yók-
wén, เว้นแต่ wén-dtɛ̀ɛ

exception *n.* (item)
ข้อยกเว้น kɔ̂ɔ-yók-wéen
[ข้อ kɔ̂ɔ]

excerpt *n.* ถ้อยคำที่คัด
ลอกมา tɔ̂i-kam-tîi-kát-
lɔ̂ɔk-maa [คำ kam]

excerpt *vt.* ตัดตอน dtàt-
dtɔɔn

excess *adj.* (extra) มากเกิน
mâak-gəən

excess *n.* (surplus)
ส่วนเกิน sùuan-gəən

excessive *adj.* เหลือเฟือ
lɯ̌ɯa-fɯɯa

exchange *n.* (act) การแลก
เปลี่ยน gaan-lɛ̂ɛk-bpliian

exchange *v.* แลก lɛ̂ɛk,
แลกเปลี่ยน lɛ̂ɛk-bpliian

exchange rate *n.* อัตรา
แลกเปลี่ยน àt-dtraa-
lɛ̂ɛk-bpliian [อัตรา àt-
dtraa]

excite *vt.* (arouse feeling
of) ปลุกเร้า bplùk-ráo |
(arouse interest of)
ทำให้_ตื่นเต้น tam-hâi-_-
dtɯ̀ɯn-dtên

excited *adj.* ตื่นเต้น
dtɯ̀ɯn-dtên

exciting *adj.* น่าตื่นเต้น
nâa-dtɯ̀ɯn-dtên

exclaim *v.* ร้องอุทาน
rɔ́ɔng-ù-taan

exclamation point *n.*
อัศเจรีย์ àt-sà~jee-rii ✗
[ตัว dtuua]

exclude *vt.* ไม่นับ mâi-
náp, เว้น wén

exclusive *adj.* (hi-so, e.g.
club) เฉพาะ chà~pɔ́ | (to
one party) แต่เพียงผู้เดียว
dtɛ̀ɛ-piiang-pûu-diiao

excrement *n.* (feces) ขี้ kîi
✎✳ [กอง gɔɔng, ก้อน
gɔ̂ɔn] | (feces) อุจจาระ ùt-
jaa-rá ❗ [กอง gɔɔng
(pile), ก้อน gɔ̂ɔn]

excrete *v.* ถ่าย tàai

excuse *n.* (pretext)
คำแก้ตัว kam-gɛ̂ɛ-dtuua
[คำ kam]

excuse *vt.* (allow to leave)
อนุญาตให้_ไปได้ à-nú-
yâat-hâi-_-bpai-dâai |
(forgive, allow) อนุญาต
à-nú-yâat

excuse me! *interj.* ขอโทษ

kɔ̌ɔ-tôot, ขออภัย kɔ̌ɔ-à~
pai ‼

excuse oneself v. ขอตัว
kɔ̌ɔ-dtuua

execute vt. (serve death
penalty) ประหาร bprà~
hǎan ‼ | (sign) เซ็นชื่อใน
sen-chɯ̂ɯ-nai

execution n.
(achievement)
การทำให้สำเร็จ gaan-
tam-hâi-sǎm-rèt

executive adj.
เกี่ยวกับการบริหาร gìiao-
gàp-gaan-bɔɔ-rí~hǎan

executive n. ผู้บริหาร
pûu-bɔɔ-rí~hǎan [คน
kon]

exemplary adj. (model)
เป็นแบบอย่าง bpen-
bɛ̀ɛp-yàang

exempt adj.
ได้รับการยกเว้น dâi-ráp-
gaan-yók-wén

exercise n. (e.g.
homework) แบบฝึกหัด
bɛ̀ɛp-fɯ̀k-hàt [ข้อ kɔ̂ɔ
(item), ชุด chút (set)]

exercise vi. (body)
ออกกำลังกาย ɔ̀ɔk-gam-
lang-gaai | (practice,
train) ซ้อม sɔ́ɔm, ฝึก fɯ̀k

exert vt. (e.g. power,
influence) ใช้ chái

exert oneself vi. โหมแรง
hǒom-rɛɛng

exhale vi. (breathe out)
หายใจออก hǎai-jai-ɔ̀ɔk

exhaust n. (e.g. car) ไอเสีย
ai-sǐia

exhaust vt. (use up all)
ใช้_หมด chái-_-mòt

exhausted adj. (fatigued)
หมดแรง mòt-rɛɛng,
อ่อนเพลีย ɔ̀ɔn-pliia

exhaust pipe n. ท่อไอเสีย
tɔ̂ɔ-ai-sǐia [ท่อ tɔ̂ɔ]

exhibit n. (e.g. at a show)
ของที่นำมาแสดง kɔ̌ɔng-
tîi-nam-maa-sà~dɛɛng
[ชิ้น chín]

exhibit v. (show) แสดง
sà~dɛɛng

exhibition n. นิทรรศการ
ní-tát-sà~gaan [ครั้ง
kráng]

exile n. (banishment)
การเนรเทศ gaan-nee-
rá~têet ‼ [ครั้ง kráng]

exist vi. (be) มี mii, มีอยู่
mii-yùu | (be alive)
มีชีวิตอยู่ mii-chii-wít-yùu

| (survive) รอดชีวิต rɔ̂ɔt-chii-wít

existent *adj.* มีอยู่ mii-yùu

exit *n.* ทางออก taang-ɔ̀ɔk [ทาง taang]

exotic *adj.* (strange) ประหลาด bprà~làat

expand *v.* ขยาย kà~yǎai

expatriate *n.* ผู้ที่อาศัยอยู่ในประเทศอื่น pûu-tîi-aa-sǎi-yùu-nai-bprà~têet-ùun [คน kon]

expect *vt.* (anticipate) คาดหวัง kâat-wǎng

expectation *n.* ความคาดหมาย kwaam-kâat-mǎai

expel *vt.* (discharge, e.g. air) ระบาย_ออก rá~baai-_-ɔ̀ɔk | (dismiss, lay off) ไล่_ออก lâi-_-ɔ̀ɔk

expense *n.* (cost, price, charge) ค่าใช้จ่าย kâa-chái-jàai [จำนวน jam-nuuan]

expensive *adj.* แพง pɛɛng

experience *n.* ประสบการณ์ bprà~sòp-gaan [ครั้ง kráng]

experience *vt.* ประสบ bprà~sòp

experienced *adj.* มีประสบการณ์ mii-bprà~sòp-gaan | (skillful) ชำนาญ cham-naan

experiment *n.* การทดลอง gaan-tót-lɔɔng [ครั้ง kráng]

experiment *vi.* (conduct an experiment) ทำการทดลอง tam-gaan-tót-lɔɔng

expert *adj.* (skilled) ชำนาญ cham-naan

expert *n.* ผู้เชี่ยวชาญ pûu-chîiao-chaan [คน kon]

expertise *n.* ความชำนาญ kwaam-cham-naan

expiration date *n.* วันหมดอายุ wan-mòt-aa-yú [วัน wan]

expire *vi.* (reach end of term) หมดอายุ mòt-aa-yú

explain *v.* อธิบาย à~tí-baai

explanation *n.* คำอธิบาย kam-à~tí-baai [คำ kam (word)]

explode *vi.* ระเบิด rá~bə̀ət

exploit *vt.* (make good use) ใช้ประโยชน์_ให้มากที่สุด chái-bprà~yòot-_-hâi-mâak-tîi-sùt | (use selfishly) เอาเปรียบ aobprìiap

explore *v.* สำรวจ sǎm-rùuat

explorer *n.* (person) นักสำรวจ nák-sǎm-rùuat [คน kon]

explosion *n.* การระเบิด gaan-rá~bə̀ət [ครั้ง kráng]

explosive *n.* วัตถุระเบิด wát-tù-rá~bə̀ət [ชิ้น chín]

export *n.* (product) สินค้าออก sǐn-káa-ɔ̀ɔk [ชนิด chá~nít]

export *vt.* ส่ง_ออก sòng-_-ɔ̀ɔk

exporter *n.* ผู้ส่งออก pûu-sòng-ɔ̀ɔk [คน kon]

expose *vt* (disclose) เปิดเผย bpə̀ət-pə̌əi | (shine light on, e.g. film) ส่องไฟใส่ sòng-fai-sài

exposed *adj.* (unprotected) ไม่มีการป้องกัน mâi-mii-gaan-bpɔ̂ng-gan

exposition *n.* (public show) นิทรรศการ ní-tát-sà~gaan [ครั้ง kráng]

express *adj.* ด่วน dùuan

express *n.* (e.g. train, bus) รถด่วน rót-dùuan [คัน kan (bus), ขบวน kà~buuan (train)]

express *vt.* (e.g. opinion) แสดง sà~dɛɛng

expression *n.* (facial) การแสดงออกทางใบหน้า gaan-sà~dɛɛng-ɔ̀ɔk-taang-bai-nâa | (idiom) สำนวน sǎm-nuuan [สำนวน sǎm-nuuan]

express mail *n.* จดหมายด่วน jòt-mǎai-dùuan [ฉบับ chà~bàp]

express oneself *vi.* แสดงออก sà~dɛɛng-ɔ̀ɔk

express train *n.* รถไฟด่วน rót-fai-dùuan [ขบวน kà~buuan]

expressway *n.* ทางด่วน taang-dùuan [สาย sǎai]

expulsion *n.* การไล่ออก gaan-lâi-ɔ̀ɔk

extend *vt.* (e.g. arm) ยื่น yûɯn | (increase in length) ต่อ dtɔ̀ɔ | (stretch out) ยืด yʉ̂ɯt

extension *n.* (cord or line) สายพ่วง sǎai-pûuang [สาย sǎai] | (part added) ส่วนที่ขยายออก sùuan-tîi-kà~yǎai-ɔ̀ɔk

extension cord *n.*

สายไฟส่วนขยาย săai-fai-sùuan-kà~yǎai [เส้น sên]

extensive *adj.* (broad) กว้างขวาง gwâang-kwǎang

extent *n.* (range) ขอบเขต kɔ̀ɔp-kèet

exterior *adj.* ข้างนอก kâang-nɔ̂ɔk

exterior *n.* ภายนอก paai-nɔ̂ɔk

external *adj.* ด้านนอก dâan-nɔ̂ɔk, ภายนอก paai-nɔ̂ɔk

extinct *adj.* (e.g. fire, volcano) ดับ dàp | (e.g. species) สูญพันธุ์ sǔun-pan

extinguish *vt.* (put out) ดับ dàp

extinguisher *n.* (device) เครื่องดับเพลิง krûuang-dàp-pləəng [เครื่อง krûuang]

extort *vt.* ข่มขู่ kòm-kùu

extortion *n.* (e.g. for money) การขู่กรรโชก gaan-kùu-gan-chôok

extra *adj.* (additional) เพิ่มเติม pɔ̂əm-dtəəm | (special) พิเศษ pí-sèet

extra *n.* (minor actor) ตัวประกอบ dtuua-bprà~gɔ̀ɔp [ตัว dtuua]

extract *vt.* (distill) สกัด sà~gàt | (e.g. tooth, tree) ถอน tɔ̌ɔn

extradite *vt.* ส่ง_ข้ามแดน sòng-_-kâam-dɛɛn

extraordinary *adj.* (e.g. costs, authority) พิเศษ pí-sèet | (remarkable) ยอดเยี่ยม yɔ̂ɔt-yîiam

extravagant *adj.* ฟุ่มเฟือย fûm-fɯɯai, สุรุ่ยสุร่าย sù~rûi-sù~râai

extreme *adj.* (ultimate) ที่สุด tîi-sùt, สุดขีด sùt-kìit

extremely *adv.* (lots) จัด jàt, ยิ่ง yîng ✒ | (overwhelmingly) อย่างมาก yàang-mâak

extremist *n.* พวกหัวรุนแรง pûak-hǔua-run-rɛɛng [คน kon]

extrovert *n.* คนชอบสังคม kon-chɔ̂ɔp-sǎng-kom [คน kon]

eye *n.* (organ of sight) ตา dtaa [ข้าง kâang (one side), คู่ kûu (pair)]

eyeball *n.* ลูกตา lûuk-dtaa

[ลูก lûuk]

eyebrow *n.* คิ้ว kíu [คู่ kûu (pair)]

eyebrow pencil *n.* ดินสอเขียนคิ้ว din-sɔ̌ɔ-kǐian-kíu [แท่ง tɛ̂ng]

eye drop *n.* ยาหยอดตา yaa-yɔ̀ɔt-dtaa

eyeglasses *n.* แว่นตา wɛ̂n-dtaa [อัน an]

eyelash *n.* ขนตา kǒn-dtaa [เส้น sên]

eyelash curler *n.* ที่ดัดขนตา tîi-dàt-kǒn-dtaa [อัน an]

eyelid *n.* เปลือกตา bplʉ̀ak-dtaa

eye liner *n.* ที่เขียนขอบตา tîi-kǐian-kɔ̀ɔp-dtaa [แท่ง tɛ̂ng]

eye shadow *n.* อายชาโดว์ aai-chaa-dôo [ตลับ dtà~làp (compact)]

eyesight *n.* สายตา sǎai-dtaa

eye socket *n.* เบ้าตา bâo-dtaa [ข้าง kâang]

eyewitness *n.* ประจักษ์พยาน bprà~jàk-pá~yaan ! [คน kon]

F

fable *n.* นิทาน ní-taan [เรื่อง rʉ̂ang]

fabric *n.* (cloth) ผ้า pâa [ชิ้น chín, ผืน pʉ̌ʉn]

face *n.* (human) หน้า nâa [หน้า nâa] | (side) ด้าน dâan [ด้าน dâan]

face *vt.* (accept) ยอมรับ yɔɔm-ráp | (confront) เผชิญหน้า pà~chəən-nâa

facelift *n.* (plastic surgery) การดึงหน้า gaan-dʉng-nâa

facet *n.* (aspect) แง่มุม ngɛ̂ɛ-mum [ด้าน dâan]

facet *vt.* (gem) เจียระไน jiia-rá~nai

facility *n.* (amenity, equipment) สิ่งอำนวยความสะดวก sìng-am-nuuai-kwaam-sà~dùuak ! [สิ่ง sìng] | (building) อาคาร aa-kaan [หลัง lǎng]

fact *n.* (one item) ข้อเท็จจริง kɔ̂ɔ-tét-jing [ข้อ kɔ̂ɔ] | (reality) เรื่องจริง rʉ̂ang-jing

[เรื่อง rûuang]

factor *n.* (element) ปัจจัย bpàt-jai [ปัจจัย bpàt-jai ⚹, อย่าง yàang]

factory *n.* โรงงาน roong-ngaan [แห่ง hèng]

factual *adj.* (real) ที่แท้จริง tîi-téɛ-jing

faculty *n.* (department) คณะ ká~ná [คณะ ká~ná] | (teaching staff) คณะอาจารย์ ká~ná-aa-jaan [คณะ ká~ná]

fade *vi.* (dim) จางลง jaang-long | (disappear gradually) เลือน lɯɯan | (lose freshness) เหี่ยว hìiao

fag see cigarette

faggot *n.* (homosexual man) กะเทย gà~təəi, เกย์ gee [คน kon]

fail *vi.* ล้มเหลว lóm-lěeo | (test) สอบตก sɔ̀ɔp-dtòk

failure *n.* ความล้มเหลว kwaam-lóm-lěeo

faint *vi.* (pass out) เป็นลม bpen-lom, หมดสติ mòt-sà~dtì ⚹

fair *adj.* (beautiful) สวย sǔuai | (color) สีอ่อน sǐi-

ว่ว่า | (just) ยุติธรรม yút-dtì-tam

fair *n.* (exhibition) งานออกร้าน ngaan-ɔ̀ɔk-ráan, งาน ngaan ⚹ [งาน ngaan]

fairness *n.* ความยุติธรรม kwaam-yú-dtì-tam

fair weather *n.* อากาศดี aa-gàat-dii

fairy *n.* นางฟ้า naang-fáa [องค์ ong]

fairy tale *n.* (story) เทพนิยาย têep-ní-yaai [เรื่อง rûuang]

faith *n.* (belief) ความเชื่อ kwaam-chɯ̂ua | (belief in religion) ศรัทธา sàt-taa

faithful *adj.* (devout) มีความศรัทธา mii-kwaam-sàt-taa | (loyal) จงรักภักดี jong-rák-pák-dii | (to lover) ใจเดียว jai-diiao, ไม่นอกใจ mâi-nɔ̂ɔk-jai

fake *adj.* ปลอม bplɔɔm, เก๊ gée ⚹

falcon *n.* (bird) เหยี่ยว yìiao [ตัว dtuua]

fall *n.* (autumn) ฤดูใบไม้ร่วง rɯ́-duu-bai-

fall vi. (drop) ตก dtòk, ตกลง dtòk-long, ร่วง rûuang

fall apart vi. (collapse, e.g. chair) พัง pang

fall asleep vi. หลับ làp

fall down vi. (e.g. building) พังลง pang-long | (tumble) ล้มลง lóm-long

falling tone n. เสียงโท sĭiang-too [เสียง sĭiang]

fall in love vi. ตกหลุมรัก dtòk-lŭm-rák

fallopian tube n. ปีกมดลูก bpìik-mót-lûuk [ข้าง kâang]

false adj. (fake) ปลอม bplɔɔm | (untrue) เท็จ tét

false teeth n. ฟันปลอม fan-bplɔɔm [ซี่ sîi (each one), ชุด chút (set)]

falsify vt. ปลอมแปลง bplɔɔm-bplɛɛng

fame n. ชื่อเสียง chûu-sĭiang

familiar adj. (intimate) สนิทสนม sà~nìt-sà~nŏm | (knowing about) คุ้นเคย kún-kəəi, รู้จัก rúu-jàk |

(well-known, common) เป็นที่รู้จักดี bpen-tîi-rúu-jàk-dii

family n. (people) ครอบครัว krɔ̂ɔp-kruua [ครอบครัว krɔ̂ɔp-kruua] | (plant or animal) พันธุ์ pan [พันธุ์ pan]

family name n. นามสกุล naam-sà~gun [อัน an]

family planning n. การวางแผนครอบครัว gaan-waang-pɛ̆ɛn-krɔ̂ɔp-kruua

famine n. ความขาดแคลนอาหาร kwaam-kàat-klɛɛn-aa-hăan

famous adj. ขึ้นชื่อ kɨ̂n-chûu, ดัง dang, เป็นที่รู้จัก bpen-tîi-rúu-jàk, มีชื่อเสียง mii-chûu-sĭiang

fan n. (electric) พัดลม pát-lom [ตัว dtuua, เครื่อง krûuang] | (hand) พัด pát [เล่ม lêm]

fan vt. (someone) พัดให้ pát-hâi

fanatic n. ผู้คลั่งไคล้ pûu-klâng-klái

fancy *adj.* (luxurious) หรูหรา rǔu-rǎa

fancy *vt.* (be attracted to) หลงใหล lǒng-lǎi | (suppose, guess) ทาย taai | (want) ต้องการ dtông-gaan

fang *n.* เขี้ยว kîiao [ซี่ sîi]

fantastic *adj.* เยี่ยมยอด yîiam-yɔ̂ɔt

fantasy *adj.* (e.g. book, movie) ที่เต็มไปด้วยความเพ้อฝัน tîi-dtem-bpai-dûuai-kwaam-pə́ə-fǎn

fantasy *n.* (wild imagination) ความเพ้อฝัน kwaam-pə́ə-fǎn

far *adj.* (distant) ไกล glai, ห่างไกล hàang-glai 🐾 | (more distant) ที่ไกลกว่า tîi-glai-gwàa

far *adv.* (to great distance) ไกล glai, ห่างไกล hàang-glai 🐾

farang *n.* (Caucasian) ฝรั่ง fà~ràng 🐾 [คน kon]

far apart *adj.* ห่างกัน hàang-gan

fare *n.* ค่าโดยสาร kâa-dooi-sǎan, ค่ารถ kâa-rót 🐾

Far East *n.* ตะวันออกไกล dtà~wan-ɔ̀ɔk-glai [แถบ tɛ̀ɛp]

farewell *n.* การลาจาก gaan-laa-jàak

farm *n.* (animal) ฟาร์ม faam [ฟาร์ม faam] | (crop) ไร่ râi [ที่ tîi, แห่ง hɛ̀ng, ผืน pʉ̌ʉn]

farm *vi.* (animal) เลี้ยงสัตว์ líiang-sàt | (crop) เพาะปลูก pɔ́-bplùuk | (rice) ทำนา tam-naa

farmer *n.* เกษตรกร gà~sèet-dtà~gɔɔn ♀ [คน kon] | (animal) เจ้าของฟาร์มสัตว์ jâo-kɔ̌ɔng-faam-sàt [คน kon] | (non-rice crop) ชาวไร่ chaao-râi [คน kon] | (rice) ชาวนา chaao-naa [คน kon]

Farsi *n.* ภาษาของชาวอิหร่าน paa-sǎa-kɔ̌ɔng-chaao-ì~ràan [ภาษา paa-sǎa]

farsighted *adj.* (longsighted) สายตายาว sǎai-dtaa-yaao

fart *n.* ตด dtòt

fart *vi.* ตด dtòt, ผายลม păai-lom ‼

farther *adj.* (more distant) ไกลกว่า glai-gwàa

farther *adv.* เลย ləəi

fascinated *adj.* (amazed) ตะลึง dtà~lɯng

fascinating *adj.* (amazing) น่าตะลึง nâa-dtà~lɯng

fashion *n.* (clothing, popularity) แฟชั่น fɛɛ-chân [ชนิด chá~nít (kind), ประเภท bprà~pêet (kind)] | (popularity) ความนิยม kwaam-ní-yom

fashionable *adj.* ทันสมัย tan-sà~măi

fast *adj.* รวดเร็ว rûuat-reo, เร็ว reo, ไว wai

fast *vi.* อดอาหาร òt-aa-hăan

fasten *vt.* (e.g. belt) รัด rát | (e.g. button) ติด dtìt | (hold tightly) ยึด yɯt

fast food *n.* อาหารจานด่วน aa-hăan-jaan-dùuan [ชนิด chá~nít, ประเภท bprà~pêet]

fat *adj.* อ้วน ûuan, ตุ้ยนุ้ย dtûi-núi ✏

fat *n.* ไขมัน kăi-man

fatal *adj.* (deadly) ถึงชีวิต tɯng-chii-wít

fate *n.* (bad luck) เคราะห์ krɔ́ | (destiny) ชะตา chá~dtaa, โชคชะตา chôok-chá~dtaa

father *n.* พ่อ pɔ̂ɔ, บิดา bì-daa ‼ [คน kon] | (Chinese Thai) ป๋า bpǎa [คน kon] | (Christian priest) บาทหลวง bàat-lŭuang, หลวงพ่อ lŭuang-pɔ̂ɔ [คน kon]

father-in-law *n.* (husband's father) พ่อปู่ pɔ̂ɔ-bpùu [คน kon] | (wife's father) พ่อตา pɔ̂ɔ-dtaa [คน kon]

Father's Day *n.* วันพ่อ wan-pɔ̂ɔ [วัน wan]

fatigue *n.* (exhaustion) ความเหน็ดเหนื่อย kwaam-nèt-nɯ̀uai

fatten *vi.* อ้วนขึ้น ûuan-kɯ̂n

fatten *vt.* ทำให้_อ้วน tam-hâi-_-ûuan

faucet *n.* ก๊อกน้ำ gɔ́k-náam [ก๊อก gɔ́k]

fault *n.* (defect)

ข้อบกพร่อง kɔ̂ɔ-bòk-prɔ̂ɔng [ข้อ kɔ̂ɔ, ประการ bprà~gaan ‼] | (mistake) ความผิดพลาด kwaam-pìt-plâat

fauna n. (of a region) สัตว์ท้องถิ่น sàt-tɔ́ɔng-tìn [ตัว dtuua]

favor n. (help) ความช่วยเหลือ kwaam-chûuai-lᵿa | (kindness) บุญคุณ bun-kun

favorable adj. เป็นที่ชื่นชอบ bpen-tîi-chᵿᵿn-chɔ̂ɔp

favorite adj. ชอบที่สุด chɔ̂ɔp-tîi-sùt, โปรด bpròot

favorite n. (thing) ของโปรด kɔ̌ɔng-bpròot [ชิ้น chín, อัน an]

fawn n. (baby deer) ลูกกวาง lûuk-gwaang [ตัว dtuua]

fax n. แฟกซ์ fɛ́k, โทรสาร too-rá~sǎan ‼ [เครื่อง krᵿᵿang (machine), แผ่น pɛ̀n (paper)]

fax vt. (someone) ส่งแฟกซ์ให้กับ sòng-fɛ́k-

hâi-gàp | (something) ส่งแฟกซ์ sòng-fɛ́k

fear v. (be afraid of) กลัว gluua, เกรงกลัว greeng-gluua ‼

fearful adj. (cowardly) ขลาด klàat

fearless adj. (brave) กล้าหาญ glâa-hǎn

feast n. (party) งานเลี้ยง ngaan-líiang [งาน ngaan]

feather n. (bird) ขนนก kǒn-nók [เส้น sên]

feature n. (of face) หน้าตา nâa-dtaa | (special characteristic) ลักษณะเฉพาะ lák-sà~nà-chà~pɔ́ [ลักษณะ lák-sà~nà]

feature vt. (highlight) ทำให้_เด่นชัด tam-hâi-_-dèn-chát

February n. กุมภาพันธ์ gum-paa-pan [เดือน dᵿᵿan]

feces n. มูล muun ‼, ขี้ kîi 💩 [กอง gɔɔng, ก้อน gɔ̂ɔn] | อุจจาระ ùt-jaa-rá ‼ [กอง gɔɔng (pile), ก้อน gɔ̂ɔn]

federal government n.

รัฐบาลกลาง rát-tà~baan-glaang

federation *n.* สหพันธรัฐ sà~hà-pan-tá~rát [กลุ่ม glùm]

fee *n.* ค่า kâa | (admission) ค่าผ่านประตู kâa-pàan-bprà~dtuu | (service charge) ค่าบริการ kâa-bɔɔ-rí~gaan

feeble *adj.* (weak) อ่อนแรง ɔ̀ɔn-rɛɛng

feed *vt.* (give food to) เลี้ยง líiang, ให้อาหาร hâi-aa-hǎan | (hand-feed) ป้อน bpɔ̂ɔn

feedback *n.* การตอบกลับ gaan-dtɔ̀ɔp glàp

feel *vi.* (e.g. angry, warm, hurt) รู้สึก rúu-sừk

feel *vt.* (examine by touch) จับ jàp, แตะ dtɛ̀, สัมผัส sǎm-pàt !

feel better *vi.* รู้สึกดีขึ้น rúu-sừk-dii-kừn

feeling *n.* (emotion) อารมณ์ aa-rom | (emotion, texture) ความรู้สึก kwaam-rúu-sừk

feel pain *vi.* เจ็บปวด jèp-bpùuat

feel worse *vi.* รู้สึกแย่ลง rúu-sừk-yɛ̂ɛ-long

feign *vt.* แกล้ง glɛ̂ɛng

fell *vt.* (e.g. a tree) โค่น kôon, ล้ม lóm

fellow *adj.* อยู่ในกลุ่มเดียวกัน yùu-nai-glùm-diiao-gan

fellow *n.* (peer, equal) คนในกลุ่มเดียวกัน kon-nai-glùm-diiao-gan [คน kon]

felony *n.* โทษอาญาสถานหนัก tôot-aa-yaa-sà~tǎan-nàk

felt *n.* (cloth) ผ้าสักหลาด pâa-sàk-gà~làat [ผืน pừn]

female *n.* (animal) ตัวเมีย dtuua-miia [ตัว dtuua] | (gender) เพศหญิง pêet-yǐng [เพศ pêet] | (woman) ผู้หญิง pûu-yǐng [คน kon]

feminist *n.* ผู้เรียกร้องสิทธิสตรี pûu-ríiak-rɔ́ɔng-sìt-tí-sà~dtrii [คน kon]

fence *n.* รั้ว rúua [รั้ว rúua, อัน an ✏]

fencing *n.* (sports)

การฟันดาบ gaan-fan-dàap

fender n. (cushioning device) เครื่องกันกระแทก krûuang-gan-grà~têek [เครื่อง krûuang] | (wheel mudguard) บังโคลนครอบล้อ bang-kloon-krɔ̂ɔp-lɔ́ɔ [อัน an]

feng shui n. ฮวงจุ้ย huuang-jûi

fennel n. ยี่หร่า yîi-ràa [ต้น dtôn (plant), ใบ bai (leave)]

ferment v. (e.g. yeast) หมัก màk

fern n. เฟิร์น fəən [ต้น dtôn (plant), ใบ bai (leaf)]

ferocious adj. (savage) ป่าเถื่อน bpàa-tùuan

Ferris wheel n. ชิงช้าสวรรค์ ching-cháa-sà~wǎn [เครื่อง krûuang]

ferry n. (boat) เรือข้ามฟาก ruua-kâam-fâak [ลำ lam]

fertile adj. (able to reproduce) ให้ลูกได้ hâi-lûuk-dâai | (e.g. soil, region) อุดมสมบูรณ์ ù-dom-sǒm-buun

fertilize vt. (impregnate) ผสมพันธุ์ pà~sǒm-pan | (spread fertilizer on) ใส่ปุ๋ย sài-bpǔi

fertilizer n. ปุ๋ย bpǔi [ชนิด chá~nít (type), กระสอบ grà~sɔ̀ɔp (sack)]

festival n. งานฉลอง ngaan-chà~lɔ̌ɔng, งานประเพณี ngaan-bprà~pee-nii, งาน ngaan ● [งาน ngaan]

festive adj. (merry) สนุกสนาน sà~nùk-sà~nǎn

fetch vt. (_ (someone) to here) พา_มา paa-_-maa | (something) ไปหยิบ_มา bpai-yìp-_-maa

fetus n. ตัวอ่อนในครรภ์ dtuua-ɔ̀ɔn-nai-kan [ตัว dtuua]

fever n. ไข้ kâi [ชนิด chá~nít]

few adj. น้อย nɔ́ɔi, เล็กน้อย lék-nɔ́ɔi, นิดเดียว nít-diiao ●

fiancé n. คู่หมั้น kûu-mân [คน kon]

fiancée see fiancé

fiber n. ไฟเบอร์ fai-bəə,

ใย yai, เส้นใย sên-yai

fiberglass *n.* ใยแก้ว yai-gɛ̂ɛo

fickle *adj.* (unfaithful) หลายใจ lǎai-jai

fiction *n.* (novel) นวนิยาย ná~wá-ní-yaai ! [เรื่อง rûuang]

fictitious *adj.* สมมุติ sǒm-mút

fiddle *n.* (violin) ซอ rɔɔ [คัน kan]

fiddle *vi.* (with hands) ส่ายมือไปมา sàai-mɯɯ-bpai-maa

fiddle with *vt.* (tinker, adjust) เล่นกับ lên-gàp

fidelity *n.* (e.g. audio, video) ความคมชัด kwaam-kom-chát | (e.g. to loved one, company) ความซื่อสัตย์ kwaam-sɯ̂ɯ-sàt

field *n.* (grounds) สนาม sà~nǎam [แห่ง hɛ̀ng] | (non-rice crop) ไร่ râi [ที่ tîi, แห่ง hɛ̀ng, ผืน pʉ̌ʉn] | (type of work) วงการ wong-gaan [วงการ wong-gaan]

fierce *adj.* (cruel) ดุร้าย

dù-ráai | (intense, e.g. winds, competition) รุนแรง run-rɛɛng | (wild, savage, hostile) ป่าเถื่อน bpàa-tʉ̀ʉan

fifteen *numb.* สิบห้า sìp-hâa

fifth *adj.* ที่ห้า tîi-hâa

fig *n.* (fruit) มะเดื่อ má~dʉ̀ʉa [ลูก lûuk]

fight *n.* (battle) สงคราม sǒng-kraam | (disagreement) ความขัดแย้ง kwaam-kàt-yɛ́ɛng | (e.g. hand-to-hand, illness) การต่อสู้ gaan-dtɔ̀ɔ-sûu

fight *vt.* (argue with) ทะเลาะกับ tá~lɔ́-gàp | (compete) สู้ sûu | (e.g. hand-to-hand, illness) ต่อสู้ dtɔ̀ɔ-sûu

fighter *n.* นักสู้ nák-sûu [คน kon]

figure *n.* (diagram, picture) ภาพประกอบ pâap-bprà~gɔ̀ɔp [อัน an] | (number) ตัวเลข dtuua-lêek [ตัว dtuua] | (person's shape) รูปร่าง rûup-râang

figure 206 **final**

figure vt. (think, suppose) คิด kít

figure out vt. (solve) คิด_ออก kít-_-ɔ̀ɔk

filament n. (fiber) เส้นใย sên-yai

file n. (folder) ไฟล์ fai ● [ไฟล์ fai] | (folder) แฟ้ม fέm [แฟ้ม fέm] | (nail, metal) ตะไบ dtà~bai [เล่ม lêm, อัน an]

file vt. (e.g. taxes, report) ยื่น yûun | (put in a folder) จัด_เข้าแฟ้ม jàt-_-kâo-fέm | (smooth with a file) ตะไบ dtà~bai

fill vi. (become full) เต็ม dtem

fill vt. (e.g. liquid, air (object is substance filled)) เติม dtəəm | (put objects into) ใส่ใน sài-nai

fillet n. (meat without bone) ชิ้นเนื้อที่ไม่มีกระดูก chín-núua-tîi-mâi-mii-grà~dùuk [ชิ้น chín]

fill in for vt. (substitute) ทำหน้าที่แทน tam-nâa-tîi-tɛɛn

filling n. (dental procedure) การอุดฟัน gaan-ùt-fan | (e.g. sweets, buns) ไส้ sâi [ชนิด chá~nít]

fill out vt. (document) กรอก grɔ̀ɔk

fill up vt. (add more (object is substance filled)) เติม dtəəm | (all the way (object is container)) ทำให้_เต็ม tam-hâi-_-dtem

film n. (for camera) ฟิล์ม fiim [แผ่น pɛ̀n (piece), ม้วน múuan (roll)] | (membrane) เยื่อบางๆ yûua-baang-baang | (movie) หนัง nǎng, ภาพยนตร์ pâap-pá~yon ● [เรื่อง rûuang]

film vt. (with camera) ถ่าย tàai

filter n. เครื่องกรอง krûuang-grɔɔng [เครื่อง krûuang]

filter v. กรอง grɔɔng

filthy adj. (dirty) โสโครก sǒo-krôok

fin n. (of a fish) ครีบปลา krîip-bplaa [ครีบ krîip]

final adj. (last, decisive)

สุดท้าย sùt-táai

final n. (exam) ไฟนอล fai-nɔɔn 🔊

finalist n. ผู้เข้ารอบสุดท้าย pûu-kâo-rɔ̂ɔp-sùt-táai [คน kon]

finally adv. ในที่สุด nai-tîi-sùt

finance n. การเงิน gaan-ngən

financial adj. ทางการเงิน taang-gaan-ngən

find vt. (by surprise, after looking) พบ póp, เจอ jəə 🔊

find out vt. (discover) ค้นพบ kón-póp

fine adj. (e.g. good, quality) ดี dii | (feeling well) สบายดี sà~baai-dii | (small-grained) ละเอียด lá~iiat

fine n. (penalty) ค่าปรับ kâa-bpràp

fine v. ปรับ bpràp

fine weather see fair weather

finger n. นิ้ว níu, นิ้วมือ níu-mɯɯ [นิ้ว níu]

fingernail n. เล็บมือ lép-mɯɯ [เล็บ lép]

fingerprint n. ลายนิ้วมือ laai-níu-mɯɯ [ลาย laai]

fingertip n. ปลายนิ้ว bplaai-níu [ที่ tîi]

finish vi. จบ jòp, สิ้นสุด sîn-sùt

finish vt. (e.g. task) ทำ_ให้เสร็จ tam-_-hâi-sèt

finish line n. เส้นชัย sên-chai [จุด jùt]

Finland n. ฟินแลนด์ fin-lɛɛn [ประเทศ bprà~têet]

fire n. ไฟ fai

fire vt. (from job) ไล่_ออก lâi-_-ɔ̀ɔk | (pull the trigger) ยิง ying

fire alarm n. สัญญาณเตือนไฟไหม้ sǎn-yaan-dtɯɯan-fai-mâi [ตัว dtuua]

firearm n. อาวุธปืน aa-wút-bpɯɯn [กระบอก grà~bɔ̀ɔk]

firecracker n. ประทัด bprà~tát [ดอก dɔ̀ɔk (one), ตับ dtàp (row)]

fired adj. (lost job) ถูกไล่ออก tùuk-lâi-ɔ̀ɔk

fire escape n. ทางหนีไฟ taang-nǐi-fai [ทาง taang]

fire extinguisher *n.*
เครื่องดับเพลิง krûuang-
dàp-pləəng [เครื่อง
krûuang]

firefighter *n.*
พนักงานดับเพลิง pá~
nák-ngaan-dàp-pləəng
[คน kon]

firefly *n.* หิ่งห้อย hìng-hɔ̂i
[ตัว dtuua]

fire hydrant *n.*
ก๊อกน้ำดับเพลิง gɔ́k-
náam-dàp-pləəng [อัน
an]

fireplace *n.* เตาผิง dtao-
pǐng [เตา dtao]

fireproof *adj.* กันไฟ gan-
fai, ทนไฟ ton-fai

fire station *n.*
สถานีดับเพลิง sà~tǎa-nii-
dàp-pləəng [สถานี sà~
tǎa-nii]

fire truck *n.* รถดับเพลิง
rót-dàp-pləəng [คัน kan]

firewood *n.* ฟืน fuun
[ท่อน tɔ̂n (piece)]

firework *n.* ดอกไม้ไฟ
dɔ̀ɔk-mái-fai [ตับ dtàp
(row), ลูก lûuk, นัด nát]

firm *adj.* (hard) แข็ง kɛ̌ng

| (stable) มั่นคง mân-
kong | (tight) แน่น nɛ̂n

firm *n.* (company) บริษัท
bɔɔ-rí~sàt [แห่ง hɛ̀ng]

first *adj.* (earlier) ก่อน
gɔ̀ɔn | (initial) แรก rɛ̂ɛk |
(number one) ที่หนึ่ง tîi-
nɯ̀ng

first *adv.* (earlier) ก่อน
gɔ̀ɔn

first aid *n.*
การปฐมพยาบาล gaan-
bpà~tǒm-pá~yaa-baan

first aid kit *n.*
ชุดปฐมพยาบาล chút-
bpà~tǒm-pá~yaa-baan
[ชุด chút]

first name *n.* ชื่อ chûɯ,
ชื่อตัว chûɯ-dtuua [ชื่อ
chûɯ]

first time *n.* ครั้งแรก
kráng-rɛ̂ɛk [ครั้ง kráng]

fiscal *adj.* (financial)
เกี่ยวกับการเงิน gìiao-
gàp-gaan-ngən

fish *n.* ปลา bplaa [ตัว
dtuua]

fish *vi.* (catch fish) ตกปลา
dtòk-bplaa

fish ball *n.* ลูกชิ้นปลา

lûuk-chín-bplaa [ลูก lûuk]

fish cake *n.* ทอดมันปลา
tɔ̂ɔt-man-bplaa [ชิ้น chín]

fisherman *n.* ชาวประมง
chaao-bprà~mong ! [คน
kon]

fishery *n.* การประมง
gaan-bprà~mong !

fish hook *n.* เบ็ดตกปลา
bèt-dtòk-bplaa [คัน kan]

fishing *n.* การตกปลา
gaan-dtòk-bplaa

fishing net *n.* แห hɛ̌ɛ, อวน
uuan [ปาก bpàak]

fishing rod *n.* คันเบ็ด
kan-bèt [คัน kan]

fish sauce *n.* น้ำปลา
nám-bplaa [ขวด kùuat
(bottle)]

fishtail *vi.* แกว่งไปมา
gwèng-bpai-maa,
ส่ายไปมา sàai-bpai-maa

fishy *adj.* (in smell) คาว
kaao | (suspicious)
น่าสงสัย nâa-sǒng-sǎi

fist *n.* กำปั้น gam-bpân
[กำปั้น gam-bpân]

fistfight *n.* การชกต่อย
gaan-chók-dtòi

fit *adj.* (in good shape)

ฟิต fít

fit *vi.* (clothes) ใส่พอดี
sài-pɔɔ-dii | (have
correct shape)
มีขนาดพอเหมาะ mii-kà~
nàat-pɔɔ-mɔ̀

fit in *vt.* (make space for)
จัดที่ให้ jàt-tîi-hâi | (make
time for) จัดเวลาให้ jàt-
wee-laa-hâi

fit in with *vt.* (match,
accord) เข้ากับ kâo-gàp

fitting *adj.* (appropriate)
เหมาะ mɔ̀

five *numb.* ห้า hâa

fix *vt.* (establish) กำหนด
gam-nòt | (repair) ซ่อม
sɔ̂m

flabby *adj.* หย่อนยาน
yɔ̀n-yaan

flag *n.* ธง tong [ผืน pǔɯn]

flake *n.* (small pieces)
ชิ้นเล็กๆ chín-lék-lék [ชิ้น
chín]

flame *n.* เปลวไฟ bpleeo-
fai [อัน an]

flannel *n.* สักหลาด sàk-
gà~làat [ผืน pǔɯn]

flap *n.* (cover) ปก bpòk
[ใบ bai, แผ่น pèn]

flap *vt.* (e.g. wings) กระพือ

grà~puu

flare n. (emergency light)
ไฟเตือนภัย fai-dtuuan-pai

flash n. (camera unit)
แฟลช flɛ́t

flash vi. (emit burst)
ส่องแสงวาบ sòng-sɛ̌ɛng-
wâap

flash card n. การ์ดคำศัพท์
gáat-kam-sàp [แผ่น pɛ̀n]

flash flood n.
น้ำท่วมฉับพลัน nám-
tûuam-chàp-plan

flashing adj. วูบวาบ
wûup-wâap

flashlight n. ไฟฉาย fai-
chǎai [กระบอก grà~bɔ̀ɔk,
อัน an]

flashy adj. (e.g. color,
clothing) ฉูดฉาด chùut-
chàat | (luxurious) หรูหรา
rǔu-rǎa

flask n. (flat container)
ขวดแบน kùuat-bɛɛn
[ขวด kùuat]

flat adj. (e.g. surface) ราบ
râap | (e.g. tire) แบน bɛn

flat n. (apartment) แฟลต
flɛ́t [หลัง lǎng, แฟลต flɛ́t]

flatter vt. (compliment)
ประจบ bprà~jòp

flaunt vt. โอ้อวด ôo-ùuat

flavor n. (taste) รส rót,
รสชาติ rót-châat [รส rót]

flavor vt. ปรุงรส bprung-
rót

flaw n. (defect) ตำหนิ
dtam-nì [แห่ง hɛ̀ng] |
(fault) ข้อกพร่อง kɔ̂ɔ-
bòk-prɔ̂ng [ข้อ kɔ̂ɔ,
ประการ bprà~gaan !]

flawless adj. ไม่มีที่ติ
mâi-mii-tîi-dtì

flea n. หมัด màt [ตัว
dtuua]

flea market n.
ตลาดขายของเก่า dtà~
làat-kǎai-kɔ̌ɔng-gào
[แห่ง hɛ̀ng]

flee v. หนี nǐi, หลบหนี
lòp-nǐi

fleet n. (military airplanes)
กองทัพอากาศ gɔɔng-
táp-aa-gàat [กอง gɔɔng]
| (military ships)
กองทัพเรือ gɔɔng-táp-
ruua [กอง gɔɔng]

flesh n. (soft part of fruit,
body) เนื้อ núua [ชิ้น chín]

flex v. งอ ngɔɔ

flexible adj. ยืดหยุ่น
yûut-yùn

flier n. (pamphlet) ใบปลิว

bai-bpliu [ใบ bai, แผ่น pèn]

flight *n.* (airplane) เที่ยวบิน tîiao-bin [เที่ยว tîiao]

flight attendant *n.* พนักงานบริการบน เครื่องบิน pá~nák-ngaan-bɔɔ-rí~gaan-bon-krûuang-bin [คน kon]

flight schedule *n.* ตารางการบิน dtaa-raang-gaan-bin [ตาราง dtaa-raang]

flimsy *adj.* (frail) บอบบาง bɔ̀ɔp-baang

fling *vt.* (throw) เหวี่ยง wìiang

flip *v.* (turn over) คว่ำ kwâm

flip *vi.* (somersault) ตีลังกา dtii-lang-gaa

flip *vt.* (e.g. coin) โยน yoon

flip-flop *n.* (shoes) รองเท้าแตะ rɔɔng-táao-dtɛ̀ [ข้าง kâang (one), คู่ kûu (pair)]

flipper *n.* (diving fin) ตีนกบ dtiin-gòp [ข้าง

kâang (one), คู่ kûu (pair)]

flirt *vi.* (woo) จีบ jìip

flirty *adj.* เจ้าชู้ jâo-chúu, ขี้หลี kîi-lǐi ☙

float *n.* (buoy) ทุ่น tûn [อัน an] | (parade) รถในขบวนแห่ rót-nai-kà~buuan-hɛ̀ɛ [คัน kan]

float *vi.* (in water, air) ลอย lɔɔi

flock *n.* (of animals) ฝูง fǔung [ฝูง fǔung]

flock *vi.* จับกันเป็นฝูง jàp-gan-bpen-fǔung

flood *n.* น้ำท่วม náam-tûuam, อุทกภัย ù-tók-gà~pai ⚠

flood *v.* (overflow) ท่วม tûuam

flooded *adj.* ท่วม tûuam

floor *n.* (of building) ชั้น chán [ชั้น chán] | (surface) พื้น púun [พื้น púun]

floppy disk *n.* แผ่นดิสก์ pèn-dít [แผ่น pèn]

flora *n.* (of a region) พืชท้องถิ่น pûut-tɔ́ɔng-tìn [ชนิด chá~nít (type), ต้น

dtôn (plant)]

florist *n.* (shop) ร้านขายดอกไม้ ráan-kǎai-dɔ̀ɔk-máai [ร้าน ráan]

flour *n.* แป้งทำอาหาร bpɛ̂ɛng-tam-aa-hǎan

flourish *vi.* (grow) งอกงาม ngɔ̀ɔk-ngaam

flow *n.* (current) กระแส grà~sɛ̌ɛ

flow *vi.* (e.g. liquid, ideas) ไหล lǎi

flower *n.* (blossom) ดอก dɔ̀ɔk, ดอกไม้ dɔ̀ɔk-máai [ดอก dɔ̀ɔk]

flowerpot *n.* กระถางดอกไม้ grà~tǎang-dɔ̀ɔk-máai [ใบ bai]

flu *n.* ไข้หวัดใหญ่ kâi-wàt-yài

fluently *adv.* (of speech) อย่างคล่องแคล่ว yàang-klɔ̂ng-klɛ̂o

fluffy *adj.* (feathery) ขนปุย kǒn-bpui, ปุย bpui | (light or airy) ฟู fuu

fluid *adj.* (liquid) เหลว lěeo

fluid *n.* (liquid) ของเหลว kɔ̌ɔng-lěeo

fluke *n.* (coincidence) ความบังเอิญ kwaam-

bang-əən

flunk *vi.* (test) สอบตก sɔ̀ɔp-dtòk

flush a toilet *vi.* กดชักโครก gòt-chák-krôok

flush toilet *n.* ชักโครก chák-krôok [อัน an]

flute *n.* ขลุ่ย klùi [เลา lao]

fly *n.* (insect) แมลงวัน má~lɛɛng-wan [ตัว dtuua]

fly *v.* บิน bin

fly a kite *vi.* ชักว่าว chák-wâao

flyover see overpass

foam *n.* (e.g. soap) ฟอง fɔɔng [ฟอง fɔɔng] | (plastic) โฟม foom

focus *n.* (central point) จุดศูนย์กลาง jùt-sǔun-glaang [จุด jùt]

focus *vi.* (concentrate) โฟกัส foo-gát ✦ | (e.g. camera) ปรับโฟกัส bpràp-foo-gát

fog *n.* หมอก mɔ̀ɔk

foggy *adj.* (e.g. mirror) ฝ้า fâa | (weather) มีหมอก mii-mɔ̀ɔk

foil *n.* (aluminum)

กระดาษอลูมิเนียม grà~
dàat-à~luu-mí-niiam
[แผ่น pèn]

fold v. พับ páp

folder n. แฟ้ม fɛ́m [แฟ้ม
fɛ́m]

folk adj. พื้นบ้าน púun-
bâan

folklore n. นิทานชาวบ้าน
ní-taan-chaao-bâan
[เรื่อง rûuang]

folk song n. (country
song) เพลงลูกทุ่ง pleeng-
lûuk-tûng [เพลง pleeng]

follow v. ตาม dtaam,
ติดตาม dtìt-dtaam |
(track, spy on) สะกดรอย
sà~gòt-rɔɔi

following adj. (later)
ต่อมา dtɔ̀ɔ-maa

follow up vi. (do more
work) ติดตามผล dtìt-
dtaam-pǒn

fond adj. (liking) ชอบ
chɔ̂ɔp

fondle vt. ลูบไล้ lûup-lái

font n. (typeface) ฟอนท์
fɔ́n [ฟอนท์ fɔ́n]

food n. ของกิน kɔ̌ɔng-gin
❀ [อย่าง yàang] | อาหาร
aa-hǎan [อย่าง yàang

(dish), ประเภท bprà~
pêet (kind)]

food poisoning n.
อาหารเป็นพิษ aa-hǎan-
bpen-pít

fool n. (dumb person)
คนโง่ kon-ngôo [คน kon]

fool vt. หลอก lɔ̀ɔk

foolish adj. (silly) ซื่อบื้อ
sûu-bûu ❀ | (stupid) โง่
ngôo

foot n. (base) ฐาน tǎan
[ฐาน tǎan] | (body part)
เท้า táao, ตีน dtiin ❀ [ข้าง
kâang (one), คู่ kûu (pair)]
| (measurement) ฟุต fút
[ฟุต fút]

football n. (American
game) อเมริกันฟุตบอล
à~mee-rí~gan-fút-bɔn
[เกม geem (game), แมตช์
mɛ̀t ❀ (match)] | (ball)
ฟุตบอล fút-bɔn [ลูก lûuk]
| (soccer game) ฟุตบอล
fút-bɔn [เกม geem
(game), แมตช์ mɛ̀t ❀
(match)]

foothill n. ตีนเขา dtiin-
kǎo ❀ [แห่ง hɛ̀ng, ที่ tîi]

footnote n. หมายเหตุ
mǎai-hèet [แห่ง hɛ̀ng]

footpath *n.* ทางเท้า taang-táao, ฟุตบาท fút-bàat [ทาง taang]

footprint *n.* รอยเท้า rɔɔi-táao, รอยตีน rɔɔi-dtiin ● [รอย rɔɔi]

for *conj.* (because) เพราะว่า prɔ́-wâa

for *prep.* (given to, sent to, for sake of) เพื่อ pûua, สำหรับ sǎm-ràp | (in favor of) เห็นด้วยกับ hěn-dûuai-gàp | (in place of) แทน tɛɛn

forbid *vt.* ห้าม hâam

force *n.* (might) แรง rɛɛng | (power, energy) กำลัง gam-lang

force *vt.* (compel) บังคับ bang-káp

forecast *n.* การพยากรณ์ gaan-pá~yaa-gɔɔn ‼

forecast *v.* ทำนาย tam-naai, ทาย taai ●, พยากรณ์ pá~yaa-gɔɔn ✖

forehead *n.* หน้าผาก nâa-pàak

foreign *adj.* ต่างชาติ dtàang-châat, ต่างประเทศ dtàang-bprà~têet

foreigner *n.* ชาวต่างชาติ chaao-dtàang-châat [คน kon]

foreman *n.* (work crew leader) หัวหน้าคนงาน hǔua-nâa-kon-ngaan [คน kon]

forensic *adj.* (used in court) ที่ใช้ในศาล tîi-chái-nai-sǎan

forensic medicine *n.* นิติเวชศาสตร์ ní-dtì-wêet-chá~sàat [วิชา wí-chaa]

forest *n.* ป่า bpàa [ป่า bpàa, แห่ง hὲng] | ป่าไม้ bpàa-máai [แห่ง hὲng]

forever *adv.* ตลอดไป dtà~lɔ̀ɔt-bpai

for example *conj.* ตัวอย่างเช่น dtuua-yàang-chên

forget *v.* ลืม lɯɯm

forgetful *adj.* ขี้ลืม kîi-lɯɯm

forgive *v.* ยกโทษ yók-tôot, ให้อภัย hâi-à~pai

fork *n.* (utensil) ส้อม sɔ̂m [คัน kan]

form *n.* (official document) แบบฟอร์ม

bὲεp-fɔɔm, ฟอร์ม fɔɔm [ใบ bai, แผ่น pὲn, ฟอร์ม fɔɔm] | (person's shape) รูปทรง rûup-song, รูปร่าง rûup-râang | (structure) รูปแบบ rûup-bὲεp [รูปแบบ rûup-bὲεp] | (structure) แบบ bὲεp [แบบ bὲεp]

form *vt.* (establish) ก่อตั้ง gɔɔ-dtâng, ตั้ง dtâng

formal *adj.* (official, proper) เป็นทางการ bpen-taang-gaan

format *n.* (appearance) รูปแบบ rûup-bὲεp [รูปแบบ rûup-bὲεp]

format *vt.* (e.g. disk, document) ฟอร์แมต fɔɔ-mὲt ✘

former *adj.* (previous) ก่อน gɔɔn, เก่า gào

formula *n.* (baby milk) นมผงสำหรับเด็ก nom-pŏng-sǎm-ràp-dèk [กระป๋อง grà~bpŏng (can)] | (e.g. chemical) สูตร sùut [สูตร sùut]

for rent *adj.* ให้เช่า hâi-châo

fort *n.* ป้อม bpɔ̂m [ป้อม

bpɔ̂m]

fortunate *adj.* โชคดี chôok-dii, เฮง heng ✿

fortune *n.* (fate) ดวง duuang | (luck) โชค chôok, โชคลาภ chôok-lâap, วาสนา wâat-sà~năa

fortuneteller *n.* หมอดู mɔ̆ɔ-duu [คน kon]

forty *numb.* สี่สิบ sìi-sìp

forum *n.* (internet) ฟอรัม fɔɔ-râm [ฟอรัม fɔɔ-râm]

forward *adv.* (not backward) ข้างหน้า kâang-nâa

forward *vt.* (e.g. letter, e-mail) ส่ง_ต่อ sòng-_-dtɔ̀ɔ

fossil *n.* (remains) ฟอสซิล fɔ́ɔt-sín [ก้อน gɔ̂ɔn, ซาก sâak]

foster child *n.* ลูกอุปถัมภ์ lûuk-ùp-bpà~tǎm [คน kon]

foster parents *n.* พ่อแม่อุปถัมภ์ pɔ̂ɔ-mε̂ε-ùp-bpà~tǎm [คน kon]

foul *adj.* (smelly) เหม็นเน่า mĕn-nâo

foul *n.* (in a game) การทำผิดกติกา gaan-tam-pìt-gà~dtì-gaa

foul *vi.* (commit a foul)
ฟาวล์ faao ✿

foundation *n.* (basis)
พื้นฐาน púun-tăan |
(cosmetics) ครีมรองพื้น
kriim-rɔɔng-púun [ชนิด
chá~nít] | (institute)
มูลนิธิ muun-lá~ní-tí
[แห่ง hèng] | (of house)
ฐาน tăan

founder *n.* ผู้ก่อตั้ง pûu-
gɔ̀ɔ-dtâng [คน kon]

fountain *n.* น้ำพุ nám-pú
[แห่ง hèng (location)]

four *numb.* สี่ sìi

fourteen *numb.* สิบสี่ sìp-
sìi

fourth *adj.* (ordinal) ที่สี่
tîi-sìi | (quarter) หนึ่งในสี่
nÙng-nai-sìi

fox *n.* หมาจิ้งจอก măa-
jîng-jɔ̀ɔk [ตัว dtuua]

fraction *n.* (numerical)
เศษส่วน sèet-sùuan
[จำนวน jam-nuuan]

fracture *n.* (break)
รอยแตก rɔɔi-dtɛ̀ɛk [รอย
rɔɔi]

fragile *adj.* (easily broken)
แตกง่าย dtɛ̀ɛk-ngâai

fragment *n.* (broken-off
part) ส่วนที่แตกออกมา
sùuan-tîi-dtɛ̀ɛk-ɔ̀ɔk-maa
[ส่วน sùuan]

fragrance *n.* (pleasant
smell) กลิ่นหอม glìn-
hɔ̌ɔm [กลิ่น glìn]

frame *n.* (e.g. picture,
window) กรอบ grɔ̀ɔp
[กรอบ grɔ̀ɔp] | (structure)
โครง kroong, โครงร่าง
kroong-râang ! [โครง
kroong]

frame *vt.* (put into a
frame) ใส่กรอบ sài-grɔ̀ɔp
| (wrongly incriminate)
ใส่ความ sài-kwaam

France *n.* ฝรั่งเศส fà~
ràng-sèet [ประเทศ
bprà~têet]

franchise *n.* (branch)
แฟรนไชส์ frɛɛn-chaai,
สาขา săa-kăa [สาขา săa-
kăa]

frank *adj.* เปิดเผย bpə̀ət-
pə̌əi

fraudulent *adj.* หลอกลวง
lɔ̀ɔk-luuang

freak *n.* (strange person)
คนประหลาด kon-bprà~

A
B
C
D
E
F
G
H
I
J
K
L
M
N
O
P
Q
R
S
T
U
V
W
X
Y
Z

làat [คน kon]

freckle n. (on the face) กระ grà [แผ่น pɛ̀n (piece), จุด jùt (spot)]

free adj. ฟรี frii ● | (independent) เป็นอิสระ bpen-ìt-sà~rà

free vt. (release) ปลดปล่อย bplòt-bplòi

freedom n. เสรีภาพ sěe-rii-pâap, อิสรภาพ ìt-sà~rá~pâap

free from adj. (without) ไร้ rái

freelance adj. อิสระ ìt-sà~rà

freephone see toll free

free radical n. อนุมูลอิสระ à-nú-muun-ìt-sà~rà

freeway n. ถนนฟรีเวย์ tà~nǒn-frii-wee ● [สาย sǎai]

free will n. ความสมัครใจ kwaam-sà~màk-jai

freeze vi. (computer) แฮ้ง hɛ́ɛng | (turns solid) แข็งตัว kěng-dtuua

freeze vt. (refrigerate) เอา_ไปแช่แข็ง ao-_-bpai-chɛ̂ɛ-kěng

freeze! interj. (don't move!) อย่าขยับ yàa-kà~

yàp

freezer n. (compartment) ช่องแช่แข็ง chɔ̂ng-chɛ̂ɛ-kěng [ช่อง chɔ̂ng]

freight n. (charge) ค่าขนส่ง kâa-kǒn-sòng

French adj. (relating to France) ฝรั่งเศส fà~ràng-sèet

French n. (language) ภาษาฝรั่งเศส paa-sǎa-fà~ràng-sèet [ภาษา paa-sǎa] | (people) ชาวฝรั่งเศส chaao-fà~ràng-sèet [คน kon]

French fry n. มันฝรั่งทอด man-fà~ràng-tɔ̂ɔt [ชิ้น chín]

French kiss n. การจูบอย่างดูดดื่ม gaan-jùup-yàang-dùut dùum

frequency n. ความถี่ kwaam-tìi [เฮิรตซ์ hə́ət]

frequent adj. ถี่ tìi, บ่อย bɔ̀i, เป็นประจำ bpen-bprà~jam

frequently adv. บ่อย bɔ̀i

fresh adj. (e.g. fruit, idea) สด sòt

freshman n. น้องใหม่

nɔ́ɔng-mài

fresh water n. น้ำจืด nám-jùut

friction n. (rubbing) การเสียดสี gaan-sìiat-sǐi

Friday n. วันศุกร์ wan-sùk [วัน wan]

fried adj. (deep fried) ทอด tɔ̂ɔt | (stir fried) ผัด pàt

friend n. เพื่อน pʉ̂ʉan, มิตร mít ☙ [คน kon]

friendly adj. เป็นมิตร bpen-mít

friendship n. มิตรภาพ mít-dtà~pâap

frighten vt. (scare) ทำให้_กลัว tam-hâi-_-gluua

frightened adj. (scared) กลัว gluua

frightening adj. น่ากลัว nâa-gluua

frill n. (of a skirt) ครุย krui, จีบ jìip

frivolous adj. ไม่จริงจัง mâi-jing-jang

frog n. กบ gòp [ตัว dtuua]

from prep. จาก jàak | (since) ตั้งแต่ dtâng-dtɛ̀ɛ

front adj. ข้างหน้า kâang-nâa, หน้า nâa

front n. (of object) ด้านหน้า dâan-nâa

frontier n. (border) ชายแดน chaai-dɛɛn, พรมแดน prom-dɛɛn [แห่ง hɛ̀ng]

front line n. แนวหน้า nɛɛo-nâa [แนว nɛɛo]

frost n. (frozen dew) น้ำค้างแข็ง nám-káang-kǐng [ก้อน gɔ̂ɔn]

frostbite n. (skin injury) แผลจากน้ำแข็ง plɛ̌ɛ-jàak-nám-kɛ̌ng [แผล plɛ̌ɛ]

frown vi. ขมวดคิ้ว kà~mùuat-kíu

frugal adj. ประหยัด bprà~yàt, มัธยัสถ์ mát-tá~yát ⚠

fruit n. (edible) ผลไม้ pǒn-lá~máai [ผล pǒn ⚠, ลูก lûuk]

fruit fly n. แมลงหวี่ má~lɛɛng-wìi [ตัว dtuua]

fruitful adj. (yielding many benefits) มีผลประโยชน์ mii-pǒn-bprà~yòot | (yielding many fruits) มีผลมาก mii-pǒn-mâak

fruitless adj. ไร้ผล rái-pǒn

frustrated *adj.*
(discouraged) ท้อแท้ tɔ́ɔ-
tɛ́ɛ

fry *n.* (French fry)
มันฝรั่งทอด man-fà~
ràng-tɔ̂ɔt [ชิ้น chín]

fry *vt.* (deep fry) ทอด tɔ̂ɔt
| (stir fry) ผัด pàt

frying pan *n.* กระทะ grà~
tá [ใบ bai]

fuck *interj.* ห่า hàa ✱

fuck *vi.* เอากัน ao-gan ✱

fuck *vt.* เย็ด yét ⚥

fuel *n.* (petrol, gasoline)
น้ำมัน nám-man
[แกลลอน gɛn-lɔn
(gallon), ลิตร lít (liter),
ขวด kùuat (bottle)]

fugitive *n.* ผู้หลบหนี pûu-
lòp-nǐi [คน kon]

full *adj.* (e.g. tank, room)
เต็ม dtem | (from eating)
อิ่ม ìm

full moon *n.*
พระจันทร์เต็มดวง prá~
jan-dtem-duuang

full of *adj.* เต็มไปด้วย
dtem-bpai-dûuai

full stop *n.* (punctuation)
จุด jùt [ตัว dtuua]

full-time *adj.* เต็มเวลา
dtem-wee-laa

fun *adj.* สนุก sà~nùk

fun *n.* (enjoyment)
ความสนุกสนาน kwaam-
sà~nùk-sà~nǎan

function *n.* (duty) ภารกิจ
paa-rá-gìt [อัน an]

function *vi.* ทำงาน tam-
ngaan, ทำหน้าที่ tam-
nâa-tîi

fund *n.* กองทุน gɔɔng-tun
[กอง gɔɔng]

fund *vt.* จัดหาทุนให้ jàt-
hǎa-tun-hâi

fundamental *adj.* (basic)
พื้นฐาน púun-tǎan

funeral *n.* งานศพ ngaan-
sòp [งาน ngaan]

fungus *n.* (e.g. infectious)
เชื้อรา chúua-raa [ตัว
dtuua] | (mildew) รา raa

funnel *n.* (utensil) กรวย
gruuai [อัน an]

funnel *vt.* (pour) กรอก
grɔ̀ɔk

funny *adj.* (humorous)
ตลก dtà~lòk, น่าขัน nâa-
kǎn | (strange) แปลก
bplɛ̀ɛk

fur *n.* ขนสัตว์ kǒn-sàt [เส้น

sên]

furious *adj.* โกรธจัด
gròot-jàt, ฉุนเฉียว chǔn-
chǐao

furnace *n.* เตาหลอม dtao-
lɔ̌ɔm [เตา dtao]

furnish *vt.* (provide _ for
_) จัดหา_ให้_ jàt-hǎa-_-
hâi-_

furniture *n.* เฟอร์นิเจอร์
fəə-ní~jɔ̀ə, เครื่องเรือน
krûuang-ruuan ! [ชิ้น
chín]

furry *adj.* (having fur)
มีขนยาว mii-kǒn-yaao

further see farther

furthermore *adv.*
ยิ่งกว่านั้น yîng-gwàa-nán

fuse *n.* (electrical, igniter)
ฟิวส์ fiu [อัน an (piece)]

fuse *vi.* (melt together)
หลอมเข้ากัน lɔ̌ɔm-kâo-
gan

fussy *adj.* (fastidious) จู้จี้
jûu-jîi

futile *adj.* (pointless)
ไม่มีประโยชน์ mâi-mii-
bprà~yòot

future *adj.* (later)
ในอนาคต nai-à~naa-kót

future *n.* อนาคต à~naa-

kót

fuzzy *adj.* (not clear)
ไม่ชัด mâi-chát

G

gable *n.* จั่ว jùua, หน้าจั่ว
nâa-jùua [จั่ว jùua, แผง
pɛ̌ɛng]

gadget *n.*
อุปกรณ์ขนาดเล็ก ùp-
bpà~gɔɔn-kà~nàat-lék
[ชิ้น chín]

gag *vi.* (choke) สำลัก sǎm-
lák

gain *n.* (profit) กำไร gam-
rai

gain *vt.* (acquire) ได้_มา
dâi-_-maa

gait *n.* ท่าเดิน tâa-dəən

galanga *n.* ข่า kàa [แง่ง
ngêng (rootstock)]

galaxy *n.* กาแล็กซี gaa-
lék-sîi [กาแล็กซี gaa-lék-
sîi]

gallery *n.* (for exhibition)
ห้องแสดงผลงาน hɔ̂ɔng-
sà~dɛɛng-pǒn-ngaan

gallon *n.* แกลลอน gɛn-lɔn

gallop *vt.* ควบ kûuap

gallows *n.* (scaffold)
ที่แขวนคอนักโทษ tîi-

kwɛ̌ɛn-kɔɔ-nák-tôot [อัน an]

gall stone *n.* นิ่ว nîu [ก้อน gɔ̂ɔn]

gamble *v.* (wager) พนัน pá~nan

gambler *n.* นักพนัน nák-pá~nan [คน kon]

gambling *n.* การพนัน gaan-pá~nan

game *n.* เกม geem [เกม geem] | (sports) กีฬา gii-laa [ชนิด chá~nít]

gang *n.* แก๊ง géng [แก๊ง géng]

gangster *n.* นักเลง nák-leeng, อันธพาล an-tá~paan [คน kon]

gap *n.* (distance) ระยะห่าง rá~yá~hàang | (space, opening) ช่อง chɔ̂ng [ช่อง chɔ̂ng]

garage *n.* (repair shop) อู่ซ่อมรถ ùu-sɔ̂m-rót [อู่ ùu] | (to store car) โรงรถ roong-rót [แห่ง hɛ̀ng]

garbage *n.* ขยะ kà~yà [ชิ้น chín (piece), กอง gɔɔng (pile)]

garbage can see trash can

garden *n.* สวน sǔuan

[สวน sǔuan]

garden *vi.* ทำสวน tam-sǔuan

gardener *n.* คนสวน kon-sǔuan [คน kon]

gargle *n.* (liquid) น้ำยาบ้วนปาก nám-yaa-bûuan-bpàak [ขวด kùuat (bottle)]

gargle *vi.* บ้วนปาก bûuan-bpàak

garland *n.* พวงมาลัย puuang-maa-lai [พวง puuang]

garlic *n.* กระเทียม grà~tiiam [หัว hǔua]

garment *n.* เสื้อผ้า sûua-pâa [ชุด chút (set), ตัว dtuua (piece)]

garnet *n.* โกเมน goo-meen ! [เม็ด mét]

gas *n.* (natural) แก๊ส gɛ́ɛt | (petrol, gasoline) น้ำมัน nám-man [แกลลอน gɛn-lɔn (gallon), ลิตร lít (liter), ขวด kùuat (bottle)]

gasoline see gas

gasp *vi.* (inhale suddenly) อ้าปากค้าง âa-bpàak-káang | (try to catch breath) หายใจหอบ hǎai-jai-hɔ̀ɔp | (under water) สำลักน้ำ săm-lák-náam

gas station n. ปั๊มน้ำมัน bpám-nám-man [ปั๊ม bpám, แห่ง hὲng]

gas stove n. เตาแก๊ส dtao-gɛ́ɛt [เตา dtao]

gate n. ประตูรั้ว bprà~ dtuu-rúua [ประตู bprà~ dtuu]

gather vi. (people) ชุมนุมกัน chum-num-gan

gather vt. (things) เก็บ_มารวมกัน gèp-_- maa-ruuam-gan

gathering n. การรวมตัว gaan-ruuam-dtuua

gaudy adj. (flashy) ฉูดฉาด chùut-chàat

gaur n. วัวกระทิง wuua- grà~ting [ตัว dtuua]

gauze n. ผ้าพันแผล pâa- pan-plɛ̆ɛ [ม้วน múuan (roll), ชิ้น chín (piece)]

gavel n. ค้อน kɔ́ɔn, ค้อนเล็ก kɔ́ɔn-lék [อัน an]

gay adj. (happy) ร่าเริง râa-rəəng | (homosexual) เกย์ gee

gay man n. กะเทย gà~

təəi, เกย์ gee [คน kon]

gaze at vt. จ้องมอง jɔ̂ng- mɔɔng

gear n. (vehicle) เกียร์ giia [ชุด chút]

gecko n. (finger-sized) จิ้งจก jîng-jòk [ตัว dtuua] | (noisy arm-sized) ตุ๊กแก dtúk-gɛɛ [ตัว dtuua]

gel n. เจล jeo | (for hair) ครีมแต่งผม kriim-dtὲng- pŏm

gem n. เพชรพลอย pét- plɔɔi [ชิ้น chín (piece), ชุด chút (set)]

Gemini n. เมถุน mee-tŭn [ราศี raa-sĭi]

gender n. เพศ pêet [เพศ pêet]

gene n. ยีน yiin [ตัว dtuua]

general adj. ทั่วไป tûua- bpai

general n. (officer) นายพล naai-pon [คน kon]

generally adv. (in general) โดยทั่วไป dooi- tûua-bpai

general manager n. ผู้จัดการทั่วไป pûu-jàt- gaan-tûua-bpai [คน kon]

generate vt. (e.g. electricity) กำเนิด gam-nəət | (e.g. problems, chemicals) สร้าง_ขึ้น sâang-_-kûn

generation n. (e.g. family, culture, design) รุ่น rûn [รุ่น rûn]

generator n. (dynamo) เครื่องกำเนิดไฟฟ้า krûuang-gam-nəət-fai-fáa [เครื่อง krûuang]

generous adj. (of things) ใจกว้าง jai-gwâang | (of things, time) มีน้ำใจ mii-nám-jai

genetics n. พันธุศาสตร์ pan-tú-sàat [วิชา wí-chaa]

genitals n. อวัยวะสืบพันธุ์ à-wai-yá~wá-sùup-pan, ของลับ kɔ̌ɔng-láp •

genius n. (person) อัจฉริยะ àt-chà-rí~yá [คน kon]

gentle adj. (e.g. wind, tap) เบา bao | (soft in manners) อ่อนโยน ʔɔ̀ɔn-yoon

gentleman n. สุภาพบุรุษ sù~pâap-bù~rút ‼ [คน kon]

genuine adj. (authentic) แท้ tɛ́ɛ

geography n. ภูมิศาสตร์ puu-mí-sàat [วิชา wí-chaa]

geology n. ธรณีวิทยา tɔɔ-rá~nii-wít-tá~yaa [วิชา wí-chaa]

geometry n. เรขาคณิต ree-kǎa-ká~nít [วิชา wí-chaa]

germ n. เชื้อโรค chúua-rôok [ชนิด chá~nít]

German n. (language) ภาษาเยอรมัน paa-sǎa-yəə rá~man [ภาษา paa-sǎa] | (person) ชาวเยอรมัน chaao-yəə-rá~man [คน kon] | (relating to Germany) เยอรมัน yəə-rá~man

Germany n. เยอรมัน yəə-rá~man [ประเทศ bprà~têet]

gesture n. (movement) ท่าทาง tâa-taang [ท่า tâa]

get vt. (receive) รับ ráp | (take) เอา ao | (take, receive) ได้ dâai | (understand) เข้าใจ kâo-jai

get along vi. เข้ากันได้ kâo-gan-dâai

get away from vt. หนีรอดจาก nǐi-rɔ̂ɔt-jàak

get back vi. (return) กลับมา glàp-maa

get back vt. (get in return, exchange) ได้_กลับมา dâai-_-glàp-maa

get dressed vi. แต่งตัว dtɛ̀ng-dtuua

get in v. (e.g. car) ขึ้น kûn

get laid vi. มีเซ็กส์ mii-sék

get lost vi. (lose one's way) หลงทาง lǒng-taang

get off v. (e.g. bus, plane) ลง long

get off vt. (e.g. boat) ออกจาก ɔ̀ɔk-jàak

get on v. (e.g. boat) ลง long | (e.g. bus, plane) ขึ้น kûn

get out vi. (leave) ออกไป ɔ̀ɔk-bpai

get out of vt. (e.g. car) ลง long

get ready vi. เตรียมพร้อม dtriiam-prɔ́ɔm

get rid of vt. กำจัด gam-jàt

get sick vi. ไม่สบาย mâi-sà~baai

get together vi. รวมตัวกัน ruuam-dtuua-gan

get up vi. (stand up) ลุก lúk | (wake up) ตื่นนอน dtùɯn-nɔɔn

get used to vt. คุ้นเคยกับ kún-kəəi-gàp, ชินกับ chin gàp

get well vi. หายป่วย hǎai-bpùai

get worse vi. ทรุดลง sút-long

geyser n. น้ำพุร้อน nám-pú-rɔ́ɔn [แห่ง hɛ̀ng]

ghetto n. เขตสลัม kèet-sà~lǎm [แห่ง hɛ̀ng]

ghost n. ปีศาจ bpii-sàat, ผี pǐi [ตัว dtuua]

ghostwriter n. นักเขียนรับจ้าง nák-kǐian-ráp-jâang [คน kon]

giant adj. มหึมา má-hɯ̀-maa

giant n. ยักษ์ yák [ตน dton]

gibbon n. ชะนี chá~nii [ตัว dtuua]

giblets n. เครื่องใน

krûuang-nai [ชิ้น chín]
gift *n.* (present) ของขวัญ
kǒong-kwǎn [ชิ้น chín] |
(talent) พรสวรรค์ pɔɔn-
sà~wǎn [อย่าง yàang]
giggle *vi.* หัวเราะคิกคัก
hǔua-rɔ́-kík-kák
gigolo *n.* จิ๊กโก๋ jík-gǒo
[คน kon]
gill *n.* เหงือก ngùuak
[เหงือก ngùuak]
gin *n.* (alcoholic
beverage) ยิน yin,
เหล้าจิน lâo-jin
ginger *n.* ขิง kǐng [แง่ง
ngêng (rootstock), หัว
hǔua (bulb)]
gingko *n.* แป๊ะก๊วย bpé-
gúuai [ต้น dtôn (plant),
ใบ bai (leave), ลูก lûuk
(nut)]
ginseng *n.* โสม sǒom [หัว
hǔua]
giraffe *n.* ยีราฟ yii-ráap
[ตัว dtuua]
girdle *n.* ผ้ารัดเอว pâa-
rát-eeo [เส้น sên] |
สายคาด sǎai-kâat [เส้น
sên, สาย sǎai]
girl *n.* เด็กหญิง dèk-yǐng

[คน kon]
girlfriend *n.* (just a friend)
เพื่อนหญิง pûuan-yǐng ❢
[คน kon] | (non-exclusive
partner) กิ๊ก gík ❀ [คน
kon] | (romantic partner)
แฟน fɛɛn, แฟนสาว fɛɛn-
sǎao [คน kon]
Girl Guide see Girl Scout
Girl Scout *n.* เนตรนารี
nêet-naa-rii [คน kon]
gist *n.* ใจความ jai-kwaam,
เนื้อหา núua-hǎa
give *vt.* ให้ hâi
give birth to *vt.* ให้กำเนิด
hâi-gam-nə̀ət ❢
give in *vi.* ยอม yɔɔm,
ยอมแพ้ yɔɔm-pɛ́ɛ
given name *n.* ชื่อตัว
chûu-dtuua, ชื่อแรก
chûu-rɛ̂ɛk [ชื่อ chûu]
give up *v.* (quit) ล้มเลิก
lóm-lə̂ək
give up *vi.* (admit defeat)
ยอมแพ้ yɔɔm-pɛ́ɛ | (lose
hope) หมดหวัง mòt-wǎng
give way *vi.* หลีกทาง lìik-
taang
glacier *n.* ธารน้ำแข็ง
taan-nám-kěng [ก้อน

gɔɔn]

glad *adj.* ดีใจ dii-jai

glance at *vt.* ชำเลืองมอง cham-lɯɯang-mɔɔng, เหลือบดู lɯ̌ɯap-duu

gland *n.* ต่อม dtɔ̀m [ต่อม dtɔ̀m]

glare *n.* (light) แสงจ้า sɛ̌ɛng-jâa

glass *n.* (drinking) แก้ว gɛ̂ɛo [ใบ bai] | (pane) กระจก grà~jòk [แผ่น pèn]

glasses *n.* (eyeglasses) แว่นตา wɛ̂n-dtaa [อัน an] | (eyeglasses) แว่น wɛ̂n [อัน an]

glaucoma *n.* ต้อหิน dtɔ̂ɔ-hǐn [โรค rôok]

glaze *v.* (coat) เคลือบ klɯ̂ɯap

glide *vi.* (slide on surface) ไถล tà~lǎi | (through the air, e.g. glider) ร่อน rɔ̂n

gloat *vi.* กระหยิ่มใจ grà~yìm-jai

global *adj.* ทั่วโลก tûua-lôok

globe *n.* (earth) โลก lôok [ใบ bai] | (spherical map) ลูกโลก lûuk-lôok [ลูก

lûuk]

gloomy *adj.* (depressed) กลุ้ม glûm

glory *n.* ความรุ่งโรจน์ kwaam-rûng-rôot

glossary *n.* ส่วนอธิบายคำศัพท์ sùuan-à~tí-baai-kam-sàp

glossy *adj.* (shiny) เป็นมันวาว bpen-man-waao

glove *n.* ถุงมือ tǔng-mɯɯ [ข้าง kâang (each), คู่ kûu (pair)]

glove compartment *n.* ที่เก็บของหน้ารถ tîi-gèp-kɔ̌ɔng-nâa-rót [ที่ tîi]

glow *n.* (radiance) แสงแวววาว sɛ̌ɛng-wɛɛo-waao

glow *vi.* (shine) มีแสงเรือง mii-sɛ̌ɛng-rɯɯang

glue *n.* กาว gaao [หลอด lɔ̀ɔt (stick)]

gnat *n.* (small insect) แมลงตัวเล็กๆ má~lɛɛng-dtuua-lék-lék [ตัว dtuua]

gnaw *v.* แทะ té

go *vi.* ไป bpai

go ahead *vi.* (do more) ทำต่อไป tam-dtɔ̀ɔ-bpai |

(move forward)
ไปข้างหน้า bpai-kâang-nâa

goal *n.* (destination) หลักชัย làk-chai [แห่ง hèng] | (objective) เป้าหมาย bpâo-mǎai [อัน an] | (soccer) ประตูฟุตบอล bprà~dtuu-fút-bɔn [ประตู bprà~dtuu]

goat *n.* แพะ pέ [ตัว dtuua]

go away! *interj.* ออกไป ɔ̀ɔk-bpai

go backward *vi.* ถอยกลับ tɔ̌ɔi-glàp, ย้อนกลับ yɔ́ɔn-glàp

go-between *n.* คนกลาง kon-glaang, นายหน้า naai-nâa [คน kon]

go beyond *vt.* ไปไกลกว่า bpai-glai-gwàa

God see god

god *n.* พระเจ้า prá~jâao [องค์ ong, พระองค์ prá-ong]

godchild *n.* ลูกอุปถัมภ์ lûuk-ùp-bpà~tǎm [คน kon]

goddess *n.* เทพธิดา têep-tí-daa [องค์ ong]

godfather *n.* พ่ออุปถัมภ์ pɔ̂ɔ-ùp-bpà~tǎm [คน kon]

godmother *n.* แม่อุปถัมภ์ mɛ̂ɛ-ùp-bpà~tǎm [คน kon]

go down *vi.* ลง long

go for a walk *vi.* เดินเล่น dəən-lên

go-getter *n.* คนมุ่งมั่น kon-mûng-mân [คน kon]

goggle *n.* (safety mask) แว่นนิรภัย wɛ̂n-ní-rá~pai [อัน an]

gold *n.* ทอง tɔɔng, ทองคำ tɔɔng-kam [บาท bàat (15 gram), กรัม gram (gram)]

golden *adj.* (color) สีทอง sǐi-tɔɔng | (of gold) เป็นทอง bpen-tɔɔng

goldfish *n.* ปลาทอง bplaa-tɔɔng [ตัว dtuua]

goldsmith *n.* ช่างทอง châng-tɔɔng [คน kon]

golf *n.* กอล์ฟ gɔ́ɔp

golf club *n.* (organization) ชมรมนักตีกอล์ฟ chom-rom-nák-dtii-gɔ́ɔp [ชมรม chom-rom] | (wood, iron) ไม้กอล์ฟ mái-gɔ́ɔp

❦ [อัน an]

golf course n. สนามกอล์ฟ sà~nǎam-gɔ́ɔp [แห่ง hèng]

gonorrhea n. หนองใน nɔ̌ɔng-nai [โรค rôok]

good adj. ดี dii

good afternoon! interj. สวัสดี sà~wàt-dii

good-bye! interj. ลาก่อน laa-gɔ̀ɔn, สวัสดี sà~wàt-dii

good day! interj. สวัสดี sà~wàt-dii

good enough adj. ดีพอ dii-pɔɔ

good evening! interj. สวัสดี sà~wàt-dii

good-looking adj. หน้าตาดี nâa-dtaa-dii

good luck n. โชคดี chôok-dii

good morning! interj. สวัสดี sà~wàt-dii, อรุณสวัสดิ์ à~run-sà~wàt ❢

good night! interj. ราตรีสวัสดิ์ raa-dtrii-sà~wàt ❢, กู๊ดไนท์ gúut-nái ❦

goods n. สินค้า sǐn-káa [ชนิด chá~nít (kind), ชิ้น

chín (piece), กล่อง glɔ̀ng (box), ห่อ hɔ̀ɔ (wrap)]

good-tempered adj. อารมณ์ดี aa-rom-dii

go off vi. (e.g. alarm) ส่งเสียงดัง sòng-sǐiang-dang | (explode) ระเบิด rá~bèət

go on vi. (continue) ทำต่อไป tam-dtɔ̀ɔ-bpai | (happen) เกิดขึ้น gə̀ət-kûn

goose n. (animal) ห่าน hàan [ตัว dtuua]

goose bumps n. ขนลุก kǒn-lúk

go out vi. (e.g. candle, power) ดับ dàp | (leave) ออกไป ɔ̀ɔk-bpai

go over v. (review) ทบทวน tóp-tuuan

gore vt. ขวิด kwìt

gorgeous adj. (beautiful) สง่างาม sà~ngàa-ngaam

gorilla n. ลิงกอริลลา ling-gɔɔ-rin-lâa [ตัว dtuua]

gossip about vt. นินทา nin-taa

go straight vt. ตรงไป dtrong-bpai

go through vt. (e.g. town, experience) ผ่าน pàan |

(e.g. tunnel) ลอด lɔ̂ɔt | (endure) ทน ton

go to bed *vi.* เข้านอน kâo-nɔɔn, ไปนอน bpai-nɔɔn

go to court *vi.* ขึ้นศาล kûn-sǎan

go under *vi.* (fail) ล้มเหลว lóm-lěeo

go up *vi.* (rise) ขึ้น kûn

gourd *n.* น้ำเต้า nám-dtâo [ลูก lûuk]

gourmet *n.* นักชิมอาหาร nák-chim-aa-hǎan [คน kon]

govern *vt.* ปกครอง bpòk-krɔɔng

governess *n.* ครูหญิงที่สอนตามบ้าน kruu-yǐng-tîi-sɔ̌ɔn-dtaam-bâan [คน kon]

government *n.* รัฐบาล rát-tà~baan [ชุด chút]

government official *n.* ข้าราชการ kâa-râat-chá~gaan [คน kon]

governor *n.* (province) ผู้ว่าราชการ pûu-wâa-râat-chá~gaan [ท่าน tân ȉ, คน kon] | (state)

ผู้ว่าการ pûu-wâa-gaan [ท่าน tân ȉ, คน kon]

gown *n.* เสื้อคลุม sûua-klum [ตัว dtuua]

grab *vt.* (grasp at) คว้า kwáa | (snatch by force) แย่ง yêng

grace *n.* (elegance) ความงดงาม kwaam-ngót-ngaam

graceful *adj.* (elegant) สง่า sà~ngàa

gracious *adj.* (well-mannered) มีมารยาท mii-maa-rá~yâat

grade *n.* (class) ชั้น chán [ชั้น chán] | (score) คะแนน ká~nɛɛn [คะแนน ká~nɛɛn]

grade school *n.* ชั้นประถม chán-bprà~tǒm [ชั้น chán]

gradually *adv.* ค่อยๆ kɔ̂i-kɔ̂i, ทีละน้อย tii-lá~nɔ́ɔi

graduate *n.* ผู้สำเร็จการศึกษา pûu-sǎm-rèt-gaan-sùk-sǎa [คน kon]

graduate *vi.* (school) เรียนจบ riian-jòp

graduation *n.* (school)

การสำเร็จการศึกษา gaan-sǎm-rèt-gaan-sùk-sǎa

grain *n.* (cereal) ธัญพืช tan-yá~pûut | (seed, sand) เม็ด mét [เม็ด mét]

gram *n.* กรัม gram [กรัม gram]

grammar *n.* ไวยากรณ์ wai-yaa-gɔɔn

grand *adj.* (dignified) ภูมิฐาน puum-tǎan | (large) ใหญ่ yài

grandchild *n.* หลาน lǎan [คน kon]

granddaughter *n.* หลานสาว lǎan-sǎao [คน kon]

grandfather *n.* (maternal) ตา dtaa [คน kon] | (paternal) ปู่ bpùu [คน kon]

grand jury *n.* คณะลูกขุนใหญ่ ká~ná~lûuk-kǔn-yài [คณะ ká~ná]

grandmother *n.* (maternal) ยาย yaai [คน kon] | (paternal) ย่า yâa [คน kon]

grandparents *n.* (maternal) ตายาย dtaa-yaai [คน kon] | (paternal)

ปู่ย่า bpùu-yâa [คน kon]

grandson *n.* หลานชาย lǎan-chaai [คน kon]

granite *n.* หินแกรนิต hǐn-grɛɛ-nìt [ก้อน gɔ̂ɔn]

grant *n.* (scholarship, fund) ทุน tun [ก้อน gɔ̂ɔn]

grant *vt.* (give) ให้ hâi

grape *n.* องุ่น à~ngùn [ลูก lûuk, พวง puang (bunch)]

grapefruit *n.* ส้มโอฝรั่ง sôm-oo-fà~ràng [ลูก lûuk]

graph *n.* กราฟ gráap [แผ่น pèn (sheet)]

graphic *adj.* (vivid) ชัดเจน chát-jeen

graphic *n.* (image) กราฟฟิก gráap-fik

graphic arts *n.* กราฟฟิกอาร์ท gráap-fik-áat

grasp *vt.* (clench in fist) กำ gam

grass *n.* หญ้า yâa [ต้น dtôn]

grasshopper *n.* ตั๊กแตน dták-gà~dtɛɛn [ตัว dtuua]

grate *vt.* (into powder) บด bòt | (into slices, strands)

ขูด kùut

grateful *adj.* รู้สึกขอบคุณ rúu-sùk-kɔ̀ɔp-kun

grating *n.* (metal) แผ่นเหล็กกั้น pɛ̀n-lèk-gân [แผ่น pɛ̀n]

gratitude *n.* ความสำนึกบุญคุณ kwaam-sǎm-nʉ́k-bun-kun | (e.g. parents) ความกตัญญู kwaam-gà~ dtan-yuu

gratuity *n.* (tip) เงินทิป ngən-típ

grave *n.* หลุมฝังศพ lǔm-fǎng-sòp [แห่ง hɛ̀ng] | หลุมศพ lǔm-sòp ✦ [แห่ง hɛ̀ng]

gravel *n.* (pebble) กรวด grùuat, ลูกรัง lûuk-rang [เม็ด mét, ก้อน gɔ̂ɔn]

graveyard *n.* ป่าช้า bpàa-cháa [แห่ง hɛ̀ng]

gravity *n.* (physics) แรงดึงดูด rɛɛng-dʉng-dùut, แรงโน้มถ่วง rɛɛng-nóom-tùuang

gravy *n.* ซ้อสราดอาหาร sɔ́ɔt-râat-aa-hǎan

gray *adj.* เทา tao, สีเทา sǐi-tao

gray hair *n.* ผมหงอก pǒm-ngɔ̀ɔk

graze *vi.* (feed on grass) เล็มหญ้า lem-yâa

grease *n.* ไข kǎi | (lubricant) สารหล่อลื่น sǎan-lɔ̀ɔ-lʉ̂ʉn

greasy *adj.* เลี่ยน lîian

great *adj.* (big) ใหญ่โต yài-dtoo | (big, notable) ยิ่งใหญ่ yîng-yài | (wonderful) ยอดเยี่ยม yɔ̂ɔt-yîiam

great! *interj.* เยี่ยม yîiam | (splendid) เจ๋ง jěng ✦

Great Britain *n.* สหราชอาณาจักร sà~hà~ râat-chá~aa-naa-jàk [ประเทศ bprà~têet]

great grandchild *n.* เหลน lěen [คน kon]

great grandfather *n.* (maternal) ตาทวด dtaa-tûuat [คน kon] | (paternal) ปู่ทวด bpùu-tûuat [คน kon]

great grandmother *n.* (maternal) ยายทวด yaai-tûuat [คน kon] | (paternal) ย่าทวด yâa-tûuat [คน kon]

great grandparent *n.*
ชวด chûuat, ทวด tûuat
[คน kon]

greed *n.* ความโลภ
kwaam-lôop

greedy *adj.* (covetous)
โลภ lôop, งก ngók ✿ |
(gluttonous) ตะกละ
dtà~glà

green *adj.* (color) เขียว
kĭiao, สีเขียว sĭi-kĭiao

greenhouse *n.*
เรือนกระจก ruuan-grà~
jòk [หลัง lăng]

green onion *n.* ต้นหอม
dtôn-hŏom [ต้น dtôn
(plant), กำ gam (bunch)]

greet *vt.* (say hello) ทัก
ták, ทักทาย ták-taai

greeting *n.* (words)
คำทักทาย kam-ták-taai
[คำ kam]

grenade *n.* ระเบิดมือ rá~
bèət-muu [ลูก lûuk]

grey see gray

grid *n.* (mesh, shape)
ตาข่าย dtaa-kàai [อัน an]

grief *n.* (distress)
ความเศร้าโศก kwaam-
sâo-sòok | (mourning)
ความอาลัย kwaam-aa-lai

grill *vt.* ย่าง yâang

grin *vi.* ยิงฟัน ying-fan,
ยิ้มกว้าง yím-gwâang

grind *vt.* บด bòt, ปั่น bpòn
| (teeth) ขบ kòp

grindstone *n.* โม่ môo [โม่
môo]

grip *n.* (firm grasp)
การยึดแน่น gaan-yút-nên

grip *vt.* (seize firmly)
เกาะ_แน่น gò~_-nên |
(with tool, chopsticks) คีบ
kîip

groan *n.* เสียงครวญคราง
sĭiang-kruuan-kraang

groan *vi.* ครวญคราง
kruuan-kraang

grocery *n.* (item) ของชำ
kŏong-cham | (store)
ร้านขายของชำ ráan-kăai-
kŏong-cham [ร้าน ráan]

groggy *adj.* (from drug)
เมายา mao-yaa | (from
lack of sleep) มึนหัว
mun-hŭua

groin *n.* ขาหนีบ kăa-nìip
[ข้าง kâang]

groom *n.* เจ้าบ่าว jâo-
bàao [คน kon]

groove *n.* ร่อง rông [ร่อง
rông]

grope *vi.* (reach about) คลำ klam

grope *vt.* (fondle sexually) ลูบไล้ lûup-lái

gross *adj.* (before deduction) รวมก่อนหักค่าใช้จ่าย ruuam-gɔ̀ɔn-hàk-kâa-chái-jàai | (disgusting) น่าสะอิดสะเอียน nâa-sà~it-sà~iian

gross *vt.* (get before deduction) ทำได้_ก่อนหักค่าใช้จ่าย tam-dâai-_-gɔ̀ɔn-hàk-kâa-chái-jàai

ground *n.* (electrical) สายดิน săai-din [สาย săai (wire)] | (floor) พื้น púun [พื้น púun] | (soil) ดิน din

ground floor *n.* ชั้นล่าง chán-lâang [ชั้น chán]

grounds *n.* (evidence) หลักฐาน làk-tăan [ชิ้น chín] | (field) สนาม sà~năam [แห่ง hèng]

group *n.* กลุ่ม glùm [กลุ่ม glùm] | พวก pûuak [พวก pûuak] | (category) จำพวก jam-pûuak [จำพวก jam-pûuak] |

(faction) ข้าง kâang [ข้าง kâang] | (faction) ฝ่าย fàai [ฝ่าย fàai]

group *v.* จัดกลุ่ม jàt-glùm

grove *n.* (small forest) ป่าละเมาะ bpàa-lá~mɔ́ [ป่า bpàa]

grow *vi.* (develop) พัฒนา pát-tá~naa | (increase in size) เติบโต dtə̀əp-dtoo | (rise) ขึ้น kûn

grow *vt.* (e.g. tree, rice) ปลูก bplùuk

grow into *vt.* (e.g. job) คุ้นเคยกับ kún-kəəi-gàp

growl *n.* เสียงคำราม sĭiang-kam-raam

growl *vi.* คำราม kam-raam

grownup *n.* ผู้ใหญ่ pûu-yài [คน kon]

growth *n.* การเติบโต gaan-dtə̀əp-dtoo

grow up *vi.* โตขึ้น dtoo-kûn

grudge *n.* (resentment) ความขุ่นแค้น kwaam-kùn-kɛ́ɛn

grumble *vi.* (complain, whine) บ่นพึมพำ bòn-pɯm-pam

grumpy *adj.* อารมณ์ไม่ดี

aa-rom-mâi-dii

grunt *vi.* ฮึดฮัด hʉ́t-hát

guarantee *vt.* (certify, assure) รับรอง ráp-rɔɔng | (e.g. products) ประกัน bprà~gan

guarantor *n.* ผู้ค้ำประกัน pûu-kám-bprà~gan [คน kon]

guaranty *n.* หลักประกัน làk-bprà~gan [อัน an]

guard *n.* (e.g. security, military) ผู้ดูแลความปลอดภัย pûu-duu-lɛɛ-kwaam-bplɔ̀ɔt-pai [คน kon]

guard *vt.* (keep an eye on) เฝ้า fâo | (protect) ป้องกัน bpɔ̂ng-gan

guardian *n.* ผู้ปกครอง pûu-bpòk-krɔɔng [คน kon]

guava *n.* ฝรั่ง fà~ràng, บักสีดา bàk-sǐi-daa ● [ลูก lûuk]

guerrilla band *n.* กองโจร gɔɔng-joon [กอง gɔɔng]

guess *n.* การเดา gaan-dao

guess *v.* (educated) คาดคะเน kâat-ká~nee, กะ gà ● | (wild) เดา dao,

ทาย taai

guest *n.* แขก kɛ̀ɛk [คน kon]

guesthouse *n.* (tourist) เกสเฮาส์ géet-háo [แห่ง hɛ̀ng, หลัง lǎng]

guidance *n.* (advice) การแนะแนว gaan-né-nɛɛo

guide *n.* ไกด์ gái, มัคคุเทศก์ mák-kú-têet ! [คน kon]

guide *v.* (lead) นำ nam, นำทาง nam-taang

guide *vt.* (advise) แนะ né

guidebook *n.* หนังสือนำเที่ยว nǎng~sʉ̌ʉ-nam-tîiao [เล่ม lêm]

guild *n.* (association) สมาคม sà~maa-kom [แห่ง hɛ̀ng]

guilty *adj.* (ashamed) ละอายใจ lá~aai-jai | (at fault) มีความผิด mii-kwaam-pìt

guinea pig *n.* (tester, animal) หนูตะเภา nǔu-dtà~pao [ตัว dtuua]

guitar *n.* กีต้าร์ gii-dtâa [ตัว dtuua]

gulf *n.* (sea) อ่าว àao [อ่าว àao]

gulp n. การกลืนคำโต gaan-gluun-kam-dtoo

gum n. (chewing) หมากฝรั่ง màak-fà~ràng [กล่อง glòng (pack), แผ่น pèn (stick), เม็ด mét (drop)] | (of teeth) เหงือก ngùuak

gun n. ปืน bpuun [กระบอก grà~bòɔk]

gunman n. มือปืน muu-bpuun [คน kon]

gunpowder n. ดินปืน din-bpuun [กล่อง glòng (box), ห่อ hɔ̀ɔ (pack)]

gunshot n. (noise, act) เสียงปืน sǐiang-bpuun [นัด nát]

gurgle vi. กลั้วคอ glûua-kɔɔ

guru n. ปรมาจารย์ bpà~rá~maa-jaan, ผู้รู้ pûu-rúu [ท่าน tân]

gust n. (wind) ลมแรง lom-rɛɛng [ระลอก rá~lɔ̂ɔk]

gut n. (bowels, entrails) ไส้พุง sâi-pung [เส้น sên]

guts n. (courage) ความกล้าหาญ kwaam-glâa-hǎan

gutter n. รางน้ำ raang-náam [ราง raang]

guy n. ผู้ชาย pûu-chaai [คน kon]

gym n. ยิม yim, โรงยิม roong-yim [ห้อง hɔ̂ng (room)]

gymnast n. นักกายกรรม nák-gaai-yá~gam [คน kon]

gymnastics n. กายกรรม gaai-yá~gam [ท่า tâa]

H

habit n. (routine) นิสัย ní-sǎi

habitat n. (animals or plants) ถิ่นที่อยู่ tìn-tîi-yùu [แห่ง hɛ̀ng]

haggle vi. (bargain) ต่อรองราคา dtɔ̀ɔ-rɔɔng-raa-kaa

hail n. (weather) ลูกเห็บ lûuk-hèp [เม็ด mét]

hair n. (body) ขน kǒn [เส้น sên] | (head) ผม pǒm [เส้น sên (strand), ทรง song (style)]

hair band n. ที่คาดผม tîi-kâat-pǒm [อัน an]

hair clip n. กิ๊บ gíp [ตัว

dtuua]

haircut n. (act) การตัดผม
gaan-dtàt-pǒm

hairdo n. ทรงผม song-
pǒm [ทรง song]

hairdresser n. ช่างทำผม
châng-tam-pǒm [คน kon]

hairpin n. กิ๊บหนีบผม gíp-
nìip-pǒm [ตัว dtuua]

hairy adj. มีขนมาก mii-
kǒn-mâak

halal adj. (food)
ที่ชาวมุสลิมกินได้ tîi-
chaao-mút-sà~lim-gin-
dâai

half n. ครึ่ง krûng

half-breed n. ลูกครึ่ง
lûuk-krûng [คน kon]

half brother n. (different
father) พี่น้องคนละพ่อ
pîi-nɔ́ɔng-kon-lá~pɔ̂ɔ
[คน kon] | (different
mother) พี่น้องคนละแม่
pîi-nɔ́ɔng-kon-lá~mɛ̂ɛ
[คน kon]

half moon n.
พระจันทร์ครึ่งดวง prá~
jan-krûng-duuang [ดวง
duuang]

half-price adj. ครึ่งราคา

krûng-raa-kaa

half sister see half brother

halfway adj. ครึ่งทาง
krûng-taang

hall n. (large room) โรง
roong [โรง roong]

hallucinate vi. เพ้อคลั่ง
pɜ́ɜ-klâng

hallway n. (corridor)
ทางเดินในตัวอาคาร
taang-dəən-nai-dtuua-
aa-kaan [ทาง taang]

halo n. รัศมี rát-sà~mǐi

halt v. (cause to stop)
ระงับ rá~ngáp

halve vt. แบ่ง_ครึ่ง bὲng-
_-krûng

ham n. (meat) หมูแฮม
mǔu-hɛm [ชิ้น chín]

hamburger n.
แฮมเบอร์เกอร์ hɛm-bəə-
gə̂ə [อัน an, ชิ้น chín]

hammer n. ค้อน kɔ́ɔn [อัน
an]

hammer v. ตอก dtɔ̀ɔk

hammock n. เปลญวน
bplee-yuuan [ปาก bpàak]

hand n. (body part) มือ
mɯɯ [ข้าง kâang] |
(clock) เข็มนาฬิกา kěm-

naa-lí~gaa [เข็ม kěm]

hand vt. (pass) ยื่น yûʉn | (send) ส่ง sòng

handbag n. กระเป๋าถือ grà~bpǎo-tʉ̌ʉ [ใบ bai]

handbook n. คู่มือ kûu-mʉʉ [เล่ม lêm]

handcuffs n. กุญแจมือ gun-jɛɛ-mʉʉ [คู่ kûu]

handful n. (fistful) กำมือหนึ่ง gam-mʉʉ-nʉ̀ng [กำ gam] | (small amount) จำนวนน้อย jam-nuuan-nɔ́ɔi [จำนวน jam-nuuan]

handicap n. (disability) ความพิการ kwaam-pí-gaan | (e.g. golf, bowling) การต่อให้ gaan-dtɔ̀ɔ-hâi

handicraft n. งานฝีมือ ngaan-fǐi-mʉʉ, หัตถกรรม hàt-tà~gam

handkerchief n. ผ้าเช็ดหน้า pâa-chét-nâa [ผืน pʉ̌ʉn]

handle n. ด้าม dâam, ที่จับ tîi-jàp [อัน an, ด้าม dâam]

handle vt. (cope with, deal) จัดการ jàt-gaan

handmade adj. ทำด้วยมือ tam-dûuai-mʉʉ

hand out vt. แจก jɛ̀ɛk

handrail n. ราว raao [ราว raao] | (on stairs) ราวบันได raao-ban-dai [ราว raao]

handshake n. การจับมือ gaan-jàp-mʉʉ

handsome adj. (men) รูปหล่อ rûup-lɔ̀ɔ, หล่อ lɔ̀ɔ

hands-on adj. มีส่วนร่วม mii-sùuan-rûuam

handwriting n. ลายมือ laai-mʉʉ [ลายมือ laai-mʉʉ]

handy adj. (easy to reach) ใกล้มือ glâi-mʉʉ | (easy to use) ใช้ง่าย chái-ngâai | (useful) เป็นประโยชน์ bpen-bprà~yòot

hang v. ห้อย hɔ̂i | (cling to) โหน hǒon

hang vt. แขวน kwɛ̌ɛn

hanger n. (clothes) ไม้แขวนเสื้อ mái-kwɛ̌ɛn-sʉ̂ʉa [อัน an]

hangnail n. จมูกเล็บ jà~mùuk-lép

hang out vi. (e.g. with friends) ใช้เวลาด้วยกัน

chái-wee-laa-dûuai-gan | (loiter) เดินเตร่จเตร่ dəən-dtrèt-dtrèe

hangover *n.* เมาค้าง mao-káang

hang up *v.* (phone) วางสาย waang-sǎai, วางหู waang-hǔu

happen *vi.* เกิด gə̀ət, เกิดขึ้น gə̀ət-kûn

happiness *n.* ความสุข kwaam-sùk

happy *adj.* ดีใจ dii-jai, มีความสุข mii-kwaam-sùk, สุข sùk

harass *vt.* (disturb, vex) รบกวน róp-guuan, รังควาญ rang-kwaan | (sexually) ลวนลาม luuan-laam

harbor *n.* (port) ท่าเรือ tâa-ruua [แห่ง hɛ̀ng]

harbor *vt.* (give sanctuary to) ให้ที่พักพิงแก่ hâi-tîi-pák-ping-gɛ̀ɛ | (hide) ปิดบัง bpìt-bang

hard *adj.* (not easy) ยาก yâak | (not soft) แข็ง kɛ̌ng | (with difficulty) ลำบาก lam-bàak

hard *adv.* หนัก nàk

hard-boiled egg *n.* ไข่ต้ม kài-dtôm [ฟอง fɔɔng]

hardcover *adj.* ปกแข็ง bpòk-kɛ̌ng

harden *vi.* (solidify) แข็งตัว kɛ̌ng-dtuua

harden *vt.* (solidify) ทำให้_แข็ง tam-hâi-_-kɛ̌ng

hardly *adv.* (almost not, barely) แทบจะไม่ tɛ̂ɛp-jà~mâi | (not so _) ไม่ค่อย mâi-kôi

hard of hearing *adj.* หูตึง hǔu-dtung, หูไม่ดี hǔu-mâi-dii

hard-on *n.* (penis) จู๋แข็ง jǔu-kɛ̌ng

hardship *n.* ความยากลำบาก kwaam-yâak-lam-bàak

hardware *n.* (computer) ฮาร์ดแวร์ háat-wɛɛ [ชิ้น chín, เครื่อง krûuang] | (construction) วัสดุ wát-sà~dù [ชิ้น chín]

hare *n.* กระต่ายป่า grà~dtàai-bpàa [ตัว dtuua]

harem *n.* ฮาเร็ม haa-rem [แห่ง hɛ̀ng]

harm n. (danger) อันตราย an-dtà~raai

harm vt. ทำร้าย tam-ráai

harmful adj. เป็นอันตราย bpen-an-dtà~raai

harmless adj. ไม่มีอันตราย mâi-mii-an-dtà~raai

harmonious adj. (melodious) ไพเราะ pai-rɔ́ ✎

harmony n. (agreement, accord) ความกลมกลืน kwaam-glom-gluun | (music) การประสานเสียง gaan-bprà~sǎan-sǐiang

harness n. (riding) บังเหียน bang-hǐian [เส้น sên, สาย sǎai]

harp n. พิณ pin [ตัว dtuua]

harpoon n. ฉมวก chà~mùuak [เล่ม lêm]

harsh adj. (e.g. condition, climate) รุนแรง run-rɛɛng | (manner) หยาบกระด้าง yàap-grà~dâang | (voice) แหบ hɛ̀ɛp

harvest n. (act) การเก็บเกี่ยว gaan-gèp-gìiao | (crop) ดอกผล dɔ̀ɔk-pǒn, ผลผลิต pǒn-pà~lìt

harvest v. เก็บเกี่ยว gèp-gìiao

hassle n. (bother) สิ่งที่น่ารำคาญ sìng-tîi-nâa-ram-kaan [อัน an]

hassle vt. (bother or harass) ก่อกวน gɔ̀ɔ-guuan

haste n. ความเร่งรีบ kwaam-rêng-rîip

hasty adj. (impatient) ใจร้อน jai-rɔ́ɔn | (rush) เร่งรีบ rêng-rîip

hat n. หมวก mùuak [ใบ bai]

hatch vi. (break open) ฟักตัว fák-dtuua

hate n. ความเกลียดชัง kwaam-glìiat-chang

hate v. เกลียด glìiat, ชัง chang ✎

haughty adj. (arrogant, conceited) หยิ่ง yìng | (disdainful) จองหอง jɔɔng-hɔ̌ɔng

haul v. (drag) ลาก lâak

haunt v. (frighten) หลอกหลอน lɔ̀ɔk-lɔ̌ɔn | (possess, inhabit) สิง sǐng

haunted adj. มีผีสิง mii-pǐi-sǐng

have v. มี mii

have a cold *vi.* เป็นหวัด bpen-wàt

have to *vi.* ต้อง dtɔ̂ng, จำเป็นต้อง jam-bpen-dtɔ̂ng ‼

hawk *n.* (bird) เหยี่ยว yìiao [ตัว dtuua]

hay *n.* (dry grass) หญ้าแห้ง yâa-hêng [กอง gɔɔng (pile), เส้น sên (strand)] | (rice chaff) ฟาง faang [กอง gɔɔng (pile), เส้น sên (strand)]

hay fever *n.* ไข้ละอองฟาง kâi-lá-ɔɔng-faang

hazardous *adj.* (perilous) เป็นอันตราย bpen-an-dtà~raai, มีภัย mii-pai | (risky) เสี่ยงโชค sìiang-chôok

he *pron.* เขา kǎo, ท่าน tân ‼ | (derogatory) มัน man ❦ | (use with friends) แก gɛɛ ❧, เค้า káo ❧

head *n.* (body part) ศีรษะ sǐi-sà ‼ [อัน an] | (body part) หัว hǔua [หัว hǔua] | (chief, boss) หัวหน้า hǔua-nâa [คน kon]

head *vi.* (go toward)

มุ่งไปทาง mûng-bpai-taang

headache *n.* ปวดหัว bpùuat-hǔua, ปวดศีรษะ bpùuat-sǐi-sà ‼

headhunter *n.* (recruiter) ผู้จัดหางาน pûu-jàt-hǎa-ngaan [คน kon]

heading *n.* (headline, topic) หัวข้อ hǔua-kɔ̂ɔ, หัวเรื่อง hǔua-rûuang [หัวข้อ hǔua-kɔ̂ɔ]

headlight *n.* (vehicle) ไฟหน้ารถ fai-nâa-rót [ดวง duuang]

headmaster *n.* ครูใหญ่ kruu-yài [คน kon]

head-on *adj.* ประสานงา bprà~sǎan-ngaa

headphone *n.* หูฟัง hǔu-fang [อัน an (piece), คู่ kûu (pair)]

headquarter *n.* (of a company) สำนักงานใหญ่ sǎm-nák-ngaan-yài [แห่ง hèng]

heads *n.* (coin) หัว hǔua [ด้าน dâan]

headstrong *adj.* ดื้อ dûu

heal *vi.* (recover) หาย hǎai

heal *vt.* (cure) รักษา rák-sǎa

health *n.* สุขภาพ sùk-kà~pâap

health insurance *n.* การประกันสุขภาพ gaan-bprà~gan-sùk-kà~pâap

healthy *adj.* แข็งแรง kěng-rɛɛng, สุขภาพดี sùk-kà~pâap-dii

hear *v.* ได้ยิน dâi-yin

hearing *n.* การได้ยิน gaan-dâi-yin | (legal) การรับฟังคดี gaan-ráp-fang-ká~dii

hearing aid *n.* เครื่องช่วยฟัง krûuang-chûuai-fang [เครื่อง krûuang]

hearsay *n.* (from third person) คำบอกเล่า kam-bɔ̀ɔk-lâo [เรื่อง rûuang] | (rumor) ข่าวลือ kàao-luu [เรื่อง rûuang (topic)]

hearse *n.* (vehicle) รถบรรทุกศพ rót-ban-túk-sòp [คัน kan]

heart *n.* (core) แก่น gɛ̀n | (organ) หัวใจ hǔua-jai

heartache *n.* (grief) ความปวดร้าวใจ kwaam-bpùuat-ráao-jai

heart attack *n.* หัวใจวาย hǔua-jai-waai

heartbreak *n.* ไข้ใจ kâi-jai ✿

heartbroken *adj.* อกหัก òk-hàk

heartburn *n.* อาการจุกเสียดท้อง aa-gaan-jùk-sìiat-tɔ́ɔng

heart disease *n.* โรคหัวใจ rôok-hǔua-jai [โรค rôok]

heat *n.* ความร้อน kwaam-rɔ́ɔn

heat *vt.* ทำให้_ร้อน tam-hâi-_-rɔ́ɔn

heater *n.* เครื่องทำความร้อน krûuang-tam-kwaam-rɔ́ɔn, ฮีทเตอร์ hiit-dtɤ̀ə [เครื่อง krûuang]

heatstroke *n.* อาการหน้ามืดเพราะความร้อน aa-gaan-nâa-mûut-prɔ́-kwaam-rɔ́ɔn

heaven *n.* สวรรค์ sà~wǎn [แห่ง hɛ̀ng]

heavy *adj.* หนัก nàk

hectic *adj.* (filled with confusion) วุ่นวาย wûn-

waai | (very busy) ยุ่งมาก
yûng-mâak

hedge n. (fence) รั้ว rúua
[รั้ว rúua, อัน an ●] | (row
of bushes) แนวพุ่มไม้
nεεo-pûm-máai [แถว
tἔεo]

heed v. เอาใจใส่ ao-jai-sài

heel n. ส้นเท้า sôn-táao,
ส้น sôn ● [ข้าง kâang]

height n. ความสูง
kwaam-sǔung | (person)
ส่วนสูง sùuan-sǔung

heir n. ทายาท taa-yâat
[คน kon]

heiress see heir

helicopter n. เฮลิคอปเตอร์
hee-lí~kɔ́p-dtəə [เครื่อง
krûuang, ลำ lam]

hell n. นรก ná~rók [ขุม
kǔm]

hello! interj. (female
speaker) สวัสดีค่ะ sà~
wàt-dii-kâ | (male
speaker) สวัสดีครับ sà~
wàt-dii-kráp

helmet n. หมวกกันน็อก
mùuak-gan-nɔ́k [ใบ bai]

help n. ความช่วยเหลือ
kwaam-chûuai-lǔua [ครั้ง

kráng]

help v. ช่วย chûuai,
ช่วยเหลือ chûuai-lǔua,
สงเคราะห์ sǒng-krɔ́ ‼

help! interj. ช่วยด้วย
chûuai-dûuai

helper n. ผู้ช่วย pûu-
chûuai [คน kon]

helpful adj. (useful)
เป็นประโยชน์ bpen-
bprà~yòot

hem n. ชายเสื้อ chaai-sûua

hemisphere n. (of the
globe) ซีกโลก sîik-lôok
[ซีก sîik]

hemorrhage n.
การตกเลือด gaan-dtòk-
lûuat

hemorrhoid n.
ริดสีดวงทวาร rít-sǐi-
duuang-tá~waan

hemp n. (plant) ปอ bpɔɔ,
ป่าน bpàan [ต้น dtôn]

hen n. (animal) แม่ไก่
mɛ̂ɛ-gài [ตัว dtuua]

hepatitis n. ตับอักเสบ
dtàp-àk-sèep [โรค rôok]

her pron. เขา kǎo, ท่าน tân
‼, แก gɛɛ ●, เค้า káo ●,
มัน man ◆

herb *n.* สมุนไพร sà~
mǔn-prai
herbal medicine *n.*
ยาสมุนไพร yaa-sà~mǔn-
prai
herbivore *n.*
สัตว์ที่กินพืชเป็นอาหาร
sàt-tîi-gin-pûut-bpen-
aa-hǎan [ตัว dtuua]
herd *n.* ฝูง fǔung, ฝูงสัตว์
fǔung-sàt [ฝูง fǔung]
herd *vt.* ต้อน dtɔ̂ɔn
here *adv.* ตรงนี้ dtrong-
níi, ที่นี่ tîi-nîi
here *pron.* นี่ nîi
heredity *n.* กรรมพันธุ์
gam-má~pan
heritage *n.* (inheritance,
cultural) มรดก mɔɔ-rá~
dòk [กอง gɔɔng, ชิ้น chín]
hermaphrodite *n.*
กะเทยแท้ gà~təəi-tɛ́ɛ
[คน kon]
hermit *n.* ฤๅษี rɯɯ-sǐi [ตน
dton]
hernia *n.* ไส้เลื่อน sâi-
lɯ̂ɯan [โรค rôok]
hero *n.* (e.g. brave
person) วีรบุรุษ wii-rá~
bù~rút [คน kon] | (e.g. in
movies) พระเอก prá-èek
[คน kon]
heroin *n.* เฮโรอีน hee-roo-
iin
heroine *n.* (e.g. brave
person) วีรสตรี wii-rá~
sà~dtrii [คน kon] | (e.g.
in movies) นางเอก
naang-èek [คน kon]
heron *n.* นกกระสา nók-
grà~sǎa [ตัว dtuua]
herring *n.* ปลาเฮอริ่ง
bplaa-həə-rîng [ตัว
dtuua]
hers *pron.* ของเขา kɔ̌ɔng-
kǎo, ของเธอ kɔ̌ɔng-təə
herself *pron.* ตัวเธอเอง
dtuua-təə-eeng
hesitant *adj.* (reluctant,
uncertain) ลังเล lang-lee
| (stammering, reluctant)
อึกอัก ùk-àk
hesitate *vi.* ลังเล lang-lee
heterosexual *adj.*
สนใจเพศตรงข้าม sǒn-
jai-pêet-dtrong-kâam
hi! *interj.* สวัสดี sà~wàt-
dii, หวัดดี wàt-dii ✿
hibernate *vi.* (animals)
จำศีล jam-sǐin
hibiscus *n.* ชบา chá~baa

[ดอก dɔ̀ɔk (flower), ต้น dtôn (plant)]

hiccup vi. สะอึก sà~ùk

hide n. (animal skin) หนังสัตว์ năng-sàt [แผ่น pèn, ผืน pʉ̆ʉn]

hide v. ซ่อน sɔ̂n, แอบ ɛ̀ɛp

hide-and-seek n. ซ่อนหา sɔ̂n-hǎa

hideout n. ที่ซ่อน tîi-sɔ̂n [ที่ tîi, แห่ง hɛ̀ng]

hiding place see hideout

hierarchy n. (by ability or status) การแบ่งชั้น gaan-bèng-chán, ศักดินา sàk-dì~naa !

high adj. (by alcohol or a drug) เมา mao | (expensive) แพง pɛɛng | (tall) สูง sǔung

high blood pressure n. ความดันเลือดสูง kwaam-dan-lʉ̂ʉat-sǔung

high-class adj. ชั้นสูง chán-sǔung, ไฮโซ hai-soo ✎

high five n. การทักทายด้วยการตีมือกัน gaan-ták-taai-dûuai-gaan-dtii-mʉʉ-gan

high frequency n.

ความถี่สูง kwaam-tìi-sǔung

high heels n. รองเท้าส้นสูง rɔɔng-táao-sôn-sǔung [ข้าง kâang (one), คู่ kûu (pair)]

highland n. ที่ราบสูง tîi-râap-sǔung [แห่ง hɛ̀ng, ที่ tîi]

highlight n. (illuminated spot) จุดเด่น jùt-dèn [จุด jùt]

highlight vt. (emphasize) เน้น néen

highly adv. อย่างมาก yàang-mâak

high school n. โรงเรียนมัธยมปลาย roong-riian-mát-tá~yom-bplaai [แห่ง hɛ̀ng]

high tide n. น้ำขึ้น náam-kʉ̂n

high tone n. เสียงตรี sǐiang-dtrii [เสียง sǐiang]

highway n. ไฮเวย์ hai-wee [ทาง taang] | ทางหลวง taang-lǔuang [สาย sǎai]

hijack n. การปล้น gaan-bplôn

hijack vt. จี้ jîi,

hijack ปล้น_กลางทาง bplôn-_-glaang-taang

hijacker *n.* โจรปล้นกลางทาง joon-bplôn-glaang-taang [คน kon] | (airplane) สลัดอากาศ sà~làt-aa-gàat [คน kon]

hike *n.* การเดินเขา gaan-dəən-kǎo

hike *v.* เดินเขา dəən-kǎo

hiking *n.* การเดินเขา gaan-dəən-kǎo, การเดินทางไกล gaan-dəən-taang-glai

hilarious *adj.* ตลกมาก dtà~lòk-mâak

hill *n.* เขา kǎo, เนินเขา nəən-kǎo [ลูก lûuk]

him *pron.* เขา kǎo, ท่าน tân 🛆, เค้า káo 🕊, มัน man 💣

himself *pron.* ตัวเขาเอง dtuua-kǎo-eeng

Hinayana Buddhism *n.* หินยาน hǐn-ná~yaan [นิกาย ní-gaai]

hind *adj.* ข้างหลัง kâang-lǎng

Hindi *n.* ภาษาฮินดู paa-sǎa-hin-duu [ภาษา paa-sǎa]

hindrance *n.* (barricade, obstacle) สิ่งกีดขวาง sìng-gìit-kwǎang, อุปสรรค ùp-bpà~sàk [สิ่ง sìng]

Hindu *adj.* ฮินดู hin-duu

Hindu *n.* ผู้นับถือศาสนาฮินดู pûu-náp-tǔu-sàat-sà~nǎa-hin-duu [คน kon]

hinge *n.* บานพับ baan-páp [ตัว dtuua, อัน an]

hint *n.* การบอกใบ้ gaan-bɔ̀ɔk-bâi

hint *vt.* บอกใบ้ให้ bɔ̀ɔk-bâi-hâi

hip *adj.* (trendy) ทันสมัย tan-sà~mǎi

hip *n.* สะโพก sà~pôok [ข้าง kâang]

hippopotamus *n.* ช้างน้ำ cháang-náam, ฮิปโป híp-bpoo 🕊 [ตัว dtuua]

hire *v.* (e.g. employee, driver) จ้าง jâang

hire *vt.* (from someone, e.g. car, bike) เช่า châo | (to someone, e.g. car, bike) ให้เช่า hâi-châo

his *pron.* ของเขา kɔ̌ɔng-kǎo

hiss *n.* เสียงฟ่อ sĭiang-fɔ̂ɔ

hiss *vi.* ทำเสียงฟู่ tam-sĭiang-fûu

historical *adj.* ทางประวัติศาสตร์ taang-bprà~wàt-dtì~sàat

history *n.* ประวัติศาสตร์ bprà~wàt-dtì~sàat [เรื่อง rûuang] | (subject) ประวัติศาสตร์ bprà~wàt-dtì~sàat [วิชา wí-chaa]

hit *adj.* (e.g. song) ฮิต hít

hit *n.* (e.g. song) สิ่งที่นิยมกัน sìng-tîi-ní-yom-gan

hit *v.* (beat) ตี dtii | (bump) กระแทก grà~têɛk | (crash into) ชน chon

hit-and-run *adj.* ชนแล้วหนี chon-lɛ́ɛo-nĭi

hitchhike *vi.* โบกรถ bòok-rót

HIV *n.* เอชไอวี ét-ai-wii

hive *n.* รังผึ้ง rang-pûng [รัง rang] | รวงผึ้ง ruuang-pûng [รวง ruuang]

hives *n.* โรคลมพิษ rôok-lom-pít [โรค rôok]

Hmong *n.* (hill tribe) แม้ว

mɛ́ɛo [เผ่า pào]

hoarse *adj.* แหบแห้ง hɛ̀ɛp-hêng

hobby *n.* งานอดิเรก ngaan-à~dì~rèek

hockey *n.* กีฬาฮอกกี้ gii-laa-hɔ́k-gîi

hoe *n.* จอบ jɔ̀ɔp [เล่ม lêm]

hog *n.* (domestic swine) หมูตอน mŭu-dtɔɔn [ตัว dtuua]

hold *vt.* (carry) ถือ tŭu | (contain) จุ jù | (seize) จับ jàp, ยึด yút

hold on! *interj.* (wait!) เดี๋ยวก่อน dĭiao-gɔ̀ɔn, รอก่อน rɔɔ-gɔ̀ɔn

hold onto *vt.* จับ_ไว้ jàp-_-wái

hold out one's hand *vi.* แบมือ bɛɛ-mɯɯ

hole *n.* ช่อง chɔ̂ɔng [ช่อง chɔ̂ɔng] | รู ruu [รู ruu, หลุม lŭm]

holiday *n.* วันหยุด wan-yùt [วัน wan, ช่วง chûuang (period)]

Holland *n.* ฮอลแลนด์ hɔn-lɛɛn [ประเทศ bprà~têet]

hollow *adj.* กลวง gluuang, เป็นโพรง bpenproong

hollow n. (cavity) โพรง proong [โพรง proong, อัน an]

holy adj. (sacred) ศักดิ์สิทธิ์ sàk-sìt

home n. บ้าน bâan [หลัง lǎng]

home economics n. คหกรรมศาสตร์ ká~hà~ gam-má~sàat [วิชา wí-chaa]

homeland n. รกราก rók-râak [แห่ง hèng]

homeless adj. ไม่มีบ้านอยู่ mâi-mii-bâan-yùu

homemade adj. ทำที่บ้าน tam-tîi-bâan

homemaker n. (housewife) แม่บ้าน mɛ̂ɛ-bâan [คน kon]

home office n. (head office) สำนักงานใหญ่ sǎm-nák-ngaan-yài [แห่ง hèng] | (office at home) สำนักงานที่อยู่ในบ้าน sǎm-nák-ngaan-tîi-yùu-nai-bâan [แห่ง hèng]

homesick adj. คิดถึงบ้าน kít-tǔng-bâan

hometown n. บ้านเกิด

bâan-gòət [แห่ง hèng, ที่ tîi]

homework n. การบ้าน gaan-bâan [อย่าง yàang]

homicide n. การฆาตกรรม gaan-kâat-dtà~gam ‼

homophobia n. การเกลียดชังพวก รักร่วมเพศ gaan-glìiat-chang-pûuak-rák-rûuam-pêet

homosexual adj. รักร่วมเพศ rák-rûuam-pêet

hone vt. (blade) ลับ láp

honest adj. ซื่อตรง sûu-dtrong

honesty n. ความซื่อสัตย์ kwaam-sûu-sàt

honey n. (bee nectar) น้ำผึ้ง nám-pûng [ขวด kùuat (bottle)] | (darling) ที่รัก tîi-rák [คน kon]

honeydew n. (melon) แตงฮันนี่ดิว dtɛɛng-han-nîi-diu [ลูก lûuk]

honeymoon n. การดื่มน้ำผึ้งพระจันทร์ gaan-dùum-nám-pûng-prá~jan

honeymoon v. ฮันนีมูน

han-nîi-muun

Hong Kong n. ฮ่องกง
hông-gong [เกาะ gɔ̀
(island)]

honk n. เสียงแตร sǐiang-
dtrɛɛ [เสียง sǐiang]

honk vi. บีบแตร bìip-dtrɛɛ

honor n. (high respect)
เกียรติ gìiat

honor vt. ให้เกียรติ hâi-
gìiat

honorable adj.
น่าเคารพนับถือ nâa-kao-
róp-náp-tǔ̈

honors n. (academic)
เกียรตินิยม gìiat-ní-yom
[อันดับ an-dàp]

hood n. (car) กระโปรงรถ
grà~bproong-rót [แผ่น
pɛ̀n, ฝา fǎa] | (e.g. jacket)
หมวกคลุม mùuak-klum
[อัน an]

hoof n. กีบ gìip,
กีบเท้าสัตว์ gìip-táao-sàt
[กีบ gìip]

hook n. ขอ kɔ̌ɔ, ตะขอ
dtà~kɔ̌ɔ [อัน an]

hook vt. เกี่ยว gìiao

hoop n. ห่วง hùuang [ห่วง
hùuang]

hop vi. กระโดด grà~dòot

hope n. ความหวัง
kwaam-wǎng

hope v. หวัง wǎng

hopeful adj. มีความหวัง
mii-kwaam-wǎng

hopeless adj.
ไม่มีความหวัง mâi-mii-
kwaam-wǎng, หมดหวัง
mòt-wǎng

horizon n. ขอบฟ้า kɔ̀ɔp-
fáa

horizontal adj. แนวนอน
nɛɛo-nɔɔn

hormone n. ฮอร์โมน
hɔɔ-moon [ชนิด chá~nít]

horn n. (animal) เขาสัตว์
kǎo-sàt, เขา kǎo ☀ [ข้าง
kâang (each), คู่ kûu
(pair)] | (musical) แตร
dtrɛɛ [ตัว dtuua]

horny adj. คล้ายเขาสัตว์
kláai-kǎo-sàt | (lustful)
มีอารมณ์ mii-aa-rom,
เงี่ยน ngîian ☀

horoscope n.
การทำนายโชคชะตา gaan-
tam-naai-chôok-chá~
dtaa, โชคชะตา chôok-
chá~dtaa

horrible adj. (dreadful)
แย่มาก yɛ̂ɛ-mâak | (scary)

น่ากลัว nâa-gluua, สยองขวัญ sà~yɔ̌ɔng-kwǎn ‼

horrified *adj.* หวาดกลัว wàat-gluua ‼

horror *n.* ความน่ากลัว kwaam-nâa-gluua, ความหวาดกลัว kwaam-wàat-gluua

hors d'oeuvre *n.* อาหารเรียกน้ำย่อย aa-hǎan-rîiak-nám-yɔ̂i [จาน jaan]

horse *n.* ม้า máa [ตัว dtuua]

horsefly *n.* เหลือบ lʉ̀uap [ตัว dtuua]

horsepower *n.* แรงม้า rɛɛng-máa [แรง rɛɛng]

horseradish *n.* (condiment) วาซาบิขาว waa-saa-bì-kǎao

horseshoe *n.* เกือกม้า gʉ̀uak-máa [อัน an]

hose *n.* (long socks) ถุงน่อง tǔng-nɔ̂ng [ข้าง kâang (each), คู่ kûu (pair)] | (rubber) สายยาง sǎai-yaang [สาย sǎai, เส้น sên]

hospitable *adj.* อัธยาศัยดี àt-tá~yaa-sǎi-dii

hospital *n.* โรงพยาบาล roong-pá~yaa-baan [แห่ง hɛ̀ng]

hospitality *n.* การต้อนรับขับสู้ gaan-dtɔ̂ɔn-ráp-kàp-sûu

hospitalize *vt.* รักษา_ในโรงพยาบาล rák-sǎa-_-nai-roong-pá~yaa-baan

host *n.* (e.g. party, ceremony, event) เจ้าภาพ jâo-pâap [คน kon]

host *v.* (e.g. party, ceremony, event) เป็นเจ้าภาพ bpen-jâo-pâap

hostage *n.* ตัวประกัน dtuua-bprà~gan [คน kon]

hostess *n.* เจ้าภาพหญิง jâo-pâap-yǐng [คน kon] | (female host) พนักงานต้อนรับหญิง pá~nák-ngaan-dtɔ̂ɔn-ráp-yǐng [คน kon]

hostile *adj.* (unfriendly) ไม่เป็นมิตร mâi-bpen-mít

hot *adj.* (sexy) เร่าร้อน râo-rɔ́ɔn ✎ | (spicy) เผ็ด pèt | (temperature) ร้อน

รั่วก

hotdog *n.* ฮ็อทด็อก hɔ́t-dɔ̀ɔk [ชิ้น chín, อัน an]

hotel *n.* โรงแรม roong-rɛɛm [แห่ง hɛ̀ng]

hot-headed *adj.* (personality) ใจร้อน jai-rɔ́ɔn

hot season *n.* ฤดูร้อน rɯ́-duu-rɔ́ɔn [ฤดู rɯ́-duu] | หน้าร้อน nâa-rɔ́ɔn ❀ [หน้า nâa]

hot spring *n.* บ่อน้ำร้อน bɔ̀ɔ-nám-rɔ́ɔn [บ่อ bɔ̀ɔ, แห่ง hɛ̀ng (location)]

hot-tempered *adj.* ใจร้อน jai-rɔ́ɔn

hound *n.* (hunting dog) หมาล่าเนื้อ mǎa-lâa-nɯ́a [ตัว dtuua]

hour *n.* ชั่วโมง chûua-moong [ชั่วโมง chûua-moong]

hourglass *n.* นาฬิกาทราย naa-lí~gaa-saai [อัน an]

hourly *adj.* (by the hour) เป็นชั่วโมง bpen-chûua-moong

hourly *adv.* (each hour) แต่ละชั่วโมง dtɛ̀ɛ-lá~

chûua-moong | (every hour) ทุกชั่วโมง túk-chûua-moong

house *n.* บ้าน bâan [หลัง lǎng]

house *vt.* (provide housing) ให้ที่อยู่ hâi-tîi-yùu

houseboat *n.* เรือนแพ rɯɯan-pɛɛ [หลัง lǎng]

household *n.* ครอบครัว krɔ̂ɔp-kruua [ครอบครัว krɔ̂ɔp-kruua] | ครัวเรือน kruua-rɯɯan ! [ครัวเรือน kruua-rɯɯan]

housekeeper *n.* คนดูแลบ้าน kon-duu-lɛɛ-bâan, แม่บ้าน mɛ̂ɛ-bâan [คน kon]

housemaid *n.* แม่บ้าน mɛ̂ɛ-bâan [คน kon]

House of Representatives *n.* สภาผู้แทนราษฎร sà~paa-pûu-tɛɛn-râat-sà~dɔɔn [แห่ง hɛ̀ng]

house registration *n.* ทะเบียนบ้าน tá~biian-bâan [ฉบับ chà~bàp]

housewarming *n.* งานขึ้นบ้านใหม่ ngaankûn-bâan-mài [งาน ngaan]

housewife *n.* แม่บ้าน mɛ̂ɛ-bâan [คน kon]

housework *n.* งานบ้าน ngaan-bâan [งาน ngaan]

how *adv.* อย่างไร yàang-rai, ยังไง yang-ngai ◖

however *conj.* อย่างไรก็ตาม yàang-rai-gɔ̂ɔ-dtaam

howl *n.* (cry of a dog) เสียงหมาหอน sǐiang-mǎa-hɔ̌ɔn

howl *v.* (e.g. a dog) หอน hɔ̌ɔn

how many *adj.* กี่ gìi

how many *n.* เท่าไร tâo-rai

hub *n.* (center) ศูนย์กลาง sǔun-glaang [ศูนย์ sǔun] | (wheel) ดุมล้อ dum-lɔ́ɔ [ดุม dum]

huddle *vi.* รวมเป็นกลุ่มก้อน ruuam-bpen-glùm-gɔ̂ɔn

hug *n.* การกอด gaan-gɔ̀ɔt

hug *v.* กอด gɔ̀ɔt

huge *adj.* ใหญ่มาก yài-mâak, มหึมา má-hʉ̀-maa ◖

hull *vt.* (remove hull of)

เอาเปลือก_ออก ao-bplʉ̀ak-_-ɔ̀ɔk

hum *n.* (sound) เสียงหึ่งๆ sǐiang-hʉ̀ng-hʉ̀ng

hum *vi.* ฮัมเพลง ham-pleeng

human *adj.* เป็นมนุษย์ bpen-má~nút ⚡

human *n.* คน kon, มนุษย์ má~nút ⚡ [คน kon]

humane *adj.* มีมนุษยธรรม mii-má~nút-sà~yá-tam

humanity *n.* มนุษยชาติ má~nút-sà~yá-châat

humble *adj.* ถ่อมตัว tɔ̀m-dtuua

humid *adj.* ชื้น chʉ́ʉn | (weather) อากาศชื้น aa-gàat-chʉ́ʉn

humidity *n.* ความชื้น kwaam-chʉ́ʉn

humiliate *vt.* (cause to feel shame) ทำให้_ขายหน้า tam-hâi-_-kǎai-nâa | (insult) เหยียดหยาม yìiat-yǎam

humility *n.* ความถ่อมตัว kwaam-tɔ̀m-dtuua

humor *n.* (amusement) ความขบขัน kwaam-kòp-kǎn, อารมณ์ขัน aa-romkǎn

humorous *adj.* ตลก dtà~
lòk

hump *n.* (e.g. camel)
หนอก nɔ̀ɔk [หนอก nɔ̀ɔk] |
(lump) ปุ่ม bpùm [ปุ่ม
bpùm]

humpback *n.* คนหลังค่อม
kon-lǎng-kɔ̂m [คน kon]

hunch *n.* (premonition)
ลางสังหรณ์ laang-sǎng-
hɔ̌ɔn

hunchback see humpback

hundred *numb.* ร้อย rɔ́ɔi,
หนึ่งร้อย nùng-rɔ́ɔi

hunger *n.* (food) ความหิว
kwaam-hǐu

hunger for *vt.*
อยากได้_มาก yàak-dâai-
_-mâak

hungry *adj.* หิว hǐu |
(desirous) อยาก yàak |
(food) หิวข้าว hǐu-kâao

hunt *n.* (act of hunting
game) การล่า gaan-lâa

hunt *v.* ล่า lâa

hunt *vi.* ล่าสัตว์ lâa-sàt

hunter *n.* (huntsman)
นายพราน naai-praan [คน
kon] | (person) นักล่า
nák-lâa [คน kon]

huntress see hunter

hurdle *n.* (barrier)
เครื่องกีดขวาง krûuang-
gìit-kwǎang [อัน an]

hurl *vt.* (throw) ขว้าง
kwâang | (wind-up
throw) เหวี่ยง wìiang

hurricane *n.* พายุเฮอริเคน
paa-yú-həə-rí~keen [ลูก
lûuk]

hurry *n.* ความเร่งรีบ
kwaam-rêng-rîip

hurry *v.* (accelerate, rush)
เร่ง rêng

hurry *vi.* (to do
something) รีบ rîip

hurt *vi.* (ache: longer-
term, less acute) ปวด
bpùuat | (pain: short-
term, acute) เจ็บ jèp

hurt *vt.* ทำให้_เจ็บปวด
tam-hâi-_-jèp-bpùuat

husband *n.* สามี sǎa-mii ⚠,
ผัว pǔua ⚫, แฟน fɛɛn ⚫
[คน kon]

husk *n.* (rice hull) แกลบ
glὲεp

hut *n.* กระท่อม grà~tɔ̂m
[หลัง lǎng]

hybrid *adj.* พันธุ์ผสม pan-
pà~sǒm

hydrogen *n.*

ก๊าซไฮโดรเจน gáat-hai-droo-jên

hydrophobia *n.* (rabies) โรคกลัวน้ำ rôok-gluua-náam, โรคพิษสุนัขบ้า rôok-pít-sù~nák-bâa ! [โรค rôok]

hyena *n.* หมาใน măa-nai [ตัว dtuua]

hygiene *n.* สุขลักษณะ sùk-kà~lák-sà~nà, อนามัย à~naa-mai

hymn *n.* เพลงสวด pleeng-sùuat [เพลง pleeng]

hyperactive *adj.* อยู่ไม่สุข yùu-mâi-sùk

hypertension *n.* ความดันโลหิตสูง kwaam-dan-loo-hìt-sǔung ! [โรค rôok]

hyphen *n.* เครื่องหมายขีด krûuang-măai-kìit [ตัว dtuua]

hypnosis *n.* การสะกดจิต gaan-sà~gòt-jìt

hypnotist *n.* นักสะกดจิต nák-sà~gòt-jìt [คน kon]

hypnotize *vt.* สะกดจิต sà~gòt-jìt

hypochondriac *n.* คนวิตกจริตเรื่องสุขภาพ kon-wí-dtòk-jà~rìt-rûuang-sùk-kà~pâap [คน kon]

hypothesis *n.* สมมุติฐาน sǒm-mút-dtì~tǎan [ข้อ kɔ̂ɔ]

hysteria *n.* ฮีสทีเรีย hìit-tii-riia [โรค rôok]

I

I *pron.* (female speaker) ฉัน chǎn, ดิฉัน dì~chǎn !, ชั้น chán ✺, ดิชั้น dì~chán ✺ | (male or female speaker) ข้าพเจ้า kâa-pá~jâao !, กู guu ✺ | (male speaker) ผม pǒm

ice *n.* น้ำแข็ง nám-kěng [ก้อน gɔ̂ɔn]

iceberg *n.* ภูเขาน้ำแข็ง puu-kǎo-nám-kěng [ลูก lûuk (mountain), ก้อน gɔ̂ɔn (piece)]

ice cream *n.* ไอศกรีม ai-sà~griim, ไอติม ai-dtim ✺ [แท่ง têng (stick), ถ้วย tûuai (bowl), ลูก lûuk (ball), รส rót (flavor)]

icicle *n.* (spike of ice)

หยาดน้ำแข็ง yàat-nám-kě̆ng [แท่ง têng]

icon n. (computers) ไอคอน ai-kɔ̂n [ไอคอน ai-kɔ̂n] | (sacred image) รูปบูชา rûup-buu-chaa [ชิ้น chín]

ICU n. ห้องไอซียู hɔ̂ng-ai-sii-yuu [ห้อง hɔ̂ng]

icy adj. (frozen) เป็นน้ำแข็ง bpen-nám-kě̆ng

idea n. (opinion) ความคิดเห็น kwaam-kít-hě̆n [อัน an] | (thought) ความคิด kwaam-kít

ideal adj. (excellent) เยี่ยม yîiam

ideal n. (standard of perfection) อุดมคติ ù-dom-ká~dtì

identical adj. (same) เหมือนกันทุกอย่าง mǔuan-gan-túk-yàang

identification n. (as suspect) การชี้ตัว gaan-chíi-dtuua

identify vt. (describe) บอกลักษณะ bɔ̀ɔk-lák-sà~nà | (e.g. suspect) ชี้ตัว chíi-dtuua | (verify)

พิสูจน์ pí-sùut

identity n. (appearance) รูปพรรณ rûup-bpà~pan | (e.g. personal, national, religious) เอกลักษณ์ èek-gà~lák

identity card n. บัตรประชาชน bàt-bprà~chaa-chon [ใบ bai]

idiom n. สำนวน sǎm-nuuan [สำนวน sǎm-nuuan]

idiot n. (foolish person) คนโง่ kon-ngôo, คนทึ่ม kon-tûm [คน kon]

idiotic adj. (foolish) โง่ ngôo, ปัญญาอ่อน bpan-yaa-ɔ̀ɔn

idle adj. (lazy) ขี้เกียจ kîi-gìiat

idle vi. (pass time) อยู่เฉยๆ yùu-chə̌əi-chə̌əi

idol n. (one who is adored) ผู้ที่มีคนคลั่งไคล้ pûu-tîi-mii-kon-klâng-klái [คน kon] | (worship image) รูปบูชา rûup-buu-chaa [รูป rûup, ใบ bai, แผ่น pèn]

i.e. idm. กล่าวคือ glàaokɯɯ, นั่นคือ nân-kɯɯ

if *conj.* ถ้า tâa, ถ้าหาก tâa-hàak, หาก hàak

igloo *n.* กระท่อมน้ำแข็ง grà~tɔ̂m-nám-kɛ̌ng [หลัง lǎng]

ignite *vi.* (burst into flame) ติดไฟ dtìt-fai

ignite *vt.* (cause to burn) ทำให้_ลุกไหม้ tam-hâi-_-lúk-mâi

ignition *n.* (catching fire) การติดไฟ gaan-dtìt-fai

ignorant *adj.* (unaware) ไม่รู้ mâi-rúu | (uneducated) ไร้การศึกษา rái-gaan-sùk-sǎa

ignore *vt.* (disregard) ไม่ใส่ใจ mâi-sài-jai, เพิกเฉยต่อ pɤ̂ɤk-chɤ̌əi-dtɔ̀ɔ ‼ | (uninterested) ไม่สนใจ mâi-sǒn-jai

iguana *n.* กิ้งก่ายักษ์ gîng-gàa-yák, อีกัวน่า ii-guua-nâa, เหี้ย hîia ✹ [ตัว dtuua]

ill *adj.* (sick) ป่วย bpùai, ไม่สบาย mâi-sà~baai

illegal *adj.* ผิดกฎหมาย pìt-gòt-mǎai, เถื่อน

tɯ̀an ✹

illegible *adj.* อ่านไม่ออก àan-mâi-ɔ̀ɔk

illiterate *adj.* (unable to read and write) ไม่รู้หนังสือ mâi-rúu-nǎng~sɯ̌ɯ

illness *n.* การเจ็บป่วย gaan-jèp-bpùai, โรคภัยไข้เจ็บ rôok-pai-kâi-jèp

illusion *n.* (concept) มายา maa-yaa | (hallucination) ภาพหลอน pâap-lɔ̌ɔn | (something causing false perception) สิ่งลวงตา sìng-luuang-dtaa

illustrate *v.* (draw) วาดภาพประกอบ wâat-pâap-bprà~gɔ̀ɔp | (explain) อธิบาย à-tí-baai

illustration *n.* (example) ตัวอย่าง dtuua-yàang [อัน an ✹, ตัวอย่าง dtuua-yàang] | (picture) ภาพประกอบ pâap-bprà~gɔ̀ɔp [ภาพ pâap]

illustrator *n.* ผู้วาดภาพประกอบ pûu-wâat-pâap-bprà~gɔ̀ɔp [คน kon]

image *n.* (picture) ภาพ

pâap [ใบ bai, แผ่น pèn, ภาพ pâap] | (reflection) เงา ngao [เงา ngao]

imagination *n.* (ability) จินตนาการ jin-dtà~naa-gaan | (fantasy) ความเพ้อฝัน kwaam-pə́ə-fǎn

imagine *v.* จินตนาการ jin-dtà~naa-gaan | (assume) สมมุติ sǒm-mút

imbalance *n.* ความไม่สมดุล kwaam-mâi-sǒm-dun

imitate *vt.* (copy, mimic) ลอกเลียน lɔ̂ɔk-liian, เลียนแบบ liian-bὲɛp

imitation *n.* (act) การลอกเลียนแบบ gaan-lɔ̂ɔk-liian-bὲɛp | (counterfeit) ของเลียนแบบ kɔ̌ɔng-liian-bὲɛp [อัน an, ชิ้น chín]

immature *adj.* ยังโตไม่เต็มที่ yang-dtoo-mâi-dtem-tîi

immediate *adj.* (close, e.g. family) ใกล้ชิด glâi-chít | (instant) ทันที tan-tii

immediately *adv.* (instantly) ทันทีทันใด tan-tii-tan-dai

immigrant *n.* ผู้อพยพ pûu-òp-pá~yóp [คน kon]

immigrate *vi.* (enter) เข้าเมือง kâo-mɯɯang | (move to) อพยพเข้า òp-pá~yóp-kâo

immigration *n.* การอพยพเข้าเมือง gaan-òp-pá~yóp-kâo-mɯɯang

immoral *adj.* ผิดศีลธรรม pìt-sǐin-tam

immortal *adj.* อมตะ am-má~dtà

immune *adj.* (protected from disease) มีภูมิคุ้มกันโรค mii-puum-kúm-gan-rôok

immunity *n.* (to disease) ภูมิคุ้มกัน puum-kúm-gan, ภูมิต้านทาน puum-dtâan-taan

impact *n.* (effect) ผลกระทบต่อ pǒn-grà~tóp-dtɔ̀ɔ

impact *vt.* (affect) มีผลกระทบต่อ mii-pǒn-grà~tóp-dtɔ̀ɔ | (strike forcefully) ปะทะกับ bpà~tá-gàp

impartial *adj.* (fair)

ยุติธรรม yút-dtì-tam |
(unbiased) ไม่มีอคติ
mâi-mii-àk-ká~dtì

impassive adj. เฉย chŏei,
ไม่ไหวติง mâi-wǎi-dting

impatient adj. (hasty,
quick-tempered) ใจร้อน
jai-rɔ́ɔn | (intolerant)
ไม่อดทน mâi-òt-ton

impeach vt. (make an
accusation) กล่าวโทษ
glàao-tôot | (try to sully
reputation)
พยายามทำให้_เสียชื่อ
pá~yaa yaam-tam-hâi-
_-sǐia-chûu

impede vt. กีดขวาง gìit-
kwǎang, หน่วงเหนี่ยว
nùuang-nìiao

imperative adj.
(necessary) เลี่ยงไม่ได้
lîiang-mâi-dâai

imperial adj. สูงส่ง
sǔung-sòng | (grand)
ยิ่งใหญ่ yîng-yài

impersonal adj. (lacking
warmth) เฉยชา chŏei-
chaa

impetuous adj. ใจร้อน jai-
rɔ́ɔn, หุนหัน hǔn-hǎn

implant vt. (e.g.

medicine) ฝัง fǎng

implore vt. (beg, plead)
วิงวอน wing-wɔɔn

imply vt. (hint) บอกเป็นนัย
bɔ̀ɔk-bpen-nai

impolite adj. ไม่สุภาพ
mâi-sù-pâap, หยาบคาย
yàap-kaai

import n. (product)
สินค้าเข้า sǐn-káa-kâo
[ชนิด chá~nít]

import vt. นำเข้า nam-kâo

importance n. ความสำคัญ
kwaam-sǎm-kan

important adj. สำคัญ
sǎm-kan

impose vt. (_ on _)
กำหนด_กับ_ gam-nòt-_-
gàp-_

impossible adj.
เป็นไปไม่ได้ bpen-bpai-
mâi-dâai, ไม่มีทาง mâi-
mii-taang ❧

impostor n.
คนที่ปลอมเป็นคนอื่น kon-
tîi-bplɔɔm-bpen-kon-
ùun [คน kon]

impotent adj. (unable to
copulate)
เป็นกามตายด้าน bpen-
gaam-dtaai-dâan |
(weak) อ่อนแอ ɔ̀ɔn-ɛɛ

impound *vt.* (seize) ริบ ríp, อายัด aa-yát

impress *n.* (act of impressing) ความประทับใจ kwaam-bprà~táp-jai

impress *vt.* ทำให้_ประทับใจ tam-hâi-_-bprà~táp-jai | (imprint) ประทับ bprà~táp

impressed *adj.* ประทับใจ bprà~táp-jai

impression *n.* (feeling) ความประทับใจ kwaam-bprà~táp-jai | (mark) รอยประทับ rɔɔi-bprà~táp [ที่ tîi]

impressive *adj.* น่าประทับใจ nâa-bprà~táp-jai

imprint *n.* (mark) รอยประทับ rɔɔi-bprà~táp [ที่ tîi] | (meaningful mark) เครื่องหมาย krûuang-mǎai [ตรา dtraa]

imprint *vt.* (make an imprint) ประทับ bprà~táp

imprison *vt.* จำคุก jam-kúk

impromptu *adj.* (without preparation) ไม่ได้เตรียมตัวมาก่อน

mâi-dâi-dtriiam-dtuua-maa-gɔɔn, สด sòt ◆

improper *adj.* (inappropriate) ไม่เหมาะสม mâi-mɔ̀-sǒm | (wrong) ไม่ถูกต้อง mâi-tùuk-dtɔ̂ng

improve *vi.* ปรับปรุง bpràp-bprung | (become better) ดีขึ้น dii-kûn

improve *vt.* ทำให้_ดีขึ้น tam-hâi-_-dii-kûn | (revise or correct) แก้ไข gɛ̂ɛ-kǎi

improvement *n.* การปรับปรุง gaan-bpràp-bprung

improvise *vt.* ไม่ได้เตรียม_มาก่อน mâi-dâi-dtriiam-_-maa-gɔɔn

imprudent *adj.* ประมาท bprà~màat

impulsive *adj.* ใจเร็ว jai-reo

impurity *n.* (condition) ความไม่บริสุทธิ์ kwaam-mâi-bɔɔ-rí~sùt

in *adv.* อยู่ใน yùu-nai

in *prep.* ใน nai | (by, at) ที่ tîi | (within) ภายใน paai-nai

inaccessible *adj.* เข้าไม่ถึง
kâo-mâi-tǔng

inaccurate *adj.*
คลาดเคลื่อน klâat-klûuan,
ไม่ถูกต้อง mâi-tùuk-dtɔ̂ng

inactive *adj.* (e.g. a
volcano) ดับ dàp |
(sluggish) เฉื่อยชา
chùuai-chaa

in addition to *prep.*
นอกจากนี้ nɔ̂ɔk-jàak-níi

in advance *adv.* ก่อนเวลา
gɔ̀ɔn-wee-laa, ล่วงหน้า
lûuang-nâa

inauspicious *adj.*
ไม่เป็นมงคล mâi-bpen-
mong-kon, อัปมงคล àp-
bpà~mong-kon ✍

incapable *adj.* ไม่สามารถ
mâi-sǎa-mâat,
ไร้ความสามารถ rái-
kwaam-sǎa-mâat

incarcerate *vt.* (confine)
กักขัง gàk-kǎng |
(imprison) จองจำ jɔɔng-
jam

in case *adv.* (in the case
of) ในกรณีของ nai-gɔɔ-
rá~nii-kɔ̌ɔng

in case *conj.* เผื่อว่า
pùua-wâa

incense *n.* (joss stick) ธูป
tûup [ดอก dɔ̀ɔk (one), ห่อ
hɔ̀ɔ (pack)]

incentive *n.* เครื่องจูงใจ
krûuang-juung-jai

incest *n.* การร่วมประเวณี
ระหว่างสายเลือด gaan-
rûuam-bprà~wee-nii-
rá~wàang-sǎai-lûuat

inch *n.* นิ้ว níu [นิ้ว níu]

incident *n.* (event)
เหตุการณ์ hèet-gaan [ครั้ง
kráng] | (occurrence)
เรื่องราว rûuang-raao
[เรื่อง rûuang]

incision *n.* (scar resulting
from such a cut) รอยผ่า
rɔɔi-pàa [รอย rɔɔi] |
(surgery) การผ่าตัด
gaan-pàa-dtàt

inclination *n.* (tendency)
ความเอนเอียง kwaam-
een-iiang

incline *n.* (slope) ทางลาด
taang-lâat [ทาง taang]

incline *vi.* (tilt) เอียง iiang

inclined to *aux.* มักจะ
mák-jà

include *vt.* (comprise)
รวมถึง ruuam-tǔng

income *n.* รายได้ raai-dâai

income tax *n.* ภาษีเงินได้ paa-sǐi-ngən-dâai

incoming *adj.* (approaching) ที่ใกล้จะมาถึง tîi-glâi-jà-maa-tǔng | (e.g. flight) ขาเข้า kǎa-kâo

incomplete *adj.* ไม่สมบูรณ์ mâi-sǒm-buun | (lacking) ขาด kàat

inconvenient *adj.* ไม่สะดวก mâi-sà~dùuak

incorporate *vi.* (form a corporation) รวมกันเป็นกลุ่มบริษัท ruuam-gan-bpen-glùm-bɔɔ-rí~sàt

incorporate *vt.* (unite) รวม_เข้าด้วยกัน ruuam-_-kâo-dûuai-gan

incorrect *adj.* (wrong) ไม่ถูกต้อง mâi-tùuk-dtɔ̂ng

increase *n.* (growth in numbers) จำนวนที่เพิ่มขึ้น jam-nuuan-tîi-pɔ̂əm-kûn

increase *v.* (augment) เพิ่ม_ขึ้น pɔ̂əm-_-kûn

increasing *adj.* เพิ่ม_ขึ้น pɔ̂əm-_-kûn, มากขึ้น mâak-kûn

incredible *adj.* ไม่น่าเชื่อ

mâi-nâa-chûua, เหลือเชื่อ lǔua-chûua

incriminate *vt.* (accuse) กล่าวโทษ glàao-tôot | (blame) ใส่ร้าย sài-ráai

incubate *vi.* (roost on eggs) ฟักไข่ fák-kài | (take form, multiply, e.g. pathogen) ฟักตัว fák-dtuua

incubator *n.* (eggs) เครื่องฟักไข่ krûuang-fák-kài [เครื่อง krûuang] | (newborns) ตู้อบสำหรับเด็กแรกเกิด dtûu-òp-sǎm-ràp-dèk-rɛ̂ɛk-gə̀ət [ตู้ dtûu]

indebted *adj.* ติดหนี้ dtìt-nîi, เป็นหนี้บุญคุณ bpen-nîi-bun-kun

indeed *adv.* (actually) จริงๆแล้ว jing-jing-lɛ́ɛo | (truly) อย่างแท้จริง yàang-tɛ́ɛ-jing

indefinite *adj.* (not fixed) ไม่กำหนดแน่นอน mâi-gam-nòt-nɛ̂ɛ-nɔɔn | (vague) คลุมเครือ klum-krɯɯa

indent *vt.* (paragraph)

ย่อหน้า yôo-nâa

independence n. อิสรภาพ ìt-sà~rá~pâap | (of a country) เอกราช èek-gà~râat

independent adj. เป็นอิสระ bpen-ìt-sà~rà, อิสระ ìt-sà~rà | (free) ฟรี frii ✻ | (of a country) เป็นเอกราช bpen-èek-gà~râat

index n. ดัชนี dàt-chá~nii [ตัว dtuua]

index finger n. นิ้วชี้ níu-chíi [นิ้ว níu]

India n. อินเดีย in-diia [ประเทศ bprà~têet]

Indian adj. (relating to India) อินเดีย in-diia

Indian n. (people) ชาวอินเดีย chaao-in-diia, แขก kèɛk ✻ [คน kon]

indicate vt. (point out) ชี้ให้เห็น chíi-hâi-hĕn | (say, measure) บ่งบอก bòng-bòok

indicator n. (turn signal) สัญญาณไฟเลี้ยว săn-yaan-fai-líiao [สัญญาณ săn-yaan]

indict vt. (charge) ฟ้องร้อง fóɔng-róɔng

indifferent adj. (having no interest) ไม่สนใจ mâi-sŏn-jai | (neutral) ไม่ลำเอียง mâi-lam-iiang | (unfriendly) เย็นชา yen-chaa

indigenous adj. (people) เกี่ยวกับชนพื้นเมือง gìiao-gàp-chon-púun-muuang

indigestion n. อาการอาหารไม่ย่อย aa-gaan-aa-hăan-mâi-yôi

indirect adj. (not direct) ทางอ้อม taang-ɔ̂ɔm, ไม่ตรง mâi-dtrong, อ้อมค้อม ɔ̂ɔm-kɔ́ɔm

individual adj. (each one) แต่ละอัน dtɛ̀ɛ-lá~an | (each person) แต่ละคน dtɛ̀ɛ-lá~kon | (private) ส่วนบุคคล sùuan-bùk-kon

individual adv. เดียว diiao

indivisible adj. (not divisible) แบ่งแยกไม่ได้ bɛ̀ng-yɛ̂ɛk-mâi-dâai

Indonesia n. อินโดนีเซีย in-doo-nii-siia [ประเทศ bprà~têet]

indoor adj. ในร่ม nai-rôm

induce vt. (cause)
ก่อให้เกิด gɔ̀ɔ-hâi-gə̀ət |
(persuade) ชักจูง chák-
juung

indulge vt. ยอมตามใจ
yɔɔm-dtaam-jai

indulgent adj. (allow
oneself) ตามใจตัว dtaam-
jai-dtuua

industrial adj.
ด้านอุตสาหกรรม dâan-
ùt-sǎa-hà~gam

industrialize vt.
ทำให้_เป็นอุตสาหกรรม
tam-hâi-_-bpen-ùt-sǎa-
hà~gam

industrious adj.
ขยันขันแข็ง kà~yǎn-kǎn-
kɛ̌ng, อุตสาหะ ùt-sǎa-hà
🙂

industry n. (manufacture
in general) อุตสาหกรรม
ùt-sǎa-hà~gam [ประเภท
bprà~pêet]

inept adj. (incompetent)
ไร้ความสามารถ rái-
kwaam-sǎa-mâat

inert adj. (chemistry) เฉื่อย
chùuai | (sluggish)
เฉื่อยชา chùuai-chaa

inevitable adj.

หลีกเลี่ยงไม่ได้ lìik-
lîiang-mâi-dâai

inexpensive adj. ถูก tùuk,
ไม่แพง mâi-pɛɛng

inexperienced adj.
ไม่มีประสบการณ์ mâi-
mii-bprà~sòp-gaan,
อ่อนหัด ɔ̀ɔn-hàt ●

infamous adj.
มีชื่อเสียงในทางไม่ดี mii-
chûu-sǐiang-nai-taang-
mâi-dii

infant n. เด็กอ่อน dèk-ɔ̀ɔn,
ทารก taa-rók [คน kon]

infatuated adj. (addicted
to) มัวเมา muua-mao |
(with) หลงใหล lǒng-lǎi

infect vt. (affect with
disease) ทำให้_ติดเชื้อ
tam-hâi-_-dtìt-chúua

infected adj. ติดเชื้อ dtìt-
chúua

infection n. การติดเชื้อ
gaan-dtìt-chúua,
การติดโรค gaan-dtìt-rôok

infectious adj. (causing
infection) ติดเชื้อ dtìt-
chúua | (contagious)
ติดต่อ dtìt-dtɔ̀ɔ

infer v. อนุมาน à-nú-

maan ✕ | (imply)
พูดเป็นนัย pûut-bpen-nai

inferior *adj.* (lower) ด้อย
dɔ̂ɔi | (worse) เลว leeo

inferiority complex *n.*
ปมด้อย bpom-dɔ̂i

infidelity *n.* (e.g. to a
spouse) การนอกใจ
gaan-nɔ̂ɔk-jai | (lack of
loyalty) ความไม่ซื่อสัตย์
kwaam-mâi-sʉ̂ʉ-sàt

infiltrate *v.* แทรกซึม
sɛ̂ɛk-sʉm

infinite *adj.* (endless)
ไม่มีที่สิ้นสุด mâi-mii-tîi-
sîn-sùt | (exceedingly
great) นับไม่ถ้วน náp-
mâi-tûuan

infinity *n.* (math)
จำนวนที่ไม่มีที่สิ้นสุด jam-
nuuan-tîi-mâi-mii-tîi-
sîn-sùt

inflamed *adj.* (infected)
อักเสบ àk-sèep |
(swollen) บวม buuam

inflammation *n.*
(infection) การอักเสบ
gaan-àk-sèep | (state of
being inflamed)
การติดไฟ gaan-dtìt-fai |
(swelling) การบวม gaan-

buuam

inflate *vi.* (swell) พองตัว
pɔɔng-dtuua

inflate *vt.* (using air)
สูบลม sùup-lom

inflation *n.* (economics)
เงินเฟ้อ ngən-fə́ə |
(swelling) การขยายตัว
gaan-kà~yǎai-dtuua

inflict *vt.* (_ on _)
ทำโทษโดย_กับ_ tam-
tôot-dooi-_-gàp-_

influence *n.* อิทธิพล ìt-tí-
pon | (impact) ผลกระทบ
pǒn-grà~tóp

influence *vt.* มีอิทธิพลต่อ
mii-ìt-tí-pon-dtɔ̀ɔ |
(affect) มีผลกระทบต่อ
mii-pǒn-grà~tóp-dtɔ̀ɔ

influential *adj.* (having
effect) มีผลกระทบ mii-
pǒn-grà~tóp | (personal
influence) มีอิทธิพล mii-
ìt-tí-pon

influenza *n.* ไข้หวัดใหญ่
kâi-wàt-yài [โรค rôok]

info see information

inform *vt.* (report) แจ้ง
jɛ̂ɛng | (report to police)
แจ้งความ jɛ̂ɛng-kwaam

informal *adj.*
ไม่เป็นทางการ mâi-bpen-

taang-gaan, กันเอง gan-eeng ✿

informant *n.* ผู้แจ้ง pûu-jɛ̂ɛng, ผู้บอก pûu-bɔ̀ɔk, นกต่อ nók-dtɔ̀ɔ ✿ [คน kon]

information *n.* (data) ข้อมูล kɔ̂ɔ-muun [ชนิด chá~nít (type), ชุด chút (set)] | (knowledge) ความรู้ kwaam-rúu | (news) ข่าวสาร kàao-sǎan [ชิ้น chín (piece), เรื่อง rɯ̂ɯang (content)]

infraction *n.* (fineable offense) โทษที่เสียเฉพาะค่าปรับ tôot-tîi-sǐia-chà~pɔ́-kâa-bpràp | (violation) การฝ่าฝืน gaan-fàa-fɯ̌ɯn

infringe *vt.* ฝ่าฝืน fàa-fɯ̌ɯn

in front *adv.* หน้า nâa

in front *prep.* ข้างหน้า kâang-nâa

in front of *adj.* หน้า nâa

in front of *adv.* ข้างหน้า kâang-nâa

in front of *prep.* ข้างหน้า kâang-nâa

in general *adv.* โดยทั่วไป dooi-tûua-bpai,

ตามธรรมดา dtaam-tam-má~daa

ingredient *n.* ส่วนประกอบ sùuan-bprà~gɔ̀ɔp, ส่วนผสม sùuan-pà~sǒm [ชนิด chá~nít ǃ, อย่าง yàang]

inhabit *vt.* อาศัยอยู่ใน aa-sǎi-yùu-nai

inhalant *n.* ยาดม yaa-dom [ชนิด chá~nít]

inhale *vi.* หายใจเข้า hǎai-jai-kâo

inhale *vt.* หายใจเอา_เข้า hǎai-jai-ao-_-kâo

inherit *v.* (take over) สืบต่อ sɯ̀ɯp-dtɔ̀ɔ

inherit *vi.* (receive a legacy) รับมรดก ráp-mɔɔ-rá~dòk

inheritance *n.* (legacy) มรดก mɔɔ-rá~dòk [กอง gɔɔng, ชิ้น chín]

inhibit *vt.* ยับยั้ง yáp-yáng

initial *adj.* (first) เริ่มแรก râ̂ɤm-rɛ̂ɛk, แรก rɛ̂ɛk

initial *n.* (first letter of a name) อักษรแรกของชื่อ àk-sɔ̌ɔn-rɛ̂ɛk-kɔ̌ɔng-chɯ̂ɯ [ตัว dtuua]

initiate *vt.* (begin) ริเริ่ม

A
B
C
D
E
F
G
H
I
J
K
L
M
N
O
P
Q
R
S
T
U
V
W
X
Y
Z

rí-rôəm ☙

initiative *n.* การริเริ่ม gaan-rí-rôəm

inject *vt.* (liquid, medicine) ฉีด chìit

injection *n.* (dose) ยาฉีด yaa-chìit [ชนิด chá~nít (type), เข็ม kěm (needle)] | (shot) การฉีดยา gaan-chìit-yaa

injure *vt.* ทำร้าย tam-ráai, ทำให้_บาดเจ็บ tam-hâi-_-bàat-jèp

injured *adj.* ได้รับบาดเจ็บ dâi-ráp-bàat-jèp, บาดเจ็บ bàat-jèp

injury *n.* (wound) การได้รับบาดเจ็บ gaan-dâi-ráp-bàat-jèp

ink *n.* หมึก mùk [ขวด kùuat (flask), หยด yòt (drop)]

inland *adv.* ภายในดินแดน paai-nai-din-dɛɛn

in-law *n.* (female) สะใภ้ sà~pái [คน kon] | (male) เขย kěəi [คน kon]

inmate *n.* (prisoner) นักโทษ nák-tôot [คน kon]

inn *n.* โรงแรมเล็ก roong-rɛɛm-lék [แห่ง hɛ̀ng]

inner *adj.* (inside) ภายใน paai-nai

innocent *adj.* (naive) ไร้เดียงสา rái-diiang-sǎa | (not guilty) บริสุทธิ์ bɔɔ-rí~sùt, ไม่ผิด mâi-pìt

innovation *n.* นวัตกรรม ná~wát-dtà~gam ❗

inoculate *v.* (vaccinate) ฉีดวัคซีน chìit-wák-siin

in order to *prep.* เพื่อที่จะ pûua-tîi-jà

inorganic *adj.* อนินทรีย์ à~nin-sii ✖

in pain *adv.* เจ็บปวด jèp-bpùuat

in practice *adv.* ในทางปฏิบัติ nai-taang-bpà-dtì~bàt

input *n.* (data) การป้อนข้อมูล gaan-bpɔ̂ɔn-kɔ̂ɔ-muun

input *vt.* (put something in) ใส่_เข้าไป sài-_-kâo-bpai

inquire *vi.* ถาม tǎam, สอบถาม sɔ̀ɔp-tǎam

inquiry *n.* (investigation) การไต่สวน gaan-dtài-sǔuan

insane *adj.* (afflicted)

สติไม่ดี sà~dtì-mâi-dii |
(crazy) บ้า bâa

insect *n.* แมลง má~lɛɛng,
แมง mɛɛng ✱ [ตัว dtuua]

insecticide *n.* ยาฆ่าแมลง
yaa-kâa-má~lɛɛng [ชนิด
chá~nít (type), ขวด
kùuat (bottle)]

insect repellent *n.*
ยาไล่แมลง yaa-lâi-má~
lɛɛng [ชนิด chá~nít
(type), ขวด kùuat
(bottle)]

insecure *adj.* (unsafe)
ไม่ปลอดภัย mâi-bplɔ̀ɔt-
pai | (unstable) ไม่มั่นคง
mâi-mân-kong

insensitive *adj.*
(emotionally, physically)
ไม่มีความรู้สึก mâi-mii-
kwaam-rúu-sùk |
(sexually) ตายด้าน dtaai-
dâan

insert *n.* (paper, sheet)
ใบแทรก bai-sɛ̂ɛk [ใบ bai]

insert *vt.* (put into) สอด
sɔ̀ɔt

inside *adj.* ภายใน paai-nai

inside *adv.* ข้างใน kâang-
nai, ภายใน paai-nai

inside *n.* ข้างใน kâang-
nai, ด้านใน dâan-nai,

ส่วนใน sùuan-nai [แห่ง
hɛ̀ng, ที่ tîi]

inside *prep.* ข้างใน
kâang-nai, ใน nai

inside out *adj.* กลับด้าน
glàp-dâan

insider *n.* คนใน kon-nai
[คน kon]

insight *n.* การเข้าใจลึกซึ้ง
gaan-kâo-jai-lúk-súng

insignificant *adj.*
(unimportant) ไม่สำคัญ
mâi-sǎm-kan

insignificant *adv.*
(unimportant) จิ๊บจ๊อย jíp-
jɔ́ɔi, ขี้ปะติ๋ว kîi-bpà~dtǐu
✱

insincere *adj.* ไม่จริงใจ
mâi-jing-jai

insist *vt.* (reiterate) ย้ำ
yám | (stand one's
ground) ยืนกราน yuun-
graan

insistent *adj.* ยืนยัน
yuun-yan | (stubborn)
หัวรั้น hǔua-rán

insoluble *adj.* (incapable
of being dissolved)
ไม่ละลาย mâi-lá~laai

insomnia *n.*

โรคนอนไม่หลับ rôok-
nɔɔn-mâi-làp [โรค rôok]

inspect v. (check)
ตรวจตรา dtrùuat-dtraa |
(examine) ตรวจสอบ
dtrùuat-sɔ̀ɔp

inspector n. (person who
inspects) ผู้ตรวจสอบ
pûu-dtrùuat-sɔ̀ɔp [คน
kon] | (police officer)
สารวัตร sǎa-rá~wát [คน
kon]

inspiration n.
แรงบันดาลใจ rɛɛng-ban-
daan-jai

inspire vt. บันดาลใจ ban-
daan-jai

install vt. (place, set up)
ติดตั้ง dtìt-dtâng

installment n. (partial
payment) เงินผ่อน ngən-
pɔ̀ɔn, ค่างวด kâa-ngûuat
❦ [งวด ngûuat]

instance n. (case) กรณี
gɔɔ-rá~nii [กรณี gɔɔ-rá~
nii ⚡, อย่าง yàang]

instant adj. (e.g. food,
beverage) กึ่งสำเร็จรูป
gùng-sǎm-rèt-rûup |
(sudden) ทันที tan-tii

instead adv. แทน tɛɛn,

แทนที่ tɛɛn-tîi

instead of adv. แทนที่
tɛɛn-tîi, แทนที่จะ tɛɛn-tîi-
jà

instinct n. สัญชาตญาณ
sǎn-châat-dtà~yaan

institute n. สถาบัน sà~
tǎa-ban [สถาบัน sà~tǎa-
ban]

institution n. (institute)
สถาบัน sà~tǎa-ban
[สถาบัน sà~tǎa-ban]

instruct vt. (advise) ชี้แนะ
chíi-né | (order) สั่ง sàng |
(teach) สอน sɔ̌ɔn, สั่งสอน
sàng-sɔ̌ɔn

instruction n. (advice)
การแนะนำ gaan-né-nam
| (order) คำสั่ง kam-sàng
[เรื่อง rûuang]

instructor n. ครู kruu,
ผู้สอน pûu-sɔ̌ɔn, อาจารย์
aa-jaan [คน kon, ท่าน tân
⚡]

instrument n. (device)
อุปกรณ์ ùp-bpà~gɔɔn
[ชิ้น chín (piece), ชุด chút
(set)] | (musical)
เครื่องดนตรี krûuang-

don-dtrii [ชิ้น chín (piece), ชุด chút (set)] | (tool) เครื่องมือ krûuang-muu [ชิ้น chín (piece), ชุด chút (set)]

insulation n. (material) ฉนวน chà~nǔuan [ชิ้น chín, อัน an]

insulin n. อินซูลิน in-suu-lin

insult n. (contempt) การดูถูก gaan-duu-tùuk

insult vt. สบประมาท sòp-bprà~màat | (look down on) ดูถูก duu-tùuk, เหยียดหยาม yìiat-yǎam

insurance n. การประกันภัย gaan-bprà~gan-pai, ประกันภัย bprà~gan-pai

insurance company n. บริษัทประกันภัย bɔɔ-rí~sàt-bprà~gan-pai [บริษัท bɔɔ-rí~sàt]

insurance policy n. กรมธรรม์ grom-má~tan [ฉบับ chà~bàp]

insure v. (buy insurance) ทำประกัน tam-bprà~gan

insure vt. (ensure, guarantee) รับประกัน ráp-bprà~gan

insured adj. มีประกัน mii-bprà~gan

insured n. (people) ผู้มีประกันภัย pûu-mii-bprà~gan-pai [คน kon]

integrate vt. (bring together) รวบรวม rûuap-ruuam | (combine, become integrated) ผสมผสาน pà~sǒm-pà~sǎan

integrity n. (condition of being whole) ความเป็นหนึ่งเดียว kwaam-bpen-nùng-diiao | (ethical code) การยึดหลักคุณธรรม gaan-yút-làk-kun-ná~tam

intellect n. สติปัญญา sà~dtì-bpan-yaa

intellectual adj. ทางสติปัญญา taang-sà~dtì-bpan-yaa

intelligence n. ความเฉลียวฉลาด kwaam-chà~lǐiao-chà~làat | (wisdom) ปัญญา bpan-yaa, สติปัญญา sà~dtì-bpan-yaa

intelligent *adj.* (clever) ฉลาด chà~làat | (sagacious) มีไหวพริบ mii-wǎi-príp | (skillful) เก่ง gèng

intend *v.* ตั้งใจ dtâng-jai, มีเจตนา mii-jèet-dtà~naa

intense *adj.* (degree or strength) เข้ม kêm, เข้มข้น kêm-kôn

intensely *adv.* อย่างแรง yàang-rɛɛng

intensity *n.* (concentration) ความเข้มข้น kwaam-kêm-kôn | (density) ความหนาแน่นของพลังงาน kwaam-nǎa-nɛ̂n-kɔ̌ɔng-pá~lang-ngaan

intensive *adj.* เข้ม kêm

intent *adj.* ตั้งใจ dtâng-jai, มุ่งมั่น mûng-mân

intent *n.* ความตั้งใจ kwaam-dtâng-jai

intention *n.* ความตั้งใจ kwaam-dtâng-jai, ความมุ่งมั่น kwaam-mûng-mân

intentional *adj.* (on purpose) เจตนา jèet-dtà~naa

interchange *vt.* (exchange) แลกเปลี่ยน_กัน lɛ̂ɛk-bplìian-_-gan

interchangeable *adj.* สลับกันได้ sà~làp-gan-dâai

intercourse *n.* (communications) การปฏิสัมพันธ์กัน gaan-bpà~dtì-sǎm-pan-gan ! | (sexual) การมีเพศสัมพันธ์ gaan-mii-pêet-sǎm-pan, การร่วมเพศ gaan-rûam-pêet

interest *n.* (benefit) ส่วนได้ส่วนเสีย sùuan-dâai-sùuan-sǐia | (fascination) ความสนใจ kwaam-sǒn-jai | (for a loan) ดอกเบี้ย dɔ̀ɔk-bîia

interest *vt.* (intrigue) ทำให้_เกิดความสนใจ tam-hâi-_-gə̀ət-kwaam-sǒn-jai

interested *adj.* สนใจ sǒn-jai

interesting *adj.* น่าสนใจ nâa-sǒn-jai

interfere *vi.* (disturb, bother) รบกวน róp-

guuan | (meddle)
ก้าวก่าย gâao-gàai, ยุ่ง
yûng
interference n. (act)
การรบกวน gaan-róp-
guuan
interim n. (intervening
time) ช่วงเวลาหยุดพัก
chûuang-wee-laa-yùt-
pák
interior adj. ภายใน paai-
nai
interjection n. (part of
speech) คำอุทาน kam-ù-
taan [คำ kam]
intermediate adj. กลาง
glaang, ชั้นกลาง chán-
glaang
intermission n.
การหยุดพัก gaan-yùt-pák
intern n. (internee)
ผู้ฝึกหัด pûu-fùk-hàt [คน
kon]
internal adj. ข้างใน
kâang-nai, ภายใน paai-
nai
international adj.
นานาชาติ naa-naa-châat,
ระหว่างประเทศ rá~
wàang-bprà~têet
internet n. อินเตอร์เน็ต
in-dtəə-nèt

interpret v. ตีความ dtii-
kwaam | (explain) อธิบาย
à-tí-baai | (translate)
แปล bplɛɛ
interpretation n. (act)
การแปล gaan-bplɛɛ |
(rendering or
explanation) การตีความ
gaan-dtii-kwaam
interpreter n. ล่าม lâam
[คน kon]
interrogate v. (ask)
สอบถาม sɔ̀ɔp-tăam |
(investigate) สอบปากคำ
sɔ̀ɔp-bpàak-kam
interrupt v. (interfere,
disturb) ขัดจังหวะ kàt-
jang-wà, รบกวน róp-
guuan
intersection n. (four-way)
สี่แยก sìi-yɛ̂ɛk [แห่ง hɛ̀ng,
ที่ tîi] | (place where
things intersect) ชุมทาง
chum-taang [แห่ง hɛ̀ng]
interval n. (amount of
time) ระยะเวลา rá~yá-
wee-laa [ระยะ rá~yá]
intervene vi. (interfere)
เข้าแทรกแซง kâo-sɛ̂ɛk-
sɛɛng | (mediate)
อยู่ระหว่างกลาง yùu-rá~
wàang-glaang

interview *n.* การสัมภาษณ์ gaan-săm-pâat

interview *v.* สัมภาษณ์ săm-pâat

intestine *n.* ลำไส้ lam-sâi, ไส้ sâi [ท่อน tɔ̂n (strip), ขด kòt (coil)]

intimacy *n.* (closeness) ความสนิทสนม kwaam-sà~nìt-sà~nŏm | (familiarity) ความคุ้นเคย kwaam-kún-kəəi | (sexual intercourse) ความสัมพันธ์ทางชู้สาว kwaam-săm-pan-taang-chúu-săao

intimate *adj.* (close) ใกล้ชิด glâi-chít | (familiar) คุ้นเคย kún-kəəi | (private) เป็นส่วนตัว bpen-sùuan-dtuua

intimidate *vt.* (coerce) บังคับ bang-káp | (scare) ทำให้_กลัว tam-hâi-_-gluua | (threaten) ข่มขู่ kòm-kùu

intimidated *adj.* กลัว gluua, ตกใจกลัว dtòk-jai-gluua

into *prep.* (inside) เข้าไป kâo-bpai | (toward) ไปยัง bpai-yang

intolerant *adj.* ไม่ผ่อนปรน mâi-pɔ̀n-bpron

intonation *n.* (pitch, tone) เสียงสูงต่ำ sĭiang-sŭung-dtàm [เสียง sĭiang]

intoxicate *vt.* ทำให้_มึนเมา tam-hâi-_-mʉn-mao

intoxicated *adj.* เมา mao

intriguing *adj.* ดึงดูดใจ dʉng-dùut-jai

introduce *vt.* (present) แนะนำ né-nam

introduction *n.* (act) การแนะนำ gaan-né-nam | (foreword) บทนำ bòt-nam [บท bòt]

introvert *n.* คนเก็บตัว kon-gèp-dtuua ✷ [คน kon]

intrude *vi.* (into life or conversation) เสือก sʉ̀uak ✷ | (trespass) บุกรุก bùk-rúk

intuition *n.* สัญชาตญาณ săn-châat-dtà~yaan

inundated *adj.* ท่วม tûuam

invade *vt.* บุกรุก bùk-rúk

invalid *adj.* (unusable) ใช้การไม่ได้ chái-gaan-mâi-dâai | (void) โมฆะ moo-ká ➤

invalid *n.* (disabled person) คนพิการ kon-pí-gaan [คน kon]

invariable *adj.* (not changing) ไม่เปลี่ยนแปลง mâi-bpliian-bplɛɛng | (stable) คงที่ kong-tîi

invasion *n.* การบุกรุก gaan-bùk-rúk, การรุกราน gaan-rúk-raan

invent *v.* ประดิษฐ์ bprà~dìt

invention *n.* (act) การประดิษฐ์ gaan-bprà~dìt | (anything invented) สิ่งประดิษฐ์ sìng-bprà~dìt [ชิ้น chín]

inventory *n.* (stock) สินค้าที่มีเก็บไว้ sǐn-káa-tîi-mii-gèp-wái [รายการ raai-gaan]

inverse *adj.* กลับกัน glàp-gan, ตรงกันข้าม dtrong-gan-kâam

invest *v.* ลงทุน long-tun

investigate *v.* (examine) สืบสวน sùup-sǔuan | (interrogate) สอบสวน sɔ̀ɔp-sǔuan

investigation *n.*

การสืบสวน gaan-sùup-sǔuan

investigator *n.* ผู้สืบสวน pûu-sùup-sǔuan [คน kon]

investment *n.* (act) การลงทุน gaan-long-tun

investor *n.* นักลงทุน nák-long-tun [คน kon]

invisible *adj.* มองไม่เห็น mɔɔng-mâi-hěn, ไม่ปรากฏ mâi-bpraa-gòt

invitation *n.* (act) การเชื้อเชิญ gaan-chúua-chəən

invite *v.* ชวน chuuan, เชิญ chəən, เชิญชวน chəən-chuuan ‼

invoice *n.* ใบเก็บเงิน bai-gèp-ngən [ใบ bai]

involve *vt.* (bring in) เอา_ไปเกี่ยวข้อง ao-_-bpai-gìiao-kɔ̂ng | (connect) พัวพันกับ puua-pan-gàp | (relate to) เกี่ยวข้องกับ gìiao-kɔ̂ng-gàp

involved *adj.* (concerned) เกี่ยวข้อง gìiao-kɔ̂ng, พัวพัน puua-pan

invulnerable *adj.*

อยู่ยงคงกระพัน yùu-yong-kong-grà~pan

iodine *n.* ไอโอดีน ai-oo-diin [สาร sǎan]

I.Q. *n.* ไอคิว ai-kiu [ไอคิว ai-kiu]

Iran *n.* อิหร่าน ì~ràan [ประเทศ bprà~têet]

Iraq *n.* อิรัก ì~rák [ประเทศ bprà~têet]

iris *n.* (of the eye) ม่านตา mâan-dtaa

iron *adj.* (made of iron) ทำด้วยเหล็ก tam-dûuai-lèk

iron *n.* (appliance) เตารีด dtao-rîit [อัน an] | (chemistry) ธาตุเหล็ก tâat-lèk [ธาตุ tâat] | (metal) เหล็ก lèk [อัน an]

iron *vi.* (clothes) รีดผ้า rîit-pâa

iron *vt.* (clothes) รีด rîit

ironic *adj.* (sarcastic) ประชด bprà~chót, แดกดัน dὲɛk-dan ●

irony *n.* (rhetoric) ถ้อยคำแดกดัน tɔ̂i-kam-dὲɛk-dan

irreconcilable *adj.* (irreparable) คืนดีกันไม่ได้

kɯɯn-dii-gan-mâi-dâai

irregular *adj.* ผิดปกติ pìt-bpà~gà~dtì, ไม่ปกติ mâi-bpà~gà~dtì

irrelevant *adj.* ไม่เกี่ยวเนื่องกัน mâi-gìiao-nɯ̂ɯang-gan

irresistible *adj.* (not resistible) ต้านทานไม่ได้ dtâan-taan-mâi-dâai | (tempting) ยั่วยวน yûua-yuuan

irresponsible *adj.* ไม่มีความรับผิดชอบ mâi-mii-kwaam-ráp-pìt-chɔ̂ɔp

irrigate *vi.* ทดน้ำ tót-náam, ชลประทาน chon-lá~bprà~taan ‼

irrigation *n.* การชลประทาน gaan-chon-lá~bprà~taan

irritate *v.* (bother, annoy) รบกวน róp-guuan | (provoke) ยั่วโมโห yûua-moo-hǒo

irritated *adj.* (annoyed) รำคาญ ram-kaan, หงุดหงิด ngùt-ngìt

is see **be**

Islam *n.* ศาสนาอิสลาม sàat-sà~nǎa-ìt-sà~laam [ศาสนา sàat-sà~nǎa]

island *n.* เกาะ gɔ̀ [เกาะ gɔ̀]

islander *n.* ชาวเกาะ chaao-gɔ̀ [คน kon]

isolate *vt.* แยก_ออกจาก_ yɛ̂ɛk-_-ɔ̀ɔk-jàak-_

isolate oneself *vi.* (depart from someone or something) ตีตัวออกห่าง dtii-dtuua-ɔ̀ɔk-hàang

Israel *n.* อิสราเอล ìt-sà~ raa-eeo [ประเทศ bprà~ têet]

issue *n.* (edition) ฉบับ chà~bàp [ฉบับ chà~bàp] | (matter) เรื่อง rûuang [เรื่อง rûuang] | (point) ประเด็น bprà~den [ประเด็น bprà~den !, จุด jùt, ข้อ kɔ̂ɔ] | (problem) ปัญหา bpan-hǎa [เรื่อง rûuang (matter), ข้อ kɔ̂ɔ (point)]

issue *v.* (publish) ตีพิมพ์ dtii-pim

it *pron.* มัน man

Italian *n.* (language) ภาษาอิตาลี paa-sǎa-ìt- dtaa-lîi [ภาษา paa-sǎa] | (people) ชาวอิตาลี chaao- ìt-dtaa-lîi [คน kon]

italic *n.* ตัวเอียง dtuua-

iiang [ตัว dtuua]

Italy *n.* อิตาลี ìt-dtaa-lîi [ประเทศ bprà~têet]

itch *v.* (scratch) เกา gao

itch *vi.* (feel itchy) คัน kan

itchy *adj.* คัน kan

it doesn't matter *idm.* ไม่เป็นไร mâi-bpen-rai

item *n.* (entry in an account) รายการ raai- gaan [รายการ raai-gaan] | (section) ข้อ kɔ̂ɔ [ข้อ kɔ̂ɔ]

itinerary *n.* (travel plan) กำหนดการเดินทาง gam- nòt-gaan-dəən-taang

its *adj.* ของมัน kɔ̌ɔng-man

it's all right. *idm.* ก็ได้ gɔ̂ɔ-dâai, ไม่เป็นไร mâi- bpen-rai

itself *pron.* ตัวมันเอง dtuua-man-eeng

it's too bad *idm.* น่าเสียดาย nâa-sǐia-daai

ivory *n.* (elephant tusk) งาช้าง ngaa-cháang [กิ่ง gìng (each), คู่ kûu (pair)]

ivy *n.* ต้นไอวี่ dtôn-ai-wîi [ต้น dtôn]

J

jab *v.* ชก chók

jab *vt.* ทิ่ม tîm

jack *n.* (for lifting) แม่แรง mɛ̂ɛ-rɛɛng [ตัว dtuua] | (socket) ปลั๊ก bplák [ตัว dtuua, อัน an]

jackal *n.* (nocturnal dog) หมาใน mǎa-nai [ตัว dtuua]

jackass *n.* (male donkey) ลาตัวผู้ laa-dtuua-pûu [ตัว dtuua] | (stupid person) คนโง่ kon-ngôo [คน kon]

jacket *n.* เสื้อแจ็คเก็ต sûua-jék-gèt [ตัว dtuua]

jackfruit *n.* ขนุน kà~nǔn [ลูก lûuk]

jackknife *n.* มีดพับ mîit-páp, มีดพับขนาดใหญ่ mîit-páp-kà~nàat-yài [เล่ม lêm]

jack-o'-lantern *n.* (Halloween) ฟักทองแกะสลักไส้เทียน fák-tɔɔng-gɛ̀-sà~làk-sâi-tiian [ลูก lûuk]

jade *n.* หยก yòk [ชิ้น chín (piece), ก้อน gɔ̂ɔn (chunk)]

jagged *adj.* เป็นฟันปลา bpen-fan-bplaa

jail *n.* (prison) คุก kúk [แห่ง hèng] | (prison) ตะราง dtà~raang [แห่ง hèng, ที่ tîi]

jail *vt.* (imprison) ขัง kǎng, จำคุก jam-kúk ⚡

jam *n.* (crammed area) จุดที่เบียดกันแน่น jùt-tîi-biiat-gan-nɛ̂n [จุด jùt] | (preserves) แยม yɛɛm [ขวด kùuat (bottle)] | (traffic jam) รถติด rót-dtìt

jam-packed *adj.* อัดแน่น àt-nɛ̂n

janitor *n.* ภารโรง paan-roong [คน kon]

January *n.* มกราคม mók-gà~raa-kom [เดือน dɯɯan]

Japan *n.* ญี่ปุ่น yîi-bpùn [ประเทศ bprà~têet]

Japanese *adj.* (relating to Japan) ญี่ปุ่น yîi-bpùn

Japanese *n.* (language) ภาษาญี่ปุ่น paa-sǎa-yîi-bpùn [ภาษา paa-sǎa] | (people) คนญี่ปุ่น kon-yîi-bpùn [คน kon]

jar *n.* (e.g. for cookie,

money) กระปุก grà~
bpùk [ใบ bai] | (water)
โอ่ง òong [ใบ bai] |
(water) ตุ่ม dtùm [ใบ bai,
ลูก lûuk]

jasmine *n.* (plant) มะลิ
má~lí [ต้น dtôn (plant),
ดอก dòok (flower)]

jaundice *n.* ดีซ่าน dii-sâan
[โรค rôok]

javelin *n.* (lance) แหลน
lɛ̌ɛn [เล่ม lêm] | (spear)
หลาว lǎao [เล่ม lêm]

jaw *n.* กราม graam [ข้าง
kâang]

jawline *n.* กราม graam

jealous *adj.* (between
lovers) หึง hǔng |
(envious) อิจฉา it-chǎa |
(possessive) หวง hǔuang

jealousy *n.* ความริษยา
kwaam-rít-sà~yǎa |
(between lovers)
ความหึงหวง kwaam-
hǔng-hǔuang

jeans *n.* (pants)
กางเกงยีนส์ gaang-
geeng-yiin [ตัว dtuua]

jeep *n.* รถจี๊ป rót-jíip [คัน
kan]

Jehovah *n.* ยะโฮวา yá~

hoo-waa [องค์ ong]

jelly *n.* เยลลี่ yen-lîi, วุ้น
wún

jellyfish *n.* แมงกะพรุน
mɛɛng-gà~prun [ตัว
dtuua]

jeopardy *n.* (hazard, peril)
ภัยอันตราย pai-an-dtà~
raai ⚡

jerk *n.* (dumb person,
dork) คนเซ่อ kon-sə̂ə [คน
kon]

jerk *v.* (twitch) กระตุก
grà~dtùk

jest *vi.* ล้อเล่น lɔ́ɔ-lên

jester *n.* ตัวตลก dtuua-
dtà~lòk [คน kon, ตัว
dtuua]

Jesus Christ *n.* คริสต์ krít,
พระเยซู prá-yee-suu, เยซู
yee-suu, พระเยซูคริสต์
prá-yee-suu-krít ⚡ [องค์
ong]

jet *n.* (plane)
เครื่องบินไอพ่น krûuang-
bin-ai-pôn [เครื่อง
krûuang]

jet lag *n.* เจ็ตแล็ก jét-lɛ́ɛk,
อาการอ่อนเพลียจาก
การเดินทางด้วยเครื่องบิน
aa-gaan-ɔ̀ɔn-pliia-jàak-

gaan-dəən-taang-
dûuai-krûuang-bin

jet plane *n.* เครื่องบินไอพ่น
krûuang-bin-ai-pôn
[เครื่อง krûuang]

Jew *n.* คนยิว kon-yiu [คน
kon]

jewel *n.* รัตนะ rát-dtà~ná
❧ [ชิ้น chín] | (gem)
เพชรพลอย pét-plɔɔi [ชิ้น
chín (piece), ชุด chút
(set)]

jeweler *n.* (store)
ร้านขายเพชรพลอย ráan-
kǎai-pét-plɔɔi [คน kon]

jewelry *n.* (accessories)
เครื่องประดับ krûuang-
bprà~dàp [ชิ้น chín
(piece), ชุด chút (set)] |
(gems) เพชรพลอย pét-
plɔɔi [ชิ้น chín (piece), ชุด
chút (set)]

Jewish *adj.* ยิว yiu

jigsaw puzzle *n.*
เกมต่อชิ้นส่วนภาพ
geem-dtɔɔ-chín-sùuan-
pâap [เกม geem]

jingle *n.* (sound produced
by metal striking
together) เสียงกรุ๊งกริ๊ง

sǐiang-grúng-gríng ❧
[เสียง sǐiang]

job *n.* (occupation) อาชีพ
aa-chîip [อาชีพ aa-chîip] |
(work) งาน ngaan [อัน an,
ชิ้น chín]

jockey *n.* (horse rider)
คนขี่ม้าแข่ง kon-kìi-máa-
kèng, จ็อกกี้ jɔ́k-gîi ❧ [คน
kon]

jog *vi.* (trot) วิ่งเหยาะๆ
wîng-yɔ̀-yɔ̀

jogging *n.* การวิ่งช้าๆ
gaan-wîng-cháa-cháa

join *vi.* (connect) ต่อกัน
dtɔɔ-gan | (put together)
ติดกัน dtìt-gan

join *vt.* (participate)
เข้าร่วม kâo-rûuam

joint *adj.* (sharing) ร่วมกัน
rûuam-gan

joint *n.* (of the body)
ข้อต่อ kɔ̂ɔ-dtɔɔ [ข้อ kɔ̂ɔ] |
(place at which things
are joined) รอยต่อ rɔɔi-
dtɔɔ [รอย rɔɔi]

joke *n.* ตลก dtà~lòk [เรื่อง
rûuang]

joke *vi.* (kid, tease) พูดเล่น
pûut-lên

joker n. (card) ไพ่โจ๊กเกอร์ pâi-jóok-gə̂ə [ใบ bai] | (comedian) ตัวตลก dtuua-dtà~lòk [คน kon, ตัว dtuua]

jolly adj. รื่นเริง rûun-rəəng

joss-stick n. ธูป tûup [ดอก dɔ̀ɔk (one), ห่อ hɔ̀ɔ (pack)]

jot vt. (take a brief note) จด_ลงสั้นๆ jòt-_-long-sân-sân

jot down vt. (take note of) จด jòt

journal n. (diary) บันทึกประจำวัน ban-túk-bprà~jam-wan [เล่ม lêm]

journalist n. นักข่าว nák-kàao, นักหนังสือพิมพ์ nák-năng~sǔu-pim, ผู้สื่อข่าว pûu-sùu-kàao ! [คน kon]

journey n. การเดินทาง gaan-dəən-taang [ครั้ง kráng]

jovial adj. (merry) เบิกบาน bə̀ək-baan

joy adj. (amused, having fun) สนุกสนาน sà~nùk-sà~nǎan | (cheerful) ร่าเริง râa-rəəng

joy n. (pleasure) ความยินดี kwaam-yin-dii

joyful adj. (cheerful) ร่าเริง râa-rəəng | (delighted) ยินดี yin-dii | (having fun) สนุก sà~nùk

jubilee n. (festival) การฉลองรื่นเริง gaan-chà~lɔ̌ɔng-rûun-rəəng [ครั้ง kráng]

Judaism n. ศาสนายิว sàat-sà~nǎa-yiu [ศาสนา sàat-sà~nǎa]

judge n. (in a contest) กรรมการ gam-má~gaan [คน kon (individual)] | (in court) ผู้พิพากษา pûu-pí-pâak-sǎa [คน kon, ท่าน tân !]

judge v. (determine, decide) ตัดสิน dtàt-sĭn

judgement see judgment

judgment n. (act) การตัดสิน gaan-dtàt-sĭn [ครั้ง kráng] | (judicial decision) คำตัดสิน kam-dtàt-sĭn, คำพิพากษา kam-pí-pâak-sǎa [ครั้ง kráng]

Judgment Day n. วันพิพากษา wan-pí-pâak-

สัา [วัน wan]

judicial *adj.*
เกี่ยวกับศาลยุติธรรม
giiao-gàp-sǎan-yút-dtì~
tam

judo *n.* ยูโด yuu-doo
[ชนิด chá~nít]

jug *n.* เหยือก yùuak [ใบ
bai]

juggle *vt.* (objects)
โยนและรับ_อย่างต่อเนื่อง
yoon-lé-ráp-_-yàang-
dtɔ̀ɔ-nûuang

juice *n.* (fruit) น้ำผลไม้
nám-pòn-lá~máai [ชนิด
chá~nít (kind), แก้ว gêɛo
(glass)]

juicy *adj.* (having juice or
water) มีน้ำ mii-náam |
(moist) ฉ่ำ chàm

jujube *n.* พุทรา pút-saa
[ลูก lûuk]

July *n.* กรกฎาคม gà~rák-
gà~daa-kom [เดือน
dɯɯan]

jumbled *adj.* ปนเป bpon-
bpee

jump *n.* การกระโดด
gaan-grà~dòot

jump *v.* โดด dòot ❀

jump *vi.* กระโดด grà~dòot

jumper see sweater

jumper cables *n.*
สายเคเบิลสำหรับสตาร์ทรถ
sǎai-kee-bên-sǎm-ràp-
sà~dtàat-rót [เส้น sên]

jump rope *n.*
เชือกที่ใช้กระโดด chûuak-
tîi-chái-grà~dòot [เส้น
sên]

junction *n.* (connecting
point) จุดเชื่อมต่อ jùt-
chûuam-dtɔ̀ɔ [จุด jùt] |
(intersection) ทางแยก
taang-yɛ̂ɛk [แห่ง hɛ̀ng] |
(place where roads
meet) ชุมทาง chum-
taang [แห่ง hɛ̀ng]

June *n.* มิถุนายน mí-tù-
naa-yon [เดือน dɯɯan]

jungle *n.* ป่าทึบ bpàa-túp
[แห่ง hɛ̀ng] | ป่า bpàa
[ป่า bpàa, แห่ง hɛ̀ng]

junior *adj.* (younger)
อ่อนกว่า ɔ̀ɔn-gwàa ❀

junior *n.* (person lesser in
rank or time of
participation) รุ่นน้อง
rûn-nɔ́ɔng [คน kon] |
(third year of college)
นักศึกษามหาวิทยาลัย

ปีสาม nák-sùk-săa-má~hăa-wít-tá~yaa-lai-bpii-săam [คน kon]

junior college n. วิทยาลัยที่ให้อนุปริญญา wít-tá~yaa-lai-tîi-hâi-à~nú-bpà~rin-yaa [แห่ง hèng]

junior high school n. โรงเรียนมัธยมต้น roong-riian-mát-tá~yom-dtôn [แห่ง hèng]

junk n. ขยะ kà~yà [ชิ้น chín (piece), กอง gɔɔng (pile)]

junk food n. อาหารขยะ aa-hăan-kà~yà

junta n. รัฐบาลทหาร rát-tà~baan-tá~hăan [ชุด chút]

Jupiter n. ดาวพฤหัส daao-pá~rʉ́-hàt [ดวง duuang]

jurisdiction n. อำนาจศาล am-nâat-săan [เขต kèet (region)]

juristic act n. นิติกรรม ní-dtì-gam

juror n. (individual) ลูกขุน lûuk-kŭn [คน kon]

jury n. (panel) คณะลูกขุน ká~ná~lûuk-kŭn [คณะ ká~ná]

jury duty n. หน้าที่ลูกขุน nâa-tîi-lûuk-kŭn [หน้าที่ nâa-tîi]

jury trial n. การพิจารณาคดีโดยคณะลูกขุน gaan-pí-jaa-rá~naa-ká~dii-dooi-ká~ná-lûuk-kŭn [ครั้ง kráng]

just adj. (fair) ยุติธรรม yút-dtì-tam | (lawful) ถูกต้องตามกฎหมาย tùuk-dtɔ̂ng-dtaam-gòt-măai

just adv. (exactly) ทีเดียว tii-diiao | (moment ago) เพิ่ง pêng, เมื่อกี้นี้ mʉ̂ua-gîi-níi | (only) เท่านั้น tâo-nán, เพียง piiang, เพียงแค่ piiang-kɛ̂ɛ ✦

just a moment adv. (little while) เดี๋ยวเดียว dĭiao-diiao

just a moment idm. แป๊บเดียวนะ bpép-diiao-ná ✦

just as adj. เหมือนกับ mʉ̌uan-gàp

just a second! interj. เดี๋ยว dĭiao

just enough adj. เพียงพอ
piiang-pɔɔ

justice n. (fairness)
ความยุติธรรม kwaam-
yú-dtì-tam

justification n.
การอ้างเหตุผล gaan-
âang-hèet-pǒn

justify v. (demonstrate a
reason) แสดงเหตุผล sà~
dɛɛng-hèet-pǒn

just now adv. เมื่อกี้
mûua-gîi, พึ่ง pûng ●

juvenile adj.
เกี่ยวกับเด็กและเยาวชน
gìiao-gàp-dèk-lé-yao-
wá~chon

juvenile n. เยาวชน yao-
wá~chon [รุ่น rûn] |
(adolescent) คนหนุ่มสาว
kon-nùm-sǎao [คน kon]

juvenile delinquency n.
การกระทำผิดของเยาวชน
gaan-grà~tam-pìt-
kǎong-yao-wá~chon

K

kaffir n. มะกรูด má~grùut
[ลูก lûuk (fruit)]

kaffir lime leaves n.
ใบมะกรูด bai-má~grùut
[ใบ bai]

kangaroo n. จิงโจ้ jing-jôo
[ตัว dtuua]

kapok n. นุ่น nûn

karate n. คาราเต้ kaa-raa-
dtêe

Karen n. (hill tribe)
กะเหรี่ยง gà~rìiang [เผ่า
pào (tribe)]

karma n. กรรม gam

keep vt. (maintain) รักษา
rák-sǎa | (save, store,
hold) เก็บ gèp

keep off v. (stay away
from) ไม่เข้าใกล้ mâi-
kâo-glâi

keep on v. (continue)
ทำ_ต่อ tam-_-dtɔ̀ɔ

keep out! interj. ห้ามเข้า
hâam-kâo

keep up with v. (catch
up) ตามทัน dtaam-tan |
(stay up to date)
ทันต่อเวลา tan-dtɔ̀ɔ-wee-
laa

keg n. (beer barrel)
ถังเบียร์ tǎng-biia [ใบ bai]

kernel n. (seed, core)
เมล็ด má~lét ⚡ [เม็ด mét,
เมล็ด má~lét ⚡]

kerosene n. น้ำมันก๊าด
nám-man-gáat [ลิตร lít]

ketchup *n.* ซอสมะเขือเทศ sɔ́ɔt-má~kǔua-têet [ขวด kùuat (bottle), ซอง sɔɔng (small pack)]

kettle *n.* กาต้มน้ำ gaa-dtôm-náam [ใบ bai]

key *adj.* สำคัญ sǎm-kan

key *n.* กุญแจ gun-jɛɛ, ลูกกุญแจ lûuk-gun-jɛɛ [ลูก lûuk, ดอก dɔ̀ɔk] | (music scale) ระดับเสียง rá~dàp-sǐiang, คีย์ kii ☙ [ระดับ rá~dàp]

keyboard *n.* คีย์บอร์ด kii-bɔ̀ɔt [อัน an] | แป้นพิมพ์ bpên-pim ☙ [อัน an, แป้น bpɛ̂ɛn]

key in *vi.* (enter info) ใส่ข้อมูล sài-kɔ̂ɔ-muun

key ring *n.* พวงกุญแจ puuang-gun-jɛɛ [พวง puuang]

keyword *n.* (word used as a reference point) คำที่อ้างถึง kam-tîi-âang-tǔng [คำ kam]

khaki *adj.* (color) กากี gaa-gii

Khmer *adj.* เขมร kà~mǔen

Khmer *n.* (language) ภาษาเขมร paa-sǎa-kà~ mǔen [ภาษา paa-sǎa] | (people) เขมร kà~mǔen [คน kon]

Khorat *n.* โคราช koo-râat ☙ [จังหวัด jang-wàt]

kick *v.* เตะ dtè

kickback *n.* (bribe) เงินใต้โต๊ะ ngən-dtâai-dtó [จำนวน jam-nuuan] | (reaction) ผลสะท้อนกลับอย่างรวดเร็ว pǒn-sà~ tɔ́ɔn-glàp-yàang-rûuat-reo

kick boxing *n.* (Thai boxing) มวยไทย muuai-tai

kick in *vi.* (take effect, e.g. drug) ออกฤทธิ์ ɔ̀ɔk-rít

kid *n.* (child) เด็ก dèk [คน kon] | (offspring) ลูก lûuk [คน kon]

kid *vi.* พูดเล่น pûut-lên

kidnap *vt.* ลักพาตัว lák-paa-dtuua

kidney *n.* ไต dtai [ข้าง kâang]

kill *vt.* ฆ่า kâa, สังหาร sǎng-hǎan ☙

killer *n.* (murderer) คนฆ่า kon-kâa, ฆาตกร kâat-dtà~gɔɔn [คน kon]

killing *n.* การฆ่า gaan-kâa

kilo *n.* (e.g. kilogram, kilometer) กิโล gì~loo ✿

kilogram *n.* กิโลกรัม gì~loo-gram

kilometer *n.* กิโลเมตร gì~loo-méet

kilowatt *n.* กิโลวัตต์ gì~loo-wàt

kin *n.* ญาติ yâat [คน kon]

kind *adj.* ใจดี jai-dii

kind *n.* (sort, type, category) ประเภท bprà~pêet [ประเภท bprà~pêet] | (sort, type, category) ชนิด chá~nít [ชนิด chá~nít]

kindergarten *n.* โรงเรียนอนุบาล roong-riian-à-nú-baan [แห่ง hèng]

kind-hearted *adj.* ใจดี jai-dii

kindle *vt.* (ignite) ทำให้_ลุก tam-hâi-_-lúk

kindly *adv.* ด้วยใจกรุณา dûuai-jai-gà~rú~naa

kindness *n.* ความกรุณา kwaam-gà~rú~naa

kind of *adv.* (little) นิดหน่อย nít-nòi

king *n.* พระเจ้าแผ่นดิน prá-jâao-pèn-din, พระมหากษัตริย์ prá-má~hăa-gà~sàt, ราชา raa-chaa ✿ [องค์ ong, พระองค์ prá-ong] | กษัตริย์ gà~sàt [องค์ ong]

king *pron.* (Thai King) ในหลวง nai-lŭuang

king cobra *n.* งูจงอาง nguu-jong-aang [ตัว dtuua]

kingdom *n.* ราชอาณาจักร râat-chá~aa-naa-jàk [แห่ง hèng]

king-lion *n.* ราชสีห์ râat-chá~sĭi ✿ [ตัว dtuua]

king-size *adj.* ขนาดใหญ่ kà~nàat-yài

kiosk *n.* แผง pĕeng [แผง pĕeng]

kiss *n.* จูบ jùup [อัน an]

kiss *v.* จูบ jùup | (sniff kiss) หอม hŏrm

kiss off! *interj.* (go away) ไปห่างๆ bpai-hàang-hàang ✿

kit *n.* (for tools) ชุดเครื่องมือ chút-krûuang-muu [ชุด chút]

kitchen *n.* ห้องครัว hôngkruua [ห้อง hông]

kite n. ว่าว wâao [ตัว dtuua]

kitten n. ลูกแมว lûuk-mɛɛo [ตัว dtuua]

kiwi n. (animal) กีวี gii-wii [ตัว dtuua] | (fruit) กีวี gii-wii [ลูก lûuk]

knapsack n. เป้ bpêe [ใบ bai]

knead v. ปั้น bpân

knead vt. นวด nûuat

knee n. หัวเข่า hǔua-kào, เข่า kào • [ข้าง kâang]

kneecap n. สะบ้าเข่า sà~bâa-kào [ข้าง kâang]

kneel vi. คุกเข่า kúk-kào, คุกเข่าลง kúk-kào-long | (crouch) หมอบ mɔ̀ɔp

knife n. มีด mîit [เล่ม lêm]

knight n. อัศวิน àt-sà~win [คน kon]

knit vt. ถัก tàk

knob n. (button) ปุ่ม bpùm [ปุ่ม bpùm] | (doorknob) ลูกบิด lûuk-bìt [อัน an, ลูก lûuk]

knock n. (sound) เสียงเคาะ sǐiang-kɔ́ [ครั้ง kráng (number of times)]

knock vt. เคาะ kɔ́

knock out v. (beat unconscious) ต่อยจนสลบ dtɔ̀i-jon-sà~lòp

knoll n. (hillock) โคก kôok [โคก kôok]

knot n. เงื่อน ngûuan [อัน an] | ปม bpom [ปม bpom] | (boat speed) นอต nɔ́t ✖ | (button) ปุ่ม bpùm [ปุ่ม bpùm]

know vi. (have knowledge) รู้ rúu, ทราบ sâap ❗ | (understand) รู้เรื่อง rúu-rûuang

know vt. (familiar with) รู้จัก rúu-jàk

know-how n. ความชำนาญ kwaam-cham-naan, ทักษะ ták-sà

know-it-all n. คนที่รู้ไปหมด kon-tîi-rúu-bpai-mòt [คน kon]

knowledge n. ความรู้ kwaam-rúu, วิทยา wít-tá~yaa ❧ | (wisdom) ปัญญา bpan-yaa

knowledgeable adj. รอบรู้ rɔ̂ɔp-rúu, รู้มาก rúu-mâak

knuckle n. ข้อนิ้ว kɔ̂ɔ-níu [ข้อ kɔ̂ɔ]

Korea n. เกาหลี gao-lĭi [ประเทศ bprà~têet]

Korean n. (language) ภาษาเกาหลี paa-săa-gao-lĭi [ภาษา paa-săa] | (people) ชาวเกาหลี chaao-gao-lĭi [คน kon]

kosher adj. (food) ที่ชาวยิวกินได้ tîi-chaao-yiu-gin-dâai

krona n. เงินโครนา ngən-kroon-naa

krone n. เงินโครน ngən-kroon

kung fu n. กังฟู gang-fuu

L

lab n. ห้องทดลอง hông-tót-lɔɔng [ห้อง hông]

label n. (sign, tag) ป้าย bpâai [ป้าย bpâai, แผ่น pèn] | (sign, tag) ฉลาก chà~làak [ใบ bai, แผ่น pèn]

label vt. (affix a label) ติดป้าย dtìt-bpâai

labor n. (in childbirth) การเจ็บท้องคลอดบุตร gaan-jèp-tɔ́ɔng-klɔ̂ɔt-bùt | (manual) กรรมกร gam-má~gɔɔn [คน kon]

| (physical effort) แรงงาน rɛɛng-ngaan

laboratory n. ห้องทดลอง hông-tót-lɔɔng, ห้องปฏิบัติการ hông-bpà~dtì-bàt-gaan [ห้อง hông]

laborer n. (manual) กรรมกร gam-má~gɔɔn [คน kon]

labyrinth n. (maze) เขาวงกต kăo-wong-gòt | (maze) ทางที่คดเคี้ยววกวน taang-tîi-kót-kíiao-wók-wiian [ทาง taang]

lace n. (cord) สายถัก săai-tàk [ลาย laai] | (ornamental fabric) ลูกไม้ lûuk-máai [ชิ้น chín (piece), ลาย laai (design)] | (string) เชือกร้อย chûuak-rɔ́ɔi [เส้น sên]

lace v. (tie shoes) ผูกเชือกรองเท้า pùuk-chûuak-rɔɔng-táao

lacerate vt. (rip, tear) ฉีก chìik, ฉีกขาด chìik-kàat

lack n. การขาดแคลน gaan-kàat-klɛɛn

lack v. (be deficient)

ขาดแคลน kàat-klɛɛn | (be missing) ขาด kàat

lacquer *n.* น้ำมันขัดเงา nám-man-kàt-ngao [กระป๋อง grà~bpɔ̌ŋ]

lad *n.* เด็กหนุ่ม dèk-nùm [คน kon]

ladder *n.* บันไดลิง ban-dai-liŋ, กระได grà~dai 🐾 [อัน an]

ladies' room *n.* ห้องน้ำหญิง hɔ̂ŋ-náam-yǐŋ, สุขาหญิง sù-kǎa-yǐŋ ⚡ [ห้อง hɔ̂ŋ]

ladle *n.* ทัพพี táp-pii [คัน kan, อัน an]

lady *n.* ผู้หญิง pûu-yǐŋ, สุภาพสตรี sù~pâap-sà~dtrii ⚡ [คน kon]

ladybug *n.* แมลงเต่าทอง má~lɛɛŋ-dtào-tɔɔŋ [ตัว dtuua]

ladyfinger *n.* (okra) กระเจี๊ยบ grà~jíiap [ต้น dtôn (plant), ลูก lûuk (fruit)]

lag *v.* (fall behind) ล้าหลัง láa-lǎŋ

lagoon *n.* บึงใหญ่ bʉŋ-yài [แห่ง hɛ̀ŋ]

Lahu *n.* (hilltribe) มูเซอ muu-sɤɤ [เผ่า pào]

laid-back *adj.* ไม่เร่งรีบ mâi-rêŋ-rîip, สบายๆ sà~baai-sà~baai

lake *n.* ทะเลสาบ tá~lee-sàap [แห่ง hɛ̀ŋ]

lamb *n.* ลูกแกะ lûuk-gɛ̀ [ตัว dtuua] | (meat) เนื้อแกะอ่อน nʉ́ua-gɛ̀-ɔ̀ɔn

lame *adj.* (crippled leg) ขาเสีย kǎa-sǐia | (disabled) พิการ pí-gaan

lamp *n.* โคมไฟ koom-fai [ใบ bai, ดวง duuang, ลูก lûuk]

lance *n.* ทวน tuuan, หอก hɔ̀ɔk [เล่ม lêm]

land *n.* ดินแดน din-dɛɛn ⚡ [แห่ง hɛ̀ŋ] | (as opposed to sea) บก bòk | (ground of the earth, nation) แผ่นดิน pɛ̀n-din [แห่ง hɛ̀ŋ, ที่ tîi] | (property) ที่ดิน tîi-din, ที่ tîi 🐾 [แปลง bplɛɛŋ, ผืน pʉ̌ʉn]

land *vi.* (e.g. an airplane) ลงสู่พื้นดิน long-sùu-pʉ́ʉn-din

landlady *n.*

เจ้าของบ้านเช่าที่เป็นผู้หญิง jâo-kɔ̌ɔng-bâan-châo-tîi-bpen-pûu-yǐng [คน kon]

landlocked *adj.*
ไม่มีทางออกทะเล mâi-mii-taang-ɔ̀ɔk-tá~lee

landlord *n.* (land owner)
เจ้าของที่ดิน jâo-kɔ̌ɔng-tîi-din [คน kon] | (rental property owner)
เจ้าของบ้านเช่า jâo-kɔ̌ɔng-bâan-châo [คน kon]

landmark *n.* (prominent spot) จุดสังเกต jùt-sǎng-gèet [จุด jùt]

land mine *n.* กับระเบิด gàp-rá~bə̀ət [ที่ tîi]

landscape *n.* (scenery) ทิวทัศน์ tiu-tát [แห่ง hɛ̀ng]

landscape *vi.* (garden) ตกแต่งสวน dtòk-dtɛ̀ng-sǔuan

landslide *n.* ดินถล่ม din-tà~lòm

lane *n.* (alley) ซอย sɔɔi [ซอย sɔɔi] | (alley) ตรอก dtrɔ̀ɔk [ตรอก dtrɔ̀ɔk] | (track) เลน leen [เลน leen]

langsat *n.* ลางสาด laang-sàat [ลูก lûuk]

language *n.* ภาษา paa-sǎa [ภาษา paa-sǎa]

lantern *n.* (portable lamp) โคม koom [ใบ bai, ดวง duuang, ลูก lûuk]

Lao *adj.* (pertaining to Laos) ลาว laao

Lao *n.* (language) ภาษาลาว paa-sǎa-laao [ภาษา paa-sǎa] | (people) คนลาว kon-laao [คน kon]

Laos *n.* (country) ลาว laao [ประเทศ bprà~têet]

Laotian see Lao

lap *n.* (body part) ตัก dtàk | (round) รอบ rɔ̂ɔp [รอบ rɔ̂ɔp]

laptop *n.* (portable computer) คอมพิวเตอร์แบบพกพา kɔm-píu-dtə̂ə-bɛ̀ɛp-pók-paa [เครื่อง krûuang]

lard *n.* (grease) น้ำมันหมู nám-man-mǔu

large *adj.* โต dtoo, ใหญ่ yài | (spacious) กว้าง gwâang

large intestine *n.* ลำไส้ใหญ่ lam-sâi-yài [ท่อน tɔ̂n (strip), ขด kòt (coil)]

large-scale *adj.* ขนาดใหญ่ kà~nàat-yài

larva *n.* ดักแด้ dàk-dɛ̂ɛ, ตัวหนอน dtuua-nɔ̌ɔn [ตัว dtuua]

larynx *n.* คอหอย kɔɔ-hɔ̌ɔi ❀ | กล่องเสียง glɔ̀ng-sǐiang [กล่อง glɔ̀ng]

laser *n.* แสงเลเซอร์ sɛ̌ɛng-lee-sə̂ə

lash *n.* (act of whipping) การเฆี่ยนตี gaan-kîian-dtii

last *adj.* (e.g. last week) ก่อน gɔ̀ɔn | (final) สุดท้าย sùt-táai

last *vi.* (be useable) ใช้ได้ chái-dâai | (remain) คงอยู่ kong-yùu

lastly *adv.* (finally) สุดท้ายนี้ sùt-táai-níi

last name *n.* นามสกุล naam-sà~gun [อัน an]

last night *n.* เมื่อคืนนี้ mûua-kʉʉn-níi

last time *n.* ครั้งที่แล้ว kráng-tîi-lɛ́ɛo

last week *n.* สัปดาห์ที่แล้ว sàp-daa-tîi-lɛ́ɛo ❢, อาทิตย์ก่อน aa-tít-gɔ̀ɔn ❀, อาทิตย์ที่แล้ว aa-tít-tîi-lɛ́ɛo ❀

last year *n.* ปีที่แล้ว bpii-tîi-lɛ́ɛo

latch *n.* กลอน glɔɔn [อัน an]

latch *v.* ใส่กลอน sài-glɔɔn

late *adj.* (recently deceased) ที่เพิ่งเสียชีวิต tîi-pə̂ng-sǐia-chii-wít

late *adv.* (delayed) มาช้า maa-cháa, ไม่ทัน mâi-tan, สาย sǎai

late at night *adv.* ดึก dʉk

late in the morning *n.* ตอนสาย dtɔɔn-sǎai

lately *adv.* เมื่อเร็วๆนี้ mûua-reo-reo-níi

later *adv.* ที่หลัง tii-lǎng, ในภายหลัง nai-paai-lǎng ❢

latest *adj.* ล่าสุด lâa-sùt, หลังสุด lǎng-sùt

Latin *adj.* ลาติน laa-dtin

Latin *n.* (language) ภาษาลาติน paa-sǎa-laa-dtin [ภาษา paa-sǎa]

latitude *n.* ละติจูด lá-dtì~jùut | เส้นรุ้ง sên-rúng, เส้นละติจูด sên-lá-dtì~jùut [เส้น sên]

latter *adj.* หลัง lăng, อันหลัง an-lăng

laugh *n.* เสียงหัวเราะ sĭiang-hŭua-rɔ́

laugh *v.* หัวเราะ hŭua-rɔ́

laughable *adj.* น่าขัน nâa-kăn, น่าหัวเราะ nâa-hŭua-rɔ́

launch *v.* (begin) เริ่ม rɵ̂ɵm | (shoot) ยิง ying

launch *vt.* (release) ปล่อย bplɔ̀i

launder *vt.* (e.g. money) ซักฟอก sák-fɔ̂ɔk | (wash and iron) ซักรีด sák-rîit

launderette *n.* ร้านซักรีด ráan-sák-rîit [ร้าน ráan]

laundromat *n.* ร้านซักรีด ráan-sák-rîit [ร้าน ráan]

laundry *n.* การซักฟอก gaan-sák-fɔ̂ɔk, การซักรีด gaan-sák-rîit

laundry room *n.* ห้องซักผ้า hɔ̂ng-sák-pâa [ห้อง hɔ̂ng]

lava *n.* ลาวา laa-wâa

lavatory *n.* (toilet) ห้องน้ำ hɔ̂ng-náam [ห้อง hɔ̂ng]

lavender *n.* (light purple) สีม่วงอ่อน sĭi-mûuang-ɔ̀ɔn [สี sĭi] | (plant) ลาเวนเดอร์ laa-wen-dɵ̂ɵ [ต้น dtôn]

lavish *adj.* ฟุ่มเฟือย fûm-fɯɯai

law *n.* กฎหมาย gòt-măai | (rules) กฎ gòt, ข้อกำหนด kɔ̂ɔ-gam-nòt [ข้อ kɔ̂ɔ] | (subject) นิติศาสตร์ ní-dtì~sàat [วิชา wí-chaa]

law and order *n.* กฎระเบียบ gòt-rá~biiap [ข้อ kɔ̂ɔ]

lawful *adj.* ถูกกฎหมาย tùuk-gòt-măai

lawn *n.* ลาน laan [ลาน laan, แห่ง hèng]

lawn mower *n.* เครื่องตัดหญ้า krɯ̂ɯang-dtàt-yâa [เครื่อง krɯ̂ɯang]

lawsuit *n.* การฟ้องร้องคดี gaan-fɔ́ɔng-rɔ́ɔng-ká~dii | คดีความ ká~dii-kwaam, ความ kwaam ✤ [คดี ká~dii, เรื่อง rɯ̂ɯang]

lawyer *n.* ทนายความ tá~naai-kwaam, นักกฎหมาย nák-gòt-măai, ทนาย tá~naai ✤ [คน kon]

laxative *n.* ยาระบาย yaa-rá~baai

lay v. (egg) วางไข่ waang-kài

lay vt. (put down) วาง waang

lay down vt. วาง_ลง waang-_-long

layer n. ชั้น chán [ชั้น chán]

lay off n. การเลิกจ้างงาน gaan-lôək-jâang-ngaan

lay off v. เลิกจ้างงาน lôək-jâang-ngaan

layout n. (plan) แผนงาน pɛ̆ɛn-ngaan [แบบ bɛ̀ɛp]

layover see stopover

lay people n. (common people) สามัญชน sǎa-man-chon [คน kon] | (laity) ฆราวาส ká~raa-wâat ❀ [คน kon]

lazy adj. ขี้เกียจ kîi-gìiat

lead n. (metal) ตะกั่ว dtà~gùua

lead v. นำ nam | (persuade) ชักจูง chák-juung

leader n. ผู้นำ pûu-nam [คน kon] | (chief) หัวหน้า hǔua-nâa [คน kon]

leadership n. ความเป็นผู้นำ kwaam-

bpen-pûu-nam

leading adj. (first-rate) เอก èek | (important) สำคัญ sǎm-kan | (outstanding) ชั้นนำ chán-nam

lead to vt. ชักนำไปสู่ chák-nam-bpai-sùu, ทำให้เกิด tam-hâi-gèət

leaf n. ใบ bai, ใบไม้ bai-máai [ใบ bai]

leaflet n. (pamphlet) ใบปลิว bai-bpliu [ใบ bai, แผ่น pèn]

league n. (alliance) สหพันธ์ sà~hà-pan [แห่ง hèng] | (sports) ลีก lìik [ลีก lìik]

leak n. (crack) รอยรั่ว rɔɔi-rûua [รอย rɔɔi]

leak v. รั่ว rûua

lean adj. (containing little fat) ไม่ค่อยมีมัน mâi-kɔ̂i-mii-man | (slender) ผอมบาง pɔ̌ɔm-baang

lean against vt. พิง ping

leap n. (act) การกระโดด gaan-grà~dòot

leap year n. ปีที่มีสามร้อยหกสิบหกวัน

bpii-tîi-mii-săam-rɔ́ɔi-
hòk-sìp-hòk-wan [ปี bpii]

learn v. เรียน riian, เรียนรู้
riian-rúu

lease n. (contract)
สัญญาเช่า săn-yaa-châo
[ฉบับ chà~bàp]

lease v. (from someone)
เช่า châo

lease vt. (to someone)
ให้_เช่า hâi-_-châo

leash n. (animal strap)
สายจูง săai-juung [เส้น
sên]

least adj. น้อยที่สุด nɔ́ɔi-
tîi-sùt

leather n. (animal) หนัง
năng ✦ [แผ่น pèn, ผืน
pʉ̆ʉn]

leave vi. (go away) ออกไป
ɔ̀ɔk-bpai

leave vt. (depart) จาก jàak
| (something) ทิ้ง_ไว้
tíng-_-wái | (something
with someone) ฝาก_ไว้
fàak-_-wái

lecture n. การบรรยาย
gaan-ban-yaai, บรรยาย
ban-yaai [ครั้ง kráng]

lecture vi. บรรยาย ban-
yaai

lecturer n. ผู้บรรยาย
pûu-ban-yaai, วิทยากร
wít-tá~yaa-gɔɔn ⚡ [ท่าน
tân ⚡, คน kon]

leech n. ทาก tâak, ปลิง
bpling [ตัว dtuua]

left adj. ซ้าย sáai

left n. (side) ด้านซ้าย
dâan-sáai [ด้าน dâan]

left-handed adj. ถนัดซ้าย
tà~nàt-sáai

left hand side adv.
ข้างซ้ายมือ kâang-sáai-
mʉʉ

leftover adj. ที่เหลือ tîi-
lʉ̆ʉa

left side n. ข้างซ้าย
kâang-sáai, ด้านซ้าย
dâan-sáai

leg n. ขา kăa [ข้าง kâang]

legacy n. มรดก mɔɔ-rá~
dòk [กอง gɔɔng, ชิ้น chín]

legal adj. (lawful)
ถูกกฎหมาย tùuk-gòt-
măai

legal adv. (pertaining to
law) ในทางกฎหมาย nai-
taang-gòt-măai

legal act n. นิติกรรม ní-
dtì-gam

legend n. (tale) ตำนาน

dtam-naan [เรื่อง rûuang (story)]

legible *adj.* อ่านง่าย àan-ngâai, อ่านออก àan-ɔ̀ɔk

legislation *n.* นิติบัญญัติ ní-dtì-ban-yàt

legislator *n.* ผู้บัญญัติกฎหมาย pûu-ban-yàt-gòt-mǎai [คน kon]

legislature *n.* สภานิติบัญญัติ sà~paa-ní-dtì-ban-yàt [สภา sà~paa]

legitimate *adj.* (lawful) ถูกต้องตามกฎหมาย tùuk-dtɔ̂ng-dtaam-gòt-mǎai

legume *n.* พืชตระกูลถั่ว pʉ̂ʉt-dtrà~guun-tùua

leisure *n.* (free time) เวลาว่าง wee-laa-wâang [ช่วง chûuang]

lemon *n.* (green) มะนาว má~naao [ลูก lûuk] | (yellow) มะนาวฝรั่ง má~naao-fà~ràng [ลูก lûuk]

lemonade *n.* น้ำมะนาว nám-má~naao [แก้ว gɛ̂ɛo]

lemongrass *n.* ตะไคร้

dtà~krái [ต้น dtôn (plant), กอ gɔɔ (bush)]

lend *v.* ให้ยืม hâi-yʉʉm

lender *n.* ผู้ให้กู้ pûu-hâi-gûu [คน kon]

length *n.* ความยาว kwaam-yaao

lengthy *adj.* ยืดเยื้อ yʉ̂ʉt-yʉ́ʉa

lenient *adj.* ปรานี bpraa-nii

lens *n.* (glasses) เลนส์ leen [ชนิด chá~nít (kind), อัน an (piece)]

lentil *n.* (legume) ถั่วแขก tùua-kɛ̀ɛk [เม็ด mét]

Leo *n.* (astrological sign) ราศีสิงห์ raa-sǐi-sǐng [ราศี raa-sǐi]

leopard *n.* เสือดาว sʉ̌ʉa-daao [ตัว dtuua]

leprosy *n.* โรคเรื้อน rôok-rʉ́ʉan [โรค rôok]

lesbian *n.* เลสเบี้ยน lêet-sà~bîian [คน kon]

less *adj.* น้อย nɔ́ɔi

less *prep.* (deduct) หักออก hàk-ɔ̀ɔk

lesser *adj.* (fewer) น้อยกว่า nɔ́ɔi-gwàa

lesson *n.* บท bòt, บทเรียน

bòt-riian [บท bòt]

lessor *n.* ผู้ให้เช่า pûu-hâi-châo [คน kon]

less than *adv.* น้อยกว่า nɔ́ɔi-gwàa

let *vt.* (allow, give) ยอมให้ yɔɔm-hâi, ให้ hâi | (permit, allow) อนุญาตให้ à-nú-yâat-hâi

let down *vt.* (disappoint) ทำให้_ผิดหวัง tam-hâi-_-pìt-wǎng

let go *v.* ปล่อย bplɔ̀i

lethal *adj.* (causing great harm) ร้ายแรง ráai-rɛɛng | (deadly) ถึงตาย tǔng-dtaai

let's *idm.* (do something) _กันเถอะ _-gan-tè

letter *n.* (mail) จดหมาย jòt-mǎai [ฉบับ chà~bàp]

leukemia *n.* (sickness) มะเร็งในเม็ดเลือดขาว má~reng-nai-mét-lûuat-kǎao, ลูคีเมีย luu-kii-miia [โรค rôok]

levee *n.* (dam) เขื่อน kùuan [เขื่อน kùuan, แห่ง hèng]

level *adj.* (flat, even) แบน bɛn, ราบเรียบ râap-rîiap

level *n.* (class, rank) ระดับ rá~dàp [ระดับ rá~dàp] | (floor, layer) ชั้น chán [ชั้น chán]

level *v.* (adjust the grade) ปรับระดับ bpràp-rá~dàp

lever *n.* (device) ชะแลง chá~lɛɛng [อัน an]

lewd *adj.* ลามก laa-mók

lexicographer *n.* คนบ้ากรำทำดิก kon-bâa-gram-tam-dìk, ผู้เขียนพจนานุกรม pûu-kǐian-pót-jà~naa-nú-grom [คน kon]

lexicon *n.* ศัพท์เฉพาะ sàp-chà~pɔ́ [คำ kam]

liability *n.* (debt) หนี้สิน nîi-sǐn [จำนวน jam-nuuan]

liable *adj.* (accountable) ต้องรับผิดชอบ dtông-ráp-pìt-chɔ̂ɔp

liaison *n.* (connection, communication) การติดต่อประสานงาน gaan-dtìt-dtɔ̀ɔ-bprà~sǎan-ngaan

liar *n.* คนโกหก kon-goo-hòk [คน kon]

liberal *adj.* (broad-minded) ใจกว้าง jai-gwâang | (politically progressive) เกี่ยวกับลัทธิเสรีนิยม gìiao-gàp-lát-tí-sěe-rii-ní-yom

liberal arts *n.* ศิลปศาสตร์ sǐn-lá~bpà~sàat [วิชา wí-chaa]

liberate *vt.* ปลดปล่อย bplòt-bplòi

liberty *n.* อิสรภาพ ìt-sà~rá~pâap

libido *n.* ความใคร่ kwaam-krâi, ความต้องการทางเพศ kwaam-dtôong-gaan-taang-pêet

Libra *n.* ราศีตุล raa-sǐi-dtun [ราศี raa-sǐi]

librarian *n.* บรรณารักษ์ ban-naa-rák [คน kon]

library *n.* ห้องสมุด hôong-sà~mùt [แห่ง hèng]

license *n.* ทะเบียน tá~biian [ใบ bai] | (permit) ใบอนุญาต bai-à~nú~yâat [ใบ bai]

license plate *n.* ป้ายทะเบียนรถ bpâai-tá~biian-rót [อัน an]

lick *v.* เลีย liia

lid *n.* ฝา fǎa [ฝา fǎa, ชิ้น chín] | ฝาปิด fǎa-bpìt [ฝา fǎa]

lie *n.* การโกหก gaan-goo-hòk

lie *v.* โกหก goo-hòk, ตอแหล dtɔɔ-lɛ̌ɛ ✿

lie down *v.* นอนลง nɔɔn-long

life *n.* ชีวิต chii-wít [ชีวิต chii-wít]

lifeboat *n.* เรือช่วยชีวิต ruua-chûuai-chii-wít [ลำ lam]

lifeguard *n.* เจ้าหน้าที่ช่วยชีวิต jâo-nâa-tîi-chûuai-chii-wít [คน kon]

life insurance *n.* การประกันชีวิต gaan-bprà~gan-chii-wít

life jacket *n.* เสื้อชูชีพ sûua-chuu-chîip [ตัว dtuua]

lifelong *adj.* ตลอดชีวิต dtà~lɔ̀ɔt-chii-wít

lifestyle *n.* วิถีดำเนินชีวิต wí-tǐi-dam-nəən-chii-wít

life vest *n.* เสื้อชูชีพ sûua-chuu-chîip [ตัว dtuua]

lift *n.* (elevator) ลิฟต์ líp

[ตัว dtuua]

lift v. (raise) ยก yók

lift vt. (end, ban) ยกเลิก yók-lêek

ligament n. (tendon) เอ็น en [เส้น sên]

light adj. (not heavy) เบา bao | (radiating light) สว่าง sà~wàang | (shade of color) อ่อน ว่วn

light n. (ray) แสง sɛ̌ɛng [แสง sɛ̌ɛng]

light vt. (ignite, e.g. candle) จุด jùt

light a fire vi. ก่อไฟ gว่ว-fai

light bulb n. หลอดไฟ lวว̀t-fai [หลอด lวว̀t]

lighten vt. (illuminate) ทำให้_สว่าง tam-hâi-_-sà~wàang | (make lighter) ทำให้_เบาลง tam-hâi-_-bao-long

lighter n. ไฟแช็ค fai-chék [อัน an]

lighthouse n. ประภาคาร bprà~paa-kaan [หลัง lǎng]

lighting n. (arranging of lights) การจัดแสงไฟ gaan-jàt-sɛ̌ɛng-fai

lightning n. (between a cloud and the ground) ฟ้าผ่า fáa-pàa [ครั้ง kráng] | (between clouds) ฟ้าแลบ fáa-lɛ̂p [ครั้ง kráng]

light-year n. ปีแสง bpii-sɛ̌ɛng [ปีแสง bpii-sɛ̌ɛng]

likable adj. น่าคบ nâa-kóp, น่าชื่นชอบ nâa-chʉ̂ʉn-chɔ̂ɔp

like adj. (similar to) เหมือน mʉ̌uan, เหมือนกับ mʉ̌uan-gàp

like prep. ปาน bpaan ☙

like v. ชอบ chɔ̂ɔp

likely adj. (possibly) น่าจะ nâa-jà

likely adv. (possibly) เป็นไปได้ bpen-bpai-dâai

liking n. ความพอใจ kwaam-pɔɔ-jai, รสนิยม rót-ní-yom

limb n. (body) แขนขา kɛ̌ɛn-kǎa [ข้าง kâang]

lime n. (citrus fruit) มะนาว má~naao [ลูก lûuk] | (mineral) ปูน bpuun

limestone n. หินปูน hǐn-bpuun

limit n. (terminal point)

ขีดจำกัด kìit-jam-gàt

limit vt. จำกัด jam-gàt

limousine n. รถลิมูซีน rót-lii-muu-siin [คัน kan]

limp adj. อ่อนแอ ɔ̀ɔn-ɛɛ

limp vi. เดินโขยกเขยก dəən-kà~yòok-kà~yèek

line n. เส้น sên [เส้น sên] | (queue, line of people) คิว kiu [คิว kiu] | (row) แถว tɛ̌ɛo [แถว tɛ̌ɛo] | (ruled line, line of text) บรรทัด ban-tát | (string) สาย sǎai [เส้น sên, สาย sǎai] | (wrinkle) รอยย่น rɔɔi-yôn [รอย rɔɔi, ที่ tîi]

lineage n. วงศ์ตระกูล wong-dtrà~guun [วงศ์ wong] | (bloodline) สายเลือด sǎai-lûuat [สาย sǎai]

linen n. ผ้าลินิน pâa-lí~nin [ชิ้น chín, ผืน pǔɯn, เมตร méet (meter)]

linger v. อ้อยอิ่ง ɔ̂ɔi-ìng

lingerie n. (nightdress) ชุดชั้นในสตรี chút-chán-nai-sà~dtrii ❢ [ชุด chút]

linguist n. นักภาษาศาสตร์ nák-paa-sǎa-sàat [คน kon]

lining n. (inner layer) ซับใน sáp-nai [ชิ้น chín]

link n. (chain) ลูกโซ่ lûuk-sôo [ห่วง hùuang]

link v. (bond) เชื่อม chûuam

link vt. (bond) ต่อ dtɔ̀ɔ

lint n. (fuzz, e.g. from laundry) ขุย kǔi

lion n. สิงโต sǐng-dtoo [ตัว dtuua (each)]

lip gloss n. ลิปกลอส líp-glɔ́ɔt [แท่ง tɛ̂ng]

lips n. ริมฝีปาก rim-fǐi-bpàak

lipstick n. ลิปสติก líp-sà~dtìk [แท่ง tɛ̂ng]

liquid adj. เป็นน้ำ bpen-náam, เหลว lěeo

liquid n. ของเหลว kɔ̌ɔng-lěeo

liquor n. สุรากลั่น sù-raa-glàn ❢, เหล้า lâo ◆ [ขวด kùuat (bottle), แก้ว gɛ̂ɛo (glass)]

list n. (of items) รายการ raai-gaan [รายการ raai-gaan] | (of names) รายชื่อ raai-chɯ̂ɯ [รายชื่อ raaichǔu]

list *v.* ลงรายการ long-raai-gaan

listen *v.* ฟัง fang

listener *n.* ผู้ฟัง pûu-fang [คน kon]

Lisu *n.* (hill tribe) ลีซอ lii-rวว [เผ่า pào]

liter *n.* ลิตร lít [ลิตร lít]

literacy *n.* การอ่านออกเขียนได้ gaan-àan-ววk-kǐian-dâai

literal *adj.* (meaning of speech) ตามตัวอักษร dtaam-dtuua-àk-sววn

literate *adj.* มีการศึกษา mii-gaan-sùk-sǎa, อ่านออกเขียนได้ àan-ววk-kǐian-dâai

literature *n.* วรรณกรรม wan-ná~gam, วรรณคดี wan-ná~ká~dii, อักษรศาสตร์ àk-sววn-sàat

litre see liter

litter *n.* (garbage) ขยะ kà~yà [ชิ้น chín (piece), กอง gววng (pile)]

litter *vi.* (scatter trash) ทิ้งเรี่ยราด tíng-rîia-râat

little *adj.* นิด nít

little bit see a little bit

little by little *adv.* ค่อยๆ kôi-kôi, ที่ละน้อย tii-lá~nว́วi

little finger *n.* นิ้วก้อย níu-gว̂วi [นิ้ว níu]

live *adj.* (alive) มีชีวิต mii-chii-wít | (fresh, happening now) สด sòt

live *v.* (dwell) อยู่ yùu

live *vi.* (dwell) อาศัย aa-sǎi !

lively *adj.* มีชีวิตชีวา mii-chii-wít-chii-waa

liver *n.* (organ) ตับ dtàp

livestock *n.* ปศุสัตว์ bpà~sù-sàt [ตัว dtuua]

living *adj.* มีชีวิต mii-chii-wít

living *n.* การครองชีพ gaan-krววng-chîip

living room *n.* ห้องนั่งเล่น hว̂ng-nâng-lên, ห้องรับแขก hว̂ng-ráp-kὲεk [ห้อง hว̂ng]

lizard *n.* (chameleon) กิ้งก่า gîng-gàa [ตัว dtuua] | (gecko) จิ้งจก jîng-jòk [ตัว dtuua]

load *n.* (burden) ภาระ paa-rá | (of work)

ปริมาณงาน bpɔɔ-rí~
maan-ngaan | (something that is
carried) ของบรรทุก
kɔ̌ɔng-ban-túk

load *vt.* (fill) ใส่ sài |
(transport) ขน kǒn

loaf *n.* (of bread)
ก้อนขนมปัง gɔ̂ɔn-kà~
nǒm-bpang [ก้อน gɔ̂ɔn]

loan *n.* การให้กู้ gaan-hâi-
gûu | (money) เงินกู้
ngən-gûu [บาท bàat]

loan *v.* ให้ยืม hâi-yʉʉm

loan *vt.* (to someone)
ให้_กู้ hâi-_-gûu

loathe *vt.* (detest) ไม่ชอบ
mâi-chɔ̂ɔp, รังเกียจ
rang-gìiat

loath to *adj.* (unwilling)
ไม่เต็มใจ mâi-dtem-jai

lobby *n.* ล็อบบี้ lɔ́p-bîi
[ห้อง hɔ̂ng]

lobby *vi.* (politician)
ล็อบบี้นักการเมือง lɔ́p-bîi-
nák-gaan-mʉʉang

lobbyist *n.* ผู้รณรงค์ pûu-
ron-ná~rong [คน kon]

lobster *n.* กุ้งมังกร gûng-
mang-gɔɔn [ตัว dtuua]

local *n.* ท้องถิ่น tɔ́ɔng-tìn,
ท้องที่ tɔ́ɔng-tîi [แห่ง hɛ̀ng
!, ที่ tîi] | (people)
คนท้องถิ่น kon-tɔ́ɔng-tìn
[คน kon]

locate *v.* (position) ตั้ง
dtâng, ตั้งอยู่ dtâng-yùu

location *n.* ที่ตั้ง tîi-dtâng
[ที่ tîi] | (address,
lodging) ที่อยู่ tîi-yùu
[แห่ง hɛ̀ng] | (site) ทำเล
tam-lee [ทำเล tam-lee]

lock *n.* แม่กุญแจ mɛ̂ɛ-gun-
jɛɛ [ตัว dtuua] | กุญแจ
gun-jɛɛ [ตัว dtuua]

lock *v.* ล็อก lɔ́k | (close)
ปิด bpìt

locker *n.* (small storage)
ล็อกเกอร์ lɔ́k-gə̂ə [อัน an]

locket *n.* ล็อกเก็ต lɔ́k-gèt
[อัน an]

locksmith *n.* ช่างทำกุญแจ
châng-tam-gun~jɛɛ [คน
kon]

lock up *vt.* (imprison)
คุมขัง kum-kǎng

locust *n.* (grasshopper)
ตั๊กแตน dták-gà~dtɛɛn

[ตัว dtuua]

lodge n. (forest cabin) บ้านพักในป่า bâan-pák-nai-bpàa [หลัง lǎng]

lodging n. (temporary place to stay) ที่พักชั่วคราว tîi-pák-chûua-kraao [แห่ง hèng]

loft n. (attic) ห้องเพดาน hɔ̂ng-pee-daan [ห้อง hɔ̂ng]

log n. ขอนไม้ kɔ̌ɔn-máai, ท่อนไม้ tɔ̂n-máai [ท่อน tɔ̂n] | (timber) ซุง sung [ท่อน tɔ̂n]

logic n. ตรรกวิทยา dtàk-gà~wít-tá~yaa, ตรรกศาสตร์ dtàk-gà~sàat [วิชา wí-chaa] | (reasoning) เหตุผล hèet-pǒn

logical adj. มีเหตุผล mii-hèet-pǒn

login v. ลอกอิน lɔ́ɔk-in

logistics n. โลจิสติกส์ loo-jís-dtìk

logo n. โลโก้ loo-gôo [อัน an]

loin n. เนื้อตะโพก nʉ́ua-dtà~pôok [ชิ้น chín]

loincloth n. ผ้าขาวม้า pâa-kǎao-máa [ผืน pʉ̌ʉn, ชิ้น chín]

lollipop n. อมยิ้ม om-yím [อัน an]

lone adj. โดดเดี่ยว dòot-diiao

lonely adj. ว้าเหว่ wáa-wèe, เหงา ngǎo

loner n. ผู้อยู่สันโดษ pûu-yùu-sǎn-dòot [คน kon]

lonesome see lonely

long adj. (distance) ไกล glai | (lengthy) ยาว yaao | (of time) นาน naan | (slow) ช้า cháa

long ago adj. นานมาแล้ว naan-maa-lɛ́ɛo

longan n. (fruit) ลำไย lam-yai [ลูก lûuk, พวง puuang (bunch)]

long-distance adj. ทางไกล taang-glai

longevity n. ความมีอายุยืน kwaam-mii-aa-yú-yʉʉn

longitude n. ลองติจูด lɔɔng-dtì~jùut, แวง wɛɛng, เส้นแวง sên-wɛɛng [เส้น sên]

long johns n.

เสื้อชั้นในสำหรับหน้าหนาว
sûua-chán-nai-săm-ràp-
nâa-năao [ตัว dtuua]

longkong n. (fruit)
ลองกอง lɔɔng-gɔɔng [ลูก
lûuk, พวง puuang
(bunch)]

long shot n.
โอกาสชนะน้อย oo-gàat-
chá~ná~nɔ́ɔi

long-term adj. ระยะยาว
rá~yá-yaao

look n. (facial feature)
หน้าตา nâa-dtaa

look v. (gaze) มอง mɔɔng
| (see) เห็น hěn | (watch)
ดู duu

look after vt. ดูแล duu-lɛɛ

look at vt. ดู duu, มอง
mɔɔng | (admire) ชม
chom ‼

look for vt. ค้นหา kón-
hăa, มองหา mɔɔng-hăa,
หา hăa

look like vt. คล้าย kláai,
ดูเหมือน duu-mŭuan

look out vi. (be careful)
ระวัง rá~wang

look up vi. (raise one's
head) เงยหน้า ngəəi-nâa

look up vt. (search for
info) ค้นหา kón-hăa

look up to idm. นับถือ
náp-tŭŭ

loom n. เครื่องทอผ้า
krûuang-tɔɔ-pâa, หูก
hùuk [เครื่อง krûuang]

loop n. ห่วง hùuang [ห่วง
hùuang]

loose adj. หลวม lŭuam

loosen v. คลาย klaai

loosen vt. แก้ gɛ̂ɛ,
ทำให้_หลวม tam-hâi-_-
lŭuam

loot v. (steal) ขโมย kà~
mooi

lord n. (duke or marquis)
ขุนนาง kŭn-naang [คน
kon] | (feudal) เจ้า jâao
[คน kon] | (god) พระเจ้า
prá~jâao [องค์ ong,
พระองค์ prá-ong]

lorry see truck

lose v. (suffer defeat) แพ้
pɛ́ɛ

lose vi. (e.g. investment)
ขาดทุน kàat-tun

lose vt. (e.g. loved one)
เสีย sĭia | (something)
ทำ_หาย tam-_-hăai

lose face vi. ขายหน้า
kăai-nâa

lose one's opportunity v. เสียโอกาส sǐia-oo-gàat

loser n. ผู้แพ้ pûu-pέε, ผู้สูญเสีย pûu-sǔun-sǐia [คน kon]

loss n. การพ่ายแพ้ gaan-pâai-pέε, การสูญเสีย gaan-sǔun-sǐia

lost adj. (defeated) แพ้ pέε | (missing) หาย hǎai | (one's way) หลงทาง lǒng-taang

lost and found office n. ที่แจ้งของสูญหาย tîi-jε̂εng-kɔ̌ɔng-sǔun-hǎai [แห่ง hὲng]

lot n. (piece of land) ที่ดิน tîi-din [แปลง bplεεng, ผืน pǔun] | (quota) ส่วนแบ่ง sùuan-bὲng [จำนวน jam-nuuan]

lotion n. ครีมบำรุงผิว kriim-bam-rung-pǐu, โลชั่น loo-chân [ขวด kùuat]

lottery n. ล็อตเตอรี่ lɔ́t-dtəə-rîi, สลากกินแบ่ง sà~làak-gin-bὲng [ใบ bai] | หวย hǔuai ✦ [ใบ bai, ฉบับ chà~bàp ❗]

lotus n. ดอกบัว dɔ̀ɔk-buua [ดอก dɔ̀ɔk] | บัว buua

loud adj. ดัง dang

loud adv. ดัง dang

loud speaker n. ลำโพง lam-poong [ตัว dtuua]

lounge n. ห้องรับรอง hɔ̂ng-ráp-rɔɔng [ห้อง hɔ̂ng]

louse n. เหา hǎo [ตัว dtuua]

lousy adj. น่ารังเกียจ nâa-rang-gìiat, แย่ yε̂ε | (having lice) มีเหา mii-hǎo

love n. ความรัก kwaam-rák

love v. รัก rák

love affair n. เรื่องรักๆใคร่ๆ rûuang-rák-rák-krâi-krâi [เรื่อง rûuang]

loved one n. คนรัก kon-rák, แฟน fεεn [คน kon]

lovely adj. น่ารัก nâa-rák, สวย sǔuai

love potion n. ยาเสน่ห์ yaa-sà~nèe [ขวด kùuat]

lover n. (girl, boyfriend) คนรัก kon-rák, แฟน fεεn [คน kon] | (in a non-serious relationship) กิ๊ก

gík ● [คน kon] | (in extra-marital relationship) ชู้ chúu [คน kon]

lovers *n.* (sweethearts) คู่รัก kûu-rák [คู่ kûu]

love triangle *n.* รักสามเส้า rák-sǎam-sâo

low *adj.* (not high) ต่ำ dtàm | (not tall) เตี้ย dtîia | (sound) ค่อย kɔ̀i

low *adv.* (sound) ค่อย kɔ̀i | (under) ใต้ dtâai

low blood pressure *n.* ความดันเลือดต่ำ kwaam-dan-lɨ̂uat-dtàm

low class *adj.* ชั้นต่ำ chán-dtàm

lower *v.* ลด lót

lower *vi.* ลดลง lót-long

lower *vt.* (e.g. volume, light level) หรี่ rìi

lowland *n.* ที่ลุ่ม tîi-lûm

low tide *n.* น้ำลง náam-long

low tone *n.* เสียงเอก sǐiang-èek [เสียง sǐiang]

loyal *adj.* ซื่อสัตย์ sɨ̂u-sàt, จงรักภักดี jong-rák-pák-dii ⚡

loyalty *n.* ความจงรักภักดี kwaam-jong-rák-pák-dii, ความซื่อสัตย์ kwaam-sɨ̂u-sàt

lozenge *n.* ยาอม yaa-om, ลูกกวาด lûuk-gwàat [เม็ด mét]

lubricate *v.* หล่อลื่น lɔ̀ɔ-lɨ̂ɨn

lucid *adj.* (clear) แจ่มแจ้ง jὲm-jɛ̂ɛng | (easily understood) เข้าใจง่าย kâo-jai-ngâai

luck *n.* โชค chôok, ดวง duuang

lucky *adj.* โชคดี chôok-dii, มีโชค mii-chôok, ฟลุ้ค flúk ●

lucrative *adj.* ที่ได้กำไรงาม tîi-dâi-gam-rai-ngaam

luggage *n.* สัมภาระ sǎm-paa-rá ⚡ [ชิ้น chín] | กระเป๋าเดินทาง grà~bpǎo-dəən-taang [ใบ bai]

lukewarm *adj.* อุ่น ùn

lull *v.* กล่อม glɔ̀m

lullaby *n.* เพลงกล่อมเด็ก pleeng-glɔ̀m-dèk [เพลง pleeng]

lumber *n.* ชิ้นไม้ chín-máai [ชิ้น chín] | ซุง sung [ท่อน tɔ̂n]

lumber v. (cut wood) ตัดไม้ dtàt-máai

lump n. (chunk) ก้อน gɔ̂ɔn, ก้อนนูน gɔ̂ɔn-nuun [ก้อน gɔ̂ɔn]

lunar adj. เกี่ยวกับพระจันทร์ gìiao-gàp-prá-jan

lunar eclipse n. จันทรุปราคา jan-tá~rú-bpà~raa-kaa [ครั้ง kráng]

lunatic adj. บ้า bâa, วิกลจริต wí-gon-jà~rìt

lunatic n. คนบ้า kon-bâa [คน kon]

lunch n. ข้าวเที่ยง kâao-tîiang, อาหารกลางวัน aa-hǎan-glaang-wan ⚡, อาหารเที่ยง aa-hǎan-tîiang ⚡ [มื้อ múu]

lung n. ปอด bpɔ̀ɔt [ข้าง kâang]

lunge n. การแทง gaan-tɛɛng

lunge v. (plunge) พุ่งไปข้างหน้า pûng-bpai-kâang-nâa

lure n. สิ่งล่อ sìng-lɔ̂ɔ

lure vt. ล่อ lɔ̂ɔ, ล่อลวง lɔ̂ɔ-luuang

luscious adj. (sweet or fragrant) หอมหวาน hɔ̌ɔm-wǎan | (tempting) ยั่วยวน yûua-yuuan

lust n. ตัณหา dtan-hǎa, ราคะ raa-ká ⚋

lustful adj. ตัณหาจัด dtan-hǎa-jàt

luxurious adj. ฟุ่มเฟือย fûm-fɯɯai, หรูหรา rǔu-rǎa, หรู rǔu ✦

luxury n. ความหรูหรา kwaam-rǔu-rǎa

lychee n. ลิ้นจี่ lín-jìi [ลูก lûuk]

lyric n. (poem) บทกวี bòt-gà~wii [บท bòt]

lyrics n. (words of a song) เนื้อเพลง núua-pleeng [บท bòt (verse)]

M

M.A. n. (Master of Arts) ศิลปศาสตร์มหาบัณฑิต sǐn-lá~bpà~sàat-má~hǎa-ban-dìt [ปริญญา bpà~rin-yaa (degree), ใบ bai (certificate)]

macaroni 304 **maiden**

macaroni *n.* มักกะโรนี mák-gà~roo-nii [เส้น sên]

machine *n.* เครื่อง krûuang [เครื่อง krûuang]

mad *adj.* (angry) โกรธ gròot, โมโห moo-hǒo | (crazy) บ้า bâa

madam *n.* คุณผู้หญิง kun-pûu-yǐng, แหม่ม mèm ✺ [คน kon] | (mamasan) แม่เล้า mêɛ-láo [คน kon]

madame *n.* มาดาม maa-daam [คน kon]

mad dog *n.* หมาบ้า mǎa-bâa [ตัว dtuua]

made from *adj.* ทำจาก tam-jàak

made of *adj.* ทำด้วย tam-dûuai

magazine *n.* นิตยสาร nít-dtà~yá~sǎan [ฉบับ chà~bàp ✺, เล่ม lêm]

magic *n.* (performance) กล gon ✺ | (sorcery) เวทมนตร์ wêet-mon

magician *n.* (illusionist) นักมายากล nák-maa-yaa-gon [คน kon]

magic spell *n.* มนต์ mon [บท bòt]

magistrate *n.* (judge in minor criminal cases) ผู้พิพากษาในคดีลหุโทษ pûu-pí~pâak-sǎa-nai-ká~dii-lá~hù-tôot [ท่าน tân ⚡, คน kon]

magnesium *n.* แมกนีเซียม mék-nii-sîiam [ธาตุ tâat]

magnet *n.* แม่เหล็ก mêɛ-lèk [แท่ง tâng, อัน an]

magnificent *adj.* ดีเลิศ dii-lə̂ət, ยอดเยี่ยม yɔ̂ɔt-yîiam

magnify *v.* ขยาย kà~yǎi, เพิ่มขนาด pə̂əm-kà~nàat

magnifying glass *n.* แว่นขยาย wên-kà~yǎi [อัน an]

Mahayana Buddhism *n.* มหายาน má~hǎa-yaan [นิกาย ní-gaai]

mahout *n.* ควาญช้าง kwaan-cháang [คน kon]

maid *n.* (female servant) สาวใช้ sǎao-chái [คน kon] | (housekeeper) แม่บ้าน mêɛ-bâan [คน kon]

maiden *n.* (young woman) หญิงสาว yǐng-sǎao [คน kon]

maiden name *n.*
นามสกุลก่อนแต่งงาน
naam-sà~gun-gòon-
dtèng-ngaan [อัน an]

maid of honor *n.*
(bridesmaid) เพื่อนเจ้าสาว
pûuan-jâo-sǎao [คน kon]

mail *vt.* ส่งทางไปรษณีย์
sòng-taang-bprai-sà~nii

mailbox *n.* ตู้ไปรษณีย์
dtûu-bprai-sà~nii [ใบ bai]

mailman *n.* บุรุษไปรษณีย์
bù-rùt-bprai-sà~nii [คน
kon]

mainland *n.* แผ่นดินใหญ่
pèn-din-yài [ผืน pǔun]

maintain *vi.* (carry on,
continue) คงอยู่ kong-yùu

maintain *vt.* (e.g. vehicle)
บำรุงรักษา bam-rung-
rák-sǎa

maintenance *n.* (e.g.
vehicle) การบำรุงรักษา
gaan-bam-rung-rák-sǎa

majesty *n.* (supreme
authority) อำนาจสูงสุด
am-nâat-sǔung-sùt

major *n.* (rank) พันตรี
pan-dtrii | (subject)
วิชาเอก wí-chaa-èek [วิชา
wí-chaa]

majority *n.* ส่วนใหญ่
sùuan-yài | (of people)
คนส่วนมาก kon-sùuan-
mâak

make *vt.* (build) สร้าง
sâang | (cause _ to be _)
ทำให้__ tam-hâi-_-_ |
(prepare) เตรียม dtriiam |
(produce, create) ทำ tam,
กระทำ grà~tam ⚡

make a bed *vi.* จัดเตียง
jàt-dtiiang

make a copy *vi.*
ถ่ายเอกสาร tàai-èek-gà~
sǎan

make a living *vi.* เลี้ยงชีพ
líiang-chîip

make a profit *vi.* ได้กำไร
dâi-gam-rai, มีกำไร mii-
gam-rai

make a reservation *v.*
จอง jɔɔng

make a statement *vi.*
กล่าว glàao ⚡

make a wish *vi.* อธิษฐาน
à~tít-tǎan

make believe *v.* เสแสร้ง
sěe-sɛ̂ɛng

make it *vi.* ทำสำเร็จ tam-
sǎm-rèt

make merit *vi.* ทำบุญ
tam-bun

make out *vi.* (have sexual intercourse) ร่วมเพศ rûuam-pêet | (kissing and caressing) เล้าโลม láo-loom

make over *vt.* (remodel) ปรับปรุงใหม่ bpràp-bprung-mài

maker *n.* (builder, producer) ผู้สร้าง pûu-sâang [คน kon] | (machine) เครื่อง krûuang [เครื่อง krûuang] | (person) คนทำ kon-tam [คน kon]

make up *vi.* (reconcile) กลับมาดีกัน glàp-maa-dii-gan

make up *vt.* (cosmetics) แต่งหน้าให้ dtèng-nâa-hâi | (put in order) จัดเตรียม jàt-dtriiam

make-up *n.* (cosmetics) เครื่องสำอาง krûuang-săm-aang [ชนิด chá~nít (type), ยี่ห้อ yîi-hôo (brand)]

malady *n.* โรค rôok [โรค rôok]

malaria *n.* ไข้ป่า kâi-bpàa, ไข้มาเลเรีย kâi-maa-lee-riia [โรค rôok]

Malaysia *n.* มาเลเซีย maa-lee-siia [ประเทศ bprà~têet]

male *n.* (animals) ตัวผู้ dtuua-pûu [ตัว dtuua] | (gender) เพศชาย pêet-chaai [เพศ pêet] | (men) ผู้ชาย pûu-chaai [คน kon]

mall *n.* มอลล์ mɔɔ [แห่ง hèng] | ห้างสรรพสินค้า hâang-sàp-pá~sĭn-káa ! [ห้าง hâang]

malnutrition *n.* ภาวะขาดสารอาหาร paa-wá-kàat-săan-aa-hăan

mammal *n.* สัตว์เลี้ยงลูกด้วยนม sàt-líiang-lûuk-dûuai-nom [ตัว dtuua, ชนิด chá~nít (kind)]

man *adj.* ชาย chaai

man *n.* ผู้ชาย pûu-chaai [คน kon]

manage *v.* (administer) บริหาร bɔɔ-rí~hăan | (handle) จัดการ jàt-gaan

manage *vt.* (take care of) ดูแล duu-lɛɛ

management *n.* (act) การจัดการ gaan-jàt-gaan

manager *n.* ผู้จัดการ pûu-jàt-gaan [คน kon]

Mandarin *n.* (language) จีนกลาง jiin-glaang [ภาษา paa-săa]

mandarin *n.* (orange) ส้มจีน sôm-jiin [ลูก lûuk]

mandatory *adj.* (compulsory) บังคับ bang-káp

mane *n.* (animal) แผงคอ pěeng-kɔɔ

maneuver *n.* (military) กลยุทธ์ทางทหาร gon-lá~yút-taang-tá~hǎan [วิธี wí-tii]

mango *n.* มะม่วง má~mûuang [ลูก lûuk]

mangosteen *n.* มังคุด mang-kút [ลูก lûuk]

manicure *n.* การทำเล็บ gaan-tam-lép

manicure *v.* แต่งเล็บ dtèng-lép

manifest *vt.* (e.g. symptom of a disease) สำแดง sǎm-dɛɛng

manifesto *n.* (e.g. communist) แถลงการณ์ tà~lěeng-gaan

manipulate *vt.* (arrange) จัดการ jàt-gaan |

(operate, use) ใช้ chái

mankind *n.* มนุษยชาติ má~nút-sà~yá-châat

man-made *adj.* ที่สร้างขึ้น tîi-sâang-kûn, ปลอม bplɔɔm

mannequin *n.* หุ่น hùn ✷ [ตัว dtuua]

manner *n.* (bearing, style) ท่าทาง tâa-taang [ท่า tâa] | (etiquette) มารยาท maa-rá~yâat | (posture, gesture) ท่า tâa [ท่า tâa] | (trait, style) กิริยา gì-rí~yaa, ลักษณะ lák-sà~nà

manpower *n.* กำลังคน gam-lang-kon, แรงงาน rɛɛng-ngaan

mansion *n.* คฤหาสน์ ká~rú-hàat ✸ [หลัง lǎng]

manual *adj.* (hand-operated) ใช้มือทำ chái-mɯɯ-tam | (pertaining to the hand) เกี่ยวกับมือ gìiao-gàp-mɯɯ

manual *n.* (handbook) คู่มือ kûu-mɯɯ [เล่ม lêm] | (textbook) ตำรา dtam-raa [เล่ม lêm]

manually *adv.* ด้วยมือ dûuai-mɯɯ

manufacture n. การผลิต gaan-pà~lìt [ครั้ง kráng]

manufacture vt. ผลิต pà~lìt

manufacturer n. ผู้ผลิต pûu-pà~lìt [คน kon]

manure n. มูลสัตว์ muun-sàt

manuscript n. (original copy) ต้นฉบับ dtôn-chà~bàp [ฉบับ chà~bàp]

many adj. มาก mâak, มากมาย mâak-maai, หลาย lǎai, เยอะ yá 🗣

map n. แผนที่ pɛ̌ɛn-tîi [แผ่น pɛ̀n (sheet), เล่ม lêm (book)]

maple n. เมเปิ้ล mee-bpên [ต้น dtôn]

marathon n. การแข่งวิ่งมาราธอน gaan-kɛ̀ng-wîng-maa-raa-tɔɔn [ครั้ง kráng]

marble n. หินอ่อน hǐn-ɔ̀ɔn [ก้อน gɔ̂ɔn (piece)]

March n. มีนาคม mii-naa-kom [เดือน dɯɯan]

march vi. เดินแถว dəən-tɛ̌ɛo

marching band n.

วงโยธวาทิต wong-yoo-tá~waa-tít [วง wong]

mare n. ม้าตัวเมีย máa-dtuua-miia [ตัว dtuua]

margarine n. เนยเทียม nəəi-tiiam [ขวด kùuat]

margarita n. เหล้าค็อกเทลรสมะนาว lâo-kɔ́k-teen-rót-má~naao

margin n. (blank space) ช่องว่าง chɔ̂ng-wâang | (border) ขอบ kɔ̀ɔp, ริม rim | (difference) ผลต่าง pǒn-dtàang

marigold n. ดาวเรือง daao-rɯɯang [ดอก dɔ̀ɔk]

marijuana n. กัญชา gan-chaa [มวน muuan (joint), ต้น dtôn (plant)]

marina n. (dock) ท่าจอดเรือ tâa-jɔ̀ɔt-rɯɯa [แห่ง hɛ̀ng]

marine adj. เกี่ยวกับทะเล gìiao-gàp-tá~lee

marine n. ทหารเรือ tá~hǎan-rɯɯa [นาย naai ⚑, คน kon]

marital adj. เกี่ยวกับการสมรส gìiao-gàp-gaan-sǒm-rót

mark *n.* (dent) รอย rɔɔi [รอย rɔɔi] | (design) ลาย laai [ลาย laai] | (spot) จุด jùt [จุด jùt] | (tally, point) คะแนน ká~nɛɛn [คะแนน ká~nɛɛn] | (written symbol) เครื่องหมาย krûuang-măai [อัน an]

mark *vt.* (give a score) ให้คะแนน hâi-ká~nɛɛn | (make a symbol or brand) ทำเครื่องหมายบน tam-krûuang-măai-bon

market *n.* ตลาด dtà~làat [แห่ง hɛ̀ng]

market *vt.* เอา_ออกตลาด ao-_-ɔ̀ɔk-dtà~làat

marketing *n.* การตลาด gaan-dtà~làat

mark up *v.* (raise the price) เพิ่มราคา pə̂əm-raa-kaa

marmalade *n.* แยมเปลือกส้ม yɛɛm-bplʉ̀ak-sôm [กระปุก grà~bpùk]

marriage *n.* การแต่งงาน gaan-dtɛ̀ng-ngaan, วิวาห์ wí-waa ☙

married *adj.* แต่งงานแล้ว dtɛ̀ng-ngaan-lɛ́ɛo

marrow *n.* (bone) ไขกระดูก kăi-grà~dùuk

marry *vt.* แต่งงานกับ dtɛ̀ng-ngaan-gàp

Mars *n.* ดาวอังคาร daao-ang-kaan [ดวง duuang]

marsh *n.* (swamp, bog) บึง bʉng, หนอง nɔ̌ɔng [แห่ง hɛ̀ng]

marshal *n.* (highest rank in military) จอมพล jɔɔm-pon [ท่าน tân]

marshy *adj.* (watery) เฉอะแฉะ chè-chè

martial art *n.* ศิลปะการป้องกันตัว sĭn-lá~bpà~gaan-bpông-gan-dtuua

martial law *n.* กฎอัยการศึก gòt-ai-yá~gaan-sʉ̀k [ข้อ kɔ̂ɔ]

martini *n.* มาร์ตินี maa-dtì~nîi

marvelous *adj.* มหัศจรรย์ má~hàt-sà~jan

mascara *n.* มาสคาร่า máas~kaa-râa [แท่ง tɛ̂ng]

mascot *n.* ตัวนำโชค dtuua-nam-chôok [ตัว dtuua]

masculine *adj.* เกี่ยวกับเพศชาย gìiao-gàp-pêet-chaai, เป็นชาย bpen-chaai

masculine n. (gender) เพศชาย pêet-chaai [เพศ pêet]

mask n. หน้ากาก nâa-gàak [อัน an]

masochist n. มาโซคิสท์ maa-soo-kít [คน kon]

mass adj. จำนวนมาก jam-nuuan-mâak

mass n. (in physics) มวล muuan

massacre n. การสังหารหมู่ gaan-săng-hǎan-mùu

massage n. การนวด gaan-nûuat

massage vt. นวด nûuat

masseur n. หมอนวดชาย mɔ̌ɔ-nûuat-chaai [คน kon]

masseuse n. หมอนวดหญิง mɔ̌ɔ-nûuat-yǐng [คน kon]

massive adj. จำนวนมาก jam-nuuan-mâak | (bulky) ขนาดใหญ่ kà~nàat-yài

mass media n. สื่อมวลชน sʉ̀ʉ-muuan-chon [สื่อ sʉ̀ʉ]

mast n. (vertical pole) เสา săo [ต้น dtôn]

master n. (expert) ผู้เชี่ยวชาญ pûu-chîiao-chaan [คน kon] | (lord) เจ้า jâao [คน kon] | (owner, boss, employer) เจ้านาย jâo-naai, นาย naai [คน kon]

master vt. (e.g. in language) เชี่ยวชาญ chîiao-chaan

Master of Arts n. ศิลปศาสตร์มหาบัณฑิต sǐn-lá~bpà~sàat-má~hǎa-ban-dìt [ปริญญา bpà~rin-yaa (degree), ใบ bai (certificate)]

master of ceremonies n. โฆษก koo-sòk, พิธีกร pí-tii-gɔɔn [คน kon]

masterpiece n. งานชิ้นเอก ngaan-chín-èek [ชิ้น chín]

master's degree n. ปริญญาโท bpà~rin-yaa-too [ปริญญา bpà~rin-yaa (degree), ใบ bai (certificate)]

masturbate vi. สำเร็จความใคร่ sǎm-rèt-kwaam-krâi, ช่วยตัวเอง chûuai-dtuua-eeng ✦

mat n. (for sitting on the

floor) เสื่อ sùua [ผืน pǔun] | (for wiping shoes or feet) พรมเช็ดเท้า prom-chét-táao [ผืน pǔun]

match n. (for lighting fire) ไม้ขีดไฟ mái-kìit-fai [กล่อง glòng (box), ห่อ hòo (pack)] | (tournament) การแข่งขัน gaan-kèng-kǎn

matchmaker n. (female) แม่สื่อ mɛ̂ɛ-sùu [คน kon] | (male) พ่อสื่อ pɔ̂ɔ-sùu [คน kon]

mate n. (friend) เพื่อน pûuan [คน kon] | (pair) คู่ kûu [คู่ kûu] | (spouse) คู่ครอง kûu-krɔɔng [คู่ kûu (pair), คน kon (person)]

material n. (apparatus, tool) อุปกรณ์ ùp-bpà~gɔɔn [ชิ้น chín (piece), ชุด chút (set)] | (e.g. for a dress) วัสดุ wát-sà~dù [ชิ้น chín] | (substance) วัตถุ wát-tù [ชิ้น chín] | (thing) ของ kɔ̌ɔng [อัน an, ชิ้น chín]

maternity n. (motherhood) ความเป็นแม่ kwaam-bpen-mɛ̂ɛ

math n. คณิตศาสตร์ ká~nít-sàat [วิชา wí-chaa]

mathematics n. คณิตศาสตร์ ká~nít-sàat [วิชา wí-chaa]

matinee n. มหรสพตอนกลางวัน má~hǒɔ-rá~sòp-dtɔɔn-glaang-wan

matrimony n. (marriage) การแต่งงาน gaan-dtèng-ngaan

matter n. (subject) เรื่องราว rûuang-raao [เรื่อง rûuang] | (substance) วัตถุ wát-tù [ชิ้น chín]

matter vi. เป็นเรื่องสำคัญ bpen-rûuang-sǎm-kan

mattress n. ที่นอน tîi-nɔɔn [แผ่น pèn, อัน an ✱] | ฟูก fûuk [ผืน pǔun, แผ่น pèn, อัน an ✱]

mature adj. (as an adult) เป็นผู้ใหญ่ bpen-pûu-yài | (ripe) สุก sùk

mature adv. (e.g. bond)

ครบกำหนด króp-gam-nòt

maximize vt. (increase or make as great as possible) เพิ่มให้_มากที่สุด pôǝm-hâi-_-mâak-tîi-sùt

maximum adj. (highest) สูงสุด sǔung-sùt | (most) มากที่สุด mâak-tîi-sùt

maximum n. (greatest quantity) จำนวนมากที่สุด jam-nuuan-mâak-tîi-sùt | (highest value) ค่าสูงสุด kâa-sǔung-sùt [ค่า kâa]

May n. พฤษภาคม prɨt-sà~paa-kom [เดือน dɨɨan]

may aux. (expresses hope) ขอให้ kɔ̌ɔ-hâi | (expresses possibility) สามารถจะ sǎa-mâat-jà, อาจจะ àat-jà

maybe adv. บางที baang-tii, อาจ àat, อาจจะ àat-jà

mayonnaise n. มายองเนส maa-yɔɔng-néet [กระปุก grà~bpùk]

mayor n. นายกเทศมนตรี naa-yók-têet-sà~mon-dtrii [ท่าน tân ♀, คน kon]

maze n. (labyrinth) ทางคดเคี้ยว taang-kót-kíiao [ทาง taang, เส้น sên]

M.D.M.A. see ecstasy

me pron. (female speaker) ฉัน chǎn, ดิฉัน dì~chǎn ♀, ดิชั้น dì~chán ♥ | (male speaker) ผม pǒm, กระผม grà~pǒm ♀

meadow n. ทุ่งหญ้า tûng-yâa [แห่ง hèng]

meal n. (eaten in one sitting) มื้ออาหาร mɨɨ-aa-hǎan [มื้อ mɨɨ] | (food) อาหาร aa-hǎan, ข้าว kâao ♥ [มื้อ mɨɨ]

mean adj. (bad) เลว leeo | (cruel) ใจร้าย jai-ráai | (evil) ชั่วร้าย chûua-ráai

mean n. (average) ค่าเฉลี่ย kâa-chà~lìia

mean vt. (be important to) มีความหมายต่อ mii-kwaam-mǎai-dtɔ̀ɔ | (have the meaning of) หมายความว่า mǎai-kwaam-wâa, หมายถึง mǎai-tɨ̌ng

meaning n. ความหมาย kwaam-mǎai | (translation) คำแปล kam-bplɛɛ [คำ kam]

meaningful *adj.*
(important) สำคัญ sǎm-kan | (significant) มีความหมาย mii-kwaam-mǎai

meantime *adv.*
ในระหว่างเวลานั้น nai-rá~wàang-wee-laa-nán

meanwhile *adv.*
ในขณะเดียวกัน nai-kà~nà~diiao-gan

measles *n.* หัด hàt [โรค rôok]

measure *v.* วัด wát

measurement *n.* การวัด gaan-wát

measuring spoon *n.*
ช้อนตวง chɔ́ɔn-dtuuang [คัน kan]

meat *n.* เนื้อ núua | (animal) เนื้อสัตว์ núua-sàt

meatball *n.* ลูกชิ้น lûuk-chín [ลูก lûuk]

mechanic *n.* ช่าง châng, ช่างกล châng-gon [คน kon] | (engineer, technician) ช่างเครื่อง châng-krûuang [คน kon]

medal *n.* เหรียญ rǐian [เหรียญ rǐian, อัน an] |

(badge) เหรียญประดับ rǐian-bprà~dàp [เหรียญ rǐian, อัน an]

meddle *vi.* จุ้นจ้าน jûn-jâan

media *n.* สื่อ sùu [สื่อ sùu]

mediate *v.* ไกล่เกลี่ย glài-glìia

mediation *v.* การไกล่เกลี่ย gaan-glài-glìia

mediator *n.* ผู้ไกล่เกลี่ย pûu-glài-glìia [คน kon] | (go-between) คนกลาง kon-glaang [คน kon]

medical *adj.* ทางการแพทย์ taang-gaan-pɛ̂ɛt

medicate *vt.* (give medicine to) ให้ยา hâi-yaa

medication *n.* (treatment) การรักษาด้วยยา gaan-rák-sǎa-dûuai-yaa | (use of medicine) การใช้ยา gaan-chái-yaa

medicine *n.* (drug) ยา yaa [ชนิด chá~nít (kind), เม็ด mét (pill), ขวด kùuat (bottle), ซอง sɔɔng (pack), แผง pɛ̌ɛng (set), หลอด lɔ̀ɔt (tube)] | (science) การแพทย์ gaan-pɛ̂ɛt [วิชา wí-chaa]

meditate vi. ทำสมาธิ tam-sà~maa-tí

meditation n. การทำสมาธิ gaan-tam-sà~maa-tí

medium adj. กลาง glaang, ปานกลาง bpaan-glaang

medium n. (means) วิธีการ wí-tii-gaan [วิธี wí-tii] | (spiritualist) คนทรง kon-song [คน kon]

meet vi. (encounter) เจอกัน jəə-gan, พบกัน póp-gan | (have a meeting) ประชุม bprà~chum

meet vt. (encounter) พบ póp, เจอ jəə ✱

meeting n. (conference) การประชุม gaan-bprà~chum | (gathering) การชุมนุม gaan-chum-num

megaphone n. เครื่องขยายเสียง krûuang-kà~yǎai-sǐiang [เครื่อง krûuang]

Mekhong River n. แม่โขง mɛ̂ɛ-kǒong [สาย sǎai]

melasma n. (skin problem) ฝ้า fâa

mellow adj. (slightly intoxicated) เมาเล็กน้อย mao-lék-nɔ́ɔi | (smooth, agreeable) กลมกล่อม glom-glɔ̀ɔm

melodious adj. ไพเราะ pai-rɔ́ ⚡

melody n. ทำนอง tam-nɔɔng [ทำนอง tam-nɔɔng]

melon n. แตง dtɛɛng [ลูก lûuk]

melt v. ละลาย lá~laai

melt vt. ทำให้_ละลาย tam-hâi-_-lá~laai, หลอม lɔ̌ɔm

member n. สมาชิก sà~maa-chík [ท่าน tân ⚡, คน kon]

member of parliament n. สมาชิกสภาผู้แทนราษฎร sà~maa-chík-sà~paa-pûu-tɛɛn-râat-sà~dɔɔn [คน kon]

membership n. การเป็นสมาชิก gaan-bpen-sà~maa-chík

memo n. โน้ต nóot, บันทึก ban-túk

memorial adj. เป็นอนุสรณ์ bpen-à~nú-rɔ̌ɔn

memorial n. อนุสรณ์ à-nú-rɔ̌ɔn ⚡ | (statue)

อนุสาวรีย์ à-nú-sǎa~wá~rii [แห่ง hèng]

memorize v. จำ jam, ท่องจำ tông-jam

memory n. (computer) หน่วยความจำ nùai-kwaam-jam [หน่วย nùai] | (recollection) ความจำ kwaam-jam

mend vt. (clothing) ปะ bpà | (correct, improve) แก้ไข gɛ̂ɛ-kǎi | (repair) แก้ gɛ̂ɛ, ซ่อม sôm, ซ่อมแซม sôm-sɛɛm

menial adj. เป็นงานชั้นต่ำ bpen-ngaan-chán-dtàm

menopause n. ช่วงวัยหมดประจำเดือน chûuang-wai-mòt-bprà~jam-duuan

menses n. ประจำเดือน bprà~jam-duuan, ระดู rá~duu ✖

men's room n. ห้องสุขาชาย hɔ̂ng-sù-kǎa-chaai [ห้อง hɔ̂ng]

menstruate v. มีประจำเดือน mii-bprà~jam-duuan

menstruation n. การมีประจำเดือน gaan-mii-bprà~jam-duuan

mental adj. เกี่ยวกับจิตใจ gìiao-gàp-jìt-jai, ทางใจ taang-jai

mental disease n. โรคจิต rôok-jìt, โรคประสาท rôok-bprà~sàat [โรค rôok]

mental health n. สุขภาพจิต sùk-kà~pâap-jìt

mention vt. (refer) พูดถึง pûut-tǔng | (state) กล่าว glàao ❗

mentor n. พี่เลี้ยง pîi-líiang ● [คน kon]

menu n. เมนู mee-nuu, รายการอาหาร raai-gaan-aa-hǎan [รายการ raai-gaan]

meow n. เสียงแมวร้อง sǐiang-mɛɛo-rɔ́ɔng [เสียง sǐiang]

meow vi. ทำเสียงแมวร้อง tam-sǐiang-mɛɛo-rɔ́ɔng

merchandise n. สินค้า sǐn-káa [ชนิด chá~nít (kind), ชิ้น chín (piece), กล่อง glɔ̀ng (box), ห่อ hɔ̀ɔ (wrap)]

merchant n. (female) แม่ค้า mɛ̂ɛ-káa [คน kon] |

(male) พ่อค้า pɔ̂ɔ-káa [คน kon] | (vendor) คนขาย kon-kăai [คน kon]

merciful *adj.* มีเมตตา mii-mêet-dtaa

Mercury *n.* ดาวพุธ daao-pút [ดวง duuang]

mercury *n.* (quicksilver) ปรอท bpà~rɔ̀ɔt [ธาตุ tâat]

mercy *n.* เมตตา mêet-dtaa

merge *vi.* (e.g. freeway) ประจบกัน bprà~jòp-gan

merge *vt.* รวม_เข้าด้วยกัน ruuam-_-kâo-dûuai-gan

meridian *n.* เส้นเมอริเดียน sên-məə-rí~dîian [เส้น sên]

merit *n.* คุณความดี kun-kwaam-dii, บุญ bun

mermaid *n.* นางเงือก naang-ngʉ̂ʉak [ตัว dtuua]

merry *adj.* เบิกบานใจ bə̀ək-baan-jai, รื่นเริง rʉ̂ʉn-rəəng

merry-go-round *n.* ม้าหมุน máa-mǔn [ตัว dtuua]

mess *n.* (condition) สภาพที่รกรุงรัง sà~pâap-tîi-rók-rung-rang

mess *vt.* (make a mess) ทำให้_รก tam-hâi-_-rók

message *n.* (news, note, letter) ข่าวสาร kàao-săan [ชิ้น chín (piece), เรื่อง rʉ̂ʉang (content)] | (news, note, letter) สาร săan ~ [ชิ้น chín, เรื่อง rʉ̂ʉang !] | (text) ข้อความ kɔ̂ɔ-kwaam [เรื่อง rʉ̂ʉang]

mess around *vi.* (waste time) เสียเวลา sǐia-wee-laa

messenger *n.* ผู้ส่งสาร pûu-sòng-săan, เมสเซนเจอร์ mét-sen-jə̂ə [คน kon]

mess up *vt.* (make dirty, untidy) ทำ_รก tam-_-rók | (perform poorly) ทำ_ได้ไม่ดี tam-_-dâai-mâi-dii

mess with *vt.* (meddle) เข้าไปยุ่ง kâo-bpai-yûng, รบกวน róp-guuan

messy *adj.* เลอะ lə́, เลอะเทอะ lə́-tə́ | (not neat) ไม่เป็นระเบียบ mâi-bpen-rá~bìiap | (sloppily for filthily) มูมมาม

muum-maam

metabolism *n.*
การเผาผลาญอาหาร
gaan-pǎo-plǎan-aa-hǎan

metal *adj.* ทำด้วยโลหะ
tam-dûuai-loo-hà

metal *n.* โลหะ loo-hà [ธาตุ
tâat]

metaphor *n.* คำอุปมา
kam-ùp-bpà~maa [คำ
kam]

meteor *n.* ดาวตก daao-
dtòk [ดวง duuang]

meteorite *n.* อุกกาบาต
ùk-gaa-bàat [ลูก lûuk]

meteorology *n.*
อุตุนิยมวิทยา ù-dtù-ní-
yom-wít-tá~yaa [วิชา wí-
chaa]

meter *n.* (e.g. taxi) มิเตอร์
míit-dtêə **|** (unit of
measure) หน่วยวัด nùai-
wát [เมตร méet]

meter see metre

metered taxi *n.*
แท็กซี่มิเตอร์ ték-sîi-míit-
dtêə [คัน kan]

methamphetamine *n.*
ยาบ้า yaa-bâa ● [เม็ด
mét]

method *n.* วิธี wí-tii [วิธี
wí-tii]

meticulous *adj.* พิถีพิถัน
pí-tǐi-pí-tǎn

metre *n.* เมตร méet [เมตร
méet]

metric *adj.*
เกี่ยวกับระบบเมตริก
gìiao-gàp-rá~bòp-mét-
dtrìk

metric system *n.*
ระบบเมตริก rá~bòp-
méet-dtrìk [ระบบ rá~
bòp]

metro *n.* รถไฟใต้ดิน rót-
fai-dtâai-din [ขบวน kà~
buuan, คัน kan]

metropolitan *adj.*
เกี่ยวกับเมืองใหญ่ gìiao-
gàp-muuang-yài

Mexico *n.* เม็กซิโก mék-
sí~goo [ประเทศ bprà~
têet]

mezzanine *n.* (of a
building, theatre) ชั้นลอย
chán-lɔɔi [ชั้น chán]

microbe *n.* จุลินทรีย์ jù-
lin-sii ‼ **|** (disease
causing) เชื้อโรค chúua-
rôok [ชนิด chá~nít]

microfilm *n.* ไมโครฟิล์ม
mai-kroo-fim [แผ่น pèn,
ม้วน múuan (roll)]

microphone n. ไมโครโฟน mai-kroo-foon, ไม mai • [ตัว dtuua]

microscope n. กล้องจุลทรรศน์ glôɔng-jun-lá~tát [ตัว dtuua]

microscopic adj. (very small) มีขนาดเล็กมาก mii-kà~nàat-lék-mâak

microwave n. ไมโครเวฟ mai-kroo-wéep [เครื่อง krûuang]

mid adj. กลาง glaang, ครึ่ง krûng

midday n. (noon) เที่ยง tîiang, เที่ยงวัน tîiang-wan

middle adj. (average) ปานกลาง bpaan-glaang | (between) ระหว่าง rá~wàang | (central) กลาง glaang, ตรงกลาง dtrong-glaang

middle-aged adj. วัยกลางคน wai-glaang-kon

middle-class n. ชนชั้นกลาง chon-chán-glaang [ชนชั้น chon-chán]

Middle East n. ตะวันออกกลาง dtà~wan-ɔ̀ɔk-glaang [แถบ tɛ̀ɛp]

middle finger n. นิ้วกลาง níu-glaang [นิ้ว níu]

middleman n. คนกลาง kon-glaang [คน kon]

middle school n. โรงเรียนมัธยม roong-riian-mát-tá~yom [แห่ง hɛ̀ng]

midnight n. เที่ยงคืน tîiang-kuun

mid tone n. เสียงสามัญ sǐiang-sǎa-man [เสียง sǐiang]

midway adj. ครึ่งทาง krûng-taang

midway adv. ครึ่งทาง krûng-taang

midwife n. หมอตำแย mɔ̌ɔ-dtam-yɛɛ [คน kon]

Mien n. (hilltribe) เย้า yáo [เผ่า pào]

might aux. สามารถจะ sǎa-mâat-jà, อาจจะ àat-jà

might n. (strength) กำลัง gam-lang | (superior power) อำนาจ am-nâat

mighty adj. ทรงพลัง song-pá~lang | (having power) มีอำนาจ mii-am-nâat

migraine *n.* ไมเกรน mai-green [โรค rôok]

migrate *vi.* อพยพ òp-pá~yóp

mild *adj.* (gentle) อ่อนโยน ɔ̀ɔn-yoon | (not spicy) ไม่เผ็ด mâi-pèt | (soft) เบา bao

mildew *n.* เชื้อรา chúua-raa

mile *n.* ไมล์ maai

milestone *n.* (distance marker) หลัก làk [หลัก làk] | (important event) เหตุการณ์สำคัญ hèet-gaan-sǎm-kan [ครั้ง kráng]

military *n.* (army) กองทัพ gɔɔng-táp [กอง gɔɔng]

military base *n.* ฐานทัพ tǎan-táp [แห่ง hèng]

milk *n.* นม nom, น้ำนม nám-nom

milk *v.* รีดนม rîit-nom

milk shake *n.* นมปั่น nom-bpàn, มิ้ลค์เชค míu-chéek [แก้ว gɛ̂ɛo]

milky *adj.* (like milk) คล้ายนม kláai-nom | (white color) มีสีขาว mii-sǐi-kǎao

Milky Way *n.* ทางช้างเผือก taang-cháang-pùuak [แห่ง hèng]

mill *n.* (millhouse) โรงสี roong-sǐi [แห่ง hèng]

mill *vt.* (granulate) โม่ môo

milligram *n.* มิลลิกรัม min-lí~gram

millimeter *n.* มิลลิเมตร min-lí~mêet

million *numb.* ล้าน láan, หนึ่งล้าน nùng-láan ⚠

millionaire *n.* เศรษฐี sèet-tǐi [คน kon]

millipede *n.* กิ้งกือ gîng-guu [ตัว dtuua]

mime *n.* (technique) ละครใบ้ lá~kɔɔn-bâi [เรื่อง rûuang]

mimic *vt.* (copy) เลียนแบบ liian-bɛ̀ɛp | (mock) ล้อเลียน lɔ́ɔ-liian

mince *vt.* สับ sàp

mind *n.* จิต jìt, จิตใจ jìt-jai, ใจ jai [ดวง duuang]

mine *n.* (e.g. coal) เหมือง mǔuang, เหมืองแร่ mǔuang-rɛ̂ɛ [เหมือง

mǔuang, แห่ง hèng]

mine *pron.* ของฉัน kɔ̌ɔng-chǎn

mine *vi.* ขุดเหมือง kùt-mǔuang

miner *n.* คนงานในเหมือง kon-ngaan-nai-mǔuang [คน kon]

mineral *n.* แร่ rɛ̂ɛ, แร่ธาตุ rɛ̂ɛ-tâat [ชนิด chá~nít]

mineral water *n.* น้ำแร่ nám-rɛ̂ɛ [ขวด kùuat]

mingle *vt.* (mix) ผสม pà~sǒm | (participate) เข้าร่วม kâo-rûuam

miniature *adj.* (tiny) เล็กมาก lék-mâak

miniature *n.* สิ่งที่ย่อส่วนลง sìng-tîi-yɔ̂ɔ-sùuan-long [อัน an]

minibus *n.* รถบัสเล็ก rót-bás-lék [คัน kan]

minimal *adj.* น้อยที่สุด nɔ́ɔi-tîi-sùt, เล็กที่สุด lék-tîi-sùt

minimum *adj.* ขั้นต่ำ kân-dtàm, ต่ำสุด dtàm-sùt

minimum *n.* จำนวนที่น้อยที่สุด jam-nuuan-tîi-nɔ́ɔi-tîi-sùt [จำนวน jam-nuuan]

minimum wage *n.* ค่าจ้างขั้นต่ำ kâa-jâang-kân-dtàm

miniskirt *n.* กระโปรงสั้น grà~bproong-sân [ตัว dtuua]

minister *n.* (cabinet member) รัฐมนตรี rát-tà~mon-dtrii [ท่าน tân !, คน kon] | (clergyman) พระ prá [รูป rûup]

ministry *n.* (bureau) กระทรวง grà~suuang [กระทรวง grà~suuang] | (cabinet) คณะรัฐมนตรี ká~ná-rát-tà~mon-dtrii [คณะ ká~ná]

mink *n.* (animal) ตัวมิ้งค์ dtuua-míng [ตัว dtuua] | (coat) เสื้อขนมิ้งค์ sɯ̂ua-kǒn-míng [ตัว dtuua] | (fur) ขนมิ้งค์ kǒn-míng

minor *adj.* (insignificant) ไม่สำคัญ mâi-sǎm-kan, เล็กน้อย lék-nɔ́ɔi

minor *n.* (juvenile) ผู้เยาว์ pûu-yao [คน kon] | (subject) วิชารอง wí-chaa-rɔɔng [วิชา wí-chaa]

minority n. (lesser part) ส่วนน้อย sùuan-nɔ́ɔi [ส่วน sùuan] | (people) คนกลุ่มน้อย kon-glùm-nɔ́ɔi [เผ่า pào (tribe), กลุ่ม glùm (group)]

minor offense n. ลหุโทษ lá~hù-tôot ✘ [ครั้ง kráng]

minor wife n. เมียน้อย miia-nɔ́ɔi [คน kon]

mint n. (plant) สะระแหน่ sà~rá~nɛ̀ɛ [ต้น dtôn (plant), ใบ bai (leaf)] | (where money is produced) โรงกษาปณ์ roong-gà~sàap [แห่ง hɛ̀ng]

minus adj. (below zero) ต่ำกว่าศูนย์ dtàm-gwàa-sǔun | (less than) ต่ำกว่า dtàm-gwàa

minus n. (sign) เครื่องหมายลบ krûuang-mǎai-lóp [ตัว dtuua]

minus prep. ลบ lóp

minute adj. (detailed) ละเอียด lá~iiat | (very small) เล็กมาก lék-mâak

minute n. นาที naa-tii [นาที naa-tii]

miracle n. ปาฏิหาริย์ bpaa-dtì-hǎan | อภินิหาร à-pí-ní-hǎan [ครั้ง kráng]

mirage n. ภาพลวงตา pâap-luuang-dtaa

mirror n. (looking glass) กระจก grà~jòk [แผ่น pèn, บาน baan]

misbehave vt. ประพฤติผิดใน bprà~prút-pìt-nai ❗

miscarriage n. (of fetus) การแท้งลูก gaan-tɛ́ɛng-lûuk

miscellaneous adj. ต่างๆ dtàang-dtàang, เบ็ดเตล็ด bèt-dtà~lèt

mischief n. (behavior) ความซุกซน kwaam-súk-son | (damage) ความเสียหาย kwaam-sǐia-hǎai

mischievous adj. (naughty) เกเร gee-ree, ซุกซน súk-son

misconduct n. (misbehavior) การประพฤติผิด gaan-bprà~prút-pìt ❗

misconduct vi. (misbehave oneself) ประพฤติผิด bprà~prút-pìt

misdemeanor n.
โทษสถานเบา tôot-sà~
tǎan-bao | ลหุโทษ lá~
hù-tôot ✖ [ครั้ง kráng]

miserable adj.
(contemptible, pitiful)
น่าสังเวช nâa-sǎng-wêet
‼ | (poor, needy)
ทุกข์ยาก túk-yâak

misery n. (poverty)
ความทุกข์ยาก kwaam-
túk-yâak | (unhappiness)
ความระทมขมขื่น kwaam-
rá~tom-kǒm-kùen ‼

misfortune n. โชคไม่ดี
chôok-mâi-dii

mishap n. (accident)
อุบัติเหตุ ù-bàt-dtì~hèet |
(bad luck) เคราะห์ร้าย
krɔ́-ráai

miss n. (title) นางสาว
naang-sǎao [คน kon]

miss vt. (e.g. school) ขาด
kàat | (e.g. the train,
plane) ตก dtòk | (fail to
hit) พลาด plâat | (regret
absence of) คิดถึง kít-
tǔng

missile n. (guided missile)
ขีปนาวุธ kǐi-bpà~naa-wút
[ลูก lûuk]

missing adj. (cannot be
found) ไม่พบ mâi-póp |
(lacking) ขาด kàat | (lost,
disappeared) หายไป
hǎai-bpai

mission n. (duty) ภารกิจ
paa-rá~gìt [อัน an]

missionary n.
หมอสอนศาสนา mɔ̌ɔ-
sɔ̌ɔn-sàat-sà~nǎa [คน
kon]

mist n. (dimness or
obscurity) ความพร่ามัว
kwaam-prâa-muua |
(fog, haze) หมอก mɔ̀ɔk

mistake n. (fault)
ความผิดพลาด kwaam-
pìt-plâat | (fault,
shortcoming) ข้อบกพร่อง
kɔ̂ɔ-bòk-prɔ̂ng [ข้อ kɔ̂ɔ,
ประการ bprà~gaan ‼] |
(misunderstanding)
การเข้าใจผิด gaan-kâo-
jai-pìt

mistake v. (make an
error) ทำผิด tam-pìt

mistress n. (female head
of a household)
เจ้านายผู้หญิง jâo-naai-
pûu-yǐng [คน kon] |
(minor wife) เมียน้อย
miia-nɔ́ɔi [คน kon]

misty *adj.* (e.g. mirror) ฝ้า fâa | (foggy) มีหมอก mii-mòok

misunderstand *vi.* เข้าใจผิด kâo-jai-pìt

misunderstanding *n.* การเข้าใจผิด gaan-kâo-jai-pìt

misuse *vt.* (misapply) ใช้_ในทางที่ผิด chái-_-nai-taang-tîi-pìt

mite *n.* (e.g. bedbug) ตัวไร dtuua-rai, ไร rai [ตัว dtuua]

mix *v.* ปน bpon, ผสม pà~sŏm

mix *vi.* (combine) รวมกัน ruuam-gan

mix *vt.* (blend, concoct) ปรุง bprung

mixed up *adj.* ยุ่งเหยิง yûng-yĕəng

mixture *n.* การผสม gaan-pà~sŏm, ส่วนผสม sùuan-pà~sŏm | (ingredients) ส่วนผสม sùuan-pà~sŏm [ชนิด chá~nít ⚡, อย่าง yàang]

moan *n.* เสียงคราง sĭiang-kraang

moan *vi.* ครวญคราง kruuan-kraang

moat *n.* (around a city) คูเมือง kuu-mɯɯang [คู kuu]

mob *n.* ฝูงชน fŭung-chon, ม็อบ mɔ́p ⚡ [กลุ่ม glùm]

mobile *adj.* เคลื่อนที่ได้ klɯ̂an-tîi-dâai

mobile phone *n.* โทรศัพท์มือถือ too-rá~sàp-mɯɯ-tɯ̌ɯ, มือถือ mɯɯ-tɯ̌ɯ ⚡ [เครื่อง krɯ̂ang]

mock *vt.* ล้อ lɔ́ɔ, ล้อเลียน lɔ́ɔ-liian

mode *n.* (computer) โหมด mòot [โหมด mòot] | (current fashion) แบบนิยม bɛ̀ɛp-ní-yom [แบบ bɛ̀ɛp]

model *n.* (female) นางแบบ naang-bɛ̀ɛp [คน kon] | (male) นายแบบ naai-bɛ̀ɛp [คน kon] | (pattern, prototype) แม่แบบ mɛ̂ɛ-bɛ̀ɛp [แบบ bɛ̀ɛp] | (preliminary work or construction) สิ่งจำลอง sìng-jam-lɔɔng

model *v.* (pose) แสดงแบบ sà~dɛɛng-bɛ̀ɛp

moderate *adj.* (medium)

ปานกลาง bpaan-glaang

moderate vi. (soften) ลดลง lót-long

moderator n. (M.C. of a panel discussion) พิธีกร pí-tii-gɔɔn [คน kon]

modern adj. ทันสมัย tan-sà~măi

modest adj. (humble) ถ่อมตัว tɔ̀m-dtuua | (polite) สุภาพ sù~pâap

modify vt. (adjust) เปลี่ยนแปลง bpliian-bplɛɛng | (correct) แก้ไข gɛ̂ɛ-kăi | (improve) ปรับปรุง bpràp-bprung

moist adj. ชุ่ม chûm | (damp) ชื้น chúun

moisture n. ความชื้น kwaam-chúun

moisturize vt. ทำให้_ชุ่มชื้น tam-hâi-_-chûm-chúun

moisturizer n. ครีมบำรุงผิว kriim-bam-rung-pĭu

molar n. ฟันกราม fan-graam [ซี่ sîi]

mold n. (cast) แม่แบบ mɛ̂ɛ-bɛ̀ɛp [แบบ bɛ̀ɛp] | (mildew) รา raa

moldy adj. (containing mold) ขึ้นรา kûn-raa | (musty) เหม็นอับ mĕn-àp

mole n. (animal) ตัวตุ่น dtuua-dtùn [ตัว dtuua] | (on the skin) ไฝ făi [เม็ด mét]

molecule n. โมเลกุล moo-lee-gun

molest vt. (annoy) รบกวน róp-guuan | (sexually) ปลุกปล้ำ bplùk-bplâm, ลวนลาม luuan-laam

mollywort n. ผักตะขาบ pàk-dtà~kàap [ต้น dtôn (plant)]

moment n. (brief period of time) ชั่วขณะ chûua-kà~nà | (specific point in time) เวลา wee-laa

momentary adj. ชั่วขณะ chûua-kà~nà

momentum n. โมเมนตัม moo-men-dtâm, แรงผลักดัน rɛɛng-plàk-dan

Mon n. (peoples) มอญ mɔɔn [คน kon]

monarch n. (king) กษัตริย์ gà~sàt ⚡ [องค์ ong]

monarchy *n.* ระบบกษัตริย์ rá~bòp-gà~sàt, ราชาธิปไตย raa-chaa-típ-bpà~dtai ☜ [ระบบ rá~bòp]

monastery *n.* อาราม aa-raam [แห่ง hèng] | วัด wát [วัด wát, แห่ง hèng]

Monday *n.* วันจันทร์ wan-jan [วัน wan]

money *n.* เงิน ngən

moneymaking *adj.* ที่ทำเงินได้ดี tîi-tam-ngən-dâi-dii

money order *n.* ธนาณัติ tá~naa-nát [ใบ bai]

mongrel *adj.* เป็นลูกผสม bpen-lûuk-pà~sǒm

monitor *n.* (person) ผู้ดูแล pûu-duu-lɛɛ [คน kon] | (screen) จอภาพ jɔɔ-pâap [จอ jɔɔ]

monitor *vt.* ดูแล duu-lɛɛ

monk *n.* พระ prá ☀ [รูป rûup]

monkey *n.* ลิง ling [ตัว dtuua]

monopoly *n.* เอกสิทธิ์ èek-gà~sìt ❗ | ระบบผูกขาด rá~bòp-pùuk-kàat [ระบบ rá~bòp]

monorail *n.* รถรางเดียว rót-raang-diiao [ขบวน kà~buuan]

monosodium glutamate *n.* ผงชูรส pǒng-chuu-rót

monotonous *adj.* จำเจ jam-jee | (repetitious) ซ้ำซาก sám-sâak

monsoon *n.* มรสุม mɔɔ-rá~sǔm [ลูก lûuk]

monster *adj.* (gigantic) มหึมา má-hù-maa

monster *n.* สัตว์ประหลาด sàt-bprà~làat [ตัว dtuua]

month *n.* เดือน dɯɯan [เดือน dɯɯan]

monthly *adj.* ทุกเดือน túk-dɯɯan, ประจำเดือน bprà~jam-dɯɯan, รายเดือน raai-dɯɯan

monthly *adv.* ทุกเดือน túk-dɯɯan

monument *n.* อนุสาวรีย์ à-nú-sǎa~wá~rii [แห่ง hèng]

moo *n.* เสียงวัว sǐiang-wuua [เสียง sǐiang]

moo *vi.* วัวร้อง wuua-rɔ́ɔng

mood *n.* อารมณ์ aa-rom

moody *adj.* (having a bad

moon) อารมณ์เสีย aa-rom-sǐia | (temperamental) เจ้าอารมณ์ jâo-aa-rom

moon n. จันทร์ jan, ดวงจันทร์ duuang-jan, พระจันทร์ prá~jan ‼ [ดวง duuang]

moonlight n. แสงจันทร์ sɛ̌ɛng-jan

moose n. กวางมูส gwaang-múus [ตัว dtuua]

mop n. ไม้ถูพื้น mái-tǔu-pʉ́ʉn [อัน an]

moral adj. ทางศีลธรรม taang-sǐin-lá~tam

moral n. ศีลธรรม sǐin-lá~tam [ข้อ kɔ̂ɔ]

morale n. กำลังใจ gam-lang-jai, ขวัญ kwǎn

morality n. จรรยา jan-yaa | ศีลธรรม sǐin-lá~tam [ข้อ kɔ̂ɔ]

morals n. หลักปฏิบัติ làk-bpà-dtì~bàt [ข้อ kɔ̂ɔ]

more adj. กว่า gwàa, มากกว่า mâak-gwàa | (again) อีก ìik

more adv. กว่า gwàa, มากกว่า mâak-gwàa | (in

addition) อีก ìik

moreover adv. ยิ่งกว่านั้น yîng-gwàa-nán

more than prep. กว่า gwàa, มากกว่า mâak-gwàa

morgue n. ที่เก็บศพ tîi-gèp-sòp [แห่ง hɛ̀ng]

morning n. เช้า cháao, ตอนเช้า dtɔɔn-cháao

morning glory n. ผักบุ้ง pàk-bûng [ต้น dtôn (plant), กำ gam (bunch)]

morning sickness n. แพ้ท้อง pɛ́ɛ-tɔ́ɔng

morphine n. มอร์ฟีน mɔɔ-fiin

mortar n. (cement) ปูน bpuun | (grinding bowl) ครก krók [ใบ bai]

mortgage n. การจำนอง gaan-jam-nɔɔng

mortgage vt. จำนอง jam-nɔɔng

mortuary n. ที่เก็บศพ tîi-gèp-sòp [แห่ง hɛ̀ng]

mosque n. มัสยิด mát-sà~yít, สุเหร่า sù-ràao [แห่ง hɛ̀ng]

mosquito n. ยุง yung [ตัว dtuua]

mosquito larva n. ลูกน้ำ lûuk-náam [ตัว dtuua]

mosquito net n. มุ้ง múng [หลัง lǎng]

mosquito repellent n. ยากันยุง yaa-gan-yung [กล่อง glòng (box)]

mosquito wire screen n. มุ้งลวด múng-lûuat [อัน an]

moss n. ตะไคร่ dtà~krâi, มอส mɔ́ɔt

most adj. ที่สุด tîi-sùt

most n. (majority) ส่วนมาก sùuan-mâak

mostly adv. (mainly) โดยมาก dooi-mâak, ส่วนมาก sùuan-mâak

motel n. โมเต็ล moo-dten [แห่ง hèng] | โรงแรมขนาดเล็ก roong-rɛɛm-kà~nàat-lék [แห่ง hèng]

moth n. แมลงกินผ้า má~lɛɛng-gin-pâa [ตัว dtuua]

mothball n. ลูกเหม็น lûuk-měn [เม็ด mét, ลูก lûuk]

mother n. แม่ mɛ̂ɛ, มารดา maan-daa ‼ [คน kon]

mother fucker! interj. เย็ดแม่ yét-mɛ̂ɛ ⚡

mother-in-law n. (husband's mother) แม่ย่า mɛ̂ɛ-yâa [คน kon] | (wife's mother) แม่ยาย mɛ̂ɛ-yaai [คน kon]

Mother's Day n. วันแม่ wan-mɛ̂ɛ [วัน wan]

mother tongue n. ภาษาแม่ paa-sǎa-mɛ̂ɛ [ภาษา paa-sǎa]

motion n. (formal proposal) ข้อเสนอ kɔ̂ɔ-sà~nǒɔ, ญัตติ yát-dtì ‼ [ข้อ kɔ̂ɔ] | (movement) การเคลื่อนไหว gaan-klûuan-wǎi

motionless adj. นิ่ง nîng, ไม่เคลื่อนไหว mâi-klûuan-wǎi

motion sickness n. การเมารถเมาเรือ gaan-mao-rót-mao-ruua

motivate v. (inspire) ดลใจ don-jai

motivate vt. (encourage, spur) กระตุ้น grà~dtûn

motivation n. แรงจูงใจ rɛɛng-juung-jai, แรงบันดาลใจ rɛɛng-ban-daan-jai

motive *n.* (inspiration)
แรงจูงใจ rɛɛng-juung-jai,
สิ่งดลใจ sìng-don-jai

motor *adj.* (driven by a
motor)
ที่ขับเคลื่อนด้วยเครื่องยนต์
tîi-kàp-klûuan-dûuai-
krûuang-yon

motor *n.* เครื่องยนต์
krûuang-yon [เครื่อง
krûuang]

motorcycle *n.* มอเตอร์ไซค์
mɔɔ-dtəə-sai,
จักรยานยนต์ jàk-grà~
yaan-yon ✦ [คัน kan]

motor home *n.*
บ้านพักในรถยนต์ bâan-
pák-nai-rót-yon [หลัง
lăng, คัน kan]

motorist *n.* ผู้ขับขี่ pûu-
kàp-kìi [คน kon]

motor oil *n.* น้ำมันเครื่อง
nám-man-krûuang [ชนิด
chá~nít]

motorway *n.* ทางด่วน
taang-dùuan [สาย săai]

motto *n.* (slogan) คำขวัญ
kam-kwăn [บท bòt]

mound *n.* (knoll) เนิน nəən

mount *v.* (go into, go up
onto, increase) ขึ้น kûn

mountain *n.* เขา kăo,
ภูเขา puu-kăo [ลูก lûuk]

mountaineer *n.* นักไต่เขา
nák-dtài-kăo [คน kon]

mourn *v.* ไว้ทุกข์ wái-túk

mouse *n.* (for computer)
เม้าส์ máo [อัน an] |
(rodent) หนู nŭu [ตัว
dtuua]

mousetrap *n.* กับดักหนู
gàp-dàk-nŭu [อัน an]

mouth *n.* ปาก bpàak

mouthwash *n.*
น้ำยาบ้วนปาก nám-yaa-
bûuan-bpàak [ขวด kùuat]

movable property *n.*
สังหาริมทรัพย์ săng-hăa-
rim-má~sáp

move *v.* เคลื่อน klûuan,
ย้าย yáai | (glide, slide)
เลื่อน lûuan

move *vi.* (house) ย้ายบ้าน
yáai-bâan

movement *n.* การเคลื่อนที่
gaan-klûuan-tîi,
การเคลื่อนไหว gaan-
klûuan-wăi

move over *v.* กระเถิบ

grà~tèp

move slightly *v.* ขยับ
kà~yàp

move up *vi.* เลื่อนขึ้น
lûuan-kûn

movie *n.* หนัง nǎng,
ภาพยนตร์ pâap-pá~yon
 ! [เรื่อง rûuang]

movie star *n.* ดารา daa-
raa [คน kon]

mow *v.* ตัดหญ้า dtàt-yâa

Mr. *n.* (male title) นาย
naai [คน kon]

Mrs. *n.* นาง naang [คน
kon]

much *adj.* มาก mâak, เยอะ
yé ✦

much *adv.* มากมาย
mâak-maai, อย่างมาก
yàang-mâak

mucus *n.* น้ำมูก nám-
mûuk, มูก mûuk

mud *n.* โคลน kloon, ตม
dtom | (muddy place)
หล่ม lòm [แห่ง hèng, ที่ tîi]

muddy *adj.* เป็นโคลน
bpen-kloon

mudguard *n.* บังโคลนรถ
bang-kloon-rót [อัน an]

mudslide *n.* ดินถล่ม din-
tà~lòm

muffin *n.* ขนมมัฟฟิน kà~
nǒm-máp-fin [ชิ้น chín]

muffler *n.* (heavy scarf)
ผ้าพันคอ pâa-pan-kɔɔ
[ผืน pǔun]

mug *n.* แก้วมัค gɛ̂ɛo-mák
✦ [ใบ bai]

mug *vt.*
ทำร้าย_เพื่อชิงทรัพย์ tam-
ráai-_-pûua ching-sáp

muggy *adj.* ร้อนชื้น rɔ́ɔn-
chúun | (hot, stuffy)
อบอ้าว òp-âao

mulberry *n.* หม่อน mɔ̀ɔn
[ต้น dtôn (plant), ใบ bai
(leaf)]

mule *n.* (animal) ล่อ lɔ̂ɔ
[ตัว dtuua]

multimillionaire *n.*
มหาเศรษฐี má~hǎa-sèet-
tǐi [คน kon]

multiple *adj.* ทวีคูณ tá~
wii-kuun, หลายเท่า lǎai-
tâo

multiple *n.* (math) ผลคูณ
pǒn-kuun [จำนวน jam-
nuuan]

multiply *v.* (increase)
ทวีคูณ tá~wii-kuun |
(math) คูณ kuun

mummy *n.* มัมมี่ mam-mîi [ตัว dtuua]

mumps *n.* คางทูม kaang-tuum [โรค rôok]

mundane *adj.* (ordinary) ธรรมดา tam-má~daa | (secular) ทางโลก taang-lôok

mung bean *n.* ถั่วเขียว tùua-kǐiao [เม็ด mét]

municipal *adj.* เทศบาล têet-sà~baan

murder *n.* ฆาตกรรม kâat-dtà~gam ‼ [ครั้ง kráng]

murder *vt.* ฆ่า kâa

murderer *n.* ฆาตกร kâat-dtà~gɔɔn [คน kon]

murmur *v.* พึมพำ pɯm-pam

muscle *n.* กล้าม glâam, กล้ามเนื้อ glâam-nɯ́ɯa [มัด mát]

muscular *adj.* มีกล้าม mii-glâam

museum *n.* พิพิธภัณฑ์ pí-pít-tá~pan [แห่ง hèng]

mush *vt.* (crush) บด bòt

mushroom *n.* เห็ด hèt [ดอก dɔ̀ɔk]

music *n.* ดนตรี don-dtrii | (tune) เพลง pleeng [เพลง pleeng]

musical *adj.* (relating to music) เกี่ยวกับดนตรี gìiao-gàp-don-dtrii

musical film *n.* หนังเพลง nǎng-pleeng [เรื่อง rɯ̂ɯang]

musical instrument *n.* เครื่องดนตรี krɯ̂ɯang-don-dtrii [ชิ้น chín (piece), ชุด chút (set)]

music box *n.* หีบเพลงชนิดไขลาน hìip-pleeng-chá~nít-kǎi-laan [กล่อง glɔ̀ng]

musician *n.* นักดนตรี nák-don-dtrii [คน kon]

Muslim *n.* ผู้นับถือศาสนาอิสลาม pûu-náp-tɯ̌ɯ-sàat-sà~nǎa-it-sà~laam [คน kon]

must *aux.* ต้อง dtɔ̂ng

must *n.* (requirement) สิ่งที่ต้องทำ sìng-tîi-dtɔ̂ng-tam

mustache *n.* หนวด nùuat [เส้น sên (strand), กระจุก grà~jùk (tuft)]

mustard *n.* มัสตาร์ด mát-

sà~dtàat [กระปุก grà~
bpùk (jar), ขวด kùuat
(bottle)]

musty *adj.* (moldy)
เหม็นอับ měn-àp, อับ àp

mutate *vi.* เปลี่ยนแปลง
bplìian-bplɛɛng

mute *adj.* (no sound)
เงียบ ngîiap | (unable to
speak) เป็นใบ้ bpen-bâi

mutton *n.* เนื้อแกะ núua-
gɛ̀ [ชิ้น chín]

mutual *adj.* ซึ่งกันและกัน
sûng-gan-lé-gan |
(together) ด้วยกัน
dûuai-gan

my *adj.* ของฉัน kɔ̌ɔng-
chǎn

Myanmar *n.* พม่า pá~
mâa, เมียนมาร์ miian-
mâa [ประเทศ bprà~têet]

myself *pron.* ตัวฉันเอง
dtuua-chǎn-eeng

mysterious *adj.* ลึกลับ
lúk-láp

mystery *n.* ความลึกลับ
kwaam-lúk-láp

myth *n.* (false collective
belief) ความเชื่อเดิม
kwaam-chûua-dəəm [อัน
an]

mythology *n.* (fairy tale)
เทพนิยาย têep-ní-yaai
[เรื่อง rûuang] | (legend)
ตำนาน dtam-naan

N

nab *vt.* (snatch) คว้า kwáa

nag *v.* ถากถาง tàak-tǎang

nail *n.* (finger or toe) เล็บ
lép [เล็บ lép] | (for
carpentry) ตะปู dtà~
bpuu [ตัว dtuua, ดอก
dɔ̀ɔk]

nail *vt.* ตอกตะปู dtɔ̀ɔk-
dtà~bpuu

nail clippers *n.* ที่ตัดเล็บ
tîi-dtàt-lép

nail file *n.* ตะไบเล็บ dtà~
bai-lép ✿ [อัน an]

nail polish *n.* ยาทาเล็บ
yaa-taa-lép [ขวด kùuat]

nail polish remover *n.*
น้ำยาล้างเล็บ nám-yaa-
láang-lép [ขวด kùuat]

naive *adj.* ไร้เดียงสา rái-
diiang-sǎa

naked *adj.* (nude) เปลือย
bpluuai, โป๊ bpóo,
ล่อนจ้อน lɔ̂n-jɔ̂n

name *n.* ชื่อ chûu [ชื่อ chûu]

name *vt.* ตั้งชื่อ dtâng-chûu

name card *n.* นามบัตร naam-bàt [ใบ bai]

name plate *n.* ป้าย bpâai [ป้าย bpâai, แผ่น pèn]

nanny *n.* พี่เลี้ยงเด็ก pîi-líiang-dèk [คน kon]

nap *n.* การงีบหลับ gaan-ngîip-làp

nap *vi.* งีบ ngîip

nape *n.* ต้นคอ dtôn-kɔɔ

napkin *n.* ผ้าเช็ดปาก pâa-chét-bpàak [แผ่น pèn (paper), ผืน pʉ̌ʉn (cloth)] | (sanitary pad) ผ้าอนามัย pâa-à~naa-mai [ชิ้น chín (piece), อัน an (piece), ห่อ hɔ̀ɔ (package), กล่อง glɔ̀ɔng (box)]

nappy see diaper

narcotic *n.* ยาเสพติด yaa-sèep-dtìt [ชนิด chá~nít]

narrate *v.* เล่า lâo

narrator *n.* ผู้บรรยาย pûu-ban-yaai [คน kon]

narrow *adj.* แคบ kɛ̂ɛp

narrow-minded *adj.*
ใจแคบ jai-kɛ̂ɛp

nasal *adj.* (relating to the nose) ทางจมูก taang-jà~mùuk

nasty *adj.* น่ารังเกียจ nâa-rang-giiat

nation *n.* ประเทศ bprà~têet [ประเทศ bprà~têet] | ชาติ châat [ชาติ châat]

national *adj.* ประจำชาติ bprà~jam-châat, แห่งชาติ hɛ̀ng-châat

national anthem *n.*
เพลงชาติ pleeng-châat [เพลง pleeng]

nationality *n.* สัญชาติ sǎn-châat [สัญชาติ sǎn-châat]

native *adj.* (by birth) แต่กำเนิด dtɛ̀ɛ-gam-nə̀ət | (indigenous) พื้นเมือง pʉ́ʉn-mʉʉang | (local) ท้องถิ่น tɔ́ɔng-tìn

natural *adj.* ธรรมชาติ tam-má~châat | (normal, usual) ปกติ bpòk-gà~dtì

naturalize *vi.* (change citizenship) เปลี่ยนสัญชาติ bpliian-sǎn-châat

natural resources *n.*
ทรัพยากร sáp-pá~yaa-

gɔɔn [ชนิด chá~nít]

nature *n.* ธรรมชาติ tam-
má~chaat | (condition)
สภาพ sà~pâap [สภาพ
sà~pâap] | (status,
condition) สภาวะ sà~
paa-wá [แห่ง hὲng]

naughty *adj.* ซน son, ดื้อ
dûu

nausea *n.* คลื่นไส้ klûun-sâi

nauseated *adj.* รู้สึกคลื่นไส้
rúu-sùk-klûun-sâi

naval *adj.* ทางเรือ taang-
ruua

naval forces *n.* กองทัพเรือ
gɔɔng-táp-ruua [กอง
gɔɔng]

navel *n.* (body) สะดือ sà~
duu

navigate *v.* (guide) นำทาง
nam-taang

navigate *vi.* (ship) เดินเรือ
dəən-ruua

navigator *n.* (person)
ผู้นำทาง pûu-nam-taang
[คน kon]

navy *n.* กองทัพเรือ gɔɔng-
táp-ruua [กอง gɔɔng]

navy blue *n.* น้ำเงินเข้ม
nám-ngən-kêm [สี sǐi]

near *adj.* ใกล้ glâi

near *adv.* ใกล้ชิด glâi-chít

near *prep.* ณ ná

nearby *adj.* ใกล้เคียง glâi-
kiiang, แถวนี้ tɛ̌εo-níi •

nearly *adv.* เกือบ gùuap,
แทบ tɛ̂εp, หวุดหวิด wùt-
wìt

nearsighted *adj.*
สายตาสั้น sǎai-dtaa-sân

neat *adj.* เป็นระเบียบ
bpen-rá~bìiap, เรียบร้อย
rîiap-rɔɔi

necessary *adj.* จำเป็น
jam-bpen

necessity *n.* ความจำเป็น
kwaam-jam-bpen |
(something necessary)
สิ่งจำเป็น sìng-jam-bpen
[อย่าง yàang]

neck *n.* คอ kɔɔ

necklace *n.* สร้อย sɔ̂i,
สร้อยคอ sɔ̂i-kɔɔ [เส้น sên]

neckline *n.* คอเสื้อ kɔɔ-
sûua

necktie *n.* เน็คไท nék-tái
[เส้น sên]

need *n.* ความต้องการ
kwaam-dtɔ̂ng-gaan

need *v.* ต้องการ dtɔ̂ng-
gaan

need vi. จำเป็น jam-bpen

needle n. เข็ม kěm [เล่ม lêm]

needy adj. ขัดสน kàt-sǒn

negative adj. (not positive) เป็นลบ bpen-lóp

neglect n. การละเลย gaan-lá-ləəi

neglect vt. ไม่สนใจ mâi-sǒn-jai, ละเลย lá-ləəi

negligent adj. ประมาท bprà~màat, ละเลย lá-ləəi, สะเพร่า sà~prâo

negotiate v. เจรจา jee-rá~jaa

negotiation n. การเจรจา gaan-jee-rá~jaa

neigh vi. ม้าร้อง máa-rɔ́ɔng

neighbor n. เพื่อนบ้าน pʉ̂an-bâan [คน kon]

neighborhood n. แถวบ้าน tɛ̌ɛo-bâan ☛ | บริเวณใกล้เคียง bɔɔ-rí~ween-glâi-kiiang [บริเวณ bɔɔ-rí~ween] | บริเวณ bɔɔ-rí~ween [แห่ง hɛ̀ng]

neighboring adj. ใกล้เคียง glâi-kiiang

neither adj. ไม่ใช่ทั้งสอง mâi-châi-táng-sɔ̌ɔng

neither conj. ไม่ใช่ทั้งสอง

mâi-châi-táng-sɔ̌ɔng

neither pron. ไม่ใช่ทั้งสอง mâi-châi-táng-sɔ̌ɔng

neon light n. ไฟนีออน fai-nii-ɔɔn [หลอด lɔ̀ɔt]

nephew n. หลานชาย lǎan-chaai, หลาน lǎan ☛ [คน kon]

Neptune n. ดาวเนปจูน daao-nép-juun [ดาว daao]

nerve n. ประสาท bprà~sàat | เส้นประสาท sên-bprà~sàat [เส้น sên]

nervous adj. (pertaining to the nerves) ทางประสาท taang-bprà~sàat | (under stress) ประหม่า bprà~màa

nest n. รัง rang [รัง rang] | (bird) รังนก rang-nók [รัง rang]

net adj. (e.g. profit) สุทธิ sùt-tí

net n. (snare, mesh) ตาข่าย dtaa-kàai [อัน an] | (used in sports, e.g. tennis) เน็ท nét [ผืน pʉ̌ʉn]

network n. เครือข่าย krʉʉa-kàai [เครือข่าย

kruua-kàai | เน็ตเวิร์ค
nét-wôok [เน็ตเวิร์ค nét-
wôok]
neurology n.
ประสาทวิทยา bprà~
sàat-wít-tá~yaa [วิชา wí-
chaa (subject)]
neutral adj. เป็นกลาง
bpen-glaang
neutron n. นิวตรอน niu-
dtrɔn
never adv. ไม่เคย mâi-kəəi
never mind idm. ไม่เป็นไร
mâi-bpen-rai
nevertheless adv.
อย่างไรก็ตาม yàang-rai-
gɔ̂ɔ-dtaam
new adj. ใหม่ mài
newborn baby n.
ทารกแรกเกิด taa-rók-
rɛ̂ɛk-gəət ♀ [คน kon]
newcomer n. คนมาใหม่
kon-maa-mài, หน้าใหม่
nâa-mài ✿ [คน kon]
newlywed n.
คนที่เพิ่งแต่งงาน kon-tîi-
pə̂ng-dtɛ̀ng-ngaan [คน
kon]
news n. ข่าว kàao [ชิ้น
chín (piece), เรื่อง rûuang
(content)] | (message,

tidings) ข่าวคราว kàao-
kraao [ชิ้น chín (piece),
เรื่อง rûuang (content)]
newscaster n. ผู้อ่านข่าว
pûu-àan-kàao [คน kon]
newsletter n. วารสารข่าว
waa-rá~sǎan-kàao [ฉบับ
chà~bàp]
newspaper n. หนังสือพิมพ์
nǎng~sǔu-pim [ฉบับ
chà~bàp]
newsstand n.
ที่ขายหนังสือพิมพ์ tîi-
kǎai-nǎng~sǔu-pim [แห่ง
hɛ̀ng]
New Testament n.
คัมภีร์ไบเบิลใหม่ kam-
pii-bai-bən-mài [เล่ม lêm]
New World n. โลกใหม่
lôok-mài [แห่ง hɛ̀ng]
New Year n. ปีใหม่ bpii-
mài [ปี bpii]
New Year's Day n.
วันปีใหม่ wan-bpii-mài
[วัน wan] | (Thai)
วันสงกรานต์ wan-sǒng-
graan [วัน wan]
New Zealand n.
นิวซีแลนด์ niu-sii-lɛɛn
[ประเทศ bprà~têet]

next *adj.* ต่อไป dtɔ̀ɔ-bpai

next time *prep.* คราวหน้า kraao-nâa

next to *prep.* ข้างๆ kâang-kâang, ติดกับ dtìt-gàp, ถัดจาก tàt-jàak

next week *adv.* สัปดาห์หน้า sàp-daa-nâa ❗, อาทิตย์หน้า aa-tít-nâa ❦

next year *adv.* ปีหน้า bpii-nâa

nibble *v.* แทะ té, เล็ม lem

nice *adj.* (cute, good-mannered) น่ารัก nâa-rák | (good) ดี dii | (pretty, beautiful) สวย sǔuai

nickname *n.* ชื่อเล่น chûu-lên [ชื่อ chûu]

niece *n.* หลานสาว lǎan-sǎao, หลาน lǎan ❦ [คน kon]

night *adj.* กลางคืน glaang-kʉʉn, ค่ำ kâm, ตอนค่ำ dtɔɔn-kâm

night *n.* กลางคืน glaang-kʉʉn [ตอน dtɔɔn] | ค่ำคืน kâm-kʉʉn ❦ [คืน kʉʉn]

night club *n.* ไนท์คลับ nái-klàp [แห่ง hɛ̀ng]

nightgown *n.* ชุดนอน chút-nɔɔn [ตัว dtuua]

nightmare *n.* ฝันร้าย fǎn-ráai [เรื่อง rʉ̂ʉang]

night owl *n.* คนกลางคืน kon-glaang-kʉʉn [คน kon]

nighttime *adj.* ตอนกลางคืน dtɔɔn-glaang-kʉʉn

nighttime *n.* วิกาล wí-gaan [คืน kʉʉn]

nighttime *prep.* ตอนกลางคืน dtɔɔn-glaang-kʉʉn

nimble *adj.* คล่องแคล่ว klɔ̂ng-klɛ̂o

nine *numb.* เก้า gâao, เลขเก้า lêek-gâao

nineteen *numb.* สิบเก้า sìp-gâao

ninety *n.* เก้าสิบ gâao-sìp

ninth *adj.* ที่เก้า tîi-gâao

nip *vt.* ขลิบ klìp, หนีบ nìip

nip off *vt.* เด็ด dèt

nippers *n.* แหนบ nɛ̀ɛp [อัน an]

nipple *n.* หัวนม hǔua-nom [หัว hǔua] | (pacifier) หัวนมยาง hǔua-nom-yaang [อัน an]

Nirvana *n.* นิพพาน níp-paan

nitrogen *n.* ไนโตรเจน nai-dtroo-jên

no *adv.* ไม่ mâi, ไม่ใช่ mâi-châi | (cannot, did not) ไม่ได้ mâi-dâai

no! *interj.* (cannot, did not) ไม่ได้ mâi-dâai | (no, not) เปล่า bplàao, ไม่ใช่ mâi-châi

Nobel prize *n.* รางวัลโนเบล raang-wan-noo-beo [รางวัล raang-wan]

noble *adj.* ชั้นสูง chán-sǔung, เป็นผู้ดี bpen-pûu-dii

nobody *n.* (unimportant person) คนไม่สำคัญ kon-mâi-sǎm-kan [คน kon]

nobody *pron.* (not anyone) ไม่มีใคร mâi-mii-krai

no contest *idm.* ไม่คัดค้าน mâi-kát-káan, ไม่ต่อสู้ mâi-dtɔ̀ɔ-sûu

nocturnal *adj.* (active at night) ชอบกลางคืน chɔ̂ɔp-glaang-kuun

nod *n.* การพยักหน้า gaan-pá~yák-nâa

nod *v.* พยักหน้า pá~yák-nâa

noise *n.* (sound) เสียง sǐiang [เสียง sǐiang]

noisy *adj.* เสียงดัง sǐiang-dang, หนวกหู nùuak-hǔu

nominate *vt.* เสนอชื่อ sà~nǝ̌ǝ-chûu

non-dairy *adj.* ที่ไม่มีนมสัตว์ tîi-mâi-mii-nom-sàt

none *adj.* ไม่มี mâi-mii

none *adv.* ไม่มี mâi-mii, ไม่เลย mâi-lǝǝi

none *pron.* ไม่มี mâi-mii

nonetheless *adv.* ถึงกระนั้น tǔng-grà~nán, แม้กระนั้นก็ดี méɛ-grà~nán-gɔ̂ɔ-dii

nonfat *adj.* ที่ไม่มีมันสัตว์ tîi-mâi-mii-man-sàt

nonfiction *n.* วรรณกรรมที่ไม่ใช่นิยาย wan-ná~gam-tîi-mâi-châi-ní-yaai

nonprofit *adj.* ไม่หวังผลกำไร mâi-wǎng-pǒn-gam-rai

nonsense *adj.* ไร้สาระ rái-
săa-rá

nonsmoker *n.*
คนที่ไม่สูบบุหรี่ kon-tîi-
mâi-sùup-bù~rìi [คน kon]

nonsmoking *adj.*
ไม่สูบบุหรี่ mâi-sùup-bù~rìi

nonstop *adj.* ไม่หยุด mâi-
yùt

noodle *n.* (egg) บะหมี่
bà~mìi [ชาม chaam
(bowl), ถ้วย tûuai (bowl),
เส้น sên (strand)] | (rice)
ก๋วยเตี๋ยว gŭuai-dtǐiao
[ชาม chaam (bowl), ถุง
tǔng (bag), ห่อ hɔ̀ɔ (pack)]

nook *n.* ซอก sɔ̂ɔk [ซอก
sɔ̂ɔk] | มุม mum [มุม
mum]

noon *n.* เที่ยง tîiang,
เที่ยงวัน tîiang-wan

no one *pron.* ไม่มีใคร
mâi-mii-krai

noontime *n.* เวลาเที่ยง
wee-laa-tîiang

norm *n.* บรรทัดฐาน ban-
tát-tăan, แบบแผน bɛ̀ɛp-
pĕɛn

normal *adj.* ธรรมดา
tam-má~daa, ปกติ

bpòk-gà~dti

north *n.* ทิศเหนือ tít-nɯ̌ɯa,
เหนือ nɯ̌ɯa [ทิศ tít]

North America *n.*
อเมริกาเหนือ à~mee-rí~
gaa-nɯ̌ɯa [ทวีป tá~wîip]

northeast *n.*
ตะวันออกเฉียงเหนือ
dtà~wan-ɔ̀ɔk-chǐiang-
nɯ̌ɯa,
ทิศตะวันออกเฉียงเหนือ
tít-dtà~wan-ɔ̀ɔk-
chǐiang-nɯ̌ɯa, อีสาน ii-
săan ๛ [ทิศ tít]

northeast of Thailand *n.*
อีสาน ii-săan | ภาคอีสาน
pâak-ii-săan [ภาค pâak]

northern *adj.* ทางเหนือ
taang-nɯ̌ɯa

Northern Hemisphere *n.*
ซีกโลกเหนือ sîik-lôok-
nɯ̌ɯa [ซีก sîik]

North Pole *n.* ขั้วโลกเหนือ
kûua-lôok-nɯ̌ɯa [ขั้ว
kûua]

North Star *n.* ดาวเหนือ
daao-nɯ̌ɯa [ดวง duuang]

northwest *n.*
ตะวันตกเฉียงเหนือ dtà~
wan-dtòk-chǐiang-nɯ̌ɯa,
ทิศตะวันตกเฉียงเหนือ tít-

dtà~wan-dtòk-chǐiang-nǔua [ทิศ tít]

Norway *n.* นอร์เวย์ nɔɔ-rá~wee [ประเทศ bprà~têet]

nose *n.* จมูก jà~mùuk

nosebleed *n.* เลือดกำเดาออก lûuat-gam-dao-ɔ̀ɔk

nose job *n.* การเสริมจมูก gaan-sɛ̌ɤm-jà~mùuk [ครั้ง kráng]

no-show *adj.* ไม่มา mâi-maa

no-show *n.* (occasion) การไม่แสดงตัว gaan-mâi-sà~dɛɛng-dtuua

nostril *n.* รูจมูก ruu-jà~mùuk [รู ruu]

nosy *adj.* สอดรู้สอดเห็น sɔ̀ɔt-rúu-sɔ̀ɔt-hěn

not *adv.* ไม่ mâi, ไม่ใช่ mâi-châi

notary *n.* พนักงานจดทะเบียน pá~nák-ngaan-jòt-tá~biian [คน kon]

notary public *n.* ผู้รับรองลายเซ็น pûu-ráp-rɔɔng-laai-sen [คน kon]

not at all *idm.* (It's not like that.) ไม่เลย mâi-lǝǝi | (it doesn't matter.) ไม่เป็นไร mâi-bpen-rai

notched *adj.* เป็นรอยบาก bpen-rɔɔi-bàak

note *n.* (memo) บันทึก ban-túk | (money) ธนบัตร tá~ná~bàt, แบงค์ béng ❧ [ใบ bai] | (music) โน้ต nóot [ตัว dtuua] | (remark) หมายเหตุ mǎai-hèet [แห่ง hèng]

note *v.* (jot down) บันทึก ban-túk | (observe) สังเกต sǎng-gèet

note *vt.* (jot down) จด jòt

notebook *n.* สมุด sà~mùt [เล่ม lêm]

nothing *adv.* ไม่มีอะไร mâi-mii-à~rai

notice *n.* (announcement) ประกาศ bprà~gàat | (observation) ข้อสังเกต kɔ̂ɔ-sǎng-gèet [ข้อ kɔ̂ɔ, ประการ bprà~gaan ❢]

notice *vt.* สังเกต sǎng-gèet

noticeable *adj.* โดดเด่น dòot-dèn

notification *n.* การแจ้ง gaan-jɛ̂ɛng, การประกาศ

gaan-bprà~gàat

notify vt. (inform) แจ้ง
jêɛng | (inform, report)
แจ้งความ jêɛng-kwaam

notorious adj.
มีชื่อเสียงในทางไม่ดี mii-
chûu-sĭiang-nai-taang-
mâi-dii

noun n. คำนาม kam-
naam, นาม naam [คำ
kam]

nourish vt. บำรุง bam-
rung

novel n. นิยาย ní-yaai,
นวนิยาย ná~wá-ní-yaai ǃ
[เรื่อง rûuang]

novelist n. นักแต่งนิยาย
nák-dtɛ̀ng-ní-yaai [คน
kon]

November n. พฤศจิกายน
prút-sà~jì-gaa-yon
[เดือน duuan]

novice n. (beginner)
ผู้เริ่มหัด pûu-rêəm-hàt
[คน kon] | (young monk)
เณร neen [รูป rûup]

now adv. เดี๋ยวนี้ dĭiao-níi,
ตอนนี้ dtɔɔn-níi

nowadays adv. ปัจจุบัน
bpàt-jù-ban, ปัจจุบันนี้

bpàt-jù-ban-níi

noway! interj. ไม่มีทาง
mâi-mii-taang

nowhere adv. ไม่มีที่ไหน
mâi-mii-tîi-nǎi

nozzle n. หัวฉีด hǔua-chìit
[หัว hǔua]

nuance n. ความแตกต่างที่
ไม่เห็นชัดเจน kwaam-
dtɛ̀ɛk-dtàang-tîi-mâi-
hĕn-chát-jeen

nuclear n. นิวเคลียร์ niu-
kliia

nuclear family n.
ครอบครัวเดี่ยว krɔ̂ɔp-
kruua-dìiao [ครอบครัว
krɔ̂ɔp-kruua]

nucleus n. นิวเคลียส niu-
klíiat | จุดศูนย์กลาง jùt-
sǔun-glaang [จุด jùt]

nude adj. เปลือย bpluuai,
ล่อนจ้อน lɔ̂n-jɔ̂n

nudge v. ถอง tɔ̌ng

nugget n. ก้อน gɔ̂ɔn [ก้อน
gɔ̂ɔn]

nuisance n. สิ่งรบกวน
sìng-róp-guuan [สิ่ง sìng]

null adj. (lacking)
ไม่มีอะไร mâi-mii-à~rai |
(without effect) เป็นโมฆะ

bpen-moo-ká

nullify v. (cancel) ยกเลิก yók-lə̂ək | (invalidate) ทำให้_โมฆะ tam-hâi-_-moo-ká

numb adj. ชา chaa

number n. (count, sum) จำนวน jam-nuuan [จำนวน jam-nuuan] | (figure, digit) ตัวเลข dtuua-lêek [ตัว dtuua] | (numeral) เบอร์ bəə ✿ [เบอร์ bəə] | (numeral) หมายเลข mǎai-lêek [หมายเลข mǎai-lêek]

number plate see license plate

numbness n. เหน็บ nèp, อาการชา aa-gaan-chaa

numeral adj. เกี่ยวกับตัวเลข gìiao-gàp-dtuua-lêek

numerous adj. มากมาย mâak-maai, หลาย lǎai

nun n. แม่ชี mɛ̂ɛ-chii, ชี chii ✿ [คน kon]

nuptial adj. เกี่ยวกับการสมรส gìiao-gàp-gaan-sǒm-rót

nurse n. พยาบาล pá~yaa-baan [คน kon]

nurse v. พยาบาล pá~yaa-

baan

nurse aid n. ผู้ช่วยพยาบาล pûu-chûuai-pá~yaa-baan [คน kon]

nursery n. (for kids) สถานรับเลี้ยงเด็ก sà~tǎan-ráp-líiang-dèk [แห่ง hɛ̀ng] | (for plants) ที่เพาะต้นไม้ tîi-pɔ́-dtôn-máai [แห่ง hɛ̀ng] | (room) ห้องเลี้ยงเด็กในบ้าน hɔ̂ng-líiang-dèk-nai-bâan [ห้อง hɔ̂ng]

nursing home n. บ้านพักคนชรา bâan-pák-kon-chá~raa [แห่ง hɛ̀ng]

nurture vt. บำรุง bam-rung

nut n. (eccentric person) คนบ้า kon-bâa [คน kon] | (hard shell fruit) ผลไม้เปลือกแข็ง pǒn-lá~mái-bplùuak-kɛ̌ng [ลูก lûuk] | (threaded fastener) หัวน็อต hǔua-nɔ́t [ตัว dtuua]

nutrient n. สารอาหาร sǎan-aa-hǎan

nutrition n. โภชนาการ poo-chá~naa-gaan

nutritious adj.

มีคุณค่าทางอาหาร mii-kun-kâa-taang-aa-hǎan

nylon *n.* ไนล่อน nai-lôn

O

oak *n.* (tree) ต้นโอ๊ก dtôn-óok [ต้น dtôn] | (wood) ไม้โอ๊ก mái-óok [ท่อน tôn, ชิ้น chín]

oar *n.* ไม้พาย mái-paai [เล่ม lêm]

oar *v.* พาย paai

oasis *n.* (in a desert) โอเอซิส oo-ee-sít [แห่ง hèng]

oat *n.* ข้าวโอ๊ต kâao-óot [ถ้วย tûuai (bowl)]

oath *n.* (pledge) คำสาบาน kam-sǎa-baan, คำปฏิญาณ kam-bpà~dtì-yaan ‼

oatmeal see oat

obedient *adj.* ที่เชื่อฟัง tîi-chûua-fang, ว่าง่าย wâa-ngâai, อยู่ในโอวาท yùu-nai-oo-wâat

obese *adj.* อ้วนพุงพลุ้ย ûuan-pung-plúi

obey *v.* เชื่อฟัง chûua-fang, ทำตามคำสั่ง tam-dtaam-kam-sàng, ปฏิบัติตาม bpà~dtì-bàt-dtaam

obituary *n.* ข่าวมรณกรรม kàao-mɔɔ-rá~ná~gam ‼ [เรื่อง rûuang]

object *n.* (grammar) กรรม gam [คำ kam] | (material) วัตถุ wát-tù [ชิ้น chín] | (thing) ของ kɔ̌ɔng, สิ่งของ sìng-kɔ̌ɔng [อัน an, ชิ้น chín]

object *v.* (oppose) คัดค้าน kát-káan

objection *n.* (disagree statement) คำคัดค้าน kam-kát-káan [คำ kam] | (disagreement) การคัดค้าน gaan-kát-káan

objection! *interj.* (in court) ขอคัดค้าน kɔ̌ɔ-kát-káan

objective *adj.* แห่งเป้าหมาย hèng-bpâo-mǎai | (impartial) เป็นกลาง bpen-glaang

objective *n.* (goal) วัตถุประสงค์ wát-tù-bprà~sǒng [ข้อ kɔ̂ɔ, อัน an] | (goal) เป้าหมาย bpâo-mǎai [อัน an]

obligate *vt.*
มีพันธะที่จะต้อง mii-pan-tá-tîi-jà-dtɔ̂ng

obligation *n.*
(commitment, strings) พันธะ pan-tá | (debt of gratitude) บุญคุณ bun-kun | (duty) ภาระหน้าที่ paa-rá-nâa-tîi

oblige *v.* (favor) กรุณา gà~rú~naa ⚡

oblige *vi.* (indebted) เป็นหนี้บุญคุณ bpen-nîi-bun-kun

oblige *vt.* (force) บังคับ bang-káp

oboe *n.* ปี่ bpìi [เลา lao]

obscene *adj.* (disgusting) ทุเรศ tú-rêet | (lewd) ลามก laa-mók, สัปดน sàp-bpà~don

obscure *adj.* (dark) มืดมน mʉ̂ʉt-mon, มืดมัว mʉ̂ʉt-muua | (vague) คลุมเครือ klum-krʉʉa, ไม่ชัดเจน mâi-chát-jeen

observation *n.* (act) การสังเกต gaan-sǎng-gèet | (remark, comment) ข้อสังเกต kɔ̂ɔ-sǎng-gèet

observe *v.* (notice) สังเกต sǎng-gèet | (obey) ปฏิบัติตาม bpà~dtì-bàt-dtaam | (watch attentively) คอยดู kɔɔi-duu, เฝ้าดู fâo-duu

obsess *vt.* ครอบงำจิตใจ krɔ̂ɔp-ngam-jìt-jai

obsession *n.* (act) การครอบงำจิตใจ gaan-krɔ̂ɔp-ngam-jìt-jai

obsolete *adj.* (no longer in use, out of date) เลิกใช้แล้ว lôək-chái-lɛ́ɛo

obstacle *n.* (hindrance) อุปสรรค ùp-bpà~sàk [อัน an] | (obstruction) สิ่งกีดขวาง sìng-gìit-kwǎang [สิ่ง sìng]

obstetrics and gynecology *n.*
แผนกสูตินรีเวช pà~nɛ̀ɛk-sǔu-dtì-ná~rii-wêet [แผนก pà~nɛ̀ɛk]

obstinate *adj.* ดื้อดึง dʉ̂ʉ-dʉng, หัวแข็ง hǔua-kěng

obstruct *vt.* ขวาง kwǎang, ขัดขวาง kàt-kwǎang, กีดขวาง gìit-kwǎang ⚡

obstruction *n.* (act) การขัดขวาง gaan-kàt-kwǎang | (barrier) อุปสรรค ùp-bpà~sàk [อัน an] | (something that obstructs) สิ่งกีดขวาง sìng-gìit-kwǎang [สิ่ง sìng]

obtain vt. (get, gain) ได้ dâai, ได้_มา dâi-_-maa

obtuse adj. (mathematics) ป้าน bpâan | (not sharp) ทื่อ tûu, ไม่คม mâi-kom, ไม่แหลม mâi-lɛ̌ɛm

obvious adj. (apparent) เด่นชัด dèn-chát | (clear) ชัด chát, ชัดแจ้ง chát-jɛ̂ɛng

occasion n. (chance) วาระ waa-rá | (chance) โอกาส oo-gàat [ครั้ง kráng] | (time) ครั้ง kráng [ครั้ง kráng]

occasional adj. (happening sometimes) เป็นครั้งคราว bpen-kráng-kraao

occupant n. (tenant) ผู้อาศัย pûu-aa-sǎi [คน kon]

occupation n. (career) อาชีพ aa-chîip [อาชีพ aa-chîip] | (taking possession) การครอบครอง gaan-krɔ̂ɔp-krɔɔng

occupied adj. (busy) ติดธุระ dtìt-tú-rá, ไม่ว่าง mâi-wâang, ยุ่ง yûng | (mind) ว้าวุ่นใจ wáa-wûn-jai

occupy vt. (dwell) อยู่ yùu | (e.g. a country) ครอบครอง krɔ̂ɔp-krɔɔng

occur vi. (happen) เกิดขึ้น gèət-kûn

occurrence n. (act) การเกิดขึ้น gaan-gèət-kûn | (event) เหตุการณ์ hèet-gaan [ครั้ง kráng]

ocean n. มหาสมุทร má~hǎa-sà~mùt [แห่ง hèng]

o'clock clf. โมง moong, นาฬิกา naa-lí~gaa ǃ | (nighttime) ทุ่ม tûm

October n. ตุลาคม dtù-laa-kom [เดือน dɯɯan]

octopus n. ปลาหมึกยักษ์ bplaa-mùk-yák [ตัว dtuua]

odd adj. (approximately) โดยประมาณ dooi-

bprà~maan | (crazy)
บ้าๆบอๆ bâa-bâa-bɔɔ-
bɔɔ ✏ | (lacking a pair)
ไม่ครบคู่ mâi-króp-kûu |
(not even) คี่ kîi |
(strange) ประหลาด bprà~
làat, แปลก bplὲεk

odd number n. เลขคี่
lêek-kîi [ตัว dtuua]

odds n. (amount that has
differences) จำนวนต่าง
jam-nuuan-dtàang
[จำนวน jam-nuuan] |
(probability or chance)
ความเป็นไปได้ kwaam-
bpen-bpai-dâai

odor n. กลิ่น glìn

of prep. (belonging to)
ของ kɔ̌ɔng

of course! interj. แน่นอน
nɛ̂ɛ-nɔɔn

off adj. (e.g. TV, radio) ปิด
bpìt | (from work)
หยุดงาน yùt-ngaan | (not
connected) หลุด lùt |
(removed) ออก ɔ̀ɔk

offend vt. (anger)
ทำให้_โกรธ tam-hâi-_-
gròot, ทำให้_ไม่พอใจ
tam-hâi-_-mâi-pɔɔ-jai |
(insult) ล่วงเกิน lûuang-

gəən | (violate) ฝ่าฝืน
fàa-fʉ̌ʉn, ละเมิด lá~mêet

offender n.
ผู้กระทำความผิด pûu-
grà~tam-kwaam-pìt [คน
kon]

offense n. (attack)
การโจมตี gaan-joom-dtii
[ครั้ง kráng] | (crime)
อาชญากรรม àat-chá~
yaa-gam | (position in
sports) ฝ่ายรุก fàai-rúk
[ฝ่าย fàai] | (violation)
การฝ่าฝืนกฎ gaan-fàa-
fʉ̌ʉn-gòt, การละเมิด
gaan-lá~mêet

offensive adj. (insulting)
ที่สบประมาท tîi-sòp-
bprà~màat | (shameful,
obscene) ทุเรศ tú-rêet

offensive n. (attack)
การโจมตี gaan-joom-dtii
[ครั้ง kráng]

offer n. (proposition)
ข้อเสนอ kɔ̂ɔ-sà~nɔ̌ɔ [ข้อ
kɔ̂ɔ]

offer vt. เสนอ sà~nɔ̌ɔ |
(give a price, bid) ให้ราคา
hâi-raa-kaa

offering n. สิ่งที่เสนอให้
sìng-tîi-sà~nɔ̌ɔ-hâi |

(worship) เครื่องเซ่นไหว้ krûuang-sên-wâai [อย่าง yàang (kind), สำหรับ săm-ráp (set)] | (worship) เครื่องบัตรพลี krûuang-bàt-plii ‼ [สำหรับ săm-ráp, ชุด chút]

office n. (bureau, center, agency) สำนักงาน săm-nák-ngaan [แห่ง hɛ̀ng] | (where work is conducted) ที่ทำงาน tîi-tam-ngaan, ออฟฟิศ ɔ́ɔp-fít ✱ [แห่ง hɛ̀ng, ที่ tîi]

officer n. เจ้าพนักงาน jâo-pá~nák-ngaan [คน kon] | (police) นายตำรวจ naai-dtam-rùuat [นาย naai ‼, คน kon] | (postholder, staff, official) เจ้าหน้าที่ jâo-nâa-tîi [คน kon]

official adj. ทางการ taang-gaan, เป็นทางการ bpen-taang-gaan

official n. เจ้าพนักงาน jâo-pá~nák-ngaan, เจ้าหน้าที่ jâo-nâa-tîi [คน kon]

offline adj. (not connected to the Internet) ไม่เชื่อมต่อกับอินเตอร์เน็ต mâi-chûuam-dtɔ̀ɔ-gàp-in-dtəə-nèt, ออฟไลน์ ɔ́ɔp-laai

offside adj. ล้ำหน้า lám-nâa

offside adv. ล้ำหน้า lám-nâa

offspring n. (descendant) ลูกหลาน lûuk-lǎan [คน kon]

off-the-record adj. ไม่บันทึกไว้ mâi-ban-túk-wái

often adv. บ่อยๆ bɔ̀i-bɔ̀i, เป็นประจำ bpen-bprà~jam, มัก mák ✍

ogre n. ยักษ์ yák [ตน dton]

oil n. น้ำมัน nám-man [แกลลอน gɛn-lɔn (gallon), ลิตร lít (liter), ขวด kùuat (bottle)] | (for painting) สีน้ำมัน sǐi-nám-man

oil vt. (lubricate) หยอดน้ำมัน yɔ̀ɔt-nám-man

oily adj. (greasy) เป็นมัน bpen-man, เลี่ยน lîian

oink *n.* เสียงหมู sĭiang-mŭu [เสียง sĭiang]

ointment *n.* ขี้ผึ้ง kîi-pûng [ชนิด chá~nít (type), หลอด lɔ̀ɔt (tube), ตลับ dtà~làp (tin)]

O.K. see okay

O.K.! see okay!

okay *adj.* (well) สบายดี sà~baai-dii | (yes, agreed) ตกลง dtòk-long

okay *vi.* (agree) ตกลง dtòk-long | (well) สบายดี sà~baai-dii

okay! *interj.* ได้ dâai, โอเค oo-kee ❀

okra *n.* กระเจี๊ยบ grà~jíiap [ต้น dtôn (plant), ลูก lûuk (fruit)]

old *adj.* (former) ก่อน gòɔn | (not new) เก่า gào | (not young) แก่ gɛ̀ɛ

older *adj.* (e.g. people, animals) แก่กว่า gɛ̀ɛ-gwàa | (e.g. people, animals, things) มีอายุมากกว่า mii-aa-yú-mâak-gwàa | (e.g. things) เก่ากว่า gào-gwàa

older brother *n.* พี่ชาย pîi-chaai [คน kon]

older sister *n.* พี่สาว pîi-săao [คน kon]

oldest *adj.* มีอายุมากที่สุด mii-aa-yú-mâak-tîi-sùt | (used with objects) เก่าที่สุด gào-tîi-sùt

old-fashioned *adj.* (conservative) หัวเก่า hŭua-gào, หัวโบราณ hŭua boo raan ❀ | (outdated) ล้าสมัย láa-sà~măi, เชย chəəi ❀

old flame *n.* ถ่านไฟเก่า tàan-fai-gào ❀ [คน kon]

old maid *n.* (spinster) สาวทึนทึก săao-tɯn-tɯ́k [คน kon]

Old Testament *n.* พระคัมภีร์เก่า prá-kam-pii-gào [เล่ม lêm]

Old World *n.* โลกเก่า lôok-gào [แห่ง hɛ̀ng]

olive *n.* มะกอก má~gɔ̀ɔk [ลูก lûuk (fruit)]

olive oil *n.* น้ำมันมะกอก nám-man-má~gɔ̀ɔk [ขวด kùuat]

Olympics *n.* กีฬาโอลิมปิก gii-laa-oo-lim-bpìk [ครั้ง kráng]

omelet _n._ ไข่เจียว kài-jiiao

omen _n._ ลาง laang | นิมิต ní-mít ⚬ [อัน an]

omission _n._ (act of omitting) การตัดออก gaan-dtàt-ɔ̀ɔk, การละเว้น gaan-lá-wéen

omit _vt._ ละเว้น lá-wén, เว้น wén | (neglect) ละเลย lá-ləəi

omniscient _adj._ ที่รอบรู้ tîi-rɔ̂ɔp-rúu

omniscient _n._ พหูสูต pá~ hǔu-sùut ⚬ [คน kon]

on _adj._ (e.g. TV, radio) กำลังทำงานอยู่ gam-lang-tam-ngaan-yùu

on _adv._ (by, at) ที่ tîi

on _prep._ (along) ตาม dtaam | (at) ที่ tîi, ณ ná ⚬ | (by means of) ด้วย dûuai | (on top) บน bon

on and on _adv._ ไม่จบสิ้น mâi-jòp-sîn

on behalf of _prep._ (for the sake of) เพื่อ pʉ̂ʉa | (in the name of) ในนามของ nai-naam-kɔ̌ɔng

once _adv._ ครั้งหนึ่ง kráng-nʉ̀ng

once _conj._ ทันทีที่ tan-tii-tîi

once _n._ ครั้งหนึ่ง kráng-nʉ̀ng, หนึ่งครั้ง nʉ̀ng-kráng [ครั้ง kráng]

once a week _adv._ สัปดาห์ละครั้ง sàp-daa-lá-kráng ⚑, อาทิตย์ละครั้ง aa-tít-lá-kráng ✿

on duty _adj._ อยู่ในหน้าที่ yùu-nai-nâa-tîi

one _adj._ (alone) เดียว diiao

one _adv._ เดียว diiao

one _numb._ หนึ่ง nʉ̀ng

one another _adv._ กัน gan

one another _pron._ ซึ่งกันและกัน sʉ̂ng-gan-lɛ́-gan

one hundred thousand _numb._ แสน sɛ̌ɛn, หนึ่งแสน nʉ̀ng-sɛ̌ɛn

one-night stand _n._ (sexual encounter) คู่นอนคืนเดียว kûu-nɔɔn-kʉʉn-diiao

one-on-one _adj._ ตัวต่อตัว dtuua-dtɔ̀ɔ-dtuua

oneself _pron._ ตนเอง dton-eeng, ตัวเอง dtuua-eeng, เอง eeng

one-sided *adj.* ข้างเดียว kâang-diiao, ฝ่ายเดียว fàai-diiao | (biased) ไม่ยุติธรรม mâi-yút-dtì-tam

one-to-one *adj.* ระหว่างสองคน rá~wàang-sɔ̌ɔng-kon

one-way *adj.* (e.g. street) ทางเดียว taang-diiao | (e.g. ticket) เที่ยวเดียว tîiao-diiao

one-way ticket *n.* ตั๋วเที่ยวเดียว dtǔua-tîiao diiao [ใบ bai]

ongoing *adj.* ต่อเนื่อง dtɔ̀ɔ-nɯ̂ɯang

onion *n.* หอม hɔ̌ɔm, หัวหอม hǔua-hɔ̌ɔm [หัว hǔua]

online *adj.* (connected to the Internet) เชื่อมต่อกับอินเตอร์เน็ต chɯ̂uam-dtɔ̀ɔ-gàp-in-dtəə-nèt ❢ | (connected to the Internet, network) ออนไลน์ ɔɔn-laai

only *adv.* (just) แค่ kɛ̂ɛ, เท่านั้น tâo-nán, เพียง piiang, เอง eeng ❧

only *conj.* (but) แต่ dtɛ̀ɛ,

เพียงแต่ piiang-dtɛ̀ɛ

on the record *idm.* เก็บบันทึกไว้ gèp-ban-tɯ́k-wái

opal *n.* มุกดา múk-daa ❧ [เม็ด mét]

opaque *adj.* (impenetrable by light) ทึบแสง tɯ́p-sɛ̌ɛng

open *adj.* เปิด bpə̀ət | (empty) โล่ง lôong | (honest) เปิดเผย bpə̀ət-pə̌əi, ไม่ปิดบัง mâi-bpìt-bang

open *n.* (space) ที่โล่ง tîi-lôong [แห่ง hɛ̀ng] | (tournament) การแข่งขัน gaan-kɛ̀ng-kǎn [ครั้ง kráng]

open *v.* (begin) เริ่ม rə̂əm | (not close) เปิด bpə̀ət | (unfold) กาง gaang

open *vt.* (turn (a key), explain, reveal) ไข kǎi

open-air *adj.* กลางแจ้ง glaang-jɛ̂ɛng

open-heart surgery *n.* การผ่าตัดหัวใจ gaan-pàa-dtàt-hǔua-jai

opening *adj.* (first) แรก rɛ̂ɛk

opening n. (act of opening) การเปิด gaan-bpèət | (beginning) ตอนเริ่มต้น dtɔɔn-rə̂əm-dtôn | (opportunity, space) ช่องทาง chɔ̂ɔng-taang [ช่อง chɔ̂ɔng] | (slot, gap) ช่อง chɔ̂ɔng [ช่อง chɔ̂ɔng]

open-minded adj. (broad-minded) ใจกว้าง jai-gwâang | (impartial) ไม่ลำเอียง mâi-lam-iiang, ยุติธรรม yút-dtì-tam

open up vi. (start) เริ่มต้น rə̂əm-dtôn

opera n. ละครดนตรี lá-kɔɔn-don-dtrii, โอเปร่า oo-bpee-râa [เรื่อง rûuang]

operate v. (surgery) ผ่าตัด pàa-dtàt | (vehicle) ขับขี่ kàp-kìi | (work) ดำเนินงาน dam-nəən-ngaan

operate vi. (e.g. equipment, machine) ทำงาน tam-ngaan, เดิน dəən ✹

operating room n. ห้องผ่าตัด hɔ̂ng-pàa-dtàt

[ห้อง hɔ̂ng]

operation n. (performance) การดำเนินการ gaan-dam-nəən-gaan | (surgery) การผ่าตัด gaan-pàa-dtàt | (surgery) ศัลยกรรม sǎn-yá~gam [ครั้ง kráng]

operator n. (telephone operator) พนักงานรับโทรศัพท์ pá~nák-ngaan-ráp-too-rá~sàp [คน kon]

opinion n. (attitude) ทัศนคติ tát-sà~ná-ká~dtì [อัน an] | (viewpoint, idea) ความคิดเห็น kwaam-kít-hěn, ทัศนะ tát-sà~ná ⍨ [อัน an]

opinionated adj. (self-opinioned) ถือทิฐิ tǔu-tít-tì | (stubborn) หัวดื้อ hǔua-dûu

opium n. ฝิ่น fìn [ต้น dtôn (plant)]

opponent adj. เป็นฝ่ายตรงข้าม bpen-fàai-dtrong-kâam

opponent n. คู่ต่อสู้ kûu-dtɔ̀ɔ-sûu [คน kon] |

ฝ่ายตรงข้าม fàai-dtrong-kâam [ฝ่าย fàai] | (enemy) ศัตรู sàt-dtruu [คน kon (person), พวก pûuak (group)]

opportunist n. คนฉวยโอกาส kon-chǔuai-oo-gàat [คน kon]

opportunity n. โอกาส oo-gàat [ครั้ง kráng]

oppose v. (conflict, refuse) โต้ dtôo | (disagree, resist) คัดค้าน kát-káan, ค้าน káan, ต่อต้าน dtɔ̀ɔ-dtâan | (disobey, resist) ขัดขืน kàt-kǔun

opposite adj. ตรงข้าม dtrong-kâam

opposite prep. (across from) อยู่คนละด้าน yùu-kon-lá~dâan

opposition n. (disagreeing) การคัดค้าน gaan-kát-káan

oppress vt. กดขี่ gòt-kìi

optic adj. เกี่ยวกับสายตา gìiao-gàp-sǎai-dtaa

optical see optic

optician n. ช่างทำแว่นตา châng-tam-wên-dtaa [คน kon]

optimistic adj. มองโลกในแง่ดี mɔɔng-lôok-nai-ngɛ̂ɛ-dii

option n. (choice) ทางเลือก taang-lûuak [ทาง taang]

optional adj. ให้เลือกได้ hâi-lûuak-dâai

optometrist n. ผู้เชี่ยวชาญด้านสายตา pûu-chîiao-chaan-dâan-sǎai-dtaa [คน kon]

opulent adj. (wealthy) มั่งคั่ง mâng-kâng

or conj. หรือ rǔu, รึ rú ●

oracle n. (fortune teller) ผู้ทำนาย pûu-tam-naai [คน kon]

oral adj. (by the mouth) ด้วยปาก dûuai-bpàak

oral sex n. การทำรักด้วยปาก gaan-tam-rák-dûuai-bpàak, ออรัลเซ็กซ์ ɔɔ-rân-sék

orange adj. สีส้ม sǐi-sôm

orange n. ส้ม sôm [ต้น dtôn (tree), ลูก lûuk (fruit)]

orange juice n. น้ำส้ม nám-sôm [แก้ว gɛ̂ɛo

(glass)]

orangutan *n.* ลิงอุรังอุตัง ling-ù~rang-ù~dtang [ตัว dtuua]

oratory *n.* (chapel) ห้องสวดมนต์ hông-sùuat-mon [ห้อง hông]

orbit *n.* วงโคจร wong-koo-jɔɔn [วง wong]

orbit *vi.* โคจร koo-jɔɔn

orchard *n.* สวนผลไม้ sŭuan-pŏn-lá~máai [ไร่ râi, สวน sŭuan]

orchestra *n.* วงออเคสตร้า wong-ɔɔ-kés-dtrâa [วง wong] | (Thai) มโหรี má~hŏo-rii [วง wong]

orchid *n.* กล้วยไม้ glûuai-máai [ช่อ chɔ̂ɔ (bunch), ดอก dɔ̀ɔk (flower)]

ordain *v.* (as a monk or priest) บวช bùuat, บรรพชา ban-pá~chaa ⚡

order *n.* (command) คำสั่ง kam-sàng [เรื่อง rûuang, อัน an ⚡] | (logical order or sequence) ลำดับ lam-dàp [ลำดับ lam-dàp, ที่ tîi] | (merchandise) ใบสั่งซื้อ

bai-sàng-súu [ใบ bai, แผ่น pèn] | (series by order of preference, grade or rank) อันดับ an-dàp [ที่ tîi]

order *v.* สั่ง sàng

ordinal *adj.* (denoting a numerical order) เกี่ยวกับลำดับ gìiao-gàp-lam-dàp | (respectively) ที่แสดงลำดับ tîi-sà~dɛɛng-lam-dàp

ordinal number *n.* เลขแสดงลำดับ lêek-sà~dɛɛng-lam-dàp [ตัว dtuua]

ordinary *adj.* (normal) ธรรมดา tam-má~daa, สามัญ sǎa-man | (usual) ปกติ bpòk-gà~dtì

ore *n.* แร่ rɛ̂ɛ, สินแร่ sĭn-rɛ̂ɛ ✾ [ชนิด chá~nít]

organ *n.* (body) อวัยวะ à~wai-yá~wá [ชิ้น chín (piece), ส่วน sùuan (part)] | (musical) หีบเพลง hìip-pleeng [เครื่อง krûuang]

organic *adj.* (no chemical) ไม่ใช้สารเคมี mâi-chái-sǎan-kee-mii

organization n. (e.g. association, company) องค์กร ong-gɔɔn [องค์กร ong-gɔɔn] | (system) ระบบ rá~bòp [ระบบ rá~bòp]

organize v. (establish) จัดตั้ง jàt-dtâng

organize vt. (make neat, systematize) จัด jàt, จัด_ให้เรียบร้อย jàt-_-hâi-rîiap-rɔ́ɔi

orgasm n. (climax) จุดสุดยอด jùt-sùt-yɔ̂ɔt [จุด jùt] | (intense excitement) อารมณ์ดีใจอย่างสุดขีด aa-rom-dii-jai-yàang-sùt-kìit

orgy n. (sexual activity) เซ็กซ์หมู่ sék-mùu

orient n. (Asian countries) ประเทศในแถบตะวันออก bprà~têet-nai-tɛ̀ɛp-dtà~wan-ɔ̀ɔk [ประเทศ bprà~têet]

Oriental adj. เกี่ยวกับชาวตะวันออก giiao-gàp-chaao-dtà~wan-ɔ̀ɔk

orientation n. (direction) ทิศทาง tít-taang [ทิศ tít] | (introductory instruction)

การอบรม gaan-òp-rom, ปฐมนิเทศน์ bpà~tǒm-ní-têet [ครั้ง kráng]

origin n. (source, root) ที่มา tîi-maa, แหล่งกำเนิด lɛ̀ng-gam-nə̀ət ! | (source, root) จุดเริ่มต้น jùt-rə̂əm-dtôn [จุด jùt]

original adj. ดั้งเดิม dâng-dəəm | (first) แรก rɛ̂ɛk, แรกเริ่ม rɛ̂ɛk-rə̂əm

original n. (authentic) ของแท้ kɔ̌ɔng-tɛ́ɛ [ชิ้น chín, อัน an] | (prototype) ต้นฉบับ dtôn-chà~bàp [อัน an]

originate v. (initiate) เริ่ม rə̂əm, เริ่มต้น rə̂əm-dtôn

ornament n. (accessory) เครื่องประดับ krûuang-bprà~dàp [ชิ้น chín (piece), ชุด chút (set)]

orphan n. เด็กกำพร้า dèk-gam-práa [คน kon]

orphanage n. สถานเลี้ยงเด็กกำพร้า sà~tǎan-líiang-dèk-gam-práa [แห่ง hɛ̀ng]

orthodox *adj.* ดั้งเดิม
dâng-dəəm

orthopedics *n.*
ศัลยกรรมกระดูก săn-yá~
gam-grà~dùuk

ostracize *vt.* (banish)
ขับไล่ kàp-lâi

ostrich *n.* (bird)
นกกระจอกเทศ nók-grà~
jɔ̀ɔk-têet [ตัว dtuua]

other *adj.* อีก ìik, อื่น อื่น,
อื่นๆ อื่น-อื่น

other *pron.* (person)
คนอื่น kon-อื่น | (thing)
สิ่งอื่น sìng-อื่น

otherwise *adv.* (in
another way) เป็นอย่างอื่น
bpen-yàang-อื่น | (or
else) มิฉะนั้น mí-chà~nán

otherwise *conj.* (if not)
มิฉะนั้น mí-chà~nán,
ไม่เช่นนั้น mâi-chên-nán

otter *n.* ตัวนาก dtuua-
nâak [ตัว dtuua]

ouch! *interj.* โอ๊ย óoi

ought to *aux.* (should)
ควรจะ kuan-jà

ounce *n.* ออนซ์ ɔɔn [ออนซ์
ɔɔn]

our *adj.* ของเรา kɔ̌ɔng-

rao, ของพวกเรา kɔ̌ɔng-
pûuak-rao ⚠

ours *adv.* ของเรา kɔ̌ɔng-
rao

ours *pron.* ของพวกเรา
kɔ̌ɔng-pûuak-rao ⚠

ourselves *pron.* ตัวเราเอง
dtuua rao-eeng

out *adj.* (e.g. light) ดับ
dàp | (finished) หมด mòt
| (inoperative) เสีย sǐia |
(not currently
fashionable) เอ้าท์ áo 🔊 |
(not inside) อยู่ข้างนอก
yùu-kâang-nɔ̂ɔk

out *adv.* (outside,
exterior, external)
ข้างนอก kâang-nɔ̂ɔk |
(used with other words,
e.g. take out, come out,
etc.) ออก ɔ̀ɔk

out! *interj.* ออกไป ɔ̀ɔk-bpai

outbreak *n.* (sudden
increase) การระบาด
gaan-rá~bàat [ครั้ง kráng]

outburst *n.* (explosion)
การระเบิด gaan-rá~bə̀ət
[ครั้ง kráng]

outburst *vi.* (of activity or
emotion) ระเบิด rá~bə̀ət

outcast *n.* (person)
คนที่สังคมไม่ยอมรับ kon-

tîi-săng-kom-mâi-yɔɔm-
ráp [คน kon]

outcome *n.*
(consequence)
ผลที่ตามมา pŏn-tîi-
dtaam-maa | (result)
ผลลัพธ์ pŏn-láp

outdated *adj.* ล้าสมัย láa-
sà~măi, เชย chəəi •

outdo *vt.* (do better)
ทำดีกว่า tam-dii-gwàa |
(overcome) เอาชนะ ao-
chá~ná

outdoor *adj.* (open air)
กลางแจ้ง glaang-jɛ̂ɛng |
(outside) ข้างนอก
kâang-nɔ̂ɔk

outer *adj.* (exterior,
external) ชั้นนอก chán-
nɔ̂ɔk | (periphery, area
outside) รอบนอก rɔ̂ɔp-
nɔ̂ɔk

outfit *n.* (clothes)
เสื้อผ้าเป็นชุด sûua-pâa-
bpen-chút [ชุด chút (set)]
| (clothes) ชุด chút [ชุด
chút]

outgoing *adj.* (leg of a
journey) ขาออก kăa-ɔ̀ɔk |
(sociable) ชอบออกสังคม
chɔ̂ɔp-ɔ̀ɔk-săng-kom

outlaw *n.* ผู้ร้าย pûu-ráai,

คนนอกกฎหมาย kon-
nɔ̂ɔk-gòt-măai ➻ [คน
kon]

outlaw *vt.* (make
unlawful)
ทำให้_เป็นสิ่งผิดกฎหมาย
tam-hâi-_-bpen-sìng-
pìt-gòt-măai | (prohibit)
ไม่อนุญาต mâi-à~nú-yâat

outlet *n.* (exit) ทางออก
taang-ɔ̀ɔk [ทาง taang] |
(of a river) ปากแม่น้ำ
bpàak-mɛ̂ɛ-náam [แห่ง
hɛ̀ng] | (socket) ปลั๊ก
bplák [ตัว dtuua, อัน an] |
(vent) ช่องระบาย chɔ̂ng-
rá~baai [ช่อง chɔ̂ng]

outline *n.* (draft, plan)
เค้าโครง káo-kroong
[เรื่อง rûuang] | (of a
story) โครงเรื่อง kroong-
rûuang [เรื่อง rûuang]

outline *vt.* (draw a line)
ร่าง râang

outlive *vt.* อายุยืนกว่า aa-
yú-yɯɯn-gwàa

outlook *n.* (attitude)
ทัศนะ tát-sà~ná ! [อัน
an] | (sight, view) ภาพ
pâap [ใบ bai, แผ่น pɛ̀n,

ภาพ pâap]

out-of-date adj. ล้าสมัย láa-sà~măi, เชย chəəi ✿, เอ้าท์ áo ✿

out of order adj. (broken) เสีย sĭia, ชำรุด cham-rút ⚡

outpatient n. ผู้ป่วยนอก pûu-bpùai-nɔ̂ɔk [ราย raai ⚡, คน kon]

output n. (product) ผลิตผล pà~lìt-dtà~pǒn [ชนิด chá~nít (kind), ชิ้น chín (piece), กล่อง glòng (box), ห่อ hɔ̀ɔ (wrap)] | (production) การผลิต gaan-pà~lìt

output vi. (e.g. computers) แสดงข้อมูล sà~dɛɛng-kɔ̂ɔ-muun

outrage n. (anger) ความโกรธจัด kwaam-gròot-jàt

outrageous adj. (violent) รุนแรง run-rɛɛng

outside adj. ข้างนอก kâang-nɔ̂ɔk, นอก nɔ̂ɔk

outside adv. ข้างนอก kâang-nɔ̂ɔk, นอก nɔ̂ɔk, ภายนอก paai-nɔ̂ɔk

outside of prep. นอกจาก nɔ̂ɔk-jàak, ยกเว้น yók-

wén

outsider n. คนนอก kon-nɔ̂ɔk [คน kon]

outskirts n. ชานเมือง chaan-mɯɯang [เขต kèet]

outsmart vt. ฉลาดกว่า chà~làat-gwàa

outspoken adj. (frank) พูดจาเปิดเผย pûut-jaa-bpə̀ət-pěəi

outstanding adj. (prominent, distinguished) เด่น dèn | (unpaid) ค้างชำระ káang-cham-rá

outward adv. (outside) ด้านนอก dâan-nɔ̂ɔk

outwards adv. ไปทางนอก bpai-taang-nɔ̂ɔk

oval adj. (egg-shaped) รูปไข่ rûup-kài

oval n. วงรี wong-rii [วง wong]

ovary n. รังไข่ rang-kài [รัง rang]

oven n. เตาอบ dtao-òp [เตา dtao, เครื่อง krɯ̂ɯang]

over adj. (finished) จบ jòp

over adv. (again) อีกครั้ง ìik-kráng

over prep. (above, on) บน

bon | (across) ข้าม kâam | (higher than) เหนือกว่า nǔua-gwàa | (more than) มากกว่า mâak-gwàa

overact v. (overdo, exaggerate) ทำเกินไป tam-gəən-bpai, โอเวอร์ oo-wə̂ə ✿

overall adj. (whole, all) ทั้งหมด táng-mòt

overall adv. (whole, all) ทั้งหมด táng-mòt

overboard v. (fall overboard) ตกเรือ dtòk-ruua | (go to extremes) ทำเกินไป tam-gəən-bpai

overcast adj. (cloudy, gloomy) ครึ้ม krúm

overcoat n. เสื้อคลุม sûua-klum, เสื้อโค้ท sûua-kóot ✿ [ตัว dtuua]

overcome v. เอาชนะ ao-chá~ná

overdo v. (go to extremes) ทำมากเกินไป tam-mâak-gəən-bpai

overdose v. (too much use) ใช้มากเกินปริมาณ chái-mâak-gəən-bpà~rí~maan

overdraft n. (amount

overdrawn) การเบิกเงินเกินบัญชี gaan-bə̀ək-ngən-gəən-ban-chii

overdraw v. (money) ถอนเงินเกิน tɔ̌ɔn-ngən-gəən

overdue adj. เกินกำหนด gəən-gam-nòt

overflow v. (flood, whelm) ท่วม tûuam, ไหลล้น lǎi-lón

overhead adj. (over one's head) เหนือหัว nǔua-hǔua, เหนือศีรษะ nǔua-sǐi-sà ⚡

over here adv. ตรงนี้ dtrong-níi, ที่นี่ tîi-níi

overlap v. เหลื่อมล้ำ lùuam-lám | (lie on top of) ทับ táp

overlapping adj. เหลื่อมล้ำ lùuam-lám

overload v. (overburden) ใช้งานมากไป chái-ngaan-mâak-bpai

overlook vt. (ignore, disregard) มองข้าม mɔɔng-kâam, ละเลย lá-ləəi

overnight adj. (during

the night) ตลอดคืน dtà~
lɔ̀ɔt-kʉʉn | (e.g. stay,
trip) ค้างคืน káang-kʉʉn
overnight adv. (during
the night) ตลอดคืน dtà~
lɔ̀ɔt-kʉʉn | (e.g. stay,
trip) ค้างคืน káang-kʉʉn
overpass n. สะพานลอย
sà~paan-lɔɔi [แห่ง hɛ̀ng]
overripe adj. สุกเกินไป
sùk-gəən-bpai
overrule v. (prevail over,
deny) ลบล้าง lóp-láang
oversea see overseas
oversea adj. (abroad)
ต่างประเทศ dtàang-
bprà~têet | (situated in
countries across the sea)
โพ้นทะเล póon-tá~lee ⚬
oversee v. (supervise)
คุมงาน kum-ngaan
oversized adj. ใหญ่เกินไป
yài-gəən-bpai
oversleep v. นอนเกินเวลา
nɔɔn-gəən-wee-laa
overspend v.
ใช้จ่ายมากเกินไป chái-
jàai-mâak-gəən-bpai
overstay v. อยู่เกินกำหนด
yùu-gəən-gam-nòt
over there adv. ตรงนั้น

dtrong-nán, ที่นั่น tîi-nân
overthrow v. (topple)
โค่นล้ม kôon-lóm
overtime n. งานล่วงเวลา
ngaan-lûuang-wee-laa ⚡,
โอที oo-tii ⚡ [กะ gà]
overturn v. (overthrow)
ล้มล้าง lóm-láang
overturn vt. (turn over)
คว่ำ kwâm
overweight adj.
น้ำหนักเกิน nám-nàk-
gəən
overwhelm v. ท่วมท้น
tûuam-tón
overwork v.
ทำงานหนักเกินไป tam-
ngaan-nàk-gəən-bpai
ovulate v. สร้างไข่ sâang-
kài
owe v. เป็นหนี้ bpen-nîi
owl n. นกฮูก nók-hûuk
[ตัว dtuua]
own adj. (belonging to
oneself) ที่เป็นของตัวเอง
tîi-bpen-kɔ̌ɔng-dtuua-
eeng
own pron. (oneself) ตัวเอง
dtuua-eeng
own v. (possess)
เป็นเจ้าของ bpen-jâo-

kɔ̌ɔng

owner n. เจ้าของ jâo-kɔ̌ɔng [คน kon]

ownership n. (fact of being an owner) ความเป็นเจ้าของ kwaam-bpen-jâo-kɔ̌ɔng | (proprietorship) กรรมสิทธิ์ gam-má~sìt ⚠

ox n. วัว wuua, โค koo ⚠ [ตัว dtuua]

oxygen n. ออกซิเจน ɔ́k-sí~jên

oyster n. หอยนางรม hɔ̌ɔi-naang-rom [ตัว dtuua]

oyster sauce n. ซอสหอยนางรม sɔ́ɔt-hɔ̌ɔi-naang-rom [ขวด kùuat (bottle)]

ozone n. โอโซน oo-soon

P

pace n. (speed of walking) อัตราการเดิน àt-dtraa-gaan-dəən | (stride) ก้าว gâao [ก้าว gâao]

pace v. (oneself) ทำตามกำลังของตัวเอง tam-dtaam-gam-lang-kɔ̌ɔng-dtuua-eeng | (step) ก้าว gâao

pacemaker n. (heart) เครื่องกระตุ้นหัวใจ krûuang-grà~dtûn-hǔua-jai, อุปกรณ์ช่วยการเต้นของหัวใจ ùp-bpà~gɔɔn-chûuai-gaan-dtên-kɔ̌ɔng-hǔua-jai [เครื่อง krûuang]

pacifier n. (plastic nipple) หัวนมยาง hǔua-nom-yaang [อัน an]

pacify v. (calm) ปลอบ bplɔ̀ɔp

pacify vt. (establish peace) ทำให้_สงบ tam-hâi-_-sà~ngòp

pack n. (e.g. of dogs) ฝูง fǔung [ฝูง fǔung] | (group) กลุ่ม glùm [กลุ่ม glùm] | (package) ห่อ hɔ̀ɔ [ห่อ hɔ̀ɔ]

pack v. (crowd) แออัด ɛɛ-àt

pack vi. (luggage) จัดกระเป๋า jàt-grà~bpǎo, เก็บของ gèp-kɔ̌ɔng ⚠

pack vt. (put in container) บรรจุ ban-jù | (wrap) ห่อ hɔ̀ɔ

package n. (pack) ห่อ hɔ̀ɔ [ห่อ hɔ̀ɔ] | (parcel) พัสดุ pát-sà~dù [กล่อง glɔ̀ng (box), ชิ้น chín (one), ห่อ hɔ̀ɔ (pack)]

package tour n. ทัวร์แบบเหมา tuua-bὲεp-mǎo

packet n. (small package) ห่อของเล็กๆ hɔ̀ɔ-kɔ̌ɔng-lék-lék [ห่อ hɔ̀ɔ]

pact n. (agreement) ข้อตกลง kɔ̂ɔ-dtòk-long, สัญญา sǎn-yaa [ฉบับ chà~bàp (whole), ข้อ kɔ̂ɔ (item)]

pad n. (cushion) เบาะ bɔ̀ [ใบ bai, ลูก lûuk] | (flat, apartment) แฟลต flὲt [หลัง lǎng, อาคาร aa-kaan] | (note paper) สมุดฉีก sà~mùt-chìik [เล่ม lêm] | (shin guard) สนับแข้ง sà~nàp-kêng [ข้าง kâang (one), คู่ kûu (pair)]

pad vt. (protect with a pad) รอง_ด้วยเบาะ rɔɔng-_-dûuai-bɔ̀ | (put in a lining) บุ bù

paddle n. (oar) ไม้พาย mái-paai [เล่ม lêm] | (ping pong) ไม้ปิงปอง mái-bping-bpɔɔng [อัน an]

paddle v. (row) พาย paai

paddle vi. (dabble in water) แกว่งขาในน้ำ gwὲng-kǎa-nai-náam | (toddle) เดินเตาะแตะ dəən-dtɔ̀-dtὲ

paddy n. (unmilled rice) ข้าวเปลือก kâao-bplὼuak [เม็ด mét]

paddy field n. ทุ่งนา tûng-naa, นา naa [ที่ tîi, แห่ง hὲng, ผืน pʉ̌ʉn]

padlock n. (U-shaped bar lock) กุญแจสายยู gun-jεε-sǎai-yuu [ชุด chút]

page n. (e.g. book) หน้า nâa, หน้าหนังสือ nâa-nǎng~sʉ̌ʉ ! [หน้า nâa]

page v. (call) เรียก rîiak

page vt. (number the page) ใส่เลขหน้า sài-lêek-nâa

pageant n. (contest) การประกวด gaan-bprà~gùuat | (procession) การแห่ gaan-hὲε

pager n. เพจเจอร์ pèet-jəə, วิทยุติดตามตัว wít-tá~yú-dtìt-dtaam-dtuua ! [เครื่อง krʉ̂uang]

pagoda n. เจดีย์ jee-dii [องค์ ong]

pail n. (bucket) ถัง tǎng [ใบ bai]

pain n. ความเจ็บปวด kwaam-jèp-bpùuat

painful adj. (aching: longer-term, less acute) ปวด bpùuat | (hurting: short-term, acute) เจ็บ jèp

painkiller n. ยาแก้ปวด yaa-gɛ̂ɛ-bpùuat [เม็ด mét]

paint n. สี sǐi [กระป๋อง grà~bpɔ̌ng (canister), สี sǐi (color)]

paint vi. ทาสี taa-sǐi

paint vt. ทา taa

paintbrush n. แปรงทาสี bprɛɛng-taa-sǐi [อัน an]

painter n. (artist) จิตรกร jìt-dtà~gɔɔn [คน kon] | (person who coats walls, etc.) ช่างทาสี châng-taa-sǐi [คน kon]

painting n. (act of drawing) การเขียนภาพ gaan-kǐian-pâap | (act of painting) การทาสี gaan-taa-sǐi | (drawing) จิตรกรรม jìt-dtà~gam ‼ | (drawing) ภาพเขียน pâap-kǐian [ภาพ pâap]

pair n. (people, animals or things) คู่ kûu [คู่ kûu]

pair vi. (form a pair) เข้าคู่ kâo-kûu

pair vt. (match) จับคู่ให้ jàp-kûu-hâi

pajamas n. ชุดนอน chút-nɔɔn [ตัว dtuua]

pal n. เพื่อน pɯ̂an, สหาย sà~hǎai ☙, เกลอ glɔɔ ⌂ [คน kon]

palace n. (Thai royal residence) พระราชวัง prá~râat-chá~wang ⚡ [หลัง lǎng] | (royal residence) วัง wang [หลัง lǎng]

palate n. (roof of the mouth) เพดานปาก pee-daan-bpàak [แผ่น pèn] | (sense of taste) ความรู้สึกในการรับรส kwaam-rúu-sɯ̀k-nai-gaan-ráp-rót

pale adj. ซีด sîit, ซีดเซียว sîit-siiao ⚡

palette n. (color) จานผสมสี jaan-pà~sǒm-sǐi, จานสี jaan-sǐi [อัน an]

Pali n. บาลี baa-lii [ภาษา

paa-săa]

palm n. (hand) ฝ่ามือ fàa-muu [ข้าง kâang] | (tree) ต้นปาล์ม dtôn-bpaam [ต้น dtôn]

pamper vt. ตามใจ dtaam-jai, เอาใจ ao-jai

pamphlet n. แผ่นพับ pèn-páp [เล่ม lêm]

pan n. กระทะ grà~tá [ใบ bai]

pan v. (e.g. for gold) ร่อน rôn

panacea n. (remedy) ยาแก้สารพัดโรค yaa-gêɛ-săa-rá~pát-rôok

pancake n. แพนเค้ก pɛɛn-kéek [ชิ้น chín]

pancreas n. ตับอ่อน dtàp-òon

panda n. หมีแพนด้า mǐi-pɛɛn-dâa [ตัว dtuua]

pane n. (window) กระจกหน้าต่าง grà~jòk-nâa-dtàang [อัน an]

panel n. (group) คณะ ká~ná [คณะ ká~ná] | (group discussion) การอภิปรายกลุ่ม gaan-à~pí~bpraai-glùm

panhandler n. ขอทาน

kǒɔ-taan [คน kon]

panic vi. (be panicked) ตกใจกลัว dtòk-jai-gluua

panic vt. (frighten) ทำให้_กลัว tam-hâi-_-gluua

panorama n. (grand view) ทัศนียภาพรวม tát-sà~nii-yá~pâap-ruuam

pant vi. (gasp) หายใจหอบ hăai-jai-hɔ̀ɔp

panther n. เสือดำ sŭua-dam [ตัว dtuua]

panties n. กางเกงใน gaang-geeng-nai [ตัว dtuua]

pantomime n. ละครใบ้ lá~kɔɔn-bâi [เรื่อง rûuang]

pantry n. (for storing food, etc.) ตู้เก็บอาหาร dtûu-gèp-aa-hăan [ตู้ dtûu]

pants n. (outergarment) กางเกง gaang-geeng, กางเกงขายาว gaang-geeng-kăa-yaao [ตัว dtuua] | (underpants) กางเกงใน gaang-geeng-nai [ตัว dtuua]

pantyhose n. ถุงน่อง

tǔng-nɔ̂ng [ข้าง kâang
(each), คู่ kûu (pair)]

pap *n*. (nipple) หัวนม
hǔua-nom [หัว hǔua]

paparazzi *n*. ช่างภาพอิสระ
châng-pâap-ìt-sà~rà [คน
kon]

papaya *n*. มะละกอ má~
lá~gɔɔ [ลูก lûuk (fruit),
ต้น dtôn (tree)]

paper *adj*. (made of
paper) กระดาษ grà~dàat

paper *n*. กระดาษ grà~
dàat [แผ่น pèn (sheet), ใบ
bai (sheet)] | (report)
รายงาน raai-ngaan [ฉบับ
chà~bàp, เรื่อง rûuang] |
(toilet paper)
กระดาษชำระ grà~dàat-
cham-rá [แผ่น pèn
(sheet), ม้วน múuan
(roll), กล่อง glɔ̀ng (box)]

paperback *n*.
หนังสือปกอ่อน nǎng~
sǔu-bpòk-ɔ̀ɔn [เล่ม lêm]

paper bag *n*. ถุงกระดาษ
tǔng-grà~dàat [ใบ bai]

paper clip *n*.
ที่หนีบกระดาษ tîi-nìip-
grà~dàat [อัน an]

paper towel *n*.

กระดาษเช็ดมือ grà~dàat-
chét-muu [แผ่น pèn
(sheet), ม้วน múuan
(roll), ชิ้น chín (piece)]

Pap test *n*.
การตรวจภายใน gaan-
dtrùuat-paai-nai

par *adj*. (average) เฉลี่ย
chà~lìia

par *n*. (golf) พาร์ paa [พาร์
paa]

parachute *n*. ร่มชูชีพ
rôm-chuu-chîip [ชุด chút]

parade *n*. (march)
การเดินขบวน gaan-
dəən-kà~buuan |
(procession)
ขบวนพาเหรด kà~
buuan-paa-rèet

parade *vi*. (go in
procession) แห่ hɛ̀ɛ

paradise *n*. สวรรค์ sà~
wǎn [แห่ง hɛ̀ng]

paradox *n*. (statement)
ข้อความที่ขัดแย้ง kɔ̂ɔ-
kwaam-tîi-kàt-yɛ́ɛng
[ข้อความ kɔ̂ɔ-kwaam]

paragon *n*. (perfect
example)
ตัวอย่างยอดเยี่ยม dtuua-
yàang-yɔ̂ɔt-yîiam

[ตัวอย่าง dtuua-yàang]

paragraph n. ย่อหน้า yɔ̂ɔ-nâa [ย่อหน้า yɔ̂ɔ-nâa]

parakeet n. นกแก้วเล็ก nók-gɛ̂ɛo-lék [ตัว dtuua]

parallel adj. ขนาน kà~nǎan

parallel n. (analogy) การเปรียบเทียบ gaan-bprìiap-tîiap | (line) เส้นขนาน sên-kà~nǎan [เส้น sên]

parallel v. (go in parallel) ขนาน kà~nǎan

parallel vt. (make parallel) ทำให้_ขนาน tam-hâi-_-kà~nǎan

paralysis n. อัมพาต am-má~pâat [โรค rôok]

paralyze vt. (affect with paralysis) ทำให้_เป็นอัมพาต tam-hâi-_-bpen-am-má~pâat

paralyzed adj. เป็นอัมพาต bpen-am-má~pâat

paramedic n. (emergency personnel) เจ้าหน้าที่ปฐมพยาบาล jâo-nâa-tîi-bpà~tǒm-pá~yaa-baan [คน kon]

paranoid adj. วิตกจริต

wí-dtòk-jà~rìt ✗

paraphrase v. ถอดความ tɔ̀ɔt-kwaam

parasite n. (of a tree, person that depends on others) กาฝาก gaa-fàak [ต้น dtôn (plant), คน kon (person)] | (worm) พยาธิ pá~yâat [ตัว dtuua]

parasol n. ร่มกันแดด rôm-gan-dɛ̀ɛt [คัน kan]

parcel n. (package) พัสดุ pát-sà~dù [กล่อง glɔ̀ɔng (box), ชิ้น chín (one), ห่อ hɔ̀ɔ (pack)] | (plot of land) ผืนดินส่วนหนึ่ง pʉ̌ʉn-din-sùuan-nʉ̀ng [แปลง bplɛɛng, ผืน pʉ̌ʉn]

parch v. (become parched) แห้งผาก hɛ̂ɛng-pàak

parch vt. (make dry) ทำให้_แห้ง tam-hâi-_-hɛ̂ɛng

pardon n. (amnesty) การอภัยโทษ gaan-à~pai-yá~tôot ⚡ | (forgiveness) การให้อภัย gaan-hâi-à~pai

pardon v. (forgive) ยกโทษ yók-tôot

pardon! *interj.* ขอโทษ kɔ̌ɔ-tôot

parent *n.* (guardian) ผู้ปกครอง pûu-bpòk-krɔɔng [คน kon]

parenthesis *n.* วงเล็บ wong-lép [ตัว dtuua (one), คู่ kûu (pair)]

parents *n.* พ่อแม่ pɔ̂ɔ-mɛ̂ɛ [คน kon]

park *n.* (national park) อุทยาน ùt-tá~yaan [แห่ง hɛ̀ng] | (public) สวนสาธารณะ sǔuan-sǎa-taa-rá~ná [แห่ง hɛ̀ng]

park *v.* (vehicle) จอด jɔ̀ɔt

parking lot *n.* ที่จอดรถ tîi-jɔ̀ɔt-rót [แห่ง hɛ̀ng, ที่ tîi]

Parkinson's disease *n.* โรคสั่นสันนิบาต rôok-sàn-sǎn-ní-bàat [โรค rôok]

parliament *n.* รัฐสภา rát-tà~sà~paa [สภา sà~paa]

parlor *n.* (for guests) ห้องรับแขก hɔ̂ng-ráp-kɛ̀ɛk [ห้อง hɔ̂ng]

parole *n.* (conditional release) การปล่อยตัวโดยมีทัณฑ์บน gaan-bplɔ̀i-dtuua-dooi-mii-tan-bon

parrot *n.* นกแก้ว nók-gɛ̂ɛo [ตัว dtuua]

parsley *n.* ผักชีฝรั่ง pàk-chii-fà~ràng [ใบ bai (leave), ต้น dtôn (plant)]

part *n.* (machinery) ชิ้นส่วน chín-sùuan, อะไหล่ à~lài [ชิ้น chín] | (piece) ชิ้น chín [ชิ้น chín] | (role) บทบาท bòt-bàat | (section) ส่วน sùuan [ส่วน sùuan]

partial *adj.* (biased) ลำเอียง lam-iiang | (not total) บางส่วน baang-sùuan

participant *adj.* (sharing) ที่มีส่วนร่วม tîi-mii-sùuan-rûuam

participant *n.* ผู้เข้าร่วม pûu-kâo-rûuam [คน kon]

participate in *v.* เข้าร่วม kâo-rûuam, มีส่วนร่วม mii-sùuan-rûuam

participation *n.* การมีส่วนร่วม gaan-mii-sùuan-rûuam

particle *n.* (dust) ฝุ่นละออง fùn-lá~ɔɔng | (linguistics) คำสร้อย

kam-sɔ̂i [คำ kam] | (science) อนุภาค à-nú-pâak ⚒

particular *adj.* (fussy) จู้จี้ jûu-jîi | (specific) เฉพาะ chà~pɔ́

particularly *adv.* (especially) โดยเฉพาะอย่างยิ่ง dooi-chà~pɔ́-yàang-yîng | (in detail) อย่างละเอียด yàang-lá~ìiat

partition *n.* (act) การแยกออก gaan-yɛ̂ɛk-ɔ̀ɔk

partition *vt.* (e.g. land, property) แบ่ง bɛ̀ng | (separate) กั้น gân

partly *adv.* บางส่วน baang-sùuan

partner *n.* (good friend, lover) คู่ขา kûu-kǎa [คน kon] | (in business) หุ้นส่วน hûn-sùuan [คน kon] | (in dancing) คู่เต้นรำ kûu-dtên-ram [คน kon] | (pair) คู่ kûu [คู่ kûu] | (spouse) คู่สมรส kûu-sǒm-rót [คู่ kûu]

partnership *n.* (state of being a partner) ความเป็นหุ้นส่วน kwaam-bpen-hûn-sùuan | (type of business) ห้างหุ้นส่วน hâang-hûn-sùuan [แห่ง hɛ̀ng]

part of speech *n.* ชนิดของคำ chá~nít-kɔ̌ɔng-kam [ชนิด chá~nít]

part-time *adj.* ไม่เต็มเวลา mâi-dtem-wee-laa, พาร์ทไทม์ páat-taam 🗣

part-time *adv.* นอกเวลา nɔ̂ɔk-wee-laa

party *n.* (e.g. birthday) งานเลี้ยง ngaan-líiang, งานปาร์ตี้ ngaan-bpaa-dtîi 🗣 [งาน ngaan] | (group) กลุ่ม glùm [กลุ่ม glùm] | (litigant) คู่กรณี kûu-gɔɔ-rá~nii [คน kon (one), ฝ่าย fàai (side)] | (political) พรรค pák [พรรค pák] | (side) ฝ่าย fàai [ฝ่าย fàai]

party organizer *n.* แม่งาน mɛ̂ɛ-ngaan [คน kon]

pass *n.* (admission ticket) บัตรผ่าน bàt-pàan [บัตร bàt]

pass *v.* (go beyond) เลย ləəi | (location, test, time,

in a card game) ผ่าน pàan

passage n. (way) ทางผ่าน
taang-pàan [ทาง taang] |
(written article) ข้อเขียน
kɔ̂ɔ-kǐian [ชิ้น chín (work),
เรื่อง rʉ̂ʉang (story)]

pass away vi. ตาย dtaai,
เสียชีวิต sǐia-chii-wít ⚡

pass by v. (pass) ผ่านไป
pàan-bpai | (walk past)
เดินผ่าน dəən-pàan

pass by vt. (overlook)
มองข้าม mɔɔng-kâam

passenger n. ผู้โดยสาร
pûu-dooi-sǎan [คน kon]

passer-by n. คนเดินผ่าน
kon-dəən-pàan [คน kon]

passion n. (desire)
ความปรารถนา kwaam-
bpràat-tà~nǎa, กิเลส gì~
lèet ✎ | (enthusiasm)
ความกระตือรือร้น
kwaam-grà~dtʉʉ-rʉʉ-
rón

passionate adj. (having
intense emotion, lustful)
อารมณ์รุนแรง aa-rom-
run-rɛɛng

passion fruit n. เสาวรส
sǎo-wá~rót [ลูก lûuk]

passive adj. (chemistry)

ไม่มีปฏิกิริยา mâi-mii-
bpà~dtì-gì-rí~yaa | (not
active) เฉื่อยชา chʉ̀ʉai-
chaa | (not reacting, e.g.
to violence) ไม่โต้ตอบ
mâi-dtôo-dtɔ̀ɔp

pass on to vt. (hand
down) ตกทอดไปยัง dtòk-
tɔ̂ɔt-bpai-yang

pass out vi. (faint) เป็นลม
bpen-lom, หมดสติ mòt-
sà~dtì ⚡

pass out vt. (give out)
แจกจ่าย jɛ̀ɛk-jàai

passport n. พาสปอร์ต
páat-sà~bpɔ̀ɔt,
หนังสือเดินทาง nǎng~
sʉ̌ʉ-dəən-taang ⚡ [ฉบับ
chà~bàp ⚡, เล่ม lêm]

password n. รหัสผ่าน rá~
hàt-pàan [ตัว dtuua]

past adj. (former) อดีต à~
dìit | (previous) ก่อน gɔ̀ɔn

past n. (ancient, former
times) สมัยก่อน sà~mǎi-
gɔ̀ɔn

past prep. (further on
than) เลย_ไป ləəi-_-bpai
| (over a given value) เกิน
gəən

pasta n. พาสต้า páat-sà~

dtâa [เส้น sên]

paste *n.* (medicine) ยาป้าย yaa-bpâai

pasteurize *vt.* ฆ่าเชื้อใน kâa-chúua-nai

pastime *n.* (hobby) งานอดิเรก ngaan-à~dì~rèek [อย่าง yàang (kind), อัน an (piece)]

pastor *n.* บาทหลวง bàat-lǔuang [คน kon]

past participle *n.* กริยาช่องสาม grì-yaa-chông-sǎam [คำ kam]

pastry *n.* ขนมปังหวาน kà~nǒm-bpang-wǎan [ชิ้น chín, ก้อน gôon]

past tense *n.* อดีตกาล à~dìit-dtà~gaan [กาล gaan]

pasture *n.* (field for animals) ทุ่งเลี้ยงสัตว์ tûng-líiang-sàt [แห่ง hèng]

pat *v.* (strike lightly) ตบ_เบาๆ dtòp-_-bao-bao

patch *n.* (eye patch) ผ้าปิดตา pâa-bpìt-dtaa [อัน an] | (used in sewing) แผ่นปะ pèn-bpà [แผ่น pèn]

patch *vt.* (mend) ปะ bpà

patch up *vi.* (cure an injury) รักษาแผล rák-sǎa-plɛ̌ɛ | (reconcile) คืนดีกัน kuun-dii-gan

patent *n.* (for an invention) สิทธิบัตร sìt-tí-bàt [ใบ bai]

patent *v.* (obtain the exclusive rights) จดสิทธิบัตร jòt-sìt-tí-bàt

paternal *adj.* (on the father's side) ทางฝ่ายพ่อ taang-fàai-pɔ̂ɔ

paternal grandmother *n.* ย่า yâa [คน kon]

paternity *n.* (fatherhood) ความเป็นพ่อ kwaam-bpen-pɔ̂ɔ

path *n.* (way) ทาง taang, เส้นทาง sên-taang [สาย sǎai, เส้น sên]

pathetic *adj.* (evoking pity) น่าสงสาร nâa-sǒng-sǎan | (piteous) น่าเวทนา nâa-wêet-tá~naa ☜

patient *adj.* อดทน òt-ton

patient *n.* คนไข้ kon-kâi, ผู้ป่วย pûu-bpùai ⚠ [ราย raai ⚠, คน kon]

patio *n.* (terrace) นอกชาน nɔ̂ɔk-chaan [แห่ง hèng]

patriot *n.* ผู้รักชาติ pûu-rák-châat [คน kon]

patriotic *adj.* รักชาติ rák-châat

patrol *n.* (act) การลาดตระเวน gaan-lâat-dtrà~ween

patrol *v.* ลาดตระเวน lâat-dtrà~ween

patron *n.* (regular customer) ลูกค้าประจำ lûuk-káa-bprà~jam [คน kon] | (supporter) ผู้อุดหนุน pûu-ùt-nǔn [คน kon]

patronize *vt.* (customer) เป็นลูกค้า bpen-lûuk-káa | (support) อุดหนุน ùt-nǔn

pattern *n.* (model) แบบ bèɛp [แบบ bèɛp] | (print) ลาย laai, ลวดลาย lûuat-laai ‼ [ลาย laai]

pause *n.* การหยุดชั่วคราว gaan-yùt-chûua-kraao

pause *vt.* (stop shortly) หยุด_ชั่วขณะ yùt-_-chûua-kà~nà

pave *v.* ปู bpuu, ปูพื้น bpuu-púɯn

pavement *n.* (paved road) ทางลาดยาง taang-lâat-yaang [ทาง taang] |

(sidewalk) ทางเดินเท้า taang-dəən-táao, บาทวิถี bàat-wí-tǐi ‼ [ทาง taang]

pavilion *n.* (rest house) ศาลา sǎa-laa [หลัง lǎng] | (temporary structure) ปะรำ bpà~ram [หลัง lǎng]

paw *n.* (animal foot) ตีนสัตว์ dtiin-sàt ❖ [ข้าง kâang] | (claw, foot) อุ้งเท้า ûng-táao [ข้าง kâang] | (claw, hand) อุ้งมือ ûng-mɯɯ [ข้าง kâang]

pawn *n.* (chess) เบี้ยหมากรุก bîia-màak-rúk [ตัว dtuua]

pawn *v.* จำนำ jam-nam

pawnshop *n.* โรงจำนำ roong-jam-nam [แห่ง hèng]

pay *n.* (compensation) ค่าตอบแทน kâa-dtɔ̀ɔp-tɛɛn

pay *v.* จ่าย jàai, ชำระ cham-rá ‼

pay attention *v.* ตั้งใจ dtâng-jai, ใส่ใจ sài-jai

payday *n.* วันจ่ายเงิน wan-jàai-ngən [วัน wan]

payment *n.* การจ่ายเงิน

pay off v. (debt)
จ่ายหนี้_หมด jàai-nîi-_-
mòt

pay off vt. (bribe)
ติดสินบน dtìt-sǐn-bon

pay phone n.
โทรศัพท์สาธารณะ too-
rá~sàp-sǎa-taa-rá~ná [ตู้
dtûu]

payroll n. (list of
employees) รายชื่อ
พนักงานที่ได้รับเงินเดือน
raai-chûu-pá~nák-
ngaan-tîi-dâi-ráp-ngən-
dɯɯan [เล่ม lêm]

pea n. ถั่ว tùua [เม็ด mét
(seed), ฝัก fàk (pod)]

peace n. ความสงบ
kwaam-sà~ngòp,
สันติภาพ sǎn-dtì-pâap ✦

peaceful adj. สงบสุข sà~
ngòp-sùk

peacekeeper n. (person)
ผู้รักษาความสงบ pûu-rák-
sǎa-kwaam-sà~ngòp
[คน kon]

peach n. ลูกท้อ lûuk-tɔ́ɔ
[ลูก lûuk]

peacock n. นกยูง nók-
yuung [ตัว dtuua]

peak n. (highest point)
จุดสูงสุด jùt-sǔung-sùt
[จุด jùt] | (top) ยอด yɔ̂ɔt
[ยอด yɔ̂ɔt]

peanut n. ถั่วลิสง tùua-lí-
sǒng [เมล็ด má~lét
(bean)]

peanuts adj.
(insignificant) ไม่สำคัญ
mâi-sǎm-kan

pear n. ลูกแพร์ lûuk-pɛɛ,
สาลี่ sǎa-lìi [ลูก lûuk]

pearl adj. (pertaining to
pearls) ไข่มุก kài-múk

pearl n. ไข่มุก kài-múk
[เม็ด mét]

pearl oyster n. หอยมุก
hɔ̌ɔi-múk [ตัว dtuua]

peasant n. (farmer)
ชาวไร่ชาวนา chaao-râi-
chaao-naa [คน kon]

pebble n. (small stone,
gravel) กรวดหิน grùuat-
hǐn [เม็ด mét, ก้อน gɔ̂ɔn]

peck v. (with a beak) จิก jìk

peculiar adj. (strange)
แปลกประหลาด bplɛ̀ɛk-
bprà~làat, พิกล pí-gon ✦

peculiar to adj. เฉพาะ chà~pɔ́ | (special) พิเศษ pí-sèet

pedal n. (e.g. of piano) ที่เหยียบ tîi-yìiap [อัน an] | (of a bicycle) บันไดรถจักรยาน ban-dai-rót-jàk-gà~yaan [อัน an]

pedal vi. (ride a bicycle) ถีบจักรยาน tìip-jàk-gà~yaan

pedestal n. (altar) แท่น tên [แท่น tên, ที่ tîi]

pedestrian n. คนเดินถนน kon-dəən-tà~nǒn, คนเดินเท้า kon-dəən-táao [คน kon]

pedestrian crossing n. ทางม้าลาย taang-máa-laai [แห่ง hὲng]

pediatrician n. หมอเด็ก mɔ̌ɔ-dèk, กุมารแพทย์ gù-maan-rá~pɛ̂ɛt ✂ [คน kon]

pedicab n. รถสามล้อ rót-sǎam-lɔ́ɔ [คัน kan]

pedigree adj. มีสายพันธุ์ดี mii-sǎai-pan-dii

pedigree n. (lineage) เชื้อสาย chúua-sǎai | (lineage) สายเลือด sǎai-lûuat [สาย sǎai]

pedophile n. ผู้ชอบร่วมเพศกับเด็ก pûu-chɔ̂ɔp-rûuam-pêet-gàp-dèk [คน kon]

pee n. ฉี่ chìi ✸, เยี่ยว yîiao ✸

pee vi. ฉี่ chìi ✸, เยี่ยว yîiao ✸

peek vi. แอบดู ὲɛp-duu

peekaboo! interj. จ๊ะเอ๋ já~ěe

peel n. เปลือก bplùuak

peel v. (skin, e.g. fruit) ปอกเปลือก bplɔ̀ɔk-bplùuak

peel off v. (e.g. skin) ลอก_ออก lɔ̂ɔk-_-ɔ̀ɔk

peep v. (glance at) แอบมอง ὲɛp-mɔɔng

peer n. (an equal) คนที่เท่าเทียมกัน kon-tîi-tâo-tiiam-gan [คน kon] | (friend) เพื่อน pûuan [คน kon]

peg n. (hook) ตะขอ dtà~kɔ̌ɔ [อัน an] | (small, round, cylindrical object) หมุด mùt [ตัว dtuua]

peg vi. (insert a peg) ตอกหมุด dtɔ̀ɔk-mùt

Peking n. ปักกิ่ง bpàk-gìng [เมือง muuang]

pelican n. นกกระทุง nók-grà~tung [ตัว dtuua]

pelvis n. กระดูกเชิงกราน grà~dùuk-chəəng-graan [ชิ้น chín]

pen n. (animal) คอก kɔ̂ɔk [คอก kɔ̂ɔk] | (writing) ปากกา bpàak-gaa [ด้าม dâam]

penalize vt. (impose a fine on) ปรับไหม bpràp-mǎi | (punish) ลงโทษ long-tôot

penalty n. (fine) ค่าปรับ kâa-bpràp | (foul) โทษ tôot | (punishment) การลงโทษ gaan-long-tôot

penalty kick n. ลูกโทษ lûuk-tôot [ลูก lûuk]

pencil n. ดินสอ din-sɔ̌ɔ [แท่ง têng]

pendant n. (necklace) จี้ jîi [อัน an]

pending adj. (undecided) ยังไม่ตัดสินใจ yang-mâi-dtàt-sǐn-jai | (unfinished) ค้าง káang

pending prep. (during) อยู่ในระหว่าง yùu-nai-rá~wàang | (until) จนกระทั่ง jon-grà~tâng

pendulum n. ลูกตุ้ม lûuk-dtûm [ลูก lûuk]

penetrate v. (infiltrate) แทรกซึม sɛ̂ɛk-sɯm | (insert a penis) สอดใส่อวัยวะเพศ sɔ̀ɔt-sài-à~wai-yá~wá-pêet ✗

penetrate vt. (pierce) แทง tɛɛng, ผ่านทะลุ pàan-tá~lú, เสียบ sìiap

penfriend n. เพื่อนทางจดหมาย pɯ̂ɯan-taang-jòt-mǎai [คน kon]

penguin n. นกเพนกวิน nók-pen-gwin [ตัว dtuua]

penicillin n. ยาเพนนิซิลิน yaa-pen-ní-sí~lin [เม็ด mét]

peninsula n. คาบสมุทร kâap-sà~mùt [คาบสมุทร kâap-sà~mùt]

penis n. อวัยวะเพศชาย à~wai-yá~wá-pêet-chaai ❗, จู๋ jǔn ✹, เจ้าโลก jâo-lôok ✹, เจี๊ยว jíiao ✹, นกเขา nók-kǎo ✹, ไอ้จู๋

âi-jǔu ♠, ไอ้เจี๊ยว âi-jíiao
♠, ควย kuuai ☜, องคชาติ
ong-ká~châat ✖ [อัน an]

pen name n. นามปากกา
naam-bpàak-gaa [นาม
naam]

penny n. หนึ่งเซนต์ nùng-
sen, เหรียญเพนนี rǐian-
pen-nii [เหรียญ rǐian]

pension n. เงินบำนาญ
ngən-bam-naan [จำนวน
jam-nuuan]

pensive adj. (thoughtful)
ครุ่นคิด krûn-kít

penthouse n. (highest
floor) ชั้นสูงสุด chán-
sǔung-sùt [ชั้น chán]

people n. (persons in
general) คน kon, ชาว
chaao ☜ [ชาว chaao
(race), กลุ่ม glùm ☜
(group), พวก pûuak
(group), คน kon
(individual)] | (populace)
ประชาชน bprà~chaa-
chon [กลุ่ม glùm ☜]

pepper n. (black) พริกไทย
prík-tai [เม็ด mét (seed),
ขวด kùuat (bottle)]

peppermint n. สะระแหน่

sà~rá~nɛ̀ɛ [ต้น dton
(plant), ใบ bai (leaf)]

per prep. (e.g. per day) ต่อ
dtɔ̀ɔ | (via) โดย dooi

perceive vt.
(comprehend) เข้าใจ kâo-
jai | (sense, experience)
รับรู้ ráp-rúu

percent n. เปอร์เซ็นต์
bpəə-sen, ร้อยละ rɔ́ɔi-lá ☝

percentage n. (per
hundred) ส่วนร้อย
sùuan-rɔ́ɔi, อัตราร้อยละ
àt-dtraa-rɔ́ɔi-lá ☝

perception n.
(awareness) การรับรู้
gaan-ráp-rúu

perceptive adj. (able to
perceive) สามารถรับรู้ได้ดี
sǎa-mâat-ráp-rúu-dâai-
dii | (understanding)
เข้าใจ kâo-jai

perch n. (pole or rod, e.g.
for birds) คอน kɔɔn [คอน
kɔɔn]

percussion n.
(instruments)
เครื่องดนตรีประเภทตี
krûuang-don-dtrii-
bprà~pêet-dtii ☝ [ชิ้น
chín, เครื่อง krûuang]

per diem *adv.* (per day)
ต่อวัน dtɔ̀ɔ-wan

per diem *n.* (daily expenses) ค่าใช้จ่ายรายวัน kâa-chái-jàai-raai-wan

perfect *adj.* (complete) สมบูรณ์ sǒm-buun | (expert) ชำนาญ cham-naan

perfect *vt.* (complete) ทำให้_สมบูรณ์ tam-hâi-_-sǒm-buun

perfection *n.* ความสมบูรณ์ kwaam-sǒm-buun

perform *v.* (act) ทำ tam, ปฏิบัติ bpà~dtì-bàt ! | (show) แสดง sà~dɛɛng

perform *vi.* (work) ทำงาน tam-ngaan

performance *n.* (action) การดำเนินการ gaan-dam-nəən-gaan | (show) การแสดง gaan-sà~dɛɛng

performer *n.* (one who performs) ผู้แสดง pûu-sà~dɛɛng [คน kon]

perfume *n.* น้ำหอม nám-hɔ̌ɔm [กลิ่น glìn (scent), ขวด kùuat (bottle)]

perhaps *adv.* (maybe)

คงจะ kong-jà, บางที baang-tii, อาจจะ àat-jà

perimeter *n.* (boundary) ขอบเขต kɔ̀ɔp-kèet

period *n.* (age) ยุค yúk [ยุค yúk] | (era) สมัย sà~mǎi [สมัย sà~mǎi] | (length, session) ระยะ rá~yá | (lesson) ชั่วโมงเรียน chûua-moong-riian [ชั่วโมง chûua-moong] | (menstruation) ประจำเดือน bprà~jam-dɯɯan | (punctuation) จุด jùt [ตัว dtuua] | (season) ฤดู rɯ́-duu [ฤดู rɯ́-duu] | (time) ตอน dtɔɔn, เวลา wee-laa

periodical *n.* (magazine) นิตยสาร nít-dtà~yá~sǎan [ฉบับ chà~bàp !, เล่ม lêm]

periphery *n.* (external boundary) ขอบนอก kɔ̀ɔp-nɔ̂ɔk

perish *vi.* (die, disappear) ตาย dtaai | (spoil) เน่าเปื่อย nâo-bpɯ̀ɯai | (to be destroyed totally) ย่อยยับ yɔ̂i-yáp

perishable *adj.* (e.g. food) บูดง่าย bùut-ngâai, เสียได้ง่าย sǐia-dâi-ngâai

perjury *n.* การให้การเท็จ gaan-hâi-gaan-tét

permanent *adj.* ถาวร tǎa-wɔɔn, ประจำ bprà~jam

permanent *n.* (hair) ผมดัด pǒm-dàt

permeate *v.* (penetrate through) ซึมซาบ sʉm-sâap, แผ่ซ่าน pɛ̀ɛ-sâan

permission *n.* การอนุญาต gaan-à~nú-yâat | (approval by committee) การอนุมัติ gaan-à~nú-mát | (consent) การยินยอม gaan-yin-yɔɔm

permit *n.* (e.g. driver's license) ใบอนุญาต bai-à-nú~yâat [ใบ bai]

permit *v.* (allow) อนุญาต à-nú-yâat | (approve by committee) อนุมัติ à-nú-mát

permit *vi.* (allow) ยินยอม yin-yɔɔm

perpendicular *adj.* (vertical) ตั้งฉาก dtâng-chàak

perpendicular *n.* (line) เส้นตั้งฉาก sên-dtâng-chàak [เส้น sên]

perpetual *adj.* (everlasting) ชั่วนิรันดร์ chûua-ní-ran ☙

perseverance *n.* ความพากเพียร kwaam-pâak-piian, ความอุตสาหะ kwaam-ùt-sǎa-hà

persevere *vi.* (endure) ทรหด tɔɔ-rá~hòt ‼ | (persist) พากเพียร pâak-piian

persimmon *n.* (fruit) พลับ pláp [ลูก lûuk (fruit), ต้น dtôn (tree)]

persist *vi.* (insist) ยืนกราน yʉʉn-graan | (last) คงอยู่ kong-yùu

persistent *adj.* (continuous) ต่อเนื่อง dtɔ̀ɔ-nʉ̂ʉang | (enduring) คงอยู่ kong-yùu | (insistent) ยืนกราน yʉʉn-graan

person *n.* (grammar) บุรุษ bù-rùt | (individual, human) คน kon, ชาว chaao, บุคคล bùk-kon ‼ [คน kon]

personal *adj.* (law) ส่วนบุคคล sùuan-bùk-kon | (of the body) ทางร่างกาย taang-râang-gaai | (private) ส่วนตัว sùuan-dtuua

personality *n.* บุคลิก bùk-ká~lík, ลักษณะเฉพาะตัว lák-sà~nà-chà~pɔ́-dtuua

personally *adv.* (acting by oneself) โดยส่วนตัว dooi-sùuan-dtuua | (without a middle party) โดยตรง dooi-dtrong

personnel *n.* (department) ฝ่ายบุคคล fàai-bùk-kon [ฝ่าย fàai (department)] | (staff) เจ้าหน้าที่ jâo-nâa-tîi, บุคลากร bùk-ká~laa-gɔɔn ! [คน kon]

perspective *n.* (picture) ภาพที่ได้สัดส่วน pâap-tîi-dâi-sàt-sùuan [ภาพ pâap] | (point of view) มุมมอง mum-mɔɔng [มุมมอง mum-mɔɔng]

perspire *vi.* (sweat) เหงื่อออก ngùua-ɔ̀ɔk

persuade *v.* (convince)

โน้มน้าว nóom-náao | (induce, invite) ชักชวน chák-chuuan, ชักนำ chák-nam

persuasion *n.* (act) การชักชวน gaan-chák-chuuan, การโน้มน้าว gaan-nóom-náao

pertain to *vt.* (relate, concern) เกี่ยวกับ gìiao-gàp

pertinent *adj.* (relating) เกี่ยวข้อง gìiao-kɔ̂ng

pertussis *n.* ไอกรน ai-gron [โรค rôok]

pervert *n.* กามวิตถาร gaam-wít-dtà~tǎan [คน kon]

pessimism *n.* การมองโลกในแง่ร้าย gaan-mɔɔng-lôok-nai-ngɛ̂ɛ-ráai

pessimistic *adj.* มองโลกในแง่ร้าย mɔɔng-lôok-nai-ngɛ̂ɛ-ráai

pest *n.* (annoying animal) สัตว์ที่รบกวน sàt-tîi-róp-guuan [ตัว dtuua] | (insect) แมลงศัตรูพืช má~lɛɛng-sàt~dtruu-pɯ̂ɯt [ตัว dtuua] | (nuisance)

สิ่งที่สร้างความรำคาญ
sìng-tîi-sâang-kwaam-
ram-kaan

pesticide n. ยาฆ่าแมลง
yaa-kâa-má~lɛɛng [ชนิด
chá~nít (type), ขวด
kùuat (bottle)]

pestle n. สาก sàak [อัน an]

pestle vt. (grind with a
pestle) ตำ dtam

pet n. (domestic animal)
สัตว์เลี้ยง sàt-líiang [ตัว
dtuua, ชนิด chá~nít
(kind)]

pet v. (pat) ลูบ lûup

petal n. กลีบดอก glìip-
dɔ̀ɔk [กลีบ glìip]

petite adj. ร่างเล็ก râang-
lék

petite n. (clothing)
เสื้อผ้าสำหรับผู้หญิงร่างเล็ก
sûua-pâa-sǎm-ràp-pûu-
yǐng-râang-lék [ชุด chút
(set), ตัว dtuua (piece)] |
(woman) ผู้หญิงร่างเล็ก
pûu-yǐng-râang-lék [คน
kon]

petition n. (request)
การยื่นคำร้อง gaan-
yûun-kam-rɔ́ɔng |
(request) คำร้อง kam-

ร้อง [ฉบับ chà~bàp] |
(to the Supreme Court)
ฎีกา dii-gaa ✘ [ใบ bai,
ฉบับ chà~bàp]

petition v. (make a
complaint) ร้องเรียน
rɔ́ɔng-riian | (make a
petition) ยื่นคำร้อง yûun-
kam-rɔ́ɔng

petrol see gas

petroleum n. ปิโตรเลียม
bpì-dtoo-lîiam

petty adj. (law)
เกี่ยวกับลหุโทษ gìiao-
gàp-lá~hù-tôot | (trivial)
เล็กน้อย lék-nɔ́ɔi

petty theft n.
การลักเล็กขโมยน้อย
gaan-lák-lék-kà~mooi-
nɔ́ɔi

phantom n. (ghost) ปีศาจ
bpii-sàat [ตัว dtuua]

pharmacist n. เภสัชกร
pee-sàt-chá~gɔɔn [คน
kon]

pharmacy n. (drug store)
ร้านขายยา ráan-kǎai-yaa
[ร้าน ráan] | (subject)
เภสัชศาสตร์ pee-sàt-chá-
sàat [วิชา wí-chaa]

pharynx n. คอหอย kɔɔhǒɔi ✿

phase *n.* (period) ระยะ
rá~yá | (stage) ขั้น kân,
ขั้นตอน kân-dtɔɔn [ขั้น
kân]

Ph.D. *n.* (degree)
ปริญญาเอก bpà~rin-yaa-
èek [ปริญญา bpà~rin-yaa
(degree), ใบ bai
(certificate)] | (degree)
ดุษฎีบัณฑิต dùt-sà~dii-
ban-dìt ✐ [ปริญญา bpà~
rin-yaa, ใบ bai
(certificate)] | (person)
ด็อกเตอร์ dɔ́k-dtêə [คน
kon]

pheasant *n.* ไก่ฟ้า gài-fáa
[ตัว dtuua]

phenomenal *adj.*
(outstanding) โดดเด่น
dòot-dèn | (pertaining to
phenomena)
เป็นปรากฏการณ์ bpen-
bpraa-gòt-dtà~gaan

phenomenon *n.*
(occurrence) ปรากฏการณ์
bpraa-gòt-dtà~gaan

philanderer *n.* คนเจ้าชู้
kon-jâo-chúu [คน kon]

philanthropy *n.*
(benevolence)

การช่วยเหลือเพื่อนมนุษย์
gaan-chûuai-lǔua-
pûuan-má~nút

Philippines *n.* ฟิลิปปินส์ fí-
líp-bpin [ประเทศ bprà~
têet]

philosopher *n.* (who
offers views or theories)
นักปรัชญา nák-bpràt-
chá~yaa [คน kon]

philosophy *n.* ปรัชญา
bpràt-chá~yaa [วิชา wí-
chaa]

phlegm *n.* เสลด sà~lèet,
เสมหะ sěem-hà ✐

phobia *n.* (strong fear)
ความหวาดกลัว kwaam-
wàat-gluua

phone *n.* โทรศัพท์ too-
rá~sàp [เครื่อง krûuang]

phone *v.* โทร too

phone book *n.*
สมุดโทรศัพท์ sà~mùt-
too-rá~sàp [เล่ม lêm]

phonetics *n.*
วิชาการออกเสียง wí-
chaa-gaan-ɔ̀ɔk-sǐiang,
สัทศาสตร์ sàt-tá~sàat ✹
[วิชา wí-chaa]

phony *adj.* (dishonest)
ไม่จริงใจ mâi-jing-jai |

(fake) ปลอม bplɔɔm, เก๊
gée ✻

phony *n.* (counterfeit)
ของปลอม kɔ̌ɔng-bplɔɔm
[ชิ้น chín]

phosphorus *n.* ฟอสฟอรัส
fɔ́ɔt-fɔɔ-rát [ธาตุ tâat]

photo *n.* รูป rûup, รูปถ่าย
rûup-tàai ⚡ [ใบ bai, แผ่น
pèn]

photocopy *n.* (copy)
สำเนาเอกสาร sǎm-nao-
èek-gà~sǎan [ฉบับ chà~
bàp]

photocopy *v.* ถ่ายเอกสาร
tàai-èek-gà~sǎan

photogenic *adj.* (looking
good in photos)
ถ่ายรูปขึ้น tàai-rûup-kɨ̂n,
ขึ้นกล้อง kɨ̂n-glɔ̂ng ✻

photograph *n.* ภาพถ่าย
pâap-tàai ⚡ [ภาพ pâap] |
รูป rûup, รูปถ่าย rûup-
tàai ⚡ [ใบ bai, แผ่น pèn]

photograph *v.* ถ่ายรูป
tàai-rûup, ถ่ายภาพ tàai-
pâap ⚡, บันทึกภาพ ban-
tɨ́k-pâap ⚡

photographer *n.* ช่างภาพ
châng-pâap, ตากล้อง
dtaa-glɔ̂ng ✻ [คน kon]

photography *n.*
การถ่ายภาพ gaan-tàai-
pâap

phrase *n.* (linguistics)
กลุ่มคำ glùm-kam, วลี
wá~lii ✖ [วลี wá~lii] |
(music) ท่อนเพลง tɔ̂n-
pleeng [ท่อน tɔ̂n]

physical *adj.* (of material
things) ทางวัตถุ taang-
wát-tù | (pertaining to
the body) ทางกาย
taang-gaai, ทางร่างกาย
taang-râang-gaai ⚡

physical *n.* (examination)
การตรวจร่างกาย gaan-
dtrùuat-râang-gaai

physical education *n.*
วิชาพละ wí-chaa-pá~lá,
พลศึกษา pá~lá~sùk-sǎa
⚡ [วิชา wí-chaa]

physical therapy *n.*
กายภาพบำบัด gaai-yá~
pâap-bam-bàt

physician *n.* หมอ mɔ̌ɔ,
นายแพทย์ naai-pɛ̂ɛt ⚡,
แพทย์ pɛ̂ɛt ⚡ [คน kon]

physicist *n.* นักฟิสิกส์ nák-
fí-sìk [คน kon]

physics *n.* ฟิสิกส์ fí-sìk
[วิชา wí-chaa]

physiology *n.* สรีรวิทยา

sà~rii-rá-wít-tá~yaa ✱ [วิชา wí-chaa]

pianist *n.* นักเปียโน nák-bpiia-noo [คน kon]

piano *n.* เปียโน bpiia-noo [หลัง lǎng]

pick *n.* (selected thing) สิ่งที่ถูกเลือก sìng-tîi-tùuk-lûuak [สิ่ง sìng, อัน an] | (selection) การเลือก gaan-lûuak

pick *v.* (dip into) จิ้ม jîm

pick *vt.* (choose) เลือก lûuak | (e.g. flowers, fruits) เด็ด dèt

pickle *n.* (e.g. cucumber) ของดอง kǒong-doong | (trouble) ความยุ่งยาก kwaam-yûng-yâak

pickle *v.* ดอง doong

pickled *adj.* ดอง doong, หมักดอง màk-doong

pick on *vt.* (criticize) ตำหนิ dtam-nì, ติ dtì ✱

pick out *vt.* (choose) คัด kát, เลือก lûuak

pickpocket *n.* นักล้วงกระเป๋า nák-lúuang-grà~bpǎo [คน kon]

pickpocket *v.* ล้วงกระเป๋า lúuang-grà~bpǎo

pick up *vt.* (by hand) เก็บ gèp | (call for someone) ไปรับ bpai-ráp | (lift) ยก_ขึ้น yók-_-kûn

pick-up truck *n.* กระบะ grà~bà, รถปิกอัพ rót-bpík-àp [คัน kan]

picky *adj.* (meticulous in one's choice) เลือกมาก lûuak-mâak

picnic *n.* ปิกนิก bpík-ník

picture *n.* (mental image derived from a narrative) ภาพพจน์ pâap-pót | (photo) ภาพ pâap [ใบ bai, แผ่น pèn, ภาพ pâap] | (photo) รูป rûup, รูปภาพ rûup-pâap ✱ [ใบ bai, แผ่น pèn]

picture *v.* (visualize) นึกภาพ núk-pâap

pie *n.* ขนมพาย kà~nǒm-paai [ชิ้น chín]

piece *n.* (chessman) ตัวหมากรุก dtuua-màak-rúk [ตัว dtuua] | (of anything) ชิ้น chín [ชิ้น chín] | (things in general use) อัน an [อัน an]

piece of land n. ที่ดิน tîi-din [แปลง bplɛɛng, ผืน pʉ̌ʉn]

pier n. (pillar) เสาหิน sǎo-hǐn [เสา sǎo, ต้น dtôn] | (wharf) ท่าเรือ tâa-rʉʉa [แห่ง hɛ̀ng]

pierce vt. (puncture) เจาะ jɔ̀, แทง tɛɛng

piercing adj. (sharp) แหลมคม lɛ̌ɛm-kom | (shrill voice) ดังแสบแก้วหู dang-sɛ̀ɛp-gɛ̂ɛo-hǔu

pig n. (animal) หมู mǔu, สุกร sù-gɔɔn ‼ [ตัว dtuua] | (greedy person) คนตะกละ kon-dtà~glà [คน kon]

pigeon n. นกพิราบ nók-pí-râap [ตัว dtuua]

pigment n. สี sǐi, เม็ดสี mét-sǐi ‼

pigtail n. (hairdo) หางเปีย hǎang-bpiia [เส้น sên] | (of a pig) หางหมู hǎang-mǔu [หาง hǎang]

pile n. (heap) กอง gɔɔng [กอง gɔɔng]

pile vt. (make a pile) กอง gɔɔng

pile up vi. (make a pile)

กองขึ้น gɔɔng-kʉ̂n

pile up vt. (make a pile) ทำให้_เป็นกอง tam-hâi-_-bpen-gɔɔng

pilgrim n. (religious devotee) ผู้แสวงบุญ pûu-sà~wɛ̌ɛng-bun [คน kon]

pill n. (medicine) ยา yaa [ชนิด chá~nít (kind), เม็ด mét (pill), ขวด kùuat (bottle), ซอง sɔɔng (pack), แผง pɛ̌ɛng (set), หลอด lɔ̀ɔt (tube)] | (tablet of medicine) ยาเม็ด yaa-mét [เม็ด mét]

pillar n. (stone pillar) เสาหิน sǎo-hǐn [เสา sǎo, ต้น dtôn]

pillow n. หมอน mɔ̌ɔn [ใบ bai, ลูก lûuk]

pillowcase n. ปลอกหมอน bplɔ̀ɔk-mɔ̌ɔn [ปลอก bplɔ̀ɔk, อัน an]

pilot adj. (experimental) สำหรับทดลอง sǎm-ràp-tót-lɔɔng

pilot n. (aviator) นักบิน nák-bin [คน kon] | (experimental trial) รายการนำร่อง raai-gaan-nam-rɔ̂ng [รายการ raai-

gaan] | (plane captain)
กัปตันเครื่องบิน gàp-
dtan-krûuang-bin [คน
kon]

pimento *n.* (pepper)
พริกหยวก prík-yùuak
[เม็ด mét]

pimp *n.* แมงดา mɛɛng-
daa [คน kon]

pimp *v.* เป็นแมงดา
bpen-mɛɛng-daa

pimple *n.* สิว sǐu [เม็ด
mét, หัว hǔua ●]

pimply *adj.* มีสิวมาก mii-
sǐu-mâak

pin *n.* (bowling) พินโบว์ลิ่ง
pin-boo-lîng [อัน an] |
(hairpin) ปิ่นปักผม bpìn-
bpàk-pǒm [อัน an] |
(safety pin, jewelry)
เข็มกลัด kěm-glàt [อัน
an] | (thumbtack, round
pin) เข็มหมุด kěm-mùt
[ตัว dtuua]

pin *vi.* (fasten with a pin)
กลัดเข็มกลัด glàt-kěm-
glàt

pin *vt.* (fasten, fix) ตรึง
dtrʉng

pincer *n.* (crab) ก้ามปู
gâam-bpuu [ก้าม gâam]

pincers *n.* (pliers) ปากคีบ
bpàak-kîip [อัน an]

pinch *vt.* (nip with finger
and thumb) หยิก yìk

pin down *vt.* (fasten, fix)
ตรึง dtrʉng

pine *n.* (tree) สน sǒn [ต้น
dtôn]

pineapple *n.* สับปะรด
sàp-bpà~rót [ลูก lûuk]

pine tree *n.* สน sǒn [ต้น
dtôn]

ping pong *n.* (ball)
ลูกปิงปอง lûuk-bping-
bpɔɔng [ลูก lûuk] | (sport)
ปิงปอง bping-bpɔɔng

pink *adj.* ชมพู chom-puu,
สีชมพู sǐi-chom-puu

pink *n.* สีชมพู sǐi-chom-
puu [สี sǐi]

pinkeye *n.* ตาแดง dtaa-
dɛɛng [โรค rôok]

pinkie *n.* นิ้วก้อย níu-gɔ̂ɔi
[นิ้ว níu]

pioneer *n.* (explorer)
ผู้บุกเบิก pûu-bùk-bə̀ək
[คน kon]

pioneer *v.* (be a pioneer)
บุกเบิก bùk-bə̀ək | (settle
a region) ตั้งรกราก

dtâng-rók-râak

pipe *n.* (conduit, hose) ท่อ
ทั่ว [ท่อ ทั่ว] | (for
smoking) กล้องยาสูบ
glông-yaa-sùup [กล้อง
glông]

piper *n.* (flute player)
คนเป่าปี่ kon-bpào-bpìi
[คน kon]

piracy *n.* (hijacking)
การปล้น gaan-bplôn |
(hijacking at sea)
การปล้นกลางทะเล gaan-
bplôn-glaang-tá~lee |
(unauthorized
reproduction)
การละเมิดลิขสิทธิ์ gaan-
lá~mâət-lík-kà~sìt

pirate *n.* โจรสลัด joon-sà~
làt [คน kon]

pirate *v.* (copy without
legal right) ละเมิดลิขสิทธิ์
lá~mâət-lík-kà~sìt

Pisces *n.* ราศีมีน raa-sǐi-
miin [ราศี raa-sǐi]

piss *n.* (urine) ปัสสาวะ
bpàt-sǎa~wá ⚡, เยี่ยว
yìiao 💧

piss *v.* (urinate) ปัสสาวะ
bpàt-sǎa~wá ⚡

piss *vi.* (urinate) ฉี่ chìi 💧,

เยี่ยว yìiao 💧

pistol *n.* ปืนพก bpʉʉn-
pók [กระบอก grà~bɔ̀ɔk]

piston *n.* ลูกสูบ lûuk-sùup
[ลูก lûuk]

pit *n.* (hole) หลุม lǔm [รู
ruu, หลุม lǔm] | (of a
fruit) เมล็ด má~lét ⚡ [เม็ด
mét, เมล็ด má~lét ⚡]

pitch *n.* (highest point)
จุดสูงสุด jùt-sǔung-sùt |
(sound) ระดับเสียง rá~
dàp-sǐiang [ระดับ rá~
dàp] | (throw) การขว้าง
gaan-kwâang

pitch *v.* (establish, set up)
ตั้ง dtâng

pitcher *n.* (e.g. baseball)
ผู้ขว้าง pûu-kwâang [คน
kon] | (jug) เหยือก yʉ̀ak
[ใบ bai]

pitfall *n.* (trap) หลุมพราง
lǔm-praang [อัน an] |
(unforeseen danger)
อันตรายที่แอบแฝง an-
dtà~raai-tîi-ɛ̀ɛp-fɛ̌ɛng

pitiful *adj.* (arousing
contemptuous pity)
น่าทุเรศ nâa-tú~rêet 💢 |
(deserving pity) น่าสงสาร

nâa-sŏng-săan, น่าเวทนา
nâa-wêet-tá~naa ➤
pity *n.* (sympathy)
ความสงสาร kwaam-
sŏng-săan
pity *vt.* สงสาร sŏng-săan
pivot *n.* (for rotating)
แกนหมุน gɛɛn-mŭn [แกน
gɛɛn]
pivot *v.* (turn around)
หมุน_รอบ mŭn-_-rɔ̂ɔp
pizza *n.* พิซซ่า pít-sâa [ชิ้น
chín (slice), ถาด tàat
(tray)]
placard *n.* ป้ายประกาศ
bpâai-bprà~gàat [ป้าย
bpâai, แผ่น pèn]
place *n.* (position)
ตำแหน่ง dtam-nèng
[ตำแหน่ง dtam-nèng] |
(site, spot) ที่ tîi, สถานที่
sà~tăan-tîi [แห่ง hèng]
place *v.* (appoint) แต่งตั้ง
dtèng-dtâng | (set) ตั้ง
dtâng
place *vt.* (put, rest)
วางไว้ที่ waang-wái-tîi
placement *n.* (act of
placing) การจัดวาง gaan-
jàt-waang | (position)
ตำแหน่ง dtam-nèng

[ตำแหน่ง dtam-nèng]
placenta *n.* รก rók
plague *n.* (epidemic
disease) โรคระบาด rôok-
rá~bàat [โรค rôok]
plain *adj.* (flat) ราบ râap |
(open, clear) โล่ง lôong |
(simple, ordinary)
เรียบง่าย rîiap-ngâai |
(unattractive) ไม่ดึงดูด
mâi-dɯng-dùut, เรียบๆ
rîiap-rîiap
plain *n.* (flatland) ที่ราบ
tîi-râap [แห่ง hèng]
plaintiff *n.* โจทก์ jòot,
เจ้าทุกข์ jâao-túk ➤ [คน
kon]
plan *n.* (design, drawing)
แบบแปลน bɛ̀ɛp-bplɛɛn
[แบบ bɛ̀ɛp (whole), แผ่น
pèn (piece)] | (diagram,
chart) ผัง păng ? [อัน an]
| (intention) แผนการ
pɛ̌ɛn-gaan ? [แผน pɛ̌ɛn,
อัน an] | (project)
โครงการ kroong-gaan
[โครงการ kroong-gaan,
อัน an]
plan *v.* (lay plan) วางแผน
waang-pɛ̌ɛn
plane *adj.* (flat) ราบ râap

plane *n.* (airplane)
เครื่องบิน krûuang-bin
[ลำ lam, เครื่อง krûuang] |
(carpentry) กบไสไม้ gòp-
săi-máai [ตัว dtuua]

plane *vt.* (carpentry) ไส săi

plane crash *n.*
เครื่องบินตก krûuang-
bin-dtòk [ครั้ง kráng]

planet *n.* ดาวเคราะห์
daao-krɔ́ [ดวง duuang]

plank *n.* (board)
แผ่นกระดาน pɛ̀n-grà~
daan [แผ่น pɛ̀n]

planner *n.* (appointment
book) สมุดบันทึกเวลานัด
sà~mùt-ban-túk-wee-
laa-nát [เล่ม lêm] | (e.g.
towns, cities)
ผู้วางโครงการ pûu-
waang-kroong-gaan [คน
kon]

plant *n.* (tree) ต้นไม้
dtôn-máai [ต้น dtôn] |
(vegetation) พืช pûut
[ชนิด chá~nít (kind), ต้น
dtôn (plant)]

plant *vt.* (cultivate)
เพาะเลี้ยง pɔ́-líiang |
(establish) ก่อตั้ง gɔ̀ɔ-

dtâng | (grow) ปลูก
bplùuk | (instill, educate)
ปลูกฝัง bplùuk-fǎng |
(put) วาง waang

plaque *n.* (engraved
plate) หินสลัก hǐn-sà~làk
[แผ่น pɛ̀n] | (on teeth)
หินปูน hǐn-bpuun [คราบ
krâap]

plasma *n.* (serum)
ปลาสมา bplaat-sà~mâa |
(whey) หางนม hǎang-
nom

plaster *n.* (band-aid)
ที่ติดแผล tîi-dtìt-plɛ̌ɛ [ชิ้น
chín (piece), กล่อง glɔ̀ng
(box)] | (powdered
gypsum) ปูนปลาสเตอร์
bpuun-bplaat-sà~dtəə

plaster *vi.* (fill with
plaster) ฉาบปูน chàap-
bpuun

plastic *adj.* (made of
plastic) ทำจากพลาสติก
tam-jàak-pláat-sà~dtìk

plastic *n.* (material)
พลาสติก pláat-sà~dtìk

plastic bag *n.* ถุงพลาสติก
tǔng-pláat-sà~dtìk [ใบ
bai]

plastic surgery *n.*
ศัลยกรรมตกแต่ง sǎn-

yá~gam-dtòk-dtèng

plate n. (coating metal) โลหะเคลือบ loo-hà-klûuap | (dish) จาน jaan [ใบ bai, ลูก lûuk] | (e.g. of vehicle) แผ่นป้าย pèn-bpâai [แผ่น pèn]

plate vt. (coat) เคลือบ klûuap

plateau n. (tableland) ที่ราบสูง tîi-râap-sǔung [แห่ง hèng, ที่ tîi]

platform n. (e.g. train, bus) ชานชาลา chaan-chaa-laa [ชาน chaan, แห่ง hèng] | (pedestal) ฐาน tǎan [ฐาน tǎan]

platinum n. ทองคำขาว tɔɔng-kam-kǎao [กรัม gram (gram)]

platter n. (plate) จานตื้นขนาดใหญ่ jaan-dtûɨn-kà~nàat-yài [ใบ bai]

play n. (drama) ละคร lá~kɔɔn [ตอน dtɔɔn (episode), ฉาก chàak (scene), เรื่อง rûɨang (story)] | (entertainment) การเล่น gaan-lên | (show) การแสดง gaan-sà~dɛɛng

play v. (games, music, etc.) เล่น lên | (movie) ฉาย chǎai | (music) บรรเลง ban-leeng ❢ | (sport) แข่งขัน kèng-kǎn

play vi. (perform) แสดง sà~dɛɛng

play vt. (have a part in a play as) แสดงเป็น sà~dɛɛng-bpen

playboy n. ชายเจ้าชู้ chaai-jâo-chúu, เพลย์บอย plee-bɔɔi ❖ [คน kon]

player n. (machine) เครื่องเล่น krûɨang-lên [เครื่อง krûɨang] | (of music) ผู้บรรเลง pûu-ban-leeng [คน kon] | (person) ผู้เล่น pûu-lên [คน kon]

playful adj. ขี้เล่น kîi-lên

playground n. สนามเด็กเล่น sà~nǎam-dèk-lên [แห่ง hèng]

playmate n. เพื่อนเล่น pûɨan-lên [คน kon]

play off n. การแข่งขันชิงชนะเลิศ gaan-kèng-kǎn-ching-chá~ná-lə̂ət [ครั้ง kráng]

plaza n. (public square) ลานกว้างสาธารณะ laan-gwâang-sǎa-taa-rá~ná [แห่ง hèng, ที่ tîi] | (shopping center) ศูนย์การค้า sǔun-gaan-káa [แห่ง hèng]

plea n. (defendant's answer) การตอบรับข้อกล่าวหา gaan-dtɔ̀ɔp-ráp-kɔ̂ɔ-glàao-hǎa | (e.g. for mercy) คำวิงวอน kam-wing-wɔɔn

plea-bargain n. การยอมความกัน gaan-yɔɔm-kwaam-gan

plead v. (answer to charges) ตอบข้อกล่าวหา dtɔ̀ɔp-kɔ̂ɔ-glàao-hǎa | (beg, implore) ขอร้อง kɔ̌ɔ-rɔ́ɔng, วิงวอน wing-wɔɔn | (make excuses) แก้ตัว gɛ̂ɛ-dtuua

pleasant adj. (e.g. weather) สบาย sà~baai | (enjoyable) สนุกสนาน sà~nùk-sà~nǎan | (satisfactory) น่าเพอใจ nâa-pɔɔ-jai

please adv. (in polite requests) โปรด bpròot, กรุณา gà~rú~naa ⚡

please vt. (give enjoyment to) ถูกใจ tùuk-jai, ทำให้_พอใจ tam-hâi-_-pɔɔ-jai

pleased adj. พอใจ pɔɔ-jai

please do _ for _ idm. ช่วย_ให้_ด้วย chûuai-_-hâi-_-dûuai ✱

pleasure n. ความยินดี kwaam-yin-dii

pleasure vt. (give pleasure) ทำให้_พอใจ tam-hâi-_-pɔɔ-jai

pleat n. (plait) รอยจีบ rɔɔi-jìip, รอยพับ rɔɔi-páp [รอย rɔɔi]

pleat v. (arrange in pleats) จับจีบ jàp-jìip

pledge n. (promise) คำมั่นสัญญา kam-mân-sǎn-yaa [ข้อ kɔ̂ɔ, ประการ bprà~gaan ⚡]

pledge v. (swear) สาบาน sǎa-baan | (vow) ปฏิญาณ bpà~dtì-yaan

pledge vi. (contract) ทำสัญญา tam-sǎn-yaa

plentiful adj. มากมาย mâak-maai

plenty adj. (numerous,

abundant) มีมากมาย mii-mâak-maai, เยอะแยะ yə́-yɛ́ ✦

plenty *n.* (abundance) ความมั่งคั่ง kwaam-mâng-kâng

pliable *adj.* (bendable) ดัดง่าย dàt-ngâai | (flexible) ยืดหยุ่น yûut-yùn

pliers *n.* คีม kiim [อัน an]

plod *n.* (heavy walk) การเดินย่ำเท้าหนักๆ gaan-dəən-yâm-táao-nàk-nàk

plot *n.* (diagram) แผนผัง pɛ̌ɛn-pǎng [อัน an] | (land) ที่ดินเป็นแปลง tîi-din-bpen-bplɛɛng [แปลง bplɛɛng] | (plan) โครงการ kroong-gaan [โครงการ kroong-gaan, อัน an] | (storyline) โครงเรื่อง kroong-rûⱨang [เรื่อง rûⱨang]

plot *vi.* (plan, scheme) วางแผน waang-pɛ̌ɛn, ออกอุบาย ɔ̀ɔk-ù-baai

plough *n.* (farming tool) คันไถ kan-tǎi [คัน kan]

plough *v.* (till, shove) ไถ tǎi

plow see plough

pluck *vi.* (feathers, hair) ถอนขน tǒɔn-kǒn

pluck *vt.* (pull) ถอน tǒɔn

plug *n.* (AC power) ปลั๊กไฟ bplák-fai [ตัว dtuua, อัน an] | (male connector) ปลั๊ก bplák, ปลั๊กตัวผู้ bplák-dtuua-pûu ✖ [ตัว dtuua, อัน an]

plug *v.* (insert a plug) เสียบปลั๊ก sìiap-bplák

plum *n.* พลัม plam [ลูก lûuk (fruit), ต้น dtôn (tree)]

plumber *n.* ช่างทำระบบท่อ châng-tam-rá~bɔ̀p-tɔ̂ɔ, ช่างประปา châng-bprà~bpaa [คน kon]

plumbing *n.* (work of a plumber) การทำระบบท่อ gaan-tam-rá~bɔ̀p-tɔ̂ɔ

plume *n.* (feather) ขนนก kǒn-nók [เส้น sên]

plummet *n.* (plumb bob) ลูกดิ่ง lûuk-dìng [ลูก lûuk]

plummet *vi.* ดิ่งลง dìng-long

plump *adj.* (chubby) จ้ำม่ำ
jâm-mâm, อวบ ùuap,
ตุ้ยนุ้ย dtûi-núi ✿

plunge *vi.* (plummet)
ดิ่งลง dìng-long,
ตกอย่างรวดเร็ว dtòk-
yàang-rûuat-reo

plural *adj.* พหูพจน์ pá~
hǔu-pót

plural *n.* (grammar)
พหูพจน์ pá~hǔu-pót [คำ
kam]

plus *adj.* (added) เพิ่ม
pêem | (positive) เป็นบวก
bpen-bùuak

plus *n.* (sign)
เครื่องหมายบวก
krûuang-mǎai-bùuak
[ตัว dtuua] | (something
additional) สิ่งที่เพิ่มเข้ามา
sìng-tîi-pêem-kâo-maa

plus *prep.* (e.g. 10 plus 2)
บวก bùuak

Pluto *n.* ดาวพลูโต daao-
pluu-dtoo [ดวง duuang]

ply *n.* (unit of yarn)
กลุ่มด้าย glùm-dâai [กลุ่ม
glùm]

plywood *n.* ไม้อัด mái-àt
[แผ่น pèn]

p.m. *adj.* หลังเที่ยง lǎng-
tîiang

pneumonia *n.* ปอดบวม
bpɔ̀ɔt-buuam [โรค rôok]

P.O. Box *n.* ตู้ ป.ณ. dtûu-
bpɔɔ-nɔɔ, ตู้ไปรษณีย์
dtûu-bprai-sà~nii [ตู้
dtûu]

pocket *n.* (pants)
กระเป๋ากางเกง grà~
bpǎo-gaang-geeng
[กระเป๋า grà~bpǎo] |
(pouch) กระเป๋า grà~
bpǎo [ใบ bai]

pocket knife *n.* มีดพก
mîit-pók [เล่ม lêm]

pod *n.* (bean or pea)
ฝักถั่ว fàk-tùua [ฝัก fàk] |
(e.g. dolphin, seal) ฝูง
fǔung [ฝูง fǔung]

podium *n.* แท่น tên ✦
[แท่น tên, ที่ tîi]

poem *n.* กลอน glɔɔn,
ร้อยกรอง rɔ́ɔi-grɔɔng [บท
bòt (verse)]

poet *n.* นักประพันธ์ nák-
bprà~pan, กวี gà~wii ✦
[คน kon]

poetry *n.* (verse)
โคลงกลอน kloong-glɔɔn,

บทกวี bòt-gà~wii,
กวีนิพนธ์ gà~wii-ní-pon
‼ [บท bòt]
point n. (decimal point)
จุดทศนิยม jùt-tót-sà~
ní~yom [จุด jùt] | (e.g.
test, contest) คะแนน
ká~nɛɛn [คะแนน ká~
nɛɛn] | (issue) ประเด็น
bprà~den [ประเด็น
bprà~den ‼, จุด jùt, ข้อ
kɔ̂ɔ] | (mark) จุด jùt [จุด
jùt] | (period) ช่วง
chûuang | (tip) ปลาย
bplaai
point v. (punctuate)
ใส่เครื่องหมายวรรคตอน
sài-krûuang-mǎai-wák-
dtɔɔn | (with finger) ชี้ chíi
pointed adj. (directed)
ตรงไปตรงมา dtrong-
bpai-dtrong-maa,
ไม่อ้อมค้อม mâi-ɔ̂ɔm-
kɔ́ɔm | (sharp) คม kom,
แหลม lɛ̌ɛm
point of view n.
(attitude) ความคิดเห็น
kwaam-kít-hěn |
(standpoint) มุมมอง
mum-mɔɔng [มุมมอง
mum-mɔɔng]

poise n. (balance)
การทรงตัว gaan-song-
dtuua | (grace)
ความสง่างาม kwaam-sà~
ngàa-ngaam
poison n. (toxic
substance) ยาพิษ yaa-pít
[ชนิด chá~nít (kind), ขวด
kùuat (bottle)]
poison vt. (feed poison)
วางยาพิษ waang-yaa-pít
poisonous adj.
(containing poison) มีพิษ
mii-pít
poke v. (bang) กระแทก
grà~tɛ̂ɛk | (jab, poke fun)
แหย่ yɛ̀ɛ | (pierce) แทง
tɛɛng | (pound) กระทุ้ง
grà~túng | (push) ดัน
dan | (with fingers, etc.)
จิ้ม jîm
poke vt. (with fingers,
etc.) จี้ jîi
poker n. (card game)
ไพ่โป๊กเกอร์ pâi-bpóok-
gɔ̂ɔ [ใบ bai (card), สำหรับ
sǎm-ráp (set), เกม geem
(game)] | (fireplace
implement) เหล็กเขี่ยไฟ
lèk-kìia-fai [อัน an]
polar adj. (relating to the

Poles) ขั้วโลก kûua-lôok

Polar Star *n.* ดาวเหนือ daao-nǔua [ดวง duuang]

pole *n.* (beam) คาน kaan [อัน an] | (electric pole) เสาไฟ sǎo-fai [เสา sǎo] | (long stick) ไม้ยาว mái-yaao [อัน an] | (of a magnet, electricity) ขั้ว kûua [ขั้ว kûua] | (of the earth) ขั้วโลก kûua-lôok [ขั้ว kûua] | (pillar, mast) เสา sǎo [ต้น dtôn]

police *n.* ตำรวจ dtam-rùuat, เจ้าหน้าที่ตำรวจ jâo-nâa-tîi-dtam-rùuat ǃ [นาย naai ǃ, คน kon]

police detective *n.* ตำรวจสืบสวน dtam-rùuat-sùup-sǔuan [นาย naai ǃ, คน kon]

policeman *n.* ตำรวจ dtam-rùuat [นาย naai ǃ, คน kon]

police officer *n.* ตำรวจ dtam-rùuat, เจ้าหน้าที่ตำรวจ jâo-nâa-tîi-dtam-rùuat ǃ [นาย naai ǃ, คน kon]

police station *n.* สถานีตำรวจ sà~tǎa-nii-dtam-rùuat [แห่ง hèng] | โรงพัก roong-pák ❋ [แห่ง hèng]

policy *n.* (insurance) กรมธรรม์ประกันภัย grom-má~tan-bprà~gan-pai [ฉบับ chà~bàp] | (plan, principles) นโยบาย ná~yoo-baai [นโยบาย ná~yoo-baai, อัน an]

polio *n.* โปลิโอ bpoo-lí~oo [โรค rôok]

polish *n.* (substance) ยาขัดเงา yaa-kàt-ngao

polish *vt.* (shine) ขัด kàt

polish up *vt.* (brush up) ฝึกฝน fùk-fǒn | (rub up) ขัดเงา kàt-ngao

polite *adj.* (courteous) มีมารยาท mii-maa-rá~yâat, สุภาพ sù~pâap

politeness *n.* ความสุภาพ kwaam-sù~pâap

political *adj.* (pertaining to politics) ทางการเมือง taang-gaan-muuang

politician *n.* นักการเมือง nák-gaan-muuang [คน kon]

politics *n.* การเมือง

gaan-mʉʉang

poll n. (survey of opinions) การสำรวจความคิดเห็น gaan-sǎm-rùuat-kwaam-kít-hěn, โพล poo ✿

poll v. (survey opinions) สำรวจความคิดเห็น sǎm-rùuat-kwaam-kít-hěn

pollen n. เกสรดอกไม้ gee-sɔ̌ɔn-dɔ̀ɔk-máai

pollute vt. (contaminate) ทำให้_เกิดมลพิษ tam-hâi-_-gə̀ət-mon-lá~pít

pollution n. มลภาวะเป็นพิษ mon-lá~paa-wá-bpen-pít

polygamy n. ลัทธินิยมการมีคู่หลายคนในเวลาเดียวกัน lát-tí-ní~yom-gaan-mii-kûu-lǎai-kon-nai-wee-laa-diiao-gan ✐, ลัทธิหลายผัวหลายเมีย lát-tí-lǎai-pǔua-lǎai-miia ✿

polytheist n. คนที่นับถือพระเจ้าหลายองค์ kon-tîi-náp-tʉ̌ʉ-prá~jâao-lǎai-ong [คน kon]

pomegranate n. ทับทิม táp-tim [เม็ด mét (seed), ลูก lûuk (fruit)]

pomelo n. ส้มโอ sôm-oo [ลูก lûuk]

pond n. (small body of water) สระน้ำ sà~náam, สระ sà ✿ [แห่ง hɛ̀ng, สระ sà]

ponder vi. (contemplate) ครุ่นคิด krûn-kít

pontiff n. (pope) สังฆราช sǎng-ká~râat, สันตะปาปา sǎn-dtà~bpaa-bpaa [องค์ ong]

pony n. (horse) ม้าพันธุ์เล็ก máa-pan-lék [ตัว dtuua]

ponytail n. ผมทรงหางม้า pǒm-song-hǎang-máa

pool n. (billiard) บิลเลียด bin-lîiat | (pond) สระน้ำ sà~náam [แห่ง hɛ̀ng, สระ sà] | (swimming pool) สระว่ายน้ำ sà-wâai-náam [แห่ง hɛ̀ng, สระ sà]

poop v. อึ ù

poor adj. (indigent) จน jon, ยากจน yâak-jon ✐ | (needy) ขัดสน kàt-sǒn | (pitiful) น่าสงสาร nâa-sǒng-sǎan

poor n. คนจน kon-jon [คน kon]

poor man *n.* คนจน kon-jon [คน kon]

pop *adv.* (sound) โพละ pló

pop *n.* (music) เพลงป๊อบ pleeng-bpɔ́p [เพลง pleeng]

pop *v.* (for ears) หูอื้อ hǔu-ɯ̂ɯ

pop *vi.* (make sharp explosive sound) ทำเสียงดังป๊อก tam-sǐiang-dang-bpɔ́k

popcorn *n.* ข้าวโพดคั่ว kâao-pôot-kûua [ถุง tǔng]

Pope *n.* สันตะปาปา sǎn-dtà~bpaa-bpaa [องค์ ong]

poppy *n.* (opium) ดอกฝิ่น dɔ̀ɔk-fìn [ดอก dɔ̀ɔk (flower), ต้น dtôn (tree)]

popular *adj.* (widely liked) เป็นที่นิยม bpen-tîi-ní-yom

popularity *n.* ความนิยม kwaam-ní-yom

population *n.* (populace) ประชากร bprà~chaa-gɔɔn ! [กลุ่ม glùm !] | (total number of persons) จำนวนประชากร jam-nuuan-bprà~chaa-gɔɔn

pop up *vi.* โผล่ plòo, ผุด pùt !

porcelain *n.* (chinaware) เครื่องลายคราม krɯ̂ɯang-laai-kraam [ชิ้น chín (piece), ชุด chút (set)]

porch *n.* (balcony) ระเบียง rá~biiang [แห่ง hὲng] | (without roof) ชาน chaan [ชาน chaan]

porcupine *n.* เม่น mên [ตัว dtuua]

pore *n.* (on skin) รูขุมขน ruu-kǔm-kǒn [รู ruu]

pork *n.* เนื้อหมู nɯ́ɯa-mǔu [ชิ้น chín]

porn *n.* (book) หนังสือโป๊ nǎng~sɯ̌ɯ-bpóo [เล่ม lêm] | (movie) หนังโป๊ nǎng-bpóo [เรื่อง rɯ̂ɯang] | (picture) ภาพโป๊ pâap-bpóo [ภาพ pâap]

pornographic *adj.* โป๊ bpóo, ลามก laa-mók

pornography see porn

porridge *n.* (oatmeal) ข้าวต้มข้าวโอ๊ต kâao-dtôm-kâao-óot

port n. (computer) พอร์ต pɔ̀ɔt [ช่อง chɔ̂ng] | (pier, wharf) ท่าเรือ tâa-ruua [แห่ง hɛ̀ng]

portable adj. พกพาได้ pók-paa-dâai | (carried by hand) หิ้วได้ hîu-dâai

porter n. (person who carries baggage) พนักงานถือกระเป๋า pá~nák-ngaan-tǔu-grà~bpǎo [คน kon]

portfolio n. (collection of work) การรวบรวมผลงาน gaan-rûuap-ruuam-pǒn-ngaan

portion n. (part) ส่วน sùuan [ส่วน sùuan] | (share) ส่วนแบ่ง sùuan-bèng [จำนวน jam-nuuan]

portrait n. รูปคน rûup-kon [รูป rûup]

portray v. (play) รับบทเป็น ráp-bòt-bpen

Portugal n. โปรตุเกส bproo-dtù~gèet [ประเทศ bprà~têet]

pose n. (posture, gesture) ท่า tâa, โพส póot ✽ [ท่า tâa]

pose vi. (e.g. for a picture) วางท่า waang-tâa, โพสท่า póot-tâa ✽

posh adj. (luxurious) หรูหรา rǔu-rǎa

position n. (post, spot, rank) ตำแหน่ง dtam-nɛ̀ng [ตำแหน่ง dtam-nɛ̀ng] | (situation) สถานะ sà~tǎa-ná [สถานะ sà~tǎa-ná]

position vi. (be located) ตั้งอยู่ dtâng-yùu

position vt. (place) วางตำแหน่ง waang-dtam-nɛ̀ng

positive adj. (in quality, degree or characteristic) เป็นบวก bpen-bùuak | (not negative) บวก bùuak | (optimistic) มองโลกในแง่ดี mɔɔng-lôok-nai-ngɛ̀ɛ-dii

positive n. (e.g. test for pregnancy) ผลเป็นบวก pǒn-bpen-bùuak | (quantity greater than zero) จำนวนนับที่มากกว่าศูนย์ jam-nuuan-náp-tîi-mâak-gwàa-sǔun [จำนวน jam-nuuan]

possess v. (own)

เป็นเจ้าของ bpen-jâo-kɔ̌ɔng

possess vt. (e.g. evil spirit) สิง sǐng | (occupy) ครอบครอง krɔ̂ɔp-krɔɔng

possession n. (act of having property) การครอบครอง gaan-krɔ̂ɔp-krɔɔng | (e.g. evil spirit) อาการถูกสิง aa-gaan-tùuk-sǐng | (ownership) ความเป็นเจ้าของ kwaam-bpen-jâo-kɔ̌ɔng | (property, assets) สมบัติ sǒm-bàt [ชิ้น chín] | (property, assets) ของ kɔ̌ɔng [อัน an, ชิ้น chín]

possessive adj. (jealous) หึง hʉ̌ng

possibility n. (state of being possible) ความเป็นไปได้ kwaam-bpen-bpai-dâai [ครั้ง kráng]

possible adj. เป็นไปได้ bpen-bpai-dâai

post n. (mail office, service) ไปรษณีย์ bprai-sà-nii [แห่ง hɛ̀ng] | (mail system) การไปรษณีย์ gaan-bprai-sà~nii

post vi. (e.g. website) โพสต์ข้อความ póot-kɔ̂ɔ-kwaam, เขียนข้อความ kǐian-kɔ̂ɔ-kwaam ‼ | (mail) ส่งจดหมาย sòng-jòt-mǎai

post vt. (e.g. an announcement) ประกาศ bprà~gàat

postage n. (stamp) แสตมป์ sà~dtɛm, ดวงตราไปรษณียากร duuang-dtraa-bprai-sà~nii-yaa-gɔɔn ‼ [ดวง duuang]

postal adj. เกี่ยวกับไปรษณีย์ gìiao-gàp-bprai-sà~nii

postbox n. ตู้ไปรษณีย์ dtûu-bprai-sà~nii [ตู้ dtûu]

postcard n. โปสการ์ด bpóot-sà~gáat, ไปรษณียบัตร bprai-sà~nii-yá~bàt ‼ [ใบ bai, แผ่น pɛ̀n]

poster n. โปสเตอร์ bpòot sà~dtəə [ใบ bai, แผ่น pɛ̀n] | (advertisement sign) ป้ายโฆษณา bpâai-

kôot-sà~naa [ป้าย bpâai,
แผ่น pèn]

postman *n.* บุรุษไปรษณีย์
bù-rùt-bprai-sà~nii [คน
kon]

postmark *n.*
ตราประทับไปรษณีย์
dtraa-bprà~táp-bprai-
sà~nii [อัน an]

post office *n.* ไปรษณีย์
bprai-sà~nii,
ที่ทำการไปรษณีย์ tîi-tam-
gaan-bprai-sà~nii ⚠ [แห่ง
hèng]

postpone *v.* (put off)
ยืดเวลา yûut-wee-laa

postpone *vt.* (put off)
เลื่อน lûuan

postscript *n.* ป.ล. bpɔɔ-
lɔɔ, ปัจฉิมลิขิต bpàt-
chǐm-lí-kìt ⚠

posture *n.* (pose, bearing)
ท่า tâa, ท่าทาง tâa-taang
[ท่า tâa]

pot *n.* (common funds)
เงินกองกลาง ngən-
gɔɔng-glaang | (cooking
pot) หม้อ mɔ̂ɔ [ใบ bai, ลูก
lûuk] | (flowerpot)
กระถาง grà~tǎang [ใบ
bai] | (teapot) กาน้ำชา

gaa-nám-chaa [ใบ bai]

potato *n.* มันฝรั่ง man-
fà~ràng [หัว hǔua]

potato chip *n.*
มันฝรั่งแผ่นทอดกรอบ
man-fà~ràng-pèn-tɔ̂ɔt-
grɔ̀ɔp [ชิ้น chín (piece),
ห่อ hɔ̀ɔ (pack), กล่อง
glɔ̀ɔng (box)]

potbelly *n.* พุงโต pung-
dtoo, พุงพลุ้ย pung-plúi

potent *adj.* (capable of
sexual intercourse)
มีสมรรถภาพทางเพศ mii-
sà~màt-tà~pâap-taang-
pêet | (mighty) มีอำนาจ
mii-am-nâat

potential *adj.* (capable)
มีความสามารถที่จะทำได้
mii-kwaam-sǎa-mâat-tîi-
jà-tam-dâai

potential *n.* ศักยภาพ
sàk-gà~yá~pâap |
(possibility)
ความเป็นไปได้ kwaam-
bpen-bpai-dâai

potion *n.* (liquid mixture)
ยาปรุง yaa-bprung

pottery *n.* เครื่องปั้นดินเผา
krûuang-bpân-din-pǎo

[ชิ้น chín]

pouch *n.* (bag) กระเป๋า
grà~bpǎo [ใบ bai] |
(sack) ถุง tǔng [ใบ bai]

poultry *n.* สัตว์ปีก sàt-
bpìik [ตัว dtuua, ชนิด
chá~nít (kind)] | เป็ดไก่
bpèt-gài ✦ [ตัว dtuua]

pound *n.* (currency, unit
of weight) ปอนด์ bpɔɔn
[ปอนด์ bpɔɔn]

pound *vi.* (heart) เต้นแรง
dtên-rɛɛng

pound *vt.* (smash) ทุบ túp
| (with a pestle) ตำ dtam

pour *vi.* (rain) ฝนเทลงมา
fǒn-tee-long-maa

pour *vt.* (from a
container) เท tee, ริน rin

pour into *v.* (fill with)
กรอก grɔ̀ɔk

pout *n.* (frown) หน้าบึ้ง
nâa-bûng

pout *vi.* (protrude the
lips) บุ้ยปาก bûi-bpàak

poverty *n.*
(impoverishment)
ความยากจน kwaam-
yâak-jon

powder *n.* (cosmetics)
แป้ง bpɛ̂ɛng [กล่อง glɔ̀ɔng

(box), ตลับ dtà~làp
(compact)] | (dust) ผง
pǒng | (fine particles) ฝุ่น
fùn

powder *vi.* (apply powder
to) ทาแป้ง taa-bpɛ̂ɛng

powdered milk *n.* นมผง
nom-pǒng [กระป๋อง
grà~bpɔ̌ng]

power *n.* (ability)
ความสามารถ kwaam-
sǎa-mâat | (energy)
พลังงาน pá~lang-ngaan |
(mathematics)
เลขยกกำลัง lêek-yók-
gam-lang | (might)
อำนาจ am-nâat |
(strength) กำลัง gam-
lang, แรง rɛɛng ✦

power *v.* (give power to)
เพิ่มพลัง pɔ̂ɔm-pá~lang

powerful *adj.* (effective)
มีประสิทธิภาพ mii-bprà~
sìt-tí~pâap | (having
power) มีกำลัง mii-gam-
lang | (influential)
มีอิทธิพล mii-ìt-tí~pon |
(mighty) มีอำนาจ mii-
am-nâat

power of attorney *n.*
ใบมอบฉันทะ bai-mɔ̂ɔp-
chǎn-tá [ใบ bai] |

หนังสือมอบอำนาจ năng~
sйй-môɔp-am-nâat [ฉบับ
chà~bàp]

practical *adj.* (pertaining
to action) ในทางปฏิบัติ
nai-taang-bpà~dtì~bàt |
(useful) นำไปปฏิบัติได้
nam-bpai-bpà~dtì~bàt-
dâai

practice *n.* (exercise, drill)
การฝึกหัด gaan-fùk-hàt |
(routine) กิจวัตร gìt-jà~
wát

practice *v.* (rehearse) ซ้อม
sɔ́ɔm, ฝึกซ้อม fùk-sɔ́ɔm ⚡
| (train, learn) ฝึก fùk, หัด
hàt, ฝึกหัด fùk-hàt ⚡

practice *vt.* (perform)
ปฏิบัติ bpà~dtì~bàt ⚡

practitioner *n.* (doctor)
แพทย์ pɛ̂ɛt ⚡ [คน kon]

pragmatic *adj.* (practical)
ในทางปฏิบัติ nai-taang-
bpà~dtì~bàt

praise *n.* (applause)
การยกย่อง gaan-yók-
yôŋ

praise *v.* (admire) ยอ yɔɔ

praise *vt.* (commend) ชม
chom

pram see baby carriage

prawn *n.* กุ้ง gûŋ [ตัว
dtuua]

pray *vi.* (e.g. to God)
สวดมนต์ sùuat-mon |
(make a wish) ภาวนา
paa-wá~naa, อธิษฐาน à~
tít-tǎan

prayer *n.* (act)
การสวดมนต์ gaan-
sùuat-mon | (person)
ผู้สวดมนต์ pûu-sùuat-
mon [คน kon] | (sacred
words) บทสวดมนต์ bòt-
sùuat-mon [บท bòt] |
(wish) คำอธิษฐาน kam-à~
tít-tǎan

preach *vi.* (deliver a
sermon) แสดงธรรม sà~
dɛɛŋ-tam, เทศนา têet-
sà~nǎa ⚡

preacher *n.* (religious
preacher) นักเทศน์ nák-
têet [คน kon]

precaution *n.* (prudent
foresight)
การป้องกันไว้ก่อน gaan-
bpɔ̂ŋ-gan-wái-gɔ̀ɔn

precede *v.* (be ahead)
นำหน้า nam-nâa | (be in
front of) อยู่ข้างหน้า yùu-
kâaŋ-nâa | (come
before) มาก่อน maa-gɔ̀ɔn

precedent *adj.* ก่อน gɔ̀ɔn

precedent *n.* (legal decision) การตัดสินทางกฎหมาย gaan-dtàt-sǐn-taang-gòt-mǎai [ครั้ง kráng]

preceding *adj.* (come before in order) นำหน้า nam-nâa | (occur before) มาก่อน maa-gɔ̀ɔn | (previous) ก่อน gɔ̀ɔn

precept *n.* (moral precepts) ศีล sǐin [ข้อ kɔ̂ɔ]

precinct *n.* (district) เขต kèet [แห่ง hɛ̀ng] | (election district) เขตเลือกตั้ง kèet-lɨ̂ɨak-dtâng [เขต kèet]

precious *adj.* (highly esteemed) ยอดเยี่ยม yɔ̂ɔt-yîiam | (valuable) มีค่า mii-kâa

precipice *n.* (cliff) หน้าผาสูงชัน nâa-pǎa-sǔung-chan [แห่ง hɛ̀ng, ที่ tîi]

precise *adj.* (accurate) แม่นยำ mɛ̂n-yam | (certain) แน่นอน nɛ̂ɛ-nɔɔn | (exact) เที่ยงตรง tîiang-dtrong

predecessor *n.* ผู้เคยดำรงตำแหน่งมาก่อน pûu-kəəi-dam-rong-dtam-nɛ̀ng-maa-gɔ̀ɔn [คน kon]

predicament *n.* (unpleasant situation) สถานการณ์ลำบาก sà~tǎa-ná~gaan-lam-bàak

predict *v.* ทำนาย tam-naai, ทาย taai ✎, พยากรณ์ pá~yaa-gɔɔn ✖

prediction *n.* (forecast) การคาดการณ์ gaan-kâat-gaan | (prophecy) การทำนาย gaan-tam-naai, การพยากรณ์ gaan-pá~yaa-gɔɔn ⚠ | (prophecy) คำทำนาย kam-tam-naai [คำ kam]

preface *n.* (introduction) คำนำ kam-nam [บท bòt] | (speech) การกล่าวนำ gaan-glàao-nam

prefer *vt.* (like better) ชอบ_มากกว่า chɔ̂ɔp-_-mâak-gwàa

preference *n.* (choice) ตัวเลือก dtuua-lɨ̂ɨak [ตัว dtuua] | (something preferred) สิ่งที่ชอบ sìng-tîi-chɔ̂ɔp | (taste) รสนิยม 42

rót-ní-yom

prefix n. (grammar) คำอุปสรรค kam-ùp-bpà~sàk ✕ [คำ kam] | (title) คำนำหน้าชื่อ kam-nam-nâa-chûu

pregnancy n. (state of being pregnant) การตั้งครรภ์ gaan-dtâng-kan, การตั้งท้อง gaan-dtâng-tóong

pregnant adj. ตั้งท้อง dtâng-tóong, มีท้อง mii-tóong, ตั้งครรภ์ dtâng-kan ✦, มีครรภ์ mii-kan ✦, ท้อง tóong ✦

prejudice n. (bias) อคติ à-ká~dtì

preliminary adj. (preparatory) ในขั้นแรก nai-kân-rêɛk, เบื้องต้น bûuang-dtôn

preliminary n. (competition) การแข่งขันคัดเลือก gaan-kèng-kǎn-kát-lûuak [ครั้ง kráng] | (elimination round) รอบคัดเลือก rɔ̂ɔp-kát-lûuak [รอบ rɔ̂ɔp]

premarital adj.

ก่อนแต่งงาน gɔ̀ɔn-dtɛ̀ng-ngaan, ก่อนสมรส gɔ̀ɔn-sǒm-rót ✦

premature adj. (ahead of time) ก่อนกำหนด gɔ̀ɔn-gam-nòt | (too soon) เร็วเกินไป reo-gəən-bpai

premature ejaculation n. การหลั่งเร็ว gaan-làng-reo

premise n. (construction) สิ่งปลูกสร้าง sìng-bplùuk-sâang ✦ [อาคาร aa-kaan ✦ (building), หลัง lǎng (building), แห่ง hɛ̀ng (location)] | (supporting a conclusion) การอ้างหลักฐาน gaan-âang-làk-tǎan [ข้อ kɔ̂ɔ]

premium adj. (having high quality) คุณภาพสูง kun-ná~pâap-sǔung

premium n. (additional fee) ค่าบริการเพิ่มเติม kâa-bɔɔ-rí-gaan-pə̂əm-dtəəm | (insurance) เบี้ยประกัน bîia-bprà~gan [จำนวน jam-nuuan]

prenuptial adj. (before marriage) ก่อนแต่งงาน gɔ̀ɔn-dtɛ̀ng-ngaan, ก่อนสมรส gɔ̀ɔn-sǒm-rót ✦

prenuptial agreement n.
สัญญาก่อนการสมรส sǎn-
yaa-gɔ̀ɔn-gaan-sǒm-rót
[ฉบับ chà~bàp]

preoccupied adj.
(absorbed) หมกมุ่น
mòk-mûn

preparation n. (act)
การเตรียมตัว gaan-
dtriiam-dtuua

prepare v. (get ready)
เตรียม dtriiam, เตรียมตัว
dtriiam-dtuua

preposition n. บุพบท
bùp-pá-bòt [คำ kam]

prescribe v. (medicine by
a doctor) สั่งจ่ายยา sàng-
jàai-yaa

prescribe vt. (establish
rules) กำหนด gam-nòt

prescription n. (slip for
remedy) ใบสั่งยา bai-
sàng-yaa [ใบ bai]

presence n. (act of being
present) การปรากฏ
gaan-bpraa-gòt |
(existence) การมีอยู่
gaan-mii-yùu

present adj. (being here)
อยู่ yùu | (modern)
ปัจจุบัน bpàt-jù-ban

present n. (gift) ของขวัญ

kɔ̌ɔng-kwǎn [ชิ้น chín] |
(time) ปัจจุบัน bpàt-jù-
ban

present v. (show) แสดง
sà~dɛɛng

present vt. (give) มอบ
mɔ̂ɔp, ให้ hâi |
(introduce) แนะนำให้รู้จัก
né-nam-hâi-rúu-jàk |
(show, display, offer)
นำเสนอ nam-sà~nǒɔ

present a proposal vt.
เสนอ sà~nǒɔ

presentation n.
(exhibition)
การแสดงผลงาน gaan-
sà~dɛɛng-pǒn-ngaan |
(performance) การแสดง
gaan-sà~dɛɛng |
(presenting a proposal)
การนำเสนอ gaan-nam-
sà~nǒɔ

presenter n. (one who
presents) พรีเซ็นเตอร์
prii-sen-dtɔ̂ɔ ✦ [คน kon]
| (one who presents an
award) ผู้มอบรางวัล
pûu-mɔ̂ɔp-raang-wan
[คน kon] | (proposal)
ผู้นำเสนอ pûu-nam-sà~
nǒɔ [คน kon]

present time n. ปัจจุบัน

bpàt-jù-ban

preservation n. (conservation) การรักษาไว้ gaan-rák-săa-wái | (food) การถนอมอาหาร gaan-tà~nɔ̌ɔm-aa-hǎan

preservative n. ยากันบูด yaa-gan-bùut

preserve vi. (fruit, etc.) หมักอาหาร màk-aa-hǎan

preserve vt. (conserve) เก็บรักษา gèp-rák-sǎa | (ferment) หมัก màk

preside v. (act as chairperson) เป็นประธาน bpen-bprà~taan

president n. (of a company) ประธาน bprà~taan [ท่าน tân ɪ̂, คน kon] | (of a country) ประธานาธิบดี bprà~taa-naa-tí-bɔɔ-dii [ท่าน tân ɪ̂, คน kon] | (of an organization) นายก naa-yók [ท่าน tân ɪ̂, คน kon]

press n. (printing press) แท่นพิมพ์ tên-pim [แท่น tên] | (reporter) นักข่าว nák-kàao [คน kon]

press v. (pressure) กดดัน gòt-dan | (push down)

กด gòt | (push forward) ดัน dan | (squeeze) บีบ bìip | (urge) เร่ง rêng

press vi. (iron) รีดผ้า rîit-pâa

press vt. (compress, iron) รีด rîit | (insist upon) ผลักดัน plàk-dan | (squash) คั้น kán

press conference n. การแถลงข่าว gaan-tà~lɛ̌ɛng-kàao

pressing adj. (insistent) ยืนกราน yʉʉn-graan | (urgent) ด่วน dùuan

press release n. การออกข่าว gaan-ɔ̀ɔk-kàao

pressure n. (e.g. of daily life) ความกดดัน kwaam-gòt-dan, แรงกดดัน rɛɛng-gòt-dan | (force per unit area) แรงดัน rɛɛng-dan

pressure vt. (press, force) กดดัน gòt-dan

prestige adj. (having dignity) มีศักดิ์ศรี mii-sàk-sǐi

prestige n. (fame) ชื่อเสียง chʉ̂ʉ-sǐiang | (honor,

glory) เกียรติยศ gìiat-
dtì~yót ❢
prestigious *adj.*
เป็นที่เคารพนับถือ bpen-
tîi-kao-róp-náp-tǔu,
มีเกียรติ mii-gìiat

presume *v.* (assume)
สันนิษฐาน sǎn-nít-tǎan |
(guess, suppose) เดา
dao, ทึกทักเอา túk-ták-ao

presumption *n.*
(assumption)
การสันนิษฐาน gaan-sǎn-
ní-tǎan

pretend *v.* (feign) แกล้ง
glêeng, แกล้งทำ glêeng-
tam

pretentious *adj.* มารยา
maan-yaa, เสแสร้ง sěe-
sêeng, ดัดจริต dàt-jà~rìt
❀ | (showy) โอ้อวด ôo-
ùuat

pretext *n.* (excuse)
ข้อแก้ตัว kɔ̂ɔ-gɛ̂ɛ-dtuua,
ข้ออ้าง kɔ̂ɔ-âang

pretrial *adj.*
ก่อนพิจารณาตัดสิน gɔ̀ɔn-
pí-jaa-rá~naa-dtàt-sǐn

pretty *adj.* (beautiful) สวย
sǔuai, งาม ngaam ❀ |
(lovely) น่ารัก nâa-rák

pretty *adv.* (quite)
ค่อนข้าง kɔ̂n-kâang

pretzel *n.*
ขนมปังกรอบเค็ม kà~
nǒm-bpang-grɔ̀ɔp-kem
[ชิ้น chín]

prevail *vi.* เป็นต่อ bpen-
dtɔ̀ɔ | (predominate)
มีอำนาจเหนือกว่า mii-
am-nâat-nǔua-gwàa |
(triumph) มีชัย mii-chai

prevent *vt.* (hinder)
ขัดขวาง kàt-kwǎang |
(keep from occurring)
ป้องกัน bpɔ̂ng-gan

prevention *n.*
(precaution) การป้องกัน
gaan-bpɔ̂ng-gan

preview *n.* (trailer)
หนังตัวอย่าง nǎng-
dtuua-yàang [เรื่อง
rûuang]

preview *v.* (view in
advance) ดูก่อน duu-gɔ̀ɔn

previous *adj.* (prior,
before) ก่อน gɔ̀ɔn

previous life *n.* ชาติก่อน
châat-gɔ̀ɔn [ชาติ châat]

previously *adv.* (before)
ก่อนหน้านี้ gɔ̀ɔn-nâa-níi

prey *n.* (hunted animal)

เหยื่อ yùua [ตัว dtuua (animal)]

prey vi. (hunt prey)

ล่าเหยื่อ lâa-yùua

price n. (bribe) เงินใต้โต๊ะ ngən-dtâai-dtó [จำนวน jam-nuuan] | (cost) ราคา raa-kaa | (value) ค่า kâa

price vt. (set price of)

ตั้งราคา dtâng-raa-kaa

priceless adj. (invaluable)

ล้ำค่า lám-kâa

prick n. (penis) นกเขา nók-kǎo ☻, ควย kuuai ☙ [อัน an]

prick vt. (stab) แทง tɛɛng

prickly heat n. (rash) ผด pòt, ผื่น pùun

pride n. (being proud) ความภูมิใจ kwaam-puum-jai | (dignity) เกียรติ gìiat | (lions) ฝูงสิงโต fǔung-sǐng-dtoo [ฝูง fǔung]

priest n. (Christian priest) บาทหลวง bàat-lǔuang [คน kon, รูป rûup ☘] | (clergyman) นักบวช nák-bùuat [คน kon, รูป rûup ☘] | (clergyman, monk)

พระ prá [รูป rûup]

primary adj. (basic)

พื้นฐาน púun-tǎan | (elementary) ประถม bprà~tǒm | (most important) สำคัญที่สุด sǎm-kan-tîi-sùt

primary school n.

โรงเรียนประถม roong-riian-bprà~tǒm [แห่ง hèng]

prime adj. (first in degree) อันดับหนึ่ง an-dàp-nùng | (important) สำคัญ sǎm-kan

prime n. (e.g. of life)

ช่วงที่ดีที่สุด chûuang-tîi-dii-tîi-sùt [ช่วง chûuang]

prime vt. (e.g. pump)

เตรียม_ให้พร้อม dtriiam-_-hâi-próom

prime minister n.

นายกรัฐมนตรี naa-yók-rát-tà~mon-dtrii [ท่าน tân ☝, คน kon]

prime number n.

เลขเฉพาะ lêek-chà~pó [ตัว dtuua]

primer n. (preliminary coat of paint) สีรองพื้น sǐi-rɔɔng-púun [สี sǐi]

primitive *adj.* (ancient)
โบราณ boo-raan |
(crude) ไม่ประณีต mâi-
bprà~nîit | (original)
ดั้งเดิม dâng-dəəm

prince *n.* เจ้าชาย jâo-chaai
[องค์ ong]

princess *n.* เจ้าหญิง jâo-
yǐng [องค์ ong]

principal *adj.* (foremost)
สูงสุด sǔung-sùt

principal *n.* (main
performer) ตัวเอก
dtuua-èek [คน kon] |
(monetary capital) เงินต้น
ngən-dtôn, เงินทุน ngən-
tun | (school) ครูใหญ่
kruu-yài [คน kon]

principle *adj.* (main) หลัก
làk

principle *n.* (moral)
หลักธรรม làk-tam [ข้อ
kɔ̂ɔ] | (practice, opinion)
หลักการ làk-gaan
[หลักการ làk-gaan] |
(regulation) กฎ gòt [ข้อ
kɔ̂ɔ]

print *n.* (fingerprint)
ลายนิ้วมือ laai-níu-mɯɯ
[ลาย laai] | (on a surface)

รอย rɔɔi [รอย rɔɔi] |
(type) ตัวพิมพ์ dtuua-pim
[ตัว dtuua]

print *v.* (fingerprint)
พิมพ์ลายนิ้วมือ pim-laai-
níu-mɯɯ | (imprint)
ประทับ bprà~táp | (on
printer, at shop) พิมพ์
pim | (photography)
ล้างรูป láang-rûup |
(publish) ตีพิมพ์ dtii-pim

print *vi.* (write neatly)
เขียนตัวบรรจง kǐian-
dtuua-ban-jong

printer *n.* (machine)
เครื่องพิมพ์ krɯ̂ɯang-pim,
ปริ๊นเตอร์ bprín-dtə̀ə •
[เครื่อง krɯ̂ɯang] |
(person) ผู้พิมพ์ pûu-pim
[คน kon]

printing *n.* (act) การพิมพ์
gaan-pim | (printed
material) สิ่งพิมพ์ sìng-
pim

printing house *n.*
โรงพิมพ์ roong-pim [แห่ง
hɛ̀ng]

print out *vt.* (make a
printed copy) พิมพ์ออกมา
pim-ɔ̀ɔk-maa

prior adj. (earlier or former) ก่อน gɔ̀ɔn

prior n. (conviction) คดีติดตัว ká~dii-dtìt-dtuua [คดี ká~dii]

priority n. (preference) สิทธิพิเศษ sìt-tí-pí-sèet, การมีสิทธิ์ก่อน gaan-mii-sìt-gɔ̀ɔn ⚡ | (something modt important to do) สิ่งที่ต้องทำก่อน sìng-tîi-dtɔ̂ŋ-tam-gɔ̀ɔn [สิ่ง sìng]

prior to prep. ก่อนหน้า gɔ̀ɔn-nâa

prism n. ปริซึม bprí-sûm [แท่ง têng]

prismatic colors n. สีรุ้ง sǐi-rúng [สี sǐi]

prison n. คุก kúk [แห่ง hèng] | เรือนจำ rɯɯan-jam ⚡ [แห่ง hèng, ที่ tîi]

prisoner n. (captive) เชลย chá~ləəi [คน kon] | (convict) นักโทษ nák-tôot, ผู้ต้องขัง pûu-dtɔ̂ng-kǎng ⚡, คนคุก kon-kúk ✿ [คน kon]

prisoner of war n. เชลยศึก chá~ləəi-sùk [คน kon]

privacy n. ความเป็นส่วนตัว kwaam-bpen-sùuan-dtuua

private adj. (individual) ส่วนตัว sùuan-dtuua, ส่วนบุคคล sùuan-bùk-kon | (not government) เอกชน èek-gà~chon | (secret) เป็นความลับ bpen-kwaam-láp, ลับ láp

private n. (military rank) พลทหาร pon-tá~hǎan [นาย naai ⚡, คน kon]

privilege n. (right) สิทธิ sìt-tí | (special right) สิทธิพิเศษ sìt-tí-pí-sèet, อภิสิทธิ์ à~pí-sìt ✖

prize n. รางวัล raang-wan [รางวัล raang-wan]

pro adj. (agreeing with) เห็นด้วย hěn-dûuai

pro n. (advantage (not a con)) ข้อดี kɔ̂ɔ-dii [ข้อ kɔ̂ɔ] | (professional) มืออาชีพ mɯɯ-aa-chîip, มือโปร mɯɯ-bproo ✿ [คน kon]

probability n. (possibility) ความเป็นไปได้ kwaam-bpen-bpai-dâai | (statistics) ความน่าจะเป็น

kwaam-nâa-jà-bpen
probable *adj.* (possible)
เป็นไปได้ bpen-bpai-dâai
probate *n.* (of a will)
การพิสูจน์พินัยกรรม
gaan-pí-sùut-pí-nai-gam
probation *n.* (act of suspending the sentence) การรอลงอาญา
gaan-rɔɔ-long-aa-yaa,
ภาคทัณฑ์ pâak-tan ✘
[ครั้ง kráng] | (act of testing) การทดสอบ
gaan-tót-sɔ̀ɔp
probation officer *n.*
เจ้าหน้าที่ภาคทัณฑ์ jâo-nâa-tîi-pâak-tan ⚡ [คน kon]
probe *vt.* (search) ค้นหา
kón-hǎa
problem *adj.* (being a problem) เป็นปัญหา
bpen-bpan-hǎa
problem *n.* (mathematics)
โจทย์ jòot [ข้อ kɔ̂ɔ] | (question) คำถาม kam-tǎam [ข้อ kɔ̂ɔ] | (trouble)
ปัญหา bpan-hǎa [เรื่อง rûuang (matter), ข้อ kɔ̂ɔ (point)]
procedure *n.* (method)

วิธีการ wí-tii-gaan [วิธี wí-tii] | (process) ขั้นตอน
kân-dtɔɔn [ขั้น kân (step)] | (process)
กระบวนการ grà~buuan-gaan ⚡ [ขั้น kân (step)]
proceed *vi.* (carry out)
ลงมือทำ long-mɯɯ-tam | (continue) ทำต่อไป tam-dtɔ̀ɔ-bpai | (go) ไป bpai
proceeds *n.* (income)
รายได้ raai-dâai | (profit)
กำไร gam-rai
process *n.*
(manufacturing) กรรมวิธี
gam-má~wí-tii [วิธี wí-tii (method)] | (step)
ขั้นตอน kân-dtɔɔn,
ขบวนการ kà~buuan-gaan ⚡ [ขั้น kân] | (summons) หมายศาล
mǎai-sǎan [ใบ bai, ฉบับ chà~bàp]
process *v.* (transform)
แปรรูป bprɛɛ-rûup
process *vi.* (proceed)
ดำเนินการ dam-nəən-gaan
procession *n.* (parade)
ขบวนแห่ kà~buuan-hɛ̀ɛ

[ขบวน kà~buuan]
proclaim v. (announce)
ประกาศ bprà~gàat |
(declare) แถลง tà~lɛ̌ɛng
procrastinate v. (delay
needlessly)
ผัดวันประกันพรุ่ง pàt-
wan-bprà~gan-prûng
procrastinate vi. (put off)
เลื่อนเวลา lɯ̂ɯan-wee-laa
procure vt. (obtain)
ได้_มา dâi-_-maa
prodigious adj.
(enormous) มหึมา má-
hɯ̀-maa ⚠ | (extremely
intelligent, genius)
ฉลาดมาก chà~làat-mâak,
อัจฉริยะ àt-chà-rí~yá ⚠
prodigy n. (child)
เด็กอัจฉริยะ dèk-àt-chà-
rí~yá [คน kon] | (person)
อัจฉริยะบุคคล àt-chà-rí~
yá-bùk-kon [คน kon]
produce n. (agricultural
product) ผลผลิต pǒn-
pà~lìt, ผลิตผล pà~lìt-
dtà~pǒn ⚠ [ชนิด chá~nít
(kind), ชิ้น chín (piece),
กล่อง glɔ̀ng (box), ห่อ hɔ̀ɔ
(wrap)]
produce vi. (yield results)
ให้ผล hâi-pǒn

produce vt. (e.g. film,
play) สร้าง sâang | (make,
create) ผลิต pà~lìt
producer n.
(manufacturer) ผู้ผลิต
pûu-pà~lìt [คน kon] |
(movie, play) ผู้สร้าง pûu-
sâang, โปรดิวเซอร์
bproo-diu-sə̂ə ⚠ [คน
kon]
product n. (farm goods,
output) ผลผลิต pǒn-pà~
lìt [ชนิด chá~nít (kind),
ชิ้น chín (piece), กล่อง
glɔ̀ng (box), ห่อ hɔ̀ɔ
(wrap)] | (goods) สินค้า
sǐn-káa [ชนิด chá~nít
(kind), ชิ้น chín (piece),
กล่อง glɔ̀ng (box), ห่อ hɔ̀ɔ
(wrap)] | (result) ผล pǒn
[อย่าง yàang]
production n. (act)
การผลิต gaan-pà~lìt |
(product) สินค้า sǐn-káa,
ผลิตภัณฑ์ pà~lìt-dtà~
pan ⚠ [ชนิด chá~nít
(kind), ชิ้น chín (piece),
กล่อง glɔ̀ng (box), ห่อ hɔ̀ɔ
(wrap)] | (result of
productivity) ผลงาน

pǒn-ngaan [ชิ้น chín]

profanity *n.* (vulgar speech) คำหยาบคาย kam-yàap-kaai [คำ kam]

profession *n.* (career) อาชีพ aa-chîip [อาชีพ aa-chîip]

professional *adj.* (for employment) ที่ทำเป็นอาชีพ tîi-tam-bpen-aa-chîip

professional *n.* (not amateur) มืออาชีพ mɯɯ-aa-chîip, มือโปร mɯɯ-bproo [คน kon]

professor *n.* (college, university) ศาสตราจารย์ sàat-dtraa-jaan [คน kon, ท่าน tân !]

proficient *adj.* (skillful) ชำนาญ châm-chɔɔng, เชี่ยวชาญ chîiao-chaan

profile *n.* (résumé) ประวัติย่อ bprà~wàt-yɔ̂ɔ | (side of a face) หน้าด้านข้าง nâa-dâan-kâang | (side view) ด้านข้าง dâan-kâang [ด้าน dâan]

profit *n.* (proceeds) กำไร gam-rai

profit *v.* (make a profit) ได้กำไร dâi-gam-rai

profitable *adj.* (yielding profit) มีกำไรดี mii-gam-rai-dii

profound *adj.* (deep, intensive) ลึก lúk, ลึกซึ้ง lúk-súng

profuse *adj.* (abundant) มากมาย mâak-maai | (extravagant) ฟุ่มเฟือย fûm-fɯɯai

program *n.* (TV or radio) รายการ raai-gaan [รายการ raai-gaan] | (TV or radio, computer, agenda) โปรแกรม bproo-grɛɛm [โปรแกรม bproo-grɛɛm] | (project, plan) โครงการ kroong-gaan [โครงการ kroong-gaan, อัน an]

program *v.* (computers) เขียนโปรแกรม kǐian-bproo-grɛɛm | (plan a program) จัดรายการ jàt-raai-gaan

progress *n.* ความก้าวหน้า kwaam-gâao-nâa

progress *v.* (move forward) ก้าวหน้า gâao-nâa

progress vi. (develop)
พัฒนา pát-tá~naa

progressive adj.
(advanced) ก้าวหน้า
gâao-nâa | (continuous)
ต่อเนื่อง dtɔ̀ɔ-nûuang

prohibit v. (forbid, ban)
ไม่อนุญาต mâi-à~nú-
yâat, ห้าม hâam,
ห้ามปราม hâam-bpraam

project n. (scheme, plan)
โครงการ kroong-gaan
[โครงการ kroong-gaan,
อัน an] | (scheme, plan)
แผน pɛ̌ɛn [อัน an] |
(scheme, plan) แผนการ
pɛ̌ɛn-gaan ! [แผน pɛ̌ɛn,
อัน an] | (scheme, plan)
โปรเจ็ค bproo-jèk ● [อัน
an]

project v. (as a ray of
light) ฉาย chǎai |
(predict) คาดการณ์ kâat-
gaan

projection n. (e.g. film)
การฉายภาพ gaan-chǎai-
pâap | (prediction)
การคาดการณ์ gaan-kâat-
gaan

projector n. (device)

เครื่องฉายภาพ krûuang-
chǎai-pâap, โปรเจ็คเตอร์
bproo-jék-dtə̂ə [เครื่อง
krûuang]

prolific adj. (e.g. author)
มีผลงานมาก mii-pǒn-
ngaan-mâak | (extremely
productive) มีลูกดก mii-
lûuk-dòk

prolong v. (in duration)
ยืดเยื้อ yʉ̂ʉt-yʉ́ʉa,
ยืดเวลา yʉ̂ʉt-wee-laa

promenade n. (area)
บริเวณสำหรับเดินเล่น
bɔɔ~rí~ween-sǎm-ràp-
dəən-lên [แห่ง hɛ̀ng] |
(stroll) การเดินเล่น gaan-
dəən-lên

prominent adj.
(important) สำคัญ sǎm-
kan | (projecting
outward) ยื่นออกมา
yʉ̂ʉn-ɔ̀ɔk-maa |
(standing out) โดดเด่น
dòot-dèn | (well-known)
มีชื่อเสียง mii-chʉ̂ʉ-sǐiang

promiscuous adj.
(sexually) สำส่อน sǎm-sɔ̀ɔn

promise n. (vow) คำสัญญา
kam-sǎn-yaa

promise vi. (to someone)

สัญญา sǎn-yaa

promote *vt.* (advance in rank, etc.)

เลื่อนตำแหน่งให้ lɯ̂ɯan-dtam-nèng-hâi | (encourage) ส่งเสริม sòng-sěrm

promotion *n.* (act)

การส่งเสริม gaan-sòng-sěrm | (e.g. work position)

การเลื่อนตำแหน่ง gaan-lɯ̂ɯan-dtam-nèng

prompt *adj.* (quick) ฉับไว chàp-wai | (without delay) ตามกำหนด dtaam-gam-nòt

prompt *n.* (reminder)

สิ่งเตือนความจำ sìng-dtɯɯan-kwaam-jam

prompt *v.* (in a play) บอกบท bɔ̀ɔk-bòt

prone *adj.* (inclined)

มีแนวโน้มที่จะ mii-nɛɛo-nóom-tîi-jà

prone *adv.* (lying face downward) นอนคว่ำ nɔɔn-kwâm

prong *n.* (pointed tine of a fork) ง่าม ngâam [ง่าม ngâam]

pronoun *n.* สรรพนาม

sàp-pá~naam [คำ kam]

pronounce *v.* (enuciate, utter) ออกเสียง ɔ̀ɔk-sǐiang

pronounce *vt.* (declare) ประกาศ bprà~gàat

pronouncement *n.* (authoritative statement) คำแถลงการณ์ kam-tà~lěng-gaan [ฉบับ chà~bàp]

pronunciation *n.*

การออกเสียง gaan-ɔ̀ɔk-sǐiang

proof *adj.* (protected from) ป้องกันได้ bpɔ̂ng-gan-dâai

proof *n.* (act of proving) การพิสูจน์ gaan-pí-sùut | (evidence) ข้อพิสูจน์ kɔ̂ɔ-pí-sùut [ข้อ kɔ̂ɔ (point)] | (evidence) หลักฐาน làk-tǎan [ชิ้น chín (piece)]

proof *v.* (proofread)

พิสูจน์อักษร pí-sùut-àk-sɔ̌ɔn

proofread *v.* พิสูจน์อักษร pí-sùut-àk-sɔ̌ɔn

proofreader *n.*

ผู้พิสูจน์อักษร pûu-pí-sùut-àk-sɔ̌ɔn [คน kon]

propaganda *n.*

การโฆษณาชวนเชื่อ gaan-kôot-sà~naa-chuuan-chûua

propeller *n.* ใบพัด bai-pát [อัน an]

proper *adj.* (appropriate) เหมาะ mɔ̀, เหมาะสม mɔ̀-sǒm ❗ | (correct) ถูกต้อง tùuk-dtɔ̂ng | (suitable) สมควร sǒm-kuuan

proper name *n.* นามเฉพาะ naam-chà~pɔ́, วิสามานยนาม wí-sǎa-maan-yá~naam ✖ [คำ kam]

proper noun see proper name

proper noun *n.* นามเฉพาะ naam-chà~pɔ́ [คำ kam]

property *n.* (land) ที่ดิน tîi-din, ที่ tîi ✎ [แปลง bplɛɛng, ผืน pǔun] | (possession) สมบัติ sǒm-bàt, ทรัพย์สิน sáp-sǐn ❗, หลักทรัพย์ làk-sáp ✖, ทรัพย์สมบัติ sáp-sǒm-bàt ➳ [ชิ้น chín] | (possession) ของ kɔ̌ɔng [อัน an, ชิ้น chín]

prophecy *n.* การพยากรณ์

gaan-pá~yaa-gɔɔn ❗ | คำทำนาย kam-tam-naai [คำ kam]

prophet *n.* ผู้ทำนาย pûu-tam-naai, ผู้พยากรณ์ pûu-pá~yaa-gɔɔn ❗ [คน kon]

proportion *n.* สัดส่วน sàt-sùuan

proposal *n.* (offer of marriage) การขอแต่งงาน gaan-kɔ̌ɔ-dtɛ̀ng-ngaan | (offer, proposition) ข้อเสนอ kɔ̂ɔ-sà~nɔ̌ɔ [ข้อ kɔ̂ɔ]

propose *v.* (marriage) ขอแต่งงาน kɔ̌ɔ-dtɛ̀ng-ngaan

propose *vt.* (present, offer) เสนอ sà~nɔ̌ɔ

proposition *n.* (proposal) ข้อเสนอ kɔ̂ɔ-sà~nɔ̌ɔ [ข้อ kɔ̂ɔ] | (proposal) ญัตติ yát-dtì ✖ [ข้อ kɔ̂ɔ]

proprietor *n.* เจ้าของ jâo-kɔ̌ɔng, ผู้ครอบครองกรรมสิทธิ์ pûu-krɔ̂ɔp-krɔɔng-gam-má~sìt ❗ [คน kon]

propriety *n.* (ownership) กรรมสิทธิ์ gam-má~sìt | (rightness) ความถูกต้อง

kwaam-tùuk-dtɔ̂ng

proscribe vt. (banish, exile) เนรเทศ nee-rá~têet

prose n. ร้อยแก้ว rɔ́ɔi-gɛ̂ɛo

prosecute v. (act as prosecutor) เป็นฝ่ายอัยการ bpen-fàai-ai-yá~gaan | (initiate civil or criminal court action) ฟ้อง fɔ́ɔng, ฟ้องร้อง fɔ́ɔng-rɔ́ɔng

prosecution n. (legal proceedings) การฟ้องร้อง gaan-fɔ́ɔng-rɔ́ɔng | (prosecuting side) ฝ่ายอัยการ fàai-ai-yá~gaan [ฝ่าย fàai]

prosecutor n. อัยการ ai-yá~gaan [คน kon]

prospect n. (expectation) การคาดหวัง gaan-kâat-wǎng | (potential customer) ผู้ที่จะมาเป็นลูกค้า pûu-tîi-jà-maa-bpen-lûuk-káa [คน kon]

prosper v. เจริญรุ่งเรือง jà~rəən-rûng-rɯɯang, เฟื่องฟู fɯ̂ɯang-fuu ✍

prosperity n. (flourishing) ความเจริญรุ่งเรือง kwaam-jà~rəən-rûng-rɯɯang

prosperous adj. (flourishing) รุ่งเรือง rûng-rɯɯang | (wealthy) มั่งคั่ง mâng-kâng

prostate adj. เกี่ยวกับต่อมลูกหมาก giiao-gàp-dtɔ̀m-lûuk-màak

prostate n. ต่อมลูกหมาก dtɔ̀m-lûuk-màak

prostitute n. (female) โสเภณี sǒo-pee-nii, ผู้หญิงหาเงิน pûu-yǐng-hǎa-ngən ✍, อีตัว ii-dtuua ✍ [คน kon] | (male) ไอ้ตัว âi-dtuua ✍ [คน kon]

prostitution n. การเป็นโสเภณี gaan-bpen-sǒo-pee-nii

protagonist n. (drama) ตัวเอกของเรื่อง dtuua-èek-kɔ̌ɔng-rɯ̂ɯang [คน kon, ตัว dtuua]

protect vt. (escort) คุ้มครอง kúm-krɔɔng | (guard) ปกป้อง bpòk-bpɔ̂ng, ป้องกัน bpɔ̂ng-gan | (preserve) รักษา rák-sǎa

protection n. การปกป้อง

gaan-bpòk-bpɔ̂ng,
การป้องกัน gaan-bpɔ̂ng-
gan

protector *n.* (guard)
ผู้คุ้มครอง pûu-kúm-
krɔɔng [คน kon]

protein *n.* โปรตีน bproo-
dtiin

protest *n.*
(demonstration)
การประท้วง gaan-bprà~
túuang [ครั้ง kráng]

protest *v.* (demonstrate)
ประท้วง bprà~túuang |
(oppose) คัดค้าน kát-káan

Protestant *n.*
นิกายโปรเตสแตนท์ ní-
gaai-bproo-dtèet-sà-
dtɛɛn [นิกาย ní-gaai
(sect)]

protocol *n.* (preliminary
treaty) โปรโตคอล
bproo-dtoo-kɔɔn,
สนธิสัญญาเบื้องต้น sǒn-tí-
sǎn-yaa-bûuang-dtôn ‼
[ฉบับ chà~bàp]

protract *v.* (postpone)
เลื่อนออก lûuan-ɔ̀ɔk |
(prolong) ยืด yûut

protrude *v.* (stick out) ยื่น
yûun

protrude *vi.* (pop out) นูน
nuun

protruding *adj.* ยื่นออกมา
yûun-ɔ̀ɔk-maa

proud *adj.* ภูมิใจ puum-jai
| (conceited, arrogant)
หยิ่ง yìng, เย่อหยิ่ง yɤ̂ə-
yìng ‼

prove *vt.* พิสูจน์ pí-sùut

proverb *n.* สุภาษิต sù-
paa-sìt [บท bòt]

provide *vt.* (make
available) ให้ hâi |
(supply) จัด_ให้ jàt-_-hâi

provided *conj.* มีข้อแม้ว่า
mii-kɔ̂ɔ-mɛ́ɛ-wâa

provider *n.* (one who
provides) ผู้จัดหา pûu-
jàt-hǎa [คน kon]

providing see provided

province *n.* จังหวัด jang-
wàt [จังหวัด jang-wàt]

provincial *adj.* (belonging
to a province)
ประจำจังหวัด bprà~jam-
jang-wàt | (relating to a
province) เกี่ยวกับจังหวัด
gìiao-gàp-jang-wàt |
(up-country, not in the
capital) ต่างจังหวัด
dtàang-jang-wàt

provision *n.* (act of supplying) การจัดหา gaan-jàt-hǎa | (proviso, stipulation) ข้อกำหนด kɔ̂ɔ-gam-nòt [ข้อ kɔ̂ɔ] | (supply) เสบียง sà~biiang

provoke *v.* (incite to anger) ยั่ว yûua | (press, goad) กระตุ้น grà~dtûn | (stir up) ยุแหย่ yú-yὲε

proximity *n.* ความใกล้ชิด kwaam-glâi-chít

prudent *adj.* (careful) รอบคอบ rɔ̂ɔp-kɔ̂ɔp | (cautious) สุขุม sù-kǔm ⬥

prune *n.* ลูกพลัมแห้ง lûuk-plam-hὲng [ลูก lûuk]

pry *n.* (crowbar) ชะแลง chá~lεεng [อัน an]

pry *v.* (lever open) งัด ngát | (peep) ลอดมอง lɔ̂ɔt-mɔɔng

P.S *n.* ป.ล. bpɔɔ-lɔɔ, ปัจฉิมลิขิต bpàt-chǐm-lí-kìt ❢

pseudonym *n.* นามแฝง naam-fὲεng [นาม naam]

psychiatrist *n.* จิตแพทย์ jìt-dtà~pɛ̂εt [คน kon]

psychic *adj.* (pertaining to nonphysical force) ทางจิตวิญญาณ taang-jìt-win-yaan | (pertaining to the human soul or mind) เกี่ยวกับจิตใจ gìiao-gàp-jìt-jai

psychic *n.* (medium) คนทรง kon-song [คน kon]

psychological *adj.* ทางด้านจิตใจ taang-dâan-jìt-jai

psychologist *n.* นักจิตวิทยา nák-jìt-dtà-wít-tá~yaa [คน kon]

psychology *n.* จิตวิทยา jìt-dtà~wít-tá~yaa [วิชา wí-chaa]

pub *n.* (bar) ร้านเหล้า ráan-lâo, ผับ pàp ⬥ [ร้าน ráan] | (bar with meals) ร้านอาหารพร้อมบาร์ ráan-aa-hǎan-prɔ́ɔm-baa [ร้าน ráan]

puberty *n.* วัยแรกรุ่น wai-rɛ̂εk-rûn [วัย wai]

pubic hair *n.* หมอย mǔɔi ⬥ [เส้น sên]

public *adj.* สาธารณะ sǎa-taa-rá~ná

public *n.* (group of people) สาธารณะ sǎa-taa-rá~ná

publication *n.* การพิมพ์
gaan-pim

public defender *n.*
ทนายความหลวง tá~
naai-kwaam-lǔuang,
ทนายอาสา tá~naai-aa-
sǎa [คน kon]

public health *n.*
สาธารณสุข sǎa-taa-rá~
ná-sùk

publicity *n.*
การประชาสัมพันธ์ gaan-
bprà~chaa-sǎm-pan

publicize *vt.* (advertise)
โฆษณา koo-sà~naa |
(give publicity to)
เผยแพร่ pǒəi-prɛ̂ɛ

public relations *n.*
ประชาสัมพันธ์ bprà~
chaa-sǎm-pan [หน่วย
nùai (unit), แผนก pà~
nɛ̀ɛk (division)]

public servant *n.*
ข้าราชการ kâa-râat-chá~
gaan [คน kon]

public utility *n.*
สาธารณูปโภค sǎa-taa-
rá~nuu-bpà~pôok

public welfare *n.*
ประชาสงเคราะห์ bprà~
chaa-sǒng-krɔ́

publish *v.* (issue publicly)

จัดพิมพ์ jàt-pim

publisher *n.* (publishing
house) สำนักพิมพ์ sǎm-
nák-pim [แห่ง hɛ̀ng]

pudding *n.* ขนมพุดดิ้ง
kà~nǒm-pút-dîng [ถ้วย
tûuai (bowl)]

puddle *n.* แอ่งน้ำ ɛ̀ng-
náam [แอ่ง ɛ̀ng, แหล่ง
hɛ̀ng]

puff *n.* (abrupt emission)
การพ่น gaan-pôn | (act
of inhaling) การสูดหายใจ
gaan-sùut-hǎai-jai |
(pastry) พัฟ páp |
(powder) แป้งพัฟ
bpɛ̂ɛng-páp [ตลับ dtà~
làp]

puff *vi.* (pant) หายใจหอบ
hǎai-jai-hɔ̀ɔp

pull *v.* ดึง dɯng | (drag)
ลาก lâak | (draw) ถอน
tɔ̌ɔn

pull another's leg *v.*
แกล้ง glɛ̂ɛng

pull back *v.* (draw back)
ถอยกลับ tɔ̌ɔi-glàp

pulley *n.* ลูกรอก lûuk-rɔ̂ɔk
[อัน an]

pulp *n.* (fruit) เนื้อผลไม้
nɯ́ɯa-pǒn-lá~máai

pulse n. (heartbeat) ชีพจร chîip-pá~jɔɔn

pump n. เครื่องสูบ krûuang-sùup, ปั้ม bpám ✿ [เครื่อง krûuang, ตัว dtuua]

pump v. สูบ sùup, ปั้ม bpám ✿

pumpkin n. ฟักทอง fák-tɔɔng [ลูก lûuk]

punch n. (fist) หมัด màt [หมัด màt] | (mixed fruit juice) น้ำผลไม้รวม nám-pǒn-lá~máai-ruuam

punch v. ชก chók, ต่อย dtɔ̀i

punctual adj. ตรงเวลา dtrong-wee-laa

punctuation mark n. เครื่องหมายวรรคตอน krûuang-mǎai-wák-dtɔɔn [ตัว dtuua]

pungent adj. (acrid, e.g. smell) ฉุน chǔn | (poignant, e.g. remarks) เจ็บแสบ jèp-sɛ̀ɛp

punish vt. ลงโทษ long-tôot, ทำโทษ tam-tôot ❗, ลงอาญา long-aa-yaa ✘

punishment n. (act)

การลงโทษ gaan-long-tôot | (penalty) โทษ tôot

pupil n. (eye) รูม่านตา ruu-mâan-dtaa | (student) นักเรียน nák-riian [คน kon]

puppet n. หุ่นกระบอก hùn-grà~bɔ̀ɔk [ตัว dtuua]

puppy n. ลูกหมา lûuk-mǎa, ลูกสุนัข lûuk-sù-nák ❗ [ตัว dtuua]

purchase n. (act) การซื้อ gaan-súu | (something bought) สิ่งที่ซื้อมา sìng-tîi-súu-maa

purchase v. (buy) ซื้อ súu

pure adj. (clean) สะอาด sà~àat | (free from extraneous matter) บริสุทธิ์ bɔɔ-rí~sùt

purely adv. (only) ล้วน lúuan

purge n. การกำจัด gaan-gam-jàt

purge vt. (eliminate) กำจัด gam-jàt

purify vt. (make pure) ทำให้_บริสุทธิ์ tam-hâi-_-bɔɔ-rí~sùt

purity n. ความบริสุทธิ์

kwaam-bɔɔ-rí~sùt

purple *adj.* ม่วง mûuang,
สีม่วง sǐi-mûuang

purpose *n.* (goal)
เป้าหมาย bpâo-mǎai [อัน
an] | (objective)
จุดประสงค์ jùt-bprà~
sǒng [ข้อ kɔ̂ɔ] |
(objective) วัตถุประสงค์
wát-tù-bprà~sǒng [ข้อ
kɔ̂ɔ, อัน an]

purse *n.* (for carrying
money) กระเป๋าเงิน grà~
bpǎo-ngən [ใบ bai] |
(handbag) กระเป๋าถือ
grà~bpǎo-tǔɯ [ใบ bai]

purse *vi.* (lips) ทำปากจู๋
tam-bpàak-jǔu

pursue *v.* (chase) ไล่ lâi |
(continue) ทำต่อไป tam-
dtɔ̀ɔ-bpai | (follow) ตาม
dtaam

pursuit *n.* (chasing, quest)
การติดตาม gaan-dtìt-
dtaam

pus *n.* หนอง nɔ̌ɔng

push *v.* (force one's way)
ดัน dan | (press) กด gòt |
(shove, drive) ผลัก plàk

push *vt.* (urge to action)
ผลักดัน plàk-dan

push cart see baby
carriage

push-up *n.* (exercise)
การวิดพื้น gaan-wít-púɯn

pussy *n.* (kitten) ลูกแมว
lûuk-mɛɛo [ตัว dtuua] |
(vagina) จิ๋ม jǐm ●

put *vt.* (add in) ใส่ sài |
(arrange) จัด jàt |
(position, place) วาง
waang

put down *vt.* (release)
วาง_ลง waang-_-long

put off *vt.* (postpone)
เลื่อน lɯ̂ɯan

put on *vt.* (wear) ใส่ sài,
สวม sǔuam ⚡, นุ่ง nûng ●

put out *vt.* (extinguish, as
a fire) ดับ dàp

put out fire *v.* ดับไฟ dàp-
fai, ดับเพลิง dàp-pləəng ⚡

put something down *vt.*
วาง_ลง waang-_-long

put together *vt.*
(assemble) ประกอบ
bprà~gɔ̀ɔp | (compile)
รวบรวม rûuap-ruuam

put up with *vt.* (tolerate)
ทนต่อ ton-dtɔ̀ɔ

puzzle *n.* (riddle) ปริศนา
bprìt-sà~nǎa [ข้อ kɔ̂ɔ]

puzzled *adj.* งง ngong, งงงวย ngong-nguuai

pyramid *n.* (monument) ปิรามิด bpì-raa-mít [แห่ง hɛ̀ng] | (shape) ทรงปิรามิด song-bpì-raa-mít

python *n.* งูเหลือม nguu-lʉ̌uam [ตัว dtuua]

Q

Q-tip see cotton swab

quack *n.* (sound of a duck) เสียงเป็ดร้อง sǐiang-bpèt-rɔ́ɔng

quadruple *adj.* สี่เท่า sìi-tâo

quail *n.* นกกระทา nók-grà~taa [ตัว dtuua]

quake *n.* (earthquake) แผ่นดินไหว pèn-din-wǎi [ครั้ง kráng]

quake *vi.* (shake) สั่น sàn

qualification *n.* คุณสมบัติ kun-ná~sǒm-bàt [อย่าง yàang]

qualified *adj.* มีคุณสมบัติ mii-kun-ná~sǒm-bàt

qualify *vi.* (be qualified) มีคุณสมบัติ mii-kun-ná~sǒm-bàt

qualify *vt.* (modify or limit, e.g. statement) ดัดแปลง dàt-bplɛɛng

quality *n.* (attribute, property) คุณลักษณะ kun-ná~lák-sà~nà | (character or nature) คุณภาพ kun-ná~pâap

quality control *n.* การควบคุมคุณภาพของสินค้า gaan-kûuap-kum-kun-ná~pâap-kɔ̌ɔng-sǐn-káa

quantity *n.* (amount) ปริมาณ bpà~rí~maan

quarantine *n.* การกักกัน gaan-gàk-gan

quarantine *vt.* กักกัน gàk-gan

quarrel *vi.* ทะเลาะกัน tá~lɔ́-gan

quarry *n.* (stone mine) เหมืองหิน mʉ̌uang-hǐn [แห่ง hɛ̀ng]

quarter *n.* (one-fourth) หนึ่งในสี่ nʉ̀ng-nai-sìi, เสี้ยว sîiao ✽ | (three months) ไตรมาส dtrai-mâat [ไตรมาส dtrai-mâat]

quarterly *adj.* ทุกสามเดือน túk-sǎam-dʉʉan

quartz *n.* (mineral)

แร่ควอตซ์ rɛ̂ɛ-kwɔ́ɔt ✖

queasy *adj.* (nauseated)
คลื่นไส้ klûun-sâi

queen *n.* พระราชินี prá-
raa-chí~nii, ราชินี raa-
chí~nii [องค์ ong]

queer *adj.* (peculiar) พิลึก
pí-lúk

quench thirst *vi.*
ดับกระหาย dàp-grà~hǎai

quest *n.* การค้นหา gaan-
kón-hǎa

question *n.* (query) คำถาม
kam-tǎam [ข้อ kɔ̂ɔ]

question *v.* (ask) ถาม
tǎam

question *vt.* (not believe)
ไม่เชื่อ mâi-chûua

questionable *adj.* น่าสงสัย
nâa-sǒng-sǎi

question mark *n.* ปรัศนี
bpràt-sà~nii ✖ [ตัว
dtuua]

questionnaire *n.*
แบบสอบถาม bɛ̀ɛp-sɔ̀ɔp-
tǎam [ชุด chút]

queue *n.* (line of people)
คิว kiu [คิว kiu]

queue up *vi.* เข้าคิว kâo-
kiu, เข้าแถว kâo-tɛ̌ɛo

quick *adj.* รวดเร็ว rûuat-

reo, เร็ว reo

quickly *adv.* (fast)
อย่างรวดเร็ว yàang-
rûuat-reo

quick-tempered *adj.*
โมโหง่าย moo-hǒo-ngâai

quiet *adj.* (light sound)
เบา bao | (silent) เงียบ
ngîiap | (still) นิ่ง nîng

quill *n.* (pen for writing)
ปากกาขนนก bpàak-gaa-
kǒn-nók [ด้าม dâam]

quilt *n.* (thick bedspread)
ผ้านวมคลุมเตียง pâa-
nuuam-klum-dtiiang [ผืน
pʉ̌ʉn]

quintet *n.* (of things)
กลุ่มที่ประกอบด้วยห้าสิ่ง
glùm-tîi-bprà~gɔ̀ɔp-
dûuai-hâa-sìng [กลุ่ม
glùm]

quit *v.* (stop, cease) เลิก
lɤ̂ɤk

quit *vi.* (resign) ลาออก
laa-ɔ̀ɔk

quit *vt.* (resign from)
ลาออกจาก laa-ɔ̀ɔk-jàak

quite *adv.* ค่อนข้าง kɔ̂n-
kâang, ทีเดียว tii-diiao ❗

quiz *n.* (exam) การทดสอบ
gaan-tót-sɔ̀ɔp [ครั้ง

kráng]

quiz *vt.* (test) ทดสอบ tót-sòɔp

quota *n.* โควต้า koo-dtâa [ส่วน sùuan]

quotation *n.* (citation) การอ้างอิงถึง gaan-âang-ing-tʉ̌ng

quotation mark *n.* อัญประกาศ an-yá~bprà~gàat ✂ [ตัว dtuua, คู่ kûu (pair)]

quote *n.* (quoted price) ราคาที่ตีไว้ raa-kaa-tîi-dtii-wái

quote *vt.* (give price for) ตีราคา dtii-raa-kaa | (repeat words from) อ้างคำพูดจาก_ âang-kam-pûut-jàak-_

R

rabbit *n.* กระต่าย grà~dtàai [ตัว dtuua]

rabies *n.* โรคกลัวน้ำ rôok-gluua-náam [โรค rôok]

race *n.* (contest of speed) การแข่งขันความเร็ว gaan-kèng-kǎn-kwaam-reo | (nationality) ชนชาติ chon-châat [ชนชาติ chon-châat] | (of human)

เชื้อชาติ chʉ́ua-châat [เชื้อชาติ chʉ́ua-châat] | (tribe) เผ่า pào [เผ่า pào]

race *vi.* แข่งขัน kèng-kǎn | (running) วิ่งแข่ง wîng-kèng

race car *n.* รถแข่ง rót-kèng [คัน kan]

racial *adj.* เกี่ยวกับเชื้อชาติ gìiao-gàp-chʉ́ua-châat

racist *n.* คนที่เหยียดผิว kon-tîi-yìiat-pǐu [คน kon]

rack *n.* (for hanging) ราว raao [ราว raao] | (shelf) ชั้น chán [ชั้น chán]

racket *n.* (sports) ไม้ตีลูก máai-dtii-lûuk [อัน an] | (tennis) ไม้เทนนิส máai-ten-nít [อัน an]

radar *n.* เรดาร์ ree-dâa

radiant *adj.* เปล่งปลั่ง bplèng-bplàng

radiate *vt.* เปล่ง bplèng

radiation *n.* การแผ่รังสี gaan-pὲɛ-rang-sǐi

radiator *n.* หม้อน้ำรถยนต์ mɔ̂ɔ-náam-rót-yon [หม้อ mɔ̂ɔ, ลูก lûuk]

radical *adj.* (extremist)

หัวรุนแรง hǔua-run-rɛɛng | (leftist) ฝ่ายซ้าย fàai-sáai

radio n. (device) วิทยุ wít-tá~yú [เครื่อง krûuang]

radioactive adj. ที่เป็นกัมมันตรังสี tîi-bpen-gam-man-dtà~rang-sǐi

radioactivity n. กัมมันตภาพรังสี gam-man-dtà~pâap-rang-sǐi

radiology n. รังสีวิทยา rang-sǐi-wít-tá~yaa

radish n. หัวไชเท้า hǔua-chai-táao [หัว hǔua]

radius n. รัศมี rát-sà~mǐi

raffle n. (prize drawing) การจับฉลากชิงโชค gaan-jàp-chà~làak-ching-chôok

raft n. แพ pɛɛ [ลำ lam]

raft vi. (travel on a raft) ล่องแพ lô̂ng-pɛɛ

rafter n. (raft punter) คนถ่อแพ kon-tɔ̀ɔ-pɛɛ [คน kon]

rag n. (scrap of cloth) เศษผ้า sèet-pâa [ชิ้น chín, ผืน pǔun] | (washcloth) ผ้าที่ใช้สำหรับล้าง pâa-tîi-chái-sǎm-ràp-láang [ชิ้น chín, ผืน pǔun]

rage n. ความคลั่งไคล้ kwaam-klâng-klái

rage vi. ลุกลาม lúk-laam, เดือดดาล dùuat-daan ✍

raid n. การโจมตี gaan-joom-dtii

raid v. โจมตี joom-dtii

rail n. (bar of wood or metal) ราว raao [ราว raao] | (track) ราง raang [ท่อน tɔ̂n, ราง raang]

railing n. (balustrade, sides of cage) ลูกกรง lûuk-grong [ซี่ sîi]

railway adj. รถไฟ rót-fai

railway n. (route) ทางรถไฟ taang-rót-fai [สาย sǎai]

railway station n. สถานีรถไฟ sà~tǎa-nii-rót-fai [แห่ง hɛ̀ng]

railway track n. รางรถไฟ raang-rót-fai [ราง raang]

rain n. ฝน fǒn [เม็ด mét]

rain vi. ฝนตก fǒn-dtòk

rainbow n. รุ้ง rúng, รุ้งกินน้ำ rúng-gin-náam ❗ [ตัว dtuua]

raincoat n. เสื้อกันฝน

sûua-gan-fǒn [ตัว dtuua]

rainforest *n.*

ป่าที่มีฝนตกมาก bpàa-
tîi-mii-fǒn-dtòk-mâak
[แห่ง hèng]

rainy *adj.* มีฝน mii-fǒn

rainy season *n.* ฤดูฝน
rʉ́-duu-fǒn [ฤดู rʉ́-duu] |
หน้าฝน nâa-fǒn ☀ [หน้า
nâa]

raise *vi.* (go up) ขึ้น kʉ̂n

raise *vt.* (e.g. child, horse)
เลี้ยงดู líiang-duu |
(increase, e.g. level)
ทำให้_เพิ่มขึ้น tam-hâi-_-
pə̂əm-kʉ̂n | (lift up, e.g.
item) ยก_ขึ้น yók-_-kʉ̂n

raisin *n.* ลูกเกด lûuk-gèet
[เม็ด mét]

rake *n.* (tool) คราด krâat
[อัน an]

rally *n.* (competition)
การแข่งขัน gaan-kèng-
kǎn | (e.g. in tennis)
การตีลูกกลับ gaan-dtii-
lûuk-glàp | (gathering)
การชุมนุม gaan-chum-
num

rally *vi.* (gather) ชุมนุมกัน
chum-num-gan

ram *n.* (sheep) แกะตัวผู้
gè-dtuua-pûu [ตัว dtuua]

rambutan *n.* เงาะ ngɔ́ [ลูก
lûuk (one), พวง puuang
(bunch)]

ramp *n.* (slope) ทางลาด
taang-lâat [ทาง taang]

rampage *v.* (act violently)
อาละวาด aa-lá~wâat

rampart *n.* ปราการ
bpraa-gaan ☜ [แห่ง hèng]

ranch *n.* (cattle) ทุ่งเลี้ยงวัว
tûng-líiang-wuua [แห่ง
hèng]

random *adj.* โดยการสุ่ม
dooi-gaan-sùm, ไม่เลือก
mâi-lʉ̂uak

range *n.* (area, scope or
sphere) ขอบเขต kɔ̀ɔp-
kèet | (distance) ระยะทาง
rá~yá-taang [กิโลเมตร
gì~loo-méet (kilo), เมตร
méet (meter), ไมล์ maai
(mile)] | (e.g. mountain)
เทือกเขา tʉ̂uak-kǎo
[เทือก tʉ̂uak] | (for
grazing) ทุ่งเลี้ยงสัตว์
tûng-líiang-sàt [แห่ง
hèng] | (series, sequence)
ลำดับ lam-dàp [ลำดับ

lam-dàp, ที่ tîi |
(shooting) สนามยิงปืน
sà~nǎam-ying-bpʉʉn
[สนาม sà~nǎam, แห่ง
hèng]

rank n. (level, grade) ชั้น
chán [ชั้น chán] |
(position, degree) ยศ yót
| (status) สถานะ sà~tǎa-
ná [สถานะ sà~tǎa-ná]

rank vt. (arrange in ranks)
จัดลำดับ jàt-lam-dàp

ransom n. (payment)
ค่าไถ่ kâa-tài

ransom vt. ไถ่ตัว tài-dtuua

rap n. (blame, censure)
การด่าว่า gaan-dàa-wâa |
(music) จังหวะแร็ป jang-
wà~rép [เพลง pleeng]

rape n. (sexual assault)
การข่มขืน gaan-kòm-
kǔʉn

rape v. ข่มขืน kòm-kǔʉn,
ปล้ำ bplâm, ขืนใจ kǔʉn-
jai !

rapid adj. เร็ว reo, ไว wai |
(e.g. river) เชี่ยว chîiao

rare adj. (cooked little)
ไม่สุกมาก mâi-sùk-mâak
| (hard to find) หายาก

hǎa-yâak

rascal n. อันธพาล an-tá~
paan [คน kon]

rash adj. (hasty) ใจร้อน
jai-rɔ́ɔn

rash n. (on the skin) ผื่น
pʉʉn | (prickly heat) ผด
pòt | (public outbreak)
การระบาด gaan-rá~bàat

raspberry n. ราสเบอรี่
râat-sà~bəə-rîi [ลูก lûuk]

rat n. (rodent) หนู nǔu [ตัว
dtuua]

rate n. (level) ระดับ rá~
dàp [ระดับ rá~dàp] |
(price) ราคา raa-kaa |
(proportion, ratio, tariff)
อัตรา àt-dtraa

rate vt. (estimate the
price of) ตีราคา dtii-raa-
kaa | (rank) จัดอันดับ jàt-
an-dàp

rather adv. (instead) ดีกว่า
dii-gwàa | (somewhat)
ค่อนข้าง kɔ̂n-kâang

ratio n. อัตราส่วน àt-
dtraa-sùuan

ration vt. (allot) ปันส่วน
bpan-sùuan

rational adj. มีเหตุผล mii-
hèet-pǒn

rattan *n.* หวาย wǎai

rattan ball *n.* ตะกร้อ dtà~grɔ̂ɔ [ลูก lûuk]

rattle *vi.* ส่งเสียงรัว sòng-sǐiang-ruua

rattlesnake *n.* งูหางกระดิ่ง nguu-hǎang-grà~dìng [ตัว dtuua]

raw *adj.* (rough) หยาบ yàap | (unripe, uncooked, crude) ดิบ dìp

ray *n.* (fish) ปลากระเบน bplaa-grà~been [ตัว dtuua] | (light beam) รังสี rang-sǐi [รังสี rang-sǐi]

rayon *n.* ผ้าเรยอง pâa-ree-yɔɔng

razor *n.* มีดโกน mîit-goon [เล่ม lêm]

razor blade *n.* ใบมีดโกน bai-mîit-goon [ใบ bai]

reach *vt.* (arrive at) ถึง tǔng | (contact) ติดต่อ dtìt-dtɔ̀ɔ | (for something) เอื้อมคว้า ûuam-kwáa

react *vi.* ตอบโต้ dtɔ̀ɔp-dtôo, มีปฏิกิริยา mii-dtì-gì-rí-yaa

reaction *n.* การโต้ตอบ gaan-dtôo-dtɔ̀ɔp, ปฏิกิริยา bpà-dtì-gì-rí-yaa

read *v.* อ่าน àan

reader *n.* (one who reads) ผู้อ่าน pûu-àan [คน kon]

ready *adj.* (finished, done) แล้ว lɛ́ɛo, เสร็จ sèt | (prepared or available) เตรียมพร้อม dtriiam-prɔ́ɔm, พร้อม prɔ́ɔm

ready-made *adj.* สำเร็จรูป sǎm-rèt-rûup

real *adj.* จริง jing, แท้ tɛ́ɛ

real estate *n.* (house and land) บ้านและที่ดิน bâan-lé-tîi-din, อสังหาริมทรัพย์ à~sǎng-hǎa-rim-má~sáp ⚡ [แห่ง hèng] | (land) ที่ tîi ✿ [แปลง bplɛɛng, ผืน pǔun]

realistic *adj.* (e.g. painting) เหมือนจริง mǔuan-jing | (e.g. plan) เป็นไปได้ bpen-bpai-dâai

reality *n.* ความเป็นจริง kwaam-bpen-jing

realize *vt.* (be or become aware of) รู้ rúu, ตระหนัก dtrà~nàk ⚡ | (obtain) ได้ dâai

really *adv.* จริงๆ jing-jing,

โดยแท้จริง dooi-tɛ́ɛ-jing !

realm *n.* อาณาจักร aa-naa-jàk [แห่ง hɛ̀ng]

realtor *n.*
นายหน้าซื้อขายหลักทรัพย์ naai-nâa-súu-kǎai-làk-sáp [คน kon]

ream *n.* (of paper) รีม riim [รีม riim]

reap *v.* (harvest) เก็บเกี่ยว gèp-giiao

rear *adj.* ข้างหลัง kâang-lǎng, หลัง lǎng

rear *n.* (back part, behind) ข้างหลัง kâang-lǎng [ข้าง kâang]

reason *n.* เหตุผล hèet-pǒn [อัน an]

reasonable *adj.* มีเหตุผล mii-hèet-pǒn, สมเหตุสมผล sǒm-hèet-sǒm-pǒn

reassure *vt.* (affirm, restore confidence to) รับรอง ráp-rɔɔng

rebate *n.* (discount) ส่วนลด sùuan-lót [เปอร์เซ็นต์ bpəə-sen] | (returned money) เงินคืน ngən-kuun

rebel *n.* (nonconformist)

คนหัวรั้น kon-hǔua-rán [คน kon] | (revolter) ผู้ก่อกบฏ pûu-gɔ̀ɔ-gà~bòt [คน kon]

rebel *vi.* (revolt) ก่อการจลาจล gɔ̀ɔ-gaan-jà~laa-jon

rebellion *n.* กบฏ gà~bòt, การจลาจล gaan-jà~laa-jon [คณะ ká~ná (group)]

rebound *vi.* (bounce back) เด้งกลับ dêng-glàp, สะท้อนกลับ sà~tɔ́ɔn-glàp

rebuff *vt.* บอกปัด bɔ̀ɔk-bpàt

rebut *v.* โต้แย้ง dtôo-yɛ́ɛng

recall *vt.* (remember) จำ_ได้ jam-_-dâai | (summon back) เรียก_กลับ riiak-_-glàp

recede *vi.* (back off, retreat) ถอย tɔ̌ɔi | (decrease) ลดถอย lót-tɔ̌ɔi

receipt *n.* ใบเสร็จ bai-sèt [ใบ bai]

receive *vt.* (guests) ได้รับ dâi-ráp, รับ ráp | (guests) ต้อนรับ dtɔ̂ɔn-ráp

receiver *n.* (of a telephone) หูโทรศัพท์ hǔu-too-rá~sàp [อัน an]

| (of electrical signals)
เครื่องรับสัญญาณ
krûuang-ráp-sǎn-yaan
[เครื่อง krûuang]

recent adj. (current)
ไม่นานมานี้ mâi-naan-maa-níi | (not long ago)
เร็วๆนี้ reo-reo-níi

recently adv. เมื่อเร็วๆนี้
mûua-reo-reo-níi

reception n. การต้อนรับ
gaan-dtɔ̂ɔn-ráp

receptionist n.
พนักงานต้อนรับ pá~nák-ngaan-dtɔ̂ɔn-ráp [คน
kon]

recess n. (interlude,
pause, break) ช่วงหยุดพัก
chûuang-yùt-pák [ช่วง
chûuang]

recession n. (slow
economy)
เศรษฐกิจชลอตัว sèet-tà~gìt-chá~lɔɔ-dtuua

recipe n. ตำรับ dtam-ràp
[ตำรับ dtam-ràp] | สูตร
sùut [สูตร sùut]

recipient n. ผู้รับ pûu-ráp
[คน kon]

reciprocal adj.
ซึ่งกันและกัน sûng-gan-lɛ́-gan

recital n. (musical)
การเล่นดนตรีเดี่ยว gaan-lên-don-dtrii-dìiao

recite v. (repeat) ท่อง tɔ̂ng

reckless adj. ประมาท
bprà~màat, ไม่ระวัง mâi-rá~wang

reckon v. (compute)
คำนวณ kam-nuuan |
(estimate) คาดคะเน
kâat-ká~nee | (think) คิด
kít

recline v. เอน een

recline on vi. พิง ping

recluse n. (hermit) ฤษี
rʉʉ-sǐi [ตน dton]

reclusive adj. สันโดษ
sǎn-dòot

recognize vt. (accept)
ยอมรับ yɔɔm-ráp |
(appreciate) เห็นคุณค่า
hěn-kun-kâa | (be
familiar with) รู้จัก rúu-jàk
| (recall) จำ_ได้ jam-_-dâai

recollect v. (remember)
จำได้ jam-dâai

recommend v. (advise)
แนะนำ nɛ́-nam

recommendation n.
การแนะนำ gaan-nɛ́-nam
| (letter) จดหมายแนะนำ

jòt-măai-né-nam [ฉบับ
chà~bàp]

reconcile *vi.* คืนดีกัน
kuun-dii-gan

reconciled *adj.* ดีกัน dii-
gan

record *n.* (for music)
แผ่นเสียง pèn-sǐiang
[แผ่น pèn] | (history)
ประวัติ bprà~wàt |
(registration) ทะเบียน
tá~biian [ใบ bai] |
(something recorded)
บันทึก ban-túk, สถิติ sà~
tì-dtì

record *v.* บันทึก ban-túk

record a sound *vi.*
บันทึกเสียง ban-túk-sǐiang

recover *vi.* (get better)
ทุเลา tú-lao, ฟื้นตัว fúun-
dtuua | (totally, from
sickness) หายเป็นปกติ
hǎai-bpen-bpòk-gà~dtì

recover *vt.* (get stolen
item back) ได้_คืน dâai-
_-kuun

recreation *n.*
(amusement, leisure)
การพักผ่อนหย่อนใจ
gaan-pák-pòn-yòn-jai

recruit *vi.* หาสมาชิกใหม่
hǎa-sà~maa-chík-mài

recruit *vt.* พา_เข้ามา paa-
_-kâo-maa

recruiter *n.*
ผู้สรรหาพนักงานใหม่ pûu-
săn-hǎa-pá~nák-
ngaan-mài [คน kon
(person), บริษัท bɔɔ-rí~
sàt (company)]

rectangle *n.* สี่เหลี่ยม sìi-
lìiam [รูป rûup] | (non-
square) สี่เหลี่ยมผืนผ้า sìi-
lìiam-pǔun-pâa [รูป rûup]

rector *n.* อธิการบดี à-tí-
gaan-bɔɔ-dii [คน kon]

rectum *n.* ช่องทวารหนัก
chɔ̂ng-tá~waan-nàk

recuperate *vi.* ฟื้นตัว
fúun-dtuua

recur *vi.* เกิดขึ้นอีก gèət-
kûn-ìik

recycle *v.* นำ_กลับมาใช้อีก
nam-_-glàp-maa-chái-
ìik, รีไซเคิล rii-sai-kên

red *adj.* แดง dɛɛng, สีแดง
sǐi-dɛɛng

red *n.* สีแดง sǐi-dɛɛng [สี
sǐi]

Red Cross *n.* กาชาด gaa-
châat, สภากาชาด sà~
paa-gaa-châat

redeem *vt.* (cash, e.g.

stocks) เอา_ไปขึ้นเงิน ao-_-bpai-kûn-ngən | (pay debt on, e.g. mortgage) ไถ่ ถัย | (restore honor of) กู้หน้า gûu-nâa ✱ | (turn in, e.g. coupons) เอา_ไปใช้ ao-_-bpai-chái

redial vi. หมุนใหม่ mǔn-mài ✱

reduce v. ลด lót

reduction n. การลดลง gaan-lót-long

redundant adj. (repeated) ซ้ำซาก sám-sâak | (unnecessary) ไม่จำเป็น mâi-jam-bpen

reed n. ต้นกก dtôn-gòk [ต้น dtôn]

reef n. (ridge of rocks) แนวหินโสโครก nɛɛo-hǐn-sǒo-krôok [แนว nɛɛo]

reel n. (e.g. film, thread) หลอด lɔ̀ɔt [หลอด lɔ̀ɔt]

reelection n. การเลือกตั้งใหม่ gaan-lûuak-dtâng-mài

referee n. กรรมการ gam-má~gaan [คน kon]

reference n. การอ้างอิง gaan-âang-ing | (document) เอกสารอ้างอิง èek-gà~sǎan-âang-ing [ฉบับ chà~bàp]

referral n. (e.g. for job, patient) การแนะนำ gaan-né-nam

refer to vt. (cite) อ้างอิงถึง âang-ing-tǔng | (e.g. dictionary) อ้างอิง âang-ing | (e.g. specialist) แนะนำให้ไปหา né-nam-hâi-bpai-hǎa | (mean) หมายถึง mǎai-tǔng

refill vt. (e.g. liquid, air (object is substance filled)) เติม dtəəm

refine vt. (purify) กลั่น glàn | (remove defects of) ขัดเกลา kàt-glao

refinery n. โรงกลั่น roong-glàn [แห่ง hɛ̀ng]

reflect v. (e.g. light, shadow) สะท้อน sà~tɔ́ɔn

reflection n. (act of reflecting) การสะท้อน gaan-sà~tɔ́ɔn | (consideration) การไตร่ตรอง gaan-dtrài-dtrɔɔng | (image) ภาพสะท้อน pâap-sà~tɔ́ɔn | (image) เงา ngao [เงา ngao]

reflex n. (reaction)

การตอบโต้โดยอัตโนมัติ gaan-dtɔ̀ɔp-dtôo-dooi-àt~dtà-noo-mát

reform n. การปฏิรูป gaan-bpà~dtì-rûup

reform vt. ปฏิรูป bpà~dtì-rûup

refrain n. (e.g. in songs) บทซ้ำ bòt-sám [บท bòt]

refrain from vt. งดเว้น ngót-wén

refresh vt. (give strength to) เติมพลังให้ dtəəm-pá~lang-hâi

refreshed adj. (e.g. from drink) สดชื่น sòt-chûun

refreshment n. เครื่องดื่ม krûuang-dùum [ชนิด chá~nít]

refrigerate v. แช่เย็น chɛ̂ɛ-yen

refrigerator n. ตู้เย็น dtûu-yen [เครื่อง krûuang]

refuel v. (gasoline, petrol) เติมน้ำมัน dtəəm-nám-man

refuge n. ที่หลบภัย tîi-lòp-pai [แห่ง hɛ̀ng]

refugee n. ผู้ลี้ภัย pûu-líi-pai [คน kon]

refund n. (amount) เงินที่คืนให้ ngən-tîi-kuun-hâi [จำนวน jam-nuuan]

refund v. คืนเงิน kuun-ngən

refusal n. การปฏิเสธ gaan-bpà~dtì~sèet | คำปฏิเสธ kam-bpà~dtì-sèet [คำ kam]

refuse n. (rubbish) ขยะ kà~yà [ชิ้น chín (piece), กอง gɔɔng (pile)]

refuse v. ปฏิเสธ bpà~dtì-sèet

refute vt. (prove to be false) หักล้าง hàk-láang | (reject as false) ปฏิเสธ bpà~dtì-sèet

regain vt. (get back) ได้_คืน dâai-_-kuun

regain consciousness vi. ฟื้นคืนสติ fúun-kuun-sà~dtì

regard vt. (consider _ as _) เห็นว่า_เป็น_ hěn-wâa-_-bpen-_ | (relate to) เกี่ยวกับ gìiao-gàp

regarding prep. เกี่ยวกับ gìiao-gàp

regardless of *prep.*
(irrespective of _)
ไม่ว่า_จะเป็นอย่างไร mâi-
wâa-_-jà-bpen-yàang-rai

regime *n.*
ระบบการปกครอง rá~
bòp-gaan-bpòk-krɔɔng
[ระบบ rá~bòp]

region *n.* (area) เขต kèet,
บริเวณ bɔɔ-rí~ween [แห่ง
hɛ̀ng] | (of the country)
ภาค pâak

register *n.* ทะเบียน tá~
biian [ใบ bai] | (formal
recording) การลงทะเบียน
gaan-long-tá~biian

register *vi.* บันทึก ban-
túk, ลงทะเบียน long-tá~
biian

registered *adj.*
บันทึกไว้แล้ว ban-túk-
wái-lɛ́ɛo

registrar *n.* นายทะเบียน
naai-tá~biian [คน kon]

registration *n.*
การจดทะเบียน gaan-jòt-
tá~biian, การลงทะเบียน
gaan-long-tá~biian,
ระเบียบ rá~biian

regret *n.* ความเสียใจ
kwaam-sǐia-jai

regret *vt.* (action, fault)

เสียใจกับ sǐia-jai-gàp |
(loss) เสียดาย sǐia-daai

regular *adj.* (established,
habitual) ประจำ bprà~
jam | (ordinary) ธรรมดา
tam-má~daa, ปกติ
bpòk-gà~dtì

regulate *vt.* กำหนด gam-
nòt

regulation *n.* กฎ gòt,
กฎเกณฑ์ gòt-geen, กติกา
gà-dtì~gaa, ระเบียบ rá~
biiap [ข้อ kɔ̂ɔ] | ข้อบังคับ
kɔ̂ɔ-bang-káp [ข้อ kɔ̂ɔ]

rehabilitate *vt.* บำบัด
bam-bàt, พักฟื้น pák-fúun

rehearsal *n.* การฝึกซ้อม
gaan-fùk-sɔ́ɔm

rehearse *v.* ซ้อม sɔ́ɔm,
ฝึกซ้อม fùk-sɔ́ɔm ⚡

reign *n.* รัชกาล rát-chá~
gaan [สมัย sà~mǎi]

reign *vi.* ครอบครอง
krɔ̂ɔp-krɔɔng | (royalty)
ครองราชย์ krɔɔng-râat

reimburse *vt.* (e.g. for
damage) ชดเชย chót-
chəəi | (e.g. for
purchase) ชำระเงินคืน
cham-rá~ngən-kuun

rein *n.* สายบังเหียน sǎaibang-hǐian [เส้น sên]

reincarnate *vi.*
กลับชาติมาเกิด glàp-
châat-maa-gèət, เกิดใหม่
gèət-mài

reincarnation *n.*
การกลับชาติมาเกิด gaan-
glàp-châat-maa-gèət

reinforce *vt.* (reiterate)
พูด_ซ้ำ pûut-_-sám |
(strengthen) เสริมกำลัง
sěəm-gam-lang

reiterate *vt.* (say again)
กล่าวซ้ำ glàao-sám

reject *vt.* ค้าน káan, ปฏิเสธ
bpa~dtì-sèet

rejoice *vi.* ดีใจ dii-jai,
ปลื้มใจ bplûum-jai, ยินดี
yin-dii

rejuvenate *vt.*
(invigorate)
ทำให้_กระปรี้กระเปร่า
tam-hâi-_-grà~bprîi-
grà~bpràao

relate *vi.* (have relevance)
เกี่ยวข้องกัน gìiao-kɔ̂ɔng-
gan

relate *vt.* (associate,
connect) เกี่ยวโยง gìiao-
yoong

related *adj.* (associated,

connected) เกี่ยวข้องกัน
gìiao-kɔ̂ɔng-gan | (in
same family) เป็นญาติกัน
bpen-yâat-gan

related to *adj.* (in same
family as) เป็นญาติกับ
bpen-yâat-gàp

relate to *vt.* (have to do
with) เกี่ยวข้องกับ gìiao-
kɔ̂ɔng-gàp

relation *n.*
การเกี่ยวข้องกัน gaan-
gìiao-kɔ̂ɔng-gan

relationship *n.*
ความสัมพันธ์ kwaam-
sǎm-pan | (romantic)
สัมพันธ์รัก sǎm-pan-rák
[ครั้ง kráng]

relative *adj.* (to
something else)
ต้องเทียบกับอันอื่น dtɔ̂ng-
tîiap-gàp-an-ùun

relative *n.* (family) ญาติ
yâat [คน kon]

relatively *adv.* (rather,
comparatively) ค่อนข้าง
kɔ̂n-kâang

relative to *prep.* (e.g.
statistic)
เมื่อเปรียบเทียบกับ
mûua-bprìiap-tîiap-gàp

relax *vi.* (loosen)
ผ่อนคลาย pɔ̀n-klaai **|**
(rest) พักผ่อน pák-pɔ̀n

relax *vt.* (loosen) คลาย
klaai

relax! *interj.* ใจเย็นๆ jai-
yen-yen

relaxation *n.*
การผ่อนคลาย gaan-pɔ̀n-
klaai

relay *vt.* (pass on) ส่ง_ผ่าน
sòng-_-pàan

release *n.* (setting free)
การปล่อย gaan-bplɔ̀i

release *vt.* ปลดปล่อย
bplòt-bplɔ̀i, ปล่อย bplɔ̀i

relevant *adj.* เกี่ยวเนื่องกัน
gìiao-nɯ̂ɯang-gan,
สัมพันธ์กัน sǎm-pan-gan

reliable *adj.* (dependable)
ไว้ใจได้ wái-jai-dâai

relief *n.* การบรรเทา gaan-
ban-tao, การผ่อนคลาย
gaan-pɔ̀n-klaai

relieve *vt.* (alleviate)
บรรเทา ban-tao **|** (free
from pain) ผ่อนคลาย
pɔ̀n-klaai **|** (lighten
burden for) ลดภาระ lót-
paa-rá

religion *n.* ศาสนา sàat-
sà~nǎa [ศาสนา sàat-sà~
nǎa]

religious *adj.* (pertaining
to religion)
เกี่ยวกับศาสนา gìiao-
gàp-sàat-sà~nǎa **|**
(pious) เคร่งศาสนา
krêng-sàat-sà~nǎa

relinquish *vt.* (release)
ปล่อย bplɔ̀i **|** (renounce)
สละ sà~là

relocate *vi.* โยกย้าย
yôok-yáai

relocate *vt.* (move) ย้าย
yáai

reluctant *adj.* (unwilling)
ไม่เต็มใจ mâi-dtem-jai

rely on *vt.* เชื่อใจ chɯ̂ɯa-jai

remain *vi.* (be left over)
เหลืออยู่ lɯ̌ɯa-yùu **|**
(continue to be _) ยัง_อยู่
yang-_-yùu **|** (not leave)
ยังอยู่ yang-yùu

remainder *n.* เศษ sèet
[ชิ้น chín]

remaining *adj.* ที่เหลือ tîi-
lɯ̌ɯa

remains *n.* (of body) ซาก
sâak [ซาก sâak]

remark *n.* (note) หมายเหตุ
mǎai-hèet [แห่ง hèng]

remark *vt.* (comment)

ให้ความเห็น hâi-kwaam-
hĕn

remarkable *adj.*
(extraordinary) ไม่ธรรมดา
mâi-tam-má~daa |
(noticeable) น่าสังเกต
nâa-săng-gèet

remarry *vi.* แต่งงานใหม่
dtèng-ngaan-mài

remedy *vt.* (correct) แก้ไข
gɛ̂ɛ-kăi | (cure) รักษา
rák-săa

remember *v.* จำ jam

remember *vt.* จำ_ได้ jam-
_-dâai

remembrance *n.*
ความทรงจำ kwaam-
song-jam

remind *vt.* เตือน dtʉʉan

reminder *n.* (thing)
สิ่งเตือนความจำ sìng-
dtʉʉan-kwaam-jam

remorse *n.* ความสำนึกผิด
kwaam-săm-nʉ́k-pìt

remote *adj.* ไกล glai,
ห่างเหิน hàang-hĕ̌ən

remote control *n.* รีโมท
rii-môot ● [ตัว dtuua]

removal *n.* การถอนออก
gaan-tɔ̆ɔn-ɔ̀ɔk,
การย้ายออก gaan-yáai-

ɔ̀ɔk

remove *vt.* (delete, erase)
ลบ_ออก lóp-_-ɔ̀ɔk | (get
rid of) กำจัด gam-jàt |
(move away, clear) ย้าย
yáai | (take off, e.g.
clothes) ถอด tɔ̀ɔt

remunerate *vt.*
(compensate) ชดเชย
chót-chəəi | (give reward
to) ให้รางวัล hâi-raang-
wan

render *vt.* (cause _ to be
_) ทำให้__ tam-hâi-_-_ |
(e.g. service, aid) จัด_ให้
jàt-_-hâi | (pay) จ่าย jàai

rendezvous *n.* (meeting)
การนัดพบ gaan-nát-póp
| (place) ที่ชุมนุม tîi-
chum-num [แห่ง hɛ̀ng]

rendezvous *vi.* นัดพบกัน
nát-póp-gan

rendition *n.*
(interpretation)
การตีความ gaan-dtii-
kwaam | (performance)
การแสดง gaan-sà~dɛɛng
[รายการ raai-gaan]

renew *v.* (e.g. contract)
ต่อ dtɔ̀ɔ | (e.g. expired
card) ต่ออายุ dtɔ̀ɔ-aa-yú |
(resume) เริ่ม_ใหม่ rɔ̂əm-

_-mài

renounce vt. ทิ้ง tíng, สละ
sà~là

renovate v. ซ่อม_ใหม่
sôm-_-mài, ทำ_ใหม่ tam-
_-mài

renown n. ชื่อเสียง chûu-
sĭiang

rent n. (payment) ค่าเช่า
kâa-châo [จำนวน jam-
nuuan]

rent v. (from someone)
เช่า châo

rent vt. (to someone)
ให้เช่า hâi-châo

rent-a-car n. การเช่ารถ
gaan-châo-rót

rental adj. สำหรับเช่า sǎm-
ràp-châo

rental n. การให้เช่า gaan-
hâi-châo

rental car n. รถเช่า rót-
châo [คัน kan]

rental fee n. ค่าเช่า kâa-
châo [จำนวน jam-nuuan]

rent out vt. ให้_เช่า hâi-_-
châo

rep see representative

repair vt. (fix, mend) แก้ไข
gɛ̂ɛ-kǎi, ซ่อม sôm

reparation n.
(compensation)

การซ่อมแซม gaan-sôm-
sɛɛm

repay vt. (compensate)
ชดเชย chót-chəəi, ชดใช้
chót-chái | (pay back _
to _) จ่าย_คืน_ jàai-_-
kɯɯn-_

repeat v. ซ้ำ sám

repeat vt. (action) ทำ_ซ้ำ
tam-_-sám | (speech)
พูด_ซ้ำ pûut-_-sám

repel vt. (force back)
ผลัก_ออกไป plàk-_-ɔ̀ɔk-
bpai

repent vi. สำนึกผิด sǎm-
núk-pìt

repetition n. การทำซ้ำ
gaan-tam-sám

replace vt. (put back in
place) แทนที่ tɛɛn-tîi |
(someone) ทำแทน tam-
tɛɛn

replacement n. (item)
ของที่ใช้แทน kɔ̌ɔng-tîi-
chái-tɛɛn | (person)
คนที่เข้าแทน kon-tîi-kâo-
tɛɛn [คน kon]

replenish vt. เติม dtəəm

replica n. ของจำลอง
kɔ̌ɔng-jam-lɔɔng

reply n. (answer) คำตอบ

kam-dtɔ̀ɔp [ข้อ kɔ̂ɔ]

reply *vi.* ตอบ dtɔ̀ɔp

report *n.* รายงาน raai-ngaan [ฉบับ chà~bàp, เรื่อง rûuang]

report *vi.* รายงาน raai-ngaan

report *vt.* แจ้ง jɛ̂ɛng | (to the police) แจ้งความ jɛ̂ɛng-kwaam

reporter *n.* (journalist) นักข่าว nák-kàao [คน kon]

represent *vt.* (act as a substitute) เป็นตัวแทน bpen-dtuua-tɛɛn

representation *n.* (having voice, influence) การมีสิทธิมีเสียง gaan-mii-sìt-mii-sǐiang

representative *n.* ตัวแทน dtuua-tɛɛn [คน kon] | (sales) ตัวแทนขาย dtuua-tɛɛn-kǎai [คน kon]

representative *adj.* เป็นแบบอย่าง bpen-bɛ̀ɛp-yàang

reprimand *vt.* ตำหนิ dtam-nì, ประณาม bprà~naam

reproach *vt.* กล่าวโทษ glàao-tôot, ตำหนิ dtam-nì

reproduce *vi.* แพร่พันธุ์ prɛ̂ɛ-pan | (for mammals) ออกลูก ɔ̀ɔk-lûuk

reproduce *vt.* (duplicate) จำลอง jam-lɔɔng

reproductive organ *n.* อวัยวะสืบพันธุ์ à-wai-yá~wá-sùup-pan

reptile *n.* สัตว์เลื้อยคลาน sàt-lúuai-klaan [ตัว dtuua, ชนิด chá~nít (kind)]

republic *n.* สาธารณรัฐ sǎa-taa-rá~ná-rát [รัฐ rát]

reputable *adj.* (renowned) มีชื่อเสียง mii-chûu-sǐiang

reputation *n.* ชื่อเสียง chûu-sǐiang

request *n.* (act) การขอร้อง gaan-kɔ̌ɔ-rɔ́ɔng | (item) ข้อเรียกร้อง kɔ̂ɔ-rîiak-rɔ́ɔng [ข้อ kɔ̂ɔ, ประการ bprà~gaan ﹗]

request *vt.* ขอ kɔ̌ɔ, ขอร้อง kɔ̌ɔ-rɔ́ɔng

require *v.* (demand) เรียกร้อง rîiak-rɔ́ɔng | (impose) กำหนด gam-nòt | (need) ต้องการ dtôŋ-gaan

requirement n. (rules, regulations) ข้อกำหนด kɔ̂ɔ-gam-nòt [ข้อ kɔ̂ɔ]

resale n. การขายใหม่ gaan-kǎai-mài

rescue n. การช่วยชีวิต gaan-chûai-chii-wít

rescue vt. ช่วยชีวิต chûai-chii-wít

research n. การวิจัย gaan-wí-jai [ครั้ง kráng]

research v. ค้นคว้า kón-kwáa, วิจัย wí-jai

researcher n. นักวิจัย nák-wí-jai [คน kon]

resemblance n. ความคล้ายคลึง kwaam-kláai-klʉng

resemble vt. คล้าย kláai, คล้ายคลึง kláai-klʉng, เหมือน mʉ̌an

resentful adj. ขุ่นเคือง kùn-kʉang, ไม่พอใจ mâi-pɔɔ-jai

resentment n. ความไม่พอใจ kwaam-mâi-pɔɔ-jai

reservation n. (doubt) ความกังขา kwaam-gang-kǎa | (e.g. hotel, air ticket) การจอง gaan-jɔɔng

reserve v. (e.g. hotel, air ticket) จอง jɔɔng

reserve vt. (conserve, save) สงวน sà~ngǔuan | (e.g. hotel, air ticket) สำรอง sǎm-rɔɔng ⚠

reserved adj. (booked) จองไว้ jɔɔng-wái | (manner) สงบเสงี่ยม sà~ngòp-sà~ngìiam

reservoir n. (of water) อ่างเก็บน้ำ àang-gèp-náam [แห่ง hèng]

reside vi. อยู่ yùu, อาศัย aa-sǎi ⚠

residence n. ที่อยู่อาศัย tîi-yùu-aa-sǎi [ที่ tîi] | ที่พัก tîi-pák [แห่ง hèng]

resident n. (inhabitant) ผู้อาศัย pûu-aa-sǎi [คน kon] | (physician in training) แพทย์ที่มาเรียนต่อเฉพาะทาง pɛ̂ɛt-tîi-maa-riian-dtɔ̀ɔ-chà~pɔ́-taang [คน kon]

residual adj. เหลืออยู่ lʉ̌a-yùu

residue n. (remains, dregs) เศษ sèet [ชิ้น chín] | (thing left over)

ส่วนที่เหลือ sùuan-tîi-lǔua
resign vi. ลาออก laa-ɔ̀ɔk
resin n. ยางสน yaang-sǒn
resist v. (defy, oppose)
ต่อต้าน dtɔ̀ɔ-dtâan,
ต้านทาน dtâan-taan |
(withstand) อดทน òt-ton
resist vt. (defy, oppose)
ขัดขวาง kàt-kwǎang
resistance n. (act)
การต้านทาน gaan-dtâan-
taan | (rebel force)
ฝ่ายต้านทาน fàai-dtâan-
taan
resistant adj. ต่อต้าน
dtɔ̀ɔ-dtâan, ทนต่อ ton-
dtɔ̀ɔ
resolution n. (act)
การแก้ปัญหา gaan-gɛ̂ɛ-
bpan-hǎa, การลงมติ
gaan-long-má-dtì |
(solution) มติ má~dtì
[เสียง sǐiang]
resolve vt. (by
committee) มีมติ mii-
má-dtì | (e.g. problem)
แก้ gɛ̂ɛ
resort n. (tourist)
ที่พักตากอากาศ tîi-pák-
dtàak-àak-gàat, รีสอร์ท
rii-sɔ̀ɔt [แห่ง hɛ̀ng]

resource n. (e.g. natural,
assets) ทรัพยากร sáp-
pá~yaa-gɔɔn [ชนิด chá~
nít]
respect n. ความเคารพ
kwaam-kao-róp
respect vt. เคารพ kao-róp,
นับถือ náp-tǔu
respectable adj. น่าเคารพ
nâa-kao-róp
respectful adj. นบนอบ
nóp-nɔ́ɔp, นอบน้อม
nɔ̂ɔp-nóom
respectively adv.
ตามลำดับ dtaam-lam-dàp
respiration n. การหายใจ
gaan-hǎai-jai
respite n. (relief)
การบรรเทา gaan-ban-tao
respond vi. ตอบ dtɔ̀ɔp,
โต้ตอบ dtôo-dtɔ̀ɔp, สนอง
sà~nɔ̌ɔng !
response n. คำตอบ kam-
dtɔ̀ɔp [คำ kam, อัน an]
responsibility n.
ความรับผิดชอบ kwaam-
ráp-pìt-chɔ̂ɔp
responsible adj.
มีความรับผิดชอบ mii-
kwaam-ráp-pìt-chɔ̂ɔp,
รับผิดชอบ ráp-pìt-chɔ̂ɔp
rest n. (pause)

การหยุดชั่วขณะ gaan-yùt-chûua-kà~nà | (relaxing) การพักผ่อน gaan-pák-pòn

rest *vi.* (relax) พักผ่อน pák-pòn | (take a break) พัก pák, หยุดพัก yùt-pák

restaurant *n.* ร้านอาหาร ráan-aa-hǎan [ร้าน ráan]

restitution *n.* (reparation for loss, damage) ค่าเสียหาย kâa-sǐia-hǎai [จำนวน jam-nuuan]

restless *adj.* กระสับกระส่าย grà~sàp-grà~sàai, อยู่ไม่สุข yùu-mâi-sùk

restore *vt.* (repair) ซ่อมแซม sôm-sɛɛm | (return) คืน kuun | (revive, bring back old) ฟื้นฟู fúun-fuu

restrain *vt.* (hold back from action) ยับยั้ง yáp-yáng, เหนี่ยวรั้ง nìiao-ráng | (imprison) กักตัว gàk-dtuua | (restrict, control) ควบคุมตัว kûuap-kum-dtuua

restrict *vt.* จำกัด jam-gàt

restriction *n.* (condition, regulation) ข้อจำกัด kôo-jam-gàt [ข้อ kôo]

restroom *n.* ห้องน้ำ hôong-náam, ห้องสุขา hôong-sù-kǎa [ห้อง hôong]

result *n.* ผล pǒn, ผลลัพธ์ pǒn-láp [ผล pǒn]

result *vi.* มีผล mii-pǒn

resume *v.* (begin again) เริ่ม_ใหม่ rêəm-_-mài | (continue) ทำ_ต่อ tam-_-dtɔ̀ɔ

résumé *n.* ประวัติย่อ bprà~wàt-yɔ̂ɔ

resurrect *vi.* (rise from the dead) คืนชีพ kuun-chîip

resurrect *vt.* (bring back) นำ_กลับมาใช้ nam-_-glàp-maa-chái

retail *n.* การขายปลีก gaan-kǎai-bpliik

retail *v.* ขายปลีก kǎai-bpliik

retailer *n.* ผู้ขายปลีก pûu-kǎai-bpliik [คน kon (person), ราย raai ! (person)]

retain *vt.* (employ) ว่าจ้าง wâa-jâang | (keep, save) เก็บ_ไว้ gèp-_-wái

retaliate *vi.* แก้แค้น gɛ̂ɛ-kɛ́ɛn

retaliate against see retaliate for

retaliate for *vt.* แก้แค้น gɛ̂ɛ-kɛ́ɛn

retard *n.* (retarded person) คนปัญญาอ่อน kon-bpan-yaa-ɔ̀ɔn [คน kon]

retard *vt.* ทำให้_ช้า tam-hâi-_-cháa

retarded *adj.* ปัญญาอ่อน bpan-yaa-ɔ̀ɔn

retina *n.* จอรับภาพ jɔɔ-ráp-pâap, เรตินา ree-dtì-nâa

retire *vi.* (from work) เกษียณ gà~sĭian, ปลดเกษียณ bplòt-gà~sĭian

retire *vt.* (take out of service) หยุดใช้ yùt-chái

retired *adj.* (from work) เกษียณ gà~sĭian

retiree *n.* ผู้เกษียณ pûu-gà~sĭian [คน kon]

retirement *n.* (e.g. from work) การเกษียณ gaan-gà~sĭian

retort *v.* (reply sharply) พูดย้อน pûut-yɔ́ɔn

retract *v.* (draw back) ดึง_กลับ dʉng-_-glàp

retract one's words *vi.* ถอนคำพูด tɔ̌ɔn-kam-pûut

retreat *n.* (e.g. for meditation) การสงบจิตใจ gaan-sà~ngòp-jìt-jai [ครั้ง kráng]

retreat *vi.* (draw back) ถอย tɔ̌ɔi | (withdraw) ถอนตัว tɔ̌ɔn-dtuua

retrieve *vt.* (get back) เอา_คืนมา ao-_-kʉʉn-maa | (rescue or save) กู้ gûu

return *n.* (e.g. merchandise) ของที่ส่งคืนมา kɔ̌ɔng-tîi-sòng-kʉʉn-maa [ชิ้น chín] | (gain, profit) ผลกำไร pŏn-gam-rai

return *vi.* (turn back, come back) กลับ glàp, กลับคืน glàp-kʉʉn

return *vt.* (give back) คืน kʉʉn

return ticket *n.* (return part of ticket) ตั๋วขากลับ dtŭua-kǎa-glàp [ใบ bai] | (round-trip ticket) ตั๋วไปกลับ dtŭua-bpai-glàp [ใบ bai]

reunite vi. รวมตัวกันใหม่ ruuam-dtuua-gan-mài

reveal vt. เปิดเผย bpèət-pǎai, แสดงให้เห็น sà~dɛɛng-hâi-hĕn

revenge n. การแก้แค้น gaan-gɛ̂ɛ-kɛ́ɛn

revenge v. แก้แค้น gɛ̂ɛ-kɛ́ɛn

revenue n. (gross income) รายได้รวมก่อนหักค่าใช้จ่าย raai-dâai-ruuam-gɔ̀ɔn-hàk-kâa-chái-jàai | (income) รายได้ raai-dâai | (tax) ภาษี paa-sǐi

revere vt. (respect) เคารพ kao-róp

reverse adj. (opposite) ตรงกันข้าม dtrong-gan-kâam

reverse n. (vehicle gear) เกียร์ถอยหลัง giia-tǒɔi-lǎng

reverse vi. (drive in reverse) ถอยรถ tǒɔi-rót

reverse vt. (put in reverse order) เรียง_กลับ riiang-_-glàp | (turn inside out) กลับ glàp

revert vi. กลับสู่สภาพเดิม

glàp-sùu-sà~pâap-dəəm

review n. (critique, evaluation) บทวิจารณ์ bòt-wí-jaan [บท bòt]

review vt. (critique) วิจารณ์ wí-jaan | (study, practice) ทบทวน tóp-tuuan

revise vt. (fix) แก้ gɛ̂ɛ, แก้ไข gɛ̂ɛ-kǎi | (improve) ปรับปรุง bpràp-bprung

revision n. (act) การปรับปรุงแก้ไข gaan-bpràp-bprung-gɛ̂ɛ-kǎi

revive vi. (regain consciousness) ฟื้นคืนสติ fúun-kuun-sà~dtì !

revive vt. (bring back to life) ชุบชีวิต chúp-chii-wít

revoke vt. (withdraw, annul) ถอน tɔ̌ɔn, ยกเลิก yók-lə̂ək

revolt n. (revolution) ปฏิวัติ bpà~dtì-wát

revolting adj. (disgusting) น่ารังเกียจ nâa-rang-gìiat

revolution n. การปฏิวัติ gaan-bpà~dtì~wát, ปฏิวัติ bpà~dtì-wát

revolve v. หมุน mǔn

revolve vi. โคจร koo-jɔɔn

�֎

revolver n. ปืนพก bpʉʉn-pók [กระบอก grà~bɔ̀ɔk]

reward n. รางวัล raang-wan [รางวัล raang-wan]

reward vt. ให้รางวัล hâi-raang-wan

rheumatism n. โรคปวดตามข้อ rôok-bpùuat-dtaam-kɔ̂ɔ [โรค rôok]

rhinoceros n. แรด rɛ̂ɛt [ตัว dtuua]

rhyme n. เสียงสัมผัส sǐiang-sǎm-pàt [เสียง sǐiang]

rhyme vi. สัมผัสกัน sǎm-pàt-gan

rhythm n. จังหวะ jang-wà [จังหวะ jang-wà]

rib n. (bone) ซี่โครง sîi-kroong [ซี่ sîi]

ribbon n. ริบบิ้น ríp-bîn, โบ boo ✿ [ม้วน múuan (roll), เส้น sên (strand)]

rice n. ข้าว kâao [เม็ด mét (grain), กระสอบ grà~sɔ̀ɔp (sack)]

rice field n. ทุ่งนา tûng-naa, นาข้าว naa-kâao, ไร่นา râi-naa [ที่ tîi, แห่ง hɛ̀ng, ผืน pʉ̌ʉn]

rice mill n. โรงสี roong-sǐi [แห่ง hɛ̀ng]

rice porridge n. ข้าวต้ม kâao-dtôm, โจ๊ก jóok [ถ้วย tûuai]

rich adj. (concentrated) เข้มข้น kêm-kôn | (wealthy) รวย ruuai

rid vt. กำจัด gam-jàt, ขจัด kà~jàt

riddle n. (puzzle) ปริศนา bprìt-sà~nǎa [ข้อ kɔ̂ɔ]

ride n. (transport to somewhere) การให้คนไปส่ง gaan-hâi-kon-bpai-sòng

ride v. (in car, boat, plane) นั่ง nâng | (on animal, bicycle) ขี่ kìi

rider n. (one who rides) ผู้ขี่ pûu-kìi [คน kon]

ridge n. สัน sǎn

ridicule vt. ล้อเลียน lɔ́ɔ-liian, หัวเราะเยาะ hǔua-rɔ́-yɔ́

ridiculous adj. (laughable) น่าขัน nâa-kǎn, น่าหัวเราะ nâa-hǔua-rɔ́

rifle *n*. ปืนยาว bpɯɯn-yaao [กระบอก grà~bɔ̀ɔk]

right *adj*. (correct) ถูก tùuk, ถูกต้อง tùuk-dtông | (opposite of left) ขวา kwǎa

right *adv*. (correctly) อย่างถูกต้อง yàang-tùuk-dtông

right *n*. (e.g. legal right) สิทธิ sìt-tí, สิทธิ์ sìt | (side) ข้างขวา kâang-kwǎa

righteous *adj*. ชอบธรรม chɔ̂ɔp-tam

right-handed *adj*. ถนัดขวา tà~nàt-kwǎa

right hand side *adj*. ข้างขวามือ kâang-kwǎa-mɯɯ

right here *adv*. ตรงนี้ dtrong-níi

right side *n*. ข้างขวา kâang-kwǎa

right there *adv*. ตรงนั้น dtrong-nán

rigid *adj*. (inflexible) ไม่ยืดหยุ่น mâi-yɯ̂ɯt-yùn | (strict) เข้มงวด kêm-ngûuat, ไม่ผ่อนปรน mâi-

pɔ̀n-bpron

rim *n*. ขอบ kɔ̀ɔp, ริม rim

rind *n*. (crust, peel) เปลือก bplɯ̀ɯak [ชิ้น chín]

ring *n*. (circle) วง wong [วง wong] | (circular band of any kind) วงแหวน wong-wɛ̌ɛn [วง wong] | (for fighting or racing) สนามแข่ง sà~nǎam-kɛ̀ng [แห่ง hɛ̀ng] | (hoop, loop) ห่วง hùuang [ห่วง hùuang] | (jewelry) แหวน wɛ̌ɛn [วง wong]

ring *v*. (e.g. a bell) สั่น sàn

ring *vt*. (call on phone) โทรศัพท์ถึง too-rá~sàp-tǔng | (encircle) ล้อม lɔ́ɔm

ring finger *n*. นิ้วนาง níu-naang [นิ้ว níu]

ringworm *n*. ขี้กลาก kîi-glàak [โรค rôok]

rink *n*. (ice) ลานสเก็ตน้ำแข็ง laan-sà~gèt-nám-kɛ̌ng [แห่ง hɛ̀ng]

rinse *vt*. ล้าง láang, ล้างสบู่ออกจาก_ láang-sà~bùu-ɔ̀ɔk-jàak-_

riot *n*. การจลาจล gaan-jà~

laa-jon

riot *vi.* ก่อการจลาจล gòɔ-gaan-jà~laa-jon

rip *n.* (tear) รอยฉีก rɔɔi-chìik [รอย rɔɔi]

rip *v.* (tear) ฉีก chìik, ผ่า pàa

ripe *adj.* สุก sùk

ripen *vt.* ทำให้_สุก tam-hâi-_-sùk

ripple *n.* ระลอกคลื่น rá~lɔ̂ɔk-klɯ̂ɯn [ลูก lûuk]

ripple *vi.* กระเพื่อม grà~pɯ̂am

rise *n.* (advancement) การเลื่อนขึ้น gaan-lɯ̂an-kɯ̂n | (increase) การเพิ่มขึ้น gaan-pɤ̂ɤm-kɯ̂n

rise *vi.* (e.g. sun, price) ขึ้น kɯ̂n | (from bed, stand up, etc.) ลุก lúk, ลุกขึ้น lúk-kɯ̂n

rising tone *n.* เสียงจัตวา sǐiang-jàt-dtà~waa [เสียง sǐiang]

risk *n.* (danger) ความเสี่ยง kwaam-sìiang

risk *v.* เสี่ยง sìiang

risky *adj.* เป็นอันตราย

bpen-an-dtà~raai, เสี่ยง sìiang

rite *n.* (formality) แบบแผน bɛ̀ɛp-pɛ̌ɛn

ritual *n.* พิธี pí-tii [พิธี pí-tii]

rival *n.* คู่แข่ง kûu-kɛ̀ng [คน kon]

river *n.* แม่น้ำ mɛ̂ɛ-náam [สาย sǎai]

roach *n.* แมลงสาบ má~lɛɛng-sàap [ตัว dtuua]

road *n.* ทาง taang [สาย sǎai, เส้น sên] | ถนน tà~nǒn [เส้น sên, สาย sǎai]

roam *vi.* ท่องเที่ยวไป tɔ̂ng-tîiao-bpai

roar *n.* เสียงคำราม sǐiang-kam-raam

roar *vi.* คำราม kam-raam

roast *n.* เนื้ออบ nɯ́a-òp [ชิ้น chín]

roast *vt.* (bake) อบ òp | (grill) ย่าง yâang | (toast) ปิ้ง bpîng

rob *vt.* จี้ jîi, ปล้น bplôn

robber *n.* โจร joon [คน kon]

robbery *n.* การปล้น gaan-bplôn, โจรกรรม joo-rá~gam

robe n. เสื้อคลุม sûua-klum [ตัว dtuua]

robot n. หุ่นยนต์ hùn-yon [ตัว dtuua]

robust adj. (muscular) กำยำ gam-yam | (sturdy) แข็งแกร่ง kěng-grèng

rock n. (music) ดนตรีร็อค don-dtrii-rɔ́k | (stone) ก้อน gɔ̂ɔn, ก้อนหิน gɔ̂ɔn-hǐn, หิน hǐn [ก้อน gɔ̂ɔn]

rock v. ไกว gwai, โยก yôok

rocker n. (chair) เก้าอี้โยก gâo-îi-yôok [ตัว dtuua]

rocket n. จรวด jà~rùuat [ลำ lam] | (bamboo) บ้องไฟ bɔ̂ng-fai [บ้อง bɔ̂ng]

rocking chair n. เก้าอี้โยก gâo-îi-yôok [ตัว dtuua]

rocky adj. (full of rocks) มีหินมาก mii-hǐn-mâak | (unstable) ไม่มั่นคง mâi-mân-kong

rod n. (fishing) คันเบ็ด kan-bèt [คัน kan]

roe n. (fish) ไข่ปลา kài-bplaa [เม็ด mét (one)]

role n. บทบาท bòt-bàat

roll n. (anything rolled up) ม้วน múuan [ม้วน múuan]

roll v. (along, e.g. wheel, pencil on table) กลิ้ง glîng

roll vt. (up into roll, e.g. carpet, scroll) ม้วน_เข้า múuan-_-kâo

roll call n. การขานชื่อ gaan-kǎan-chûu

roller n. (small wheel) ลูกกลิ้ง lûuk-glîng [อัน an]

roller coaster n. รถไฟเหาะ rót-fai-hɔ̀ [เครื่อง krûuang]

roller skate n. รองเท้าสเก็ต rwong-táao-sà~gét [ข้าง kâang (one), คู่ kûu (pair)]

roll-on n. (deodorant) ลูกกลิ้ง lûuk-glîng [ขวด kùuat]

roll out vt. (unroll) ม้วน_ออก múuan-_-ɔ̀ɔk

roll up vi. ม้วนตัว múuan-dtuua

roll up vt. ม้วน_เข้า múuan-_-kâo | (e.g. sleeve, pant leg) ถลก tà~lòk

Roman Catholic n. นิกายโรมันคาทอลิก ní-

gaai-roo-man-kaa-tɔɔ-lìk
[นิกาย ní-gaai]

romance *n.* การรักใคร่
gaan-rák-krâi

romantic *adj.* โรแมนติก
roo-mɛɛn-dtìk

roof *n.* หลังคา lǎng-kaa
[หลังคา lǎng-kaa]

room *n.* (chamber of any
kind) ห้อง hɔ̂ng [ห้อง
hɔ̂ng] | (open space)
ที่ว่าง tîi-wâang

room *v.* พักอยู่ pák-yùu

roommate *n.*
เพื่อนร่วมห้อง pɯ̂uan-
rûuam-hɔ̂ng [คน kon]

room service *n.*
บริการในห้องพัก bɔɔ-rí~
gaan-nai-hɔ̂ng-pák

roomy *adj.* กว้าง gwâang

roost *n.* (perch) คอน kɔɔn
[คอน kɔɔn]

roost *vi.* (e.g. birds)
เกาะนอน gɔ̀-nɔɔn

rooster *n.* ไก่ตัวผู้ gài-
dtuua-pûu, พ่อไก่ pɔ̂ɔ-gài
[ตัว dtuua]

root *n.* (ancestor) รากเหง้า
râak-ngâo | (e.g. of
plant) ราก râak [ราก râak]

root *vi.* (grow roots)

งอกราก ngɔ̂ɔk-râak

rope *n.* เชือก chɯ̂uak [เส้น
sên (cord)]

rose *n.* กุหลาบ gù-làap
[ช่อ chɔ̂ɔ (bunch), ดอก
dɔ̀ɔk (flower), ต้น dtôn
(plant)]

rosemary *n.* โรสแมรี่
róos-mɛɛ-rîi [ต้น dtôn]

rosy *adj.* (color) สีกุหลาบ
sǐi-gù-làap

rot *vi.* เน่าเปื่อย nâo-
bpɯ̀uai, ผุ pù

rotate *v.* (spin) หมุน mǔn

rotate *vi.* (take turns)
สับเปลี่ยน sàp-bplìian,
หมุนเวียน mǔn-wiian

rotation *n.* การหมุนเวียน
gaan-mǔn-wiian

rotten *adj.* เน่า nâo, บูด
bùut, ผุ pù

rouge *n.* ที่ทาแก้ม tîi-taa-
gɛ̂ɛm, รูจ rúut

rough *adj.* (bumpy)
ขรุขระ krù-krà | (crude)
หยาบ yàap | (e.g. draft)
คร่าวๆ krâao-krâao

round *adj.* (circular) กลม
glom, เป็นวงกลม bpen-
wong-glom

round *n.* (boxing) ยก yók [ยก yók] **|** (sports) รอบ rɔ̂ɔp [รอบ rɔ̂ɔp]

round *prep.* (around) รอบๆ rɔ̂ɔp-rɔ̂ɔp

roundabout *adj.* วกวน wók-won, อ้อม ʔɔ̂ɔm

roundabout *n.* (traffic circle) วงเวียน wong-wiian [แห่ง hɛ̀ng]

round down *vt.* (to whole number) ปัด_ลง bpàt-_-long

round-the-clock *adj.* ตลอดเวลา dtà~lɔ̀ɔt-wee-laa

round trip *adj.* ไปกลับ bpai-glàp

round-trip ticket *n.* ตั๋วไปกลับ dtǔua-bpai-glàp [ใบ bai]

round up *vt.* (e.g. herd) ต้อน dtɔ̂ɔn **|** (to whole number) ปัด_ขึ้น bpàt-_-kûn

rouse *vt.* (stimulate) กระตุ้น grà~dtûn

route *n.* ทาง taang, เส้นทาง sên-taang [สาย sǎai, เส้น sên]

routine *adj.* (habitual) เป็นกิจวัตร bpen-gìt-jà~wát

routine *n.* กิจวัตร gìt-jà~wát

row *n.* แถว tɛ̌ɛo [แถว tɛ̌ɛo]

row *v.* พาย paai

row a boat *vi.* พายเรือ paai-ruua

royal *adj.* หลวง lǔuang

royalty *n.* (e.g. for author, composer) ค่าลิขสิทธิ์ kâa-lík-kà~sìt

rub *vt.* (scrub) ขัด kàt, ถู tǔu

rubber *adj.* ยาง yaang

rubber *n.* (elastic substance) ยาง yaang **|** (eraser) ยางลบ yaang-lóp [อัน an]

rubber band *n.* ยางรัด yaang-rát [เส้น sên]

rubbish *n.* (trash) ขยะ kà~yà [ชิ้น chín (piece), กอง gɔɔng (pile)]

rubella *n.* หัดเยอรมัน hàt-yəən-rá~man [โรค rôok]

rub it in *vi.* ซ้ำเติม sám-dtəəm

ruby *n.* (gem) ทับทิม táp-tim [เม็ด mét]

rude *adj.* หยาบ yàap,

หยาบคาย yàap-kaai

rug *n.* พรม prom [ผืน pǔɯn]

rugby *n.* (sport) รักบี้ rák-bîi

ruin *n.* (remains) ซากปรักหักพัง sâak-bpà~rák-hàk-pang [ชิ้น chín]

ruin *vt.* (destroy) ทำลาย tam-laai

rule *n.* กฎ gòt, กฎระเบียบ gòt-rá~bìiap ! [ข้อ kɔ̂ɔ] | (in sports) กติกา gà-dtì~gaa [ข้อ kɔ̂ɔ] | (principle, standard) หลักเกณฑ์ làk-geen [หลัก làk] | (regulation) ข้อบังคับ kɔ̂ɔ-bang-káp [ข้อ kɔ̂ɔ]

rule *vi.* (govern) ปกครอง bpòk-krɔɔng | (in court) ตัดสิน dtàt-sǐn

ruler *n.* (leader) ผู้ปกครอง pûu-bpòk-krɔɔng [ท่าน tân !, คน kon] | (measuring) ไม้บรรทัด máai-ban-tát [อัน an, เล่ม lêm]

ruling *n.* (verdict) คำตัดสิน kam-dtàt-sǐn

rum *n.* เหล้ารัม lâo-ram

[ขวด kùuat (bottle), แก้ว gɛ̂ɛo (glass)]

rumor *n.* ข่าวลือ kàao-lɯɯ [ข่าว kàao, เรื่อง rɯ̂ɯang]

rumor *vt.* ลือ lɯɯ

rump *n.* (buttocks) สะโพก sà~pôok

run *v.* (jog) วิ่ง wîng

run *vt.* (computer program) เปิด bpəət | (have duration) ใช้เวลา chái-wee-laa

run an errand *vi.* วิ่งทำธุระ wîng-tam-tú-rá

run away *vi.* วิ่งหนี wîng-nǐi

run for *vt.* (office) เข้าชิงตำแหน่ง kâo-ching-dtam-nὲng

run into *vt.* พบ_โดยบังเอิญ póp-_-dooi-bang-əən

runner *n.* นักวิ่ง nák-wîng [คน kon]

runner-up *n.* รองชนะเลิศ rɔɔng-chá~ná~lə̂ət [คน kon]

run out *vi.* (be used up) หมด mòt | (jog out) วิ่งออกไป wîng-ɔ̀ɔk-bpai

runway *n.* (airplane)

ทางบินขึ้นลง taang-bin-kûn-long [ทาง taang]

rural *adj.* ชนบท chon-ná~bòt, บ้านนอก bâan-nɔ̂ɔk ☙

rural area *n.* ชนบท chon-ná~bòt [แห่ง hɛ̀ng]

ruse *n.* เล่ห์กล lêe-gon, อุบาย ù-baai [อัน an]

rush *n.* ความเร่งรีบ kwaam-rêng-rîip

rush *v.* เร่ง rêng

rush hour *n.* ชั่วโมงเร่งด่วน chûua-moong-rêng-dùuan

Russia *n.* รัสเซีย rát-siia [ประเทศ bprà~têet]

Russian *n.* (language) ภาษารัสเซีย paa-sǎa-rát-siia [ภาษา paa-sǎa] | (people) ชาวรัสเซีย chaao-rát-siia [คน kon]

rust *n.* สนิม sà~nǐm

rust *vi.* เป็นสนิม bpen-sà~nǐm

rustic *adj.* (of rural area) บ้านนอก bâan-nɔ̂ɔk ☙

rustic *n.* (bumpkin) คนบ้านนอก kon-bâan-nɔ̂ɔk [คน kon]

rusty *adj.* เป็นสนิม bpen-

sà~nǐm | (out of practice) ขาดการฝึกฝน kàat-gaan-fùk-fǒn

ruthless *adj.* โหดเหี้ยม hòot-hîiam

rye *n.* ข้าวไรย์ kâao-rai

S

sack *n.* (bag) ถุง tǔng [ใบ bai] | (for rice) กระสอบ grà~sɔ̀ɔp [ใบ bai] | (satchel) ย่าม yâam [ใบ bai]

sacred *adj.* (consecrated) เป็นที่บูชา bpen-tîi-buu-chaa | (holy) ศักดิ์สิทธิ์ sàk-sìt

sacrifice *n.* (item offered to god) เครื่องเซ่น krûuang-sên [อย่าง yàang (kind), สำรับ sǎm-ráp (set)] | (offer to god) การบวงสรวง gaan-buuang-sǔuang

sacrifice *v.* (devote) เสียสละ sǐia-sà~là | (kill as a sacrifice) บูชายัญ buu-chaa-yan | (offer to god) บวงสรวง buuang-sǔuang

sad *adj.* เศร้า sâo, เสียใจ

sĭia-jai

sadden *vt.* ทำให้_เสียใจ tam-hâi-_-sĭia-jai

saddle *n.* (e.g. bicycle, motorcycle) อานรถ aan-rót [อัน an] | (for horse) อานม้า aan-máa [อัน an]

sadistic *adj.* ซาดิสต์ saa-dìt

sadness *n.* ความเศร้า kwaam-sâo, ความเสียใจ kwaam-sĭia-jai, โทมนัส toom-má~nát ✍

safe *adj.* (not dangerous) ปลอดภัย bplɔ̀ɔt-pai

safe-deposit box *n.* ตู้เซฟ dtûu-séep, ตู้นิรภัย dtûu-ní-rá~pai ‼ [ใบ bai]

safe sex *n.* การมีเพศสัมพันธ์ที่ปลอดภัย gaan-mii-pêet-sǎm-pan-tîi-bplɔ̀ɔt-pai

safety *adj.* (preventing harm) นิรภัย ní-rá~pai

safety *n.* (being safe) ความปลอดภัย kwaam-bplɔ̀ɔt-pai

safety belt *n.* เข็มขัดนิรภัย kĕm-kàt-ní-rá~pai [เส้น sên]

safety pin *n.* เข็มกลัด kĕm-glàt [ตัว dtuua]

sag *vi.* (hang down unevenly) หย่อนลง yɔ̀n-long

sage *n.* (herb) ผกากรอง pà~gaa-grɔɔng [ต้น dtôn] | (wise man) นักปราชญ์ nák-bpràat [คน kon]

Sagittarius *n.* ราศีธนู raa-sĭi-tá~nuu [ราศี raa-sĭi]

sago *n.* สาคู sǎa-kuu [เม็ด mét]

sail *n.* (boat) ใบเรือ bai-ruua [ใบ bai]

sail *vi.* (cruise) แล่นเรือ lɛ̂n-ruua

sailboat *n.* เรือใบ ruua-bai [ลำ lam]

sailor *n.* (crew) กะลาสี gà~laa-sĭi, ลูกเรือ lûuk-ruua [คน kon]

saint *n.* นักบุญ nák-bun [รูป rûup]

sake *n.* (benefit) ผลประโยชน์ pǒn-bprà~yòot | (drink) เหล้าสาเก lâo-sǎa-gee [ขวด kùuat (bottle)]

salad *n.* สลัด sà~làt [จาน jaan (plate)]

salary *n.* เงินเดือน ngən-

duuan [จำนวน jam-
nuuan]
sale *n.* (act) การขาย
gaan-kǎai | (discount)
การขายของลดราคา
gaan-kǎai-kǒɔng-lót-
raa-kaa [ครั้ง kráng]
salesperson *n.* คนขาย
kon-kǎai, พนักงานขาย
pá~nák-ngaan-kǎai ‼
[คน kon]
sales representative *n.*
ตัวแทนฝ่ายขาย dtuua-
tɛɛn-fàai-kǎai [คน kon]
sales tax *n.* ภาษีการขาย
paa-sǐi-gaan-kǎai
saline solution *n.* น้ำเกลือ
nám-gluua [ขวด kùuat
(bottle)]
saliva *n.* น้ำลาย nám-laai
salmon *n.* ปลาแซลมอน
bplaa-sɛɛn-mɔ̂n [ตัว
dtuua (whole), ชิ้น chín
(piece)]
salon *n.* (beauty)
ร้านเสริมสวย ráan-sɤ̌ɤm-
sǔai [ร้าน ráan] | (hall)
ห้องโถง hɔ̂ng-tǒong [ห้อง
hɔ̂ng]
salt *n.* (table salt) เกลือ
gluua [ถุง tǔng (bag),

เม็ด mét (drop)]
salt water *n.* น้ำเค็ม nám-
kem
salty *adj.* เค็ม kem
salute *v.* (greet, bow)
คำนับ kam-náp
salvage *v.* กู้ gûu
same *adj.* (similar)
เหมือนกัน mǔuan-gan |
(unchanged) เหมือนเดิม
mǔuan-dɤɤm
same as *adv.* เช่นเดียวกับ
chên-diiao-gàp
sample *n.* ตัวอย่าง dtuua-
yàang [อัน an ✿, ตัวอย่าง
dtuua-yàang]
sanction *vt.* (approve)
อนุมัติ à-nú-mát |
(punish) ลงโทษ long-tôot
sand *n.* ทราย saai [เม็ด
mét (grain)]
sandal *n.* รองเท้าแตะ
rɔɔng-táao-dtɛ̀ [ข้าง
kâang (one), คู่ kûu (pair)]
sandpaper *n.*
กระดาษทราย grà~dàat-
saai [แผ่น pɛ̀n]
sandwich *n.* แซนด์วิช
sɛɛn-wít [อัน an]
sandwich *vt.* (_ between
_) ประกบ_ระหว่าง_

bprà~gòp-_-rá~wàang-_
sandy *adj.* (full of sand)
มีทรายมาก mii-saai-mâak
sane *adj.* (not mad) ไม่บ้า
mâi-bâa | (sensible)
มีเหตุผล mii-hèet-pǒn
sanitary *adj.*
ถูกหลักอนามัย tùuk-làk-
à~naa-mai
sanitary napkin *n.*
ผ้าอนามัย pâa-à~naa-mai
[แผ่น pèn]
Sanskrit *n.* สันสกฤต săn-
sà~grìt [ภาษา paa-săa]
Santa Claus *n.*
ซานตาคลอส saan-dtaa-
klɔ́ɔs [คน kon]
santol *n.* กระท้อน grà~
tɔ́ɔn [ลูก lûuk]
sapota *n.* ละมุด lá~mút
[ลูก lûuk]
sapphire *n.* นิลสีคราม
nin-sǐi-kraam [เม็ด mét,
ก้อน gɔ̂ɔn]
sarcastic *adj.* เสียดสี sìiat-
sǐi
sardine *n.* ปลาซาร์ดีน
bplaa-saa-diin [ตัว dtuua]
sarong *n.* โสร่ง sà~ròong
[ผืน pǔun]
sash *n.* สายคาด sǎai-kâat

[เส้น sên, สาย sǎai]
sashimi *n.* ซาชิมิ saa-
chí~mí [ชิ้น chín]
Satan *n.* ซาตาน saa-dtaan
[ตน dton]
satchel *n.* ย่าม yâam [ใบ
bai]
satellite *n.* (astronomy)
ดาวบริวาร daao-bɔɔ-rí~
waan [ดวง duuang] |
(man-made) ดาวเทียม
daao-tiiam [ดวง duuang]
satin *n.* ผ้าต่วน pâa-
dtùuan [ผืน pǔun]
satire *n.* การเสียดสี gaan-
sìiat-sǐi
satisfaction *n.*
(contentment) ความพอใจ
kwaam-pɔɔ-jai
satisfactory *adj.* น่าพอใจ
nâa-pɔɔ-jai
satisfied *adj.* พอใจ pɔɔ-jai
| (fulfilled) สะใจ sà-jai
satisfy *vt.* (please)
ทำให้_พอใจ tam-hâi-_-
pɔɔ-jai
saturate *vt.* (fill
completely) ทำให้_อิ่มตัว
tam-hâi-_-ìm-dtuua |
(make wet) ทำให้_โชก
tam-hâi-_-chôok

Saturday *n.* วันเสาร์ wan-sǎo [วัน wan]

Saturn *n.* ดาวเสาร์ daao-sǎo [ดวง duuang]

sauce *n.* ซอส rɔ́ɔt, น้ำจิ้ม nám-jîm [ขวด kùuat (bottle)]

saucer *n.* ถ้วยรอง tûuai-rɔɔng [ใบ bai]

sausage *n.* ไส้กรอก sâi-grɔ̀ɔk [ชิ้น chín]

savage *adj.* (barbarous) ป่าเถื่อน bpàa-tὺuan | (fierce) ดุร้าย dù-ráai

save *vt.* (keep, store) เก็บ_ไว้ gèp-_-wái | (life of) ช่วยชีวิต chûuai-chii-wít | (situation or face) กู้ gûu

save money *vi.* เก็บเงิน gèp-ngən

savings account *n.* บัญชีเงินฝากออมทรัพย์ ban-chii-ngən-fàak-ɔɔm-sáp [บัญชี ban-chii]

savior *n.* (rescuer) ผู้ช่วยชีวิต pûu-chûuai-chii-wít [คน kon]

savor *vt.* (enjoy) เพลิดเพลินกับ plə̂ət-pləən-gàp

saw *n.* เลื่อย lὺuai [ปื้น bpὺɯn]

saw *v.* เลื่อย lὺuai

sawdust *n.* ขี้เลื่อย kîi-lὺuai

saxophone *n.* แซกโซโฟน sék-soo-foon [เครื่อง krὺuang]

say *vt.* (state) บอก bɔ̀ɔk, กล่าว glàao ⚡, ว่า wâa ✸

saying *n.* (proverb) คำพังเพย kam-pang-pəəi [บท bòt]

scab *n.* (wound) สะเก็ดแผล sà~gèt-plɛ̌ɛ [สะเก็ด sà~gèt]

scabies *n.* หิด hìt [โรค rôok (disease)]

scale *n.* (fish) เกล็ด glèt [เกล็ด glèt] | (music) บันไดเสียง ban-dai-sǐiang [ขั้น kân] | (weighing) ตาชั่ง dtaa-châng [คัน kan, เครื่อง krὺuang] | (weighing) เครื่องชั่งน้ำหนัก krὺuang-châng-nám-nàk [เครื่อง krὺuang]

scallop *n.* หอยพัด hɔ̌ɔi-pát

[ตัว dtuua]

scalp n. หนังหัว nǎng-hǔua, หนังศีรษะ nǎng-sǐi-sà

scan vt. (computing) สแกน sà~gɛɛn | (glance) ดู_เผินๆ duu-_-pǒen-pǒen

scandal n. เรื่องอื้อฉาว rûuang-ûu-chǎao [เรื่อง rûuang]

scanner n. เครื่องสแกน krûuang-sà~gɛɛn [เครื่อง krûuang]

scapegoat n. แพะรับบาป pé-ráp-bàap [ตัว dtuua (goat), คน kon (human)]

scar n. แผลเป็น plɛ̌ɛ-bpen [แห่ง hɛ̀ng, ที่ tîi]

scar vt. ทำให้_เป็นแผลเป็น tam-hâi-_-bpen-plɛ̌ɛ-bpen

scarce adj. (deficient) ขาดแคลน kàat-klɛɛn

scare vt. ทำให้_กลัว tam-hâi-_-gluua

scarecrow n. หุ่นไล่กา hùn-lâi-gaa [ตัว dtuua]

scared adj. กลัว gluua, ตกใจกลัว dtòk-jai-gluua, หวาดกลัว wàat-gluua ‼

scarf n. ผ้าพันคอ pâa-pan-kɔɔ [ผืน pǔɯn]

scarlet adj. สีเลือดหมู sǐi-lûuat-mǔu

scary adj. น่ากลัว nâa-gluua, สยองขวัญ sà~yɔ̌ɔng-kwǎn ‼

scatter vi. เกลื่อน glùuan, เกลื่อนกลาด glùuan-glàat ‼

scatter vt. กระจาย grà~jaai

scene n. (in story) ฉาก chàak [ฉาก chàak] | (place where something happens) จุดเกิดเหตุ jùt-gòet-hèet [แห่ง hɛ̀ng]

scenery n. (spectacle) ทิวทัศน์ tiu-tát [แห่ง hɛ̀ng]

scent n. (odor) กลิ่น glìn | (perfume) น้ำหอม nám-hɔ̌ɔm [กลิ่น glìn (scent), ขวด kùuat (bottle)]

schedule n. (agenda) รายการ raai-gaan [รายการ raai-gaan (list or list item)] | (timetable) ตารางเวลา dtaa-raang-wee-laa [ตาราง dtaa-raang (table), รายการ raai-gaan (item)]

schedule *vt.* (make a schedule) จัดตาราง jàt-dtaa-raang | (plan) วางแผน waang-pĕen

scheme *n.* (nefarious plan) แผนร้าย pĕen-ráai [แผน pĕen] | (program) โครงการ kroong-gaan [โครงการ kroong-gaan, อัน an]

schizophrenia *n.* จิตฟั่นเฟือน jìt-fân-fɯɯan

scholar *n.* (academic) นักวิชาการ nák-wí-chaa-gaan [คน kon] | (college student) นักศึกษา nák-sɯ̀k-sǎa [คน kon] | (student awarded money) นักเรียนทุน nák-riian-tun [คน kon]

scholarship *n.* ทุนการศึกษา tun-gaan-sɯ̀k-sǎa [ทุน tun]

school *n.* โรงเรียน roong-riian [แห่ง hɛ̀ng] | (college) วิทยาลัย wít-tá~yaa-lai [แห่ง hɛ̀ng]

science *n.* วิทยาศาสตร์ wít-tá~yaa-sàat [วิชา wí-chaa]

scientific *adj.*

ทางวิทยาศาสตร์ taang-wít-tá~yaa-sàat

scientist *n.* นักวิทยาศาสตร์ nák-wít-tá~yaa-sàat [คน kon]

scissors *n.* กรรไกร gan-grai, ตะไกร dtà~grai ✿ [เล่ม lêm]

scold *vt.* ด่า dàa, ดุ dù, ดุด่า dù-dàa

scone *n.* ขนมปังสโคน kà~nǒm-bpang-sà~koon [ชิ้น chín]

scoop *n.* (news) ข่าวด่วน kàao-dùuan [เรื่อง rɯ̂ɯang] | (utensil) ที่ตัก tîi-dtàk [อัน an]

scoop *vt.* (e.g. rice, curry, sand) ตัก dtàk

scooter *n.* (motor) มอเตอร์ไซค์เล็ก mɔɔ-dtəə-sai-lék [คัน kan]

scope *n.* (range) ขอบเขต kɔ̀ɔp-kèet [ขอบเขต kɔ̀ɔp-kèet] | (range) ขอบข่าย kɔ̀ɔp-kàai [ขอบข่าย kɔ̀ɔp-kàai]

score *n.* (e.g. test, game) คะแนน ká~nɛɛn [คะแนน ká~nɛɛn] | (music)

โน้ตเพลง nóot-pleeng [เพลง pleeng (song), แผ่น pèn (CD, sheet of music)]

score vi. (gain point) ทำคะแนน tam-ká~nɛɛn | (keep score) นับแต้ม náp-dtɛ̂ɛm

scorn vt. (disdain) ดูหมิ่น duu-mìn

Scorpio n. ราศีพิจิก raa-sǐi-pí-jìk [ราศี raa-sǐi]

scorpion n. แมงป่อง mɛɛng-bpɔ̀ng [ตัว dtuua]

Scotch tape n. เทปติดกระดาษ téep-dtìt-grà~dàat, สก๊อตเทป sà~gɔ́t-téep ● [ม้วน múuan]

scoundrel n. คนชั่ว kon-chûua [คน kon]

scout n. (seeker, e.g. talent scout) แมวมอง mɛɛo-mɔɔng [คน kon]

scout v. (spy on) สอดแนม sɔ̀ɔt-nɛɛm

scrabble n. (game) สแครบเบิ้ล sà~krép-bên [เกม geem]

scramble vt. (egg) ตี dtii | (mix) ผสม pà~sǒm

scrap n. (small piece) เศษ sèet [ชิ้น chín]

scrape vt. ขูด kùut, ถาก tàak

scrape off vt. ขูด_ออก kùut-_-ɔ̀ɔk

scratch n. (mark) รอยข่วน rɔɔi-kùuan [รอย rɔɔi]

scratch vt. เกา gao | (e.g. with fingernails) ข่วน kùuan | (scrape with a pen) ขีด kìit

scratch out vt. (cross out) ขีดฆ่า kìit-kâa

scream n. เสียงกรีดร้อง sǐiang-grìit-rɔ́ɔng

scream vi. กรีดร้อง grìit-rɔ́ɔng

screen n. (curtain) ม่าน mâan [ผืน pǔɯn] | (monitor) จอ jɔɔ [จอ jɔɔ, ผืน pǔɯn] | (mosquito) มุ้งลวด múng-lûuat [อัน an]

screen vt. (select) คัดเลือก kát-lɯ̂ɯak

screw n. (metal) ตะปูควง dtà~bpuu-kuuang, สกรู sà~gruu [ตัว dtuua]

screw vt. (have sex with) มีเซ็กส์กับ mii-sék-gàp |

(rotate, e.g. fastener) ขัน
kăn

screwdriver *n.* ไขควง
kăi-kuuang [อัน an, เล่ม
lêm]

scribble *vt.* (writing)
เขียน_หวัด kĭian-_-wàt

script *n.* (manuscript)
ต้นฉบับ dtôn-chà~bàp
[ฉบับ chà~bàp] | (play)
บทละคร bòt-lá~kɔɔn [บท
bòt]

scrub *vt.* (rub) ขัด kàt, ถู
tŭu

scrutinize *vt.*
ตรวจ_อย่างละเอียด
dtrùuat-_-yàang-lá~iiat

scuba diver *n.*
นักประดาน้ำ nák-bprà~
daa-náam ⚠ [คน kon]

sculptor *n.* (carver)
ช่างแกะสลัก châang-gὲ-
sà~làk [คน kon]

sculpture *n.* (art work)
รูปแกะสลัก rûup-gὲ-sà~
làk [ชิ้น chín]

scurvy *n.*
โรคเลือดออกตามไรฟัน
rôok-lûuat-ɔ̀ɔk-dtaam-
rai-fan [โรค rôok]

sea *n.* ทะเล tá~lee [แห่ง
hὲng]

seafood *n.* อาหารทะเล
aa-hăan-tá~lee [ชนิด
chá~nít (type)]

seahorse *n.* ม้าน้ำ máa-
náam [ตัว dtuua]

seal *n.* (animal) แมวน้ำ
mɛɛo-náam [ตัว dtuua] |
(stamp) ตรา dtraa [ตรา
dtraa] | (stamp)
ตราประทับ dtraa-bprà~
táp ⚠ [ตรา dtraa, อัน an]

seal *vt.* (e.g. a letter)
ปิดผนึก bpìt-pà~nừk |
(mark with a seal)
ประทับตรา bprà~táp-
dtraa

sea lion *n.* สิงห์โตทะเล
sĭng-dtoo-tá~lee [ตัว
dtuua]

seam *n.* ตะเข็บผ้า dtà~
kèp-pâa [ตะเข็บ dtà~kèp]

seaman *n.* ชาวทะเล
chaao-tá~lee [คน kon]

seamstress *n.* หญิงเย็บผ้า
yĭng-yép-pâa [คน kon]

search *n.* (act) การค้นหา
gaan-kón-hăa

search for *vt.* ค้น kón,
ค้นหา kón-hăa

searchlight *n.* ไฟฉาย fai-chǎai [กระบอก grà~bɔ̀ɔk, อัน an]

search warrant *n.* หมายค้น mǎai-kón [ฉบับ chà~bàp]

seashore *n.* ชายทะเล chaai-tá~lee [แห่ง hὲng]

seasick *adj.* เมาคลื่น mao-klûɯn, เมาเรือ mao-rɯɯa

seaside *adj.* ชายทะเล chaai-tá~lee

season *n.* ฤดู rɯ́-duu [ฤดู rɯ́-duu] | หน้า nâa [หน้า nâa]

season *vt.* (flavor) ปรุงรส bprung-rót

seasonal *adj.* ตามฤดูกาล dtaam-rɯ́-duu-gaan

seat *n.* ที่นั่ง tîi-nâng [ที่ tîi]

seat *vt.* (provide with seats) จัดที่นั่งให้ jàt-tîi-nâng-hâi

seat belt *n.* เข็มขัดนิรภัย kěm-kàt-ní-rá~pai [เส้น sên]

seawater *n.* น้ำทะเล nám-tá~lee

seaweed *n.* สาหร่ายทะเล sǎa-ràai-tá~lee [แผ่น pèn]

secluded *adj.* (isolated) เก็บตัว gèp-dtuua,

สันโดษ sǎn-dòot

second *adj.* ที่สอง tîi-rʉ̌ɯng

second *n.* (time) วินาที wí-naa-tii [วินาที wí-naa-tii]

secondary *adj.* (minor) ไม่สำคัญมาก mâi-sǎm-kan-mâak, รอง rɔɔng

secondary school *n.* โรงเรียนมัธยมต้น roong-riian-mát-tá~yom-dtôn [แห่ง hὲng]

second-hand *adj.* มือสอง mɯɯ-sʉ̌ɯng

secret *adj.* เป็นความลับ bpen-kwaam-láp, ลับ láp

secretary *n.* เลขา lee-kǎa, เลขานุการ lee-kǎa-nú-gaan ! [คน kon]

sect *n.* (religious) นิกาย ní-gaai [นิกาย ní-gaai]

section *n.* (chapter, part) ตอน dtɔɔn [ตอน dtɔɔn] | (division) ภาค pâak | (item) ข้อ kɔ̂ɔ [ข้อ kɔ̂ɔ] | (part) ส่วน sùuan [ส่วน sùuan]

sector *n.* (division) ภาค pâak

secular *adj.* ทางโลก taang-lôok

secure *adj.* (firm) มั่นคง mân-kong | (safe) ปลอดภัย bplɔ̀ɔt-pai

secure *vt.* (guarantee) รับรอง ráp-rɔɔng | (make safe) ทำให้_ปลอดภัย tam-hâi-_-bplɔ̀ɔt-pai

security *n.* (guarantee) หลักประกัน làk-bprà~gan [อัน an] | (stability) ความมั่นคง kwaam-mân-kong

security guard *n.* ยาม yaam, ผู้รักษาความปลอดภัย pûu-rák-sǎa kwaam bplɔ̀ɔt-pai ❗ [คน kon]

sedan *n.* รถเก๋ง rót-gěng [คัน kan]

sedation *n.* (tranquilization) การระงับประสาท gaan-rá~ngáp-bprà~sàat

sediment *n.* ตะกอน dtà~gɔɔn

seduce *vt.* (lure) หลอกล่อ lɔ̀ɔk-lɔ̂ɔ | (tempt) ยั่วยวน yûua-yuuan

see *vt.* (get to know, date) คบหา kóp-hǎa | (visit) เยี่ยม yîiam | (with eyes) มอง mɔɔng, เห็น hěn

seed *n.* (grain) เมล็ด má~lét ❗ [เม็ด mét, เมล็ด má~lét ❗] | (grain) เม็ด mét [เม็ด mét]

seek *vt.* (search for) ค้นหา kón-hǎa

seem *vt.* ดูเหมือนว่า duu-mǔuan-wâa, ราวกับว่า raao-gàp-wâa

seesaw *n.* กระดานหก grà~daan-hòk [อัน an]

segment *n.* (division) ตอน dtɔɔn [ตอน dtɔɔn] | (part) ส่วน sùuan [ส่วน sùuan]

segregate *vt.* (separate) แบ่งแยก bɛ̀ng-yɛ̂ɛk

seize *vt.* (capture) จับกุม jàp-gum | (confiscate) ยึด yʉ́t | (snatch) แย่ง yɛ̂ng

seizure *n.* (attack) อาการชัก aa-gaan-chák | (capture) การจับกุม gaan-jàp-gum

seldom *adv.* นานๆครั้ง naan-naan-kráng, ไม่ค่อยจะ mâi-kɔ̂i-jà

select *v.* เลือก lʉ̂ʉak, คัดเลือก kát-lʉ̂ʉak ❗

selection *n.* (item)
ตัวเลือก dtuua-lûuak [ตัว dtuua]
self *n* (one's own self) ตน dton | (one's own self) ตัว dtuua, ตัวเอง dtuua-eeng [ตัว dtuua]
self-centered *adj.*
เห็นแก่ตัว hěn-gɛ̀ɛ-dtuua
self-confident *adj.*
มั่นใจในตนเอง mân-jai-nai-dton-eeng
self-defense *n.*
การป้องกันตัว gaan-bpɔ̂ng-gan-dtuua
self-employed *adj.*
ทำงานอิสระ tam-ngaan-ìt-sà-rà
self-help *n.*
การช่วยเหลือตนเอง gaan-chûuai-lǔua-dton-eeng
selfish *adj.* เห็นแก่ตัว hěn-gɛ̀ɛ-dtuua
self-made *adj.*
สำเร็จด้วยตัวเอง sǎm-rèt-dûuai-dtuua-eeng ⚡
self-respect *n.*
การเคารพตัวเอง gaan-kao-róp-dtuua-eeng
self-service *adj.*
บริการตัวเอง bɔɔ-rí-

gaan-dtuua-eeng
sell *v.* ขาย kǎai, จำหน่าย jam-nàai ⚡
seller *n* คนขาย kon-kǎai [คน kon]
semen *n.* น้ำกาม nám-gaam, น้ำอสุจิ nám-à-sù~ji ⚡
semester *n.* ภาคเรียน pâak-riian [ภาค pâak] | เทอม təəm [เทอม təəm]
semi- *pref.* กึ่ง gùng- ⚡
semicolon *n.* อัฒภาค àt-tá~pâak ✂ [ตัว dtuua]
seminar *n.* การสัมมนา gaan-sǎm-má~naa
semiweekly *adj.*
สัปดาห์ละสองครั้ง sàp-daa-lá~rʉ̌ʉng-kráng ⚡, อาทิตย์ละสองครั้ง aa-tít-lá~rʉ̌ʉng-kráng ✦
senate *n.* สภาสูง sà~paa-sǔung, วุฒิสภา wút-tí-sà~paa ⚡ [สภา sà~paa]
senator *n.* วุฒิสมาชิก wút-tí-sà~maa-chík, ส.ว. rʉ̌ʉ-wʉʉ ✦ [คน kon]
send *vt.* ส่ง sòng
senile *adj.* (failing mentally) ขี้หลงขี้ลืม kîi-

lǒng-kîi-luum | (old) แก่
gɛ̀ɛ

senior n. (college)
นักศึกษาชั้นปีสุดท้าย nák-
sùk-sǎa-chán-bpii-sùt-
táai [คน kon] | (elder)
ผู้สูงอายุ pûu-sǔung-aa-
yú [คน kon]

seniority n. อาวุโส aa-wú-
sǒo

sensation n. (feeling)
ความรู้สึก kwaam-rúu-sèk

sense n. (i.e. sight, touch,
taste, sound, smell)
ประสาทสัมผัส bprà~sàat-
sǎm-pàt [อย่าง yàang]

sense vt. (realize) รับรู้
ráp-rúu

sensitive adj. (easy to
trigger strong emotion)
อ่อนไหว ɔ̀ɔn-wǎi |
(irritable) โกรธง่าย
gròot-ngâai

sensor n. (device)
เครื่องเซ็นเซอร์ krûuang-
sen-sɔ̀ɔ [เครื่อง krûuang]

sensual adj. (relating to
physical feeling)
เกี่ยวกับความรู้สึกทางกาย
gìiao-gàp-kwaam-rúu-
sèk-taang-gaai | (sexual)

ในทางกาม nai-taang-
gaam

sensuality n. (arousal)
ความกำหนัด kwaam-
gam-nàt ✍

sentence n. (grammar)
ประโยค bprà~yòok
[ประโยค bprà~yòok] |
(ruling) การตัดสิน gaan-
dtàt-sǐn

sentence vt. (condemn to
punishment)
ตัดสินลงโทษ dtàt-sǐn-
long-tôot

separate vt. แบ่งแยก
bèng-yɛ̂ɛk, แยก yɛ̂ɛk

separated adj. (apart)
แยกจากกัน yɛ̂ɛk-jàak-gan
| (e.g. spouses)
แยกกันอยู่ yɛ̂ɛk-gan-yùu

September n. กันยายน
gan-yaa-yon [เดือน
duuan]

sequence n. (order) ลำดับ
lam-dàp [ลำดับ lam-dàp,
ที่ tîi]

serene adj. (tranquil) สงบ
sà~ngòp

sergeant n. นายสิบ naai-
sìp [นาย naai ✍, คน kon] |
จ่า jàa [นาย naai, คน kon]

serial adj. (sequential)

ที่ต่อเนื่องกัน tîi-dtɔ̀ɔ-nɯ̂ɯang-gan

series n. (order) ลำดับ lam-dàp [ลำดับ lam-dap, ที่ tîi] | (set) ชุด chút [ชุด chút]

serious adj. (e.g. tense situation) ตึงเครียด dtʉng-krîiat | (important) สำคัญ sǎm-kan | (somber, sincere) จริงจัง jing-jang

sermon n. การเทศนา gaan-têet-sà~nǎa

serpent n. (snake) งูใหญ่ nguu-yài [ตัว dtuua]

serum n. เซรุ่ม see-rûm

servant n. คนใช้ kon-chái, ขี้ข้า kîi-kâa ❀ [คน kon]

serve v. บริการ bɔɔ-rí~gaan

serve vi. (e.g. as soldier, servant) รับใช้ ráp-chái | (in sports) เสิร์ฟลูก sɤ̀ɤp-lûuk

server n. (computer) เครื่องเซิร์ฟเวอร์ krɯ̂ɯang-sɤ̀ɤp-wɤ̂ɤ [เครื่อง krɯ̂ɯang] | (sports) ผู้เสิร์ฟลูก pûu-

sɤ̀ɤp-lûuk [คน kon] | (waiter) พนักงานเสิร์ฟ pá~nák-ngaan-sɤ̀ɤp [คน kon]

service n. การบริการ gaan-bɔɔ-rí~gaan

service vt. (repair) ซ่อม sɔ̂m

sesame n. งา ngaa [เม็ด mét (seed)]

session n. ระยะ rá~yá | (semester) ภาคเรียน pâak-riian [ภาค pâak]

set n. (group) กลุ่ม glùm [กลุ่ม glùm] | (of play) ฉาก chàak [ฉาก chàak] | (of sports games) เซต sét [เซต sét]

set vi. (sun) ตก dtòk

set vt. (place, put in place, set watch, clock) ตั้ง dtâng | (prescribe) กำหนด gam-nòt | (put, place) วาง waang

set one's alarm vi. ตั้งเวลาปลุก dtâng-wee-laa-bplùk

set out vt. (arrange) จัด jàt

settle vi. (sink to bottom) นอนก้น nɔɔn-gôn

settle vt. (case) สะสาง sà-sǎang | (migrate to)

อพยพเข้า òp-pá~yóp-kâo

settle down *vi.* (live long-term) ตั้งรกราก dtâng-rók-râak

settlement *n.* (amount from legal case) จำนวนที่ตกลงกัน jam-nuuan-tîi-dtòk-long-gan | (community) ชุมชน chum-chon [ชุมชน chum-chon]

settler *n.* ผู้ตั้งรกราก pûu-dtâng-rók-râak [คน kon]

set up *vt.* (install, configure) ติดตั้ง dtìt-dtâng

setup *n.* การติดตั้ง gaan-dtìt-dtâng

seven *numb.* เจ็ด jèt

seventeen *numb.* สิบเจ็ด sìp-jèt

seventh *adj.* ที่เจ็ด tîi-jèt

seventy *numb.* เจ็ดสิบ jèt-sìp

sever *vt.* (cut off) ตัด_ขาด dtàt-_-kàat | (separate) แยก_ออก yɛ̂ɛk-_-ɔ̀ɔk

several *adj.* มาก mâak, มากมาย mâak-maai, หลาย lǎai

severe *adj.* (harsh,

serious) รุนแรง run-rɛɛng

severely *adv.* อย่างรุนแรง yàang-run-rɛɛng

sew *v.* เย็บ yép

sewage *n.* สิ่งโสโครก sìng-sǒo-krôok

sewer *n.* (pipe) ท่อน้ำเสีย tɔ̂ɔ-nám-sǐia [ท่อ tɔ̂ɔ] | (waste) ของเสีย kɔ̌ɔng-sǐia

sewing machine *n.* จักรเย็บผ้า jàk-yép-pâa [คัน kan]

sex *n.* (gender) เพศ pêet [เพศ pêet] | (intercourse) การมีเพศสัมพันธ์ gaan-mii-pêet-sǎm-pan

sexism *n.* การแบ่งแยกเพศ gaan-bèng-yɛ̂ɛk-pêet

sexual *adj.* เกี่ยวกับเพศ gìiao-gàp-pêet

sexual desire *n.* ความต้องการทางเพศ kwaam-dtɔ̂ng-gaan-taang-pêet, กามารมณ์ gaa-maa-rom ✍

sexual harassment *n.* การคุกคามทางเพศ gaan-kúk-kaam-taang-pêet

sexual intercourse *n.* การร่วมเพศ gaan-rûuam-pêet, ประเวณี

bprà~wee-nii ☞

sexy adj. เซ็กซี่ sék-sîi

shade n. (color) เฉดสี chèet-sǐi [เฉด chèet] | (cover) ที่ร่ม tîi-rôm, ร่ม rôm [ที่ tîi]

shade awning n. ผ้าใบ pâa-bai [ผืน pǔun, แผ่น pèn]

shadow n. (cast image) เงา ngao [เงา ngao]

shady adj. (giving shade) ให้ร่มเงา hâi-rôm-ngao | (suspicious) น่าสงสัย nâa-sǒng-sǎi

shaft n. (axle) เพลา plao [เพลา plao] | (tube, e.g. mine, vent) ปล่อง bplòng [ปล่อง bplòng]

shake n. (drink) น้ำปั่น nám-bpàn [แก้ว gɛ̂ɛo (glass)]

shake vi. (vibrate, quiver) สั่น sàn

shake vt. (cause to rock) เขย่า kà~yào

shake hands with vt. จับมือ jàp-muu

shaky adj. (unsteady) ไม่มั่นคง mâi-mân-kong

shall aux. จะ jà, จะต้อง jà-dtɔ̂ng, น่าจะ nâa-jà

shallot n. หอมแดง hɔ̌ɔm-dɛɛng [หัว hǔua]

shallow adj. (not deep) ตื้น dtûun | (superficial) ผิวเผิน pǐu-pǒon

sham n. (deceiving) การหลอกลวง gaan-lɔ̀ɔk-luuang

shame n. (embarrassment) ความอับอาย kwaam-àp-aai

shameful adj. (disgraceful) น่าขายหน้า nâa-kǎai-nâa, น่าอาย nâa-aai

shameless adj. (showing no shame) ไร้ยางอาย rái-yaang-aai, หน้าด้าน nâa-dâan ☜

shampoo n. แชมพู chem-puu, ยาสระผม yaa-sà~ pǒm [ขวด kùuat (bottle)]

shape n. (figure, form) ร่าง râang, รูปร่าง rûup-râang, หุ่น hùn, สัณฐาน sǎn-tǎan ⚡, ฟอร์ม fɔɔm ☜

share n. (stock of business) หุ้นส่วน hûn-sùuan [หุ้น hûn]

share *vt.* (divide) แบ่ง bὲng

shareholder *n.* ผู้ถือหุ้น pûu-tǔu-hûn [คน kon]

shark *n.* ปลาฉลาม bplaa-chà~lǎam [ตัว dtuua]

sharp *adj.* (clever) ฉลาด chà~làat | (e.g. knife) คม kom | (e.g. picture) ชัด chát

sharpen *vt.* (e.g. blade) ลับ láp | (e.g. pencil) เหลา lǎo

sharpener *n.* (pencil) กบเหลาดินสอ gòp-lǎo-din-sɔ̌ɔ [อัน an] | (stone for blade) หินลับมีด hǐn-láp-mîit [อัน an]

sharpshooter *n.* นักแม่นปืน nák-mɛ̂n-bpuun [คน kon]

shatter *vi.* แตกละเอียด dtὲɛk-lá~iiat

shatter *vt.* ทำให้_แตกละเอียด tam-hâi-_-dtὲɛk-lá~iiat

shave *v.* (e.g. beard, hair) โกน goon

shawl *n.* ผ้าคลุมไหล่ pâa-klum-lài [ผืน pǔun]

she *pron.* เขา kǎo |

(derogatory) มัน man ❀ | (use with friends) แก gɛɛ ❀, เค้า káo ❀, หล่อน lɔ̀n ❀

shear *vt.* (cut) ตัด dtàt

sheath *n.* (knife) ปลอกมีด bplɔ̀ɔk-mîit [ปลอก bplɔ̀ɔk] | (sword) ฝักดาบ fàk-dàap [ฝัก fàk]

shed *n.* (storage) เพิงเก็บของ pəəng-gèp-kɔ̌ɔng [หลัง lǎng]

shed *vt.* (e.g. tears) หลั่ง làng

sheep *n.* แกะ gὲ [ตัว dtuua]

sheer *adj.* (transparent) บางใส baang-sǎi

sheet *n.* (bed) ผ้าปูที่นอน pâa-bpuu-tîi-nɔɔn [ผืน pǔun] | (broad, thin piece, e.g. paper) แผ่น pὲn [แผ่น pὲn]

shelf *n.* หิ้ง hîng [หิ้ง hîng] | ชั้น chán [ชั้น chán]

shell *n.* (conch) สังข์ sǎng [ขอน kɔ̌ɔn] | (of crustaceans) กระดอง grà~dɔɔng [ฝา fǎa] | (of eggs) เปลือก bplùuak [อัน an, ชิ้น chín] | (of

shellfish) เปลือกหอย
bplùuak-hɔ̌ɔi [ชิ้น chín]

shell vt. (remove shell of)
กะเทาะ gà~tɔ́

shellfish n. (oyster,
mussel) หอย hɔ̌ɔi [ตัว
dtuua] | (shrimp, lobster)
กุ้ง gûng [ตัว dtuua]

shelter n. (dwelling place)
ที่พักอาศัย tîi-pák-aa-sǎi
[ที่ tîi]

shelter vt. (protect)
ปกป้อง bpòk-bpɔ̂ng

shepherd n. (of sheep)
คนเลี้ยงแกะ kon-líiang-
gɛ̀ [คน kon]

sherbet n. น้ำผลไม้แช่แข็ง
nám-pǒn-lá~máai-chɛ̂ɛ-
kɛ̌ng [แก้ว gɛ̂ɛo]

sheriff n. นายอำเภอ naai-
am-pəə [คน kon]

shield n. (armor) โล่ lôo
[อัน an]

shield vt. (hide) ซ่อน sɔ̂n |
(shelter) ปกป้อง bpòk-
bpɔ̂ng

shift n. (work time) กะ gà
[กะ gà]

shift v. (move) เคลื่อน
klûuan

shift vi. (change vehicle
gear) เปลี่ยนเกียร์
bplìian-giia

shift key n. ปุ่มชิฟท์
bpùm-chíp [ปุ่ม bpùm]

shilling n. ชิลลิ่ง chin-lîng

shin n. หน้าแข้ง nâa-kêng
[ข้าง kâang]

shine vi. (emit light)
ส่องแสง sɔ̀ng-sɛ̌ɛng

shine vt. (point, e.g.
flashlight) ฉาย chǎai |
(polish) ขัด ให้ขึ้นเงา
kàt-_-hâi-kʉ̂n-ngao

shining adj. (bright) สว่าง
sà~wàang | (glittering)
เป็นประกาย bpen-bprà~
gaai

ship n. (vessel) เรือ rʉʉa
[ลำ lam]

ship vt. (send) ส่ง sòng

shipment n. (shipping
goods) การขนส่งสินค้า
gaan-kǒn-sòng-sǐn-káa

shipwreck n. เรือล่ม rʉʉa-
lôm [ครั้ง kráng]

shirt n. เสื้อเชิ้ต sʉ̂ʉa-
chə́ət, เสื้อ sʉ̂ʉa ✦ [ตัว
dtuua]

shit n. ขี้ kîi ✦ [กอง

gɔɔng, ก้อน gɔ̂ɔn] |
อุจจาระ ùt-jaa-rá ⚠ [กอง
gɔɔng (pile), ก้อน gɔ̂ɔn] |
(nonsense) เรื่องเหลวไหล
rûuang-lěeo-lǎi

shit v. (defecate)
ถ่ายอุจจาระ tàai-ùt-jaa-rá
⚠, ขี้ kîi ⚠

shit! interj. ถุย tǔi ⚠

shiver n. (symptom)
อาการสั่น aa-gaan-sàn

shiver vi. (shake) สั่น sàn

shock n. (condition)
อาการช็อก aa-gaan-chɔ́k

shock vt. ช็อก chɔ́k |
(surprise)
ทำให้_สะดุ้งตกใจ tam-
hâi-_-sà~dûng-dtòk-jai

shocked adj. ช็อก chɔ́k |
(startled, stunned)
ตกใจสุดขีด dtòk-jai-sùt-
kìit

shoddy adj. (of poor
quality) กระจอก grà~jɔ̀ɔk

shoe n. รองเท้า rɔɔng-
táao [ข้าง kâang (one), คู่
kûu (pair)]

shoehorn n. ที่ช้อนรองเท้า
tîi-chɔ́ɔn-rɔɔng-táao [อัน
an]

shoelace n.
เชือกผูกรองเท้า chûuak-
pùuk-rɔɔng-táao [เส้น
sên]

shoe polish n.
ยาขัดเงารองเท้า yaa-kàt-
ngao-rɔɔng-táao [กล่อง
glɔ̀ng (case), ขวด kùuat
(caster)]

shoestring see shoelace

shoot n. (sprout) หน่อ nɔ̀ɔ
[หน่อ nɔ̀ɔ]

shoot vi. (e.g. gun) ลั่น lân

shoot vt. (e.g. gun) ยิง
ying | (e.g. photograph,
video) ถ่าย tàai

shooting n. (with gun)
การยิงปืน gaan-ying-
bpʉʉn [ครั้ง kráng]

shooting star n. ดาวตก
daao-dtòk [ดวง duuang]

shop n. (store) ร้าน ráan,
ร้านค้า ráan-káa [ร้าน
ráan]

shop vi. จ่ายตลาด jàai-
dtà~làat, ช็อปปิ้ง chɔ́p-
bpîng, ซื้อของ sʉ́ʉ-kɔ̌ɔng

shoplifting n.
การขโมยของตามร้าน
gaan-kà~mooi-kɔ̌ɔng-
dtaam-ráan

shop owner n. เจ้าของร้าน jâo-kǒ̌ong-ráan [คน kon]

shopping n. (act) การซื้อของ gaan-súu-kǒ̌ong, ช้อปปิ้ง chɔ́p-bpîng

shore n. ชายฝั่ง chaai-fàng, ฝั่ง fàng [แห่ง hèng, ฝั่ง fàng]

short adj. (duration) ไม่นาน mâi-naan | (height) เตี้ย dtîia | (length) สั้น sân | (low) ต่ำ dtàm

short circuit n. การลัดวงจร gaan-lát-wong-jɔɔn

shortcut n. ทางลัด taang-lát [ทาง taang]

shorten vt. ทำให้_สั้นลง tam-hâi-_-sân-long

shorthand n. ชวเลข chá~wá~lêek

short-lived adj. อายุสั้น aa-yú-sân

shorts n. (outergarment) กางเกงขาสั้น gaang-geeng-kǎa-sân [ตัว dtuua]

short story n. เรื่องสั้น rûuang-sân [เรื่อง rûuang]

short-tempered adj. ใจร้อน jai-rɔ́ɔn

short-term adj. ระยะสั้น rá~yá-sân

shortwave n. คลื่นสั้น klûun-sân

shot n. (gunshot) การยิงปืน gaan-ying-bpuun [นัด nát] | (heavy ball) บอลน้ำหนัก bɔn-nám-nàk [ลูก lûuk] | (in sports) การยิงลูก gaan-ying-lûuk | (injection) การฉีดยา gaan-chìit-yaa | (of alcohol) เป๊ก bpék [เป๊ก bpék] | (photograph) รูปภาพ rûup-pâap [ใบ bai, แผ่น pèn]

shotgun n. ปืนลูกซอง bpuun-lûuk-sɔɔng [กระบอก grà~bɔ̀ɔk]

should aux. (ought to) ควร kuuan, ควรจะ kuuan-jà | (probably will) น่า nâa, น่าจะ nâa-jà

shoulder n. บ่า bàa, ไหล่ lài [ข้าง kâang]

shout n. (act) การตะโกน

gaan-dtà~goon |
(sound) เสียงตะโกน
sǐiang-dtà~goon

shout vi. ตะโกน dtà~goon

shovel n. (for scooping)
พลั่ว plûua [เล่ม lêm] |
(spade, for digging)
เสียม sǐiam [เล่ม lêm]

show n. (TV program)
รายการทีวี raai-gaan-tii-
wii [รายการ raai-gaan] |
(exhibition) นิทรรศการ
ní-tát-sà~gaan [ครั้ง
kráng] | (performance)
การแสดง gaan-sà~dɛɛng,
โชว์ choo ❊ [ครั้ง kráng]

show vi. (be visible) โชว์
choo ❊

show vt. (_ to _) เอา_ให้_ดู
ao-_-hâi-_-duu | (display,
perform) โชว์ choo ❊ |
(express) แสดงออกถึง
sà~dɛɛng-ɔ̀ɔk-tǔng

showcase n. (display
case) ตู้แสดงสินค้า dtûu-
sà~dɛɛng-sǐn-káa [ใบ bai]

shower n. (fixture) ฝักบัว
fàk-buua [อัน an] | (light
rain) ฝนตกปรอยๆ fǒn-
dtòk-bprɔɔi-bprɔɔi

shower vi. (take a

shower) อาบน้ำฝักบัว
àap-nám-fàk-buua

show off v. อวด ùuat

show respect vi.
ให้ความเคารพ hâi-
kwaam-kao-róp

showroom n. โชว์รูม
choo-ruum [แห่ง hɛ̀ng]

shred n. (bit) เศษ sèet [ชิ้น
chín]

shred vt. (cut into small
pieces) ตัด_เป็นชิ้นๆ
dtàt-_-bpen-chín-chín

shriek vi. กรีดร้อง grìit-
rɔ́ɔng

shrimp n. กุ้ง gûng [ตัว
dtuua]

shrine n. (sacred place)
ศาลเจ้า sǎan-jâao [แห่ง
hɛ̀ng]

shrink vi. หดตัว hòt-dtuua

shrink vt. ทำให้_หดตัว
tam-hâi-_-hòt-dtuua

shrinkage n. การหดตัว
gaan-hòt-dtuua

shroud n. (over corpse)
ผ้าห่อศพ pâa-hɔ̀ɔ-sòp
[ผืน pǔʉn]

shrub n. พุ่มไม้ pûm-máai
[พุ่ม pûm]

shrug vi. ยักไหล่ yák-lài

shuffle *vt.* (rearrange)
ย้าย_ไปมา yáai-_-bpai-
maa

shuffle cards *vi.* สับไพ่
sàp-pâi

shun *vt.* หลีกเลี่ยง lìik-
lîiang

shut *v.* (close) ปิด bpìt

shut down *vi.* (business)
ปิดกิจการ bpìt-gìt-jà~
gaan | (e.g. computer)
ปิดเครื่อง bpìt-krûuang

shut off *vi.* (turn off)
หยุดทำงาน yùt-tam-
ngaan

shut off *vt.* (turn off) ปิด
bpìt

shutter *n.* (camera)
ชัตเตอร์กล้อง chát-dtôə-
glông

shuttle *n.* (bus) รถนำส่ง
rót-nam-sòng [คัน kan]

shuttlecock *n.* ลูกขนไก่
lûuk-kǒn-gài [ลูก lûuk]

shut up! *interj.* หุบปาก
hùp-bpàak ◆

shy *adj.* (timid) ขี้อาย kîi-
aai, อาย aai

Siam *n.* สยาม sà~yǎam
[ประเทศ bprà~têet]

Siamese twins *n.*

แฝดสยาม fὲɛt-sà~yǎam
[คู่ kûu]

sibling *n.* พี่น้อง pîi-nɔ́ɔng
[คน kon]

sick *adj.* ป่วย bpùai,
ไม่สบาย mâi-sà~baai

sickle *n.* (scythe) เคียว
kiiao [เล่ม lêm]

sick leave *n.* การลาป่วย
gaan-laa-bpùai

sickness *n.* (ailment)
ความเจ็บป่วย kwaam-
jèp-bpùai | (disease) โรค
rôok [โรค rôok]

sick person *n.* คนป่วย
kon-bpùai [ราย raai ⚠,
คน kon]

side *adj.* (subordinate)
รอง rɔɔng

side *n.* (lateral part) ข้าง
kâang, ด้านข้าง dâan-
kâang [ข้าง kâang] |
(surface) ด้าน dâan [ด้าน
dâan] | (team, party,
faction) ฝ่าย fàai [ฝ่าย
fàai]

sideburn *n.* จอน jɔɔn [ข้าง
kâang]

side by side *conj.*
เคียงข้างกัน kiiang-
kâang-gan

side effect *n.* ผลข้างเคียง pŏn-kâang-kiiang

sidewalk *n.* ทางเดินเท้า taang-dəən-táao, บาทวิถี bàat-wí-tǐi ⚠ [ทาง taang]

side with *vt.* เข้าข้าง kâo-kâang

siege *vt.* (assault) โจมตี joom-dtii | (surround) โอบล้อม òop-lɔ́ɔm

sieve *n.* (strainer) ตะแกรง dtà~grɛɛng [ใบ bai]

sieve *vt.* (sift solids) ร่อน rɔ̂n | (strain a liquid) กรอง grɔɔng

sift *v.* (sort with sieve) ร่อน rɔ̂n

sigh *n.* (act) การถอนหายใจ gaan-tɔ̌ɔn-hǎai-jai

sigh *vi.* (e.g. from relief) ถอนหายใจ tɔ̌ɔn-hǎai-jai

sight *n.* (eyesight) สายตา sǎai-dtaa | (gun) จุดเล็ง jùt-leng [จุด jùt] | (spectacle) ทิวทัศน์ tiu-tát [แห่ง hɛ̀ng]

sightseeing *n.* การเที่ยวชม gaan-tîiao-chom, การทัศนาจร gaan-tát-sà~naa-jɔɔn ⚠

sign *n.* (omen) ลาง laang |

(seal) ตรา dtraa [ตรา dtraa] | (street sign, label) ป้าย bpâai [ป้าย bpâai, แผ่น pèn] | (symbol) สัญลักษณ์ sǎn-yá~lák [อัน an] | (symptom) อาการ aa-gaan | (trace) รอย rɔɔi [รอย rɔɔi]

sign *vi.* (one's name) เซ็น sen, ลงชื่อ long-chûu, ลงนาม long-naam ⚠

signal *n.* สัญญาณ sǎn-yaan [สัญญาณ sǎn-yaan] | (traffic light) ไฟจราจร fai-jà-raa-jɔɔn [จุด jùt]

signal *vi.* (make a signal) ให้สัญญาณ hâi-sǎn-yaan

signature *n.* ลายเซ็น laai-sen, ลายมือชื่อ laai-mɯɯ-chûu ⚠ [อัน an] | (music) เพลงประกอบ pleeng-bprà~gɔ̀ɔp [เพลง pleeng]

significant *adj.* (important) สำคัญ sǎm-kan | (meaningful) มีความหมาย mii-kwaam-mǎai

sign language *n.* ภาษาใบ้ paa-sǎa-bâi ✦ [ภาษา

paa-sǎa]

silence n. ความเงียบ
kwaam-ngîiap

silent adj. เงียบ ngîiap

silicon n. ซิลิคอน sí-lí-kɔɔn

silk n. (cloth) ผ้าไหม
pâa-mǎi [ผืน pǔɯn] |
(thread) ไหม mǎi [เส้น
sên (thread), หลอด lɔ̀ɔt
(reel)]

silkworm n. ตัวไหม
dtuua-mǎi [ตัว dtuua]

silky adj. (silk-like)
เหมือนไหม mǔɯan-mǎi |
(smooth) ลื่น lɯ̂ɯn | (soft)
นิ่ม nîm

silly adj. (foolish) งี่เง่า
ngîi-ngâo | (nonsense)
ไร้สาระ rái-sǎa-rá |
(stupid) โง่ ngôo

silo n. (barn) ยุ้งข้าว
yúng-kâao [หลัง lǎng] |
(military)
หลุมใต้ดินเก็บอาวุธ lǔm-
dtâai-din-gèp-aa-wút
[แห่ง hὲng]

silver adj. (color) สีเงิน
sǐi-ngən

silver n. เงิน ngən

silverware n. เครื่องเงิน

krûɯang-ngən [ชุด chút]

similar adj. คล้าย kláai,
เหมือน mǔɯan

similarity n.
ความคล้ายคลึง kwaam-
kláai-klɯng, ความเหมือน
kwaam-mǔɯan

simmer v. (stew) เคี่ยว
kîiao

simmer vt. (stew) ตุ๋น dtǔn

simple adj. (easy) ง่าย
ngâai | (not complicated)
ไม่ซับซ้อน mâi-sáp-sɔ́ɔn |
(not luxurious) เรียบง่าย
rîiap-ngâai

simplify vt. ทำให้_ง่าย
tam-hâi-_-ngâai

simultaneous adj.
ในเวลาเดียวกัน nai-wee-
laa-diiao-gan

sin n. บาป bàap [อัน an]

since adv. (ago) ก่อน
gɔ̀ɔn, มาแล้ว maa-lɛ́ɛo

since conj. (because)
เนื่องจาก nɯ̂ɯang-jàak

since prep. (from) ตั้งแต่
dtâng-dtὲɛ

sincere adj. จริงใจ jing-jai

sincerity n. ความจริงใจ
kwaam-jing-jai

sinful *adj.* เป็นบาป bpen-bàap

sing *v.* (e.g. birds) ร้อง rɔ́ɔng | (song) ร้องเพลง rɔ́ɔng-pleeng, ขับร้อง kàp-rɔ́ɔng ‼

Singapore *n.* สิงคโปร์ sǐng-ká~bpoo [ประเทศ bprà~têet]

singer *n.* นักร้อง nák-rɔ́ɔng [คน kon]

single *adj.* (alone, sole) คนเดียว kon-diiao, เดียว diiao, ลำพัง lam-pang | (individual) เดี่ยว dìiao | (unmarried) โสด sòot

singular *n.* (grammar) เอกพจน์ èek-gà~pót [คำ kam]

sink *n.* อ่าง àang [ใบ bai] | (wash basin) ที่ล้างหน้า tîi-láang-nâa [ที่ tîi]

sink *vi.* (drown) จม jom, จมน้ำ jom-náam

sinner *n.* คนบาป kon-bàap [คน kon]

sinus *n.* ไซนัส sai-nát [โพรง proong]

sip *v.* จิบ jìp

sir *pron.* คุณ kun, ท่าน tân

‼

siren *n.* สัญญาณเตือนภัย sǎn-yaan-dtʉʉan-pai, เสียงหวอ sǐiang-wɔ̌ɔ [เสียง sǐiang (sound)]

sister *n.* (older) พี่สาว pîi-sǎao [คน kon] | (younger) น้องสาว nɔ́ɔng-sǎao [คน kon]

sister-in-law *n.* (older) พี่สะใภ้ pîi-sà~pái [คน kon] | (younger) น้องสะใภ้ nɔ́ɔng-sà~pái [คน kon]

sit *vi.* นั่ง nâng

sitcom *n.* ละครตลกสั้น lá~kɔɔn-dtà~lòk-sân [เรื่อง rûʉang]

sit down *vi.* นั่งลง nâng-long

site *n.* (location) ที่ตั้ง tîi-dtâng [ที่ tîi] | (location) ทำเล tam-lee [ทำเล tam-lee]

situation *n.* (circumstance) สถานการณ์ sà~tǎa-ná-gaan [สถานการณ์ sà~tǎa-ná-gaan]

six *numb.* หก hòk

six hundred *numb.*
หกร้อย hòk-rɔ́ɔi

sixteen *numb.* สิบหก sìp-hòk

sixth *adj.* ที่หก tîi-hòk

sixth sense *n.* สัมผัสที่หก săm-pàt-tîi-hòk

sixty *numb.* หกสิบ hòk-sìp

size *n.* ขนาด kà~nàat [ขนาด kà~nàat]

sizzle *n.* (frying sound) เสียงทอด sǐiang-tɔ̂ɔt

sizzle *vi.* (make a hissing sound) ทำเสียงดังฉ่าๆ tam-sǐiang-dang-chàa-chàa

skate *n.* (shoes) รองเท้าสเก็ต rɔɔng-táao-sà~gét [ข้าง kâang (one), คู่ kûu (pair)]

skate *vi.* เล่นสเก็ต lên-sà~gèt

skeleton *adj.* (pertaining to a skeleton) เกี่ยวกับโครงกระดูก gìiao-gàp-kroong-grà~dùuk

skeleton *n.* (body) โครงกระดูก kroong-grà~dùuk [โครง kroong] | (outline) โครงร่าง

kroong-râang [โครง kroong]

skeptical *adj.* (suspecting something) สงสัย sŏng-sǎi

sketch *n.* ภาพร่าง pâap-râang [ภาพ pâap]

sketch *v.* วาดคร่าวๆ wâat-krâao-krâao

skewer *n.* เหล็กเสียบเนื้อเวลาย่าง lèk-sìiap-núua-wee-laa-yâang [อัน an]

ski *n.* สกี sà~gii [คู่ kûu (pair)]

ski *vi.* เล่นสกี lên-sà~gii

skid *n.* (mark) รอยลื่นไถล rɔɔi-lûun-tà~lǎi [รอย rɔɔi]

skid *vi.* (glide, slide along) ลื่นไถล lûun-tà~lǎi

skier *n.* นักเล่นสกี nák-lên-sà~gii [คน kon]

skill *n.* ทักษะ ták-sà, ฝีมือ fǐi-muu ✎

skillful *adj.* ชำนาญ cham-naan, มีทักษะ mii-ták-sà

skim *vt.* (e.g. book) ดู_อย่างเผินๆ duu-_-yàang-pěən-pěən

skim milk *n.* นมที่สกัดไขมันออก nomtîi-sà~gàt-kǎi-man-ɔ̀ɔk

skin *n.* ผิว pǐu, ผิวหนัง

pǐu-nǎng [ชั้น chán
(layer)] | (animal)
หนังสัตว์ nǎng-sàt [แผ่น
pɛ̀n, ผืน pǔɯn] | (crust,
peel) เปลือก bplɯ̀ak [อัน
an, ชิ้น chín]
skin *vt.* (remove skin of)
ถลกหนัง tà~lòk-nǎng
skinny *adj.* (very thin)
ผอมมาก pɔ̌ɔm-mâak
skip *n.* (act of jumping)
การกระโดด gaan-grà~
dòot
skip *vi.* (hop, jump)
กระโดด grà~dòot
skip *vt.* (avoid, e.g. class)
ขาด kàat | (pass over,
leave out) ข้าม kâam
skirt *n.* กระโปรง grà~
bproong [ตัว dtuua]
skit *n.* (short play)
ละครสั้น lá~kɔɔn-sân
[ตอน dtɔɔn (episode),
เรื่อง rɯ̂ɯang (story)]
skull *n.* กะโหลก gà~lòok,
หัวกะโหลก hǔua-gà~
lòok [ใบ bai]
skunk *n.* ตัวเหม็น dtuua-

měn, สกั๊งค์ sà~gáng [ตัว
dtuua]
sky *n.* ท้องฟ้า tɔ́ɔng-fáa,
ฟ้า fáa [ผืน pǔɯn]
skyscraper *n.* ตึกระฟ้า
dtɯ̀k-rá~fáa [หลัง lǎng,
ตึก dtɯ̀k]
sky train *n.* รถไฟฟ้า rót-
fai-fáa [ขบวน kà~buuan,
คัน kan]
slack *adj.* (loose, e.g.
rope) หย่อน yɔ̀n
slack *n.* (rimmed hat)
ลุงพอ lung-pɔɔ [ใบ bai]
slacks *n.* กางเกงใส่เล่น
gaang-geeng-sài-lên [ตัว
dtuua]
slam *n.* (noise)
เสียงกระแทก sǐiang-grà~
tɛ̂ɛk
slam *vt.* (shut loudly)
ปิด_เสียงดัง bpìt-_-
sǐiang-dang
slang *n.* คำสแลง kam-sà~
lɛɛng [คำ kam]
slant *n.* (slanting)
การเอียงลาด gaan-iiang-
lâat
slant *vi.* (lean, incline)
เอียง iiang
slanted *adj.* (tilted) เฉ

chěe

slap *vt.* (on face) ตบหน้า dtòp-nâa | (smack) ตบ dtòp

slash *n.* (cut mark) รอยฟัน rɔɔi-fan [รอย rɔɔi] | (punctuation) เครื่องหมายทับ krûuang-măai-táp ✍ [ตัว dtuua]

slash *v.* (slice) เฉือน chǔuan

slate *n.* (rock) หินชนวน hǐn-chá~nuuan [ก้อน gɔ̂ɔn] | (thin plate) กระดานชนวน grà~daan-chá~nuuan [แผ่น pèn]

slaughter *n.* (killing) การฆ่า gaan-kâa

slaughter *v.* ฆ่า kâa, สังหาร sǎng-hǎan ✍

slaughterhouse *n.* โรงฆ่าสัตว์ roong-kâa-sàt [แห่ง hὲng]

slave *n.* ทาส tâat [คน kon]

slavery *n.* ความเป็นทาส kwaam-bpen-tâat

slay *v.* (murder) ฆ่า kâa, สังหาร sǎng-hǎan ✍

sleep *n.* (state) การนอนหลับ gaan-nɔɔn-làp

sleep *vi.* นอน nɔɔn, นอนหลับ nɔɔn-làp, หลับ làp

sleeping bag *n.* ถุงนอน tǔng-nɔɔn [อัน an]

sleeping pill *n.* ยานอนหลับ yaa-nɔɔn-làp [เม็ด mét (tablet)]

sleepwalk *vi.* เดินละเมอ dəən-lá~məə

sleepy *adj.* (drowsy) ง่วง ngûuang, ง่วงนอน ngûuang-nɔɔn

sleet *n.* หิมะฝน hì~má-fǒn

sleeve *n.* แขนเสื้อ kɛ̌ɛn-sûua [ข้าง kâang]

sleigh *n.* รถเลื่อนบนหิมะ rót-lûuan-bon-hì~má [คัน kan]

slender *adj.* (slim) ผอมบาง pɔ̌ɔm-baang | (tapering) เรียว riiao

slice *n.* (piece) ชิ้น chín [ชิ้น chín] | (thin slice) แผ่นบาง pèn-baang [แผ่น pèn]

slice *v.* (chop) หั่น hàn | (cut thin) เฉือน chǔuan | (fruit) ฝาน fǎan

slide *n.* (photography)

ภาพสไลด์ pâap-sà~lái
[ภาพ pâap] |
(playground) สไลเดอร์
sà~lái-dəə [ชุด chút (set),
แผ่น pèn (board)]

slide *vi.* (skid) ไถล tà~lǎi |
(slip) ลื่น lûⁿn

slight *adj.* (few) น้อย nɔ́ɔi
| (small amount) เล็กน้อย
lék-nɔ́ɔi

slight *n.* (affront) การดูถูก
gaan-duu-tùuk

slim *adj.* (people, animals)
ผอม pɔ̌ɔm, ผอมบาง
pɔ̌ɔm-baang | (things)
บาง baang

slime *n.* (liquid) เมือก
mûⁿak | (mud) โคลน
kloon

slimy *adj.* (covered with
slime) เป็นเมือก bpen-
mûⁿak | (elusive) ลื่นไหล
lûⁿn-lǎi

sling *n.* (strap, e.g. gun,
bandage) สายสะพาย
sǎai-sà~paai [เส้น sên]

sling *vt.* (suspend) โยง
yoong | (throw) ขว้าง
kwâang

slingshot *n.* หนังสติ๊ก

nǎng-sà~dtík [อัน an,
เส้น sên]

slip *n.* (act of sliding)
การลื่น gaan-lûⁿn |
(lingerie) ซับใน sáp-nai
[ตัว dtuua] | (mistake)
ความผิดพลาด kwaam-
pìt-plâat

slip *vi.* (glide) ลื่น lûⁿn

slip *vt.* (slide) เลื่อน lûⁿan

slipper *n.* รองเท้าแตะ
rɔɔng-táao-dtɛ̀,
รองเท้าใส่ในบ้าน rɔɔng-
táao-sài-nai-bâan ⚠ [ข้าง
kâang (one), คู่ kûu (pair)]

slippery *adj.* ลื่น lûⁿn

slit *n.* (cut) รอยผ่า rɔɔi-pàa
[รอย rɔɔi]

slit *vt.* ผ่า pàa

sliver *n.* (splinter) เสี้ยน
sîian [อัน an] | (wood)
เศษไม้ sèet-máai [ชิ้น
chín]

slob *n.* (lazy person)
คนขี้เกียจ kon-kîi-gìiat
[คน kon]

slogan *n.* สโลแกน sà~
loo-gɛɛn, คำขวัญ kam-
kwǎn ⚠ [บท bòt]

slope n. (act) การลาดเอียง gaan-lâat-iiang | (incline) ทางลาดเอียง taang-lâat-iiang [แห่ง hèng (location)] | (incline) ที่ลาด tîi-lâat [ทาง taang, ที่ tîi]

slope v. ลาดเอียง lâat-iiang

sloping adj. ลาด lâat, เอียง iiang

sloppy adj. (careless) มักง่าย mák-ngâai, สะเพร่า sà~prâo | (messy) ไม่เป็นระเบียบ mâi-bpen-rá~biiap, เลอะเทอะ lə́-tə́

slot n. ช่อง chông, ช่องเล็ก chông-lék [ช่อง chông]

slot machine n. (gambling machine) ตู้พนัน dtûu-pá~nan [เครื่อง krûuang]

slow adj. ช้า cháa | (long time) นาน naan

slow down vi. (become slower) ชะลอตัว chá~lɔɔ-dtuua

slow down vt. (make slower) ทำให้_ช้าลง tam-hâi-_-cháa-long

slowly adv. ช้าๆ cháa-cháa, อย่างช้าๆ yàang-cháa-cháa

slug n. (animal) ตัวทาก dtuua-tâak, ทาก tâak [ตัว dtuua]

sluggish adj. เฉื่อย chùuai, เชื่องช้า chûuang-cháa, อืด ùut | (business) ซบเซา sóp-sao

slum n. แหล่งเสื่อมโทรม lèng-sùuam-soom ⚠, สลัม sà~lǎm ❋ [แห่ง hèng]

slurp v. (e.g. soup) ซด sót | (eat noisily) กิน_เสียงดัง gin-_-sǐiang-dang

slut n. อีตัว ii-dtuua ⬦, ดอกทอง dɔ̀ɔk-tɔɔng ⚥, อีดอก ii-dɔ̀ɔk ⚥ [คน kon] | (dirty woman) หญิงสกปรก yǐng-sòk-gà~bpròk [คน kon]

sly adj. เจ้าเล่ห์ jâo-lêe

smack vt. (kiss) จูบ_เสียงดัง jùup-_-sǐiang-dang | (slap) ตบ dtòp

small adj. (few) น้อย nɔ́ɔi | (tiny) เล็ก lék

small intestine n. ลำไส้เล็ก lam-sâi-lék

[ท่อน tɔ̂n (strip), ขด kòt (coil)]

smallpox *n.* ฝีดาษ fǐi-dàat, ไข้ทรพิษ kâi-tɔɔ-rá~pít ‼

smart *adj.* เก่ง gèng, ฉลาด chà~làat | (elegant, stylish) สมาร์ต sà~máat

smash *vt.* (break into pieces) แตก_เป็นเสี่ยงๆ dtɛ̀ɛk-_-bpen-sìiang-bpen-sìiang | (destroy) ทำลาย tam-laai | (pound) ทุบ túp

smear *n.* (smudge) รอยเปื้อน rɔɔi-bpûuan [จุด jùt]

smear *vt.* (spread, paint) ทา taa | (vilify) ทำให้_เสื่อมเสีย tam-hâi-_-sùuam-sǐia

smell *n.* กลิ่น glìn

smell *vt.* (perceive smell of) ได้กลิ่น dâi-glìn | (sniff) ดม dom

smell bad *vi.* เหม็น měn

smell good *vi.* หอม hɔ̌ɔm

smelly *adj.* เหม็น měn

smelt *vt.* (ore) ถลุง tà~lǔng

smile *n.* ยิ้ม yím, รอยยิ้ม

rɔɔi-yím

smile *vi.* ยิ้ม yím

smock *n.* (coverall) เสื้อคลุมหลวมๆ sûua-klum-lǔuam-lǔuam [ตัว dtuua]

smog *n.* ควันพิษ kwan-pít, หมอกควัน mɔ̀ɔk-kwan

smoggy *adj.* เต็มไปด้วยหมอกควัน dtem-bpai-dûuai-mɔ̀ɔk-kwan

smoke *n.* ควัน kwan

smoke *vi.* (emit smoke) ปล่อยควัน bplɔ̀ɔi-kwan

smoke *vt.* (e.g. cigarette) สูบ sùup | (e.g. salmon) รมควัน rom-kwan

smoke cigarettes *vi.* สูบบุหรี่ sùup-bù~rìi

smoker *n.* คนสูบบุหรี่ kon-sùup-bù~rìi [คน kon]

smoky *adj.* มีควันมาก mii-kwan-mâak

smooth *adj.* (flat) ราบ râap, เรียบ rîiap | (free from difficulties, etc.) ราบรื่น râap-rûun

smooth *vt.* ทำให้_เรียบ tam-hâi-_-rîiap

smuggle v. ลักลอบ lák-lɔ̂ɔp

smuggler n. คนลักลอบ kon-lák-lɔ̂ɔp [คน kon]

snack n. ขนม kà~nǒm [อัน an (piece), ชิ้น chín (piece), ถ้วย tûuai (bowl)] | (refreshments) ของว่าง kɔ̌ɔng-wâang [อัน an (piece), ชิ้น chín (piece), จาน jaan (plate)]

snail n. หอยทาก hɔ̌ɔi-tâak [ตัว dtuua]

snake n. งู nguu [ตัว dtuua]

snap vi. (fingers) ดีดนิ้ว dìit-níu | (make abrupt sound) เกิดเสียงดังแหลม gə̀ət-sǐiang-dang-lɛ̌ɛm

snapshot n. (photo) รูปถ่าย rûup-tàai ⚡ [ใบ bai, แผ่น pɛ̀n]

snare n. บ่วง bùuang [อัน an] | แร้ว rɛ́ɛo [คัน kan]

snatch vt. คว้า kwáa, แย่ง yɛ̂ɛng, แย่งชิง yɛ̂ɛng-ching

sneak vi. (walk quietly) แอบ ɛ̀ɛp

sneak vt. (_ into _) แอบเอา_ไป_ ɛ̀ɛp-ao-_-bpai-_

sneaker n. (shoe) รองเท้าผ้าใบ rɔɔng-táao-pâa-bai [ข้าง kâang (one), คู่ kûu (pair)]

sneaky adj. ไม่ซื่อ mâi-sน̂น

sneer vi. ยิ้มเยาะ yím-yɔ́

sneeze n. การจาม gaan-jaam

sneeze vi. จาม jaam

sniff n. การสูดกลิ่น gaan-sùut-glìn

sniff v. ดม dom, สูดกลิ่น sùut-glìn ⚡

sniff kiss v. หอม hɔ̌ɔm

snob n. คนหัวสูง kon-hǔua-sǔung [คน kon]

snobbish adj. หยิ่ง yìng, อวดดี ùuat-dii

snoop vi. (spy) สอดแนม sɔ̀ɔt-nɛɛm

snooze n. การงีบหลับ gaan-ngîip-làp

snooze vi. งีบหลับ ngîip-làp

snore n. เสียงกรน sǐiang-gron

snore vi. กรน gron

snort vi. (e.g. pig, horse) พ่นลมทางจมูก pôn-lom-taang-jà~mùuk

snort vt. (inhale, e.g.

drugs) ดูด dùut

snot *n.* (mucus) น้ำมูก
nám-mûuk, ขี้มูก kîi-
mûuk ✿

snow *n.* หิมะ hì-má

snow *vi.* หิมะตก hì~má-
dtòk

snow pea *n.* ถั่วลันเตา
tùua-lan-dtao [ต้น dtôn
(plant), ฝัก fàk (pod)]

snowy *adj.* (full of snow)
มีหิมะมาก mii-hì~má-
mâak

snuggle *vi.* กระแซะ grà~
sέ, กอดกัน gɔ̀ɔt-gan

so *adv.* (extremely) มาก
mâak | (in the way, like
that) แบบนั้น bὲεp-nán

so *conj.* (therefore) จึง
jɯng, ดังนั้น dang-nán

soak *v.* (in container, tub)
แช่ chêε

soak *vt.* (saturate, e.g.
clothes) ทำให้_เปียก
tam-hâi-_-bpìiak

soaked *adj.* (saturated,
e.g. clothes, ground) ชุ่ม
chûm

soap *n.* สบู่ sà~bùu [ก้อน
gɔ̂ɔn]

soap opera *n.* เรื่องน้ำเน่า
rûuang-nám-nâo [เรื่อง
rûuang]

soapy *adj.* เป็นฟอง bpen-
fɔɔng, มีฟองสบู่ mii-
fɔɔng-sà~bùu

soar *vi.* (float) ลอย lɔɔi |
(fly upwards) บินสูงขึ้น
bin-sǔung-kûn

sob *vi.* คร่ำครวญ krâm-
kruuan, สะอื้น sà~ûɯn

sober *adj.* (from alcohol)
สร่างเมา sàang-mao |
(stopped drinking)
หยุดดื่ม yùt-dùɯm

soccer *n.* ฟุตบอล fút-bɔn

sociable *adj.* เข้ากับคนง่าย
kâo-gàp-kon-ngâai

social *adj.* สังคม sǎng-kom

socialism *n.* สังคมนิยม
sǎng-kom-ní-yom [ระบบ
rá~bòp]

socialist *n.* นักสังคมนิยม
nák-sǎng-kom-ní-yom
[คน kon]

socialize *vi.* (with others)
คบหาสมาคม kóp-hǎa-
sà~maa-kom

social science *n.*
สังคมศาสตร์ sǎng-kom-

má~sàat [วิชา wí-chaa]

social security *n.*
ประกันสังคม bprà~gan-
sǎng-kom

social worker *n.*
นักสังคมสงเคราะห์ nák-
sǎng-kom-sǒng-krɔ́ [คน
kon]

society *n.* สังคม sǎng-
kom [สังคม sǎng-kom]

sociology *n.* สังคมวิทยา
sǎng-kom-wít-tá~yaa
[วิชา wí-chaa]

sock *n.* ถุงเท้า tǔng-táao
[ข้าง kâang (each), คู่ kûu
(pair)]

socket *n.* (female
connector) ปลั๊ก bplák,
ปลั๊กตัวเมีย bplák-
dtuua-miia ✖ [ตัว dtuua,
อัน an]

soda *n.* โซดา soo-daa |
(carbonated drink)
น้ำอัดลม nám-àt-lom
[ขวด kùuat]

sodium *n.* โซเดียม soo-
diiam [ธาตุ tâat]

sodomy *n.*
การร่วมเพศทางทวารหนัก
gaan-rûuam-pêet-
taang-tá~waan-nàk

sofa *n.* โซฟา soo-faa [ตัว
dtuua]

soft *adj.* (in sound) เบา
bao | (to the touch) นิ่ม
nîm, นุ่ม nûm, อ่อน ɔ̀ɔn

softball *n.* (game)
ซอฟท์บอล sɔ́ɔp-bɔn [เกม
geem]

soft-boiled egg *n.* ไข่ลวก
kài-lûuak [ฟอง fɔɔng]

soften *vi.* อ่อนโยน ɔ̀ɔn-
yoon

soften *vt.* ทำให้_อ่อนลง
tam-hâi-_-ɔ̀ɔn-long

softly *adv.* (gently)
อย่างเบาๆ yàang-bao-
bao, ค่อยๆ kɔ̂i-kɔ̂i ✦

softness *n.* ความอ่อนนุ่ม
kwaam-ɔ̀ɔn-nûm

software *n.* ซอฟต์แวร์
sɔ́ɔp-wɛɛ [โปรแกรม
bproo-grɛɛm]

soggy *adj.* (wet) เปียกโชก
bpiiak-chôok

soi *n.* (lane) ซอย sɔɔi [ซอย
sɔɔi] | (lane) ตรอก dtrɔ̀ɔk
[ตรอก dtrɔ̀ɔk]

soil *n.* ดิน din, พื้นดิน
púun-din

solar *adj.* (pertaining to
sun) เกี่ยวกับดวงอาทิตย์

giiao-gàp-duuang-aa-tít

solar eclipse *n.* สุริยุปราคา
sù-rí~yúp-bpà~raa-kaa
[ครั้ง kráng]

sold *adj.* ขายแล้ว kăai-lɛ́ɛo

soldier *n.* ทหาร tá~hăan
[นาย naai ⚣, คน kon]

sold out *adj.* ขายหมดแล้ว
kăai-mòt-lɛ́ɛo

sole *adj.* เดียว diiao, เดี่ยว
dìiao

sole *n.* (of foot) ฝ่าเท้า
fàa-táao [ข้าง kâang] |
(of shoe) พื้นรองเท้า
púun-rɔɔng-táao [แผ่น
pɛ̀n]

solemn *adj.* เคร่งขรึม
krêng-krǔm, เอาจริงเอาจัง
ao-jing-ao-jang

solicitor see lawyer

solid *adj.* (firm) มั่นคง
mân-kong | (not hollow)
ตัน dtan

solid *n.* (not liquid)
ของแข็ง kɔ̌ɔng-kɛ̌ng

solitary *adj.* โดดเดี่ยว
dòot-dìiao, สันโดษ sǎn-
dòot

solitude *n.* ความสันโดษ
kwaam-sǎn-dòot

solo *adv.* เดี่ยว dìiao

solo *n.* (performance by
one singer or
instrumentalist)
การแสดงเดี่ยว gaan-sà~
dɛɛng-dìiao

soluble *adj.* (can be
dissolved) ละลายได้ lá~
laai-dâai | (solvable)
แก้ได้ gɛ̂ɛ-dâai

solution *n.* (answer)
คำตอบ kam-dtɔ̀ɔp |
(substance) สารละลาย
sǎan-lá~laai

solve *vt.* (e.g. problem)
แก้ gɛ̂ɛ

solve a problem *vi.*
แก้ปัญหา gɛ̂ɛ-bpan-hǎa

solvent *adj.* (able to pay
debts) จ่ายหนี้ได้ jàai-nîi-
dâai

solvent *n.* (e.g. cleaner)
น้ำยา nám-yaa

somber *adj.* (dark) มืดมน
mûut-mon

some *adj.* บาง baang

some *adv.* บ้าง bâang

somebody *pron.* (as
object) คน kon | (as
subject) มีคนที่ mii-kon-tîi

someday *adv.*

someday วันใดวันหนึ่ง wan-dai-wan-nùng | (sooner or later) สักวัน sàk-wan

somehow *adv.* ด้วยวิธีใดก็ตาม dûuai-wí-tii-dai-gɔ̂ɔ-dtaam

someone see somebody

some people *pron.* บางคน baang-kon

some places *n.* บางแห่ง baang-hɛ̀ng

somersault *vi.* ตีลังกา dtii-lang-gaa

something *pron.* (as object) สิ่ง sìng | (as object, in question) อะไร à~rai | (as subject) มีอะไรที่ mii-à~rai-tîi

some things *pron.* บางสิ่ง baang-sìng, บางอย่าง baang-yàang

sometime *adv.* ในอนาคต nai-à~naa-kót

sometimes *adv.* บางครั้ง baang-kráng

somewhat *adv.* ค่อนข้าง kɔ̂n-kâang

somewhere *adv.* (as object) สักที่หนึ่ง sàk-tîi-nùng | (as object, in question) ที่ไหน tîi-năi |

(as subject) ที่ไหน tîi-năi

so much *adv.* อย่างมาก yàang-mâak

son *n.* ลูกชาย lûuk-chaai [คน kon]

song *n.* เพลง pleeng [เพลง pleeng]

Songkran Day *n.* วันสงกรานต์ wan-sŏng-graan [วัน wan]

sonic *adj.* เกี่ยวกับเสียง gìiao-gàp-sĭiang

son-in-law *n.* ลูกเขย lûuk-kə̌əi [คน kon]

soon *adv.* ในเร็วๆนี้ nai-reo-reo-níi, อีกไม่นาน ìik-mâi-naan

soot *n.* เขม่า kà~mào

soothe *v.* (relieve) บรรเทา ban-tao

sophisticated *adj.* (worldly) ช่ำชองโลก châm-chɔɔng-lôok

sophomore *n.* นักศึกษาปีสอง nák-sùk-săa-bpii-sɔ̌ɔng [คน kon]

soprano *n.* (voice) เสียงโซปราโน sĭiang-soo-bpraa-nôo

sorcerer *n.* หมอผี mɔ̌ɔ-pĭi [คน kon]

sorceress see sorcerer

sore *adj.* ปวดเมื่อย bpùuat-mûuai

sore throat *n.* อาการเจ็บคอ aa-gaan-jèp-kɔɔ

sorrow *n.* ความเสียใจ kwaam-sĭia-jai

sorrowful *adj.* เศร้าโศก sâo

sorry *adj.* เสียใจ sĭia-jai

sorry! *interj.* ขอโทษ kŏɔ-tôot

sort *n.* (kind) ชนิด chá~nít [ชนิด chá~nít] | (type, category) ประเภท bprà~pêet [ประเภท bprà~pêet]

sort *v.* แยก yɛ̂ɛk

sort out *vt.* จัดลำดับ jàt-lam-dàp

so-so *adj.* งั้นๆ ngán-ngán, เฉยๆ chɤ̌ɤi-chɤ̌ɤi

so that *conj.* เพื่อว่า pûɯa-wâa

soul *n.* วิญญาณ win-yaan [ดวง duuang]

soulmate *n.* เนื้อคู่ nɯ́ɯa-kûu, บุพเพสันนิวาส bùp-pee-săn-ní~wâat ☞ [คน kon]

sound *n.* เสียง sĭiang [เสียง sĭiang]

sound like *vt.* (makes the sound) ออกเสียง ว่วก-sĭiang

soundtrack *n.* (from a film) เสียงในฟิล์ม sĭiang-nai-fiim [เสียง sĭiang]

soup *n.* แกง gɛɛng, ซุป súp [ถ้วย tûuai (bowl)]

sour *adj.* เปรี้ยว bprîiao

source *n.* (of data) แหล่งข้อมูล lɛ̀ng-kɔ̂ɔ-muun [แหล่ง lɛ̀ng, แห่ง hɛ̀ng] | (origin) ที่มา tîi-maa | (origin) แหล่งที่มา lɛ̀ng-tîi-maa [แหล่ง lɛ̀ng]

south *adj.* ใต้ dtâai, ทางใต้ taang-dtâai

south *n.* (direction) ใต้ dtâai, ทิศใต้ tít-dtâai [ทิศ tít] | (region) ภาคใต้ pâak-dtâai [ภาค pâak]

South America *n.* อเมริกาใต้ à~mee-rí~gaa-dtâai [ทวีป tá~wîip]

southeast *n.* ตะวันออกเฉียงใต้ dtà~wan-ɔ̀ɔk-chĭiang-dtâai, ทิศตะวันออกเฉียงใต้ tít-dtà~wan-ɔ̀ɔk-chĭiang-dtâai [ทิศ tít]

Southeast Asia *n.*
เอเชียตะวันออกเฉียงใต้
ee-chiia dtà-·wan-ɔ̀ɔk-
chǐiang-dtâai [แถบ tɛ̀ɛp]

Southern Africa *n.*
แอฟริกาใต้ ɛ́p-frí-gaa-
dtâai [แถบ tɛ̀ɛp]

Southern Asia *n.* เอเชียใต้
ee-chiia-dtâai [แถบ tɛ̀ɛp]

Southern Europe *n.*
ยุโรปใต้ yú-ròop-dtâai
[แถบ tɛ̀ɛp]

South Korea *n.* เกาหลีใต้
gao-lǐi-dtâai [ประเทศ
bprà~têet]

South Pole *n.* ขั้วโลกใต้
kûua-lôok-dtâai [ขั้ว
kûua]

southwest *n.*
ตะวันตกเฉียงใต้ dtà~
wan-dtòk-chǐiang-dtâai,
ทิศตะวันตกเฉียงใต้ tít-
dtà~wan-dtòk-chǐiang-
dtâai [ทิศ tít]

souvenir *n.* ของที่ระลึก
kɔ̌ɔng-tîi-rá~lʉ́k [อัน an,
ชิ้น chín]

sow *vt.* (e.g. seeds) หว่าน
wàan

soy *n.* ถั่วเหลือง tùua-
lʉ̌uang [เมล็ด má~lét
(bean)]

soybean *n.* เมล็ดถั่วเหลือง
má~lét-tùua-lʉ̌uang
[เมล็ด má~lét]

soybean sauce see soy
sauce

soy sauce *n.* ซอสถั่วเหลือง
sɔ́ɔt-tùua-lʉ̌uang, ซีอิ๊ว
sii-íu [ขวด kùuat (bottle)]

spa *n.* สปา sà-bpaa [แห่ง
hɛ̀ng] | (hot tub) บ่อน้ำแร่
bɔ̀ɔ-nám-rɛ̂ɛ [แห่ง hɛ̀ng]

space *n.* (area) เนื้อที่
nʉ́ua-tîi | (astronomical)
อวกาศ à~wá~gàat |
(blank space) ช่องว่าง
chɔ̂ng-wâang [ช่อง
chɔ̂ng] | (gap) ระยะห่าง
rá~yá~hàang

spaceship *n.* ยานอวกาศ
yaan-à~wá~gàat

spacious *adj.* กว้าง
gwâang, กว้างขวาง
gwâang-kwǎang,
มีเนื้อที่มาก mii-nʉ́ua-
tîi-mâak

spade *n.* (card) โพธิ์ดำ
poo-dam | (pickaxe, for

digging) เสียม sĭiam [เล่ม lêm] | (shovel, for scooping) พลั่ว plûua [เล่ม lêm]

spaghetti *n.* สปาเก็ตตี้ sà~bpaa-gét-dtîi [เส้น sên]

Spain *n.* สเปน sà~bpeen [ประเทศ bprà~têet]

spam *n.* สแปม sà~bpɛɛm [ครั้ง kráng, อัน an]

span *n.* (time or distance) ระยะ rá~yá [ระยะ rá~yá] | (time or distance) ช่วง chûuang [ช่วง chûuang]

Spanish *n.* (language) ภาษาสเปน paa-sǎa-sà~bpeen [ภาษา paa-sǎa]

spank *vt.* ตีก้น dtii-gôn

spare *adj.* (backup) สำรอง sǎm-rɔɔng

spare *vt.* (lend) ให้ยืม hâi-yuuem | (show mercy to) มีเมตตาต่อ mii-mêet-dtaa-dtɔ̀ɔ

spare tire *n.* (e.g. for cars) ยางอะหลั่ย yaang-à~lài [ล้อ lɔ́ɔ] | (stomach) พุง pung ✽ [พุง pung]

spark *n.* ประกาย bprà~gaai

spark *vi.* เป็นประกาย bpen-bprà~gaai

sparkle *vi.* ส่องแสงแวววาว sɔ̀ng-sɛ̌ɛng-wɛɛo-waao

sparrow *n.* นกกระจอก nók-grà~jɔ̀ɔk [ตัว dtuua]

sparse *adj.* ประปราย bprà~bpraai

spasm *n.* กล้ามเนื้อกระตุก glâam-núua-grà~dtùk

spatula *n.* (flipper used for frying) ตะหลิว dtà~lǐu [อัน an]

speak *v.* (e.g. Thai, slowly, the truth) พูด pûut

speak *vi.* (chat) คุย kui

speaker *n.* (loud speaker) ลำโพง lam-poong [ตัว dtuua] | (one who speaks) ผู้พูด pûu-pûut [คน kon]

speak of *vt.* พูดถึง pûut-tǔng

spear *n.* หลาว lǎao, หอก hɔ̀ɔk [เล่ม lêm]

special *adj.* พิเศษ pí-sèet

specialist *n.* ผู้เชี่ยวชาญ pûu-chîiao-chaan [คน kon]

specialize *vi.* เป็นผู้เชี่ยวชาญ bpen-pûu-chîiao-chaan

specialty n.
ความชำนาญพิเศษ
kwaam-cham-naan-pí-sèet

species n. (type, kind)
ชนิด chá~nít [ชนิด chá~nít]

specific adj. เจาะจง jɔ̀-jong, เฉพาะ chà~pɔ́

specification n. (details)
รายละเอียด raai-lá~ìiat
[อัน an]

specify vt. กำหนด gam-nòt, เจาะจง jɔ̀-jong

specimen n. ตัวอย่าง
dtuua-yàang [ตัว dtuua
🖊, ตัวอย่าง dtuua-yàang]

speck n. จุดด่าง jùt-dàang
[จุด jùt]

spectacles n. แว่นตา
wên-dtaa [อัน an]

spectacular adj. น่าดูน่าชม
nâa-duu-nâa-chom

spectator n. ผู้ชม pûu-chom [คน kon]

speculate vi. (do high-risk, high-reward business)
เสี่ยงโชคในธุรกิจ sìiang-chôok-nai-tú-rá-gìt |
(guess) เดา dao

speech n. (act) การพูด
gaan-pûut | (public address) คำปราศรัย
kam-bpraa-săi,
สุนทรพจน์ sŭn-tɔɔ-rá~pót 🖊 [คำ kam]

speechless adj. พูดไม่ออก
pûut-mâi-ɔ̀ɔk

speed n. (drug) ยาม้า
yaa-máa | (rapidity)
ความเร็ว kwaam-reo

speed vt. (expedite)
เร่งความเร็ว rêng-kwaam-reo

speedboat n. เรือยนต์เร็ว
ruua-yon-reo [คัน kan]

speed limit n.
การจำกัดความเร็ว gaan-jam-gàt-kwaam-reo

speedometer n.
เครื่องวัดความเร็ว
krûuang-wát-kwaam-reo
[เครื่อง krûuang]

speedy adj. รวดเร็ว rûuat-reo

spell n. (charm) มนต์สะกด
mon-sà~gòt, เสน่ห์ sà~nèe

spell v. สะกด sà~gòt

spend v. (expend) ใช้ chái
| (pay) จ่าย jàai

spendthrift adj. ฟุ่มเฟือย fûm-fɯɯai

spendthrift n. (person) คนสุรุ่ยสุร่าย kon-sù~rûi-sù~râai [คน kon]

spend time vi. ใช้เวลา chái-wee-laa

sperm n. อสุจิ à-sù~jì [ตัว dtuua]

spermicide n. สารฆ่าอสุจิ sǎan-kâa-à~sù~jì

sphere n. (round figure) รูปทรงกลม rûup-song-glom [รูป rûup]

sphinx n. สฟิงซ์ sà~fing [ตัว dtuua]

spice n. (e.g. cinnamon) เครื่องเทศ krɯ̂ɯang-têet [ชนิด chá~nít]

spice vt. (add flavor to) เพิ่มรสชาติ pə̂əm-rót-châat

spicy adj. เผ็ด pèt, รสจัด rót-jàt

spider n. แมงมุม mɛɛng-mum [ตัว dtuua]

spike n. (abrupt increase) การขึ้นอย่างรวดเร็ว gaan-kɯ̂n-yàang-rûuat-reo | (sharp-pointed object) สิ่งแหลมคม sìng-lɛ̌ɛm-kom

spill vi. (liquid) ล้น lón

spill vt. (liquid) ทำ_หก tam-_-hòk

spin v. ปั่น bpàn, หมุน mǔn

spinach n. ผักขม pàk-kǒm [ต้น dtôn]

spine n. (of body) กระดูกสันหลัง grà~dùuk-sǎn-lǎng [ชิ้น chín] | (of book) สันหนังสือ sǎn-nǎng~sɯ̌ɯ

spinster n. (old maid) สาวทึนทึก sǎao-tɯn-túk [คน kon]

spiny adj. (thorny) มีหนาม mii-nǎam

spiral n. (shape) เกลียว gliiao [เกลียว gliiao]

spirit n. (enthusiasm) ความมุ่งมั่น kwaam-mûng-mân | (ghost) ผี pǐi [ตัว dtuua] | (liquor) เหล้า lâo [ขวด kùuat (bottle), แก้ว gɛ̂ɛo (glass)] | (mood, feeling) อารมณ์ aa-rom

spiritual adj. (pertaining to spirit or soul) เกี่ยวกับจิตใจ gìiao-gàp-

jìt-jai | (sacred)
เกี่ยวกับสิ่งศักดิ์สิทธิ์
giiao-gàp-sìng-sàk-sìt

spit vi. บ้วนน้ำลาย bûuan-nám-laai, ถ่มน้ำลาย tòm-nám-laai ⚡

spite vt. เย้ย yéəi

spittoon n. กระโถน grà~tŏon [ใบ bai]

splash vi. กระเด็น grà~den

splash vt. สาด sàat

spleen n. (organ) ม้าม máam [อัน an]

splendid adj. (grand) โอ่โถง òo-tŏong | (wonderful) ยอดเยี่ยม yôɔt-yîiam

splinter n. (sliver) เสี้ยน sîian [อัน an]

split n. (crack) รอยแยก rɔɔi-yɛ̂ɛk [รอย rɔɔi] | (separation) การแตกแยก gaan-dtɛ̀ɛk-yɛ̂ɛk

split vi. (crack) แตก dtɛ̀ɛk

split vt. (with sharp blow) ผ่า pàa

split up vi. แยกกัน yɛ̂ɛk-gan

spoil vi. (become bad) เสีย sĭia

spoil vt. (e.g. food) ทำให้_เสีย tam-hâi-_-sĭia | (someone) ตามใจ dtaam jai

spokesperson n. โฆษก koo-sòk [คน kon]

sponge n. ฟองน้ำ fɔɔng-náam [ชิ้น chín (piece)]

sponge vt. เช็ดถู_ด้วยฟองน้ำ chét-tǔu-_-dûuai-fɔɔng-náam

spongy adj. (like a sponge) เป็นเหมือนฟองน้ำ bpen-mǔuan-fɔɔng-náam

sponsor n. (e.g. advertising) สปอนเซอร์ sà~bpɔɔn-sə̂ə ✿ [คน kon, ราย raai ⚡] | (one who supports) ผู้อุปถัมภ์ pûu-ùp-bpà~tăm [คน kon]

spontaneous adj. (acting upon impulse) โดยทันที dooi-tan-tii | (self-acting, natural) เป็นไปเอง bpen-bpai-eeng

spook n. (ghost) ผี pǐi [ตัว dtuua]

spooky adj. น่ากลัว nâa-gluua

spool n. หลอด lɔ̀ɔt [หลอด

lɔ̀ɔt] | (for thread)
หลอดด้าย lɔ̀ɔt-dâai [หลอด
lɔ̀ɔt]

spoon *n.* ช้อน chɔ́ɔn [คัน
kan]

spoon *vt.* ตัก_ด้วยช้อน
dtàk-_-dûuai-chɔ́ɔn

spoonful *n.* เต็มช้อน
dtem-chɔ́ɔn

sporadic *adj.* (scattered)
กระจัดกระจาย grà~jàt-
grà~jaai | (time)
เป็นระยะ bpen-rá~yá

spore *n.* สปอร์ sà~bpɔɔ

sport *n.* กีฬา gii-laa [ชนิด
chá~nít]

spot *n.* (place) สถานที่ sà~
tǎan-tîi [แห่ง hɛ̀ng] |
(point) จุด jùt [จุด jùt] |
(stain) รอย rɔɔi [รอย rɔɔi]

spotless *adj.* หมดจด mòt-
jòt

spotlight *n.* สปอตไลท์
sà~bpɔ̀t-lái [อัน an, ดวง
duuang]

spotted *adj.* เป็นจุดๆ
bpen-jùt-jùt

spouse *n.* (mate) คู่ครอง
kûu-krɔɔng [คู่ kûu (pair),
คน kon (person)] | (one's
husband or wife) คู่สมรส

kûu-sǒm-rót [คู่ kûu]

spout *n.* (e.g. of squeeze
bottle) ปากพ่น bpàak-
pôn [อัน an] | (of kettle)
พวยกา puuai-gaa [พวย
puuai] | (water faucet)
ก๊อกน้ำ gɔ́ɔk-náam [ก๊อก
gɔ́ɔk]

sprain *n.* (symptom)
อาการเคล็ดขัดยอก aa-
gaan-klét-kàt-yɔ̂ɔk

sprain *v.* (e.g. leg, ankle)
บิด bìt

spray *n.* (substance
sprayed) สเปรย์ sà~bpree

spray *v.* พ่น pôn

spray *vt.* ฉีด chìit

spread *n.* (act)
การแพร่กระจาย gaan-
prɛ̂ɛ-grà~jaai | (bed
cover) ผ้าปู pâa-bpuu
[ผืน pǔ̀ɯn]

spread *v.* (disperse)
กระจาย grà~jaai | (e.g.
legs, compass) ถ่าง tàang

spread *vi.* (e.g. news, fire)
ลาม laam

spread out *v.* (expand)
ขยาย kà~yǎai

spread out *vt.* (e.g. wings,
arms) กาง_ออก gaang-_-
ɔ̀ɔk

spring *n.* (elastic device) สปริง sà~bpring [ตัว dtuua] | (fountain) น้ำพุ nám-pú [แห่ง hὲng (location)] | (season) ฤดูใบไม้ผลิ rú-duu-bai-máai-plì [ฤดู rú-duu] | (water source) ต้นน้ำ dtôn-náam [แห่ง hὲng]

spring *vi.* (bounce) เด้ง dêng, สปริงตัว sà~bpring-dtuua

spring onion see green onion

spring roll *n.* เปาะเปี๊ยะ bpɔ́-bpíia

sprinkle *n.* (light rain) ฝนที่ตกปรอยๆ fǒn-tîi-dtòk-bprɔɔi-bprɔɔi

sprinkle *vt.* (liquid) พรม prom | (liquid or powder) โรย rooi

sprinkler *n.* เครื่องพ่น krûuang-pôn [เครื่อง krûuang]

sprint *vi.* (run at full speed) วิ่งเต็มฝีเท้า wîng-dtem-fíi-táao

sprout *n.* (bean sprout) ถั่วงอก tùua-ngɔ̂ɔk [เส้น sên (sprout)] | (bud) หน่อ nɔ̀ɔ [หน่อ nɔ̀ɔ]

sprout *vi.* งอก ngɔ̂ɔk, แตกหน่อ dtὲεk-nɔ̀ɔ

spur *n.* (for horse, of rooster) เดือย duuai [เดือย duuai] | (sharp projection) ที่ยื่นแหลมออกมา tîi-yûun-lɛ̌εm-ɔ̀ɔk-maa

spur *vt.* (accelerate) เร่ง rêng

spy *n.* (detective) นักสืบ nák-sùup, สายลับ sǎai-láp [คน kon]

spy on *vt.* สืบ sùup

squad *n.* (group) หมู่ mùu [หมู่ mùu] | (police unit) กลุ่มตำรวจ glùm-dtam-rùuat [กลุ่ม glùm]

square *adj.* (at a right angle) ตั้งฉากกัน dtâng-chàak-gan | (four sides equal) จตุรัส jà-dtù~ràt

square *adv.* (e.g. square foot) ตาราง dtaa-raang

square *n.* (plaza) สแควร์ sà~kwεε [แห่ง hὲng] | (rectangle) สี่เหลี่ยมจตุรัส sìi-lìiam-jà~dtù~ràt |

(second power) กำลังสอง gam-lang-sɔ̌ɔng

square root *n.* รากที่สอง râak-tîi-sɔ̌ɔng

squash *n.* (plant) แตง dtɛɛng, ฟัก fák [ลูก lûuk]

squash *vt.* (crush) คั้น kán, บีบ bìip

squat *vi.* (crouch down) นั่งยองๆ nâng-yɔɔng-yɔɔng

squeaky *adj.* ที่ร้องเสียงแหลม tîi-rɔ́ɔng-sǐiang-lɛ̌ɛm

squeeze *vt.* (crush) คั้น kán, บีบ bìip

squid *n.* ปลาหมึก bplaa-mɨ̀k [ตัว dtuua]

squint *vi.* (with part-closed eyes) หรี่ตา rìi-dtaa

squirrel *n.* กระรอก grà~rɔ̂ɔk [ตัว dtuua]

squirt *n.* (liquid squirted) ของเหลวที่พุ่งออกมา kɔ̌ɔng-lěeo-tîi-pûng-ɔ̀ɔk-maa

squirt *v.* พ่น pôn

squirt out *vi.* พ่นออก pôn-ɔ̀ɔk

stab *vt.* แทง tɛɛng

stable *adj.* (e.g. tripod, job, economy) มั่นคง mân-kong, อยู่ตัว yùu-dtuua •

stable *n.* (horse) โรงม้า roong-máa [แห่ง hɛ̀ng]

stack *n.* (pile, heap) กอง gɔɔng [กอง gɔɔng]

stack *vt.* กอง gɔɔng, ตั้ง_ซ้อนกัน dtâng-_-sɔ́ɔn-gan

stadium *n.* (sports) สนามกีฬา sà~nǎam-gii-laa [แห่ง hɛ̀ng]

staff *n.* (baton, club) กระบอง grà~bɔɔng [อัน an] | (personnel) คณะผู้ทำงาน ká~ná-pûu-tam-ngaan [คณะ ká~ná]

stag *n.* (male deer) กวางตัวผู้ gwaang-dtuua-pûu [ตัว dtuua]

stage *n.* (of development) ขั้น kân [ขั้น kân] | (performance) เวที wee-tii [แห่ง hɛ̀ng]

stagger *vi.* (walk unsteadily) เดินโซเซ dəən-soo-see

stagger *vt.* (distribute, alternate) สับหลีก sàp-lìik

stagnant *adj.* (e.g. economy) ซบเซา sóp-sao | (still) หยุดนิ่ง yùt-nîng

stagnate *vi.* (become still) หยุดนิ่ง yùt-nîng | (cease to be active) ซบเซา sóp-sao

stain *n.* (blot, speck) รอยเปื้อน rɔɔi-bpûuan [จุด jùt]

stain *vt.* (make dirty) ทำให้_เปื้อน tam-hâi-_-bpûuan

stained *adj.* (dirty) เปื้อน bpûuan, สกปรก sòk-gà~bpròk

stair *n.* (step) ขั้นบันได kân-ban-dai [ขั้น kân]

staircase *n.* บันได ban-dai [อัน an, แห่ง hèng]

stairway see staircase

stake *n.* (money or property risked) ส่วนได้เสีย sùuan-dâai-sǐia | (pole) เสาหลัก sǎo-làk [ต้น dtôn]

stalactite *n.* หินย้อย hǐn-yɔ́ɔi [ก้อน gɔ̂ɔn]

stalagmite *n.* หินงอก hǐn-ngɔ̂ɔk [ก้อน gɔ̂ɔn]

stale *adj.* (musty, e.g. air) เหม็นอับ měn-àp, อับ àp | (not fresh) ไม่สด mâi sòt

stalk *n.* (stem) ก้าน gâan [ก้าน gâan] | (trunk) ต้น dtôn [ต้น dtôn]

stalk *v.* (follow secretly) ย่องตาม yɔ̂ng-dtaam

stall *n.* (booth) แผงลอย pěng-lɔɔi [แผง pěng] | (store) ร้าน ráan [ร้าน ráan]

stamina *n.* ความทรหด kwaam-tɔɔ-rá~hòt

stamp *n.* (postage) แสตมป์ sà~dtɛm [ดวง duuang] | (seal) ตรา dtraa [ตรา dtraa]

stamp *vt.* (e.g. with seal) ตีตรา dtii-dtraa | (with foot) กระทืบ grà~tʉ̂ʉp

stampede *n.* การวิ่งอลหม่าน gaan-wîng-on-lá~màan

stand *n.* (support frame, easel) ขาตั้ง kǎa-dtâng [ขา kǎa]

stand *vi.* (be standing: people) ยืน yʉʉn | (be standing: things) ตั้งอยู่

dtâng-yùu

stand *vt.* (endure) ทน_ได้
ton-_-dâai

standard *adj.*
เป็นมาตรฐาน bpen-
mâat-dtra~tăan

standard *n.* (criterion)
เกณฑ์ geen, มาตรฐาน
mâat-dtra~tăan

standardize *v.*
ทำให้_เป็นมาตรฐาน tam-
hâi-_-bpen-mâat-dtra~
tăan

stand for *vt.* (e.g.
abbreviation) ย่อมาจาก
yɔ̂ɔ-maa-jàak

stand-in *n.* ตัวแทน
dtuua-tɛɛn [คน kon]

stand out *vi.* (be
extraordinary and
different) เด่นชัด dèn-
chát

stand up *vi.* (get up)
ยืนขึ้น yʉʉn-kʉ̂n

staple *adj.* (basic, chief)
เป็นหลัก bpen-làk

staple *n.* (e.g. rice, bread)
อาหารหลัก aa-hăan-làk |
(for paper) ลูกสแตปเปิล
lûuk-sà~dtép-bpên [ลูก
lûuk (one), แถว tɛ̆ɛo
(row)]

staple *vt.* (use stapler on)
ติดสแตปเปิลบน dtìt-sà~
dtép-bpên-bon

stapler *n.* ที่เย็บกระดาษ
tîi-yép-grà~dàat,
สแต็ปเปิ้ล sà~dtép-bpên
[อัน an]

star *n.* (in a movie) ดารา
daa-raa [คน kon] | (in
the sky) ดาว daao [ดวง
duuang]

star *vi.* (perform) แสดง
sà~dɛɛng

starch *n.* แป้ง bpɛ̂ɛng
[กล่อง glɔ̀ng (box)]

stare *vi.* จ้อง jɔ̂ng, จ้องมอง
jɔ̂ng-mɔɔng

starfish *n.* ปลาดาว bplaa-
daao [ตัว dtuua]

starry *adj.* เต็มไปด้วยดาว
dtem-bpai-dûuai-daao

start *n.* (starting point)
จุดเริ่มต้น jùt-rɑ̂əm-dtôn
[จุด jùt]

start *v.* (begin) เริ่ม rɑ̂əm |
(turn on, e.g. machinery)
ติด dtìt

start engine *vi.* ติดเครื่อง
dtìt-krʉ̂uang

starter see appetizer

startle *vt.* ทำให้_ตกใจ

tam-hâi-_-dtòk-jai,
ทำให้_สะดุ้ง tam-hâi-_-
sà~dûng

startled *adj.* ตกใจ dtòk-
jai, สะดุ้ง sà~dûng
starve *vi.* หิวจัด hǐu-jàt |
(to death) อดตาย òt-dtaai
starving *adj.* หิวจัด hǐu-jàt
| (to death) อดอยาก òt-
yàak
state *n.* (condition) สภาพ
sà~pâap [สภาพ sà~
pâap] | (e.g. California)
รัฐ rát [รัฐ rát, แห่ง hèng]
state *vt.* กล่าว glàao ⚠
state enterprise *n.*
รัฐวิสาหกิจ rát-wí-sǎa-
hà-gìt
statement *n.* (e.g. bank)
ใบแจ้งรายการ bai-jɛ̂ɛng-
raai-gaan [ใบ bai] |
(words) คำให้การ kam-
hâi-gaan
statesman *n.* รัฐบุรุษ rát-
tà~bù-rút [คน kon]
static *n.* (electricity)
ไฟฟ้าสถิต fai-fáa-sà~tìt
⚒ | (noise) เสียงซ่า
sǐiang-sâa
station *n.* (e.g. TV, radio,
train) สถานี sà~tǎa-nii

[สถานี sà~tǎa-nii]
stationary *adj.* คงที่
konq-tîi, ไม่เคลื่อนที่ mâi-
klûuan-tîi
stationery *n.* เครื่องเขียน
krûuang-kǐian [ชิ้น chín]
statistics *n.* สถิติ sà~tì-dtì
status *n.* (circumstance,
condition) สภาวะ sà~
paa-wá [สภาวะ sà~paa-
wá, แห่ง hèng] | (rank,
position) สถานะ sà~tǎa-
ná [สถานะ sà~tǎa-ná]
statute of limitations *n.*
อายุความ aa-yú-kwaam
stay *vi.* (remain) อยู่ yùu |
(reside, lodge) พักอยู่
pák-yùu
stay away from *vt.*
ไม่มาใกล้ mâi-maa-glâi,
ออกห่าง ɔ̀ɔk-hàang
stay overnight *vi.* ค้างคืน
káang-kɯɯn
stay put *vi.* คงที่ kong-tîi,
ไม่ขยับ mâi-kà~yàp
steady *adj.* (constant)
สม่ำเสมอ sà~màm-sà~
mǝ̌ǝ | (firm) มั่นคง mân-
kong
steak *n.* สเต็ค sà~dtéek

[ชิ้น chín]

steal *v.* ขโมย kà~mooi

steam *n.* ไอน้ำ ai-náam

steam *vt.* (cook over steam) นึ่ง nûng | (double boil) ตุ๋น dtǔn

steamboat *n.* เรือกลไฟ ruua-gon-fai [ลำ lam]

steamship see steamboat

steamy *adj.* (e.g. mirror) ฝ้า fâa | (hot and humid) ร้อนอบอ้าว rɔ́ɔn-òp-âao

steel *n.* เหล็กกล้า lèk-glâa

steep *adj.* สูงชัน sǔung-chan

steer *vi.* (car) ถือพวงมาลัย tǔu-puang-maa-lai

steering wheel *n.* พวงมาลัย puang-maa-lai [อัน an]

stem *n.* (leaf or fruit stalk) ก้าน gâan, ขั้ว kûua [ก้าน gâan]

step *n.* (footstep) ก้าว gâao [ก้าว gâao] | (in a procedure) ขั้นตอน kân-dtɔɔn [ขั้น kân] | (of ladder, stairs) ขั้น kân [ขั้น kân]

step *vi.* ก้าว gâao

stepbrother *n.* พี่เลี้ยง pîi-líiang, พี่เลี้ยงชาย pîi-líiang-chaai [คน kon]

stepchild *n.* ลูกเลี้ยง lûuk-líiang [คน kon]

stepdaughter see stepson

stepfather *n.* พ่อเลี้ยง pɔ̂ɔ-líiang [คน kon]

stepmother *n.* แม่เลี้ยง mɛ̂ɛ-líiang [คน kon]

step on *vt.* เหยียบ yìiap

step over *vt.* ข้าม kâam

stepparent *n.* (father) พ่อเลี้ยง pɔ̂ɔ-líiang [คน kon] | (mother) แม่เลี้ยง mɛ̂ɛ-líiang [คน kon]

stepsister *n.* พี่เลี้ยง pîi-líiang, พี่เลี้ยงหญิง pîi-líiang-yǐng [คน kon]

stepson *n.* ลูกเลี้ยง lûuk-líiang [คน kon]

stereo *n.* (sound equipment) เครื่องเสียง krûuang-sǐiang, สเตริโอ sà~dtee-rí~oo [เครื่อง krûuang]

stereotype *n.* (sociology)

ทัศนคติทางสังคม tát-sà~
ná~ká~dtì-taang-săng-
kom

sterile *adj.* (childless)
เป็นหมัน bpen-măn |
(germ free) ปลอดเชื้อ
bplòɔt-chúua

sterilize *vt.* (kill germs in)
ฆ่าเชื้อใน kâa-chúua-nai |
(make infertile)
ทำให้_เป็นหมัน tam-hâi-
_-bpen-măn

sterling silver *n.*
โลหะเงินบริสุทธิ์ loo-hà-
ngən-bɔɔ-rí~sùt

stethoscope *n.*
หูฟังของแพทย์ hŭu-fang-
kɔ̌ɔng-pɛ̂ɛt [อัน an]

stew *n.* สตู sà~dtuu

stew *v.* เคี่ยว kîiao

steward *n.* (air) สจ๊วต sà~
júuat [คน kon]

stewardess *n.* (on the
plane) แอร์โฮสเตส ɛɛ-
hóot-sà~dtèet [คน kon]

stick *n.* (log, piece of
wood) ท่อนไม้ tɔ̂n-máai
[ท่อน tɔ̂n]

stick *vi.* (adhere, attach)
ติดกัน dtìt-gan

sticker *n.* สติ๊กเกอร์ sà~

dtík-gəə [แผ่น pèn]

stick in *vt.* (put it)
ใส่_เข้าไป sài-_-kâo-bpai

stick out *vi.* ยื่นออกมา
yûun-ɔ̀ɔk-maa

sticky *adj.* เหนียว nǐiao

sticky rice *n.* ข้าวเหนียว
kâao-nǐiao [กระสอบ
grà~sɔ̀ɔp (sack), ถุง tǔng
(bag)]

stiff *adj.* (e.g. manner)
แข็งทื่อ kĕng-tûu | (e.g.
muscle) เกร็ง greng |
(hard) แข็ง kĕng | (rigid)
เข้มงวด kêm-ngûuat

stigma *n.* มลทิน mon-tin

stigmatism *n.* สายตาเอียง
sǎai-dtaa-iiang

still *adj.* (calm, quiet)
เงียบสงบ ngîiap-sà~
ngòp | (motionless) นิ่ง
nîng

still *adv.* (yet) ยัง yang

stimulant *n.* (drug) ยาโด๊ป
yaa-dóop | (e.g. coffee)
สารกระตุ้น sǎan-grà~dtûn

stimulate *vt.* กระตุ้น
grà~dtûn, เร้า ráo

sting *vi.* (feel a sharp
pain) แสบ sɛ̀ɛp

sting *vt.* (e.g. bee) ต่อย dtòi | (other insects) กัด gàt

stingy *adj.* ขี้เหนียว kîi-nǐiao, งก ngók ✦

stink *vi.* เหม็น měn

stinky *adj.* เหม็น měn

stipulate *vt.* วางเงื่อนไข waang-ngûuan-kǎi

stipulation *n.* (agreement between lawyers) ข้อตกลงระหว่างทนาย kɔ̂ɔ-dtòk-long-rá~ wàang-tá~naai [ข้อ kɔ̂ɔ] | (condition) เงื่อนไข ngûuan-kǎi [ข้อ kɔ̂ɔ]

stir *v.* (blend) กวน guuan, คน kon

stitch *v.* (sew) เย็บ yép

stitching *n.* (sewing) การเย็บผ้า gaan-yép-pâa

stock *n.* (inventory) สต๊อก sà~dtɔ́k | (share of business) หุ้นส่วน hûn-sùuan [หุ้น hûn]

stock *vt.* (furnish with a stock) ใส่สต๊อก sài-sà~ dtɔ́ɔk

stockbroker *n.* นายหน้าซื้อขายหุ้น naai-

nâa-sʉ́ʉ-kǎai-hûn [คน kon]

stockholder *n.* ผู้ถือหุ้น pûu-tʉ̌ʉ-hûn [คน kon]

stocking *n.* ถุงน่อง tǔng-nɔ̂ng [ข้าง kâang (each), คู่ kûu (pair)]

stock market *n.* ตลาดหุ้น dtà~làat-hûn [แห่ง hɛ̀ng]

stocky *adj.* กำยำ gam-yam, ล่ำสัน lâm-sǎn

stomach *n.* ท้อง tɔ́ɔng | (organ) กระเพาะ grà~pɔ́ ✖ [กระเพาะ grà~pɔ́]

stomachache *n.* ปวดท้อง bpùuat-tɔ́ɔng, อาการปวดท้อง aa-gaan-bpùuat-tɔ́ɔng

stone *n.* ก้อนหิน gɔ̂ɔn-hǐn, หิน hǐn [ก้อน gɔ̂ɔn]

stool *n.* (chair) ม้านั่ง máa-nâng [ตัว dtuua] | (feces) อุจจาระ ùt-jaa-rá ‼ [กอง gɔɔng (pile), ก้อน gɔ̂ɔn]

stoop *vi.* (bend) ก้มตัวลง gôm-dtuua-long | (condescend) ถ่อมตัว tɔ̀m-dtuua

stop *v.* (e.g. car, talking,

machine) หยุด yùt **|** (e.g. workday, smoking, slavery) เลิก lə̂ək

stop vi. (rest, pause) พัก pák

stop vt. (prohibit) ห้าม hâam

stopover n. (in a journey) การหยุดระหว่างทาง gaan-yùt-rá~wàang-taang [ครั้ง kráng]

storage n. (act) การเก็บรักษา gaan-gèp-rák-sǎa **|** (for storing) ที่เก็บของ tîi-gèp-kɔ̌ɔng [ที่ tîi]

store n. (shop) ร้าน ráan [ร้าน ráan]

store vt. (keep, reserve) เก็บ_ไว้ gèp-_-wái

storehouse n. (warehouse) โกดัง goo-dang ✦ [แห่ง hɛ̀ng (location)]

storeroom n. ห้องเก็บของ hɔ̂ng-gèp-kɔ̌ɔng [ห้อง hɔ̂ng]

storm n. (weather) พายุ paa-yú, มรสุม mɔɔ-rá~sǔm ✦ [ลูก lûuk]

stormy adj. (e.g.

relationship) สับสนวุ่นวาย sàp-sǒn-wûn-waai **|** (weather) มีลมพายุ mii-lom-paa-yú

story n. (fable, tale) นิทาน ní-taan [เรื่อง rûuang] **|** (of building) ชั้น chán [ชั้น chán] **|** (situation, narrative) เรื่อง rûuang [เรื่อง rûuang]

stout adj. (sturdy) บึกบึน bʉ̀k-bʉn, ล่ำ lâm

stove n. เตา dtao [ใบ bai, ลูก lûuk]

stow v. (put in place) เก็บ_ให้เรียบร้อย gèp-_-hâi-rîiap-rɔ́ɔi

straight adj. (alcohol) ไม่ใส่อย่างอื่น mâi-sài-yàang-ʉ̀ʉn **|** (heterosexual) ชายจริงหญิงแท้ chaai-jing-yǐng-tɛ́ɛ ✦ **|** (not bent, candid) ตรง dtrong

straight adv. (candidly) ตรงไปตรงมา dtrong-bpai-dtrong-maa **|** (directly) ตรงดิ่ง dtrong-dìng

straight ahead adv.

ตรงไป dtrong-bpai

straighten *vt.* ทำให้_ตรง tam-hâi-_-dtrong

strain *n.* (injury to a muscle, etc.) การเคล็ดขัดยอก gaan-klét-kàt-yɔ̂ɔk

strain *vt.* (cause tension in) ทำให้_ตึงเครียด tam-hâi-_-dtʉng-krîiat | (filter) กรอง grɔɔng | (remove water from) ทำให้_สะเด็ดน้ำ tam-hâi-_-sà~dèt-náam

strait *n.* ช่องแคบ chông-kɛ̂ɛp [ช่อง chông]

strand *n.* (of rope) เกลียวเชือก gliiao-chʉ̂ak [เส้น sên]

stranded *adj.* โดนปล่อยเกาะ doon-bplɔ̀i-gɔ̀

strange *adj.* ประหลาด bprà~làat, แปลก bplɛ̀ɛk

stranger *n.* คนแปลกหน้า kon-bplɛ̀ɛk-nâa [คน kon]

strangle *vt.* (neck of) บีบคอ bìip-kɔɔ

strap *n.* (for fastening) สายรัด sǎai-rát [เส้น sên] | (leather) สายหนัง sǎai-

nǎng [เส้น sên]

strapless *adj.* ไม่มีสายหิ้วรั้ง mâi-mii-sǎai-hîu-ráng

strapless *n.* เสื้อเกาะอก sʉ̂a-gɔ̀-òk [ตัว dtuua]

strategize *vi.* วางแผน waang-pɛ̌ɛn

strategy *n.* (tactics) ชั้นเชิง chán-chəəng, ยุทธศาสตร์ yút-tá~sàat [อัน an]

straw *n.* (for drinks) หลอดดูด lɔ̀ɔt-dùut, หลอด lɔ̀ɔt ● [หลอด lɔ̀ɔt] | (hay) ฟาง faang [กอง gɔɔng (pile), เส้น sên (strand)]

strawberry *n.* สตรอเบอรี่ sà~dtrɔɔ-bəə-r̂ii [ลูก lûuk (fruit), ต้น dtôn (tree)]

stray *vi.* หลงทาง lǒng-taang

stream *n.* ลำธาร lam-taan, สายน้ำ sǎai-náam [สาย sǎai]

stream *vi.* ไหล lǎi

street *n.* ถนน tà~nǒn [เส้น sên, สาย sǎai]

streetwalker *n.* (prostitute) โสเภณี sǒo-pee-nii [คน kon]

strength *n.* (power) กำลัง gam-lang, เรี่ยวแรง rîiao-rɛɛng, แรง rɛɛng ✿, พลัง pá~lang ⚫

strengthen *vt.* (make stronger) ทำให้_แข็งแรง tam-hâi-_-kɛ̌ng-rɛɛng

strenuous *adj.* (energetic) แข็งขัน kɛ̌ng-kǎn, เหนื่อยยาก nùuai-yâak | (laborious) ที่ต้องออกแรง tîi-dtɔ̂ng-ɔ̀ɔk-rɛɛng

stress *n.* (on syllables) การเน้นเสียง gaan-nén-sǐiang | (tension) ความเครียด kwaam-krîiat

stress *vt.* (emphasize) เน้น néen

stressed *adj.* เครียด krîiat

stressful *adj.* ตึงเครียด dtʉng-krîiat

stretch *vi.* (body) ยืดเส้นยืดสาย yʉ̂ʉt-sên-yʉ̂ʉt-sǎai

stretch *vt.* (lengthen, widen, extend, enlarge) ยืด yʉ̂ʉt | (tighten) ทำให้_ตึง tam-hâi-_-dtʉng

stretcher *n.* (for carrying people) เตียงหาม dtiiang-hǎam [อัน an]

stretch out *vi.* ขยายออก kà~yǎai-ɔ̀ɔk

strict *adj.* เข้มงวด kêm-ngûat, เคร่งครัด krêng-krát

stride *n.* (long step) ก้าวยาว gâao-yaao ✿ [ก้าว gâao]

stride *v.* เดินก้าวยาว dəən-gâao-yaao

strike *n.* (work protest) การหยุดงานประท้วง gaan-yùt-ngaan-bprà~túuang ⚡, สไตรค์ sà~dtrái ✿

strike *vi.* (work protest) หยุดงานประท้วง yùt-ngaan-bprà~túuang

strike *vt.* (hit) ตี dtii

striking *adj.* (attractive) สวยสะดุดตา sǔuai-sà~dùt-dtaa | (noticeable) สะดุดตา sà~dùt-dtaa

string *n.* เชือก chʉ̂ʉak [เส้น sên (cord)]

string bean *n.* ถั่วฝักยาว tùua-fàk-yaao [ฝัก fàk]

strip *n.* (long piece) แผ่นยาว pɛ̀n-yaao [แถบ tɛ̀ɛp]

strip v. (remove clothing)
แก้ผ้า gɛ̀ɛ-pâa

stripe n. (line) ลายทางยาว
laai-taang-yaao [ลาย laai]

striptease n.
การเต้นระบำเปลื้องผ้า
gaan-dtên-rá~bam-
bplʉ̂ang-pâa

strive vi. ต่อสู้ dtɔ̀ɔ-sûu,
พากเพียร pâak-piian ✏

stroke n. (act of striking)
การตี gaan-dtii | (brain)
หลอดเลือดในสมองตีบ
lɔ̀ɔt-lʉ̂at-nai-sà~
mɔ̌ɔng-dtìip [โรค rôok] |
(swimming) ท่าว่ายน้ำ
tâa-wâai-náam

stroke vt. (touch lightly)
ลูบคลำ lûup-klam

stroll vi. เดินเล่น dəən-lên

stroller see baby carriage

strong adj. (body)
แข็งแรง kɛ̌ng-rɛɛng |
(emotion) เข้มแข็ง kêm-
kɛ̌ng | (hard) แข็ง kɛ̌ng |
(light) จ้า jâa

structure n. โครงสร้าง
kroong-sâang [โครงสร้าง
kroong-sâang]

struggle n. การต่อสู้
gaan-dtɔ̀ɔ-sûu

struggle vi. ดิ้นรน dîn-
ron, ต่อสู้ dtɔ̀ɔ-sûu

stub n. (e.g. ticket, check)
หาง hǎang [ใบ bai]

stubborn adj. ดื้อรั้น dʉ̂ʉ-
rán, หัวแข็ง hǔua-kɛ̌ng

student n. นักเรียน nák-
riian, ลูกศิษย์ lûuk-sìt ✏
[คน kon]

studio n. (apartment)
ห้องชุดขนาดเล็ก hɔ̂ng-
chút-kà~nàat-lék [ห้อง
hɔ̂ng] | (workroom)
สตูดิโอ sà~dtuu-dì~oo
[ห้อง hɔ̂ng]

studious adj. (in learning)
ขยันเรียน kà~yǎn-riian |
(industrious) อุตสาหะ ùt-
sǎa-hà ✏

study n. การเรียน gaan-
riian

study v. เรียน riian, ศึกษา
sʉ̀k-sǎa ⚠

study vi. เรียนหนังสือ
riian-nǎng~sʉ̌ʉ

stuff n. (things) ของ
kɔ̌ɔng, สิ่งของ sìng-kɔ̌ɔng
[อัน an, ชิ้น chín]

stuff vt. (_ into _)
ยัดไส้_ใส่_ yát-sâi-_-sài-_

stuffing n. (e.g. sweets, buns) ไส้ sâi [ชนิด chá~nít]

stuffy adj. (nose) คัดจมูก kát-jà~mùuk | (poorly ventilated) อบอ้าว òp-âao

stumble vi. (make mistake) ทำพลาด tam-plâat | (trip) สะดุด sà~dùt

stumble across vt. (person or thing) พบ_โดยบังเอิญ póp-_-dooi-bang-əən

stump n. (tree stump) ตอ dtɔɔ [ตอ dtɔɔ]

stun vt. (amaze) ทำให้_ตะลึงงัน tam-hâi-_-dtà~lʉng-ngan

stunned adj. (amazed) ตะลึง dtà~lʉng | (confused) งง ngong

stunning adj. (astonishing) น่าทึ่ง nâa-tûng | (of striking beauty) สวยจนต้องตะลึง sǔuai-jon-dtông-dtà~lʉng

stunt n. (dangerous feat) การแสดงโลดโผน gaan-sà~dɛɛng-lôot-pǒon

stuntman n. (stand-in) ตัวแสดงแทน dtuua-sà~dɛɛng-tɛɛn [คน kon, ตัว dtuua]

stupa n. เจดีย์ jee-dii, สถูป sà·tùup [องค์ ong]

stupid adj. โง่ ngôo, เซ่อ sə̂ə ☜

sturdy adj. (durable) แข็งแกร่ง kɛ̌ng-grɛ̀ng

stutter vi. พูดติดอ่าง pûut-dtìt-àang

sty n. (animal) คอก kɔ̂ɔk [คอก kɔ̂ɔk] | (eyelid) กุ้งยิง gûng-ying [โรค rôok]

style n. สไตล์ sà~dtaai [สไตล์ sà~dtaai]

stylist n. (in hair salon) ผู้ออกแบบทรงผม pûu-ɔ̀ɔk-bɛ̀ɛp-song-pǒm [คน kon]

subconscious n. จิตใต้สำนึก jìt-dtâai-sǎm-nʉ́k

subdistrict n. ตำบล dtam-bon [ตำบล dtam-bon]

subdivision n. การแบ่งย่อย gaan-bɛ̀ng-yɔ̂i

subject n. (citizen) ข้า kâa [คน kon] | (course) วิชา

wí-chaa [วิชา wí-chaa] |
(grammar)
ประธานของประโยค
bprà~taan-kɔ̌ɔng~
bprà~yôok | (matter,
story) เรื่อง rûuang [เรื่อง
rûuang] | (theme) หัวข้อ
hǔua-kɔ̂ɔ [หัวข้อ hǔua-
kɔ̂ɔ]
subjective adj.
(intangible, unmeasured)
เกี่ยวกับนามธรรม gìiao-
gàp-naam-má~tam
sublease vt. เช่าช่วง châo-
chûuang
sublet vt. เช่า_ต่อ châo-_-
dtɔ̀ɔ, แบ่ง_ให้เช่า bèng-_-
hâi-châo
sublime adj. (highest)
สูงสุด sǔung-sùt |
(splendid) ดีเลิศ dii-lə̂ət
submarine n. เรือดำน้ำ
ruua-dam-náam [ลำ lam]
submerge vi. (go under
water) ดำน้ำ dam-náam
submerge vt. (dip into
water) จุ่ม jùm
submissive adj.
ยอมทำตาม yɔɔm-tam-
dtaam, ว่าง่าย wâa-ngâai
submit vt. (hand in) มอบ

mɔ̂ɔp, ยื่น yûun |
(present) เสนอ sà~nɔ̌ɔ
subordinate adj.
(secondary) รอง rɔɔng
subordinate n. (at work)
ผู้อยู่ใต้บังคับบัญชา pûu-
yùu-dtâai-bang-káp-
ban-chaa [คน kon] |
(inferior, junior) ลูกน้อง
lûuk-nɔ́ɔng [คน kon]
subpoena n. หมายศาล
mǎai-sǎan [ใบ bai, ฉบับ
chà~bàp]
subscribe to vt. (e.g.
magazine) เป็นสมาชิก
bpen-sà~maa-chík
subsequent adj. ต่อมา
dtɔ̀ɔ-maa, ภายหลัง paai-
lǎng
subside vi. (diminish)
ลดลง lót-long | (e.g.
pain) บรรเทา ban-tao |
(sink) จมลง jom-long
subsidiary adj. (minor)
เป็นรอง bpen-rɔɔng
subsidiary n. (company)
บริษัทสาขา bɔɔ-rí~sàt-
sǎa-kǎa [แห่ง hèng]
subsidize vt. ให้เงินอุดหนุน
hâi-ngən-ùt-nǔn
subsidy n. เงินอุดหนุน
ngən-ùt-nǔn

substance *n.* (gist, essence) เนื้อหา núua-hǎa, สาระ sǎa-rá | (physical) สาร sǎan

substantial *adj.* (meaningful) มีแก่นสาร mii-gɛ̀n-sǎan | (significant) สำคัญ sǎm-kan

substitute *n.* (person) ตัวแทน dtuua-tɛɛn [คน kon]

substitute for *vt.* แทน tɛɛn

subtitle *n.* (movie) คำแปลหนัง kam-bplɛɛ-nǎng ✴ | (under title) หัวข้อย่อย hǔua-kɔ̂ɔ-yɔ̂i [เรื่อง rûuang]

subtle *adj.* (hard to understand) เข้าใจยาก kâo-jai-yâak | (implied) ที่บอกเป็นนัยๆ tîi-bɔ̀ɔk-bpen-nai-nai

subtract *vt.* ลบ_ออก lóp-_ɔ̀ɔk

suburb *n.* ชานเมือง chaan-muuang [เขต kèet]

subway *n.* (train) รถไฟใต้ดิน rót-fai-dtâai-din [ขบวน kà~buuan, คัน kan]

succeed *vi.* (achieve success) สำเร็จ sǎm-rèt

succeed *vt.* (e.g. inherit role or business from) สืบทอด sùup-tɔ̂ɔt

success *n.* (achievement) ความสำเร็จ kwaam-sǎm-rèt

successful *adj.* มีชัยชนะ mii-chai-chá~ná

succession *n.* (royal) การสืบสันตติวงศ์ gaan-sùup-sǎn-dtà-dtì-wong ǃ

such *adj.* เช่นนี้ chên-níi

such *pron.* (person) คนนี้ kon-níi | (thing) สิ่งนี้ sìng-níi

such as *adv.* เช่น chên

such as *conj.* (for example) ตัวอย่างเช่น dtuua-yàang-chên

suck *v.* ดูด dùut

suck *vi.* (be very bad) แย่มาก yɛ̂ɛ-mâak ✴

suction *n.* การดูด gaan-dùut

sudden *adj.* กะทันหัน gà~tan-hǎn, ทันที tan-tii

suddenly *adv.* โดยทันทีทันใด dooi-tan-tii-tan-dai, อย่างรวดเร็ว yàang-rûuat-reo

suds *n.* ฟองสบู่ fɔɔng-sà~bùu

sue *v.* ฟ้อง fɔɔng, ฟ้องร้อง fɔɔng-rɔ́ɔng

suede *n.* หนังนิ่ม năng-nîm

suffer *v.* ทนทุกข์ ton-túk, อดทน òt-ton

suffering *adj.* ที่ทุกข์ทรมาน tîi-túk-tɔɔ-rá~maan

suffering *n.* (hardship) ความทุกข์ยาก kwaam-túk-yâak

sufficient *adj.* พอ pɔɔ, เพียงพอ piiang-pɔɔ

suffix *n.* คำต่อท้าย kam-dtɔɔ-tái [คำ kam]

suffocate *vi.* (be unable to breathe) หายใจไม่ออก hăai-jai-mâi-ɔɔk

suffocate *vt.* (prevent from breathing) ทำให้_หายใจไม่ออก tam-hâi-_-hăai-jai-mâi-ɔɔk

sugar *n.* น้ำตาล nám-dtaan [ช้อน chɔɔn (spoonful)]

sugarcane *n.* อ้อย ɔ̂ɔi [ต้น dtôn (plant)]

sugar daddy *n.* ป๋า bpăa 🐾 [คน kon]

sugary *adj.* (containing sugar) ใส่น้ำตาล sài-nám-dtaan | (sweet) หวาน wăan

suggest *vt.* (advise) แนะนำ né-nam

suggestion *n.* (advice) คำแนะนำ kam-né-nam [อัน an]

suicide *n.* การฆ่าตัวตาย gaan-kâa-dtuua-dtaai

suit *n.* (card) ชุดไพ่สีเดียวกัน chút-pâi-sĭi-diiao-gan [สำหรับ săm-ráp] | (garment) ชุดสูท chút-sùut [ชุด chút] | (lawsuit) คดีความ ká~dii-kwaam, ความ kwaam 🐾 [คดี ká~dii, เรื่อง rûuang]

suit *v.* เหมาะกับ mò-gàp

suitable *adj.* สมควร sŏm-kuuan, เหมาะสม mò-sŏm

suitcase *n.* กระเป๋าเดินทาง grà~bpăo-dəən-taang [ใบ bai]

suite *n.* (group of things) ชุด chút [ชุด chút] | (room) ห้องชุด hɔ̂ɔng-chút [ห้อง hɔ̂ɔng]

sulfur *n.* กำมะถัน gam-má~tăn

sulky *adj.* บึ้งตึง bûng-dtung, ไม่พูดไม่จา mâi-pûut-mâi-jaa

sum *n.* (math) ผลบวก pŏn-bùuak | (total) ยอด yɔ̂ɔt ✱

summarize *v.* สรุป sà~rùp

summary *n.* บทสรุป bòt-sà~rùp [บท bòt]

summer *n.* ฤดูร้อน rɤ́-duu-rɔ́ɔn [ฤดู rɤ́-duu] | หน้าร้อน nâa-rɔ́ɔn ✱ [หน้า nâa]

summit *n.* จุดสูงสุด jùt-sŭung-sùt

summon *vt.* (order to appear) ออกหมายเรียก ɔ̀ɔk-măai-rîiak

summons *n.* (subpoena) หมายเรียกตัว măai-rîiak-dtuua [ใบ bai, ฉบับ chà~bàp]

sum up *v.* สรุป sà~rùp

sun *n.* ดวงอาทิตย์ duuang-aa-tít, อาทิตย์ aa-tít, พระอาทิตย์ prá~aa-tít ❢ [ดวง duuang]

sun *vi.* ตากแดด dtàak-dὲɛt

sunblind *n.* ม่านกันแดด mâan-gan-dὲɛt [อัน an]

sunburn *n.* ผิวเกรียมแดด pĭu-griiam-dὲɛt

Sunday *n.* วันอาทิตย์ wan-aa-tít [วัน wan]

sundial *n.* นาฬิกาแดด naa-lí~gaa-dὲɛt [เรือน ruuan]

sunflower *n.* ทานตะวัน taan-dtà~wan [ต้น dtôn (tree), ดอก dɔ̀ɔk (flower)]

sunglasses *n.* แว่นกันแดด wɛ̂n-gan-dὲɛt [อัน an]

sunlight *n.* แสงแดด sɛ̌ɛng-dὲɛt

sunny *adj.* (bright) แดดออก dὲɛt-ɔ̀ɔk, มีแสงแดด mii-sɛ̌ɛng-dὲɛt

sunny side-up egg *n.* ไข่ดาว kài-daao [ใบ bai]

sunrise *n.* พระอาทิตย์ขึ้น prá~aa-tít-kûn

sunscreen *n.* (cream) ครีมกันแดด kriim-gan-dὲɛt [หลอด lɔ̀ɔt (tube)] | (shade awning) ผ้าใบ pâa-bai [ผืน pŭɯn, แผ่น pὲn]

sunset *n.* พระอาทิตย์ตก prá~aa-tít-dtòk

sunshine *n.* แสงแดด

sɛ̌ɛng-dɛ̀ɛt

sunstroke *n.* ลมแดด
lom-dɛ̀ɛt [โรค rôok]

super *adj.* (above normal)
เกินธรรมดา gəən-tam-
má~daa | (wonderful)
วิเศษ wí-sèet, สุดขีด sùt-
kiit ✿, สุดยอด sùt-yɔ̂ɔt ✿

superb *adj.* (elegant)
หรูหรา rǔu-rǎa |
(excellent) ดีเลิศ dii-lə̂ət

superficial *adj.* (external,
near the surface) ผิวเผิน
pǐu-pə̌ən

superior *n.* (in rank)
ผู้บังคับบัญชา pûu-bang-
káp-ban-chaa [คน kon]

superior to *prep.* (better
than) เหนือกว่า nʉ̌a-
gwàa | (in rank) สูงกว่า
sǔung-gwàa

superlative *adj.* (highest,
greatest) สูงสุด sǔung-sùt

supermarket *n.*
ซูเปอร์มาร์เก็ต súp-
bpəə-maa-gét [แห่ง hɛ̀ng]

supernatural *adj.*
เหนือธรรมชาติ nʉ̌a-
tam-má~châat

superpower *n.* มหาอำนาจ
má~hǎa-am-nâat

supersede *vt.* แทนที่ tɛɛn-

tîi

superstitious *adj.*
เชื่อโชคลาง chʉ̂a-
chôok-laang

supervise *v.* ดูแล duu-lɛɛ

supervise *vt.* ควบคุม
kûap-kum

supervisor *n.* (overseer,
boss) หัวหน้างาน hǔa-
nâa-ngaan [คน kon]

supper *n.* อาหารค่ำ aa-
hǎan-kâm [มื้อ mʉ́ʉ]

supplement *n.* (addition)
ส่วนเพิ่มเติม sùuan-
pə̂əm-dtəəm | (e.g.
vitamins) อาหารเสริม aa-
hǎan-sə̌əm

supplement *vt.* เสริม sə̌əm

supplementary *adj.*
ที่ช่วยเสริม tîi-chûai-
sə̌əm, ที่เพิ่มเติม tîi-
pə̂əm-dtəəm

supplier *n.* ผู้จัดหาให้ pûu-
jàt-hǎa-hâi [คน kon]

supply *n.* เสบียง sà~biiang

supply *vi.* (provide _ for _)
จัดหา_ให้_ jàt-hǎa-_-hâi_

support *n.* (act)
การสนับสนุน gaan-sà~
nàp-sà~nǔn

support *vt.* (back up)

support

สนับสนุน sà~nàp-sà~nǔn | (provide for) ช่วยเหลือ chûuai-lǔ̌ua | (withstand, e.g. weight) ค้ำ kám

supporter n. ผู้สนับสนุน pûu-sà~nàp-sà~nǔn [คน kon]

supportive adj. ช่วยเป็นกำลังใจ chûuai-bpen-gam-lang-jai, สนับสนุน sà~nàp-sà~nǔn

suppose vt. (assume) สมมุติ sǒm-mút | (guess) เดา dao, ทึกทักเอา túk-ták-ao

suppository n. ยาเหน็บ yaa-nèp [เม็ด mét]

suppress vt. (e.g. feelings, smile) กลั้น glân | (e.g. press, symptoms) ระงับ rá~ngáp | (e.g. uprising, crime) ปราบปราม bpràap-bpraam

supreme adj. (highest) สูงสุด sǔung-sùt

supreme court n. ศาลฎีกา sǎan-dii-gaa [ศาล sǎan]

sure adj. (certain, definite) แน่นอน nɛ̂ɛ-nɔɔn | (convinced) แน่ใจ nɛ̂ɛ-jai

surf vi. (ride a surfboard)

เล่นกระดานโต้คลื่น lên-grà~daan-dtôo-klûʉn

surface n. ผิวหน้า pǐu-nâa, พื้นผิว pʉ́ʉn-pǐu

surge n. (sudden increase) การเพิ่มขึ้นอย่างรวดเร็ว gaan-pə̂əm-kʉ̂n-yàang-rûuat-reo

surge vi. (rise and fall) ขึ้นๆลงๆ kʉ̂n-kʉ̂n-long-long

surgeon n. ศัลยแพทย์ sǎn-yá~pɛ̂ɛt, หมอผ่าตัด mɔ̌ɔ-pàa-dtàt ● [คน kon]

surgery n. การผ่าตัด gaan-pàa-dtàt, ศัลยกรรม sǎn-yá~gam [ครั้ง kráng]

surgical adj. (of surgery) ศัลยกรรม sǎn-yá~gam

surname n. นามสกุล naam-sà~gun [อัน an]

surpass vt. เกินกว่า gəən-gwàa, ล้ำหน้า lám-nâa

surplus n. (excess) จำนวนที่เกิน jam-nuuan-tîi-gəən

surprise n. (astonishment) ความประหลาดใจ

surprise n.
kwaam-bprà~làat-jai

surprise v.
ทำให้_ประหลาดใจ tam-
hâi-_-bprà~làat-jai

surprised adj. ประหลาดใจ
bprà~làat-jai

surprising adj.
น่าประหลาดใจ nâa-bprà~
làat-jai

surrender n. (act)
การส่งมอบตัว gaan-
sòng-mɔ̂ɔp-dtuua

surrender vi. (give in)
ยอมแพ้ yɔɔm-pɛ́ɛ | (to
the police) มอบตัว
mɔ̂ɔp-dtuua

surrogate n. (mother)
หญิงที่รับอุ้มท้องแทน
yǐng-tîi-ráp-ûm-tɔ́ɔng-
tɛɛn [คน kon]

surround vt. ล้อม lɔ́ɔm,
ห้อมล้อม hɔ̂ɔm-lɔ́ɔm

surrounding adj. แวดล้อม
wɛ̂ɛt-lɔ́ɔm

surrounding n.
(environment) สิ่งแวดล้อม
sìng-wɛ̂ɛt-lɔ́ɔm [แห่ง
hèng]

surveillance n. (close
observation)
การสะกดรอย gaan-sà~
gòt-rɔɔi

survey n. การสำรวจ gaan-
sǎm-rùuat

survey v. สำรวจ sǎm-rùuat

survival n. การอยู่รอด
gaan-yùu-rɔ̂ɔt

survive vi. (remain alive)
รอด rɔ̂ɔt, รอดตาย rɔ̂ɔt-
dtaai, อยู่รอด yùu-rɔ̂ɔt

survive vt. (live through,
e.g. misery) สู้ชีวิตกับ
sûu-chii-wít-gàp

survivor n. ผู้รอดชีวิต
pûu-rɔ̂ɔt-chii-wít [คน
kon]

suspect n. (accused)
ผู้ต้องหา pûu-dtɔ̂ng-hǎa
[คน kon, ราย raai !]

suspect vt. สงสัย sǒng-sǎi

suspend vt. (e.g. from
school, job) ให้หยุดพัก
hâi-yùt-pák | (hang,
dangle) แขวน kwɛ̌ɛn |
(postpone) เลื่อน lɯ̂an

suspenders n. (pants)
สายโยงกางเกง sǎai-
yoong-gaang-geeng
[สาย sǎai]

suspense n. (awaiting
with excitement)
ความใจจดใจจ่อ kwaam-
jai-jòt-jai-jɔ̀ɔ

suspension n. (e.g. from

school) การให้หยุดพัก gaan-hâi-yùt-pák |

(postponement) การเลื่อน gaan-lûuan

suspicious *adj.* น่าสงสัย nâa-sǒng-sǎi, ระแวง rá~wɛɛng

sustain *vt.* (e.g. injuries) ประสบ bprà~sòp | (maintain, e.g. job, level) รักษา_ไว้ได้ rák-sǎa-_-wái-dâai | (support) ค้ำจุน kám-jun

swab *n.* (absorbent cloth) ผ้าซับ pâa-sáp [ผืน pǔɯn]

swab *vt.* (with cotton) ทา_ด้วยสำลี taa-_-dûuai-sǎm-lii

swallow *n.* (bird) นกนางแอ่น nók-naang-ɛ̀n [ตัว dtuua]

swallow *vt.* (down throat) กลืน glɯɯn

swallow one's words *vi.* กลับคำ glàp-kam

swamp *n.* (bog, marsh) บึง bɯng, หนอง nɔ̌ɔng [แห่ง hɛ̀ng]

swamp *v.* (inundate) ทำให้_ท่วม tam-hâi-_-tûuam

swan *n.* หงส์ hǒng [ตัว dtuua]

swap *n.* (exchange) การแลกเปลี่ยน gaan-lɛ̂ɛk-bpliian

swap *v.* แลกเปลี่ยน lɛ̂ɛk-bpliian

swarm *n.* (e.g. bees, insects) ฝูง fǔung [ฝูง fǔung]

swarm *vi.* (crowd together) จับเป็นกลุ่ม jàp-bpen-glùm

sway *vi.* แกว่งไกว gwɛ̀ng-gwai, ส่าย sàai

swear *vi.* (curse) สาปแช่ง sàap-chɛ̂ng

swear *vt.* (vow) สาบาน sǎa-baan

sweat *n.* (perspiration) เหงื่อ ngùɯa

sweat *vi.* (perspire) เหงื่อออก ngùɯa-ɔ̀ɔk

sweater *n.* เสื้อกันหนาว sûɯa-gan-nǎao, เสื้อสเวตเตอร์ sûɯa-sà~wêet-dtəə [ตัว dtuua]

Sweden *n.* สวีเดน sà~wii-deen [ประเทศ bprà~têet]

sweep *v.* (with broom) กวาด gwàat

sweep *vt.* (get rid of) กวาดล้าง gwàat-láang

sweet *adj.* (lovable) น่ารัก nâa-rák | (sound) ไพเราะ pai-rɔ́ ! | (taste) หวาน wǎan

sweetheart *n.* (loved one) คนรัก kon-rák, แฟน fɛɛn [คน kon] | (my darling) ที่รัก tîi-rák [คน kon] | (sweet person) คนน่ารัก kon-nâa-rák [คน kon]

sweethearts *n.* คู่รัก kûu-rák [คู่ kûu]

sweet potato *n.* มันเทศ man-têet [หัว hǔua]

sweets *n.* ขนม kà~nǒm, ของหวาน kɔ̌ɔng-wǎan [อัน an (piece), ชิ้น chín (piece), ถ้วย tûuai (bowl)]

swell *vi.* (be inflamed) บวม buuam | (increase in size) พอง pɔɔng

swelling *n.* (from infection) การขยายตัว gaan-kà~yǎai-dtuua, การบวม gaan-buuam

swerve *vi.* (turn aside abruptly) หักเลี้ยวอย่างเร็ว hàk-líiao-yàang-reo

swift *adj.* (fast) เร็ว reo, ว่องไว wông-wai ! | (sudden) ทันที tan-tii

swim *vi.* ว่ายน้ำ wâai-náam, ว่าย wâai ●

swimmer *n.* นักว่ายน้ำ nák-wâai-náam [คน kon]

swimming *n.* การว่ายน้ำ gaan-wâai-náam

swimming pool *n.* สระว่ายน้ำ sà-wâai-náam [แห่ง hɛ̀ng, สระ sà]

swimsuit *n.* ชุดว่ายน้ำ chút-wâai-náam [ชุด chút]

swing *n.* (to sit on) ชิงช้า ching-cháa [อัน an]

swing *v.* (rock) ไกว gwai

swing *vi.* (back and forth) แกว่งไปมา gwɛ̀ng-bpai-maa

swipe *vt.* (e.g. card) รูด rûut | (hit hard) ตี_อย่างแรง dtii-_-yàang-rɛɛng

switch *n.* (for turning on and off) ที่เปิดปิด tîi-bpə̀ət-bpìt, สวิตช์ sà~wìt [อัน an, ตัว dtuua]

switch *v.* เปลี่ยน bplìian,

สับเปลี่ยน sàp-bplìian
switch off *vt.* (turn off)
ปิด bpìt
Switzerland *n.*
สวิตเซอร์แลนด์ sà~wíit-
səə-lɛɛn [ประเทศ bprà~
têet]
swollen *adj.* (increased in
size) พอง pɔɔng |
(inflamed) บวม buuam
sword *n.* ดาบ dàap [เล่ม
lêm]
syllable *n.* พยางค์ pá~
yaang [พยางค์ pá~yaang]
symbol *n.* สัญลักษณ์ sǎn-
yá~lák [อัน an]
symbolic *adj.*
เป็นสัญลักษณ์ bpen-sǎn-
yá~lák
symbolize *vt.*
เป็นสัญลักษณ์ของ bpen-
sǎn-yá~lák-kʉ̌ɔng
symmetry *n.*
ความสมมาตร kwaam-
sǒm-mâat
sympathetic *adj.* สงสาร
sǒng-sǎan, เห็นอกเห็นใจ
hěn-òk-hěn-jai
sympathize *vi.* เห็นใจ
hěn-jai
sympathy *n.*

ความเห็นอกเห็นใจ
kwaam-hěn-òk-hěn-jai
symphony *n.* (music)
ดนตรีประสานเสียง don-
dtrii-bprà~sǎan-sǐiang
symptom *n.* (sign,
indication) อาการ aa-gaan
synagogue *n.* โบสถ์ยิว
bòot-yiu ● [โบสถ์ bòot]
syndrome *n.* (group of
symptoms) อาการของโรค
ที่เกิดขึ้นพร้อมกัน aa-
gaan-kʉ̌ɔng-rôok-tîi-
gə̀ət-kʉ̂n-prɔ́ɔm-gan
[อาการ aa-gaan]
synonym *n.*
คำพ้องความหมาย kam-
pɔ́ɔng-kwaam-mǎai [คำ
kam]
synopsis *n.* ใจความสำคัญ
jai-kwaam-sǎm-kan
syntax *n.* การสร้างประโยค
gaan-sâang-bprà~yòok
synthesize *vt.* สังเคราะห์
sǎng-krɔ́
syphilis *n.* ซิฟิลิส sí-fí-lít
[โรค rôok]
syringe *n.* (medical
instrument) กระบอกฉีดยา
grà~bɔ̀ɔk-chìit-yaa,
เข็มฉีดยา kěm-chìit-yaa

[เข็ม kĕm, อัน an ✱]

syrup n. (drink sweetener) น้ำเชื่อม nám-chûuam [ขวด kùuat] | (medicine) ยาน้ำเชื่อม yaa-nám-chûuam [ขวด kùuat]

system n. ระบบ rá~bòp [ระบบ rá~bòp]

T

tab n. (computer keyboard) แท็บ tép ✱ [ปุ่ม bpùm] | (flap, short strip) แถบ tɛ̀ɛp [แถบ tɛ̀ɛp]

table n. (chart) ตาราง dtaa-raang [ตาราง dtaa-raang, อัน an] | (furniture) โต๊ะ dtó [ตัว dtuua]

tablecloth n. ผ้าปูโต๊ะ pâa-bpuu-dtó [ผืน pʉ̌ʉn]

tablespoon n. ช้อนโต๊ะ chɔ́ɔn-dtó [คัน kan]

tablet n. (pill) ยาเม็ด yaa-mét [เม็ด mét] | (scratch pad) สมุดฉีก sà~mùt-chìik [เล่ม lêm] | (stone) หินสลัก hǐn-sà~làk [แผ่น pɛ̀n]

table tennis n. ปิงปอง bping-bpɔɔng

taboo adj. ต้องห้าม dtɔ̂ng-hâam

taboo n. (something prohibited) สิ่งต้องห้าม sìng-dtɔ̂ng-hâam [อย่าง yàang]

tack n. (e.g. for paper) หมุด mùt [ตัว dtuua] | (flat-top nail) ตะปูหัวแบน dtà~bpuu-hǔua-bɛɛn [ตัว dtuua, ดอก dɔ̀ɔk]

tack vt. (fasten, pin) ติดตะขอ dtìt-dtà~kɔ̌ɔ

tactic n. (secret technique) เคล็ดลับ klét-láp [ข้อ kɔ̂ɔ] | (trick) ชั้นเชิง chán-chəəng [อัน an]

tadpole n. ลูกกบ lûuk-gòp, ลูกอ๊อด lûuk-ɔ́ɔt ✱ [ตัว dtuua]

Taechew adj. (Chinese group) แต้จิ๋ว dtɛ̂ɛ-jǐu

taekwondo n. เทควันโด tee-kwan-doo

tag n. (label) ฉลาก chà~làak, สลาก sà~làak [ใบ bai, แผ่น pɛ̀n] | (sign) ป้าย bpâai [ป้าย bpâai, แผ่น pɛ̀n]

tag vt. (label) ติดป้าย dtìt-bpâai

tail *adj.* ข้างท้าย kâang-táai

tail *n.* (buttocks) บั้นท้าย bân-táai | (e.g. animal) หาง hǎang [หาง hǎang] | (e.g. plane, speech) ส่วนท้าย sùuan-táai

tail *vt.* (follow close behind) ตามติด dtaam-dtìt

tailgate *v.* (drive closely) ขับรถตามติดๆ kàp-rót-dtaam-dtìt-dtìt

taillight *n.* ไฟท้าย fai-táai [ดวง duuang]

tailor *n.* ช่างตัดเสื้อ châng-dtàt-sûua [คน kon]

tails *n.* (coin) ก้อย gôoi [ด้าน dâan]

Taiwan *n.* ไต้หวัน dtâi-wǎn [ประเทศ bprà~têet]

take *vt.* (ꞈ (someone) from here (to)) พา_ไป paa-_-bpai | (ꞈ (someone) here (to)) พา_มา paa-_-maa | (something, some vehicle) from here (to)) เอา_ไป ao-_-bpai | (ꞈ (something, some vehicle) here (to)) เอา_มา ao-_-maa | (choose) เลือก lûuak | (e.g. medicine, meal) ทาน taan ⚡, กิน gin 🔊 | (endure) ทน_ได้ ton-_-dâai | (get, grab) เอา ao | (study) เรียน riian

take an oath *vi.* สาบานตน sǎa-baan-dton

take apart *vt.* แยกชิ้นส่วน_ออก yɛ̂ɛk-chín-sùuan-_-ɔ̀ɔk

take a picture *vi.* ถ่ายรูป tàai-rûup, ถ่ายภาพ tàai-pâap ⚡

take a trip *vi.* เดินทาง dəən-taang, ไปเที่ยว bpai-tîiao

take away *vt.* (item) เอา_ไปที่อื่น ao-_-bpai-tîi-ùun | (person) พา_ไปที่อื่น paa-_-bpai-tîi-ùun

takeaway see takeout

take back *vt.* (return for exchange) เอา_ไปคืน ao-_-bpai-kuun

take back one's words *vi.* ถอนคำพูด tǔan-kam-pûut

take care of *vt.* (deal

with) จัดการกับ jàt-gaan-gàp | (look after, treat) ดูแล duu-lɛɛ, รักษา rák-sǎa

take charge of *vt.* (be responsible) รับผิดชอบ ráp-pìt-chɔ̂ɔp | (oversee, control) ควบคุมดูแล kûuap-kum-duu-lɛɛ

take medicine *vi.* ทานยา taan-yaa ⚠

take off *vi.* (for a trip) ออกเดินทาง ɔ̀ɔk-dəən-taang

take off *vt.* (e.g. clothes, shoes) ถอด tɔ̀ɔt | (take as vacation) หยุด yùt

take out *vt.* (extract or remove) เอา_ออก ao-_-ɔ̀ɔk

takeout *adj.* (food) ที่ห่อกลับบ้าน tîi-hɔ̀ɔ-glàp-bâan

take over *vi.* (assume control) รับช่วงต่อ ráp-chûuang-dtɔ̀ɔ

take place *vi.* เกิดขึ้น gə̀ət-kûn

take space *vt.* กินที่ gin-tîi

take time *vi.* ใช้เวลา chái-wee-laa

take time *vt.* กินเวลา gin-wee-laa ⚠

take turns *vi.* ผลัดกัน plàt-gan, สลับกัน sà~làp-gan

talc *n.* แป้งผง bpɛ̂ɛng-pǒng [กระป๋อง grà~bpɔ̌ng (can)]

tale *n.* (story, fable) นิทาน ní-taan, เรื่องเล่า rûuang-lâo [เรื่อง rûuang]

talent *n.* (natural gift) ความสามารถพิเศษ kwaam-sǎa-mâat-pí-sèet, พรสวรรค์ pɔɔn-sà~wǎn [อย่าง yàang]

talented *adj.* มีพรสวรรค์ mii-pɔɔn-sà~wǎn

talk *vi.* (chat, converse) คุย kui, พูด pûut, พูดคุย pûut-kui ⚠, สนทนา sǒn-tá~naa ⚠

talkative *adj.* ช่างคุย châng-kui, พูดเก่ง pûut-gèng

talk show *n.* ทอล์คโชว์ tɔ̂ɔk-choo ⚠ [รายการ raai-gaan]

tall *adj.* (in height) สูง sǔung

tamarind *n.* (fruit) มะขาม má~kǎam [ฝัก fàk (fruit),

ต้น dtôn (tree)]

tamarind sauce n.
น้ำมะขาม nám-má~kăam

tame adj. (animal) เชื่อง chûuang | (submissive) ว่าง่าย wâa-ngâai

tame v. ทำให้_เชื่อง tam-hâi-_-chûuang

tampon n.
ผ้าอนามัยแบบสอด pâa-à~naa-mai-bÈɛp-sɔ̀ɔt [อัน an, แท่ง tÊɛng]

tan adj. มีผิวสีน้ำตาล mii-pĭu-sĭi-nám-dtaan

tan n. (color) สีน้ำตาลไหม้ sĭi-nám-dtaan-mâi [สี sĭi]

tangerine n. (orange) ส้มเขียวหวาน sôm-kĭiao-wăan [ลูก lûuk]

tangible adj. (capable of being touched) จับต้องได้ jàp-dtɔ̂ng-dâai, สัมผัสได้ săm-pàt-dâai

tangle vi. พัวพัน puua-pan, ยุ่งเหยิง yûng-yə̆əng

tangle vt. ทำให้_ยุ่งเหยิง tam-hâi-_-yûng-yə̆əng

tank n. (combat vehicle) รถถัง rót-tăng [คัน kan] | (container) ถัง tăng [ใบ

bai]

tanker n. (cargo ship) เรือบรรทุก ruua-ban-túk [ลำ lam] | (truck to carry petrol) รถบรรทุกน้ำมัน rót-ban-túk-nám-man [คัน kan]

tank top n. เสื้อแขนกุด sûua-kĕɛn-gùt [ตัว dtuua]

Taoism n. ลัทธิเต๋า lát-tí-dtăo [ลัทธิ lát-tí]

tap adj. (e.g. water) ก๊อก gɔ́k

tap n. (faucet) ก๊อกน้ำ gɔ́k-náam [ก๊อก gɔ́k]

tap vt. (pat lightly) ตบ_เบาๆ dtòp-_-bao-bao | (strike, e.g. with fingers) เคาะ kɔ́

tape n. (adhesive) กระดาษกาว grà~dàat-gaao [ม้วน múuan (roll), แผ่น pÈn (sheet)] | (cassette) เทป téep [ม้วน múuan] | (measuring) สายวัด săai-wát [เส้น sên]

tape vt. (record a sound) บันทึกเสียง ban-túk-sĭiang

tape player n.
เครื่องเล่นเทป krûuang-

lên-téep [เครื่อง krûuang]

taper v. (become thin)
เรียวลง riiao-long

tape recorder n.
เครื่องเล่นเทป krûuang-
lên-téep [เครื่อง krûuang]

tapestry n. (woven
material) สิ่งทอ sìng-tɔɔ
[ชิ้น chín]

tapeworm n. พยาธิตัวตืด
pá~yâat-dtuua-dtùut
[ตัว dtuua]

tapioca n. (flour)
แป้งมันสำปะหลัง
bpɛ̂ɛng-man-sǎm-bpà~
lǎng | (pudding)
ขนมพุดดิ้ง kà~nǒm-pút-
dîng, สาคู sǎa-kuu [ถ้วย
tûuai (bowl)]

tar adj. (e.g. asphalt road)
ราดยาง râat-yaang

tar n. (coal tar) น้ำมันดิน
nám-man-din [แกลลอน
gɛn-lɔn (gallon), ลิตร lít
(liter)] | (in cigarette)
สารเสพย์ติดในบุหรี่ sǎan-
sèep-dtìt-nai-bù~rìi

tardy adj. (late) ล่าช้า lâa-
cháa

target n. (e.g. shooting)

เป้า bpâo [อัน an] |
(objective) วัตถุประสงค์
wát-tù-bprà~sǒng [อัน
an]

tariff n. (bill, cost, charge)
อัตราค่าบริการ àt-dtraa-
kâa-bɔɔ-rí~gaan |
(customs) ภาษีศุลกากร
paa-sǐi-sǔn-lá~gaa-gɔɔn

tarnish vt. ทำให้_มัวหมอง
tam-hâi-_-muua-mǒng

taro n. เผือก pùuak [หัว
hǔua]

tart adj. (taste, e.g.
underripe fruit) ฝาด fàat

tart n. (pastry) ขนมทาร์ท
kà~nǒm-tâat [ชิ้น chín]

tartar n. (on the teeth)
หินปูน hǐn-bpuun

task n. (any piece of
work) งาน ngaan [อัน an,
ชิ้น chín] | (duty) ภารกิจ
paa-rá~gìt [อัน an]

taste n. (aesthetics)
รสนิยม rót-ní~yom |
(flavor) รส rót, รสชาติ
rót-châat [รส rót]

taste vt. (eat, drink) ชิม
chim

tasteless adj. (lacking
aesthetic taste)

ไม่มีรสนิยม mâi-mii-rót-sà~ní-yom | (lacking flavor) จืด jùut, ไม่มีรสชาติ mâi-mii-rót-châat

tasty *adj.* อร่อย à~rɔ̀i

tattoo *n.* ลายสัก laai-sàk [ลาย laai]

Taurus *n.* ราศีพฤษภ raa-sǐi-prút [ราศี raa-sǐi]

tavern *n.* (inn) โรงแรมเล็กๆ roong-rɛɛm-lék-lék, โรงเตี๊ยม roong-dtíiam ✦ [แห่ง hɛ̀ng] | (where liquor is sold) โรงขายเหล้า roong-kǎai-lâo [ร้าน ráan]

tax *n.* ภาษี paa-sǐi

tax-free *adj.* ปลอดภาษี bplɔ̀ɔt-paa-sǐi

taxi *n.* แท็กซี่ ték-sîi [คัน kan]

taxi meter see metered taxi

taxpayer *n.* ผู้เสียภาษี pûu-sǐia-paa-sǐi [คน kon, ราย raai ⚡]

tea *n.* (beverage) ชา chaa [ซอง sɔɔng (bag), ถ้วย tûuai (cup)]

teach *v.* (instruct) สอน

sɔ̌ɔn, สั่งสอน sàng-sɔ̌ɔn

teacher *n.* ครู kruu, อาจารย์ aa-jaan, คุณครู kun-kruu ⚡ [คน kon, ท่าน tân ⚡]

teak *n.* (tree) ต้นสัก dtôn-sàk [ต้น dtôn] | (wood) ไม้สัก mái-sàk

team *n.* คณะ ká~ná [คณะ ká~ná] | ทีม tiim [ทีม tiim]

teapot *n.* กาน้ำชา gaa-nám-chaa [ใบ bai]

tear *n.* (from eyes) น้ำตา nám-dtaa [หยด yòt] | (rip) รอยฉีก rɔɔi-chìik [รอย rɔɔi]

tear *v.* (rip) ฉีก chìik

tear down *vt.* พัง pang, รื้อ_ออก rúu-_-ɔ̀ɔk

teardrop *n.* หยดน้ำตา yòt-nám-dtaa [หยด yòt]

tear up *vt.* ฉีก_ทิ้ง chìik-_-tíng

tease *n.* (person) คนชอบหยอก kon-chɔ̂ɔp-yɔ̀ɔk [คน kon]

tease *v.* (make fun of) ล้อเลียน lɔ́ɔ-liian, หยอกล้อ yɔ̀ɔk-lɔ́ɔ, แหย่ yɛ̀ɛ ✦

teaspoon *n.* ช้อนชา chɔ́ɔn-chaa [คัน kan]

technical *adj.* ทางเทคนิค taang-têek-ník

technician *n.* ช่างเทคนิค châng-ték-nìk, นายช่าง naai-châng ✱ [คน kon]

technique *n.* (method) กลวิธี gon-lá~wí-tii [แบบ bɛ̀ɛp, อย่าง yàang]

technology *n.* เทคโนโลยี têek-noo-loo-yîi

teddy bear *n.* ตุ๊กตาหมี dtúk-gà~dtaa-mǐi [ตัว dtuua]

teenage *adj.* รุ่นหนุ่มสาว rûn-nùm-sǎao

teenager *n.* วัยรุ่น wai-rûn, วัยโจ๋ wai-jǒo ✱ [คน kon]

telecommunication *n.* โทรคมนาคม too-rá-ká~má~naa-kom

telegram *n.* โทรเลข too-rá~lêek [ฉบับ chà~bàp]

telepathy *n.* โทรจิต too-rá~jìt

telephone *n.* โทรศัพท์ too-rá~sàp [เครื่อง krûuang]

telephone *v.* โทรศัพท์

too-rá~sàp, โทร too ✱

telephone booth *n.* ตู้โทรศัพท์ dtûu-too-rá~sàp [ตู้ dtûu]

telephone number *n.* เบอร์โทรศัพท์ bəə-too-rá~sàp, เบอร์โทร bəə-too ✱ [เบอร์ bəə]

telephone receiver *n.* หูโทรศัพท์ hǔu-too-rá~sàp [อัน an]

telescope *n.* กล้องโทรทรรศน์ glɔ̂ɔng-too-rá~tát ✖ [กล้อง glɔ̂ɔng] | กล้องส่องทางไกล glɔ̂ɔng-sɔ̀ɔng-taang-glai [ตัว dtuua]

televise *vt.* ถ่ายทอดโทรทัศน์ tàai-tɔ̂ɔt-too-rá~tát

television *n.* โทรทัศน์ too-rá~tát, ทีวี tii-wii ✱ [เครื่อง krûuang]

tell *vt.* (e.g. story) บอก bɔ̀ɔk, เล่า lâo, แจ้ง jɛ̂ɛng ✦

tell a lie *v.* โกหก goo-hòk

tell apart *vt.* (distinguish _ and _) แยกแยะ_จาก_ yɛ̂ɛk-yɛ́-_-jàak-_

tell a story *vi.* เล่าเรื่อง

lâo-rûuang

teller n. (bank) พนักงานรับจ่ายเงิน pá~ nák-ngaan-ráp-jàai-ngən [คน kon]

tell if vt. (be certain whether _ or not) บอกได้ว่า_หรือไม่ bɔ̀ɔk-dâi-wâa-_-rɯ̌ɯ-mâi

temper n. (outburst of anger) อารมณ์โกรธ aa-rom-gròot

temperament n. (disposition) นิสัยใจคอ ní-sǎi-jai-kɔɔ, อัธยาศัย àt-tá~yaa-sǎi ‼ | (mood) อารมณ์ aa-rom

temperature n. อุณหภูมิ un-hà~puum [องศา ong-sǎa (degree)] | (fever) ไข้ kâi

template n. (computer) เทมเพล็ต tem-plèt [ไฟล์ fai, อัน an] | (for pattern) แผ่นลอกแบบ pɛ̀n-lɔ̂ɔk-bὲɛp [แผ่น pɛ̀n] | (woodworking) แผ่นไม้รอง pɛ̀n-máai-rɔɔng [แผ่น pɛ̀n]

temple n. (Buddhist) วัด wát [วัด wát, แห่ง hὲng] |

(on the head) ขมับ kà~màp [ข้าง kâang]

tempo n. (rhythm) จังหวะ jang wà [จังหวะ jang wà] | (speed) ความเร็ว kwaam-reo

temporary adj. ชั่วขณะ chûua-kà~nà, ชั่วคราว chûua-kraao

temporary n. (employee) พนักงานชั่วคราว pá~nák-ngaan-chûua-kraao [คน kon]

tempt vt. (appeal strongly to) ยั่วยวน yûua-yuuan, ล่อ lɔ̂ɔ | (try to seduce) ล่อลวง lɔ̂ɔ-luuang

ten numb. สิบ sìp

tenant n. คนเช่า kon-châo, ผู้เช่า pûu-châo [คน kon]

tendency n. (inclination) แนวโน้ม nɛɛo-nóom

tender adj. (kindhearted) ขี้สงสาร kîi-sǒng-sǎan | (meat) เปื่อย bpὲuai | (sensitive) มีความรู้สึกไว mii-kwaam-rúu-sὲk-wai | (soft) นุ่ม nûm, อ่อน ɔ̀ɔn, อ่อนโยน ɔ̀ɔn-yoon ☙

tender *n.* (bidding)
การยื่นประมูล gaan-
yʉ̂ʉn-bprà~muun

tender *vi.* (bid) ยื่นประมูล
yʉ̂ʉn-bprà~muun

tenderness *n.*
ความนิ่มนวล kwaam-
nîm-nuuan, ความอ่อนโยน
kwaam-ɔ̀ɔn-yoon

tendon *n.* เส้นเอ็น sên-en,
เอ็น en [เส้น sên]

tend to *aux.* (be inclined
to) มักจะ mák-jà

tennis *n.* กีฬาเทนนิส gii-
laa-ten-nís, เทนนิส ten-
nís [ชนิด chá~nít]

tennis shoes *n.*
รองเท้าผ้าใบ rɔɔng-táao-
pâa-bai [ข้าง kâang
(one), คู่ kûu (pair)]

tense *adj.* (serious,
critical) ตึงเครียด dtʉng-
krîiat

tense *n.* (grammar) กาล
gaan

tension *n.* (of the mind)
ความตึงเครียด kwaam-
dtʉng-krîiat | (tightness)
ความตึง kwaam-dtʉng

tent *n.* เต็นท์ dtén,
กระโจม grà~joom ⚡ [หลัง

lăng]

tenth *adj.* ที่สิบ tîi-sìp

ten thousand *numb.* หมื่น
mʉ̀ʉn

term *n.* (agreement
lifespan) อายุสัญญา aa-
yú-săn-yaa | (condition)
เงื่อนไข ngʉ̂ʉan-kăi [ข้อ
kɔ̂ɔ] | (occasion) คราว
kraao [คราว kraao] |
(semester) ภาคเรียน
pâak-riian [ภาค pâak] |
(semester) เทอม təəm
[เทอม təəm] | (time
period) ระยะเวลา rá~
yá-wee-laa | (word)
คำศัพท์ kam-sàp [คำ kam]

terminal *adj.* (end of line,
e.g. station) ปลายทาง
bplaai-taang | (gravely
sick) อยู่ในขั้นสุดท้าย
yùu-nai-kân-sùt-táai

terminal *n.* (airport
terminal) อาคารผู้โดยสาร
aa-kaan-pûu-dooi-săan
[หลัง lăng] | (station, e.g.
subway) สถานี sà~tăa-nii
[สถานี sà~tăa-nii]

terminate *vi.* (come to an
end) สิ้นสุด sîn-sùt

terminate *vt.* (get rid of,

kill) กำจัด gam-jàt ✦ |
(lay off) ให้_ออกจากงาน
hâi-_-ɔ̀ɔk-jàak-ngaan
termination *n.*
(employment)
การให้ออกจากงาน gaan-
hâi-ɔ̀ɔk-jàak-ngaan |
(ending) การสิ้นสุด gaan-
sîn-sùt
terminology *n.*
(nomenclature) คำศัพท์
kam-sàp,
คำศัพท์เฉพาะทาง kam-
sàp-chà~pɔ́-taang [คำ
kam]
termite *n.* ปลวก bplùuak
[ตัว dtuua]
terrace *n.* (on the roof)
ดาดฟ้า dàat-fáa [แห่ง
hὲng]
terrible *adj.* (scary) น่ากลัว
nâa-gluua | (severe,
fierce) รุนแรง run-rɛɛng |
(very bad) แย่มาก yɛ̂ɛ-
mâak, เลวร้าย leeo-ráai
terrific *adj.* (grand)
ยิ่งใหญ่ yîng-yài |
(wonderful) ยอดเยี่ยม
yɔ̂ɔt-yîiam
terrify *vt.* (horrify)
ทำให้_หวาดกลัว tam-hâi-

_-wàat-gluua
territory *n.* (boundary)
ดินแดน din-dɛɛn,
อาณาเขต aa-naa-kèet ⚠
[แห่ง hὲng]
terror *n.* (fright, horror)
ความหวาดกลัว kwaam-
wàat-gluua
terrorism *n.* การก่อการร้าย
gaan-gɔ̀ɔ-gaan-ráai
terrorist *adj.* ก่อการร้าย
gɔ̀ɔ-gaan-ráai
terrorist *n.* ผู้ก่อการร้าย
pûu-gɔ̀ɔ-gaan-ráai [คน
kon]
test *n.* (e.g. in school)
การสอบ gaan-sɔ̀ɔp | (e.g.
medical) การตรวจ gaan-
dtrùuat | (e.g. of device)
การตรวจสอบ gaan-
dtrùuat-sɔ̀ɔp | (paper,
e.g. in school) ข้อสอบ
kɔ̂ɔ-sɔ̀ɔp [ข้อ kɔ̂ɔ
(question), ชุด chút (set)]
test *v.* (e.g. in school) สอบ
sɔ̀ɔp
test *vt.* (check, e.g. body,
machine) ตรวจ dtrùuat |
(try out) ลอง lɔɔng
testament *n.* (of the
Bible) พระคัมภีร์ prá-
kam-pii [เล่ม lêm] | (will)

พินัยกรรม pí-nai-gam
[ฉบับ chà~bàp]

testicle *n.* ลูกอัณฑะ lûuk-an-tá, ไข่ห่ำ kài-hǎm ❀, ห่ำ hǎm ❀ [ลูก lûuk]

testify *vi.* (bear witness) เป็นพยาน bpen-pá~yaan | (give evidence) ให้การ hâi-gaan

testimony *n.* (in court) คำให้การ kam-hâi-gaan

tetanus *n.* บาดทะยัก bàat-tá~yák [โรค rôok]

text *n.* (message) ข้อความ kɔ̂ɔ-kwaam [เรื่อง rɯ̂ɯang]

text *vt.* (send a message to) ส่งข้อความให้ sòng-kɔ̂ɔ-kwaam-hâi

textbook *n.* หนังสือเรียน nǎng~sɯ̌ɯ-riian, แบบเรียน bɛ̀ɛp-riian !, ตำรา dtam-raa ❀ [เล่ม lêm]

textile *n.* ผ้า pâa, สิ่งทอ sìng-tɔɔ [ชิ้น chín]

texture *n.* (of cloth) เนื้อผ้า nɯ́ɯa-pâa | (surface) พื้นผิว pɯ́ɯn-pǐu

Thai *adj.* (relating to Thailand) ไทย tai

Thai *n.* (language) ภาษาไทย paa-sǎa-tai | (people) คนไทย kon-tai, ชาวไทย chaao-tai [คน kon]

Thai boxing *n.* มวยไทย muuai-tai

Thailand *n.* (country) ประเทศไทย bprà~têet-tai, ไทย tai ❀ [ประเทศ bprà~têet] | (country) เมืองไทย mɯɯang-tai ❀ [เมือง mɯɯang]

than *prep.* กว่า gwàa

thank *vt.* ขอบคุณ kɔ̀ɔp-kun | (used with friends, younger people) ขอบใจ kɔ̀ɔp-jai

thankful *adj.* (grateful) รู้สึกขอบคุณ rúu-sɯ̀k-kɔ̀ɔp-kun

thanks *n.* ความขอบคุณ kwaam-kɔ̀ɔp-kun

Thanksgiving Day *n.* วันขอบคุณพระเจ้า wan-kɔ̀ɔp-kun-prá~jâao [วัน wan]

thank you! *interj.* ขอบคุณ kɔ̀ɔp-kun | (to peers and inferiors) ขอบใจ kɔ̀ɔp-jai

that *adj.* นั่น nân, นั้น nán,

โน่น nôon

that *adv.* นั่น nân, นั้น nán, โน่น nôon

that *conj.* ว่า wâa

that *pron.* สิ่งนั้น sìng-nán

that's all right *idm.* ไม่เป็นไร mâi-bpen-rai

that's right *idm.* ใช่ châi

that's why! *interj.* มิน่า mí-nâa

thaw *vi.* (liquid) ละลาย lá~laai | (solid, e.g. food) อ่อนตัวลง ʔɔ̀ɔn-dtuua-long

thaw *vt.* (liquid) ทำให้_ละลาย tam-hâi-_-lá~laai | (solid, e.g. food) อุ่น_ให้อ่อนลง ʔùn-_-hâi-ʔɔ̀ɔn-long

theater *n.* (movie) โรงหนัง roong-nǎng ☜ [แห่ง hɛ̀ng] | (play) โรงละคร roong-lá~kɔɔn [แห่ง hɛ̀ng]

theft *n.* การขโมย gaan-kà~mooi, การลักทรัพย์ gaan-lák-sáp ⚠

their *adj.* ของพวกเขา kɔ̌ɔng-pûuak-kǎo

theirs *pron.* ของพวกเขา kɔ̌ɔng-pûuak-kǎo

them *pron.* พวกเขา pûuak-kǎo

theme *n.* (topic, subject) หัวข้อ hǔua-kɔ̂ɔ [หัวข้อ hǔua-kɔ̂ɔ]

themselves *pron.* พวกเขา pûuak-kǎo

then *adv.* (after that) ต่อจากนั้น dtɔ̀ɔ-jàak-nán | (at that time) ในตอนนั้น nai-dtɔɔn-nán | (next in order of time) แล้วก็ lɛ́ɛo-gɔ̂ɔ

then *n.* (that time) เวลานั้น wee-laa-nán ⚠

theology *n.* เทววิทยา tee-wá-wít-tá~yaa [วิชา wí-chaa]

theory *n.* ทฤษฎี trít-sà~dii [ทฤษฎี trít-sà~dii]

therapeutic *adj.* เกี่ยวกับการรักษาโรค gìao-gàp-gaan-rák-sǎa-rôok

therapy *n.* การบำบัดโรค gaan-bam-bàt-rôok

Theravada Buddhism *n.* หินยาน hǐn-ná~yaan [นิกาย ní-gaai]

there *adv.* (over there) ตรงนั้น dtrong-nán, ที่นั่น tîi-nân, นั่น nân, โน่น

nôon, โน้น nóon

there *pron.* นั่น nân, โน่น nôon

there! *interj.* นั่นไง nân-ngai

there are see there is

therefore *adv.* ดังนั้น dang-nán, เพราะฉะนั้น prɔ́-chà~nán ⚠

there is *v.* มี mii

thermometer *n.* เทอร์โมมิเตอร์ təə-moo-mí-dtəə, ปรอท bpà~rɔ̀ɔt ⚫ [อัน an]

thermos bottle *n.* กระติกน้ำร้อน grà~dtìk-nám-rɔ́ɔn [ใบ bai]

these *adj.* เหล่านี้ lào-níi

these *pron.* พวกนี้ pûuak-níi, เหล่านี้ lào-níi

thesis *n.* (academic research) วิทยานิพนธ์ wít-tá~yaa-ní-pon [ฉบับ chà~bàp (whole), เรื่อง rûuang (title)]

they *pron.* พวกเขา pûuak-kǎo

thick *adj.* (e.g. hair, smoke) หนา nǎa | (e.g.

liquid) ข้น kôn

thief *n.* ขโมย kà~mooi [คน kon]

thigh *n.* ต้นขา dtôn-kǎa, ขาอ่อน kǎa-ɔ̀ɔn ⚫ [คู่ kûu (pair)]

thin *adj.* (e.g. fog) เบาบาง bao-baang | (for people, animals) บอบบาง bɔ̀ɔp-baang, ผอม pɔ̌ɔm | (for things) บาง baang

thing *n.* (event, matter) เรื่อง rûuang [เรื่อง rûuang] | (object, item) ของ kɔ̌ɔng, สิ่งของ sìng-kɔ̌ɔng [อัน an, ชิ้น chín] | (object, thought, statement) สิ่ง sìng [อัน an, ชิ้น chín] | (task) งาน ngaan [อัน an, ชิ้น chín]

think *v.* คิด kít, นึก núk

think about *vt.* คิดถึง kít-tŭng

think of *vt.* (consider, reminisce about) คิดถึง kít-tŭng | (invent, create) คิดค้น kít-kón

third *adj.* (one-third) หนึ่งในสาม nùng-nai-sǎam | (ordinal) ที่สาม

tîi-sǎam

third party n. บุคคลที่สาม
bùk-kon-tîi-sǎam,
บุคคลภายนอก bùk-kon-
paai-nɔ̂ɔk [คน kon
(person), กลุ่ม glùm
(group)]

third person n.
(grammar) บุรุษที่สาม bù-
rùt-tîi-sǎam ✹

thirst n. (for water)
ความกระหายน้ำ kwaam-
grà~hǎai-náam

thirst vi. (desire) กระหาย
grà~hǎai ✺

thirsty adj. หิวน้ำ hǐu-
náam, กระหายน้ำ grà~
hǎai-náam ❗

this adj. นี้ nîi, นี้ níi

this pron. นี้ nîi, สิ่งนี้ sìng-
níi

this evening n. คืนนี้
kɯɯn-níi

this week n. สัปดาห์นี้
sàp-daa-níi ❗

thong n. (G-string) จีสตริง
jii-sà~dtring [ตัว dtuua] |
(shoe or slipper)
รองเท้าแตะ rɔɔng-táao-
dtɛ̀ [ข้าง kâang (one), คู่

kûu (pair)]

thorn n. (e.g. of a rose)
หนาม nǎam [อัน an]

thorough adj. (detailed)
ละเอียดถี่ถ้วน lá~iiat-tîi-
tûuan

thoroughly adv.
อย่างละเอียดถี่ถ้วน yàang-
lá~iiat-tìi-tûuan

those pron. เหล่านั้น lào-
nán

thou pron. (you) คุณ kun,
ท่าน tân ✺

though adv.
(nevertheless)
อย่างไรก็ตาม yàang-rai-
gɔ̂ɔ-dtaam

though conj. (although,
even if) ถึงแม้ว่า tǔng-
mɛ́ɛ-wâa, แม้ mɛ́ɛ

thought n. ความคิด
kwaam-kít | (opinion,
idea) ความคิดเห็น
kwaam-kít-hěn [อัน an]

thoughtful adj. (careful)
รอบคอบ rɔ̂ɔp-kɔ̂ɔp |
(thinking of others)
เห็นใจคนอื่น hěn-jai-
kon-ùɯn

thousand numb. หนึ่งพัน
nùng-pan

thrash vt. (beat) เฆี่ยน kîian

thread n. (for sewing) ด้าย dâai, เส้นด้าย sên-dâai [เส้น sên (string)] | (screw thread) เกลียว gliiao [เกลียว gliiao]

threat n. การขู่เข็ญ gaan-kùu-kěn

threaten vt. ข่มขู่ kòm-kùu

three numb. สาม sǎam

thresh vt. (separate the grain or seeds) นวด nûuat

threshold n. (entrance) ประตูทางเข้า bprà~dtuu-taang-kâo [ทาง taang]

thrifty adj. ประหยัด bprà~yàt

thrill n. (something thrilling) สิ่งเร้าใจ sìng-ráo-jai [สิ่ง sìng]

thrill vt. ทำให้_หวาดเสียว tam-hâi-_-wàat-sǐiao

thrilled adj. (stirred emotionally) เร้าใจ ráo-jai

thrive vi. (of plants) งอกงาม ngɔ̂ɔk-ngaam | (prosper, flourish) เติบโต dtə̀əp-dtoo

throat n. คอ kɔɔ, คอหอย kɔɔ-hɔ̌ɔi ✎

throne n. บัลลังก์ ban-lang [บัลลังก์ ban-lang]

through adj. (direct, no layover) ที่เดินทางต่อเดียว tîi-dəən-taang-dtɔ̀ɔ-diiao | (done, finished) เสร็จแล้ว sèt-lɛ́ɛo

through adv. (throughout) โดยตลอด dooi-dtà~lɔ̀ɔt

through prep. (by way of) โดย dooi | (e.g. through page 23) จนถึง jon-tǔng | (in one side and out the other) ทะลุ tá~lú | (throughout) ตลอด dtà~lɔ̀ɔt

throughout adv. ตลอด dtà~lɔ̀ɔt

throughout prep. (all over) ทั่ว tûua

throw n. การโยน gaan-yoon

throw vt. (e.g. kiss) ส่ง sòng | (e.g. lance) พุ่ง pûng | (e.g. party) จัด jàt | (toss) ขว้าง kwâang, โยน yoon

throw away vt. ทิ้ง tíng

throw up vi. อาเจียน aa-jiian, อ้วก ûuak

thru see through

thrust v. ดัน_อย่างแรง dan-_-yàang-rεεng

thumb n. นิ้วหัวแม่มือ níu-hǔua-mɛ̂ɛ-mʉʉ, นิ้วโป้ง níu-bpôong [นิ้ว níu]

thumbprint n. ลายนิ้วหัวแม่มือ laai-níu-hǔua-mɛ̂ɛ-mʉʉ

thunder n. ฟ้าร้อง fáa-rɔ́ɔng [ครั้ง kráng (clap)]

thunderbolt n. ฟ้าผ่า fáa-pàa [ครั้ง kráng]

Thursday n. วันพฤหัส wan-pá~rʉ́-hàt, วันพฤหัสบดี wan-pá~rʉ́-hàt-sà~bɔɔ-dii [วัน wan]

thus adv. ดังนี้ dang-níi

thyroid n. ต่อมไธรอยด์ dtɔ̀m-tai-rɔɔi

tick n. (bloodsucking animal) เห็บ hèp [ตัว dtuua] | (e.g. checkmark, X) เครื่องหมาย krʉ̂ʉang-mǎai [อัน an] | (sound) เสียงดังติ๊กๆ sǐiang-dang-dtík-dtík

tick v. (make a mark) ขีด kìit

ticket n. (e.g. movie, train) ตั๋ว dtǔua [ใบ bai] | (written summons, e.g. for speeding) ใบสั่ง bai-sàng [ใบ bai]

ticket vt. (e.g. give traffic ticket to) ให้ใบสั่ง hâi-bai-sàng

tickle v. จั๊กจี้ ják-gà~jíi

ticklish adj. จั๊กจี้ ják-gà~jíi

tidal wave n. คลื่นยักษ์ klʉ̂ʉn-yák, สึนามิ sù-naa-mí [ลูก lûuk]

tide n. (current) กระแสน้ำ grà~sɛ̌ɛ-náam [กระแส grà~sɛ̌ɛ] | (periodic ebb and flow) กระแสน้ำขึ้นน้ำลง grà~sɛ̌ɛ-nám-kʉ̂n-nám-long

tidy adj. (orderly) เรียบร้อย rîiap-rɔ́ɔi

tie n. (neckwear) เน็คไท nék-tái [เส้น sên]

tie vi. (be even) เสมอกัน sà~mə̌ə-gan

tie vt. (e.g. bundle, bondage) มัด mát | (e.g.

sail, boat, horse) ผูก
pùuk | (fix with fastener,
e.g. zip tie) รัด rát

tier *n.* (layer) ชั้น chán [ชั้น
chán] | (level) ระดับ rá~
dàp [ระดับ rá~dàp]

tie up *vt.* (e.g. animal)
ล่าม lâam | (e.g. traffic)
ทำให้_ติดขัด tam-hâi-_-
dtìt-kàt | (make
occupied) ทำให้_มีงานยุ่ง
tam-hâi-_-mii-ngaan-
yûng

tiger *n.* เสือ sǔua [ตัว
dtuua]

tiger cub *n.* ลูกเสือ lûuk-
sǔua [ตัว dtuua]

tight *adj.* (e.g. dress) คับ
káp | (e.g. rope) ตึง
dtʉng | (e.g. screw,
bottle top) แน่น nɛ̂n |
(e.g. space) คับแคบ káp-
kɛ̂ɛp | (e.g. valve,
budget) ฝืด fʉ̀ʉt

tighten *vt.* ทำให้_แน่น
tam-hâi-_-nɛ̂n

tightly *adv.* สนิท sà~nìt

tights *n.* (sportswear)
เสื้อกางเกงยืดแนบเนื้อ
sʉ̂ua-gaang-geeng-
yʉ̂ʉt-nɛ̂ɛp-nʉ́ua [ตัว

dtuua (piece), ชุด chút
(suit)] | (stockings)
ถุงน่อง tǔng-nɔ̂ng [ข้าง
kâang (each), คู่ kûu
(pair)]

tile *n.* กระเบื้อง grà~
bʉ̂ʉang [แผ่น pɛ̀n]

till *conj.* จนกระทั่ง jon-
grà~tâng

tilt *v.* (lean) เอียง iiang

timber *n.* (log) ท่อนไม้
tɔ̂n-máai [ท่อน tɔ̂n]

time *adj.* (relating to
time) เกี่ยวกับเวลา gìiao-
gàp-wee-laa

time *n.* (e.g. at this time)
ตอน dtɔɔn [ตอน dtɔɔn] |
(occurrence number, e.g.
third time) ครั้ง kráng |
(passing of time) เวลา
wee-laa

time *vt.* (record a speed
or duration) จับเวลา jàp-
wee-laa

time is up *idm.* หมดเวลา
mòt-wee-laa

timely *adj.* ถูกเวลา tùuk-
wee-laa, เหมาะกับเวลา
mɔ̀-gàp-wee-laa

timer *n.* (machine)
เครื่องจับเวลา krʉ̂uang-

jàp-wee-laa [เครื่อง krûuang] | (person) ผู้จับเวลา pûu-jàp-wee-laa [คน kon]

times *n.* (e.g. did it four times) ครั้ง kráng | (e.g. three times faster) เท่า tâo

times *vt.* (e.g. three times four) คูณ kuun

timetable *n.* ตารางเวลา dtaa-raang-wee-laa [ตาราง dtaa-raang]

timid *adj.* (cowardly) ขี้ขลาด kîi-klàat

timing *n.* การกะเวลา gaan-gà-wee-laa

tin *n.* (can) กระป๋อง grà~bpɔ̌ng [ใบ bai] | (mineral) ดีบุก dii-bùk [แร่ rɛ̂ɛ]

tingle *vi.* (feel tingling sensation) รู้สึกซ่า rúu-sùk-sâa

tingling *adj.* เสียว sǐiao

tint *n.* (for the hair) สีย้อมผม sǐi-yɔ́ɔm-pǒm [สี sǐi]

tiny *adj.* เล็กมาก lék-mâak

tip *n.* (ending point) ปลาย bplaai [จุด jùt] | (gratuity) ทิป típ | (suggestion) ข้อแนะนำ kɔ̂ɔ-nɛ́-nam [ข้อ kɔ̂ɔ] | (top) ยอด yɔ̂ɔt [ยอด yɔ̂ɔt]

tip *v.* (give gratuity) ให้เงินทิป hâi-ngən-típ

tiptoe *adv.* เขย่ง kà~yèng

tiptoe *n.* ปลายเท้า bplaai-táao

tire *n.* (for cars) ยางรถ yaang-rót [เส้น sên]

tire *vt.* (exhaust) ทำให้_เหนื่อย tam-hâi-_-nùuai | (make bored) ทำให้_เบื่อ tam-hâi-_-bùua

tired *adj.* (e.g. muscles) เมื่อย mûuai | (exhausted) เหนื่อย nùuai

tired of *adj.* (bored, annoyed with) เบื่อ bùua | (weary) เหนื่อย nùuai

tiresome *adj.* (boring, annoying) น่าเบื่อ nâa-bùua

tissue *n.* (cells) เนื้อเยื่อ núua-yûua | (fiber, film) เยื่อ yûua

tissue paper *n.* กระดาษชำระ grà~dàat-cham-rá [แผ่น pèn

(sheet), ม้วน múuan (roll), กล่อง glòng (box)]

title *n.* (deed, e.g. land) โฉนด chà~nòot [ฉบับ chà~bàp] | (heading) หัวเรื่อง hǔua-rûuang [เรื่อง rûuang] | (job title) ตำแหน่ง dtam-nèng [ตำแหน่ง dtam-nèng] | (of book, movie, song, story) ชื่อ chûue [ชื่อ chûue]

to *prep.* (e.g. give to) กับ gàp, แก่ gὲε ‼ | (e.g. go to) ที่ tîi | (e.g. to this day) ถึง tǔng

toad *n.* (animal) คางคก kaang-kók [ตัว dtuua]

toast *n.* (bread) ขนมปังปิ้ง kà~nǒm-bpang-bpîng [ชิ้น chín]

toast *vt.* (drink to honor of) ดื่มอวยพรให้ dùum-uuai-pɔɔn-hâi | (roast) ปิ้ง bpîng

toaster *n.* (appliance) เครื่องปิ้งขนมปัง krûuang-bpîng-kà~nǒm-bpang [เครื่อง krûuang]

tobacco *n.* ยาสูบ yaa-sùup [มวน muuan (roll), ใบ bai (leaf)]

today *adv.* (nowadays) ปัจจุบันนี้ bpàt-jù-ban-níi

today *n.* วันนี้ wan-níi

to-do *adj.* ที่ต้องทำ tîi-dtɔ̂ng-tam

toe *n.* นิ้วเท้า níu-táao [นิ้ว níu]

toenail *n.* เล็บเท้า lép-táao [เล็บ lép]

toffee *n.* ลูกอม lûuk-om [เม็ด mét]

tofu *n.* เต้าหู้ dtâo-hûu [ชิ้น chín]

together *adv.* (at the same time) พร้อมกัน prɔ́ɔm-gan | (in company with) ด้วยกัน dûuai-gan

together with *prep.* พร้อมด้วย prɔ́ɔm-dûuai

toil *vi.* ทำงานหนัก tam-ngaan-nàk

toilet *n.* (room) ห้องน้ำ hɔ̂ng-náam, ห้องส้วม hɔ̂ng-sûuam ✦ [ห้อง hɔ̂ng] | (room, fixture)

ส้วม sûuam ✦ [ที่ tîi]

toilet paper *n.*
กระดาษชำระ grà~dàat-
cham-rá [แผ่น pèn
(sheet), ม้วน múuan
(roll), กล่อง glòng (box)]

token *n.* (coin) เหรียญ
rǐian [เหรียญ rǐian, อัน an]
| (symbol) สัญลักษณ์ sǎn-
yá~lák [อัน an]

tolerance *n.* (fortitude)
ความอดทน kwaam-òt-
ton | (freedom from
bigotry)
อิสระในการยอมรับ ìt-sà~
rà-nai-gaan-yɔɔm-ráp

tolerate *vt.* (endure)
อดทน òt-ton

toll *n.* (for road)
ค่าผ่านทาง kâa-pàan-
taang

toll free *adj.* (phone
number) โทรฟรี too-frii

toll road *n.* ทางด่วน
taang-dùuan [สาย sǎai]

tomato *n.* มะเขือเทศ
má~kǔua-têet [ลูก lûuk
(fruit), ต้น dtôn (plant)]

tomato juice *n.*
น้ำมะเขือเทศ nám-má~
kǔua-têet [แก้ว gɛ̂ɛo

(glass), กล่อง glòng (box),
ขวด kùuat (bottle)]

tomb *n.* หลุมฝังศพ lǔm-
fǎng-sòp [แห่ง hɛ̀ng]

tomboy *n.* ทอมบอย tɔm-
bɔɔi [คน kon]

tomorrow *n.* (day) พรุ่งนี้
prûng-níi, วันพรุ่งนี้ wan-
prûng-níi [วัน wan] |
(future) อนาคต à~naa-kót

ton *n.* (large amount)
จำนวนมาก jam-nuuan-
mâak | (unit of weight)
ตัน dtan

tonal language *n.*
ภาษาที่มีเสียงสูงต่ำ paa-
sǎa-tîi-mii-sǐiang-
sǔung-dtàm [ภาษา paa-
sǎa]

tone *n.* (pitch) เสียงสูงต่ำ
sǐiang-sǔung-dtàm [เสียง
sǐiang] | (shade, hue)
โทนสี toon-sǐi [โทน toon]

tone *vt.* (e.g. the body)
ทำให้_แข็งแรง tam-hâi-
_kɛ̌ng-rɛɛng

toner *n.* (cosmetics)
โลชั่นสมานผิว loo-chân-
sà~mǎan-pǐu [ขวด
kùuat] | (printer, copy

machine) โทนเนอร์ toon-nə̀ə [อัน an (cartridge)]

tongs n. (tool) คีม kiim [อัน an]

tongue n. (in the mouth) ลิ้น lín [ลิ้น lín]

tonic n. (medicine) ยาบำรุงกำลัง yaa-bam-rung-gam-lang | (soda water) น้ำโทนิค nám-too-ník [ขวด kùuat]

tonight n. คืนนี้ kʉʉn-níi

tonsil n. ต่อมทอนซิล dtɔ̀ɔm-tɔn-sin, ทอนซิล tɔn-sin [ต่อม dtɔ̀ɔm]

tonsilitis n. ต่อมทอนซิลอักเสบ dtɔ̀ɔm-tɔn-sin-àk-sèep

too adv. (also) ก็ gɔ̂ɔ, ด้วย dûuai, เหมือนกัน mʉ̌ʉan-gan | (excessively) เกิน gəən, เกินไป gəən-bpai

tool n. (hand tool, device) เครื่องมือ krʉ̂uang-mʉʉ [ชิ้น chín (piece), ชุด chút (set)]

too much adv. มากเกินไป mâak-gəən-bpai

toot vi. (blow horn) เป่าแตร bpào-dtrɛɛ

tooth n. ฟัน fan [ซี่ sîi (piece), ชุด chút (set)]

toothache n. ปวดฟัน bpùuat-fan

toothbrush n. แปรงสีฟัน bprɛɛng-sǐi-fan [อัน an]

toothpaste n. ยาสีฟัน yaa-sǐi-fan [หลอด lɔ̀ɔt]

toothpick n. ไม้จิ้มฟัน mái-jîm-fan [อัน an]

top adj. (of the highest degree) สูงสุด sǔung-sùt

top n. (highest rank) ตำแหน่งสูงสุด dtam-nɛ̀ng-sǔung-sùt [ตำแหน่ง dtam-nɛ̀ng] | (peak) ยอด yɔ̂ɔt [ยอด yɔ̂ɔt] | (spinning) ลูกข่าง lûuk-kàang [ลูก lûuk] | (uppermost part) ส่วนบน sùuan-bon [ส่วน sùuan]

topaz n. บุษราคัม bùt-sà~raa-kam [เม็ด mét (piece)]

topic n. (subject) เรื่อง rʉ̂uang [เรื่อง rʉ̂uang] | (theme) หัวข้อ hǔua-kɔ̂ɔ [หัวข้อ hǔua-kɔ̂ɔ]

topping n. (food)

เครื่องโรยหน้าอาหาร krûuang-rooi-nâa-aa-hǎan

topple vt. (e.g. government) โค่นล้ม kôon-lóm | (e.g. objects) ทำให้_ล้มลง tam-hâi-_-lóm-long

torch n. (flashlight) ไฟฉาย fai-chǎai [กระบอก grà~bɔ̀ɔk, อัน an] | (with flame) คบ kóp, คบไฟ kóp-fai [คบ kóp]

torn adj. ขาด kàat

tornado n. (twister) พายุทอร์นาโด paai-yú-tɔɔ-naa-doo, พายุหมุน paa-yú-mǔn [ลูก lûuk]

torso n. (trunk of human body) ลำตัว lam-dtuua

tortoise n. เต่า dtào [ตัว dtuua]

torture n. (act) การทรมาน gaan-tɔɔ-rá~maan

torture vt. (torment) ทรมาน tɔɔ-rá~maan, ทารุณ taa-run ✏

toss vi. (e.g. in bed) กระสับกระส่าย grà~sàp-grà~sàai

toss vt. (throw, pitch)

ขว้าง kwâang, โยน yoon | (turn over) พลิก_กลับ plík-_-glàp

tot n. (small child) เด็กเล็ก dèk-lék [คน kon]

total adj. (aggregate) รวมทั้งหมด ruuam-táng-mòt

total n. (sum) สุทธิ sùt-tí ✏

touch n. (communication) การติดต่อสื่อสาร gaan-dtìt-dtɔ̀ɔ-sʉ̀ʉ-sǎan

touch vi. สัมผัสกัน sǎm-pàt-gan

touch vt. (affect, e.g. feelings) กระทบ grà~tóp | (come into contact) จับ jàp, แตะ dtè, สัมผัส sǎm-pàt ✏

touching adj. (strong emotion) สะเทือนใจ sà~tʉʉan-jai

touchy adj. (easy to trigger strong emotion) ขี้น้อยใจ kîi-nɔ́ɔi-jai | (irritable) ขี้โมโห kîi-moo-hǒo | (requiring caution) ต้องระมัดระวังมาก dtɔ̂ng-rá~mát-rá~wang-mâak

tough adj. (durable)

ทนทาน ton-taan | (fierce, violent, mean) ดุ dù | (not tender, sticky) เหนียว nǐiao | (strong) แข็งแรง kǎeng-rεεng

toughen vt. (strengthen, make durable) ทำให้_แข็งแรง tam-hâi-_-kǎeng-rεεng

tour n. (e.g. concert) การเดินสายแสดง gaan-dəən-sǎai-sà~dεεng [ครั้ง kráng] | (sight-seeing) ทัศนาจร tát-sà~naa-jɔɔn ! [ครั้ง kráng]

tour v. ท่องเที่ยว tɔ̂ng-tîiao

tour guide n. ไกด์ gái [คน kon]

tourism n. การท่องเที่ยว gaan-tɔ̂ng-tîiao

tourist n. นักท่องเที่ยว nák-tɔ̂ng-tîiao [คน kon]

tournament n. การแข่งขัน gaan-kèng-kǎn

tow v. (haul) พ่วง pûuang, ลาก lâak

toward prep. ไปทาง bpai-taang

towel n. (for body) ผ้าเช็ดตัว pâa-chét-

dtuua, ผ้าขนหนู pâa-kǒn-nǔu ● [ผืน pǔun] | (paper for wiping) กระดาษเช็ดมือ grà~dàat-chét-mɯɯ [แผ่น pèn (sheet), ม้วน múuan (roll), ชิ้น chín (piece)]

tower n. หอคอย hǎɔ-kɔɔi [แห่ง hèng]

town n. เมือง mɯɯang [เมือง mɯɯang]

town house n. ทาวน์เฮาส์ taao-háo [หลัง lǎng]

toxic adj. เป็นพิษ bpen-pít, มีพิษ mii-pít

toxin n. สารพิษ sǎan-pít

toy n. ของเล่น kɔ̌ɔng-lên [ชิ้น chín]

toy with vt. เล่นกับ lên-gàp

trace n. (e.g. footprint) รอย rɔɔi [รอย rɔɔi]

trace vt. (follow trail of) ตามรอย dtaam-rɔɔi

track n. (e.g. on CD) แทร็ค trèk | (e.g. track and field) การวิ่งแข่ง gaan-wîng-kèng | (race) ลู่แข่ง lûu-kèng [ลู่ lûu] | (railway) รางรถไฟ raang-

track rót-fai [ราง raang] | (way, rail, road) เส้นทาง sên-taang [สาย sǎai, เส้น sên]

track vt. (follow) ติดตาม dtìt-dtaam

track-and-field n. กรีฑา grii-taa [ชนิด chá~nít]

tractor n. รถแทรกเตอร์ rót-trék-dtə̂ə • [คัน kan] | (field) รถไถนา rót-tǎi-naa [คัน kan]

trade n. (commerce) การค้า gaan-káa | (exchange) การแลกเปลี่ยน gaan-lɛ̂ɛk-bpliian

trade v. (buy and sell, do business) ค้าขาย káa-kǎai, ซื้อขาย súu-kǎai | (exchange) แลกเปลี่ยน lɛ̂ɛk-bpliian

trademark n. เครื่องหมายการค้า krûuang-mǎai-gaan-káa [เครื่องหมาย krûuang-mǎai]

tradition n. ธรรมเนียม tam-niiam, ประเพณี bprà~pee-nii, ขนบธรรมเนียม kà~nòp-tam-niiam ‼ [แบบ bɛ̀ɛp,

อย่าง yàang]

traditional adj. ดั้งเดิม dâng-dəəm, เป็นประเพณี bpen-bprà~pee-nii

traffic n. (on street) จราจร jà~raa-jɔɔn

traffic circle n. วงเวียน wong-wiian [แห่ง hɛ̀ng]

traffic in vt. (deal illegally in) ลักลอบค้า lák-lɔ̂ɔp-káa

traffic jam n. รถติด rót-dtìt, การจราจรติดขัด gaan-jà~raa-jɔɔn-dtìt-kàt ‼

traffic light n. ไฟจราจร fai-jà~raa-jɔɔn [จุด jùt]

tragedy n. (sad story) ละครโศก lá~kɔɔn-sòok, โศกนาฏกรรม sòok-gà~nâat-dtà~gam [เรื่อง rûuang]

tragic adj. น่าสลดใจ nâa-sà~lòt-jai

trail n. (path, walkway) ทางเดิน taang-dəən [ทาง taang]

trail vt. (be behind) ตามหลัง dtaam-lǎng | (follow trail of) ตามรอย dtaam-rɔɔi

trailer n. (drawn by

vehicle) รถพ่วง rót-pûuang [คัน kan] | (movie preview) ตัวอย่างหนัง dtuua-yàang-nǎng

train *n.* (railroad) รถไฟ rót-fai [ขบวน kà~buuan]

train *vi.* (drill) ฝึกหัด fʉ̀k-hàt ‼

train *vt.* (educate, guide) อบรม òp-rom

trainer *n.* ครูฝึก kruu-fʉ̀k [คน kon]

training *n.* การฝึกหัด gaan-fʉ̀k-hàt

traitor *n.* ผู้หักหลัง pûu-hàk-lǎng, ผู้ทรยศ pûu-tɔɔ-rá-yót ‼ [คน kon]

tram *n.* (streetcar) รถราง rót-raang [คัน kan]

trample *vt.* ย่ำ yâm

tranquility *n.* ความเงียบสงบ kwaam-ngîiap-sà~ngòp

tranquilize *vt.* (calm) ทำให้_สงบ tam-hâi-_-sà~ngòp | (sedate by drug) กล่อมประสาท glɔ̀m-bprà~sàat

tranquilizer *n.* ยากล่อมประสาท yaa-glɔ̀m-bprà~sàat [เม็ด mét]

transact *vi.* (conduct business) ทำการค้า tam-gaan-káa

transact *vt.* (conduct) จัดการ jàt-gaan

transaction *n.* (action) การดำเนินการ gaan-dam-nəən-gaan [ครั้ง kráng] | (business) การค้าธุรกิจ gaan-káa-tú-rá~gìt [ครั้ง kráng]

transcend *vt.* เหนือกว่า nʉ̌ua-gwàa

transcribe *vt.* (e.g. court reporter) ถอดความ tɔ̀ɔt-kwaam | (spell out phonetically) ถ่ายเสียง_เป็นตัวอักษร tàai-sǐiang-_-bpen-dtuua-àk-sɔ̌ɔn

transcript *n.* (school record) ใบรับรองผลการศึกษา bai-ráp-rɔɔng-pǒn-gaan-sʉ̀k-sǎa [ใบ bai]

transfer *n.* (money) การโอนเงิน gaan-oon-ngən | (ownership) การเปลี่ยนเจ้าของ gaanbpliian-jâao-kǔɔng

transfer vt. (move _ to _)
ย้าย_ไป_ yáai-_-bpai-_,
เคลื่อนย้าย_ไป_ klûuan-
yáai-_-bpai-_ ! |
(ownership, control of _
to _) โอน_ให้_ oon-_-hâi-_

transformer n. (electrical)
หม้อแปลง mɔ̂ɔ-bplɛɛng
[หม้อ mɔ̂ɔ, ลูก lûuk]

transform into vt.
เปลี่ยนเป็น bpliian-bpen

transfusion n. (blood)
การถ่ายเลือด gaan-tàai-
lûuat

transit n. การเดินทางผ่าน
gaan-dəən-taang-pàan

transition n. (change)
การเปลี่ยนแปลง gaan-
bpliian-bplɛɛng

translate v. (language)
แปล bplɛɛ

translation n. (meaning)
คำแปล kam-bplɛɛ [คำ
kam]

translator n. ผู้แปล pûu-
bplɛɛ [คน kon]

transliterate vt. (write
using different system)
ถ่ายตัวอักษร tàai-dtuua-
àk-sɔ̌ɔn

transmission n. (act)

การกระจาย gaan-grà~
jaai | (vehicle)
เครื่องถ่ายกำลัง krûuang-
tàai-gam-lang

transmit v. (broadcast)
ถ่ายทอด tàai-tɔ̂ɔt | (pass
on, e.g. germ) แพร่เชื้อ
prɛ̂ɛ-chúua

transparent adj. โปร่งแสง
bpròong-sɛ̌ɛng, ใส sǎi

transplant n. (of organ)
การเปลี่ยนอวัยวะ gaan-
bpliian-à-wai-yá-wá

transplant vt. (e.g. hair)
ปลูกถ่าย bplùuk-tàai

transport vt. ขน kǒn,
ขนส่ง kǒn-sòng

transportation n.
การขนส่ง gaan-kǒn-sòng

transsexual n. กะเทย gà~
təəi [คน kon] | (got
surgery) กะเทยแปลงเพศ
gà~təəi-bplɛɛng-pêet
[คน kon] | (having
instinct to be other sex)
ผู้ที่มีจิตใจเหมือนเพศตรง
ข้าม pûu-tîi-mii-jìt-jai-
mǔuan-pêet-dtrong-
kâam [คน kon]

transvestite n. กะเทย
gà~təəi [คน kon] |

(cross-dresser) ผู้ที่ชอบ
แต่งตัวเป็นเพศตรงข้าม
pûu-tîi-chɔ̂ɔp-dtɛ̀ng-
dtuua-bpen-pêet-
dtrong-kâam [คน kon]

trap n. กับดัก gàp-dàk [อัน
an]

trap vt. ดักจับ dàk-jàp

trash n. (garbage) ขยะ
kà~yà [ชิ้น chín (piece),
กอง gɔɔng (pile)]

trash vt. (throw out) ทิ้ง
tíng

trash can n. ถังขยะ tǎng-
kà~yà [ใบ bai]

trauma n. (emotional)
ความบอบช้ำทางใจ
kwaam-bɔ̀ɔp-chám-
taang-jai | (physical)
ความบอบช้ำทางกาย
kwaam-bɔ̀ɔp-chám-
taang-gaai

travel vi. เดินทาง dəən-
taang

travel agency n.
บริษัทท่องเที่ยว bɔɔ-rí~
sàt-tɔ̂ng-tîiao [แห่ง hɛ̀ng]

traveler n. (one who
travels) นักเดินทาง nák-
dəən-taang [คน kon] |

(tourist) นักท่องเที่ยว
nák-tɔ̂ng-tîiao [คน kon]

traveler's check n.
เช็คเดินทาง chék-dəən-
taang [ใบ bai]

travel to vt. เดินทางไป
dəən-taang-bpai

tray n. ถาด tàat [ใบ bai]

tread n. (for tires or
shoes) ดอกยาง dɔ̀ɔk-
yaang

tread vi. (step, walk)
ก้าวย่าง gâao-yâang

tread on vt. (step or walk
on) เหยียบ yìiap

treason n. (against state)
การกบฏ gaan-gà~bòt

treasure n. (e.g. buried)
ขุมทรัพย์ kǔm-sáp [ขุม
kǔm] | (property,
possessions) สมบัติ
sǒm-bàt [ชิ้น chín] |
(valuable things) ของมีค่า
kɔ̌ɔng-mii-kâa

treasurer n. (of company
or association) เหรัญญิก
hěe-ran-yík [คน kon]

treasury n. (national)
ท้องพระคลัง tɔ́ɔng-prá-
klang ‼ [แห่ง hɛ̀ng]

treat n. (item given)

ของน่าทาน kɔ̌ɔng-nâa-
taan [อย่าง yàang (sort),
ชิ้น chín (piece)]

treat *vt.* (_ (person) _ (e.g.
well, badly)) ทำกับ__
tam-gàp-_-_ | (care for,
cure) รักษา rák-sǎa |
(consider _ to be _)
นับว่า__ náp-wâa-_-_ |
(give free meal, etc. to)
เลี้ยง líiang

treatment *n.* การรักษา
gaan-rák-sǎa

treaty *n.* (e.g. between
nations) สนธิสัญญา sǒn-
tí-sǎn-yaa [ฉบับ chà~bàp]

tree *n.* ต้นไม้ dtôn-máai
[ต้น dtôn]

tree stump *n.* ตอ dtɔɔ [ตอ
dtɔɔ]

trek *vi.* (hike) เดินป่า
dəən-bpàa

tremble *vi.* (vibrate,
quiver) สั่น sàn

tremendous *adj.* (in
number or degree)
มากมาย mâak-maai | (in
size) ใหญ่โตมาก yài-
dtoo-mâak

trench *n.* (ditch) ท้องร่อง
tɔ́ɔng-rɔ̂ng [ร่อง rɔ̂ng] |

(in warfare) สนามเพลาะ
sà~nǎam-plɔ́ [แห่ง hɛ̀ng]

trend *n.* (current style)
สมัยนิยม sà~mǎi-ní-yom
[แบบ bɛ̀ɛp]

trendy *adj.* (fashionable)
นำสมัย nam-sà~mǎi

trespass *vi.* (enter
wrongfully) บุกรุก bùk-rúk

trial *adj.* (experimental)
ทดลอง tót-lɔɔng

trial *n.* (experiment)
การทดลอง gaan-tót-
lɔɔng [ครั้ง kráng] | (in a
court of law)
การพิจารณาคดี gaan-pí-
jaa-rá~naa-ká-dii [ครั้ง
kráng]

triangle *n.* (shape)
สามเหลี่ยม sǎam-lìiam
[รูป rûup, อัน an]

tribe *n.* (e.g. hilltribe) เผ่า
pào [เผ่า pào]

tribute *n.* (to another
country) บรรณาการ ban-
naa-gaan | (to
praiseworthy quality)
การสรรเสริญ gaan-sǎn-
sɤ̌ən

trick *n.* กลอุบาย gon-ù-
baai, เล่ห์เหลี่ยม lêe-lìiam

[อัน an]

trick *vt.* หลอก lɔ̀ɔk

tricky *adj.* (cunning) เจ้าเล่ห์ jâo-lêe, มีเล่ห์เหลี่ยม mii-lêe-lìiam | (difficult) ยาก yâak

trifle *n.* (insignificant issue) เรื่องเล็กน้อย rûuang-lék-nɔ́ɔi [เรื่อง rûuang]

trigger *n.* ไกปืน gai-bpʉʉn [อัน an]

trim *vt.* (e.g. hair) เล็ม lem | (grass) ดาย daai

trio *n.* (group of three people) กลุ่มสามคน glùm-sǎam-kon [กลุ่ม glùm (group)] | (group of three things) กลุ่มที่มีสามสิ่ง glùm-tîi-mii-sǎam-sìng [กลุ่ม glùm]

trip *n.* (journey) การเดินทาง gaan-dəən-taang

trip *vi.* (stumble or fall) สะดุด sà~dùt

tripe *n.* (intestines) เครื่องใน krûuang-nai [ชิ้น chín]

triple *adj.* (three times more) สามเท่า sǎam-tâo

triple *vt.* (make three times more) ทำให้_เป็นสามเท่า tam-hâi-_-bpen-sǎam-tâo

tripod *n.* (for camera) ขาตั้งกล้องถ่ายรูป kǎa-dtâng-glɔ̂ng-tàai-rûup [อัน an]

triumph *n.* (victory) ชัยชนะ chai-chá~ná

trivial *adj.* (unimportant) ไม่สำคัญ mâi-sǎm-kan

trolley *n.* (streetcar) รถราง rót-raang [คัน kan]

troop *n.* (group of soldiers) กองทหาร gɔɔng-tá~hǎan [กอง gɔɔng]

trophy *n.* (prize) ถ้วยรางวัล tûuai-raang-wan [ถ้วย tûuai, ใบ bai, ลูก lûuk]

tropic *n.* เขตร้อน kèet-rɔ́ɔn

tropical *adj.* เขตร้อน kèet-rɔ́ɔn

trot *vi.* (horse) วิ่งเหยาะๆ wîng-yɔ̀-yɔ̀

trouble *n.* (difficulty) ความลำบาก kwaam-lam-bàak | (issue, problem)

ปัญหา bpan-hǎa [เรื่อง rûuang (matter), ข้อ kɔ̂ɔ (point)]

trouble *vt.* (bother) รบกวน róp-guuan

troublesome *adj.* น่ารำคาญ nâa-ram-kaan

trousers *n.* (outergarment) กางเกงขายาว gaang-geeng-kǎa-yaao, กางเกง gaang-geeng ✦ [ตัว dtuua]

truck *n.* รถบรรทุก rót-ban-túk [คัน kan]

true *adj.* (not false) ถูก tùuk | (real) จริง jing

truly *adv.* อย่างแท้จริง yàang-téɛ-jing

trumpet *n.* แตร dtrɛɛ [ตัว dtuua]

trunk *n.* (luggage) หีบใส่ของ hìip-sài-kɔ̌ɔng [ใบ bai] | (of a car) กระโปรงหลังรถ grà-proong-lǎng-rót [ที่ tîi] | (of a tree) ลำต้น lam-dtôn [ลำ lam] | (of an elephant) งวงช้าง nguuang-cháang [งวง nguuang]

trust *n.* (in integrity, motives) ความไว้วางใจ kwaam-wái-waang-jai | (legal entity for holding assets) ทรัสต์ trás

trust *vt.* (in integrity, motives) เชื่อใจ chûua-jai, ไว้ใจ wái-jai | (in strength, ability) มั่นใจ mân-jai

trustee *n.* ผู้พิทักษ์ทรัพย์สิน pûu-pí-ták-sáp-sǐn [คน kon]

trustworthy *adj.* น่าไว้วางใจ nâa-wái-waang-jai

truth *n.* ความจริง kwaam-jing

truthful *adj.* (of person) จริงใจ jing-jai

try *vi.* (make an effort) พยายาม pá~yaa-yaam, ลอง lɔɔng, ลองดู lɔɔng-duu ✦

try *vt.* (sample, test) ลอง lɔɔng | (taste) ชิม chim

try on *vt.* ลอง lɔɔng

T-shirt *n.* เสื้อยืด sûua-yûut [ตัว dtuua]

tsunami *n.* คลื่นยักษ์ klûun-yák, สึนามิ sù-naa-mí [ลูก lûuk]

tub *n.* (container, jar) อ่าง àang [ใบ bai]

tube *n.* (container, e.g. for toothpaste) หลอด lɔ̀ɔt [หลอด lɔ̀ɔt] | (pipe, hollow cylinder) ท่อ tɔ̂ɔ [ท่อ tɔ̂ɔ] | (plastic tube, hose) สายยาง sǎai-yaang [สาย sǎai, เส้น sên]

tuberculosis *n.* วัณโรค wan-ná~rôok [โรค rôok]

Tuesday *n.* วันอังคาร wan-ang-kaan [วัน wan]

tuft *n.* (cluster) กระจุก grà~jùk [อัน an]

tug *vt.* (drag, pull) ลาก lâak | (pull) ดึง dɯng

tugboat *n.* เรือโยง rɯɯa-yoong [ลำ lam]

tug-of-war *n.* ชักเย่อ chák-gà~yə̂ə

tuition *n.* ค่าเล่าเรียน kâa-lâo-riian [จำนวน jam-nuuan]

tuk-tuk *n.* ตุ๊กๆ dtúk-dtúk, รถตุ๊กๆ rót-dtúk-dtúk [คัน kan]

tulip *n.* (flower) ทิวลิป tiu-lìp [ดอก dɔ̀ɔk] | (plant) ต้นทิวลิป dtôn-tiu-lìp [ต้น

dtôn (plant), หัว hǔua (bulb)]

tumble down *vi.* (collapse) ล้ม lóm

tummy *n.* ท้อง tɔ́ɔng

tumor *n.* เนื้องอก nɯ́ɯa-ngɔ̂ɔk [ก้อน gɔ̂ɔn]

tuna *n.* ปลาทูน่า bplaa-tuu-nâa [ตัว dtuua, กระป๋อง grà~bpɔ̌ng (can)]

tune *n.* (harmony) ความสอดคล้อง kwaam-sɔ̀ɔt-klɔ́ɔng | (melody) ทำนองเพลง tam-nɔɔng-pleeng [ทำนอง tam-nɔɔng]

tune *vt.* (e.g. radio, TV) ปรับ bpràp

tunnel *n.* อุโมงค์ ù-moong [อุโมงค์ ù-moong]

turbulence *n.* (disorder) ความวุ่นวาย kwaam-wûn-waai | (strong wind) ลมแรงจัด lom-rɛɛng-jàt

turf *n.* (artificial) หญ้าเทียม yâa-tiiam | (natural) สนามหญ้า sà~nǎam-yâa [สนาม sà~nǎam, แห่ง hɛ̀ng]

turkey *n.* ไก่งวง gài-nguuang [ตัว dtuua]

turmeric *n.* ขมิ้น kà~mîn [หัว hǔua (bulb)]

turn *n.* (e.g. my turn) ที tii [ที tii] | (e.g. my turn) ตา dtaa [ตา dtaa (shift)] | (road bend) โค้ง kóong [โค้ง kóong]

turn *v.* (e.g. a car while driving) เลี้ยว líiao | (for person, e.g. head) หัน hǎn | (spin) หมุน mǔn

turn *vt.* (page, body) พลิก plík

turn around *vi.* (go the way one came) กลับ glàp

turn away *vt.* (prevent from entering) ไม่ให้_เข้า mâi-hâi-_-kâo

turn back see turn around

turn back *vi.* (for person, e.g. head) หันกลับ hǎn-glàp

turn down *vt.* (decline) ปฏิเสธ bpà~dtì-sèet | (e.g. volume, light level) หรี่ rìi

turn in *vt.* (e.g. criminal) มอบตัว mɔ̂ɔp-dtuua | (e.g. homework, results) ส่ง sòng

turn inside out *vt.* กลับ glàp

turn into *vt.* กลายเป็น glaai-bpen

turnip *n.* หัวผักกาด hǔua-pàk-gàat [หัว hǔua]

turn off *vt.* (e.g. light, machine) ปิด bpìt | (e.g. sexually) ทำให้_เสียอารมณ์ tam-hâi-_-sǐia-aa-rom

turn on *vt.* (e.g. light, machine) เปิด bpə̀ət | (e.g. sexually) ทำให้_มีอารมณ์ tam-hâi-_-mii-aa-rom

turn oneself in *v.* (to police) มอบตัว mɔ̂ɔp-dtuua

turn out *vi.* (appear) ปรากฏว่า bpraa-gòt-wâa

turn over *vi.* (flip upside down) พลิกตัว plík-dtuua

turn over *vt.* (flip upside down) คว่ำ kwâm | (page, body) พลิก plík

turnover *n.* (employee) การเปลี่ยนพนักงาน gaan-bplìian-pá~nák-ngaan

turn signal *n.* สัญญาณเลี้ยว sǎn-yaan-líiao [สัญญาณ sǎn-yaan]

A
B
C
D
E
F
G
H
I
J
K
L
M
N
O
P
Q
R
S
T
U
V
W
X
Y
Z

turntable *n.*
(phonograph)
เครื่องเล่นแผ่นเสียง
krûuang-lên-pèn-sĭiang
[เครื่อง krûuang]

turn up *vi.* (arrive) มาถึง
maa-tŭng | (lay face up)
หงาย ngǎai

turn upside down see
turn over

turpentine *n.* น้ำมันสน
nám-man-sŏn [กระป๋อง
grà~bpŏng (can)]

turquoise *n.* (stone)
หินเทอร์ควอยซ์ hĭn-təə-
kwɔ́ɔi [ก้อน gɔ̂ɔn]

turtle *n.* เต่า dtào [ตัว
dtuua]

tusk *n.* (elephant) งาช้าง
ngaa-cháang [กิ่ง gìng
(each), คู่ kûu (pair)]

tutor *n.* ครูพิเศษ kruu-pí-
sèet [คน kon]

tutor *v.* สอนพิเศษ sɔ̌ɔn-
pí-sèet, ติว dtiu ✎

tuxedo *n.* ทักซิโด้ ták-sí~
dôo [ชุด chút]

tweezers *n.* แหนบ nɛ̀ɛp
[อัน an]

twelve *numb.* สิบสอง sìp-
sɔ̌ɔng

twenty *numb.* ยี่สิบ yîi-sìp

twice *adv.* (on two
occasions) สองครั้ง
sɔ̌ɔng-kráng | (two times
more) สองเท่า sɔ̌ɔng-tâo

twig *n.* (small branch) กิ่ง
gìng [กิ่ง gìng]

twilight *n.* พลบค่ำ plóp-
kâm, เวลาโพล้เพล้ wee-
laa-plóo-plée,
แสงอาทิตย์ตอนเย็น
sɛ̌ɛng-aa-tít-dtɔɔn-yen

twin *adj.* เป็นคู่กัน bpen-
kûu-gan, แฝด fɛ̀ɛt

twin *n.* ฝาแฝด fǎa-fɛ̀ɛt,
แฝด fɛ̀ɛt [คู่ kûu]

twin bed *n.* (small bed)
เตียงขนาดเล็ก dtiiang-
kà~nàat-lék [เตียง
dtiiang]

twine *vt.* (twist together)
บิด_เป็นเกลียว bìt-_-
bpen-gliiao

twinkle *n.* (light)
แสงแวววาว sɛ̌ɛng-wɛɛo-
waao

twinkle *vi.* (sparkle)
ประกาย bprà~gaai

Twins *n.* (astrological
sign) ราศีเมถุน raa-sĭi-
mee-tŭn [ราศี raa-sĭi]

twirl *vi.* หมุนรอบ mŭn-rôop

twirl *vt.* ทำให้_หมุน tam-hâi-_-mŭn

twist *n.* (dance) การเต้นจังหวะทวิสต์ gaan-dtên-jang-wà-tá~wít

twist *v.* บิด bìt

twist *vt.* บิด_ให้เป็นเกลียว bìt-_-hâi-bpen-gliiao

twisted *adj.* (e.g. string) เกลียว gliiao | (not straight) เก gee | (sprained, e.g. ankle) แพลง plɛɛng

two *numb.* สอง sǒong

two-fold *adj.* ทวีคูณ tá~wii-kuun, สองเท่า sǒong-tâo

two hundred *numb.* สองร้อย sǒong-rɔ́ɔi

two-timer *n.* (lover or spouse) คนที่ไม่ซื่อสัตย์ต่อคู่รัก kon-tîi-mâi-sûe-sàt-dtɔ̀ɔ-kûu-rák [คน kon]

tycoon *n.* นักธุรกิจที่ร่ำรวย nák-tú-rá-gìt-tîi-râm-ruuai [คน kon]

type *n.* (class) ประเภท bprà~pêet [ประเภท bprà~pêet] | (kind) ชนิด chá~nít [ชนิด chá~nít] | (pattern, style, form) แบบ bɛ̀ɛp [แบบ bɛ̀ɛp]

type *v.* (print, type on keyboard) พิมพ์ pim

type *vt.* (push keyboard key) กด gòt

typewriter *n.* เครื่องพิมพ์ดีด krûeang-pim-dìit [เครื่อง krûeang]

typhoid *n.* ไข้รากสาดน้อย kâi-râak-sàat-nɔ́ɔi, ไทฟอยด์ tai-fɔɔi [โรค rôok]

typhoon *n.* ไต้ฝุ่น dtâai-fùn, พายุไต้ฝุ่น paa-yú-dtâi-fùn ! [ลูก lûuk]

typical *adj.* (conforming to a type) เป็นแบบฉบับ bpen-bɛ̀ɛp-chà~bàp | (exemplifying) เป็นตัวอย่าง bpen-dtuua-yàang

typist *n.* พนักงานพิมพ์ดีด pá~nák-ngaan-pim-dìit ! [คน kon]

tyrannize *vt.* (oppress) ข่มขี่ kòm-kìi

tyranny *n.* (governing with absolute power)

การปกครองแบบเผด็จการ
gaan-bpòk-krɔɔng-
bὲὲp-pà~dèt-gaan |
(tyrannical act) การข่มเหง
gaan-kòm-hěeng
tyrant *n.* (dictator)
ผู้ปกครองแบบเผด็จการ
pûu-bpòk-krɔɔng-bὲὲp-
pà~dèt-gaan [คน kon]
tyre see tire

U

UFO *n.* จานบิน jaan-bin
[ลำ lam]
ugly *adj.* (displeasing)
น่าเกลียด nâa-glìiat |
(unattractive) ขี้เหร่ kîi-rèe
UK *n.* สหราชอาณาจักร sà~
hà-râat-chá~aa-naa-jàk
[ประเทศ bprà~têet]
ulcer *n.* แผลอักเสบ plὲὲ-
àk-sèep [แห่ง hèng]
ultimate *adj.* (most
extreme, highest) ที่สุด
tîi-sùt
ultrasound *n.* อุลตราซาวด์
un-dtrâa-saao
umbrella *n.* ร่ม rôm [คัน
kan]
unable *adj.* ไม่สามารถ
mâi-sǎa-mâat
unable to *aux.* ทำ_ไม่ได้

tam-_-mâi-dâai,
ทำ_ไม่ไหว tam-_-mâi-wǎi
🐾
unabridged *adj.*
ไม่ตัดตอน mâi-dtàt-dtɔɔn
unanimous *adj.*
เป็นเอกฉันท์ bpen-èek-
gà~chǎn
unarmed *adj.* ไม่มีอาวุธ
mâi-mii-aa-wút
unavoidable *adj.*
หลีกเลี่ยงไม่ได้ lìik-
lìiang-mâi-dâai
unaware *adj.* (not aware,
unconscious) ไม่รู้ตัว
mâi-rúu-dtuua | (not
knowing) ไม่รู้ mâi-rúu
unbalanced *adj.* ไม่สมดุล
mâi-sǒm-dun
unbearable *adj.* ทนไม่ได้
ton-mâi-dâai, ทนไม่ไหว
ton-mâi-wǎi
unbelievable *adj.*
ไม่น่าเชื่อ mâi-nâa-chûua
uncertain *adj.* (not
certain) ไม่แน่นอน mâi-
nὲὲ-nɔɔn | (not sure)
ไม่แน่ใจ mâi-nὲὲ-jai
unchanged *adj.*
ไม่เปลี่ยนแปลง mâi-
bplìian-bplὲὲng

uncivilized *adj.*
(barbarous) ป่าเถื่อน
bpàa-tèuan

uncle *n.* (father or
mother's older brother)
ลุง lung [คน kon] |
(father's younger
brother) อา aa [คน kon] |
(mother's younger
brother) น้า náa [คน kon]

unclear *adj.* (ambiguous)
กำกวม gam-guuam |
(cloudy) มัว muua | (not
clear) ไม่ชัดเจน mâi-chát-
jeen

uncomfortable *adj.* (not
comfortable) ไม่สบาย
mâi-sà~baai | (uneasy)
อึดอัด ùt-àt

uncommon *adj.*
ไม่ธรรมดา mâi-tam-
má~daa

unconcerned *adj.*
(unworried) ไม่กังวล
mâi-gang-won

unconditional *adj.*
ไม่มีเงื่อนไข mâi-mii-
ngûuan-kăi

unconscious *adj.* ไม่ได้สติ
mâi-dâi-sà~dtì

unconventional *adj.*
ผิดธรรมเนียม pìt-tam-
niiam

uncountable *adj.* นับไม่ได้
náp-mâi-dâai

uncover *vt.* เปิดเผย
bpə̀ət-pə̆əi

undecided *adj.*
ยังไม่ตัดสินใจ yang-mâi-
dtàt-sǐn-jai

undefeatable *adj.*
ไม่มีใครเอาชนะได้ mâi-
mii-krai-ao-chá~ná-dâai

under *prep.* (below in
degree, rank) ข้างล่าง
kâang-lâang | (beneath,
below the surface of) ใต้
dtâai

undercover *adj.* สายลับ
sǎai-láp

underdeveloped *adj.*
ล้าหลัง láa-lǎng

underdog *n.* (one who is
expected to lose)
ผู้เสียเปรียบในการแข่งขัน
pûu-sǐia-bpriiap-nai-
gaan-kèng-kǎn [คน kon]

underestimate *v.*
ประเมินค่า_ต่ำไป bprà~
məən-kâa-_-dtàm-bpai

undergarment *n.*
เสื้อชั้นใน sûua-chán-nai
[ตัว dtuua]

undergo *vt.* (experience)

ประสบ bprà~sòp

undergraduate n.
นักศึกษาปริญญาตรี nák-
sùk-săa-bpà~rin-yaa-
dtrii [คน kon]

underground adj.
(beneath the surface of
the ground) ใต้ดิน dtâai-
din | (hidden or secret)
ใต้ดิน dtâai-din

underline n. เส้นใต้ sên-
dtâai [เส้น sên]

underline vt.
(underscore) ขีดเส้นใต้
kìit-sên-dtâai

underlying adj. (hidden,
implicit) ที่ซ่อนอยู่ tîi-sôn-
yùu

undermine vt. (weaken)
ตัดกำลัง dtàt-gam-lang

underneath adj. ข้างใต้
kâang-dtâai, ล่าง lâang

underneath prep. ข้างใต้
kâang-dtâai, ข้างล่าง
kâang-lâang

underpants n. กางเกงใน
gaang-geeng-nai,
กางเกงลิง gaang-geeng-
ling ✴ [ตัว dtuua]

underpay vt.
จ่าย_ต่ำกว่าที่ควร jàai-_-

dtàm-gwàa-tîi-kuuan

undersea adj. ใต้ทะเล
dtâai-tá~lee

undershirt n. เสื้อกล้าม
sûua-glâam [ตัว dtuua]

understand v. เข้าใจ kâo-
jai

understand vi. รู้เรื่อง rúu-
rûuang ✴

understandable adj.
(comprehensible)
ที่เข้าใจได้ tîi-kâo-jai-dâai

understanding n.
(comprehension)
ความเข้าใจ kwaam-kâo-
jai | (mutual agreement)
ข้อตกลงร่วมกัน kôo-dtòk-
long-rûuam-gan

undertake vt. (perform)
ดำเนินการ dam-nəən-
gaan | (take charge)
รับผิดชอบ ráp-pìt-chôop

undertaker n. (funeral
director) ผู้จัดการศพ pûu-
jàt-gaan-sòp [คน kon]

under-the-counter adj.
(illegal) ผิดกฎหมาย pìt-
gòt-măai

underwear n. (panties,
boxers, jockeys)
กางเกงใน gaang-geeng-

nai [ตัว dtuua]

underworld n. (e.g. mafia) สังคมของพวกนอกกฎหมาย săng-kom-kŭong-pûuak-nɔ̂ɔk-gòt-măai [สังคม săng-kom] | (hell) นรก ná~rók [ขุมkŭm]

underwrite vt. (insure) รับประกัน ráp-bprà~gan | (one's name on) ลงชื่อใน long-chûu-nai

undeveloped adj. ด้อยพัฒนา dɔ̂ɔi-pát-tá~naa

undo vt. (cancel) ยกเลิกyók-lɔ̂ək | (reverse) เปลี่ยน_กลับ bplìian-_-glàp | (untie, loosen) แก้gɛ̂ɛ

undone adj. (not completed) ไม่สมบูรณ์mâi-sŏm-buun | (unfinished) ค้างไว้káang-wái

undress vi. ถอดเสื้อผ้าtɔ̀ɔt-sû̂ua-pâa, แก้ผ้าgɛ̂ɛ-pâa ✿

undress vt. (remove) ถอด_ออก tɔ̀ɔt-_-ɔ̀ɔk

uneasy adj. (restless)

กระสับกระส่าย grà~sàp-grà~sàai | (uncomfortable) ไม่สบายmâi-sà~baai

unemployed adj. ไม่มีงานทำ mâi-mii-ngaan-tam

unequal adj. ไม่เท่ากันmâi-tâo-gan

unequal adv. (e.g. rank, position) เหลื่อมล้ำlùuam-lám

uneven adj. (not level) ไม่เรียบ mâi-rîiap | (varying, not uniform) ไม่สม่ำเสมอ mâi-sà~màm-sà~mɔ̆ɔ

unexpected adj. ไม่คาดคิด mâi-kâat-kít

unfair adj. ไม่ยุติธรรม mâi-yút-dtì-tam

unfaithful adj. (disloyal) ไม่ซื่อสัตย์ mâi-sûu-sàt

unfamiliar adj. ไม่คุ้นเคย mâi-kún-kəəi

unfinished adj. (incomplete) ไม่สมบูรณ์ mâi-sŏm-buun | (unaccomplished) ไม่สำเร็จ mâi-săm-rèt

unfold v. (open) กาง

gaang

unfold vt. (reveal, disclose in words) เปิดโปง bpèət-bpoong

unforgettable adj. ลืมไม่ได้ luum-mâi-dâai, ไม่อาจลืมได้ mâi-àat-luum-dâai ⚡

unforgivable adj. ให้อภัยไม่ได้ hâi-à~pai-mâi-dâai

unfortunate adj. (unlucky) โชคไม่ดี chôok-mâi-dii

unfortunately adv. (regrettably) น่าเสียดาย nâa-sǐia-daai

unfriendly adj. ไม่เป็นมิตร mâi-bpen-mít

unfurnished adj. ไม่มีเฟอร์นิเจอร์ mâi-mii-fəə-ní~jəə

ungrateful adj. (not displaying gratitude) อกตัญญู à~gà~dtan-yuu

unhappy adj. ไม่มีความสุข mâi-mii-kwaam-sùk

unharmed adj. (unhurt) ไม่ได้รับบาดเจ็บ mâi-dâi-ráp-bàat-jèp

unhealthy adj. (unhealthful) สุขภาพไม่ดี sùk-kà~pâap-mâi-dii

uniform adj. (consistent, constant) สม่ำเสมอ sà~màm-sà~mǒə

uniform n. เครื่องแบบ krûuang-bὲεp [ชุด chút]

unify vi. รวมกัน ruuam-gan

unify vt. รวม_เข้าด้วยกัน ruuam-_-kâo-dûuai-gan

unimportant adj. ไม่สำคัญ mâi-sǎm-kan

uninteresting adj. (not interesting) ไม่น่าสนใจ mâi-nâa-sǒn-jai

union n. (being united) การรวมกัน gaan-ruuam-gan | (e.g. labor union) สหภาพ sà~hà-pâap [แห่ง hὲng]

unique adj. มีเอกลักษณ์ mii-èek-gà~lák

unisex adj. ใช้ได้ทั้งสองเพศ chái-dáai-táng-sǒuwng-pêet

unit n. (one of a number of things, etc.) หน่วย nùai [หน่วย nùai]

unite vi. รวมกัน ruuam-gan

unite vt. (join, combine)

รวม_ให้เป็นหนึ่งเดียว
ruuam-_-hâi-bpen-
nùng-diiao ‼

United Kingdom n.
สหราชอาณาจักร sà~hà-
râat-chá~aa-naa-jàk
[ประเทศ bprà~têet]

United Nations n.
สหประชาชาติ sà~hà-
bprà~chaa-châat
[องค์การ ong-gaan]

**United States of
America** n. สหรัฐอเมริกา
sà~hà-rát-à~mee-rí~gaa
‼ [ประเทศ bprà~têet]

unity n. (harmony) สามัคคี
sǎa-mák-kii | (oneness)
ความเป็นเอกภาพ
kwaam-bpen-èek-gà~
pâap

universal adj. (worldwide,
used by all) สากล sǎa-gon

universe n. จักรวาล jàk-
grà~waan [แห่ง hèng]

university n. มหาวิทยาลัย
má~hǎa-wít-tá~yaa-lai
[แห่ง hèng]

unkind adj. ใจร้าย jai-ráai

unknown adj. (not
discovered) ที่ยังไม่ค้นพบ
tîi-yang-mâi-kón-póp |

(not famous) ไม่มีชื่อเสียง
mâi-mii-chûu-sǐiang

unlawful adj. ผิดกฎหมาย
pìt-gòt-mǎai

unless conj. นอกจาก nɔ̂ɔk-
jàak, เว้นเสียแต่ว่า wén-
sǐia-dtɛ̀ɛ-wâa

unlike adj. ไม่เหมือนกัน
mâi-mǔuan-gan

unlike prep. แตกต่างจาก
dtɛ̀ɛk-dtàang-jàak

unlikely adj.
ไม่น่าเป็นไปได้ mâi-nâa-
bpen-bpai-dâai

unlimited adj. ไม่จำกัด
mâi-jam-gàt

unload v. ขน_ลง kǒn-_-
long

unlock v. (open) เปิด_ออก
bpə̀ət-_-ɔ̀ɔk

unlucky adj. โชคร้าย
chôok-ráai

unmarried adj.
ยังไม่ได้แต่งงาน yang-
mâi-dâi-dtɛ̀ng-ngaan,
โสด sòot

unnatural adj. (not
natural) ไม่เป็นธรรมชาติ
mâi-bpen-tam-má~châat

unnecessary adj. ไม่จำเป็น
mâi-jam-bpen

unpack vi. เอาของออก

ao-kǒɔng-ɔ̀ɔk
unpack *vt.* เอา_ออก ao-_-
ɔ̀ɔk
unpaid *adj.* (Serving
without pay) ไม่ได้ค่าจ้าง
mâi-dâi-kâa-jâang | (not
yet paid) ยังไม่ได้ชำระ
yang-mâi-dâi-cham-rá
unplug *vt.* ถอดปลั๊ก tɔ̀ɔt-
bplák
unpopular *adj.*
ไม่เป็นที่นิยม mâi-bpen-
tîi-ní-yom
unpredictable *adj.*
คาดไม่ได้ kâat-mâi-dâai
unreal *adj.* ไม่จริง mâi-jing
unrealistic *adj.*
ไม่มองดูสภาพจริงๆ mâi-
mɔɔng-duu-sà~pâap-
jing-jing
unreasonable *adj.*
ไม่สมเหตุสมผล mâi-
sǒm-hèet-sǒm-pǒn
unreliable *adj.*
ไม่น่าไว้วางใจ mâi-nâa-
wái-waang-jai
unrest *n.* ความไม่สงบ
kwaam-mâi-sà~ngòp
unripe *adj.* ไม่สุก mǎi-sùk
| (raw) ดิบ dìp
unsafe *adj.* ไม่ปลอดภัย

mâi-bplɔ̀ɔt-pai
unstable *adj.* ไม่มั่นคง
mâi-mân-kong
unsteady *adj.* ไม่มั่นคง
mâi-mân-kong
unsure *adj.* ไม่แน่ใจ mâi-
nɛ̂ɛ-jai
untamed *adj.* ไม่เชื่อง
mâi-chûuang
untidy *adj.* ไม่เป็นระเบียบ
mâi-bpen-rá~biiap
until *prep.* จน jon,
จนกระทั่ง jon-grà~tâng,
จนถึง jon-tǔng
untrue *adj.* (not true)
ไม่จริง mâi-jing |
(unfaithful) ไม่ซื่อสัตย์
mâi-sûu-sàt
unusual *adj.* ผิดปกติ pìt-
bpà-gà~dtì, ไม่ธรรมดา
mâi-tam-má~daa
unwilling *adj.* (reluctant)
ไม่เต็มใจ mâi-dtem-jai
unworthy *adj.* (not
deserving) ไม่คู่ควร mâi-
kûu-kuuan
unwrap *v.* แก้ห่อ_ออก
gɛ̂ɛ-hɔ̀ɔ-_-ɔ̀ɔk
up *adv.* (above, higher)
ข้างบน kâang-bon | (e.g.

go up, come up) ขึ้น kûn
| (upright) ตั้งตรง dtâng-
dtrong

upbringing n. การเลี้ยงดู
gaan-líiang-duu

update vt. (e.g.
computer) ใส่ข้อมูลใหม่ใน
sài-kôo-muun-mài-nai |
(person, organization,
etc.) ให้ข้อมูลใหม่กับ hâi-
kôo-muun-mài-gàp

upgrade vt. ยกระดับ yók-
rá~dàp

upheaval n. ความไม่สงบ
kwaam-mâi-sà~ngòp

uphold vt. (raise) ยก_ขึ้น
yók-_-kûn | (support, e.g.
law) สนับสนุน sà~nàp-
sà~nǔn

upon prep. (at the time)
ในเวลา nai-wee-laa | (on)
บน bon

upper adj. ที่สูงกว่า tîi-
sǔung-gwàa

upper-class n. สังคมชั้นสูง
sǎng-kom-chán-sǔung
[ชั้น chán]

upper layer n. ชั้นบน
chán-bon [ชั้น chán]

upper story n. ชั้นบน
chán-bon [ชั้น chán]

upright adj. (vertical)
ตั้งตรง dtâng-dtrong

uprising n. การจลาจล
gaan-jà~laa-jon

uproar n. ความวุ่นวาย
kwaam-wûn-waai

upset adj. (angry) โกรธ
gròot | (in a bad mood)
อารมณ์เสีย aa-rom-sǐia

upset n. (loss) การพ่ายแพ้
gaan-pâai-pέε

upset vt. (defeat superior
enemy) โค่นล้ม kôon-
lóm, ล้ม lóm ● | (disturb)
ทำให้_ไม่พอใจ tam-hâi-
_-mâi-pɔɔ-jai

upset stomach adj. (any
stomach discomfort)
ท้องไม่ดี tɔ́ɔng-mâi-dii |
(nauseous) คลื่นไส้อาเจียน
klʉ̂ʉn-sâi-aa-jiian

upshift vi. (vehicle)
เปลี่ยนเป็นเกียร์สูง
bplìian-bpen-giia-sǔung

upside down adj. (turn
over) คว่ำลง kwâm-long

upstairs n. ชั้นบน chán-
bon [ชั้น chán]

uptight *adj.* ตึงเครียด dtʉng-krîiat

up to *adj.* (as many as) ถึง tʉ̌ng

up to *vt.* (dependent on) แล้วแต่ lɛ́ɛo-dtɛ̀ɛ

up-to-date *adj.* ทันสมัย tan-sà~mǎi

upward *adv.* เหนือขึ้นไป nʉ̌ʉa-kʉ̂n-bpai

Uranus *n.* ดาวยูเรนัส daao-yuu-ree-nát [ดวง duuang]

urban *adj.* เกี่ยวกับเมือง gìiao-gàp-mʉʉang

urchin *n.* (sea urchin) หอยเม่น hɔ̌ɔi-mên [ตัว dtuua]

urge *v.* (impel, drive, insist) กระตุ้น grà~dtûn, เร่งเร้า rêng-ráo

urge *vi.* (persuade) ชักนำ chák-nam

urgent *adj.* เร่งด่วน rêng-dùuan

urinal *n.* ที่ปัสสาวะ tîi-bpàt-sǎa~wá [ที่ tîi]

urinate *vi.* ปัสสาวะ bpàt-sǎa~wá ⚠, ฉี่ chìi ●, เยี่ยว yîiao ◆

urine *n.* ปัสสาวะ bpàt-

sǎa~wá ⚠, ฉี่ chìi ●, เยี่ยว yîiao ◆

urn *n.* (for ashes) โกศ gòot [ใบ bai]

us *pron.* พวกเรา pûuak-rao, เรา rao

USA *n.* อเมริกา à~mee-rí~gaa, สหรัฐอเมริกา sà~hà-rát-à~mee-rí~gaa ⚠ [ประเทศ bprà~têet]

usable *adj.* (capable of being used) มีประโยชน์ mii-bprà~yòot | (utilizable) ใช้ได้ chái-dâai

usage *n.* (act) การใช้ gaan-chái | (use) ประโยชน์ bprà~yòot [อย่าง yàang]

use *n.* (act) การใช้ gaan-chái

use *vt.* ใช้ chái

used *adj.* (has been used) ใช้แล้ว chái-lɛ́ɛo

used to *idm.* เคยชินกับ kəəi-chin-gàp, คุ้นเคยกับ kún-kəəi-gàp ⚠

used up *adj.* หมด mòt

useful *adj.* มีประโยชน์ mii-bprà~yòot

useless *adj.* ไม่มีประโยชน์

mâi-mii-bprà~yòot

user n. ผู้ใช้ pûu-chái [คน
kon]

user-friendly adj. (easy
to use) ใช้ง่าย chái-ngâai

use up vt. ใช้_หมด chái-
_-mòt

usher n. (who escorts
people to seats)
พนักงานที่พาไปยังที่นั่ง
pá~nák-ngaan-tîi-paa-
bpai-yang-tîi-nâng [คน
kon]

usual adj. ปกติ bpòk-gà~
dtì

usually adv. ตามธรรมดา
dtaam-tam-má~daa, มัก
mák, มักจะ mák-jà

utensil n. (tool, e.g.
spoon, fork)
เครื่องมือเครื่องใช้
krûuang-muu-krûuang-
chái [ชิ้น chín]

uterus n. มดลูก mót-lûuk

utility n. (for the public)
สาธารณูปโภค sǎa-taa-
rá~nuu-bpà~pôok

utilize vt. (use)
ใช้_ให้เป็นประโยชน์ chái-
_-hâi-bpen-bprà~yòot

utmost adj. (extreme)

สุดขีด sùt-kìit | (ultimate,
best) ที่สุด tîi-sùt

utter v. (send forth with
the voice, make sounds)
เปล่งเสียง bplèng-sǐiang

U-turn vi. กลับรถ glàp-
rót, ยูเทิร์น yuu-təən ✦

uvula n. ลิ้นไก่ lín-gài [อัน
an]

V

vacancy n. (emptiness)
ความว่าง kwaam-wâang |
(empty room) ห้องว่าง
hɔ̂ng-wâang

vacant adj. (free, empty)
ว่าง wâang

vacate vt. (make empty)
ทำให้_ว่าง tam-hâi-_-
wâang | (remove)
ถอน_ออก tɔ̌ɔn-_-ɔ̀ɔk

vacation n. (for schools)
ช่วงปิดภาคเรียน
chûuang-bpìt-pâak-riian
[ช่วง chûuang] | (holiday)
วันหยุด wan-yùt [วัน wan,
ช่วง chûuang (period)]

vaccinate vt. ฉีดวัคซีนให้
chìit-wák-siin-hâi

vaccine n. วัคซีน wák-siin
[ชนิด chá~nít]

vacuum v. (use a vacuum cleaner on) ดูดฝุ่น dùut-fùn

vacuum cleaner n. เครื่องดูดฝุ่น krûuang-dùut-fùn [เครื่อง krûuang]

vagabond n. คนพเนจร kon-pá~nee-jɔɔn [คน kon]

vagina n. จิ๋ม jǐm ●, ไข่แดง kài-dɛɛng ☀, หี hǐi ♨, ช่องคลอด chɔ̂ng-klɔ̂ɔt ✖

vague adj. คลุมเครือ klum-kruua, ไม่ชัดเจน mâi-chát-jeen

vain adj. (conceited) ถือตัว tɯ̌ɯ-dtuua | (of no substance) ไร้สาระ rái-sǎa-rá

Valentine's Day n. วันแห่งความรัก wan-hɛ̀ng-kwaam-rák [วัน wan]

valet n. (attendant who parks cars) ผู้บริการจอดรถ pûu-bɔɔ-rí~gaan-jɔ̀ɔt rót [คน kon] | (male servant) คนรับใช้ชาย kon-ráp-chái-chaai [คน kon]

valid adj. (official) เป็นทางการ bpen-taang-gaan | (useable) ใช้ได้ chái-dâai

valley n. หุบเขา hùp-kǎo [แห่ง hɛ̀ng]

valuable adj. (having value) มีค่า mii-kâa

value n. (cost, price) มูลค่า muun-lá~kâa ⚠ | (worth) ค่า kâa

value vt. (give importance to) ให้ความสำคัญ hâi-kwaam-sǎm-kan

value-added tax n. ภาษีมูลค่าเพิ่ม paa-sǐi-muun-lá~kâa-pə̂əm, แวต wɛ́t ● [จำนวน jam-nuuan]

valve n. (e.g. for engine, heart, etc.) ลิ้นปิดเปิด lín-bpìt-bpə̀ət [อัน an]

vampire n. (bat) ค้างคาวดูดเลือด káang-kaao-dùut-lɯ̂at [ตัว dtuua] | (dracula) ผีดูดเลือด pǐi-dùut-lɯ̂at [ตัว dtuua]

van n. รถตู้ rót-dtûu [คัน kan]

vanguard n. แนวหน้า nɛɛo-nâa [แนว nɛɛo]

vanilla *adj.* วนิลา wá~ní-laa

vanish *vi.* หายไป hǎai-bpai

vanity *n.* (being vain) ความหยิ่งยโส kwaam-yìng-yá~sǒo

vapor *n.* (smog, fog, steam) ไอ ai

variable *adj.* (changeable) เปลี่ยนแปลงได้ bplìian-bplɛɛng-dâai

variable *n.* (factor) ตัวแปร dtuua-bprɛɛ [ตัว dtuua]

variation *n.* (change) การเปลี่ยนแปลง gaan-bplìian-bplɛɛng | (difference) ความแตกต่าง kwaam-dtɛ̀ɛk-dtàang

variety *n.* (diversity) ความหลากหลาย kwaam-làak-lǎai

various *adj.* (different) ต่างๆกัน dtàang-dtàang-gan | (many forms) หลากหลาย làak-lǎai | (of diverse kinds) ต่างๆนานา dtàang-dtàang-naa-naa ⚠

vary *vi.* (undergo change) แตกต่าง dtɛ̀ɛk-dtàang

vase *n.* แจกัน jɛɛ-gan [ใบ bai]

vast *adj.* (wide and spacious) กว้างใหญ่ gwâang-yài

vault *n.* (act) การกระโดดข้ามสิ่งกีดขวาง gaan-grà~dòot-kâam-sìng-gìit-kwǎang | (underground room) ห้องใต้ดิน hɔ̂ng-dtâai-din [ห้อง hɔ̂ng]

veal *n.* เนื้อลูกวัว nɯ́ua-lûuk-wuua [ชิ้น chín]

vegetable *n.* ผัก pàk [ชนิด chá~nít (kind), ต้น dtôn (plant)]

vegetable oil *n.* น้ำมันพืช nám-man-pɯ̂ɯt [ชนิด chá~nít (kind), ขวด kùuat (bottle)]

vegetarian *adj.* เจ jee, ไม่กินเนื้อสัตว์ mâi-gin-nɯ́ua-sàt

vegetarian *n.* กินเจ gin-jee ✿ [คน kon]

vegetation *n.* (plants) พืชผัก pɯ̂ɯt-pàk [ชนิด chá~nít (kind), ต้น dtôn (plant)]

vehicle *n.* รถ rót, พาหนะ paa-hà~ná ⚠ [คัน kan]

veil *n.* (face cover)

ผ้าคลุมหน้า pâa-klum-nâa [ผืน pǔun]

vein n. (blood vessel) เส้นเลือด sên-lûuat [เส้น sên]

velocity n. ความเร็ว kwaam-reo

velvet adj. กำมะหยี่ gam-má~yìi

vending machine n. ตู้ขายสินค้าแบบหยอดเหรียญ dtûu-kǎai-sǐn-káa-bɛ̀ɛp-yɔ̀ɔt-rǐian [เครื่อง krûuang]

vendor n. (seller) คนขายของ kon-kǎai-kɔ̌ɔng [คน kon]

venerate vt. นับถือ náp-tǔu

venereal disease n. กามโรค gaam-má~rôok [โรค rôok]

vengeance n. การแก้แค้น gaan-gɛ̂ɛ-kɛ́ɛn

vengeful adj. พยาบาท pá~yaa-bàat

venison n. เนื้อกวาง núua-gwaang [ชิ้น chín]

venom n. (poison, toxin) พิษ pít

vent n. (outlet for air)

ช่องลม chɔ̂ng-lom [ช่อง chɔ̂ng]

ventilate vt. (provide _ with fresh air) ระบายอากาศใน rá~baai-aa-gàat-nai

venture v. (risk, take a risk) เสี่ยงภัย sìiang-pai

Venus n. (planet) ดาวศุกร์ daao-sùk [ดวง duuang]

veranda n. ระเบียง rá~biiang [แห่ง hɛ̀ng]

verandah see veranda

verb n. คำกริยา kam-grì-yaa [คำ kam]

verbal adj. (as opposed to actions) เป็นวาจา bpen-waa-jaa | (pertaining to words) เกี่ยวกับถ้อยคำ gìiao-gàp-tɔ̂i-kam

verdict n. (judgment) คำพิพากษา kam-pí-pâak-sǎa

verify vt. (check) ตรวจสอบ dtrùuat-sɔ̀ɔp | (prove) พิสูจน์ pí-sùut

vermicelli n. เส้นหมี่ sên-mìi [เส้น sên (strand), ห่อ hɔ̀ɔ (pack)]

versatile adj. (can be used for several

purposes) อเนกประสงค์
à~nèek-bprà~sŏng

verse *n.* (poem, poetry)
โคลงกลอน kloong-glɔɔn,
บทกวี bòt-gà~wii [บท
bòt]

version *n.* (in computer
science) เวอร์ชั่น wəə-
chân [เวอร์ชั่น wəə-chân]
| (translated work)
บทแปล bòt-bplɛɛ [บท
bòt]

versus *prep.* กับ gàp

vertical *adj.* แนวตั้ง ŋɛɛo-
dtâng

very *adv.* มาก mâak,
อย่างมาก yàang-mâak

very good *adj.* ดีมาก dii-
mâak

very much *adv.* มาก mâak

vessel *n.* (container)
ภาชนะ paa-chá~ná [ใบ
bai, ชิ้น chín] | (tube)
หลอด lɔ̀ɔt [หลอด lɔ̀ɔt] |
(vein) หลอดเลือด lɔ̀ɔt-
lɨ̂at [หลอด lɔ̀ɔt]

vest *n.* (waistcoat) เสื้อกั๊ก
sɨ̂a-gák [ตัว dtuua]

vet *n.* สัตวแพทย์ sàt-pɛ̂ɛt
❀ [คน kon]

veteran *n.* (who has
served in the military)
ทหารผ่านศึก tá~hǎan-
pàan-sɨk [นาย naai !, คน
kon]

veterinarian *n.* สัตวแพทย์
sàt-dtà~wà~pɛ̂ɛt [คน
kon]

veto *vt.* (oppose) คัดค้าน
kát-káan

vexed *adj.* (annoyed)
หัวเสีย hǔua-sǐia ❀

via *prep.* โดยทาง dooi-
taang, ทาง taang

vibrant *adj.* (energetic)
มีชีวิตชีวา mii-chii-wít-
chii-waa

vibrate *vi.* สั่น sàn

vibration *n.*
การสั่นสะเทือน gaan-sàn-
sà~tɨɨan

vice *n.* (evil habit)
นิสัยไม่ดี ní-sǎi-mâi-dii
[อัน an]

vice *prep.* (in place of) รอง
rɔɔng

vice president *n.* (of a
country) รองประธานาธิบดี
rɔɔng-bprà~taa-naa-
típ-bɔɔ-dii [คน kon]

vice versa *adv.*
ในทางกลับกัน nai-taang-

glàp-gan

vicinity n. บริเวณใกล้เคียง bɔɔ-rí~ween-glâi-kiiang [บริเวณ bɔɔ-rí~ween]

vicious adj. (malicious) ชั่วร้าย chûua-ráai

victim n. (person who suffers from some adverse circumstance) ผู้เคราะห์ร้าย pûu-krɔ́-ráai [คน kon] | (prey, who is harmed or killed by another) เหยื่อ yʉ̀ʉa [คน kon]

victory n. ชัยชนะ chai-chá~ná

video adj. วิดีโอ wii-dii-oo

videotape n. เทปวิดีโอ téep-wii-dii-oo [เทป téep, ม้วน múuan (roll)]

videotape vt. บันทึก ภาพของ_ลงบนวิดีโอ ban-tʉ́k-pâap-kɔ̌ɔng-_-long-bon-wii-dii-oo

Vietnam n. เวียดนาม wîiat-naam [ประเทศ bprà~têet]

Vietnamese adj. เวียดนาม wîiat-naam, ญวน yuuan ●

Vietnamese n. (person) ชาวเวียดนาม chaao-wîiat-naam [คน kon]

view n. (picture of a landscape) ทิวทัศน์ tiu-tát [แห่ง hɛ̀ng]

view vt. (watch, see) ดู duu

viewer n. ผู้ชม pûu-chom [คน kon]

viewpoint n. (place of view) จุดดูวิว jùt-duu-wiu [จุด jùt]

vigil n. การเฝ้ายาม gaan-fâo-yaam

vigor n. (strength, force) กำลัง gam-lang

vigorous adj. (energetic) กระฉับกระเฉง grà~chàp-grà~chěeng

villa n. บ้านพักตากอากาศ bâan-pák-dtàak-aa-gàat [หลัง lǎng]

village n. หมู่บ้าน mùu-bâan [หมู่บ้าน mùu-bâan]

villager n. ชาวบ้าน chaao-bâan [คน kon]

villain n. (evil person) คนชั่วร้าย kon-chûua-ráai [คน kon]

vindicate vt. (avenge) แก้แค้น gɛ̂ɛ-kɛ́ɛn

vine n. (creeping plant) ไม้เถา mái-tǎo [เถา tǎo]

vinegar n. น้ำส้มสายชู nám-sôm-sǎai-chuu [ขวด kùuat]

vineyard n. ไร่องุ่น râi-à~ngùn [ไร่ râi]

vinyl n. สารไวนิล sǎan-wai-nin [ชนิด chá~nít]

violate vt. (law, rule, agreement) ฝ่าฝืน fàa-fǔun | (right, privacy) ละเมิด lá~mêɤt

violation n. การฝ่าฝืน gaan-fàa-fǔun

violence n. ความรุนแรง kwaam-run-rɛɛng

violent adj. รุนแรง run-rɛɛng

violet n. (flower) ดอกไวโอเลต dɔ̀ɔk-wai-oo-lèt [ดอก dɔ̀ɔk] | (tree) ไวโอเลต wai-oo-lèt [ต้น dtôn]

violin n. ไวโอลิน wai-oo-lin [คัน kan]

viper n. งูพิษ nguu-pít [ตัว dtuua]

Virgin n. (mother of Jesus) พระมารดาของพระเยซู prá-maan-daa-kɔ̌ɔng-prá-yee-suu [พระนาง prá~naang]

virgin n. (chaste woman) สาวบริสุทธิ์ sǎao-bɔɔ-rí~sùt [คน kon]

Virgo n. ราศีกันย์ raa-sǐi-gan [ราศี raa-sǐi]

virtual adj. (simulated) เหมือนจริง mǔuan-jing

virtue n. (goodness) คุณความดี kun-kwaam-dii

virtuous adj. (having virtue) มีศีลธรรม mii-sǐin-lá~tam

virus n. ไวรัส wai-rát [เชื้อ chúua]

visa n. วีซ่า wii-sâa [ตรา dtraa]

visible adj. (can be seen) เห็นได้ hěn-dâai

vision n. (eyesight) สายตา sǎai-dtaa | (foresight) วิสัยทัศน์ wí~sǎi-tát

visit n. การเยี่ยมเยือน gaan-yîiam-yuuan !

visit v. เยี่ยม yîiam | (come visit) มาเยี่ยม maa-yîiam | (go visit) ไปเยี่ยม bpai-yîiam

visitor n. ผู้มาเยี่ยม pûu-maa-yîiam [คน kon] |

(guest) แขก kɛ̀ɛk [คน kon]

visual *adj.* (pertaining to sight) เกี่ยวกับสายตา giiao-gàp-sǎai-dtaa

vital *adj.* (essential) สำคัญ sǎm-kan

vital statistics *n.* (measurements of a woman's figure) สัดส่วน sàt-sùuan ❧

vitamin *n.* วิตามิน wí-dtaa-min, ไวตามิน wai-dtaa-min [ยี่ห้อ yîi-hɔ̂ɔ (brand), ขวด kùuat (bottle), ชนิด chá~nít (kind)]

vocabulary *n.* คำศัพท์ kam-sàp [คำ kam] | ศัพท์ sàp [คำ kam]

vocal *adj.* (pertaining to the voice) เกี่ยวกับเสียงพูด giiao-gàp-sǐiang-pûut

vocal *n.* (sound) เสียงที่เปล่งออกมา sǐiang-tîi-bplèng-ɔ̀ɔk-maa

vocation *n.* (profession, career) อาชีพ aa-chîip [อาชีพ aa-chîip]

vodka *n.* เหล้ารัสเซีย lâo-rát-siia [แก้ว gɛ̂ɛo (glass),

ขวด kùuat (bottle)]

voice *n.* (vocal sound) เสียง sǐiang [เสียง sǐiang]

voice box *n.* (larynx) กล่องเสียง glɔ̀ng-sǐiang [กล่อง glɔ̀ng]

voice mail *n.* ข้อความที่บันทึกเป็นเสียง kɔ̂ɔ-kwaam-tîi-ban-túk-bpen-sǐiang

voice-over *n.* (voice of an off-screen narrator) เสียงของผู้บรรยาย sǐiang-kɔ̌ɔng-pûu-ban-yaai

void *adj.* (having no legal force) โมฆะ moo-ká

volatile *adj.* (changeable) เปลี่ยนแปลงง่าย bpliian-bplɛɛng-ngâai

volcano *n.* ภูเขาไฟ puu-kǎo-fai [ลูก lûuk]

volleyball *n.* วอลเลย์บอล wɔn-lêe-bɔn [เกม geem (game), แมตช์ mɛ̀t (match)]

volume *n.* (capacity (in cubic units)) ปริมาตร bpà~rí~máat | (loudness) ระดับเสียง rá~dàp-sǐiang [เดซิเบล dee-sí~beo (decibel),

ระดับ rá~dàp (level)]

volunteer *n.* อาสาสมัคร aa-sǎa-sà~màk [คน kon]

volunteer *vi.* สมัครใจ sà~màk-jai, อาสา aa-sǎa ✿

vomit *vi.* อาเจียน aa-jiian, อ้วก ûuak ✿

vote *n.* (number of votes cast) คะแนนเสียง ká~nɛɛn-sǐiang [คะแนน ká~nɛɛn]

vote *vi.* เลือกตั้ง lûuak-dtâng, ออกเสียง ɔ̀ɔk-sǐiang

vote for *vt.* (elect) เลือก lûuak

voucher *n.* (coupon) คูปอง kuu-bpɔɔng [ใบ bai] | (evidence, proof) ใบสำคัญจ่าย bai-sǎm-kan-jàai [ใบ bai]

vow *v.* (swear) ปฏิญาณ bpà~dtì-yaan, สาบาน sǎa-baan

vowel *n.* สระ sà~rà [ตัว dtuua, เสียง sǐiang (sound)]

voyage *n.* การเดินทาง gaan-dəən-taang [ครั้ง kráng]

vulgar *adj.* หยาบคาย yàap-kaai

vulnerable *adj.* (susceptible to physical injury) บาดเจ็บได้ง่าย bàat-jèp-dâi-ngâai

vulture *n.* แร้ง rɛ́ɛng [ตัว dtuua]

vulva *n.* ปากช่องคลอด bpàak-chɔ̂ng-klɔ̂ɔt

W

wacky *adj.* (crazy, silly) ติ๊งต๊อง dtíng-dtɔ́ng ✿ | (eccentric) พิลึก pí-lʉ́k

wade *vi.* (in water) ลุยน้ำ lui-náam

waffle *n.* วาฟเฟิล wáap-fə̂n [อัน an, แผ่น pɛ̀n]

wag *vt.* (e.g. tail) กระดิก grà~dìk

wage *n.* ค่าจ้าง kâa-jâang, ค่าแรง kâa-rɛɛng [จำนวน jam-nuuan]

wager *v.* (gamble) เดิมพัน dəəm-pan, พนัน pá~nan

wagon *n.* (child's toy) รถลากของเล่น rót-lâak-kɔ̌ɔng-lên [คัน kan] | (horse-drawn vehicle) รถม้า rót-máa [คัน kan]

wail *vi.* (mourn bitterly)

ร้องโหยหวน rɔ́ɔng-hǒoi-hǔuan

waist n. เอว eeo [นิ้ว níu]

waistcoat n. เสื้อกั๊ก sûua-gák [ตัว dtuua]

wait n. การรอคอย gaan-rɔɔ-kɔɔi

wait vi. คอย kɔɔi, รอ rɔɔ

wait! interj. เดี๋ยวก่อน dǐiao-gɔ̀ɔn

waiter n. (in a restaurant) พนักงานเสิร์ฟ pá~nák-ngaan-sə̀əp [คน kon]

wait for vt. คอย kɔɔi, รอ rɔɔ

waiting list n. รายชื่อของคนที่รอคิวอยู่ raai-chûu-kɔ̌ɔng-kon-tîi-rɔɔ-kiu-yùu [อัน an]

waiting room n. ห้องนั่งรอ hɔ̂ng-nâng-rɔɔ [ห้อง hɔ̂ng]

wait on vt. (serve) บริการ bɔɔ-rí~gaan

waitress n. พนักงานเสิร์ฟหญิง pá~nák-ngaan-sə̀əp-yǐng [คน kon]

waive vt. (give up, relinquish) สละ sà~là | (postpone) เลื่อน lûuan

waive one's right vi. สละสิทธิ์ sà~là-sìt

waive time vi. เลื่อนเวลา lûuan-wee-laa

wake n. (deathwatch) การเฝ้าศพก่อนฝัง gaan-fâo-sòp-gɔ̀ɔn-fǎng

wake vt. (someone up) ปลุก bplùk

wake up vi. (get up) ตื่น dtùun, ตื่นนอน dtùun-nɔɔn

wake up! interj. (get up!) ตื่น dtùun

walk n. (for pleasure) การเดินเล่น gaan-dəən-lên

walk vi. เดิน dəən

walk away from vt. เดินหนี dəən-nǐi

walker n. (support device) อุปกรณ์ช่วยเดิน ùp-bpà~gɔɔn-chûuai-dəən [เครื่อง krûuang]

walkie-talkie n. วิทยุมือถือ wít-tá~yú-muu-tǔu [เครื่อง krûuang]

walking stick n. ไม้เท้า mái-táao [อัน an]

walkout n. (strike)

การหยุดงานเพื่อประท้วง
gaan-yùt-ngaan-pนิ~ua-
bprà~túuang

wall *n.* (e.g. fortress,
property line) กำแพง
gam-pɛɛng [แห่ง hὲng] |
(e.g. house, room) ผนัง
pà~năng [ด้าน dâan]

wallet *n.* กระเป๋าเงิน grà~
bpăo-ngən [ใบ bai]

wall-to-wall *adj.*
(completely covering a
floor) คลุมทั้งพื้น klum-
táng-púun

walnut *n.* มันฮ่อ man-hɔ̂ɔ
[ลูก lûuk]

walrus *n.* สิงโตทะเล sĭng-
dtoo-tá~lee [ตัว dtuua]

waltz *n.* (ballroom dance)
การเต้นวอลซ์ gaan-
dtên-wɔ́ɔn

wand *n.* (e.g. for witches)
ไม้กายสิทธิ์ mái-gaa-yá~
sìt [อัน an]

wander *vi.* (go aimlessly)
ร่อนเร่ rɔ̂n-rêe, พเนจร
pá~nee-jɔɔn ✍

wandering *adj.* ไร้จุดหมาย
rái-jùt-măai

waning moon *n.*
พระจันทร์ข้างแรม prá~

jan-kâang-rɛɛm [ดวง
duuang]

want *n.* ความต้องการ
kwaam-dtɔ̂ng-gaan

want *v.* ปรารถนา bpràat-
tà~năa ✍

want *vi.* อยากทำ yàak-tam

want *vt.* (thing) อยากได้
yàak-dâai

want ad *n.* (for jobs)
ประกาศรับสมัครงาน
bprà~gàat-ráp-sà~màk-
ngaan [เรื่อง rûuang]

want out of *vt.* อยากเลิก
yàak-lə̂ək

want to *vt.* (do
something) อยาก yàak

war *n.* สงคราม sŏng-
kraam, ศึก sùk ✍

ward *n.* (division or
district) เขต kèet [แห่ง
hὲng] | (of hospital)
ตึกคนไข้ dtùk-kon-kâi
[ตึก dtùk]

wardrobe *n.* ตู้เสื้อผ้า
dtûu-sนิ̂ua-pâa [ใบ bai]

ware *n.* (container, e.g.
food ware) ภาชนะ paa-
chá~ná [ใบ bai, ชิ้น chín]

warehouse *n.* คลังสินค้า
klang-sĭn-káa [หลัง lăng

(building), แห่ง hèng (location)] | โกดัง goo-dang ✽ [แห่ง hèng (location)]

war game n. การซ้อมรบ gaan-sɔ́ɔm-róp

warlord n. แม่ทัพ mɛ̂ɛ-táp [คน kon]

warm adj. อบอุ่น òp-ùn, อุ่น ùn

warm v. (make warm, become warm) อุ่น ùn

warm-blooded adj. เลือดอุ่น lɨ̂ɨat-ùn

warm-hearted adj. ใจดี jai-dii

warm-up n. การอุ่นเครื่อง gaan-ùn-krɨ̂ɨang

warn vt. (caution, remind) เตือน dtɨɨan

warning n. (act of warning) การเตือน gaan-dtɨɨan | (word of caution) คำเตือน kam-dtɨɨan

warrant n. (assurance or confirmation) การรับรอง qaan-ráp-rɔɔng

warrant vt. (guarantee) รับประกัน ráp-bprà~gan

warrant of arrest see arrest warrant

warranty n. (guarantee) การรับประกัน gaan-ráp-bprà~gan

warrior n. นักรบ nák-róp [คน kon]

warship n. เรือรบ rɨɨa-róp [ลำ lam]

wart n. (on skin) หูด hùut [เม็ด mét]

was see be

wash n. (clothes to be washed) เสื้อผ้าที่ต้องซัก sɨ̂ɨa-pâa-tîi-dtɔ̂ng-sák

wash v. (e.g. dishes, car) ล้าง láang

wash vt. (e.g. dishes, car) ล้าง_ด้วยสบู่ láang-_-dûuai-sà~bùu

wash basin n. อ่างล้างมือ àang-láang-mɨɨ [อัน an]

washcloth n. ผ้าที่ใช้สำหรับล้าง pâa-tîi-chái-sǎm-ràp-láang [ชิ้น chín, ผืน pɨ̌ɨn]

wash clothes vi. ซักผ้า sák-pâa

wash hair vi. สระ sà

washing machine n. เครื่องซักผ้า krɨ̂ɨang-sák-pâa [เครื่อง krɨ̂ɨang]

washtub *n.* อ่างซักผ้า
àang-sák-pâa [ใบ bai]

wasp *n.* ตัวต่อ dtuua-dtɔ̀ɔ
[ตัว dtuua]

waste *n.* (garbage) ขยะ
kà~yà [ชิ้น chín (piece),
กอง gɔɔng (pile)]

waste *vt.* (lose, e.g.
energy, time) เสีย sǐia

wasteful *adj.*
(extravagant) ฟุ่มเฟือย
fûm-fɯɯai | (useless)
สูญเปล่า sǔun-bplàao ǃ

wastepaper *n.*
เศษกระดาษ sèet-grà~
dàat [ชิ้น chín]

watch *n.* (lookout)
การเฝ้าดู gaan-fâo-duu |
(timepiece) นาฬิกา naa-
lí~gaa [เรือน rɯɯan]

watch *v.* (look) ดู duu |
(wait expectantly) เฝ้า fâo

watchman *n.* (guard) ยาม
yaam [คน kon]

watch out! *interj.* ระวัง
rá~wang

watch out for *vt.* (be
careful of) ระวัง rá~wang

water *adj.* น้ำ náam

water *n.* น้ำ náam

water *vi.* (drool)
น้ำลายไหล nám-laai-lǎi

water *vt.* (e.g. plant) รด
rót | (make wet)
ทำให้_เปียก tam-hâi-_-
bpiiak

water buffalo *n.* ควาย
kwaai [ตัว dtuua]

water chestnut *n.* แห้ว
hɛ̂o [หัว hǔua]

water closet *n.* ห้องส้วม
hɔ̂ng-sûuam [ส้วม
sûuam] | สุขา sù-kǎa ǃ
[ห้อง hɔ̂ng]

watercolor *n.* สีน้ำ sǐi-
náam [สี sǐi (color), หลอด
lɔ̀ɔt (tube)]

waterfall *n.* น้ำตก nám-
dtòk [แห่ง hɛ̀ng]

water filter *n.*
เครื่องกรองน้ำ krɯ̂ɯang-
grɔɔng-náam [เครื่อง
krɯ̂ɯang]

water heater *n.*
เครื่องทำน้ำอุ่น krɯ̂ɯang-
tam-nám-ùn [เครื่อง
krɯ̂ɯang]

watering can *n.* บัวรดน้ำ
buua-rót-náam [ใบ bai]

watermelon *n.* แตงโม dtɛɛng-moo [ลูก lûuk]

waterproof *adj.* กันน้ำ gan-náam

waterspout *n.* (pipe) ท่อระบายน้ำ tɔ̂ɔ-rá~baai-náam [ท่อ tɔ̂ɔ]

water supply *n.* การประปา gaan-bprà~bpaa

watery *adj.* (containing much water) แฉะ chè

watt *n.* วัตต์ wàt

wave *n.* (in the ocean) คลื่น klûun [ลูก lûuk]

wave *vi.* โบกมือ bòok-muu

wave *vt.* โบก bòok

waver *vi.* (vacillate) วอกแวก wɔ̂ɔk-wɛ̂ɛk

wavy *adj.* (e.g. hair) หยิก yìk | (having lots of waves) มีคลื่นมาก mii-klûun-mâak

wax *n.* (beeswax) ขี้ผึ้ง kîi-pûng [ชนิด chá~nít (type), หลอด lɔ̀ɔt (tube), ตลับ dtà~làp (tin)]

way *n.* (course, direction) แนวทาง nɛɛo-taang [แนว nɛɛo] | (direction) ทิศทาง tít-taang [ทิศ tít] |

(manner) ทำนอง tam-nɔɔng [ทำนอง tam-nɔɔng] | (method) วิธี wí-tii [วิธี wí-tii] | (path or course) ทาง taang, เส้นทาง sên-taang [สาย sǎai, เส้น sên]

way out *n.* ทางออก taang-ɔ̀ɔk [ทาง taang]

we *pron.* พวกเรา pûuak-rao, เรา rao

weak *adj.* (not strong, frail) อ่อนแอ ɔ̀ɔn-ɛɛ

weaken *vi.* อ่อนแอลง ɔ̀ɔn-ɛɛ-long

weaken *vt.* ทำให้_อ่อนแอ tam-hâi-_-ɔ̀ɔn-ɛɛ

weakness *n.* (lack of strength) ความอ่อนแอ kwaam-ɔ̀ɔn-ɛɛ

wealth *n.* (state of being abundant) ความมั่งมี kwaam-mâng-mii

wealthy *adj.* มั่งคั่ง mâng-kâng, ร่ำรวย râm-ruuai

wean *vt.* (gradually deprive) ค่อยๆออกห่างจาก kɔ̂i-kɔ̂i-ɔ̀ɔk-hàang-jàak

weapon *n.* อาวุธ aa-wút [ชิ้น chín]

wear *vt.* ใส่ sài, นุ่ง nûng ✦

wear out *vt.* (use something until it wears out) ใช้_จนเสีย chái-_-jon-sĭia

weather *n.* อากาศ aa-gàat

weather forecast *n.* พยากรณ์อากาศ pá~yaa-gɔɔn-aa-gàat [ครั้ง kráng]

weave *v.* (cloth) ทอ tɔɔ

weave *vi.* (proceed in a winding course) โซเซ soo-see

weave *vt.* (spin, e.g. web) ชัก chák

web *n.* ใยแมงมุม yai-mɛɛng-mum [ใย yai]

website *n.* เว็บไซท์ wép-sái [เว็บ wép]

wed *vt.* แต่งงานกับ dtɛ̀ng-ngaan-gàp, สมรสกับ sŏm-rót-gàp ❗

wedding *n.* งานแต่งงาน ngaan-dtɛ̀ng-ngaan [งาน ngaan]

wedding ring *n.* แหวนแต่งงาน wɛ̆ɛn-dtɛ̀ng-ngaan [วง wong]

wedge *n.* ลิ่ม lîm [อัน an]

Wednesday *n.* วันพุธ wan-pút [วัน wan]

weed *n.* (marijuana) กัญชา gan-chaa [มวน muuan (joint), ต้น dtôn (plant)] | (unwanted plant) วัชพืช wát-chá~pûut [ต้น dtôn]

week *n.* สัปดาห์ sàp-daa [สัปดาห์ sàp-daa] | อาทิตย์ aa-tít ✦ [อาทิตย์ aa-tít]

weekday *n.* (working day) วันทำงาน wan-tam-ngaan [วัน wan]

weekend *n.* (Saturday and Sunday) เสาร์อาทิตย์ săo-aa-tít [วัน wan] | (end of a week) สุดสัปดาห์ sùt-sàp-daa ❗ [วัน wan]

weekly *adv.* (per week) ต่ออาทิตย์ dtɔ̀ɔ-aa-tít, อาทิตย์ละครั้ง aa-tít-lá-kráng

weep *vi.* ร้องไห้ rɔ́ɔng-hâi

weevil *n.* มอด mɔ̂ɔt [ตัว dtuua]

weigh *vi.* (have weight) หนัก nàk

weigh *vt.* (measure, e.g. on scale) ชั่ง châng

weight *n.* น้ำหนัก nám-nàk

weird *adj.* (strange)
ประหลาด bprà~làat

welcome *n.* (reception)
การรับรอง gaan-ráp-rɔɔng

welcome *vt.* ต้อนรับ
dtɔ̂ɔn-ráp

welcome! *interj.*
ยินดีต้อนรับ yin-dii-
dtɔ̂ɔn-ráp

weld *vt.* เชื่อม chûuam

welder *n.* ช่างเชื่อม
châng-chûuam [คน kon]

welfare *n.* (social)
สังคมสงเคราะห์ sǎng-
kom-sǒng-krɔ́

well *adv.* (skillfully) ได้ดี
dâai-dii

well *n.* บ่อน้ำ bɔ̀ɔ-náam
[บ่อ bɔ̀ɔ]

well! *interj.* (Oh!) เอ้า âo

well-being *n.* (welfare)
ความผาสุข kwaam-pǎa-
sùk

well-done *adj.* (cooked)
สุก sùk | (excellent)
ทำได้ดี tam-dâi-dii

well-known *adj.* มีชื่อเสียง
mii-chûu-sǐiang

well-mannered *adj.*
(courteous) มารยาทดี
maa-rá~yâat-dii

well-off *adj.* (rich) ร่ำรวย
râm-ruuai | (wealthy)
มั่งคั่ง mâng-kâng

were see be

werewolf *n.* มนุษย์หมาป่า
má~nút-mǎa-bpàa [ตัว
dtuua]

west *n.* ตะวันตก dtà~
wan-dtòk, ทิศตะวันตก
tít-dtà~wan-dtòk [ทิศ tít]

western *adj.* ตะวันตก
dtà~wan-dtòk

western *n.* (movie)
หนังคาวบอย nǎng-kaao-
bɔɔi [เรื่อง rûuang]

westerner *n.* ชาวตะวันตก
chaao-dtà~wan-dtòk
[คน kon]

wet *adj.* เปียก bpìiak, แฉะ
chè ✱

wet dream *n.* ฝันเปียก
fǎn-bpìiak

whale *n.* ปลาวาฬ bplaa-
waan [ฝูง fǔung (pod),
ตัว dtuua (each)]

wharf *n.* ท่าเรือ tâa-ruua
[แห่ง hɛ̀ng]

what *adj.* อะไร à~rai

what *adv.* อะไร à~rai

what *pron.* อะไร à~rai

what a pity *idm.*
น่าเสียดาย nâa-sǐia-daai

whatever *adj.* อะไรก็ได้
à~rai-gɔ̂ɔ-dâai

whatever *pron.* อะไรก็ได้
à~rai-gɔ̂ɔ-dâai

wheat *n.* ข้าวสาลี kâao-
sǎa-lii

wheel *n.* ล้อ lɔ́ɔ [ล้อ lɔ́ɔ]

wheel *vt.* (move on wheels) เข็น kěn

wheelchair *n.* รถเข็น rót-
kěn [คัน kan]

when *adv.* เมื่อไหร่ mûua-
rài

when *conj.* ตอนที่ dtɔɔn-
tîi, เมื่อ mûua ⚡

when *pron.* เมื่อไหร่
mûua-rài

whenever *conj.*
เมื่อใดก็ตาม mûua-dai-
gɔ̂ɔ-dtaam

where *adv.* ที่ไหน tîi-nǎi,
ไหน nǎi, ตรงไหน
dtrong-nǎi ❁

where *conj.* ตรงที่ dtrong-
tîi

whereabouts *n.*
ตำแหน่งที่อยู่ dtam-nèng-
tîi-yùu [ตำแหน่ง dtam-
nèng]

wherever *conj.*
ที่ไหนก็ตาม tîi-nǎi-gɔ̂ɔ-
dtaam, ที่ไหนก็ได้ tîi-nǎi-
gɔ̂ɔ-dâai ❁

whether or not *conj.*
ไม่ว่าจะ_หรือไม่ mâi-wâa-
jà-_-rǔu-mâi ⚡

which *adj.* ไหน nǎi,
อันไหน an-nǎi

which *pron.* ใด dai, ที่ tîi,
ซึ่ง sûng ⚡

whichever *pron.*
อันไหนก็ได้ an-nǎi-gɔ̂ɔ-
dâai ❁

which way *pron.* ทางไหน
taang-nǎi

while *conj.* ขณะที่ kà~nà-
tîi

while *n.* ชั่วขณะ chûua-
kà~nà

whine *vi.* (in a childish
fashion) อ้อน ɔ̂ɔn | (make
a moaning sound) คราง
kraang

whip *n.* แส้ sɛ̂ɛ [เส้น sên]

whip *vt.* เฆี่ยน kîian

whipped cream *n.* วิปครีม
wíp-kriim

whirl *vi.* หมุน mǔn

whirlpool *n.* น้ำวน nám-won [แห่ง hèng]

whirlwind *n.* ลมบ้าหมู lom-bâa-mǔu ❧ [ลูก lûuk]

whisker *n.* หนวด nùuat [เส้น sên (strand), กระจุก grà~jùk (tuft)]

whisky *n.* วิสกี้ wít-sà~gîi [แก้ว gɛ̂ɛo (glass), ขวด kùuat (bottle)]

whisper *v.* กระซิบ grà~síp

whistle *n.* (acoustic device) นกหวีด nók-wìit [อัน an]

whistle *vi.* (blow) เป่านกหวีด bpào-nók-wìit | (through the mouth) ผิวปาก pǐu-bpàak

white *adj.* ขาว kǎao, สีขาว sǐi-kǎao

white *n.* (color) สีขาว sǐi-kǎao [สี sǐi]

white blood cell *n.* เม็ดเลือดขาว mét-lûuat-kǎao [เม็ด mét]

whiteboard *n.* กระดานขาว grà~daan-kǎao [แผ่น pèn]

White House *n.* ทำเนียบขาว tam-nîiap-kǎao [หลัง lǎng]

who *pron.* (person who) ผู้ที่ pûu-tîi | (which person) ใคร krai, ผู้ใด pûu-dai ⚑

whoa! *interj.* อุ๊ย úui

whoever *pron.* ใครก็ตาม krai-gɔ̂ɔ-dtaam

whole *adj.* ทั้งหมด táng-mòt | (all, complete) ครบ króp

wholegrain *n.* (unprocessed grain) โฮลเกรน hoo-green [ชนิด chá~nít]

wholesale *n.* การขายส่ง gaan-kǎai-sòng

wholesale *v.* ขายส่ง kǎai-sòng

whom *pron.* (one who) ผู้ที่ pûu-tîi | (question word) ใคร krai

whooping cough *n.* (pertussis) ไอกรน ai-gron [โรค rôok]

whore *n.* โสเภณี sǒo-pee-nii, อีตัว ii-dtuua ❧ [คน kon]

whorehouse *n.* ซ่อง sɔ̂ng [แห่ง hèng]

whose *pron.* (ones

belonging to) ของผู้ที่
kɔ̌ɔng-pûu-tîi | (question
word) ของใคร kɔ̌ɔng-krai

why *adv.* ทำไม tam-mai,
เพราะอะไร prɔ́-à~rai ☙

wicked *adj.* (evil) ชั่วร้าย
chûua-ráai

wicker *n.* เครื่องจักสาน
krûuang-jàk-sǎan [ชนิด
chá~nít (type), ชิ้น chín
(piece)]

wickerwork see wicker

wide *adj.* กว้าง gwâang

widen *vt.* (make wide)
ทำให้_กว้าง tam-hâi-_-
gwâang

widespread *adj.* แพร่หลาย
prɛ̂ɛ-lǎai

widow *n.* แม่ม่าย mɛ̂ɛ-
mâai [คน kon]

widower *n.* พ่อม่าย pɔ̂ɔ-
mâai [คน kon]

width *n.* ความกว้าง
kwaam-gwâang

wife *n.* เมีย miia, ภรรยา
pan-rá~yaa ⚠, แฟน fɛɛn
☙ [คน kon]

wig *n.* ผมปลอม pǒm-
bplɔɔm [อัน an]

wild *adj.* (crazy) บ้าคลั่ง

bâa-klâng | (e.g. animal)
ป่า bpàa

wildlife *n.* สัตว์ป่า sàt-
bpàa [ตัว dtuua, ชนิด
chá~nít (kind)]

will *aux.* จะ jà

will *n.* (determination)
ความตั้งใจ kwaam-dtâng-
jai | (legal document)
พินัยกรรม pí-nai-gam
[ฉบับ chà~bàp]

willing *adj.* เต็มใจ dtem-jai

willingness *n.* ความเต็มใจ
kwaam-dtem-jai

win *v.* (e.g. game, battle)
ชนะ chá~ná

wind *n.* ลม lom

wind *vt.* (curl) พัน pan |
(e.g. a watch) ไข kǎi

windbreaker *n.* เสื้อกันลม
sûua-gan-lom [ตัว dtuua]

winding *adj.* คดเคี้ยว kót-
kíiao

windmill *n.* กังหัน gang-
hǎn [ตัว dtuua]

window *n.* หน้าต่าง nâa-
dtàang [บาน baan]

window frame *n.* บานกบ
baan-gòp ⚒ [แผ่น pɛ̀n]

windowpane *n.*
กระจกหน้าต่าง grà~jòk-

nâa-dtàang [บาน baan]

window-shop vi.
เดินดูสินค้าโดยไม่ซื้อ dəən-duu-sĭn-káa-dooi-mâi-súu

windshield n. (of a vehicle) กระจกหน้ารถ grà~jòk-nâa-rót [บาน baan]

windshield wiper n. ที่ปัดน้ำฝน tîi-bpàt-nám-fŏn [อัน an]

windy adj. ลมแรง lom-rɛɛng

wine n. ไวน์ waai [แก้ว gɛ̂ɛo (glass), ขวด kùuat (bottle)]

wing n. (extension, of a bird) ปีก bpìik [ปีก bpìik, ข้าง kâang] | (political) ฝ่าย fàai [ฝ่าย fàai]

wink vi. (make a wink) หลิ่วตา lìu-dtaa

winner n. ผู้ชนะ pûu-chá~ná [คน kon]

winter n. ฤดูหนาว rʉ́-duu-nǎao [ฤดู rʉ́-duu] | หน้าหนาว nâa-nǎao ✿ [หน้า nâa]

wipe vt. (brush away) ปัด_ออก bpàt-_-ɔ̀ɔk |

(rub and clean) เช็ด chét | (scrub) ถู tŭu

wipe off vt. (remove by wiping) เช็ด_ออก chét-_-ɔ̀ɔk

wire n. (metal) ลวด lûuat [เส้น sên (strand), ขด kòt (coil), ม้วน múuan (roll)]

wireless adj. ไร้สาย rái-sǎai

wireless n. (radio) วิทยุ wít-tá~yú [เครื่อง krʉ̂ʉang]

wire tap n. เครื่องดักฟัง krʉ̂ʉang-dàk-fang [เครื่อง krʉ̂ʉang]

wisdom n. (intellect) ปัญญา bpan-yaa

wisdom tooth n. ฟันคุด fan-kút [ซี่ sîi]

wise adj. (erudite, omniscient) รอบรู้ rɔ̂ɔp-rúu

wish n. ความปรารถนา kwaam-bpràat-tà~nǎa

wish v. (desire) ต้องการ dtɔ̂ng-gaan ‼

wish vt. (express a wish) ขอให้ kɔ̌ɔ-hâi

wit n. ไหวพริบ wǎi-príp

witch n. แม่มด mɛ̂ɛ-mót

[ตน dton]

witch doctor *n.* หมอผี mɔ̌ɔ-pǐi [คน kon]

with *prep.* (accompanying or against someone) กับ gàp | (by the use of, e.g. fork) ด้วย dûuai

withdraw *vt.* ถอน tɔ̌ɔn

withdrawal *n.* (money) การถอนเงิน gaan-tɔ̌ɔn-ngən

withdraw money *vi.* ถอนเงิน tɔ̌ɔn-ngən

wither *vi.* เหี่ยวแห้ง hìiao-hɛ̂ng, ร่วงโรย rûuang-rooi

withhold *vt.* (hold back restrain) ระงับ rá~ngáp

withholding tax *n.* การหักภาษี ณ ที่จ่าย gaan-hàk-paa-sǐi-ná-tîi-jàai

within *prep.* ข้างใน kâang-nai, ภายใน paai-nai

without *prep.* ปราศจาก bpràat-sà~jàak, ไร้ rái ‼

withstand *vi.* (resist) ต่อต้าน dtɔ̀ɔ-dtâan

witness *n.* พยาน pá~yaan [ปาก bpàak ‼, คน kon]

witness *vi.* เป็นพยาน bpen-pá~yaan

witness *vt.* เห็น hěn

witness stand *n.* คอกพยาน kɔ̂ɔk-pá~yaan [แห่ง hɛ̀ng]

witty *adj.* (astute) มีไหวพริบ mii-wǎi-príp

wizard *n.* พ่อมด pɔ̂ɔ-mót [ตน dton]

wobble *vi.* (move from side to side) โคลงเคลง kloong-kleeng

wok *n.* กระทะ grà~tá [ใบ bai]

wolf *n.* หมาป่า mǎa-bpàa [ตัว dtuua]

woman *n.* ผู้หญิง pûu-yǐng, สตรี sà~dtrii ‼ [คน kon]

womanizer *n.* ผู้ชายเจ้าชู้ pûu-chaai-jâo-chúu [คน kon]

womb *n.* มดลูก mót-lûuk, ครรภ์ kan ‼

wonder *vi.* (doubt) ข้องใจ kɔ̂ng-jai

wonderful *adj.* (marvelous) เลิศ lɤ̂ɤt, วิเศษ wí-sèet

wonderful! *interj.* เยี่ยม

yîiam

wonton *n.* เกี๊ยว gíiao [ชิ้น chín]

woo *vt.* (court) จีบ jìip

wood *n.* (timber or lumber) ไม้ máai [อัน an, ท่อน tɔ̂n (piece), แผ่น pèn (sheet), ต้น dtôn (log)]

wooden *adj.* (made of wood) ทำด้วยไม้ tam-dûuai-máai

woodpecker *n.* นกหัวขวาน nók-hǔua-kwǎn [ตัว dtuua]

woods *n.* (forest) ป่า bpàa [ป่า bpàa, แห่ง hèng] | (forest) ป่าไม้ bpàa-máai [แห่ง hèng]

wood tick *n.* เห็บที่อยู่ในป่า hèp-tîi-yùu-nai-bpàa [ตัว dtuua]

wool *n.* (animal yarn) ขนสัตว์ kǒn-sàt [เส้น sên]

word *n.* (lyrics) เนื้อเพลง núua-pleeng [บท bòt (verse)] | (something said, combination of sounds) คำ kam [คำ kam] | (speech, remark) คำพูด kam-pûut [คำ kam] | (vocabulary) คำศัพท์ kam-sàp [คำ kam]

word *vt.* (e.g. contract) ใช้ภาษาใน chái-paa-sǎa-nai

word of mouth *n.* การบอกเล่า gaan-bɔ̀ɔk-lâo

work *n.* (accomplishment, result of work) ผลงาน pǒn-ngaan [ชิ้น chín] | (in general) การงาน gaan-ngaan [อัน an] | (job, career) งาน ngaan [ชิ้น chín]

work *vi.* ทำงาน tam-ngaan | (function) ใช้การได้ chái-gaan-dâai

workaholic *n.* คนบ้างาน kon-bâa-ngaan [คน kon]

worker *n.* คนงาน kon-ngaan [คน kon]

work out *vi.* (end nicely) ลงเอยด้วยดี long-əəi-dûuai-dii | (exercise) ออกกำลังกาย ɔ̀ɔk-gam-lang-gaai

workshop *n.* (educational seminar) การอบรม gaan-òp-rom [ครั้ง kráng] | (where work is done) ห้องทำงาน hɔ̂ng-tam-ngaan [ห้อง hɔ̂ng]

world *n*. โลก lôok [ใบ bai]

world-class *adj*. ระดับโลก rá~dàp-lôok

world-famous *adj*. ดังทั่วโลก dang-tûua-lôok

worldly *adj*. (sophisticated) เจนโลก jeen-lôok

World War I *n*. สงครามโลกครั้งที่หนึ่ง sŏng-kraam-lôok-kráng-tîi-nùeng [ครั้ง kráng]

worldwide *adj*. ทั่วโลก tûua-lôok

worm *n*. (caterpillar) หนอน nŏon [ตัว dtuua] | (earthworm) ไส้เดือน sâi-duuan [ตัว dtuua] | (parasite) พยาธิ pá~yâat [ตัว dtuua]

worn out *adj*. (exhausted) เพลีย pliia | (torn) ขาด kàat

worn-out *adj*. (no longer usable) ใช้จนเสีย chái-jon-sĭia

worried *adj*. (about someone or something) ห่วง hùuang | (be anxious) กังวล gang-won

worry *n*. ความวิตกกังวล kwaam-wí-dtòk-gang-won

worry *vt*. ทำให้_เป็นห่วง tam-hâi-_-bpen-hùuang

worse *adj*. แย่ลง yɛ̂ɛ-long, เลวลง leeo-long

worsen *v*. ทำให้_แย่ลง tam-hâi-_-yɛ̂ɛ-long

worship *n*. การนับถือ gaan-náp-tŭe

worship *vt*. (sacred objects) บูชา buu-chaa

worst *adj*. แย่ที่สุด yɛ̂ɛ-tîi-sùt, เลวที่สุด leeo-tîi-sùt

worth *n*. (value) คุณค่า kun-kâa

worth *prep*. (deserving of) ควรที่จะ kuuan-tîi-jà | (having a value of) มีค่า mii-kâa

worthless *adj*. ไม่มีราคา mâi-mii-raa-kaa, ไร้ค่า rái-kâa

worth reading *adj*. น่าอ่าน nâa-àan

worth seeing *adj*. น่าดู nâa-duu

worthwhile *adj*. คุ้มค่า kúm-kâa

worthy *adj*. (deserving) คู่ควร kûu-kuuan

would *aux.* จะ jà

would like *v.* ต้องการ dtôɔng-gaan

wound *n.* แผล plɛ̌ɛ, บาดแผล bàat-plɛ̌ɛ ! [แห่ง hɛ̀ng, ที่ tîi]

wound *vt.* ทำให้_บาดเจ็บ tam-hâi-_-bàat-jèp

wow! *interj.* โอ้โห ôo-hǒo

wrap *n.* (shawl) ผ้าคลุม pâa-klum [ผืน pǔɯn]

wrap *vt.* ห่อ hɔ̀ɔ

wrap around *vt.* พันรอบ pan-rɔ̂ɔp

wrap up *vt.* (cover with paper) ห่อ hɔ̀ɔ | (finish) ทำ_ให้เสร็จ tam-_-hâi-sèt

wrath *n.* ความโมโห kwaam-moo-hǒo

wreath *n.* พวงหรีด puuang-rìit [พวง puuang]

wreck *n.* (wreckage) ซาก sâak [ซาก sâak]

wreck *vt.* (e.g. car) ทำ_พัง tam-_-pang ✦

wrecked *adj.* (boat) อับปาง àp-bpaang | (e.g. car, TV) พัง pang

wrench *n.* (tool for gripping and turning) ประแจ bprà~jɛɛ, คีม kiim

✦ [อัน an]

wrench *vt.* (e.g. the knee) บิด bìt

wrestle *vi.* (engage in wrestling) ปล้ำกัน bplâm-gan

wrestle *vt.* (force by wrestling) ต่อสู้ dtɔ̀ɔ-sûu

wrestling *n.* มวยปล้ำ muuai-bplâm

wriggle *vi.* (writhe) บิดตัวไปมา bìt-dtuua-bpai-maa

wring *vt.* (twist and compress) บิด bìt

wrinkle *n.* (on face or skin) รอยย่น rɔɔi-yôn [รอย rɔɔi, ที่ tîi]

wrinkled *adj.* ย่น yôn

wrist *n.* ข้อมือ kɔ̂ɔ-mɯɯ [ข้อ kɔ̂ɔ, ข้าง kâang (each side)]

wristwatch *n.* นาฬิกาข้อมือ naa-lí~gaa-kɔ̂ɔ-mɯɯ [เรือน rɯɯan]

write *v.* เขียน kǐian

write down *vt.* จด_ลง jòt-_-long | (record) บันทึก ban-túk

writer *n.* นักเขียน nák-kǐian, ผู้แต่ง pûu-dtɛ̀ng

[คน kon]

writhe *vi.* บิดตัว bìt-dtuua

writing *n.* (act) การเขียน gaan-kǐian | (handwriting) ลายมือ laai-muu [ลายมือ laai-muu]

wrong *adj.* (awry) ผิดพลาด pìt-plâat | (incorrect, not suitable) ผิด pìt

X

xenophobia *n.* (of foreigners) โรคหวาดกลัวชาวต่างชาติ rôok-wàat-gluua-chaao-dtàang-châat | (of new things) ความกลัวของใหม่ kwaam-gluua-kǒng-mài

X-rated *adj.* (adults only) เฉพาะผู้ใหญ่ chà~pó-pûu-yài | (sexually explicit) ลามก laa-mók

x-ray *n.* รังสีเอ็กซ์ rang-sǐi-ék, เอ็กซ์เรย์ ék-sà~ree ✲ [ภาพ pâap (image)]

x-ray *vt.* เอ็กซ์เรย์ ék-sà~ree

xylophone *n.* ระนาด rá~nâat [ชุด chút

(instrument)]

Y

yacht *n.* เรือยอชท์ ruua-yɔ́ɔt [ลำ lam]

yak *n.* วัวจามรี wuua-jaam-má~rii [ตัว dtuua]

yam *n.* (sweet potato) มัน man, มันเทศ man-têet [หัว hǔua]

yap *vi.* (bark) เห่า hào

yard *n.* (lawn, courtyard) ลาน laan [ลาน laan, แห่ง hὲng] | (unit of measure) หลา lǎa [หลา lǎa]

yarn *n.* เส้นด้าย sên-dâai [เส้น sên (string)]

yawn *vi.* หาว hǎao

year *n.* ปี bpii [ปี bpii]

yearly *adj.* ประจำปี bprà~jam-bpii

year-round *adj.* ตลอดปี dtà~lɔ̀ɔt-bpii

yeast *n.* (e.g. baking, brewing) เชื้อหมัก chúua-màk ‼ [เชื้อ chúua] | (e.g. brewing) ส่าเหล้า sàa-lâo [เชื้อ chúua] | (e.g. infection) เชื้อรา chúua-raa [เชื้อ chúua]

yell *vi.* ตะโกน dtà~goon

yellow *adj.* (color) เหลือง lɯ̌ang | (cowardly) ขี้ขลาด kîi-klàat

yellow *n.* (color) สีเหลือง sɪ̌i-lɯ̌ang [สี sɪ̌i]

yellow fever *n.* ไข้เหลือง kâi-lɯ̌ang [โรค rôok]

yen *n.* เงินเยน ngɤn-yeen

yes! *interj.* (for female speakers) ค่ะ kâ | (for male speakers) ครับ kráp | (mainly for male speakers) ฮะ há ●

yesterday *adv.* เมื่อวานนี้ mɯ̂a-waan-níi

yesterday *n.* เมื่อวานนี้ mɯ̂a-waan-níi [วัน wan]

yet *adv.* (moreover) ยังคง yang-kong | (still, thus far) ยัง yang

yet *conj.* (nevertheless) อย่างไรก็ตาม yàang-rai-gɔ̂-dtaam

yield *n.* (something yielded) ผลที่ได้ pǒn-tîi-dâai [จำนวน jam-nuuan]

yield *vi.* (give way) ให้ทาง hâi-taang | (surrender) ยอม yɔɔm

yield *vt.* (e.g. fruit, labor) ให้ hâi

yoga *n.* โยคะ yoo-ká [ท่า tâa (pose)]

yogurt *n.* นมเปรี้ยว nom-bprîiao, โยเกิร์ต yoo-gɤ̀ɤt ● [รส rót (flavor), ถ้วย tûuai (cup)]

yoke *n.* (device to pair animals) แอก ɛ̀ɛk [อัน an, ตัว dtuua] | (frame for carrying) คานหาบ kaan-hàap [คัน kan]

yoke *vt.* (harness) เทียม tiiam

yolk *n.* ไข่แดง kài-dɛɛng

you *pron.* แก gɛɛ ● | (used generally) คุณ kun | (used to address someone older) พี่ pîi | (used to address someone younger) น้อง nɔ́ɔng

young *adj.* (immature, unripe) อ่อน ɔ̀ɔn | (used with men) หนุ่ม nùm | (used with women) สาว sǎao | (youthful) อายุน้อย aa-yú-nɔ́ɔi

younger brother *n.* น้อง nɔ́ɔng, น้องชาย nɔ́ɔng-

chaai [คน kon]
younger generation n.
คนรุ่นหลัง kon-rûn-lǎng
[รุ่น rûn]
younger sibling n. น้อง
nɔ́ɔng [คน kon]
younger sister n. น้อง
nɔ́ɔng, น้องสาว nɔ́ɔng-
sǎao [คน kon]
youngest child n.
ลูกสุดท้อง lûuk-sùt-tɔ́ɔng
[คน kon]
young people n. หนุ่มสาว
nùm-sǎao [คน kon]
your adj. ของคุณ kɔ̌ɔng-
kun
you're welcome idm.
ไม่เป็นไร mâi-bpen-rai
yours pron. ของคุณ
kɔ̌ɔng-kun
yourself pron. ตัวคุณเอง
dtuua-kun-eeng
yourselves see yourself
youth n. (generation)
เยาวชน yao-wá~chon
[รุ่น rûn] | (people)
คนหนุ่มสาว kon-nùm-
sǎao [คน kon]
yuan n. เงินหยวน ngən-
yǔuan, หยวน yǔuan
[หยวน yǔuan]

yucky adj. (disgusting)
น่ารังเกียจ nâa-rang-gìiat
yucky! interj. น่าเกลียด
nâa-glìiat

Z

zebra crossing n.
ทางม้าลาย taang-máa-
laai [แห่ง hɛ̀ng]
Zen n. นิกายเซน ní-gaai-
sen [นิกาย ní-gaai]
zero n. (nothing) ไม่มีอะไร
mâi-mii-à~rai
zero numb. ศูนย์ sǔun
zest n. (enthusiasm)
ความกระตือรือร้น
kwaam-grà~dtuu-ruu-
rón
zigzag adj. คดเคี้ยว kót-
kíiao, ซิกแซก sík-sék ♣
zigzag n. (shape)
รูปฟันปลา rûup-fan-
bplaa [รูป rûup]
zigzag vi. ซิกแซก sík-sék
♣
zinc n. สังกะสี sǎng-gà~sǐi
zip n. (zipper) ซิป síp [อัน
an, เส้น sên]
zip code n. รหัสไปรษณีย์
rá~hàt-bprai-sà~nii [รหัส
rá~hàt]

zipper *n.* ซิป síp [อัน an, เส้น sên]

zip up *v.* รูดซิป rûut-síp

zit *n.* สิว sǐu [เม็ด mét, หัว hǔua ☙]

zodiac *n.* จักรราศี jàk-raa-sǐi [ราศี raa-sǐi]

zodiac sign *n.* ราศี raa-sǐi [ราศี raa-sǐi]

zombie *n.* ผีดิบ pǐi-dìp [ตัว dtuua]

zone *n.* (area) บริเวณ bɔɔ-rí~ween [แห่ง hèng] | (region) เขต kèet [แห่ง hèng]

zoo *n.* สวนสัตว์ sǔuan-sàt [แห่ง hèng]

zoom in *vi.* ซูมเข้า suum-kâo ☙

zoom lens *n.* เลนส์ซูม leen-suum [เลนส์ leen]

zoom out *v.* ซูมออก suum-ɔ̀ɔk ☙

Section Two: Thai Script

For each Thai word in this section, we list one or more English translations. Sometimes, the Thai word covers only certain meanings of an English word provided. In these cases, we clarify the meaning of the Thai word by providing multiple English words that focus the meaning down, or by narrowing down the meaning of individual English words with some extra details inside parentheses (just as we do in the English section: see © on p. 2). For example:

> หน้า **nâa** *adv.* ahead, in front
> หน้า **nâa** *n.* face, page (e.g. book), season [หน้า nâa]

From this entry, you can conclude that หน้า **nâa** means "page" in the sense of "page of a book;" we do not say anything about other meanings of "page," such as "servant or attendant."

See p. 2 for more information about reading entries.

See p. 21 to learn about reading and writing Thai script.

See p. 40 to learn about Thai script dictionary order.

ก ข ฃ ค ฅ ฆ ง จ ฉ ช ซ ฌ ญ ฎ ฏ ฐ ฑ ฒ ณ ด ต ถ ท ธ น บ ป ผ ฝ พ ฟ ภ ม ย ร ฤ ล ว ศ ษ ส ห ฬ อ ฮ

ก

ก gɔɔ *let.* ก. ไก่ gɔɔ-gài, a consonant of the Thai alphabet (mid consonant) [ตัว dtuua]

ก็ gɔ̂ *adv.* also, too

กก gòk *n.* reed [ต้น dtôn]

ก๊ก gók *n.* group (nation, party) ◆ [ก๊ก gók]

กง gong *n.* ribs of a wooden boat

กงสุล gong-sǔn *n.* consul [คน kon, ท่าน tân ⚥]

กฎ gòt *n.* law (rules) [ข้อ kɔ̂ɔ]

กฎหมาย gòt-mǎai *n.* law

กด gòt *v.* press (push down), push

กดขี่ gòt-kìi *vt.* oppress

กดดัน gòt-dan *v.* press (pressure)

กดดัน gòt-dan *vt.* pressure (press, force)

ก็ดี gɔ̂-dii *adv.* quite good

ก็ได้ gɔ̂-dâai *adv.* can also

ก็ตาม gɔ̂-dtaam *adv.* no matter, whatever

กติกา gà-dtì~gaa *n.* regulation, rule (in sports) [ข้อ kɔ̂ɔ]

ก้น gôn *n.* bottom (lowest part) [ก้น gôn]

กบ gòp *n.* frog [ตัว dtuua]

กบฏ gà~bòt *n.* rebellion [คณะ ká~ná (group)]

ก้ม gôm *vi.* bend over (bow)

กรกฎาคม gà~rák-gà~daa-kom, gɔɔ-rák-gà~daa-kom *n.* July [เดือน dʉʉan]

กรง grong *n.* cage (e.g. bird) [ใบ bai]

กรณี gɔɔ-rá~nii, gà~rá~nii *n.* case (law or medicine) [กรณี gɔɔ-rá~nii ⚥, อย่าง yàang]

กรด gròt *n.* acid [ตัว dtuua]

กรม grom *n.* division (government) [กรม grom]

กรมธรรม์ grom-má~tan *n.* insurance policy [ฉบับ chà~bàp]

กรรไกร gan-grai *n.* scissors [เล่ม lêm]

กรรม gam *n.* karma

กรรมกร gam-má~gɔɔn *n.* labor (manual) [คน kon]

กรรมการ gam-má~gaan *n.* judge (in a contest)

[คน kon (individual)]

กรรมพันธุ์ gam-má~pan *n.* heredity

กรรมวิธี gam-má~wí-tii *n.* process (manufacturing) [วิธี wí-tii (method)]

กรรมสิทธิ์ gam-má~sìt *n.* ownership (proprietorship) ‼

กรวด grùuat *n.* gravel (pebble) [เม็ด mét, ก้อน gɔ̂ɔn]

กรวย gruuai *n.* cone (shape) [อัน an, กรวย gruuai]

กรอก grɔ̀ɔk *v.* pour into (fill with)

กรอก grɔ̀ɔk *vt.* fill out (document)

กรอง grɔɔng *v.* filter

กรอง grɔɔng *vt.* strain (filter)

กรอบ grɔ̀ɔp *adj.* crispy

กรอบ grɔ̀ɔp *n.* frame (e.g. picture, window) [กรอบ grɔ̀ɔp]

กระ grà *n.* freckle (on the face) [แผ่น pèn (piece), จุด jùt (spot)]

กระจก grà~jòk *n.* mirror (looking glass) [แผ่น pèn, บาน baan]

กระจกตา grà~jòk-dtaa *n.* cornea

กระจอก grà~jɔ̀ɔk *adj.* shoddy (of poor quality)

กระจับ grà~jàp *n.* water chestnut [ลูก lûuk]

กระจาด grà~jàat *n.* basket (shallow) [ใบ bai]

กระจาย grà~jaai *v.* spread (disperse)

กระจาย grà~jaai *vt.* scatter

กระจุก grà~jùk *n.* cluster, tuft [อัน an]

กระเจี๊ยบ grà~jíiap *n.* ladyfinger, okra [ต้น dtôn (plant), ลูก lûuk (fruit)]

กระโจม grà~joom *n.* tent ‼ [หลัง lăng]

กระฉับกระเฉง grà~chàp-grà~chěeng *adj.* active (energetic)

กระชับ grà~cháp *adj.* fastened firmly

กระชาก grà~châak *v.* pull (haul, tug)

กระซิบ grà~síp *v.* whisper

กระดอง grà~dɔɔng *n.* shell (of crustaceans) [ฝา făa]

กระด้าง grà~dâang *adj.* coarse (harsh)

กระดาน grà~daan *n.* board (plank of wood) [แผ่น pèn]

กระดานข่าว grà~daan-kàao *n.* bulletin board [แผ่น pèn]

กระดานหก grà~daan-hòk *n.* seesaw [อัน an]

กระดาษ grà~dàat *n.* paper [แผ่น pèn (sheet), ใบ bai (sheet)]

กระดาษชำระ grà~dàat-cham-rá *n.* toilet paper [แผ่น pèn (sheet), ม้วน múuan (roll), กล่อง glòng (box)]

กระดิก grà~dìk *vt.* wiggle fingers or toes

กระดิ่ง grà~dìng *n.* doorbell [อัน an]

กระดุม grà~dum *n.* button (e.g. shirt, blouse) [เม็ด mét (piece)]

กระดูก grà~dùuk *n.* bone (of person, animal, but not fish) [ซี่ sîi, ชิ้น chín]

กระดูกสันหลัง grà~dùuk-săn-lăng *n.* spine (of body) [ชิ้น chín]

กระเด็น grà~den *vi.* splash

กระโดด grà~dòot *vi.* bound (leap), hop, jump, skip

กระได grà~dai *n.* ladder [อัน an]

กระได grà~dai *n.* staircase/stairway [อัน an, แห่ง hèng]

กระต่าย grà~dtàai *n.* rabbit [ตัว dtuua]

กระติก grà~dtìk *n.* canteen (water container) [ใบ bai]

กระตือรือร้น grà~dtuu-ruu-rón *adj.* eager, enthusiastic

กระตุก grà~dtùk *v.* jerk (twitch)

กระตุ้น grà~dtûn *v.* urge (impel, drive, insist)

กระตุ้น grà~dtûn *vt.* motivate (encourage, spur), stimulate

กระถาง grà~tăang *n.* pot (flowerpot) [ใบ bai]

กระเถิบ grà~tòep *v.* move over

กระโถน grà~tŏon *n.* spittoon [ใบ bai]

กระทง grà~tong *n.* small container made from banana leaves, small boat floated on Loy Kratong [ใบ bai]

กระทบ grà~tóp *vt.* collide with, contact with

กระทรวง grà~suuang *n.* ministry (bureau) [กระทรวง grà~suuang]

กระท้อน grà~tɔ́ɔn *n.* santol [ลูก lûuk]

กระท่อม grà~tɔ̂m *n.* cottage, hut [หลัง lǎng]

กระทะ grà~tá *n.* frying pan, pan, wok [ใบ bai]

กระทั่ง grà~tâng *conj.* till

กระทำ grà~tam *vt.* do/does/did ✏, make (produce, create) ✏

กระเทียม grà~tiiam *n.* garlic [หัว hǔua]

กระแทก grà~têɛk *vt.* bump (bang, slam)

กระนั้น grà~nán *adv.* still, thus far, nevertheless ✏

กระบวนการ grà~buuan-gaan *n.* procedure (process) ✏ [ขั้น kân (step)]

กระบอก grà~bɔ̀ɔk *n.* cylinder [กระบอก grà~bɔ̀ɔk]

กระบอง grà~bɔɔng *n.* baton (club), staff (baton, club) [อัน an]

กระบะ grà~bà *n.* pick-up truck [คัน kan]

กระบี่ grà~bìi *n.* Krabi province [จังหวัด jang-wàt]

กระเบียด grà~bìiat *n.* quarter of an inch

กระเบื้อง grà~bûuang *n.* tile [แผ่น pèn]

กระป๋อง grà~bpɔ̌ng *n.* can, tin [ใบ bai]

กระปุก grà~bpùk *n.* jar (e.g. for cookie, money) [ใบ bai]

กระเป๋า grà~bpǎo *n.* bag (hand luggage), pocket, pouch [ใบ bai]

กระเป๋าเงิน grà~bpǎo-ngən *n.* wallet [ใบ bai]

กระเป๋าเดินทาง grà~bpǎo-dəən-taang *n.* suitcase [ใบ bai]

กระเป๋าเอกสาร grà~bpǎo-èek-gà~sǎan *n.* briefcase [ใบ bai]

กระโปรง grà~bproong *n.* skirt [ตัว dtuua]

กระโปรงรถ grà~bproong-rót *n.* hood/bonnet (car) [แผ่น pèn, ฝา fǎa]

กระโปรงหลังรถ grà~proong-lǎng-rót *n.* trunk (of a car) [ที่ tîi]

กระผม grà~pǒm *pron.* me (male speaker) ‼

กระพือ grà~puu *vt.* flap (e.g. wings)

กระเพรา grà~prao see กะเพรา

กระเพาะ grà~pɔ́ *n.* stomach (organ) ✘ [กระเพาะ grà~pɔ́]

กระเพาะปัสสาวะ grà~pɔ́-bpàt-sǎa~wá *n.* bladder

กระรอก grà~rɔ̂ɔk *n.* squirrel [ตัว dtuua]

กระสอบ grà~sɔ̀ɔp *n.* bag (rice sack), sack (for rice) [ใบ bai]

กระสับกระส่าย grà~sàp-grà~sàai *adj.* restless, uneasy

กระสือ grà~sǔu *n.* filth-eating spirit [ตัว dtuua]

กระสุนปืน grà~sǔn-bpuun *n.* cartridge (e.g. gun) [นัด nát, ลูก lûuk]

กระแส grà~sɛ̌ɛ *n.* flow (current)

กระแสน้ำขึ้นน้ำลง grà~sɛ̌ɛ-náam-kûn-náam-long *n.* tide (periodic ebb and flow)

กระหาย grà~hǎai *adj.* eager (desiring intensely)

กระหายน้ำ grà~hǎai-náam *adj.* thirsty ‼

กรัม gram *n.* gram [กรัม gram]

กราฟ gráap *n.* graph [แผ่น pèn (sheet)]

กราม graam *n.* jawline

กริ่ง grìng *n.* doorbell [อัน an]

กริยา grì-yaa *n.* verb [คำ kam]

กรีฑา grii-taa *n.* track-and-field [ชนิด chá~nít]

กรีดร้อง grìit-rɔ́ɔng *vi.* scream, shriek

กรุงเทพ grung-têep *n.* Bangkok [เมือง muuang]

กรุณา gà~rú~naa *adv.* please (in polite requests) ‼

กรุณา gà~rú~naa *v.* oblige (favor) 🖋

กล gon *n.* juggling, ruse, magic (performance) 🐾

กลไก gon-gai *n.* mechanism

กลบ glòp *vt.* bury

กลม glom *adj.* circular (shape), round

กลมกล่อม glom-glòm *adj.* mellow (smooth, agreeable)

กลวง gluuang *adj.* hollow

กล้วย glûuai *n.* banana [ลูก lûuk (one), หวี wǐi (bunch)]

กล้วยไม้ glûuai-máai *n.* orchid [ช่อ chɔ̂ɔ (bunch), ดอก dɔ̀ɔk (flower)]

กลวิธี gon-lá~wí-tii *n.* technique (method) [แบบ bὲɛp, อย่าง yàang]

กลอง glɔɔng *n.* drum (musical) [ใบ bai]

กล่อง glòng *clf.* e.g. boxes, cases, cartons, packages, etc.

กล่อง glòng *n.* box (e.g. cardboard) [ใบ bai]

กล้อง glɔ̂ng *n.* camera [กล้อง glɔ̂ng]

กล้องส่องทางไกล glɔ̂ng-sɔ̀ng-taang-glai *n.* binoculars [ตัว dtuua]

กล่องเสียง glɔ̀ng-sǐiang *n.* larynx, voice box [กล่อง glɔ̀ng]

กลอน glɔɔn *n.* poem [บท bòt (verse)]

กลอน glɔɔn *n.* latch [อัน an]

กล่อม glɔ̀m *v.* lull

กลอุบาย gon-ù-baai *n.* trick [อัน an]

กลั่น glàn *vt.* distill, refine (purify)

กลั้น glân *vt.* restrain (hold back from action)

กลับ glàp *vi.* return (turn back, come back)

กลับคืน glàp-kuun *vi.* return (turn back, come back)

กลัว gluua *v.* dread (afraid), fear (be afraid of)

กลั้วคอ glûua-kɔɔ *vi.* gurgle

กล้า glâa *adj.* bold, brave, strong (body)

กลาง glaang *adj.* central, middle

กลางคืน glaang-kuun *n.*

night [ตอน dtɔɔn]

กลางแจ้ง glaang-jɛ̂ɛng *adj.* open-air

กล้าม glâam *n.* muscle [มัด mát]

กลายเป็น glaai-bpen *vt.* become, turn into

กล่าว glàao *vt.* mention ⚡, say ⚡, state ⚡

กล่าวโทษ glàao-tôot *vt.* blame (condemn)

กล่าวหา glàao-hǎa *vt.* accuse (charge)

กล้าหาญ glâa-hǎan *adj.* brave ⚡, fearless

กลิ้ง glîng *v.* roll (along, e.g. wheel, pencil on table)

กลิ่น glìn *n.* odor, smell

กลิ่นหอม glìn-hɔ̌ɔm *n.* aroma

กลีบดอก glìip-dɔ̀ɔk *n.* petal [กลีบ glìip]

กลืน gluun *vt.* match in color, swallow (down throat)

กลุ่ม glùm *clf.* for groups

กลุ่ม glùm *n.* group, pack, set [กลุ่ม glùm]

กวน guuan *v.* stir (blend)

กวน guuan *vt.* disturb (bother)

ก๋วยเตี๋ยว gǔuai-dtǐiao *n.* noodle (rice) [ชาม chaam (bowl), ถุง tǔng (bag), ห่อ hɔ̀ɔ (pack)]

กว่า gwàa *prep.* more than

กวาง gwaang *n.* deer (animal) [ตัว dtuua]

กว้าง gwâang *adj.* broad, large, spacious, wide

กว้างขวาง gwâang-kwǎang *adj.* large, spacious

กว้างใหญ่ gwâang-yài *adj.* vast (wide and spacious)

กวาด gwàat *v.* sweep (with broom)

กวี gà~wii *n.* poet ⚡ [คน kon]

กษัตริย์ gà~sàt *n.* king, monarch ⚡ [องค์ ong]

กสิกรรม gà~sì~gam *n.* agriculture (planting)

กอ gɔɔ *n.* cluster of plants [กอ gɔɔ]

ก่อ gɔ̀ɔ *vt.* build (originate), create

ก๊อกน้ำ gɔ́k-náam *n.* tap (faucet) [ก๊อก gɔ́k]

ก่อกวน gɔ̀ɔ-guuan *vt.*

hassle (bother or harass)

ก่อการร้าย gɔ̀ɔ-gaan-ráai *adj.* terrorist

กอง gɔɔng *vt.* pile (make a pile), stack

กองขึ้น gɔɔng-kûn *vi.* pile up (make a pile)

กองโจร gɔɔng-joon *n.* guerrilla band [กอง gɔɔng]

กองทหาร gɔɔng-tá~hǎn *n.* troop (group of soldiers) [กอง gɔɔng]

กองทัพ gɔɔng-táp *n.* military (army) [กอง gɔɔng]

กองทุน gɔɔng-tun *n.* fund [กอง gɔɔng]

กองหน้า gɔɔng-nâa *n.* avant-garde [กอง gɔɔng]

กอด gɔ̀ɔt *v.* embrace, hug

ก่อตั้ง gɔ̀ɔ-dtâng *vt.* establish, form

ก่อน gɔ̀ɔn *adj.* first (earlier), former (previous), last (e.g. last week)

ก่อน gɔ̀ɔn *adv.* ago, before, first (earlier), since

ก่อน gɔ̀ɔn *prep.* before

ก้อน gɔ̂ɔn *clf.* e.g. bars of soap, stones, chunks, etc.

ก้อน gɔ̂ɔn *n.* bar (e.g. soap), chunk, lump, rock (stone) [ก้อน gɔ̂ɔn]

ก่อนกำหนด gɔ̀ɔn-gam-nòt *adj.* premature (ahead of time)

ก้อนหิน gɔ̂ɔn-hǐn *n.* rock, stone [ก้อน gɔ̂ɔn]

กอบ gɔ̀ɔp *v.* gather up with both hands

ก่อไฟ gɔ̀ɔ-fai *vi.* light a fire

ก้อย gɔ̂ɔi *n.* tails (coin) [ด้าน dâan]

กอล์ฟ gɔ́ɔp *n.* golf

ก่อสร้าง gɔ̀ɔ-sâang *vt.* build ❢, construct ❢

กะ gà *conj.* and ✦

กะ gà *n.* shift (work time) [กะ gà]

กะ gà *v.* estimate (speculate) ✦

กะทะ gà~tá see กระทะ

กะทัดรัด gà~tát-rát *adj.* brief (succinct), compact (packable)

กะทันหัน gà~tan-hǎn *adj.* sudden

กะทิ gà~tí *n.* coconut cream/coconut milk [กล่อง glɔ̀ng (box)]

กะเทย gà~təəi *n.* gay

man, transsexual,
transvestite [คน kon]

กะเทยแปลงเพศ gà~
təəi-bplɛɛng-pêet *n.*
transsexual (got surgery)
[คน kon]

กะเทาะ gà~tɔ́ *vt.* shell
(remove shell of)

กะบังลม gà~bang-lom *n.*
diaphragm (body part)

กะปิ gà~bpì *n.* shrimp
paste [กระปุก grà~bpùk]

กะพริบ gà~príp *vi.* blink
(light)

กะพริบตา gà~príp-dtaa
vi. blink (eyes)

กะเพรา gà~prao *n.* holy
basil [ต้น dtôn (plant), ใบ
bai (leaf)]

กะรัต gà~ràt *n.* carat
[กะรัต gà~ràt]

กะละมัง gà~lá~mang *n.*
enameled bowl or basin
[ใบ bai, ลูก lûuk]

กะละแม gà~lá~mɛɛ *n.*
caramel [อัน an, ชิ้น chín]

กะลา gà~laa *n.* coconut
shell [ใบ bai, ซีก sîik]

กะลาสี gà~laa-sǐi *n.* sailor
(crew) [คน kon]

กะหรี่ gà~rìi *n.* female

prostitute ✿ [คน kon]

กะหล่ำดอก gà~làm-dɔ̀ɔk
n. cauliflower [หัว hǔua]

กะหล่ำปลี gà~làm-bplii *n.*
cabbage [หัว hǔua]

กะเหรี่ยง gà~rìiang *n.*
Karen (hill tribe) [เผ่า pào
(tribe)]

กะโหลก gà~lòok *n.* skull
[ใบ bai]

กัก gàk *vt.* restrict

กักกัน gàk-gan *vt.*
quarantine, restrict

กักขัง gàk-kǎng *vt.*
incarcerate (confine)

กังขา gang-kǎa *vt.*
suspect ✐

กังฟู gang-fuu *n.* kung fu

กังวล gang-won *adj.*
worried (be anxious)

กังหัน gang-hǎn *n.*
windmill [ตัว dtuua]

กัญชา gan-chaa *n.*
marijuana/cannabis,
weed [มวน muuan
(joint), ต้น dtôn (plant)]

กัด gàt *v.* bite

กัด gàt *vt.* sting (other
insects)

กัดกร่อน gàt-grɔ̀n *adj.*

corrosive

กัดเซาะ gàt-sɔ́ *adj.* abrasive (material)

กัน gan *pron.* each other

กัน gan *v.* protect from

กัน gan *vt.* obstruct

กั้น gân *vt.* bar, block (shut off)

กันชน gan-chon *n.* bumper (e.g. car) • [อัน an]

_กันเถอะ _-gan-tè *idm.* let's (do something)

กันน้ำ gan-náam *adj.* waterproof

กันบูด gan-bùut *adj.* preservative

กันไฟ gan-fai *adj.* fireproof

กันยายน gan-yaa-yon *n.* September [เดือน dɯɯan]

กันเอง gan-eeng *adj.* informal •

กับ gàp *conj.* and

กับ gàp *prep.* to (e.g. give to), versus, with (accompanying or against someone)

กับข้าว gàp-kâao *n.* dish (food to eat with rice) [อย่าง yàang (kind), จาน jaan (plate)]

กับดัก gàp-dàk *n.* pitfall, trap [อัน an]

กับระเบิด gàp-rá~bèət *n.* land mine [ที่ tîi]

กัปตัน gàp-dtan *n.* captain [คน kon]

กัมพูชา gam-puu-chaa *n.* Cambodia ✝ [ประเทศ bprà~têet]

กัมมันตรังสี gam-man-dtà~rang-sǐi *adj.* radioactive

กา gaa *n.* pot, teapot [ใบ bai]

กา gaa *n.* crow [ตัว dtuua]

กา gaa *v.* make a mark

กาก gàak *n.* refuse (rubbish) [ชิ้น chín (piece), กอง gɔɔng (pile)]

กากบาท gaa-gà~bàat *n.* plus or multiplication sign (+, x) [ตัว dtuua]

กากี gaa-gii *adj.* khaki (color)

กาง gaang *v.* open (unfold)

ก้าง gâang *n.* bone (fish) [ชิ้น chín]

กางเกง gaang-geeng *n.* pants (outergarment)

ข
ข
ค
ค
ฆ
ง
จ
ฉ
ช
ซ
ฌ
ญ
ฎ
ฏ
ฐ
ฑ
ฒ
ณ
ด
ต
ถ
ท
ธ
น
บ
ป
ผ
ฝ
พ
ฟ
ภ
ม
ย
ร
ฤ
ล
ฦ
ว
ศ
ษ
ส
ห
ฬ
อ
ฮ

[ตัว dtuua]

กางเกงขาสั้น gaang-geeng-kǎa-sân *n.* shorts (outergarment) [ตัว dtuua]

กางเกงใน gaang-geeng-nai *n.* underpants, underwear (panties, boxers, jockeys) [ตัว dtuua]

ก้างปลา gâang-bplaa *n.* fish bone [ชิ้น chín]

กาชาด gaa-châat *n.* Red Cross

ก๊าซ gáat *n.* gas/gasoline/petrol

กาญจนบุรี gaan-jà~ná-bù~rii *n.* Kanchanaburi province [จังหวัด jang-wàt]

ก้าน gâan *n.* stalk, stem (leaf or fruit stalk) [ก้าน gâan]

กาน้ำ gaa-náam *n.* kettle [ใบ bai]

กาฝาก gaa-fàak *n.* parasite (of a tree, person that depends on others) [ต้น dtôn (plant), คน kon (person)]

กาแฟ gaa-fεε *n.* coffee

[ถ้วย tûuai (cup)]

กามเทพ gaam-má~têep *n.* cupid [ตน dton]

ก้ามปู gâam-bpuu *n.* pincer (crab) [ก้าม gâam]

กามโรค gaam-má~rôok *n.* venereal disease [โรค rôok]

กามวิตถาร gaam-wít-dtà~tǎan *n.* pervert [คน kon]

กามารมณ์ gaa-maa-rom *n.* sexual desire ☙

กาย gaai *n.* physical form

กายกรรม gaai-yá~gam *n.* gymnastics [ท่า tâa]

กายภาพบำบัด gaai-yá~pâap-bam-bàt *n.* physical therapy

การ gaan- *pref.* placed before nouns or verbs to form noun derivatives meaning "affairs of..., matters of..."

การแข่งขัน gaan-kèng-kǎn *n.* rally (competition)

การงาน gaan-ngaan *n.* work (in general) [อัน an]

การจลาจล gaan-jà~laa-jon *n.* riot

การ์ตูน gaa-dtuun *n.*

cartoon [เรื่อง rûuang (story)]

การเมือง gaan-mɯɯang *n.* politics

การันต์ gaa-ran *n.* mark ̱ placed above a letter to indicate that it is silent [ตัว dtuua]

กาล gaan *n.* tense (grammar)

กาแล็กซี gaa-lɛ́k-sîi *n.* galaxy [กาแล็กซี gaa-lɛ́k-sîi]

กาว gaao *n.* glue [หลอด lɔ̀ɔt (stick)]

ก้าว gâao *n.* step (footstep) [ก้าว gâao]

ก้าวก่าย gâao-gàai *vi.* interfere (meddle)

ก้าวย่าง gâao-yâang *vi.* tread (step, walk)

ก้าวร้าว gâao-ráao *adj.* aggressive

ก้าวหน้า gâao-nâa *adj.* advanced (improved)

ก๊าส gáat, gáas *n.* kerosene

กาฬสินธุ์ qaa-lá~sĭn *n.* Kalasin province [จังหวัด jang-wàt]

กำ gam *n.* bunch

(vegetables), bundle (handful) [กำ gam]

กำ gam *vt.* grasp (clench in fist)

กำกวม gam-guuam *adj.* ambiguous, unclear

กำกับ gam-gàp *v.* supervise

กำกับ gam-gàp *vt.* direct (e.g. movie)

กำจัด gam-jàt *vt.* eliminate (get rid of)

กำชับ gam-cháp *v.* warn or order repeatedly

กำนัน gam-nan *n.* sub-district headman [คน kon]

กำเนิด gam-nə̀ət *adj.* born ̯

กำเนิด gam-nə̀ət *vt.* generate (e.g. electricity)

กำปั้น gam-bpân *n.* fist [กำปั้น gam-bpân]

กำพร้า gam-práa *adj.* orphaned

กำแพง gam-pɛɛng *n.* wall (e.g. fortress, property line) [แห่ง hɛ̀ng]

กำแพงเพชร gam-pɛɛng-pét *n.* Kamphaeng Phet province [จังหวัด jang-wàt]

กำมะถัน gam-má~tăn *n.* sulfur

กำมะหยี่ gam-má~yìi *adj.* velvet

กำมือ gam-mɯɯ *v.* clench the hand

กำยำ gam-yam *adj.* stocky, well-built

กำไร gam-rai *n.* gain, proceeds, profit

กำลัง gam-lang *adv.* adverb indicating action going on

กำลัง gam-lang *n.* energy (power, strength)

กำลังคน gam-lang-kon *n.* manpower

กำลังสอง gam-lang-sɔ̌ɔng *n.* square (second power)

กำไล gam-lai *n.* bracelet [วง wong]

กำไลเท้า gam-lai-táao *n.* anklet [วง wong]

กำหนด gam-nòt *v.* require (impose)

กำหนด gam-nòt *vt.* define, fix (establish), regulate, specify

กำหนดเวลา gam-nòt-

wee-laa *n.* deadline [ครั้ง kráng]

กำหนัด gam-nàt *n.* excitement

กิ๊ก gík *n.* boyfriend, girlfriend, lover in a non-serious relationship ✹ [คน kon]

กิ่ง gìng *n.* branch (of a tree) [กิ่ง gìng]

กิ้งก่า gîng-gàa *n.* lizard (chameleon) [ตัว dtuua]

กิ้งกือ gîng-gɯɯ *n.* millipede [ตัว dtuua]

กิจกรรม gìt-jà~gam *n.* activity [ครั้ง kráng]

กิจการ gìt-jà~gaan *n.* cause [ครั้ง kráng]

กิจวัตร gìt-jà~wát *n.* practice, routine

กิน gin *v.* drink ✹, eat ✹

กินข้าว gin-kâao *v.* dine (have a meal) ✹, eat ✹

กินเจ gin-jee *n.* vegetarian ✹ [คน kon]

กินได้ gin-dâai *adj.* edible

กินยา gin-yaa *vt.* take medicine

กิ๊บ gíp *n.* bobby pin, hair

clip [ตัว dtuua]

กิริยา gì-rí~yaa *n.* manner (trait, style)

กิเลส gì~lèet *n.* passion (desire) ❧

กิโล gì~loo *n.* kilo (e.g. kilogram, kilometer) ✹

กิโลกรัม gì~loo-gram *n.* kilogram

กิโลเมตร gì~loo-méet *n.* kilometer

กิโลวัตต์ gì~loo-wàt *n.* kilowatt

กี่ gìi *adj.* how many

กี่ gìi *n.* loom [เครื่อง krûuang, หลัง lǎng]

กีดขวาง gìit-kwǎang *vt.* impede, obstruct ❗

กีต้าร์ gii-dtâa *n.* guitar [ตัว dtuua]

กีบ gìip *n.* hoof [กีบ gìip]

กีบเท้าสัตว์ gìip-táao-sàt *n.* hoof [กีบ gìip]

กีวี gii-wii *n.* kiwi (fruit) [ลูก lûuk]

กีวี gii-wii *n.* kiwi (animal) [ตัว dtuua]

กีฬา gii-laa *n.* game (sports) [ชนิด chá~nít]

กึกก้อง gùk-gông *adj.* loud

กึ่ง gùng- *pref.* semi- ❗

กุ๊ก gúk *n.* cook (male) ✹ [คน kon]

กุ้ง gûng *n.* prawn, shrimp [ตัว dtuua]

กุ้งยิง gûng-ying *n.* sty (eyelid) [โรค rôok]

กุญแจ gun-jɛɛ *n.* key [ลูก lûuk, ดอก dɔ̀ɔk]

กุญแจมือ gun-jɛɛ-muu *n.* handcuffs [คู่ kûu]

กุนเชียง gun-chiiang *n.* Chinese sausage [อัน an]

กุมภาพันธ์ gum-paa-pan *n.* February [เดือน duuan]

กุศล gù-sǒn *n.* merit

กู guu *pron.* I (male or female speaker) ☞

กู้ gûu *vt.* borrow (money at interest), rescue, save (situation or face)

เก gee *adj.* crippled (lame), disfigured (slanted)

เก๊ gée *adj.* counterfeit ✹, fake ✹, phony ✹

เก่ง gèng *adj.* able (good at), clever, smart

เกณฑ์ geen *n.* standard (criterion)

เกณฑ์ geen *vt.* draft (soldier)

เก็บ gèp *vt.* keep (save, store, hold), pick up (by hand)

เก็บเกี่ยว gèp-gìiao *v.* harvest, reap

เก็บของ gèp-kɔ̌ɔng *vi.* clean up (put things away)

เก็บตัว gèp-dtuua *adj.* secluded (isolated)

เก็บรักษา gèp-rák-sǎa *v.* conserve

เก็บรักษา gèp-rák-sǎa *vt.* preserve (conserve)

เกม geem *n.* game [เกม geem]

เกย์ gee *adj.* gay (homosexual)

เกรง greeng *v.* be in awe of, revere

เกร็ง greng *adj.* stiff (e.g. muscle)

เกรงกลัว greeng-gluua *v.* fear (be afraid of) ⚡

เกรงใจ greeng-jai *v.* be reluctant to impose (upon)

เกร็ด grèt *n.* anecdote [อัน an]

เกราะ grɔ̀ *n.* armor [ชุด chút (suit)]

เกเร gee-ree *adj.* mischievous (naughty)

เกล็ด glèt *n.* scale (fish) [เกล็ด glèt]

เกลี้ยกล่อม glîia-glɔ̀m *v.* coax (persuade)

เกลี้ยง glîiang *adj.* clean

เกลียด glìiat *v.* hate

เกลียว glìiao *adj.* coiled, twisted (e.g. string)

เกลียว glìiao *n.* spiral (shape), thread (screw thread) [เกลียว glìiao]

เกลียวเชือก glìiao-chʉ̂ak *n.* strand (of rope) [เส้น sên]

เกลือ glʉʉa *n.* salt (table salt) [ถุง tǔng (bag), เม็ด mét (drop)]

เกลื่อน glʉ̀an *vi.* scatter

เกลื้อน glʉ̂an *n.* chloasma (skin disease) [โรค rôok]

เกลื่อนกลาด glʉ̀an-glàat *vi.* scatter ⚡

เกลือป่น glʉʉa-bpòn *n.* refined salt [ถุง tǔng]

เกวียน gwiian *n.* cart

(drawn by animals) [เล่ม lêm]

เกษตรกร gà~sèet-dtà~gɔɔn *n.* farmer ⚠ [คน kon]

เกษตรกรรม gà~sèet-dtà~gam *n.* agriculture (livestock and crops) ⚠

เกษียณ gà~sǐian *adj.* retired (from work)

เกสร gee-sɔ̌ɔn *n.* pollen

เกสเฮาส์ géet-háo *n.* guesthouse (tourist) [แห่ง hèng, หลัง lǎng]

เกา gao *v.* itch (scratch)

เก่า gào *adj.* former (previous), old (not new)

เก้า gâao *numb.* nine

เกาหลี gao-lǐi *n.* Korea [ประเทศ bprà~têet]

เกาหลีใต้ gao-lǐi-dtâai *n.* South Korea [ประเทศ bprà~têet]

เก้าอี้ gâo-îi *n.* chair (to sit on) [ตัว dtuua]

เกาะ gɔ̀ *n.* island [เกาะ gɔ̀]

เกาะ gɔ̀ *vt.* cling to (grab, hold)

เกิด gə̀ət *adj.* born

เกิดขึ้น gə̀ət-kûn *vi.* happen, occur, take place

เกิดใหม่ gə̀ət-mài *vi.* reincarnate

เกิน gəən *prep.* past (over a given value)

เกินกำหนด gəən-gam-nòt *adj.* overdue

เกินไป gəən-bpai *adv.* too (excessively)

เกียร์ giia *n.* gear (vehicle) [ชุด chút]

เกียรติ gìiat *n.* dignity, honor (high respect)

เกียรตินิยม gìiat-ní-yom *n.* honors (academic) [อันดับ an-dàp]

เกียรติยศ gìiat-dtì~yót *n.* prestige (honor, glory) ⚠

เกี่ยว gìiao *v.* caught in, cut (with a sickle)

เกี่ยว gìiao *vt.* hook

เกี๊ยว gíiao *n.* wonton [ชิ้น chín]

เกี่ยวกับ gìiao-gàp *prep.* about (relating to)

เกี่ยวโยง gìiao-yoong *vt.* relate (associate, connect)

เกี๊ยะ gía *n.* wooden slippers [คู่ kûu (pair)]

เกือกม้า gùuak-máa *n.* horseshoe [อัน an]

เกือบ gùuap *adv.* almost, nearly

เกือบตาย gùuap-dtaai *adj.* near death

แก gɛɛ *pron.* he (use with friends) ✴, her ✴, she (use with friends) ✴, you ✴

แก่ gɛ̀ɛ *adj.* dark (color), old (not young), senile, vigorous (energetic)

แก่ gɛ̀ɛ *vi.* age

แก้ gɛ̂ɛ *vt.* correct, cure (remedy), loosen, mend (repair), revise (fix), solve (e.g. problem), take off (clothes)

แก้ไข gɛ̂ɛ-kǎi *vt.* amend, correct, edit (revise or correct), mend (correct, improve)

แก้แค้น gɛ̂ɛ-kɛ́ɛn *vi.* retaliate

แก้แค้น gɛ̂ɛ-kɛ́ɛn *vt.* vindicate (avenge)

แกง gɛɛng *n.* curried food, curry (dish), soup [ถ้วย tûuai (bowl)]

แก๊ง géng *n.* gang [แก๊ง géng]

แกงจืด gɛɛng-jùut *n.* mild curry

แก้ตัว gɛ̂ɛ-dtuua *v.* make an excuse

แก้ต่าง gɛ̂ɛ-dtàang *vt.* defend (verbally)

แกน gɛɛn *n.* axis (e.g. earth, graph), core (central part) [แกน gɛɛn]

แก้ปัญหา gɛ̂ɛ-bpan-hǎa *vi.* solve a problem

แก้ม gɛ̂ɛm *n.* cheek [ข้าง kâang]

แกล้ง glɛ̂ɛng *v.* do out of spite, do on purpose (make a pretense)

แกลบ glɛ̀ɛp *n.* chaff (of rice), husk (rice hull)

แกลลอน gɛn-lɔɔn *n.* gallon

แก้ว gɛ̂ɛo *clf.* for numbers of glasses or cups of water, tea, beer, etc.

แก้ว gɛ̂ɛo *n.* glass (drinking) [ใบ bai]

แกว่ง gwɛ̀ng *vi.* swing (back and forth)

แกว่งไกว gwɛ̀ng-gwai *vi.* sway

แก้วหู gɛ̂ɛo-hǔu *n.* eardrum [ชิ้น chín]

แก๊ส gɛ́ɛt, gɛ́ɛs *n.* gas/gasoline/petrol (natural)

แกะ gɛ̀ *n.* sheep [ตัว

dtuua]

แกะดำ gὲ-dam *n.* black sheep [ตัว dtuua (animal), คน kon (human)]

แกะสลัก gὲ-sà~làk *v.* carve (sculpture)

โกโก้ goo-gôo *n.* cocoa [แก้ว gɛ̂εo (glass)]

โกง goong *adj.* cheating, corrupt

โกดัง goo-dang *n.* warehouse ✸ [แห่ง hὲng (location)]

โกเต็กซ์ goo-dték *n.* female sanitary pad [แผ่น pὲn]

โกน goon *v.* shave (e.g. beard, hair)

โกรธ gròot *adj.* angry, mad

โกศ gòot *n.* urn (for ashes) [ใบ bai]

โกหก goo-hòk *v.* lie, tell a lie

ใกล้ glâi *adj.* close, near

ใกล้ glâi *prep.* around (in same area)

ใกล้เคียง glâi-kiiang *adj.* nearby, neighboring

ใกล้ชิด glâi-chít *adj.*

immediate (close, e.g. family)

ไก่ gài *n.* chicken [ตัว dtuua]

ไก่งวง gài-nguuang *n.* turkey [ตัว dtuua]

ไกด์ gái *n.* tour guide [คน kon]

ไก่ตะเภา gài-dtà~pao *n.* Cochin (chicken) [ตัว dtuua]

ไกปืน gai-bpɯɯn *n.* trigger [อัน an]

ไก่ฟ้า gài-fáa *n.* pheasant [ตัว dtuua]

ไกล glai *adv.* far (to great distance)

ไกว gwai *v.* rock, swing

ข

ข kɔ̌ɔ *let.* ข. ไข่ kɔ̌ɔ-kài, a consonant of the Thai alphabet (high consonant) [ตัว dtuua]

ขจัด kà-jàt *vt.* rid, wipe out (remove, get rid of)

ขณะ kà~nà *adv.* meanwhile

ขณะที่ kà~nà-tîi *conj.* while

ขณะนี้ kà~nà-níi *adv.* now

ขด kòt *n.* circle, coil [ขด kòt]

ขน kǒn *n.* hair (body) [เส้น sên]

ขน kǒn *vt.* load, transport

ข้น kôn *adj.* concentrated, thick (e.g. liquid)

ขนตา kǒn-dtaa *n.* eyelash [เส้น sên]

ขนนก kǒn-nók *n.* down (bird feathers) [เส้น sên]

ขนบธรรมเนียม kà~nòp-tam-niiam *n.* tradition ! [แบบ bɛɛp, อย่าง yàang]

ขนปุย kǒn-bpui *adj.* fluffy (feathery)

ขนม kà~nǒm *n.* snack, sweets [อัน an (piece), ชิ้น chín (piece), ถ้วย tûuai (bowl)]

ขนมจีน kà~nǒm-jiin *n.* Thai vermicelli [ถ้วย tûuai (bowl)]

ขนมปัง kà~nǒm-bpang *n.* bread [แถว tɛ̌ɛo (loaf), ก้อน gɔ̂ɔn (round), แผ่น pèn (piece)]

ขน_ลง kǒn-_-long *v.* unload

ขนลุก kǒn-lúk *n.* goose bumps

ขนส่ง kǒn-sòng *vt.* transport

ขนสัตว์ kǒn-sàt *n.* fur, wool (animal yarn) [เส้น sên]

ขนาด kà~nàat *n.* size [ขนาด kà~nàat]

ขนาน kà~nǎn *adj.* parallel

ขนาบ kà~nàap *adj.* sandwiched

ขนุน kà~nǔn *n.* jackfruit [ลูก lûuk]

ขบ kòp *vt.* grind (teeth)

ขบวน kà~buuan *clf.* for long lines, e.g. parades, trains

ขบวนการ kà~buuan-gaan *n.* process (step) ! [ขั้น kân]

ขบวนแห่ kà~buuan-hɛ̀ɛ *n.* procession (parade) [ขบวน kà~buuan]

ขม kǒm *adj.* bitter (taste)

ข่มขี่ kòm-kìi *vt.* tyrannize (oppress)

ข่มขืน kòm-kǔun *v.* rape

ข่มขู่ kòm-kùu *vt.* extort, intimidate, threaten

ขมวดคิ้ว kà~mùuat-kíu *vi.* frown

ข่มเหง kòm-hěeng *vt.*
abuse (bully, mistreat)

ขมับ kà~màp *n.* temple
(on the head) [ข้าง kâang]

ขมิ้น kà~mîn *n.* turmeric
[หัว hǔua (bulb)]

ขโมย kà~mooi *n.* burglar,
thief [คน kon]

ขโมย kà~mooi *v.* steal

ขยะ kà~yà *n.* garbage,
litter, trash [ชิ้น chín
(piece), กอง gɔɔng (pile)]

ขยะแขยง kà~yà-kà~
yɛ̌ɛng *adj.* disgusted

ขยัน kà~yǎn *adj.* diligent

ขยันขันแข็ง kà~yǎn-kǎn-
kɛ̌ng *adj.* industrious

ขยับ kà~yàp *v.* move
slightly

ขยาย kà~yǎai *v.* enlarge
(expand), spread out
(expand)

ขยำ kà~yǎm *vt.* crumple
(e.g. paper)

ขยิบ kà~yìp *vi.* wink
(make a wink) ✎

ขยี้ kà~yîi *vt.* crumple (e.g.
paper)

ขรุขระ krù-krà *adj.*
bumpy, rough

ขลาด klàat *adj.* fearful
(cowardly)

ขลิบ klìp *vt.* nip

ขลุ่ย klùi *n.* flute [เลา lao]

ขวด kùuat *clf.* for bottles,
flasks, casters

ขวด kùuat *n.* bottle [ขวด
kùuat]

ข่วน kùuan *vt.* scratch
(e.g. with fingernails)

ขวบ kùuap *n.* year (of
age, for mainly children)
✎ [ขวบ kùuap]

ขวัญ kwǎn *n.* courage,
morale

ขวัญ kwǎn *n.* whorl of
hair on top of the head
[ขวัญ kwǎn]

ขวา kwǎa *adj.* right
(opposite of left)

ขวาง kwǎang *v.* lie across

ขวาง kwǎang *vt.* obstruct

ขว้าง kwâang *vt.* hurl,
throw (toss)

ขวางกั้น kwǎang-gân *vt.*
hinder, obstruct

ขวางทาง kwǎang-taang *v.*
block the way

ขวาน kwǎan *n.* ax/axe
[เล่ม lem]

ขวิด kwìt *vt.* gore

ขอ kɔ̌ɔ *n.* hook [อัน an]

ขอ kɔ̌ɔ *v.* beg

ขอ kɔ̌ɔ *vt.* request

ข้อ kɔ̂ɔ *clf.* for joints, contract items, questions, rules, opinions, etc.

ข้อ kɔ̂ɔ *n.* item, section [ข้อ kɔ̂ɔ]

ข้อกำหนด kɔ̂ɔ-gam-nòt *n.* requirement (rules, regulations) [ข้อ kɔ̂ɔ]

ข้อแก้ตัว kɔ̂ɔ-gɛ̂ɛ-dtuua *n.* pretext (excuse)

ข้อเขียน kɔ̂ɔ-kǐian *n.* passage (written article) [ชิ้น chín (work), เรื่อง rûuang (story)]

ข้อความ kɔ̂ɔ-kwaam *n.* message (text) [เรื่อง rûuang]

ข้อคิดเห็น kɔ̂ɔ-kít-hěn *n.* comment (opinion) [ประเด็น bprà~den ✦, ข้อ kɔ̂ɔ]

ข้อเคล็ด kɔ̂ɔ-klét *n.* dislocated joint

ของ kɔ̌ɔng *n.* object (thing), stuff (things) [อัน an, ชิ้น chín]

ของ kɔ̌ɔng *prep.* of (belonging to)

ของกิน kɔ̌ɔng-gin *n.* food

✦ [อย่าง yàang]

ของเก่า kɔ̌ɔng-gào *n.* antique [ตัว dtuua (furniture), ชิ้น chín (piece)]

ของขวัญ kɔ̌ɔng-kwǎn *n.* gift (present) [ชิ้น chín]

ของแข็ง kɔ̌ɔng-kěng *n.* solid (not liquid)

ของคาว kɔ̌ɔng-kaao *n.* dish of the main course [จาน jaan]

ของใคร kɔ̌ɔng-krai *pron.* whose (question word)

ข้องใจ kɔ̂ɔng-jai *vi.* wonder (doubt)

ของชำ kɔ̌ɔng-cham *n.* grocery (item)

ของใช้ kɔ̌ɔng-chái *n.* useful articles [ชิ้น chín]

ของดอง kɔ̌ɔng-dɔɔng *n.* pickle (e.g. cucumber)

ของที่ระลึก kɔ̌ɔng-tîi-rá~lúk *n.* souvenir [อัน an, ชิ้น chín]

ของเทียม kɔ̌ɔng-tiiam *n.* dildo ✦ [อัน an]

ของแท้ kɔ̌ɔng-tɛ́ɛ *n.* original (authentic) [ชิ้น

chín, อัน an]

ของปลอม kɔ̌ɔng-bplɔɔm *n.* phony (counterfeit) [ชิ้น chín]

ของมีค่า kɔ̌ɔng-mii-kâa *n.* treasure (valuable things)

ของลับ kɔ̌ɔng-láp *n.* genitals ✱

ของเล่น kɔ̌ɔng-lên *n.* toy [ชิ้น chín]

ของว่าง kɔ̌ɔng-wâang *n.* snack (refreshments) [อัน an (piece), ชิ้น chín (piece), จาน jaan (plate)]

ของสด kɔ̌ɔng-sòt *n.* raw foods (of any kind)

ของเสีย kɔ̌ɔng-sǐia *n.* sewer (waste)

ของหวาน kɔ̌ɔng-wǎan *n.* candy, dessert, sweets [อัน an (piece), ชิ้น chín (piece), ถ้วย tûuai (bowl)]

ของเหลว kɔ̌ɔng-lěeo *n.* fluid, liquid

ข้อจำกัด kâo-jam-gàt *n.* restriction (condition, regulation) [ข้อ kâo]

ข้อดี kâo-dii *n.* advantage (good point), pro (advantage (not a con)) [ข้อ kâo]

ข้อตกลง kâo-dtòk-long *n.* pact (agreement) [ฉบับ chà~bàp (whole), ข้อ kâo (item)]

ข้อต่อ kâo-dtɔ̀ɔ *n.* joint (of the body) [ข้อ kâo]

ขอตัว kɔ̌ɔ-dtuua *v.* excuse oneself

ขอแต่งงาน kɔ̌ɔ-dtὲng-ngaan *v.* propose (marriage)

ขอทาน kɔ̌ɔ-taan *n.* beggar, panhandler [คน kon]

ข้อเท็จจริง kâo-tét-jing *n.* fact (one item) [ข้อ kâo]

ข้อเท้า kâo-táao *n.* ankle [ข้อ kâo]

ขอโทษ kɔ̌ɔ-tôot *v.* excuse me! pardon me!, ask for forgiveness, ask for pardon

ขอน kɔ̌ɔn *n.* log [ท่อน tɔ̂n]

ขอนแก่น kɔ̌n-gὲn *n.* Khon Kaen province [จังหวัด jang-wàt]

ข้อนิ้ว kâo-níu *n.* knuckle [ข้อ kâo]

ข้อแนะนำ kâo-nέ-nam *n.* tip (suggestion) [ข้อ kâo]

ขอบ kɔ̀ɔp *n.* edge, margin

ก
ข
ค
ฆ
ง
จ
ฉ
ช
ซ
ฌ
ญ
ฎ
ฏ
ฐ
ฑ
ฒ
ณ
ด
ต
ถ
ท
ธ
น
บ
ป
ผ
ฝ
พ
ฟ
ภ
ม
ย
ร
ฤ
ล
ว
ศ
ษ
ส
ห
อ
ฮ

(border), rim

ข้อบกพร่อง kɔ̂ɔ-bòk-prôŋ n. fault (defect), flaw [ข้อ kɔ̂ɔ, ประการ bprà~gaan ⚡]

ขอบข่าย kɔ̀ɔp-kàai n. scope (range) [ขอบข่าย kɔ̀ɔp-kàai]

ขอบเขต kɔ̀ɔp-kèet n. scope (range) [ขอบเขต kɔ̀ɔp-kèet]

ขอบคุณ kɔ̀ɔp-kun interj. thank you!

ขอบใจ kɔ̀ɔp-jai interj. thank you! (to peers and inferiors)

ขอบถนน kɔ̀ɔp-tà~nǒn n. curb (along the edge of a street) [ที่ tîi]

ขอบนอก kɔ̀ɔp-nɔ̂ɔk n. periphery (external boundary)

ขอบฟ้า kɔ̀ɔp-fáa n. horizon

ข้อบังคับ kɔ̂ɔ-bang-káp n. rule (regulation) [ข้อ kɔ̂ɔ]

ข้อบังคับ kɔ̂ɔ-bang-káp n. regulation [ข้อ kɔ̂ɔ]

ข้อพิสูจน์ kɔ̂ɔ-pí-sùut n. proof (evidence) [ข้อ kɔ̂ɔ (point)]

ข้อมือ kɔ̂ɔ-mɯɯ n. wrist [ข้อ kɔ̂ɔ, ข้าง kâaŋ (each side)]

ข้อมูล kɔ̂ɔ-muun n. data, information/info [ชนิด chá~nít (type), ชุด chút (set)]

ขอยืม kɔ̌ɔ-yɯɯm vt. borrow (item)

ขอร้อง kɔ̌ɔ-rɔ́ɔŋ vt. request

ข้อสอบ kɔ̂ɔ-sɔ̀ɔp n. test (paper, e.g. in school) [ข้อ kɔ̂ɔ (question), ชุด chút (set)]

ข้อสังเกต kɔ̂ɔ-sǎng-gèet n. notice (observation) [ข้อ kɔ̂ɔ, ประการ bprà~gaan ⚡]

ข้อเสนอ kɔ̂ɔ-sà~nə̌ə n. proposal (offer, proposition) [ข้อ kɔ̂ɔ]

ข้อเสีย kɔ̂ɔ-sǐia n. con, disadvantage (bad point) [ข้อ kɔ̂ɔ]

ขอแสดงความยินดี kɔ̌ɔ-sà~dɛɛŋ-kwaam-yin-dii interj. congratulations! ⚡

ข้อหา kɔ̂ɔ-hǎa n. allegation (charge) [ข้อ kɔ̂ɔ]

ขอให้ kɔ̌ɔ-hâi *vt.* wish (express a wish)

ขออภัย kɔ̌ɔ-à~pai *interj.* excuse me! ‼

ข้ออ้าง kɔ̂ɔ-âang *n.* pretext (excuse)

ขัง kǎng *vt.* jail (imprison)

ขัด kàt *vt.* feel sore or broken, polish (shine), rub, scrub

ขัดเกลา kàt-glao *vt.* refine (remove defects of)

ขัดขวาง kàt-kwǎang *vt.* get in the way, obstruct

ขัดขืน kàt-kʉ̌ʉn *v.* oppose (disobey, resist)

ขัดเงา kàt-ngao *vt.* polish up (rub up)

ขัดจังหวะ kàt-jang-wà *v.* interrupt (interfere, disturb)

ขัดใจ kàt-jai *vt.* dissatisfy, displease

ขัดแย้ง kàt-yɛ́ɛng *adj.* contrary (obstinate)

ขัดแย้งกัน kàt-yɛ́ɛng-gan *vi.* conflict (disagree)

ขัดสน kàt-sǒn *adj.* be in need of, needy, poor

ขัน kǎn *n.* basin, bowl (water) [ใบ bai]

ขัน kǎn *vi.* coo (e.g.

doves), crow (e.g. rooster)

ขัน kǎn *vt.* tighten by turning or twisting, screw (rotate, e.g. fastener)

ขั้น kân *n.* phase, stage (of development), step (of ladder, stairs) [ขั้น kân]

ขั้นตอน kân-dtɔɔn *n.* phase (stage), process (step) [ขั้น kân]

ขั้นต่ำ kân-dtàm *adj.* minimum

ขันโตก kǎn-dtòok *n.* wooden utensil in northern Thailand [ใบ bai]

ขันที kǎn-tii *n.* eunuch [คน kon]

ขับ kàp *v.* drive

ขับขี่ kàp-kìi *v.* operate (vehicle)

ขับถ่าย kàp-tàai *v.* defecate ‼

ขับร้อง kàp-rɔ́ɔng *v.* sing (song) ‼

ขับไล่ kàp-lâi *vt.* chase away, evict (expel)

ขั้ว kûua *n.* pole (of a magnet, electricity) [ขั้ว

kûua]

ขั้ว kûua *n.* stem (leaf or fruit stalk) [ก้าน gâan]

ขั้วโลก kûua-lôok *n.* pole (of the earth) [ขั้ว kûua]

ขา kǎa *n.* leg [ข้าง kâang]

ข่า kàa *n.* galanga [แง่ง ngêng (rootstock)]

ข้า kâa *n.* subject (citizen) [คน kon]

ขากลับ kǎa-glàp *n.* return trip [ขา kǎa]

ขาไก่ kǎa-gài *n.* drumstick (chicken) [ขา kǎa]

ขาเข้า kǎa-kâo *adj.* incoming (e.g. flight)

ข้าง kâang *clf.* for each side of a pair

ข้าง kâang *n.* side (lateral part) [ข้าง kâang]

ข้าง kâang *prep.* beside, by (next to)

ข้างขวา kâang-kwǎa *n.* right (side)

ข้างขึ้น kâang-kûn *adj.* waxing (moon)

ข้างเคียง kâang-kiiang *adj.* by the side of

ข้างซ้าย kâang-sáai *n.* left side

ข้างเดียว kâang-diiao *adj.* one-sided

ข้างต้น kâang-dtôn *prep.* above-mentioned (i.e. text), at the beginning

ข้างใต้ kâang-dtâai *adj.* underneath

ข้างใต้ kâang-dtâai *prep.* underneath

ข้างท้ายเรือ kâang-táai-ruua *adv.* aft (of a ship)

ข้างนอก kâang-nɔ̂ɔk *adj.* outside

ข้างนอก kâang-nɔ̂ɔk *adv.* out (outside, exterior, external), outside

ข้างใน kâang-nai *prep.* inside, within

ข้างบน kâang-bon *adv.* up (above, higher)

ข้างแรม kâang-rɛɛm *adj.* waning (moon)

ข้างล่าง kâang-lâang *prep.* below/beneath (physically), under (below in degree, rank), underneath

ข้างหน้า kâang-nâa *adv.* in front of

ข้างหลัง kâang-lǎng *n.* rear (back part, behind) [ข้าง kâang]

ขาด kàat *adj.* absent, broken (torn), missing (lacking)

ขาด kàat *vt.* miss (e.g. school)

ขาดใจ kàat-jai *vi.* die

ขาดทุน kàat-tun *vi.* lose (e.g. investment)

ขาดน้ำ kàat-náam *adj.* dehydrated (lacking sufficient water)

ขาตั้ง kǎa-dtâng *n.* stand (support frame, easel) [ขา kǎa]

ขาไป kǎa-bpai *n.* outgoing trip [ขา kǎa]

ข้าพเจ้า kâa-pá~jâao *pron.* I (male or female speaker) ⚠

ข้าม kâam *v.* cross (e.g. street)

ข้าม kâam *vt.* step over

ขาย kǎai *v.* sell

ขายดี kǎai-dii *adj.* best-selling

ขายตัว kǎai-dtuua *v.* be a prostitute ☀

ขายปลีก kǎai-bpliik *v.* retail

ขายส่ง kǎai-sòng *v.* wholesale

ขายหน้า kǎai-nâa *adj.* ashamed (at losing face)

ข้าราชการ kâa-râat-chá~gaan *n.* bureaucrat, civil servant [คน kon]

ขาว kǎao *adj.* white

ข่าว kàao *n.* news [ชิ้น chín (piece), เรื่อง rûuang (content)]

ข้าว kâao *n.* meal (food) ☀ [มื้อ múu]

ข้าว kâao *n.* rice [เม็ด mét (grain), กระสอบ grà~sòop (sack)]

ข้าวเกรียบ kâao-grìiap *n.* crispy rice cake [แผ่น pèn]

ข้าวแกง kâao-gɛɛng *n.* rice with curry (eaten as complete meal) [จาน jaan]

ข่าวคราว kàao-kraao *n.* news (message, tidings) [ชิ้น chín (piece), เรื่อง rûuang (content)]

ข้าวเจ้า kâao-jâao *n.* non-glutinous rice

ข้าวเช้า kâao-cháao *n.* breakfast [มื้อ múu]

ข้าวซ้อมมือ kâao-sɔ́ɔm-muu *n.* brown rice [เม็ด

mét]

ข้าวต้ม kâao-dtôm *n.* rice porridge [ถ้วย tûuai]

ข้าวเที่ยง kâao-tîiang *n.* lunch [มื้อ múu]

ข้าวเปลือก kâao-bplùuak *n.* paddy (unmilled rice) [เม็ด mét]

ข้าวโพด kâao-pôot *n.* corn (plant) [ต้น dtôn (plant), ฝัก fàk (cob)]

ข้าวเย็น kâao-yen *n.* dinner [มื้อ múu]

ข่าวลือ kàao-luu *n.* rumor [ข่าว kàao, เรื่อง rûuang]

ข้าวสวย kâao-sǔuai *n.* cooked white rice

ข่าวสาร kàao-sǎan *n.* information/info (news), message (news, note, letter) [ชิ้น chín (piece), เรื่อง rûuang (content)]

ข้าวสาร kâao-sǎan *n.* husked rice, uncooked rice [เม็ด mét (seed), กระสอบ grà~sɔ̀ɔp (sack)]

ข้าวสาลี kâao-sǎa-lii *n.* wheat

ข้าวสุก kâao-sùk *n.* cooked rice

ข้าวหลาม kâao-lǎam *n.* rice in bamboo [กระบอก grà~bɔ̀ɔk]

ข้าวหลามตัด kâao-lǎam-dtàt *n.* diamond (suit) [ใบ bai]

ข้าวเหนียว kâao-nǐiao *n.* sticky rice [กระสอบ grà~sɔ̀ɔp (sack), ถุง tǔng (bag)]

ข้าศึก kâa-sùk *n.* enemy [คน kon (person), พวก pûuak (group)]

ขาเสีย kǎa-sǐia *adj.* lame (crippled leg)

ขาหนีบ kǎa-nìip *n.* groin [ข้าง kâang]

ขาหัก kǎa-hàk *v.* have a broken leg

ขาออก kǎa-ɔ̀ɔk *adj.* outgoing (leg of a journey)

ขาอ่อน kǎa-ɔ̀ɔn *n.* thigh ✦ [คู่ kûu (pair)]

ขำ kǎm *adj.* funny (humorous) ✦

ขิง kǐng *n.* ginger [แง่ง ngêng (rootstock), หัว hǔua (bulb)]

ขิม kǐm *n.* kind of Thai classical stringed

instrument [ตัว dtuua]

ขี่ kìi v. ride (on animal, bicycle)

ขี้ kîi- *pref.* meaning "characterized by, given to, having tendency to, habitually"

ขี้ kîi *n.* dirt (residue), feces ☙, shit ☙ [กอง goong, ก้อน gôon]

ขี้กลาก kîi-glàak *n.* ringworm [โรค rôok]

ขี้เกียจ kîi-gìiat *adj.* idle, lazy

ขี้โกง kîi-goong *adj.* cheating ☙

ขี้ขลาด kîi-klàat *adj.* timid (cowardly)

ขี้ข้า kîi-kâa *n.* servant ☙ [คน kon]

ขีด kìit *n.* bar (e.g. on phone for signal strength) [ขีด kìit]

ขีด kìit *v.* draw (line figure)

ขีด kìit *vt.* scratch (scrape with a pen)

ขีดฆ่า kìit-kâa *vt.* scratch out (cross out)

ขีดเส้นใต้ kìit-sên-dtâai *vt.* underline (underscore)

ขี้ตู่ kîi-dtùu *v.* claim falsely ☙

ขี้เถ้า kîi-tâo *n.* ash (fire residue) [ผง pǒng]

ขี้น้อยใจ kîi-nɔ́ɔi-jai *adj.* touchy (easy to trigger strong emotion)

ขีปนาวุธ kìi-bpà~naa-wút *n.* missile (guided missile) [ลูก lûuk]

ขี้ผึ้ง kîi-pʉ̂ng *n.* wax (beeswax) [ชนิด chá~nít (type), หลอด lɔ̀ɔt (tube), ตลับ dtà~làp (tin)]

ขี้ฟัน kîi-fan *n.* decaying food particles between the teeth

ขี้มูก kîi-mûuk *n.* snot (mucus) ☙

ขี้ไม้ kîi-máai *adj.* boastful

ขี้โมโห kîi-moo-hǒo *adj.* easily mad; irritable

ขี้ยา kîi-yaa *n.* drug addict (person) ☙ [คน kon]

ขี้ร้อน kîi-rɔ́ɔn *adj.* sensitive to hot weather

ขี้ลืม kîi-lʉʉm *adj.* forgetful

ขี้เล่น kîi-lên *adj.* playful

ขี้เลื่อย kîi-lûuai *n.* sawdust

ขี้สงสาร kîi-sǒng-sǎan *adj.* overly sympathetic, tender (kindhearted)

ขี้หลงขี้ลืม kîi-lǒng-kîi-luum *adj.* senile (failing mentally)

ขี้หลี kîi-lǐi *adj.* flirty ●

ขี้หู kîi-hǔu *n.* earwax [ก้อน gɔ̂ɔn]

ขี้เหนียว kîi-nǐiao *adj.* stingy

ขี้เหร่ kîi-rèe *adj.* ugly (unattractive)

ขี้อวด kîi-ùuat *adj.* boastful

ขี้อาย kîi-aai *adj.* shy (timid)

ขึ้น kûn *adv.* up (e.g. go up, come up)

ขึ้น kûn *vi.* raise (go up), rise (e.g. sun, price)

ขึ้นกล้อง kûn-glɔ̂ng *adj.* photogenic (looking good in photos) ●

ขึ้นเงิน kûn-ngən *v.* redeem for cash

ขึ้นใจ kûn-jai *v.* remember vividly

ขึ้นฉ่าย kûn-chàai *n.* celery [ต้น dtôn (plant)]

ขึ้นชื่อ kûn-chûu *adj.* famous

ขึ้นเตียง kûn-dtiiang *vi.* have sex ●

ขึ้นปีใหม่ kûn-bpii-mài *vi.* start a new year

ขึ้นฝั่ง kûn-fàng *vi.* disembark (go ashore from a ship)

ขึ้นรถ kûn-rót *v.* take a car, train or bus

ขึ้นรา kûn-raa *adj.* moldy (containing mold)

ขึ้นรา kûn-raa *v.* mildew

ขึ้นศาล kûn-sǎan *vi.* go to court

ขืนใจ kǔun-jai *v.* rape ⚠

ขื่อ kùu *n.* horizontal roof beam: tie beam, joist [ตัว dtuua]

ขุด kùt *v.* dig (with tool)

ขุดค้น kùt-kón *v.* excavate

ขุดทอง kùt-tɔɔng *vi.* looking for a fortune ●

ขุดเหมือง kùt-mǔuang *vi.* mine

ขุน kǔn *adj.* large

ขุ่น kùn *adj.* cloudy (e.g. water)

ขุ่นเคือง kùn-kɯɯang *adj.* resentful

ขุนนาง kŭn-naang *n.* lord (duke or marquis) [คน kon]

ขุนแผน kŭn-pɛ̌ɛn *n.* Casanova [คน kon]

ขุนศึก kŭn-sèk *n.* powerful military leader [คน kon]

ขุย kŭi *n.* flaky crust, scaly or powdery residue

ขู่ kùu *vt.* threaten

ขู่เข็ญ kùu-kĕn *vt.* coerce by intimidation

ขูด kùut *vt.* grate (into slices, strands), scrape

ขูด_ออก kùut-_-ɔ̀ɔk *vt.* scrape off

เขก kèek *vt.* hit with the knuckles

เข่ง kèng *n.* kind of bamboo basket [ใบ bai]

เขต kèet *clf.* for region, area, district within Bangkok

เขต kèet *n.* area (district, e.g. election) [แห่ง hèng]

เขตแดน kèet-dɛɛn *n.* boundary (territory) [เขต kèet]

เขตร้อน kèet-rɔ́ɔn *n.* tropic

เขตเลือกตั้ง kèet-lɯ̂ak-dtâng *n.* precinct (election district) [เขต kèet]

เข็น kĕn *vt.* wheel (move on wheels)

เข็ม kĕm *n.* needle [เล่ม lêm]

เข้ม kêm *adj.* concentrated (rich), intensive

เข็มกลัด kĕm-glàt *n.* brooch (pin), safety pin [ตัว dtuua]

เข้มข้น kêm-kôn *adj.* intense (degree or strength)

เข็มขัด kĕm-kàt *n.* belt [เส้น sên]

เข็มขัดนิรภัย kĕm-kàt-ní-rá~pai *n.* safety belt, seat belt [เส้น sên]

เข้มแข็ง kêm-kĕng *adj.* strong (emotion)

เข้มงวด kêm-ngûat *adj.* stiff (rigid), strict

เข็มฉีดยา kĕm-chìit-yaa *n.* syringe (medical

ข

ข
ค
ฅ
ฆ
ง
จ
ฉ
ช
ซ
ฌ
ญ
ฎ
ฏ
ฐ
ฑ
ฒ
ณ
ด
ต
ถ
ท
ธ
น
บ
ป
ผ
ฝ
พ
ฟ
ภ
ม
ย
ร
ฤ
ล
ฦ
ว
ศ
ษ
ส
ห
อ
ฮ

instrument) [เข็ม kěm, อัน an ◆]

เข็มทิศ kěm-tít *n.* compass (device) [อัน an]

เขม่น kà~mèn *v.* muscle twitch

เข็มนาฬิกา kěm-naa-lí~gaa *n.* hand (clock) [เข็ม kěm]

เข็มเย็บผ้า kěm-yép-pâa *n.* sewing needle [เล่ม lêm]

เขมร kà~měen *adj.* Cambodian, Khmer

เข็มหมุด kěm-mùt *n.* pin (thumbtack, round pin) [ตัว dtuua]

เขม่า kà~mào *n.* carbon deposit (as in car engine), soot

เขย kěəi *n.* in-law (male) [คน kon]

เขยก kà~yèek *vi.* limp

เขย่ง kà~yèng *adv.* tiptoe

เขย่า kà~yào *vt.* shake (cause to rock)

เขลา klǎo *adj.* stupid

เขว kwěe *adv.* astray

เขา kǎo *n.* horn (animal) ◆ [ข้าง kâang (each), คู่ kûu (pair)]

เขา kǎo *n.* hill, mountain [ลูก lûuk]

เขา kǎo *pron.* he, her, him, she

เข่า kào *n.* knee ◆ [ข้าง kâang]

เข้า kâo *prep.* come into contact with

เข้า kâo *v.* enter

เข้ากันได้ kâo-gan-dâai *vi.* get along

เข้าเกียร์ kâo-giia *vi.* engage the gears

เข้าใกล้ kâo-glâi *v.* approach (come near), get close

เข้าข้าง kâo-kâang *vt.* side with

เข้าคิว kâo-kiu *vi.* queue up

เข้าคู่ kâo-kûu *vi.* pair (form a pair)

เข้าใจ kâo-jai *v.* understand

เข้าใจผิด kâo-jai-pìt *vi.* misunderstand

เข้าถึง kâo-těng *vt.* access

เข้าแถว kâo-těɛo *vi.* queue up

เข้านอน kâo-nɔɔn *vi.* go to bed

เข้าไป kâo-bpai *prep.* into (inside)

เข้ามา kâo-maa *v.* come in

เข้าเมือง kâo-mɯɯang *vi.* immigrate (enter)

เข้าร่วม kâo-rûuam *v.* attend (participate in)

เข้าเรียน kâo-riian *vi.* attend (school)

เขาวงกต kǎo-wong-gòt *n.* labyrinth (maze)

เข้าสู่ kâo-sùu *v.* enter in, to, toward

เข้าหา kâo-hǎa *vt.* approach (go see)

เขี่ย kìia *v.* flick off (e.g. ashes from cigarette)

เขียง kǐiang *n.* cutting board [อัน an, เขียง kǐiang]

เขียด kìiat *n.* small green frog [ตัว dtuua]

เขียน kǐian *v.* write

เขียน_หวัด kǐian-_-wàt *vt.* scribble (writing)

เขียว kǐiao *adj.* green (color)

เขี้ยว kîiao *n.* fang [ซี่ sîi]

เขื่อน kɯ̀ɯan *n.* dam, levee [เขื่อน kɯ̀ɯan, แห่ง hɛ̀ng]

แขก kɛ̀ɛk *n.* Middle Easterners, guest, Indian (people) ✿, visitor [คน kon]

แข็ง kǎeng *adj.* firm, hard (not soft), stiff, strong

แข้ง kɛ̂ng *n.* shin [ข้าง kâang]

แข็งขัน kǎeng-kǎn *adj.* diligent, strenuous (energetic)

แข่งขัน kɛ̀ng-kǎn *vi.* compete, contest

แข็งใจ kǎeng-jai *v.* steel oneself (force oneself)

แข็งตัว kǎeng-dtuua *vi.* erect (get hard), freeze (turns solid)

แข็งทื่อ kǎeng-tɯ̂ɯ *adj.* stiff (e.g. manner)

แข็งแรง kǎeng-rɛɛng *adj.* healthy, tough (strong)

แขน kɛ̌ɛn *n.* arm (body part) [ข้าง kâang]

แขนขา kɛ̌ɛn-kǎa *n.* limb (body) [ข้าง kâang]

แขนเสื้อ kɛ̌ɛn-sɯ̂ɯa *n.* sleeve [ข้าง kâang]

แขวง kwɛ̌ɛng *n.* county, district (precinct) [แขวง kwɛ̌ɛng]

แขวน kwĕen *vt.* dangle, hang, suspend

โขก kòok *vt.* rap (knock, tap)

โขน kŏon *n.* Ramayana drama play [ตัว dtuua (character), โรง roong (hall)]

ไข kăi *n.* grease

ไข kăi *vt.* open (turn (a key), explain, reveal), wind (e.g. a watch)

ไข่ kài *n.* egg [ฟอง fɔɔng]

ไข้ kâi *n.* fever [ชนิด chá~nít]

ไขกระดูก kăi-grà~dùuk *n.* marrow (bone)

ไข่ขาว kài-kăao *n.* egg white

ไขควง kăi-kuuang *n.* screwdriver [อัน an, เล่ม lêm]

ไข่เจียว kài-jiiao *n.* omelet

ไข่ดาว kài-daao *n.* sunny side-up egg [ใบ bai]

ไข่แดง kài-dɛɛng *n.* egg yolk, vagina ✺, yolk

ไข่ต้ม kài-dtôm *n.* hard-boiled egg [ฟอง fɔɔng]

ไข้ทรพิษ kâi-tɔɔ-rá~pít *n.*

smallpox ⚠

ไข่ปลา kài-bplaa *n.* fish roe [เม็ด mét (one)]

ไข้ป่า kâi-bpàa *n.* malaria [โรค rôok]

ไขมัน kăi-man *n.* fat

ไข่มุก kài-múk *n.* pearl [เม็ด mét]

ไข่ลวก kài-lûuak *n.* soft-boiled egg [ฟอง fɔɔng]

ไข้เลือดออก kâi-lûuat-ɔ̀ɔk *n.* dengue fever

ไข้หวัด kâi-wàt *n.* cold (disease), common cold

ไข้หวัดนก kâi-wàt-nók *n.* avian flu/bird flu

ไข้หวัดใหญ่ kâi-wàt-yài *n.* influenza [โรค rôok]

ไข่หำ kài-hăm *n.* testicle ✺ [ลูก lûuk]

ไข้เหลือง kâi-lɯ̆ɯang *n.* yellow fever [โรค rôok]

ฃ

ฃ kɔ̆ɔ *let.* ฃ. ขวด kɔ̆ɔ-kùuat, a consonant of the Thai alphabet (high consonant) (obsolete) [ตัว dtuua]

ค

ค kɔɔ *let.* ค. ควาย kɔɔ-kwaaı, a consonant of the Thai alphabet (low consonant) [ตัว dtuua]

คง kong *adj.* last, permanent

คงจะ kong-jà *adv.* perhaps (maybe)

คงทน kong-ton *adj.* enduring (durable)

คงที่ kong-tîi *adj.* constant, stationary

คณบดี ká~ná-bɔɔ-dii *n.* dean (e.g. in college) [คน kon]

คณะ ká~ná *n.* faculty (department), panel (group) [คณะ ká~ná]

คณะกรรมการ ká~ná~gam-má~gaan *n.* board (committee) [คณะ ká~ná]

คณะรัฐมนตรี ká~ná-rát-tà~mon-dtrii *n.* council of ministers [คณะ ká~ná]

คณะลูกขุน ká~ná~lûuk-kǔn *n.* jury (panel) [คณะ ká~ná]

คณิตศาสตร์ ká~nít-sàat, ká~nít-dtà~sàat *n.* math [วิชา wí-chaa]

คด kót *adj.* dishonored

(dishonest)

คดเคี้ยว kót-kíiao *adj.* winding

คดี ká~dii *n.* case (law), charge (legal) [คดี ká~dii]

คดีแพ่ง ká~dii-pêng *n.* civil case [คดี ká~dii]

คดีอาญา ká~dii-aa-yaa *n.* criminal case [คดี ká~dii]

คติ ká~dtì *n.* ethical teaching [ข้อ kɔ̂ɔ]

คน kon *clf.* for human, person

คน kon *n.* mankind, human, man, person (individual, human) [คน kon]

คน kon *pron.* somebody/someone (as object)

คน kon *v.* stir (blend)

ค้น kón *vt.* search for

คนกลาง kon-glaang *n.* middleman [คน kon]

คนขับรถ kon-kàp-rót *n.* driver [คน kon]

คนขาย kon-kǎai *n.* merchant (vendor) [คน kon]

คนไข้ kon-kâi *n.* patient [ราย raai ⍭, คน kon]

ค้นคว้า kón-kwáa *v.*

ก
ข
ฃ
ค
ฅ
ฆ
ง
จ
ฉ
ช
ซ
ฌ
ญ
ฎ
ฏ
ฐ
ฑ
ฒ
ณ
ด
ต
ถ
ท
ธ
น
บ
ป
ผ
ฝ
พ
ฟ
ภ
ม
ย
ร
ฤ
ล
ฦ
ว
ศ
ษ
ส
ห
ฬ
อ
ฮ

research

คนคุก kon-kúk *n.* prisoner (convict) ✦ [คน kon]

คนแคระ kon-krɛ́ *n.* dwarf [คน kon]

คนงาน kon-ngaan *n.* worker [คน kon]

คนเช่า kon-châo *n.* tenant [คน kon]

คนใช้ kon-chái *n.* user, servant [คน kon]

คนเดินเท้า kon-dəən-táao *n.* pedestrian [คน kon]

คนเดียว kon-diiao *adj.* alone (one person), single (alone, sole)

คนโต kon-dtoo *n.* eldest [คน kon]

คนทรง kon-song *n.* medium (spiritualist), psychic [คน kon]

คนทำ kon-tam *n.* doer [คน kon]

คนนอก kon-nɔ̂ɔk *n.* outsider [คน kon]

คนใน kon-nai *n.* insider [คน kon]

คนป่วย kon-bpùai *n.* sick person [ราย raai ⚠, คน kon]

ค้นพบ kón-póp *vt.* discover, find out

คนพิการ kon-pí-gaan *n.* cripple [คน kon]

คนรัก kon-rák *n.* loved one [คน kon]

ค้นหา kón-hǎa *vt.* look for, look up (search for info), seek (search for)

คบ kóp *n.* torch (with flame) [คบ kóp]

คบ kóp *v.* associate or be friend with

คบหา kóp-hǎa *vt.* associate with (interact with socially)

คม kom *adj.* pointed, sharp (e.g. knife)

คม kom *n.* edge of blade

คมนาคม kom-má~naa-kom, ká~má~naa-kom *n.* communication

ครก krók *n.* mortar (grinding bowl) [ใบ bai]

ครบ króp *adj.* due, whole (all, complete)

ครบกำหนด króp-gam-nòt *adv.* mature (e.g. bond)

ครบถ้วน króp-tûuan *adj.* complete (having all parts)

ครรภ์ kan *n.* womb ‼

ครอง krɔɔng *vt.* govern

ครอบครอง krɔ̂ɔp-krɔɔng *vi.* reign

ครอบครอง krɔ̂ɔp-krɔɔng *vt.* possess (occupy)

ครอบครัว krɔ̂ɔp-kruua *n.* family (people) [ครอบครัว krɔ̂ɔp-kruua]

ครอบฟัน krɔ̂ɔp-fan *n.* crown (tooth) [ซี่ sîi]

ครั้ง kráng *clf.* for event, number of times, etc.

ครั้ง kráng *n.* occasion (time) [ครั้ง kráng]

ครั้งหนึ่ง kráng-nùng *n.* once [ครั้ง kráng]

ครับ kráp *part.* for male speakers

ครัว kruua *n.* kitchen ✹ [ห้อง hɔ̂ng]

ครัวเรือน kruua-ruuan *n.* household ‼ [ครัวเรือน kruua-ruuan]

คราง kraang *vi.* whine (make a moaning sound)

คราด krâat *n.* rake (tool) [อัน an]

คร่าวๆ krâao-krâao *adj.* rough (e.g. draft)

คราวหน้า kraao-nâa *prep.* next time

คร่ำครวญ krâm-kruuan *vi.* sob

คริสต์ krít *n.* Jesus Christ [องค์ ong]

คริสต์ศักราช krít-dtà~sàk-gà~râat *n.* A.D. [ปี bpii]

ครีบปลา krîip-bplaa *n.* fin (of a fish) [ครีบ krîip]

ครีม kriim *adj.* cream-colored

ครีม kriim *n.* cream

ครึ่ง krûng- *pref.* semi-

ครึ่ง krûng *adj.* mid

ครึ่ง krûng *n.* half

ครึ่งทาง krûng-taang *adv.* midway

ครึ้ม krúm *adj.* overcast (cloudy, gloomy)

ครุ่นคิด krûn-kít *vi.* ponder (contemplate)

ครุย krui *n.* frill (of a skirt)

ครู kruu *n.* teacher [คน kon, ท่าน tân ‼]

ครูฝึก kruu-fùk *n.* coach (trainer) [คน kon]

ครูพิเศษ kruu-pí-sèet *n.*

tutor [คน kon]

ครูใหญ่ kruu-yài *n.* headmaster, principal (school) [คน kon]

คฤหาสน์ ká~rú-hàat *n.* mansion ! [หลัง lǎng]

คลอง klɔɔng *n.* canal [คลอง klɔɔng, สาย sǎai]

คล่อง klɔ̂ng *adj.* fluent (smooth)

คล่องแคล่ว klɔ̂ng-klɛ̂o *adj.* active (fast, agile)

คล่องตัว klɔ̂ng-dtuua *adj.* flexible, easy to handle

คลอด klɔ̂ɔt *v.* deliver (baby)

คละกัน klá-gan *adj.* assorted

คลัง klang *n.* treasury (for valuables) [แห่ง hèng]

คลั่ง klâng *adj.* crazy, delirious

คลั่งไคล้ klâng-klái *adj.* avid (desirous), crazy about

คลังพัสดุ klang-pát-sà~dù *n.* depot (for supplies) [แห่ง hèng]

คลังสินค้า klang-sǐn-káa *n.* warehouse [หลัง lǎng (building), แห่ง hèng

(location)]

คลังอาวุธ klang-aa-wút *n.* arsenal

คลัตช์ klát *n.* clutch (vehicle) [แผ่น pèn, ชุด chút (set)]

คลาดเคลื่อน klâat-klûuan *adj.* inaccurate

คลาน klaan *vi.* crawl (e.g. babies)

คล้าย kláai *adj.* close, similar

คล้าย kláai *vt.* look like

คล้ายคลึง kláai-klʉng *vt.* resemble

คลาสสิก klâat-sìk *adj.* classic

คลำ klam *vt.* look for something by touching

คลิก klík *v.* click (computing)

คลิตอริส klí-dtɔɔ-rít *n.* clitoris ✘ [ปุ่ม bpùm, จุด jùt]

คลินิก klí-ník *n.* clinic [แห่ง hèng]

คลื่น klʉ̂ʉn *n.* wave (in the ocean) [ลูก lûuk]

คลื่นยักษ์ klʉ̂ʉn-yák *n.* tidal wave, tsunami [ลูก lûuk]

คลื่นไส้ klûɯn-sâi *adj.*
nauseated

คลื่นไส้ klûɯn-sâi *n.*
nausea

คลุก klúk *v.* mix together

คลุม klum *vt.* cover (wrap)

คลุ้มคลั่ง klúm-klâng *adj.*
delirious

คลุมเครือ klum-krɯɯa *adj.*
indefinite (vague)

ควง kuuang *vt.* go on a
date with

ควบ kûuap *vt.* gallop

ควบคุม kûuap-kum *vt.*
control, supervise

ควบคุมตัว kûuap-kum-
dtuua *vt.* restrain
(restrict, control)

ควบม้า kûuap-máa *vi.*
gallop a horse

ควย kuuai *n.* cock (penis)
👤 [อัน an]

ควร kuuan *adj.* proper
(suitable)

ควร kuuan *aux.* should
(ought to)

ควรจะ kuuan-jà *aux.*
ought to, should (ought
to)

ควัน kwan *n.* smoke

ควันพิษ kwan-pít *n.* smog

คว้า kwáa *vt.* nab, reach
for, snatch

คว้าง kwáang *adv.*
floating aimlessly

ควาญช้าง kwaan-cháang
n. mahout [คน kon]

คว้าน kwáan *vt.* take out
from the inside

ความ kwaam- *pref.* to
form a noun from a verb
or adjective

ความ kwaam *n.* lawsuit 👤,
legal case [คดี ká~dii,
เรื่อง rɯ̂ɯang]

ความกดดัน kwaam-gòt-
dan *n.* pressure (e.g. of
daily life)

ความก้าวหน้า kwaam-
gâao-nâa *n.* progress

ความเข้าใจ kwaam-kâo-
jai *n.* understanding
(comprehension)

ความคิด kwaam-kít *n.*
thought

ความคิดเห็น kwaam-kít-
hěn *n.* idea (opinion) [อัน
an]

ความเคารพ kwaam-kao-
róp *n.* respect

ความใคร่ kwaam-krâi *n.*
lust, libido

ก ข ฃ ค ฅ ฆ ง จ ฉ ช ซ ฌ ญ ฎ ฏ ฐ ฑ ฒ ณ ด ต ถ ท ธ น บ ป ผ ฝ พ ฟ ภ ม ย ร ฤ ล ฦ ว ศ ษ ส ห อ ฮ

ก
ข
ฃ
ค
ฅ
ฆ
ง
จ
ฉ
ช
ซ
ฌ
ญ
ฎ
ฏ
ฐ
ฑ
ฒ
ณ
ด
ต
ถ
ท
ธ
น
บ
ป
ผ
ฝ
พ
ฟ
ภ
ม
ย
ร
ฤ
ล
ฦ
ว
ศ
ษ
ส
ห
อ
ฮ

ความงาม kwaam-ngaam *n.* beauty (quality)

ความจริง kwaam-jing *n.* truth

ความเจ็บปวด kwaam-jèp-bpùuat *n.* pain

ความช่วยเหลือ kwaam-chûuai-lěua *n.* help [ครั้ง kráng]

ความเชื่อ kwaam-chûua *n.* belief (opinion) [อัน an]

ความซื่อสัตย์ kwaam-sûu-sàt *n.* honesty

ความดันเลือด kwaam-dan-lûuat *n.* blood pressure

ความต้องการ kwaam-dtông-gaan *n.* demand, need, requirement

ความตั้งใจ kwaam-dtâng-jai *n.* intention

ความตาย kwaam-dtaai *n.* death

ความถี่ kwaam-tìi *n.* frequency [เฮิรตซ์ héet]

ความประพฤติ kwaam-bprà~prút *n.* behavior (action)

ความปลอดภัย kwaam-bplòot-pai *n.* safety (being safe)

ความเป็นจริง kwaam-bpen-jing *n.* reality

ความผิดพลาด kwaam-pìt-plâat *n.* error

ความฝัน kwaam-fǎn *n.* dream [อัน an]

ความพยายาม kwaam-pá~yaa-yaam *n.* effort

ความพอใจ kwaam-pɔɔ-jai *n.* satisfaction (contentment)

ความภูมิใจ kwaam-puum-jai *n.* pride (being proud)

ความมั่นใจ kwaam-mân-jai *n.* confidence

ความยาว kwaam-yaao *n.* length

ความยุติธรรม kwaam-yú-dtì-tam *n.* fairness

ความเย็น kwaam-yen *n.* coldness

ความร้อน kwaam-rɔɔn *n.* heat

ความรัก kwaam-rák *n.* love

ความรับผิดชอบ kwaam-ráp-pìt-chôop *n.* responsibility

ความรู้ kwaam-rúu *n.* knowledge

ความรู้สึก kwaam-rúu-sùk *n.* emotion

ความเร็ว kwaam-reo *n.* speed (rapidity)

ความเศร้า kwaam-sâo *n.* sadness

ความสงบ kwaam-sà~ngòp *n.* peace

ความสนใจ kwaam-sǒn-jai *n.* interest (fascination)

ความสะดวก kwaam-sà~dùuak *n.* convenience

ความสัมพันธ์ kwaam-sǎm-pan *n.* relationship

ความสามารถ kwaam-sǎa-mâat *n.* ability, capacity

ความสำคัญ kwaam-sǎm-kan *n.* importance

ความสุข kwaam-sùk *n.* happiness

ความเสี่ยง kwaam-sìiang *n.* risk (danger)

ความเสียหาย kwaam-sǐia-hǎai *n.* damage

ความหลัง kwaam-lǎng *n.* past (ancient, former times)

ความหวัง kwaam-wǎng *n.* hope

ควาย kwaai *n.* buffalo, water buffalo [ตัว dtuua]

คว่ำ kwâm *v.* flip (turn over)

คว่ำบาตร kwâm-bàat *vt.* boycott

คว่ำลง kwâm-long *adj.* upside down (turn over)

คอ kɔɔ *n.* neck, throat

คอก kɔ̂ɔk *n.* sty (animal) [คอก kɔ̂ɔk]

คอตีบ kɔɔ-dtìip *n.* diphtheria [โรค rôok]

คอน kɔɔn *n.* perch (pole or rod, e.g. for birds) [คอน kɔɔn]

ค้อน kɔ́ɔn *n.* hammer [อัน an]

ค่อนข้าง kɔ̂n-kâang *adv.* quite, rather (somewhat)

คอนดอม kɔn-dɔm *n.* condom [อัน an, ชิ้น chín]

คอนโดมิเนียม kɔɔn-doo-mí-niiam *n.* condominium [หลัง lǎng (building), ห้อง hɔ̂ng (room)]

คอนแทค kɔɔn-tɛ̂ɛk *n.* contact lens ✽ [คู่ kûu]

คอนเสิร์ต kɔn-sə̀ət *n.* concert [ครั้ง kráng (event), วง wong (band)]

คอมพิวเตอร์ kɔm-píu-dtêə *n.* computer [เครื่อง krʉ̂ang]

คอย kɔɔi *vi.* wait

ค่อย kɔ̂i *adj.* low (sound)

ค่อย kɔ̂i *adv.* low (sound)

ค่อยๆ kɔ̂i-kɔ̂i *adv.* little by little, softly (gently) ✸

คอร์ด kɔ̀ɔt *n.* chord [เส้น sên]

คอลัมน์ kɔɔ-lâm *n.* column (article) [คอลัมน์ kɔɔ-lâm]

คอเลสเตอรอล kɔɔ-lées-dtəə-rɔ̂n *n.* cholesterol

คอเสื้อ kɔɔ-sʉ̂a *n.* collar (e.g. shirt, coat) [คอ kɔɔ]

คอหอย kɔɔ-hɔ̌i *n.* larynx ✸, throat ✸

คะ ká *part.* for female speakers

ค่ะ kâ *interj.* yes! (for female speakers)

ค่ะ kâ *part.* for female speakers

คะน้า ká~náa *n.* broccoli (Chinese kale, kai lan) [ต้น dtôn (plant), ใบ bai (leaf)]

คะแนน ká~nɛɛn *n.* grade (score) [คะแนน ká~nɛɛn]

คะแนนเสียง ká~nɛɛn-sǐiang *n.* vote (number of votes cast) [คะแนน ká~nɛɛn]

คัด kát *v.* choose (select)

คัดค้าน kát-káan *v.* contradict, object (oppose)

คัดจมูก kát-jà~mùuk *adj.* stuffy (nose)

คัดเลือก kát-lʉ̂ak *v.* select !

คัด_ออก kát-_-ɔ̀ɔk *vt.* eliminate (select out)

คัน kan *adj.* itchy

คัน kan *clf.* for forks, umbrellas, vehicles, rod, bow

คัน kan *vi.* itch (feel itchy)

คั้น kán *vt.* press (squash), squeeze (crush)

คันไถ kan-tǎi *n.* plough/ plow (farming tool) [คัน kan]

คันเบ็ด kan-bèt *n.* rod (fishing) [คัน kan]

คันเร่ง kan-rêng *n.* accelerator (gas pedal) [อัน an]

คับ káp *adj.* jammed, tight (e.g. dress)

คับขัน káp-kăn *adj.* critical, emergency

คับแคบ káp-kɛ̂ɛp *adj.* tight (e.g. space)

คัพ káp *n.* cup (of bra)

คัมภีร์ kam-pii *n.* sacred book [เล่ม lêm]

คัมภีร์ไบเบิ้ล kam-pii-bai-bên *n.* Bible [เล่ม lêm]

คา kaa *vi.* remain stuck (e.g. car in mud, key in door)

ค่า kâa *n.* fee, price, value (worth)

ค้า káa *v.* do business (in)

ค้าขาย káa-kǎai *v.* trade (buy and sell, do business)

ค่าครองชีพ kâa-krɔɔng-chíip *n.* cost of living

คาง kaang *n.* chin [คาง kaang]

ค้าง káang *adj.* incomplete (stuck), pending (unfinished)

คางคก kaang-kók *n.* toad (animal) [ตัว dtuua]

ค้างคาว káang-kaao *n.* bat (animal) [ตัว dtuua]

ค้างคืน káang-kʉʉn *adj.* overnight (e.g. stay, trip)

คางทูม kaang-tuum *n.* mumps [โรค rôok]

ค้างไว้ káang-wái *adj.* undone (unfinished)

ค่าจ้าง kâa-jâang *n.* wage [จำนวน jam-nuuan]

ค่าเฉลี่ย kâa-chà~lìia *n.* mean (average)

ค่าชดใช้ kâa-chót-chái *n.* damages (legal)

ค่าเช่า kâa-châo *n.* rental fee [จำนวน jam-nuuan]

คาดการณ์ kâat-gaan *v.* project (predict)

คาดคะเน kâat-ká~nee *v.* estimate (speculate)

คาดหวัง kâat-wăng *vt.* expect (anticipate)

ค่าโดยสาร kâa-dooi-sǎan *n.* cost of passage, fare

ค่าตอบแทน kâa-dtɔ̀ɔp-tɛɛn *n.* pay (compensation)

ค่าตัว kâa-dtuua *n.* price for one's service, wage [จำนวน jam-nuuan]

คาถา kaa-tǎa *n.* sacred words (spell)

ค่าไถ่ kâa-tài *n.* ransom (payment)

ค่าทำขวัญ kâa-tam-kwǎn

n. consolation money

คาน kaan *n.* beam (long piece of wood) [อัน an]

ค้าน káan *v.* object (oppose)

ค้าน káan *vt.* dispute (politely), reject

คานหาบ kaan-hàap *n.* yoke (frame for carrying) [คัน kan]

ค่านายหน้า kâa-naai-nâa *n.* commission (fee or percentage)

คาบ kâap *vt.* clamp (with teeth or beak)

คาบเกี่ยว kâap-gìiao *v.* extend over (into)

ค่าบริการ kâa-bɔɔ-rí~gaan *n.* fee (service charge)

คาบสมุทร kâap-sà~mùt *n.* peninsula [คาบสมุทร kâap-sà~mùt]

ค่าปรับ kâa-bpràp *n.* fine, penalty

ค่าผ่านทาง kâa-pàan-taang *n.* toll (for road)

ค่าผ่านประตู kâa-pàan-bprà~dtuu *n.* fee (admission)

คาเฟอีน kaa-fee-iin *n.* caffeine

ค่าย kâai *n.* camp [ค่าย kâai]

ค่ารถ kâa-rót *n.* fare 🖘

คาร์บอน kaa-bɔ̂n *n.* carbon [กลุ่ม glùm]

ค่าแรง kâa-rɛɛng *n.* wage [จำนวน jam-nuuan]

ค่าเล่าเรียน kâa-lâo-riian *n.* tuition [จำนวน jam-nuuan]

คาว kaao *adj.* fishy (in smell)

คาสิโน kaa-sì~noo *n.* casino [แห่ง hɛ̀ng]

ค่าเสียหาย kâa-sĭia-hăai *n.* restitution (reparation for loss, damage) [จำนวน jam-nuuan]

ค่าโสหุ้ย kâa-sŏo-hûi *n.* cost or expenses [จำนวน jam-nuuan]

คำ kam *clf.* for words, terms, bite of food

คำ kam *n.* bite (of food) [คำ kam]

ค่ำ kâm *adj.* night

ค้ำ kám *vt.* brace (hold up, support), support (withstand, e.g. weight)

คำขวัญ kam-kwăn *n.* motto, slogan ! [บท bòt]

ค่ำคืน kâm-kɯɯn *n.* night ‼ [คืน kɯɯn]

คำคุณศัพท์ kam-kun-ná~ sàp *n.* adjective [คำ kam]

ค้ำจุน kám-jun *vt.* sustain (support)

คำต่อท้าย kam-dtɔ̀ɔ-táai *n.* suffix [คำ kam]

คำตอบ kam-dtɔ̀ɔp *n.* answer [ข้อ kɔ̂ɔ]

คำตัดสิน kam-dtàt-sĭn *n.* judgment/judgement (judicial decision) [ครั้ง kráng]

คำเตือน kam-dtɯɯan *n.* caution (warning)

คำถาม kam-tăam *n.* problem, question (query) [ข้อ kɔ̂ɔ]

คำทักทาย kam-ták-taai *n.* address (greeting)

คำทำนาย kam-tam-naai *n.* prediction (prophecy) [คำ kam]

คำนวณ kam-nuuan *v.* calculate, compute

คำนับ kam-náp *v.* salute (greet, bow)

คำนาม kam-naam *n.* noun [คำ kam]

คำนำ kam-nam *n.* preface (introduction) [บท bòt]

คำแนะนำ kam-né-nam *n.* suggestion (advice) [อัน an]

คำแปล kam-bplɛɛ *n.* meaning (translation) [คำ kam]

คำพังเพย kam-pang-pəəi *n.* saying (proverb) [บท bòt]

คำพิพากษา kam-pí-pâak- săa *n.* verdict (judgment)

คำพูด kam-pûut *n.* word (speech, remark) [คำ kam]

คำร้อง kam-rɔ́ɔng *n.* petition (request) [ฉบับ chà~bàp]

คำราม kam-raam *vi.* growl, roar

คำวิเศษณ์ kam-wí-sèet *n.* adjective [คำ kam]

คำศัพท์ kam-sàp *n.* term (word), vocabulary [คำ kam]

คำสร้อย kam-sɔ̂i *n.* particle (linguistics) [คำ kam]

คำสแลง kam-sà~lɛɛng *n.*

slang [คำ kam]

คำสั่ง kam-sàng *n.* command, order [เรื่อง rûuang, อัน an ✹]

คำสัญญา kam-săn-yaa *n.* promise (vow)

คำสันธาน kam-săn-taan *n.* conjunction (part of speech) [คำ kam]

คำสารภาพ kam-săa-rá~pâap *n.* admission (confession)

คำให้การ kam-hâi-gaan *n.* testimony (in court)

คำอธิบาย kam-à~tí-baai *n.* explanation [คำ kam (word)]

คำอุทาน kam-ù-taan *n.* interjection (part of speech) [คำ kam]

คิด kít *v.* think

คิดค้น kít-kón *vt.* think of (invent, create)

คิดถึง kít-tǔng *vt.* miss (regret absence of)

คิดถึงบ้าน kít-tǔng-bâan *adj.* homesick

คิดว่า kít-wâa *v.* think that...

คิด_ออก kít-_-ʔɔ̀ɔk *vt.* figure out (solve)

คิว kiu *n.* queue (line of people) [คิว kiu]

คิ้ว kíu *n.* eyebrow [คู่ kûu (pair)]

คี่ kîi *adj.* odd (not even)

คีบ kîip *vt.* grip (with tool, chopsticks)

คีม kiim *n.* pliers, tongs (tool) [อัน an]

คีย์ kii *n.* key (music scale) ✹ [ระดับ rá~dàp]

คืน kuun *vt.* return (give back)

คืนดีกัน kuun-dii-gan *vi.* patch up, reconcile

คืนนี้ kuun-níi *n.* this evening, tonight

คือ kuu *v.* be/is/am/are/was/were/been (as follows)

คือ kuu *vt.* equal

คุก kúk *n.* jail, prison [แห่ง hèng]

คุกกี้ kúk-gîi *n.* cookie [ชิ้น chín, อัน an ✹]

คุกเข่า kúk-kào *vi.* kneel

คุกคาม kúk-kaam *vt.* extort

คุณ kun *pron.* title used before the first name,

you (used generally)

คุณค่า kun-kâa *n.* worth (value)

คุณธรรม kun-ná~tam *n.* moral principles

คุณนาย kun-naai *n.* madame (Thai well-to-do lady of the house) [คน kon]

คุณภาพ kun-ná~pâap *n.* quality (character or nature)

คุณลักษณะ kun-ná~lák-sà~nà *n.* quality (attribute, property)

คุณลักษณะ kun-ná~lák-sà~nà *n.* qualities [ข้อ kɔ̂ɔ]

คุณสมบัติ kun-ná~sǒm-bàt *n.* qualification [อย่าง yàang]

คุณหญิง kun-yǐng *n.* woman of higher class [คน kon]

คุ้น kún *v.* be tame

คุ้นเคย kún-kəəi *adj.* familiar (knowing about), fitting closely

คุม kum *vt.* take charge of (oversee, control)

คุ้ม kúm *vt.* protect (guard)

คุ้มกัน kúm-gan *v.* escort (for protection)

คุมขัง kum-kǎng *vt.* imprison, lock up

คุ้มครอง kúm-krɔɔng *vt.* protect (escort)

คุ้มคลั่ง kúm-klâng *adj.* insane

คุ้มค่า kúm-kâa *adj.* worthwhile

คุมงาน kum-ngaan *v.* oversee (supervise)

คุย kui *vi.* chat, speak, talk (chat, converse)

คุ้ย kúi *v.* scratch the ground (as a chicken)

คุยโต kui-dtoo *vi.* boast, brag

คุยโม้ kui-móo *vi.* boast

คู kuu *n.* small canal, ditch (trench, moat) [คู kuu]

คู่ kûu *adj.* dual (paired)

คู่ kûu *clf.* for pairs

คู่ kûu *n.* couple (pair), mate (pair) [คู่ kûu]

คู่กรณี kûu-gɔɔ-rá~nii *n.* party (litigant) [คน kon (one), ฝ่าย fàai (side)]

คู่ขา kûu-kǎa *n.* partner (good friend, lover) [คน

kon]

คู่ครอง kûu-krɔɔng *n.* spouse (mate) [คู่ kûu (pair), คน kon (person)]

คู่ควร kûu-kuuan *adj.* worthy (deserving)

คู่ความ kûu-kwaam *n.* parties to a legal case [คน kon]

คู่คี่ kûu-kîi *adj.* be about even

คูณ kuun *vt.* times (e.g. three times four)

คู่ต่อสู้ kûu-dtɔ̀ɔ-sûu *n.* opponent [คน kon]

คู่บ่าวสาว kûu-bàao-sǎao *n.* bride and groom [คู่ kûu]

คูปอง kuu-bpɔɔng *n.* coupon, voucher [ใบ bai]

คู่มือ kûu-mɯɯ *n.* handbook [เล่ม lêm]

คูเมือง kuu-mɯɯang *n.* moat (around a city) [คู kuu]

คู่รัก kûu-rák *n.* lovers, sweethearts [คู่ kûu]

คู่สมรส kûu-sǒm-rót *n.* partner, spouse (one's husband or wife) [คู่ kûu]

คู่หมั้น kûu-mân *n.* fiancé/fiancée [คน kon]

คู่หู kûu-hǔu *n.* one's trusted companion ☜ [คน kon]

เค้ก kéek *n.* cake [ชิ้น chín (piece), ก้อน gɔ̂ɔn (whole)]

เค้น kén *v.* coerce

เคเบิล kee-bên *n.* cable, electric wire [สาย sǎai]

เค็ม kem *adj.* salty

เคมี kee-mii *n.* chemistry [วิชา wí-chaa]

เคมีบำบัด kee-mii-bam-bàt *n.* chemotherapy

เคย kəəi *adv.* ever (at some time)

เคยตัว kəəi-dtuua *vi.* get into the habit of

เคร่ง krêng *adj.* serious (e.g. tense situation), strict

เคร่งครัด krêng-krát *adj.* strict

เครา krao *n.* beard [กระจุก grà~jùk (tuft)]

เคราะห์ krɔ́ *n.* fate (bad luck)

เคราะห์กรรม krɔ́-gam *n.* destiny (karma)

เครียด krîiat *adj.* stressed

เครือ kruua *n.* lineage [เครือ kruua]

เครือข่าย kruua-kàai *n.* network [เครือข่าย kruua-kàai]

เครื่อง krûuang *clf.* for machines, electronic devices, etc.

เครื่อง krûuang *n.* engine, machine [เครื่อง krûuang]

เครื่องกรองน้ำ krûuang-grɔɔng-náam *n.* water filter [เครื่อง krûuang]

เครื่องแกง krûuang-gɛɛng *n.* curry spices [ชนิด chá~nít]

เครื่องขยายเสียง krûuang-kà~yǎai-sǐiang *n.* amplifier, microphone, speaker [เครื่อง krûuang]

เครื่องเขียน krûuang-kǐian *n.* stationery, writing supplies [ชิ้น chín]

เครื่องคิดเลข krûuang-kít-lêek *n.* calculator [เครื่อง krûuang]

เครื่องเงิน krûuang-ngən *n.* silverware [ชุด chút]

เครื่องใช้ krûuang-chái *n.* device (appliance) [ชิ้น chín (piece), ชุด chút (set)]

เครื่องซักผ้า krûuang-sák-pâa *n.* washing machine [เครื่อง krûuang]

เครื่องดนตรี krûuang-don-dtrii *n.* instrument (musical) [ชิ้น chín (piece), ชุด chút (set)]

เครื่องดับเพลิง krûuang-dàp-pləəng *n.* fire extinguisher [เครื่อง krûuang]

เครื่องดื่ม krûuang-dùum *n.* beverage [ชนิด chá~nít]

เครื่องดูดฝุ่น krûuang-dùut-fùn *n.* vacuum cleaner [เครื่อง krûuang]

เครื่องแต่งกาย krûuang-dtèng-gaai *n.* costume, dress (clothing) ! [ชุด chút (set), ตัว dtuua (piece)]

เครื่องถ่ายเอกสาร krûuang-tàai-èek-gà~sǎan *n.* copier (copy

machine) [เครื่อง krûuang]

เครื่องทำน้ำอุ่น krûuang-tam-nám-ùn *n.* water heater [เครื่อง krûuang]

เครื่องเทศ krûuang-têet *n.* spice (e.g. cinnamon) [ชนิด chá~nít]

เครื่องนุ่งห่ม krûuang-nûng-hòm *n.* clothes/clothing ! [ชุด chút (set), ตัว dtuua (piece)]

เครื่องใน krûuang-nai *n.* entrails, tripe (intestines) [ชิ้น chín]

เครื่องบิน krûuang-bin *n.* airplane, plane [ลำ lam, เครื่อง krûuang]

เครื่องแบบ krûuang-bɛ̀ɛp *n.* uniform [ชุด chút]

เครื่องประดับ krûuang-bprà~dàp *n.* accessory, jewelry (accessories) [ชิ้น chín (piece), ชุด chút (set)]

เครื่องปรับอากาศ krûuang-bpràp-aa-gàat *n.* air conditioner [เครื่อง

krûuang]

เครื่องปั้นดินเผา krûuang-bpân-din-pǎo *n.* pottery [ชิ้น chín]

เครื่องพิมพ์ดีด krûuang-pim-dìit *n.* typewriter [เครื่อง krûuang]

เครื่องมือ krûuang-muu *n.* tool (hand tool, device) [ชิ้น chín (piece), ชุด chút (set)]

เครื่องยนต์ krûuang-yon *n.* engine, motor [เครื่อง krûuang]

เครื่องราง krûuang-raang *n.* amulet [ชิ้น chín, อัน an]

เครื่องเล่น krûuang-lên *n.* player (machine) [เครื่อง krûuang]

เครื่องสำอาง krûuang-sǎm-aang *n.* cosmetics [ชนิด chá~nít (type), ยี่ห้อ yîi-hɔ̂ɔ (brand)]

เครื่องสูบ krûuang-sùup *n.* pump [เครื่อง krûuang, ตัว dtuua]

เครื่องเสียง krûuangsĭiang *n.* stereo (sound equipment) [เครื่อง krûuang]

เครื่องหมาย krûuang-măai *n.* mark (written symbol), tick (e.g. checkmark, X) [อัน an]

เคล็ดลับ klét-láp *n.* tactic (secret technique) [ข้อ kôo]

เคลิ้ม klə́əm *adj.* half asleep

เคลื่อน klûuan *v.* move

เคลื่อนที่ klûuan-tîi *vi.* be moving

เคลื่อนที่ได้ klûuan-tîi-dâai *adj.* mobile

เคลื่อนย้าย_ไป_ klûuan-yáai-_-bpai-_ *vt.* transfer (move _ to _) ⚠

เคลื่อนไหว klûuan-wăi *vi.* move about

เคลือบ klûuap *vt.* coat, plate

เค้า káo *pron.* he (use with friends) ❋, she (use with friends) ❋

เค้าโครง káo-kroong *n.* outline (draft, plan) [เรื่อง rûuang]

เคารพ kao-róp *vt.* respect, revere

เคาะ kó *vt.* knock, tap (strike, e.g. with fingers)

เคียง kiiang *adj.* side, close, adjacent

เคียว kiiao *n.* sickle (scythe) [เล่ม lêm]

เคี่ยว kîiao *v.* simmer, stew

เคี้ยว kíiao *v.* chew

เคือง kuuang *adj.* annoyed

แค่ kêɛ *adv.* as far, as long, only (just)

แค่ kêɛ *prep.* to the extent of, as long

แคตตาลอก két-dtaa-lɔ́k *n.* catalog [เล่ม lêm]

แค้น kɛ́ɛn *adj.* vindictive

แค้น kɛ́ɛn *v.* harbor feelings of anger

แค้นเคือง kɛ́ɛn-kuuang *v.* feel resentful

แคนตาลูป kɛɛn-dtaa-lúup *n.* cantaloupe [ลูก lûuk]

แคบ kɛ̂ɛp *adj.* narrow

แคปซูล kɛ́p-suun *n.* capsule [เม็ด mét]

แคม kɛɛm *n.* gunwale of a boat [แคม kɛɛm]

แคร่หาม krɛ̂ɛ-hăam *n.* stretcher [คัน kan]

แครอท kɛɛ-rɔ̀t *n.* carrot
[หัว hǔua (whole), ชิ้น
chín (piece)]

แคลเซี่ยม kɛn-sîiam *n.*
calcium

แคลอรี่ kɛɛ-lɔɔ-rîi *n.*
calorie ✖ [แคลอรี่ kɛɛ-
lɔɔ-rîi]

แคว้น kwɛ́ɛn *n.* region
[แคว้น kwɛ́ɛn]

โค koo *n.* ox ❗ [ตัว dtuua]

โคก kôok *n.* knoll (hillock)
[โคก kôok]

โคเคน koo-keen *n.*
cocaine

โค้ง kóong *adj.* curved
(e.g. line)

โค้ง kóong *vi.* bow (bend
down)

โคจร koo-jɔɔn *vi.* orbit,
revolve ✖

โค่น kôon *vt.* fell (e.g. a
tree)

โคนขา koon-kǎa *n.* thigh
[คู่ kûu (pair)]

โค่นล้ม kôon-lóm *vt.*
topple (e.g. government)

โคม koom *n.* lantern
(portable lamp) [ใบ bai,

ดวง duuang, ลูก lûuk]

โคมไฟ koom-fai *n.* lamp
[ใบ bai, ดวง duuang, ลูก
lûuk]

โครง kroong *n.* frame
(structure) [โครง kroong]

โครงกระดูก kroong-grà~
dùuk *n.* skeleton (body)
[โครง kroong]

โครงการ kroong-gaan *n.*
program (project, plan)
[โครงการ kroong-gaan,
อัน an]

โครงร่าง kroong-râang *n.*
frame (structure) ❗,
skeleton (outline) [โครง
kroong]

โครงเรื่อง kroong-rûuang
n. outline (of a story)
[เรื่อง rûuang]

โครงสร้าง kroong-sâang
n. structure [โครงสร้าง
kroong-sâang]

โคราช koo-râat *n.*
colloquial name of
Nakhon Ratchasima
province, Khorat ✦
[จังหวัด jang-wàt]

โคลง kloong *n.* kind of
Thai poem [บท bòt]

โคลงกลอน kloong-glɔɔn *n.* poetry (verse) [บท bòt]

โคลน kloon *n.* mud, slime

โคลน kloon *vt.* clone

โควต้า koo-dtâa *n.* quota [ส่วน sùuan]

ใคร krai *pron.* anybody/anyone (in question), who (which person), whom (question word)

ใครๆ krai-krai *pron.* anybody/anyone ❁

ใครก็ได้ krai-gɔ̂ɔ-dâai *pron.* anybody/anyone

ใคร่ครวญ krâi-kruuan *v.* consider carefully

ค

ค kɔɔ *let.* ค. คน kɔɔ-kon, a consonant of the Thai alphabet (low consonant) (obsolete) [ตัว dtuua]

ฆ

ฆ kɔɔ *let.* ฆ. ระฆัง kɔɔ-rá~kang, a consonant of the Thai alphabet (low consonant) [ตัว dtuua]

ฆราวาส ká~raa-wâat *n.* lay people (laity) ❁ [คน kon]

ฆ่า kâa *vt.* kill, murder

ฆ่าเชื้อ kâa-chúua *vt.* sterilize (kill germs in)

ฆาตกร kâat-dtà~gɔɔn *n.* murderer [คน kon]

ฆาตกรรม kâat-dtà~gam *n.* murder ! [ครั้ง kráng]

ฆ่าตัวตาย kâa-dtuua-dtaai *vi.* commit suicide

เฆี่ยน kîian *vt.* thrash (beat), whip

โฆษก koo-sòk *n.* announcer, master of ceremonies [คน kon]

โฆษณา koo-sà~naa, kôot-sà~naa *n.* commercial (on radio or TV) [ชิ้น chín]

โฆษณา koo-sà~naa, kôot-sà~naa *v.* advertise

โฆษณา koo-sà~naa, kôot-sà~naa *vt.* publicize (advertise)

ง

ง ngɔɔ *let.* ง. งู ngɔɔ-nguu, a consonant of the Thai alphabet (low consonant) [ตัว dtuua]

งก ngók *adj.* greedy (covetous) ❁, stingy ❁

งง ngong *adj.* puzzled, stunned (confused)

งงงวย ngong-nguuai *adj.* puzzled

งด ngót *v.* cancel (discontinue, stop)

งดงาม ngót-ngaam *adj.* beautiful ✐

งดเว้น ngót-wén *vt.* refrain from

งบประมาณ ngóp-bprà~maan *n.* budget [จำนวน jam-nuuan]

งม ngom *v.* grope in the water for

งมงาย ngom-ngaai *adj.* beyond reason, stupid

ง่วง ngûuang *adj.* drowsy, sleepy

งวงช้าง nguuang-cháang *n.* trunk (of an elephant) [งวง nguuang]

ง่วงนอน ngûuang-nɔɔn *adj.* sleepy (drowsy)

งวด ngûuat *n.* fixed period of time for payment [งวด ngûuat]

งอ ngɔɔ *adj.* bent, curved (e.g. line)

งอ ngɔɔ *v.* bend

ง้อ ngɔ́ɔ *v.* seek reconciliation with, make up to

งอก ngɔ̂ɔk *vi.* bud, sprout

งอกงาม ngɔ̂ɔk-ngaam *vi.* flourish (grow)

งอกราก ngɔ̂ɔk-râak *vi.* root (grow roots)

งอแง ngɔɔ-ngɛɛ *adj.* crying like a baby, clumsy, fussy

งอน ngɔɔn *adj.* bent

งอน ngɔɔn *v.* curve upward

งอบ ngɔ̂ɔp *n.* kind of hat made of palm leaves [ใบ bai]

งอม ngɔɔm *adj.* overripe, very old

ง่อย ngɔ̂i *adj.* crippled (for hands), lame

งั่ง ngâng *adj.* dull (stupid)

งัด ngát *v.* raise with a lever, pry (lever open)

งัดแงะ ngát-ngɛ́ *vi.* break in (burgle)

งั้นๆ ngán-ngán *adj.* so-so

งา ngaa *n.* sesame [เม็ด mét (seed)]

ง้าง ngáang *v.* lift up to open

งาช้าง ngaa-cháang *n.* elephant tusk [กิ่ง gìng (each), คู่ kûu (pair)]

งาน ngaan *n.* job (work)
[อัน an, ชิ้น chín]

งาน ngaan *n.* affair (anything requiring action) [งาน ngaan]

งานกุศล ngaan-gù~sǒn *n.* benefit (charity event) [งาน ngaan]

งานฉลอง ngaan-chà~lɔɔng *n.* celebration, festival [งาน ngaan]

งานแต่งงาน ngaan-dtɛ̀ng-ngaan *n.* wedding [งาน ngaan]

งานบ้าน ngaan-bâan *n.* chore (house), housework [งาน ngaan]

งานประเพณี ngaan-bprà~pee-nii *n.* festival [งาน ngaan]

งานปีใหม่ ngaan-bpii-mài *n.* New Year festival [งาน ngaan]

งานฝีมือ ngaan-fǐi-mɯɯ *n.* handicraft

งานเลี้ยง ngaan-líiang *n.* feast, party (e.g. birthday) [งาน ngaan]

งานศพ ngaan-sòp *n.* funeral [งาน ngaan]

งานอดิเรก ngaan-à~dì~rèek *n.* hobby

งาม ngaam *adj.* beautiful ☜, graceful

ง่าม ngâam *n.* prong (pointed tine of a fork) [ง่าม ngâam]

ง่าย ngâai *adj.* easy, simple

ง่ายดาย ngâai-daai *adj.* very easy, very simple

ง้าว ngáao *n.* pike with curved blade [เล่ม lêm]

งี่เง่า ngîi-ngâo *adj.* silly (foolish)

งีบ ngîip *vi.* nap

งีบหลับ ngîip-làp *vi.* doze (nap), snooze

งุนงง ngun-ngong *adj.* bewildered

งุ่มง่าม ngûm-ngâam *adj.* awkward (clumsy)

งู nguu *n.* snake [ตัว dtuua]

งูๆปลาๆ nguu-nguu-bplaa-bplaa *adj.* knowing very little about something

งูเขียว nguu-kǐiao *n.* common green snake [ตัว dtuua]

งูจงอาง nguu-jong-aang *n.* king cobra [ตัว dtuua]

งูพิษ nguu-pít *n.* viper [ตัว dtuua]

ก
ข
ฃ
ค
ฅ
ฆ
ง
จ
ฉ
ช
ซ
ฌ
ญ
ฎ
ฏ
ฐ
ฑ
ฒ
ณ
ด
ต
ถ
ท
ธ
น
บ
ป
ผ
ฝ
พ
ฟ
ภ
ม
ย
ร
ฤ
ล
ฦ
ว
ศ
ษ
ส
ห
อ
ฮ

งูเหลือม nguu-lɯ̌ɯam *n.* boa (snake), python [ตัว dtuua]

งูเห่า nguu-hào *n.* cobra [ตัว dtuua]

เงยหน้า ngəəi-nâa *vi.* look up (raise one's head)

เงา ngao *n.* shadow (cast image) [เงา ngao]

เงาะ ngɔ́ *n.* rambutan [ลูก lûuk (one), พวง puuang (bunch)]

เงิน ngən *n.* money, silver

เงินกู้ ngən-gûu *n.* loan (money) [บาท bàat]

เงินใช้สอย ngən-chái-sɔ̌ɔi *n.* allowance (money) [จำนวน jam-nuuan]

เงินดาวน์ ngən-daao *n.* down payment [จำนวน jam-nuuan]

เงินเดือน ngən-dɯɯan *n.* income (salary) [จำนวน jam-nuuan]

เงินต้น ngən-dtôn *n.* principal (monetary capital)

เงินตรา ngən-dtraa *n.* currency (money)

เงินทอน ngən-tɔɔn *n.* change (money returned) [จำนวน jam-nuuan]

เงินทุน ngən-tun *n.* principal (monetary capital)

เงินประกัน ngən-bprà~ gan *n.* bail (money amount)

เงินปันผล ngən-bpan-pǒn *n.* dividend

เงินผ่อน ngən-pɔ̀n *n.* installment (partial payment) [งวด ngûuat]

เงินเฟ้อ ngən-fɤ́ɤ *n.* inflation (economics)

เงินมัดจำ ngən-mát-jam *n.* deposit (down payment, security) [จำนวน jam-nuuan]

เงินสด ngən-sòt *n.* cash [แบงค์ béng (bill), เหรียญ rǐian (coin)]

เงินอุดหนุน ngən-ùt-nǔn *n.* subsidy

เงี่ยน ngîian *adj.* horny (lustful) ⚥

เงี่ยน ngîian *vt.* have a craving for ⚥

เงียบ ngîiap *adj.* mute (no sound), quiet, silent

เงียบสงบ ngîiap-sà~ngòp *adj.* still (calm, quiet)

เงือก ngน̂uak *n.* mermaid [ตัว dtuua]

เงื่อน ngน̂uan *n.* clue, knot [อัน an]

เงื่อนไข ngน̂uan-kăi *n.* condition (stipulation), term [ข้อ kɔ̂ɔ]

แง่บวก ngɛ̂ɛ-bùuak *adj.* positive (optimistic)

แง้ม ngɛ́ɛm *v.* open slightly

แง่มุม ngɛ̂ɛ-mum *n.* aspect (point of view) [มุม mum]

โง่ ngôo *adj.* dumb (stupid), silly (stupid)

โงเง ngoo-ngee *adj.* drowsy (sleepy)

โง่เง่า ngôo-ngâo *adj.* idiotic (foolish)

จ

จ jɔɔ *let.* จ. จาน jɔɔ-jaan, a consonant of the Thai alphabet (mid consonant) [ตัว dtuua]

จงรักภักดี jong-rák-pák-dii *adj.* faithful, loyal ❗

จด jòt *vt.* jot down (take note of)

จด_ลง jòt-_-long *vt.* write down

จดหมาย jòt-măai *n.* letter (mail) [ฉบับ chà~bàp]

จตุจักร jà~dtù-jàk *n.* Chatuchak district [เขต kèet]

จตุรัส jà-dtù~ràt *adj.* square (four sides equal)

จน jon *adj.* poor (indigent)

จน jon *prep.* until

จนกระทั่ง jon-grà~tâng *prep.* pending, until

จนกว่า jon-gwàa *conj.* as long as

จนถึง jon-tŭng *prep.* until

จนปัญญา jon-bpan-yaa *adj.* beyond one's knowledge

จนมุม jon-mum *vi.* have no way out ✎

จบ jòp *adj.* over (finished)

จม jom *vi.* sink (drown)

จมน้ำ jom-náam *vi.* sink (drown)

จมน้ำตาย jom-náam-dtaai *vi.* drown

จมลง jom-long *vi.* subside (sink)

จมูก jà~mùuk *n.* nose

จมูกเล็บ jà~mùuk-lép *n.* hangnail

จรรยา jan-yaa *n.* morality

จรวด jà~rùuat *n.* rocket [ลำ lam]

จระเข้ jɔɔ-rá~kêe *n.* crocodile [ตัว dtuua]

จราจร jà~raa-jɔɔn *n.* traffic (on street)

จริง jing *adj.* actual, authentic, true (real)

จริงๆ jing-jing *adv.* really

จริงจัง jing-jang *adj.* serious (somber, sincere)

จริงใจ jing-jai *adj.* sincere, truthful (of person)

จริยธรรม jà~rí-yá-tam *n.* ethics (system of moral principles)

จ้วง jûuang *v.* stab with full force

จวน juuan *adv.* very near

จอ jɔɔ *n.* Year of the Dog [ปี bpii]

จอ jɔɔ *n.* screen (monitor) [จอ jɔɔ, ผืน pʉ̌ʉn]

จ่อ jɔ̀ɔ *v.* place against

จ้อ jɔ̂ɔ *adv.* talkatively ●

จอก jɔ̀ɔk *n.* small cup or glass [ใบ bai]

จอง jɔɔng *v.* book (reserve)

จ้อง jɔ̂ng *vi.* stare

จองจำ jɔɔng-jam *vt.* incarcerate (imprison)

จ้องมอง jɔ̂ng-mɔɔng *vi.* stare

จองหอง jɔɔng-hɔ̌ɔng *adj.* haughty (disdainful)

จอเงิน jɔɔ-ngən *n.* movie ● [จอ jɔɔ]

จอด jɔ̀ɔt *v.* park (vehicle)

จอน jɔɔn *n.* sideburn [ข้าง kâang]

จอบ jɔ̀ɔp *n.* hoe [เล่ม lêm]

จ๊อบ jɔ́ɔp *n.* job or temporary work ● [ชิ้น chín]

จอภาพ jɔɔ-pâap *n.* monitor (screen) [จอ jɔɔ]

จอม jɔɔm *n.* chief (leader) ● [คน kon]

จอมปลวก jɔɔm-bplùuak *n.* termite hill [จอม jɔɔm]

จอมพล jɔɔm-pon *n.* marshal (highest rank in military) [ท่าน tân]

จ๋อย jɔ̌ɔi *adj.* yellow (color)

จ๋อย jɔ̌ɔi *adv.* extremely (lots) ●

จะ jà *aux.* shall, will, would

จ๊ะ já *part.* used in questions, to urge or suggest

จะเข้ jà~kêe *n.* Thai classical music instrument [ตัว dtuua]

จ๊ะเอ๋ já~ĕe *interj.* peekaboo!

จัก jàk *v.* split, cleave, e.g. bamboo

จักจั่น jàk-gà~jàn *n.* cicada [ตัว dtuua]

จั๊กจี้ ják-gà~jîi *v.* tickle

จั๊กจี้ ják-gà~jîi *adj.* ticklish

จักร jàk *n.* engine [ตัว dtuua, เครื่อง krûuang]

จักร jàk *n.* circle ✺ [อัน an, วง wong]

จักรพรรดิ jàk-grà~pát *n.* emperor [พระองค์ prá-ong]

จักรยาน jàk-grà~yaan *n.* bicycle, bike [คัน kan]

จักรยานยนต์ jàk-grà~yaan-yon *n.* motorcycle ⚡ [คัน kan]

จักรเย็บผ้า jàk-yép-pâa *n.* sewing machine [คัน kan]

จักรราศี jàk-raa-sǐi *n.* zodiac [ราศี raa-sǐi]

จักรวรรดิ jàk-grà~wàt *n.* empire ⚡ [แห่ง hèng]

จักรวาล jàk-grà~waan *n.* universe [แห่ง hèng]

จักรี jàk-grii *n.* Chakri Dynasty, god Krishna

จัง jang *adv.* quite

จังหวะ jang-wà *n.* beat (rhythm) [จังหวะ jang-wà]

จังหวัด jang-wàt *n.* province [จังหวัด jang-wàt]

จัญไร jan-rai *adj.* damned (accursed)

จัด jàt *adj.* violent

จัด jàt *adv.* extremely (lots)

จัด jàt *vt.* arrange (manage, prepare)

จัดตั้ง jàt-dtâng *v.* organize (establish)

จัดพิมพ์ jàt-pim *v.* publish (issue publicly)

จัด_ให้ jàt-_-hâi *vt.* provide (supply)

จัตวา jàt-dtà~waa *adj.* four, fourth (ordinal)

จันทบุรี jan-tá-bù~rii *n.* Chantaburi province [จังหวัด jang-wàt]

จันทร์ jan *n.* moon [ดวง duuang]

จันทร์ jan *n.* Monday ⚫ [วัน wan]

กขฃคฅฆงจฉชซฌญฎฏฐฑฒณดตถทธนบปผฝพฟภมยรฤลวศษสหอฮ

จันทรุปราคา jan-tá~rú-bpà~raa-kaa *n.* lunar eclipse [ครั้ง kráng]

จับ jàp *vt.* arrest (e.g. police), catch (capture, seize)

จับกุม jàp-gum *vt.* seize (capture)

จั่ว jùua *n.* gable [จั่ว jùua, แผง pɛ̌ɛng]

จ่า jàa *n.* sergeant [นาย naai, คน kon]

จ้า jâa *adj.* bright (annoyingly)

จาก jàak *n.* nipa palm (plant) [ต้น dtôn]

จาก jàak *prep.* from

จาก jàak *vt.* leave (depart)

จากนั้น jàak-nán *adv.* afterward/afterwards (subsequently)

จ้าง jâang *vt.* employ (hire)

จางลง jaang-long *vi.* fade (dim)

จาน jaan *n.* dish, plate [ใบ bai, ลูก lûuk]

จานบิน jaan-bin *n.* UFO [ลำ lam]

จานสี jaan-sǐi *n.* palette (color) [อัน an]

จ๊าบ jáap *adj.* cool (good)

จาม jaam *vi.* sneeze

จ่าย jàai *v.* pay, spend

จ่ายตลาด jàai-dtà~làat *vi.* shop

จารกรรม jaa-rá~gam *n.* espionage [ครั้ง kráng]

จ่าศาล jàa-sǎan *n.* bailiff (in courtroom) [คน kon]

จ่าหน้า jàa-nâa *v.* provide with a heading

จ่าหน้าซอง jàa-nâa-sɔɔng see จ่าหน้า

จำ jam *v.* memorize, remember

จำกัด jam-gàt *vt.* limit, restrict

จำคุก jam-kúk *vt.* imprison, jail ❗

จำเจ jam-jee *adj.* monotonous

จำ_ได้ jam-_-dâai *vt.* recognize (recall), remember

จำนวน jam-nuuan *n.* number (count, sum) [จำนวน jam-nuuan]

จำนวนเต็ม jam-nuuan-dtem *n.* whole number [จำนวน jam-nuuan]

จำนวนมาก jam-nuuan-mâak *adj.* mass

จำนอง jam-nɔɔng *vt.* mortgage

จำนำ jam-nam *v.* pawn

จำปา jam-bpaa *n.* magnolia [ดอก dɔɔk]

จำเป็น jam-bpen *adj.* essential, necessary

จำเป็นต้อง jam-bpen-dtɔ̂ng *vi.* have to ⚡

จำพวก jam-pûuak *n.* group (category) [จำพวก jam-pûuak]

จ้ำม่ำ jâm-mâm *adj.* plump (chubby)

จำลอง jam-lɔɔng *vt.* reproduce (duplicate)

จำเลย jam-ləəi *n.* defendant (in court) [คน kon]

จำศีล jam-sǐin *v.* to stay at one place for a long time 💥

จำศีล jam-sǐin *vi.* hibernate (animals)

จำหน่าย jam-nàai *vt.* distribute (pass out) ⚡

จิก jik *v.* peck (with a beak)

จิ๊กโก๋ jík-gǒo *n.* gigolo [คน kon]

จิ้งจก jîng-jòk *n.* house lizard [ตัว dtuua]

จิงโจ้ jing-jôo *n.* kangaroo [ตัว dtuua]

จิ้งหรีด jîng-rìit *n.* cricket (insect) [ตัว dtuua]

จิต jit *n.* mind [ดวง duuang]

จิตใจ jit-jai *n.* mind and spirit

จิตใต้สำนึก jìt-dtâai-sǎm-núk *n.* subconscious

จิตแพทย์ jìt-dtà~pɛ̂ɛt *n.* psychiatrist [คน kon]

จิตฟั่นเฟือน jìt-fân-fɯɯan *n.* schizophrenia

จิตรกร jìt-dtà~gɔɔn *n.* painter (artist) [คน kon]

จิตรกรรม jìt-dtà~gam *n.* painting (drawing) ⚡

จิตวิทยา jìt-dtà~wít-tá~yaa *n.* psychology [วิชา wí-chaa]

จินตนาการ jin-dtà~naa-gaan *n.* imagination (ability)

จิบ jìp *vt.* taste (sip)

จิ้ม jîm *v.* dip in, pick (dip into)

จิ๋ม jǐm *n.* pussy 💥, vagina 💥

จิ๋ว jǐu *adj.* tiny •

จี้ jîi *n.* pendant (necklace) [อัน an]

จี้ jîi *vt.* poke (with fingers, etc.), rob

จีน jiin *adj.* Chinese

จีน jiin *n.* China [ประเทศ bprà~têet]

จีนกลาง jiin-glaang *n.* Mandarin (language) [ภาษา paa-sǎa]

จีบ jìip *n.* frill (of a skirt)

จีบ jìip *v.* court (woo)

จีวร jii-wɔɔn *n.* robe of a Buddhist monk [ผืน pʉ̌ʉn]

จึง jʉng *adv.* therefore

จึง jʉng *conj.* so (therefore)

จืด jʉ̀ʉt *adj.* dull, flat in taste

จุ jù *vt.* hold (contain)

จุด jùt *clf.* for points, spots, etc.

จุด jùt *n.* dot, point (mark) [จุด jùt]

จุด jùt *vt.* light (ignite, e.g. candle)

จุดเชื่อมต่อ jùt-chʉ̂ʉam-dtɔ̀ɔ *n.* junction

(connecting point) [จุด jùt]

จุดด่าง jùt-dàang *n.* speck [จุด jùt]

จุดเด่น jùt-dèn *n.* highlight (illuminated spot) [จุด jùt]

จุดทศนิยม jùt-tót-sà~ní~yom *n.* decimal point [จุด jùt]

จุดบอด jùt-bɔ̀ɔt *n.* blind spot [จุด jùt]

จุดประสงค์ jùt-bprà~sǒng *n.* purpose (objective) [ข้อ kɔ̂ɔ]

จุดเริ่มต้น jùt-rɤ̂ɤm-dtôn *n.* origin (source, root), start (starting point) [จุด jùt]

จุดศูนย์กลาง jùt-sǔun-glaang *n.* focus (central point) [จุด jùt]

จุดสังเกต jùt-sǎng-gèet *n.* landmark (prominent spot) [จุด jùt]

จุดสำคัญ jùt-sǎm-kan *n.* essence (important element) [จุด jùt]

จุดสุดยอด jùt-sùt-yɔ̂ɔt *n.* orgasm (climax) [จุด jùt]

จุดสูงสุด jùt-sǔung-sùt *n.* pitch (highest point)

จุ้นจ้าน jûn-jâan *vi.* meddle

จุ่ม jùm *vt.* dip (into liquid)

จุลภาค jun-lá~pâak *n.* comma ✗ [ตัว dtuua]

จุลินทรีย์ jù-lin-sii *n.* microbe ❗

จู๋ jǔu *n.* penis ❀ [อัน an]

จูง juung *v.* lead by the hand, lead

จู้จี้ jûu-jîi *adj.* fussy (fastidious), particular

จูบ jùup *n.* kiss [อัน an]

จูบ jùup *v.* kiss

เจ jee *adj.* vegetarian

เจ้ jée *n.* older sister [คน kon]

เจ๊ง jéng *adj.* going out of business ❀

เจ๋ง jěng *adj.* cool (good) ❀

เจ๋ง jěng *interj.* awesome! ❀

เจ็ด jèt *numb.* seven

เจดีย์ jee-dii *n.* pagoda, stupa [องค์ ong]

เจตนา jèet-dtà~naa *adj.* intentional (on purpose)

เจตนา jèet-dtà~naa *v.* do on purpose

เจนโลก jeen-lôok *adj.* worldly (sophisticated)

เจ็บ jèp *vi.* hurt (pain: short-term, acute)

เจ็บใจ jèp-jai *vi.* mentally hurt

เจ็บปวด jèp-bpùuat *adj.* painful ❗

เจรจา jee-rá~jaa *v.* negotiate

เจริญ jà~rəən *adj.* civilized

เจริญ jà~rəən *v.* progress (develop), prosper

เจล jeo *n.* gel

เจอ jəə *vt.* meet (encounter) ❀

เจอกัน jəə-gan *vi.* meet (encounter)

เจ้า jâao *n.* lord (feudal) [คน kon]

เจ้าของ jâo-kǒong *n.* owner, proprietor [คน kon]

เจ้าของร้าน jâo-kǒong-ráan *n.* shop owner [คน kon]

เจ้าขุนมูลนาย jâo-kǔn-muun-naai *n.* bureaucrat [คน kon]

เจ้าชาย jâo-chaai *n.*

ก
ข
ค
ฆ
ง
จ
ฉ
ช
ซ
ฌ
ญ
ฎ
ฏ
ฐ
ฑ
ฒ
ณ
ด
ต
ถ
ท
ธ
น
บ
ป
ผ
ฝ
พ
ฟ
ภ
ม
ย
ร
ฤ
ล
ว
ศ
ษ
ส
ห
อ
ฮ

prince [องค์ ong]

เจ้าชู้ jâo-chúu *adj.* flirty

เจ้าตัว jâo-dtuua *n.*
person in question [คน
kon]

เจ้าทุกข์ jâao-túk *n.*
plaintiff ✱ [คน kon]

เจ้านาย jâo-naai *n.* boss,
master (owner, boss,
employer) [คน kon]

เจ้าบ่าว jâo-bàao *n.*
groom [คน kon]

เจ้าพนักงาน jâo-pá~nák-
ngaan *n.* officer, official
[คน kon]

เจ้าภาพ jâo-pâap *n.* host
(e.g. party, ceremony,
event) [คน kon]

เจ้าเล่ห์ jâo-lêe *adj.* sly,
tricky (cunning)

เจ้าโลก jâo-lôok *n.* penis
✱ [อัน an]

เจ้าสาว jâo-sǎao *n.* bride
[คน kon]

เจ้าหญิง jâo-yǐng *n.*
princess [องค์ ong]

เจ้าหน้าที่ jâo-nâa-tîi *n.*
authority (official), officer
(post-holder, staff,
official) [คน kon]

เจ้าหนี้ jâo-nîi *n.* creditor
[คน kon, ราย raai ⚡]

เจ้าอารมณ์ jâo-aa-rom
adj. moody
(temperamental)

เจ้าอาวาส jâo-aa-wâat *n.*
abbot [รูป rûup]

เจาะ jɔ̀ *v.* drill (cut a hole)

เจาะ jɔ̀ *vt.* pierce
(puncture)

เจาะจง jɔ̀-jong *vt.* specify

เจียระไน jiia-rá~nai *vt.*
facet (gem)

เจี๊ยว jíiao *n.* penis ✱ [อัน
an]

เจียวไข่ jiiao-kài *v.* make
an omelet

เจี๊ยวจ๊าว jíiao-jáao *adj.*
noisy ✱

แจก jὲɛk *vt.* hand out

แจกจ่าย jὲɛk-jàai *vt.* allot
(distribute)

แจกแจง jὲɛk-jɛɛng *v.*
explain thoroughly

แจกไพ่ jὲɛk-pâi *vi.* deal
(cards)

แจกัน jɛɛ-gan *n.* vase [ใบ
bai]

แจ้ง jɛ̂ɛng *adj.* clear
(obvious) ☙

แจ้ง jɛ̂ɛng *vt.* notify

(inform)

แจ้งความ jêɛng-kwaam *vt.* notify (inform, report), report (to the police)

แจ่ม jèm *adj.* bright, distinct

แจ่มแจ้ง jèm-jɛ̂ɛng *adj.* bright (explicit, clear) ‼

แจ่มใส jèm-sǎi *adj.* clear (weather)

แจ๋ว jěo *adj.* clear (transparent)

แจวเรือ jɛɛo-rɨɨa *vi.* row a boat

โจก jòok *n.* chief (leader) ☙ [คน kon]

โจ๊ก jóok *n.* rice porridge [ถ้วย tûai]

โจทก์ jòot *n.* plaintiff [คน kon]

โจทย์ jòot *n.* problem (mathematics) [ข้อ kɔ̂ɔ]

โจน joon *v.* jump ☙

โจม joom *n.* canopy [หลัง lǎng]

โจมตี joom-dtii *v.* attack (physically), raid

โจร joon *n.* robber [คน kon]

โจรกรรม joo-rá~gam *n.* robbery

โจรสลัด joon-sà~làt *n.* pirate [คน kon]

ใจ jai *n.* mind [ดวง duuang]

ใจกล้า jai-glâa *adj.* bold, brave

ใจกลางเมือง jai-glaang-mɨɨang *n.* downtown [แห่ง hɛ̀ng]

ใจกว้าง jai-gwâang *adj.* broad-minded

ใจความ jai-kwaam *n.* substance (gist, essence)

ใจแคบ jai-kɛ̂ɛp *adj.* narrow-minded

ใจง่าย jai-ngâai *adj.* cheap (e.g. women)

ใจชื้น jai-chɨ́ɨn *adj.* cheerful, relieved

ใจดี jai-dii *adj.* kind, kind-hearted

ใจเดียว jai-diiao *adj.* faithful (to lover)

ใจบุญ jai-bun *adj.* charitable

ใจเย็น jai-yen *adj.* calm (mind), cool-hearted

ใจเย็นๆ jai-yen-yen *interj.* calm down!, relax!

ใจร้อน jai-rɔ́ɔn *adj.* hasty

กขฃคฅฆง**จ**ฉชซฌญฎฏฐฑฒณดตถทธนบปผฝพฟภมยรฤลฦวศษสหฬอฮ

(impatient), short-tempered

ใจร้าย jai-ráai *adj.* cruel, mean

ใจเร็ว jai-reo *adj.* impulsive

ใจลอย jai-lɔɔi *adj.* absent-minded

ใจหาย jai-hǎai *adj.* stunned with fear

ฉ

ฉ chɔ̌ɔ *let.* ฉ. ฉิ่ง chɔ̌ɔ-chìng, a consonant of the Thai alphabet (high consonant) [ตัว dtuua]

ฉก chòk *vt.* strike (snake)

ฉกรรจ์ chà~gan *adj.* strong (body) ‼

ฉกาจ chà~gàat *adj.* bold, brave, daring

ฉนวน chà~nǔuan *n.* insulation (material) [ชิ้น chín, อัน an]

ฉบับ chà~bàp *clf.* for newspapers and documents

ฉบับ chà~bàp *n.* issue (edition) [ฉบับ chà~bàp]

ฉบับร่าง chà~bàp-râang *n.* draft (of written work) [ฉบับ chà~bàp]

ฉมวก chà~mùuak *n.* harpoon [เล่ม lêm]

ฉลอง chà~lɔ̌ɔng *v.* celebrate

ฉลาก chà~làak *n.* label (sign, tag) [ใบ bai, แผ่น pèn]

ฉลาด chà~làat *adj.* intelligent (clever)

ฉลาม chà~lǎam *n.* shark [ตัว dtuua]

ฉลุ chà~lù *v.* make an intricate pattern on a scroll

ฉลู chà~lǔu *n.* ox [ตัว dtuua]

ฉวย chǔuai *vt.* grab (snatch by force)

ฉ้อโกง chɔ̂ɔ-goong *vi.* cheat (e.g. on test) ‼

ฉอเลาะ chɔ̌ɔ-lɔ́ *vi.* speak cajolingly

ฉะ chà *v.* hit (strike)

ฉะฉาน chà~chǎan *adj.* fluent (clear)

ฉะเชิงเทรา chà~chəəng-sao *n.* Chachoengsao province [จังหวัด jang-wàt]

ฉัตรมงคล chàt-mong-kon *n.* celebration of Coronation Day [วัน wan]

 ฉัน chǎn *pron.* I (female speaker)

ฉัน chǎn *v.* eat ✿

ฉันท์ chǎn *n.* Thai verse form [บท bòt]

ฉันเพล chǎn-peen *vi.* have food before noon ✿

ฉับไว chàp-wai *adj.* prompt (quick)

ฉาก chàak *n.* carpenter's or draftsman's square [อัน an]

ฉาก chàak *n.* scene (in story) [ฉาก chàak]

ฉาง chǎang *n.* barn, silo [หลัง lǎng]

ฉ่าง chàang *n.* sound of clanking of metal objects

ฉาบ chàap *n.* cymbal (large) [ข้าง kâang (piece), คู่ kûu (pair)]

ฉาบปูน chàap-bpuun *vi.* plaster (fill with plaster)

ฉาย chǎai *v.* play (movie)

ฉาย chǎai *vt.* shine (point, e.g. flashlight)

ฉายหนัง chǎai-nǎng *v.* show a movie

ฉายา chǎa-yaa *n.* Pali name of a priest

ฉาว chǎao *adj.* widespread ✿⋙

ฉ่ำ chàm *adj.* damp, juicy (moist), wet (soaked)

ฉำฉา chǎm-chǎa *n.* wood of pine and other conifers [ต้น dtôn]

ฉิ่ง chìng *n.* cymbal (small) [ข้าง kâang (piece), คู่ kûu (pair)]

ฉิว chǐu *adj.* angry ✿⋙

ฉี่ chìi *vi.* pee ✿⋙, piss ✿⋙, urinate ✿⋙

ฉีก chìik *v.* rip, tear

ฉีกขาด chìik-kàat *vt.* lacerate (rip, tear)

ฉีด chìit *vt.* inject (liquid, medicine), spray

ฉุ chù *adj.* fat

ฉุกเฉิน chùk-chěən *adj.* critical (emergency)

ฉุด chùt *v.* haul (drag)

ฉุน chǔn *adj.* angry ✿⋙, strong (odor)

ฉุนเฉียว chǔn-chǐiao *adj.* furious

ฉูดฉาด chùut-chàat *adj.* gaudy (flashy)

เฉ chěe *adj.* deviated, slanted (tilted)

เฉดสี chèet-sǐi *n.* shade (color) [เฉด chèet]

เฉพาะ chà~pɔ́ *adj.*

การ ก ข ฃ ค ฅ ฆ ง จ **ฉ** ช ซ ฌ ญ ฎ ฏ ฐ ฑ ฒ ณ ด ต ถ ท ธ น บ ป ผ ฝ พ ฟ ภ ม ย ร ฤ ล ว ศ . ษ ส ห ฬ อ ฮ

particular (specific)

เฉย chǒoi *adj.* calm (still), impassive

เฉยๆ chǒoi-chǒoi *adj.* so-so

เฉยชา chǒoi-chaa *adj.* impersonal (lacking warmth)

เฉลิม chà~lěəm *vt.* commemorate

เฉลี่ย chà~lìia *adj.* par (average)

เฉลียว chà~lǐiao *adj.* truly wise or clever

เฉิดฉาย chə̀ət-chǎai *adj.* bright

เฉียง chǐiang *adj.* deflected

เฉียด chìiat *v.* just miss, pass near

เฉียบ chìiap *adj.* very acute

เฉียว chǐiao *adj.* strong (body)

เฉี่ยว chìiao *v.* pass swiftly

เฉือน chǔ̌an *v.* slash (slice)

เฉื่อย chù̂ai *adj.* inert (chemistry), sluggish

เฉื่อยชา chù̂ai-chaa *adj.* inert (sluggish), passive (not active)

แฉ chɛ̌ɛ *vt.* reveal

แฉก chɛ̀ɛk *adj.* jagged, notched

แฉล้ม chà~lɛ̂ɛm *adj.* lovely, pretty (beautiful)

แฉะ chɛ̀ *adj.* humid, watery (containing much water), wet 🔊

โฉนด chà~nòot *n.* deed (e.g. land), title (deed, e.g. land) [ฉบับ chà~bàp]

โฉบ chòop *vt.* swoop down on and snatch away

โฉมงาม chǒom-ngaam *adj.* beautiful

โฉลก chà~lòok *n.* chance 🔊, luck

ไฉไล chǎi-lai *adj.* pretty (beautiful) 🔊

ช

ช chɔɔ *let.* ช. ช้าง chɔɔ-cháang, a consonant of the Thai alphabet (low consonant) [ตัว dtuua]

ชก chók *v.* jab, punch

ชกต่อย chók-dtɔ̀i *vi.* box (fight) 🔊

ชกมวย chók-muuai *vi.* box (fight) 🔊

ชง chong *v.* soak in a

liquid

ชฎา chá~daa *n.* crown, headdress [อัน an]

ชดเชย chót-chəəi *v.* compensate

ชดใช้ chót-chái *vt.* repay (compensate)

ชน chon *v.* hit (crash into)

ชนกัน chon-gan *vi.* collide (hit), crash (e.g. car)

ชนชั้น chon-chán *n.* caste (class) [กลุ่ม glùm (group)]

ชนชาติ chon-châat *n.* race (nationality) [ชนชาติ chon-châat]

ชนบท chon-ná~bòt *adj.* rural

ชนบท chon-ná~bòt *n.* countryside [แห่ง hèng]

ชนะ chá~ná *v.* win (e.g. game, battle)

ชนิด chá~nít *n.* kind (sort, type, category) [ชนิด chá~nít]

ชบา chá~baa *n.* hibiscus [ดอก dɔ̀ɔk (flower), ต้น dtôn (plant)]

ชม chom *vt.* look at (admire) ⚠, praise (commend)

ชมเชย chom-chəəi *vt.* compliment ⚠

ชมพู chom-puu *adj.* pink

ชมพู่ chom-pûu *n.* rose apple [ลูก lûuk (fruit)]

ชมรม chom-rom *n.* club (association) [ชมรม chom-rom]

ชรา chá~raa *adj.* aged ⚠

ชล chon *n.* water ☙

ชลบุรี chon-bù~rii *n.* Chonburi province [จังหวัด jang-wàt]

ชลประทาน chon-lá~bprà~taan *vi.* irrigate ⚠

ช่วง chûang *n.* point (period)

ชวด chûat *n.* Year of the Rat

ชวด chûat *n.* great grandparent [คน kon]

ชวน chuuan *v.* invite

ช่วย chûai *v.* assist, help

ช่วยด้วย chûai-dûuai *interj.* help!

ช่วยตัวเอง chûuai-dtuua-eeng *vi.* masturbate ⚠

ช่วยเหลือ chûuai-lǔua *v.* abet, help

ช่วยเหลือ chûuai-lǔua *vt.* aid

ชวเลข chá~wá~lêek *n.*

shorthand

ช่อ chôo *n.* bunch (flowers) [ช่อ chôo]

ช็อค chók *adj.* shocked

ช็อค chók *vt.* shock

ช่อง chông *n.* channel (e.g. TV), opening (slot, gap) [ช่อง chông]

ช่องคลอด chông-klôot *n.* vagina ✖

ช่องแคบ chông-kêɛp *n.* strait [ช่อง chông]

ช่องทาง chông-taang *n.* opening (opportunity, space) [ช่อง chông]

ช่องระบาย chông-rá~baai *n.* outlet (vent) [ช่อง chông]

ช่องลม chông-lom *n.* vent (outlet for air) [ช่อง chông]

ช่องเล็ก chông-lék *n.* slot [ช่อง chông]

ช่องว่าง chông-wâang *n.* space (blank space) [ช่อง chông]

ช่อดอกไม้ chôo-dòɔk-máai *n.* bouquet [ช่อ chôo]

ช็อต chót *v.* electrocute (shock)

ช้อน chɔ́ɔn *n.* spoon [คัน kan]

ช้อนชา chɔ́ɔn-chaa *n.* teaspoon [คัน kan]

ช้อนตวง chɔ́ɔn-dtuuang *n.* measuring spoon [คัน kan]

ช้อนโต๊ะ chɔ́ɔn-dtó *n.* tablespoon [คัน kan]

ช้อนส้อม chɔ́ɔn-sɔ̂m *n.* spoon and fork [คู่ kûu (pair)]

ชอบ chɔ̂ɔp *adj.* fond (liking)

ชอบ chɔ̂ɔp *v.* like

ชอบกล chɔ̂ɔp-gon *adj.* strange

ชอบใจ chɔ̂ɔp-jai *adj.* amused (pleased)

ชอบที่สุด chɔ̂ɔp-tîi-sùt *adj.* favorite

ชอบธรรม chɔ̂ɔp-tam *adj.* righteous

ช็อปปิ้ง chɔ́p-bpîng *vi.* shop

ชอล์ก chɔ́k *n.* chalk [แท่ง têng]

ชะงัก chá~ngák *v.* stop abruptly

ชะเง้อ chá~ngə́ə *v.* stretch one's neck out to

see

ชะโงก chá~ngôok v. poke (one's head) out

ชะตา chá~dtaa n. fate (destiny), horoscope

ชะนี chá~nii n. gibbon [ตัว dtuua]

ชะลอตัว chá~lɔɔ-dtuua vi. slow down (become slower)

ชะแลง chá~lɛɛng n. crowbar, lever (device), pry [อัน an]

ชัก chák v. have spasms or convulsions, pull (haul, tug)

ชัก chák vt. weave (spin, e.g. web)

ชักโครก chák-krôok n. flush toilet [อัน an]

ชักจูง chák-juung v. lead (persuade)

ชักชวน chák-chuuan v. persuade (induce, invite)

ชักช้า chák-cháa vi. hesitate

ชักนำ chák-nam v. persuade (induce, invite)

ชักนำ chák-nam vi. urge (persuade)

ชักเย่อ chák-gà~yə̂ə n. tug-of-war

ชักใย chák-yai v. control behind the scenes ✺

ชักว่าว chák-wâao vi. fly a kite, masturbate (male) ✺

ชัง chang v. detest, hate ⤳

ชัง chang vt. dislike

ชั่ง châng vt. weigh (measure, e.g. on scale)

ชั่งใจ châng-jai v. weigh the pros and cons

ชัด chát adj. clear (easily seen), obvious, sharp (e.g. picture)

ชัดเจน chát-jeen adj. clear (obvious), distinct

ชัดแจ้ง chát-jɛ̂ɛng adj. clear ❗, obvious

ชั้น chán n. class (social, school), floor (of building), grade, layer, rack, shelf [ชั้น chán]

ชั้น chán pron. I (female speaker) ✺

ชั้นกลาง chán-glaang adj. intermediate

ชั้นเชิง chán-chəəng n. strategy (tactics), tactic (trick) [อัน an]

ชั้นต่ำ chán-dtàm adj. low class

ก
ข
ฃ
ค
ฅ
ฆ
ง
จ
ฉ
ช
ซ
ฌ
ญ
ฎ
ฏ
ฐ
ฑ
ฒ
ณ
ด
ต
ถ
ท
ธ
น
บ
ป
ผ
ฝ
พ
ฟ
ภ
ม
ย
ร
ฤ
ล
ฦ
ว
ศ
ษ
ส
ห
อ
ฮ

ชั้นนอก chán-nɔ̂ɔk *adj.* outer (exterior, external)

ชั้นใน chán-nai *n.* inner layer, the inside [ชั้น chán]

ชั้นบน chán-bon *n.* upper layer, upper story, upstairs [ชั้น chán]

ชั้นยอด chán-yɔ̂ɔt *adj.* first-class, top grade, leading

ชั้นลอย chán-lɔɔi *n.* mezzanine (of a building, theatre) [ชั้น chán]

ชั้นล่าง chán-lâang *adj.* downstairs

ชั้นล่าง chán-lâang *n.* downstairs, ground floor [ชั้น chán]

ชั้นสูง chán-sǔung *adj.* noble

ชันสูตรศพ chan-ná~sùut-sòp *v.* perform an autopsy

ชัยชนะ chai-chá~ná *n.* triumph (victory)

ชัยนาท chai-nâat *n.* Chainat province [จังหวัด jang-wàt]

ชัยภูมิ chai-yá~puum *n.* Chaiyaphum Province [จังหวัด jang-wàt]

ชั่วขณะ chûua-kà~nà *adj.* momentary, temporary

ชั่วขณะ chûua-kà~nà *n.* while

ชั่วคราว chûua-kraao *adj.* temporary

ชั่วครู่ chûua-krûu *adv.* awhile, briefly

ชั่วนิรันดร์ chûua-ní-ran *adj.* perpetual (everlasting) ♥

ชั่วโมง chûua-moong *n.* hour [ชั่วโมง chûua-moong]

ชั่วร้าย chûua-ráai *adj.* despicable, mean (evil), vicious (malicious)

ชา chaa *adj.* numb

ชา chaa *n.* tea (beverage) [ซอง sɔɔng (bag), ถ้วย tûuai (cup)]

ชา chaa *v.* feel numb

ช้า cháa *adj.* long, slow

ช้าๆ cháa-cháa *adv.* slowly

ช่าง châng *adv.* have a liking for, be prone to

ช่าง châng *n.* mechanic

[คน kon]

ช้าง cháang *n.* elephant [ตัว dtuua (wild), เชือก chûuak (tamed)]

ช่างกล châng-gon *n.* mechanic [คน kon]

ช่างก่อสร้าง châng-gɔ̀ɔ-sâang *n.* builder (construction worker) [คน kon]

ช่างเชื่อม châng-chûuam *n.* welder [คน kon]

ช่างตัดผม châng-dtàt-pǒm *n.* barber [คน kon]

ช่างตัดเสื้อ châng-dtàt-sûua *n.* dressmaker, tailor [คน kon]

ช่างทำผม châng-tam-pǒm *n.* hairdresser [คน kon]

ช้างน้ำ cháang-náam *n.* hippopotamus [ตัว dtuua]

ช่างประปา châng-bprà~bpaa *n.* plumber [คน kon]

ช้างเผือก cháang-pùuak *n.* white elephant [เชือก chûuak (tamed), ตัว dtuua (wild)]

ช่างฝีมือ châng-fǐi-mɯɯ *n.* craftsman (artisan) [คน kon]

ช่างไฟฟ้า châng-fai-fáa *n.* electrician [คน kon]

ช่างภาพ châng-pâap *n.* camera man [คน kon]

ช่างไม้ châng-máai *n.* carpenter [คน kon]

ช่างเหล็ก châng-lèk *n.* blacksmith [คน kon]

ชาดก chaa-dòk *n.* existence of the Lord Buddha [เรื่อง rûuang]

ชาติ châat *n.* nation [ชาติ châat]

ชาติก่อน châat-gɔ̀ɔn *n.* previous life [ชาติ châat]

ชาน chaan *n.* porch (without roof) [ชาน chaan]

ชานชาลา chaan-chaa-laa *n.* platform (e.g. train, bus) [ชาน chaan, แห่ง hɛ̀ng]

ชานเมือง chaan-mɯɯang *n.* outskirts [เขต kèet]

ชาม chaam *n.* bowl (food) [ใบ bai]

ชาย chaai *adj.* man

ชายคา chaai-kaa *n.* eaves

ชายจริงหญิงแท้ chaai-jing-yǐng-tɛ́ɛ *adj.* straight (heterosexual) ஐ

ก
ข
ฃ
ค
ฅ
ฆ
ง
จ
ฉ
ช
ซ
ฌ
ญ
ฎ
ฏ
ฐ
ฑ
ฒ
ณ
ด
ต
ถ
ท
ธ
น
บ
ป
ผ
ฝ
พ
ฟ
ภ
ม
ย
ร
ฤ
ล
ฦ
ว
ศ
ษ
ส
ห
อ
ฮ

ชายแดน chaai-dɛɛn *n.* border (e.g. country), frontier [แห่ง hɛ̀ng]

ชายทะเล chaai-tá~lee *adj.* seaside

ชายฝั่ง chaai-fàng *n.* coast, shore [แห่ง hɛ̀ng, ฝั่ง fàng]

ชายเสื้อ chaai-sûua *n.* hem

ชายโสด chaai-sòot *n.* bachelor (single man) [คน kon]

ชายหาด chaai-hàat *n.* beach [แห่ง hɛ̀ng]

ชาร์จ cháat *v.* charge (electricity) ●

ชาว chaao *n.* people (persons in general) ⚠ [ชาว chaao (race), กลุ่ม glùm ⚠ (group), พวก pûuak (group), คน kon (individual)]

ชาวเกาะ chaao-gɔ̀ *n.* islander [คน kon]

ชาวตะวันตก chaao-dtà~wan-dtòk *n.* westerner [คน kon]

ชาวต่างชาติ chaao-dtàang-châat *n.* foreigner [คน kon]

ชาวต่างด้าว chaao-dtàang-dâao *n.* alien (immigrant) [ชาว chaao]

ชาวไทย chaao-tai *n.* Thai (people) [คน kon]

ชาวนา chaao-naa *n.* farmer (rice) [คน kon]

ชาวบ้าน chaao-bâan *n.* villager [คน kon]

ชาวประมง chaao-bprà~mong *n.* fisherman ⚠ [คน kon]

ชาวพุทธ chaao-pút *n.* Buddhist [คน kon]

ชาวไร่ chaao-râi *n.* farmer (non-rice crop) [คน kon]

ช่ำชอง châm-chɔɔng *adj.* proficient (skillful)

ชำนาญ cham-naan *adj.* experienced, skillful

ชำร่วย cham-rûuai *n.* little gift [อัน an, ชิ้น chín]

ชำระ cham-rá *v.* pay ⚠

ชำระ cham-rá *vt.* cleanse ⚠

ชำรุด cham-rút *adj.* defective (damaged) ⚠

ชำแหละ cham-lὲ *v.* cut open

ชิ่ง chîng *v.* run away quickly ●

ชิงชัง ching-chang *v.* hate

ชิงช้า ching-cháa *n.* swing (to sit on) [อัน an]

ชิงช้าสวรรค์ ching-cháa-sà~wǎn *n.* Ferris wheel [เครื่อง krûuang]

ชิด chít *adj.* close (next to)

ชิน chin *adj.* accustomed to

ชิ้น chín *clf.* for piece

ชิ้น chín *n.* piece (of anything) [ชิ้น chín]

ชินกับ chin-gàp *adj.* accustomed to

ชิ้นไม้ chín-máai *n.* lumber [ชิ้น chín]

ชิ้นส่วน chín-sùuan *n.* part (machinery) [ชิ้น chín]

ชิพ chíp *n.* chip (e.g. computer) [ชิ้น chín]

ชิม chim *vt.* taste (eat, drink), try

ชิลลิ่ง chin-lîng *n.* shilling

ชี chii *n.* nun ● [คน kon]

ชี้ chíi *v.* point (with finger)

ชี้ตัว chíi-dtuua *vt.* identify (e.g. suspect)

ชีพ chîip *n.* life

ชีพจร chîip-pá~jɔɔn *n.* pulse (heartbeat)

ชีวประวัติ chii-wá-bprà~wàt *n.* biography [เรื่อง rûuang]

ชีววิทยา chii-wá-wít-tá~yaa *n.* biology [วิชา wí-chaa]

ชีวิต chii-wít *n.* life [ชีวิต chii-wít]

ชี้ให้เห็น chíi-hâi-hěn *vt.* indicate (point out)

ชื่น chûun *adv.* joyfully, happily, cheerfully

ชื้น chúun *adj.* damp, humid, moist

ชื่นชม chûun-chom *vt.* admire

ชื่อ chûu *n.* first name, name [ชื่อ chûu]

ชื่อตัว chûu-dtuua *n.* first name [ชื่อ chûu]

ชื่อเล่น chûu-lên *n.* nickname [ชื่อ chûu]

ชื่อเสียง chûu-sǐiang *n.* fame, renown

ชุด chút *clf.* for sets, groups of things, dresses, etc.

ก
ข
ค
ฅ
ฆ
ง
จ
ฉ
ช
ซ
ฌ
ญ
ฎ
ฏ
ฐ
ฑ
ฒ
ณ
ด
ต
ถ
ท
ธ
น
บ
ป
ผ
ฝ
พ
ฟ
ภ
ม
ย
ร
ฤ
ล
ฦ
ว
ศ
ษ
ส
ห
ฬ
อ
ฮ

ชุด chút *n.* batch (group), outfit (clothes) [ชุด chút]

ชุดนอน chút-nɔɔn *n.* nightgown [ตัว dtuua]

ชุดไพ่ chút-pâi *n.* deck (of cards) [สำรับ sǎm-ráp]

ชุดราตรี chút-raa-dtrii *n.* evening dress [ชุด chút]

ชุดว่ายน้ำ chút-wâai-náam *n.* swimsuit [ชุด chút]

ชุดสูท chút-sùut *n.* suit (garment) [ชุด chút]

ชุบ chúp *vt.* dip (into liquid)

ชุบชีวิต chúp-chii-wít *vt.* revive (bring back to life)

ชุ่ม chûm *adj.* moist, soaked (saturated, e.g. clothes, ground)

ชุมชน chum-chon *n.* settlement (community) [ชุมชน chum-chon]

ชุ่มชื่น chûm-chʉ̂ʉn *adj.* happy

ชุมทาง chum-taang *n.* junction (place where roads meet) [แห่ง hèng]

ชุมนุมกัน chum-num-gan *vi.* rally (gather)

ชุมพร chum-pɔɔn *n.* Chumphon province [จังหวัด jang-wàt]

ชุลมุน chun-lá~mun *adj.* chaotic

ชู chuu *v.* raise up high

ชู้ chúu *n.* adulterer/adulteress, lover (in extra-marital relationship) [คน kon]

ชูชีพ chuu-chîip *n.* buoy (float) [อัน an]

ชูรส chuu-rót *v.* enhance the flavor

เช็ค chék *n.* check (bank draft) [ใบ bai (piece), ฉบับ chà~bàp ! (piece)]

เช็ค chék *v.* check (verify)

เช็คเดินทาง chék-dəən-taang *n.* traveler's check [ใบ bai]

เช็ด chét *vt.* wipe (rub and clean)

เช่น chên *adv.* such as

เช่นกัน chên-gan *adv.* also

เช่นเคย chên-kəəi *adv.* as usual

เช่นเดียวกับ chên-diiao-gàp *adv.* same as

เช่นนี้ chên-níi *adj.* such

เช่นว่า chên-wâa *prep.* as mentioned

เชฟ chép *n.* chef ✸ [คน kon]

เชย chəəi *adj.* old-fashioned (outdated) ✸

เชลย chá~ləəi *n.* captive, prisoner [คน kon]

เช่า châo *v.* rent (from someone)

เช่า châo *vt.* hire (from someone, e.g. car, bike)

เช้า cháao *n.* morning

เช่า_ต่อ châo-_-dtɔ̀ɔ *vt.* sublet

เช้ามืด cháao-mûut *n.* dawn/daybreak

เชิงกราน chəəng-graan *n.* pelvis [ชิ้น chín]

เชิงเทียน chəəng-tiian *n.* candlestick [อัน an]

เชิญ chəən *v.* invite

เชิญชวน chəən-chuuan *v.* invite ❗

เชิดหุ่น châət-hùn *v.* perform puppet dance

เชียงราย chiiang-raai *n.* Chiang Rai province [จังหวัด jang-wàt]

เชียงใหม่ chiiang-mài *n.* Chiang Mai province

[จังหวัด jang-wàt]

เชียร์ chiia *vi.* cheer (make sound) ✸

เชี่ยว chîiao *adj.* rapid (e.g. river)

เชี่ยวชาญ chîiao-chaan *adj.* proficient (skillful)

เชื่อ chûua *v.* believe (in something)

เชื้อ chúua *n.* race (lineage) [เชื้อ chúua]

เชือก chûuak *n.* rope, string [เส้น sên (cord)]

เชื่อง chûuang *adj.* docile, tame (animal)

เชื่องช้า chûuang-cháa *adj.* sluggish

เชื่อใจ chûua-jai *vt.* rely on

เชื้อชาติ chúua-châat *n.* race (of human) [เชื้อชาติ chúua-châat]

เชื่อด chûuat *v.* cut forcefully (slice)

เชื่อถือ chûua-tǔu *vt.* trust (in ability)

เชื่อถือได้ chûua-tǔu-dâai *adj.* credible

เชื่อฟัง chûua-fang *v.* obey

กขฃคฅฆงจฉชซฌญฎฏฐฑฒณดตถทธนบปผฝพฟภมยรฤลฦวศษสหฬอฮ

เชื่อม chûuam *v.* cook in thick syrup

เชื่อมต่อกัน chûuam-dtɔ̀ɔ-gan *vi.* connect (join)

เชื้อรา chúua-raa *n.* fungus (e.g. infectious) [ตัว dtuua]

เชื้อโรค chúua-rôok *n.* bacteria, germ [ชนิด chá~nít]

เชื้อสาย chúua-sǎai *n.* family line

เชื้อหมัก chúua-màk *n.* yeast (e.g. baking, brewing) ‼ [เชื้อ chúua]

แช่ chɛ̂ɛ *v.* soak (in container, tub)

แช่ง chɛ̂ŋ *v.* put a curse

แชมพู chɛm-puu *n.* shampoo [ขวด kùuat (bottle)]

แช่เย็น chɛ̂ɛ-yen *v.* refrigerate

โชค chôok *n.* luck

โชคชะตา chôok-chá~dtaa *n.* fate (destiny)

โชคดี chôok-dii *adj.* lucky

โชติ chôot *n.* prosperity (state of growth with rising profits)

โชว์ choo *vi.* show (be visible) ✎

ใช่ châi *idm.* all right (yes), that's right

ใช้ chái *v.* spend (expend)

ใช้ chái *vt.* use

ใช้ได้ chái-dâai *adj.* usable (utilizable), valid (useable)

ใช้แล้ว chái-lɛ́ɛo *adj.* used (has been used)

ใช้เวลา chái-wee-laa *vi.* spend time, take time

ใช้_หมด chái-_-mòt *vt.* use up

ไช chai *vt.* form by drilling or digging

ไชโย chai-yoo *interj.* bravo!, cheers!

ซ

ซ rɔɔ *let.* ซ. โซ่ rɔɔ-sôo, a consonant of the Thai alphabet (low consonant) [ตัว dtuua]

ซด sót *v.* slurp (e.g. soup)

ซน son *adj.* naughty

ซบเซา sóp-sao *adj.* sluggish (business)

ซบเซา sóp-sao *vi.* stagnate (cease to be active)

ซอ ซɔɔ *n.* fiddle (violin) [คัน kan]

ซอก sɔ̂ɔk *n.* nook [ซอก sɔ̂ɔk]

ซอง sɔɔng *clf.* for envelopes, cases, small packs, e.g. cigarette, ketchup, etc.

ซอง sɔɔng *n.* envelope [ซอง sɔɔng]

ซอง sɔɔng *n.* case (pouch) [ซอง sɔɔng, อัน an ●]

ซ่อง sɔ̂ng *n.* brothel, whorehouse [แห่ง hɛ̀ng]

ซ่อน sɔ̂n *v.* hide

ซ่อน sɔ̂n *vt.* conceal (hide), shield (hide)

ซ่อนเร้น sɔ̂n-rén *vt.* hide (conceal)

ซ่อนหา sɔ̂n-hǎa *n.* hide-and-seek

ซอฟต์แวร์ sɔ́ɔp-wɛɛ *n.* software [โปรแกรม bproo-grɛɛm]

ซอฟท์บอล sɔ́ɔp-bɔn *n.* softball (game) [เกม geem]

ซ่อม sɔ̂m *vt.* fix (repair), service (repair)

ซ้อม sɔ́ɔm *v.* practice, rehearse

ซ่อมแซม sɔ̂m-sɛɛm *vt.* mend (repair)

ซอย sɔɔi *n.* alley, lane, soi [ซอย sɔɔi]

ซอส sɔ́ɔt *n.* sauce [ขวด kùuat (bottle)]

ซัก sák *vi.* inquire ☞

ซักผ้า sák-pâa *vi.* wash clothes

ซักฟอก sák-fɔ̂ɔk *vt.* launder (e.g. money)

ซักรีด sák-rîit *vt.* launder (wash and iron)

ซักแห้ง sák-hêng *vt.* dry-clean

ซัด sát *vi.* dash (rush)

ซับซ้อน sáp-sɔ́ɔn *adj.* complex, complicated

ซับใน sáp-nai *n.* lining (inner layer) [ชิ้น chín]

ซ่า sâa *adj.* tingling

ซาก sâak *n.* dead body, remains (of body), wreck (wreckage) [ซาก sâak]

ซากศพ sâak-sòp *n.* corpse [ซาก sâak]

ซาชิมิ saa-chí~mí *n.* sashimi [ชิ้น chín]

ซาดิสต์ saa-dìt *adj.* sadistic

ซาตาน saa-dtaan *n.* Satan [ตน dton]

ซ่าน sâan *v.* permeate

(penetrate through)

ซ้าย sáai *adj.* left

ซาลาเปา saa-laa-bpao *n.* steamed, stuffed bun [ใบ bai, ลูก lûuk]

ซ้ำ sám *v.* repeat

ซ้ำซาก sám-sâak *adj.* monotonous (repetitious)

ซ้ำเติม sám-dtəəm *vi.* rub it in

ซิ sí *part.* intensive to modify a verb in the imperative mood

ซิกแซก sík-sék *adj.* zigzag ✦

ซิการ์ sí-gâa *n.* cigar [มวน muuan]

ซิ่ง sîng *adj.* brave and hip in expressing oneself ✦

ซิ่น sîn *n.* sarong [ผืน pʉ̌ʉn, ตัว dtuua]

ซิป síp *n.* zip, zipper [อัน an, เส้น sên]

ซิลิคอน sí-lí-kɔɔn *n.* silicon

ซี่ sîi *clf.* for teeth, ribs, bars of a cage

ซีกโลก sîik-lôok *n.* hemisphere (of the globe) [ซีก sîik]

ซีเกมส์ sii-geem *n.* SEA

GAMES [ครั้ง kráng]

ซี่โครง sîi-kroong *n.* rib (bone) [ซี่ sîi]

ซีด sîit *adj.* pale

ซีดเซียว sîit-siiao *adj.* withered (pale) ⚠

ซีอิ๊ว sii-íu *n.* soy sauce/ soybean sauce [ขวด kùuat (bottle)]

ซึง sʉng *n.* northern Thai stringed instrument [คัน kan]

ซึ่ง sʉ̂ng *pron.* which ⚠

ซึ้ง sʉ́ng *adj.* profound (deep, intensive)

ซึ้ง sʉ́ng *n.* kind of food steamer [ใบ bai]

ซึ่งกันและกัน sʉ̂ng-gan-lɛ́-gan *adj.* mutual

ซึม sʉm *vt.* absorb

ซึมซาบ sʉm-sâap *v.* permeate (penetrate through)

ซื่อ sʉ̂ʉ *adj.* truthful (of person)

ซื้อ sʉ́ʉ *v.* buy, purchase

ซื้อของ sʉ́ʉ-kɔ̌ɔng *vi.* shop

ซื้อขาย sʉ́ʉ-kǎai *v.* trade (buy and sell, do

business)

ชื่อตรง sûu-dtrong *adj.* honest

ชื่อบื้อ sûu-bûu *adj.* foolish (silly) •

ซื่อสัตย์ sûu-sàt *adj.* loyal

ซุกซน súk-son *adj.* mischievous (naughty)

ซุง sung *n.* log (timber) [ท่อน tɔ̂n]

ซุบซิบ súp-síp *v.* whisper

ซุป súp *n.* soup [ถ้วย tûuai (bowl)]

ซุ่มโจมตี sûm-joom-dtii *vt.* ambush

ซุ่มซ่าม sûm-sâam *adj.* careless •, clumsy •

ซูบซีด sûup-sîit *adj.* emaciated and pale

ซูบผอม sûup-pɔ̌ɔm *adj.* pale and skinny

ซูมเข้า suum-kâo *vi.* zoom in •

ซูมออก suum-ɔ̀ɔk *v.* zoom out •

เซ็กซ์หมู่ sék-mùu *n.* orgy (sexual activity)

เซ็กซี่ sék-sîi *adj.* sexy

เซ็ง seng *adj.* dull (bored, boring) •, tasteless

(lacking flavor)

เซต sét *n.* set (of sports games) [เซต sét]

เซ็น sen *vi.* sign (one's name)

เซ่น sên *v.* make offering or sacrifice to the spirit

เซ็นชื่อใน sen-chûu-nai *vt.* execute (sign)

เซ็นเซอร์ sen-sôə *v.* censor

เซ็นต์ sen *n.* cent [เซ็นต์ sen]

เซรุ่ม see-rûm *n.* serum

เซลเซียส seo-sîiat *n.* Celsius [องศา ong-sǎa]

เซลล์ seo *n.* cell (in the body) [เซลล์ seo]

เซ่อ sôə *adj.* foolish (silly) •, stupid •

เซ้าซี้ sáo-síi *vi.* persist (insist)

เซียมซี siiam-sii *n.* wooden lots shaken to tell fortune in Chinese tradition [ใบ bai]

เซียว siiao *adj.* wrinkled

แซนด์วิช sɛɛn-wít *n.* sandwich [อัน an]

แซ่บ sêp *adj.* delicious •

โซ่ sôo *n.* chain (metal)

[เส้น sên, สาย sǎai]

โซเซ soo-see *vi.* stagger (walk unsteadily)

โซดา soo-daa *n.* soda

โซฟา soo-faa *n.* sofa [ตัว dtuua]

ไซ sai *n.* fish trap [ลูก lûuk]

ไซ้ sái *adj.* whatsoever ☙

ไซ้ sái *vi.* dig for food with the beak

ไซโคลน sai-kloon *n.* cyclone

ไซนัส sai-nát *n.* sinus [โพรง proong]

ฌ

ฌ choo *let.* ฌ. กะเฌอ gà~chəə, a consonant of the Thai alphabet (low consonant) [ตัว dtuua]

ฌาน chaan *n.* sect in Buddhism, transcendent insight

ญ

ญ yoo *let.* ญ. หญิง yǐng, a consonant of the Thai alphabet (low consonant) [ตัว dtuua]

ญวน yuuan *adj.* Vietnamese ●

ญัตติ yát-dtì *n.* motion (formal proposal) ❗ [ข้อ kôo]

ญาณ yaan *n.* transcendent insight

ญาติ yâat *n.* kin, relative (family) [คน kon]

ญี่ปุ่น yîi-bpùn *n.* Japan [ประเทศ bprà~têet]

ฎ

ฎ doo *let.* ฎ. ชฎา doo-chá~daa, a consonant of the Thai alphabet (mid consonant) [ตัว dtuua]

ฎีกา dii-gaa *n.* petition (to the Supreme Court) ✕ [ใบ bai, ฉบับ chà~bàp]

ฏ

ฏ dtoo *let.* ฏ. ปฏัก dtoo-bpà~dtàk, a consonant of the Thai alphabet (mid consonant) [ตัว dtuua]

ฐ

ฐ tǒo *let.* ฐ. ฐาน tǒo-tǎan, a consonant of the Thai alphabet (high consonant) [ตัว dtuua]

ฐาน tǎan *n.* base (foundation), platform (pedestal) [ฐาน tǎan]

ฐานข้อมูล tǎan-kɔ̂ɔ-muun *n.* database ✗ [ชุด chút]

ฐานทัพ tǎan-táp *n.* base (military) [แห่ง hὲng]

ฐานะ tǎa-ná *n.* status (social rank) [ฐานะ tǎa-ná]

ฐานันดร tǎa-nan-dɔɔn *n.* rank of nobility, title

ฐิติ tí-dtì *n.* certainty, status, way of living

ฑ

ฑ tɔɔ *let.* ฑ. มณโฑ tɔɔ-mon-too, a consonant of the Thai alphabet (low consonant) [ตัว dtuua]

ฒ

ฒ tɔɔ *let.* ฒ. ผู้เฒ่า tɔɔ-pûu-tâo, a consonant of the Thai alphabet (low consonant) [ตัว dtuua]

เฒ่า tâo *adj.* very old

เฒ่าแก่ tâo-gὲɛ *n.* go-between who arranges a marriage [คน kon]

เฒ่าหัวงู tâo-hǔua-nguu *n.* dirty old man ☀ [คน kon]

ณ

ณ nɔɔ *let.* ณ. เณร nɔɔ-neen, a consonant of the Thai alphabet (low consonant) [ตัว dtuua]

ณ ná *prep.* by ⚡, in (by, at) ☜, near, on (at) ☜

เณร neen *n.* Buddhist novice [รูป rûup]

ด

ด dɔɔ *let.* ด. เด็ก dɔɔ-dèk, a consonant of the Thai alphabet (mid consonant) [ตัว dtuua]

ดง dong *n.* jungle ☜ [แห่ง hὲng, ดง dong]

ด้น dôn *v.* sew a seam by hand

ดนตรี don-dtrii *n.* music

ดม dom *vt.* smell (sniff)

ดรรชนี dàt-chá~nii see ดัชนี

ดลใจ don-jai *v.* motivate (inspire)

ดวง duuang *clf.* for stars, lights, stamps

ดวง duuang *n.* round object

ดวง duuang *n.* fortune (fate), luck

ดวงจันทร์ duuang-jan *n.*

moon [ดวง duuang]

ดวงใจ duuang-jai *n.* heart [ดวง duuang]

ดวงชะตา duuang-chá~ dtaa see ดวง

ดวงตา duuang-dtaa *n.* eye [ดวง duuang]

ดวงอาทิตย์ duuang-aa-tít *n.* sun [ดวง duuang]

ด่วน dùuan *adj.* express, pressing (urgent)

ด้วน dûuan *adj.* amputated

ด้วน dûuan *v.* cut short

ด้วย dûuai *adv.* also, as well, too

ด้วย dûuai *prep.* by (using, e.g. fork, hand), on (by means of), with (by the use of, e.g. fork)

ด้วยกัน dûuai-gan *adv.* together (in company with)

ด้วยตัวเอง dûuai-dtuua-eeng *adv.* by oneself

ดอก dɔ̀ɔk *clf.* e.g. flowers, nails, keys

ดอก dɔ̀ɔk *n.* flower (blossom) [ดอก dɔ̀ɔk]

ดอกจัน dɔ̀ɔk-jan *n.* asterisk symbol (*) [ตัว dtuua]

ดอกจันทน์ dɔ̀ɔk-jan *n.* mace [ดอก dɔ̀ɔk]

ดอกจิก dɔ̀ɔk-jìk *n.* club (card suit)

ดอกตูม dɔ̀ɔk-dtuum *n.* bud (undeveloped flower) [ดอก dɔ̀ɔk]

ด็อกเตอร์ dɔ́k-dtə̀ə *n.* Ph.D. (person) [คน kon]

ดอกทอง dɔ̀ɔk-tɔɔng *n.* slut ⚥ [คน kon]

ดอกบัว dɔ̀ɔk-buua *n.* lotus [ดอก dɔ̀ɔk]

ดอกเบี้ย dɔ̀ɔk-bîia *n.* interest (for a loan)

ดอกผล dɔ̀ɔk-pǒn *n.* harvest (crop)

ดอกฝิ่น dɔ̀ɔk-fìn *n.* poppy (opium) [ดอก dɔ̀ɔk (flower), ต้น dtôn (tree)]

ดอกไม้ dɔ̀ɔk-máai *n.* flower (blossom) [ดอก dɔ̀ɔk]

ดอกไม้ไฟ dɔ̀ɔk-mái-fai *n.* firework [ตับ dtàp (row), ลูก lûuk, นัด nát]

ดอกยาง dɔ̀ɔk-yaang *n.* tread (for tires or shoes)

ดอง dɔɔng *adj.* pickled

ดอง dɔɔng *v.* pickle

ดอนเมือง dɔɔn-mɯɯang

pron. Don Mueang airport

ดอย dɔɔi *n.* hill [ลูก lûuk]

ด้อยพัฒนา dɔ̂ɔi-pát-tá~naa *adj.* undeveloped

ดอยสะเก็ด dɔɔi-sà~gèt *n.* Doi Saket district

ดอยอินทนนท์ dɔɔi-in-tá~non *n.* Doi Inthanon mountain [ดอย dɔɔi]

ดอลล่าร์ dɔn-lâa *n.* dollar (bill) [ใบ bai]

ดัก dàk *vt.* trap

ดักแด้ dàk-dɛ̂ɛ *n.* cocoon (larvae) [ตัว dtuua]

ดัง dang *adj.* famous, loud

ดั่ง dàng *adj.* like ☜

ดังกล่าว dang-glàao *adv.* as mentioned

ดั้งจมูก dâng-jà~mùuk *n.* bridge of nose [ดั้ง dâng]

ดังเช่น dang-chên *conj.* for example

ดั้งเดิม dâng-dəəm *adj.* original, traditional

ดังต่อไปนี้ dang-dtɔ̀ɔ-bpai-níi *adv.* as follows

ดังที่ dang-tîi *conj.* as

ดังนั้น dang-nán *adv.*

therefore

ดังนั้น dang-nán *conj.* so (therefore)

ดังนี้ dang-níi *adv.* thus

ดัชนี dàt-chá~nii *n.* index [ตัว dtuua]

ดัด dàt *vt.* bend

ดัดง่าย dàt-ngâai *adj.* pliable (bendable)

ดัดจริต dàt-jà~rìt *adj.* pretentious ☜

ดัดแปลง dàt-bplɛɛng *vt.* adapt (modify), qualify (modify or limit, e.g. statement)

ดัน dan *v.* poke (push), press (push forward)

ดับ dàp *adj.* extinct (e.g. fire, volcano), inactive (e.g. a volcano)

ดับ dàp *vi.* die, lose one's fame

ดับ dàp *vt.* blow out (e.g. candle), extinguish (put out)

ดับกระหาย dàp-grà~hǎai *vi.* quench thirst

ดับเพลิง dàp-pləəng *v.* put out fire ❗

ดับไฟ dàp-fai *v.* put out fire

ด่า dàa *v.* curse

ด่า dàa *vt.* scold

ดาก dàak *n.* anus ⚥

ด่าง dàang *n.* alkali

ดาดฟ้า dàat-fáa *n.* deck (e.g. ship) [แห่ง hèng, ดาดฟ้า dàat-fáa]

ด่าน dàan *n.* official station or post [ด่าน dàan]

ด้าน dâan *adj.* dull

ด้าน dâan *n.* face, side (surface) [ด้าน dâan]

ด้านข้าง dâan-kâang *n.* side (lateral part) [ข้าง kâang]

ด้านซ้าย dâan-sáai *n.* left (side) [ด้าน dâan]

ด้านนอก dâan-nɔ̂ɔk *adv.* outward (outside)

ด้านใน dâan-nai *n.* inside [แห่ง hèng, ที่ tîi]

ดาบ dàap *n.* sword [เล่ม lêm]

ดาม daam *vt.* strengthen (brace)

ด้าม dâam *n.* handle [อัน an, ด้าม dâam]

ดาย daai *v.* cut away, mow

ด้าย dâai *n.* thread (for sewing) [เส้น sên (string)]

ดารา daa-raa *n.* star (in a movie) [คน kon]

ดาราศาสตร์ daa-raa-sàat *n.* astronomy [วิชา wí-chaa]

ดาว daao *n.* star (in the sky) [ดวง duuang]

ดาวเคราะห์ daao-krɔ́ *n.* planet [ดวง duuang]

ดาวตก daao-dtòk *n.* meteor, shooting star [ดวง duuang]

ดาวเทียม daao-tiiam *n.* satellite (man-made) [ดวง duuang]

ดาวน์โหลด daao-lòot *v.* download

ดาวบริวาร daao-bɔɔ-rí~waan *n.* satellite (astronomy) [ดวง duuang]

ดาวเรือง daao-ruuang *n.* marigold [ดอก dɔ̀ɔk]

ดาวฤกษ์ daao-rɤ̂ɤk *n.* fixed star [ดวง duuang]

ดาวหาง daao-hǎang *n.* comet [ดวง duuang]

ดำ dam *adj.* black

ดำน้ำ dam-náam *vi.* dive

ดำเนินการ dam-nəən-gaan *vi.* process

(proceed)

ดำเนินคดี dam-nəən-ká~dii *vt.* indict (charge)

ดิค dìk *n.* dictionary • [เล่ม lêm]

ดิฉัน dì~chǎn *pron.* I (female speaker) !

ดิชั้น dì~chán *pron.* I (female speaker) •

ดิน din *n.* earth (ground, soil), ground (soil)

ดิน din *n.* dirt (soil) [กอง gɔɔng, ก้อน gɔ̂ɔn]

ดิ้น dîn *vi.* dance (disco, no step) •

ดินแดน din-dɛɛn *n.* land !, territory (boundary) [แห่ง hɛ̀ng]

ดินถล่ม din-tà~lòm *n.* landslide, mudslide

ดิ้นรน dîn-ron *vi.* struggle

ดินระเบิด din-rá~bə̀ət *n.* dynamite [ลูก lûuk]

ดินสอ din-sɔ̌ɔ *n.* pencil [แท่ง tɛ̂ng]

ดินสอสี din-sɔ̌ɔ-sǐi *n.* crayon [แท่ง tɛ̂ng]

ดินเหนียว din-nǐiao *n.* clay (soil) [ก้อน gɔ̂ɔn (chunk)]

ดิบ dìp *adj.* raw (unripe, uncooked, crude)

ดี dii *adj.* fine (e.g. good, quality)

ดี dii *n.* gallbladder [ถุง tǔng]

ดีกว่า dii-gwàa *adj.* better (than something)

ดีกว่า dii-gwàa *adv.* rather (instead)

ดีกัน dii-gan *adj.* reconciled

ดีขึ้น dii-kûn *adj.* better (than before)

ดีใจ dii-jai *adj.* glad, happy

ดีใจ dii-jai *vi.* rejoice

ดีซ่าน dii-sâan *n.* jaundice [โรค rôok]

ดีเซล dii-seo *n.* diesel (gasoline)

ดีที่สุด dii-tîi-sùt *adj.* best

ดีบุก dii-bùk *n.* tin (mineral) [แร่ rɛ̂ɛ]

ดีพอ dii-pɔɔ *adj.* good enough

ดีมาก dii-mâak *adj.* very good

ดีเลิศ dii-lə̂ət *adj.* ideal (excellent), magnificent

ดึก dùk *adv.* late at night

ดึง dʉng *vt.* tug (pull)

ดึงดูด dɯng-dùut *vt.* draw in (attract, e.g. customers)

ดึงดูดใจ dɯng-dùut-jai *vt.* appeal to (attract)

ดื่ม dùɯm *v.* drink

ดื้อ dûɯ *adj.* naughty

ดื้อรั้น dûɯ-rán *adj.* stubborn

ดุ dù *adj.* tough (fierce, violent, mean)

ดุกดิก dùk-dìk *vi.* move about

ดุด่า dù-dàa *vt.* scold

ดุมล้อ dum-lɔ́ɔ *n.* hub (wheel) [ดุม dum]

ดุร้าย dù-ráai *adj.* savage (fierce)

ดุล dun *n.* balance (accounting)

ดู duu *v.* look (watch)

ดู duu *vt.* look at, view (watch, see)

ดูด dùut *v.* suck

ดูดซึม dùut-sɯm *vt.* absorb ❗

ดูดฝุ่น dùut-fùn *v.* vacuum (use a vacuum cleaner on)

ดูถูก duu-tùuk *vt.* insult (look down on)

ดูแล duu-lɛɛ *vt.* keep an eye on, care for (take care of)

ดูหมิ่น duu-mìn *vt.* scorn (disdain)

ดูเหมือน duu-mɯ̌an *vt.* look like

เด็ก dèk *n.* child (young person), kid [คน kon]

เด็กๆ dèk-dèk *n.* children [คน kon]

เด็กกำพร้า dèk-gam-práa *n.* orphan [คน kon]

เด็กชาย dèk-chaai *n.* boy [คน kon]

เด็กอ่อน dèk-ɔ̀ɔn *n.* baby, infant [คน kon]

เด้ง dêng *vi.* spring (bounce)

เด็ด dèt *vt.* nip off, snap apart

เด็ดขาด dèt-kàat *adj.* absolute (e.g. power, ruler)

เดท dèet *v.* date (romantic) ❖

เด่นชัด dèn-chát *adj.* apparent, obvious

เดา dao *v.* guess (wild)

เดิน dəən *vi.* operate (e.g. equipment, machine) ❖

walk

เดินทาง dəən-taang *vi.* travel

เดินทางไป dəən-taang-bpai *vt.* travel to

เดินป่า dəən-bpàa *vi.* trek (hike)

เดินผ่าน dəən-pàan *v.* pass by (walk past)

เดินเรือ dəən-ruua *vi.* navigate (ship)

เดินละเมอ dəən-lá~məə *vi.* sleepwalk

เดินเล่น dəən-lên *vi.* go for a walk, stroll

เดินหนี dəən-nǐi *vt.* walk away from

เดิมพัน dəəm-pan *n.* bet (wager) [ครั้ง kráng]

เดียว diiao *adj.* one (alone), sole

เดียว diiao *adv.* one

เดี่ยว dìiao *adv.* solo

เดี๋ยว dǐiao *adv.* in a moment

เดี๋ยว dǐiao *interj.* just a second!

เดียวกัน diiao-gan *adj.* same

เดี๋ยวนี้ dǐiao-níi *adv.* now

เดี๊ยะ día *adv.* exactly (just perfectly) ✸

เดือด dùuat *vi.* boil

เดือดดาล dùuat-daan *vi.* rage ☙

เดือน duuan *n.* month [เดือน duuan]

เดือย duuai *n.* spur (for horse, of rooster) [เดือย duuai]

แดก dɛ̀ɛk *v.* eat 💣

แดกดัน dɛ̀ɛk-dan *adj.* ironic (sarcastic) ✸

แดง dɛɛng *adj.* red

แดด dɛ̀ɛt *n.* sunlight ✸

แดดออก dɛ̀ɛt-ɔ̀ɔk *adj.* sunny (bright)

โด่ง dòong *adj.* high up in the air

โดด dòot *v.* jump ✸

โดดเด่น dòot-dèn *adj.* conspicuous

โดดเดี่ยว dòot-dìiao *adj.* lone, solitary

โดน doon *v.* strike (hit)

โดย dooi *prep.* by (created by), by (vehicle, e.g. car, plane)

โดยการสุ่ม dooi-gaan-sùm *adj.* random

ก
ข
ฃ
ค
ฅ
ฆ
ง
จ
ฉ
ช
ซ
ฌ
ญ
ฎ
ฏ
ฐ
ฑ
ฒ
ณ
ด
ต
ถ
ท
ธ
น
บ
ป
ผ
ฝ
พ
ฟ
ภ
ม
ย
ร
ฤ
ล
ว
ศ
ษ
ส
ห
ฬ
อ
ฮ

โดยเฉพาะ dooi-chà~pɔ́ *adj.* specific

โดยตรง dooi-dtrong *adv.* directly

ใด dai *adj.* any (whatsoever) ⚡, whatever

ใด dai *adv.* what ⚡

ใด dai *pron.* which

ได้ dâai *aux.* can (able to)

ได้ dâai *vt.* able to, get (take, receive), obtain (get, gain)

ได้กำไร dâi-gam-rai *vt.* earn (get as profit)

ได้_คืน dâai-_-kɯɯn *vt.* regain (get back)

ได้ดี dâai-dii *adj.* become successful ⚡

ไดโนเสาร์ dai-noo-sǎo *n.* dinosaur [ตัว dtuua]

ได้_มา dâi-_-maa *vt.* obtain (get, gain)

ได้ยิน dâi-yin *v.* hear

ได้รับ dâi-ráp *vt.* receive

ต

ต dtɔɔ *let.* ต. เต่า dtɔɔ-dtào, a consonant of the Thai alphabet (mid consonant) [ตัว dtuua]

ตก dtòk *vi.* crash (e.g. plane, stock market), fall (drop), set (sun)

ตก dtòk *vt.* miss (e.g. the train, plane)

ตกใจ dtòk-jai *adj.* startled

ตกแต่ง dtòk-dtɛ̀ng *v.* decorate

ตกปลา dtòk-bplaa *vi.* fish (catch fish)

ตกลง dtòk-long *vi.* agree (accept, promise), drop, fall, okay/O.K.

ตกหลุมรัก dtòk-lǔm-rák *vi.* fall in love

ตด dtòt *vi.* fart

ตน dton *n.* body (self)

ต้น dtôn *adj.* beginning

ต้น dtôn *clf.* for trees, plants

ต้น dtôn *n.* stalk (trunk) [ต้น dtôn]

ต้นกำเนิด dtôn-gam-nə̀ət *n.* birth (origin) [แห่ง hɛ̀ng]

ต้นขา dtôn-kǎa *n.* thigh [คู่ kûu (pair)]

ต้นคอ dtôn-kɔɔ *n.* nape of neck

ต้นฉบับ dtôn-chà~bàp *n.* manuscript (original copy) [ฉบับ chà~bàp]

ต้นน้ำ dtôn-náam *n.* spring (water source) [แห่ง hèng]

ต้นไม้ dtôn-máai *n.* plant, tree [ต้น dtôn]

ตนเอง dton-eeng *pron.* oneself

ตบ dtòp *vt.* slap, smack

ตบตา dtòp-dtaa *v.* bluff

ตบมือ dtòp-mɯɯ *v.* clap hands

ตม dtom *n.* mud

ต้ม dtôm *vt.* deceive ✷, boil

ตรง dtrong *adj.* accurate, exact, straight (not bent, candid)

ตรงกลาง dtrong-glaang *adj.* middle (central)

ตรงข้าม dtrong-kâam *adj.* opposite

ตรงที่ dtrong-tîi *conj.* where

ตรงไป dtrong-bpai *vt.* go straight

ตรงเวลา dtrong-wee-laa *adj.* punctual

ตรงไหน dtrong-nǎi *adv.* where ✷

ตรรกศาสตร์ dtàk-gà~sàat *n.* logic [วิชา wí-chaa]

ตรวจ dtrùuat *v.* check (verify)

ตรวจ dtrùuat *vt.* test (check, e.g. body, machine)

ตรวจตรา dtrùuat-dtraa *v.* inspect (check)

ตรวจวัด dtrùuat-wát *v.* measure

ตรวจสอบ dtrùuat-sɔ̀ɔp *v.* inspect (examine)

ตรอก dtrɔ̀ɔk *n.* lane (alley), soi [ตรอก dtrɔ̀ɔk]

ตระหง่าน dtrà~ngàan *adj.* high ✷

ตระหนัก dtrà~nàk *vi.* know (have knowledge) ✷

ตรัง dtrang *n.* Trang province [จังหวัด jang-wàt]

ตรัย dtrai *numb.* three ✷

ตรัสรู้ dtràt-sà~rúu *adj.* enlightened (e.g. Lord Buddha)

ตรา dtraa *n.* sign (seal), trademark [ตรา dtraa]

ตรากตรำ dtràak-dtram *vi.* endure (persevere) ⚠

ตราด dtràat *n.* Trat province [จังหวัด jang-wàt]

ก
ข
ข
ค
ค
ฆ
ง
จ
ฉ
ช
ซ
ฌ
ญ
ฎ
ฏ
ฐ
ฑ
ฒ
ณ
ต
ถ
ท
ธ
น
บ
ป
ผ
ฝ
พ
ฟ
ภ
ม
ย
ร
ฤ
ล
ฦ
ว
ศ
ษ
ส
ห
ฬ
อ
ฮ

ก
ข
ฃ
ค
ฅ
ฆ
ง
จ
ฉ
ช
ซ
ฌ
ญ
ฎ
ฏ
ฐ
ฑ
ฒ
ณ
ด
ต
ถ
ท
ธ
น
บ
ป
ผ
ฝ
พ
ฟ
ภ
ม
ย
ร
ฤ
ล
ฦ
ว
ศ
ษ
ส
ห
ฬ
อ
ฮ

ตรายาง dtraa-yaang *n.* rubber stamp [อัน an]

ตราหน้า dtraa-nâa *vt.* brand (stigmatize)

ตรี dtrii *numb.* three

ตรึกตรอง dtrɯ̀k-dtrɔɔng *v.* consider carefully

ตรึง dtrɯng *vt.* be held in place

ตรู่ dtrùu *n.* dawn/ daybreak 👑

ตลก dtà~lòk *adj.* comic, funny, humorous

ตลอด dtà~lɔ̀ɔt *adv.* all, all over, throughout

ตลอด dtà~lɔ̀ɔt *prep.* through/thru (throughout)

ตลอดจน dtà~lɔ̀ɔt-jon *conj.* including

ตลอดไป dtà~lɔ̀ɔt-bpai *adv.* forever

ตลอดเวลา dtà~lɔ̀ɔt-wee-laa *adv.* all the time, always

ตลาด dtà~làat *n.* market [แห่ง hɛ̀ng]

ตวาด dtà~wàat *v.* scold harshly

ตอ dtɔɔ *n.* tree stump [ตอ dtɔɔ]

ต่อ dtɔ̀ɔ *n.* wasp [ตัว dtuua]

ต่อ dtɔ̀ɔ *prep.* per (e.g. per day), versus

ต่อ dtɔ̀ɔ *v.* haggle (price)

ต่อ dtɔ̀ɔ *vt.* connect (join), connect to (e.g. over phone, network), extend (increase in length)

ตอก dtɔ̀ɔk *v.* hammer

ตอกตะปู dtɔ̀ɔk-dtà~bpuu *vt.* nail

ต้อกระจก dtɔ̂ɔ-grà~jòk *n.* cataract (eye) [อัน an (piece)]

ต่อกัน dtɔ̀ɔ-gan *vi.* join (connect)

ต้อง dtɔ̂ng *aux.* must

ต้องการ dtɔ̂ng-gaan *v.* need, would like

ต้องห้าม dtɔ̂ng-hâam *adj.* taboo

ตอด dtɔ̀ɔt *v.* nibble

ต่อต้าน dtɔ̀ɔ-dtâan *prep.* against (e.g. wind, institution)

ต่อต้าน dtɔ̀ɔ-dtâan *vi.* defy (resist)

ตอน dtɔɔn *n.* chapter (part), episode (e.g. in a show), segment (division), time (e.g. at this time) [ตอน dtɔɔn]

ตอน dtɔɔn *vt.* castrate

ต้อน dtɔ̂n *vt.* herd, round up (e.g. herd)

ต้อนรับ dtɔ̂ɔn-ráp *vt.* receive (guests)

ต่อเนื่อง dtɔ̀ɔ-nɨ̂aŋ *adj.* continual (continuous), ongoing

ตอบ dtɔ̀ɔp *v.* answer

ตอบ dtɔ̀ɔp *vi.* reply, respond

ตอบโต้ dtɔ̀ɔp-dtôo *vi.* react

ต่อไป dtɔ̀ɔ-bpai *adj.* next

ต่อไปนี้ dtɔ̀ɔ-bpai-níi *conj.* as follows

ต่อม dtɔ̀m *n.* gland [ต่อม dtɔ̀m]

ต่อมลูกหมาก dtɔ̀m-lûuk-màak *n.* prostate

ต่อมา dtɔ̀ɔ-maa *adj.* subsequent

ต่อย dtɔ̀i *v.* punch

ต่อย dtɔ̀i *vi.* box (fight)

ต่อย dtɔ̀i *vt.* sting (e.g. bee)

ต่อราคา dtɔ̀ɔ-raa-kaa *vi.* bargain (haggle)

ต่อสู้ dtɔ̀ɔ-sûu *vt.* fight (e.g. hand-to-hand, illness), wrestle (force by wrestling)

ต้อหิน dtɔ̂ɔ-hǐn *n.* glaucoma [โรค rôok]

ตอแหล dtɔɔ-lɛ̌ɛ *interj.* bullshit!/B.S.! ❀

ตอแหล dtɔɔ-lɛ̌ɛ *v.* lie ❀

ต่ออายุ dtɔ̀ɔ-aa-yú *v.* renew (e.g. expired card)

ตะกร้อ dtà~grɔ̂ɔ *n.* rattan ball [ลูก lûuk]

ตะกร้า dtà~grâa *n.* basket (deep) [ใบ bai]

ตะกละ dtà~glà *adj.* greedy (gluttonous)

ตะกอน dtà~gɔɔn *n.* sediment

ตะกั่ว dtà~gùua *n.* lead (metal)

ตะเกียบ dtà~gìiap *n.* chopsticks [ข้าง kâaŋ (piece), คู่ kûu (pair)]

ตะแกรง dtà~grɛɛŋ *n.* sieve (strainer) [ใบ bai]

ตะโก dtà~goo *n.* ebony (tree) [ต้น dtôn]

ตะโก้ dtà~gôo *n.* Thai coconut pudding [ชิ้น chín]

ตะโกน dtà~goon *vi.* shout, yell

ตะขอ dtà~kɔ̌ɔ *n.* hook [อัน an]

ตะขาบ dtà~kàap *n.* centipede [ตัว dtuua]

ตะเข็บผ้า dtà~kèp-pâa *n.* seam [ตะเข็บ dtà~kèp]

ตะคริว dtà~kriu *n.* cramp (muscular)

ตะครุบ dtà~krúp *v.* snap up (pounce upon and seize)

ตะคอก dtà~kɔ̂ɔk *v.* scold harshly

ตะไคร่ dtà~krâi *n.* moss

ตะไคร้ dtà~krái *n.* lemongrass [ต้น dtôn (plant), กอ gɔɔ (bush)]

ตะบองเพชร dtà~bɔɔng-pét *n.* cactus [ต้น dtôn]

ตะไบ dtà~bai *n.* file (nail, metal) [เล่ม lêm, อัน an]

ตะปู dtà~bpuu *n.* nail (for carpentry) [ตัว dtuua, ดอก dɔ̀ɔk]

ตะพาบ dtà~pâap *n.* soft-shelled turtle [ตัว dtuua]

ตะราง dtà~raang *n.* jail (prison) [แห่ง hɛ̀ng, ที่ tîi]

ตะลึง dtà~lʉng *adj.* fascinated (amazed)

ตะวันตก dtà~wan-dtòk *n.* west [ทิศ tít]

ตะวันตกเฉียงใต้ dtà~wan-dtòk-chǐiang-dtâai *n.* southwest [ทิศ tít]

ตะวันตกเฉียงเหนือ dtà~wan-dtòk-chǐiang-nʉ̌ua *n.* northwest [ทิศ tít]

ตะวันออก dtà~wan-ɔ̀ɔk *n.* east [ทิศ tít]

ตะวันออกเฉียงใต้ dtà~wan-ɔ̀ɔk-chǐiang-dtâai *n.* southeast [ทิศ tít]

ตะวันออกเฉียงเหนือ dtà~wan-ɔ̀ɔk-chǐiang-nʉ̌ua *n.* northeast [ทิศ tít]

ตะหลิว dtà~lǐu *n.* spatula (flipper used for frying) [อัน an]

ตัก dtàk *n.* lap (body part)

ตัก dtàk *vt.* scoop (e.g. rice, curry, sand)

ตักเตือน dtàk-dtʉʉan *vt.* admonish (caution, remind)

ตั๊กแตน dták-gà~dtɛɛn *n.* grasshopper [ตัว dtuua]

ตักบาตร dtàk-bàat *v.* present food to a Buddhist monk

ตั้ง dtâng *vt.* form

(establish), set (place, put in place, set watch, clock)

ตั้งครรภ์ dtâng-kan *adj.* pregnant ‼

ตั้งใจ dtâng-jai *v.* intend, pay attention

ตั้งฉาก dtâng-chàak *adj.* perpendicular (vertical)

ตั้งฉากกัน dtâng-chàak-gan *adj.* square (at a right angle)

ตั้งชื่อ dtâng-chûu *vt.* name

ตั้งตรง dtâng-dtrong *adv.* up (upright)

ตั้งแต่ dtâng-dtɛ̀ɛ *prep.* from, since

ตั้งท้อง dtâng-tɔ́ɔng *adj.* pregnant

ตั้งมั่น dtâng-mân *v.* establish firmly

ตั้งรกราก dtâng-rók-râak *vi.* settle down (live long-term)

ตั้งอยู่ dtâng-yùu *vi.* position (be located)

ตัณหา dtan-hǎa *n.* lust, passion (desire) ‼

ตัด dtàt *v.* chop, cut

ตัดกัน dtàt-gan *vi.* clash (colors)

ตัดงบ dtàt-ngóp *v.* cut the budget

ตัดชีวิต dtàt-chii-wít *vt.* kill ‼

ตัดญาติกับ dtàt-yâat-gàp *vt.* disown (as family)

ตัดตอน dtàt-dtɔɔn *vt.* excerpt

ตัดสาย dtàt-sǎai *vt.* disconnect (cut off phone)

ตัดสิน dtàt-sǐn *v.* judge (determine, decide)

ตัดสินใจ dtàt-sǐn-jai *v.* make up one's mind

ตัน dtan *adj.* solid (not hollow)

ตัน dtan *n.* ton (unit of weight)

ตับ dtàp *n.* liver (organ)

ตับอ่อน dtàp-ɔ̀ɔn *n.* pancreas

ตับอักเสบ dtàp-àk-sèep *n.* hepatitis [โรค rôok]

ตัว dtuua *clf.* e.g. animals, alphabets, numbers, marks, piece of clothes etc.

ตัว dtuua *n.* body, self (one's own self) [ตัว

dtuua]

ตั๋ว dtǔua *n.* ticket (e.g. movie, train) [ใบ bai]

ตัวการ dtuua-gaan *n.* culprit (responsible person) [ตัว dtuua, คน kon]

ตัวตลก dtuua-dtà~lòk *n.* clown, jester [คน kon, ตัว dtuua]

ตัวต่อตัว dtuua-dtɔ̀ɔ-dtuua *adj.* one-on-one

ตัวถัง dtuua-tǎng *n.* body of a car [คัน kan]

ตัวแทน dtuua-tɛɛn *n.* agency (representative) [คน kon (person), แห่ง hɛ̀ng (place)]

ตัวนำ dtuua-nam *n.* leader [คน kon]

ตัวนำไฟฟ้า dtuua-nam-fai-fáa *n.* conductor (electrical) [ชนิด chá~nít, ตัว dtuua ●]

ตัวประกัน dtuua-bprà~gan *n.* hostage [คน kon]

ตัวแปร dtuua-bprɛɛ *n.* variable (factor) [ตัว dtuua]

ตั๋วไปกลับ dtǔua-bpai-glàp *n.* round-trip ticket

[ใบ bai]

ตัวผู้ dtuua-pûu *n.* male (animals) [ตัว dtuua]

ตัวพิมพ์ dtuua-pim *n.* print (type) [ตัว dtuua]

ตัวเมีย dtuua-miia *n.* female (animal) [ตัว dtuua]

ตัวย่อ dtuua-yɔ̂ɔ *n.* abbreviation (letter) [ตัว dtuua]

ตัวไร dtuua-rai *n.* mite (e.g. bedbug) [ตัว dtuua]

ตัวละคร dtuua-lá~kɔɔn *n.* character (in a play) [คน kon, ตัว dtuua]

ตัวเลข dtuua-lêek *n.* number (figure, digit) [ตัว dtuua]

ตัวเลือก dtuua-lûuak *n.* choice (of people or things) [ตัว dtuua]

ตัวสะกด dtuua-sà~gòt *n.* final consonant [ตัว dtuua]

ตัวหนังสือ dtuua-nǎng~sǔu *n.* alphabet [ตัว dtuua]

ตัวอย่าง dtuua-yàang *n.* illustration (example), sample [อัน an ●,

ตัวอย่าง dtuua-yàang]

ตัวอย่างหนัง dtuua-yàang-năng *n.* trailer (movie preview)

ตัวอ่อน dtuua-ɔ̀ɔn *n.* embryo (animal or human) [ตัว dtuua]

ตัวอักษร dtuua-àk-sɔ̌ɔn *n.* alphabet [ตัว dtuua]

ตัวเอก dtuua-èek *n.* principal (main performer) [คน kon]

ตัวเอง dtuua-eeng *pron.* oneself, own

ตัวเอียง dtuua-iiang *n.* italic [ตัว dtuua]

ตา dtaa *n.* eye (organ of sight) [ข้าง kâang (one side), คู่ kûu (pair)]

ตา dtaa *n.* turn (e.g. my turn) [ตา dtaa (shift)]

ตา dtaa *n.* grandfather (maternal), old man [คน kon]

ตาก dtàak *n.* Tak province [จังหวัด jang-wàt]

ตาก dtàak *vt.* dry (in sun, e.g. fruit)

ตากแดด dtàak-dὲὲt *vi.* expose to the sun

ตากุ้งยิง dtaa-gûng-ying *n.* sty (eyelid) [โรค rôok]

ตาข่าย dtaa-kàai *n.* net (snare, mesh) [อัน an]

ตาขาว dtaa-kǎao *n.* white of the eye

ตาเข dtaa-kěe *adj.* cross-eyed

ต่าง dtàang *adj.* different (not same)

ต่างๆ dtàang-dtàang *adj.* diverse (various)

ต่างจังหวัด dtàang-jang-wàt *adj.* provincial (up-country, not in the capital)

ต่างชาติ dtàang-châat *adj.* of another nationality, foreign

ต่างประเทศ dtàang-bprà~têet *adj.* foreign, overseas/oversea (abroad)

ตาชั่ง dtaa-châng *n.* scale (weighing) [คัน kan, เครื่อง krûuang]

ตาแดง dtaa-dɛɛng *n.* pinkeye [โรค rôok]

ตาตุ่ม dtaa-dtùm *n.* anklebone [ข้าง kâang (of one leg), คู่ kûu (of both legs)]

กขฃคฅฆงจฉชซฌญฎฏฐฑฒณดตถทธนบปผฝพฟภมยรฤลวศษสหฬอฮ

ตาถั่ว dtaa-tùua *adj.* be careless •

ตาทวด dtaa-tûuat *n.* great grandfather (maternal) [คน kon]

ตาทิพย์ dtaa-típ *adj.* clairvoyant

ต้านทาน dtâan-taan *v.* resist (defy, oppose)

ตาน้ำ dtaa-náam *n.* mouth of a spring [ตา dtaa, แห่ง hèng]

ตาบอด dtaa-bɔ̀ɔt *adj.* blind

ตาปลา dtaa-bplaa *n.* bunion [อัน an, ที่ tîi]

ตาม dtaam *prep.* along (e.g. road), on

ตาม dtaam *v.* follow, pursue

ตามเข็มนาฬิกา dtaam-kĕm-naa-lí-gaa *adv.* clockwise

ตามใจ dtaam-jai *vt.* pamper, spoil (someone)

ตามเดิม dtaam-dəəm *adv.* as before

ตามทัน dtaam-tan *vt.* catch up with

ตามที่ dtaam-tîi *prep.* according to

ตามนั้น dtaam-nán *adv.* accordingly

ตามมา dtaam-maa *v.* follow

ตามรอย dtaam-rɔɔi *vt.* trace (follow trail of)

ตามลำดับ dtaam-lam-dàp *adv.* respectively

ตามหลัง dtaam-lăng *vt.* trail (be behind)

ตาย dtaai *adj.* dead (not alive)

ตายตัว dtaai-dtuua *adj.* fix-priced

ตายาย dtaa-yaai *n.* grandparents (maternal) [คน kon]

ตาราง dtaa-raang *adv.* square (e.g. square foot)

ตาราง dtaa-raang *n.* table (chart) [ตาราง dtaa-raang, อัน an]

ตารางวา dtaa-raang-waa *n.* square-yard (Thai measurement equivalent to two meters squared) [ตาราง dtaa-raang]

ตาล dtaan *n.* sugar palm [ต้น dtôn (tree), ลูก lûuk (fruit)]

ตำ dtam *vt.* pierce (puncture), pound (with

a pestle)

ต่ำ dtàm *adj.* low (not high), short

ตำนาน dtam-naan *n.* legend (tale) [เรื่อง rûuang (story)]

ตำบล dtam-bon *n.* subdistrict [ตำบล dtam-bon]

ตำรวจ dtam-rùuat *n.* police officer [นาย naai ♀, คน kon]

ตำรับ dtam-ràp *n.* recipe [ตำรับ dtam-ràp]

ตำรา dtam-raa *n.* manual, textbook ✎ [เล่ม lêm]

ตำลึง dtam-lʉng *n.* East Indian spinach [เถา tǎo (plant)]

ต่ำสุด dtàm-sùt *adj.* minimum

ตำหนัก dtam-nàk *n.* house or residence of royalty [หลัง lǎng]

ตำหนิ dtam-nì *n.* defect (scar, flaw) [ที่ tîi]

ตำหนิ dtam-nì *vt.* pick on (criticize), reprimand

ตำแหน่ง dtam-nɛ̀ng *n.* position (post, spot, rank) [ตำแหน่ง dtam-nɛ̀ng]

ติ dtì *vt.* pick on (criticize) ♦

ติ้งต๊อง dtíng-dtóng *adj.* wacky (crazy, silly) ♦

ติ่งหู dtìng-hǔu *n.* earlobe

ติด dtìt *v.* get stuck, start (turn on, e.g. machinery)

ติด dtìt *vi.* connect (e.g. over phone, network)

ติดกัน dtìt-gan *vi.* join (put together), stick (adhere, attach)

ติดกับ dtìt-gàp *prep.* against (in contact with)

ติดขัด dtìt-kàt *v.* get stuck

ติดเครื่อง dtìt-krʉ̂uang *vi.* start engine

ติดเชื้อ dtìt-chʉ́ua *adj.* infected

ติดดิน dtìt-din *idm.* down-to-earth (not pretentious) ♦

ติดต่อ dtìt-dtɔ̀ɔ *adj.* infectious (contagious)

ติดต่อ dtìt-dtɔ̀ɔ *vt.* contact (communicate with), contract (disease)

ติดตั้ง dtìt-dtâng *vt.* install (place, set up)

ติดตาม dtìt-dtaam *vt.* track (follow)

ติดพัน dtìt-pan *adj.* engaged (engrossed)

ติดไฟ dtìt-fai *vi.* ignite (burst into flame)

ติดยา dtìt-yaa *adj.* addicted (to drug)

ติดสินบน dtìt-sǐn-bon *vt.* pay off (bribe)

ติดหนี้ dtìt-nîi *adj.* indebted

ติดอ่าง dtìt-àang *vi.* stutter

ติเตียน dtì-dtiian *vt.* blame (criticize)

ติว dtiu *v.* tutor ✦

ตี dtii *vt.* beat (hit, mix), strike (hit)

ตีความ dtii-kwaam *v.* interpret

ตีตรา dtii-dtraa *vt.* stamp (e.g. with seal)

ตีน dtiin *n.* foot (body part) ✦ [ข้าง kâang (one), คู่ kûu (pair)]

ตีนกา dtiin-gaa *n.* crow's-feet [รอย rɔɔi]

ตีพิมพ์ dtii-pim *v.* print (publish)

ตีราคา dtii-raa-kaa *vt.* price (set price of)

ตีลังกา dtii-lang-gaa *vi.* flip, somersault

ตึก dtʉ̀k *n.* building [หลัง lǎng]

ตึกระฟ้า dtʉ̀k-rá~fáa *n.* skyscraper [หลัง lǎng, ตึก dtʉ̀k]

ตึง dtʉng *adj.* tight (e.g. rope)

ตึงเครียด dtʉng-krîiat *adj.* serious (e.g. tense situation), stressful

ตืด dtʉ̀ʉt *n.* tapeworm [ตัว dtuua]

ตื่น dtʉ̀ʉn *vi.* wake up (get up)

ตื้น dtʉ̂ʉn *adj.* shallow (not deep)

ตื่นตัว dtʉ̀ʉn-dtuua *adj.* alert

ตื่นเต้น dtʉ̀ʉn-dtên *adj.* excited

ตื่นนอน dtʉ̀ʉn-nɔɔn *vi.* wake up (get up)

ตุ๊กๆ dtúk-dtúk *n.* small motor tricycle or boat, tuk-tuk [คัน kan]

ตุ๊กแก dtúk-gɛɛ *n.* large house-lizard [ตัว dtuua]

ตุ๊กตา dtúk-gà~dtaa *n.* doll [ตัว dtuua]

ตุ๊ด dtút *n.* gay man who

acts feminine ● [คน kon]

ตุ๋น dtǔn *vt.* double boil, simmer, stew

ตุ่ม dtùm *n.* jar (water) [ใบ bai, ลูก lûuk]

ตุ้ม dtûm *n.* suspend object [ลูก lûuk, ตัว dtuua]

ตุ้มหู dtûm-hǔu *n.* earring [คู่ kûu (pair)]

ตุ้ยนุ้ย dtûi-núi *adj.* fat ●, plump (chubby) ●

ตุลาคม dtù-laa-kom *n.* October [เดือน duuan]

ตู่ dtùu *v.* claim falsely

ตู้ dtûu *n.* cabinet, chest, cupboard [ใบ bai]

ตูด dtùut *n.* anus ✱, ass (bottom) ✱

ตู้ ป.ณ. dtûu-bpɔɔ-nɔɔ *n.* P.O. Box [ตู้ dtûu]

ตู้ปลา dtûu-bplaa *n.* aquarium (fish bowl) [ตู้ dtûu]

ตู้ไปรษณีย์ dtûu-bprai-sà~nii *n.* mailbox [ใบ bai]

ตู้ไปรษณีย์ dtûu-bprai-sà~nii *n.* P.O. Box [ตู้ dtûu]

ตูม dtuum *adj.* budding

ตู้เย็น dtûu-yen *n.* refrigerator [เครื่อง krûuang]

ตู้เสื้อผ้า dtûu-sûua-pâa *n.* wardrobe [ใบ bai]

เต้น dtên *vi.* beat (e.g. heart), dance (modern)

เต็นท์ dtén *n.* tent [หลัง lǎng]

เต้นรำ dtên-ram *vi.* dance (ballroom)

เต็ม dtem *adj.* full (e.g. tank, room)

เต็มใจ dtem-jai *adj.* willing

เตรียม dtriiam *v.* prepare (get ready)

เตรียมตัว dtriiam-dtuua *v.* prepare (get ready)

เตรียมพร้อม dtriiam-prɔ́ɔm *vi.* get ready

เตะ dtè *v.* kick

เตา dtao *n.* stove [ใบ bai, ลูก lûuk]

เต่า dtào *n.* tortoise, turtle [ตัว dtuua]

เต้าเจี้ยว dtâo-jîiao *n.* bean paste [ขวด kùuat (bottle)]

เต้านม dtâo-nom *n.*

breast (woman's) ⚢ [เต้า dtâo]

เตาผิง dtao-pǐng *n.* fireplace [เตา dtao]

เตารีด dtao-rîit *n.* iron (appliance) [อัน an]

เตาหลอม dtao-lɔ̌ɔm *n.* furnace [เตา dtao]

เต้าหู้ dtâo-hûu *n.* tofu [ชิ้น chín]

เตาอบ dtao-òp *n.* oven [เตา dtao, เครื่อง krûuang]

เติบโต dtə̀əp-dtoo *vi.* grow (increase in size), thrive (prosper, flourish)

เติม dtəəm *vt.* fill up (add more (object is substance filled)), replenish

เตี้ย dtîia *adj.* low (not tall), short (height)

เตียง dtiiang *n.* bed (furniture) [เตียง dtiiang]

เตียงคู่ dtiiang-kûu *n.* two small beds in a hotel room

เตียงหาม dtiiang-hǎam *n.* stretcher (for carrying people) [อัน an]

เตือน dtuuan *vt.* remind, warn (caution, remind)

แต่ dtɛ̀ɛ *conj.* but, only

แตก dtɛ̀ɛk *adj.* broken (shattered, e.g. glass)

แตก dtɛ̀ɛk *vi.* split (crack)

แตกต่าง dtɛ̀ɛk-dtàang *adj.* distinct (different, separate)

แตกหน่อ dtɛ̀ɛk-nɔ̀ɔ *vi.* bud (produce buds)

แต่กำเนิด dtɛ̀ɛ-gam-nə̀ət *adj.* native (by birth)

แตง dtɛɛng *n.* melon, squash (plant) [ลูก lûuk]

แต่ง dtɛ̀ng *vt.* beautify (decorate), compose (e.g. music), dress (decorate)

แตงกวา dtɛɛng-gwaa *n.* cucumber [ลูก lûuk]

แต่งงานกับ dtɛ̀ng-ngaan-gàp *vt.* marry, wed

แต่งตั้ง dtɛ̀ng-dtâng *v.* place (appoint)

แต่งตัว dtɛ̀ng-dtuua *vi.* get dressed

แตงโม dtɛɛng-moo *n.* watermelon [ลูก lûuk]

แต้จิ๋ว dtɛ̂ɛ-jǐu *adj.* Taechew (Chinese group)

แต่เช้า dtɛ̀ɛ-cháao *adj.* early (in the morning)

แตด dtὲεt *n.* clitoris ⚲
แตร dtrεε *n.* bugle, trumpet [ตัว dtuua]
แต่แรก dtὲε-rêεk *adv.* at first
แต่ละ dtὲε-lá *adj.* each
แต๋ว dtěo *n.* gay queen ❀ [คน kon]
แต่ว่า dtὲε-wâa *conj.* but
แตะ dtὲ *vt.* touch (come into contact)
โต dtoo *adj.* big, large
โต้ dtôo *v.* oppose (conflict, refuse)
โต้เถียง dtôo-tǐiang *v.* debate (argue about)
โต้แย้ง dtôo-yέεng *v.* rebut
โต้แย้ง dtôo-yέεng *vt.* contest (disagree with)
โต้วาที dtôo-waa-tii *v.* debate (formally)
โต๊ะ dtó *n.* desk, table (furniture) [ตัว dtuua]
ใต้ dtâai *adj.* south
ใต้ dtâai *n.* south (direction) [ทิศ tít]
ใต้ dtâai *prep.* under (beneath, below the surface of)
ใต้ดิน dtâai-din *adj.*

underground (hidden or secret)
ไต dtai *n.* kidney [ข้าง kâang]
ไต่ dtài *vi.* creep
ไต้ dtâai *n.* torch (with flame) [ลูก lûuk, เล่ม lêm]
ไต้ฝุ่น dtâai-fùn *n.* typhoon [ลูก lûuk]
ไตร่ตรอง dtrài-dtrɔɔng *v.* consider (think over)
ไตรมาส dtrai-mâat *n.* quarter (three months) [ไตรมาส dtrai-mâat]
ไต้หวัน dtâai-wǎn *n.* Taiwan [ประเทศ bprà~têet]

ถ

ถ tɔ̌o *let.* ถ. ถุง tʉ̌ng, a consonant of the Thai alphabet (high consonant) [ตัว dtuua]
ถก tòk *v.* pull (draw)
ถด tòt *vi.* retreat
ถนน tà~nǒn *n.* avenue, road, street [เส้น sên, สาย sǎai]
ถนอม tà~nɔ̌ɔm *vt.* cherish (look after)
ถนัด tà~nàt *adj.*

ก
ข
ข
ค
ค
ฆ
ง
จ
ฉ
ช
ซ
ฌ
ญ
ฎ
ฏ
ฐ
ฑ
ฒ
ณ
ด
ต
ถ
ท
ธ
น
บ
ป
ผ
ฝ
พ
ฟ
ภ
ม
ย
ร
ฤ
ล
ว
ศ
ษ
ส
ห
ฬ
อ
ฮ

dexterous (skillful)

ถนัดขวา tà~nàt-kwǎa *adj.* right-handed

ถนัดซ้าย tà~nàt-sáai *adj.* left-handed

ถนัดทั้งสองมือ tà~nàt-táng-sɔ̌ɔng-mʉʉ *adj.* ambidextrous

ถ่ม tòm *vi.* spit

ถ่มน้ำลาย tòm-nám-laai *vi.* spit ⚠

ถลก tà~lòk *vt.* roll up (e.g. sleeve, pant leg)

ถลุง tà~lǔng *vt.* punch, hit, smelt (ore)

ถ่วงน้ำ tùuang-náam *v.* throw in water

ถ้วย tûuai *clf.* for small bowls, cups, trophies

ถ้วย tûuai *n.* bowl (food), cup (container), small bowl [ใบ bai]

ถ้วยรางวัล tûuai-raang-wan *n.* trophy (prize) [ถ้วย tûuai, ใบ bai, ลูก lûuk]

ถ่อ tɔ̀ɔ *n.* barge pole [ลำ lam, เล่ม lêm]

ถ่อ tɔ̀ɔ *vt.* make a special effort, drag

ถอง tʉ̌ɔng *v.* nudge

ถอด tɔ̀ɔt *vt.* remove (take off, e.g. clothes)

ถอดความ tɔ̀ɔt-kwaam *v.* paraphrase, translate (language)

ถอดปลั๊ก tɔ̀ɔt-bplák *vt.* unplug

ถอดรหัส tɔ̀ɔt-rá~hàt *v.* decode

ถอด_ออก tɔ̀ɔt-_-ɔ̀ɔk *vt.* undress (remove)

ถอน tʉ̌ɔn *v.* pull (draw)

ถอน tʉ̌ɔn *vt.* withdraw

ถอนคำพูด tʉ̌ɔn-kam-pûut *vi.* take back one's words

ถอนเงิน tʉ̌ɔn-ngən *vi.* withdraw money

ถอนหายใจ tʉ̌ɔn-hǎai-jai *vi.* sigh (e.g. from relief)

ถ่อมตัว tɔ̀m-dtuua *adj.* modest (humble)

ถอย tʉ̌ɔi *vi.* retreat (draw back)

ถอยกลับ tʉ̌ɔi-glàp *v.* pull back (draw back)

ถอยรถ tʉ̌ɔi-rót *vi.* reverse (drive in reverse)

ถอยหลัง tʉ̌ɔi-lǎng *vi.* back up (vehicle, oneself)

ถัก tàk *vt.* knit

ถัง tǎng *n.* pail (bucket) [ใบ bai]

ถังขยะ tăng-kà~yà *n.* trash can/garbage can/bin [ใบ bai]

ถังแตก tăng-dtɛ̀ɛk *adj.* broke (penniless) ✱

ถังน้ำแข็ง tăng-nám-kĕng *n.* cooler (ice container) [ถัง tăng]

ถัดจาก tàt-jàak *prep.* next to

ถั่ว tùua *n.* pea [เม็ด mét (seed), ฝัก fàk (pod)]

ถั่ว tùua *n.* bean [เม็ด mét]

ถั่วเขียว tùua-kĭiao *n.* mung bean [เม็ด mét]

ถั่วงอก tùua-ngɔ̂ɔk *n.* bean sprout [เส้น sên (sprout)]

ถั่วฝักยาว tùua-fàk-yaao *n.* string bean [ฝัก fàk]

ถั่วลันเตา tùua-lan-dtao *n.* snow pea [ต้น dtôn (plant), ฝัก fàk (pod)]

ถั่วลิสง tùua-lí-sŏng *n.* peanut [เมล็ด má~lét (bean)]

ถั่วเหลือง tùua-lŭuang *n.* soy [เมล็ด má~lét (bean)]

ถ้า tâa *conj.* if

ถาก tàak *vt.* scrape

ถากถาง tàak-tăang *v.* nag

ถาง tăang *v.* cut away

ถ่าง tàang *v.* spread (e.g. legs, compass)

ถาด tàat *n.* tray [ใบ bai]

ถ่าน tàan *n.* battery (e.g. camera), charcoal [ก้อน gɔ̂ɔn]

ถ่านไฟเก่า tàan-fai-gào *n.* old flame ✱ [คน kon]

ถ่านหิน tàan-hĭn *n.* coal ⚡ [ก้อน gɔ̂ɔn]

ถาม tăam *v.* ask (question)

ถ่าย tàai *v.* excrete

ถ่าย tàai *vt.* shoot (e.g. photograph, video), transfuse (e.g. blood)

ถ่ายทอด tàai-tɔ̂ɔt *v.* broadcast, transmit

ถ่ายเท tàai-tee *vt.* transfuse (diffuse through)

ถ่ายภาพ tàai-pâap *vi.* take a picture ⚡

ถ่ายรูป tàai-rûup *vi.* take a picture

ถ่ายหนัง tàai-năng *vi.* shoot a movie

ถ่ายเอกสาร tàai-èek-gà~săan *vi.* make a copy

ถาวร tăa-wɔɔn *adj.* permanent

ถ้ำ tâm *n.* den (animal) [แห่ง hὲng, ถ้ำ tâm]

ถ้ามอง tâm-mɔɔng *n.* peek at someone else's activities ● [คน kon]

ถิ่น tìn *n.* home (locality) [ถิ่น tìn]

ถี่ tìi *adj.* frequent

ถึง tŭng *prep.* to (e.g. to this day)

ถึง tŭng *vi.* arrive

ถึงกระนั้น tŭng-grà~nán *adv.* nonetheless

ถึงแก่กรรม tŭng-gὲε-gam *vi.* die ⚠

ถึงชีวิต tŭng-chii-wít *adj.* fatal (deadly)

ถึงตายได้ tŭng-dtaai-dâai *adj.* deadly (lethal)

ถึงแม้ว่า tŭng-mέε-wâa *conj.* though (although, even if)

ถือ tŭu *vt.* carry (hold)

ถือตัว tŭu-dtuua *adj.* conceited (haughty)

ถือว่า tŭu-wâa *vt.* deem (consider)

ถุง tŭng *clf.* of bags, gallbladders, pouches, etc.

ถุง tŭng *n.* sack (bag) [ใบ bai]

ถุงกระดาษ tŭng-grà~ dàat *n.* paper bag [ใบ bai]

ถุงเท้า tŭng-táao *n.* sock [ข้าง kâang (each), คู่ kûu (pair)]

ถุงน่อง tŭng-nɔ̂ng *n.* tights (stockings) [ข้าง kâang (each), คู่ kûu (pair)]

ถุงนอน tŭng-nɔɔn *n.* sleeping bag [อัน an]

ถุงมือ tŭng-mɯɯ *n.* glove [ข้าง kâang (each), คู่ kûu (pair)]

ถุงยาง tŭng-yaang *n.* condom [อัน an, ชิ้น chín]

ถุย tŭi *interj.* shit! ●

ถู tŭu *vt.* wipe (scrub)

ถูก tùuk *adj.* inexpensive, right (correct)

ถูกกฎหมาย tùuk-gòt-măai *adj.* legal (lawful)

ถูกใจ tùuk-jai *vt.* please (give enjoyment to)

ถูกชะตา tùuk-chá~dtaa *adj.* compatible (get

along well) ✱

ถูกต้อง tùuk-dtɔ̂ng *adj.*
accurate (correct)

เถอะ tà *part.* for
indicating command,
urging

เถ้าแก่ tâo-gɛ̀ɛ *n.* business
owner (male) ✱ [คน kon]

เถาะ tɔ̀ *n.* Year of the
Rabbit

เถิด tə̀ət *part.* used to
make a request or
command

เถียงกัน tǐiang-gan *vi.*
argue (talk back, dispute)

เถื่อน tɨ̀uan *adj.* illegal ✱

แถบ tɛ̀ɛp *n.* tab (flap,
short strip) [แถบ tɛ̀ɛp]

แถลง tà~lɛ̌ɛng *v.* proclaim
(declare)

แถลงการณ์ tà~lɛ̌ɛng-
gaan *n.* manifesto (e.g.
communist)

แถว tɛ̌ɛo *n.* area (vicinity,
zone) ✱ [แห่ง hɛ̀ng]

แถว tɛ̌ɛo *n.* row [แถว tɛ̌ɛo]

แถวนี้ tɛ̌ɛo-níi *adj.* nearby
✱

โถ tǒo *n.* earthen jar [ใบ
bai]

โถส้วม tǒo-sûuam *n.*
toilet [โถ tǒo]

ไถ tǎi *v.* plough/plow (till,
shove)

ไถ่ tài *v.* purchase back

ไถ่ตัว tài-dtuua *vt.* ransom

ไถล tà~lǎi *vi.* glide (slide
on surface)

ท

ท tɔɔ *let.* ท. ทหาร tá-hǎan,
a consonant of the Thai
alphabet (low
consonant) [ตัว dtuua]

ทด tót *n.* dike, dam

ทด tót *vt.* compensate
for, carry (in arithmetic)

ทดน้ำ tót-náam *vi.* irrigate

ทดลอง tót-lɔɔng *adj.* trial
(experimental)

ทดลอง tót-lɔɔng *vt.*
experiment with, test
(experiment with)

ทดสอบ tót-sɔ̀ɔp *vt.* quiz
(test)

ทน ton *vt.* endure (for
thing), go through

ทน_ได้ ton-_-dâai *vt.*
stand (endure)

ทนต่อ ton-dtɔ̀ɔ *adj.*
resistant

ทนทาน ton-taan *adj.*
durable (withstands wear
and tear)

ทนทุกข์ ton-túk *v.* suffer

ทนไฟ ton-fai *adj.* fireproof

ทนไม่ไหว ton-mâi-wǎi *adj.* unbearable

ทนาย tá~naai *n.* lawyer/ solicitor ✤ [คน kon]

ทนายความ tá~naai-kwaam *n.* lawyer/ solicitor [คน kon]

ทนายอาสา tá~naai-aa-sǎa *n.* public defender [คน kon]

ทบทวน tóp-tuuan *vt.* review (study, practice)

ทยอย tá~yɔɔi *vi.* come or go in succession

ทแยงมุม tá~yɛɛng-mum *adj.* diagonal

ทรง song *n.* form, figure, style [ทรง song]

ทรง song *v.* used before verb for royal words ♔

ทรงผม song-pǒm *n.* hairdo [ทรง song]

ทรมาน tɔɔ-rá~maan *vt.* torture (torment)

ทรยศ tɔɔ-rá~yót *vt.* betray (be disloyal to)

ทรรศนะ tát-sà~ná see ทัศนะ

ทรวง suuang *n.* breast (chest)

ทรหด tɔɔ-rá~hòt *vi.* persevere (endure) ❗

ทรัพย์ sáp *n.* property (possession) [ชิ้น chín]

ทรัพย์สมบัติ sáp-sǒm-bàt *n.* property (possession) ✤ [ชิ้น chín]

ทรัพย์สิน sáp-sǐn *n.* asset ❗, estate ❗, property (possession) ❗ [ชิ้น chín]

ทรัพย์สินส่วนรวม sáp-sǐn-sùuan-ruuam *n.* community property [ชิ้น chín]

ทรัพยากร sáp-pá~yaa-gɔɔn *n.* resource (e.g. natural, assets) [ชนิด chá~nít]

ทรัพยากรธรรมชาติ sáp-pá~yaa-gɔɔn-tam-má~châat *n.* natural resources

ทราบ sâap *vi.* know (have knowledge) ❗

ทราม saam *adj.* mean (evil)

ทราย saai *n.* sand [เม็ด mét (grain)]

ทรุดลง sút-long *vi.* get worse

ทฤษฎี trít-sà~dii *n.*

theory [ทฤษฎี trít-sà~dii]

ทลาย tá~laai *vi.* tumble down (collapse)

ทวง tuuang *v.* solicit the return of a borrowed article

ท้วง túuang *v.* protest (oppose)

ท่วงทำนอง tûuang-tam-nɔɔng *n.* style (manner, mode) ⚠

ท่วงที tûuang-tii *n.* manner

ทวด tûuat *n.* great grandparent [คน kon]

ทวน tuuan *n.* lance [เล่ม lêm]

ทวนเข็มนาฬิกา tuuan-kěm-naa-lí~gaa *adj.* counterclockwise/ anticlockwise

ทวนน้ำ tuuan-náam *v.* move against the tide

ทวนลม tuuan-lom *v.* go against the wind

ท่วม tûuam *adj.* flooded, inundated

ท่วม tûuam *v.* flood, overflow (flood, whelm)

ท่วมท้น tûuam-tón *v.* overwhelm

ทวาร tá~waan *n.* door ⚠

[บาน baan]

ทวารหนัก tá~waan-nàk *n.* anus, asshole

ทวี tá~wii *adv.* twice (two times more) ⚠

ทวีคูณ tá~wii-kuun *adj.* two-fold

ทวีคูณ tá~wii-kuun *v.* multiply (increase)

ทวีคูณ tá~wii-kuun *vi.* double

ทวีป tá~wîip *n.* continent [ทวีป tá~wîip]

ทศ tót *numb.* ten ⚠

ทศวรรษ tót-sà~wát *n.* decade [ทศวรรษ tót-sà~wát]

ทหาร tá~hǎan *n.* soldier [นาย naai ⚠, คน kon]

ทหารผ่านศึก tá~hǎan-pàan-sùk *n.* veteran (who has served in the military) [นาย naai ⚠, คน kon]

ทหารเรือ tá~hǎan-ruua *n.* marine [นาย naai ⚠, คน kon]

ทหารอากาศ tá~hǎan-aa-gàat *n.* air force officer

ทอ tɔɔ *v.* weave (cloth)

ท่อ tɔ̂ɔ *n.* tube (pipe, hollow cylinder) [ท่อ tɔ̂ɔ]

ทอง tɔɔng *n.* gold [บาท bàat (15 gram), กรัม gram (gram)]

ท่อง tɔ̂ng *v.* recite (repeat)

ท้อง tɔ́ɔng *adj.* pregnant ●

ท้อง tɔ́ɔng *n.* stomach

ท้องแขน tɔ́ɔng-kɛ̆ɛn *n.* inside part of the arm [ข้าง kâang]

ทองคำ tɔɔng-kam *n.* gold [บาท bàat (15 gram), กรัม gram (gram)]

ทองคำขาว tɔɔng-kam-kǎao *n.* platinum [กรัม gram (gram)]

ท่องจำ tɔ̂ng-jam *v.* learn by rote, memorize

ทองแดง tɔɔng-dɛɛng *n.* copper

ท้องถิ่น tɔ́ɔng-tìn *adj.* native (local)

ท้องถิ่น tɔ́ɔng-tìn *n.* local [แห่ง hɛ̀ng ●, ที่ tîi]

ท้องที่ tɔ́ɔng-tîi *n.* local [แห่ง hɛ̀ng ●, ที่ tîi]

ท่องเที่ยว tɔ̂ng-tîiao *v.* tour

ทองแท่ง tɔɔng-tɛ̂ng *n.* gold bar, bullion [แท่ง tɛ̂ng, ลิ่ม lîm]

ทองใบ tɔɔng-bai *n.* gold leaf [แผ่น pɛ̀n]

ท้องผูก tɔ́ɔng-pùuk *n.* constipation

ท้องฟ้า tɔ́ɔng-fáa *n.* sky [ผืน pɯ̌ɯn]

ทองม้วน tɔɔng-múuan *n.* rolled wafer [อัน an, ม้วน múuan, แผ่น pɛ̀n]

ท้องร่อง tɔ́ɔng-rɔ̂ng *n.* trench (ditch) [ร่อง rɔ̂ng]

ท้องเสีย tɔ́ɔng-sɯ̌ia *n.* diarrhea [อาการ aa-gaan]

ทองหยอด tɔɔng-yɔ̀ɔt *n.* eggdrop sweet [เม็ด mét, ลูก lûuk]

ทองหยิบ tɔɔng-yìp *n.* kind of Thai sweetmeat [ดอก dɔ̀ɔk, หยิบ yìp]

ทองเหลือง tɔɔng-lɯ̌ang *n.* brass, bronze (metal)

ทอด tɔ̂ɔt *adj.* deep-fried, fried (deep fried)

ทอด tɔ̂ɔt *vt.* fry (deep fry)

ทอดทิ้ง tɔ̂ɔt-tíng *v.* abandon (desert)

ทอดมันปลา tɔ̂ɔt-man-bplaa *n.* fish cake [ชิ้น chín]

ท้อแท้ tɔ́ɔ-tɛ́ɛ *adj.* down

hearted, frustrated (discouraged)

ทอน tɔɔn *v.* give change

ทอนเงิน tɔɔn-ngən *v.* give change

ท่อนไม้ tɔ̂n-máai *n.* log, stick (log, piece of wood) [ท่อน tɔ̂n]

ท่อน้ำเสีย tɔ̂ɔ-nám-sĭia *n.* sewer (pipe) [ท่อ tɔ̂ɔ]

ทอฟฟี่ tɔ́p-fîi *n.* toffee [เม็ด mét, อัน an, ห่อ hɔ̀ɔ (pack)]

ท่อระบาย tɔ̂ɔ-rá~baai *n.* drain pipe [ท่อ tɔ̂ɔ]

ท่อระบายน้ำ tɔ̂ɔ-rá~baai-náam *n.* waterspout (pipe) [ท่อ tɔ̂ɔ]

ท่อไอเสีย tɔ̂ɔ-ai-sĭia *n.* exhaust pipe [ท่อ tɔ̂ɔ]

ทะนง tá~nong *adj.* arrogant

ทะนุถนอม tá~nú-tà~nɔ̌ɔm *vt.* cherish (care for)

ทะเบียน tá~biian *n.* license, record (registration) [ใบ bai]

ทะเบียนบ้าน tá~biian-bâan *n.* house registration [ฉบับ chà~bàp]

ทะเบียนสมรส tá~biian-sŏm-rót *n.* certificate of marriage [ใบ bai]

ทะยอย tá~yɔɔi *v.* follow gradually

ทะเยอทะยาน tá~yəə-tá~yaan *adj.* ambitious

ทะลัก tá~lák *adj.* filled to overflowing

ทะลุ tá~lú *adj.* pierced through

ทะลุ tá~lú *prep.* through/thru (in one side and out the other)

ทะลุ tá~lú *vt.* break through (penetrate)

ทะเล tá~lee *n.* sea [แห่ง hɛ̀ng]

ทะเลทราย tá~lee-saai *n.* desert [แห่ง hɛ̀ng]

ทะเลสาบ tá~lee-sàap *n.* lake [แห่ง hɛ̀ng]

ทะเลาะกัน tá~lɔ́-gan *vi.* clash (argue), quarrel

ทะเลาะกับ tá~lɔ́-gàp *vt.* fight (argue with)

ทัก ták *vt.* greet (say hello)

ทักทาย ták-taai *vt.* greet (say hello)

ทักษะ ták-sà *n.* know-how, skill

ทั้ง táng *adj.* entire, whole

ก ข ฃ ค ฅ ฆ ง จ ฉ ช ซ ฌ ญ ฎ ฏ ฐ ฑ ฒ ณ ด ต ถ ท ธ น บ ป ผ ฝ พ ฟ ภ ม ย ร ล ว ศ ษ ส ห อ ฮ

ทั้งๆ ที่ táng-táng-tîi *conj.* even though

ทั้งคืน táng-kʉʉn *adv.* all night

ทั้งคู่ táng-kûu *adj.* both

ทั้งที่ táng-tîi *conj.* although ☚

ทั้งนี้ táng-níi *conj.* so that, in order that ✒

ทั้งวัน táng-wan *adv.* all day long

ทั้งสอง táng-sɔ̌ɔng *pron.* both

ทั้งสิ้น táng-sîn *adv.* entirely (altogether) ☚

ทั้งหมด táng-mòt *adj.* entire, whole

ทั้งหมด táng-mòt *adv.* entirely (altogether), overall (whole, all)

ทั้งหลาย táng-lǎai *adj.* various, numerous

ทัณฑ์ tan *n.* penalty (foul)

ทันใจ tan-jai *adv.* as quickly as desired

ทันต่อเวลา tan-dtɔ̀ɔ-wee-laa *v.* keep up with (stay up to date)

ทันที tan-tii *adj.*

immediate, instant (sudden)

ทันที tan-tii *n.* instance

ทันทีทันใด tan-tii-tan-dai *adv.* immediately (instantly)

ทันทีที่ tan-tii-tîi *conj.* as soon as, once

ทันสมัย tan-sà~mǎi *adj.* fashionable, modern, up-to-date

ทับ táp *v.* overlap (lie on top of)

ทับทิม táp-tim *n.* pomegranate [เม็ด mét (seed), ลูก lûuk (fruit)]

ทับทิม táp-tim *n.* ruby (gem) [เม็ด mét]

ทัพพี táp-pii *n.* coconut-shell spoon, ladle [คัน kan, อัน an]

ทั่ว tûua *prep.* all over (throughout)

ทั่วไป tûua-bpai *adj.* general

ทั่วโลก tûua-lôok *adj.* global, worldwide

ทัศน์ tát *n.* vision

ทัศนคติ tát-sà~ná-ká~dtì *n.* attitude (of mind or feeling) [อัน an]

ทัศนะ tát-sà~ná *n.* opinion (viewpoint, idea) ‼ [อัน an]

ทัศนาจร tát-sà~naa-jɔɔn *n.* tour (sight-seeing) ‼ [ครั้ง kráng]

ทา taa *vt.* apply (e.g. cream or medicine), apply on (e.g. medicine), paint

ท่า tâa *n.* pose (posture, gesture) [ท่า tâa]

ทาก tâak *n.* leech, slug (animal) [ตัว dtuua]

ทาง taang *n.* way (path or course) [สาย sǎai, เส้น sên]

ทาง taang *prep.* by (route, e.g. ground, air), via

ทางการ taang-gaan *adj.* official

ทางไกล taang-glai *adj.* long-distance

ทางเข้า taang-kâo *n.* entrance [ทาง taang]

ทางคดเคี้ยว taang-kót-kíiao *n.* maze (labyrinth) [ทาง taang, เส้น sên]

ทางโค้ง taang-kóong *n.* curve (road) [แห่ง hèng, ที่ tîi]

ทางใจ taang-jai *adj.* mental

ทางช้างเผือก taang-cháang-pùuak *n.* Milky Way [แห่ง hèng]

ทางด่วน taang-dùuan *n.* expressway [สาย sǎai]

ทางเดิน taang-dəən *n.* trail (path, walkway) [ทาง taang]

ทางเดินเท้า taang-dəən-táao *n.* pavement (sidewalk) [ทาง taang]

ทางเดียว taang-diiao *adj.* one-way (e.g. street)

ทางตัน taang-dtan *n.* dead end [ทาง taang]

ทางทะเล taang-tá~lee *adv.* by sea

ทางเท้า taang-táao *n.* footpath [ทาง taang]

ทางใน taang-nai *n.* transcendental meditation

ทางบก taang-bòk *adv.* by land

ทางเบี่ยง taang-bìiang *n.* diversion (detour) [ทาง taang]

ทางไปรษณีย์ taang-bprai-sà~nii *adv.* by mail

ก
ข
ค
ฅ
ฆ
ง
จ
ฉ
ช
ซ
ฌ
ญ
ฎ
ฏ
ฐ
ฑ
ฒ
ณ
ด
ต
ถ
ท
ธ
น
บ
ป
ผ
ฝ
พ
ฟ
ภ
ม
ย
ร
ฤ
ล
ฦ
ว
ศ
ษ
ส
ห
ฬ
อ
ฮ

ทางผ่าน taang-pàan *n.* passage (way) [ทาง taang]

ทางม้าลาย taang-máa-laai *n.* crosswalk, zebra crossing [แห่ง hèng]

ทางแยก taang-yêɛk *n.* junction (intersection) [แห่ง hèng]

ทางรถไฟ taang-rót-fai *n.* railway (route) [สาย sǎai]

ทางลัด taang-lát *n.* shortcut [ทาง taang]

ทางลาด taang-lâat *n.* ramp (slope) [ทาง taang]

ทางลาดยาง taang-lâat-yaang *n.* pavement (paved road) [ทาง taang]

ทางเลี่ยง taang-lîiang *n.* diversion (detour) [ทาง taang]

ทางเลือก taang-lûuak *n.* option (choice) [ทาง taang]

ทางโลก taang-lôok *adj.* secular

ทางหลวง taang-lǔuang *n.* highway [สาย sǎai]

ทางออก taang-ɔ̀ɔk *n.* way out [ทาง taang]

ทางอ้อม taang-ɔ̂ɔm *n.* bypass (detour) [ทาง taang]

ทางอากาศ taang-aa-gàat *adv.* by air

ท่าเดิน tâa-dəən *n.* gait

ท่าทาง tâa-taang *n.* gesture (movement), manner (bearing, style) [ท่า tâa]

ท้าทาย táa-taai *v.* challenge

ทาน taan *n.* donation

ทาน taan *v.* eat

ท่าน tân *clf.* for someone in a high rank or position ⚡

ท่าน tân *pron.* second and third person pronoun used to address someone with respect ⚡

ทานตะวัน taan-dtà~wan *n.* sunflower [ต้น dtôn (tree), ดอก dɔ̀ɔk (flower)]

ทาบ tâap *vt.* place over

ท่ามกลาง tâam-glaang *prep.* among/amongst (surrounded by)

ทาย taai *v.* forecast ⚡, guess (wild)

ท้าย táai *n.* end (rear)

ทายาท taa-yâat *n.* descendant, heir/heiress

[คน kon]

ทารก taa-rók *n.* baby [คน kon]

ทารุณ taa-run *vt.* torture (torment) ☙

ท่าเรือ tâa-ruua *n.* port (pier, wharf) [แห่ง hèng]

ทาส tâat *n.* slave [คน kon]

ทาสี taa-sǐi *vi.* paint

ทำ tam *vt.* do/does/did, make (produce, create)

ทำขวัญ tam-kwǎn *v.* perform ceremony for strength and encouragement

ทำงาน tam-ngaan *vi.* be on (working, not off), perform (work)

ทำจาก tam-jàak *adj.* made from

ทำ_ซ้ำ tam-_-sám *vt.* repeat (action)

ทำด้วย tam-dûuai *adj.* made of

ทำ_ตก tam-_-dtòk *vt.* drop

ทำ_ต่อ tam-_-dtɔ̀ɔ *v.* carry on (do more)

ทำต่อไป tam-dtɔ̀ɔ-bpai *vi.* proceed (continue)

ทำตัว tam-dtuua *vi.* act (behave)

ทำตาม tam-dtaam *vi.* comply (do as told)

ทำโทษ tam-tôot *vt.* punish ‼

ทำนบ tam-nóp *n.* dam [แห่ง hèng]

ทำนอง tam-nɔɔng *n.* melody [ทำนอง tam-nɔɔng]

ทำนา tam-naa *vi.* farm (rice)

ทำนาย tam-naai *v.* predict

ทำเนียบขาว tam-nîiap-kǎao *n.* White House [หลัง lǎng]

ทำบุญ tam-bun *vi.* make merit

ทำไม tam-mai *adv.* why

ทำร้าย tam-ráai *vt.* injure

ทำลาย tam-laai *vt.* destroy (ruin)

ทำลายสถิติ tam-laai-sà-dtì~dtì *v.* break a record

ทำเล tam-lee *n.* location (site) [ทำเล tam-lee]

ทำสวน tam-sǔuan *vi.* garden

ทำ_สำเร็จ tam-_-sǎm-rèt *vt.* accomplish

ทำหน้าที่ tam-nâa-tîi *vi.* function

ทำ_หาย tam-_-hǎai *vt.* lose (something)

ทำอาหาร tam-aa-hǎan *vi.* cook (make food)

ทิ้ง tíng *vt.* discard (throw away), dump (empty out)

ทิ้ง_ไว้ tíng-_-wái *vt.* leave (something)

ทิฐิ tí-tì *n.* pride (conviction)

ทิป típ *n.* tip (gratuity)

ทิ่ม tîm *vt.* jab, prick (stab)

ทิวทัศน์ tiu-tát *n.* scenery (spectacle), view (picture of a landscape) [แห่ง hèng]

ทิศ tít *n.* direction (e.g. north) [ทิศ tít]

ทิศใต้ tít-dtâai *n.* south (direction) [ทิศ tít]

ทิศทาง tít-taang *n.* direction, way [ทิศ tít]

ทิศเหนือ tít-nɨɨa *n.* north [ทิศ tít]

ที tii *n.* turn (e.g. my turn) [ที tii]

ที่ tîi *adv.* on (by, at)

ที่ tîi *n.* place (site, spot) [แห่ง hèng]

ที่ tîi *n.* land ✿, property

✿, real estate ✿ [แปลง bplɛɛng, ผืน pʉ̌ʉn]

ที่ tîi *prep.* as (that, which), at (place), in (by, at), on, to (e.g. go to)

ที่ tîi *pron.* which

ที่เก็บของ tîi-gèp-kɔ̌ɔng *n.* storage (for storing) [ที่ tîi]

ที่เก้า tîi-gâao *adj.* ninth

ที่เขี่ยบุหรี่ tîi-kìia-bù~rìi *n.* ashtray [อัน an]

ที่คาดผม tîi-kâat-pǒm *n.* hair band [อัน an]

ที่จอดรถ tîi-jɔ̀ɔt-rót *n.* parking lot/car park [แห่ง hèng, ที่ tîi]

ที่จะ tîi-jà *conj.* that, which

ที่ชาร์จ tîi-cháat *n.* charger ✿ [อัน an]

ที่ดัดขนตา tîi-dàt-kǒn-dtaa *n.* eyelash curler [อัน an]

ที่ดิน tîi-din *n.* land (property), piece of land [แปลง bplɛɛng, ผืน pʉ̌ʉn]

ที่เดียว tii-diiao *adv.* just (exactly), quite ❗

ที่ตั้ง tîi-dtâng *n.* location, site [ที่ tîi]

ที่ตัดเล็บ tîi-dtàt-lép *n.* nail clippers

ที่ทำงาน tîi-tam-ngaan *n.* office (where work is conducted) [แห่ง hɛ̀ng, ที่ tîi]

ที่ทิ้งขยะ tîi-tíng-kà~yà *n.* dump (where trash is dumped) [ที่ tîi]

ที่นอน tîi-nɔɔn *n.* mattress [แผ่น pɛ̀n, อัน an ●]

ที่นั่ง tîi-nâng *n.* seat [ที่ tîi]

ที่นั่น tîi-nân *adv.* over there, there (over there)

ที่นี่ tîi-nîi *adv.* here, over here

ที่ปรึกษา tîi-bprùk-sǎa *n.* counselor (advisor) [ท่าน tân ⚡, คน kon]

ที่ปัดน้ำฝน tîi-bpàt-nám-fǒn *n.* windshield wiper [อัน an]

ที่พัก tîi-pák *n.* accommodation (lodging), residence [แห่ง hɛ̀ng]

ที่พักอาศัย tîi-pák-aa-sǎi *n.* shelter (dwelling place) [ที่ tîi]

ทีม tiim *n.* team [ทีม tiim]

ที่ม้วนผม tîi-múuan-pǒm *n.* curler [อัน an]

ที่มา tîi-maa *n.* origin (source, root), source

ที่ร่ม tîi-rôm *n.* shade (cover) [ที่ tîi]

ที่รองแก้ว tîi-rɔɔng-gɛ̂ɛo *n.* coaster (e.g. for cups) [อัน an]

ที่รัก tîi-rák *n.* darling, dear (loved one) [คน kon]

ที่ราบ tîi-râap *n.* plain (flatland) [แห่ง hɛ̀ng]

ที่ราบลุ่ม tîi-râap-lûm *n.* basin (e.g. river basin), low plain [แห่ง hɛ̀ng]

ที่ราบสูง tîi-râap-sǔung *n.* highland [แห่ง hɛ̀ng, ที่ tîi]

ทีละ tii-lá *adj.* each, one by one

ทีละ tii-lá *prep.* at a time

ทีละน้อย tii-lá~nɔ́ɔi *adv.* gradually, little by little

ที่ล้างหน้า tîi-láang-nâa *n.*

sink (wash basin) [ที่ tîi]

ที่ลาด tîi-lâat *n.* slope (incline) [ทาง taang, ที่ tîi]

ที่ลุ่ม tîi-lûm *n.* lowland

ที่โล่ง tîi-lôong *n.* open (space) [แห่ง hɛ̀ng]

ที่ว่าง tîi-wâang *n.* room (open space)

ทีวี tii-wii *n.* television • [เครื่อง krɯ̂ɯang]

ที่สร้างสรรค์ tîi-sâang-sǎn *adj.* creative

ที่สุด tîi-sùt *adj.* to the end, most

ที่หนีบ tîi-nìip *n.* clip (clasp) [อัน an]

ทีหลัง tii-lǎng *adv.* later

ที่เหยียบ tîi-yìiap *n.* pedal (e.g. of piano) [อัน an]

ที่เหลือ tîi-lɯ̌ɯa *adj.* leftover

ที่ไหน tîi-nǎi *adv.* somewhere (as object, in question), somewhere (as subject), where

ที่ไหนก็ได้ tîi-nǎi-gɔ̂ɔ-dâai *adv.* anywhere

ที่ไหนก็ตาม tîi-nǎi-gɔ̂ɔ- dtaam *conj.* wherever

ที่อยู่ tîi-yùu *n.* address (for mailing), dwelling, location (address, lodging) [แห่ง hɛ̀ng]

ที่อยู่อาศัย tîi-yùu-aa-sǎi *n.* residence [ที่ tîi]

ที่อื่น tîi-ɯ̀ɯn *adv.* elsewhere

ทึบ tʉ́p *adj.* dense (e.g. jungle)

ทึบแสง tʉ́p-sɛ̌ɛng *adj.* opaque (impenetrable by light)

ทึ่ม tʉ̂m *adj.* retarded

ทื่อ tʉ̂ɯ *adj.* blunt (not sharp)

ทุก túk *adj.* all, each, entire, every

ทุกๆ túk-túk *adj.* every (all)

ทุกข์ túk *n.* difficulty (suffering)

ทุกข์ใจ túk-jai *adj.* sad

ทุกข์ยาก túk-yâak *adj.* miserable (poor, needy)

ทุกคน túk-kon *pron.* all, everybody/everyone

ทุกครั้ง túk-kráng *adv.* every time

ทุกเดือน túk-duuan *adv.* every month, monthly

ทุกที túk-tii *adv.* every time

ทุกที่ túk-tîi *adv.* everywhere

ทุกปี túk-bpii *adj.* annual

ทุกวัน túk-wan *adv.* daily, every day

ทุกเวลา túk-wee-laa *adv.* anytime

ทุกสัปดาห์ túk-sàp-daa *adv.* every week ‼

ทุกแห่ง túk-hèng *adv.* everywhere

ทุกอย่าง túk-yàang *pron.* everything

ทุกอาทิตย์ túk-aa-tít *adv.* every week

ทุ่งนา tûng-naa *n.* paddy field, rice field [ที่ tîi, แห่ง hèng, ผืน pǔun]

ทุ่งเลี้ยงสัตว์ tûng-líiang-sàt *n.* pasture (field for animals) [แห่ง hèng]

ทุ่งหญ้า tûng-yâa *n.* meadow [แห่ง hèng]

ทุจริต tút-jà~rìt *adj.* corrupt

ทุน tun *n.* capital

(investment) [ก้อน gɔ̂ɔn]

ทุ่น tûn *n.* float (buoy) [อัน an]

ทุนการศึกษา tun-gaan-sùk-sǎa *n.* scholarship [ทุน tun]

ทุนนิยม tun-ní-yom *n.* capitalism

ทุ่นระเบิด tûn-rá~bə̀ət *n.* explosive mine [ทุ่น tûn, ลูก lûuk]

ทุ่นแรง tûn-rɛɛng *v.* save labor

ทุบ túp *vt.* pound, smash

ทุพพลภาพ túp-pon-lá~pâap *adj.* crippled ‼

ทุ่ม tûm *clf.* o'clock (nighttime)

ทุ้ม túm *n.* lowest tone of an instrument [เสียง sǐiang]

ทุ่มเท tûm-tee *v.* lavish, throw all one's resources

ทุย tui *n.* buffalo ✹ [ตัว dtuua]

ทุเรศ tú-rêet *adj.* disgusting, obscene, offensive (shameful, obscene)

ทุเรียน tú-riian *n.* durian (fruit) [ลูก lûuk]

ก ข ฃ ค ฅ ฆ ง จ ฉ ช ซ ฌ ญ ฎ ฏ ฐ ฑ ฒ ณ ด ต ถ **ท** ธ น บ ป ผ ฝ พ ฟ ภ ม ย ร ฤ ล ว ศ ษ ส ห อ ฮ

ทุลักทุเล tú-lák-tú-lee *adj.* struggling

ทุเลา tú-lao *vi.* recover (get better)

ทูต tûut *n.* diplomatic agent [ท่าน tân ‼, คน kon]

ทูน tuun *v.* hold over the head

เท tee *vt.* pour (from a container)

เท่ têe *adj.* smart looking ‼

เทคโนโลยี têek-noo-loo-yîi *n.* technology

เท็จ tét *adj.* false (untrue)

เททิ้ง tee-tíng *vt.* empty (pour off)

เทป téep *n.* tape (cassette) [ม้วน múuan]

เทปกาว téep-gaao *n.* adhesive tape [ชนิด chá~nít]

เทพ têep *n.* angel [องค์ ong]

เทพธิดา têep-tí-daa *n.* goddess [องค์ ong]

เทพนิยาย têep-ní-yaai *n.* fairy tale (story) [เรื่อง rûuang]

เทพพระเจ้า têep-prá~

jâao *n.* divine being ‼ [องค์ ong]

เทพยดา têep-pá~yá~daa *n.* elf (fairy) [ตน dton]

เทพี tee-pii *n.* beauty queen ‼ [คน kon]

เทมปุระ tem-bpù-rá *n.* kind of Japanese food

เทวดา tee-wá~daa *n.* angel (male) [องค์ ong]

เทววิทยา tee-wá-wít-tá~yaa *n.* theology [วิชา wí-chaa]

เทศกาล têet-sà~gaan *n.* carnival [งาน ngaan]

เทศน์ têet *n.* sermon [กัณฑ์ gan]

เทศน์ têet *vi.* preach (deliver a sermon)

เทศนา têet-sà~năa *vi.* preach (deliver a sermon) ‼

เทศบาล têet-sà~baan *adj.* municipal

เทศบาล têet-sà~baan *n.* municipality (municipal government) [เทศบาล têet-sà~baan, ที่ tîi, แห่ง hèng]

เทอม təəm *n.* semester, term [เทอม təəm]

เทอะทะ té-tá *adj.* bulky

เทา tao *adj.* gray/grey

เท่า tâo *n.* times (e.g. three times faster)

เท้า táao *n.* foot (body part) [ข้าง kâang (one), คู่ kûu (pair)]

เท่ากัน tâo-gan *adj.* equal, equivalent

เท่ากับ tâo-gàp *adj.* equivalent

เท่ากับ tâo-gàp *vt.* equal

เท่าที่ tâo-tîi *conj.* as long as

เท่าที่ tâo-tîi *prep.* as far, as far as

เท่านั้น tâo-nán *adv.* just, only

เท้าเปล่า táao-bplàao *adv.* barefoot

เท่าไร tâo-rai *n.* how many

เที่ยง tîiang *adj.* accurate

เที่ยง tîiang *n.* midday, noon

เที่ยงคืน tîiang-kɯɯn *n.* midnight

เที่ยงตรง tîiang-dtrong *adj.* precise (exact)

เที่ยงวัน tîiang-wan *n.* midday, noon

เทียน tiian *n.* candle [เล่ม lêm]

เทียบฝั่ง tîiap-fàng *adv.* ashore

เทียม tiiam *adj.* artificial (fake)

เทียม tiiam *vt.* yoke (harness)

เทียว tiiao *v.* go back and forth

เที่ยว tîiao *v.* make a pleasure tour

เที่ยวเดียว tîiao-diiao *adj.* one-way (e.g. ticket)

เที่ยวบิน tîiao-bin *n.* flight (airplane) [เที่ยว tîiao]

เทือกเขา tɯ̂ɯak-kǎo *n.* range (e.g. mountain) [เทือก tɯ̂ɯak]

แท้ tɛ́ɛ *adj.* authentic, genuine, real

แท็กซี่ tɛ́k-sîi *n.* taxi [คัน kan]

แทง tɛɛng *vt.* jab, penetrate, pierce (puncture), stab

แท่ง tɛ̂ng *n.* chunk (long bar) [แท่ง tɛ̂ng]

แท้จริง tɛ́ɛ-jing *adj.* true (real)

แทน tɛɛn *adv.* instead

ก ข ข ค ค ฅ ฆ ง จ ฉ ช ซ ฌ ญ ฎ ฏ ฐ ฑ ฒ ณ ด ต ถ ท ธ น บ ป ผ ฝ พ ฟ ภ ม ย ร ฤ ล ฦ ว ศ ษ ส ห อ ฮ

ก
ข
ฃ
ค
ฅ
ฆ
ง
จ
ฉ
ช
ซ
ฌ
ญ
ฎ
ฏ
ฐ
ฑ
ฒ
ณ
ด
ต
ถ
ท
ธ
น
บ
ป
ผ
ฝ
พ
ฟ
ภ
ม
ย
ร
ฤ
ล
ฦ
ว
ศ
ษ
ส
ห
ฬ
อ
ฮ

แทน tɛɛn *vt.* substitute for

แท่น tên *n.* pedestal (altar), podium ❢ [แท่น tên, ที่ tîi]

แทนที่ tɛɛn-tîi *adv.* instead, instead of

แทนที่ tɛɛn-tîi *vt.* replace (put back in place), supersede

แท่นพิมพ์ tên-pim *n.* press (printing press) [แท่น tên]

แทบ tɛ̂ɛp *adv.* nearly

แทบจะไม่ tɛ̂ɛp-jà~mâi *adv.* hardly (almost not, barely)

แทรกซึม sɛ̂ɛk-sɯm *v.* infiltrate, penetrate

แทร็ค trέk *n.* track (e.g. on CD)

แทะ tέ *v.* chew on (gnaw, e.g. bone), gnaw, nibble

โท too *adj.* second, two ✗

โทนสี toon-sǐi *n.* tone (shade, hue) [โทน toon]

โทมนัส toom-má~nát *n.* sadness ✍

โทร too *v.* phone, telephone ✽

โทรกลับ too-glàp *vi.* call back

โทรคมนาคม too-rá-ká~má~naa-kom *n.* telecommunication

โทรจิต too-rá~jìt *n.* telepathy

โทรทัศน์ too-rá~tát *n.* television [เครื่อง krûuang]

โทรฟรี too-frii *adj.* toll free/freephone (phone number)

โทรเลข too-rá~lêek *n.* telegram [ฉบับ chà~bàp]

โทรศัพท์ too-rá~sàp *n.* phone, telephone [เครื่อง krûuang]

โทรศัพท์ too-rá~sàp *v.* telephone

โทรสาร too-rá~sǎan *n.* fax ❢ [เครื่อง krûuang (machine), แผ่น pèn (paper)]

โทษ tôot *n.* penalty (foul), punishment

โทษทัณฑ์ tôot-tan *n.* penalty (foul) ✗

โทษประหาร tôot-bprà~hǎan *n.* capital punishment [ครั้ง kráng]

ไท tai *n.* freedom ✍

ไทย tai *adj.* Thai (relating to Thailand)

ไทย tai *n.* Thailand (country) ✦ [ประเทศ bprà~têet]

ธ

ธ tɔɔ *let.* ธ. ธง tɔɔ-tong, a consonant of the Thai alphabet (low consonant) [ตัว dtuua]

ธง tong *n.* banner, flag [ผืน pʉ̌ʉn]

ธนบัตร tá~ná~bàt *n.* banknote [ใบ bai]

ธนบุรี ton-bù-rii *n.* Thon Buri district [เขต kèet]

ธนาคาร tá~naa-kaan *n.* bank (money institution) [แห่ง hɛ̀ng]

ธนาณัติ tá~naa-nát *n.* money order [ใบ bai]

ธรณีวิทยา tɔɔ-rá~nii-wít-tá~yaa *n.* geology [วิชา wí-chaa]

ธรรม tam *n.* Buddhist teaching

ธรรมชาติ tam-má~châat *n.* nature

ธรรมดา tam-má~daa *adj.* common (normal), everyday (ordinary), regular (ordinary)

ธรรมเนียม tam-niiam *n.* tradition [แบบ bɛ̀ɛp, อย่าง yàang]

ธรรมะ tam-má *n.* Dharma [ข้อ kɔ̂ɔ]

ธัญพืช tan-yá~pʉ̂ʉt *n.* grain (cereal)

ธันวาคม tan-waa-kom *n.* December [เดือน dʉʉan]

ธาตุ tâat *n.* element (substance) [ชนิด chá~nít, ตัว dtuua ✦]

ธานี taa-nii *n.* city ✍ [แห่ง hɛ̀ng]

ธารน้ำแข็ง taan-nám-kɛ̌ng *n.* glacier [ก้อน gɔ̂ɔn]

ธิดา tí-daa *n.* daughter ✍ [คน kon]

ธุรกิจ tú-rá~gìt *n.* business (commerce)

ธุระ tú-rá *n.* business (errand, personal affairs) [เรื่อง rʉ̂ʉang, อัน an ✦]

ธุลี tú-lii *n.* dust (dry particles) ✍

ธูป tûup *n.* incense (joss stick) [ดอก dɔ̀ɔk (one), ห่อ hɔ̀ɔ (pack)]

ก ข ฃ ค ฅ ฆ ง จ ฉ ช ซ ฌ ญ ฎ ฏ ฐ ฑ ฒ ณ ด ต ถ **ท ธ** น บ ป ผ ฝ พ ฟ ภ ม ย ร ฤ ล ว ศ ษ ส ห อ ฮ

โธ่ tôo *interj.* Alas! What a pity!

น

น กวว *let.* น. หนู กวว-nŭn, a consonant of the Thai alphabet (low consonant) [ตัว dtuua]

นก nók *n.* bird [ตัว dtuua]

นกหวีด nók-wìit *n.* whistle (acoustic device) [อัน an]

นกฮูก nók-hûuk *n.* owl [ตัว dtuua]

นครราชสีมา ná-kɔɔn-râat-chá~sǐi-maa *n.* Nakhon Ratchasima province [จังหวัด jang-wàt]

นนทบุรี non-tá-bù~rii *n.* Nonthaburi province [จังหวัด jang-wàt]

นบ nóp *v.* make a gesture of respect

นบนอบ nóp-nɔ̂ɔp *adj.* respectful

นม nom *n.* milk

นม nom *n.* breast (woman's) [เต้า dtâo]

นมเปรี้ยว nom-bprîiao *n.* yogurt [รส rót (flavor), ถ้วย tûuai (cup)]

นมผง nom-pǒng *n.* powdered milk [กระป๋อง grà~bpǒng]

นมัสการ ná~mát-sà~gaan *n.* act of showing respect to a monk

นโยบาย ná~yoo-baai *n.* policy (plan, principles) [นโยบาย ná~yoo-baai, อัน an]

นรก ná~rók *n.* hell [ขุม kǔm]

นวด nûuat *vt.* knead, massage

นวนิยาย ná~wá-ní-yaai *n.* fiction ⚡, novel ⚡ [เรื่อง rûɯang]

นวม nuuam *n.* boxing glove [คู่ kûu (pair), ข้าง kâang (one)]

น่วม nûuam *adj.* soft (to the touch)

นวล nuuan *adj.* cream-colored

นวัตกรรม ná~wát-dtà~gam *n.* innovation ⚡

นอก nɔ̂ɔk *adj.* outside

นอกจาก nɔ̂ɔk-jàak *prep.* besides, beyond, but, except, outside of

นอกจากนี้ nɔ̂ɔk-jàak-níi *prep.* in addition to

นอกใจ nɔ̂ɔk-jai *vi.* cheat (on one's lover)

นอกเวลา nɔ̂ɔk-wee-laa *adv.* part-time

น่อง nɔ̂ng *n.* calf (body part) [ข้าง kâang, อัน an (for animal)]

น้อง nɔ́ɔng *n.* younger sibling [คน kon]

น้อง nɔ́ɔng *pron.* you (used to address someone younger)

น้องเขย nɔ́ɔng-kɤ̌ɤi *n.* brother-in-law (younger) [คน kon]

น้องชาย nɔ́ɔng-chaai *n.* younger brother [คน kon]

น้องสะใภ้ nɔ́ɔng-sà~pái *n.* sister-in-law (younger) [คน kon]

น้องสาว nɔ́ɔng-sǎao *n.* younger sister [คน kon]

น้องใหม่ nɔ́ɔng-mài *n.* freshman

นอต nɔ́t *n.* nut [ตัว dtuua]

นอน nɔɔn *vi.* sleep

นอนก้น nɔɔn-gôn *vi.* settle (sink to bottom)

นอนหลับ nɔɔn-làp *adj.* asleep

นอบน้อม nɔ̂ɔp-nɔ́ɔm *vi.* show respect

น้อย nɔ́ɔi *adj.* few, less, slight, small

น้อยกว่า nɔ́ɔi-gwàa *prep.* below/beneath (less than)

น้อยใจ nɔ́ɔi-jai *v.* feel inferior, feel neglected

น้อยหน่า nɔ́ɔi-nàa *n.* sugar apple [ลูก lûuk]

นะ ná *part.* used to make an utterance gentler

น่ะ nâ *part.* used to express urging

นัก nák *n.* person (individual, human) [คน kon]

นัก nák- *pref.* expert, participant in

นักข่าว nák-kàao *n.* journalist [คน kon]

นักเขียน nák-kǐian *n.* author, writer [คน kon]

นักท่องเที่ยว nák-tɔ̂ng-tîiao *n.* tourist [คน kon]

นักโทษ nák-tôot *n.* inmate, prisoner (convict) [คน kon]

นักธุรกิจ nák-tú-rá-gìt *n.* businessperson [คน kon]

นักบิน nák-bin *n.* pilot

กขฃคฅฆงจฉชซฌญฎฏฐฑฒณดตถทธ**น**บปผฝพฟภมยรลวศษสหฬอฮ

(aviator) [คน kon]

นักร้อง nák-rɔ́ɔng *n.* singer [คน kon]

นักเรียน nák-riian *n.* pupil, student [คน kon]

นักศึกษา nák-sɯ̀k-sǎa *n.* college student [คน kon]

นักสืบ nák-sɯ̀ɯp *n.* detective, spy [คน kon]

นักแสดง nák-sà~dɛɛng *n.* cast (actors) [ชุด chút]

นั่ง nâng *v.* ride (in car, boat, plane)

นั่ง nâng *vi.* sit

นั่งลง nâng-long *vi.* sit down

นัด nát *v.* make an appointment

นั่น nân *adj.* that

นั้น nán *adj.* that

นับ náp *v.* count

นับแต้ม náp-dtɛ̂ɛm *vi.* score (keep score)

นับถือ náp-tɯ̌ɯ *vt.* believe (in a religion), respect

นับว่า náp-wâa *vt.* consider (count as, reckon as)

นา naa *n.* paddy field [ที่ tîi, แห่ง hɛ̀ng, ผืน pɯ̌ɯn]

น่า nâa- *pref.* for verbs or adjectives to intensify their meanings, or mean "worthy of"

น้า náa *n.* mother's younger brother or sister [คน kon]

นาก nâak *n.* otter [ตัว dtuua]

น่ากลัว nâa-gluua *adj.* frightening, scary

น่ากิน nâa-gin *adj.* tasty-looking

น่าเกลียด nâa-glìiat *adj.* ugly (displeasing)

นาค nâak *n.* legendary serpent (Naga) [ตัว dtuua]

นาค nâak *n.* man entering priesthood [คน kon (person)]

นาง naang *n.* Mrs. [คน kon]

นาง naang *n.* woman [นาง naang, คน kon]

นางงาม naang-ngaam *n.* beauty queen [คน kon]

นางเงือก naang-ngɯ̂ɯak *n.* mermaid [ตัว dtuua]

นางแบบ naang-bɛ̀ɛp *n.* model (female) [คน kon]

นางฟ้า naang-fáa *n.* angel

ก ข ฃ ค ฅ ฆ ง จ ฉ ช ซ ฌ ญ ฎ ฏ ฐ ฑ ฒ ณ ด ต ถ ท ธ น บ ป ผ ฝ พ ฟ ภ ม ย ร ล ว ศ ษ ส ห อ ฮ

(female), fairy [องค์ ong]

นางสาว naang-sǎao *n.* young lady, miss (title) [คน kon]

นางเอก naang-èek *n.* heroine (e.g. in movies) [คน kon]

นาที naa-tii *n.* minute [นาที naa-tii]

นาน naan *adj.* long (of time), slow (long time)

น่าน nâan *n.* Nan province [จังหวัด jang-wàt]

นานา naa-naa *adj.* different (not same), various

นานาชาติ naa-naa-châat *adj.* international

น่าฟัง nâa-fang *adj.* pleasant to listen to

นาม naam *n.* noun [คำ kam]

นามบัตร naam-bàt *n.* business card, name card [ใบ bai]

นามปากกา naam-bpàak-gaa *n.* pen name [นาม naam]

นามสกุล naam-sà~gun *n.* last name [อัน an]

นาย naai *n.* master

(owner, boss, employer), Mr. (male title) [คน kon]

นายก naa-yók *n.* chief leader, president (of an organization) [ท่าน tân ꞏ, คน kon]

นายกเทศมนตรี naa-yók-têet-sà~mon-dtrii *n.* mayor [ท่าน tân ꞏ, คน kon]

นายกรัฐมนตรี naa-yók-rát-tà~mon-dtrii *n.* prime minister [ท่าน tân ꞏ, คน kon]

นายจ้าง naai-jâang *n.* boss (who pays you), employer [คน kon]

นายทะเบียน naai-tá~biian *n.* registrar [คน kon]

นายทุน naai-tun *n.* capitalist (one with capital) [คน kon]

นายแบบ naai-bὲεp *n.* model (male) [คน kon]

นายประกัน naai-bprà~gan *n.* bailsman [คน kon]

นายพล naai-pon *n.* general (officer) [คน kon]

นายหน้า naai-nâa *n.* broker, go-between [คน kon]

นายอำเภอ naai-am-pəə

ก
ข
ข
ค
ฅ
ฆ
ง
จ
ฉ
ช
ซ
ฌ
ญ
ฎ
ฏ
ฐ
ฑ
ฒ
ณ
ด
ต
ถ
ท
ธ
น
บ
ป
ผ
ฝ
พ
ฟ
ภ
ม
ย
ร
ฤ
ล
ฦ
ว
ศ
ษ
ส
ห
อ
ฮ

n. head official of a district, sheriff [คน kon]

น่ารัก nâa-rák *adj.* cute, lovely

น่ารังเกียจ nâa-rang-gìiat *adj.* disgusting (yucky, revolting), nasty, yucky

น่ารำคาญ nâa-ram-kaan *adj.* annoying

น้าว náao *v.* bend

น่าสงสัย nâa-sŏng-săi *adj.* suspicious

น่าสงสาร nâa-sŏng-săan *adj.* pitiful (deserving pity)

น่าเสียดาย nâa-sĭia-daai *adv.* unfortunately (regrettably)

นาฬิกา naa-lí~gaa *clf.* o'clock ‼

นาฬิกา naa-lí~gaa *n.* clock, watch (timepiece) [เรือน ruuan]

นาฬิกาปลุก naa-lí~gaa-bplùk *n.* alarm clock [เรือน ruuan]

นำ nam *v.* guide, lead

น้ำ náam *n.* water

น้ำกรด nám-gròt *n.* acid

น้ำขึ้น náam-kûn *n.* high tide

นำเข้า nam-kâo *vt.* import

น้ำแข็ง nám-kĕng *n.* ice [ก้อน gɔ̂ɔn]

น้ำค้าง nám-káang *n.* dew (water droplets) [หยด yòt]

น้ำเค็ม nám-kem *n.* salt water

น้ำเงิน nám-ngən *adj.* blue (navy blue)

น้ำจิ้ม nám-jîm *n.* sauce [ขวด kùuat (bottle)]

น้ำจืด nám-jὺut *n.* fresh water

น้ำใจ nám-jai *n.* spirit (kindness, good will, thoughtfulness)

น้ำเชื่อม nám-chὺuam *n.* syrup (drink sweetener) [ขวด kùuat]

น้ำตก nám-dtòk *n.* waterfall [แห่ง hὲng]

น้ำตา nám-dtaa *n.* tear (from eyes) [หยด yòt]

น้ำตาล nám-dtaan *adj.* brown

น้ำตาล nám-dtaan *n.* sugar [ช้อน chɔ́ɔn (spoonful)]

น้ำเต้า nám-dtâo *n.* gourd [ลูก lûuk]

น้ำท่วม náam-tûuam *n.* flood

น้ำทะเล nám-tá~lee *n.* seawater

นำทาง nam-taang *v.* guide (lead)

น้ำประปา nám-bprà~bpaa *n.* city water

น้ำปลา nám-bplaa *n.* fish sauce [ขวด kùuat (bottle)]

น้ำผึ้ง nám-pûng *n.* honey (bee nectar) [ขวด kùuat (bottle)]

น้ำพริก nám-prík *n.* hot chili paste sauce [ถ้วย tûuai]

น้ำพุ nám-pú *n.* spring (fountain) [แห่ง hɛ̀ng (location)]

น้ำมนต์ nám-mon *n.* holy water

น้ำมะขาม nám-má~kǎam *n.* tamarind sauce

น้ำมัน nám-man *n.* fuel (petrol, gasoline), oil [แกลลอน gɛn-lɔɔn (gallon), ลิตร lít (liter), ขวด kùuat (bottle)]

น้ำมันหมู nám-man-mǔu *n.* lard (grease)

น้ำมือ nám-mɯɯ *n.* action, one's own deed

น้ำมูก nám-mûuk *n.* mucus, snot

น้ำยา nám-yaa *n.* solvent (e.g. cleaner)

น้ำแร่ nám-rɛ̂ɛ *n.* mineral water [ขวด kùuat]

น้ำลง náam-long *n.* low tide

น้ำลาย nám-laai *n.* saliva

น้ำลายไหล nám-laai-lǎi *vi.* drool (let saliva run)

น้ำวน nám-won *n.* whirlpool [แห่ง hɛ̀ng]

น้ำส้ม nám-sôm *n.* orange juice [แก้ว gɛ̂ɛo (glass)]

น้ำส้มสายชู nám-sôm-sǎai-chuu *n.* vinegar [ขวด kùuat]

นำสมัย nam-sà~mǎi *adj.* trendy (fashionable)

น้ำเสียง nám-sǐiang *n.* tone of voice

น้ำหนัก nám-nàk *n.* weight

นำหน้า nam-nâa *v.* precede (be ahead)

น้ำหวาน nám-wǎan *n.* flavored syrup

น้ำหอม nám-hɔ̌ɔm *n.* perfume [กลิ่น glìn (scent), ขวด kùuat (bottle)]

น้ำอัดลม nám-àt-lom *n.* soda (carbonated drink) [ขวด kùuat]

นิกาย ní-gaai *n.* sect (religious) [นิกาย ní-gaai]

นิโคลัส ní-koo-lát *n.* Cochin (chicken) [ตัว dtuua]

นิ่ง nîng *adj.* motionless, quiet, still

นิด nít *adj.* little

นิดเดียว nít-diiao *adj.* few ✿

นิดหน่อย nít-nɔ̀i *adv.* a little bit/little bit

นิตยสาร nít-dtà~yá~sǎan *n.* magazine [ฉบับ chà~bàp ✐, เล่ม lêm]

นิติ ní-dtì *n.* law

นิติกรรม ní-dtì-gam *n.* juristic act, legal act

นิติบัญญัติ ní-dtì-ban-yàt *n.* legislation

นิติศาสตร์ ní-dtì~sàat *n.* law (subject) [วิชา wí-chaa]

นิทรรศการ ní-tát-sà~gaan *n.* exhibition [ครั้ง kráng]

นิทรา nít-traa *n.* drowsiness ✍

นิทาน ní-taan *n.* fable, story, tale [เรื่อง rûuang]

นินทา nin-taa *vt.* gossip about

นิพพาน níp-paan *n.* Nirvana

นิ่ม nîm *adj.* silky (soft)

นิมนต์ ní-mon *v.* invite a Buddhist monk

นิมิต ní-mít *n.* omen ✍ [อัน an]

นิยาม ní-yaam *n.* definition (explanation)

นิยาย ní-yaai *n.* novel [เรื่อง rûuang]

นิรนาม ní-rá~naam *adj.* anonymous

นิรภัย ní-rá~pai *adj.* safety (preventing harm)

นิรันดร์ ní-ran *adj.* permanent ✍

นิโรธ ní-rôot *n.* death

นิล nin *adj.* black ⬥

นิล nin *n.* black or dark precious stone

นิ่ว nîu *n.* gall stone [ก้อน gɔ̂ɔn]

นิ้ว níu *n.* finger, inch [นิ้ว níu]

นิ้วกลาง níu-glaang *n.* middle finger [นิ้ว níu]

นิ้วก้อย níu-gɔ̂ɔi *n.* little finger, pinkie [นิ้ว níu]

นิวเคลียร์ niu-kliia *n.* nuclear

นิ้วชี้ níu-chíi *n.* index finger [นิ้ว níu]

นิ้วเท้า níu-táao *n.* toe [นิ้ว níu]

นิ้วนาง níu-naang *n.* ring finger [นิ้ว níu]

นิ้วโป้ง níu-bpôong *n.* thumb ⬥ [นิ้ว níu]

นิ้วมือ níu-mɯɯ *n.* finger [นิ้ว níu]

นิสัย ní-sǎi *n.* character (nature, habit)

นิสัยใจคอ ní-sǎi-jai-kɔɔ *n.* temperament (disposition)

นิสิต ní-sìt *n.* college student [คน kon]

นี่ nîi *pron.* here, this

นี้ níi *adj.* this

นึก núk *v.* think

นึง nɯng *idm.* one, just

นึ่ง nɯ̂ng *vt.* steam (cook over steam)

นุ่ง nûng *vt.* put on (wear) ⬥

นุ่น nûn *n.* kapok

นุ่ม nûm *adj.* soft (to the touch), tender

นูน nuun *vi.* curve out, protrude (pop out)

นู่น nûun *adv.* that (one) over there

นู้น núun see นู่น

เน็ท nét *n.* net (used in sports, e.g. tennis) [ผืน pɯ̌ɯn]

เน้น néen *vt.* emphasize, highlight, stress

เนย nəəi *n.* butter [กล่อง glɔ̀ng (box)]

เนยแข็ง nəəi-kɛ̌ng *n.* cheese [ชิ้น chín (piece)]

เนยเทียม nəəi-tiiam *n.*

margarine [ขวด kùuat]

เนรเทศ nee-rá~têet *vt.* proscribe (banish, exile)

เน่า nâo *adj.* rotten

เน่าเปื่อย nâo-bpùuai *vi.* decay, perish (spoil), rot

เนิน nəən *n.* mound (knoll)

เนินเขา nəən-kǎo *n.* hill [ลูก lûuk]

เนื้อ núua *n.* meat

เนื้อคู่ núua-kûu *n.* soulmate [คน kon]

เนื่องจาก nûuang-jàak *prep.* because of (due to)

เนื้องอก núua-ngɔ̂ɔk *n.* tumor [ก้อน gɔ̂ɔn]

เนื้อที่ núua-tîi *n.* space (area)

เนื้อผ้า núua-pâa *n.* texture (of cloth)

เนื้อเพลง núua-pleeng *n.* lyrics (words of a song) [บท bòt (verse)]

เนื้อเยื่อ núua-yûua *n.* tissue (cells)

เนื้อเรื่อง núua-rûuang *n.* essential part of a story [เรื่อง rûuang]

เนื้อวัว núua-wuua *n.* beef

[ชิ้น chín]

เนื้อสัตว์ núua-sàt *n.* meat (animal)

เนื้อหมู núua-mǔu *n.* pork [ชิ้น chín]

เนื้อหา núua-hǎa *n.* content (e.g. of book, article), gist

เนื้ออบ núua-òp *n.* roast [ชิ้น chín]

แน่ใจ nɛ̂ɛ-jai *adj.* certain, sure (convinced)

แน่น nɛ̂n *adj.* firm, jammed, tight (e.g. screw, bottle top)

แน่นอน nɛ̂ɛ-nɔɔn *adj.* certain (definite, inevitable), definite

แนบ nɛ̂ɛp *vt.* attach (e.g. document)

แนวตั้ง nɛɛo-dtâng *adj.* vertical

แนวทาง nɛɛo-taang *n.* way (course, direction) [แนว nɛɛo]

แนวนอน nɛɛo-nɔɔn *adj.* horizontal

แน่วแน่ nɛ̂o-nɛ̂ɛ *adj.* decisive (unwavering)

แนวโน้ม nɛɛo-nóom *n.*

tendency (inclination)

แนวหน้า nεεɔ-nâa *n.* front line [แนว nεεɔ]

แนะ né *vt.* guide (advise)

แนะนำ né-nam *vt.* introduce (present), suggest (advise)

โน้ต nóot *n.* note (music) [ตัว dtuua]

โน่น nôon *pron.* there

โน้น nóon *adv.* that (one) over there

โน้มน้าว nóom-náao *v.* persuade (convince)

ใน nai *prep.* at (place), in, inside

ในขณะที่ nai-kà~nà-tîi *conj.* while

ในที่สุด nai-tîi-sùt *adv.* at last, eventually, finally

ในหลวง nai-lǔuang *pron.* His Majesty the king, king (Thai King)

ในอนาคต nai-à~naa-kót *adv.* sometime

บ

บ bɔɔ *let.* บ. ใบไม้ bɔɔ-bai-máai, a consonant of the Thai alphabet (mid consonant) [ตัว dtuua]

บ่ bɔɔ *adj.* no, never, not

บก bòk *n.* land (as opposed to sea)

บ่งบอก bòng-bɔ̀ɔk *vt.* indicate (say, measure)

บด bòt *vt.* grind

บท bòt *n.* chapter (section) [บท bòt]

บทกวี bòt-gà~wii *n.* lyric (poem), poetry (verse) [บท bòt]

บทความ bòt-kwaam *n.* article (e.g. newspaper) [เรื่อง rûuang]

บทนำ bòt-nam *n.* introduction (foreword) [บท bòt]

บทบาท bòt-bàat *n.* role

บทเพลง bòt-pleeng *n.* lyrics (words of a song) [บท bòt]

บทเรียน bòt-riian *n.* lesson [บท bòt]

บทสนทนา bòt-sǒn-tá~naa *n.* conversation, dialogue [บท bòt]

บทสรุป bòt-sà~rùp *n.* summary [บท bòt]

บน bon *prep.* over (above, on), upon (on)

บ่น bòn *vi.* complain (whine)

บ่ม bòm v. ripen

บรรจุ ban-jù vt. contain, pack (put in container)

บรรณาธิการ ban-naa-tí-gaan n. editor [คน kon]

บรรณารักษ์ ban-naa-rák n. librarian [คน kon]

บรรดา ban-daa n. entire

บรรทัด ban-tát n. line (ruled line, line of text)

บรรทัดฐาน ban-tát-tăan n. norm

บรรเทา ban-tao vt. alleviate

บรรพบุรุษ ban-pá-bù~rùt n. ancestor

บรรยากาศ ban-yaa-gàat n. atmosphere

บรรยาย ban-yaai vt. depict

บรรเลง ban-leeng v. play (music) ♪

บริการ bɔɔ-rí~gaan v. serve

บริจาค bɔɔ-rí~jàak v. contribute, donate

บริบท bɔɔ-rí~bòt n. context (linguistics)

บริโภค bɔɔ-rí~pôok v. consume (eat, spend) ✖

บริวาร bɔɔ-rí~waan n. follower (disciple) [คน kon]

บริเวณ bɔɔ-rí~ween n. area (vicinity, zone) [แห่ง hèng]

บริษัท bɔɔ-rí~sàt n. company, firm [แห่ง hèng]

บริสุทธิ์ bɔɔ-rí~sùt adj. innocent (not guilty), pure (free from extraneous matter)

บริหาร bɔɔ-rí~hăan v. manage (administer)

บวก bùuak adj. positive (not negative)

บวก bùuak prep. plus (e.g. 10 plus 2)

บวก bùuak vt. add (numbers)

บ่วง bùuang n. snare [อัน an]

บวงสรวง buuang-sŭuang v. sacrifice (offer to god)

บวช bùuat v. ordain (as a monk or priest)

บ้วน bûuan v. spit out

บ้วนน้ำลาย bûuan-nám-laai vi. spit

บ้วนปาก bûuan-bpàak vi. gargle

บวบ bùuap n. dishrag gourd [ลูก lûuk]

บวม buuam adj. inflamed,

swollen

บ๊วย búuai *n.* kind of fruit [ลูก lûuk]

บอก bɔ̀ɔk *vt.* say (state), tell (e.g. story)

บ้อง bɔ̂ŋ *n.* hollow cylindrical piece of wood [บ้อง bɔ̂ŋ]

บ๊อง bɔ́ɔŋ *adj.* crazy

บ้องไฟ bɔ̂ŋ-fai *n.* rocket (bamboo) [บ้อง bɔ̂ŋ]

บอด bɔ̀ɔt *adj.* blind, blinded

บ่อน bɔ̀n *n.* casino [บ่อน bɔ̀n, แห่ง hɛ̀ŋ]

บ่อน้ำ bɔ̀ɔ-náam *n.* well [บ่อ bɔ̀ɔ]

บอบบาง bɔ̀ɔp-baang *adj.* flimsy (frail), thin (for people, animals)

บ่อย bɔ̀i *adv.* frequently

บ๋อย bɔ̌i *n.* bellboy ✹, server (waiter) ✹ [คน kon]

บ่อยๆ bɔ̀i-bɔ̀i *adv.* often

บอระเพ็ด bɔɔ-rá~pét *n.* species of climbing vine [ต้น dtôn]

บอลลูน bɔn-luun *n.* balloon [ลูก lûuk]

บะหมี่ bà~mìi *n.* egg

noodle [ชาม chaam (bowl), ถ้วย tûuai (bowl), เส้น sên (strand)]

บักสีดา bàk-sǐi-daa *n.* guava ✹ [ลูก lûuk]

บังกะโล bang-gà~loo *n.* bungalow [หลัง lǎng]

บังคับ bang-káp *vt.* coerce, compel, force

บังคับบัญชา bang-káp-ban-chaa *v.* command, direct, order

บังโคลนรถ bang-kloon-rót *n.* mudguard [อัน an]

บั้งไฟ bâng-fai *n.* bamboo rocket [บั้ง bâng, ลูก lûuk]

บังเหียน bang-hǐian *n.* harness (riding) [เส้น sên, สาย sǎai]

บังเอิญ bang-əən *adv.* by chance

บัญชี ban-chii *n.* account [เล่ม lêm]

บัญญัติ ban-yàt *vt.* enact (law)

บัณฑิต ban-dìt *n.* university graduate [คน kon]

บัดซบ bàt-sóp *adj.* idiotic

บัตร bàt *n.* card (e.g.

credit, I.D.) [ใบ bai]

บัตรเครดิต bàt-kree-dìt *n.* credit card [ใบ bai]

บัตรเชิญ bàt-chəən *n.* invitation card [บัตร bàt, ใบ bai, แผ่น pèn]

บัตรประชาชน bàt-bprà~ chaa-chon *n.* identity card [ใบ bai]

บัตรผ่าน bàt-pàan *n.* pass (admission ticket) [บัตร bàt]

บั่น bàn *v.* cut into pieces

บันดาล ban-daan *vt.* cause ✍

บันได ban-dai *n.* staircase/stairway [อัน an, แห่ง hèng]

บันไดลิง ban-dai-ling *n.* ladder [อัน an]

บันไดเลื่อน ban-dai-lûuan *n.* escalator [ตัว dtuua]

บั้นท้าย bân-táai *n.* tail (buttocks)

บันทึก ban-túk *v.* note (jot down), record

บัลลังก์ ban-lang *n.* throne [บัลลังก์ ban-lang]

บัว buua *n.* lotus

บ่า bàa *n.* shoulder [ข้าง kâang]

บ้า bâa *adj.* crazy, crazy about, insane, mad

บ้าๆบอๆ bâa-bâa-bɔɔ-bɔɔ *adj.* crazy ✿, odd ✿

บาง baang *adj.* any, slim (things), some, thin (for things)

บ้าง bâang *adv.* any (to some extent), some

บางคน baang-kon *pron.* some people

บางครั้ง baang-kráng *adv.* sometimes

บางที baang-tii *adv.* maybe, perhaps

บางส่วน baang-sùuan *adj.* partial (not total)

บางสิ่ง baang-sìng *pron.* some things

บางแห่ง baang-hèng *n.* some places

บางอย่าง baang-yàang *pron.* some things

บาด bàat *v.* make a cut

บาดเจ็บ bàat-jèp *adj.* injured

บาดทะยัก bàat-tá~yák *n.* tetanus [โรค rôok]

บาดแผล bàat-plἕɛ *n.* cut

(wound) [แห่ง hὲng, ที่ tîi]

บาดหมาง bàat-măang *adj.* estranged

บาดาล baa-daan *n.* abyss of hell

บาตร bàat *n.* Buddhist monk's round alms-bowl [ใบ bai, ลูก lûuk]

บาท bàat *n.* baht [บาท bàat]

บาทวิถี bàat-wí-tĭi *n.* sidewalk ! [ทาง taang]

บาทหลวง bàat-lŭuang *n.* Christian priest [คน kon]

บาน baan *vi.* bloom

บ้าน bâan *n.* home, house [หลัง lăng]

บานกบ baan-gòp *n.* window frame ✄ [แผ่น pὲn]

บ้านเกิด bâan-gə̀ət *n.* hometown [แห่ง hὲng, ที่ tîi]

บ้านนอก bâan-nɔ̂ɔk *n.* rural area ● [แห่ง hὲng]

บ้านพักตากอากาศ bâan-pák-dtàak-aa-gàat *n.* villa [หลัง lăng]

บานพับ baan-páp *n.* hinge [ตัว dtuua, อัน an]

บ้านเมือง bâan-mɯɯang

n. country

บาป bàap *n.* sin [อัน an]

บ่าย bàai *n.* afternoon [ตอน dtɔɔn]

บาร์ baa *n.* bar (where drinks are served) [แห่ง hὲng, ร้าน ráan]

บารมี baa-rá~mii *n.* merit

บาลี baa-lii *n.* Pali [ภาษา paa-săa]

บาศก์ bàat *n.* dice [ลูก lûuk]

บำนาญ bam-naan *n.* pension [จำนวน jam-nuuan]

บำบัด bam-bàt *vt.* rehabilitate

บำรุง bam-rung *vt.* nourish, nurture

บำรุงรักษา bam-rung-rák-săa *vt.* maintain (e.g. vehicle)

บำเหน็จ bam-nèt *n.* retirement allowance

บิณฑบาต bin-tá~bàat *v.* go about with an alms bowl to receive food

บิด bìt *v.* sprain (e.g. leg, ankle), twist

บิดเบือน bìt-bɯɯan *adj.* distorted

บิดา bì-daa *n.* father !

ก ข ฃ ค ฅ ฆ ง จ ฉ ช ซ ฌ ญ ฎ ฏ ฐ ฑ ฒ ณ ด ต ถ ท ธ น **บ** ป ผ ฝ พ ฟ ภ ม ย ร ล ฦ ว ศ ษ ส ห ฬ อ ฮ

[คน kon]

บิน bin *v.* fly

บิล bin *n.* bill, check (food bill) [ใบ bai]

บีบ bìip *v.* press (squeeze)

บีบ bìip *vt.* compress (squeeze, e.g. computer file, herb)

บีบคอ bìip-kɔɔ *vt.* choke (strangle)

บีบแตร bìip-dtrɛɛ *vi.* honk

บึกบึน bʉk-bʉn *adj.* stout (sturdy)

บึง bʉng *n.* bog, marsh (swamp, bog) [แห่ง hɛ̀ng]

บึ้งตึง bʉ̂ng-dtʉng *adj.* sulky

บุ bù *vt.* pad (put in a lining)

บุกรุก bùk-rúk *vi.* intrude (trespass)

บุกรุก bùk-rúk *vt.* invade

บุคคล bùk-kon *n.* person (individual, human) ‼ [คน kon]

บุคลากร bùk-ká~laa-gɔɔn *n.* personnel (staff) ‼ [คน kon]

บุคลิก bùk-ká~lík *n.* personality

บุคลิกภาพ bùk-ká~lík-

gà~pâap *n.* characteristic (nature, habit) ‼

บุ้ง bûng *n.* caterpillar (hairless variety) [ตัว dtuua]

บุญ bun *n.* merit

บุญคุณ bun-kun *n.* favor (kindness), obligation (debt of gratitude)

บุปผา bùp-pǎa *n.* flower (blossom) ⚘ [ดอก dɔ̀ɔk]

บุพบท bùp-pá-bòt *n.* preposition [คำ kam]

บุพเพสันนิวาส bùp-pee-sǎn-ní~wâat *n.* soulmate ⚘ [คน kon]

บุ๋ม bǔm *adj.* dented, dimpled

บุรีรัมย์ bù~rii-ram *n.* Buri Ram province [จังหวัด jang-wàt]

บุรุษ bù~rùt *n.* person (grammar)

บุรุษไปรษณีย์ bù~rùt-bprai-sà~nii *n.* mailman [คน kon]

บุษราคัม bùt-sà~raa-kam *n.* topaz [เม็ด mét (piece)]

บุหงา bù~ngǎa *n.* flower (blossom) ⚘ [ดอก dɔ̀ɔk]

บุหรี่ bù~rìi *n.* cigarette/

fag [ซอง sɔɔng (pack), มวน muuan (each)]

บูชา buu-chaa *vt.* worship (sacred objects)

บูด bùut *adj.* rotten

บูดง่าย bùut-ngâai *adj.* perishable (e.g. food)

บูท búut *v.* boot (computer) ✎

เบ็ด bèt *n.* fish hook [คัน kan]

เบ็ดเตล็ด bèt-dtà~lèt *adj.* miscellaneous

เบรค brèek *n.* brake (e.g. car) [ตัว dtuua]

เบา bao *adj.* gentle (e.g. wind, tap), light (not heavy), mild (soft), quiet (light sound)

เบ้าตา bâo-dtaa *n.* eye socket [ข้าง kâang]

เบาบาง bao-baang *adj.* thin (e.g. fog)

เบาหวาน bao-wǎan *n.* diabetes [โรค rôok]

เบาะ bɔ̀ *n.* pad (cushion) [ใบ bai, ลูก lûuk]

เบิกบาน bə̀ək-baan *adj.* jovial (merry)

เบิกพยาน bə̀ək-pá~yaan *v.* call in witnesses

เบี้ย bîia *n.* chip (gambling) [อัน an]

เบี้ยประกัน bîia-bprà~gan *n.* premium (insurance) [จำนวน jam-nuuan]

เบียร์ biia *n.* beer [กระป๋อง grà~bpɔ̌ng (can), ขวด kùuat (bottle), แก้ว gɛ̂ɛo (glass)]

เบี้ยว bîiao *adj.* out of line (not in a straight line)

เบี้ยหมากรุก bîia-màak-rúk *n.* pawn (chess) [ตัว dtuua]

เบื่อ bùua *adj.* tired of (bored, annoyed with)

เบื้อง bûuang- *pref.* side

เบื้องต้น bûuang-dtôn *adj.* elementary (primary)

เบื่อหน่าย bùua-nàai *adj.* fed up

แบก bɛ̀ɛk *vt.* carry on the shoulder

แบ่ง bɛ̀ng *vt.* divide (separate into parts), share

แบงค์ béng *n.* note (money) ✎ [ใบ bai]

แบ่ง_ครึ่ง bɛ̀ng-_-krʉ̂ng

vt. halve

แบ่งประเภท bèng-bprà~pêet *vt.* classify

แบ่งแยก bèng-yɛ̂ɛk *vt.* segregate, separate

แบตเตอรี่ bɛ̀t-dtəə-rîi *n.* battery (e.g. for car) [ใบ bai]

แบน bɛn *adj.* flat (e.g. tire), level (flat, even)

แบบ bɛ̀ɛp *n.* form (structure), pattern (model) [แบบ bɛ̀ɛp]

แบบแปลน bɛ̀ɛp-bplɛɛn *n.* drawing (plan, design) [แบบ bɛ̀ɛp (whole), แผ่น pɛ̀n (piece)]

แบบแผน bɛ̀ɛp-pɛ̌ɛn *n.* norm, rite (formality)

แบบฝึกหัด bɛ̀ɛp-fʉ̀k-hàt *n.* exercise (e.g. homework) [ข้อ kɔ̂ɔ (item), ชุด chút (set)]

แบบพิมพ์ bɛ̀ɛp-pim *n.* form, printed form [ฉบับ chà~bàp, แบบ bɛ̀ɛp, แผ่น pɛ̀n]

แบบเรียน bɛ̀ɛp-riian *n.* textbook ! [เล่ม lêm]

แบบสอบถาม bɛ̀ɛp-sɔ̀ɔp-tǎam *n.* questionnaire [ชุด chút]

แบมือ bɛɛ-mʉʉ *vi.* hold out one's hand

โบ๋ bǒo *adj.* containing holes

โบก bòok *vt.* wave

โบราณ boo-raan *adj.* ancient (antiquated), antique, old, primitive

โบราณคดี boo-raan-ná~ká~dii *n.* archaeology [วิชา wí-chaa]

โบราณวัตถุ boo-raan-ná~wát-tù *n.* antique ! [ตัว dtuua (furniture), ชิ้น chín (piece)]

โบว์ลิ่ง boo-lîng *n.* bowling (game)

โบสถ์ bòot *n.* Buddhist temple, church [แห่ง hɛ̀ng (location), หลัง lǎng (building)]

ใบ bai *clf.* for leaves, fruits, various kinds of containers, slips of sheets of paper

ใบ bai *n.* leaf [ใบ bai]

ใบ้ bâi *adj.* dumb, mute (unable to speak)

ใบเกิด bai-gə̀ət *n.* birth certificate [ใบ bai]

ใบขับขี่ bai-kàp-kìi *n.* driver's license [ใบ bai]

ใบตอง bai-dtɔɔng *n.* banana leaf [พับ páp, แหนบ nὲεp, ทาง taang]

ใบแทรก bai-sɛ̂ɛk *n.* insert (paper, sheet) [ใบ bai]

ใบประกาศ bai-bprà~gàat *n.* certificate ✱ [ใบ bai, แผ่น pὲn]

ใบปลิว bai-bpliu *n.* flier (pamphlet) [ใบ bai, แผ่น pὲn]

ใบพัด bai-pát *n.* propeller [อัน an]

ใบมอบฉันทะ bai-mɔ̂ɔp-chǎn-tá *n.* power of attorney [ใบ bai]

ใบมะกรูด bai-má~grùut *n.* kaffir lime leaves [ใบ bai]

ใบมีด bai-mîit *n.* blade [ใบ bai]

ใบไม้ bai-máai *n.* leaf [ใบ bai]

ใบรับรอง bai-ráp-rɔɔng *n.* certificate [ใบ bai, แผ่น pὲn]

ใบสมัคร bai-sà~màk *n.* application form [ใบ bai]

ใบสั่ง bai-sàng *n.* ticket (written summons, e.g. for speeding) [ใบ bai]

ใบสั่งยา bai-sàng-yaa *n.* prescription (slip for remedy) [ใบ bai]

ใบเสร็จ bai-sèt *n.* receipt [ใบ bai]

ใบหย่า bai-yàa *n.* divorce certificate [ใบ bai]

ใบอนุญาต bai-à-nú~yâat *n.* license, permit (e.g. driver's license) [ใบ bai]

ป

ป bpɔɔ *let.* ป. ปลา bpɔɔ-bplaa, a consonant of the Thai alphabet (mid consonant) [ตัว dtuua]

ป.ล. bpɔɔ-lɔɔ *n.* postscript, P.S

ปก bpòk *n.* cover (e.g. book) [ใบ bai, แผ่น pὲn]

ปกแข็ง bpòk-kĕng *adj.* hardcover

ปกครอง bpòk-krɔɔng *vi.* rule (govern)

ปกติ bpòk-gà~dtì, bpà~gà~dtì *adj.* normal, ordinary (usual), regular

ปกป้อง bpòk-bpông *vt.* protect (guard)

ปกปิด bpòk-bpìt *vt.* conceal (hide)

ปฏิ bpà~dtì- *pref.* anti- ⚑

ปฏิกิริยา bpà~dtì-gì-rí-yaa *n.* reaction

ปฏิชีวนะ bpà~dtì-chii-wá~ná *adj.* antibiotic

ปฏิญาณ bpà~dtì-yaan *v.* pledge, vow (swear)

ปฏิทิน bpà~dtì-tin *n.* calendar [แผ่น pèn (wall)]

ปฏิบัติ bpà~dtì-bàt *vt.* practice (perform) ⚑

ปฏิบัติตาม bpà~dtì-bàt-dtaam *v.* observe (obey)

ปฏิรูป bpà~dtì-rûup *vt.* reform

ปฏิวัติ bpà~dtì-wát *n.* revolt, revolution

ปฏิเสธ bpà~dtì-sèet *vt.* deny (refuse), reject

ปฐมนิเทศน์ bpà~tŏm-ní-têet *n.* orientation (introductory instruction) [ครั้ง kráng]

ปทานุกรม bpà~taa-nú-grom *n.* dictionary [เล่ม lêm]

ปทุมธานี bpà~tum-taa-nii *n.* Pathum thani province [จังหวัด jang-wàt]

ปน bpon *v.* mingle, mix

ป่น bpòn *vt.* grind

ป่นปี้ bpòn-bpîi *adv.* completely crushed ⚑

ปนเป bpon-bpee *adj.* jumbled

ปม bpom *n.* clue [อัน an]

ปม bpom *n.* knot [ปม bpom]

ปมด้อย bpom-dôi *n.* inferiority complex

ปรบมือ bpròp-muu *vi.* applaud (clap)

ปรมาจารย์ bpà~rá~maa-jaan *n.* guru [ท่าน tân]

ปรอท bpà~rɔ̀ɔt *n.* mercury (quicksilver) [ธาตุ tâat]

ปรอท bpà~rɔ̀ɔt *n.* thermometer ⚑ [อัน an]

ประกบ_ระหว่าง_ bprà~gòp-_-rá~wàang-_ *vt.* sandwich (_ between _)

ประกวด bprà~gùat *vi.* contest (compete)

ประกอบ bprà~gɔ̀ɔp *vt.* put together (assemble)

ประกอบด้วย bprà~gɔ̀ɔp-dûai *vt.* consist of

(comprise), contain (include)

ประกัน bprà~gan *vt.* assure (guarantee, insure)

ประกันตัว bprà~gan-dtuua *vt.* bail (legal)

ประกันภัย bprà~gan-pai *n.* insurance

ประกันสังคม bprà~gan-săng-kom *n.* social security

ประกาย bprà~gaai *n.* spark

ประการ bprà~gaan *clf.* for items, counts, points, kinds, sorts, ways !

ประกาศ bprà~gàat *vt.* declare (proclaim), pronounce

ประกาศนียบัตร bprà~gàat-sà~nii-yá~bàt, bprà~gaa-sà~nii-yá~bàt *n.* diploma (for graduation) [ใบ bai]

ประคบ bprà~kóp *v.* massage with hot press

ประคำ bprà~kam *n.* string of beads [ลูก lûuk (grain), สาย săai (string)]

ประจบ bprà~jòp *vt.* flatter (compliment)

ประจบกัน bprà~jòp-gan *vi.* merge (e.g. freeway)

ประจวบเหมาะกัน bprà~jùuap-mɔ̀-gan *vi.* coincide (happen at same time)

ประจักษ์พยาน bprà~jàk-pá~yaan *n.* eyewitness ! [คน kon]

ประจำ bprà~jam *adj.* on duty, permanent, regular (established, habitual)

ประจำเดือน bprà~jam-dɯɯan *adj.* monthly

ประจำเดือน bprà~jam-dɯɯan *n.* menses, period (menstruation)

ประจำปี bprà~jam-bpii *adj.* annual, yearly

ประจำวัน bprà~jam-wan *adv.* daily

ประแจ bprà~jɛɛ *n.* wrench (tool for gripping and turning) [อัน an]

ประชด bprà~chót *adj.* ironic (sarcastic)

ประชากร bprà~chaa-gɔɔn *n.* population (populace) ! [กลุ่ม glùm !]

ประชาชน bprà~chaa-chon *n.* people (populace) [กลุ่ม glùm !]

ประชาธิปไตย bprà~

กขฃคฅฆงจฉชซฌญฎฏฐฑฒณดตถทธนบ **ป** ผฝพฟภมยรฤลฦวศษสหฬอฮ

chaa-típ-bpà~dtai *n.*
democracy

ประชาสงเคราะห์ bprà~
chaa-sǒng-krɔ́ *n.* public
welfare

ประชาสัมพันธ์ bprà~
chaa-sǎm-pan *n.* public
relations [หน่วย nùai
(unit), แผนก pà~nɛ̀ɛk
(division)]

ประชุม bprà~chum *vi.*
convene (meet)

ประณาม bprà~naam *vt.*
condemn (reproach)

ประณีต bprà~nîit *adj.*
delicate (finely crafted)

ประดับ bprà~dàp *v.*
decorate

ประดา bprà~daa *v.* dive
and remain submerged

ประดิษฐ์ bprà~dìt *v.*
invent

ประเด็น bprà~den *n.*
issue, point [ประเด็น
bprà~den ฺ, จุด jùt, ข้อ
kɔ̂ɔ]

ประตู bprà~dtuu *n.* door,
gate [ประตู bprà~dtuu]

ประตูรั้ว bprà~dtuu-rúua
n. gate [ประตู bprà~dtuu]

ประถม bprà~tǒm *adj.*

primary (elementary),
prime

ประท้วง bprà~túuang *vi.*
demonstrate (protest)

ประทัด bprà~tát *n.*
firecracker [ดอก dɔ̀ɔk
(one), ตับ dtàp (row)]

ประทับ bprà~táp *vt.*
impress, imprint (make
an imprint)

ประทับใจ bprà~táp-jai
adj. impressed

ประทับตรา bprà~táp-
dtraa *vt.* seal (mark with
a seal)

ประเทศ bprà~têet *n.*
country, nation [ประเทศ
bprà~têet]

ประธาน bprà~taan *n.*
subject (grammar)

ประธาน bprà~taan *n.*
chair, president (of a
company) [ท่าน tân ฺ, คน
kon]

ประธานาธิบดี bprà~taa-
naa-tí-bɔɔ-dii *n.*
president (of a country)
[ท่าน tân ฺ, คน kon]

ประนม bprà~nom *v.*
bring both hands
together in obeisance or
respect

ประนีประนอม bprà~nii-bprà~nɔɔm *vi.* compromise (conciliate, reconcile)

ประปราย bprà~bpraai *adj.* sparse

ประปา bprà~bpaa *n.* water supply

ประพฤติ bprà~prút *vi.* behave ⚠

ประพฤติผิดใน bprà~prút-pìt-nai *vt.* misbehave ⚠

ประเพณี bprà~pee-nii *n.* custom, tradition [แบบ bɛ̀ɛp, อย่าง yàang]

ประเภท bprà~pêet *clf.* for kind, type, sort, category

ประเภท bprà~pêet *n.* class (category), kind (sort, type, category) [ประเภท bprà~pêet]

ประมวลผล bprà~muuan-pǒn *v.* evaluate

ประมาณ bprà~maan *adv.* about (approx.)

ประมาณ bprà~maan *v.* approximate (estimate)

ประมาท bprà~màat *adj.* careless, reckless

ประมูล bprà~muun *vi.* bid

ประเมิน bprà~məən *vt.* appraise, evaluate

ประเมินผล bprà~məən-pǒn *v.* assess, estimate

ประยุกต์ bprà~yúk *adj.* applied

ประโยค bprà~yòok *n.* sentence (grammar) [ประโยค bprà~yòok]

ประโยชน์ bprà~yòot *n.* benefit (advantage), usage (use) [อย่าง yàang]

ประลัย bprà~lai *n.* death

ประวัติ bprà~wàt *n.* record (history)

ประวัติย่อ bprà~wàt-yɔ̂ɔ *n.* curriculum vitae/C.V., profile, résumé

ประวัติศาสตร์ bprà~wàt-dtì~sàat *n.* history [เรื่อง rûuang]

ประเวณี bprà~wee-nii *n.* sexual intercourse ⚘

ประสบ bprà~sòp *vt.* find (by surprise, after looking), undergo (experience)

ประสบการณ์ bprà~sòp-gaan *n.* experience [ครั้ง kráng]

ประสบความสำเร็จ bprà~sòp-kwaam-sǎm-rèt *vi.* succeed (achieve success)

ประสา bprà~sǎa *n.*

manner

ประสาท bprà~sàat *n.*
nerve

ประสานงา bprà~sǎan-
ngaa *adj.* head-on

ประสานงาน bprà~sǎan-
ngaan *vi.* coordinate
(organize)

ประสิทธิภาพ bprà~sìt-
tí~pâap *n.* efficiency

ประเสริฐ bprà~sə̀ət *adj.*
excellent ⚡

ประหม่า bprà~màa *adj.*
nervous (under stress)

ประหยัด bprà~yàt *adj.*
economical (thrifty)

ประหลาด bprà~làat *adj.*
strange, weird

ประหลาดใจ bprà~làat-jai
adj. amazed, surprised

ประหาร bprà~hǎan *vt.*
execute (serve death
penalty) ⚡

ปรัชญา bpràt-chá~yaa,
bpràt-yaa *n.* philosophy
[วิชา wí-chaa]

ปรับ bpràp *v.* fine

ปรับ bpràp *vt.* adjust

ปรับตัว bpràp-dtuua *vi.*
adapt (oneself)

ปรับปรุง bpràp-bprung *vt.*
modify (improve), revise

(improve)

ปรับไหม bpràp-mǎi *vt.*
penalize (impose a fine
on)

ปรับอากาศ bpràp-aa-
gàat *adj.* air-conditioned

ปรัศนี bpràt-sà~nii *n.*
question mark ✗ [ตัว
dtuua]

ปรากฏว่า bpraa-gòt-wâa
vi. turn out (appear)

ปรากฏ bpraa-gòt *vi.*
appear (be in sight)

ปรากฏการณ์ bpraa-gòt-
dtà~gaan *n.*
phenomenon
(occurrence)

ปรากฏตัว bpraa-gòt-
dtuua *vi.* appear (present
oneself)

ปราการ bpraa-gaan *n.*
rampart ⚡ [แห่ง hèng]

ปรางค์ bpraang *n.* stupa
[องค์ ong]

ปราจีนบุรี bpraa-jiin-bù~
rii *n.* Prachin Buri
province [จังหวัด jang-
wàt]

ปราชัย bpraa-chai *adj.*
defeated ⚡

ปราณ bpraan *n.* breath
(air) ⚡

ปราณี bpraa-nii *adj.* show pity of ✏

ปราดเปรียว bpràat-bpriiao *adj.* brisk (fast)

ปรานี bpraa-nii *adj.* lenient

ปราบปราม bpràap-bpraam *vt.* suppress (e.g. uprising, crime)

ปราม bpraam *v.* prohibit (forbid, ban)

ปราโมทย์ bpraa-môot *n.* joy

ปรารถนา bpràat-tà~nǎa *v.* want ✏

ปราศจาก bpràat-sà~jàak *prep.* without

ปราสาท bpraa-sàat *n.* castle [หลัง lǎng (building)]

ปริซึม bprí-sǔm *n.* prism [แท่ง têng]

ปริญญา bpà~rin-yaa *n.* degree (e.g. B.A., M.A.) [ใบ bai]

ปริมาณ bpà~rí~maan *n.* quantity (amount)

ปริมาตร bpà~rí~máat *n.* volume (capacity (in cubic units))

ปริศนา bprìt-sà~nǎa *n.* puzzle, riddle [ข้อ kôɔ]

ปรึกษา bprʉk-sǎa *vt.* consult with

ปรุง bprung *vt.* mix (blend, concoct)

ปรุงรส bprung-rót *vt.* flavor, season

ปลด bplòt *vt.* detach (unfasten)

ปลดเกษียณ bplòt-gà~ sǐian *vi.* retire (from work)

ปลดปล่อย bplòt-bplòi *vt.* free, release

ปลดอาวุธ bplòt-aa-wút *vi.* disarm

ปล้น bplôn *vt.* rob

ปลวก bplùuak *n.* termite [ตัว dtuua]

ปลอกคอ bplɔ̀ɔk-kɔɔ *n.* collar (animal wears around its neck) [อัน an]

ปลอกมีด bplɔ̀ɔk-mîit *n.* sheath (knife) [ปลอก bplɔ̀ɔk]

ปลอกหมอน bplɔ̀ɔk-mɔ̌ɔn *n.* pillowcase [ปลอก bplɔ̀ɔk, อัน an]

ปล่อง bplɔ̀ng *n.* shaft (tube, e.g. mine, vent) [ปล่อง bplɔ̀ng]

ปล่องไฟ bplɔ̀ng-fai *n.* chimney [ปล่อง bplɔ̀ng]

ปลอด bplɔ̀ɔt *adj.* free from, safe from

ปลอดเชื้อ bplɔ̀ɔt-chʉ́ʉa *adj.* sterile (germ free)

ปลอดภัย bplɔ̀ɔt-pai *adj.* secure (safe)

ปลอดภาษี bplɔ̀ɔt-paa-sǐi *adj.* duty-free, tax-free

ปลอบ bplɔ̀ɔp *v.* pacify (calm)

ปลอบ bplɔ̀ɔp *vt.* console

ปลอบใจ bplɔ̀ɔp-jai see ปลอบ

ปลอบโยน bplɔ̀ɔp-yoon *vt.* comfort (soothe, console)

ปลอม bplɔɔm *adj.* fake, phony

ปลอมแปลง bplɔɔm-bplɛɛng *vt.* falsify

ปล่อย bplɔ̀i *v.* let go

ปล่อย bplɔ̀i *vt.* launch, release, relinquish

ปล่อยลง bplɔ̀i-long *v.* let down

ปลั๊ก bplák *n.* jack (socket), plug (male connector) [ตัว dtuua, อัน an]

ปลั๊กตัวผู้ bplák-dtuua-pûu *n.* plug (male connector) ⚒ [ตัว dtuua, อัน an]

ปลั๊กตัวเมีย bplák-dtuua-miia *n.* socket (female connector) ⚒ [ตัว dtuua, อัน an]

ปลั๊กไฟ bplák-fai *n.* plug (AC power) [ตัว dtuua, อัน an]

ปลา bplaa *n.* fish [ตัว dtuua]

ปลาดุก bplaa-dùk *n.* catfish [ตัว dtuua]

ปลาทอง bplaa-tɔɔng *n.* goldfish [ตัว dtuua]

ปลาย bplaai *n.* end (edge, point), point (tip)

ปลายทาง bplaai-taang *adj.* terminal (end of line, e.g. station)

ปลายทาง bplaai-taang *n.* destination (place) [ที่ tîi]

ปลาโลมา bplaa-loo-maa *n.* dolphin [ตัว dtuua]

ปลาวาฬ bplaa-waan *n.* whale [ฝูง fǔung (pod), ตัว dtuua (each)]

ปลาสมา bpláat-sà~mâa *n.* plasma (serum)

ปลาหมึก bplaa-mʉ̀k *n.* squid [ตัว dtuua]

ปลาไหล bplaa-lǎi *n.* eel

[ตัว dtuua]

ปล้ำ bplâm *v.* wrestle, rape

ปลิง bpling *n.* leech [ตัว dtuua]

ปลิว bpliu *adj.* carried by wind

ปลีก bplìik *vt.* separate

ปลื้มใจ bplêuem-jai *vi.* rejoice

ปลุก bplùk *vt.* arouse (sexually), wake (someone up)

ปลุกเร้า bplùk-ráo *vt.* excite (arouse feeling of)

ปลูก bplùuk *vt.* cultivate, grow (e.g. tree, rice), plant

ปลูกถ่าย bplùuk-tàai *vt.* transplant (e.g. hair)

ปลูกฝัง bplùuk-fǎng *vt.* plant (instill, educate)

ปวกเปียก bpùuak-bpiiak *adj.* limp (lacking rigidity)

ปวง bpuuang *adj.* entire

ปวด bpùuat *vi.* ache

ปวดท้อง bpùuat-tɔ́ɔng *n.* stomachache

ปวดฟัน bpùuat-fan *n.* toothache

ปวดศีรษะ bpùuat-sǐi-sà *n.* headache ‼

ปวดหัว bpùuat-hǔua *n.* headache

ปวดหู bpùuat-hǔu *n.* earache

ป่วย bpùai *adj.* ailing (very sick), ill, sick

ปศุสัตว์ bpà~sù-sàt *n.* livestock [ตัว dtuua]

ปอ bpɔɔ *n.* hemp (plant) [ต้น dtôn]

ปอกเปลือก bpɔ̀ɔk-bplùuak *v.* peel (skin, e.g. fruit)

ป่อง bpòng *adj.* bloated

ป้อง bpɔ̂ng *vt.* protect (guard)

ป้องกัน bpɔ̂ng-gan *vt.* defend (physically), protect (guard)

ปอด bpɔ̀ɔt *n.* lung [ข้าง kâang]

ปอดบวม bpɔ̀ɔt-buuam *n.* pneumonia [โรค rôok]

ป้อน bpɔ̂ɔn *vt.* feed (hand-feed)

ปอนด์ bpɔɔn *n.* pound (currency, unit of weight) [ปอนด์ bpɔɔn]

ป้อม bpɔ̂m *n.* fort [ป้อม bpɔ̂m]

ปะ bpà *vt.* mend

ก
ข
ฃ
ค
ฅ
ฆ
ง
จ
ฉ
ช
ซ
ฌ
ญ
ฎ
ฏ
ฐ
ฑ
ฒ
ณ
ด
ต
ถ
ท
ธ
น
บ
ป
ผ
ฝ
พ
ฟ
ภ
ม
ย
ร
ฤ
ล
ฦ
ว
ศ
ษ
ส
ห
อ
ฮ

ก
ข
ฃ
ค
ฅ
ฆ
ง
จ
ฉ
ช
ซ
ฌ
ญ
ฎ
ฏ
ฐ
ฑ
ฒ
ณ
ด
ต
ถ
ท
ธ
น
บ
ป
ผ
ฝ
พ
ฟ
ภ
ม
ย
ร
ฤ
ล
ว
ศ
ษ
ส
ห
อ
ฮ

(clothing), patch

ปะการัง bpà~gaa-rang *n.*
coral [ต้น dtôn (plant),
กิ่ง gìng (piece)]

ปะทะ bpà~tá *v.* contact
with

ปะทะกัน bpà~tá-gan *vi.*
collide (hit)

ปะปน bpà-bpon *v.*
mingle (mix)

ปะรำ bpà~ram *n.* pavilion
(temporary structure)
[หลัง lǎng]

ปักกิ่ง bpàk-gìng *n.*
Peking [เมือง muuang]

ปัจจัย bpàt-jai *n.* factor
(element), motive [ปัจจัย
bpàt-jai ⚡, อย่าง yàang]

ปัจจุบัน bpàt-jù-ban *adj.*
current, present (modern)

ปัจฉิมลิขิต bpàt-chǐm-lí-
kìt *n.* postscript ⚡, P.S ⚡

ปัญญา bpan-yaa *n.*
intelligence (wisdom)

ปัญญาอ่อน bpan-yaa-ɔ̀ɔn
adj. idiotic (foolish),
retarded

ปัญหา bpan-hǎa *n.* issue,
problem, trouble [เรื่อง
rûuang (matter), ข้อ kɔ̂ɔ
(point)]

ปัดฝุ่น bpàt-fùn *vi.* dust
(wipe)

ปัด_ออก bpàt-_-ɔ̀ɔk *vt.*
wipe (brush away)

ปั่น bpàn *v.* spin

ปั้น bpân *v.* knead

ปั้นจั่น bpân-jàn *n.* crane
(machine) [ตัว dtuua]

ปั๊ม bpám *n.* pump ⚡
[เครื่อง krûuang, ตัว
dtuua]

ปั๊ม bpám *v.* pump ⚡

ปั๊มน้ำมัน bpám-nám-
man *n.* gas station [ปั๊ม
bpám, แห่ง hèng]

ปัสสาวะ bpàt-sǎa~wá *n.*
piss ⚡, urine ⚡

ปา bpaa *vt.* throw (toss)

ป่า bpàa *adj.* wild (e.g.
animal)

ป่า bpàa *n.* forest, jungle,
woods [ป่า bpàa, แห่ง
hèng]

ป้า bpâa *n.* father or
mother's older sister [คน
kon]

ป๊า bpǎa *n.* father
(Chinese Thai) [คน kon]

ปาก bpàak *n.* entrance ⚡,

mouth

ปากกา bpàak-gaa *n.* pen (writing) [ด้าม dâam]

ปากมดลูก bpàak-mót-lûuk *n.* cervix

ปากแม่น้ำ bpàak-mɛ̂ɛ-náam *n.* delta (river) [แห่ง hɛ̀ng]

ป่าช้า bpàa-cháa *n.* cemetery [แห่ง hɛ̀ng]

ปาฏิหาริย์ bpaa-dtì-hǎan *n.* miracle

ปาฐกถา bpaa-tà-gà~tǎa *n.* lecture (sermon) ✍ [ครั้ง kráng]

ปาด bpàat *v.* smooth or level off

ป่าเถื่อน bpàa-tɥ̀an *adj.* barbarous, savage

ป่าทึบ bpàa-túp *n.* jungle ⚡ [แห่ง hɛ̀ng]

ปาน bpaan *n.* birth mark [แห่ง hɛ̀ng ⚡, ที่ tîi]

ปาน bpaan *prep.* like ✍

ป่าน bpàan *n.* hemp (plant) [ต้น dtôn]

ป้าน bpâan *adj.* blunt, obtuse (mathematics)

ปานกลาง bpaan-glaang *adj.* medium, middle

(average), moderate

ปาย bpaai *n.* Pai district [อำเภอ am-pəə]

ป่าย bpàai *v.* climb

ป้าย bpâai *n.* notice board, sign (street sign, label), tag [ป้าย bpâai, แผ่น pèn]

ป้าย bpâai *v.* brush or wipe with a sweeping motion, dab

ป้ายรถเมล์ bpâai-rót-mee *n.* bus stop [ป้าย bpâai]

ปิ้ง bpîng *vt.* broil (grill), roast, toast

ปิ๊ง bpíng *v.* click (with someone) 🔔

ปิงปอง bping-bpɔɔng *n.* table tennis

ปิด bpìt *adj.* closed (not open), off (e.g. TV, radio)

ปิด bpìt *vt.* switch off (turn off)

ปิดกิจการ bpìt-gìt-jà~gaan *vi.* shut down (business)

ปิดบัง bpìt-bang *vt.* harbor (hide)

ปิรามิด bpì-raa-mít *n.* pyramid (monument) [แห่ง hɛ̀ng]

ปี bpii *n.* year [ปี bpii]

ปี่ bpìi *n.* oboe [เลา lao]

ปีก bpìik *n.* wing (extension, of a bird) [ปีก bpìik, ข้าง kâang]

ปีกมดลูก bpìik-mót-lûuk *n.* fallopian tube [ข้าง kâang]

ปีกลาย bpii-glaai *n.* last year

ปีน bpiin *v.* climb (tree, mountain)

ปี๊บ bpíip *n.* kerosene can, bucket [ใบ bai, ลูก lûuk]

ปีศาจ bpii-sàat *n.* demon, devil [ตัว dtuua]

ปีแสง bpii-sɛ̌ɛng *n.* light-year [ปีแสง bpii-sɛ̌ɛng]

ปีใหม่ bpii-mài *n.* New Year [ปี bpii]

ปืน bpʉʉn *n.* gun [กระบอก grà~bɔ̀ɔk]

ปืนพก bpʉʉn-pók *n.* pistol, revolver [กระบอก grà~bɔ̀ɔk]

ปืนยาว bpʉʉn-yaao *n.* rifle [กระบอก grà~bɔ̀ɔk]

ปืนลูกซอง bpʉʉn-lûuk-sɔɔng *n.* shotgun [กระบอก grà~bɔ̀ɔk]

ปืนใหญ่ bpʉʉn-yài *n.* cannon [กระบอก grà~bɔ̀ɔk]

ปุ่ม bpùm *n.* button (e.g. phone), hump (lump), knob [ปุ่ม bpùm]

ปุ่มกระสัน bpùm-grà~sǎn *n.* clitoris [ปุ่ม bpùm, จุด jùt]

ปุย bpui *adj.* fluffy (feathery)

ปุ๋ย bpǔi *n.* fertilizer [ชนิด chá~nít (type), กระสอบ grà~sɔ̀ɔp (sack)]

ปู bpuu *n.* crab [ตัว dtuua]

ปู bpuu *v.* pave

ปู่ bpùu *n.* grandfather (paternal) [คน kon]

ปูชนียวัตถุ bpuu-chá~nii-yá-wát-tù *n.* object worthy of worship [ชิ้น chín]

ปูชนียสถาน bpuu-chá~nii-yá-sà~tǎan *n.* place worthy of worship [แห่ง hɛ̀ng]

ปู่ทวด bpùu-tûuat *n.* great grandfather (paternal) [คน kon]

ปูน bpuun *n.* lime (mineral), mortar

(cement)

ปูนซีเมนต์ bpuun-sii-men *n.* cement [กระสอบ grà~sɔ̀ɔp (sack)]

ปู่ย่า bpùu-yâa *n.* grandparents (paternal) [คน kon]

เป้ bpêe *n.* backpack, knapsack [ใบ bai]

เป๋ bpěe *adj.* twisted (distorted) ✦

เป๊ก bpék *n.* shot (of alcohol) [เป๊ก bpék]

เป็ด bpèt *n.* duck [ตัว dtuua]

เป็น bpen *adj.* alive (living)

เป็น bpen *v.* become, to know how to, be/is/am/are/was/were/been (something)

เป็น bpen *vi.* exist (be)

เป็นกลาง bpen-glaang *adj.* neutral

เป็นของ bpen-kɔ̌ɔng *vt.* belong to (someone)

เป็นจริง bpen-jing *vi.* come true

เป็นเจ้าของ bpen-jâo-kɔ̌ɔng *v.* possess (own)

เป็นต้น bpen-dtôn *idm.* et cetera/etc.

เป็นประจำ bpen-bprà~jam *adv.* often

เป็นไปได้ bpen-bpai-dâai *adj.* possible

เป็นพยาน bpen-pá~yaan *vi.* testify (bear witness)

เป็นพิษ bpen-pít *adj.* toxic

เป็นมิตร bpen-mít *adj.* friendly

เป็นระเบียบ bpen-rá~bìiap *adj.* neat

เป็นลม bpen-lom *vi.* faint (pass out), pass out

เป็นหนี้ bpen-nîi *v.* owe

เป็นหมัน bpen-mǎn *adj.* sterile (childless)

เป็นหวัด bpen-wàt *vi.* have a cold

เป็นเหตุให้ bpen-hèet-hâi *vt.* cause

เปรต bprèet *n.* demon [ตัว dtuua]

เปราะ bprɔ̀ *adj.* brittle (fragile)

เปรียบเทียบ bprìiap-tîiap *vt.* compare

เปรี้ยว bprîiao *adj.* sexy, confident and expressive ✦, sour

ก
ข
ฃ
ค
ฅ
ฆ
ง
จ
ฉ
ช
ซ
ฌ
ญ
ฎ
ฏ
ฐ
ฑ
ฒ
ณ
ด
ต
ถ
ท
ธ
น
บ
ป
ผ
ฝ
พ
ฟ
ภ
ม
ย
ร
ฤ
ล
ว
ศ
ษ
ส
ห
ฬ
อ
ฮ

เปล bplee *n.* hammock [ปาก bpàak]

เปล่ง bplèng *vt.* emit (sound, light), radiate

เปล่งปลั่ง bplèng-bplàng *adj.* radiant

เปลวไฟ bpleeo-fai *n.* flame [อัน an]

เปล่า bplàao *adj.* bare (e.g. hands, walls), empty (containing nothing)

เปล่า bplàao *interj.* no! (no, not)

เปลี่ยน bpliian *v.* alter (modify), change

เปลี่ยน_กลับ bpliian-_-glàp *vt.* undo (reverse)

เปลี่ยนแปลง bpliian-bplɛɛng *vt.* modify (adjust)

เปลี่ยนมือ bpliian-mɯɯ *vi.* change hands

เปลี่ยนสัญชาติ bpliian-sǎn-châat *v.* change one's citizenship

เปลือก bplɯ̀ɯak *n.* shell (of eggs), skin (crust, peel) [อัน an, ชิ้น chín]

เปลือกตา bplɯ̀ɯak-dtaa *n.* eyelid

เปลื้อง bplɯ̂ɯang *vt.* strip off (clothes)

เปลือย bplɯɯai *adj.* bare, naked, nude

เปอร์เซ็นต์ bpəə-sen *n.* percent

เป๊ะ bpé *adv.* exactly (precisely) ☜

เป่า bpào *vi.* blow (with lungs)

เป้า bpâo *n.* target (e.g. shooting) [อัน an]

เป้าหมาย bpâo-mǎai *n.* aim, goal, objective [อัน an]

เป้าหลอก bpâo-lɔ̀ɔk *n.* decoy (object) [เป้า bpâo]

เปาะเปี๊ยะ bpɔ́-bpíia *n.* spring roll

เปิด bpə̀ət *adj.* open

เปิด bpə̀ət *vt.* turn on (e.g. light, machine)

เปิดตัว bpə̀ət-dtuua *vi.* come out (reveal one's sexuality)

เปิดเผย bpə̀ət-pə̌əi *vt.* disclose, expose, reveal, uncover

เปีย bpiia *n.* pigtail (hairdo) [เส้น sên]

เปียก bpìiak *adj.* damp,

wet

เปียกโชก bpìiak-chôok *adj.* soggy (wet)

เปื้อน bpûuan *adj.* stained (dirty)

เปื่อย bpùuai *adj.* rotten, tender (meat)

แป้ง bpε̂εng *n.* powder (cosmetics) [กล่อง glɔ̀ng (box), ตลับ dtà~làp (compact)]

แป้ง bpε̂εng *n.* starch [กล่อง glɔ̀ng (box)]

แป้งผง bpε̂εng-pǒng *n.* talc [กระป๋อง grà~bpɔ̌ng (can)]

แปด bpὲεt *numb.* eight

แป้น bpε̂εn *adj.* round and flat

แป้นพิมพ์ bpε̂εn-pim *n.* keyboard ‼ [อัน an, แป้น bpε̂εn]

แปร๊บ bpέεp *adv.* one little moment ✦

แปรง bpreεng *n.* brush [อัน an]

แปรงสีฟัน bpreεng-sǐi-fan *n.* toothbrush [อัน an]

แปรรูป bpreε-rûup *v.* process (transform)

แปล bplεε *v.* interpret,

translate (language)

แปลก bplὲεk *adj.* funny, odd, strange

แปลง bplεεng *vt.* modify (adjust)

แปลงที่ดิน bplεεng-tîi-din *n.* plot of land [แปลง bplεεng]

แปลบ bplὲεp *vi.* flash (e.g. lightning)

โป๊ bpóo *adj.* naked (nude), pornographic

โป้ง bpôong *adj.* boastful

โปร่งแสง bpròong-sε̌εng *adj.* transparent

โปรเจ็ค bproo-jὲk *n.* project (scheme, plan) ✦ [อัน an]

โปรด bpròot *adj.* favorite

โปรด bpròot *adv.* please (in polite requests)

โปรตีน bproo-dtiin *n.* protein

โปรย bprooi *vt.* sow (e.g. seeds)

ไป bpai *vi.* go

ไปกลับ bpai-glàp *adj.* round trip

ไปด้วย bpai-dûuai *v.* accompany (go with)

ก ข ฃ ค ฅ ฆ ง จ ฉ ช ซ ฌ ญ ฎ ฏ ฐ ฑ ฒ ณ ด ต ถ ท ธ น บ ป ผ ฝ พ ฟ ภ ม ย ร ฤ ล ฦ ว ศ ษ ส ห อ ฮ

ก
ข
ฃ
ค
ฅ
ฆ
ง
จ
ฉ
ช
ซ
ฌ
ญ
ฎ
ฏ
ฐ
ฑ
ฒ
ณ
ด
ต
ถ
ท
ธ
น
บ
ป
ผ
ฝ
พ
ฟ
ภ
ม
ย
ร
ฤ
ล
ฦ
ว
ศ
ษ
ส
ห
อ
ฮ

ไปถึง bpai-tǔng *vi.* arrive

ไปทัน bpai-tan *vt.* catch (e.g. bus)

ไปทาง bpai-taang *prep.* toward

ไปเที่ยว bpai-tîiao *vi.* take a trip

ไปยัง bpai-yang *prep.* into (toward)

ไปยาลน้อย bpai-yaan-nɔ́ɔi *n.* symbol ฯ used to shorten words [ตัว dtuua]

ไปยาลใหญ่ bpai-yaan-yài *n.* symbol ฯลฯ meaning et cetera [ตัว dtuua]

ไปเยี่ยม bpai-yîiam *v.* visit (go visit)

ไปรษณีย์ bprai-sà-nii *n.* post office [แห่ง hɛ̀ng]

ไปรษณียบัตร bprai-sà~nii-yá~bàt *n.* postcard ! [ใบ bai, แผ่น pɛ̀n]

ไปรษณีย์อากาศ bprai-sà~nii-aa-gàat *n.* airmail

ไปรับ bpai-ráp *vt.* pick up (call for someone)

ไปส่ง bpai-sòng *vt.* drop off (deliver)

ไปหา bpai-hǎa *v.* go see someone

ผ

ผ pɔ̌ɔ *let.* ผ. ผึ้ง pɔ̌ɔ-pûng, a consonant of the Thai alphabet (high consonant) [ตัว dtuua]

ผกากรอง pà~gaa-grɔɔng *n.* sage (herb) [ต้น dtôn]

ผง pǒng *n.* dirt, dust (dry particles), powder

ผงกะหรี่ pǒng-gà~rìi *n.* curry powder

ผงชูรส pǒng-chuu-rót *n.* monosodium glutamate

ผงซักฟอก pǒng-sák-fɔ̂ɔk *n.* detergent [ถุง tǔng (bag), กล่อง glɔ̀ng (box), ห่อ hɔ̀ɔ (pack)]

ผด pòt *n.* prickly heat (rash)

ผนัง pà~nǎng *n.* wall (e.g. house, room) [ด้าน dâan]

ผนึก pà~nʉ̀k *vt.* seal (e.g. a letter)

ผม pǒm *n.* hair (head) [เส้น sên (strand), ทรง song (style)]

ผม pǒm *pron.* I (male speaker)

ผมปลอม pǒm-bplɔɔm *n.* wig [อัน an]

ผมเปีย pǒm-bpiia *n.*

braid (hair) [เส้น sên]

ผมหงอก pŏm-ngɔ̀ɔk *n.* gray hair

ผมหยิก pŏm-yìk *n.* curl (hair) [ลอน lɔɔn]

ผล pŏn *clf.* for fruits, results

ผล pŏn *n.* product (result) [อย่าง yàang]

ผล pŏn *n.* result [ผล pŏn]

ผล pŏn *n.* fruit (edible) [ผล pŏn, ลูก lûuk]

ผลงาน pŏn-ngaan *n.* work (accomplishment, result of work) [ชิ้น chín]

ผลประโยชน์ pŏn-bprà~ yòot *n.* benefit (reward), sake

ผลผลิต pŏn-pà~lìt *n.* product (farm goods, output) [ชนิด chá~nít (kind), ชิ้น chín (piece), กล่อง glɔ̀ŋ (box), ห่อ hɔ̀ɔ (wrap)]

ผลไม้ pŏn-lá~máai *n.* fruit (edible) [ผล pŏn ⚡, ลูก lûuk]

ผลลัพธ์ pŏn-láp *n.* result [ผล pŏn]

ผลัก plàk *v.* push (shove, drive)

ผลักดัน plàk-dan *vt.* press (insist upon)

ผลัด plàt *vi.* take turns

ผลัด plàt *vt.* relay (pass on)

ผลิ plì *vi.* bud, sprout

ผลิต pà~lìt *vt.* produce (make, create)

ผลิตผล pà~lìt-dtà~pŏn *n.* product (farm goods, output) ⚡ [ชนิด chá~nít (kind), ชิ้น chín (piece), กล่อง glɔ̀ŋ (box), ห่อ hɔ̀ɔ (wrap)]

ผลิตภัณฑ์ pà~lìt-dtà~pan *n.* production (product) ⚡ [ชนิด chá~nít (kind), ชิ้น chín (piece), กล่อง glɔ̀ŋ (box), ห่อ hɔ̀ɔ (wrap)]

ผสม pà~sŏm *v.* mix

ผสมเทียม pà~sŏm-tiiam *n.* artificial insemination

ผสมผสาน pà~sŏm-pà~ sǎan *vt.* integrate (combine, become integrated)

ผสมพันธุ์ pà~sŏm-pan *vt.* fertilize (impregnate)

ผ่อนคลาย pɔ̀n-klaai *vi.* relax (loosen)

ผอม pɔ̌ɔm *adj.* slim

(people, animals), thin (for people, animals)

ผอมบาง pɔ̌ɔm-baang *adj.* lean, slender, slim (people, animals)

ผัก pàk *n.* vegetable [ชนิด chá~nít (kind), ต้น dtôn (plant)]

ผักขม pàk-kǒm *n.* spinach [ต้น dtôn]

ผักชี pàk-chii *n.* cilantro [ใบ bai (leave), ต้น dtôn (plant)]

ผักตะขาบ pàk-dtà~kàap *n.* mollywort [ต้น dtôn (plant)]

ผักบุ้ง pàk-bûng *n.* morning glory [ต้น dtôn (plant), กำ gam (bunch)]

ผัง pǎng *n.* plan (diagram, chart) ⚠ [อัน an]

ผัด pàt *adj.* fried (stir fried)

ผัด pàt *vt.* fry (stir fry)

ผัน pǎn *vi.* deviate (change)

ผับ pàp *n.* pub (bar) ⚠ [ร้าน ráan]

ผัว pǔua *n.* husband ⚠ [คน kon]

ผัวะ pùa *n.* clap (sound of slapping)

ผา pǎa *n.* cliff [แห่ง hèng]

ผ่า pàa *v.* rip (tear)

ผ่า pàa *vt.* slit

ผ้า pâa *n.* cloth, fabric [ชิ้น chín, ผืน pǔun]

ผ้ากันเปื้อน pâa-gan-bpûuan *n.* apron [ผืน pǔun]

ผ้าขนหนู pâa-kǒn-nǔu *n.* towel (for body) ⚠ [ผืน pǔun]

ผ้าขาวม้า pâa-kǎao-máa *n.* loincloth [ผืน pǔun, ชิ้น chín]

ผ้าขี้ริ้ว pâa-kîi-ríu *n.* rag (ragged clothing) [ผืน pǔun, ชิ้น chín]

ผ้าคลุม pâa-klum *n.* wrap (shawl) [ผืน pǔun]

ผ้าเช็ดตัว pâa-chét-dtuua *n.* towel (for body) [ผืน pǔun]

ผ้าเช็ดหน้า pâa-chét-nâa *n.* handkerchief [ผืน pǔun]

ผ่าตัด pàa-dtàt *v.* operate (surgery)

ผ้าถุง pâa-tǔng *n.* sarong-like skirt [ผืน pǔun]

ผ่าน pàan v. pass (location, test, time, in a card game)

ผ่าน pàan vi. walk pass

ผ่านทะลุ pàan-tá~lú vt. penetrate (pierce)

ผ่านไป pàan-bpai v. pass by (pass)

ผ้านวม pâa-nuuam n. comforter (quilt) [ผืน pʉ̌ʉn]

ผ้าใบ pâa-bai n. awning (shade), canvas [ผืน pʉ̌ʉn, แผ่น pɛ̀n]

ผ้าพันคอ pâa-pan-kɔɔ n. scarf [ผืน pʉ̌ʉn]

ผ้าพันแผล pâa-pan-plɛ̌ɛ n. gauze [ม้วน múuan (roll), ชิ้น chín (piece)]

ผายปอด pǎai-bpɔɔt v. perform CPR

ผายลม pǎai-lom vi. fart ⚡

ผ้ายาง pâa-yaang n. rubber cloth [ผืน pʉ̌ʉn, แผ่น pɛ̀n]

ผาสุก pǎa-sùk n. happiness ⚘, peace ⚘

ผ้าห่ม pâa-hòm n. blanket [ผืน pʉ̌ʉn]

ผ้าไหม pâa-mǎi n. silk (cloth), silk cloth [ผืน pʉ̌ʉn]

ผ้าอนามัย pâa-à~naa-mai n. sanitary napkin [แผ่น pɛ̀n]

ผ้าอ้อม pâa-ɔ̂ɔm n. diaper/nappy [ผืน pʉ̌ʉn]

ผิง pǐng vt. bake

ผิด pìt adj. wrong (incorrect, not suitable)

ผิดกฎหมาย pìt-gòt-mǎai adj. illegal

ผิดปกติ pìt-bpà-gà~dtì adj. abnormal, unusual

ผิดประเวณี pìt-bprà~wee-nii vi. commit adultery ⚡

ผิดพลาด pìt-plâat adj. wrong (awry)

ผิดรูปร่าง pìt-rûup-râang adj. deformed (disfigured)

ผิดศีลธรรม pìt-sǐin-tam, pìt-sǐin-lá~tam adj. immoral

ผิดหวัง pìt-wǎng adj. disappointed

ผิว pǐu n. skin [ชั้น chán (layer)]

ผิวปาก pǐu-bpàak vi. whistle (through the mouth)

ผิวเผิน pǐu-pǒən *adj.* shallow (superficial)

ผิวหน้า pǐu-nâa *n.* surface

ผี pǐi *n.* ghost, spirit [ตัว dtuua]

ผีดิบ pǐi-dìp *n.* zombie [ตัว dtuua]

ผีสิง pǐi-sǐng *adj.* haunted

ผีเสื้อ pǐi-sûua *n.* butterfly (animal) [ตัว dtuua]

ผึ่ง pùng *vt.* dry (in sun, e.g. towel)

ผึ้ง pûng *n.* bee (animal) [ตัว dtuua (each one), ฝูง fǔung (swarm)]

ผืน pǔun *clf.* for cloths, thin pieces, e.g. mats, towels etc.

ผื่น pùun *n.* prickly heat, rash (on the skin)

ผุ pù *adj.* rotten

ผุด pùt *vi.* pop up ⚡

ผู้ pûu *n.* one who does..., person (individual, human) [คน kon]

ผู้ pûu *pron.* who (person who)

ผูก pùuk *vt.* bind, tie (e.g. sail, boat, horse)

ผู้ก่อการร้าย pûu-gɔ̀ɔ-gaan-ráai *n.* terrorist [คน kon]

ผู้กำกับ pûu-gam-gàp *n.* director (e.g. manager at work, movie director) [คน kon]

ผู้เข้าประกวด pûu-kâo-bprà~gùuat *n.* contestant (e.g. beauty contest) [คน kon]

ผู้เข้าร่วม pûu-kâo-rûuam *n.* participant [คน kon]

ผู้ค้ำประกัน pûu-kám-bprà~gan *n.* guarantor [คน kon]

ผู้เคราะห์ร้าย pûu-krɔ́-ráai *n.* victim (person who suffers from some adverse circumstance) [คน kon]

ผู้จัดการ pûu-jàt-gaan *n.* manager [คน kon]

ผู้จัดหา pûu-jàt-hǎa *n.* provider (one who provides) [คน kon]

ผู้ชนะ pûu-chá~ná *n.* winner [คน kon]

ผู้ชนะเลิศ pûu-chá~ná-lə̂ət *n.* champion ⚡ [คน kon]

ผู้ชม pûu-chom *n.* viewer

[คน kon]

ผู้ช่วย pûu-chûuai *n.* assistant, helper [คน kon]

ผู้ชาย pûu-chaai *n.* guy, male (men), man [คน kon]

ผู้เชี่ยวชาญ pûu-chîiao-chaan *n.* expert [คน kon]

ผู้โดยสาร pûu-dooi-sǎan *n.* passenger [คน kon]

ผู้ใด pûu-dai *pron.* who (which person) ⚠

ผู้ต้องหา pûu-dtɔ̂ng-hǎa *n.* suspect (accused) [คน kon, ราย raai ⚠]

ผู้แต่ง pûu-dtɛ̀ng *n.* author, writer [คน kon]

ผู้ที่ pûu-tîi *pron.* whom (one who)

ผู้นำ pûu-nam *n.* leader [คน kon]

ผู้บริหาร pûu-bɔɔ-rí~hǎan *n.* executive [คน kon]

ผู้ปกครอง pûu-bpòk-krɔɔng *n.* guardian, parent [คน kon]

ผู้ป่วย pûu-bpùai *n.* patient ⚠ [ราย raai ⚠, คน kon]

ผู้แปล pûu-bplɛɛ *n.* translator [คน kon]

ผู้ผลิต pûu-pà~lìt *n.* manufacturer [คน kon]

ผู้พิพากษา pûu-pí-pâak-sǎa *n.* judge (in court) [คน kon, ท่าน tân ⚠]

ผู้เยาว์ pûu-yao *n.* minor (juvenile) [คน kon]

ผู้รอดชีวิต pûu-rɔ̂ɔt-chii-wít *n.* survivor [คน kon]

ผู้รับเหมา pûu-ráp-mǎo *n.* contractor (e.g. construction) [คน kon]

ผู้ร้าย pûu-ráai *n.* outlaw [คน kon]

ผู้ลี้ภัย pûu-líi-pai *n.* refugee [คน kon]

ผู้ว่าการ pûu-wâa-gaan *n.* governor (state) [ท่าน tân ⚠, คน kon]

ผู้ว่าราชการ pûu-wâa-râat-chá~gaan *n.* governor (province) [ท่าน tân ⚠, คน kon]

ผู้ส่งออก pûu-sòng-ɔ̀ɔk *n.* exporter [คน kon]

ผู้สมัคร pûu-sà~màk *n.* candidate [คน kon]

ผู้สอน pûu-rʉ̌an *n.* instructor [คน kon, ท่าน

ก
ข
ฃ
ค
ฅ
ฆ
ง
จ
ฉ
ช
ซ
ฌ
ญ
ฎ
ฏ
ฐ
ฑ
ฒ
ณ
ด
ต
ถ
ท
ธ
น
บ
ป
ผ
ฝ
พ
ฟ
ภ
ม
ย
ร
ฤ
ล
ว
ศ
ษ
ส
ห
อ
ฮ

tân ǃ]

ผู้สื่อข่าว pûu-sùu-kàao *n.* journalist ǃ [คน kon]

ผู้แสดง pûu-sà~dɛɛng *n.* performer (one who performs) [คน kon]

ผู้หญิง pûu-yǐng *n.* female, lady, woman [คน kon]

ผู้หญิงหาเงิน pûu-yǐng-hǎa-ngən *n.* prostitute (female) ● [คน kon]

ผู้ใหญ่ pûu-yài *n.* adult, grownup [คน kon]

ผู้อพยพ pûu-òp-pá~yóp *n.* emigrant, immigrant [คน kon]

ผู้อาวุโส pûu-aa-wú-sǒo *n.* elder (senior) [คน kon]

ผู้อำนวยการ pûu-am-nuuai-gaan *n.* director (executive, e.g. headmaster, C.E.O.) [คน kon]

ผู้อื่น pûu-ùun *pron.* others

เผชิญหน้า pà~chəən-nâa *vt.* face (confront)

เผชิญหน้ากับ pà~chəən-nâa-gàp *vt.* confront

เผ็ด pèt *adj.* hot, spicy

เผด็จการ pà~dèt-gaan *n.*

dictator [คน kon]

เผ่น pèn *vi.* leap (act quickly), spring (jump)

เผย pə̌əi *vt.* disclose

เผยแพร่ pə̌əi-prêɛ *vt.* broadcast (make known)

เผา pǎo *vt.* burn

เผ่า pào *n.* race, tribe (e.g. hilltribe) [เผ่า pào]

เผาศพ pǎo-sòp *v.* cremate a body

เผือก pùuak *n.* taro [หัว hǔua]

เผื่อว่า pùua-wâa *conj.* in case

แผ่ pɛ̀ɛ *vi.* spread out (unfold)

แผงคอ pɛ̌ɛng-kɔɔ *n.* mane (animal)

แผงลอย pɛ̌ɛng-lɔɔi *n.* stall (booth) [แผง pɛ̌ɛng]

แผน pɛ̌ɛn *n.* project (scheme, plan) [อัน an]

แผ่น pèn *clf.* for thin, flat objects, e.g. sheets of paper, boards, etc.

แผ่น pèn *n.* sheet (broad, thin piece, e.g. paper) [แผ่น pèn]

แผนก pà~nɛ̀ɛk *n.* department, division [แผนก pà~nɛ̀ɛk]

ก
ข
ฃ
ค
ฅ
ฆ
ง
จ
ฉ
ช
ซ
ฌ
ญ
ฎ
ฏ
ฐ
ฑ
ฒ
ณ
ด
ต
ถ
ท
ธ
น
บ
ป
ผ
ฝ
พ
ฟ
ภ
ม
ย
ร
ล
ฦ
ว
ศ
ษ
ส
ห
อ
ฮ

แผนการ phǎen-gaan *n.* project (scheme, plan) ‼ [แผน phǎen, อัน an]

แผ่นซีดี phàen-sii-dii *n.* CD [แผ่น phàen]

แผ่นดิน phàen-din *n.* land (ground of the earth, nation) [แห่ง hàeng, ที่ tîi]

แผ่นดินไหว phàen-din-wǎi *n.* earthquake [ครั้ง kráng]

แผ่นดิสก์ phàen-dít, phàen-dís *n.* CD [แผ่น phàen]

แผนที่ phǎen-tîi *n.* map [แผ่น phàen (sheet), เล่ม lêm (book)]

แผนผัง phǎen-phǎng *n.* plot (diagram) [อัน an]

แผนภาพ phǎen-phâap *n.* diagram (chart, graph) [แผ่น phàen]

แผนร้าย phǎen-ráai *n.* scheme (nefarious plan) [แผน phǎen]

แผล phlǎe *n.* wound [แห่ง hàeng, ที่ tîi]

แผลเป็น phlǎe-bpen *n.* scar [แห่ง hàeng, ที่ tîi]

โผล่ phlòo *vi.* emerge (come out), pop up

ไผ่ phài *n.* bamboo

(material) [มัด mát (bundle), เส้น sên (piece)]

ฝ

ฝ fɔ̌ɔ *let.* ฝ. ฝา fɔ̌ɔ-fǎa, a consonant of the Thai alphabet (high consonant) [ตัว dtuua]

ฝน fǒn *n.* rain [เม็ด mét]

ฝนตก fǒn-dtòk *vi.* rain

ฝรั่ง fà~ràng *n.* Caucasian (Westerner) ✦, farang ✦ [คน kon]

ฝรั่ง fà~ràng *n.* guava [ลูก lûuk]

ฝรั่งเศส fà~ràng-sèet *n.* France [ประเทศ bprà~têet]

ฝอย fɔ̌ɔi *n.* trivial details, droplet, frill (trimming)

ฝอยทอง fɔ̌ɔi-tɔɔng *n.* Thai sweetmeat [ชิ้น chín]

ฝัก fàk *n.* case, pod [ฝัก fàk, อัน an ✦]

ฝักถั่ว fàk-tùua *n.* pod (bean or pea) [ฝัก fàk]

ฝักบัว fàk-buua *n.* shower (fixture) [อัน an]

ฝัง fǎng *vt.* bury, implant (e.g. medicine)

ก ข ฃ ค ฅ ฆ ง จ ฉ ช ซ ฌ ญ ฎ ฏ ฐ ฑ ฒ ณ ด ต ถ ท ธ น บ ป ผ **ฝ** พ ฟ ภ ม ย ร ฤ ล ว ศ ษ ส ห ฬ อ ฮ

ฝั่ง fàng *n.* bank (shore), coast (e.g. West Coast) [แห่ง hɛ̀ng, ฝั่ง fàng]

ฝังเข็ม făng-kěm *v.* perform acupuncture to

ฝั่งทะเล fàng-tá~lee *n.* coast [แห่ง hɛ̀ng, ฝั่ง fàng]

ฝัน făn *n.* dream [อัน an]

ฝัน făn *v.* dream

ฝันถึง făn-tǔng *vt.* dream of

ฝันเปียก făn-bpìiak *n.* wet dream

ฝันร้าย făn-ráai *n.* nightmare [เรื่อง rûuang]

ฝันร้าย făn-ráai *v.* have a bad dream

ฝา făa *n.* cap, cover (e.g. jar), lid [ฝา făa, ชิ้น chín]

ฝ้า fâa *adj.* foggy (e.g. mirror)

ฝ้า fâa *n.* melasma (skin problem)

ฝาก fàak *v.* deposit (money)

ฝาก fàak *vt.* put something in the care of

ฝากเงิน fàak-ngən *vi.* deposit money

ฝากฝัง fàak-făng *v.* put into the care of

ฝาก_ไว้ fàak-_-wái *vt.* leave (something with someone)

ฝาด fàat *adj.* tart (taste, e.g. underripe fruit)

ฝาเท้า fàa-táao *n.* sole (of foot) [ข้าง kâang]

ฝาน fǎan *v.* cut thin, slice (fruit)

ฝาปิด fǎa-bpìt *n.* lid [ฝา fǎa]

ฝ่าฝืน fàa-fǔɯn *vt.* infringe, violate (law, rule, agreement)

ฝาแฝด fǎa-fɛ̀ɛt *n.* twin [คู่ kûu]

ฝ่าฟัน fàa-fan *vi.* strive

ฝ่าไฟแดง fàa-fai-dɛɛng *vi.* run the red light

ฝ่ามือ fàa-mɯɯ *n.* palm (hand) [ข้าง kâang]

ฝาย fǎai *n.* small dam [ฝาย fǎai]

ฝ่าย fàai *n.* group (faction), side (team, party, faction) [ฝ่าย fàai]

ฝ้าย fâai *n.* cotton (plant) [ต้น dtôn]

ฝ่ายรับ fàai-ráp *n.* defense (in sports) [ฝ่าย fàai]

ฝ่ายรุก fàai-rúk *n.* offense (position in sports) [ฝ่าย fàai]

ฝิ่น fìn *n.* opium [ต้น dtôn (plant)]

ฝีดาษ fǐi-dàat *n.* smallpox

ฝีปาก fǐi-bpàak *n.* verbal skill

ฝีมือ fǐi-mɯɯ *n.* skill ☞

ฝึก fʉk *vi.* exercise (practice, train)

ฝึกซ้อม fʉk-sɔ́ɔm *v.* practice ♪, rehearse ♪

ฝึกฝน fʉk-fǒn *vt.* polish up (brush up)

ฝึกหัด fʉk-hàt *v.* practice (train, learn) ♪

ฝึกหัด fʉk-hàt *vi.* train (drill) ♪

ฝืด fʉ̀ʉt *adj.* difficult to move, tight (e.g. valve, budget)

ฝืน fʉ̌ʉn *v.* do against

ฝุ่น fùn *n.* dirt, dust (dry particles)

ฝูง fǔung *n.* flock (of animals), herd, swarm (e.g. bees, insects) [ฝูง fǔung]

ฝูงชน fǔung-chon *n.* crowd (people), mob

[กลุ่ม glùm]

ฝูงสัตว์ fǔung-sàt *n.* herd [ฝูง fǔung]

เฝ้า fâo *vt.* guard (keep an eye on)

เฝ้าดู fâo-duu *v.* observe (watch attentively)

เฝือก fʉ̀ʉak *n.* cast (medical) [อัน an]

แฝง fɛ̌ɛng *vt.* conceal (hide)

แฝด fɛ̀ɛt *n.* twin [คู่ kûu]

แฝดสยาม fɛ̀ɛt-sà~yǎam *n.* Siamese twins [คู่ kûu]

ใฝ่ fài *v.* hope

ใฝ่ใจ fài-jai *adj.* keenly interested in

ไฝ fǎi *n.* mole (on the skin) [เม็ด mét]

พ

พ pɔɔ *let.* พ. พาน pɔɔ-paan, a consonant of the Thai alphabet (low consonant) [ตัว dtuua]

พ.ศ. pɔɔ-sɔ̌ɔ *n.* Buddhist Era [ปี bpii]

พก pók *v.* carry or hide on the body

พจนานุกรม pót-jà~naa-nú-grom *n.* dictionary

[เล่ม lêm]

พญา pá~yaa *n.* lord [ท่าน tân ฺ, คน kon]

พ่น pôn *v.* spray, squirt

พ้น pón *v.* pass beyond

พนม pá~nom *vt.* palms together in the attitude of salutation

พ่นออก pôn-ɔ̀ɔk *vi.* squirt out

พนัก pá~nák *n.* back of a chair [พนัก pá~nák]

พนัน pá~nan *v.* bet, gamble, wager

พเนจร pá~nee-jɔɔn *vi.* wander (go aimlessly) ๛

พบ póp *vt.* find (by surprise, after looking), meet (encounter), see

พบกัน póp-gan *vi.* meet (encounter)

พม่า pá~mâa *n.* Burma, Myanmar [ประเทศ bprà~têet]

พยศ pá~yót *v.* fling and throw, refuse to obey

พยักหน้า pá~yák-nâa *v.* nod

พยัญชนะ pá~yan-chá~ná *n.* consonant [ตัว dtuua]

พยากรณ์ pá~yaa-gɔɔn *v.* forecast ✖, predict ✖

พยางค์ pá~yaang *n.* syllable [พยางค์ pá~yaang]

พยาธิ pá~yaa-tí *n.* ailment ๛

พยาธิ pá~yâat *n.* parasite, worm [ตัว dtuua]

พยาน pá~yaan *n.* witness [ปาก bpàak ฺ, คน kon]

พยาบาท pá~yaa-bàat *adj.* vengeful

พยาบาล pá~yaa-baan *n.* nurse [คน kon]

พยายาม pá~yaa-yaam *v.* make an effort

พยายาม pá~yaa-yaam *vi.* try (make an effort)

พร pɔɔn *n.* blessing (something blessed) [ข้อ kɔ̂ɔ, ประการ bprà~gaan ฺ]

พรม prom *n.* carpet, rug [ผืน pʉ̌ʉn]

พรม prom *vt.* sprinkle (liquid)

พรมแดน prom-dɛɛn *n.* frontier (border) [แห่ง hɛ̀ŋ]

พรรค pák *n.* party (political) [พรรค pák]

พรรษา pan-sǎa *n.* Buddhist Lent

พรสวรรค์ pɔɔn-sà~wǎn *n.* gift, talent (natural gift) [อย่าง yàang]

พรหม prom *n.* Brahma (Hindu god) [องค์ ong]

พรหมลิขิต prom-lí-kìt *n.* destiny (fate)

พร้อม prɔ́ɔm *adj.* ready (prepared or available)

พร้อมกัน prɔ́ɔm-gan *adv.* together (at the same time)

พร้อมกับ prɔ́ɔm-gàp *conj.* together with

พร้อมด้วย prɔ́ɔm-dûuai *prep.* together with

พร้อมทั้ง prɔ́ɔm-táng *conj.* along with, together with

พระ prá *n.* minister (clergyman), monk ✸ [รูป rûup]

พระคัมภีร์ prá-kam-pii *n.* testament (of the Bible) [เล่ม lêm]

พระจันทร์ prá~jan *n.* moon ⚠ [ดวง duuang]

พระเจ้า prá~jâao *n.* god/ God, lord [องค์ ong, พระองค์ prá-ong]

พระพุทธเจ้า prá-pút-tá~ jâao *n.* Buddha [องค์ ong, พระองค์ prá-ong]

พระพุทธรูป prá-pút-tá~ rûup *n.* Buddha image [องค์ ong]

พระมหากษัตริย์ prá-má~ hǎa-gà~sàt *n.* king [องค์ ong, พระองค์ prá-ong]

พระเยซู prá-yee-suu *n.* Jesus Christ [องค์ ong]

พระเยซูคริสต์ prá-yee- suu-krít *n.* Jesus Christ ⚠ [องค์ ong]

พระราชบัญญัติ prá~râat- chá~ban-yàt *n.* bill (legislative act) [ฉบับ chà~bàp (version), มาตรา mâat-dtraa (section)]

พระราชวัง prá~râat- chá~wang *n.* palace (Thai royal residence) ⚠ [หลัง lǎng]

พระราชินี prá-raa-chí~nii *n.* queen [องค์ ong]

พระสงฆ์ prá-sǒng *n.* Buddhist monk [รูป rûup]

พระอาทิตย์ prá~aa-tít *n.* sun ⚠ [ดวง duuang]

พระเอก prá-èek *n.* hero

ก ข ฃ ค ฅ ฆ ง จ ฉ ช ซ ฌ ญ ฎ ฏ ฐ ฑ ฒ ณ ด ต ถ ท ธ น บ ป ผ ฝ **พ** ฟ ภ ม ย ร ล ว ศ ษ ส ห อ ฮ

ก
ข
ข
ค
ฅ
ฆ
ง
จ
ฉ
ช
ซ
ฌ
ญ
ฎ
ฏ
ฐ
ฑ
ฒ
ณ
ด
ต
ถ
ท
ธ
น
บ
ป
ผ
ฝ
ฟ
ภ
ม
ย
ร
ฤ
ล
ฦ
ว
ศ
ษ
ส
ห
ฬ
อ
ฮ

(e.g. in movies) [คน kon]

พราก_จาก_ prâak-_-jàak-_ *vt.* deprive (take _ away from _)

พราน praan *n.* hunter/huntress (huntsman) [คน kon]

พราหมณ์ praam *n.* Brahmin [คน kon]

พรำ pram *adj.* (of rain) falling or drizzling

พริก prík *n.* chilli/chili [เม็ด mét (seed), ต้น dtôn (plant)]

พริกไทย prík-tai *n.* pepper (black) [เม็ด mét (seed), ขวด kùuat (bottle)]

พริกป่น prík-bpòn *n.* cayenne pepper

พริกหยวก prík-yùuak *n.* bell pepper, pimento (pepper) [เม็ด mét]

พริ้ง príng *adj.* pretty (beautiful) ☜

พรุ่งนี้ prûng-níi *n.* tomorrow (day) [วัน wan]

พฤกษศาสตร์ prúk-sà~sàat *n.* botany [วิชา wí-chaa]

พฤติการณ์ prút-dtì-gaan *n.* behavior, action ⚠

พฤศจิกายน prút-sà~jì-gaa-yon *n.* November [เดือน dʉʉan]

พฤษภาคม prút-sà~paa-kom *n.* May [เดือน dʉʉan]

พฤหัส pá~rʉ́-hàt *n.* Thursday [วัน wan]

พลทหาร pon-tá~hǎan *n.* private (military rank) [นาย naai ⚠, คน kon]

พลบ plóp *n.* dusk

พลบค่ำ plóp-kâm *n.* twilight

พลเมือง pon-lá~mʉʉang *n.* citizen [คน kon]

พลเรือน pon-lá~rʉʉan *n.* civilian [คน kon]

พลศึกษา pá~lá-sʉ̀k-sǎa *n.* physical education ⚠ [วิชา wí-chaa]

พละ pá~lá *n.* physical education [วิชา wí-chaa]

พลัง pá~lang *n.* strength (power) ☜

พลังงาน pá~lang-ngaan *n.* energy (e.g. electrical), power

พลับ pláp *n.* persimmon (fruit) [ลูก lûuk (fruit), ต้น dtôn (tree)]

พลั่ว plûua *n.* shovel (for

scooping) [เล่ม lêm]

พลาด plâat *vi.* fail, fail to join

พลาด plâat *vt.* miss (fail to hit)

พลาย plaai *n.* elephant male ⚣ [เชือก chûuak]

พลาสติก pláat-sà~dtìk *n.* plastic (material)

พลิก plík *vt.* turn (page, body)

พลิก_กลับ plík-_-glàp *vt.* toss (turn over)

พลุ plú *n.* firework (cannon cracker) [ตับ dtàp (row), ลูก lûuk, นัด nát]

พวก pûuak *n.* group [พวก pûuak]

พวกเขา pûuak-kǎo *pron.* them, themselves, they

พวกนี้ pûuak-níi *pron.* these

พวกเรา pûuak-rao *pron.* us, we

พวง puuang *n.* bunch (e.g. grapes), garland [พวง puuang]

พ่วง pûuang *v.* tow (haul)

พวงกุญแจ puuang-gun-jɛɛ *n.* key ring [พวง puuang]

พวงมาลัย puuang-maa-lai *n.* garland [พวง puuang]

พวงมาลัย puuang-maa-lai *n.* steering wheel [อัน an]

พวงหรีด puuang-rìit *n.* wreath [พวง puuang]

พวยกา puuai-gaa *n.* spout (of kettle) [พวย puuai]

พหูพจน์ pá~hǔu-pót *adj.* plural

พหูสูต pá~hǔu-sùut *n.* omniscient ⚡ [คน kon]

พอ pɔɔ *adj.* enough, sufficient

พอ pɔɔ *conj.* as soon as ☙

พ่อ pɔ̂ɔ *n.* polite form of addressing a boy or younger man, dad, father [คน kon]

พ้อ pɔ́ɔ *vi.* complain (whine)

พอก pɔ̂ɔk *v.* put on in layers

พ่อครัว pɔ̂ɔ-kruua *n.* cook (male) [คน kon]

พ่อค้า pɔ̂ɔ-káa *n.* merchant (male) [คน kon]

พอง pɔɔng *adj.* swollen (increased in size)

ก
ข
ฃ
ค
ฅ
ฆ
ง
จ
ฉ
ช
ซ
ฌ
ญ
ฎ
ฏ
ฐ
ฑ
ฒ
ณ
ด
ต
ถ
ท
ธ
น
บ
ป
ผ
ฝ
พ
ฟ
ภ
ม
ย
ร
ฤ
ล
ฦ
ว
ศ
ษ
ส
ห
อ
ฮ

พ้อง pɔ́ɔng *vi.* coincide

พองตัว pɔɔng-dtuua *vi.* inflate (swell)

พอใจ pɔɔ-jai *adj.* pleased, satisfied

พ่อตา pɔ̂ɔ-dtaa *n.* father-in-law (wife's father) [คน kon]

พ่อบ้าน pɔ̂ɔ-bâan *n.* head of the family, husband [คน kon]

พ่อปู่ pɔ̂ɔ-bpùu *n.* father-in-law (husband's father) [คน kon]

พอเพียง pɔɔ-piiang *adj.* adequate

พ่อมด pɔ̂ɔ-mót *n.* wizard [ตน dton]

พ่อม่าย pɔ̂ɔ-mâai *n.* widower [คน kon]

พ่อแม่ pɔ̂ɔ-mɛ̂ɛ *n.* parents [คน kon]

พ่อเลี้ยง pɔ̂ɔ-líiang *n.* stepfather [คน kon]

พอแล้ว pɔɔ-lɛ́ɛo *interj.* enough already!

พอสมควร pɔɔ-sǒm-kuuan *adj.* decent (adequate), moderate

พ่อสื่อ pɔ̂ɔ-sɯ̀ɯ *n.* matchmaker (male) [คน kon]

พะแนง pá~nɛɛng *n.* thick curry with large pieces of roast meat [ถ้วย tûuai]

พะเยา pá~yao *n.* Phayao province [จังหวัด jang-wàt]

พะวง pá~wong *adj.* worried (be anxious)

พัก pák *vi.* rest (take a break)

พักผ่อน pák-pɔ̀n *vi.* rest (relax)

พักฟื้น pák-fɯ́ɯn *vt.* rehabilitate

พักอยู่ pák-yùu *vi.* stay (reside, lodge)

พัง pang *adj.* wrecked (e.g. car, TV)

พัง pang *vi.* crash (e.g. computer), fall apart (collapse, e.g. chair)

พัง pang *vt.* tear down

พังงา pang-ngaa *n.* Phangnga province [จังหวัด jang-wàt]

พัฒน์พงษ์ pát-pong *n.* Patpong [ย่าน yâan]

พัฒนา pát-tá~naa *vi.* grow (develop), progress (develop)

พัด pát *vi.* blow (e.g. wind,

fan)

พัดลม pát-lom *n.* fan (electric) [ตัว dtuua, เครื่อง krûuang]

พัดให้ pát-hâi *vt.* fan (someone)

พัทยา pát-tá~yaa *n.* Pattaya [เขต kèet]

พัน pan *numb.* thousand

พัน pan *vt.* wind (curl)

พันตรี pan-dtrii *n.* major (rank)

พันธมิตร pan-tá~mít *n.* alliance [กลุ่ม glùm]

พันธะ pan-tá *n.* obligation (commitment, strings)

พันธุ์ pan *n.* breed, family (plant or animal) [พันธุ์ pan]

พันล้าน pan-láan *numb.* billion (thousand million)

พันเอก pan-èek *n.* colonel (in the marines) [นาย naai ❗, คน kon]

พับ páp *v.* fold

พับเพียบ páp-pîiap *v.* sit with both legs tucked back to one side

พัวพันกับ puua-pan-gàp *vt.* involve (connect)

พัสดุ pát-sà~dù *n.* package, parcel [กล่อง glòng (box), ชิ้น chín (one), ห่อ h̀ɔ (pack)]

พากเพียร pâak-piian *vi.* persevere (persist)

พากย์ pâak *n.* language of soundtrack in movie

พาน paan *n.* tray with pedestal [ใบ bai, ลูก lûuk, พาน paan]

พา_ไป paa-_-bpai *vt.* take (_ (someone) from here (to))

พา_มา paa-_-maa *vt.* bring (_ (someone) here (to))

พาย paai *v.* oar, row

พายัพ paa-yáp *n.* northwest ⚡ [ทิศ tít]

พายุ paa-yú *n.* storm (weather) [ลูก lûuk]

พายุหมุน paa-yú-mǔn *n.* tornado (twister) [ลูก lûuk]

พายุหิมะ paa-yú-hì~má *n.* blizzard

พาสปอร์ต páat-sà~bpɔ̀ɔt *n.* passport [ฉบับ chà~bàp ❗, เล่ม lêm]

พาหนะ paa-hà~ná *n.*

พาหนะ vehicle ‼ [คัน kan]

ำนัก pam-nák *vt.* house (provide housing)

พิกล pí-gon *adj.* peculiar (strange) ✎

พิการ pí-gaan *adj.* lame (disabled)

พิง ping *vt.* lean against

พิจารณา pí-jaa-rá~naa *v.* consider (think over)

พิจิตร pí-jìt *n.* Phichit province [จังหวัด jang-wàt]

พิณ pin *n.* harp [ตัว dtuua]

พิถีพิถัน pí-tǐi-pí-tǎn *adj.* meticulous

พิธี pí-tii *n.* ceremony, ritual [พิธี pí-tii]

พิธีกร pí-tii-gɔɔn *n.* master of ceremonies [คน kon]

พิธีกรรม pí-tii-gam *n.* rite, ritual [พิธี pí-tii]

พินัยกรรม pí-nai-gam *n.* will (legal document) [ฉบับ chà~bàp]

พินาศ pí-nâat *n.* destruction (annihilation) ✎

พิพิธภัณฑ์ pí-pít-tá~pan *n.* museum [แห่ง hɛ̀ng]

พิมพ์ pim *v.* print (on printer, at shop), type (print, type on keyboard)

พิมาย pí-maai *n.* Phimai district [อำเภอ am-pəə]

พิโรธ pí-rôot *vi.* rage ♔

พิลึก pí-lʉ́k *adj.* queer (peculiar), strange

พิเศษ pí-sèet *adj.* extra, special

พิษ pít *n.* venom (poison, toxin)

พิษณุโลก pít-sà~nú-lôok *n.* Phitsanulok province [จังหวัด jang-wàt]

พิสดาร pít-sà~daan *adj.* strange

พิสูจน์ pí-sùut *vt.* identify, prove, verify

พี่ pîi *n.* her, she, him, he, prefix to the name of an older sibling [คน kon]

พี่เขย pîi-kə̌əi *n.* brother-in-law (older) [คน kon]

พีชคณิต pii-chá-ká~nít *n.* algebra [วิชา wí-chaa]

พี่ชาย pîi-chaai *n.* brother (older) [คน kon]

พี่น้อง pîi-nɔ́ɔng *n.* brothers, sibling [คน kon]

พี่เลี้ยง pîi-líiang *n.* nurse maid, stepbrother, stepsister [คน kon]

พี่เลี้ยง pîi-líiang *n.* mentor ❀ [คน kon]

พี่เลี้ยงเด็ก pîi-líiang-dèk *n.* nanny [คน kon]

พี่สะใภ้ pîi-sà~pái *n.* sister-in-law (older) [คน kon]

พี่สาว pîi-sǎao *n.* sister (older) [คน kon]

พึ่ง pûng *adv.* a moment ago, just now ❀

พึ่งพา pûng-paa *vt.* depend on (rely on for support)

พึมพำ pʉm-pam *v.* murmur

พืช pʉ̂ʉt *n.* plant (vegetation) [ชนิด chá~nít (kind), ต้น dtôn (plant)]

พื้น pʉ́ʉn *n.* floor (surface) [พื้น pʉ́ʉn]

พื้นฐาน pʉ́ʉn-tǎan *adj.* basic, primary

พื้นดิน pʉ́ʉn-din *n.* soil

พื้นที่ pʉ́ʉn-tîi *n.* area (surface area) [แห่ง hɛ̀ng]

พื้นผิว pʉ́ʉn-pǐu *n.* surface, texture

พื้นเมือง pʉ́ʉn-mʉʉang *adj.* native (indigenous)

พู pú *vi.* break out (erupt)

พุง pung *n.* belly ❀ [พุง pung]

พุ่ง pûng *vt.* throw (e.g. lance)

พุงพลุ้ย pung-plúi *n.* potbelly

พุทธ pút *adj.* Buddhist

พุทธศักราช pút-tá~sàk-gà~ràat *n.* Buddhist Era ⚡ [ปี bpii]

พุทรา pút-saa *n.* jujube [ลูก lûuk]

พุธ pút *n.* Wednesday ❀ [วัน wan]

พุ่ม pûm *n.* bush [พุ่ม pûm]

พุ่มไม้ pûm-máai *n.* bush, shrub [พุ่ม pûm]

พู่กัน pûu-gan *n.* brush (for painting)

พูด pûut *v.* speak (e.g. Thai, slowly, the truth)

พูดเก่ง pûut-gèng *adj.* talkative

พูดคุย pûut-kui *vi.* chat ⚡,

talk (chat, converse) ǃ

พูด_ซ้ำ pûut-_-sám *vt.* repeat (speech)

พูดถึง pûut-tǔng *vt.* mention (refer)

พูดเล่น pûut-lên *vi.* joke (kid, tease)

เพ่ง pêng *v.* stare at

เพชร pét *n.* diamond (mineral) [เม็ด mét (stone), กะรัต gà~ràt (carat)]

เพชรพลอย pét-plɔɔi *n.* gem, jewel, jewelry (gems) [ชิ้น chín (piece), ชุด chút (set)]

เพดาน pee-daan *n.* ceiling [แผ่น pèn]

เพราะ prɔ́ *adj.* beautiful (for music), melodious

เพราะ prɔ́ *conj.* because

เพราะฉะนั้น prɔ́-chà~nán *adv.* therefore ǃ

เพราะว่า prɔ́-wâa *conj.* because, due to

เพราะอะไร prɔ́-à~rai *adv.* why ✦

เพล peen *n.* midday meal-time for Buddhist monk [มื้อ mɯ́ɯ]

เพลง pleeng *n.* music

(tune), song [เพลง pleeng]

เพลงชาติ pleeng-châat *n.* anthem (national) [เพลง pleeng]

เพลา plao *n.* axle (shaft of machine), shaft [เพลา plao]

เพลิดเพลิน plə̂ət-pləən *adj.* amused (by performance)

เพลิดเพลินกับ plə̂ət-pləən-gàp *vt.* savor (enjoy)

เพลิน pləən *vi.* be lost in thought, be oblivious

เพลีย pliia *adj.* tired (exhausted)

เพลี้ย plíia *n.* plant louse [ตัว dtuua]

เพศ pêet *n.* sex (gender) [เพศ pêet]

เพศชาย pêet-chaai *n.* male (gender) [เพศ pêet]

เพศหญิง pêet-yǐng *n.* female (gender) [เพศ pêet]

เพ้อคลั่ง pə́ə-klâng *vi.* hallucinate

เพ้อเจ้อ pə́ə-jə̂ə *adj.* delirious

เพาะปลูก pɔ́-bplùuk *vi.*

farm (crop)

เพาะเลี้ยง pɔ́-líiang *vt.* plant (cultivate)

เพิกถอน pə̂ək-tʉ̌ɔn *v.* cancel (annul)

เพิ่ง pə̂ng *adv.* just (moment ago)

เพิ่ม pə̂əm *vt.* add (fill up, increase)

เพิ่ม_ขึ้น pə̂əm-_-kʉ̂n *v.* increase (augment)

เพิ่มเติม pə̂əm-dtəəm *adj.* extra (additional)

เพียง piiang *adv.* as far as, equal to, just, only

เพียงแค่ piiang-kɛ̂ɛ *adv.* just (only) ‼

เพียงใด piiang-dai *adv.* how far

เพียงแต่ piiang-dtɛ̀ɛ *conj.* only (but)

เพียงพอ piiang-pɔɔ *adj.* enough, just enough

เพื่อ pʉ̂ʉa *prep.* for (given to, sent to, for sake of), on behalf of (for the sake of)

เพื่อที่จะ pʉ̂ʉa-tîi-jà *prep.* in order to

เพื่อน pʉ̂ʉan *n.* companion, friend, mate,

pal, peer [คน kon]

เพื่อนเจ้าบ่าว pʉ̂ʉan-jâo-bàao *n.* best man [คน kon]

เพื่อนเจ้าสาว pʉ̂ʉan-jâo-sǎao *n.* bridesmaid, maid of honor [คน kon]

เพื่อนชาย pʉ̂ʉan-chaai *n.* boyfriend (just a friend) ‼ [คน kon]

เพื่อนบ้าน pʉ̂ʉan-bâan *n.* neighbor [คน kon]

เพื่อนร่วมงาน pʉ̂ʉan-rûuam-ngaan *n.* colleague [คน kon]

เพื่อนร่วมชั้น pʉ̂ʉan-rûuam-chán *n.* classmate [คน kon]

เพื่อนสนิท pʉ̂ʉan-sà~nìt *n.* buddy, one's trusted companion [คน kon]

เพื่อนหญิง pʉ̂ʉan-yǐng *n.* girlfriend (just a friend) ‼ [คน kon]

เพื่อว่า pʉ̂ʉa-wâa *conj.* so that

เพื่อให้ pʉ̂ʉa-hâi *conj.* so that, in order to

เพื่ออะไร pʉ̂ʉa-à~rai *adv.* for what reason

แพ pɛɛ n. raft [ลำ lam]

แพ้ pɛ́ɛ adj. allergic (to something)

แพ้ pɛ́ɛ v. lose (suffer defeat)

แพง pɛɛng adj. dear, expensive, high

แพ่ง pêng n. civil case

แพทย์ pɛ̂ɛt n. doctor ⚕, physician ⚕ [คน kon]

แพ้ท้อง pɛ́ɛ-tɔ́ɔng n. morning sickness

แพร prɛɛ n. silk cloth [ผืน pʉ̌ʉn]

แพร่ prɛ̂ɛ n. Phrae province [จังหวัด jang-wàt]

แพร่เชื้อ prɛ̂ɛ-chʉ́ʉa v. transmit (pass on, e.g. germ)

แพร่พันธุ์ prɛ̂ɛ-pan vi. breed (procreate), reproduce

แพร่หลาย prɛ̂ɛ-lǎai adj. widespread

แพลง plɛɛng adj. twisted (sprained, e.g. ankle)

แพะ pɛ́ n. goat [ตัว dtuua]

แพะรับบาป pɛ́-ráp-bàap n. scapegoat [ตัว dtuua (goat), คน kon (human)]

โพธิ์ poo n. bo tree, pipal tree [ต้น dtôn]

โพธิ์ดำ poo-dam n. spade (card)

โพ้น póon adv. there (over there)

โพ้นทะเล póon-tá~lee adj. overseas/oversea (situated in countries across the sea) 🐋

โพรง proong n. cavity (hole), hollow [โพรง proong, อัน an]

โพล้เพล้ plóo-plée n. twilight

โพละ pló adv. pop (sound)

โพส póot n. pose (posture, gesture) ✊ [ท่า tâa]

โพสท่า póot-tâa vi. pose (e.g. for a picture) ✊

ไพ่ pâi n. card (playing) [ใบ bai (card), สำรับ sǎm-ráp (deck)]

ไพร prai n. forest 🐋 [แห่ง hɛ̀ng]

ไพร่ prâi n. subjects of a king [คน kon]

ไพเราะ pai-rɔ́ adj. melodious ⚕

ฟ

ฟ fɔɔ *let.* ฟ. ฟัน fɔɔ-fan, a consonant of the Thai alphabet (low consonant) [ตัว dtuua]

ฟรี frii *adj.* free ✧, independent ✧

ฟลุ๊ค flúk *adj.* lucky ✧

ฟอกสบู่ fɔ̂ɔk-sà~bùu *v.* wash with soap

ฟอง fɔɔng *clf.* for eggs, bubbles

ฟอง fɔɔng *n.* foam (e.g. soap) [ฟอง fɔɔng]

ฟ้อง fɔ́ɔng *v.* sue, take into court

ฟองน้ำ fɔɔng-náam *n.* sponge [ชิ้น chín (piece)]

ฟ้องร้อง fɔ́ɔng-rɔ́ɔng *v.* charge (legal), prosecute (initiate civil or criminal court action), sue

ฟ้อน fɔ́ɔn *vi.* dance (traditional)

ฟอร์ม fɔɔm *n.* form (official document) [ใบ bai, แผ่น pɛ̀n, ฟอร์ม fɔɔm]

ฟอร์แมต fɔɔ-mɛ̀t *vt.* format (e.g. disk, document) ✗

ฟอสซิล fɔ́ɔt-sîn *n.* fossil (remains) [ก้อน gɔ̂ɔn, ซาก sâak]

ฟัก fák *n.* vegetable of the squash or melon family [ลูก lûuk]

ฟักไข่ fák-kài *vi.* incubate (roost on eggs)

ฟักตัว fák-dtuua *vi.* hatch (break open)

ฟักทอง fák-tɔɔng *n.* pumpkin [ลูก lûuk]

ฟัง fang *v.* listen

ฟัน fan *n.* tooth [ซี่ sîi (piece), ชุด chút (set)]

ฟัน fan *v.* chop (e.g. piece of wood)

ฟันดาบ fan-dàap *v.* male and male anal intercourse ✧

ฟันปลอม fan-bplɔɔm *n.* false teeth [ซี่ sîi (each one), ชุด chút (set)]

ฟันผุ fan-pù *n.* cavity (dental) [ซี่ sîi]

ฟ้า fáa *n.* sky [ผืน pʉ̌ʉn]

ฟาง faang *n.* hay (rice chaff), straw [กอง gɔɔng (pile), เส้น sên (strand)]

ฟาด fâat *v.* strike (hit)

ฟ้าผ่า fáa-pàa *n.* lightning (between a cloud and the ground), thunderbolt [ครั้ง kráng]

ฟ้าร้อง fáa-rɔ́ɔng *n.* thunder [ครั้ง kráng (clap)]

ฟ้าแลบ fáa-lɛ̂p *n.* lightning (between clouds) [ครั้ง kráng]

ฟิล์ม fiim *n.* film (for camera) [แผ่น pèn (piece), ม้วน múuan (roll)]

ฟิวส์ fiu *n.* fuse (electrical, igniter) [อัน an (piece)]

ฟิสิกส์ fí-sìk *n.* physics [วิชา wí-chaa]

ฟืน fɯɯn *n.* firewood [ท่อน tɔ̂n (piece)]

ฟื้น fɯ́ɯn *vi.* come to (regain consciousness)

ฟื้นตัว fɯ́ɯn-dtuua *vi.* recover (get better), recuperate

ฟื้นฟู fɯ́ɯn-fuu *vt.* restore (revive, bring back old)

ฟุต fút *n.* foot (measurement) [ฟุต fút]

ฟุตบอล fút-bɔn *n.* football (ball) [ลูก lûuk]

ฟุตบาท fút-bàat *n.* footpath [ทาง taang]

ฟุบ fúp *v.* fall face down

ฟุ่มเฟือย fûm-fɯɯai *adj.* extravagant, lavish, luxurious

ฟู fuu *adj.* fluffy (light or airy)

ฟูก fûuk *n.* mattress [ผืน pʉ̌ʉn, แผ่น pèn, อัน an ✦]

เฟือง fɯɯang *adj.* diffused

เฟื่องฟู fɯ̂ɯang-fuu *v.* prosper ✦

แฟกซ์ fɛ́k *n.* fax [เครื่อง krʉ̂ʉang (machine), แผ่น pèn (paper)]

แฟน fɛɛn *n.* husband ✦, loved one, lover (girl, boyfriend), wife ✦ [คน kon]

แฟ้ม fɛ́m *n.* file, folder [แฟ้ม fɛ́m]

แฟลช flɛ̀t *n.* flash (camera unit)

แฟลต flɛ̀t *n.* flat (apartment) [หลัง lǎng, แฟลต flɛ̀t]

โฟกัส foo-gát *vi.* focus (concentrate) ✦

ก ข ฃ ค ฅ ฆ ง จ ฉ ช ซ ฌ ญ ฎ ฏ ฐ ฑ ฒ ณ ด ต ถ ท ธ น บ ป ผ ฝ **พ** ฟ ภ ม ย ร ฤ ล ฦ ว ศ ษ ส ห ฬ อ ฮ

โฟม foom *n.* foam (plastic)
ไฟ fai *n.* fire
ไฟจราจร fai-jà-raa-jɔɔn *n.* signal (traffic light), traffic light [จุด jùt]
ไฟฉาย fai-chǎai *n.* flashlight, searchlight, torch [กระบอก grà~bɔ̀ɔk, อัน an]
ไฟแช็ค fai-chɛ́k *n.* lighter [อัน an]
ไฟดับ fai-dàp *n.* blackout (power failure)
ไฟท้าย fai-táai *n.* taillight [ดวง duuang]
ไฟฟ้า fai-fáa *n.* electricity
ไฟฟ้าสถิต fai-fáa-sà~tìt *n.* static (electricity) ⚒
ไฟล์ fai *n.* file (folder) 🗣 [ไฟล์ fai]

ภ

ภ pɔɔ *let.* ภ. สำเภา pɔɔ-sǎm-pao, a consonant of the Thai alphabet (low consonant) [ตัว dtuua]
ภรรยา pan-rá~yaa, pan-yaa *n.* wife ❗ [คน kon]
ภักดี pák-dii *adj.* loyal
ภัย pai *n.* accident, danger ❧
ภาค pâak *n.* region (of the country), sector (division)
ภาคใต้ pâak-dtâai *n.* south (region) [ภาค pâak]
ภาคทัณฑ์ pâak-tan *n.* probation (act of suspending the sentence) ⚒ [ครั้ง kráng]
ภาคผนวก pâak-pà~nùuak *n.* appendix (addendum) [ส่วน sùuan, ภาค pâak]
ภาคเรียน pâak-riian *n.* semester, term [ภาค pâak]
ภาควิชา pâak-wí-chaa *n.* academic department [ภาควิชา pâak-wí-chaa]
ภาคเหนือ pâak-nʉ̌ʉa *n.* northern region [ภาค pâak]
ภาคอีสาน pâak-ii-sǎan *n.* northeast of Thailand [ภาค pâak]
ภาชนะ paa-chá~ná *n.* container [ใบ bai, ชิ้น chín]
ภาพ pâap *n.* image (picture) [ใบ bai, แผ่น pɛ̀n, ภาพ pâap]

ก
ข
ฃ
ค
ฅ
ฆ
ง
จ
ฉ
ช
ซ
ฌ
ญ
ฎ
ฏ
ฐ
ฑ
ฒ
ณ
ด
ต
ถ
ท
ธ
น
บ
ป
ผ
ฝ
พ
ฟ
ภ
ม
ย
ร
ฤ
ล
ฦ
ว
ศ
ษ
ส
ห
ฬ
อ
ฮ

ภาพเขียน pâap-kǐian *n.* painting (drawing) [ภาพ pâap]

ภาพถ่าย pâap-tàai *n.* photograph ⚡ [ภาพ pâap]

ภาพประกอบ pâap-bprà~gòɔp *n.* figure (diagram, picture) [อัน an]

ภาพพจน์ pâap-pót *n.* picture (mental image derived from a narrative)

ภาพยนตร์ pâap-pá~yon *n.* film (movie) ⚡ [เรื่อง rûuang]

ภาพร่าง pâap-râang *n.* sketch [ภาพ pâap]

ภาพวาด pâap-wâat *n.* drawing (picture) [ภาพ pâap]

ภาพหลอน pâap-lɔ̌ɔn *n.* illusion (hallucination)

ภายนอก paai-nɔ̂ɔk *adj.* external

ภายใน paai-nai *adj.* inside, internal

ภายใน paai-nai *prep.* in, within

ภายหลัง paai-lǎng *adv.* after

ภารกิจ paa-rá-gìt *n.* function (duty), task (duty) [อัน an]

ภารโรง paan-roong *n.* janitor [คน kon]

ภาระ paa-rá *n.* burden (responsibility, duty) [อัน an]

ภาระหน้าที่ paa-rá-nâa-tîi *n.* obligation (duty)

ภาวนา paa-wá~naa *vi.* pray (make a wish)

ภาษา paa-sǎa *n.* language [ภาษา paa-sǎa]

ภาษากลาง paa-sǎa-glaang *n.* common language [ภาษา paa-sǎa]

ภาษาถิ่น paa-sǎa-tìn *n.* dialect [ภาษา paa-sǎa]

ภาษาไทย paa-sǎa-tai *n.* Thai (language)

ภาษาใบ้ paa-sǎa-bâi *n.* sign language ✦ [ภาษา paa-sǎa]

ภาษาพูด paa-sǎa-pûut *adj.* colloquial

ภาษาแม่ paa-sǎa-mɛ̂ɛ *n.* mother tongue [ภาษา paa-sǎa]

ภาษาอังกฤษ paa-sǎa-ang-grìt *n.* English (language) [ภาษา paa-sǎa]

ภาษี paa-sǐi *n.* duty,

revenue, tax

ภาษีมูลค่าเพิ่ม paa-sǐi-muun-lá~kâa-pôəm *n.* value-added tax [จำนวน jam-nuuan]

ภิกษุ pík-sù *n.* Buddhist monk [รูป rûup]

ภูกระดึง puu-grà~dɯng *n.* Phu Kradueng [อำเภอ am-pəə (district)]

ภูเก็ต puu-gèt *n.* Phuket province [จังหวัด jang-wàt]

ภูเขา puu-kǎo *n.* mountain [ลูก lûuk]

ภูเขาไฟ puu-kǎo-fai *n.* volcano [ลูก lûuk]

ภูมิ puum *n.* land

ภูมิคุ้มกัน puum-kúm-gan *n.* immunity (to disease)

ภูมิใจ puum-jai *adj.* proud

ภูมิฐาน puum-tǎan *adj.* grand (dignified)

ภูมิต้านทาน puum-dtâan-taan *n.* immunity (to disease)

ภูมิปัญญา puum-bpan-yaa *n.* intelligence (knowledge)

ภูมิลำเนา puum-lam-nao *n.* native habitat

ภูมิศาสตร์ puu-mí-sàat *n.* geography [วิชา wí-chaa]

ภูมิหลัง puum-lǎng *n.* background (history)

ภูมิอากาศ puu-mí-aa-gàat *n.* climate (in geography)

เภสัชกร pee-sàt-chá~gɔɔn *n.* pharmacist [คน kon]

โภชนา poo-chá~naa *n.* diet (food or drink) ✖

โภชนาการ poo-chá~naa-gaan *n.* dietetics, nutrition

ม

ม mɔɔ *let.* ม. ม้า mɔɔ-máa, a consonant of the Thai alphabet (low consonant) [ตัว dtuua]

มกราคม mók-gà~raa-kom, má~gà~raa-kom *n.* January [เดือน dɯɯan]

มงกุฎ mong-gùt *n.* crown (headgear) [องค์ ong 👑 (for king), มงกุฎ mong-gùt]

มงคล mong-kon *n.* cotton band worn on the head [วง wong]

มณี má~nii *n.* gem ✦ [ชิ้น

chín]

มด mót *n.* ant [ตัว dtuua]

มดลูก mót-lûuk *n.* uterus, womb

มติ má~dtì *n.* resolution (solution) [เสียง sǐiang]

มนต์ mon *n.* sacred words (magic spell) [บท bòt]

มนตร์ mon see มนต์

มนต์สะกด mon-sà~gòt *n.* spell (charm)

มนต์เสน่ห์ mon-sà~nèe *n.* charm (magic spell)

มนัส má~nát *n.* mind ✌ [ดวง duuang]

มนุษย์ má~nút *n.* human ❗ [คน kon]

มนุษยชาติ má~nút-sà~yá-châat *n.* mankind

มรกต mɔɔ-rá~gòt *n.* emerald [เม็ด mét, ก้อน gɔ̂ɔn (not cut)]

มรณภาพ mɔɔ-rá~ná-pâap *vi.* die ✿

มรณะ mɔɔ-rá~ná *vi.* die ❗

มรดก mɔɔ-rá~dòk *n.* heritage (inheritance, cultural) [กอง gɔɔng, ชิ้น chín]

มรรยาท man-yâat see

มารยาท

มรสุม mɔɔ-rá~sǔm *n.* monsoon, storm (weather) ✌ [ลูก lûuk]

มลทิล mon-tin *n.* stigma

ม่วง mûuang *adj.* purple

มวน muuan *clf.* for cigars, cigarettes

ม้วน múuan *n.* roll (anything rolled up) [ม้วน múuan]

ม้วน múuan *vt.* roll (up into roll, e.g. carpet, scroll)

ม้วน_เข้า múuan-_-kâo *vt.* roll up

ม้วนตัว múuan-dtuua *vi.* roll up

ม้วน_ออก múuan-_-ɔ̀ɔk *vt.* roll out (unroll)

ม้วย múuai *vi.* die ✌

มวยไทย muuai-tai *n.* Thai boxing

มวยปล้ำ muuai-bplâm *n.* wrestling

มวยผม muuai-pǒm *n.* bun (of the hair) [มวย muuai, ลูก lûuk]

มวล muuan *adj.* total (all of)

มวล muuan *n.* mass (in physics)

มหา má~hǎa *adj.* large, many, much

มหากาพย์ má~hǎa-gàap *n.* epic [เรื่อง rûueang]

มหาดไทย má-hàat-tai *n.* Ministry of the Interior [กระทรวง grà~suuang]

มหายาน má~hǎa-yaan *n.* Mahayana Buddhism [นิกาย ní-gaai]

มหาวิทยาลัย má~hǎa-wít-tá~yaa-lai *n.* university [แห่ง hèng]

มหาเศรษฐี má~hǎa-sèet-tǐi *n.* multimillionaire [คน kon]

มหาสมุทร má~hǎa-sà~mùt *n.* ocean [แห่ง hèng]

มหาสารคาม má~hǎa-sǎa-rá~kaam *n.* Maha Sarakham province [จังหวัด jang-wàt]

มหาอำนาจ má~hǎa-am-nâat *n.* superpower

มหึมา má-hù-maa *adj.* enormous, giant, prodigious !

มโหรี má~hǒo-rii *n.* Thai orchestra [วง wong]

มอง mɔɔng *v.* look (gaze)

มอง mɔɔng *vt.* look at, see (with eyes)

มองข้าม mɔɔng-kâam *vt.* overlook (ignore, disregard), pass by

มองหา mɔɔng-hǎa *vt.* look for

มอญ mɔɔn *n.* Peguans (Mon (peoples)) [คน kon]

มอด mɔɔt *n.* weevil [ตัว dtuua]

มอเตอร์ mɔɔ-dtɔ̂ɔ *n.* motor [ตัว dtuua, ลูก lûuk]

มอเตอร์ไซค์ mɔɔ-dtɔɔ-sai *n.* bike, motorcycle [คัน kan]

มอบ mɔ̂ɔp *vt.* submit (hand in)

มอบตัว mɔ̂ɔp-dtuua *vi.* surrender (to the police)

มอบหมาย mɔ̂ɔp-mǎai *vt.* assign (designate)

มะกรูด má~grùut *n.* kaffir [ลูก lûuk (fruit)]

มะกอก má~gɔ̀ɔk *n.* olive [ลูก lûuk (fruit)]

มะขาม má~kǎam *n.* tamarind (fruit) [ฝัก fàk (fruit), ต้น dtôn (tree)]

มะเขือ má~kǔuea *n.* eggplant [ลูก lûuk]

ก
ข
ค
ฅ
ฆ
ง
จ
ฉ
ช
ซ
ฌ
ญ
ฎ
ฏ
ฐ
ฑ
ฒ
ณ
ด
ต
ถ
ท
ธ
น
บ
ป
ผ
ฝ
พ
ฟ
ภ
ม
ย
ร
ฤ
ล
ฦ
ว
ศ
ษ
ส
ห
อ
ฮ

มะเขือเทศ má~kǔua-têet *n.* tomato [ลูก lûuk (fruit), ต้น dtôn (plant)]

มะเขือเผา má~kǔua-pǎo *n.* soft penis ●

มะเขือยาว má~kǔua-yaao *n.* long penis ●

มะเดื่อ má~dùua *n.* fig (fruit) [ลูก lûuk]

มะนาว má~naao *n.* lemon (green), lime (citrus fruit) [ลูก lûuk]

มะปราง má~bpraang *n.* plum mango [ลูก lûuk]

มะพร้าว má~práao *n.* coconut [ลูก lûuk]

มะม่วง má~mûuang *n.* mango [ลูก lûuk]

มะม่วงหิมพานต์ má~mûuang-hǐm-má~paan *n.* cashew [ลูก lûuk]

มะเมีย má~miia *n.* Year of the Horse [ปี bpii]

มะแม má~mɛɛ *n.* Year of the Goat [ปี bpii]

มะยม má~yom *n.* country gooseberry [ลูก lûuk (fruit), ต้น dtôn (tree)]

มะระ má~rá *n.* bitter melon [ลูก lûuk]

มะรืน má~ruuen *n.* day after tomorrow [วัน wan]

มะเร็ง má~reng *n.* cancer

มะโรง má~roong *n.* Year of the Dragon [ปี bpii]

มะละกอ má~lá~gɔɔ *n.* papaya [ลูก lûuk (fruit), ต้น dtôn (tree)]

มะลิ má~lí *n.* jasmine (plant) [ต้น dtôn (plant), ดอก dɔ̀ɔk (flower)]

มะเส็ง má~sěng *n.* Year of the Snake [ปี bpii]

มัก mák *adj.* prone (liable)

มัก mák *adv.* often ⚘, usually

มักง่าย mák-ngâai *adj.* sloppy (careless)

มักจะ mák-jà *adv.* commonly, usually

มัคคุเทศก์ mák-kú-têet *n.* guide ! [คน kon]

มังกร mang-gɔɔn *n.* dragon [ตัว dtuua]

มั่งคั่ง mâng-kâng *adj.* wealthy, well-off

มังคุด mang-kút *n.* mangosteen [ลูก lûuk]

มั่งมี mâng-mii *adj.* rich

มังสวิรัติ mang-sà~wí-rát

n. vegetarianism

มัจฉะ mát-chà *n.* fish ฅ [ตัว dtuua]

มัจฉา mát-chǎa see มัจฉะ

มัด mát *vt.* bind, bundle, tie (e.g. bundle, bondage)

มัธยม mát-tá~yom *n.* middle school, high school [ชั้น chán]

มัธยัสถ์ mát-tá~yát *adj.* economical (thrifty) ¡

มัน man *n.* yam (sweet potato) [หัว hǔua]

มัน man *pron.* he (derogatory) ✹, her ✹, him ✹, it, she (derogatory) ✹

มั่น mân *adj.* certain

มันแกว man-gɛɛo *n.* kind of sweet potato, jicama [หัว hǔua]

มั่นคง mân-kong *adj.* firm, secure, solid, stable (e.g. tripod, job, economy), steady

มั่นใจ mân-jai *adj.* confident

มั่นใจ mân-jai *vt.* trust (in strength, ability)

มันเทศ man-têet *n.* sweet potato [หัว hǔua]

มันฝรั่ง man-fà~ràng *n.* potato [หัว hǔua]

มัมมี่ mam-mîi *n.* mummy [ตัว dtuua]

มั้ย mái *part.* to form a question

มัว muua *adj.* blurry, dim (not bright)

มัวเมา muua-mao *adj.* infatuated (addicted to)

มัสมั่น mát-sà~màn *n.* kind of highly seasoned curry

มัสยิด mát-sà~yít *n.* mosque [แห่ง hɛ̀ng]

มา maa *vi.* come (reach, arrive)

ม่า mâa *n.* Chinese mother [คน kon]

ม้า máa *n.* horse [ตัว dtuua]

มาก mâak *adj.* a lot of, many, much, several

มาก mâak *adv.* a lot, so (extremely), very

มากกว่า mâak-gwàa *adv.* more

มากเกินไป mâak-gəən-bpai *adv.* too much

มากที่สุด mâak-tîi-sùt *adj.* maximum (most)

มากมาย mâak-maai *adj.* numerous, tremendous (in number or degree)

มากมาย mâak-maai *adv.* much

มาก่อน maa-gɔ̀ɔn *adj.* preceding (occur before)

มาช้า maa-cháa *adv.* late (delayed)

มาตรการ mâat-dtrà~gaan *n.* measure (standard) [มาตรการ mâat-dtrà~gaan]

มาตรฐาน mâat-dtrà~tǎan *n.* standard (criterion)

มาถึง maa-tǔng *vi.* arrive

ม่าน mâan *n.* curtain, screen [ผืน pǔɯn]

ม่านตา mâan-dtaa *n.* iris (of the eye)

ม้านั่ง máa-nâng *n.* bench (seat), stool (chair) [ตัว dtuua]

ม้าน้ำ máa-náam *n.* seahorse [ตัว dtuua]

มาพบ maa-póp *v.* come to see ‼

ม้าม máam *n.* spleen (organ) [อัน an]

ม้ามืด máa-mûɯt *n.* dark horse [คน kon (person),

ตัว dtuua (animal)]

ม่าย mâai *n.* widow, widower [คน kon]

มายา maa-yaa *n.* illusion (concept)

มาเยี่ยม maa-yîiam *v.* visit (come visit)

มารดา maan-daa *n.* mother ‼ [คน kon]

มารยา maan-yaa *adj.* pretentious

มารยาท maa-rá~yâat *n.* courtesy (decency), etiquette, manner

ม้าร้อง máa-rɔ́ɔng *vi.* neigh

มารับ maa-ráp *v.* come to meet

มาลัย maa-lai *n.* garland, lei, wreath [พวง puuang]

มาแล้ว maa-lɛ́ɛo *adv.* ago, since

ม้าหมุน máa-mǔn *n.* carousel (merry-go-round) [ตัว dtuua]

มาหา maa-hǎa *vi.* come over (visit)

มิ mí *adv.* not ✍

มิฉะนั้น mí-chà~nán *adv.* otherwise (or else)

มิฉะนั้น mí-chà~nán *conj.*

otherwise (if not)

มิด mít *adv.* entirely, submerged completely

มิตร mít *n.* friend ➤ [คน kon]

มิตรภาพ mít-dtà~pâap *n.* friendship

มิติ mí-dtì *n.* dimension [มิติ mí-dtì]

มิเตอร์ míit-dtêə *n.* meter (e.g. taxi)

มิถุนายน mí-tù-naa-yon *n.* June [เดือน dʉʉan]

มิน่า mí-nâa *interj.* that's why!

มี mii *v.* have, there is/there are

มี mii *vi.* exist (be)

มีกำไร mii-gam-rai *vi.* make a profit

มีคนที่ mii-kon-tîi *pron.* somebody/someone (as subject)

มีครรภ์ mii-kan *adj.* pregnant ⚠

มีความสุข mii-kwaam-sùk *adj.* happy

มีค่า mii-kâa *adj.* precious (valuable)

มีชีวิต mii-chii-wít *adj.* alive (living)

มีชีวิตชีวา mii-chii-wít-chii-waa *adj.* lively, vibrant (energetic)

มีชีวิตอยู่ mii-chii-wít-yùu *vi.* exist (be alive)

มีชื่อเสียง mii-chʉ̂ʉ-sǐiang *adj.* famous

มีชู้ mii-chúu *vi.* commit adultery ⚠

มีโชค mii-chôok *adj.* lucky

มีด mîit *n.* knife [เล่ม lêm]

มีดโกน mîit-goon *n.* razor [เล่ม lêm]

มีดพก mîit-pók *n.* pocket knife [เล่ม lêm]

มีดพับ mîit-páp *n.* jackknife [เล่ม lêm]

มีท้อง mii-tɔ́ɔng *adj.* pregnant

มีทักษะ mii-ták-sà *adj.* skillful

มีธุระ mii-tú-rá *adj.* busy (having work or errand)

มีนาคม mii-naa-kom *n.* March [เดือน dʉʉan]

มีมารยาท mii-maa-rá~yâat *adj.* polite (courteous)

มีสติ mii-sà~dtì *adj.* conscious (awake)

มีสมาธิ mii-sà~maa-tí *vi.*

concentrate (focus the mind, be composed)

มีส่วน mii-sùuan *vi.* take part

มีสิทธิ์ mii-sìt *adj.* eligible (have a right)

มีเสน่ห์ mii-sà~nèe *adj.* attractive (charming)

มีเหตุผล mii-hèet-pǒn *adj.* sane (sensible)

มีอยู่ mii-yùu *adj.* available (not run out yet), existent

มีอะไรที่ mii-à~rai-tîi *pron.* something (as subject)

มีอายุ mii-aa-yú *adj.* aged (of the age of, having lived long)

มีอารมณ์ mii-aa-rom *v.* get horny

มึน mʉn *adj.* dazed (stunned)

มึนหัว mʉn-hǔua *adj.* groggy (from lack of sleep)

มืด mʉ̂ut *adj.* dark (light level)

มืดมน mʉ̂ut-mon *adj.* obscure (dark)

มืดมัว mʉ̂ut-muua *adj.* obscure (dark)

มือ mʉʉ *n.* hand (body part) [ข้าง kâang]

มื้อ mʉ́ʉ *n.* meal (eaten in one sitting) [มื้อ mʉ́ʉ]

มือถือ mʉʉ-tʉ̌ʉ *n.* mobile phone ● [เครื่อง krʉ̂ʉang]

มือปืน mʉʉ-bpʉʉn *n.* gunman [คน kon]

มือเปล่า mʉʉ-bplàao *adj.* empty-handed

มือโปร mʉʉ-bproo *n.* professional (not amateur) ● [คน kon]

มือสมัครเล่น mʉʉ-sà~màk-lên *n.* amateur [คน kon]

มือสอง mʉʉ-sɔ̌ɔng *adj.* second-hand

มืออาชีพ mʉʉ-aa-chîip *n.* pro, professional (not amateur) [คน kon]

มุก múk *adj.* pearl (pertaining to pearls)

มุกดา múk-daa *n.* opal ● [เม็ด mét]

มุกดาหาร múk-daa-hǎan *n.* pearl ● [เม็ด mét]

มุกดาหาร múk-daa-hǎan *n.* Mukdahan province [จังหวัด jang-wàt]

มุง mung *v.* put on a roof, crowd around

มุ่ง mûng *v.* intend

มุ้ง múng *n.* mosquito net [หลัง lǎng]

มุ่งมั่น mûng-mân *adj.* intent

มุ่งร้าย mûng-ráai *v.* intend to do harm

มุ้งลวด múng-lûuat *n.* screen (mosquito) [อัน an]

มุ่งหมาย mûng-mǎai *v.* have a definite purpose

มุด mút *v.* crawl under

มุม mum *n.* angle, corner, nook [มุม mum]

มุมมอง mum-mɔɔng *n.* point of view (standpoint) [มุมมอง mum-mɔɔng]

มุสา mú-sǎa *v.* lie ☙

มูก mûuk *n.* mucus

มูเซอ muu-səə *n.* Lahu (hilltribe) [เผ่า pào]

มูมมาม muum-maam *adj.* messy (sloppily for filthily)

มูล muun *n.* feces ⚠ [กอง gɔɔng, ก้อน gɔ̂ɔn]

มูลค่า muun-lá~kâa, muun-kâa *n.* value (cost, price) ⚠

มูลฐาน muun-tǎan *n.* basis (fundamental element)

มูลนิธิ muun-lá~ní-tí *n.* foundation (institute) [แห่ง hɛ̀ng]

มูลฝอย muun-fɔ̌ɔi *n.* waste matter

มูลสัตว์ muun-sàt *n.* manure

เม็กซิโก mék-sí~goo *n.* Mexico [ประเทศ bprà~têet]

เมฆ mêek *n.* cloud [กลุ่ม glùm (cluster), ก้อน gɔ̂ɔn (mass)]

เม็ด mét *clf.* e.g. seeds, buttons, gems, pills, candies, etc.

เม็ด mét *n.* seed (grain) [เม็ด mét]

เม็ดสี mét-sǐi *n.* pigment ⚠

เมตตา mêet-dtaa *n.* kindness, mercy

เมตร méet *n.* metre/ meter [เมตร méet]

เมถุน mee-tǔn *n.* Gemini [ราศี raa-sǐi]

เม่น mên *n.* porcupine

[ตัว dtuua]

เมรุ meen, mee-rú *n.* crematorium [แห่ง hèng]

เมล็ด má~lét *n.* seed (grain) ‼ [เม็ด mét, เมล็ด má~lét ‼]

เมษายน mee-sǎa-yon *n.* April [เดือน duuan]

เมา mao *adj.* affected with motion sickness, intoxicate, drunk

เม่า mâo *n.* species of insect or rice [ตัว dtuua]

เมาคลื่น mao-klûun *adj.* seasick

เมาค้าง mao-káang *n.* hangover

เมารถ mao-rót *adj.* carsick

เมาเรือ mao-ruua *adj.* seasick

เมาเหล้า mao-lâo *adj.* drunk

เมิน məən *v.* turn the face away from

เมีย miia *n.* wife [คน kon]

เมี่ยง mîiang *n.* kind of Thai appetizer [คำ kam]

เมียนมาร์ miian-mâa *n.* Myanmar [ประเทศ bprà~têet]

เมียน้อย miia-nɔ́ɔi *n.* minor wife, mistress (minor wife) [คน kon]

เมียหลวง miia-lǔuang *n.* legal wife [คน kon]

เมื่อ mûua *conj.* when ‼

เมือก mûuak *n.* slime (liquid)

เมื่อก่อน mûua-gɔ̀ɔn *adv.* before (formerly)

เมื่อกี้ mûua-gîi *adv.* a moment ago, just now

เมื่อกี๊ mûua-gíi see เมื่อกี้

เมื่อคืนนี้ mûua-kuun-níi *n.* last night

เมือง muuang *n.* city, town [เมือง muuang]

เมืองขึ้น muuang-kûn *n.* colony [เมือง muuang]

เมืองไทย muuang-tai *n.* Thailand (country) ❧ [เมือง muuang]

เมืองนอก muuang-nɔ̂ɔk *n.* foreign country ❧ [ประเทศ bprà~têet]

เมืองหลวง muuang-lǔuang *n.* capital (city) [แห่ง hèng]

เมื่อใดก็ตาม mûua-dai-gɔ̂ɔ-dtaam *conj.* whenever

เมื่อย mûuai *adj.* tired (e.g. muscles)

เมื่อรืนนี้ mûua-ruun-níi *n.* day after tomorrow [วัน wan]

เมื่อวานนี้ mûua-waan-níi *n.* yesterday [วัน wan]

เมื่อไหร่ mûua-rài *adv.* when

เมื่อไหร่ mûua-rài *pron.* when

เมื่อไหร่ก็ได้ mûua-rài-gɔ̂ɔ-dâai *adv.* anytime ✦

แม่ mɛ̂ɛ *n.* mother [คน kon]

แม้ mɛ́ɛ *conj.* though (although, even if)

แม่ไก่ mɛ̂ɛ-gài *n.* hen (animal) [ตัว dtuua]

แม่โขง mɛ̂ɛ-kǒong *n.* kind of Thai whiskey, Mekhong River [สาย sǎai]

แม่ครัว mɛ̂ɛ-kruua *n.* female cook [คน kon]

แม่ค้า mɛ̂ɛ-káa *n.* market woman, merchant (female) [คน kon]

แมง mɛɛng *n.* insect ✦ [ตัว dtuua]

แมง mɛɛng- *pref.* for the names of certain animals

แมงกะพรุน mɛɛng-gà~ prun *n.* jellyfish [ตัว dtuua]

แมงดา mɛɛng-daa *n.* pimp [คน kon]

แมงดานา mɛɛng-daa-naa *n.* water strider [ตัว dtuua]

แมงป่อง mɛɛng-bpɔ̀ng *n.* scorpion [ตัว dtuua]

แมงมุม mɛɛng-mum *n.* spider [ตัว dtuua]

แมงลัก mɛɛng-lák *n.* hairy basil [ต้น dtôn]

แม่งาน mɛ̂ɛ-ngaan *n.* party organizer [คน kon]

แม่ชี mɛ̂ɛ-chii *n.* nun [คน kon]

แม้แต่ mɛ́ɛ-dtɛ̀ɛ *adv.* even

แม่ทัพ mɛ̂ɛ-táp *n.* warlord [คน kon]

แมน mɛɛn *adj.* being masculine ✦

แม่นยำ mɛ̂n-yam *adj.* accurate, exact, precise

แม่น้ำ mɛ̂ɛ-náam *n.* river [สาย sǎai]

แม่บ้าน mɛ̂ɛ-bâan *n.* housewife, maid (housekeeper) [คน kon]

ก ข ข ค ฅ ฆ ง จ ฉ ช ซ ฌ ญ ฎ ฏ ฐ ฑ ฒ ณ ด ต ถ ท ธ น บ ป ผ ฝ พ ฟ ภ ม ย ร ฤ ล ว ศ ษ ส ห อ

ก
ข
ค
ฅ
ฆ
ง
จ
ฉ
ช
ซ
ฌ
ญ
ฎ
ฏ
ฐ
ฑ
ฒ
ณ
ด
ต
ถ
ท
ธ
น
บ
ป
ผ
ฝ
พ
ฟ
ภ
ม
ย
ร
ฤ
ล
ว
ศ
ษ
ส
ห
อ
ฮ

แม่แบบ mɛ̂ɛ-bɛ̀ɛp *n.* model (pattern, prototype) [แบบ bɛ̀ɛp]

แม่มด mɛ̂ɛ-mót *n.* witch [ตน dton]

แม่ม่าย mɛ̂ɛ-mâai *n.* widow [คน kon]

แม่ย่า mɛ̂ɛ-yâa *n.* mother-in-law (husband's mother) [คน kon]

แม่ยาย mɛ̂ɛ-yaai *n.* mother-in-law (wife's mother) [คน kon]

แม่แรง mɛ̂ɛ-rɛɛng *n.* jack (for lifting) [ตัว dtuua]

แมลง má~lɛɛng *n.* bug, insect [ตัว dtuua]

แมลงปอ má~lɛɛng-bpɔɔ *n.* dragonfly [ตัว dtuua]

แมลงปีกแข็ง má~lɛɛng-bpìik-kɛ̌ng *n.* beetle [ตัว dtuua]

แมลงวัน má~lɛɛng-wan *n.* fly (insect) [ตัว dtuua]

แมลงสาบ má~lɛɛng-sàap *n.* cockroach [ตัว dtuua]

แมลงหวี่ má~lɛɛng-wìi *n.* fruit fly [ตัว dtuua]

แม่เล้า mɛ̂ɛ-láo *n.* madam (mamasan) [คน kon]

แม่เลี้ยง mɛ̂ɛ-líiang *n.* stepmother [คน kon]

แมว mɛɛo *n.* cat [ตัว dtuua]

แม้ว mɛ́ɛo *n.* Hmong (hill tribe) [เผ่า pào]

แมวน้ำ mɛɛo-náam *n.* seal (animal) [ตัว dtuua]

แมวมอง mɛɛo-mɔɔng *n.* scout (seeker, e.g. talent scout) [คน kon]

แม้ว่า mɛ́ɛ-wâa *conj.* even if

แม่สื่อ mɛ̂ɛ-sùu *n.* matchmaker (female) [คน kon]

แม่เหล็ก mɛ̂ɛ-lèk *n.* magnet [แท่ง tɛ̂ng, อัน an]

แม่ฮ่องสอน mɛ̂ɛ-hɔ̂ng-sɔ̌ɔn *n.* Mae Hong Son province [จังหวัด jang-wàt]

โม่ môo *n.* grindstone [โม่ môo]

โม่ môo *vt.* mill (granulate)

โม้ móo *vi.* brag ✦

โม้ móo *vt.* flaunt ✦

โมฆะ moo-ká *adj.* invalid ✦, void (having no legal force)

โมง moong *clf.* o'clock

โมทนา moo-tá~naa *adj.* pleased

โมโห moo-hǒo *adj.* angry, mad

โมะ mó *n.* small vagina ✿

ไม่ mâi *adv.* no, not

ไม่ mâi *aux.* doesn't, do not/don't (negation)

ไม้ máai *n.* wood (timber or lumber) [อัน an, ท่อน tôn (piece), แผ่น pèn (sheet), ต้น dtôn (log)]

ไม่_ก็_ mâi-_-gɔ̂ɔ-_ *conj.* either...or

ไม้กระดาน mái-grà~daan *n.* board (plank of wood) [แผ่น pèn]

ไม้กวาด mái-gwàat *n.* broom [อัน an]

ไม้กากบาท mái-gaa-gà~bàat *n.* cross, X mark [ตัว dtuua]

ไม้กางเขน mái-gaang-kěen *n.* cross (in Christianity) [อัน an]

ไม้กายสิทธิ์ mái-gaa-yá~sìt *n.* wand (e.g. for witches) [อัน an]

ไม้ขีดไฟ mái-kìit-fai *n.* match (for lighting fire) [กล่อง glòng (box), ห่อ hɔ̀ɔ (pack)]

ไม้แขวนเสื้อ mái-kwɛ̌ɛn-sûua *n.* hanger (clothes) [อัน an]

ไม่ค่อย mâi-kôi *adv.* not quite, not very

ไม่เคย mâi-kəəi *adv.* never

ไม้จัตวา mái-jàt-dtà~waa *n.* fourth tone mark ๋ [ตัว dtuua]

ไม้จิ้มฟัน mái-jîm-fan *n.* toothpick [อัน an]

ไม้ใจ mâi-jai *adj.* coward ✿

ไม่ใช่ mâi-châi *adv.* no, not

ไม้ดัด mái-dàt *n.* dwarfed tree [ต้น dtôn]

ไม่ได้ mâi-dâai *adv.* no (cannot, did not)

ไม่ได้ mâi-dâai *aux.* didn't

ไม่ได้ mâi-dâai *interj.* no! (cannot, did not)

ไม้ตรี mái-dtrii *n.* third tone mark ๊ [ตัว dtuua]

ไม่ต้อง mâi-dtɔ̂ng *v.* not to have to

ไม้ตีกลอง mái-dtii-glɔɔng *n.* drumstick (musical)

ก ข ฃ ค ฅ ฆ ง จ ฉ ช ซ ฌ ญ ฎ ฏ ฐ ฑ ฒ ณ ด ต ถ ท ธ น บ ป ผ ฝ พ ฟ ภ ม ย ร ฤ ล ฦ ว ศ ษ ส ห ฬ อ ฮ

[อัน an]

ไม้ไต่คู้ mái-dtài-kúu *n.* vowel-shortening mark ˉ [ตัว dtuua]

ไม้ถูพื้น mái-tǔu-púɯn *n.* mop [อัน an]

ไม้เถา mái-tǎo *n.* vine (creeping plant) [เถา tǎo]

ไม้เท้า mái-táao *n.* cane (for walking) [อัน an]

ไม้โท mái-too *n.* second tone mark ˊ [ตัว dtuua]

ไม่น่าเชื่อ mâi-nâa-chûɯa *adj.* unbelievable

ไม้บรรทัด máai-ban-tát *n.* ruler (measuring) [อัน an, เล่ม lêm]

ไม่เป็นไร mâi-bpen-rai *idm.* not at all (it doesn't matter.), that's all right, you're welcome

ไม้ไผ่ mái-pài *n.* bamboo (tree) [ลำ lam (piece), ต้น dtôn (tree), กอ gɔɔ (group)]

ไม้พาย mái-paai *n.* oar [เล่ม lêm]

ไม้หันลาย mái-má~laai *n.* vowel mark (ั) [ตัว dtuua]

ไม้ม้วน mái-múuan *n.* vowel mark (ใ) [ตัว dtuua]

ไม่มี mâi-mii *pron.* none

ไม่มีที่ไหน mâi-mii-tîi-nǎi *adv.* nowhere

ไม่มีอะไร mâi-mii-à~rai *adv.* nothing

ไม้ยมก mái-yá~mók *n.* symbol indicating repetition of words or phrases (ๆ) [ตัว dtuua]

ไม้ยาว mái-yaao *n.* pole (long stick) [อัน an]

ไม้เรียว mái-riiao *n.* cane (flogging rod) [อัน an]

ไมล์ maai *n.* mile

ไม่เลย mâi-ləəi *adv.* none

ไม่ว่า mâi-wâa *adv.* regardless of

ไม่สบาย mâi-sà~baai *adj.* sick

ไม่สามารถ mâi-sǎa-mâat *adj.* unable

ไม้หันอากาศ mái-hǎn-aa-gàat *n.* short ""a"" vowel mark ˆ [ตัว dtuua]

ไม่ไหว mâi-wǎi *aux.* cannot/can't ●

ไม่อยู่ mâi-yùu *adj.* absent

ไม้อัด mái-àt *n.* plywood
[แผ่น pèn]

ไม้เอก mái-èek *n.* first
tone mark ◌่ [ตัว dtuua]

ย

ย yɔɔ *let.* ย. ยักษ์ yɔɔ-yák,
a consonant of the Thai
alphabet (low
consonant) [ตัว dtuua]

ยก yók *n.* round (boxing)
[ยก yók]

ยก yók *v.* lift (raise)

ยก_ขึ้น yók-_-kûn *vt.*
boost (raise), pick up (lift)

ยกทรง yók-song *n.* bra/
brassiere ❖ [ตัว dtuua]

ยกโทษ yók-tôot *v.*
forgive, pardon

ยกฟ้อง yók-fɔ́ɔng *vt.*
dismiss (legal case)

ยกระดับ yók-rá~dàp *vt.*
upgrade

ยกเลิก yók-lə̂ək *v.* cancel
(call off)

ยกเลิก yók-lə̂ək *vt.* lift
(end, ban)

ยกเว้น yók-wén *prep.*
except, outside of

ย่น yôn *adj.* wrinkled

ยนต์ yon *n.* engine

ยนต์ yon *n.* machine
[เครื่อง krûuang]

ยมฑูต yom-má~tûut *n.*
messenger of death [ตน
dton]

ยศ yót *n.* rank (position,
degree)

ยโส yá-sŏo *adj.* arrogant

ยโสธร yá-sŏo-tɔɔn *n.*
Yasothon province
[จังหวัด jang-wàt]

ยอ yɔɔ *v.* praise (admire)

ย่อ yɔ̂ɔ *vt.* abbreviate

ยอก yɔ̂ɔk *vt.* prick (stab)

ย่อง yɔ̂ng *vi.* creep up,
walk on tiptoes

ยอด yɔ̂ɔt *n.* sum (total) ❖

ยอด yɔ̂ɔt *n.* peak, tip, top
[ยอด yɔ̂ɔt]

ยอดเขา yɔ̂ɔt-kǎo *n.*
mountain top [ยอด yɔ̂ɔt]

ยอดเยี่ยม yɔ̂ɔt-yîiam *adj.*
excellent, terrific
(wonderful)

ย้อน yɔ́ɔn *v.* retort (reply
sharply)

ย้อนกลับ yɔ́ɔn-glàp *vi.* go
backward

ยอม yɔɔm *vi.* yield
(surrender)

ย่อม yɔ̂m *adj.* tiny, quite

ก ข ข ค ค ฆ ง จ ฉ ช ซ ฌ ญ ฎ ฏ ฐ ฑ ฒ ณ ด ต ถ ท ธ น บ ป ผ ฝ พ ฟ ภ ม ย ร ฤ ล ฦ ว ศ ษ ส ห ฬ อ ฮ

small, little

ย้อม yɔ́ɔm *v.* dye

ยอมความ yɔɔm-kwaam *vi.* compromise (settle legal case)

ยอมตายเพื่อ yɔɔm-dtaai-pʉ̂ʉa *v.* die for

ยอมแพ้ yɔɔm-pɛ́ɛ *vi.* give in, give up (admit defeat), surrender (give in)

ยอมรับ yɔɔm-ráp *v.* accept

ยอมให้ yɔɔm-hâi *vt.* let (allow, give)

ย่อมาจาก yɔ̂ɔ-maa-jàak *vt.* stand for (e.g. abbreviation)

ย่อย yɔ̂i *adj.* insignificant (unimportant), minor

ย่อยยับ yɔ̂i-yáp *vi.* perish (to be destroyed totally)

ย่อยสลาย yɔ̂i-sà~lǎai *vi.* decompose (disintegrate)

ย่อยอาหาร yɔ̂i-aa-hǎan *vi.* digest (food)

ย่อหน้า yɔ̂ɔ-nâa *vt.* indent (paragraph)

ยะลา yá-laa *n.* Yala province [จังหวัด jang-wàt]

ยะโฮวา yá~hoo-waa *n.* Jehovah [องค์ ong]

ยักยอก yák-yɔ̂ɔk *vt.* embezzle

ยักษ์ yák *n.* giant [ตน dton]

ยักไหล่ yák-lài *vi.* shrug

ยัง yang *adv.* yet (still, thus far)

ยังคง yang-kong *adv.* yet (moreover)

ยังไง yang-ngai *adv.* how ❀

ยังไงก็ตาม yang-ngai-gɔ̂ɔ-dtaam *adv.* anyhow ❀, anyway ❀

ยัง_อยู่ yang-_-yùu *vi.* remain (continue to be _)

ยังอยู่ yang-yùu *vi.* remain (not leave)

ยัดไส้_ใส่_ yát-sâi-_-sài-_ *vt.* stuff (_ into _)

ยับยั้ง yáp-yáng *vt.* inhibit, restrain (hold back from action)

ยั่ว yûua *v.* provoke (incite to anger)

ยั่วยวน yûua-yuuan *vt.* seduce, tempt (appeal strongly to)

ยา yaa *n.* drug (medicine) [ชนิด chá~nít (kind), เม็ด mét (pill), ขวด kùuat (bottle), ซอง sɔɔng (pack), แผง pɛ̌ɛng (set), หลอด lɔ̀ɔt (tube)]

ย่า yâa *n.* paternal grandmother [คน kon]

ยาก yâak *adj.* difficult (not easy)

ยากจน yâak-jon *adj.* poor (indigent) !

ยากันยุง yaa-gan-yung *n.* mosquito repellent [กล่อง glòng (box)]

ยาแก้ปวด yaa-gɛ̂ɛ-bpùuat *n.* painkiller [เม็ด mét]

ยาแก้แพ้ yaa-gɛ̂ɛ-pɛ́ɛ *n.* antihistamine

ยาแก้อักเสบ yaa-gɛ̂ɛ-àk-sèep *n.* anti-inflammatory

ยาแก้ไอ yaa-gɛ̂ɛ-ai *n.* cough medicine [ขวด kùuat (bottle)]

ยาคุมกำเนิด yaa-kum-gam-nə̀ət *n.* contraceptive [เม็ด mét (pill), แผง pɛ̌ɛng (mat)]

ยาฆ่าแมลง yaa-kâa-má~lɛɛng *n.* insecticide [ชนิด chá~nít (type), ขวด kùuat (bottle)]

ยาง yaang *adj.* rubber

ย่าง yâang *vt.* broil, grill, roast

ย่างก้าว yâang-gâao *v.* take a slow step

ยางยืด yaang-yʉ̂ʉt *n.* elastic band [เส้น sên]

ยางรถ yaang-rót *n.* tire/tyre (for cars) [เส้น sên]

ยางรัด yaang-rát *n.* rubber band [เส้น sên]

ยางลบ yaang-lóp *n.* rubber (eraser) [อัน an]

ยางสน yaang-sǒn *n.* resin

ยางอะหลั่ย yaang-à~lài *n.* spare tire (e.g. for cars) [ล้อ lɔ́ɔ]

ยาจก yaa-jòk *n.* poor person [คน kon]

ยาชา yaa-chaa *n.* anesthetic

ยาดม yaa-dom *n.* inhalant [ชนิด chá~nít]

ยาดับกลิ่น yaa-dàp-glìn *n.* deodorant (room) [ขวด kùuat]

ย่าทวด yâa-tûuat *n.* great grandmother (paternal) [คน kon]

ยาทาเล็บ yaa-taa-lép *n.* nail polish [ขวด kùuat]

ยาน yaan *adj.* flabby

ยานพาหนะ yaan-paa-hà~ná *n.* carrier (vehicle) ❗ [คัน kan]

ยานอนหลับ yaa-nɔɔn-làp *n.* sleeping pill [เม็ด mét (tablet)]

ยานอวกาศ yaan-à~wá~gàat *n.* spaceship

ยาบ้า yaa-bâa *n.* methamphetamine ● [เม็ด mét]

ยาพิษ yaa-pít *n.* poison (toxic substance) [ชนิด chá~nít (kind), ขวด kùuat (bottle)]

ยาม yaam *n.* period (time)

ยาม yaam *n.* security guard [คน kon]

ย่าม yâam *n.* bag (cloth), sack, satchel [ใบ bai]

ยาม้า yaa-máa *n.* speed (drug)

ยาเม็ด yaa-mét *n.* tablet (pill) [เม็ด mét]

ยาย yaai *n.* form of addressing an old woman, maternal grandmother [คน kon]

ย้าย yáai *v.* move

ยายทวด yaai-tûuat *n.* great grandmother

(maternal) [คน kon]

ย้ายบ้าน yáai-bâan *vi.* move (house)

ย้าย_ไป_ yáai-_-bpai-_ *vt.* transfer (move _ to _)

ย้าย_ออก yáai-_-ɔ̀ɔk *vt.* clear (remove)

ยาระบาย yaa-rá~baai *n.* laxative

ยาลดกรด yaa-lót-gròt *n.* antacid [ขวด kùuat (bottle)]

ยาลดไข้ yaa-lót-kâi *n.* medicine for fever

ยาว yaao *adj.* long (lengthy)

ยาสระผม yaa-sà~pǒm *n.* shampoo [ขวด kùuat (bottle)]

ยาสีฟัน yaa-sǐi-fan *n.* toothpaste [หลอด lɔ̀ɔt]

ยาสูบ yaa-sùup *n.* tobacco [มวน muuan (roll), ใบ bai (leaf)]

ยาเสน่ห์ yaa-sà~nèe *n.* love potion [ขวด kùuat]

ยาเสพติด yaa-sèep-dtìt *n.* drug (narcotic) [ชนิด chá~nít]

ยาหม่อง yaa-mɔ̀ng *n.* balm [ตลับ dtà~làp (tin)]

ยาหยอดตา yaa-yɔ̀ɔt-dtaa *n.* eye drop

ยาหยอดหู yaa-yɔ̀ɔt-hǔu *n.* ear drop

ยาเหน็บ yaa-nèp *n.* suppository [เม็ด mét]

ยาอม yaa-om *n.* lozenge [เม็ด mét]

ยาอี yaa-ii *n.* ecstasy/ M.D.M.A. (drug), ephedrine

ยำ yam *n.* Thai salad [จาน jaan]

ย่ำ yâm *vt.* trample

ย้ำ yám *vt.* insist (reiterate)

ยิง ying *vt.* blast, shoot (e.g. gun)

ยิ่ง yîng *adj.* excessive, many, much

ยิ่งกว่านั้น yîng-gwàa-nán *adv.* moreover

ยิ่งขึ้น yîng-kʉ̂n *adv.* even more, further

ยิ่งใหญ่ yîng-yài *adj.* great (big, notable)

ยิน yin *v.* hear

ยินดี yin-dii *adj.* delighted

ยินดี yin-dii *vi.* rejoice

ยินดีด้วย yin-dii-dûuai *interj.* congratulations!

ยินดีต้อนรับ yin-dii-dtɔ̂ɔn-ráp *interj.* welcome!

ยินยอม yin-yɔɔm *vi.* approve (agree), consent, permit (allow)

ยิม yim *n.* gym [ห้อง hɔ̂ng (room)]

ยิ้ม yím *n.* smile

ยิ้ม yím *vi.* smile

ยิ้มเยาะ yím-yɔ́ *vi.* sneer

ยิว yiu *adj.* Jewish

ยี่ yîi *adj.* two (twice)

ยีน yiin *n.* gene [ตัว dtuua]

ยีราฟ yii-ráap *n.* giraffe [ตัว dtuua]

ยีสต์ yíit *n.* yeast (e.g. baking, brewing) [เชื้อ chʉ́ua]

ยี่สิบ yîi-sìp *numb.* twenty

ยี่หร่า yîi-ràa *n.* fennel [ต้น dtôn (plant), ใบ bai (leave)]

ยี่ห้อ yîi-hɔ̂ɔ *n.* brand (trademark) [ยี่ห้อ yîi-hɔ̂ɔ]

ยืด yʉ́t *vt.* cling to (grab, hold), confiscate, seize

ยืด yʉ̂ut *v.* protract (prolong)

ก
ข
ฃ
ค
ฅ
ฆ
ง
จ
ฉ
ช
ซ
ฌ
ญ
ฎ
ฏ
ฐ
ฑ
ฒ
ณ
ด
ต
ถ
ท
ธ
น
บ
ป
ผ
ฝ
พ
ฟ
ภ
ม
ย
ร
ฤ
ล
ฦ
ว
ศ
ษ
ส
ห
อ
ฮ

ยืด yûut *vt.* extend (stretch out)

ยืดยาด yûut-yâat *adj.* slow-moving

ยืดเยื้อ yûut-yúua *adj.* lengthy

ยืดเวลา yûut-wee-laa *v.* defer (postpone)

ยืดเส้นยืดสาย yûut-sên-yûut-sǎai *vi.* stretch (body)

ยืดหยุ่น yûut-yùn *adj.* flexible, pliable

ยืน yuun *vi.* stand (be standing: people)

ยื่น yûun *v.* protrude (stick out)

ยื่น yûun *vt.* extend (e.g. arm), submit (hand in)

ยืนกราน yuun-graan *vi.* persist (insist)

ยืนขึ้น yuun-kûn *vi.* stand up (get up)

ยื่นคำร้อง yûun-kam-rɔ́ɔng *v.* petition (make a petition)

ยืนยัน yuun-yan *vt.* confirm (affirm)

ยืม yuum *vt.* borrow (item)

ยุ yú *vt.* stimulate

ยุค yúk *n.* age, era, period

[ยุค yúk]

ยุง yung *n.* mosquito [ตัว dtuua]

ยุ่ง yûng *adj.* busy, confusing, occupied

ยุ่ง yûng *vi.* interfere (meddle)

ยุ้ง yúng *n.* granary, barn, silo [หลัง lǎng]

ยุ่งเหยิง yûng-yěong *adj.* chaotic, entangled

ยุติ yút-dtì *vi.* end ⚬

ยุติธรรม yút-dtì-tam *adj.* fair, impartial, just

ยุทธศาสตร์ yút-tá~sàat *n.* strategy (tactics) [อัน an]

ยุบ yúp *v.* diminish in size

ยุบสภา yúp-sà~paa *vi.* dissolve parliament

ยุ่ย yûi *adj.* tender (soft) ✊

ยุโรป yú-ròop *n.* Europe [ทวีป tá~wîip]

ยุแหย่ yú-yɛ̀ɛ *v.* provoke (stir up)

ยูโด yuu-doo *n.* judo [ชนิด chá~nít]

ยู่ยี่ yûu-yîi *adj.* crumpled ✊, wrinkled ✊

ยูโร yuu-roo *n.* Euro [จำนวน jam-nuuan]

เยซู yee-suu *n.* Jesus Christ [องค์ ong]

เย็ด yét *vt.* fuck ⚥

เยน yeen *n.* yen

เย็น yen *adj.* cold (cool, chilly)

เย็น yen *n.* evening

เย็นชา yen-chaa *adj.* cold (emotion)

เย็นชืด yen-chûut *adj.* cold ●

เย็บ yép *v.* sew, stitch

เย็บปักถักร้อย yép-bpàk-tàk-rɔ́ɔi *n.* embroidery

เย้ย yɔ́ɔi *vt.* spite

เยอรมัน yəə-rá~man *n.* Germany [ประเทศ bprà~têet]

เย่อหยิ่ง yə̂ə-yìng *adj.* proud (conceited, arrogant) ⚠

เยอะ yə́ *adj.* abundant ●, many ●, much ●

เยอะแยะ yə́-yɛ́ *adj.* plenty (numerous, abundant) ●

เย้า yáo *n.* Mien (hilltribe) [เผ่า pào]

เยาว์ yao *adj.* juvenile (youthful)

เยาวชน yao-wá~chon *n.* juvenile [รุ่น rûn]

เยาะเย้ย yɔ́-yə́əi *adj.* cynical

เยี่ยง yîiang *adj.* such, like

เยี่ยม yîiam *adj.* ideal (excellent)

เยี่ยม yîiam *v.* visit

เยี่ยมยอด yîiam-yɔ̂ɔt *adj.* fantastic

เยี่ยมเยือน yîiam-yɯɯan *v.* pay a visit

เยี่ยว yîiao *n.* pee ●, piss ●, urine ●

เยียวยา yiiao-yaa *v.* heal (cure)

เยื่อ yɯ̂ɯa *n.* tissue (fiber, film)

เยือน yɯɯan *v.* visit

แย่ yɛ̂ɛ *adv.* ill

แย้ yɛ́ɛ *n.* kind of ground lizard [ตัว dtuua]

แยก yɛ̂ɛk *v.* divide up, sort

แยก yɛ̂ɛk *vt.* separate

แยกกัน yɛ̂ɛk-gan *vi.* split up

แยกกันอยู่ yɛ̂ɛk-gan-yùu *adj.* separated (e.g. spouses)

แยกประเภท yɛ̂ɛk-bprà~pêet *vt.* categorize

ก
ข
ฃ
ค
ฅ
ฆ
ง
จ
ฉ
ช
ซ
ฌ
ญ
ฎ
ฏ
ฐ
ฑ
ฒ
ณ
ด
ต
ถ
ท
ธ
น
บ
ป
ผ
ฝ
พ
ฟ
ภ
ม
ย
ร
ฤ
ล
ฦ
ว
ศ
ษ
ส
ห
ฬ
อ
ฮ

แย่ง yêng *vt.* seize, snatch

แย้ง yέεng *v.* contradict, protest (demonstrate)

แย่งชิง yêng-ching *vt.* snatch

แย่มาก yέε-mâak *adj.* awful, terrible (very bad)

แย่มาก yέε-mâak *vi.* suck (be very bad) ☞

แย่ลง yέε-long *adj.* worse

โยก yôok *v.* shake from side to side, rock

โยกย้าย yôok-yáai *vi.* relocate

โยคะ yoo-ká *n.* yoga [ท่า tâa (pose)]

โยง yoong *v.* tie to a post

โยง yoong *vt.* sling (suspend)

โย่ง yôong *adj.* tall and thin

โยธา yoo-taa *n.* construction work

โยน yoon *vt.* flip (e.g. coin), throw (toss)

โยม yoom *n.* Buddhist monk's form of addressing laymen [คน kon]

ใย yai *n.* fiber

ใยแมงมุม yai-mεεng-mum *n.* web [ใย yai]

ร

ร rɔɔ *let.* ร. เรือ rɔɔ-rɯɯa, a consonant of the Thai alphabet (low consonant) [ตัว dtuua]

รก rók *n.* placenta

รกราก rók-râak *n.* homeland [แห่ง hὲng]

รด rót *vt.* water (e.g. plant)

รถ rót *n.* automobile, bus, car, vehicle [คัน kan]

รถเก๋ง rót-gěng *n.* car, sedan [คัน kan]

รถเข็น rót-kěn *n.* cart (e.g. shopping), dolly, wheelchair [คัน kan]

รถแข่ง rót-kὲng *n.* race car [คัน kan]

รถจี๊ป rót-jíip *n.* jeep [คัน kan]

รถเช่า rót-châo *n.* rental car [คัน kan]

รถด่วน rót-dùuan *n.* express (e.g. train, bus) [คัน kan (bus), ขบวน kà~buuan (train)]

รถดับเพลิง rót-dàp-pləəng *n.* fire truck [คัน kan]

รถติด rót-dtìt *n.* jam (traffic jam)

รถตู้ rót-dtûu *n.* van [คัน kan]

รถถัง rót-tǎng *n.* tank (combat vehicle) [คัน kan]

รถบรรทุก rót-ban-túk *n.* truck/lorry [คัน kan]

รถบัส rót-bás, rót-bát *n.* bus [คัน kan]

รถพยาบาล rót-pá~yaa-baan *n.* ambulance [คัน kan]

รถพ่วง rót-pûuang *n.* trailer (drawn by vehicle) [คัน kan]

รถไฟ rót-fai *n.* train (railroad) [ขบวน kà~buuan]

รถไฟด่วน rót-fai-dùuan *n.* express train [ขบวน kà~buuan]

รถไฟใต้ดิน rót-fai-dtâai-din *n.* metro, subway (train) [ขบวน kà~buuan, คัน kan]

รถไฟฟ้า rót-fai-fáa *n.* electric train [ขบวน kà~buuan, คัน kan]

รถม้า rót-máa *n.* carriage (horse-drawn vehicle)

[คัน kan]

รถยนต์ rót-yon *n.* automobile, car [คัน kan]

รถราง rót-raang *n.* tram (streetcar) [คัน kan]

รถสามล้อ rót-sǎam-lɔ́ɔ *n.* pedicab [คัน kan]

ร่น rôn *vi.* retreat

รบ róp *v.* make war

รบกวน róp-guuan *v.* interrupt (interfere, disturb)

รบเร้า róp-ráo *vi.* persist (insist) ⚠

ร่ม rôm *n.* shade (cover) [ที่ tîi]

ร่ม rôm *n.* umbrella [คัน kan]

รมควัน rom-kwan *vt.* smoke (e.g. salmon)

ร่มชูชีพ rôm-chuu-chîip *n.* parachute [ชุด chút]

รวง ruuang *n.* ear (e.g. rice, corn) [รวง ruuang]

ร่วง rûuang *vi.* fall (drop)

รวงผึ้ง ruuang-pɯ̂ng *n.* hive [รวง ruuang]

ร่วงโรย rûuang-rooi *vi.* wither ⟳

รวดเร็ว rûuat-reo *adj.*

fast, quick, speedy

ร่วน rûuan *adj.* brittle (loose)

รวบรวม rûuap-ruuam *vt.* compile (put together)

รวบรัด rûuap-rát *adj.* brief (succinct)

รวม ruuam *vt.* add (mix in)

รวมกัน ruuam-gan *vi.* mix (combine), unify, unite

ร่วมกัน rûuam-gan *adj.* joint (sharing)

ร่วมกัน rûuam-gan *vi.* coordinate (organize)

รวมถึง ruuam-tʉ̌ng *vt.* include (comprise)

รวมทั้งหมด ruuam-táng-mòt *adj.* altogether (total)

ร่วมเพศ rûuam-pêet *vi.* make out (have sexual intercourse)

ร่วมมือ rûuam-mʉʉ *vi.* cooperate

ร่วมลงนาม rûuam-long-naam *vi.* cosign ❗

ร่วมสมัย rûuam-sà~mǎi *adj.* contemporary (same age, time)

รวย ruuai *adj.* rich (wealthy)

รส rót *n.* flavor, taste [รส rót]

รสจัด rót-jàt *adj.* spicy

รสชาติ rót-châat *n.* flavor, taste [รส rót]

รสนิยม rót-ní-yom, rót-sà~ní-yom *n.* liking, taste (aesthetics)

รหัส rá~hàt *n.* code [ตัว dtuua]

รหัสไปรษณีย์ rá~hàt-bprai-sà~nii *n.* zip code [รหัส rá~hàt]

รหัสผ่าน rá~hàt-pàan *n.* password [ตัว dtuua]

รอ rɔɔ *vi.* wait

รอก rɔ̂ɔk *n.* pulley [อัน an]

รอง rɔɔng *adj.* secondary (minor), side, subordinate

รอง rɔɔng *prep.* vice (in place of)

รอง rɔɔng *vt.* support (place under)

ร่อง rɔ̂ng *n.* groove, path (ditch) [ร่อง rɔ̂ng]

ร้อง rɔ́ɔng *v.* sing (e.g. birds)

ร้อง rɔ́ɔng *vi.* cry

ร้องขอ rɔ́ɔng-kɔ̌ɔ *vt.* beg for

รองชนะเลิศ rɔɔng-chá~ná~lə̂ət *n.* runner-up [คน kon]

ร้องทุกข์ rɔ́ɔng-túk *vi.* complain (make a complaint)

รองเท้า rɔɔng-táao *n.* shoe [ข้าง kâang (one), คู่ kûu (pair)]

รองเท้าแตะ rɔɔng-táao-dtɛ̀ *n.* flip-flop (shoes), sandal [ข้าง kâang (one), คู่ kûu (pair)]

รองเท้าผ้าใบ rɔɔng-táao-pâa-bai *n.* sneaker (shoe) [ข้าง kâang (one), คู่ kûu (pair)]

รองเท้าสเก็ต rɔɔng-táao-sà~gét *n.* skate (shoes) [ข้าง kâang (one), คู่ kûu (pair)]

รองประธานาธิบดี rɔɔng-bprà~taa-naa-típ-bɔɔ-dii *n.* vice president (of a country) [คน kon]

ร้องเพลง rɔ́ɔng-pleeng *v.* chant, sing (song)

ร่องรอย rɔ̂ng-rɔɔi *n.* clue [อัน an]

รองรับ rɔɔng-ráp *v.* stand by, support

ร้องเรียน rɔ́ɔng-riian *v.* petition (make a complaint)

ร้องไห้ rɔ́ɔng-hâi *vi.* cry

ร้องอุทาน rɔ́ɔng-ù-taan *v.* exclaim

รอด rɔ̂ɔt *adj.* saved

รอด rɔ̂ɔt *vi.* survive (remain alive)

รอดตาย rɔ̂ɔt-dtaai *vi.* survive (remain alive)

ร่อน rôn *v.* pan (e.g. for gold), sift (sort with sieve)

ร้อน rɔ́ɔn *adj.* hot (temperature)

ร้อนใจ rɔ́ɔn-jai *adj.* anxious (eager)

ร้อนชื้น rɔ́ɔn-chúun *adj.* muggy

ร้อนรน rɔ́ɔn-ron *adj.* anxious ☛

ร่อนเร่ rôn-rêe *vi.* wander (go aimlessly)

ร้อนอบอ้าว rɔ́ɔn-òp-âao *adj.* steamy (hot and humid)

รอบ rɔ̂ɔp *n.* cycle (rotation, anniversary), lap, round (sports) [รอบ rɔ̂ɔp]

รอบ rɔ̂ɔp *prep.* around (in circle, around edge)

รอบๆ rɔ̂ɔp-rɔ̂ɔp *prep.* round (around)

รอบคอบ rɔ̂ɔp-kɔ̂ɔp *adj.*

ก
ข
ฃ
ค
ฅ
ฆ
ง
จ
ฉ
ช
ซ
ฌ
ญ
ฎ
ฏ
ฐ
ฑ
ฒ
ณ
ด
ต
ถ
ท
ธ
น
บ
ป
ผ
ฝ
พ
ฟ
ภ
ม
ย
ร
ฤ
ล
ฦ
ว
ศ
ษ
ส
ห
ฬ
อ
ฮ

careful, prudent

รอบด้าน rɔ̂ɔp-dâan *adj.* all-around/all-round (broadly)

รอบนอก rɔ̂ɔp-nɔ̂ɔk *adj.* outer (periphery, area outside)

รอบรู้ rɔ̂ɔp-rúu *adj.* knowledgeable

รอย rɔɔi *n.* dent (on a surface), mark, trace (e.g. footprint) [รอย rɔɔi]

ร้อย rɔ́ɔi *numb.* hundred

ร้อยกรอง rɔ́ɔi-grɔɔng *n.* poem [บท bòt (verse)]

ร้อยแก้ว rɔ́ɔi-gɛ̂ɛɔ *n.* prose

รอยขว่น rɔɔi-kùuan *n.* scratch (mark) [รอย rɔɔi]

รอยจีบ rɔɔi-jìip *n.* pleat (plait) [รอย rɔɔi]

รอยฉีก rɔɔi-chìik *n.* tear (rip) [รอย rɔɔi]

รอยช้ำ rɔɔi-chám *n.* bruise (contusion) [รอย rɔɔi]

รอยต่อ rɔɔi-dtɔ̀ɔ *n.* joint (place at which things are joined) [รอย rɔɔi]

รอยตีน rɔɔi-dtiin *n.* footprint ● [รอย rɔɔi]

รอยเท้า rɔɔi-táao *n.* footprint [รอย rɔɔi]

รอยประทับ rɔɔi-bprà~táp *n.* imprint (mark) [ที่ tîi]

รอยเปื้อน rɔɔi-bpûuan *n.* stain (blot, speck) [จุด jùt]

รอยพับ rɔɔi-páp *n.* crease (e.g. paper, clothes) [รอย rɔɔi]

รอยฟัน rɔɔi-fan *n.* slash (cut mark) [รอย rɔɔi]

รอยย่น rɔɔi-yôn *n.* wrinkle (on face or skin) [รอย rɔɔi, ที่ tîi]

รอยยิ้ม rɔɔi-yím *n.* smile

รอยแยก rɔɔi-yɛ̂ɛk *n.* split (crack) [รอย rɔɔi]

รอยรั่ว rɔɔi-rûua *n.* leak (crack) [รอย rɔɔi]

รอยร้าว rɔɔi-ráao *n.* crack (split line) [รอย rɔɔi]

ร้อยละ rɔ́ɔi-lá *n.* percent ❗

รอยแหว่ง rɔɔi-wɛ̀ng *n.* indent (notch)

ร้อยเอก rɔ́ɔi-èek *n.* army captain [นาย naai ❗, คน kon]

ร้อยเอ็ด rɔ́ɔi-èt *n.* Roi Et province [จังหวัด jang-wàt]

ระกา rá~gaa *n.* Year of

the Cock [ปี bpii]

ระคาย rá~kaai *v.* cause itching

ระฆัง rá~kang *n.* bell (cast metal) [ใบ bai, ลูก lûuk]

ระงับ rá~ngáp *vt.* suppress (e.g. press, symptoms), withhold (hold back restrain)

ระดับ rá~dàp *n.* level (class, rank) [ระดับ rá~dàp]

ระดับโลก rá~dàp-lôok *adj.* world-class

ระดู rá~duu *n.* menses ✕

ระทึก rá~túk *adj.* (of the heart) beating fast from fear

ระนอง rá~nɔɔng *n.* Ranong province [จังหวัด jang-wàt]

ระนาด rá~nâat *n.* xylophone [ชุด chút (instrument)]

ระบบ rá~bòp *n.* organization, system [ระบบ rá~bòp]

ระบาด rá~bàat *vi.* be dispersed, be scattered

ระบาย rá~baai *v.* color (paint)

ระบาย rá~baai *vi.* drain (liquid)

ระบายอากาศใน rá~baai-aa-gàat-nai *vt.* ventilate (provide _ with fresh air)

ระบำ rá~bam *n.* stage dance [ชุด chút (show), วง wong (band)]

ระเบิด rá~bə̀ət *n.* bomb [ลูก lûuk]

ระเบิด rá~bə̀ət *vi.* burst, explode

ระเบิดปรมาณู rá~bə̀ət-bpà~rá~maa-nuu *n.* atomic bomb [ลูก lûuk]

ระเบิดมือ rá~bə̀ət-muu *n.* grenade [ลูก lûuk]

ระเบียง rá~biiang *n.* corridor, porch (balcony) [แห่ง hɛ̀ng]

ระเบียน rá~biian *n.* registration

ระเบียบ rá~bìiap *n.* regulation [ข้อ kɔ̂ɔ]

ระมัดระวัง rá~mát-rá~wang *adj.* careful, cautious

ระยอง rá~yɔɔng *n.* Rayong province [จังหวัด jang-wàt]

ระยะ rá~yá *n.* period (length, session), phase

ระยะทาง rá~yá-taang *n.*

distance [กิโลเมตร gì~loo-méet (kilo), เมตร méet (meter), ไมล์ maai (mile)]

ระยะเวลา rá~yá-wee-laa *n.* interval (amount of time) [ระยะ rá~yá]

ระลอกคลื่น rá~lɔ̂ɔk-klʉ̂ʉn *n.* ripple [ลูก lûuk]

ระลึก rá~lʉ́k *vt.* recall (remember) ⁉

ระวัง rá~wang *vi.* look out (be careful)

ระวัง rá~wang *vt.* watch out for (be careful of)

ระแวง rá~wɛɛŋ *adj.* suspicious

ระหว่าง rá~wàaŋ *prep.* among/amongst (in the midst of), between, during (at one moment in a period)

ระเหย rá~hə̌əi *vi.* evaporate (vaporize)

รัก rák *v.* love

รักใคร่ rák-krâi *vt.* care for (be fond of)

รักชาติ rák-châat *adj.* patriotic

รักร่วมเพศ rák-rûuam-pêet *adj.* homosexual

รักแร้ rák-rɛ́ɛ *n.* armpit

[ข้าง kâaŋ]

รักษา rák-sǎa *vt.* cure (treat), heal, protect (preserve), take care of (look after, treat)

รักษาการ rák-sǎa-gaan *adj.* deputy (substitute, stand-in)

รัง rang *n.* nest [รัง rang]

รั้ง ráng *v.* pull (haul, tug)

รังแก rang-gɛɛ *vt.* bully (molest)

รังไข่ rang-kài *n.* ovary [รัง rang]

รังควาญ rang-kwaan *vt.* harass (disturb, vex)

รังแค rang-kɛɛ *n.* dandruff

รังนก rang-nók *n.* nest (bird) [รัง rang]

รังผึ้ง rang-pʉ̂ŋ *n.* beehive, hive [รัง rang]

รังสี rang-sǐi *n.* ray (light beam) [รังสี rang-sǐi]

รัชกาล rát-chá~gaan *n.* reign [สมัย sà~mǎi]

รัฐ rát *n.* state (e.g. California) [รัฐ rát, แห่ง hèŋ]

รัฐธรรมนูญ rát-tà~tam-má~nuun *n.* constitution

[ฉบับ chà~bàp]

รัฐบาล rát-tà~baan *n.* government [ชุด chút]

รัฐประหาร rát-tà~bprà~hǎan *n.* coup/coup d'état

รัฐมนตรี rát-tà~mon-dtrii *n.* minister (cabinet member) [ท่าน tân ǐ, คน kon]

รัฐวิสาหกิจ rát-wí-sǎa-hà~gìt *n.* state enterprise

รัฐสภา rát-tà~sà~paa *n.* parliament [สภา sà~paa]

รัด rát *vt.* fasten (e.g. belt), tie (fix with fastener, e.g. zip tie)

รัดคอ rát-kɔɔ *vt.* suffocate (strangle)

รัตนะ rát-dtà~ná *n.* gem ✎ [ชิ้น chín]

รับ ráp *v.* answer (phone)

รับ ráp *vt.* get, receive

รับจ้าง ráp-jâang *v.* take employment

รับประกัน ráp-bprà~gan *vt.* insure (ensure, guarantee), underwrite

รับประทาน ráp-bprà~taan *v.* eat ǐ

รับผิดชอบ ráp-pìt-chɔ̂ɔp *vt.* take charge of (be responsible), undertake (take charge)

รับรอง ráp-rɔɔng *vt.* confirm, guarantee (certify, assure)

รับรองแขก ráp-rɔɔng-kɛ̀ɛk *vi.* entertain (host guests)

รับรู้ ráp-rúu *vt.* sense (realize)

รับสารภาพ ráp-sǎa-rá~pâap *vt.* admit (confess)

รั่ว rûua *v.* leak

รั้ว rúua *n.* fence [รั้ว rúua, อัน an ✎]

รัศมี rát-sà~mǐi *n.* halo, radius

รา raa *n.* fungus (mildew)

ราก râak *n.* root (e.g. of plant) [ราก râak]

รากที่สอง râak-tîi-sɔ̌ɔng *n.* square root

รากเหง้า râak-ngâo *n.* root (ancestor)

ราคะ raa-ká *n.* lust ✎, passion (desire) ✎

ราคา raa-kaa *n.* cost, price, rate

ราง raang *n.* rail (track) [ท่อน tɔ̂n, ราง raang]

ร่าง râang *n.* shape (figure, form)

ร่าง râang *vt.* draft (e.g. letter), outline (draw a line)

ร้าง ráang *adj.* deserted (abandoned)

ร่างกาย râang-gaai *n.* body ! [ตัว dtuua]

รางน้ำ raang-náam *n.* gutter [ราง raang]

รางรถไฟ raang-rót-fai *n.* railway track [ราง raang]

รางวัล raang-wan *n.* award, prize [รางวัล raang-wan]

ราชทูต râat-chá~tûut *n.* ambassador [ท่าน tân !, คน kon]

ราชบุรี râat-chá~bù-rii *n.* Ratchaburi province [จังหวัด jang-wàt]

ราชวงศ์ râat-chá~wong *n.* dynasty [ราชวงศ์ râat-chá~wong]

ราชสีห์ râat-chá~sǐi *n.* king-lion ๛ [ตัว dtuua]

ราชอาณาจักร râat-chá~aa-naa-jàk *n.* kingdom [แห่ง hèng]

ราชา raa-chaa *n.* king ๛ [องค์ ong, พระองค์ prá-ong]

ราชาภิเษก raa-chaa-pí-sèek *n.* coronation

ราชินี raa-chí~nii *n.* queen [องค์ ong]

ราดยาง râat-yaang *adj.* tar (e.g. asphalt road)

ราตรี raa-dtrii *n.* night ๛ [คืน kuun]

ราตรีสวัสดิ์ raa-dtrii-sà~wàt *interj.* good night! !

ร่าน rân *adj.* lustful

ร้าน ráan *n.* shop, stall, store [ร้าน ráan]

ร้านกาแฟ ráan-gaa-fɛɛ *n.* cafe, coffee shop [ร้าน ráan]

ร้านขายยา ráan-kǎai-yaa *n.* drugstore [ร้าน ráan]

ร้านค้า ráan-káa *n.* shop (store) [ร้าน ráan]

ร้านซักรีด ráan-sák-rîit *n.* launderette [ร้าน ráan]

ร้านตัดผม ráan-dtàt-pǒm *n.* barbershop [ร้าน ráan]

ร้านเสริมสวย ráan-sɜ̌ɜm-sǔuai *n.* beauty parlor [ร้าน ráan]

ร้านอาหาร ráan-aa-hǎan *n.* restaurant [ร้าน ráan]

ราบ râap *adj.* plane (flat),

smooth (flat)

ราบรื่น râap-rûun *adj.* smooth (free from difficulties, etc.)

ราบเรียบ râap-rîiap *adj.* level (flat, even)

ราย raai *n.* individual (person, case, each) [ราย raai]

ร้าย ráai *adj.* evil, wicked (fierce)

รายการ raai-gaan *n.* schedule (agenda) [รายการ raai-gaan (list or list item)]

รายการ raai-gaan *n.* list (of items) [รายการ raai-gaan]

รายการอาหาร raai-gaan-aa-hǎan *n.* menu [รายการ raai-gaan]

รายงาน raai-ngaan *n.* paper, report [ฉบับ chà~bàp, เรื่อง rûuang]

รายงาน raai-ngaan *vi.* report

รายจ่าย raai-jàai *n.* expenses, spending [จำนวน jam-nuuan]

รายชื่อ raai-chûu *n.* list (of names) [รายชื่อ raai-chûu]

รายเดือน raai-duuan *adj.*

monthly

รายได้ raai-dâai *n.* earning (revenue), income, proceeds

รายปี raai-bpii *adj.* yearly

ร้ายแรง ráai-rɛɛng *adj.* lethal (causing great harm)

รายล้อม raai-lɔ́ɔm *v.* crowd around ⚠

รายละเอียด raai-lá~ìiat *n.* detail [อัน an]

ร่าเริง râa-rəəng *adj.* cheerful, joyful

ราว raao *n.* bar (metal or wood pole) [ราว raao]

ร้าว ráao *adj.* cracked

ร้าว ráao *vi.* crack (split)

ราวๆ raao-raao *adv.* about (approx.)

ราวกับ raao-gàp *conj.* as though

ราศี raa-sǐi *n.* zodiac sign [ราศี raa-sǐi]

ราษฎร râat-sà~dɔɔn *n.* citizen ⚠ [คน kon]

รำ ram *vi.* dance (traditional)

รำข้าว ram-kâao *n.* bran

รำคาญ ram-kaan *adj.* annoyed, irritated

ร่ำรวย râm-ruuai *adj.* wealthy, well-off (rich)

รำวง ram-wong *v.* perform Thai folk-dance

ริดสีดวงทวาร rít-sĭi-duuang-tá~waan *n.* hemorrhoid

ริน rin *vt.* pour (from a container)

ริบ ríp *vt.* confiscate, impound (seize)

ริบบิ้น ríp-bîn *n.* ribbon [ม้วน múuan (roll), เส้น sên (strand)]

ริม rim *n.* edge, margin (border), rim

ริมฝีปาก rim-fĭi-bpàak *n.* lips

ริเริ่ม rí-rôอm *vt.* initiate (begin) ๛

ริ้วรอย ríu-rɔɔi *n.* blemish (e.g. on face) [แห่ง hèng]

รีด rîit *vt.* iron (clothes), press (compress, iron)

รีดนม rîit-nom *v.* milk

รีบ rîip *vi.* hurry (to do something)

รีสอร์ท rii-sɔ̀ɔt *n.* resort (tourist) [แห่ง hèng]

รึ rɯ́ *conj.* or ๛

รื่นเริง rɯ̂ɯn-rəəng *adj.* jolly, merry

รื้อ rɯ́ɯ *vt.* pull down, demolish

รื้อถอน rɯ́ɯ-tɔ̌ɔn *vi.* demolish (tear down)

รุ่ง rûng *n.* dawn/daybreak

รุ้ง rúng *n.* rainbow [ตัว dtuua]

รุ้งกินน้ำ rúng-gin-náam *n.* rainbow ๋ [ตัว dtuua]

รุ่งเช้า rûng-cháao *n.* dawn/daybreak ๛

รุ่งเรือง rûng-rɯɯang *v.* prosper

รุด rút *v.* hurry (accelerate, rush)

รุ่น rûn *n.* generation (e.g. family, culture, design) [รุ่น rûn]

รุนแรง run-rɛɛng *adj.* fierce (intense, e.g. winds, competition), terrible (severe, fierce), violent

รุ่นหนุ่มสาว rûn-nùm-sǎao *adj.* teenage

รุม rum *v.* crowd around

รู ruu *n.* hole [รู ruu, หลุม lǔm]

รู้ rúu *vi.* know (have knowledge)

รู้ rúu *vt.* realize (be or become aware of)

รูก้น ruu-gôn *n.* asshole ●

รูขุมขน ruu-kŭm-kŏn *n.* pore (on skin) [รู ruu]

รูจมูก ruu-jà~mùuk *n.* nostril [รู ruu]

รู้จัก rúu-jàk *adj.* familiar (knowing about)

รู้จัก rúu-jàk *vt.* know (familiar with)

รูด rûut *v.* slide smoothly

รูด rûut *vt.* swipe (e.g. card)

รูดซิป rûut-síp *v.* zip up

รู้ตัว rúu-dtuua *adj.* aware (conscious)

รูป rûup *n.* photo, picture [ใบ bai, แผ่น pèn]

รูปไข่ rûup-kài *adj.* oval (egg-shaped)

รูปถ่าย rûup-tàai *n.* photograph ⚡ [ใบ bai, แผ่น pèn]

รูปทรง rûup-song *n.* form (person's shape)

รูปแบบ rûup-bɛ̀ɛp *n.* form (structure) [รูปแบบ rûup-bɛ̀ɛp]

รูปพรรณ rûup-bpà~pan *n.* identity (appearance)

รูปภาพ rûup-pâap *n.* picture (photo) ⚡ [ใบ bai, แผ่น pèn]

รูปร่าง rûup-râang *n.* figure (person's shape)

รูปลอก rûup-lɔ̀ɔk *n.* decal [แผ่น pèn (sheet), รูป rûup (picture)]

รูปหล่อ rûup-lɔ̀ɔ *adj.* handsome (men)

รู้เรื่อง rúu-rûueang *vi.* know, understand ●

รู้สึก rúu-sùk *vi.* feel (e.g. angry, warm, hurt)

รู้สึกตัว rúu-sùk-dtuua *adj.* conscious (awake)

รู้สึกผิด rúu-sùk-pìt *adj.* ashamed (guilty about transgression)

เรขา ree-kǎa *n.* drawing, graphic

เรขาคณิต ree-kǎa-ká~nít *n.* geometry [วิชา wí-chaa]

เร่ง rêng *v.* hurry (accelerate, rush), press (urge)

เร่งเครื่อง rêng-krûueang *v.* speed up the engine

เร่งด่วน rêng-dùuan *adj.*

urgent

เร่งรีบ rêng-rîip *vi.* rush

เร่งเร้า rêng-ráo *v.* urge (impel, drive, insist)

เร็ว reo *adj.* fast, quick, rapid, swift

เร็วๆนี้ reo-reo-níi *adj.* recent (not long ago)

เรอ rəə *vi.* burp

เรา rao *pron.* us, we

เร้า ráo *vt.* stimulate

เร้าใจ ráo-jai *adj.* thrilled (stirred emotionally)

เร่าร้อน râo-rɔ́ɔn *adj.* be in heat, hot (sexy) ⚹

เริ่ม rɤ̂ɤm *v.* commence, originate (initiate), start (begin)

เริ่ม rɤ̂ɤm *vi.* come on (e.g. disease)

เรียก rîiak *v.* call, page

เรียก_กลับ rîiak-_-glàp *vt.* recall (summon back)

เรียกร้อง rîiak-rɔ́ɔng *v.* demand (require)

เรียกว่า rîiak-wâa *adj.* called (named)

เรียง riiang *v.* place in a row

เรียงความ riiang-kwaam *n.* essay [เรื่อง rûʉang]

เรียน riian *v.* learn, study

เรียนรู้ riian-rúu *v.* learn

เรียนหนังสือ riian-nǎng~ sʉ̌ʉ *vi.* study

เรียบ rîiap *adj.* even (flat), smooth (flat)

เรียบๆ rîiap-rîiap *adj.* plain (unattractive)

เรียบง่าย rîiap-ngâai *adj.* plain (simple, ordinary)

เรียบร้อย rîiap-rɔ́ɔi *adj.* neat, tidy (orderly)

เรียว riiao *adj.* slender (tapering)

เรี่ยวแรง rîiao-rɛɛng *n.* strength (power)

เรือ rʉʉa *n.* boat, ship (vessel) [ลำ lam]

เรือกลไฟ rʉʉa-gon-fai *n.* steamboat/steamship [ลำ lam]

เรือข้ามฟาก rʉʉa-kâam-fâak *n.* ferry (boat) [ลำ lam]

เรื่อง rûʉang *clf.* for movies, plays, stories

เรื่อง rûʉang *n.* story (situation, narrative), thing (event, matter), topic (subject) [เรื่อง rûʉang]

เรื่องจริง rûuang-jing *n.* fact (reality) [เรื่อง rûuang]

เรื่องราว rûuang-raao *n.* matter (subject) [เรื่อง rûuang]

เรื่องเล่า rûuang-lâo *n.* tale (story, fable) [เรื่อง rûuang]

เรื่องสั้น rûuang-sân *n.* short story [เรื่อง rûuang]

เรือดำน้ำ ruua-dam-náam *n.* submarine [ลำ lam]

เรือน ruuan *n.* dwelling place, house [หลัง lǎng, เรือน ruuan]

เรื้อน rúuan *n.* leprosy [โรค rôok]

เรือนจำ ruuan-jam *n.* prison ! [แห่ง hèng, ที่ tîi]

เรือนแพ ruuan-pɛɛ *n.* houseboat [หลัง lǎng]

เรือนหอ ruuan-hɔ̌ɔ *n.* bridal house [หลัง lǎng]

เรือบรรทุก ruua-ban-túk *n.* barge, tanker (cargo ship) [ลำ lam]

เรือใบ ruua-bai *n.* sailboat [ลำ lam]

เรื่อย rûuai *adj.* continual (continuous)

เรือโยง ruua-yoong *n.* tugboat [ลำ lam]

เรือรบ ruua-róp *n.* warship [ลำ lam]

เรื้อรัง rúua-rang *adj.* chronic

เรือล่ม ruua-lôm *n.* shipwreck [ครั้ง kráng]

แร่ rɛ̂ɛ *n.* mineral, ore [ชนิด chá~nít]

แรก rɛ̂ɛk *adj.* first, initial, original, primary

แรกเริ่ม rɛ̂ɛk-rôəm *adj.* original (first)

แรง rɛɛng *n.* force (might), power (strength) ✱

แร้ง rɛ́ɛng *n.* vulture [ตัว dtuua]

แรงกดดัน rɛɛng-gòt-dan *n.* pressure (e.g. of daily life)

แรงกระตุ้น rɛɛng-grà~dtûn *n.* drive (motivation)

แรงงาน rɛɛng-ngaan *n.* labor (physical effort)

แรงจูงใจ rɛɛng-juung-jai *n.* motivation

แรงดัน rɛɛng-dan *n.*

pressure (force per unit area)

แรงดึงดูด rεεng-dɯng-dùut *n.* gravity (physics)

แรงบันดาลใจ rεεng-ban-daan-jai *n.* inspiration

แรงม้า rεεng-máa *n.* horsepower [แรง rεεng]

แรด rêet *n.* rhinoceros [ตัว dtuua]

แร่ธาตุ rε̂ε-tâat *n.* mineral [ชนิด chá~nít]

แร้ว rέεo *n.* snare [คัน kan]

โรค rôok *n.* disease, malady [โรค rôok]

โรคกลัวน้ำ rôok-gluua-náam *n.* rabies [โรค rôok]

โรคติดต่อ rôok-dtìt-dtɔ̀ɔ *n.* contagious disease [โรค rôok]

โรคประสาท rôok-bprà~sàat *n.* mental disease [โรค rôok]

โรคภัยไข้เจ็บ rôok-pai-kâi-jèp *n.* illness

โรคระบาด rôok-rá~bàat *n.* epidemic (disease) [โรค rôok]

โรคะ roo-ká *n.* disease ☙

โรง roong *clf.* e.g. schools, buildings, factory

โรง roong *n.* house [หลัง lăng, เรือน rɯɯan]

โรง roong *n.* hall (large room) [โรง roong]

โรงกลั่น roong-glàn *n.* refinery [แห่ง hèng]

โรงงาน roong-ngaan *n.* factory [แห่ง hèng]

โรงจำนำ roong-jam-nam *n.* pawnshop [แห่ง hèng]

โรงพยาบาล roong-pá~yaa-baan *n.* hospital [แห่ง hèng]

โรงพัก roong-pák *n.* police station ☙ [แห่ง hèng]

โรงพิมพ์ roong-pim *n.* printing house [แห่ง hèng]

โรงรถ roong-rót *n.* garage (to store car) [แห่ง hèng]

โรงเรียน roong-riian *n.* school [แห่ง hèng]

โรงแรม roong-rεεm *n.* hotel [แห่ง hèng]

โรงละคร roong-lá~kɔɔn *n.* theater (play) [แห่ง hèng]

โรงสี roong-sǐi *n.* rice mill [แห่ง hὲng]

โรงหนัง roong-nǎng *n.* cinema (movie theater) ● [แห่ง hὲng]

โรงอาหาร roong-aa-hǎan *n.* canteen (cafeteria) [แห่ง hὲng]

โรย rooi *vt.* sow (e.g. seeds), sprinkle (liquid or powder)

ไร rai *adj.* which

ไร rai *n.* bedbug [ตัว dtuua]

ไร rai *pron.* which

ไร่ râi *n.* farm (crop), field (non-rice crop) [ที่ tîi, แห่ง hὲng, ผืน pǔ̈n]

ไร้ rái *adj.* free from (without)

ไร้ rái *prep.* without ⚡

ไร้กังวล rái-gang-won *adj.* carefree

ไร้ค่า rái-kâa *adj.* worthless

ไร้จุดหมาย rái-jùt-mǎai *adj.* wandering

ไร้เดียงสา rái-diiang-sǎa *adj.* childish (innocent), naive

ไร่นา râi-naa *n.* rice field

[ที่ tîi, แห่ง hὲng, ผืน pǔ̈n]

ไร้ผล rái-pǒn *adj.* fruitless

ไร้ยางอาย rái-yaang-aai *adj.* shameless (showing no shame)

ไร้สาย rái-sǎai *adj.* wireless

ไร้สาระ rái-sǎa-rá *adj.* crap, nonsense, silly

ไร่องุ่น râi-à~ngùn *n.* vineyard [ไร่ râi]

ฤ

ฤดู rɨ́-duu *n.* period (season) [ฤดู rɨ́-duu]

ฤดูใบไม้ผลิ rɨ́-duu-bai-máai-plì *n.* spring (season) [ฤดู rɨ́-duu]

ฤดูใบไม้ร่วง rɨ́-duu-bai-máai-rûuang *n.* fall (autumn) [ฤดู rɨ́-duu]

ฤดูฝน rɨ́-duu-fǒn *n.* rainy season [ฤดู rɨ́-duu]

ฤดูร้อน rɨ́-duu-rɔ́ɔn *n.* hot season, summer [ฤดู rɨ́-duu]

ฤดูหนาว rɨ́-duu-nǎao *n.* winter [ฤดู rɨ́-duu]

ฤทธิ์ rít *n.* effect, energy, power (might)

ก
ข
ฃ
ค
ฅ
ฆ
ง
จ
ฉ
ช
ซ
ฌ
ญ
ฎ
ฏ
ฐ
ฑ
ฒ
ณ
ด
ต
ถ
ท
ธ
น
บ
ป
ผ
ฝ
พ
ฟ
ภ
ม
ย
ร
ฤ
ล
ฦ
ว
ศ
ษ
ส
ห
อ
ฮ

ฤทัย rú-tai *n.* mind ☙, soul ☙ [ดวง duuang]

ฤษี rʉʉ-sǐi *n.* hermit, recluse [ตน dton]

ล

ล lɔɔ *let.* ล. ลิง lɔɔ-lɪng, a consonant of the Thai alphabet (low consonant) [ตัว dtuua]

ลง long *v.* descend (go down), get off (e.g. bus, plane)

ลง long *vi.* go down

ลงเขา long-kǎo *adv.* downhill (down a hill)

ลงคะแนน long-ká~nɛɛn *vi.* cast a ballot

ลงชื่อ long-chʉ̂ʉ *vi.* sign (one's name)

ลงชื่อใน long-chʉ̂ʉ-nai *vt.* underwrite (one's name on)

ลงทะเบียน long-tá~biian *v.* enroll (register)

ลงทะเบียน long-tá~biian *vi.* register

ลงท้าย long-táai *adj.* be at the end

ลงทุน long-tun *v.* invest

ลงโทษ long-tôot *vt.* penalize, punish

ลงนาม long-naam *vi.* sign (one's name) ‼

ลงพุง long-pung *v.* have a big belly

ลงมือ long-mʉʉ *vt.* undertake (start)

ลงแรง long-rɛɛng *v.* expend energy

ลงวันที่ใน long-wan-tîi-nai *vt.* date (write the date on)

ลงอาญา long-aa-yaa *vt.* punish ⚔

ลงเอยที่ long-əəi-tîi *vi.* end up at ✦

ลด lót *v.* lower, reduce

ลดชั้น lót-chán *vt.* demote (reduce level or class)

ลดฐานะ lót-tǎa-ná *vt.* downgrade (lower in status)

ลดต่ำลง lót-dtàm-long *vi.* decline (go down)

ลดราคา lót-raa-kaa *v.* discount (reduce price of)

ลดลง lót-long *vi.* decrease, reduce

ลน lon *v.* hold over a flame

ล้น lón *vi.* spill (liquid)

ลบ lóp *prep.* minus

ลบล้าง lóp-láang *v.* overrule (prevail over, deny)

ลบ_ออก lóp-_-ɔ̀ɔk *vt.* erase, subtract

ลพบุรี lóp-bù~rii *n.* Lop Buri province [จังหวัด jang-wàt]

ลม lom *n.* air (in tires), wind

ล้ม lóm *vt.* fell (e.g. a tree)

ลมแดด lom-dɛ̀ɛt *n.* sunstroke [โรค rôok]

ลมบ้าหมู lom-bâa-mǔu *n.* epilepsy [โรค rôok]

ลมบ้าหมู lom-bâa-mǔu *n.* whirlwind ✿ [ลูก lûuk]

ลมแรง lom-rɛɛng *adj.* windy

ล้มลง lóm-long *vi.* fall down (tumble)

ล้มละลาย lóm-lá~laai *adj.* bankrupt

ล้มล้าง lóm-láang *v.* overturn (overthrow)

ล้มเลิก lóm-lə̂ək *v.* cancel (call off)

ลมหายใจ lom-hǎai-jai *n.* breath (air)

ล้มเหลว lóm-lěeo *vi.* fail, go under

ลวก lûuak *v.* cook briefly

ล้วงกระเป๋า lúuang-grà~bpǎo *v.* pickpocket

ล่วงเกิน lûuang-gəən *v.* trespass against, show disrespect to

ล่วงล้ำ lûuang-lám *vi.* intrude (trespass)

ล่วงหน้า lûuang-nâa *adv.* beforehand, in advance

ลวด lûuat *n.* wire (metal) [เส้น sên (strand), ขด kòt (coil), ม้วน múuan (roll)]

ลวดลาย lûuat-laai *n.* skills of a person

ลวดลาย lûuat-laai *n.* decorative design ‼, pattern (print) ‼ [ลาย laai]

ลวดหนาม lûuat-nǎam *n.* barbed wire [เส้น sên (strand), ม้วน múuan (roll)]

ล้วน lúuan *adv.* purely (only)

ลวนลาม luuan-laam *vt.* harass (sexually)

ลหุโทษ lá~hù-tôot *n.* minor offense ✖ [ครั้ง kráng]

ล่อ lɔ̂ɔ *n.* mule (animal) [ตัว dtuua]

ล่อ ล่อ *vt.* lure, tempt (appeal strongly to)

ล้อ ล้อ *n.* wheel [ล้อ ล้อ]

ล้อ ล้อ *vt.* mock

ลอก ลอก *vi.* make a copy

ลอกคราบ ลอก-krâap *v.* shed e.g. snake

ลอกเลียน ลอก-liian *vt.* imitate (copy, mimic)

ลอก_ออก ลอก-_-ออก *v.* peel off (e.g. skin)

ลอง ลอง *vi.* try (make an effort)

ลอง ลอง *vt.* try (sample, test)

ล่อง ล่อง *v.* cause to float along

ลองกอง ลอง-กอง *n.* longkong (fruit) [ลูก lûuk, พวง puuang (bunch)]

ลองใจ ลอง-jai *v.* test one's feelings

ลองดู ลอง-duu *vi.* try (make an effort) 🔊

ล่องแพ ล่อง-pεε *vi.* raft (travel on a raft)

ล่องลอย ล่อง-ลอย *vi.* wander (go aimlessly)

ลอด ลอด *v.* pass through or under, crawl under

ลอด ลอด *vt.* go through (e.g. tunnel)

ลอดช่อง ลอด-chông *n.* Thai sweetmeat made of short noodles and coconut milk [ตัว dtuua (strand), ถ้วย tûuai (bowl)]

ล็อตเตอรี่ ล็อต-dtəə-rîi *n.* lottery [ใบ bai]

ลอน ลอน *n.* curl, wave

ล่อนจ้อน ล่อน-jôn *adj.* naked, nude

ลอบ ลอบ *n.* fish trap made of rattan [ลูก lûuk]

ลอบฆ่า ลอบ-kâa *vt.* assassinate

ลอบทำร้าย ลอบ-tam-ráai *vt.* ambush

ล้อม ล้อม *vt.* besiege, enclose (surround, e.g. fence)

ลอย ลอย *vi.* float (in water, air), soar

ลอยกระทง ลอย-grà~tong *n.* Thai annual floating festival [เทศกาล têet-sà~gaan]

ล่อลวง ล่อ-luuang *vt.* entice, lure

ล้อเล่น ล้อ-lên *vi.* jest

ล้อเลียน ล้อ-liian *vt.* mimic, mock, ridicule

ล่อหลอก ล่อ-ลอก *vt.* draw

in (lure, e.g. victims)

ละ lá *part.* used often with mildly corroborative force

ละก็ lá~gɔ̂ɔ *part.* and then, otherwise

ละคร lá~kɔɔn *n.* play (drama) [ตอน dtɔɔn (episode), ฉาก chàak (scene), เรื่อง rûuang (story)]

ละครสัตว์ lá~kɔɔn-sàt *n.* circus [คณะ ká~ná]

ละทิ้ง lá~tíng *v.* abandon (relinquish)

ละมั่ง lá~mâng *n.* deer (animal) [ตัว dtuua]

ละมุด lá~mút *n.* sapota [ลูก lûuk]

ละเมอ lá~məə *v.* talk in one's sleep

ละเมาะ lá~mɔ́ *n.* grove [ป่า bpàa]

ละเมิด lá~mêət *vt.* offend, violate (right, privacy)

ละเมิดลิขสิทธิ์ lá~mêət-lík-kà~sìt *v.* pirate (copy without legal right)

ละลาย lá~laai *v.* melt

ละลาย lá~laai *vi.* dissolve (e.g. salt), thaw (liquid)

ละลายน้ำแข็ง lá~laai-nám-kɛ̌ng *vi.* defrost

ละเลย lá~ləəi *vt.* neglect

ละเว้น lá~wén *vt.* omit

ละออง lá~ɔɔng *n.* fine particle

ละอายใจ lá~aai-jai *adj.* ashamed (guilty about transgression)

ละเอียด lá~ìiat *adj.* crushed, detailed, fine (small-grained)

ละเอียดถี่ถ้วน lá~ìiat-tìi-tûuan *adj.* thorough (detailed)

ลักพาตัว lák-paa-dtuua *vt.* kidnap

ลักยิ้ม lák-yím *n.* dimple (on cheek) [แห่ง hɛ̀ng]

ลักลอบ lák-lɔ̂ɔp *v.* smuggle

ลักษณนาม lák-sà~nà-naam *n.* classifier (Thai part of speech) [ประเภท bprà~pêet (category), คำ kam (word)]

ลักษณะ lák-sà~nà *n.* appearance (look), manner (trait, style)

ลักษณะ lák-sà~nà *n.* character (appearance) [ลักษณะ lák-sà~nà]

ลัง lang *clf.* e.g. wooden boxes, crates, etc.

ลัง lang *n.* wooden box [ใบ bai]

ลังเล lang-lee *adj.* hesitant (reluctant, uncertain)

ลังเล lang-lee *vi.* hesitate

ลัด lát *v.* take a short cut

ลัดวงจร lát-wong-jɔɔn *v.* have an electric short-circuit

ลัทธิ lát-tí *n.* doctrine (religion) [ลัทธิ lát-tí]

ลั่น lân *vi.* explode, shoot (e.g. gun)

ลับ láp *adj.* confidential, private, secret

ลับ láp *vt.* sharpen (e.g. blade)

ลา laa *n.* ass, donkey [ตัว dtuua]

ลา laa *v.* request to take leave, say good-bye

ล่า lâa *v.* hunt

ลาก lâak *vt.* tug (drag, pull)

ลาก่อน laa-gɔɔn *interj.* bye-bye!/bye!

ลาง laang *n.* omen, sign

ล่าง lâang *adj.* underneath

ล้าง láang *v.* wash (e.g. dishes, car)

ล้าง láang *vt.* rinse

ล้างผลาญ láang-plǎan *vt.* devastate (ravage)

ล้างรูป láang-rûup *v.* print (photography)

ล้างรูป láang-rûup *vi.* develop pictures

ล้างสมอง láang-sà~mɔɔng *vt.* brainwash

ลางสังหรณ์ laang-sǎng-hɔ̌ɔn *n.* hunch (premonition)

ลางสาด laang-sàat *n.* langsat [ลูก lûuk]

ล่างสุด lâang-sùt *adj.* bottom (lowest part)

ล่าช้า lâa-cháa *adj.* delayed

ลาด lâat *adj.* sloping

ลาด lâat *v.* pave (spread)

ลาดตระเวน lâat-dtrà~ween *v.* patrol

ลาดยาง lâat-yaang *v.* paved with asphalt

ลาดเอียง lâat-iiang *v.* slope

ลาตัวผู้ laa-dtuua-pûu *n.* jackass (male donkey) [ตัว dtuua]

ลาติน laa-dtin *adj.* Latin

ลาน laan *n.* courtyard,

yard (lawn, courtyard)
[ลาน laan, แห่ง hèng]

ล้าน láan *adj.* bald

ล้าน láan *numb.* million

ลาบ lâap *n.* minced meat
[จาน jaan]

ลาภ lâap *n.* piece of good
fortune [ชิ้น chín]

ลาม laam *vi.* spread (e.g.
news, fire)

ล่าม lâam *n.* interpreter
[คน kon]

ล่าม lâam *v.* put a rope
around

ล่าม lâam *vt.* tie up (e.g.
animal)

ลามก laa-mók *adj.* dirty,
lewd, obscene

ล่ามโซ่ lâam-sôo *vt.* chain
(tether, restrain)

ลาย laai *n.* design (style),
mark, pattern (print) [ลาย
laai]

ลายเซ็น laai-sen *n.*
signature [อัน an]

ลายนิ้วมือ laai-níu-mɯɯ *n.*
fingerprint [ลาย laai]

ลายมือ laai-mɯɯ *n.*
handwriting, writing
[ลายมือ laai-mɯɯ]

ลายมือชื่อ laai-mɯɯ-chɯ̂ɯ

n. signature **!** [อัน an]

ลายสัก laai-sàk *n.* tattoo
[ลาย laai]

ลาว laao *n.* Laos (country)
[ประเทศ bprà~têet]

ล้าสมัย láa-sà~mǎi *adj.*
old-fashioned
(outdated), out-of-date

ล่าสัตว์ lâa-sàt *vi.* hunt

ล่าสุด lâa-sùt *adj.* latest

ล้าหลัง láa-lǎng *adj.*
underdeveloped

ล้าหลัง láa-lǎng *v.* lag (fall
behind)

ล่าเหยื่อ lâa-yɯ̀ɯa *vi.* prey
(hunt prey)

ลาออก laa-ɔ̀ɔk *vi.* quit,
resign

ลำ lam *n.* body (trunk) [ตัว
dtuua]

ล่ำ lâm *adj.* muscular,
stout (sturdy)

ล้ำค่า lám-kâa *adj.* very
precious

ลำเค็ญ lam-ken *adj.* poor
(suffering hardship)

ล่ำซำ lâm-sam *adj.* rich **!**

ลำดับ lam-dàp *n.* order
(logical order or
sequence), series [ลำดับ

lam-dàp, ที่ tîi]

ลำต้น lam-dtôn *n.* trunk (of a tree) [ลำ lam]

ลำตัว lam-dtuua *n.* torso (trunk of human body)

ลำธาร lam-taan *n.* brook, creek, stream [สาย săai]

ลำบาก lam-bàak *adj.* difficult (causing hardship)

ลำปาง lam-bpaang *n.* Lampang province [จังหวัด jang-wàt]

ลำพัง lam-pang *adv.* alone (by oneself)

ลำพูน lam-puun *n.* Lamphun province [จังหวัด jang-wàt]

ลำโพง lam-poong *n.* loud speaker [ตัว dtuua]

ลำไย lam-yai *n.* longan (fruit) [ลูก lûuk, พวง puuang (bunch)]

ลำเลียง lam-liiang *vt.* convey (transport)

ล่ำสัน lâm-săn *adj.* athletic (fit), stocky

ลำแสง lam-sɛ̌ɛng *n.* beam (light) [ลำ lam]

ลำไส้ lam-sâi *n.* bowel, intestine [ท่อน tɔ̂ɔn (strip),

ขด kòt (coil)]

ลำไส้ใหญ่ lam-sâi-yài *n.* large intestine [ท่อน tɔ̂ɔn (strip), ขด kòt (coil)]

ล้ำหน้า lám-nâa *adj.* offside

ล้ำหน้า lám-nâa *vt.* surpass

ลำเอียง lam-iiang *adj.* biased, partial

ลิเก lí-gee *n.* Thai musical folk dramas [คณะ ká~ná]

ลิขสิทธิ์ lí-kà~sìt, lík-kà~ sìt *n.* copyright [ฉบับ chà~bàp]

ลิง ling *n.* ape, monkey [ตัว dtuua]

ลิตร lít *n.* liter/litre [ลิตร lít]

ลิ้น lín *n.* tongue (in the mouth) [ลิ้น lín]

ลิ้นไก่ lín-gài *n.* uvula [อัน an]

ลิ้นจี่ lín-jìi *n.* lychee [ลูก lûuk]

ลิ้นชัก lín-chák *n.* drawer (of furniture) [ลิ้นชัก lín-chák]

ลิบ líp *adj.* distant, remote

ลิปสติก líp-sà~dtik *n.* lipstick [แท่ง tɛ̂ng]

ลิฟต์ líp *n.* elevator, lift [ตัว dtuua]

ลิ่ม lîm *n.* wedge [อัน an]

ลีก lîik *n.* league (sports) [ลีก lîik]

ลีซอ lii-sɔɔ *n.* Lisu (hill tribe) [เผ่า pào]

ลีบ lîip *adj.* parched (withered)

ลีลาศ lii-lâat *n.* ballroom dance

ลึก lúk *adj.* deep

ลึกซึ้ง lúk-súng *adj.* profound (deep, intensive)

ลึกลับ lúk-láp *adj.* mysterious

ลึงค์ lʉng *n.* penis ⚹ [อัน an]

ลื่น lʉ̂ʉn *adj.* silky (smooth), slippery

ลื่น lʉ̂ʉn *vi.* slide, slip (glide)

ลืม lʉʉm *v.* forget

ลืมตา lʉʉm-dtaa *v.* open the eyes

ลือ lʉʉ *v.* spread as a rumor

ลือ lʉʉ *vt.* rumor

ลุก lúk *vi.* rise (from bed, stand up, etc.)

ลุกขึ้น lúk-kʉ̂n *vi.* rise (from bed, stand up, etc.)

ลุกลาม lúk-laam *vi.* rage

ลุง lung *n.* term for addressing a middle-aged man, father or mother's older brother [คน kon]

ลุงพอ lung-pɔɔ *n.* slack (rimmed hat) [ใบ bai]

ลุยน้ำ lui-náam *vi.* wade (in water)

ลุล่วง lú-lûuang *adj.* done

ลูก lûuk *clf.* e.g. fruits, balls, containers, waves, storms, hills, etc.

ลูก lûuk *n.* child (son or daughter) [คน kon]

ลูกกรง lûuk-grong *n.* bar of a cage [ซี่ sîi]

ลูกกรอก lûuk-grɔ̀ɔk *n.* stillborn fetus [ตัว dtuua]

ลูกกลิ้ง lûuk-glîng *n.* roll-on (deodorant) [ขวด kùuat]

ลูกกลิ้ง lûuk-glîng *n.* roller (small wheel) [อัน an]

ลูกกวาด lûuk-gwàat *n.* lozenge [เม็ด mét]

ก
ข
ฃ
ค
ฅ
ฆ
ง
จ
ฉ
ช
ซ
ฌ
ญ
ฎ
ฏ
ฐ
ฑ
ฒ
ณ
ด
ต
ถ
ท
ธ
น
บ
ป
ผ
ฝ
พ
ฟ
ภ
ม
ย
ร
ฤ
ล
ฦ
ว
ศ
ษ
ส
ห
อ
ฮ

ก ข ข ค ค ฅ ฆ ง จ ฉ ช ซ ฌ ญ ฎ ฏ ฐ ฑ ฒ ณ ด ต ถ ท ธ น บ ป ผ ฝ พ ฟ ภ ม ย ร **ล** ฦ ว ศ ษ ส ห ฬ อ ฮ

ลูกกุญแจ lûuk-gun-jɛɛ *n.* key [ลูก lûuk, ดอก dɔɔk]

ลูกเกด lûuk-gèet *n.* raisin [เม็ด mét]

ลูกไก่ lûuk-gài *n.* chick (baby chicken) [ตัว dtuua]

ลูกขนไก่ lûuk-kŏn-gài *n.* shuttlecock [ลูก lûuk]

ลูกข่าง lûuk-kàang *n.* top (spinning) [ลูก lûuk]

ลูกขุน lûuk-kŭn *n.* juror (individual) [คน kon]

ลูกเขย lûuk-kěoi *n.* son-in-law [คน kon]

ลูกครึ่ง lûuk-krûng *n.* half-breed [คน kon]

ลูกความ lûuk-kwaam *n.* lawyer's client [คน kon]

ลูกค้า lûuk-káa *n.* client, customer [คน kon]

ลูกคิด lûuk-kít *n.* abacus [ราง raang, ลูก lûuk]

ลูกจ้าง lûuk-jâang *n.* employee [คน kon]

ลูกชาย lûuk-chaai *n.* son [คน kon]

ลูกชิ้น lûuk-chín *n.* meatball [ลูก lûuk]

ลูกโซ่ lûuk-sôo *n.* link (chain) [ห่วง hùuang]

ลูกดอก lûuk-dɔɔk *n.* dart [ลูก lûuk]

ลูกดิ่ง lûuk-dìng *n.* plummet (plumb bob) [ลูก lûuk]

ลูกตา lûuk-dtaa *n.* eyeball [ลูก lûuk]

ลูกตาล lûuk-dtaan *n.* sugar-plum nut [ลูก lûuk]

ลูกตุ้ม lûuk-dtûm *n.* pendulum [ลูก lûuk]

ลูกเต๋า lûuk-dtǎo *n.* dice [ลูก lûuk]

ลูกท้อ lûuk-tɔ́ɔ *n.* peach [ลูก lûuk]

ลูกโทษ lûuk-tôot *n.* penalty kick [ลูก lûuk]

ลูกธนู lûuk-tá~nuu *n.* arrow (weapon) [ดอก dɔɔk]

ลูกน้อง lûuk-nɔ́ɔng *n.* subordinate (inferior, junior) [คน kon]

ลูกน้ำ lûuk-náam *n.* mosquito larva [ตัว dtuua]

ลูกบอล lûuk-bɔn *n.* ball (sports) [ลูก lûuk]

ลูกบ้าน lûuk-bâan *n.*

villager [คน kon]

ลูกบาศก์ lûuk-bàat *n.* cube [ลูก lûuk]

ลูกบิด lûuk-bìt *n.* knob (doorknob) [อัน an, ลูก lûuk]

ลูกปัด lûuk-bpàt *n.* bead (small, round object) [ลูก lûuk (seed), เม็ด mét (seed)]

ลูกปืน lûuk-bpɯɯn *n.* bullet [ลูก lûuk, นัด nát]

ลูกโป่ง lûuk-bpòong *n.* balloon (toy, decoration) [ใบ bai]

ลูกแฝด lûuk-fɛ̀ɛt *n.* twin [คู่ kûu]

ลูกพี่ลูกน้อง lûuk-pîi-lûuk-nɔ́ɔng *n.* cousin [คน kon]

ลูกมือ lûuk-mɯɯ *n.* helper or assistant ✦ [คน kon]

ลูกแมว lûuk-mɛɛo *n.* kitten, pussy [ตัว dtuua]

ลูกไม้ lûuk-máai *n.* lace (ornamental fabric) [ชิ้น chín (piece), ลาย laai (design)]

ลูกรอก lûuk-rɔ̂ɔk *n.* pulley [อัน an]

ลูกระเบิด lûuk-rá~bə̀ət *n.* bomb [ลูก lûuk]

ลูกรัง lûuk-rang *n.* gravel (pebble) [เม็ด mét, ก้อน gɔ̂ɔn]

ลูกเรือ lûuk-rɯɯa *n.* sailor (crew) [คน kon]

ลูกเลี้ยง lûuk-líiang *n.* stepchild [คน kon]

ลูกโลก lûuk-lôok *n.* globe (spherical map) [ลูก lûuk]

ลูกศร lûuk-sɔ̌ɔn *n.* arrow (symbol) [ตัว dtuua]

ลูกศิษย์ lûuk-sìt *n.* student ✦ [คน kon]

ลูกสะใภ้ lûuk-sà~pái *n.* daughter-in-law [คน kon]

ลูกสัตว์ lûuk-sàt *n.* cub (young animal) [ตัว dtuua]

ลูกสาว lûuk-sǎao *n.* daughter [คน kon]

ลูกสุดท้อง lûuk-sùt-tɔ́ɔng *n.* youngest child [คน kon]

ลูกสูบ lûuk-sùup *n.* piston [ลูก lûuk]

ลูกเสือ lûuk-sɯ̌ɯa *n.* boy scout [คน kon]

ลูกเสือ lûuk-sɯ̌ɯa *n.* cub

(baby tiger) [ตัว dtuua]

ลูกหนี้ lûuk-nîi *n.* debtor [ราย raai ⚡, คน kon]

ลูกหลาน lûuk-lǎan *n.* offspring (descendant) [คน kon]

ลูกหิน lûuk-hǐn *n.* marble [ลูก lûuk]

ลูกเห็บ lûuk-hèp *n.* hail (weather) [เม็ด mét]

ลูกเหม็น lûuk-měn *n.* mothball [เม็ด mét, ลูก lûuk]

ลูกอม lûuk-om *n.* candy, toffee [เม็ด mét]

ลูกอมแก้ไอ lûuk-om-gɛ̂ɛ-ai *n.* cough drop [เม็ด mét]

ลูกอ๊อด lûuk-ɔ́ɔt *n.* tadpole ✹ [ตัว dtuua]

ลูกอัณฑะ lûuk-an-tá *n.* testicle [ลูก lûuk]

ลูกอุปถัมภ์ lûuk-ùp-bpà~tǎm *n.* foster child, godchild [คน kon]

ลู่แข่ง lûu-kèng *n.* track (race) [ลู่ lûu]

ลูบ lûup *v.* pet (pat)

ลูบคลำ lûup-klam *vt.*

stroke (touch lightly)

ลูบไล้ lûup-lái *vt.* fondle, rub lightly

เล็ก lék *adj.* small (tiny)

เล็กที่สุด lék-tîi-sùt *adj.* minimal

เล็กน้อย lék-nɔ́ɔi *adj.* few, petty (trivial)

เล็กมาก lék-mâak *adj.* miniature, tiny

เลขคณิต lêek-ká~nít *n.* arithmetic [วิชา wí-chaa]

เลขคี่ lêek-kîi *n.* odd number [ตัว dtuua]

เลขคู่ lêek-kûu *n.* even number [ตัว dtuua]

เลขา lee-kǎa *n.* secretary [คน kon]

เลขานุการ lee-kǎa-nú-gaan *n.* secretary ⚡ [คน kon]

เล็ง leng *vt.* aim (e.g. gun)

เลน leen *n.* lane (track) [เลน leen]

เล่น lên *v.* amuse oneself, gamble, play (games, music, etc.)

เล่นกับ lên-gàp *vt.* fiddle with (tinker, adjust)

เล่นตัว lên-dtuua *v.* play hard to get

เล่นไพ่ lên-pâi *v.* play cards

เล่นละคร lên-lá~kɔɔn *v.* put on an act

เลนส์ leen *n.* lens (glasses) [ชนิด chá~nít (kind), อัน an (piece)]

เล็บ lép *n.* nail (finger or toe) [เล็บ lép]

เล็บเท้า lép-táao *n.* toenail [เล็บ lép]

เล็บมือ lép-mɯɯ *n.* fingernail [เล็บ lép]

เล็ม lem *v.* cut a little, nibble

เล่ม lêm *clf.* for books, knives, candles, etc.

เล็มหญ้า lem-yâa *vi.* graze (feed on grass)

เลย ləəi *adv.* at all, farther/further, more

เลย ləəi *n.* Loei province [จังหวัด jang-wàt]

เลย ləəi *prep.* beyond (further away than), past (further on than)

เลว leeo *adj.* bad, mean

เลวร้าย leeo-ráai *adj.* terrible (very bad)

เลวลง leeo-long *adj.* worse

เล่ห์กล lêe-gon *n.* trick [อัน an]

เล่ห์เหลี่ยม lêe-lìiam *n.* trick [อัน an]

เลอะ lə *adj.* messy, stained

เลอะเทอะ lə-tə *adj.* messy, sloppy

เล่า lâo *v.* narrate

เล่า lâo *vt.* tell (e.g. story)

เล้า láo *n.* coop (small animals) [เล้า láo]

เล่านิทาน lâo-ní-taan *vi.* tell a story

เล่าเรียน lâo-riian *v.* learn ✎

เล่าเรื่อง lâo-rɯ̂ɯang *vi.* tell a story

เล้าโลม láo-loom *vt.* caress ✎

เลาะ lɔ́ *v.* go along the edge of, take the hem out

เลิก lə̂ək *v.* quit (stop, cease), stop (e.g. workday, smoking, slavery)

เลิกกัน lə̂ək-gan *vi.* break up (relationship)

เลินเล่อ ləən-lə̂ə *adj.* careless

เลิศ lə̂ət *adj.* awesome

(wonderful)

เลีย liia *v.* seek favors by flattering, lick

เลียง liiang *n.* kind of mild vegetable curry

เลี่ยง lîiang *v.* sneak away

เลี้ยง líiang *vt.* breed (raise, e.g. horses), feed (give food to)

เลี้ยงชีพ líiang-chîip *vi.* make a living

เลี้ยงดู líiang-duu *vt.* bring up (raise a child)

เลี้ยงส่ง líiang-sòng *v.* give a farewell party

เลี้ยงสัตว์ líiang-sàt *vi.* farm (animal)

เลี่ยน lîian *adj.* greasy, oily

เลียบ lîiap *v.* go along the edge of

เลี่ยม lîiam *v.* covered with a thin sheet of metal

เลี้ยว líiao *v.* turn (e.g. a car while driving)

เลือก lûuak *vt.* pick (choose), vote for (elect)

เลือกตั้ง lûuak-dtâng *vi.* vote

เลื่องลือ lûuang-luu *adj.* spread far and wide

เลือด lûuat *n.* blood

เลือดเย็น lûuat-yen *adj.* cold-blooded

เลือดไหล lûuat-lăi *vi.* bleed

เลือดออก lûuat-ɔ̀ɔk *vi.* bleed

เลือดอุ่น lûuat-ùn *adj.* warm-blooded

เลือน luuan *adj.* dim (faintly outlined)

เลือน luuan *vi.* fade (disappear gradually)

เลื่อน lûuan *v.* move (glide, slide)

เลื่อน lûuan *vt.* change position, postpone (put off)

เลื่อนขึ้น lûuan-kûn *vi.* move up

เลื่อนเวลา lûuan-wee-laa *vi.* waive time

เลื่อนออก lûuan-ɔ̀ɔk *v.* protract (postpone)

เลื่อย lûuai *n.* saw [ปั้น bpûun]

เลื่อย lûuai *v.* saw

เลื้อย lúuai *vi.* creep (e.g. plants)

แล lɛɛ *v.* look ➳

แล่ lɛ̂ɛ *v.* cut open, cut thin

แลก lɛ̂ɛk *v.* exchange

แลกเงิน lɛ̂ɛk-ngən *vi.* change money

แลกเปลี่ยน lɛ̂ɛk-bplìian *v.* exchange, swap, trade

แล้ง lɛ́ɛng *adj.* dry (no rain)

แล่นเรือ lɛ̂n-ruua *vi.* cruise (in ship), sail

แลบ lɛ̂ɛp *vi.* flash (e.g. lightning), stick out

แล้ว lɛ́ɛo *adv.* already

แล้วก็ lɛ́ɛo-gɔ̂ *adv.* then (next in order of time)

แล้วแต่ lɛ́ɛo-dtɛ̀ɛ *vt.* up to (dependent on)

และ lɛ́ *adv.* also

และ lɛ́ *conj.* and

และหรือ lɛ́-rǔu *prep.* and/or

และอื่นๆ อีก lɛ́-ùun-ùun-ìik *idm.* et cetera/etc.

โล่ lôo *n.* shield (armor) [อัน an]

โลก lôok *n.* earth, globe, world [ใบ bai]

โลกีย์ loo-gii *n.* worldly matter

โล่ง lôong *adj.* open (empty), plain (open, clear)

โล่งเตียน lôong-dtiian *adj.* cleared (clearcut) ⚑

โลงศพ loong-sòp *n.* coffin [โลง loong, ใบ bai]

โล่งอก lôong-òk *v.* feel relieved

โลภ lôop *adj.* greedy (covetous)

โลม loom *vt.* caress ✑

โลมา loo-maa *n.* dolphin [ตัว dtuua]

โลเล loo-lee *adj.* ever-changing

โลหะ loo-hà *n.* metal [ธาตุ tâat]

โลหิต loo-hìt *n.* blood ⚑

ไล่ lâi *vt.* chase (pursue rapidly)

ไล่ออก lâi-_-ɔ̀ɔk *vt.* dismiss (fire, kick out)

ว

ว wɔɔ *let.* ว. แหวน wɔɔ-wɛ̌ɛn, a consonant of the Thai alphabet (low consonant) [ตัว dtuua]

วกกลับ wók-glàp *v.* return to the starting point

วกวน wók-won *adj.* roundabout

วง wong *n.* ring (circle) [วง wong]

วงกต wong-gòt *n.* maze (labyrinth) [ทาง taang, เส้น sên]

วงกลม wong-glom *n.* circle (ring, round object, etc.) [วง wong]

วงการ wong-gaan *n.* field (type of work) [วงการ wong-gaan]

วงโคจร wong-koo-jɔɔn *n.* orbit [วง wong]

วงจร wong-jɔɔn *n.* cycle (e.g. life) [วงจร wong-jɔɔn]

วงดนตรี wong-don-dtrii *n.* band (music) [วง wong]

วงโยธวาทิต wong-yoo-tá~waa-tít *n.* marching band [วง wong]

วงรี wong-rii *n.* oval [วง wong]

วงเล็บ wong-lép *n.* parenthesis [ตัว dtuua (one), คู่ kûu (pair)]

วงเวียน wong-wiian *n.* roundabout (traffic circle) [แห่ง hèng]

วงศ์ wong *n.* lineage (clan) [วงศ์ wong]

วงศ์ตระกูล wong-dtrà~guun *n.* lineage [วงศ์ wong]

วงแหวน wong-wěɛn *n.* ring (circular band of any kind) [วง wong]

วรรณ wan *n.* color ✍

วรรณกรรม wan-ná~gam *n.* literature

วรรณคดี wan-ná~ká~dii *n.* literature

วรรณะ wan-ná~ná *n.* caste (in India) [ชั้น chán]

วลี wá~lii *n.* phrase (linguistics) ✗ [วลี wá~lii]

วอก wɔ̂ɔk *n.* Year of the Monkey [ปี bpii]

วอกแวก wɔ̂ɔk-wɛ̂ɛk *vi.* waver (vacillate)

ว่องไว wôŋ-wai *adj.* swift (fast) ⚡

วอนขอ wɔɔn-kɔ̌ɔ *vt.* beg for ✍

วัคซีน wák-siin *n.* vaccine [ชนิด chá~nít]

วัง wang *n.* palace (royal residence) [หลัง lǎng]

วัชพืช wát-chá~pûut *n.* weed (unwanted plant) [ต้น dtôn]

วัฒนธรรม wát-tá~ná~tam *n.* culture (customs) [อัน an]

วัณโรค wan-ná~rôok *n.* tuberculosis [โรค rôok]

วัด wát *n.* temple (Buddhist) [วัด wát, แห่ง hèng]

วัด wát *v.* measure

วัตต์ wàt *n.* watt

วัตถุ wát-tù *n.* material (substance), object [ชิ้น chín]

วัตถุประสงค์ wát-tù-bprà~sǒng *n.* purpose (objective) [ข้อ kɔ̂ɔ, อัน an]

วัน wan *n.* day of the week, day [วัน wan]

วันก่อน wan-gɔ̀ɔn *n.* day before yesterday [วัน wan]

วันเกิด wan-gə̀ət *n.* birthday [วัน wan]

วันจันทร์ wan-jan *n.* Monday [วัน wan]

วันที่ wan-tîi *n.* date (calendar day) [วัน wan]

วันนี้ wan-níi *n.* today

วันปีใหม่ wan-bpii-mài *n.* New Year's Day [วัน wan]

วันพฤหัสบดี wan-pá~rɥ́-hàt-sà~bɔɔ-dii *n.* Thursday ! [วัน wan]

วันพ่อ wan-pɔ̂ɔ *n.* Father's Day [วัน wan]

วันพุธ wan-pút *n.* Wednesday [วัน wan]

วันแม่ wan-mɛ̂ɛ *n.* Mother's Day [วัน wan]

วันศุกร์ wan-sùk *n.* Friday [วัน wan]

วันสงกรานต์ wan-sǒng-graan *n.* New Year's Day (Thai), Songkran Day [วัน wan]

วันเสาร์ wan-sǎo *n.* Saturday [วัน wan]

วันหมดอายุ wan-mòt-aa-yú *n.* expiration date [วัน wan]

วันหยุด wan-yùt *n.* holiday, vacation [วัน wan, ช่วง chûuang (period)]

วันอังคาร wan-ang-kaan *n.* Tuesday [วัน wan]

วันอาทิตย์ wan-aa-tít *n.* Sunday [วัน wan]

ก
ข
ฃ
ค
ฅ
ฆ
ง
จ
ฉ
ช
ซ
ฌ
ญ
ฎ
ฏ
ฐ
ฑ
ฒ
ณ
ด
ต
ถ
ท
ธ
น
บ
ป
ผ
ฝ
พ
ฟ
ภ
ม
ย
ร
ฤ
ล
ฦ
ว
ศ
ษ
ส
ห
ฬ
อ
ฮ

ก
ข
ฃ
ค
ฅ
ฆ
ง
จ
ฉ
ช
ซ
ฌ
ญ
ฎ
ฏ
ฐ
ฑ
ฒ
ณ
ด
ต
ถ
ท
ธ
น
บ
ป
ผ
ฝ
พ
ฟ
ภ
ม
ย
ร
ฤ
ล
ฦ
ว
ศ
ษ
ส
ห
ฬ
อ
ฮ

วับ wáp *adv.* flashingly

วัย wai *n.* age (e.g. young age, middle age, old age) [วัย wai]

วัยกลางคน wai-glaang-kon *adj.* middle-aged

วัยโจ๋ wai-jǒo *n.* teenager ✹ [คน kon]

วัยเด็ก wai-dèk *n.* childhood

วัยรุ่น wai-rûn *n.* adolescent, teenager [คน kon]

วัยแรกรุ่น wai-rɛ̂ɛk-rûn *n.* puberty [วัย wai]

วัว wuua *n.* cow, ox [ตัว dtuua]

วัวควาย wuua-kwaai *n.* cattle [ฝูง fǔung (herd)]

วัวจามรี wuua-jaam-má~rii *n.* yak [ตัว dtuua]

วัวตัวผู้ wuua-dtuua-pûu *n.* bull (male cattle or ox) [ตัว dtuua]

วัสดุ wát-sà~dù *n.* material (e.g. for a dress) [ชิ้น chín]

วา waa *n.* Thai linear measure equivalent to two meters [วา waa]

ว่า wâa *conj.* that

ว่า wâa *v.* criticize (censure) ✹

ว่า wâa *vt.* say (state) ✹

วาง waang *vt.* lay (put down), put (position, place)

ว่าง wâang *adj.* vacant (free, empty)

วางไข่ waang-kài *v.* lay (egg)

วางใจ waang-jai *adj.* confident

วางใจ waang-jai *vt.* trust (in integrity, motives)

วางท่า waang-tâa *vi.* pose (e.g. for a picture)

ว่างเปล่า wâang-bplàao *adj.* blank (empty) ❗

วางแผน waang-pɛ̌ɛn *vi.* plot (plan, scheme), strategize

วางยา waang-yaa *vt.* drug (against one's will)

วาง_ลง waang-_-long *vt.* lay down, put something down

วางสาย waang-sǎai *v.* hang up (phone)

วางหู waang-hǔu *v.* hang up (phone)

ว่าง่าย wâa-ngâai *adj.* submissive, tame

วาด wâat *v.* draw (picture)

วาตภัย waa-dtà~pai *n.* disaster from a wind storm

วานซืน waan-sɯɯn *n.* day before yesterday [วัน wan]

วาบ wâap *adj.* flashing

ว่าย wâai *vi.* swim ✎

ว่ายน้ำ wâai-náam *vi.* swim

วารสาร waa-rá~sǎan *n.* periodical (journal) [ฉบับ chà~bàp ⚡, เล่ม lêm]

วาระ waa-rá *n.* event, period (length, session) ✂

ว่าว wâo *n.* kite [ตัว dtuua]

ว้าวุ่นใจ wáa-wûn-jai *adj.* occupied (mind)

วาสนา wâat-sà~nǎa *n.* fortune (luck)

ว้าเหว่ wáa-wèe *adj.* lonely/lonesome

วิกฤต wí-grìt *adj.* critical (emergency)

วิกฤตการณ์ wí-grìt-dtà~gaan *n.* crisis ⚡

วิกลจริต wí-gon-jà~rìt *adj.* lunatic

วิกาล wí-gaan *n.* nighttime [คืน kɯɯn]

วิเคราะห์ wí-krɔ́ *vt.* analyze

วิ่ง wîng *v.* run (jog)

วิ่งแข่ง wîng-kèng *vi.* race (running)

วิงวอน wing-wɔɔn *vt.* implore (beg, plead)

วิงเวียน wing-wiian *adj.* dizzy

วิ่งหนี wîng-nǐi *vi.* run away

วิ่งเหยาะๆ wîng-yɔ̀-yɔ̀ *vi.* jog (trot)

วิจัย wí-jai *v.* research

วิจารณ์ wí-jaan *v.* criticize

วิจารณ์ wí-jaan *vt.* review (critique)

วิชา wí-chaa *clf.* for subjects, branches of science, technology, and knowledge

วิชา wí-chaa *n.* subject (course) [วิชา wí-chaa]

วิญญาณ win-yaan *n.* soul [ดวง duuang]

วิดีโอ wii-dii-oo *adj.* video

วิตกจริต wí-dtòk-jà~rìt *adj.* paranoid ✖

วิตถาร wít-tǎan, wít-dtà~tǎan *adj.* strange

วิตามิน wí-dtaa-min *n.* vitamin [ยี่ห้อ yîi-hɔ̂ɔ

(brand), ขวด kùuat
(bottle), ชนิด chá~nít
(kind)]

วิถี wí-tǐi *n.* path (circle)

วิทยา wít-tá~yaa *n.*
knowledge ✍

วิทยากร wít-tá~yaa-gɔɔn
n. lecturer ☝ [ท่าน tân ☝,
คน kon]

วิทยานิพนธ์ wít-tá~yaa-
ní-pon *n.* thesis
(academic research)
[ฉบับ chà~bàp (whole),
เรื่อง rûuang (title)]

วิทยาลัย wít-tá~yaa-lai *n.*
college (for education),
school [แห่ง hɛ̀ng]

วิทยาศาสตร์ wít-tá~yaa-
sàat *n.* science [วิชา wí-
chaa]

วิทยุ wít-tá~yú *n.* radio
(device), wireless [เครื่อง
krûuang]

วิธี wí-tii *n.* method, way
[วิธี wí-tii]

วิธีการ wí-tii-gaan *n.*
approach (means,
method) [วิธี wí-tii]

วินัย wí-nai *n.* discipline
(self control, rule) [ข้อ
kɔ̂ɔ]

วินาที wí-naa-tii *n.* second
(time) [วินาที wí-naa-tii]

วินิจฉัย wí-nít-chǎi *vt.*
diagnose (make a
diagnosis of)

วิบัติ wí-bàt *n.* destruction
(annihilation)

วิบาก wí-bàak *n.* hardship

วิปัสสนา wí-bpàt-sà~nǎa
n. meditation

วิวัฒนาการ wí-wát-tá~
naa-gaan *n.* evolution (in
nature)

วิวาท wí-wâat *vt.* dispute
(angrily) ✍

วิวาห์ wí-waa *n.* marriage
✍

วิศวกร wít-sà~wá~gɔɔn
n. engineer [คน kon]

วิศวกรรม wít-sà~wá-gam
n. engineering

วิเศษ wí-sèet *adj.* super
(wonderful)

วิสัยทัศน์ wí-sǎi-tát *n.*
vision (foresight)

วิสามัญ wí-sǎa-man *adj.*
extraordinary
(remarkable) ✂

วิสาหกิจ wí-sǎa-hà~gìt *n.*
enterprise (venture)

วีซ่า wii-sâa *n.* visa [ตรา
dtraa]

วีรบุรุษ wii-rá-bù~rút *n.* hero (e.g. brave person) [คน kon]

วีรสตรี wii-rá~sà~dtrii *n.* heroine (e.g. brave person) [คน kon]

วุฒิ wút-tí *adj.* elderly ➤

วุฒิสภา wút-tí-sà~paa *n.* senate ! [สภา sà~paa]

วุฒิสมาชิก wút-tí-sà~maa-chík *n.* senator [คน kon]

วุ้น wún *n.* jelly

วุ่นวาย wûn-waai *adj.* confusing

วุ้นเส้น wún-sên *n.* cellophane noodles (glass noodles, bean threads) [เส้น sên (strand), ห่อ hɔ̀ɔ (pack)]

วูบ wûup *v.* disappear instantly

วูบวาบ wûup-wâap *adj.* flashing

เวทนา wêet-tá~naa *vt.* pity

เวทมนตร์ wêet-mon *n.* magic (sorcery)

เวที wee-tii *n.* stage (performance) [แห่ง hɛ̀ng]

เว้น wén *vt.* exclude, omit

เว้นแต่ wén-dtɛ̀ɛ *prep.* but, except

เว้นเสียแต่ว่า wén-sǐia-dtɛ̀ɛ-wâa *conj.* unless

เวลา wee-laa *n.* period, time (passing of time)

เวลาเที่ยง wee-laa-tîiang *n.* noontime

เวลานั้น wee-laa-nán *n.* then (that time) !

เวลาเย็น wee-laa-yen *n.* eve

เวลาว่าง wee-laa-wâang *n.* leisure (free time) [ช่วง chûuang]

เว้า wáo *adj.* concave (e.g. lens)

เวียดนาม wîiat-naam *n.* Vietnam [ประเทศ bprà~têet]

เวียน wiian *vi.* revolve ➤

แวง wɛɛng *n.* longitude [เส้น sên]

แวด wɛ̂ɛt *vt.* surround

แวดล้อม wɛ̂ɛt-lɔ́ɔm *adj.* surrounding

แว่น wên *n.* glasses (eyeglasses) ✦ [อัน an]

แว่นกันแดด wên-gan-dɛ̀ɛt *n.* sunglasses [อัน an]

แว่นขยาย wên-kà~yǎai *n.*

magnifying glass [อัน an]

แว่นตา wên-dtaa *n.* eyeglasses [อัน an]

แวะมา wé-maa *v.* come by (drop by) ●

แวะหา wé-hǎa *vt.* visit (drop by to see)

โว woo *adj.* boastful

โวหาร woo-hǎan *n.* idiom [สำนวน sǎm-nuuan]

ไว wai *adj.* fast, rapid

ไว้ wái *v.* preserve (keep)

ไว้ใจ wái-jai *vt.* depend on, trust (in integrity, motives)

ไว้ทุกข์ wái-túk *v.* mourn

ไวน์ waai *n.* wine [แก้ว gɛ̂ɛo (glass), ขวด kùuat (bottle)]

ไวยากรณ์ wai-yaa-gɔɔn *n.* grammar

ไวรัส wai-rát *n.* virus [เชื้อ chúua]

ไว้วางใจ_เรื่อง_ wái-waang-jai-_-rûuang-_ *vt.* entrust (someone with something)

ศ

ศ rɔ́ɔ *let.* ศ. ศาลา rɔ́ɔ-sǎa-laa, a consonant of the

Thai alphabet (high consonant) [ตัว dtuua]

ศก sòk *n.* era (age, period) ☞, year ☞ [ศก sòk]

ศตวรรษ sàt~dtà~wát *n.* century [ศตวรรษ sàt~dtà~wát]

ศพ sòp *n.* corpse (dead body) [ศพ sòp]

ศร rɔ́ɔn *n.* arrow (weapon) ☞

ศรัทธา sàt-taa *n.* faith (belief in religion), trust (in integrity, motives)

ศรี sǐi *n.* dignity (glory, fame, fortune)

ศรีสะเกษ sǐi-sà~gèet *n.* Si Sa Ket province [จังหวัด jang-wàt]

ศอก sɔ̀ɔk *n.* elbow [ข้อ kɔ̂ɔ, ข้าง kâang]

ศักดินา sàk-dì~naa *n.* hierarchy (by ability or status) ⓘ

ศักดิ์สิทธิ์ sàk-sìt *adj.* divine, holy, sacred

ศักยภาพ sàk-gà~yá~pâap *n.* potential

ศักราช sàk-gà~ràat *n.* era (age, period) ⓘ [ศักราช sàk-gà~ràat]

ศัตรู sàt-dtruu *n.* enemy, opponent [คน kon (person), พวก pûuak (group)]

ศัพท์ sàp *n.* vocabulary [คำ kam]

ศัลยกรรม săn-yá~gam *n.* operation (surgery) [ครั้ง kráng]

ศัลยกรรมตกแต่ง săn-yá~gam-dtòk-dtɛ̀ng *n.* plastic surgery

ศัลยแพทย์ săn-yá~pɛ̂ɛt *n.* surgeon [คน kon]

ศาล săan *n.* court (of law), court house [ศาล săan]

ศาลเจ้า săan-jâao *n.* shrine (sacred place) [แห่ง hɛ̀ng]

ศาลฎีกา săan-dii-gaa *n.* supreme court [ศาล săan]

ศาลา săa-laa *n.* pavilion (rest house) [หลัง lăng]

ศาลากลาง săa-laa-glaang *n.* city hall [หลัง lăng (building), แห่ง hɛ̀ng (location)]

ศาสดา sàat-sà~daa *n.* religious founder [ท่าน tân, องค์ ong (king)]

ศาสตราจารย์ sàat-dtraa-jaan *n.* professor (college, university) [คน kon, ท่าน tân !]

ศาสนา sàat-sà~năa *n.* religion [ศาสนา sàat-sà~năa]

ศาสนาคริสต์ sàat-sà~năa-krít *n.* Christianity [ศาสนา sàat-sà~năa]

ศาสนาพุทธ sàat-sà~năa-pút *n.* Buddhism [ศาสนา sàat-sà~năa]

ศิลปศาสตร์ sĭn-lá~bpà~sàat *n.* liberal arts [วิชา wí-chaa]

ศิลปศาสตร์มหาบัณฑิต sĭn-lá~bpà~sàat-má~hăa-ban-dìt *n.* M.A. (Master of Arts), Master of Arts [ปริญญา bpà~rin-yaa (degree), ใบ bai (certificate)]

ศิลปะ sĭn-lá~bpà *n.* art

ศิลปิน sĭn-lá~bpin *n.* artist [คน kon]

ศิลา sì-laa *n.* stone ☞ [ก้อน gɔ̂ɔn]

ศิษย์ sìt *n.* pupil !, student ☞ [คน kon]

ศิษย์เก่า sìt-gào *n.* alumni [คน kon]

ก
ข
ฃ
ค
ฅ
ฆ
ง
จ
ฉ
ช
ซ
ฌ
ญ
ฎ
ฏ
ฐ
ฑ
ฒ
ณ
ด
ต
ถ
ท
ธ
น
บ
ป
ผ
ฝ
พ
ฟ
ภ
ม
ย
ร
ฤ
ล
ฦ
ว
ศ
ษ
ส
ห
ฬ
อ
ฮ

ศีรษะ sǐi-sà *n.* head (body part) ‼ [อัน an]

ศีล sǐin *n.* precept (moral precepts) [ข้อ kɔ̂ɔ]

ศีลธรรม sǐin-lá~tam, sǐin-tam *n.* moral, morality [ข้อ kɔ̂ɔ]

ศึก sùk *n.* war ☙

ศึกษา sùk-sǎa *v.* learn ‼, study ‼

ศุกร์ sùk *n.* Venus (planet) [ดวง duuang]

ศุกร์ sùk *n.* Friday ✹ [วัน wan]

ศุลกากร sǔn-lá~gaa-gɔɔn *n.* customs [แผนก pà~nɛ̀ɛk]

ศูนย์ sǔun *numb.* zero

ศูนย์กลาง sǔun-glaang *n.* center, hub [ศูนย์ sǔun]

ศูนย์การค้า sǔun-gaan-káa *n.* plaza (shopping center) [แห่ง hɛ̀ng]

เศรษฐกิจ sèet-tà~gìt *n.* economy

เศรษฐศาสตร์ sèet-tà~sàat *n.* economics [วิชา wí-chaa]

เศรษฐี sèet-tǐi *n.* millionaire [คน kon]

เศร้า sâo *adj.* sad, sorrowful

เศษ sèet *n.* bit (small piece), crumb (remnant), residue (remains, dregs), scrap (small piece) [ชิ้น chín]

เศษ sèet *n.* numerator of a fraction [จำนวน jam-nuuan]

เศษผ้า sèet-pâa *n.* rag (scrap of cloth) [ชิ้น chín, ผืน pʉ̌ʉn]

เศษไม้ sèet-máai *n.* sliver (wood) [ชิ้น chín]

เศษส่วน sèet-sùuan *n.* fraction (numerical) [จำนวน jam-nuuan]

โศกนาฏกรรม sòok-gà~nâat-dtà~gam *n.* tragedy (sad story) [เรื่อง rʉ̂ʉang]

ษ

ษ rʉɯ *let.* ษ. ฤษี rʉɯ-sǐi, a consonant of the Thai alphabet (high consonant) [ตัว dtuua]

ษมา sà~maa *v.* beg (for pardon) ☙

ษมาโทษ sà~maa-tôot *v.*

ask for pardon for sin or wrong-doings

ส

ส รว้ว *let.* ส. เสือ รว้ว-sǔua, a consonant of the Thai alphabet (high consonant) [ตัว dtuua]

ส.ว. รว้ว-wɔɔ *n.* senator ✿ [คน kon]

สกปรก sòk-gà~bpròk, sòk-gà~bpòk *adj.* stained (dirty)

สกรู sà~gruu *n.* screw (metal) [ตัว dtuua]

สกัด sà~gàt *vt.* extract (distill)

สกี sà~gii *n.* ski [คู่ kûu (pair)]

ส่ง sòng *vt.* ship (send), turn in (e.g. homework, results)

สงกรานต์ sǒng-graan *n.* Thai New Year, April 13th [งาน ngaan]

ส่ง_กลับ sòng-_-glàp *vt.* return (send back)

สงขลา sǒng-klǎa *n.* Songkhla province [จังหวัด jang-wàt]

สงคราม sǒng-kraam *n.* fight (battle), war

สงเคราะห์ sǒng-krɔ́ *v.*

help !

ส่งจดหมาย sòng-jòt-mǎai *vi.* post (mail)

ส่ง_ต่อ sòng-_-dtɔ̀ɔ *vt.* forward (e.g. letter, e-mail)

สงบ sà~ngòp *adj.* calm (quiet), serene (tranquil)

สงบสุข sà~ngòp-sùk *adj.* peaceful

สงวน sà~ngǔuan *vt.* reserve (conserve, save)

สงสัย sǒng-sǎi *vi.* be uncertain

สงสัย sǒng-sǎi *vt.* be uncertain about, doubt (suspect: object is expected outcome), suspect

สงสาร sǒng-sǎan *vt.* pity

ส่งเสริม sòng-sɤ̌ɤm *vt.* boost (encourage, promote)

ส่ง_ออก sòng-_-ɔ̀ɔk *vt.* export

สง่า sà~ngàa *adj.* dignified (graceful)

สง่างาม sà~ngàa-ngaam *adj.* elegant (graceful)

สด sòt *adj.* fresh (e.g. fruit, idea), live (fresh, happening now)

สดชื่น sòt-chûun *adj.*

refreshed (e.g. from drink)

สดใส sòt-săi *adj.* bright (color)

สดุด sà~dùt *vi.* trip (stumble or fall)

สตรี sà~dtrii *n.* woman ! [คน kon]

สตางค์ sà~dtaang *n.* Thai coin equal to one hundredth of a baht [สตางค์ sà~dtaang, เหรียญ rǐian]

สติ sà~dtì *n.* conscience (awareness)

สติปัญญา sà~dtì-bpan-yaa *n.* intelligence (wisdom)

สติไม่ดี sà~dtì-mâi-dii *adj.* insane (afflicted)

สตู sà~dtuu *n.* stew

สตูล sà~dtuun *n.* Satun province [จังหวัด jang-wàt]

สเต็กเนื้อ sà~dtéek-núua *n.* beefsteak [ชิ้น chín]

สไตรค์ sà~dtrái *n.* strike (work protest) ✿

สไตล์ sà~dtaai *n.* style [สไตล์ sà~dtaai]

สถาน sà~tăan *n.* place

(site, spot)

สถานกงสุล sà~tăan-gong-sŭn *n.* consulate [แห่ง hèng]

สถานการณ์ sà~tăa-ná-gaan *n.* situation (circumstance) [สถานการณ์ sà~tăa-ná-gaan]

สถานที่ sà~tăan-tîi *n.* place (site, spot) [แห่ง hèng]

สถานที่เกิด sà~tăan-tîi-gèət *n.* birth place ! [ที่ tîi]

สถานทูต sà~tăan-tûut *n.* embassy [แห่ง hèng]

สถานะ sà~tăa-ná *n.* status (rank, position) [สถานะ sà~tăa-ná]

สถานี sà~tăa-nii *n.* station (e.g. TV, radio, train) [สถานี sà~tăa-nii]

สถานีตำรวจ sà~tăa-nii-dtam-rùuat *n.* police station [แห่ง hèng]

สถานีรถไฟ sà~tăa-nii-rót-fai *n.* railway station [แห่ง hèng]

สถานีรถเมล์ sà~tăa-nii-rót-mee *n.* bus station

[สถานี sà~tǎa-nii]

สถาบัน sà~tǎa-ban *n.* institute, institution [สถาบัน sà~tǎa-ban]

สถาปนิก sà~tǎa-bpà~ník *n.* architect (building) [คน kon]

สถาปัตยกรรม sà~tǎa-bpàt-dtà~yá~gam *n.* architecture [วิชา wí-chaa]

สถิติ sà~tì-dtì *n.* record (something recorded), statistics

สถูป sà~tùup *n.* stupa [องค์ ong]

สน sǒn *n.* pine tree [ต้น dtôn]

ส้น sôn *n.* heel ✿ [ข้าง kâang]

สนใจ sǒn-jai *vt.* care about (be interested in)

สนทนา sǒn-tá~naa *vi.* talk (chat, converse) ❗

สนเทศ sǒn-têet *n.* news

ส้นเท้า sôn-táao *n.* heel [ข้าง kâang]

สนธยา sǒn-tá~yaa *n.* twilight ☙

สนธิ sǒn-tí *n.* intercourse (joint)

สนธิสัญญา sǒn-tí-sǎn-yaa *n.* treaty (e.g. between nations) [ฉบับ chà~bàp]

สนม sà~nǒm *n.* royal concubine [คน kon]

ส้นสูง sôn-sǔung *n.* high heels [ข้าง kâang (one), คู่ kûu (pair)]

สนอง sà~nǒwng *vi.* respond ❗

สนั่น sà~nàn *adj.* very loud

สนับแข้ง sà~nàp-kêng *n.* pad (shin guard) [ข้าง kâang (one), คู่ kûu (pair)]

สนับสนุน sà~nàp-sà~nǔn *vt.* back (support)

สนาม sà~nǎam *n.* field (grounds) [แห่ง hèng]

สนามกีฬา sà~nǎam-gii-laa *n.* arena, stadium (sports) [แห่ง hèng]

สนามแข่ง sà~nǎam-kèng *n.* ring (for fighting or racing) [แห่ง hèng]

สนามเด็กเล่น sà~nǎam-dèk-lên *n.* playground [แห่ง hèng]

สนามบิน sà~nǎam-bin *n.* airport [แห่ง hèng]

สนามรบ sà~nǎam-róp *n.* battlefield [แห่ง hèng]

สนามหญ้า sà~nǎam-yâa *n.* turf (natural) [สนาม

ก ข ฃ ค ฅ ฆ ง จ ฉ ช ซ ฌ ญ ฎ ฏ ฐ ฑ ฒ ณ ด ต ถ ท ธ น บ ป ผ ฝ พ ฟ ภ ม ย ร ฤ ล ฦ ว ศ ษ **ส** ห ฬ อ ฮ

ก ข ค ฅ ฆ ง จ ฉ ช ซ ฌ ญ ฎ ฏ ฐ ฑ ฒ ณ ด ต ถ ท ธ น บ ป ผ ฝ พ ฟ ภ ม ย ร ฤ ล ฦ ว ศ ษ **ส** ห ฬ อ ฮ

sà~năam, แห่ง hèng]

สนิท sà~nìt *adj.* close (e.g. friend), sound (e.g. sleep)

สนิท sà~nìt *adv.* tightly

สนิทสนม sà~nìt-sà~nŏm *adj.* familiar (intimate)

สนิม sà~nĭm *n.* rust

สนุก sà~nùk *adj.* amusing (entertaining), joyful (having fun)

สนุกสนาน sà~nùk-sà~năan *adj.* joy (amused, having fun)

สบง sà~bong *n.* piece of cloth worn by Buddhist monks [ผืน pŭun]

สบตา sòp-dtaa *v.* meet the eyes of

สบประมาท sòp-bprà~màat *vt.* insult

สบาย sà~baai *adj.* comfortable, pleasant (e.g. weather)

สบายๆ sà~baai-sà~baai *adj.* chilled out, easygoing (relaxed)

สบายใจ sà~baai-jai *adj.* contented (be joyous)

สบายดี sà~baai-dii *adj.* fine (feeling well)

สบู่ sà~bùu *n.* soap [ก้อน gôon]

สไบ sà~bai *n.* shawl, wrap [ผืน pŭun]

สปริง sà~bpring *n.* spring (elastic device) [ตัว dtuua]

สปา sà-bpaa *n.* spa [แห่ง hèng]

สเปน sà~bpeen *n.* Spain [ประเทศ bprà~têet]

สเปรย์ sà~bpree *n.* spray (substance sprayed)

สแปม sà~bpɛɛm *n.* spam [ครั้ง kráng, อัน an]

สภา sà~paa *n.* council (board) [แห่ง hèng, สภา sà~paa]

สภานิติบัญญัติ sà~paa-ní-dtì-ban-yàt *n.* legislature [สภา sà~paa]

สภาผู้แทนราษฎร sà~paa-pûu-tɛɛn-râat-sà~dɔɔn *n.* House of Representatives [แห่ง hèng]

สภาพ sà~pâap *n.* state (condition) [สภาพ sà~pâap]

สภาวะ sà~paa-wá *n.* status (circumstance, condition) [สภาวะ sà~paa-wá, แห่ง hèng]

สภาสูง sà~paa-sǔung *n.* senate [สภา sà~paa]

สม sǒm *adj.* suitable, well matched

ส้ม sôm *n.* orange [ต้น dtôn (tree), ลูก lûuk (fruit)]

สมการ sà~má~gaan *n.* equation (in math) [สมการ sà~má~gaan]

สมควร sǒm-kuuan *adj.* appropriate (proper)

สมควรได้รับ sǒm-kuuan-dâi-ráp *vt.* deserve, earn

สมจริง sǒm-jing *adj.* truthful, corresponding with reality

สมณะ sà~má~ná *n.* monk [รูป rûup, คณะ ká~ná (group), หมู่ mùu (group)]

สมดุล sǒm-dun *adj.* balanced

สมดุล sǒm-dun *n.* balance (equilibrium)

สมดุลยภาพ sǒm-dun-lá~yá~pâap *n.* equilibrium

สมเด็จ sǒm-dèt *n.* His or Her Majesty, title of high rank of a Buddhist monk [ท่าน tân]

ส้มตำ sôm-dtam *n.* Thai papaya salad [จาน jaan]

สมน้ำหน้า sǒm-nám-nâa *vi.* serve somebody right

สมบัติ sǒm-bàt *n.* possession (property, assets) [ชิ้น chín]

สมบูรณ์ sǒm-buun *adj.* complete (having all parts), fat, perfect

สมมาตร sǒm-mâat *n.* symmetry

สมมุติ sǒm-mút *vt.* suppose (assume)

สมมุติฐาน sǒm-mút-dtì~tǎan *n.* hypothesis [ข้อ kôo]

สมรสกับ sǒm-rót-gàp *vt.* wed ⚡

สมอง sà~mǒong *n.* brain [ก้อน gôon]

สมอเรือ sà~mɔ̌o-ruua *n.* anchor [ตัว dtuua]

ส้มโอ sôm-oo *n.* pomelo [ลูก lûuk]

สมัคร sà~màk *vt.* apply for (e.g. a job)

สมัครใจ sà~màk-jai *vi.* volunteer

สมัย sà~mǎi *n.* era (age, period) [สมัย sà~mǎi]

สมัยก่อน sà~mǎi-gɔ̀ɔn *n.* past (ancient, former times)

สมาคม sà~maa-kom *n.* association (society) [แห่ง hɛ̀ng]

สมาชิก sà~maa-chík *n.* member [ท่าน tân ⚡, คน kon]

สมาชิกสภาผู้แทนราษฎร sà~maa-chík-sà~paa-pûu-tɛɛn-râat-sà~dɔɔn *n.* member of parliament [คน kon]

สมาธิ sà~maa-tí *n.* concentration (mental focus)

สมาพันธ์ sà~maa-pan *n.* confederation [กลุ่ม glùm]

สม่ำเสมอ sà~màm-sà~mɤ̌ɤ *adj.* steady (constant), uniform (consistent, constant)

สมุด sà~mùt *n.* notebook [เล่ม lêm]

สมุดฉีก sà~mùt-chìik *n.* pad (note paper) [เล่ม lêm]

สมุดโทรศัพท์ sà~mùt-too-rá~sàp *n.* phone book [เล่ม lêm]

สมุดบันทึก sà~mùt-ban-tʉ́k *n.* diary [เล่ม lêm]

สมุดแผนที่ sà~mùt-pʉ̌ɛn-tîi *n.* atlas (map book) [เล่ม lêm]

สมุทรปราการ sà~mùt-bpraa-gaan *n.* Samut Prakan province [จังหวัด jang-wàt]

สมุทรสงคราม sà~mùt-sǒng-kraam *n.* Samut Songkhram province [จังหวัด jang-wàt]

สมุทรสาคร sà~mùt-sǎa-kɔɔn *n.* Samut Sakhon province [จังหวัด jang-wàt]

สมุทัย sà~mù-tai *n.* cause ⚡

สมุนไพร sà~mǔn-prai *n.* herb, medicinal herbs

สยองขวัญ sà~yɔ̌ɔng-kwǎn *adj.* horrible (scary) ⚡

สยาม sà~yǎam *n.* Siam [ประเทศ bprà~têet]

สรงน้ำ sǒng-náam *vi.* bathe

สรรพนาม sàp-pá~naam *n.* pronoun [คำ kam]

สรวล sǔan *v.* laugh

สร้อย sôi *n.* necklace [เส้น sên]

สร้อยคอ sôi-kɔɔ *n.* necklace [เส้น sên]

สระ sà~rà *n.* vowel [ตัว dtuua, เสียง sĭiang (sound)]

สระ sà *n.* pond (small body of water) ✻ [แห่ง hèng, สระ sà]

สระ sà *vi.* wash hair

สระน้ำ sà~náam *n.* pond (small body of water), pool [แห่ง hèng, สระ sà]

สระบุรี sà~rà-bù~rii *n.* Saraburi province [จังหวัด jang-wàt]

สระว่ายน้ำ sà-wâai-náam *n.* swimming pool [แห่ง hèng, สระ sà]

สร้าง sâang *vt.* construct, create (build)

สร้างไข่ sâang-kài *v.* ovulate

สร่างเมา sàang-mao *adj.* sober (from alcohol)

สร้างสรรค์ sâang-săn *adj.* creative

สรีรวิทยา sà~rii-rá-wít-tá~yaa *n.* physiology ✗ [วิชา wí-chaa]

สรีระ sà~rii-rá *n.* body ✗

สรุป sà~rùp *v.* conclude (summarize)

สลบ sà~lòp *vi.* black out (pass out)

สละ sà~là *vt.* relinquish (renounce)

สละสิทธิ์ sà~là-sìt *vi.* waive one's right

สลัก sà~làk *n.* bolt [ตัว dtuua, อัน an]

สลัก sà~làk *v.* engrave

สลักประตู sà~làk-bprà~dtuu *n.* latch [อัน an]

สลักหลัง sà~làk-lăng *vt.* endorse (sign name on back of)

สลัด sà~làt *n.* salad [จาน jaan (plate)]

สลัดอากาศ sà~làt-aa-gàat *n.* hijacker (airplane) [คน kon]

สลับกัน sà~làp-gan *vi.* alternate

สลัม sà~lăm *n.* slum ✻ [แห่ง hèng]

สลาก sà~làak *n.* tag (label) [ใบ bai, แผ่น pèn]

สลากกินแบ่ง sà~làak-gin-bèng *n.* lottery [ใบ bai]

ก ข ฃ ค ฅ ฆ ง จ ฉ ช ซ ฌ ญ ฎ ฏ ฐ ฑ ฒ ณ ด ต ถ ท ธ น บ ป ผ ฝ พ ฟ ภ ม ย ร ล ฦ ว ศ ษ ส ห ฬ อ ฮ

สลึง sà~lĕng *n.* small Thai coin equal to one fourth of a baht [เหรียญ rĭian]

สวด sùuat *v.* chant (pray)

สวดมนต์ sùuat-mon *vi.* pray (e.g. to God)

สวน sŭuan *n.* garden [สวน sŭuan]

สวน sŭuan *vi.* pass in opposite directions

ส่วน sùuan *n.* part, section [ส่วน sùuan]

ส่วนกลาง sùuan-glaang *n.* center, core [ส่วน sùuan]

ส่วนเกิน sùuan-gəən *n.* excess (surplus)

ส่วนโค้ง sùuan-kóong *n.* arc (curve) [ส่วน sùuan]

ส่วนได้ส่วนเสีย sùuan-dâai-sùuan-sĭia *n.* interest (benefit)

ส่วนตัว sùuan-dtuua *adj.* personal, private (individual)

ส่วนน้อย sùuan-nว́ววi *n.* minority (lesser part) [ส่วน sùuan]

ส่วนใน sùuan-nai *n.* inside [แห่ง hèng, ที่ tîi]

ส่วนบน sùuan-bon *n.* top

(uppermost part) [ส่วน sùuan]

ส่วนบุคคล sùuan-bùk-kon *adj.* private (individual)

ส่วนแบ่ง sùuan-bèng *n.* lot (quota), portion (share) [จำนวน jam-nuuan]

ส่วนประกอบ sùuan-bprà~gว̀วp *n.* component [ส่วน sùuan, ชิ้น chín]

ส่วนผสม sùuan-pà~sŏm *n.* ingredient [ชนิด chá~nít ⚡, อย่าง yàang]

ส่วนมาก sùuan-mâak *adv.* mostly (mainly)

ส่วนรวม sùuan-ruuam *n.* people at large, public

ส่วนราชการ sùuan-râat-chá~gaan *n.* government agency

ส่วนลด sùuan-lót *n.* discount [จำนวน jam-nuuan (amount)]

สวนสนุก sŭuan-sà~nùk *n.* amusement park [แห่ง hèng]

สวนสัตว์ sŭuan-sàt *n.* zoo [แห่ง hèng]

สวนสาธารณะ sŭuan-sǎa-

taa-rá~ná *n.* park
(public) [แห่ง hèng]

ส่วนสูง sùuan-sǔung *n.*
height (person)

ส่วนใหญ่ sùuan-yài *n.*
majority

ส่วนไหน sùuan-nǎi *adj.*
which

สวม sǔuam *vt.* put on
(wear) ♪

ส้วม sûuam *n.* toilet
(room, fixture) ♪, water
closet ♪ [ที่ tîi]

สวย sǔuai *adj.* attractive
(beautiful)

ส่วย sùai *n.* tribute (to
another country)

สวยงาม sǔuai-ngaam *adj.*
beautiful ♪

สวรรค์ sà~wǎn *n.* heaven
[แห่ง hèng]

สวัสดี sà~wàt-dii *interj.*
bye-bye!/bye!, good day!

สว่าง sà~wàang *adj.*
bright (light intensity)

สว่าน sà~wàan *n.* drill
(tool) [ตัว dtuua]

สวีเดน sà~wii-deen *n.*
Sweden [ประเทศ bprà~
têet]

สหกรณ์ sà~hà~gɔɔn *n.*

co-op, cooperative [แห่ง
hèng]

สหประชาชาติ sà~hà~
bprà~chaa-châat *n.*
United Nations [องค์การ
ong-gaan]

สหพันธ์ sà~hà-pan *n.*
league (alliance) [แห่ง
hèng]

สหพันธรัฐ sà~hà-pan-
tá~rát *n.* federation [กลุ่ม
glùm]

สหภาพ sà~hà-pâap *n.*
union (e.g. labor union)
[แห่ง hèng]

สหรัฐอเมริกา sà~hà-rát-
à~mee-rí~gaa *n.* United
States of America ♪
[ประเทศ bprà~têet]

สหศึกษา sà~hà-sùk-sǎa
adj. co-ed

สหาย sà~hǎai *n.* pal ♪
[คน kon]

สอง sɔ̌ɔng *numb.* two

ส่อง sɔ̀ng *v.* look in a
mirror

สองครั้ง sɔ̌ɔng-kráng *adv.*
twice (on two occasions)

สองเท่า sɔ̌ɔng-tâo *adj.*
double (two times more)

ส่องนก sɔ̀ng-nók *vi.*
birdwatch

ก
ข
ฃ
ค
ฅ
ฆ
ง
จ
ฉ
ช
ซ
ฌ
ญ
ฎ
ฏ
ฐ
ฑ
ฒ
ณ
ด
ต
ถ
ท
ธ
น
บ
ป
ผ
ฝ
พ
ฟ
ภ
ม
ย
ร
ฤ
ล
ฦ
ว
ศ
ษ
ส
ห
ฬ
อ
ฮ

สองร้อย sɔ̌ɔng-rɔ́ɔi *numb.* two hundred

ส่องแสง sɔ̀ng-sɛ̌ɛng *vi.* shine (emit light)

ส่องแสงแวววาว sɔ̀ng-sɛ̌ɛng-wɛɛɛ-waao *vi.* sparkle

สอด sɔ̀ɔt *vt.* insert (put into)

สอดคล้องกัน sɔ̀ɔt-klɔ́ɔng-gan *vi.* correspond (relate)

สอดแนม sɔ̀ɔt-nɛɛm *vi.* snoop (spy)

สอดรู้สอดเห็น sɔ̀ɔt-rúu-sɔ̀ɔt-hěn *adj.* nosy

สอน sɔ̌ɔn *vt.* instruct (teach)

สอนพิเศษ sɔ̌ɔn-pí-sèet *v.* tutor

สอบ sɔ̀ɔp *v.* test (e.g. in school)

สอบตก sɔ̀ɔp-dtòk *vi.* fail (test), flunk (test)

สอบถาม sɔ̀ɔp-tǎam *vi.* inquire

สอบปากคำ sɔ̀ɔp-bpàak-kam *v.* interrogate (investigate)

สอบสวน sɔ̀ɔp-sǔuan *v.* investigate (interrogate)

ส้อม sɔ̂m *n.* fork (utensil)

[คัน kan]

สะกด sà~gòt *v.* spell

สะกดจิต sà~gòt-jìt *vt.* hypnotize

สะกดรอย sà~gòt-rɔɔi *v.* follow tracks

สะกิด sà~gìt *v.* nudge gently

สะใจ sà-jai *adj.* satisfied (fulfilled)

สะดวก sà~dùuak *adj.* convenient

สะดวกสบาย sà~dùuak-sà~baai *adj.* comfortable !

สะดือ sà~dɯɯ *n.* belly button, navel (body)

สะดุ้ง sà~dûng *adj.* startled

สะดุด sà~dùt *vi.* stumble (trip)

สะดุดตา sà~dùt-dtaa *adj.* striking (noticeable)

สะเด็ด sà~dèt *adj.* dried

สะเด็ดน้ำ sà~dèt-náam *vi.* strain (remove water)

สะท้อน sà~tɔ́ɔn *v.* echo (sound), reflect (e.g. light, shadow)

สะท้อนใจ sà~tɔ́ɔn-jai *adj.* disheartened

สะเทือนใจ sà~tɨɨan-jai *adj.* touching (strong emotion)

สะบั้น sà~bân *adj.* broken off

สะบ้าเข่า sà~bâa-kào *n.* kneecap [ข้าง kâang]

สะพาน sà~paan *n.* bridge (for crossing) [แห่ง hὲng]

สะพานลอย sà~paan-lɔɔi *n.* overpass/flyover [แห่ง hὲng]

สะพาย sà~paai *vt.* carry (on the shoulder)

สะเพร่า sà~prâo *adj.* negligent, sloppy (careless)

สะโพก sà~pôok *n.* hip [ข้าง kâang]

สะใภ้ sà~pái *n.* in-law (female) [คน kon]

สะระแหน่ sà~rá~nὲ *n.* mint (plant) [ต้น dtôn (plant), ใบ bai (leaf)]

สะสม sà~sŏm *vt.* accumulate, collect

สะสาง sà~sǎang *vt.* solve (e.g. problem)

สะอาด sà~àat *adj.* clean, pure

สะอึก sà~ɨk *vi.* hiccup

สะอื้น sà~ɨ̂ɨn *vi.* sob

สัก sàk *n.* teak (tree) [ต้น dtôn]

สักที่นึ่ง sàk-tîi-nὺng *adv.* somewhere (as object)

สักวัน sàk-wan *adv.* someday (sooner or later)

สักหลาด sàk-gà~làat *n.* flannel [ผืน pɨ̌ɨn]

สั่ง sàng *v.* command, order

สั่ง sàng *vt.* instruct (order)

สังกะสี săng-gà~sǐi *n.* zinc

สังกะสี săng-gà~sǐi *n.* galvanized iron [แผ่น pèn]

สังกัด săng-gàt *vt.* belong to (government entity)

สั่งการ sàng-gaan *vi.* dictate (give orders)

สังเกต săng-gèet *v.* note, observe (notice)

สังข์ săng *n.* conch, shell [ขอน kɔ̌ɔn]

สังขยา săng-kà~yǎa *n.* Thai custard pudding

สังคม săng-kom *adj.* social

สังคม săng-kom *n.* society [สังคม săng-kom]

สังคมวิทยา săng-kom-wít-tá~yaa *n.* sociology [วิชา wí-chaa]

สังคมศาสตร์ săng-kom-má~sàat *n.* social science [วิชา wí-chaa]

สังคมสงเคราะห์ săng-kom-sŏng-krɔ́ *n.* welfare (social)

สังเคราะห์ săng-krɔ́ *adj.* artificial (synthetic)

สังฆทาน săng-ká~taan *n.* alms (for monks) [ชุด chút]

สังฆนายก săng-ká~naa-yók *n.* chief of all the Buddhists [รูป rûup]

สังฆราช săng-ká~râat *n.* pontiff (pope) [องค์ ong]

สังฆะ săng-ká *n.* monk [รูป rûup]

สั่งซื้อ sàng-sɯ́ɯ *v.* order a purchase

สังวร săng-wɔɔn *n.* caution ✺, constraint ✺

สังสรรค์ săng-sǎn *v.* have an informal conversation

สั่งสอน sàng-sɔ̌ɔn *v.* educate (teach)

สังหรณ์ săng-hɔ̌ɔn *v.* have a bad feeling

สังหรณ์ใจ săng-hɔ̌ɔn-jai *v.* have a premonition

สังหาร săng-hǎan *v.* slay (murder) ✺

สังหาริมทรัพย์ săng-hǎa-rim-má~sáp *n.* movable property

สัจจะ sàt-jà *n.* truthfulness, oath

สัญจร săn-jɔɔn *n.* path (passage, course) [สาย sǎai, เส้น sên, ทาง taang]

สัญชาตญาณ săn-châat-dtà~yaan *n.* instinct

สัญชาติ săn-châat *n.* citizenship [สัญชาติ săn-châat]

สัญญา săn-yaa *n.* agreement [ข้อ kɔ̂ɔ (clause), ฉบับ chà~bàp (whole)]

สัญญา săn-yaa *vi.* promise (to someone)

สัญญาณ săn-yaan *n.* signal [สัญญาณ săn-yaan]

สัญญาณเลี้ยว săn-yaan-líiao *n.* turn signal [สัญญาณ săn-yaan]

สัญลักษณ์ săn-yá~lák *n.* sign, symbol [อัน an]

สัณฐาน săn-tǎan *n.* shape (figure, form) ❗

สัดส่วน sàt-sùuan *n.* proportion

สัตย์ sàt *n.* honesty, oath ⚘

สัตว์ sàt *n.* animal, creature [ตัว dtuua, ชนิด chá~nít (kind)]

สัตว์ครึ่งบกครึ่งน้ำ sàt-krûng-bòk-krûng-náam *n.* amphibian (animal) [ตัว dtuua, ชนิด chá~nít (kind)]

สัตว์ป่า sàt-bpàa *n.* wildlife [ตัว dtuua, ชนิด chá~nít (kind)]

สัตว์ปีก sàt-bpìik *n.* poultry, winged animal [ตัว dtuua, ชนิด chá~nít (kind)]

สัตวแพทย์ sàt-dtà~wà~pɛ̂ɛt *n.* veterinarian [คน kon]

สัตว์เลี้ยง sàt-líiang *n.* pet (domestic animal) [ตัว dtuua, ชนิด chá~nít (kind)]

สัตว์เลี้ยงลูกด้วยนม sàt-líiang-lûuk-dûuai-nom *n.* mammal [ตัว dtuua, ชนิด chá~nít (kind)]

สัตว์เลื้อยคลาน sàt-

lúuai-klaan *n.* reptile [ตัว dtuua, ชนิด chá~nít (kind)]

สัทศาสตร์ sàt-tá~sàat *n.* phonetics ✿ [วิชา wí-chaa]

สัน sǎn *n.* ridge

สั่น sàn *vi.* quake, shake (vibrate, quiver), shiver

สั้น sân *adj.* brief, short (length)

สันดอนแม่น้ำ sǎn-dɔɔn-mɛ̂ɛ-náam *n.* delta (river) ⚘ [แห่ง hɛ̀ng]

สันดาน sǎn-daan *n.* in-born traits

สันโดษ sǎn-dòot *adj.* secluded (isolated)

สันตะปาปา sǎn-dtà~bpaa-bpaa *n.* pontiff (pope), Pope [องค์ ong]

สันติภาพ sǎn-dtì-pâap *n.* peace ❗

สันทัด sǎn-tát *adj.* proficient (skillful)

สันนิษฐาน sǎn-nít-tǎan *v.* assume, presume

สันสกฤต sǎn-sà~grìt *n.* Sanskrit [ภาษา paa-sǎa]

สั่นสะเทือน sàn-sà~tuuan *vi.* vibrate ❗

สันหนังสือ sǎn-nǎng~sǔu *n.* spine (of book)

สับ sàp *vt.* mince

สับปะรด sàp-bpà~rót *n.* pineapple [ลูก lûuk]

สับเปลี่ยน sàp-bpliian *vi.* rotate (take turns)

สับไพ่ sàp-pâi *vi.* shuffle cards

สับสน sàp-sǒn *adj.* confused, confusing

สับหลีก sàp-lìik *vt.* stagger (distribute, alternate)

สัปดน sàp-bpà~don *adj.* obscene (lewd)

สัปดาห์ sàp-daa *n.* week [สัปดาห์ sàp-daa]

สัปหงก sàp-bpà~ngòk *vi.* doze (nod off)

สัปเหร่อ sàp-bpà~ràə *n.* undertaker (mortician) [คน kon]

สัพเพเหระ sàp-pee-hěe-rá *adj.* insignificant (too small to be important)

สัมผัส sǎm-pàt *vt.* contact (touch), feel (examine by touch) ⚠

สัมผัสกัน sǎm-pàt-gan *vi.* rhyme, touch

สัมพันธ์รัก sǎm-pan-rák *n.* relationship (romantic) [ครั้ง kráng]

สัมภาระ sǎm-paa-rá *n.* luggage ⚠ [ชิ้น chín]

สัมภาษณ์ sǎm-pâat *v.* interview

สัมมนา sǎm-má~naa *v.* seminar ⚠

ส่า sàa *n.* yeast (e.g. baking, brewing) ◆ [เชื้อ chúua]

สาก sàak *n.* pestle [อัน an]

สากล sǎa-gon *adj.* universal (worldwide, used by all)

สาเก sǎa-gee *n.* sake (drink) [ขวด kùuat (bottle)]

สาขา sǎa-kǎa *n.* branch (e.g. bank or restaurant), franchise [สาขา sǎa-kǎa]

สาคู sǎa-kuu *n.* tapioca (pudding) [ถ้วย tûuai (bowl)]

สาง sǎang *n.* demon [ตัว dtuua]

สาด sàat *vt.* splash

สาทร sǎa-tɔɔn *n.* Sathon district [เขต kèet]

สาธยาย sǎa-tá~yaai *v.*

explain ‼

สาธารณประโยชน์ sǎa-taa-rá~ná-bprà~yòot *n.* public interest

สาธารณรัฐ sǎa-taa-rá~ná-rát *n.* republic [รัฐ rát]

สาธารณสุข sǎa-taa-rá~ná-sùk *n.* public health

สาธารณะ sǎa-taa-rá~ná *adj.* public

สาธารณะ sǎa-taa-rá~ná *n.* public (group of people)

สาธารณูปโภค sǎa-taa-rá~nuu-bpà~pôok *n.* public utility

สาธิต sǎa-tít *vi.* demonstrate (by example)

สาธุ sǎa-tú *interj.* amen!, Buddhist amen!

สานุศิษย์ sǎa-nú-sìt *n.* disciple [คน kon]

สาบาน sǎa-baan *v.* pledge (swear), vow (swear)

สาบาน sǎa-baan *vt.* swear (vow)

สาบานตน sǎa-baan-dton *vi.* take an oath

สาป sàap *v.* put a curse

สาปแช่ง sàap-chêng *v.* curse

สาปแช่ง sàap-chêng *vi.* swear (curse)

สาม sǎam *numb.* three

สามเหลี่ยม sǎam-lìiam *n.* triangle (shape) [รูป rûup, อัน an]

สามัคคี sǎa-mák-kii *n.* unity (harmony)

สามัญ sǎa-man *adj.* ordinary (normal)

สามัญชน sǎa-man-chon *n.* commoner, lay people (common people) [คน kon]

สามัญสำนึก sǎa-man-sǎm-núk *n.* common sense

สามารถ sǎa-mâat *adj.* efficient

สามารถ sǎa-mâat *aux.* can (able to) ‼

สามี sǎa-mii *n.* husband ‼ [คน kon]

สามีภรรยา sǎa-mii-pan-rá~yaa *n.* couple (husband and wife) [คู่ kûu]

สาย sǎai *adv.* late (delayed)

สาย sǎai *n.* late in the morning

สาย sǎai *n.* cord, line (string) [เส้น sên, สาย sǎai]

ส่าย sàai *vi.* sway

สายการบิน sǎai-gaan-bin *n.* airline [สาย sǎai]

สายคาด sǎai-kâat *n.* girdle, sash [เส้น sên, สาย sǎai]

สายดิน sǎai-din *n.* ground (electrical) [สาย sǎai (wire)]

สายเดี่ยว sǎai-dìiao *n.* spaghetti strap top ✦ [ตัว dtuua]

สายตา sǎai-dtaa *n.* eyesight, sight, vision

สายตายาว sǎai-dtaa-yaao *adj.* farsighted (longsighted)

สายตาสั้น sǎai-dtaa-sân *adj.* nearsighted

สายตาเอียง sǎai-dtaa-iiang *n.* stigmatism

สายน้ำ sǎai-náam *n.* stream [สาย sǎai]

สายบัว sǎai-buua *n.* water-lily stem [สาย sǎai]

สายพ่วง sǎai-pûuang *n.* extension (cord or line) [สาย sǎai]

สายพาน sǎai-paan *n.* carousel (revolving belt) [เส้น sên]

สายไฟ sǎai-fai *n.* cord (electrical) [เส้น sên]

สายยาง sǎai-yaang *n.* tube (plastic tube, hose) [สาย sǎai, เส้น sên]

สายรัด sǎai-rát *n.* band (fastener) [เส้น sên]

สายรุ้ง sǎai-rúng *n.* rainbow [ตัว dtuua]

สายลับ sǎai-láp *n.* agent, spy (detective) [คน kon]

สายเลือด sǎai-lûuat *n.* lineage (bloodline) [สาย sǎai]

สายวัด sǎai-wát *n.* tape (measuring) [เส้น sên]

สายหนัง sǎai-nǎng *n.* strap (leather) [เส้น sên]

สาร sǎan *n.* substance (physical)

สาร sǎan *n.* message (news, note, letter) ✎ [ชิ้น chín, เรื่อง rûuang ❗]

สารคดี sǎa-rá-ká~dii *n.* documentary [เรื่อง rûuang]

สารเคมี sǎan-kee-mii *n.*

chemical substance [ชนิด chá~nít]

สารถี săa-rá~tĭi *n.* driver ☸ [คน kon]

สารบัญ săa-rá~ban *n.* contents (table of contents) [สารบัญ săa-rá~ban]

สารพิษ săan-pít *n.* toxin

สารภาพ săa-rá~pâap *v.* confess

สารละลาย săan-lá~laai *n.* solution (substance)

สารวัตร săa-rá~wát *n.* inspector (police officer) [คน kon]

สารอาหาร săan-aa-hăan *n.* nutrient

สาระ săa-rá *n.* substance (gist, essence)

สารานุกรม săa-raa-nú-grom *n.* encyclopedia [เล่ม lêm]

สาลี่ săa-lîi *n.* pear [ลูก lûuk]

สาว săao *adj.* young (used with women)

สาว săao *n.* young woman [คน kon]

สาวก săa-wók *n.* disciple (in religion) [องค์ ong ☸, คน kon]

สาวใช้ săao-chái *n.* maid (female servant) [คน kon]

สาวทึนทึก săao-tɯn-tɯ́k *n.* old maid (spinster) [คน kon]

สาวน้อย săao-nɔ́ɔi *n.* chick (young woman) ☸ [คน kon]

สาวบริสุทธิ์ săao-bɔɔ-rí~sùt *n.* virgin (chaste woman) [คน kon]

สาวโสด săao-sòot *n.* single woman [คน kon]

สาส์น săan *n.* document ☝ [ฉบับ chà~bàp]

สาหร่าย săa-ràai *n.* algae [ชนิด chá~nít]

สาหร่ายทะเล săa-ràai-tá~lee *n.* seaweed [แผ่น pèn]

สาหัส săa-hàt *adj.* acute (e.g. injury)

สาเหตุ săa-hèet *n.* cause [ข้อ kɔ̂ɔ]

สำคัญ săm-kan *adj.* critical, crucial, essential, important

สำแดง săm-dɛɛng *vt.* declare (at customs)

สำนวน săm-nuuan *n.* expression (idiom) [สำนวน săm-nuuan]

กขฃคฅฆงจฉชซฌญฎฏฐฑฒณดตถทธนบปผฝพฟภมยรฤลวศษ**ส**หฬอฮ

สำนัก săm-nák *n.* bureau (institute, agency) [สำนัก săm-nák]

สำนักงาน săm-nák-ngaan *n.* office (bureau, center, agency) [แห่ง hèng]

สำนักงานใหญ่ săm-nák-ngaan-yài *n.* home office (head office) [แห่ง hèng]

สำนักพิมพ์ săm-nák-pim *n.* publisher (publishing house) [แห่ง hèng]

สำนึกผิด săm-núk-pìt *vi.* repent

สำเนา săm-nao *n.* duplicate (copy) [แผ่น pèn (piece), ฉบับ chà~bàp (whole)]

สำเนียง săm-niiang *n.* accent (dialect, pronunciation) [สำเนียง săm-niiang]

สำมะโนครัว săm-má~noo-kruua *n.* census [ครั้ง kráng]

สำรวจ săm-rùuat *v.* explore, survey

สำรวม săm-ruuam *adj.* careful 📣

สำรอง săm-rɔɔng *adj.* spare (backup)

สำรอง săm-rɔɔng *vt.* reserve (e.g. hotel, air ticket) ▮

สำรับ săm-ráp *clf.* for playing cards, pack, suit

สำราญ săm-raan *adj.* cheerful 📣

สำเร็จ săm-rèt *vi.* achieve, succeed (achieve success)

สำเร็จความใคร่ săm-rèt-kwaam-krâi *vi.* masturbate

สำเร็จรูป săm-rèt-rûup *adj.* ready-made

สำลัก săm-lák *vi.* choke (e.g. on water, food)

สำลักน้ำ săm-lák-náam *vi.* gasp (under water)

สำลี săm-lii *n.* cotton (wool) [ก้อน gɔ̂ɔn (piece), แผ่น pèn (sheet)]

สำลีแท่ง săm-lii-têng *n.* cotton swab/baby bud/Q-tip [ก้าน gâan, อัน an]

สำส่อน săm-sɔ̀ɔn *adj.* promiscuous (sexually)

สำหรับ săm-ràp *prep.* for (given to, sent to, for sake of)

สำออย săm-ɔɔi *vi.* pretend to cry to gain

sympathy 🎵

สิ sì *part.* indicating definiteness or emphasis

สิง sǐng *v.* haunt (possess, inhabit)

สิ่ง sìng *n.* thing (object, thought, statement) [อัน an, ชิ้น chín]

สิ่ง sìng *pron.* something (as object)

สิ่งของ sìng-kǒng *n.* thing (object, item) [อัน an, ชิ้น chín]

สิงคโปร์ sǐng-ká~bpoo *n.* Singapore [ประเทศ bprà~têet]

สิ่งเจือปน sìng-jʉʉa-bpon *n.* additive

สิงโต sǐng-dtoo *n.* lion [ตัว dtuua (each)]

สิงโตทะเล sǐng-dtoo-tá~lee *n.* walrus [ตัว dtuua]

สิ่งทอ sìng-tɔɔ *n.* textile [ชิ้น chín]

สิ่งมีชีวิต sìng-mii-chii-wít *n.* living things

สิ่งล่อใจ sìng-lɔ̂ɔ-jai *n.* bait (tempting item) [สิ่ง sìng]

สิ่งแวดล้อม sìng-wɛ̂ɛt-lɔ́ɔm *n.* surrounding (environment) [แห่ง hɛ̀ng]

สิงห์ sǐng *n.* lion [ตัว dtuua (each)]

สิงห์โตทะเล sǐng-dtoo-tá~lee *n.* sea lion [ตัว dtuua]

สิงหาคม sǐng-hǎa-kom *n.* August [เดือน dʉʉan]

สิทธิ sìt-tí *n.* privilege, right (e.g. legal right)

สิทธิ์ sìt *n.* right (e.g. legal right)

สิทธิบัตร sìt-tí-bàt *n.* patent (for an invention) [ใบ bai]

สิทธิพิเศษ sìt-tí-pí-sèet *n.* privilege (special right)

สิน sǐn *n.* property (possession) [ชิ้น chín]

สินค้า sǐn-káa *n.* merchandise, product (goods) [ชนิด chá~nít (kind), ชิ้น chín (piece), กล่อง glòng (box), ห่อ hɔ̀ɔ (wrap)]

สินค้าเข้า sǐn-káa-kâo *n.* import (product) [ชนิด chá~nít]

สินค้าออก sĭn-káa-ɔ̀ɔk *n.* export (product) [ชนิด chá~nít]

สินบน sĭn-bon *n.* bribe [อัน an]

สินแร่ sĭn-rɛ̂ɛ *n.* ore ⚒ [ชนิด chá~nít]

สินสอด sĭn-sɔ̀ɔt *n.* dowry [จำนวน jam-nuuan (amount), ชิ้น chín (piece)]

สิ้นสุด sîn-sùt *vi.* terminate (come to an end)

สิบ sìp *numb.* ten

สิบโท sìp-too *n.* corporal (in the marines) [คน kon]

สิบสอง sìp-sɔ̌ɔng *adj.* dozen (twelve)

สิริมงคล sì-rì-mong-kon *n.* luck ☙

สิว sĭw *n.* acne, pimple [เม็ด mét, หัว hŭua ❋]

สิ่ว sìw *n.* chisel [อัน an, ปาก bpàak]

สี sĭi *adj.* color (e.g. TV)

สี sĭi *n.* pigment

สี sĭi *n.* color [สี sĭi]

สี sĭi *n.* paint [กระป๋อง grà~bpɔ̌ng (canister), สี sĭi (color)]

สี่ sìi *numb.* four

สีกา sĭi-gaa *n.* female layman ⚘ [คน kon]

สีขาว sĭi-kăao *adj.* white

สีเขียว sĭi-kǐiao *adj.* green (color)

สีชมพู sĭi-chom-puu *adj.* pink

สีดำ sĭi-dam *n.* black [สี sĭi]

สีแดง sĭi-dɛɛng *adj.* red

สีทอง sĭi-tɔɔng *adj.* golden (color)

สีทองแดง sĭi-tɔɔng-dɛɛng *adj.* bronze (color)

สีเทา sĭi-tao *adj.* gray/grey

สี่เท่า sìi-tâo *adj.* quadruple

สีน้ำ sĭi-náam *n.* watercolor [สี sĭi (color), หลอด lɔ̀ɔt (tube)]

สีน้ำเงิน sĭi-nám-ngən *adj.* blue (navy blue)

สีน้ำตาล sĭi-nám-dtaan *adj.* brown

สีผิว sĭi-pĭu *n.* complexion (skin color)

สีฟ้า sĭi-fáa *adj.* blue (sky blue)

สีม่วง sĭi-mûuang *adj.* purple

สีย้อม sǐi-yɔ́ɔm *n.* dye [สี sǐi, ชนิด chá~nít (kind)]

สี่แยก sìi-yɛ̂ɛk *n.* intersection (four-way) [แห่ง hɛ̀ŋ, ที่ tîi]

สีรุ้ง sǐi-rúŋ *n.* prismatic colors [สี sǐi]

สีสดใส sǐi-sòt-sǎi *adj.* colorful

สีส้ม sǐi-sôm *adj.* orange

สี่สิบ sìi-sìp *numb.* forty

สีแสด sǐi-sɛ̀ɛt *n.* red orange [สี sǐi]

สี่เหลี่ยม sìi-lìiam *n.* rectangle [รูป rûup]

สีเหลือง sǐi-lɯ̌aŋ *n.* yellow (color) [สี sǐi]

สีอ่อน sǐi-ʔɔ̀ɔn *adj.* fair (color)

สึก sɯ̀k *vi.* disrobe (from monkhood) ✿

สึกกร่อน sɯ̀k-grɔ̀n *vi.* erode (wear away)

สึนามิ sù-naa-mí *n.* tidal wave, tsunami [ลูก lûuk]

สืบ sɯ̀ɯp *v.* search for the facts

สืบ sɯ̀ɯp *vt.* spy on

สืบค้น sɯ̀ɯp-kón *v.* investigate, search for, seek

สืบต่อ sɯ̀ɯp-dtɔ̀ɔ *v.* inherit (take over)

สืบทอด sɯ̀ɯp-tɔ̂ɔt *vt.* succeed (e.g. inherit role or business from)

สืบสวน sɯ̀ɯp-sǔuan *v.* investigate (examine)

สืบหา sɯ̀ɯp-hǎa *vt.* detect (search)

สื่อ sɯ̀ɯ *n.* media [สื่อ sɯ̀ɯ]

สื่อมวลชน sɯ̀ɯ-muuan-chon *n.* mass media [สื่อ sɯ̀ɯ]

สื่อสาร sɯ̀ɯ-sǎan *v.* communicate

สุก sùk *adj.* done (cooked, well done)

สุกร sù-gɔɔn *n.* pig (animal) ⚠ [ตัว dtuua]

สุกใส sùk-sǎi *adj.* bright, brilliant (very intense light)

สุข sùk *adj.* happy

สุขภาพ sùk-kà~pâap *n.* health

สุขภาพจิต sùk-kà~pâap-jìt *n.* mental health

สุขลักษณะ sùk-kà~lák-sà~nà *n.* hygiene

สุขา sù-kǎa *n.* water

closet ⚠ [ห้อง hɔ̂ng]

สุขี sù-kǐi *adj.* happy ✎

สุขุม sù-kǔm *adj.* prudent (cautious) ✎

สุขุมวิท sù-kǔm-wít *n.* Sukhumvit Road [ถนน tà~nǒn]

สุโขทัย sù-kǒo-tai *n.* Sukhothai province [จังหวัด jang-wàt]

สุด sùt *adj.* last

สุดขีด sùt-kìit *adj.* extreme (ultimate)

สุดท้าย sùt-táai *adj.* final (last, decisive), last

สุดยอด sùt-yɔ̂ɔt *adj.* superlative (highest, greatest)

สุดสัปดาห์ sùt-sàp-daa *n.* weekend (end of a week) ⚠ [วัน wan]

สุทธิ sùt-tí *adj.* net (e.g. profit)

สุทธิ sùt-tí *n.* total (sum) ⚠

สุนทรพจน์ sǔn-tɔɔ-rá~pót *n.* speech (public address) ⚠ [คำ kam]

สุนทรี sǔn-tá~rii *adj.* beautiful

สุนัข sù~nák *n.* dog ⚠ [ตัว dtuua]

สุภาพ sù~pâap *adj.* polite (courteous)

สุภาพบุรุษ sù~pâap-bù~rút *n.* gentleman ⚠ [คน kon]

สุภาพสตรี sù~pâap-sà~dtrii *n.* lady ⚠ [คน kon]

สุภาษิต sù~paa-sìt *n.* proverb [บท bòt]

สุ่ม sùm *n.* coop (poultry) [ใบ bai]

สุ่ม sùm *v.* make a wild guess

สุรา sù-raa *n.* liquor [ขวด kùuat (bottle), แก้ว gɛ̂ɛo (glass)]

สุราษฎร์ธานี sù-râat-taa-nii *n.* Surat Thani province [จังหวัด jang-wàt]

สุรินทร์ sù-rin *n.* Surin province [จังหวัด jang-wàt]

สุริยุปราคา sù-rí~yúp-bpà~raa-kaa *n.* solar eclipse [ครั้ง kráng]

สุรุ่ยสุร่าย sù~rûi-sù~râai *adj.* extravagant

สุวรรณภูมิ sù-wan-ná~puum *n.* Suvarnabhumi airport [แห่ง hὲng]

สุสาน sù-sǎan *n.* graveyard ! [แห่ง hὲng]

สุเหร่า sù-rào *n.* mosque [แห่ง hὲng]

สู้ sûu *vt.* fight (compete)

สู่ขอ sùu-kɔ̌ɔ *v.* ask a girl to marry

สูง sǔung *adj.* high, tall (in height)

สูงกว่า sǔung-gwàa *prep.* superior to (in rank)

สูงชัน sǔung-chan *adj.* steep

สูงส่ง sǔung-sòng *adj.* imperial

สูงสุด sǔung-sùt *adj.* superlative (highest, greatest)

สูงอายุ sǔung-aa-yú *adj.* elderly !

สูจิบัตร sǔu-jì-bàt *n.* agenda (program) [ฉบับ chà~bàp ! (piece), เล่ม lêm (book)]

สูญเปล่า sǔun-bplàao *adj.* wasteful (useless) !

สูญพันธุ์ sǔun-pan *adj.* extinct (e.g. species)

สูดกลิ่น sùut-glìn *v.* sniff !

สูตร sùut *n.* formula (e.g. chemical) [สูตร sùut]

สูติบัตร sǔu-dtì-bàt *n.* birth certificate ! [ฉบับ chà~bàp]

สูบ sùup *v.* pump

สูบ sùup *vt.* smoke (e.g. cigarette)

สูบบุหรี่ sùup-bù-rìi *vi.* smoke cigarettes

สู้รบกับ sûu-róp-gàp *vt.* combat

เสก sèek *v.* pronounce religious or magical formula

เสกสรร sèek-sǎn *v.* invent

เส้น sên *clf.* for lines, strings, hair, roads, long things, etc.

เส้น sên *n.* cord (string), line [เส้น sên]

เส้นขนาน sên-kà~nǎan *n.* parallel (line) [เส้น sên]

เส้นโค้ง sên-kóong *n.* curve (line) [เส้น sên]

เส้นชัย sên-chai *n.* finish line [จุด jùt]

เส้นด้าย sên-dâai *n.* thread (for sewing), yarn [เส้น sên (string)]

เส้นตาย sên-dtaai *n.* deadline ● [ครั้ง kráng]

ก
ข
ข
ค
ค
ฆ
ง
จ
ฉ
ช
ซ
ฌ
ญ
ฎ
ฏ
ฐ
ฑ
ฒ
ณ
ด
ต
ถ
ท
ธ
น
บ
ป
ผ
ฝ
พ
ฟ
ภ
ม
ย
ร
ฤ
ล
ฦ
ว
ศ
ษ
ส
ห
ฬ
อ
ฮ

เส้นใต้ sên-dtâai *n.*
underline [เส้น sên]

เส้นทาง sên-taang *n.*
track (way, rail, road)
[สาย sǎai, เส้น sên]

เส้นประสาท sên-bprà~
sàat *n.* nerve [เส้น sên]

เส้นผ่าศูนย์กลาง sên-
pàa-sǔun-glaang *n.*
diameter [เส้น sên]

เส้นใย sên-yai *n.* fiber,
filament

เส้นรอบวง sên-rɔ̂ɔp-
wong *n.* circumference
[เส้น sên]

เส้นรุ้ง sên-rúng *n.*
latitude [เส้น sên]

เส้นเลือด sên-lɯ̂at *n.*
blood vessel [เส้น sên]

เส้นแวง sên-wɛɛng *n.*
longitude [เส้น sên]

เส้นศูนย์สูตร sên-sǔun-
sùut *n.* equator [เส้น sên]

เสน่ห์ sà~nèe *n.*
enchantment (magical
spell), spell (charm)

เส้นหมี่ sên-mìi *n.*
vermicelli [เส้น sên
(strand), ห่อ hɔ̀ɔ (pack)]

เสน่หา sà~nèe-hǎa *v.* love
☙

เสนอ sà~nɤ̌ə *vt.* offer

เสนอชื่อ sà~nɤ̌ə-chɯ̂ɯ *vt.*
nominate

เสนียด sà~nìiat *n.* evil ☙,
misfortune

เสบียง sà~biiang *n.*
provision, supply

เสพย์ sèep *v.* eat

เสมหะ sěem-hà *n.*
phlegm ☝

เสมอ sà~mɤ̌ə *adj.* even
(equal)

เสมอ sà~mɤ̌ə *adv.* always

เสมอกัน sà~mɤ̌ə-gan *vi.*
tie (be even)

เสมียน sà~mǐian *n.* clerk
(in an office) [คน kon]

เสร็จ sèt *adj.* complete
(done, finished)

เสร็จ sèt *vi.* come (have
an orgasm) ☙, complete

เสร็จแล้ว sèt-lɛ́ɛo *adj.*
done (finished)

เสริม sɤ̌əm *vt.* supplement

เสริมกำลัง sɤ̌əm-gam-
lang *vt.* reinforce
(strengthen)

เสริมสร้าง sɤ̌əm-sâang *v.*
reinforce, strengthen

เสรี sěe-rii *adj.* independent (free)

เสรีภาพ sěe-rii-pâap *n.* freedom

เสลด sà~lèet *n.* phlegm

เสแสร้ง sěe-sɛ̂ɛng *adj.* pretentious

เสแสร้ง sěe-sɛ̂ɛng *v.* make believe

เสา sǎo *n.* pole (pillar, mast) [ต้น dtôn]

เสาไฟ sǎo-fai *n.* pole (electric pole) [เสา sǎo]

เสาร์ sǎo *n.* Saturday ● [วัน wan]

เสาร์อาทิตย์ sǎo-aa-tít *n.* weekend (Saturday and Sunday) [วัน wan]

เสาวรส sǎo-wá~rót *n.* passion fruit [ลูก lûuk]

เสาหลัก sǎo-làk *n.* stake (pole) [ต้น dtôn]

เสาหิน sǎo-hǐn *n.* pier (pillar) [เสา sǎo, ต้น dtôn]

เสาอากาศ sǎo-aa-gàat *n.* antenna (transmission) [ต้น dtôn]

เสีย sǐia *adj.* broken (not functioning), out of order

เสีย sǐia *vi.* pass away, spoil (become bad)

เสีย sǐia *vt.* lose (e.g. loved one), waste (lose, e.g. energy, time)

เสี่ย sìia *n.* wealthy Chinese man [คน kon]

เสียง sǐiang *n.* noise, sound [เสียง sǐiang]

เสี่ยง sìiang *adj.* risky

เสี่ยง sìiang *v.* risk

เสียงก้อง sǐiang-gɔ̂ng *n.* echo (sound)

เสียงเคาะ sǐiang-kɔ́ *n.* knock (sound) [ครั้ง kráng (number of times)]

เสียงจัตวา sǐiang-jàt-dtà~waa *n.* rising tone [เสียง sǐiang]

เสียงดัง sǐiang-dang *adj.* noisy

เสียงตรี sǐiang-dtrii *n.* high tone [เสียง sǐiang]

เสียงต่ำ sǐiang-dtàm *adj.* bass (sound)

เสียงแตร sǐiang-dtrɛɛ *n.* beep (vehicle horn) [เสียง sǐiang]

เสียงโท sǐiang-too *n.* falling tone [เสียง sǐiang]

เสียงพึมพำ sǐiang-pɯm-pam *n.* buzz

ก
ข
ฃ
ค
ฅ
ฆ
ง
จ
ฉ
ช
ซ
ฌ
ญ
ฎ
ฏ
ฐ
ฑ
ฒ
ณ
ด
ต
ถ
ท
ธ
น
บ
ป
ผ
ฝ
พ
ฟ
ภ
ม
ย
ร
ฤ
ล
ว
ศ
ษ
ส
ห
ฬ
อ
ฮ

เสี่ยงภัย sìiang-pai v. fight danger, venture (risk, take a risk)

เสียงสามัญ sǐiang-sǎa-man n. mid tone [เสียง sǐiang]

เสียงสูงต่ำ sǐiang-sǔung-dtàm n. intonation (pitch, tone) [เสียง sǐiang]

เสียงเอก sǐiang-èek n. low tone [เสียง sǐiang]

เสียใจ sǐia-jai adj. sad, sorry

เสียโฉม sǐia-chǒom adj. disfigured

เสียชีวิต sǐia-chii-wít vi. die !

เสียดสี sìiat-sǐi adj. sarcastic

เสียดาย sǐia-daai vt. regret (loss)

เสียตัว sǐia-dtuua vi. lose one's virginity

เสี้ยน sîian n. sliver (splinter) [อัน an]

เสียบ sìiap vt. penetrate (pierce)

เสียบปลั๊ก sìiap-bplák v. plug (insert a plug)

เสียม sǐiam n. pickaxe, shovel (spade, for digging) [เล่ม lêm]

เสียว sǐiao adj. tingling

เสียว sǐiao v. feel a thrill of fear, have sexual sensations ●

เสี้ยว sîiao n. quarter (one-fourth) ●

เสียโอกาส sǐia-oo-gàat v. lose one's opportunity

เสือ sǔua n. tiger [ตัว dtuua]

เสื่อ sùua n. mat (for sitting on the floor) [ผืน pǔun]

เสื้อ sûua n. shirt ●, upper garment [ตัว dtuua]

เสือก sùuak vi. butt in (meddle) ●

เสื้อกล้าม sûua-glâam n. undershirt [ตัว dtuua]

เสื้อกั๊ก sûua-gák n. waistcoat [ตัว dtuua]

เสื้อกันฝน sûua-gan-fǒn n. raincoat [ตัว dtuua]

เสื้อกันลม sûua-gan-lom n. windbreaker [ตัว dtuua]

เสื้อกันหนาว sûua-gan-nǎao n. cardigan,

ก
ข
ฃ
ค
ฅ
ฆ
ง
จ
ฉ
ช
ซ
ฌ
ญ
ฎ
ฏ
ฐ
ฑ
ฒ
ณ
ด
ต
ถ
ท
ธ
น
บ
ป
ผ
ฝ
พ
ฟ
ภ
ม
ย
ร
ล
ฦ
ว
ศ
ษ
ส
ห
ฬ
อ
ฮ

sweater/jumper [ตัว dtuua]

เสื้อคลุม sûua-klum *n.* cloak, dressing gown, robe [ตัว dtuua]

เสื้อโค้ท sûua-kóot *n.* coat [ตัว dtuua]

เสื้อชั้นใน sûua-chán-nai *n.* bra/brassiere, undergarment [ตัว dtuua]

เสื้อชูชีพ sûua-chuu-chîip *n.* life vest [ตัว dtuua]

เสื้อเชิ้ต sûua-chə́ət *n.* shirt [ตัว dtuua]

เสือดาว sʉ̌ua-daao *n.* leopard [ตัว dtuua]

เสื้อผ้า sûua-pâa *n.* clothes/clothing, garment [ชุด chút (set), ตัว dtuua (piece)]

เสื่อม sʉ̀uam *vi.* decay (fall into ruin, decline)

เสื่อมเสีย sʉ̀uam-sǐia *adj.* disgraceful

เสื้อยืด sûua-yʉ̂ʉt *n.* T-shirt [ตัว dtuua]

แส้ sɛ̂ɛ *n.* whip [เส้น sên]

แสกกลาง sɛ̀ɛk-glaang *adj.* parted in the middle

แสง sɛ̌ɛng *n.* light (ray) [แสง sɛ̌ɛng]

แสงจันทร์ sɛ̌ɛng-jan *n.* moonlight

แสงจ้า sɛ̌ɛng-jâa *n.* glare (light)

แสงแดด sɛ̌ɛng-dɛ̀ɛt *n.* daylight, sunlight

แสด sɛ̀ɛt *adj.* orange yellow, red orange

แสดง sà~dɛɛng *vi.* act (e.g. on TV), play (perform)

แสดงความยินดีกับ sà~dɛɛng-kwaam-yin-dii-gàp *vt.* congratulate

แสดงธรรม sà~dɛɛng-tam *vi.* give a dharma talk

แสดงแบบ sà~dɛɛng-bɛ̀ɛp *v.* model (pose)

แสดงเป็น sà~dɛɛng-bpen *vt.* play (have a part in a play as)

แสดงผล sà~dɛɛng-pǒn *v.* show the result

แสดงให้เห็น sà~dɛɛng-hâi-hĕn *vt.* reveal

แสดงออก sà~dɛɛng-ɔ̀ɔk *vi.* express oneself

แสตมป์ sà~dtɛm *n.* stamp (postage) [ดวง duuang]

แสน sɛ̌ɛn *numb.* one hundred thousand

แสบ sɛ̀ɛp *vi.* sting (feel a sharp pain)

โสโครก sǒo-krôok *adj.* filthy (dirty)

โสด sòot *adj.* single, unmarried

โสน sà~nǒo *n.* species of tall marsh

โสเภณี sǒo-pee-nii *n.* prostitute (female) [คน kon]

โสม sǒom *n.* ginseng [หัว hǔua]

โสมม sǒo-mom *adj.* dirty (filthy)

โสร่ง sà~ròong *n.* garment worn by Thai women, sarong [ผืน pʉ̌ʉn]

ใส sǎi *adj.* clear (free from clouds, dust, etc.)

ใส่ sài *vt.* contain, load (fill), put (add in), wear

ใส่กลอน sài-glɔɔn *v.* latch

ใส่ความ sài-kwaam *vt.* frame (wrongly incriminate)

ใส่ใจ sài-jai *v.* pay attention

ใส่ร้าย sài-ráai *vt.* incriminate (blame)

ใส่เสื้อผ้าให้ sài-sʉ̂ua-pâa-hâi *vt.* clothe (dress)

ไส sǎi *vt.* plane (carpentry)

ไส้ sâi *n.* core (fruit)

ไส้ sâi *n.* filling (e.g. sweets, buns) [ชนิด chá~nít]

ไส้ sâi *n.* intestine [ท่อน tɔ̂n (strip), ขด kòt (coil)]

ไส้กรอก sâi-grɔ̀ɔk *n.* sausage [ชิ้น chín]

ไส้เดือน sâi-dʉuan *n.* earthworm [ตัว dtuua]

ไส้ติ่ง sâi-dtìng *n.* appendix (body part) [ก้อน gɔ̂ɔn, อัน an]

ไส้ติ่งอักเสบ sâi-dtìng-àk-sèep *n.* appendicitis [ก้อน gɔ̂ɔn]

ไส้เทียน sâi-tiian *n.* candlewick [เส้น sên]

ไส้พุง sâi-pung *n.* gut (bowels, entrails) [เส้น sên]

ไส้เลื่อน sâi-lʉ̂uan *n.* hernia [โรค rôok]

ไส้ศึก sâi-sʉ̀k *n.* spy

(detective) [คน kon]

ห

ห hɔ̌ɔ *let.* ห. หีบ hɔ̌ɔ-hìip, a consonant of the Thai alphabet (high consonant) [ตัว dtuua]

หก hòk *numb.* six

หงส์ hǒng *n.* swan [ตัว dtuua]

หงอก ngɔ̀ɔk *adj.* silver gray (hair color)

หงอน ngɔ̌ɔn *n.* crest (e.g. bird) [หงอน ngɔ̌ɔn]

หงาย ngǎai *vi.* turn up (lay face up)

หงิก ngìk *adj.* wrinkled

หงุดหงิด ngùt-ngìt *adj.* irritated (annoyed)

หญ้า yâa *n.* grass [ต้น dtôn]

หญ้าเทียม yâa-tiiam *n.* turf (artificial)

หญ้าแห้ง yâa-hêng *n.* hay (dry grass) [กอง gɔɔng (pile), เส้น sên (strand)]

หญิงสาว yǐng-sǎao *n.* maiden (young woman) [คน kon]

หด hòt *vi.* contract (shrink)

หดตัว hòt-dtuua *vi.* shrink

หดหู่ hòt-hùu *adj.* depressed (sad)

หนวกหู nùuak-hǔu *adj.* noisy

หน่วงเหนี่ยว nùuang-nìiao *vt.* impede

หนวด nùuat *n.* mustache [เส้น sên (strand), กระจุก grà~jùk (tuft)]

หน่วย nùai *n.* unit (one of a number of things, etc.) [หน่วย nùai]

หน่วยกิต nùai-gìt *n.* credit (e.g. college) [หน่วย nùai]

หน่วยวัด nùai-wát *n.* meter (unit of measure) [เมตร méet]

หน่อ nɔ̀ɔ *n.* shoot (sprout) [หน่อ nɔ̀ɔ]

หนอก nɔ̀ɔk *n.* hump (e.g. camel) [หนอก nɔ̀ɔk]

หนอง nɔ̌ɔng *n.* pus

หนอง nɔ̌ɔng *n.* swamp (bog, marsh) [แห่ง hèng]

หนองคาย nɔ̌ɔng-kaai *n.* Nong Khai province [จังหวัด jang-wàt]

หนองใน nɔ̌ɔng-nai *n.* gonorrhea [โรค rôok]

หนอน nɔ̌ɔn *n.* worm (caterpillar) [ตัว dtuua]

ก
ข
ฃ
ค
ฅ
ฆ
ง
จ
ฉ
ช
ซ
ฌ
ญ
ฎ
ฏ
ฐ
ฑ
ฒ
ณ
ด
ต
ถ
ท
ธ
น
บ
ป
ผ
ฝ
พ
ฟ
ภ
ม
ย
ร
ล
ฤ
ว
ศ
ษ
ส
ห
ฬ
อ
ฮ

หน่อไม้ nɔ̀ɔ-máai *n.* young bamboo shoot [หน่อ nɔ̀ɔ]

หน่อย nɔ̀i *adv.* bit (somewhat)

หนัก nàk *adj.* hard, heavy

หนัก nàk *vi.* weigh (have weight)

หนักใจ nàk-jai *adj.* anxious (worried)

หนักหนา nàk-nǎa *adv.* very much

หนัง nǎng *n.* film (movie) [เรื่อง rûuang]

หนัง nǎng *n.* leather (animal) ☞ [แผ่น pèn, ผืน pǔɯn]

หนัง nǎng *n.* skin [ชั้น chán (layer)]

หนังศีรษะ nǎng-sǐi-sà *n.* scalp ‼

หนังสัตว์ nǎng-sàt *n.* hide (animal skin) [แผ่น pèn, ผืน pǔɯn]

หนังสือ nǎng~sǔɯ *n.* book [เล่ม lêm]

หนังสือเดินทาง nǎng~sǔɯ-dəən-taang *n.* passport ‼ [ฉบับ chà~bàp ‼, เล่ม lêm]

หนังสือโป๊ nǎng~sǔɯ-bpóo *n.* porn/ pornography (book) [เล่ม lêm]

หนังสือพิมพ์ nǎng~sǔɯ-pim *n.* newspaper [ฉบับ chà~bàp]

หนังสือมอบอำนาจ nǎng~sǔɯ-mɔ̂ɔp-am-nâat *n.* power of attorney [ฉบับ chà~bàp]

หนังสือเรียน nǎng~sǔɯ-riian *n.* textbook [เล่ม lêm]

หนังหัว nǎng-hǔua *n.* scalp

หนา nǎa *adj.* thick (e.g. hair, smoke)

หน้า nâa *adj.* front

หน้า nâa *adv.* ahead (in front), in front

หน้า nâa *n.* face (human), page (e.g. book), season [หน้า nâa]

หน้ากาก nâa-gàak *n.* mask [อัน an]

หน้าแข้ง nâa-kêng *n.* shin [ข้าง kâang]

หน้าจั่ว nâa-jùua *n.* gable [จั่ว jùua, แผง pɛɛng]

หน้าด้าน nâa-dâan *adj.* shameless (showing no shame) ✦

หน้าตา nâa-dtaa *n.* feature (of face)

หน้าต่าง nâa-dtàang *n.* window [บาน baan]

หน้าที่ nâa-tîi *n.* duty (responsibility) [หน้าที่ nâa-tîi]

หน้านา nâa-naa *n.* rice-planting season [หน้า nâa]

หนาแน่น nǎa-nên *adj.* dense (small and heavy)

หน้าบ้าน nâa-bâan *n.* area in front of a house [บริเวณ bɔɔ-rí~ween]

หน้าบึ้ง nâa-bûng *n.* pout (frown)

หน้าปก nâa-bpòk *n.* cover, e.g. book [ใบ bai, แผ่น pèn]

หน้าปัด nâa-bpàt *n.* dial (face of a clock) [อัน an]

หน้าผาก nâa-pàak *n.* brow, forehead

หน้าฝน nâa-fǒn *n.* rainy season ✦ [หน้า nâa]

หนาม nǎam *n.* barb, thorn (e.g. of a rose) [อัน an]

หน้าร้อน nâa-rɔ́ɔn *n.* hot season ✦ [หน้า nâa]

หน้าแล้ง nâa-lέɛng *n.* dry season [หน้า nâa]

หนาว nǎao *adj.* cool (chilly)

หนาวเย็น nǎao-yen *adj.* bleak (cold and piercing)

หนาวสั่น nǎao-sàn *vi.* chill (shiver)

หน้าหนังสือ nâa-nǎng~sǔu *n.* page (e.g. book) ❗ [หน้า nâa]

หน้าหนาว nâa-nǎao *n.* cold season ✦ [หน้า nâa]

หน้าหลัง nâa-lǎng *n.* back page (e.g. of a newspaper) [หน้า nâa]

หน้าใหม่ nâa-mài *n.* newcomer ✦ [คน kon]

หน้าอก nâa-òk *n.* breast, bust, chest

หนี nǐi *vi.* break out (escape)

หนีตาม nǐi-dtaam *vi.* elope (run away with a lover)

หนีบ nìip *vt.* nip

หนี้สิน nîi-sǐn *n.* debt [จำนวน jam-nuuan]

หนึ่ง nùng *numb.* one

หนึ่งครั้ง nùng-kráng *n.* once [ครั้ง kráng]

หนึ่งในสี่ nùng-nai-sìi *n.* quarter (one-fourth)

หนึ่งพันล้าน nùng-pan-láan *numb.* billion (thousand million)

หนึ่งล้าน nùng-láan *numb.* million !

หนุน nǔn *vt.* support (back up)

หนุนหลัง nǔn-lǎng *vt.* back (support)

หนุ่ม nùm *adj.* young (used with men)

หนุ่มสาว nùm-sǎao *n.* young people [คน kon]

หนู nǔu *n.* rat (rodent) [ตัว dtuua]

หนูน้อย nǔu-nɔ́ɔi *n.* little child, little one [คน kon]

หมก mòk *v.* cover over, hide (bury)

หมกมุ่น mòk-mûn *adj.* preoccupied (absorbed)

หมด mòt *adj.* out (finished)

หมด mòt *vi.* run out (be used up)

หมดกำลังใจ mòt-gam-lang-jai *adj.* discouraged

หมดเกลี้ยง mòt-glîiang *adj.* cleaned out (empty of content)

หมดจด mòt-jòt *adj.* cleaned out

หมดตัว mòt-dtuua *adj.* broke (penniless)

หมดแรง mòt-rɛɛng *adj.* exhausted (fatigued)

หมดเวลา mòt-wee-laa *idm.* time is up

หมดสติ mòt-sà~dtì *vi.* pass out (faint) !

หมดหวัง mòt-wǎng *adj.* hopeless

หมดอายุ mòt-aa-yú *vi.* expire (reach end of term)

หม่น mòn *adj.* dull (depressed)

หมวก mùuak *n.* cap (hat) [ใบ bai]

หมวกกันน็อก mùuak-gan-nɔ́k *n.* helmet [ใบ bai]

หมวกคลุม mùuak-klum *n.* hood/bonnet (e.g. jacket) [อัน an]

ก ข ข ค ฅ ฆ ง จ ฉ ช ซ ฌ ญ ฎ ฏ ฐ ฑ ฒ ณ ด ต ถ ท ธ น บ ป ผ ฝ พ ฟ ภ ม ย ร ฤ ล ว ศ ษ ส **ห** ฬ อ ฮ

หมวดหมู่ mùuat-mùu *n.* category (group, section) [หมวด mùuat]

หมวย mŭuai *n.* young Chinese woman [คน kon]

หมอ mŏo *n.* doctor, fellow (guy) [คน kon]

หม้อ mɔ̂ɔ *clf.* e.g. radiators, pot-like containers etc.

หม้อ mɔ̂ɔ *n.* pot (cooking pot) [ใบ bai, ลูก lûuk]

หมอก mɔ̀ɔk *n.* mist (fog, haze)

หมอกควัน mɔ̀ɔk-kwan *n.* smog

หมอง mɔ̌ɔng *adj.* depressed (sad), dull

หมอดู mŏo-duu *n.* fortuneteller [คน kon]

หมอเด็ก mŏo-dèk *n.* pediatrician [คน kon]

หมอตำแย mŏo-dtam-yɛɛ *n.* midwife [คน kon]

หมอน mŏɔn *n.* pillow [ใบ bai, ลูก lûuk]

หม่อน mɔ̀n *n.* mulberry [ต้น dtôn (plant), ใบ bai (leaf)]

หมอนวด mŏo-nûuat *n.* masseur, masseuse [คน kon]

หมอนั่น mŏo-nân *n.* that guy ✤ [คน kon]

หมอบ mɔ̀ɔp *vi.* kneel (crouch)

หม้อแปลง mɔ̂ɔ-bplɛɛng *n.* transformer (electrical) [หม้อ mɔ̂ɔ, ลูก lûuk]

หมอผี mŏo-pǐi *n.* witch doctor [คน kon]

หมอฟัน mŏo-fan *n.* dentist [คน kon]

หมอย mŏoi *n.* pubic hair ✤ [เส้น sên]

หมัก màk *vt.* preserve (ferment)

หมักดอง màk-dɔɔng *v.* preserve or pickle by slow fermentation

หมัด màt *n.* flea [ตัว dtuua]

หมัด màt *n.* punch (fist) [หมัด màt]

หมั่น màn *adj.* diligent

หมั้นกับ mân-gàp *vt.* engage (for marriage)

หมั่นไส้ màn-sâi *v.* cause disgust

หมา mǎa *n.* dog [ตัว dtuua]

หมาก màak *n.* betel nut

[ลูก lûuk (fruit), ต้น dtôn (tree)]

หมากฝรั่ง màak-fà~ràng *n.* gum (chewing) [กล่อง glòng (pack), แผ่น pèn (stick), เม็ด mét (drop)]

หมากรุก màak-rúk *n.* chess [กระดาน grà~daan (board), ตัว dtuua (piece), ชุด chút (set)]

หมางใจ mǎang-jai *adj.* estranged

หมาจิ้งจอก mǎa-jîng-jɔ̀ɔk *n.* fox [ตัว dtuua]

หมาตัวเมีย mǎa-dtuua-miia *n.* bitch (female dog) [ตัว dtuua]

หมาใน mǎa-nai *n.* hyena [ตัว dtuua]

หมาบ้า mǎa-bâa *n.* mad dog [ตัว dtuua]

หมาป่า mǎa-bpàa *n.* wolf [ตัว dtuua]

หมาย mǎai *vt.* expect (aim at), mark (make a mark)

หม้าย mâai see ม่าย

หมายค้น mǎai-kón *n.* search warrant [ฉบับ chà~bàp]

หมายความว่า mǎai-kwaam-wâa *v.* mean that

หมายจับ mǎai-jàp *n.* arrest warrant/warrant of arrest [ใบ bai, ฉบับ chà~bàp ⚡]

หมายตา mǎai-dtaa *v.* take notice of

หมายถึง mǎai-tǔng *vt.* mean (have the meaning of)

หมายเรียกตัว mǎai-rîiak-dtuua *n.* summons (subpoena) [ใบ bai, ฉบับ chà~bàp]

หมายเลข mǎai-lêek *n.* number (numeral) [หมายเลข mǎai-lêek]

หมายศาล mǎai-sǎan *n.* subpoena [ใบ bai, ฉบับ chà~bàp]

หมายเหตุ mǎai-hèet *n.* remark (note) [แห่ง hèng]

หมาหมู่ mǎa-mùu *n.* pack of dogs [กลุ่ม glùm]

หม่ำ màm *v.* drink ⚡

หมิ่น mìn *v.* look down upon

หมี mǐi *n.* bear [ตัว dtuua]

หมี่ mìi *n.* fine noodles [เส้น sên]

หมึก mùk *n.* ink [ขวด kùuat (flask), หยด yòt (drop)]

หมื่น mùʉn *numb.* ten thousand

หมุด mùt *n.* small screw, peg (small, round, cylindrical object), tack (e.g. for paper) [ตัว dtuua]

หมุน mǔn *v.* revolve, turn (spin)

หมุนเวียน mǔn-wiian *vi.* circulate (e.g. air, person, handout), rotate (take turns)

หมู mǔu *adj.* easy ☞

หมู mǔu *n.* pig (animal) [ตัว dtuua]

หมู่ mùu *n.* squad (group) [หมู่ mùu]

หมู่เกาะ mùu-gɔ̀ *n.* archipelago [แห่ง hὲng]

หมู่บ้าน mùu-bâan *n.* village [หมู่บ้าน mùu-bâan]

หมูป่า mǔu-bpàa *n.* boar (wild boar) [ตัว dtuua]

หยก yòk *n.* jade [ชิ้น chín (piece), ก้อน gɔ̂ɔn (chunk)]

หยด yòt *vi.* drip (fall in drops)

หยดน้ำตา yòt-nám-dtaa *n.* teardrop [หยด yòt]

หยวน yǔuan *n.* yuan [หยวน yǔuan]

หยอกล้อ yɔ̀ɔk-lɔ́ɔ *v.* tease (make fun of)

หย่อน yɔ̀n *adj.* slack (loose, e.g. rope)

หย่อนยาน yɔ̀n-yaan *adj.* flabby

หย่อนลง yɔ̀n-long *vi.* sag (hang down unevenly)

หยักศก yàk-sòk *adj.* curly (hair)

หยั่ง yàng *v.* measure

หย่า yàa *v.* divorce

หยากไย่ yàak-yâi *n.* cobweb [ใย yai]

หยาด yàat *n.* drip ☞

หยาบคาย yàap-kaai *adj.* impolite, rude, vulgar

หย่าร้าง yàa-ráang *adj.* divorced

หยิก yìk *adj.* wavy (e.g. hair)

หยิ่ง yìng *adj.* proud (conceited, arrogant)

หยิบ yìp *vt.* take hold of

หยี yǐi *adj.* squinting

หยุด_ชั่วขณะ yùt-_-chûua-kà~nà *vt.* pause (stop shortly)

หยุดทำงาน yùt-tam-ngaan *adj.* dead (not working)

หยุดทำงาน yùt-tam-ngaan *vi.* shut off (turn off)

หยุดนิ่ง yùt-nîng *adj.* stagnant (still)

หยุดพัก yùt-pák *vi.* break (stop or rest)

หยุดยั้ง yùt-yáng *vt.* suppress (e.g. press, symptoms)

หรี่ rìi *vt.* lower (e.g. volume, light level)

หรี่ตา rìi-dtaa *vi.* squint (with part-closed eyes)

หรือ rʉ̌ʉ *conj.* either...or

หรือ rʉ̌ʉ *part.* used to form a question

หรู rʉ̌u *adj.* beautiful ✦, luxurious ✦

หรูหรา rʉ̌u-rǎa *adj.* fancy (luxurious)

หลงทาง lǒng-taang *vi.* get lost (lose one's way)

หลงรัก lǒng-rák *vt.* be passionately in love with

หลงใหล lǒng-lǎi *adj.* crazy about, infatuated (with)

หลน lǒn *n.* stew

หลบ lòp *vi.* duck (avoid collision)

หลบ lòp *vt.* slip or sneak away

หลบเลี่ยง lòp-lîiang *v.* evade

หลบหนี lòp-nǐi *v.* escape, flee

หลบหลีก lòp-lìik *adj.* evasive

หล่ม lòm *n.* mud (muddy place) [แห่ง hèng, ที่ tîi]

หลวง lǔuang- *pref.* used to add respect to a title

หลวง lǔuang *adj.* royal

หลวงพ่อ lǔuang-pɔ̂ɔ *n.* father (Christian priest) [คน kon]

หลวม lǔuam *adj.* loose

หล่อ lɔ̀ɔ *adj.* handsome (men)

หล่อ lɔ̀ɔ *vt.* cast (in a mold)

หลอก lɔ̀ɔk *v.* deceive (fool)

หลอก lɔ̀ɔk *vt.* trick

หลอกลวง lɔ̀ɔk-luuang *vt.* cheat (deceive)

หลอกหลอน lɔ̀ɔk-lɔ̌ɔn *v.* haunt (frighten)

หลอด lɔ̀ɔt *clf.* for tubes, straws, reels, etc.

หลอด lɔ̀ɔt *n.* reel (e.g. film, thread), tube (container, e.g. for toothpaste) [หลอด lɔ̀ɔt]

หลอดด้าย lɔ̀ɔt-dâai *n.* spool (for thread) [หลอด lɔ̀ɔt]

หลอดดูด lɔ̀ɔt-dùut *n.* straw (for drinks) [หลอด lɔ̀ɔt]

หลอดไฟ lɔ̀ɔt-fai *n.* bulb (light bulb) [หลอด lɔ̀ɔt]

หลอดเลือด lɔ̀ɔt-lʉ̂at *n.* vessel (vein) [หลอด lɔ̀ɔt]

หลอดอาหาร lɔ̀ɔt-aa-hǎan *n.* esophagus [หลอด lɔ̀ɔt]

หลอน lɔ̌ɔn *v.* haunt (frighten)

หล่อน lɔ̀n *pron.* she (use with friends) ●, you (used to address a female in a derogatory way)

หล่อลื่น lɔ̀ɔ-lʉ̂ʉn *v.* lubricate

หละหลวม là-lǔam *adj.* careless

หลัก làk *adj.* chief, principle (main)

หลัก làk *n.* digit (place,

e.g. 1s, 10s, 100s) [หลัก làk]

หลักการ làk-gaan *n.* principle (practice, opinion) [หลักการ làk-gaan]

หลักเกณฑ์ làk-geen *n.* rule (principle, standard) [หลัก làk]

หลักชัย làk-chai *n.* goal (destination) [แห่ง hɛ̀ŋ]

หลักฐาน làk-tǎan *n.* proof (evidence) [ชิ้น chín (piece)]

หลักทรัพย์ làk-sáp *n.* property (possession) ✘ [ชิ้น chín]

หลักธรรม làk-tam *n.* principle (moral) [ข้อ kɔ̂ɔ]

หลักประกัน làk-bprà~gan *n.* security (guarantee) [อัน an]

หลักสูตร làk-sùut *n.* curriculum [หลักสูตร làk-sùut]

หลักแหล่ง làk-lɛ̀ŋ *n.* place where one settles down to live [แห่ง hɛ̀ŋ]

หลัง lǎŋ *adj.* latter, rear

หลัง lǎŋ *clf.* e.g. buildings, houses, piano

หลัง lăng *n.* back (body part)

หลั่ง làng *vt.* shed (e.g. tears), sprinkle (liquid)

หลังคา lăng-kaa *n.* roof [หลังคา lăng-kaa]

หลังจาก lăng-jàak *adv.* after

หลังเที่ยง lăng-tîiang *adj.* p.m.

หลังสุด lăng-sùt *adj.* latest

หลับ làp *adj.* asleep

หลับตา làp-dtaa *vi.* close one's eyes

หลับใน làp-nai *v.* daydream

หลา lăa *n.* yard (unit of measure) [หลา lăa]

หล้า lâa *n.* earth (ground, soil) ✍

หลาก làak *adj.* different (not same), various

หลาน lăan *n.* grandchild, nephew ♂, niece ♀ [คน kon]

หลาบ làap *vi.* have learned one's lesson

หลาม lăam *n.* python [ตัว dtuua]

หลาย lăai *adj.* many, numerous, several

หลายใจ lăai-jai *adj.* fickle (unfaithful)

หลาว lăao *n.* javelin, spear [เล่ม lêm]

หลิ่วตา lìu-dtaa *vi.* wink (make a wink)

หลีกทาง lìik-taang *vi.* give way

หลีกเลี่ยง lìik-lîiang *vt.* avoid

หลุด lùt *adj.* off (not connected)

หลุดมือ lùt-mʉʉ *v.* slip from the hand

หลุม lŭm *n.* cavity (in earth), pit (hole) [รู ruu, หลุม lŭm]

หลุมฝังศพ lŭm-făng-sòp *n.* grave [แห่ง hèng]

หลุมพราง lŭm-praang *n.* pitfall (trap) [อัน an]

หวง hŭuang *adj.* jealous (possessive)

ห่วง hùuang *adj.* worried (about someone or something)

ห่วง hùuang *n.* ring (hoop, loop) [ห่วง hùuang]

ห่วงใย hùuang-yai *adj.* concerned about

หวงแหน hǔuang-hěɛn *vt.* cherish (value highly)

หวด hùuat *n.* earthenware steamer [ใบ bai]

ห้วน hûuan *adj.* brief (blunt)

หวนกลับ hǔuan-glàp *vi.* come back (return) ✎

หวย hǔuai *n.* lottery ✿ [ใบ bai, ฉบับ chà~bàp ‼]

ห่วย hùai *adj.* no good

ห่วยแตก hùai-dtɛ̀ɛk *adj.* cranky (e.g. trucks) ✿

หวอ wɔ̌ɔ *adj.* exposed (unprotected) ✿

หวอ wɔ̌ɔ *n.* siren [เสียง sǐiang (sound)]

หวัง wǎng *v.* hope

หวัดดี wàt-dii *interj.* hi! ✿

หวั่น wàn *adj.* fearful (frightened)

หว่างขา wàang-kǎa *n.* crotch (between the legs)

หวาดกลัว wàat-gluua *adj.* horrified ‼, scared ‼

หวาน wǎan *adj.* sugary, sweet (taste)

หว่าน wàan *vt.* sow (e.g. seeds)

หวาย wǎai *n.* wicker/ wickerwork (rattan palm)

✿ [ชนิด chá~nít (kind), ชิ้น chín (piece)]

หวี wǐi *n.* bunch (bananas) [หวี wǐi]

หวี wǐi *n.* comb (hair) [เล่ม lêm]

หวี wǐi *vt.* comb (hair)

หวุดหวิด wùt-wìt *adv.* nearly

หวุดหวิด wùt-wìt *n.* close call (narrow escape) ✿

หอ hɔ̌ɔ *n.* dorm/ dormitory [หลัง lǎng (building)]

ห่อ hɔ̀ɔ *clf.* for packs, packages, packets, etc.

ห่อ hɔ̀ɔ *n.* bundle, pack, package [ห่อ hɔ̀ɔ]

ห่อ hɔ̀ɔ *vt.* pack, wrap

หอก hɔ̀ɔk *n.* lance, spear [เล่ม lêm]

หอการค้า hɔ̌ɔ-gaan-káa *n.* chamber of commerce [แห่ง hɛ̀ng]

หอคอย hɔ̌ɔ-kɔɔi *n.* tower [แห่ง hɛ̀ng]

ห้อง hɔ̂ng *n.* chamber, compartment (room) [ห้อง hɔ̂ng]

ห้องครัว hɔ̂ng-kruua *n.* kitchen [ห้อง hɔ̂ng]

ห้องคลอด hɔ̂ng-klɔ̂ɔt *n.* delivery room (baby) [ห้อง hɔ̂ng]

ห้องฉุกเฉิน hɔ̂ng-chùk-chɵ̌ɵn *n.* emergency room [ห้อง hɔ̂ng]

ห้องชุด hɔ̂ng-chút *n.* suite (room) [ห้อง hɔ̂ng]

ห้องใต้ดิน hɔ̂ng-dtâai-din *n.* basement, vault (underground room) [ห้อง hɔ̂ng]

ห้องโถง hɔ̂ng-tǒong *n.* salon (hall) [ห้อง hɔ̂ng]

ห้องทำงาน hɔ̂ng-tam-ngaan *n.* workshop (where work is done) [ห้อง hɔ̂ng]

ห้องนอน hɔ̂ng-nɔɔn *n.* bedroom [ห้อง hɔ̂ng]

ห้องนั่งเล่น hɔ̂ng-nâng-lên *n.* living room [ห้อง hɔ̂ng]

ห้องน้ำ hɔ̂ng-náam *n.* bathroom, restroom, toilet (room) [ห้อง hɔ̂ng]

ห้องรับแขก hɔ̂ng-ráp-kɛ̀ɛk *n.* living room [ห้อง hɔ̂ng]

ห้องเรียน hɔ̂ng-riian *n.* classroom [ห้อง hɔ̂ng]

ห้องสมุด hɔ̂ng-sà~mùt *n.* library [แห่ง hɛ̀ng]

ห้องส้วม hɔ̂ng-sûuam *n.* toilet (room) ✿ [ห้อง hɔ̂ng]

หอน hɔ̌ɔn *v.* howl (e.g. a dog)

หอบ hɔ̀ɔp *v.* pant (gasp)

หอประชุม hɔ̌ɔ-bprà~chum *n.* auditorium (convention hall) [แห่ง hɛ̀ng]

หอพัก hɔ̌ɔ-pák *n.* dorm/dormitory [หลัง lǎng (building)]

หอม hɔ̌ɔm *n.* onion [หัว hǔua]

หอม hɔ̌ɔm *v.* kiss (sniff kiss)

หอม hɔ̌ɔm *vi.* smell good

หอมแดง hɔ̌ɔm-dɛɛng *n.* shallot [หัว hǔua]

ห้อมล้อม hɔ́ɔm-lɔ́ɔm *vt.* surround

หอมเล็ก hɔ̌ɔm-lék *n.* chives [หัว hǔua]

หอย hɔ̌ɔi *n.* shellfish (oyster, mussel), snail [ตัว dtuua]

ห้อย hɔ̂i *adj.* pendant

(hanging)

ห้อย hôi *v.* hang

หอยทาก hɔ̌ɔi-tâak *n.* snail [ตัว dtuua]

หอยนางรม hɔ̌ɔi-naang-rom *n.* oyster [ตัว dtuua]

หอยมุก hɔ̌ɔi-múk *n.* pearl oyster [ตัว dtuua]

หัก hàk *adj.* broken (split, e.g. wood)

หัก hàk *v.* deduct (subtract)

หัก hàk *vt.* break (bend and break)

หักง่าย hàk-ngâai *adj.* brittle (fragile)

หักบัญชี hàk-ban-chii *vt.* debit (from account)

หักล้าง hàk-láang *vt.* refute (prove to be false)

หักหน้า hàk-nâa *v.* cause someone to lose face ♦

หักโหม hàk-hǒom *v.* overexert oneself

หักออก hàk-ɔ̀ɔk *vt.* break off (piece)

หัด hàt *n.* measles [โรค rôok]

หัด hàt *v.* practice (train, learn)

หัตถกรรม hàt-tà~gam *n.* handicraft

หัน hǎn *v.* turn (for person, e.g. head)

หั่น hàn *v.* cut (chop), slice (chop)

หันกลับ hǎn-glàp *vi.* turn back (for person, e.g. head)

หันเห hǎn-hěe *vi.* deviate (swerve, change course)

หัว hǔua *n.* heads (coin) [ด้าน dâan]

หัว hǔua *n.* bulb (plant), head (body part) [หัว hǔua]

หัวกะทิ hǔua-gà~tí *n.* elite (best of anything) ♦ [คน kon]

หัวกะโหลก hǔua-gà~lòok *n.* skull [ใบ bai]

หัวเก่า hǔua-gào *adj.* old-fashioned (conservative)

หัวข้อ hǔua-kɔ̂ɔ *n.* subject, theme, topic [หัวข้อ hǔua-kɔ̂ɔ]

หัวเข่า hǔua-kào *n.* knee [ข้าง kâang]

หัวแข็ง hǔua-kɛ̌ng *adj.* obstinate, stubborn

หัวใจ hǔua-jai *n.* heart (organ)

หัวใจวาย hǔua-jai-waai *n.*

ก ข ฃ ค ฅ ฆ ง จ ฉ ช ซ ฌ ญ ฎ ฏ ฐ ฑ ฒ ณ ด ต ถ ท ธ น บ ป ผ ฝ พ ฟ ภ ม ย ร ล ฦ ว ศ ษ ส **ห** ฬ อ ฮ

heart attack

หัวฉีด hǔua-chìit *n.* nozzle [หัว hǔua]

หัวไชเท้า hǔua-chai-táao *n.* radish [หัว hǔua]

หัวเทียน hǔua-tiian *n.* spark plug [ตัว dtuua]

หัวนม hǔua-nom *n.* nipple, pap [หัว hǔua]

หัวผักกาด hǔua-pàk-gàat *n.* turnip [หัว hǔua]

หัวแม่มือ hǔua-mɛ̂ɛ-muu *n.* thumb [นิ้ว níu]

หัวรั้น hǔua-rán *adj.* insistent (stubborn)

หัวรุนแรง hǔua-run-rɛɛng *adj.* radical (extremist)

หัวเราะ hǔua-rɔ́ *v.* laugh

หัวเราะเยาะ hǔua-rɔ́-yɔ́ *vt.* ridicule

หัวเรื่อง hǔua-rûuang *n.* title (heading) [เรื่อง rûuang]

หัวล้าน hǔua-láan *adj.* bald, bald head

หัวเสีย hǔua-sǐia *adj.* vexed (annoyed) ✷

หัวหน้า hǔua-nâa *n.* boss, leader (chief) [คน kon]

หัวหอม hǔua-hɔ̌ɔm *n.* onion [หัว hǔua]

หัวหิน hǔua-hǐn *n.* Hua Hin district [อำเภอ am-pəə]

หา hǎa *vt.* look for

ห่า hàa *interj.* fuck ✷

ห่า hàa *n.* heavy fall of rain, cholera ✷, evil spirit

ห้า hâa *numb.* five

หาก hàak *conj.* if

หาง hǎang *n.* stub (e.g. ticket, check) [ใบ bai]

หาง hǎang *n.* tail (e.g. animal) [หาง hǎang]

ห่าง hàang *adj.* away

ห้าง hâang *n.* department store, firm (store) [ห้าง hâang]

ห่างกัน hàang-gan *adj.* far apart

ห่างไกล hàang-glai *adj.* distant ❗, far ✎

หางเครื่อง hǎang-krûuang *n.* dancer (in a band) [คน kon]

หางจระเข้ hǎang-jɔɔ-rá~ kêe *n.* aloe [ต้น dtôn]

หางเปีย hǎang-bpiia *n.* pigtail (hairdo) [เส้น sên]

ห้างหุ้นส่วน hâang-hûn-sùuan *n.* partnership

(type of business) [แห่ง hɛ̀ng]

ห่างเหิน hàang-hə̌ən *adj.* remote

หาดทราย hàat-saai *n.* sandy beach [หาด hàat]

หาดใหญ่ hàat-yài *n.* Hat Yai district [อำเภอ am-pəə]

หาได้ hǎa-dâai *adj.* available (obtainable)

ห่าน hàan *n.* goose (animal) [ตัว dtuua]

หาบ hàap *n.* load [หาบ hàap]

หาบ hàap *vt.* carry at both ends of a pole on one's shoulder

หาม hǎam *vt.* bear (carry)

ห่าม hàam *adj.* almost ripe (fruit)

ห้าม hâam *vt.* ban, forbid, stop (prohibit)

ห้ามเข้า hâam-kâo *interj.* keep out!

หาย hǎai *adj.* lost (missing)

หาย hǎai *vi.* be healed or cured, be lost from sight

หายใจ hǎai-jai *v.* breathe

หายใจเข้า hǎai-jai-kâo *vi.* inhale

หายใจหอบ hǎai-jai-hɔ̀ɔp *vi.* pant (gasp)

หายใจออก hǎai-jai-ɔ̀ɔk *vi.* exhale (breathe out)

หายตัว hǎai-dtuua *vi.* disappear (vanish from sight)

หายนะ hǎa-yá~ná *n.* calamity, disaster

หายป่วย hǎai-bpùai *vi.* get well

หายไป hǎai-bpai *vi.* vanish

หายาก hǎa-yâak *adj.* rare (hard to find)

หาร hǎn *v.* divide (math)

หาเรื่อง hǎa-rʉ̂ʉang *v.* pick a quarrel

หาเลี้ยงชีพ hǎa-líiang-chîip *vi.* earn a living

หาว hǎao *vi.* yawn

หำ hǎm *n.* testicle ● [ลูก lûuk]

หิ้ง hîng *n.* shelf [หิ้ง hîng]

หิ่งห้อย hìng-hôi *n.* firefly [ตัว dtuua]

หิด hìt *n.* scabies [โรค rôok (disease)]

หิน hǐn *n.* rock, stone [ก้อน gɔ̂ɔn]

หินงอก hǐn-ngɔ̂ɔk *n.*

ก
ข
ค
ฆ
ง
จ
ฉ
ช
ซ
ฌ
ญ
ฎ
ฏ
ฐ
ฑ
ฒ
ณ
ด
ต
ถ
ท
ธ
น
บ
ป
ผ
ฝ
พ
ฟ
ภ
ม
ย
ร
ล
ว
ศ
ษ
ส
ห
อ
ฮ

stalagmite [ก้อน gɔ̂ɔn]

หินปูน hǐn-bpuun *n.* plaque (on teeth) [คราบ krâap]

หินย้อย hǐn-yɔ́ɔi *n.* stalactite [ก้อน gɔ̂ɔn]

หินยาน hǐn-ná~yaan *n.* Theravada Buddhism [นิกาย ní-gaai]

หินอ่อน hǐn-ɔ̀ɔn *n.* marble [ก้อน gɔ̂ɔn (piece)]

หิมะ hì-má *n.* snow

หิมะตก hì~má-dtòk *vi.* snow

หิว hǐu *adj.* hungry

หิวข้าว hǐu-kâao *adj.* hungry (food)

หิวจัด hǐu-jàt *adj.* starving

หิ้วได้ hîu-dâai *adj.* portable (carried by hand)

หิวน้ำ hǐu-náam *adj.* thirsty

หี hǐi *n.* cunt ☙, vagina ☙

หีบ hìip *clf.* for trunk-like boxes, coffins

หีบ hìip *n.* chest (cabinet), trunk (luggage) [ใบ bai]

หีบศพ hìip-sòp *n.* casket (coffin) [หีบ hìip]

หึง hǔng *adj.* envious (between lovers)

หุงข้าว hǔng-kâao *v.* cook rice

หุ่น hùn *n.* shape (figure, form)

หุ่น hùn *n.* mannequin ☙ [ตัว dtuua]

หุ่นกระบอก hùn-grà~bɔ̀ɔk *n.* puppet [ตัว dtuua]

หุ่นยนต์ hùn-yon *n.* robot [ตัว dtuua]

หุ่นไล่กา hùn-lâi-gaa *n.* scarecrow [ตัว dtuua]

หุ้นส่วน hûn-sùuan *n.* stock (share of business) [หุ้น hûn]

หุ้นส่วน hûn-sùuan *n.* partner (in business) [คน kon]

หุนหัน hǔn-hǎn *adj.* impetuous

หุบเขา hùp-kǎo *n.* valley [แห่ง hèng]

หุบปาก hùp-bpàak *interj.* shut up! ☙

หุ้ม hûm *vt.* wrap around

หู hǔu *n.* ear (organ) [หู hǔu, ข้าง kâang]

หู่ hùu *adj.* wrinkled

หูก hùuk *n.* loom [เครื่อง krʉ̂ʉang]

หูกระต่าย hǔu-grà~dtàai *n.* bow (ribbon) [อัน an]

หูด hùut *n.* wart (on skin) [เม็ด mét]

หูติดเชื้อ hǔu-dtìt-chʉ́ʉa *n.* ear infection [ข้าง kâang]

หูตึง hǔu-dtʉng *adj.* hard of hearing

หูโทรศัพท์ hǔu-too-rá~sàp *n.* telephone receiver [อัน an]

หูฝาด hǔu-fàat *adj.* hear mistakenly

หูฟัง hǔu-fang *n.* earphone [อัน an (piece), คู่ kûu (pair)]

หูหนวก hǔu-nùuak *adj.* deaf

หูอื้อ hǔu-ʉ̂ʉ *v.* pop (for ears)

เหงา ngǎo *adj.* lonely/lonesome

เหงื่อ ngʉ̀ʉa *n.* sweat (perspiration)

เหงือก ngʉ̀ʉak *n.* gum (of teeth)

เหงือก ngʉ̀ʉak *n.* gill [เหงือก ngʉ̀ʉak]

เหงื่อออก ngʉ̀ʉa-ɔ̀ɔk *vi.* perspire, sweat

เห็ด hèt *n.* mushroom [ดอก dɔ̀ɔk]

เหตุการณ์ hèet-gaan *n.* incident (event) [ครั้ง kráng]

เหตุผล hèet-pǒn *n.* reason [อัน an]

เห็น hěn *v.* look (see)

เห็นแก่ตัว hěn-gɛ̀ɛ-dtuua *adj.* selfish

เห็นใจ hěn-jai *vi.* sympathize

เห็นด้วย hěn-dûuai *v.* agree (with someone)

เหน็บ nèp *n.* numbness

เหน็บ nèp *vt.* insert (attach)

เห็นอกเห็นใจ hěn-òk-hěn-jai *adj.* sympathetic

เหนียว nǐiao *adj.* tough (not tender, sticky)

เหนี่ยว nìiao *v.* pull (haul, tug)

เหนี่ยวรั้ง nìiao-ráng *vt.* restrain (hold back from action)

เหนือ nǔua *n.* north [ทิศ tít]

เหนือ nǔua *prep.* above, over (higher than)

เหนือกว่า nǔua-gwàa *prep.* superior to (better than)

เหนื่อย nùuai *adj.* tired (exhausted)

เหนื่อยใจ nùuai-jai *v.* feel weary

เหนื่อยยาก nùuai-yâak *adj.* strenuous (energetic)

เหนื่อยอ่อน nùuai-ɔ̀ɔn *v.* droop (sag, be weakened)

เหนือหัว nǔua-hǔua *adj.* overhead (over one's head)

เห็บ hèp *n.* tick (bloodsucking animal) [ตัว dtuua]

เหม็น měn *adj.* smelly

เหม็น měn *vi.* stink

เหม็นตด měn-dtòt *vi.* smell a fart

เหม็นเน่า měn-nâo *adj.* foul (smelly)

เหม็นอับ měn-àp *adj.* moldy, musty

เหมา mǎo *v.* buy or sell as a whole, contract for work

เหมาะ mɔ̀ *adj.* fitting (appropriate)

เหมาะสม mɔ̀-sǒm *adj.* appropriate, suitable

เหมือง mǔuang *n.* mine (e.g. coal) [เหมือง mǔuang, แห่ง hɛ̀ng]

เหมือน mǔuan *adj.* like (similar to), similar

เหมือน mǔuan *v.* be the same as

เหมือน mǔuan *vt.* resemble

เหมือนกัน mǔuan-gan *adj.* equal to, same (similar)

เหมือนกัน mǔuan-gan *adv.* alike, also, as well

เหมือนกับ mǔuan-gàp *adj.* like (similar to)

เหมือนกับ mǔuan-gàp *adv.* as (in the same manner, equally)

เหมือนจริง mǔuan-jing *adj.* realistic (e.g. painting), virtual (simulated)

เหมือนเดิม mǔuan-dəəm *adj.* same (unchanged)

เหมือนไหม mǔuan-mǎi

เหย้า yâo *n.* dwelling place [แห่ง hèng]

เหยียดหยาม yìiat-yǎam *vt.* insult (look down on)

เหยียบ yìiap *vt.* tread on (step or walk on)

เหยี่ยว yìiao *n.* hawk (bird) [ตัว dtuua]

เหยื่อ yùua *n.* victim (prey, who is harmed or killed by another) [คน kon]

เหยื่อ yùua *n.* bait (e.g. fish) [อัน an]

เหยือก yùuak *n.* jug, pitcher [ใบ bai]

เหรัญญิก hěe-ran-yík *n.* treasurer (of company or association) [คน kon]

เหรียญ rǐian *n.* coin, medal, token [เหรียญ rǐian, อัน an]

เหล็ก lèk *n.* iron (metal) [อัน an]

เหล็กกล้า lèk-glâa *n.* steel

เหลน lěen *n.* great grandchild [คน kon]

เหลว lěeo *adj.* fluid, liquid

เหลา lǎo *vt.* sharpen (e.g. pencil)

เหล้า lâo *n.* alcohol, liquor ● [ขวด kùuat (bottle), แก้ว gêeo (glass)]

เหล่านั้น lào-nán *pron.* those

เหล่านี้ lào-níi *adj.* these

เหลิง lěong *v.* carry too far beyond a proper limit (of behavior)

เหลียวหลัง lǐiao-lǎng *v.* look back

เหลือ lǔua *adj.* remaining

เหลือก lùuak *v.* roll the eyes up

เหลือง lǔuang *adj.* yellow (color)

เหลือเชื่อ lǔua-chûua *adj.* incredible

เหลือบ lùuap *n.* horsefly [ตัว dtuua]

เหลือบดู lùuap-duu *vt.* glance at

เหลือเฟือ lǔua-fuua *adj.* excessive

เหลือม lǔuam *n.* python [ตัว dtuua]

เหลื่อมล้ำ lùuam-lám *adv.* unequal (e.g. rank, position)

เหลืออยู่ lǔua-yùu *vi.* remain (be left over)

เหวี่ยง wìiang *vt.* fling (throw)

เห่อ hə̀ə *vi.* gloat

เหา hǎo *n.* louse [ตัว dtuua]

เห่า hào *vi.* bark, yap

เหาะ hɔ̀ *vi.* soar into the air

เหี้ย hîia *n.* iguana ✿, water lizard [ตัว dtuua]

เหี่ยว hìiao *adj.* withered (dried up)

เหี่ยว hìiao *vi.* fade (lose freshness)

เหี่ยวแห้ง hìiao-hêng *vi.* wither

แห hɛ̌ *n.* fishing net [ปาก bpàak]

แห่ hɛ̀ *vi.* parade (go in procession)

แห่ง hɛ̀ng *clf.* for places, location

แห่ง hɛ̀ng *n.* place (site, spot)

แห้ง hɛ̂ng *adj.* dried, dry

แห้งแล้ง hɛ̂ng-lɛ́ɛng *adj.* barren (dry)

แหน nɛ̌ *n.* duckweed

แหนบ nɛ̀ɛp *n.* nippers, tweezers [อัน an]

แหนม nɛ̌ɛm *n.* kind of Thai condiment made

from fermented pork

แหบ hɛ̀ɛp *adj.* dry, harsh (voice)

แหบแห้ง hɛ̀ɛp-hɛ̂ng *adj.* hoarse

แหม mɛ̌ɛ *interj.* well! (Oh my goodness!)

แหม่ม mɛ̀m *n.* Caucasian woman, madam ✿ [คน kon]

แหย่ yɛ̀ *v.* poke (jab, poke fun), tease (make fun of) ✿

แหลก lɛ̀ɛk *adj.* crushed

แหล่ง lɛ̀ng *n.* place (site, spot)

แหล่งกำเนิด lɛ̀ng-gam-nə̀ət *n.* origin (source, root) ⚠

แหล่งที่มา lɛ̀ng-tîi-maa *n.* source (origin) [แหล่ง lɛ̀ng]

แหลน lɛ̌ɛn *n.* javelin (lance) [เล่ม lêm]

แหลม lɛ̌ɛm *adj.* pointed (sharp)

แหลม lɛ̌ɛm *n.* cape (peninsula) [แห่ง hɛ̀ng]

แหลมคม lɛ̌ɛm-kom *adj.* piercing (sharp)

แหละ lɛ̀ *part.* used at the end of a statement for

emphasis

แห้ว hêo *n.* water chestnut [หัว hŭua]

แหว่ง wèng *adj.* partly broken

แหวน wĕen *n.* ring (jewelry) [วง wong]

โหงวเฮ้ง ngŏo-héng *n.* characteristic (physical feature) •

โหดร้าย hòot-ráai *adj.* brutal, cruel

โหดเหี้ยม hòot-hîiam *adj.* ruthless

โหน hŏon *vi.* swing from by the hands

โหนก nòok *n.* bump (something protruding) [อัน an]

โหม hŏom *vi.* exert oneself

โหม่ง mòong *v.* hit (strike)

โหย hŏoi *v.* exhausted

โหยหิว hŏoi-hĭu *adj.* fatigue with hunger

โหระพา hŏo-rá~paa *n.* basil (sweet) [ต้น dtôn (plant), ใบ bai (leaf)]

โหราศาสตร์ hŏo-raa-sàat *n.* astrology [วิชา wí-chaa]

โหล lŏo *n.* dozen

ให้ hâi *vt.* give, grant, let (allow, give), present

ให้การ hâi-gaan *vi.* testify (give evidence)

ให้กำลังใจ hâi-gam-lang-jai *vt.* cheer (encourage)

ให้_กู้ hâi-_-gûu *vt.* loan (to someone)

ให้เกียรติ hâi-gìiat *vt.* honor

ให้เช่า hâi-châo *adj.* for rent

ให้เช่า hâi-châo *vt.* hire (to someone, e.g. car, bike), rent (to someone)

ใหญ่ yài *adj.* big, large

ใหญ่โต yài-dtoo *adj.* great (big)

ให้ผล hâi-pŏn *vi.* produce (yield results)

ให้พร hâi-pɔɔn *vt.* bless

ใหม่ mài *adj.* new

ใหม่ mài *adv.* again •

ใหม่เอี่ยม mài-ìiam *adj.* brand new

ให้ยืม hâi-yʉʉm *v.* lend, loan

ให้สินบน hâi-sĭn-bon *vt.* bribe

ให้อภัย hâi-à~pai *v.*

forgive

ให้อาหาร hâi-aa-hǎan *vt.* feed (give food to)

ไห hǎi *n.* earthen jar [ใบ bai]

ไหน nǎi *adj.* any, which

ไหน nǎi *adv.* where

ไหม mǎi *n.* silk (thread) [เส้น sên (thread), หลอด lɔ̀ɔt (reel)]

ไหม mǎi *part.* used to convert a statement into a yes-or-no question

ไหม้ mâi *vi.* burn

ไหล lǎi *vi.* coast, flow (e.g. liquid, ideas), stream

ไหล่ lài *n.* shoulder [ข้าง kâang]

ไหว้ wâai *v.* salute by placing the hands palm against palm and raising them to the face

ไหวพริบ wǎi-príp *n.* wit

ฬ

ฬ lɔɔ *let.* ฬ. จุฬา lɔɔ-jù-laa, a consonant of the Thai alphabet (low consonant) [ตัว dtuua]

อ

อ ɔɔ *let.* อ. อ่าง ɔɔ-àang, a

consonant of the Thai alphabet (mid consonant) [ตัว dtuua]

อก òk *n.* bosom (breast, chest)

อกตัญญู à~gà~dtan-yuu *adj.* ungrateful (not displaying gratitude)

อกหัก òk-hàk *adj.* heartbroken

อกุศล à~gù-sǒn *adj.* inauspicious

อคติ à-ká~dtì *n.* bias (prejudice)

องค์กร ong-gɔɔn *n.* organization (e.g. association, company) [องค์กร ong-gɔɔn]

องคชาติ ong-ká~châat *n.* cock ⚡, penis ✗ [อัน an]

องค์ประกอบ ong-bprà~gɔ̀ɔp *n.* constituent (component) [ส่วน sùuan, ชิ้น chín]

องครักษ์ ong-ká~rák *n.* watcher (protector) [คน kon]

องศา ong-sǎa *n.* degree (temperature) [องศา ong-sǎa]

องุ่น à~ngùn *n.* grape [ลูก lûuk, พวง puuang

(bunch)]

อด òt *vt.* abstain from ❧

อดทน òt-ton *adj.* patient

อดทน òt-ton *vi.* endure (persevere)

อดทนต่อ òt-ton-dtɔ̀ɔ *vt.* endure (for person)

อดอยาก òt-yàak *adj.* starving (to death)

อดอาหาร òt-aa-hǎan *vi.* fast

อดิเรก à-dì~rêek *n.* hobby

อดีต à~dìit *adj.* past (former)

อดีตกาล à~dìit-dtā~gaan *n.* past tense [กาล gaan]

อธรรม à~tam *n.* evil ❧

อธิการบดี à-tí-gaan-bɔɔ-dii *n.* rector [คน kon]

อธิบดี à~típ-bɔɔ-dii *n.* head of a department

อธิบาย à-tí-baai *v.* explain, illustrate, interpret

อธิษฐาน à~tít-tǎan *vi.* make a wish

อนาคต à~naa-kót *n.* future, tomorrow

อนามัย à~naa-mai *n.* hygiene

อนินทรีย์ à~nin-sii *adj.* inorganic ✖

อนึ่ง à~nùng *prep.* besides ⚡, in addition to

อนุญาต à-nú-yâat *vt.* excuse (forgive, allow)

อนุบาล à-nú-baan *n.* kindergarten ❧ [แห่ง hɛ̀ng]

อนุภาค à-nú-pâak *n.* particle (science) ✖

อนุมัติ à-nú-mát *v.* permit (approve by committee)

อนุมาน à-nú-maan *v.* infer ✖

อนุมูลอิสระ à-nú-muun-ìt-sà~rà *n.* free radical

อนุโมทนา à-nú-moo-tá~naa *vi.* express gratitude ⚡

อนุรักษ์ à-nú-rák *v.* conserve (e.g. natural resources)

อนุโลม à-nú-loom *vi.* defer (yield)

อนุสรณ์ à-nú-rɔ̌ɔn *n.* memorial ⚡, remembrance ⚡

อนุสาวรีย์ à-nú-sǎa~wá~rii *n.* monument [แห่ง hɛ̀ng]

อเนก à~nèek *adj.* several

อเนกประสงค์ à~nèek-

กขฃคฅฆงจฉชซฌญฎฏฐฑฒณดตถทธนบปผฝพฟภมยรฤลวศษสหฬอฮ

อเนกประสงค์ bprà~sǒng *adj.* versatile (can be used for several purposes)

อบ òp *vt.* bake, roast

อบเชย òp-chəəi *n.* cinnamon

อบรม òp-rom *vt.* train (educate, guide)

อบอ้าว òp-âao *adj.* muggy (hot, stuffy)

อบอุ่น òp-ùn *adj.* warm

อบายมุข à~baai-yá~múk *n.* path of ruining one's self [อย่าง yàang]

อพยพ òp-pá~yóp *vi.* evacuate, migrate

อพยพเข้า òp-pá~yóp-kâo *vt.* settle (migrate to)

อภัยโทษ à~pai-yá~tôot *n.* pardon (amnesty)

อภินันทนาการ à~pí-nan-tá~naa-gaan *adj.* complimentary (given free)

อภินิหาร à~pí-ní-hǎan *n.* miracle [ครั้ง kráng]

อภิสิทธิ์ à~pí-sìt *n.* privilege (special right) ✗

อม om *v.* keep in the mouth

อมตะ am-má~dtà *adj.* immortal

อมนุษย์ à~má~nút *n.* non-human being [ตน dton]

อมยิ้ม om-yím *n.* lollipop [อัน an]

อเมริกา à~mee-rí~gaa *n.* America, USA [ประเทศ bprà~têet]

อย่า yàa *aux.* do not/don't (forbiddance)

อย่า yàa *v.* prohibit (forbid, ban)

อยาก yàak *vt.* want to (do something)

อยากได้ yàak-dâai *vt.* desire, want (thing)

อยากรู้อยากเห็น yàak-rúu-yàak-hěn *adj.* curious (nosy)

อย่าง yàang *n.* kind (sort, type, category) [อย่าง yàang]

อย่างแท้จริง yàang-téɛ-jing *adv.* truly

อย่างยิ่ง yàang-yîng *adv.* extremely (very much)

อย่างไรก็ตาม yàang-rai-gɔ̂ɔ-dtaam *conj.* however, yet (nevertheless)

อยุธยา a-yút-tá~yaa *n.*

Ayutthaya province [จังหวัด jang-wàt]

อยู่ yùu *adj.* present (being here)

อยู่ yùu *v.* be/is/am/are/was/were/been (somewhere), live (dwell)

อยู่ yùu *vi.* reside, stay (remain)

อยู่ยงคงกระพัน yùu-yong-kong-grà~pan *adj.* invulnerable

อยู่ยาม yùu-yaam *v.* to be on guard ✎

อยู่รอด yùu-rɔ̂ɔt *vi.* survive (remain alive)

อรหันต์ ɔɔ-rá~hǎn, à~rá~hǎn *n.* Buddha (Arhanta) [องค์ ong]

อร่อย à~rɔ̀i *adj.* delicious, tasty

อริ à~rì *n.* enemy ✎ [คน kon (person), พวก pûuak (group)]

อรุณ à~run *n.* dawn/daybreak ✎

อรุณสวัสดิ์ à~run-sà~wàt *interj.* good morning! ❢

อลหม่าน on-lá~màan *adj.* busy (chaotic)

อโลหะ à~loo-hà *n.* non-material

อ้วก ûuak *vi.* throw up ✎, vomit ✎

อวกาศ à~wá~gàat *n.* space (astronomical)

อวด ùuat *vi.* boast

อวดดี ùuat-dii *adj.* arrogant, snobbish

อวตาร à~wá~dtaan *v.* descend from heaven ✎

อวน uuan *n.* fishing net, purse net [ปาก bpàak]

อ้วน ûuan *adj.* fat

อวบ ùuap *adj.* plump (chubby)

อวสาน à~wá~sǎan *vi.* end ✎

อวัยวะ à~wai-yá~wá *n.* organ (body) [ชิ้น chín (piece), ส่วน sùuan (part)]

อวัยวะเพศชาย à~wai-yá~wá-pêet-chaai *n.* penis ❢ [อัน an]

อวัยวะสืบพันธุ์ à~wai-yá~wá-sùup-pan *n.* genitals, reproductive organ

อโศก à~sòok *n.* Indian flowering plant [ต้น dtôn]

อสรพิษ à-rɔ̌ɔ-rá~pít *n.* creatures with poisonous fangs

อสังหาริมทรัพย์ à~sǎng-hǎa-rim-má~sáp *n.* real estate (house and land) ‼ [แห่ง hèng]

อสุจิ à-sù~jì *n.* sperm [ตัว dtuua]

อหิวาต์ à~hì-waa *n.* cholera

ออก ɔ̀ɔk *adj.* off (removed)

ออก ɔ̀ɔk *adv.* out (used with other words, e.g. take out, come out, etc.)

ออกกฎหมาย ɔ̀ɔk-gòt-mǎai *vi.* make law

ออกกำลังกาย ɔ̀ɔk-gam-lang-gaai *vi.* exercise (body), work out

ออกจาก ɔ̀ɔk-jàak *vt.* depart, get off (e.g. boat)

ออกซิเจน ɔ́k-sí~jên *n.* oxygen

ออกเดินทาง ɔ̀ɔk-dəən-taang *vi.* depart, take off (for a trip)

ออกนอกเรื่อง ɔ̀ɔk-nɔ̂ɔk-rûuang *vi.* digress

ออกแบบ ɔ̀ɔk-bɛ̀ɛp *v.* design

ออกไป ɔ̀ɔk-bpai *vi.* get out, leave (go away)

ออกผล ɔ̀ɔk-pǒn *vi.* bear fruit, yield fruit

ออกพรรษา ɔ̀ɔk-pan-sǎa *vi.* come out of Buddhist Lent

ออกมา ɔ̀ɔk-maa *vi.* come out (result as, e.g. photo, vote)

ออกฤทธิ์ ɔ̀ɔk-rít *vi.* kick in (take effect, e.g. drug)

ออกลูก ɔ̀ɔk-lûuk *vi.* give birth ✿, reproduce (for mammals)

ออกเสียง ɔ̀ɔk-sǐiang *v.* pronounce (enuciate, utter)

ออกเสียง ɔ̀ɔk-sǐiang *vi.* vote

ออกเสียง ɔ̀ɔk-sǐiang *vt.* sound like (makes the sound)

ออกหัด ɔ̀ɔk-hàt *v.* break out with measles

ออกห่าง ɔ̀ɔk-hàang *vt.* stay away from

ออกอากาศ ɔ̀ɔk-aa-gàat *v.* air (broadcast)

อ่อน ɔ̀ɔn *adj.* light (shade of color), soft (to the touch), tender

อ้อน ɔ̂ɔn *vi.* whine (in a childish fashion)

อ่อนใจ ɔ̀ɔn-jai *v.* feel weary

ออนซ์ ɔɔn *n.* ounce [ออนซ์

ววก]

อ่อนเพลีย ɔ̀ɔn-pliia *adj.* exhausted (fatigued)

อ่อนเยาว์ ɔ̀ɔn-yao *adj.* be juvenile

อ่อนโยน ɔ̀ɔn-yoon *adj.* gentle (soft in manners), mild

อ่อนโยน ɔ̀ɔn-yoon *vi.* soften

อ่อนแรง ɔ̀ɔn-rɛɛng *adj.* feeble (weak)

อ้อนวอน ɔ̂ɔn-wɔɔn *vt.* appeal to (beg)

อ่อนหัด ɔ̀ɔn-hàt *adj.* inexperienced ✿

อ่อนไหว ɔ̀ɔn-wǎi *adj.* sensitive (easy to trigger strong emotion)

อ่อนแอ ɔ̀ɔn-ʔɛɛ *adj.* limp, weak (not strong, frail)

ออฟฟิศ ɔ́ɔp-fít *n.* office (where work is conducted) ✿ [แห่ง hɛ̀ng, ที่ tîi]

อ้อม ɔ̂ɔm *adj.* roundabout

อ้อมค้อม ɔ̂ɔm-kɔ́ɔm *adj.* indirect (not direct)

อ่อย ɔ̀i *vt.* lure ✿

อ้อย ɔ̂i *n.* sugarcane [ต้น dtôn (plant)]

อะตอม à~dtɔm *n.* atom [อะตอม à~dtɔm]

อะไร à~rai *adj.* what

อะไร à~rai *adv.* what

อะไร à~rai *pron.* anything (in question), something (as object, in question), what

อะไรก็ได้ à~rai-gɔ̂ɔ-dâai *adj.* whatever

อะไรก็ได้ à~rai-gɔ̂ɔ-dâai *pron.* anything, whatever

อะไรก็ตาม à~rai-gɔ̂ɔ-dtaam *pron.* anything ⚡

อะหลั่ย à~lài see อะไหล่

อะไหล่ à~lài *n.* spare parts (cars, etc.) [ชิ้น chín]

อักขระ àk-kà~rà *n.* letter of the alphabet [ตัว dtuua]

อักษร àk-sɔ̌ɔn *n.* alphabet

อักษรศาสตร์ àk-sɔ̌ɔn-sàat *n.* literature

อักเสบ àk-sèep *adj.* inflamed (infected)

อัคคีภัย àk-kii-pai *n.* disaster caused by fire

อังกฤษ ang-grìt *n.* England [ประเทศ bprà~têet]

ก
ข
ข
ค
ค
ฆ
ง
จ
ฉ
ช
ซ
ฌ
ญ
ฎ
ฏ
ฐ
ฑ
ฒ
ณ
ด
ต
ถ
ท
ธ
น
บ
ป
ผ
ฝ
พ
ฟ
ภ
ม
ย
ร
ฤ
ล
ว
ศ
ษ
ส
ห
ฬ
อ
ฮ

อังคาร ang-kaan *n.* Mars [ดวง duuang]

อังคาร ang-kaan *n.* Tuesday ☀ [วัน wan]

อั้งเปา âng-bpao *n.* red envelope [ซอง sɔɔng]

อัจฉริยะ àt-chà-rí-yá *n.* genius (person) [คน kon]

อัญประกาศ an-yá-bprà-gàat *n.* quotation mark ✵ [ตัว dtuua, คู่ kûu (pair)]

อัฐ àt *n.* obsolete unit of Thai currency, money ⬠

อัฐิ àt-tì *n.* ash (from cremation) [ผง pǒng (dust), ชิ้น chín (piece)]

อัฒภาค àt-tá-pâak *n.* semicolon ✵ [ตัว dtuua]

อัด àt *vt.* compress (pressurize)

อัดแน่น àt-nên *adj.* jam-packed

อัดรูป àt-rûup *v.* print a photograph

อัตโนมัติ àt-dtà-noo-mát *adj.* automatic

อัตรา àt-dtraa *n.* rate (proportion, ratio, tariff)

อัตราร้อยละ àt-dtraa-rɔ́ɔi-lá *n.* percentage (per

hundred) ⚠

อัตราแลกเปลี่ยน àt-dtraa-lɛ̂ɛk-bpliian *n.* exchange rate [อัตรา àt-dtraa]

อัตราส่วน àt-dtraa-sùuan *n.* ratio

อัธยาศัย àt-tá-yaa-sǎi *n.* temperament (disposition) ⚠

อัธยาศัยดี àt-tá-yaa-sǎi-dii *adj.* hospitable

อัน an *clf.* for small or long objects

อันดับ an-dàp *n.* order (series by order of preference, grade or rank) [ที่ tîi]

อันใดอันหนึ่ง an-dai-an-nὺng *pron.* either (each)

อันตราย an-dtà-raai *adj.* dangerous

อันตราย an-dtà-raai *n.* danger, harm

อันธพาล an-tá-paan *n.* gangster, rascal [คน kon]

อันไหน an-nǎi *adj.* which

อับ àp *adj.* musty (moldy)

อับปาง àp-bpaang *adj.* wrecked (boat)

อับอาย àp-aai *adj.*

embarrassed (ashamed)

อัปมงคล àp-bpà~mong-kon *adj.* inauspicious ๛

อัมพาต am-má~pâat *n.* paralysis [โรค rôok]

อัยการ ai-yá~gaan *n.* prosecutor [คน kon]

อัลบั้ม aa-lá~bâm *n.* album [เล่ม lêm]

อัศเจรีย์ àt-sà~jee-rii *n.* exclamation point ✄ [ตัว dtuua]

อัศวิน àt-sà~win *n.* knight [คน kon]

อา aa *n.* father's younger brother or sister [คน kon]

อ้า âa *v.* open wide

อากร aa-gɔɔn *n.* revenue

อาการ aa-gaan *n.* symptom (sign, indication)

อากาศ aa-gàat *n.* air (outside air), climate, weather

อาข่า aa-kàa *n.* Akha (hilltribe) [เผ่า pào]

อาคาร aa-kaan *n.* building, facility [หลัง lăng]

อ่าง àang *n.* basin (sink), tub (container, jar) [ใบ bai]

อ้าง âang *vt.* claim (assert)

อ่างเก็บน้ำ àang-gèp-náam *n.* reservoir (of water) [แห่ง hèng]

อ่างซักผ้า àang-sák-pâa *n.* washtub [ใบ bai]

อ้างถึง âang-tŭng *vt.* cite (quote)

อ่างทอง àang-tɔɔng *n.* Angthong province [จังหวัด jang-wàt]

อ่างล้างมือ àang-láang-mɯɯ *n.* wash basin [อัน an]

อ่างอาบน้ำ àang-àap-náam *n.* bathtub [อ่าง àang]

อ้างอิง âang-ing *vt.* refer to (e.g. dictionary)

อาจ àat *adj.* bold, brave

อาจ àat *adv.* maybe

อาจจะ àat-jà *adv.* maybe, perhaps

อาจารย์ aa-jaan *n.* instructor, teacher [คน kon, ท่าน tân ‼]

อาจารย์ใหญ่ aa-jaan-yài *n.* principal (school) [ท่าน tân ‼]

อาเจียน aa-jiian *vi.* vomit

ก
ข
ข
ค
ค
ฆ
ง
จ
ฉ
ช
ช
ฌ
ญ
ฎ
ฏ
ฐ
ฑ
ฒ
ณ
ด
ต
ถ
ท
ธ
น
บ
ป
ผ
ฝ
พ
ฟ
ภ
ม
ย
ร
ฤ
ล
ว
ศ
ษ
ส
ห
อ
ฮ

อาชญากร àat-chá~yaa-goon n. criminal [คน kon]

อาชญากรรม àat-chá~yaa-gam n. crime, offense

อาชีพ aa-chîip n. career (profession), occupation [อาชีพ aa-chîip]

อาณาเขต aa-naa-kèet n. boundary (territory) ! [แห่ง hɛ̀ng]

อาณาจักร aa-naa-jàk n. empire, realm [แห่ง hɛ̀ng]

อาทิ aa-tí conj. for instance !

อาทิ aa-tí n. example !

อาทิตย์ aa-tít n. sun [ดวง duuang]

อาทิตย์ aa-tít n. week ✸ [อาทิตย์ aa-tít]

อาน aan n. saddle [อัน an]

อ่าน àan v. read

อ่านง่าย àan-ngâai adj. legible

อ่านออก àan-ɔ̀ɔk adj. legible

อาบ àap vi. bathe

อาบน้ำ àap-náam vi. bathe

อาบัติ aa-bàt n. violation ✿

อ้าปากค้าง âa-bpàak-káang vi. gasp (inhale suddenly)

อาพาธ aa-pâat adj. ill (sick) ✿

อาพาร์ตเมนท์ aa-páat-mén n. apartment [ห้อง hɔ̂ng]

อาฟริกา áa-frí-gaa n. Africa [ทวีป tá~wîip]

อาเมน aa-men interj. amen!

อาย aai adj. ashamed (embarrassed at mistake), shy (timid)

อายัด aa-yát vt. deactivate, impound (seize)

อายุ aa-yú n. age (number of years old)

อายุความ aa-yú-kwaam n. statute of limitations

อายุน้อย aa-yú-nɔ́ɔi adj. young (youthful)

อายุสั้น aa-yú-sân adj. short-lived

อารบิค aa-rá~bìk adj. Arabic

อารมณ์ aa-rom n. emotion, feeling, mood

อารมณ์ค้าง aa-rom-káang vi. done with sex but have not reached an orgasm ✸

ก ข ฃ ค ฅ ฆ ง จ ฉ ช ซ ฌ ญ ฎ ฏ ฐ ฑ ฒ ณ ด ต ถ ท ธ น บ ป ผ ฝ พ ฟ ภ ม ย ร ฤ ล ฦ ว ศ ษ ส ห ฬ ๏ อ ฮ

อารมณ์เสีย aa-rom-sǐia *adj.* moody (having a bad mood)

อารยธรรม aa-rá~yá-tam *n.* civilization

อาราม aa-raam *n.* monastery [แห่ง hèng]

อาละวาด aa-lá~wâat *v.* rampage (act violently)

อ่าว àao *n.* bay, gulf (sea) [อ่าว àao]

อ้าว âao *adj.* hot (temperature)

อาวาส aa-wâat *n.* monastery ✍ [แห่ง hèng]

อาวุธ aa-wút *n.* arm, weapon [ชิ้น chín]

อาวุธปืน aa-wút-bpɯɯn *n.* firearm [กระบอก grà~bɔ̀ɔk]

อาวุโส aa-wú-sǒo *adj.* elderly

อาศัย aa-sǎi *vi.* live (dwell) ⚡, reside ⚡

อาศัยอยู่ใน aa-sǎi-yùu-nai *vt.* inhabit

อาสัญ aa-sǎn *vi.* die ✍

อาสาสมัคร aa-sǎa-sà~màk *n.* volunteer [คน kon]

อาหาร aa-hǎan *n.* meal

(food) [มื้อ mɯ́ɯ]

อาหาร aa-hǎan *n.* cuisine, food [อย่าง yàang (dish), ประเภท bprà~pêet (kind)]

อาหารกลางวัน aa-hǎan-glaang-wan *n.* lunch ⚡ [มื้อ mɯ́ɯ]

อาหารขยะ aa-hǎan-kà~yà *n.* junk food

อาหารค่ำ aa-hǎan-kâm *n.* supper [มื้อ mɯ́ɯ]

อาหารเช้า aa-hǎan-cháao *n.* breakfast ⚡ [มื้อ mɯ́ɯ]

อาหารทะเล aa-hǎan-tá~lee *n.* seafood [ชนิด chá~nít (type)]

อาหารเที่ยง aa-hǎan-tîiang *n.* lunch ⚡ [มื้อ mɯ́ɯ]

อาหารเป็นพิษ aa-hǎan-bpen-pít *n.* food poisoning

อาหารเย็น aa-hǎan-yen *n.* dinner ⚡ [มื้อ mɯ́ɯ]

อาหารเสริม aa-hǎan-sɤ̌ɤm *n.* supplement (e.g. vitamins)

อาหารหลัก aa-hǎan-làk *n.* staple (e.g. rice, bread)

ก ข ฃ ค ฅ ฆ ง จ ฉ ช ซ ฌ ญ ฎ ฏ ฐ ฑ ฒ ณ ด ต ถ ท ธ น บ ป ผ ฝ พ ฟ ภ ม ย ร ฤ ล ว ศ ษ ส ห **อ** ฮ

กขฃคฅฆงจฉชซฌญฎฏฐฑฒณดตถทธนบปผฝพฟภมยรฤลวศษสหฬอฮ

อำนาจ am-nâat *n.* authority, might (superior power), power

อำนาจศาล am-nâat-sǎan *n.* jurisdiction [เขต kèet (region)]

อำนาจสูงสุด am-nâat-sǔung-sùt *n.* majesty (supreme authority)

อำพัน am-pan *n.* amber (fossil resin) [ก้อน gɔ̂ɔn]

อำเภอ am-pəə *n.* district office [อำเภอ am-pəə]

อิง ing *vt.* rest against

อิจฉา it-chǎa *adj.* envious, jealous

อิจฉา it-chǎa *vt.* envy

อิฐ ìt *n.* brick (clay) [ก้อน gɔ̂ɔn (block)]

อิตาลี it-dtaa-lîi *n.* Italy [ประเทศ bprà~têet]

อิทธิพล ìt-tí-pon *n.* influence

อิทธิฤทธิ์ ìt-tí-rít *n.* power (might)

อินเดีย in-diia *n.* India [ประเทศ bprà~têet]

อินโดนีเซีย in-doo-nii-siia *n.* Indonesia [ประเทศ bprà~têet]

อินทผลัม in-tá~pà~lam *n.* date (fruit) [ลูก lûuk]

อินทรี in-sii *n.* eagle [ตัว dtuua]

อิ่ม ìm *adj.* full (from eating)

อิรัก ì~rák *n.* Iraq [ประเทศ bprà~têet]

อิสรภาพ ìt-sà~rá~pâap *n.* freedom

อิสระ ìt-sà~rà *adj.* independent

อิสราเอล ìt-sà~raa-eeo *n.* Israel [ประเทศ bprà~têet]

อิหร่าน ì~ràan *n.* Iran [ประเทศ bprà~têet]

อี ii- *pref.* (derogatory) title used with first names of women, bound element in names of birds and animals

อีก ìik *adv.* again, more (in addition)

อีกต่อไป ìik-dtɔ̀ɔ-bpai *adv.* anymore

อีควาย ii-kwaai *interj.* stupid! (female) ❦

อีจู้ ii-jûu *n.* fish trap [ใบ bai]

อีดอก ii-dɔ̀ɔk *n.* slut ⚥ [คน kon]

อีตัว ii-dtuua *n.* whore ☄ [คน kon]

อีโต้ ii-dtôo *n.* cleaver [เล่ม lêm]

อีเมล์ ii-meo *n.* email ✿ [ฉบับ chà~bàp]

อีสาน ii-sǎan *n.* northeast of Thailand

อีสาน ii-sǎan *n.* northeast ✿ [ทิศ tít]

อีสุกอีใส ii-sùk-ii-sǎi *n.* chicken pox

อีห่า ii-hàa *interj.* damn you! ✿

อีแอบ ii-ὲɛp *n.* in the closet gay ✿ [คน kon]

อี้ ̀ *n.* fecal matter [ก้อน gɔ̂ɔn, กอง gɔɔng (pile)]

อี้ ̀ *v.* defecate

อีกทึก ̀k-gà~túk *adj.* noisy

อึ่งอ่าง ̀ng-àang *n.* bullfrog [ตัว dtuua]

อืด ̀t *vt.* suppress (e.g. feelings, smile)

อืดอัด ̀t-àt *adj.* uncomfortable (uneasy)

อึ๋ม ̌m *n.* breast (woman's) ✿ [เต้า dtâo]

อืด ̀t *adj.* sluggish, swollen

อืดอาด ̀t-àat *adj.* slow-moving

อื่น ̀n *adj.* another, different (not same), else (other, e.g. ask someone else), other

อื่น ̀n *adv.* else (other, e.g. how else?)

อื่นๆ ̀n-ùun *adj.* other

อื้อ ̂ *adj.* loud, noisy

อุกกาบาต ùk-gaa-bàat *n.* meteorite [ลูก lûuk]

อุ้งเท้า ûng-táao *n.* paw (claw, foot) [ข้าง kâang]

อุ้งมือ ûng-mɯɯ *n.* paw (claw, hand) [ข้าง kâang]

อุ้งเล็บ ûng-lép *n.* claw (of animals with toes) [ข้าง kâang]

อุจจาระ ùt-jaa-rá *n.* excrement ⚡, feces ⚡, shit ⚡ [กอง gɔɔng (pile), ก้อน gɔ̂ɔn]

อุณหภูมิ un-hà~puum *n.* temperature [องศา ong-sǎa (degree)]

อุด ùt *v.* caulk

อุดตัน ùt-dtan *v.* clog (e.g. pores, pipes)

อุดปาก ùt-bpàak *vt.* suffocate (strangle)

อุดมคติ ù-dom-ká~dtì *n.* ideal (standard of perfection)

อุดมสมบูรณ์ ù-dom-sǒm-buun *adj.* abundant, fertile (e.g. soil, region)

อุดรธานี ù-dɔɔn-taa-nii *n.* Udon Thani province [จังหวัด jang-wàt]

อุดหนุน ùt-nǔn *vt.* patronize (support), subsidize

อุตรดิตถ์ ùt-dtà-rà~dìt *n.* Uttaradit province [จังหวัด jang-wàt]

อุตสาหกรรม ùt-sǎa-hà~gam *n.* industry (manufacture in general) [ประเภท bprà~pêet]

อุตสาหะ ùt-sǎa-hà *adj.* industrious ✍

อุตุนิยมวิทยา ù-dtù-ní-yom-wít-tá~yaa *n.* meteorology [วิชา wí-chaa]

อุทกภัย ù-tók-gà~pai *n.* flood ⚡

อุทธรณ์ ùt-tɔɔn, ù-tɔɔn *vi.* appeal (request new hearing)

อุทยาน ùt-tá~yaan *n.* park (national park) [แห่ง hɛ̀ng]

อุทาน ù-taan *n.* exclamation (forceful utterance)

อุทาหรณ์ ù-taa-hɔ̌ɔn *n.* example ✍

อุทิศ ù-tít *vt.* dedicate, devote (time, money)

อุ่น ùn *adj.* lukewarm, warm

อุบลราชธานี ù-bon-râat-chá~taa-nii *n.* Ubon Ratchathani province [จังหวัด jang-wàt]

อุบัติเหตุ ù-bàt-dtì~hèet *n.* accident (e.g. car) [ครั้ง kráng]

อุบาทว์ ù-bàat *adj.* wicked (hellish)

อุบาย ù-baai *n.* ruse [อัน an]

อุบาสก ù-baa-sòk *n.* devout layman [คน kon]

อุบาสิกา ù-baa-sì~gaa *n.* devout laywoman [คน kon]

อุโบสถ ù-boo-sòt *n.* Buddhist building [หลัง lǎng]

อุปกรณ์ ùp-bpà~gɔɔn *n.*

accessory (part), equipment [ชิ้น chín (piece), ชุด chút (set)]

อุปถัมภ์ ù-bpà-tǎm *vt.* support (provide for) ⚡

อุปโภค ùp-bpà~pôok *v.* consume (spend) ✖

อุปสมบท ùp-bpà~sǒm-bòt *adj.* ordained as a Buddhist monk

อุปสรรค ùp-bpà~sàk *n.* obstacle (hindrance) [อัน an]

อุปาทาน ùp-bpaa~taan *v.* adhere to wrong beliefs, prejudice (bias)

อุ้ม ûm *v.* carry in one's arms

อุ้ม ûm *vt.* carry (cradle in arms)

อุโมงค์ ù-moong *n.* tunnel [อุโมงค์ ù-moong]

อุลตราซาวด์ un-dtrâa-saao *n.* ultrasound

อู่ ùu *n.* cradle (for baby) [อู่ ùu]

อู่ ùu *n.* dock (shipyard) [อู่ ùu]

อู้งาน ûu-ngaan *v.* work with unnecessary delay

อู่ซ่อมรถ ùu-sôm-rót *n.* body shop (for autos) [อู่ ùu]

อูฐ ùut *n.* camel [ตัว dtuua]

อู๊ย úui *interj.* whoa!

อู่เรือ ùu-ruua *n.* dock (shipyard) [อู่ ùu]

เอก èek *adj.* leading (first-rate), prime (first)

เอกฉันท์ èek-gà~chǎn *n.* unanimity

เอกชน èek-gà~chon *adj.* private (not government)

เอ็กซ์เรย์ ék-sà~ree *n.* x-ray ● [ภาพ pâap (image)]

เอกพจน์ èek-gà~pót *n.* singular (grammar) [คำ kam]

เอกราช èek-gà~râat *n.* independence (of a country)

เอกลักษณ์ èek-gà~lák *n.* entity, identity (e.g. personal, national, religious)

เอกสาร èek-gà~sǎan *n.* document [ฉบับ chà~bàp]

เอกสิทธิ์ èek-gà~sìt *n.* monopoly ⚡

เอกอัครราชทูต èek-àk-ká~râat-chá~tûut *n.* ambassador [ท่าน tân ⚐, คน kon]

เอง eeng *adv.* only (just) ⚐

เอง eeng *pron.* oneself

เอชไอวี ét-ai-wii *n.* HIV

เอเชีย ee-chiia *n.* Asia [ทวีป tá~wîip]

เอเชียตะวันออกเฉียงใต้ ee-chiia-dtà~wan-ɔ̀ɔk-chǐiang-dtâai *n.* Southeast Asia [แถบ tɛ̀ɛp]

เอเชียใต้ ee-chiia-dtâai *n.* Southern Asia [แถบ tɛ̀ɛp]

เอซ èet, èes *n.* ace (in playing cards) [ใบ bai]

เอ็ด èt *numb.* one (used after tens, hundreds, etc.)

เอน een *v.* recline

เอ็น en *n.* ligament (tendon) [เส้น sên]

เอนไซม์ en-saai *n.* enzyme [ชนิด chá~nít]

เอ็นดู en-duu *v.* have compassion and affection for

เอ่ย ə̀əi *v.* utter

เอ่ยถึง ə̀əi-tǔng *vt.* speak of

เอเย่นต์ ee-yên *n.* agent

(representative) [คน kon (person), แห่ง hɛ̀ng (place)]

เอว eeo *n.* waist [นิ้ว níu]

เออ əə *interj.* expressing agreement

เอา ao *vt.* get, take (get, grab)

เอ้า âo *interj.* well! (Oh!)

เอากัน ao-gan *vi.* have sex ⚐, fuck ⚐

เอาใจ ao-jai *vt.* appease (satisfy, please), pamper

เอาใจใส่ ao-jai-sài *v.* heed

เอาชนะ ao-chá~ná *v.* defeat (conquer, win over), overcome

เอาเปรียบ ao-bpriiap *v.* take advantage of

เอา_ไป ao-_-bpai *vt.* take (_ (something, some vehicle) from here (to))

เอา_มา ao-_-maa *vt.* bring (_ (something, some vehicle) here (to))

เอา_ออก ao-_-ɔ̀ɔk *vt.* take out (extract or remove)

เอียง iiang *adj.* sloping

เอียง iiang *vi.* incline (tilt)

เอี้ยง îiang *n.* singing myna [ตัว dtuua]

เอียน iian *adj.* sickly sweet, too oily

เอี๊ยม íiam *n.* kind of apron [ตัว dtuua, ผืน pǔun]

เอื้อน ûuan *v.* draw out the voice or sounds

เอื้อมคว้า ûuam-kwáa *vt.* reach (for something)

แอก ɛ̀ɛk *n.* yoke (device to pair animals) [อัน an, ตัว dtuua]

แอ่ง ɛ̀ng *n.* basin (e.g. river basin) [แอ่ง ɛ̀ng, แห่ง hɛ̀ng]

แอ่งน้ำ ɛ̀ng-náam *n.* puddle [แอ่ง ɛ̀ng, แห่ง hɛ̀ng]

แอ่น ɛ̀n *v.* bend the body backward, bend out

แอนตาร์คติกา ɛɛn-dtáak-dtì~gâa *n.* Antarctica [ทวีป tá~wîip]

แอบ ɛ̀ɛp *v.* hide

แอบดู ɛ̀ɛp-duu *vi.* peek

แอบฟัง ɛ̀ɛp-fang *v.* eavesdrop (listen in)

แอบมอง ɛ̀ɛp-mɔɔng *v.* peep (glance at)

แอปเปิล ɛ́p-bpên *n.* apple [ลูก lûuk (fruit)]

แอมป์ ɛm *n.* ampere/amp

แอร์ ɛɛ *n.* air conditioner ✤ [เครื่อง krûuang]

แอลกอฮอล์ ɛn-gɔɔ-hɔɔ *n.* alcohol (chemical)

แอสไพริน ɛ̀ɛs-pai-rin *n.* aspirin [เม็ด mét]

แออัด ɛɛ-àt *adj.* congested (packed or crowded)

โอ oo *n.* small bowl [ใบ bai]

โอ่ òo *vi.* boast

โอ๋ ǒo *vt.* comfort (pamper) ✤

โอกาส oo-gàat *n.* chance (opportunity), occasion [ครั้ง kráng]

โอเค oo-kee *interj.* okay!/O.K.! ✤

โอ่ง òong *n.* jar (water) [ใบ bai]

โองการ oong-gaan *n.* command [โองการ oong-gaan]

โอชา oo-chaa *adj.* delicious ✤

โอ่โถง òo-tǒong *adj.* splendid (grand)

โอที oo-tii *n.* overtime ❀ [กะ gà]

โอนกรรมสิทธิ์ oon-gam-má-sìt *v.* transfer ownership

โอนสัญชาติ oon-sǎn-châat *vi.* change one's citizenship

โอน_ให้_ oon-_-hâi-_ *vt.* transfer (ownership, control of _ to _)

โอบ òop *v.* embrace (hug)

โอบกอด òop-gɔ̀ɔt *vt.* cuddle

โอบล้อม òop-lɔ́ɔm *vt.* siege (surround)

โอ๊ย óoi *interj.* ouch!

โอลิมปิก oo-lim-bpìk *n.* Olympics [ครั้ง kráng]

โอเวอร์ oo-wə̂ə *v.* overact (overdo, exaggerate) ❀

โอหัง oo-hǎng *adj.* arrogant ☙, daring

โอ้โห ôo-hǒo *interj.* wow!

โอ้อวด ôo-ùat *adj.* pretentious (showy)

โอ้อวด ôo-ùat *vi.* brag

โอ่อ่า òo-àa *adj.* dignified and pretty

โอ้เอ้ ôo-êe *v.* linger

(delay)

ไอ ai *n.* vapor (smog, fog, steam)

ไอ ai *vi.* cough

ไอ้ âi- *pref.* derogatory title used with first names of men and also for insult

ไอกรน ai-gron *n.* pertussis, whooping cough [โรค rôok]

ไอ้ควาย âi-kwaai *interj.* stupid! (male) ❀

ไอคิว ai-kiu *n.* I.Q. [ไอคิว ai-kiu]

ไอ้จู๋ âi-jǔu *n.* penis ❀ [อัน an]

ไอ้เจี๊ยว âi-jíiao *n.* penis ❀ [อัน an]

ไอ้ตัว âi-dtuua *n.* prostitute (male) ♂❀ [คน kon]

ไอติม ai-dtim *n.* ice cream ❀ [แท่ง tɛ̂ng (stick), ถ้วย tûuai (bowl), ลูก lûuk (ball), รส rót (flavor)]

ไอน้ำ ai-náam *n.* steam

ไอศกรีม ai-sà~griim *n.* ice cream [แท่ง tɛ̂ng (stick), ถ้วย tûuai (bowl),

ลูก lûuk (ball), รส rót (flavor)]

ไอ้สัตว์ âi-sàt *interj.* you animal! ♟

ไอเสีย ai-sǐia *n.* exhaust (e.g. car), exhaust fumes

ไอ้หนู âi-nǔu *n.* small penis ●

ไอ้ห่า âi-hàa *interj.* damn you! ●

ไอโอดีน ai-oo-diin *n.* iodine [สาร sǎan]

ฮ

ฮ hɔɔ *let.* ฮ. นกฮูก hɔɔ-nók-hûuk, a consonant of the Thai alphabet (low consonant) [ตัว dtuua]

ฮวงจุ้ย huuang-jûi *n.* feng shui

ฮวงซุ้ย huuang-súi *n.* Chinese cemetery [แห่ง hɛ̀ng, ที่ tîi]

ฮ่อ hɔ̀ *adj.* Chinese tribe, from Yunnan province of China

ฮ่องกง hɔ̂ng-gong *n.* Hong Kong [เกาะ gɔ̀ (island)]

ฮ่องเต้ hɔ̂ng-dtêe *n.* Chinese emperor [องค์ ong]

ฮะ há *interj.* yes! (mainly for male speakers) ●

ฮะ há *part.* variant of "yes"

ฮัมเพลง ham-pleeng *vi.* hum

ฮา haa *adj.* funny (humorous) ●

ฮาเร็ม haa-rem *n.* harem [แห่ง hɛ̀ng]

ฮิต hít *adj.* hit (e.g. song)

ฮินดู hin-duu *adj.* Hindu

ฮิปโป híp-bpoo *n.* hippopotamus ● [ตัว dtuua]

ฮึกเหิม húk-hǒəm *adj.* bold

ฮึด hút *v.* make up one's mind to fight

ฮึดฮัด hút-hát *vi.* grunt

ฮือ hɯɯ *n.* crying or groaning sound

ฮือ hɯɯ *vi.* suddenly burst into flame

ฮูก hûuk *n.* owl [ตัว dtuua]

เฮง heng *adj.* fortunate ●, lucky ●

เฮงซวย heng-suuai *interj.* crap!

เฮ่ย hêi *interj.* hey!

เฮโรอีน hee-roo-iin *n.*

heroin

เฮลิคอปเตอร์ hee-lí~ kóp-dtôə *n.* helicopter

[เครื่อง krûuang, ลำ lam]

เฮโล hee-loo *v.* flock in large numbers

เฮฮา hee-haa *adj.* hilarious

เฮี้ยน híian *adj.* manifesting the power of an evil spirit ✸

แฮ้ง hÉeng *vi.* have a headache from drinking ✸, freeze (computer)

แฮม hɛm *n.* ham (meat)

[ชิ้น chín]

โฮ hoo *interj.* boohoo!

ไฮโซ hai-soo *adj.* high-class ✸

ไฮโดรเจน hai-droo-jên *n.* hydrogen

ไฮโล hai-loo *n.* kind of gambling played with dice

ไฮเวย์ hai-wee *n.* highway

[ทาง taang]

ก
ข
ข
ค
ค
ฆ
ง
จ
ฉ
ช
ซ
ฌ
ญ
ฎ
ฏ
ฐ
ฑ
ฒ
ณ
ด
ต
ถ
ท
ธ
น
บ
ป
ผ
ฝ
พ
ฟ
ภ
ม
ย
ร
ฤ
ล
ฦ
ว
ศ
ษ
ส
ห
ฬ
อ

Section Three: Thai Sound

See p. 14 for some tips on finding words in this section.

See p. 3 for an introduction to speaking and understanding Thai words, including the Paiboon[+] system.

a

aa 883
âa 883
aa-bàt 884
âa-bpàak-káang 884
aa-chîip 884
áa-frí-gaa 884
aa-gaan 883
aa-gàat 883
aa-gɔɔn 883
aa-hăan 885
aa-hăan-bpen-pít
.... 885
aa-hăan-cháao 885
aa-hăan-glaang-
   wan 885
aa-hăan-kâm 885
aa-hăan-kà~yà .. 885
aa-hăan-làk 885
aa-hăan-sĕəm .. 885
aa-hăan-tá~lee 885
aa-hăan-tîiang .. 885
aa-hăan-yen 885
aai 884
aa-jaan 883
aa-jaan-yài 883
aa-jiian 883
aa-kàa 883
aa-kaan 883
aa-lá~bâm 883
aa-lá~wâat 885
aa-men 884
aan 884
àan 884
aa-naa-jàk 884
aa-naa-kèet 884
àang 883
âang 883
àang-àap-náam 883
àang-gèp-náam 883

âang-ing 883
àang-láang-mʉʉ
.... 883
àang-sák-pâa 883
aang-tɔɔng 883
âang-tʉ̆ng 883
àan-ngâai 884
àan-ɔ̀ɔk 884
àao 885
âao 885
àap 884
aa-pâat 884
aa-pâat-mén 884
àap-náam 884
aa-raam 885
aa-rá~bìk 884
aa-rá~yá-tam 885
aa-rom 884
aa-rom-káang 884
aa-rom-sĭia 885
aa-săa-sà~màk 885
aa-săi 885
aa-săi-yùu-nai .. 885
aa-săn 885
àat 883
àat-chá~yaa-gam
.... 884
àat-chá~yaa-gɔɔn
.... 884
aa-tí 884
aa-tít 884
àat-jà 883
aa-wâat 885
aa-wú-sŏo 885
aa-wút 885
aa-wút-bpʉʉn 885
aa-yát 884
aa-yú 884
aa-yú-kwaam 884
aa-yú-nɔ́ɔi 884
aa-yú-sân 884

à~baai-yá~múk 878
à~dìit 877
à~dìit-dtà~gaan
.... 877
à~dì~rêek 877
à~dtɔm 881
à~gà~dtan-yuu 876
à~gù~sŏn 876
à~hì-waa 880
ai 892
âi 892
ai-dtim 892
âi-dtuua 892
ai-gron 892
âi-hàa 893
âi-jíiao 892
âi-jŭu 892
ai-kiu 892
âi-kwaai 892
ai-náam 892
âi-nŭu 893
ai-oo-diin 893
ai-sà~griim 892
âi-sàt 893
ai-sĭia 893
ai-yá~gaan 893
à-ká~dtì 876
àk-kà~rà 881
àk-kii-pai 881
àk-sèep 881
àk-sɔ̆ɔn 881
àk-sɔ̆ɔn-sàat 881
à~lài 881
à~loo-hà 879
à-má~nút 878
à-mee-rí~gaa 878
am-má~dtà 878
am-má~pâat 883
am-nâat 886
am-nâat-săan ... 886

am-nâat-sǔung-sùt
...... 886
am-pan 886
am-pəə 886
an 882
à~naa-kót 877
à~naa-mai 877
an-dai-an-nʉ̀ng 882
an-dàp 882
an-dtà~raai 882
à~nèek 877
à~nèek-bprà~sǒng
...... 877
âng-bpao 882
ang-grìt 881
ang-kaan 882
à~ngùn 876
à~nin-sii 877
an-nǎi 882
an-tá~paan 882
à-nú-baan 877
à-nú-loom 877
à-nú-maan 877
à-nú-mát 877
à-nú-moo-tá~naa
...... 877
à-nú-muun-ìt-sà~rà
...... 877
à-nú-pâak 877
à-nú-rák 877
à-nú-sǎa~wá~rii
...... 877
à-nú-sɔ̌ɔn 877
à-nú-yâat 877
à~nʉ̀ng 877
an-yá~bprà~gàat
...... 882
ao 890
âo 890
ao-_-bpai 890
ao-bpriiap 890

ao-chá~ná 890
ao-gan 890
ao-jai 890
ao-jai-sài 890
ao-_-maa 890
ao-_-ɔ̀ɔk 890
àp 882
àp-aai 882
à~pai-yá~tôot 878
àp-bpaang 882
àp-bpà~mong-kon
...... 883
à~pí-nan-tá~naa-
gaan 878
à-pí-ní-hǎan 878
à~pí-sìt 878
à~rá~hǎn 879
à~rai 881
à~rai-gɔ̂ɔ-dâai .. 881
à~rai-gɔ̂ɔ-dtaam
...... 881
à~rì 879
à~rɔ̀i 879
à~run 879
à~run-sà~wàt .. 879
à~sǎng-hǎa-rim-
má~sáp 880
à~sòok 879
à-sɔ̌ɔ-rá~pít 879
à-sù~jì 880
àt 2x882
à~tam 877
àt-chà-rí~yá 882
àt-dtà~noo-mát
...... 882
àt-dtraa 882
àt-dtraa-lɛ̂ɛk-bpliian
...... 882
àt-dtraa-rɔ́ɔi-lá 882
àt-dtraa-sùuan 882
à-tí-baai 877

à-tí-gaan-bɔɔ-dii
...... 877
à~típ-bɔɔ-dii 877
à~tít-tǎan 877
àt-nên 882
àt-rûup 882
àt-sà~jee-rii 883
àt-sà~win 883
àt-tá~pâak 882
àt-tá~yaa-sǎi 882
àt-tá~yaa-sǎi-dii
...... 882
àt-tì 882
à~wá~dtaan 879
à~wá~gàat 879
à~wai-yá~wá 879
à~wai-yá~wá-
pêet-chaai 879
à~wai-yá~wá-
sùup-pan 879
à~wá~sǎan 879
a-yút-tá~yaa 878

b

baa 723
bàa 722
bâa 722
bâa-bâa-bɔɔ-
ccɔ 722
baa-daan 723
bàai 723
baa-lii 723
baan 723
bâan 723
baang 722
bâang 722
bâan-gə̀ət 723
baang-hèng 722
baang-kon 722
baang-kráng 722
baan-gòp 723

baang-sìng 722	bà~mìi 721	bàt 721
baang-sùuan 722	bam-naan 723	bàt-bprà~chaa-
baang-tii 722	bam-nèt 723	chon 722
baang-yàang 722	bam-rung 723	bàt-chəən 722
bâan-muuang .. 723	bam-rung-rák-săa	bàt-kree-dìt 722
bâan-nɔ̂ɔk 723	 723	bàt-pàan 722
bâan-pák-dtàak-	bàn 722	bàt-sóp 721
aa-gàat 723	ban-chii 721	bèt 725
baan-páp 723	ban-daa 720	bèt-dtà~lèt 725
bàap 723	ban-daan 722	bɛ̀ɛk 725
baa-rá~mii 723	ban-dai 722	bɛɛ-muu 726
bàat 722, 3x723	ban-dai-ling 722	bɛ̀ɛp 726
bàat-jèp 722	ban-dai-lûuan .. 722	bɛ̀ɛp-bplɛɛn 726
bàat-lǔuang 723	ban-dìt 721	bɛ̀ɛp-fùk-hàt 726
bàat-măang 723	bang-əən 721	bɛ̀ɛp-pěen 726
bàat-plɛ̌ɛ 722	bâng-fai 721	bɛ̀ɛp-pim 726
bàat-tá~yák 722	bang-gà~loo 721	bɛ̀ɛp-riian 726
bàat-wí~tǐi 723	bang-hǐian 721	bɛ̀ɛp-sɔ̀ɔp-tăam 726
bai 726	bang-káp 721	bɛn 726
bâi 726	bang-káp-ban-chaa	bèng 725
bai-à-nú~yâat .. 727	 721	béng 725
bai-bpliu 727	bang-kloon-rót .. 721	bèng-bprà~pêet
bai-bprà~gàat .. 727	ban-jù 720	 726
bai-dtɔɔng 727	ban-lang 722	bèng-_-krûng 725
bai-gèət 726	ban-leeng 720	bèng-yɛ̂ɛk 726
bai-kàp-kìi 727	ban-naa-rák 720	bèt-dtəə-rîi 726
bai-máai 727	ban-naa-tí-gaan	bə̀ək-baan 725
bai-má~grùut ... 727	 720	bə̀ək-pá~yaan .. 725
bai-mîit 727	ban-pá-bù~rùt 720	bì-daa 723
bai-mɔ̂ɔp-chăn-tá	bân-táai 722	biia 725
.... 727	ban-tao 720	bîia 725
bai-pát 727	ban-tát 720	bîia-bprà~gan ... 725
bai-ráp-rɔɔng 727	ban-tát-tăan 720	bîia-màak-rúk ... 725
bai-sà~màk 727	ban-túk 722	bîiao 725
bai-sàng 727	ban-yaa-gàat 720	bìip 724
bai-sàng-yaa 727	ban-yaai 720	bìip-dtrɛɛ 724
bai-sèt 727	ban-yàt 721	bìip-kɔɔ 724
bai-sɛ̂ɛk 727	bao 725	bin 2x724
bai-yàa 727	bao-baang 725	bin-tá~bàat 723
bàk-sǐi-daa 721	bâo-dtaa 725	bìt 725
bam-bàt 723	bao-wăan 725	bìt-buuan 723

bòk 719
bòm 720
bon 719
bòn 719
bòng-bɔ̀ɔk 719
bŏo 726
bòok 726
boo-lîng 726
boo-raan 726
boo-raan-ná~ká~
dii 726
boo-raan-ná~wát-
tù 726
bòot 726
bòt 2x719
bòt-bàat 719
bòt-gà~wii 719
bòt-kwaam 719
bòt-nam 719
bòt-pleeng 719
bòt-riian 719
bòt-sà~rùp 719
bòt-sŏn-tá~naa 719
bɔ̀ 725
bɔ̀i 721
bɔ̌i 721
bɔ̌i-bɔ̀i 721
bɔ̀n 721
bɔng 721
bɔng-fai 721
bɔn-luun 721
bɔ̀ɔ 719
bɔ̀ɔk 721
bɔ̀ɔ-náam 721
bɔ́ɔng 721
bɔ̀ɔp-baang 721
bɔɔ-rá~pét 721
bɔɔ-rí~bòt 720
bɔɔ-rí~gaan 720
bɔɔ-rí~hǎan 720
bɔɔ-rí~jàak 720

bɔɔ-rí~pôok 720
bɔɔ-rí~sàt 720
bɔɔ-rí~sùt 720
bɔɔ-rí~waan 720
bɔɔ-rí~ween 720
bɔ̀ɔt 721
brèek 725
bù 724
bùk-ká~laa-gɔɔn
.... 724
bùk-ká~lík 724
bùk-ká~lík-gà~
pâap 724
bùk-kon 724
bùk-rúk 724
bŭm 724
bun 724
bŭng 724
bù-ngǎa 724
bun-kun 724
bùp pǎa 724
bùp-pá-bòt 724
bùp-pee-sǎn-ní~
wâat 724
bù~rìi 724
bù~rii-ram 724
bù-rùt 724
bù-rùt-bprai-sà~nii
.... 724
bùt-sà~raa-kam 724
buua 722
búuai 721
bùuak 720
buuam 720
bûuan 720
bûuan-bpàak 720
bùuang 720
buuang-sŭuang 720
bûuan-nám-laai 720
bùuap 720
bùuat 720

buu-chaa 725
bùut 725
búut 725
bùut-ngâai 725
bʉ̀k-bʉn 724
bʉng 724
bʉ̌ng-dtʉng 724
bʉ̀ua 725
bʉ̀ua-nàai 725
bʉ̂ʉang 725
bʉ̂ʉang-dtôn 725

bp

bpà 735
bpaa 736
bpàa 736
bpâa 736
bpǎa 736
bpàa-cháa 737
bpaa-dtì-hǎan .. 737
bpaai 737
bpàai 737
bpâai 737
bpâai-rót-mee .. 737
bpàak 736
bpàak-gaa 737
bpàak-mɛ̂ɛ-náam
.... 737
bpàak-mót-lûuk
.... 737
bpaan 737
bpàan 737
bpâan 737
bpaan-glaang ... 737
bpàat 737
bpaa-tà-gà~tǎa 737
bpàa-túp 737
bpàa-tùuan 737
bpà-bpon 736
bpà~dtì 728
bpà~dtì-bàt 728

bpà~dtì-bàt-dtaam
.... 728
bpà~dtì-chii-wá~ná
.... 728
bpà-dtì-gì-rí-yaa
.... 728
bpà~dtì-rûup 728
bpà~dtì-sèet 728
bpà~dtì-tin 728
bpà~dtì-wát 728
bpà~dtì-yaan 728
bpà~gaa-rang .. 736
bpà~gà~dtì 727
bpai 741
bpai-dûuai 741
bpai-glàp 741
bpai-hǎa 742
bpai-ráp 742
bpai-sòng 742
bpai-taang 742
bpai-tan 742
bpai-tîiao 742
bpai-tǔng 742
bpai-yaan-nɔ́ɔn 742
bpai-yaan-yài 742
bpai-yang 742
bpai-yîiam 742
bpàk-gìng 736
bpám 736
bpám-nám-man
.... 736
bpàn 736
bpân 736
bpan-hǎa 736
bpân-jàn 736
bpan-yaa 736
bpan-yaa-ɔ́ɔn ... 736
bpào 740
bpâo 740
bpâo-lɔ̀ɔk 740
bpâo-mǎai 740

bpà~ram 736
bpà~rá~maa-jaan
.... 728
bpà~rí~maan ... 733
bpà~rí~máat 733
bpà~rin-yaa 733
bpà~rɔ̀ɔt 728
bpà~sù-sàt 735
bpà~tá 736
bpà~taa-nú-grom
.... 728
bpà~tá-gan 736
bpàt-chǐm-lí-kìt 736
bpàt-fùn 736
bpàt-jai 736
bpàt-jù-ban 736
bpà~tǒm-ní-têet
.... 728
bpàt-_-ɔ̀ɔk 736
bpàt-sǎa~wá 736
bpà~tum-taa-nii
.... 728
bpé 740
bpêe 739
bpěe 739
bpék 739
bpen 739
bpen-bpai-dâai 739
bpen-bprà~jam 739
bpen-dtôn 739
bpen-glaang 739
bpen-hèet-hâi .. 739
bpen-jâo-kɔ̌ɔng 739
bpen-jing 739
bpen-kɔ̌ɔng 739
bpen-lom 739
bpen-mǎn 739
bpen-mít 739
bpen-nîi 739
bpen-pá~yaan .. 739
bpen-pít 739

bpen-rá~bìiap .. 739
bpen-wàt 739
bpèt 739
bpêɛn 741
bpêɛng 741
bpêɛng-pǒng 741
bpéɛp 741
bpèɛt 741
bpên-pim 741
bpəə-sen 740
bpèət 740
bpèət-dtuua 740
bpèət-pǎei 740
bpii 738
bpìi 738
bpiia 740
bpìiak 740
bpìiak-chôok 741
bpii-glaai 738
bpìik 738
bpìik-mót-lûuk 738
bpii-mài 738
bpiin 738
bpíip 738
bpii-sàat 738
bpii-sɛ́ɛng 738
bpìng 737
bpíng 737
bping-bpɔng 737
bpì-raa-mít 737
bpìt 737
bpìt-bang 737
bpìt-gìt-jà~gaan
.... 737
bplaa 734
bplaa-dùk 734
bplaai 734
bplaai-taang 734
bplaa-lǎi 734
bplaa-loo-maa ... 734
bplaa-mùk 734

bplàao 740
bplaa-toong 734
bpláat-sà~mâa 734
bplaa-waan 734
bplák 734
bplák-dtuua-miia
.... 740
bplák-dtuua-pûu
.... 734
bplák-fai 734
bplâm 735
bplee 740
bpleeo-fai 740
bplèng 740
bplèng-bplàng 740
bplɛɛ 741
bplɛ̀ɛk 741
bplɛɛng 741
bplɛɛng-tîi-din .. 741
bplɛ̀ɛp 741
bplìian 740
bplìian-bplɛɛng 740
bplìian-_-glàp 740
bplìian-mʉʉ 740
bplìian-sǎn-châat
.... 740
bplìik 735
bpling 735
bpliu 735
bplôn 733
bplòt 733
bplòt-aa-wút 733
bplòt-bplòi 733
bplòt-gà~sǐian 733
bplòi 734
bplòi-long 734
bplòng 733
bplòng-fai 733
bplɔ̀ɔk-kɔɔ 733
bplɔ̀ɔk-mîit 733
bplɔ̀ɔk-mɔ̌ɔn 733

bplɔɔm 734
bplɔɔm-bplɛɛng 734
bplɔ̀ɔp 734
bplɔ̀ɔp-jai 734
bplɔ̀ɔp-yoon 734
bplɔ̀ɔt 733
bplɔ̀ɔt-chʉ́ʉa 734
bplɔ̀ɔt-paa-sǐi 734
bplɔ̀ɔt-pai 734
bplùk 735
bplùk-ráo 735
bplùuak 733
bplùuk 735
bplùuk-fǎng 735
bplùuk-tàai 735
bplʉ̀ʉai 740
bplʉ̀ʉak 740
bplʉ̀ʉak-dtaa 740
bplʉ̌ʉang 740
bplʉ̌ʉm-jai 735
bpòk 727
bpòk-bpìt 728
bpòk-bpông 728
bpòk-gà~dtì 727
bpòk-kɛ̌ng 727
bpòk-krɔɔng 727
bpom 728
bpom-dôi 728
bpon 728
bpòn 728
bpon-bpee 728
bpòn-bpîi 728
bpóo 741
bpôong 741
bpó-bpíia 740
bpôm 735
bpòng 735
bpông 735
bpông-gan 735
bpɔɔ 735
bpɔ̀ɔk-bplʉ̀ʉak 735

bpɔɔ-lɔɔ 727
bpɔɔn 735
bpôɔn 735
bpɔ̀ɔt 735
bpɔ̀ɔt-buuam 735
bpraa-chai 732
bpraa-gaan 732
bpraa-gòt 732
bpraa-gòt-dtà~
gaan 732
bpraa-gòt-dtuua
.... 732
bpraa-gòt-wâa 732
bpraa-jiin-bù~rii
.... 732
bpraam 733
bpraa-môot 733
bpraan 732
bpraang 732
bpraa-nii 2x733
bpràap-bpraam 733
bpraa-sàat 733
bpràat-bpriiao .. 733
bpràat-sà~jàak 733
bpràat-tà~nǎa .. 733
bprà~bpaa 731
bprà~bpraai 731
bprà~chaa-chon
.... 729
bprà~chaa-gɔɔ
.... 729
bprà~chaa-sǎm-
pan 729
bprà~chaa-sǒng-
krɔ́ 730
bprà~chaa-típ-
bpà~dtai 729
bprà~chót 729
bprà~chum 730
bprà~daa 730
bprà~dàp 730

bprà~den 730
bprà~dìt 730
bprà~dtuu 730
bprà~dtuu-rúua 730
bprà~gaai 729
bprà~gaan 729
bprà~gaa-sà~nii-
  yá~bàt 729
bprà~gàat 729
bprà~gàat-sà~nii-
  yá~bàt 729
bprà~gan 729
bprà~gan-dtuua
  729
bprà~gan-pai ... 729
bprà~gan-sǎng-
  kom 729
bprà~gòp-_-rá~
  wàang-_ 728
bprà~gɔ̀ɔp 728
bprà~gɔ̀ɔp-dûuai
  728
bprà~gùuat 728
bprà~hǎan 732
bprai-sà~nii 742
bprai-sà~nii-aa-
  gàat 742
bprai-sà~nii-yá~bàt
  742
bprà~jàk-pá~yaan
  729
bprà~jam 729
bprà~jam-bpii .. 729
bprà~jam-dɯɯan
  729
bprà~jam-wan 729
bprà~jɛɛ 729
bprà~jɔ̀p 729
bprà~jɔ̀p-gan ... 729
bprà~jùuap-mɔ̀-gan
  729

bprà~kam 729
bprà~kóp 729
bprà~làat 732
bprà~làat-jai 732
bprà~lai 731
bprà~màa 732
bprà~maan 731
bprà~màat 731
bprà~mɛɛn 731
bprà~mɛɛn-pǒn
  731
bprà~muuan-pǒn
  731
bprà~muun 731
bprà~naam 730
bprà~nii-bprà~
  nɔɔm 730
bprà~nîit 730
bprà~nom 730
bpràp 732
bpràp-aa-gàat .. 732
bpràp-bprung .. 732
bpràp-dtuua 732
bprà~pee-nii 731
bprà~pêet 731
bpràp-mǎi 732
bprà~prút 731
bprà~prút-pìt-nai
  731
bprà~sǎa 731
bprà~sǎan-ngaa
  732
bprà~sǎan-ngaan
  732
bprà~sàat 732
bprà~sə̀ət 732
bprà~sìt-tí~pâap
  732
bprà~sòp 731
bprà~sòp-gaan 731

bprà~sòp-kwaam-
  sǎm-rèt 731
bprà~taan 730
bprà~taa-naa-tí-
  bɔɔ-dii 730
bprà~táp 730
bprà~táp-dtraa 730
bprà~táp-jai 730
bprà~tát 730
bpràt-chá~yaa 732
bprà~têet 730
bprà~tǒm 730
bpràt-sà~nii 732
bprà~túuang 730
bpràt-yaa 732
bprà~wàt 731
bprà~wàt-dtì~sàat
  731
bprà~wàt-yɔ̂ɔ ... 731
bprà~wee-nii ... 731
bprà~yàt 732
bprà~yòok 731
bprà~yòot 731
bprà~yúk 731
bprèet 739
bprɛɛng 741
bprɛɛng-sǐi-fan 741
bprɛɛ-rûup 741
bprîiao 739
bprìiap-tîiap 739
bprí-sə̀m 733
bprìt-sà~nǎa 733
bproo-dtiin 741
bprooi 741
bproo-jèk 741
bpròong-sěeng 741
bpròot 741
bpròp-mɯɯ 728
bprɔ̀ 739
bprung 733
bprung-rót 733

bprɯ̀k-săa 733	chaai-dɛɛn 660	cháat 660
bpùai 735	chaai-fàng 660	châat-gɔ̀ɔn 659
bpui 738	chaai-hàat 660	chăa-yaa 653
bpŭi 738	chaai-jing-yǐng-tɛ́ɛ	chá~baa 655
bpùm 738	 659	chà~bàp 652
bpùm-grà~săn ... 738	chaai-kaa 659	chà~bàp-râang ... 652
bpuu 738	chăai-năng 653	chà~chăan 652
bpùu 738	chaai-sòot 660	chà~chəəng-sao
bpùuak-bpìiak .. 735	chaai-sɯ̀ɯa 660	 652
bpùuang 735	chaai-tá~lee 660	chá~daa 655
bpùuat 735	chàak 653	chá~dtaa 657
bpùuat-fan 735	chaam 659	chà~gàat 652
bpùuat-hŭu 735	chaan 659, 668	chà~gan 652
bpùuat-hŭua 735	chaan-chaa-laa ... 659	chai 664
bpùuat-sǐi-sà 735	chàang 653	châi 664
bpùuat-tɔ́ɔng 735	cháang 653	chái 664
bpuu-chá~nii-yá-	chăang 653	chai-chá~ná 658
sà~tăan 738	cháang-náam ... 659	chái-dâai 664
bpuu-chá~nii-yá-	cháang-pɯ̀ɯak .. 659	chăi-lai 654
wát-tù 738	chaan-mɯɯang ... 659	chái-lɛ́ɛo 664
bpuun 738	chaao 660	chai-_-mòt 664
bpuun-sǐi-men ... 739	cháao 663	chai-nâat 658
bpùu-tûuat 738	chăao 653	chái-wee-laa 664
bpùu-yâa 739	chaao-bâan 660	chai-yá~puum .. 658
bpɯ̀ɯai 741	chaao-bprà~mong	chai-yoo 664
bpɯ̀ɯan 741	 660	chák 657
bpɯɯn 738	chaao-dtàang-châat	chák-cháa 657
bpɯɯn-lûuk-sɔɔng	 660	chák-chuuan 657
.... 738	chaao-dtàang-dâao	chák-gà~yə̂ə 657
bpɯɯn-pók 738	 660	chák-juung 657
bpɯɯn-yaao 738	chaao-dtà~wan-	chák-krôok 657
bpɯɯn-yài 738	dtòk 660	chák-nam 657
	chaao-gɔ̀ 660	chák-wâao 657
ch	cháao-mɯ̂ɯt 663	chák-yai 657
	chaao-naa 660	chà~làak 652
chà 652	chaao-pút 660	chà~lăam 652
chaa 658	chaao-râi 660	chà~làat 652
cháa 658	chaao-tai 660	chà~lɛ̂ɛm 654
cháa-cháa 658	chàap 653	chá~lɛɛng 657
chaa-dòk 659	chàap-bpuun 653	chá~ləəi 663
chaai 659	châat 659	chà~lə̆əm 654
chăai 653		

chà~lìia 654
chà~lìiao 654
chà~lòok 654
chá~lɔɔ-dtuua .. 657
chà~lɔ̌ɔng 652
chà~lù 652
chà~lǔu 652
chàm 653
chăm-chǎa 653
châm-chɔɔng 660
cham-lè 660
cham-naan 660
cham-rá 660
cham-rút 660
cham-rûuai 660
chà~mùuak 652
chán 657
chăn 2x653
chá~ná 655
chán-bon 658
chán-chəəng 657
chán-dtàm 657
chang 657
châng 657, 658
chá~ngák 656
châng-bprà~bpaa
.... 659
châng-chǔuam .. 659
châng-dtàt-pǒm
.... 659
châng-dtàt-sǔua
.... 659
chá~ngə̌ə 656
châng-fai-fáa 659
châng-fǐi-mɯɯ .. 659
châng-gon 659
châng-gɔ̀ɔ-sâang
.... 659
châng-jai 657
chán-glaang 657
châng-lèk 659

châng-máai 659
chá~ngôok 657
châng-pâap 659
châng-tam-pǒm
.... 659
chá~nii 657
chá~nít 655
chán-lâang 658
chán-lɔɔi 658
chán-nai 658
chan-ná~sùut-sòp
.... 658
chán-nɔ̂ɔk 658
chà~nòot 654
chăn-peen 653
chán-sǔung 658
chà~nǔuan 652
chán-yɔ̂ɔt 658
châo 663
châo-_-dtɔɔ 663
chà~pɔ́ 653
chàp-wai 653
chá~raa 655
chát 657
chát-jeen 657
chát-jɛ̂ɛng 657
chàt-mong-kon .. 652
chá~wá~lêek 655
chěe 653
chèet-sǐi 653
chék 662
chék-dəən-taang
.... 662
chèn 662
chèn-diiao-gàp .. 662
chèn-gan 662
chèn-kəəi 662
chèn-níi 662
chèn-wâa 663
chép 663
chét 662

chè 654
chêɛ 664
chěɛ 654
chèɛk 654
chêɛ-yen 664
chɛm-puu 664
chêng 664
chəəi 663
chə̌əi 654
chə̌əi-chaa 654
chə̌əi-chə̌əi 654
chəən 663
chəən-chuuan ... 663
chəəng-graan ... 663
chəəng-tiian 663
chə̀ət-chǎai 654
chə̂ət-hûn 663
chii 661
chìi 653
chíi 661
chiia 663
chǐiang 654
chiiang-mài 663
chiiang-raai 663
chìiao 654
chîiao 663
chǐiao 654
chîiao-chaan 663
chìiap 654
chìiat 654
chíi-dtuua 661
chíi-hâi-hěn 661
chìik 653
chìik-kàat 653
chîip 661
chîip-pá~jɔɔn 661
chìit 653
chii-wá-bprà~wàt
.... 661
chii-wá-wít-tá~yaa
.... 661

chii-wít	661	
chim	661	
chin	661	
chín	661	
chìng	653	
chîng	660	
chin-gàp	661	
ching-cháa	661	
ching-cháa-sà~wǎn	661	
ching-chang	660	
chin-lîng	661	
chín-máai	661	
chín-sùuan	661	
chíp	661	
chít	661	
chǐu	653	
chòk	652	
chók	654	
chók-dtòi	654	
chók-muuai	654	
chom	655	
chom-chəəi	655	
chom-puu	655	
chom-pûu	655	
chom-rom	655	
chon	2x655	
chon-bù~rii	655	
chon-châat	655	
chon-chán	655	
chong	654	
chon-gan	655	
chon-lá~bprà~taan	655	
chon-ná~bòt	655	
choo	664	
chôok	664	
chôok-chá~dtaa	664	
chôok-dii	664	
chǒom-ngaam	654	
chòop	654	
chôot	664	
chót-chái	655	
chót-chəəi	655	
chɔ̀k	2x656	
chɔ̂ng	656	
chɔ̂ng-kɛ̂ɛp	656	
chɔ̂ng-klɔ̀ɔt	656	
chɔ̂ng-lék	656	
chɔ̂ng-lom	656	
chɔ̂ng-rá~baai	656	
chɔ̂ng-taang	656	
chɔ̂ng-wâang	656	
chɔ̂ɔ	656	
chɔ̂ɔ-dɔ̀ɔk-máai	656	
chɔ̂ɔ-goong	652	
chɔ̌ɔ-lɔ́	652	
chɔ́ɔn	656	
chɔ́ɔn-chaa	656	
chɔ́ɔn-dtó	656	
chɔ́ɔn-dtuuang	656	
chɔ́ɔn-sôm	656	
chɔ̂ɔp	656	
chɔ̂ɔp-gon	656	
chɔ̂ɔp-jai	656	
chɔ̂ɔp-tam	656	
chɔ̂ɔp-tîi-sùt	656	
chɔ́p-bpîng	656	
chɔ́t	656	
chù	653	
chùk-chə̌ən	653	
chûm	662	
chum-chon	662	
chǔm-chʉ́ʉn	662	
chum-num-gan	662	
chum-pɔɔn	662	
chum-taang	662	
chǔn	653	
chǔn-chǐiao	653	
chun-lá~mun	662	
chúp	662	
chúp-chii-wít	662	
chùt	653	
chút	662	
chút-nɔɔn	662	
chút-pâi	662	
chút-raa-dtrii	662	
chút-sùut	662	
chút-wâai-náam	662	
chuu	662	
chúu	662	
chûuai	655	
chǔuai	652	
chûuai-dtuua-eeng	655	
chûuai-dûuai	655	
chûuai-lʉ̌ʉa	655	
chûua-kà~nà	658	
chûua-kraao	658	
chûua-krûu	658	
chûua-moong	658	
chuuan	655	
chûuang	655	
chûua-ní-ran	658	
chûua-ráai	658	
chûuat	655	
chuu-chîip	662	
chuu-rót	662	
chùut-chàat	653	
chʉ̌ʉ	661	
chʉ̂ʉa	663	
chʉ́ʉa	663	
chʉ́ʉa-châat	663	
chʉ́ʉa-fang	663	
chʉ̂ʉai	654	
chʉ̂ʉai-chaa	654	
chʉ́ʉa-jai	663	
chʉ́ʉak	663	
chʉ́ʉam	664	
chʉ́ʉa-màk	664	
chʉ̌am-dtɔ̀ɔ-gan	664	

chǔʉan 654
chǔʉang 663
chǔʉang-cháa .. 663
chúʉa-raa 664
chúʉa-rôok 664
chúʉa-sǎai 664
chûʉat 663
chúʉa-tǔʉ 663
chúʉa-tǔʉ-dâai 663
chûʉ-dtuua 661
chǔʉ-lên 661
chúʉn 661
chúʉn 661
chúʉn-chom 661
chǔʉ-sǐiang 661

d

dàa 672
daai 672
dâai 672, 676
dâai-dii 676
dâai-_-kʉʉn 676
dàak 672
daam 672
dâam 672
dàan 672
dâan 672
dàang 672
dâan-kâang 672
dâan-nai 672
dâan-nɔ̂ɔk 672
dâan-sáai 672
daao 672
daao-bɔɔ-rí~waan
.... 672
daao-dtòk 672
daao-hǎang 672
daao-krɔ́ 672
daao-lòot 672
daao-rʉ̂ək 672
daao-rʉʉang 672

daao-tiiam 672
dàap 672
daa-raa 672
daa-raa-sàat 672
dàat-fáa 672
dai 676
dâi-gam-rai 676
dâi-_-maa 676
dai-noo-sǎo 676
dâi-ráp 676
dâi-yin 676
dàk 671
dàk-dɛ̂ɛ 671
dam 672
dam-náam 672
dam-nəən-gaan 672
dam-nəən-ká~dii
.... 673
dan 671
dang 671
dàng 671
dang-chên 671
dâng-dəəm 671
dang-dtɔɔ-bpai-níi
.... 671
dang-glàao 671
dâng-jà~mùuk 671
dang-nán 671
dang-níi 671
dang-tîi 671
dao 674
dàp 671
dàp-fai 671
dàp-grà~hǎai ... 671
dàp-pləəng 671
dàt 671
dàt-bplɛɛng 671
dàt-chá~nii 671
dàt-jà~rìt 671
dàt-ngâai 671
dèet 674

dèk 674
dèk-chaai 674
dèk-dèk 674
dèk-gam-práa .. 674
dèk-ɔ̀ɔn 674
dèn-chát 674
dêng 674
dèt 674
dèt-kàat 674
dɛ̀ɛk 675
dɛ̀ɛk-dan 675
dɛɛng 675
dɛ̀ɛt 675
dɛ̀ɛt-ɔ̀ɔk 675
dəəm-pan 675
dəən 674
dəən-bpàa 675
dəən-lá~məə 675
dəən-lên 675
dəən-nʼi 675
dəən-pàan 675
dəən-rʉʉa 675
dəən-taang 675
dəən-taang-bpai
.... 675
día 675
dì~chán 673
dì~chǎn 673
dii 673
diiao 675
dìiao 675
dǐiao 675
diiao-gan 675
dǐiao-níi 675
dii-bùk 673
dii-gaa 668
dii-gan 673
dii-gwàa 673
dii-jai 673
dii-kʉ̂n 673
dii-lâət 673

dii-mâak	673
dii-pɔɔ	673
dii-sâan	673
dii-seo	673
dii-tǐi-sùt	673
dìk	673
din	673
dîn	673
din-dɛɛn	673
din-nǐiao	673
din-rá~bèət	673
dîn-ron	673
din-sɔ́ɔ	673
din-sɔ́ɔ-sǐi	673
din-tà~lòm	673
dìp	673
dom	669
dôn	669
don-dtrii	669
dong	669
don-jai	669
dooi	675
dooi-chà~pɔ́	676
dooi-dtrong	676
dooi-gaan-sùm	675
doon	675
dòong	675
dòot	675
dòot-dèn	675
dòot-dìiao	675
dɔ́k-dtə̂ə	670
dɔn-lâa	671
dɔɔi	671
dɔɔi-in-tá~non	671
dɔ̂ɔi-pát-tá~naa	671
dɔɔi-sà~gèt	671
dɔ̀ɔk	670
dɔ̀ɔk-bîia	670
dɔ̀ɔk-buua	670
dɔ̀ɔk-dtuum	670
dɔ̀ɔk-fin	670

dɔ̀ɔk-jan	2x670
dɔ̀ɔk-jìk	670
dɔ̀ɔk-máai	670
dɔ̀ɔk-mái-fai	670
dɔ̀ɔk-pǒn	670
dɔ̀ɔk-tɔɔng	670
dɔ̀ɔk-yaang	670
dɔɔng	670
dɔɔn-muuang	670
dù	674
dù-dàa	674
dùk-dìk	674
dum-lɔ́ɔ	674
dun	674
dù-ráai	674
duu	674
dûuai	670
dûuai-dtuua-eeng	
	670
dûuai-gan	670
dùuan	670
dûuan	670
duuang	2x669
duuang-aa-tít	670
duuang-chá~dtaa	
	669
duuang-dtaa	670
duuang-jai	670
duuang-jan	669
duu-lɛɛ	674
duu-mìn	674
duu-mǔuan	674
dùut	674
dùut-fùn	674
dùut-sum	674
duu-tùuk	674
dùk	673
dung	673
dung-dùut	674
dung-dùut-jai	674
dûu	674

duuai	675
duuan	675
duuat	675
dùuat-daan	675
dùum	674
dûu-rán	674

dt

dtaa	683
dtaa-bɔ̀ɔt	684
dtaa-bplaa	684
dtaa-châng	683
dtaa-dɛɛng	683
dtaa-dtùm	683
dtaa-gûng-ying	683
dtaai	684
dtâai	2x689
dtâai-din	689
dtaai-dtuua	684
dtâai-fùn	689
dtàak	683
dtaa-kàai	683
dtaa-kǎao	683
dtàak-dèet	683
dtaa-kěe	683
dtaam	684
dtaam-dəəm	684
dtaam-jai	684
dtaam-kěm-naa-lí-gaa	684
dtaam-lam-dàp	684
dtaam-lǎng	684
dtaam-maa	684
dtaam-nán	684
dtaam-rɔɔi	684
dtaam-tan	684
dtaam-tîi	684
dtaan	684
dtaa-náam	684
dtàang	683

a
b
bp
ch
d
dt
e
ɛ
ə
f
g
h
i
j
k
l
m
n
ng
o
ɔ
p
r
s
t
u
ʉ
w
y

dtàang-bprà~têet 683
dtàang-châat 683
dtàang-dtàang 683
dtàang-jang-wàt 683
dtâan-taan 684
dtaa-raang 684
dtaa-raang-waa 684
dtaa-típ 684
dtaa-tùua 684
dtaa-tûuat 684
dtaa-yaai 684
dtà~bai 680
dtà~bɔɔng-pét 680
dtà~bpuu 680
dtà~gìiap 679
dtà~glà 679
dtà~goo 679
dtà~gôo 679
dtà~goon 679
dtà~gɔɔn 679
dtà~grâa 679
dtà~grɛɛng 679
dtà~grɔ̂ɔ 679
dtà~gùua 679
dtai 689
dtài 689
dtâi-wǎn 689
dtàk 680
dtà~kàap 680
dtàk-bàat 680
dtàk-dtʉʉan 680
dtà~kèp-pâa 680
dták-gà~dtɛɛn 680
dtàk-gà~sàat 677
dtà~kɔ̌ɔ 680
dtà~kɔ̀ɔk 680
dtà~krâi 680
dtà~krái 680
dtà~kriu 680

dtà~krúp 680
dtà~làat 678
dtà~lǐu 680
dtà~lòk 678
dtà~lɔ̀ɔt 678
dtà~lɔ̀ɔt-bpai 678
dtà~lɔ̀ɔt-jon 678
dtà~lɔ̀ɔt-wee-laa
.... 678
dtà~lʉng 680
dtam 684
dtàm 685
dtam-bon 685
dtam-lʉng 685
dtam-naan 685
dtam-nàk 685
dtam-nèng 685
dtam-nì 685
dtam-raa 685
dtam-ràp 685
dtam-rùuat 685
dtàm-sùt 685
dtan 681
dtâng 680
dtâng-chàak 681
dtâng-chàak-gan
.... 681
dtâng-chʉʉ 681
dtâng-dtɛ̀ɛ 681
dtâng-dtrong 681
dtâng-jai 681
dtâng-kan 681
dtâng-mân 681
dtâng-rók-râak 681
dtâng-tɔ́ɔng 681
dtâng-yùu 681
dtan-hǎa 681
dtao 687
dtào 687
dtâo-hûu 688
dtâo-jîiao 687

dtao-lɔ̌ɔm 688
dtâo-nom 687
dtao-òp 688
dtao-pǐng 688
dtao-rîit 688
dtàp 681
dtà~pâap 680
dtàp-àk-sèep 681
dtàp-ɔ̀ɔn 681
dtà~raang 680
dtàt 681
dtàt-chii-wít 681
dtàt-dtɔɔn 681
dtàt-gan 681
dtàt-ngóp 681
dtàt-sǎai 681
dtàt-sǐn 681
dtàt-sǐn-jai 681
dtàt-yâat-gàp 681
dtà~wàat 678
dtà~wan-dtòk 680
dtà~wan-dtòk-
    chǐiang-dtâai .. 680
dtà~wan-dtòk-
    chǐiang-nʉ̌ʉa .. 680
dtà~wan-ɔ̀ɔk 680
dtà~wan-ɔ̀ɔk-
    chǐiang-dtâai .. 680
dtà~wan-ɔ̀ɔk-
    chǐiang-nʉ̌ʉa .. 680
dtè 687
dtem 687
dtem-jai 687
dtên 687
dtén 687
dtên-ram 687
dtɛ̀ 689
dtɛ̂ɛ 688
dtɛ̂ɛ-cháao 688
dtɛ̂ɛ-gam-nə̀ət 688
dtêɛ-jǐu 688

dtèɛk 688	dtìt-fai 686	dtông 678
dtèɛk-dtàang 688	dtìt-gan 685	dtông-gaan 678
dtèɛk-nɔɔ 688	dtìt-gàp 685	dtông-hâam 678
dtèɛ-lá 689	dtìt-kàt 685	dtɔɔ 678
dtɛɛng 688	dtìt-krûuang 685	dtɔ̀ɔ 678
dtɛɛng-gwaa 688	dtìt-nîi 686	dtɔ̀ɔ-aa-yú 679
dtɛɛng-moo 688	dtìt-pan 686	dtɔ̀ɔ-bpai 679
dtɛ̀ɛ-rɛ̂ɛk 689	dtìt-sǐn-bon 686	dtɔ̀ɔ-bpai-níi 679
dtɛ̀ɛt 689	dtìt-yaa 686	dtɔ̀ɔ-dtâan 678
dtɛ̀ɛ-wâa 689	dtiu 686	dtɔ̀ɔ-gan 678
dtèng 688	dtó 689	dtɔ̀ɔ-grà~jòk 678
dtèng-dtǎng 688	dtòk 676	dtɔ̀ɔ-hǐn 679
dtèng-dtuua 688	dtòk-bplaa 676	dtɔ̀ɔk 678
dtèng-ngaan-gàp	dtòk-dtèng 676	dtɔ̀ɔk-dtà~bpuu 678
.... 688	dtòk-jai 676	dtɔɔ-lɛ̌ɛ 679
dtěo 689	dtòk-long 676	dtɔ̀ɔ-maa 679
dtəəm 688	dtòk-lǔm-rák 676	dtɔɔn 679
dtə̀əp-dtoo 688	dtom 677	dtɔ̌ɔn 679
dtì 685	dtôm 677	dtɔ̀ɔn-ráp 679
dtì-dtiian 686	dton 676	dtɔ̀ɔ-nûuang 679
dtii 686	dtôn 676	dtɔ̀ɔp 679
dtîia 688	dtôn-chà~bàp .. 676	dtɔ̀ɔp-dtôo 679
dtiiang 688	dton-eeng 677	dtɔ̀ɔ-raa-kaa 679
dtiiang-hǎam 688	dtôn-gam-nə̀ət 676	dtɔ̀ɔ-sûu 679
dtiiang-kûu 688	dtôn-kǎa 676	dtɔ̀ɔt 678
dtii-dtraa 686	dtôn-kɔɔ 676	dtraa 677
dtii-kwaam 686	dtôn-máai 677	dtràak-dtram 677
dtii-lang-gaa 686	dtôn-náam 677	dtraa-nâa 678
dtiin 686	dtoo 689	dtràat 677
dtiin-gaa 686	dtôo 689	dtraa-yaang 678
dtii-pim 686	dtôo-tǐiang 689	dtrai 677
dtii-raa-kaa 686	dtôo-waa-tii 689	dtrài-dtrɔɔng 689
dtíng-dtɔ́ng 685	dtôo-yɛ́ɛng 689	dtrai-mâat 689
dtìng-hǔu 685	dtòp 677	dtrà~nàk 677
dtìt 685	dtòp-dtaa 677	dtrang 677
dtìt-àang 686	dtòp-muu 677	dtrà~ngàan 677
dtìt-chúua 685	dtòt 676	dtràt-sà~rúu 677
dtìt-din 685	dtɔ̀i 679	dtrɛɛ 689
dtìt-dtaam 685	dtɔ̀m 679	dtrii 678
dtìt-dtâng 685	dtɔ̀m-lûuk-màak	dtriiam 687
dtìt-dtɔ̀ɔ 685	 679	dtriiam-dtuua ... 687

dtriiam-prɔ́ɔm .. 687
dtrong 677
dtrong-bpai 677
dtrong-glaang .. 677
dtrong-kâam 677
dtrong-nǎi 677
dtrong-tîi 677
dtrong-wee-laa 677
dtrɔ̀ɔk 677
dtrùu 678
dtrùuat 677
dtrùuat-dtraa 677
dtrùuat-sɔ̀ɔp 677
dtrùuat-wát 677
dtrʉ̀k-dtrɔɔng ... 678
dtrʉng 678
dtûi-núi 687
dtúk-dtúk 686
dtúk-gà~dtaa ... 686
dtúk-gɛɛ 686
dtù-laa-kom 687
dtùm 687
dtûm 687
dtûm-hǔu 687
dtǔn 687
dtút 686
dtùu 687
dtûu 687
dtuua 681
dtǔua 682
dtuua-àk-sɔ̌ɔn .. 683
dtǔua-bpai-glàp 682
dtuua-bprà~gan 682
dtuua-bprɛɛ 682
dtuua-dtà~lòk 682
dtuua-dtɔ̀ɔ-dtuua 682
dtuua-èek 683
dtuua-eeng 683
dtuua-gaan 682
dtuua-iiang 683
dtuua-lá~kɔɔn .. 682
dtuua-lêek 682
dtuua-lʉ̂ʉak 682
dtuua-miia 682
dtuua-nam 682
dtuua-nam-fai-fáa 682
dtuua-nǎng~sʉ̌ʉ 682
dtuua-ɔ̀ɔn 683
dtuua-pim 682
dtuua-pûu 682
dtuua-rai 682
dtuua-sà~gòt ... 682
dtuua-tǎng 682
dtuua-tɛɛn 682
dtuua-yàang 682
dtuua-yàang-nǎng 683
dtuua-yɔ̂ɔ 682
dtûu-bplaa 687
dtûu-bpɔɔ-nɔɔ 687
dtûu-bprai-sà~nii 687
dtuum 687
dtûu-sʉ̂ʉa-pâa 687
dtùut 687
dtûu-yen 687
dtʉ̀k 686
dtʉ̀k-rá~fáa 686
dtʉng 686
dtʉng-krîiat 686
dtʉʉan 688
dtʉ̀ʉn 686
dtʉ̂ʉn 686
dtʉ̀ʉn-dtên 686
dtʉ̀ʉn-dtuua 686
dtʉ̀ʉn-nɔɔn 686
dtʉ̀ʉt 686

e

ee-chiia 890
ee-chiia-dtâai ... 890
ee-chiia-dtà~wan-ɔ̀ɔk-chǐiang-dtâai 890
èek 889
èek-àk-ká~râat-chá~tûut 889
èek-gà~chǎn 889
èek-gà~chon 889
èek-gà~lák 889
èek-gà~pót 889
èek-gà~râat 889
èek-gà~sǎan 889
èek-gà~sìt 889
een 890
eeng 890
eeo 890
èes 890
èet 890
ee-yên 890
ék-sà~ree 889
en 890
en-duu 890
en-saai 890
èt 890
ét-ai-wii 890

ɛ

ɛɛ 891
ɛɛ-àt 891
ɛ̀ɛk 891
ɛɛn-dtáak-dtì~gâa 891
ɛ̀ɛp 891
ɛ̀ɛp-duu 891
ɛ̀ɛp-fang 891
ɛ̀ɛp-mɔɔng 891
ɛ́ɛs-pai-rin 891

ɛm	891
èn	891
èng	891
èng-náam	891
ɛn-gɔɔ-hɔɔ	891
ép-bpên	891

ə

əə	890
əèi	890
əèi-tǔng	890

f

fâa	750
fáa	763
fǎa	750
fǎa-bpìt	750
fàa-fai-dɛɛng	750
fǎa-fan	750
fǎa-fèɛt	750
fàa-fǔun	750
fàai	750
fâai	750
fǎai	750
fàai-ráp	750
fàai-rúk	751
fàak	750
fàak-fǎng	750
fàak-ngən	750
fàak-_-wái	750
fáa-lêp	764
fàa-mɯɯ	750
fǎan	750
faang	763
fáa-pàa	764
fáa-rɔ́ɔng	764
fàat	750
fâat	763
fàa-táao	750
fai	2x765
fài	751

fǎi	751
fai-chǎai	765
fai-chék	765
fai-dàp	765
fai-fáa	765
fai-fáa-sà~tìt	765
fài-jai	751
fai-jà-raa-jɔɔn	765
fai-táai	765
fàk	749
fák	763
fàk-buua	749
fák-dtuua	763
fák-kài	763
fák-tɔɔng	763
fàk-tùua	749
fan	763
fǎn	750
fǎn-bpìiak	750
fan-bplɔɔm	763
fan-dàap	763
fang	763
fàng	750
fǎng	749
fǎng-kěm	750
fàng-tá~lee	750
fan-pù	763
fǎn-ráai	750
fǎn-tɯng	750
fâo	751
fâo-duu	751
fà~ràng	749
fà~ràng-sèet	749
fɛɛn	764
fɛ̌ɛng	751
fèɛt	751
fèɛt-sà~yǎam	751
fèk	764
fém	764
fǐi-bpàak	751
fǐi-dàat	751

fiim	764
fǐi-mɯɯ	751
fin	751
fí-sìk	764
fiu	764
flɛ̀t	2x764
flúk	763
fǒn	749
fǒn-dtòk	749
foo-gát	764
foom	765
fɔ́ɔi	749
fɔ́ɔi-tɔɔng	749
fɔ́ɔk-sà~bùu	763
fɔɔm	763
fɔɔ-mèt	763
fɔ́ɔn	763
fɔɔng	763
fɔ́ɔng	763
fɔ́ɔng-náam	763
fɔ́ɔng-rɔ́ɔng	763
fɔ́ɔt-sîu	763
frii	763
fûm-fɯɯai	764
fùn	751
fúp	764
fút	764
fút-bàat	764
fút-bɔn	764
fuu	764
fûuk	764
fǔung	751
fǔung-chon	751
fǔung-sàt	751
fùk	751
fùk-fǒn	751
fùk-hàt	751
fùk-sɔ́ɔm	751
fɯ̀ɯak	751
fûuang	764
fûuang-fuu	764

fʉʉn 764
fúʉn 764
fʉ̌ʉn 751
fúʉn-dtuua 764
fúʉn-fuu 764
fùʉt 751

g

gà 595
gaa 597
gaa-châat 598
gaa-dtuun 598
gaa-fàak 598
gaa-fɛɛ 598
gaa-gà~bàat 597
gaa-gii 597
gaai 598
gaai-yá~gam 598
gaai-yá~pâap-
  bam-bàt 598
gàak 597
gaa-lá~sǐn 599
gaa-lék-sǐi 599
gaa-maa-rom 598
gâam-bpuu 598
gaam-má~rôok .. 598
gaam-má~têep ... 598
gaam-wít-dtà~tǎan
  598
gaan 598, 599
gâan 598
gaa-náam 598
gaang 597
gâang 597
gâang-bplaa 598
gaang-geeng 597
gaang-geeng-kǎa-
  sân 598
gaang-geeng-nai
  598
gaan-jà~laa-jon 598

gaan-jà~ná-bù~rii
  598
gaan-kɛ̀ng-kǎn 598
gaan-mʉʉang .. 599
gaan-ngaan 598
gaao 599
gâao 599, 603
gâao-gàai 599
gâao-nâa 599
gâao-ráao 599
gâao-yâang 599
gaa-ran 599
gáas 599
gáat 598, 599
gà~bang-lom 596
gà~bòt 588
gà~bpì 596
gà-dtì~gaa 588
gài 605
gái 605
gai-bpʉʉn 605
gài-dtà~pao 605
gài-fáa 605
gài-nguuang 605
gàk 596
gàk-gan 596
gàk-kǎng 596
gà~laa 596
gà~laa-sǐi 596
gà~lá~mang 596
gà~làm-bplii 596
gà~làm-dɔ̀ɔk 596
gà~lá~mɛɛ 596
gà~lòok 596
gam 588, 599
gam-bpân 599
gam-cháp 599
gam-gàp 599
gam-guuam 599
gam-jàt 599

gam-lai 600
gam-lai-táao 600
gam-lang 600
gam-lang-kon .. 600
gam-lang-sɔ̌ɔng 600
gam-má~gaan .. 588
gam-má~gɔɔn .. 588
gam-man-dtà~
  rang-sǐi 597
gam-má~pan ... 589
gam-má~sìt 589
gam-má~tǎn 600
gam-má~wí-tii 589
gam-má~yìi 600
gam-mʉʉ 600
gam-nan 599
gam-nàt 600
gam-nɛ̀ɛt 599
gam-nòt 600
gam-nòt-wee-laa
  600
gam-pɛɛng 599
gam-pɛɛng-pét 599
gam-práa 599
gam-puu-chaa 597
gam-rai 600
gam-yam 600
gan 597
gân 597
gan-bùut 597
gan-chaa 596
gan-chon 597
gan-eeng 597
gan-fai 597
gang-fuu 596
gang-hǎn 596
gang-kǎa 596
gan-grai 588
gang-won 596
gan-náam 597
_-gan-tɛ̀ 597

gan-yaa-yon 597
gao 603
gào 603
gâo-îi 603
gao-lǐi 603
gao-lǐi-dtâai 603
gàp 597
gàp-dàk 597
gàp-dtan 597
gàp-kâao 597
gàp-rá~bəət 597
gà~prao 596
gà~príp 596
gà~príp-dtaa 596
gà~rák-gà~daa-
    kom 588
gà~rá~nii 588
gà~ràt 596
gà~rìi 596
gà~rìiang 596
gà~rú~naa 593
gà~sàt 594
gà~sèet-dtà~gam
    603
gà~sèet-dtà~gɔɔn
    603
gà~sì~gam 594
gà~sǐian 603
gàt 596
gà~tá 591
gà~tan-hǎn 595
gà~tát-rát 595
gà~təəi 595
gà~təəi-bplɛɛng-
    pêet 596
gàt-grɔ̀n 596
gà~tí 595
gà~tɔ́ 596
gàt-sɔ́ 597
gà~wii 594
gee 601, 602

gée 601
geem 602
geen 602
gee-ree 602
gee-sɔ̌ɔn 603
géet-háo 603
gèng 601
gèp 602
gèp-dtuua 602
gèp-gìiao 602
gèp-kɔ̌ɔng 602
gèp-rák-sǎa 602
gɛ̀ 604
gɛ̀-dam 605
gɛɛ 604
gɛ̀ɛ 604
gɛ̂ɛ 604
gɛ̀ɛ-bpan-hǎa 604
gɛ̀ɛ-dtàang 604
gɛ̀ɛ-dtuua 604
gɛ̀ɛ-kǎi 604
gɛ̀ɛ-kɛ́ɛn 604
gɛ̂ɛm 604
gɛɛn 604
gɛɛng 604
gɛɛng-jʉ̀ʉt 604
gɛ̂ɛo 604
gɛ̂ɛo-hǔu 604
gɛ́ɛs 604
gɛ́ɛt 604
géng 604
gɛn-lɔn 604
gɛ̀-sà~làk 605
gəən 603
gəən-bpai 603
gəən-gam-nòt 603
gə̀ət 603
gə̀ət-kʉ̀n 603
gə̀ət-mài 603
gía 603
gìi 601

giia 603
gìiao 603
gíiao 603
gìiao-gàp 603
gìiao-yoong 603
gìiat 603
gìiat-dtì~yót 603
gìiat-ní~yom 603
gii-dtâa 601
gii-laa 601
gìip 601
gìip-táao-sàt 601
gìit-kwǎang 601
gii-wii 601
gík 600
gì~lèet 601
gì~loo 601
gì~loo-gram 601
gì~loo-méet 601
gì~loo-wàt 601
gin 600
gin-dâai 600
gìng 600
gîng-gàa 600
gîng-gʉʉ 600
gin-jee 600
gin-kâao 600
gin-yaa 600
gíp 600
gi-rí~yaa 601
gìt-jà~gaan 600
gìt-jà~gam 600
gìt-jà~wát 600
glâa 593
glâa-hǎan 594
glaai-bpen 594
glâam 594
glaang 593
glaang-jɛ̂ɛng 594
glaang-kʉʉn 593

glàao 594
glàao-hăa 594
glàao-tôot 594
glai 605
glâi 605
glâi-chít 605
glâi-kiiang 605
glàn 593
glân 593
glàp 593
glàp-kʉʉn 593
glèt 602
glɛ̂ɛng 604
glɛ̀ɛp 604
glîia-glɔ̌m 602
glîiang 602
gliiao 602
gliiao-chʉ̀ʉak 602
glîiat 602
glìip-dɔ̀ɔk 594
glìn 594
glîng 594
glìn-hɔ̌ɔm 594
glom 593
glom-glɔ̌m 593
glòp 593
glɔ̌m 593
glɔ̀ng 593
glɔ̂ng 593
glɔ̀ng-sĭiang 593
glɔ̂ng-sɔ̀ng-taang-
  glai 593
glɔ̀ɔn 593
glɔɔng 593
glùm 594
gluua 593
glûuai 593
glûuai-máai 593
glûua-kɔɔ 593
gluuang 593

gluua 602
gluua-bpòn 602
glʉ̀uan 602
glʉ̌uan 602
glʉ̀uan-glàat 602
glʉʉn 594
gòk 588
gók 588
gôm 588
gon 593
gôn 588
gong 588
gon-gai 593
gong-sŭn 588
gon-lá~wí-tii 593
gon-ù-baai 593
goo-dang 605
goo-dték 605
goo-gôo 605
goo-hòk 605
goon 605
goong 605
gòot 605
gòp 588
gòt 2x588
gòt-dan 588
gòt-kìi 588
gòt-măai 588
gɔ̀ 603
gɔ́k-náam 594
gɔɔ 594
gɔ̀ɔ 594
gɔ̂ɔ 588
gɔ̀ɔ-dâai 588
gɔ̂ɔ-dii 588
gɔ̂ɔ-dtaam 588
gɔ̀ɔ-dtâng 595
gɔ̀ɔ-fai 595
gɔ̀ɔ-gaan-ráai ... 595
gɔ̀ɔ-guuan 594
gɔ̂ɔi 595

gɔ̀ɔn 595
gɔ̂ɔn 595
gɔɔng 595
gɔ̀ɔn-gam-nòt .. 595
gɔɔng-joon 595
gɔɔng-kûn 595
gɔɔng-nâa 595
gɔɔng-tá~hăan 595
gɔɔng-táp 595
gɔɔng-tun 595
gɔ̂ɔn-hĭn 595
gɔ̀ɔp 595
gɔ́ɔp 595
gɔɔ-rák-gà~daa-
  kom 588
gɔɔ-rá~nii 588
gɔ̀ɔ-sâang 595
gɔ́ɔt 595
grà 589
graam 592
gráap 592
grà~bà 591
grà~bìi 591
grà~bìiat 591
grà~bɔ̀ɔk 591
grà~bɔɔng 591
grà~bpăo 591
grà~bpăo-dəən-
  taang 591
grà~bpăo-èek-gà~
  săan 591
grà~bpăo-ngən 591
grà~bpɔ̌ng 591
grà~bproong 592
grà~bproong-rót
  592
grà~bpùk 591
grà~buuan-gaan
  591
grà~bʉ̌uang 591
grà~châak 589

grà~cháp 589
grà~chàp-grà~
  chĕeng 589
grà~daan 590
grà~dâang 590
grà~daan-hòk .. 590
grà~daan-kàao 590
grà~dàat 590
grà~dàat-cham-rá
  590
grà~dai 590
grà~den 590
grà~dìk 590
grà~dìng 590
grà~dòot 590
grà~dɔɔng 589
grà~dtàai 590
grà~dtìk 590
grà~dtùk 590
grà~dtûn 590
grà~dtʉʉ-rʉʉ-rón
  590
grà~dum 590
grà~dùuk 590
grà~dùuk-săn-lăng
  590
grà~hăai 592
grà~hăai-náam 592
grà~jaai 589
grà~jàat 589
grà~jàp 589
grà~jíiap 589
grà~jòk 589
grà~jòk-dtaa 589
grà~joom 589
grà~jɔɔk 589
grà~jùk 589
gram 592
grà~nán 591
grà~pǒm 592

grà~pɔ́ 592
grà~pɔ́-bpàt-săa~
  wá 592
grà~prao 596
grà~proong-lăng-
  rót 592
grà~pʉʉ 592
grà~rɔ̂ɔk 592
grà~sàp-grà~sàai
  592
grà~sĕɛ 592
grà~sĕɛ-nám-kĕn-
  nám-long 592
grà~síp 589
grà~sɔ̀ɔp 592
grà~sŭn-bpʉʉn 592
grà~suuang 591
grà~sʉʉ 592
grà~tá 591
grà~tăang 590
grà~tam 591
grà~tâng 591
grà~tɛ̂ɛk 591
grà~tɛ̀p 590
grà~tiiam 591
grà~tong 591
grà~tŏon 590
grà~tóp 591
grà~tôm 591
grà~tɔ́ɔn 591
greeng 602
greeng-gluua ... 602
greeng-jai 602
greng 602
grèt 602
grii-taa 592
grìit-rɔ́ɔng 592
grìng 592
grì-yaa 592
grom 588
grom-má~tan ... 588

grong 588
gròot 605
gròt 588
grɔ̀ 602
grɔ̀ɔk 589
grɔɔng 589
grɔ̀ɔp 589
grung-têep 592
gruuai 589
grùuat 589
gúk 601
gum-paa-pan ... 601
gun-chiiang 601
gûng 601
gûng-ying 601
gun-jɛɛ 601
gun-jɛɛ-mʉʉ 601
gù-sǒn 601
guu 601
gûu 601
gǔuai-dlǐiao 594
guuan 594
gùk-gông 601
gùng 601
gùuak-máa 603
gùuap 604
gùuap-dtaai 604
gwàa 594
gwaang 594
gwâang 594
gwâang-kwăang
  594
gwâang-yài 594
gwàat 594
gwai 605
gwèng 604
gwèng-gwai 604
gwiian 602

h

há 893

haa 893	hâi 875
hàa 868	hǎi 876
hâa 868	hâi-aa-hǎan 876
hǎa 868	hâi-à~pai 875
hǎa-dâai 869	hâi-châo 875
hǎai 869	hai-droo-jên 894
hǎai-bpai 869	hâi-gaan 875
hǎai-bpùai 869	hâi-gam-lang-jai
hǎai-dtuua 869	 875
hǎai-jai 869	hâi-gìiat 875
hǎai-jai-hɔ̀ɔp 869	hâi-_-gûu 875
hǎai-jai-kâo 869	hai-loo 894
hǎai-jai-ɔ̀ɔk 869	hâi-pǒn 875
hàak 868	hâi-pɔɔn 875
hǎa-líiang-chîip ... 869	hâi-sǐn-bon 875
hàam 869	hai-soo 894
hâam 869	hai-wee 894
hǎam 869	hâi-yʉʉm 875
hâam-kâo 869	hàk 867
hàan 869	hàk-ban-chii 867
hǎan 869	hàk-hǒom 867
hàang 868	hàk-láang 867
hâang 868	hàk-nâa 867
hǎang 868	hàk-ngâai 867
hǎang-bpiia 868	hàk-ɔ̀ɔk 867
hàang-gan 868	hǎm 869
hàang-glai 868	ham-pleeng 893
hàang-hěǝn 869	hàn 867
hâang-hûn-sùuan	hǎn 867
.... 868	hǎn-glàp 867
hǎang-jɔɔ-rá~kêe	hǎn-hěe 867
	hào 874
hǎang-krʉ̀ʉang ... 868	hǎo 874
hǎao 869	hàt 867
hàap 869	hàt-tà~gam 867
haa-rem 893	hee-haa 894
hǎa-rʉ̀ʉang 869	hee-lí~kɔ́p-dtâǝ ... 894
hàat-saai 869	hee-loo 894
hàat-yài 869	hěe-ran-yík 873
hǎa-yâak 869	hee-roo-iin 893
hǎa-yá~ná 869	hèet-gaan 871
hèet-pǒn 871
hěn 871
hěn-dûuai 871
heng 893
hěn-gɛ̀ɛ-dtuua 871
heng-suuai 893
hěn-jai 871
hěn-òk-hěn-jai 871
hèp 872
hèt 871
hɛ̀ɛ 874
hɛ́ɛ 874
héɛng 894
hɛ̀ɛp 874
hɛ̀ɛp-hěng 874
hɛm 894
hèng 874
hěng 874
hêng-lɛ́ɛng 874
hêo 875
hàǝ 874
hài 893
hǐi 870
hǐia 874
hǐian 894
hìiao 874
hìiao-hêng 874
hìip 870
hiip-sòp 870
hì-má 870
hì~má-dtòk 870
hǐn 869
hǐn-bpuun 870
hin-duu 893
hîng 869
hîng-hɔ̌i 869
hǐn-ná~yaan 870
hǐn-ngɔ̂ɔk 869
hǐn-ɔ̀ɔn 870
hǐn-yɔ́ɔi 870
híp-bpoo 893

hìt	869
hít	893
hǐu	870
hǐu-dâai	870
hǐu-jàt	870
hǐu-kâao	870
hǐu-náam	870
hòk	855
hǒng	855
hoo	894
hǒoi	875
hǒoi-hǐu	875
hǒom	875
hǒon	875
hǒo-raa-sàat	875
hǒo-rá~paa	875
hòot-hîiam	875
hòot-ráai	875
hòt	855
hòt-dtuua	855
hòt-hùu	855
hɔ̀	874
hɔ̀i	867
hɔ̌ng	865
hɔ̌ng-chùk-chǎ~ən	866
hɔ̌ng-chút	866
hɔ̌ng-dtâai-din	866
hɔ̌ng-dtêe	893
hɔ̌ng-gong	893
hɔ̌ng-klɔ̀ɔt	866
hɔ̌ng-kruua	865
hɔ̌ng-náam	866
hɔ̌ng-nâng-lên	866
hɔ̌ng-nɔɔn	866
hɔ̌ng-ráp-kɛ̀ɛk	866
hɔ̌ng-riian	866
hɔ̌ng-sà~mùt	866
hɔ̌ng-sûuam	866
hɔ̌ng-tam-ngaan	866
hɔ̌ng-tɔ̌ong	866
hɔ̀ɔ	865
hɔ̂ɔ	893
hɔ̌ɔ	865
hɔ̌ɔ-bprà~chum	866
hɔ̌ɔ-gaan-káa	865
hɔ̌ɔi	866
hɔ̌ɔi-múk	867
hɔ̌ɔi-naang-rom	867
hɔ̌ɔi-tâak	867
hɔ̀ɔk	865
hɔ̀ɔ-kɔɔi	865
hɔ̌ɔm	866
hɔ̌ɔm-dɛɛng	866
hɔ̌ɔm-lék	866
hɔ̌ɔm-lɔɔm	866
hɔ̌ɔn	866
hɔ̀ɔp	866
hɔ̌ɔ-pák	866
hùai	865
hùai-dtɛ̀ɛk	865
hûm	870
hùn	870
hǔng-kâao	870
hùn-grà~bɔ̀ɔk	870
hǔn-hǎn	870
hùn-lâi-gaa	870
hûn-sùuan	870
hùn-yon	870
hùp-bpàak	870
hùp-kǎo	870
hùu	871
hǔu	870
hǔua	867
hǔua-chai-táao	868
hǔua-chìit	868
hǔua-gà~lòok	867
hǔua-gào	867
hǔua-gà~tí	867
hǔua-hǐn	868
hǔua-hɔ̌ɔm	868
hǔuai	865
hǔua-jai	867
hǔua-jai-waai	867
hǔua-kào	867
hǔua-kěng	867
hǔua-kɔ̂ɔ	867
hǔua-láan	868
hǔua-mêɛ-mʉʉ	868
hûuan	865
hǔua-nâa	868
hùuang	864
hǔuang	864
hǔuang-hɛ̌ɛn	865
huuang-jǔi	893
hǔuan-glàp	865
huuang-súi	893
hùuang-yai	864
hǔua-nom	868
hǔua-pàk-gàat	868
hǔua-rán	868
hǔua-rɔ́	868
hǔua-rɔ́-yɔ́	868
hǔua-run-rɛɛng	868
hǔua-rʉ̂ʉang	868
hǔua-sǐia	868
hǔuat	865
hǔua-tiian	868
hǔu-dtìt-chʉ́ʉa	871
hǔu-dtʉng	871
hǔu-fàat	871
hǔu-fang	871
hǔu-grà~dtàai	871
hùuk	871
hûuk	893
hǔu-nùuak	871
hùut	871
hǔu-too-rá~sàp	871
hǔu-ʉ̂ʉ	871
hʉ́k-hǎ~əm	893
hʉ̌ng	870
hút	893

hút-hát 893	jàa 646	jàk 2x645
huu 893	jâa 646	jà~kêe 645
i	jàai 646	jàk-gà~jàn 645
	jàai-dtà~làat 646	ják-gà~jîi 645
ii 886	jàak 646	ják-gà~jíi 645
íiam 891	jàak-nán 646	jàk-grà~pát 645
iian 891	jaam 646	jàk-grà~waan ... 645
iiang 890	jaan 646	jàk-grà~wàt 645
îiang 890	jàa-nâa 646	jàk-grà~yaan 645
ii-dɔ̀ɔk 886	jàa-nâa-sɔɔŋ ... 646	jàk-grà~yaan-yon
ii-dtôo 887	jaan-bin 646	 645
ii-dtuua 886	jâang 646	jàk-grii 645
ii-ɛ̀ɛp 887	jaang-long 646	jàk-raa-sǐi 645
ii-hàa 887	jaan-sǐi 646	jàk-yép-pâa 645
ii-jûu 886	jâao 649	jam 646
iik 886	jâao-túk 650	jam-bpaa 647
iik-dtɔ̀ɔ-bpai 886	jáap 646	jam-bpen 647
ii-kwaai 886	jaa-rá~gam 646	jam-bpen-dtông
ii-meo 887	jàa-sǎan 646	 647
ii-sǎan 887	jà~dtù-jàk 643	jam-_-dâai 646
ii-sùk-ii-sǎi 887	jà-dtù~ràt 643	jam-gàt 646
ìm 886	já~ěe 645	jam-jee 646
in-diia 886	jai 651	jam-kúk 646
in-doo-nii-siia ... 886	jai-bun 651	jam-ləəi 647
ing 886	jai-chúun 651	jam-lɔɔng 647
in-sii 886	jai-dii 651	jâm-mâm 647
in-tá~pà~lam 886	jai-diiao 651	jam-nàai 647
ì~ràan 886	jai-glâa 651	jam-nam 647
ì~rák 886	jai-glaang-muuang	jam-nɔɔng 647
ìt 886	 651	jam-nuuan 646
ìt-chǎa 886	jai-gwâang 651	jam-nuuan-dtem
ìt-dtaa-lîi 886	jai-hǎai 652	 646
ìt-sà~rà 886	jai-kêɛp 651	jam-nuuan-mâak
ìt-sà~raa-eeo 886	jai-kwaam 651	 646
ìt-sà~rá~pâap .. 886	jai-lɔɔi 652	jam-pûuak 647
ìt-tí-pon 886	jai-ngâai 651	jam-sǐin 647
ìt-tí-rít 886	jai-ráai 652	jà~mùuk 643
j	jai-reo 652	jà~mùuk-lép 643
	jai-rɔ́ɔn 651	jan 645
jà 644	jai-yen 651	jang 645
já 644	jai-yen-yen 651	jang-wà 645

jang-wàt 645	jeen-lôok 649	jing-jang 644
jan-rai 645	jee-rá~jaa 649	jing-jing 644
jan-tá-bù~rii 645	jèet-dtà~naa 649	jǐng-jòk 647
jan-tá~rú-bpà~	jéng 649	jing-jôo 647
raa-kaa 646	jěng 649	jîng-rìit 647
jan-yaa 644	jeo 649	jìp 647
jâo-aa-rom 650	jèp 649	jit 647
jâo-aa-wâat 650	jèp-bpùuat 649	jìt-dtâai-sǎm-nùk
jâo-bàao 650	jèp-jai 649	 647
jâo-chaai 649	jèt 649	jìt-dtà~gam 647
jâo-chúu 650	jɛɛ-gan 650	jìt-dtà~gɔɔn 647
jâo-dtuua 650	jɛ̀ɛk 650	jìt-dtà~pɛ̂ɛt 647
jâo-kǒɔng 649	jɛ̀ɛk-jàai 650	jìt-dtà~wít-tá~yaa
jâo-kǒɔng-ráan ... 649	jɛ̀ɛk-jɛɛng 650	 647
jâo-kǔn-muun-naai	jɛ̀ɛk-pâi 650	jìt-fân-fɯɯan 647
.... 649	jɛ̂ɛng 650	jìt-jai 647
jâo-lêe 650	jɛ̂ɛng-kwaam 651	jǐu 648
jâo-lôok 650	jɛɛo-rɯɯa 651	jom 643
jâo-naai 650	jɛm 651	jom-long 643
jâo-nâa-tîi 650	jɛm-jêɛng 651	jom-náam 643
jâo-nîi 650	jɛm-sǎi 651	jom-náam-dtaai 643
jâo-pâap 650	jěo 651	jon 643
jâo-pá~nák-ngaan	jəə 649	jon-bpan-yaa 643
.... 650	jəə-gan 649	jong-rák-pák-dii
jâo-sǎao 650	jîi 648	 643
jâo-yǐng 650	jíiao 650	jon-grà~tâng 643
jàp 646	jíiao-jáao 650	jon-gwàa 643
jàp-gum 646	jiiao-kài 650	jon-mum 643
jà~raa-jɔɔn 644	jiia-rá~nai 650	jon-tǔng 643
jà~rəən 649	jiin 648	jòok 651
jà~rí-yá-tam 644	jiin-glaang 648	jóok 651
jà~rùuat 644	jiip 648	joom 651
jàt 645	jii-wɔɔn 648	joom-dtii 651
jàt-dtâng 645	jìk 647	joon 2x651
jàt-dtà~waa 645	jík-gǒo 647	joon-sà~làt 651
jàt-_-hâi 645	jîm 647	joo-rá~gam 651
jàt-pim 645	jǐm 647	jòot 2x651
jee 649	jin-dtà~naa-gaan	jòp 643
jée 649	 647	jòt 643
jee-dii 649	jing 644	jòt-_-long 643
	jing-jai 644	jòt-mǎai 643

jɔ̀ 650
jɔ̀-jong 650
jǒng 644
jǒng-mɔɔng 644
jɔɔ 644
jɔ̀ɔ 644
jɔ̂ɔ 644
jɔ́ɔi 644
jɔ̂ɔk 644
jɔɔm 644
jɔɔm-bplùuak 644
jɔɔm-pon 644
jɔɔn 644
jɔɔng 644
jɔɔng-ngən 644
jɔɔng-hǔng 644
jɔɔng-jam 644
jɔ̂ɔp 644
jɔ́ɔp 644
jɔɔ-pâap 644
jɔɔ-rá~kêe 644
jɔ̂ɔt 644
jù 648
jù-lin-sii 649
jùm 649
jûn-jâan 649
jun-lá~pâak 649
jùt 648
jùt-bɔ̀ɔt 648
jùt-bprà~sǒng 648
jùt-chʉ̂ʉam-dtɔ̀ɔt
.... 648
jùt-dàang 648
jùt-dèn 648
jùt-rɨ̂əm-dtôn 648
jùt-sǎm-kan 648
jùt-sǎng-gèet 648
jùt-sùt-yɔ̂ɔt 648
jùt-sǔun-glaang ... 648
jùt-sǔung-sùt 649

jùt-tót-sà~ní~yom
.... 648
jǔu 649
jùua 646
juuan 644
jûuang 644
jûu-jîi 649
juung 649
jùup 649
jung 648
jʉ̀ʉt 648

k

kâ 628
ká 628
kaa 629
kàa 612
kâa 612, 629, 639
káa 629
kǎa 612
kaa-bɔ̂n 630
kâa-bɔɔ-rí~gaan
.... 630
kǎa-bpai 613
kâa-bpràp 630
kâa-chà~lìia 629
kâa-châo 629
kâa-chót-chái ... 629
kâa-chʉ̀ʉa 639
kâa-dooi-sǎan ... 629
kǎa-dtâng 613
kâa-dtɔ̀ɔp-tɛɛn .. 629
kâa-dtuua 629
kâa-dtuua-dtaai . 639
kaa-fee-iin 630
kǎa-gài 612
kǎa-glàp 612
kǎa-hàk 614
kǎai 630
kǎai 613
kǎai-bplìik 613

kǎai-dii 613
kǎai-dtuua 613
kǎai-nâa 613
kǎai-sòng 613
kâa-jâang 629
káa-kǎai 629
kǎa-kâo 612
kâa-krɔɔng-chîip
.... 629
kâa-lâo-riian 630
kâam 613
kaan 630
káan 630
kâa-naai-nâa 630
kaang 629
kâang 612
káang 629
kâang-bon 612
kâang-diiao 612
kâang-dtâai 612
kâang-dtôn 612
káang-kaao 629
kâang-kiiang 612
kaang-kók 629
kâang-kʉ̀n 612
kâang-kʉʉn 612
kâang-kwǎa 612
kâang-lâang 612
kâang-lǎng 612
kâang-nâa 612
kâang-nai 612
kâang-nɔ̂ɔk 612
kâang-rɛɛm 612
kâang-sáai 612
kâang-táai-rʉʉa .. 612
kaang-tuum 629
káang-wái 629
kaan-hàap 630
kǎa-nìip 614
kaao 630
kàao 613

kâao	613	kâa-sùk	614	kâi-wàt-yài	620
kăao	613	kàat	613	kà~jàt	605
kâao-bplu̯ak	614	kaa-tăa	629	kam	630
kâao-cháao	613	kâa-tài	629	kâm	630
kâao-dtôm	614	kâa-tam-kwăn	629	kăm	630
kâao-gɛɛng	613	kâat-dtà~gam	639	kăm	614
kâao-grìiap	613	kâat-dtà~gɔɔn	639	ká~má~naa-kom
kâao-jâao	613	kâat-gaan	629		622
kàao-kraao	613	kàat-jai	613	kà~mào	618
kâao-lăam	614	kâat-ká~nee	629	kà~màp	607
kâao-lăam-dtàt	614	kàat-náam	613	kam-à~tí-baai	632
kàao-luu	614	kàat-tun	613	kam-bplɛɛ	631
kâao-nǐiao	614	kâat-wăng	629	kam-dtàt-sǐn	631
kâao-pôot	614	kà~buuan	606	kam-dtɔɔp	631
kâao-săa-lii	614	kà~buuan-gaan	606	kam-dtɔɔ-táai	631
kàao-săan	614	kà~buuan-hɛ̀ɛ	606	kam-dtuuan	631
kâao-săan	614	ká~dii	621	kà~mĕen	618
kâao-sɔɔm-muu		ká~dii-aa-yaa	621	kà~mèn	618
	613	ká~dii-pĕng	621	kam-hâi-gaan	632
kâao-sùk	614	ká~dtì	621	kà~mîn	607
kâao-sŭuai	614	kài	620	kám-jun	631
kâao-tîiang	614	kâi	620	kam-kun-ná~sàp
kâao-yen	614	kăi	620		631
kăa-ɔ̀ɔk	614	kâi-bpàa	620	kâm-kuun	631
kăa-ɔ̀ɔn	614	kài-bplaa	620	kam-kwăn	631
kâap	630	kài-daao	620	kam-naam	631
kâa-pàan-bprà~		kài-dɛɛng	620	kam-nam	631
dtuu	630	kài-dtôm	620	kam-náp	631
kâa-pàan-taang	630	kăi-grà~dùuk	620	kam-né-nam	631
kâa-pá~jâao	613	kài-hăm	620	kam-nuuan	631
kâap-gìiap	630	kài-jiiao	620	kà~mooi	607
kâap-sà~mùt	630	kài-kăao	620	kam-pang-pəəi	631
kaa-raa-dtêe	630	kăi-kuuang	620	kam-pii	629
kâa-râat-chá~gaan		kài-lûuak	620	kam-pii-bai-bên	629
	613	kâi-lŭuang	620	kam-pí-pâak-săa
kâa-rɛɛng	630	kâi-lɯ̀ɯat-ɔ̀ɔk	620		631
kâa-rót	630	kăi-man	620	kam-pûut	631
kăa-sĭia	614	kài-múk	620	kam-raam	631
kâa-sĭia-hăai	630	kâi-tɔɔ-rá~pít	620	kam-rɔ́ɔng	631
kaa-sì~noo	630	kâi-wàt	620	kam-săa-rá~pâap
kâa-sŏo-hûi	630	kâi-wàt-nók	620		632

kam-sà~lɛɛng ... 631
kam-sàng 632
kam-săn-taan ... 632
kam-săn-yaa 632
kam-sàp 631
kam-sôi 631
kam-tăam 631
kam-ták-taai 631
kam-tam-naai ... 631
kam-ù-taan 632
kà~mùuat-kíu ... 606
kam-wí-sèet 631
kan 623, 628
kân 611
kán 628
kăn 611
kà~nà 605
ká~ná 621
ká~náa 628
kà~năan 606
kà~nàap 606
kà~nàat 606
ká~ná-bɔɔ-dii ... 621
ká~ná~gam-má~
   gaan 621
ká~ná-lûuk-kŭn
   621
kà~nà-níi 605
ká~ná-rát-tà~
   mon-dtrii 621
kà~nà-tîi 605
kan-bèt 628
kân-dtàm 611
kăn-dtòok 611
kân-dtɔɔn 611
ká~nɛɛn 628
ká~nɛɛn-sĭiang .. 628
kăng 611
ká~nít-dtà~sàat
   621
ká~nít-sàat 621

kà~nŏm 606
kà~nŏm-bpang .. 606
kà~nŏm-jiin 606
kà~nòp-tam-niiam
   606
kan-rêng 628
kan-tăi 628
kăn-tii 611
kà~nŭn 606
kào 618
kăo 618
káo 637
kăo 618
kâo-bpai 619
kâo-gan-dâai 618
kâo-giia 618
kâo-glâi 618
kâo-hăa 619
kâo-jai 618
kâo-jai-pìt 618
kâo-kâang 618
kâo-kiu 618
káo-kroong 637
kâo-kûu 618
kâo-maa 619
kâo-mʉʉang 619
kâo-nɔɔn 618
kâo-riian 619
kao-róp 637
kâo-rûuam 619
kâo-sùu 619
kâo-tɛ̌ɛo 618
kâo-tŭng 618
kăo-wong-gòt .. 619
kàp 611
káp 628, 629
káp-kăn 629
káp-kɛ̂ɛp 629
káp-kìi 611
kàp-lâi 611
kàp-rɔ́ɔng 611

kàp-tàai 611
ká~raa-wâat 639
ká~rú-hàat 624
kàt 611
kát 628
kàt-glao 611
kàt-jai 611
kát-jà~mùuk 628
kàt-jang-wà 611
kát-káan 628
kàt-kŭun 611
kàt-kwăang 611
kát-lûuak 628
kàt-ngao 611
kát-_-ɔ̀ɔk 628
kàt-sŏn 611
kàt-yɛ́ɛng 611
kàt-yɛ́ɛng-gan .. 611
kà~yà 607
kà~yăai 607
kà~yà-kà~yɛ̌ɛng
   607
kà~yăm 607
kà~yăn 607
kà~yăn-kăn-kĕng
   607
kà~yào 618
kà~yàp 607
kà~yèek 618
kà~yèng 618
kà~yîi 607
kà~yìp 607
kee-bôn 634
kèek 617
kéek 634
kee-mii 634
kee-mii-bam-bàt
   634
kèet 617
kèet-dɛɛn 617

a
b
bp
ch
d
dt
e
ɛ
ə
f
g
h
i
j
k
l
m
n
ng
o
ɔ
p
r
s
t
u
ʉ
w
y

kèet-lûuak-dtâng
.... 617
kèet-rɔ́ɔn 617
kem 634
kêm 617
kěm 617
kěm-chìit-yaa 617
kěm-glàt 617
kěm-kàt 617
kěm-kàt-ní-rá~pai
.... 617
kêm-kěng 617
kêm-kôn 617
kěm-mùt 618
kěm-naa-lí~gaa 618
kêm-ngûuat 617
kěm-tít 618
kěm-yép-pâa 618
kén 634
kěn 617
kèng 617
kɛ̂ɛ 637
kɛ̀ɛk 619
kɛɛ-lɔɔ-rîi 638
kɛɛm 637
kɛ́ɛn 637
kɛ̌ɛn 619
kɛɛn-dtaa-lúup 637
kɛ̌ɛn-kǎa 619
kɛ́ɛn-kuuang 637
kɛ̌ɛn-sûua 619
kɛ̂ɛp 637
kɛ̌ɛ-rɔ̀t 638
kěng 619
kěng 619
kěng-dtuua 619
kěng-jai 619
kèng-kǎn 619
kěng-kǎn 619
kěng-rɛɛng 619
kěng-tûu 619

kɛn-sîiam 638
kép-suun 637
két-dtaa-lɔ́k 637
kəəi 634
kǎəi 618
kəəi-dtuua 634
kii 632
kìi 615
kîi 2x615, 632
kîia 619
kîi-aai 616
kîian 639
kǐian 619
kiiang 637
kǐiang 619
kǐian-_-wàt 619
kiiao 637
kîiao 619, 637
kíiao 637
kǐiao 619
kìiat 619
kîi-bpà~naa-wút
.... 615
kîi-dtùu 615
kîi-fan 615
kîi-gìiat 615
kîi-glàak 615
kîi-goong 615
kîi-hǔu 616
kîi-kâa 615
kîi-klàat 615
kîi-lên 615
kîi-lîi 616
kîi-lǒng-kîi-luum
.... 616
kîi-lûuai 616
kîi-luum 615
kiim 632
kîi-móo 615
kîi-moo-hǒo 615
kîi-mûuk 615

kîi-nǐiao 616
kîi-nɔ́ɔi-jai 615
kǐip 632
kîi-pûng 615
kîi-rèe 616
kîi-rɔ́ɔn 615
kîi-sǒng-sǎan 616
kìit 615
kîi-tâo 615
kìit-kâa 615
kìit-sên-dtâai 615
kîi-ùuat 616
kîi-yaa 615
kǐm 614
kǐng 614
kít 632
kít-kón 632
kít-_-ɔ̀ɔk 632
kít-tǔng 632
kít-tǔng-bâan ... 632
kít-wâa 632
kiu 632
kíu 632
kláai 624
kláai-klung 624
klaan 624
klàat 607
klâat-klûuan 624
klâat-sìk 624
klá-gan 624
klam 624
klang 624
klâng 624
klang-aa-wút 624
klâng-klái 624
klang-pát-sà~dù
.... 624
klang-sǐn-káa 624
klǎo 618
klát 624
klét-láp 637

a
b
bp
ch
d
dt
e
ɛ
ə
f
g
h
i
j
k
l
m
n
ng
o
ɔ
p
r
s
t
u
ʉ
w
y

kléəm 637	kɔ̌n-bpui 606	kɔ̌on 620
klí-dtɔɔ-rít 624	kon-chái 622	kóong 638
klík 624	kon-châo 622	koon-kǎa 638
klí-ník 624	kon-dəən-táao 622	kôon-lóm 638
klìp 607	kon-diiao 622	koo-râat 638
kloon 639	kɔ̌n-dtaa 606	koo-sà~naa 639
kloong 638	kon-dtoo 622	koo-sòk 639
kloong-glɔɔn ... 639	kong 621	kôot-sà~naa 639
klɔ̂ng 624	kong-jà 621	kòp 606
klɔ̂ng-dtuua 624	kon-glaang 621	kóp 622
klɔ̂ng-klêo 624	kong-tǐi 621	kóp-hǎa 622
klɔɔng 624	kong-ton 621	kòt 606
klɔ̂ɔt 624	kón-hǎa 622	kót 621
klùi 607	kon-kǎai 621	kót-kíiao 621
klúk 625	kon-kâi 621	kɔ́ 637
klum 625	kon-kàp-rót 621	kôi 628
klúm-klâng 625	kon-krɛ́ 622	kɔ̂i-kɔ̂i 628
klum-krʉʉa 625	kon-kúk 622	kɔm-píu-dtêə 628
klûʉan 637	kón-kwáa 621	kɔn-dôm 627
klûʉan-tǐi 637	kɔ̌n-_-long 606	kɔ̌n-gèn 609
klûʉan-tǐi-dâai 637	kɔ̌n-lúk 606	kɔ̂ng-jai 608
klûʉan-wǎi 637	kon-nai 622	kɔ̂n-kâang 627
klûʉan-yáai-_- bpai-_ 637	kon-ngaan 622	kɔn-sə̀ət 627
klûʉap 637	kɔ̌n-nók 606	kɔɔ 627
klûʉn 624	kon-nɔ̂ɔk 622	kɔ́ɔ 608
klûʉn-sâi 625	kon-pí-gaan 622	kɔ̌ɔ 608
klûʉn-yák 624	kón-póp 622	kɔ̂ɔ-âang 611
kom 622	kon-rák 622	kɔ̂ɔ-à~pai 611
kɔ̌m 606	kɔ̌n-sàt 606	kɔ̂ɔ-bang-káp ... 610
kòm-hěeng 607	kon-song 622	kɔ̂ɔ-bòk-prŏng .. 610
kòm-kìi 606	kɔ̌n-sòng 606	kɔ̂ɔ-dii 609
kòm-kùu 606	kon-tam 622	kɔ̌ɔ-dtèng-ngaan 609
kòm-kǔʉn 606	koo 638	
kom-má~naa-kom 622	koo-dtâa 639	kɔɔ-dtìip 627
kon 621	koo-jɔɔn 638	kɔ̂ɔ-dtòk-long ... 609
kôn 606	kòok 620	kɔ̂ɔ-dtɔ̀ɔ 609
kón 621	kôok 638	kɔ̂ɔ-dtuua 609
kɔ̌n 606	koo-keen 638	kɔ̂ɔ-gam-nòt 608
kon-bpùai 622	koom 638	kɔ̂ɔ-gɛ̂ɛ-dtuua ... 608
	koom-fai 638	kɔ̂ɔ-hǎa 610
	kôon 638	kɔ̌ɔ-hâi 611

a
b
bp
ch
d
dt
e
ɛ
ə
f
g
h
i
j
k
l
m
n
ng
o
ɔ
p
r
s
t
u
ʉ
w
y

kɔɔ-hɔ̌ɔi 628	kɔ̂ɔ-níu 609	krîiat 635
kɔɔi 628	kɔɔn-têɛk 627	kriim 623
kɔ̂ɔ-jam-gàt 609	kɔ̀ɔp 609	krîip-bplaa 623
kɔ̂ɔk 627	kɔ̀ɔp-fáa 610	krít 623
kɔ̂ɔ-kĭian 608	kɔ̀ɔp-pí-sùut 610	krít-dtà~sàk-gà~
kɔ̂ɔ-kít-hĕn 608	kɔ̀ɔp-jai 610	ràat 623
kɔ̂ɔ-klét 608	kɔ̀ɔp-kàai 610	krók 622
kɔ̂ɔ-kwaam 608	kɔ̀ɔp-kèet 610	kroong 638
kɔɔ-lâm 628	kɔ̀ɔp-kun 610	kroong-gaan 638
kɔɔ-lées-dtəə-rôn	kɔ̀ɔp-nôok 610	kroong-grà~dùuk
.... 628	kɔ̀ɔp-tà~nŏn 610	 638
kɔ̂ɔ-muun 610	kɔ̌ɔ-rɔ́ɔng 610	kroong-râang ... 638
kɔ̂ɔ-mʉʉ 610	kɔɔ-sà~dɛɛng-	kroong-rʉ̌ʉang .. 638
kɔɔn 627	kwaam-yin-dii 610	kroong-sâang ... 638
kɔ́ɔn 627	kɔ̂ɔ-sà~nə̌ə 610	króp 622
kɔ̌ɔn 609	kɔ̂ɔ-sǎng-gèet .. 610	króp-gam-nòt .. 622
kɔɔn-doo-mí-niiam	kɔ̂ɔ-sĭia 610	króp-tûuan 622
.... 627	kɔ̌ɔ-sɔ̀ɔp 610	krɔ́ 634
kɔ̂ɔ-né-nam 609	kɔɔ-sʉ̂ʉa 628	krɔ́-gam 634
kɔ̌ɔng 608	kɔ̀ɔt 628	krɔɔng 623
kɔ̌ɔng-bplɔɔm ... 609	kɔ̂ɔ-taan 609	krɔ̂ɔp-fan 623
kɔ̌ɔng-chái 608	kɔ̂ɔ-táao 609	krɔ̂ɔp-krɔɔng 623
kɔ̌ɔng-cham 608	kɔ̂ɔ-tét-jing 609	krɔ̂ɔp-kruua 623
kɔ̌ɔng-dɔɔng 608	kɔ̂ɔ-tôot 609	krui 623
kɔ̌ɔng-gào 608	kɔ̌ɔ-yʉʉm 610	krù-krà 607
kɔ̌ɔng-gin 608	kraang 623	krûn-kít 623
kɔ̌ɔng-kaao 608	krâao-krâao 623	kruu 623
kɔ̌ɔng-kĕng 608	kraao-nâa 623	kruua 623
kɔ̌ɔng-krai 608	krâat 623	kruua-rʉʉan 623
kɔ̌ɔng-kwǎn 608	krai 639	kruu-fʉ̀k 623
kɔ̌ɔng-láp 609	krai-gɔ̂ɔ-dâai 639	kruu-pí-sèet 623
kɔ̌ɔng-lĕeo 609	krai-krai 639	kruu-yài 624
kɔ̌ɔng-lên 609	krâi-kruuan 639	krʉ́m 623
kɔ̌ɔng-mii-kâa ... 609	krâm-kruuan 623	krʉ̀ng 2x623
kɔ̌ɔng-sĭia 609	kráng 623	krʉ̀ng-taang 623
kɔ̌ɔng-sòt 609	kráng-nʉ̀ng 623	krʉʉa 635
kɔ̌ɔng-tɛ́ɛ 608	krao 634	krʉʉa-kàai 635
kɔ̌ɔng-tiiam 608	kráp 623	krûʉang 635
kɔ̌ɔng-tîi-rá~lʉ́k 608	krêng 634	krûʉang-bὲɛp ... 636
kɔ̌ɔng-wǎan 609	krêng-krát 634	krûʉang-bin 636
kɔ̌ɔng-wâang 609	krɛ̂ɛ-hǎam 637	

krûuang-bpân-din-pǎo 636
krûuang-bprà~dàp 636
krûuang-bpràp-aa-gàat 636
krûuang-chái 635
krûuang-dàp-pləəng 635
krûuang-don-dtrii 635
krûuang-dtèng-gaai 635
krûuang-dùut-fùn 635
krûuang-dùum 635
krûuang-gɛɛng 635
krûuang-grɔɔng-náam 635
krûuang-kà~yǎai-sǐiang 635
krûuang-kǐian ... 635
krûuang-kít-lêek 635
krûuang-lên 636
krûuang-mǎai ... 637
krûuang-mɯɯ ... 636
krûuang-nai 636
krûuang-ngən .. 635
krûuang-nûng-hòm 636
krûuang-pim-dìit 636
krûuang-raang 636
krûuang-sák-pâa 635
krûuang-sǎm-aang 636
krûuang-sǐiang 636
krûuang-sùup .. 636

krûuang-tàai-èek-gà~sǎan 635
krûuang-tam-nám-ùn 636
krûuang-têet 636
krûuang-yon 636
kui 633
kúi 633
kǔi 617
kui-dtoo 633
kui-móo 633
kúk 632
kúk-gîi 632
kúk-kaam 632
kúk-kào 632
kum 633
kúm 633
kúm-gan 633
kúm-kâa 633
kum-kǎng 633
kúm-klâng 633
kúm-krɔɔng 633
kum-ngaan 633
kun 632
kùn 617
kún 633
kǔn 616
kun-kâa 633
kún-kəəi 633
kùn-kɯɯang 617
kun-naai 633
kǔn-naang 617
kun-ná~lák-sà~nà 633
kun-ná~pâap 633
kun-ná~sǒm-bàt 633
kun-ná~tam 633
kǔn-pěɛn 617
kǔn-sùk 617
kun-yǐng 633

kùt 616
kùt-kón 616
kùt-mɯɯang 616
kùt-tɔɔng 616
kuu 633
kùu 617
kûu 633
kûua 612
kuuai 625
kûua-lôok 612
kuuan 625
kùuan 607
kuuang 625
kuuan-jà 625
kùuap 607
kûuap 625
kûuap-kum 625
kûuap-kum-dtuua 625
kûuap-máa 625
kùuat 607
kûu-bàao-sǎao 634
kuu-bpɔɔng 634
kûu-dtɔ̀ɔ-sûu ... 634
kûu-gɔɔ-rá~nii ... 633
kûu-hǔu 634
kûu-kǎa 633
kùu-kěn 617
kûu-kîi 634
kûu-krɔɔng 634
kûu-kuuan 634
kûu-kwaam 634
kûu-mân 634
kûu-mɯɯ 634
kuu-mɯɯang 634
kuun 634
kûu-rák 634
kûu-sǒm-rót 634
kùut 617
kùut-_-ɔ̀ɔk 617
kûn 616

kùn-bpii-mài 616
kùn-chàai 616
kùn-chûu 616
kùn-dtiiang 616
kùn-fàng 616
kùn-glông 616
kùn-jai 616
kùn-ngən 616
kùn-raa 616
kùn-rót 616
kùn-sǎan 616
kʉʉ 632
kʉ̀ʉ 619
kʉ̀ʉan 619
kʉ̀ʉang ,............. 637
kʉʉn 632
kʉʉn-dii-gan 632
kʉʉn-jai 616
kʉʉn-níi 632
kwáa 625
kwǎa 607
kwaai 627
kwaam 2x625
kwaam-bpen-jing
.... 626
kwaam-bplɔ̀ɔt-pai
.... 626
kwaam-bprà~prʉ́t
.... 626
kwaam-chûuai-lʉ̌ua
.... 626
kwaam-chûua ... 626
kwaam-dan-lʉ̀uat
.... 626
kwaam-dtaai 626
kwaam-dtâng-jai
.... 626
kwaam-dtông-gaan
.... 626
kwaam-fǎn 626

kwaam-gâao-nâa
.... 625
kwaam-gòt-dan 625
kwaam-jèp-bpùuat
.... 626
kwaam-jing 625
kwaam-kâo-jai 625
kwaam-kao-róp 625
kwaam-kít 625
kwaam-kít-hěn 625
kwaam-krâi 625
kwaam-lǎng 627
kwaam-mân-jai 626
kwaam-ngaam 626
kwaam-pá~yaa-
yaam 626
kwaam-pìt-plâat
.... 626
kwaam-pɔɔ-jai . 626
kwaam-puum-jai
.... 626
kwaam-rák 626
kwaam-ráp-pìt-
chɔ̂ɔp 626
kwaam-reo 627
kwaam-rɔ́ɔn 626
kwaam-rúu 626
kwaam-rúu-sʉ̀k 627
kwaam-sǎa-mâat
.... 627
kwaam-sà~dùuak
kwaam-sǎm-kan
.... 627
kwaam-sǎm-pan
.... 627
kwaam-sà~ngòp
.... 627
kwaam-sâo 627
kwaam-sǐia-hǎai 627
kwaam-sìiang ... 627

kwaam-sǒn-jai .. 627
kwaam-sùk 627
kwaam-sʉ̀ʉ-sàt 626
kwaam-tìi 626
kwaam-wǎng ... 627
kwaam-yaao 626
kwaam-yen 626
kwaam-yú-dtì-tam
.... 626
kwáan 625
kwǎan 607
kwaan-cháang .. 625
kwâang 607
kwáang 625
kwǎang 607
kwǎang-gân 607
kwǎang-taang .. 607
kwâm 627
kwâm-bàat 627
kwâm-long 627
kwaŋ 625
kwǎn 607
kwan-pít 625
kwěe 618
kwɛ́ɛn 638
kwɛ̌ɛn 620
kwɛ̌ɛng 619
kwìt 607

lá 807
laa 808
lâa 808, 864
lǎa 864
lá~aai-jai 807
lâa-cháa 808
laa-dtin 808
laa-dtuua-pûu .. 808
laa-gɔ̀ɔn 808
laai 809
lǎai 864

lăai-jai 864
laai-mʉʉ 809
laai-mʉʉ-chʉ́ʉ 809
laai-níu-mʉʉ 809
laai-sàk 809
laai-sen 809
làak 864
lâak 808
láa-lăng 809
laam 809
lâam 809
lăam 864
laa-mók 809
lâam-sôo 809
laan 808
láan 809
lăan 864
laang 808
lâang 808
láang 808
láang-plăan 808
láang-rûup 808
laang-sàat 808
láang-sà~mʉ̌ong
.... 808
laang-săng-hʉ̌on
.... 808
lâang-sùt 808
laao 809
lăao 864
laa-ɔ̀ɔk 809
làap 864
lâap 2x809
láa-sà~măi 809
lâa-sàt 809
lâa-sùt 809
lâat 808
lâat-dtrà~ween 808
lâat-iiang 808
lâat-yaang 808
lâa-yʉ̀ua 809

lá~gôɔ 807
lá~hù-tôot 805
lài 876
lâi 817
lăi 876
lá~ìiat 807
lá~ìiat-tìi-tûuan 807
lâi-_-ɔ̀ɔk 817
làk 863
làk-bprà~gan ... 863
làk-chai 863
làk-gaan 863
làk-geen 863
làk-lèng 863
lák-lɔ̀ɔp 807
lá~kɔɔn 807
lá~kɔɔn-sàt 807
lák-paa-dtuua ... 807
lák-sà~nà 807
lák-sà~nà-naam
.... 807
làk-sáp 863
làk-sùut 863
làk-tăan 863
làk-tam 863
lák-yím 807
lá~laai 807
lá~laai-nám-kĕng
.... 807
lá~ləəi 807
là-lŭuam 863
lam 809
lâm 809
lá~mâng 807
lam-bàak 810
lam-bpaang 810
lam-dàp 809
lam-dtôn 810
lam-dtuua 810
lá~məə 807
lá~mêət 807

lá~mêət-lík-kà~sìt
.... 807
lam-iiang 810
lám-kâa 809
lam-ken 809
lam-liiang 810
lám-nâa 810
lá~mɔ́ 807
lam-pang 810
lam-poong 810
lam-puun 810
lam-sâi 810
lam-sâi-yài 810
lâm-sam 809
lâm-săn 810
lam-sĕɛng 810
lam-taan 810
lá~mút 807
lam-yai 810
lân 808
lang 808
làng 864
lăng 864
lăng-jàak 864
lăng-kaa 864
lang-lee 808
lăng-sùt 864
lăng-tĭiang 864
lâo 815, 873
láo 815
lăo 873
láo-loom 815
lào-nán 873
lào-níi 873
lâo-ní-taan 815
lâo-riian 815
lâo-rʉ̂uang 815
lá~ɔɔng 807
làp 864
láp 808
làp-dtaa 864

làp-nai 864
lát 808
lá~tíng 807
lát-tí 808
lát-wong-jɔɔn ... 808
lá-wén 807
lêe-gon 815
lee-kǎa 814
lee-kǎa-nú-gaan
.... 814
lêek-ká~nít 814
lêek-kîi 814
lêek-kûu 814
lêe-lìiam 815
leen 814, 815
lěen 873
leeo 815
lěeo 873
leeo-long 815
leeo-ráai 815
lèk 873
lék 814
lèk-glâa 873
lék-mâak 814
lék-nɔɔi 814
lék-tîi-sùt 814
lem 815
lêm 815
lem-yâa 815
lên 814
lên-dtuua 814
leng 814
lên-gàp 814
lên-lá~kɔɔn 815
lên-pâi 815
lép 815
lép-mɯɯ 815
lép-táao 815
lè 874
lɛ́ 817
lɛɛ 816

lêɛ 817
lɛ̂ɛk 874
lɛ̂ɛk 817
lɛ̂ɛk-bplìian 817
lɛ̂ɛk-ngən 817
lɛ̌ɛm 874
lɛ̌ɛm-kom 874
lɛ̌ɛn 874
lɛ́ɛng 817
lɛ́ɛo 817
lɛ́ɛo-dtɛɛ 817
lɛ́ɛo-gɔ̂ɔ 817
lɛ̂ɛp 817
lèng 874
lèng-gam-nə̀ət ... 874
lèng-tîi-maa 874
lên-rɯɯa 817
lɛ́-rɯ̌ɯ 817
lɛ́-ɯ̀ɯn-ɯ̀ɯn-ìik .. 817
lə̂ 815
ləəi 815
lə̂ək 815
lə̂ək-gan 815
lə̌əng 873
ləən-lə̂ə 815
lə̂ət 815
lə́-tə́ 815
lí-gee 810
liia 816
lîiam 816
lîian 816
liiang 816
lîiang 816
líiang 816
líiang-chǐip 816
líiang-duu 816
líiang-sàt 816
líiang-sòng 816
líiao 816
lîiao-lǎng 873
lîiap 816

lìik 811
lìik-lîiang 864
lìik-taang 864
lii-lâat 811
lîip 811
lii-sɔɔ 811
lí-kà~sìt 810
lík-kà~sìt 810
lîm 811
lín 810
lín-chák 810
ling 810
lín-gài 810
lín-jìi 810
líp 810, 811
líp-sà~dtìk 810
lít 810
lìu-dtaa 864
lom 805
lòm 862
lóm 805
lom-bâa-mǔu 805
lom-dɛ̀ɛt 805
lom-hǎai-jai 805
lóm-láang 805
lóm-lá~laai 805
lóm-lěeo 805
lóm-lə̂ək 805
lóm-long 805
lom-rɛɛng 805
lon 804
lón 804
lǒn 862
long 804
long-aa-yaa 804
long-chǔu 804
long-chǔu-nai ... 804
long-ə̀əi-tîi 804
long-ká~nɛɛn 804
long-kǎo 804
lǒng-lǎi 862

a
b
bp
ch
d
dt
e
ɛ
ə
f
g
h
i
j
k
l
m
n
ng
o
ɔ
p
r
s
t
u
ɯ
w
y

long-mɨɨ 804
long-naam 804
long-pung 804
lŏng-rák 862
long-rɛɛng 804
long-táai 804
lŏng-taang 862
long-tá~biian ... 804
long-tôot 804
long-tun 804
long-wan-tĭi-nai 804
lôo 817
lŏo 875
loo-gii 817
loo-hà 817
loo-hìt 817
lôok 817
loo-lee 817
loom 817
loo-maa 817
lôong 817
lôong-dtiian ... 817
lôong-òk 817
loong-sòp 817
lôop 817
lòp 862
lóp 804
lóp-bù~rii 805
lóp-láang 805
lòp-lĭiang 862
lòp-lìik 862
lòp-nĭi 862
lóp-_-ɔ̀ck 805
lót 804
lót-chán 804
lót-dtàm-long ... 804
lót-long 804
lót-raa-kaa 804
lót-tăa-ná 804
lɔ́ 815
lɔn 806

lɔ̀n 863
lɔ̆ng 806
lɔ̆ng-lɔɔi 806
lɔ̂ng-pɛɛ 806
lɔ̆n-jôn 806
lɔ̂ɔ 862
lɔ̆ɔ 806
lɔ́ɔ 806
lɔɔi 806
lɔɔi-grà~tong ... 806
lɔ̂ɔk 862
lɔ̆ɔk 806
lɔ̆ɔk-krâap 806
lɔ̆ɔk-liian 806
lɔ̆ɔk-lɔ̆ɔn 862
lɔ̂ɔk-luuang 862
lɔ̆ɔk-_-ɔ̀ɔk 806
lɔ̆ɔ-lên 806
lɔ̆ɔ-liian 806
lɔ̂ɔ-lɔ̆ɔk 806
lɔ̆ɔ-luuang 806
lɔ̆ɔ-lɨ̆ɨn 863
lɔ̆ɔm 806
lɔ̆ɔn 863
lɔɔng 806
lɔɔng-duu 806
lɔɔng-gɔɔng ... 806
lɔɔng-jai 806
lɔ̂ɔp 806
lɔ̂ɔp-kâa 806
lɔ̂ɔp-tam-ráai ... 806
lɔ̂ɔt 863
lɔ̂ɔt 806
lɔ̂ɔt-aa-hăan 863
lɔ̂ɔt-chông 806
lɔ̀ɔt-dâai 863
lɔ̂ɔt-dùut 863
lɔ̀ɔt-fai 863
lɔ̂ɔt-lɨ̆ɨat 863
lɔ̂ɔt-dtəə-rĭi 806
lui-náam 811

lúk 811
lúk-kɨ̀n 811
lúk-laam 811
lú-lûuang 811
lŭm 864
lŭm-făng-sòp ... 864
lŭm-praang 864
lung 811
lung-pɔɔ 811
lùt 864
lùt-mɨɨ 864
lûuak 805
lŭuam 862
lúuan 805
lûuang 2x862
lûuang-gəən 805
lúuang-grà~bpăo
.... 805
lûuang-lám 805
lûuang-nâa 805
lŭuang-pɔ̂ɔ 862
luuan-laam 805
lûuat 805
lûuat-laai 805
lûuat-năam 805
lûuk 811
lûuk-an-tá 814
lûuk-bâan 812
lûuk-bàat 813
lûuk-bìt 813
lûuk-bɔn 812
lûuk-bpàt 813
lûuk-bpòong 813
lûuk-bpɨɨn 813
lûuk-chaai 812
lûuk-chín 812
lûuk-dìng 812
lûuk-dɔ̀ɔk 812
lûuk-dtaa 812
lûuk-dtaan 812
lûuk-dtăo 812

lûuk-dtûm 812
lûu-kèng 814
lûuk-fὲεt 813
lûuk-gài 812
lûuk-gèet 812
lûuk-glîng 811
lûuk-grong 811
lûuk-grɔ̀ɔk 811
lûuk-gun-jɛɛ 812
lûuk-gwàat 811
lûuk-hèp 814
lûuk-hǐn 814
lûuk-jâang 812
lûuk-káa 812
lûuk-kàang 812
lûuk-kǝ̌ǝi 812
lûuk-kít 812
lûuk-kǒn-gài 812
lûuk-krɯ̌ng 812
lûuk-kǔn 812
lûuk-kwaam 812
lûuk-lǎan 814
lûuk-líiang 813
lûuk-lôok 813
lûuk-máai 813
lûuk-mɛ̌n 814
lûuk-mɛɛɔ 813
lûuk-mɯɯ 813
lûuk-náam 812
lûuk-nîi 814
lûuk-nɔ́ɔng 812
lûuk-om 814
lûuk-om-gɛ̂ɛ-ai .. 814
lûuk-ɔ́ɔt 814
lûuk-pîi-lûuk-nɔ́ɔng
.... 813
lûuk-rá~bɜ̀ɜt 813
lûuk-rang 813
lûuk-rɔ̂ɔk 813
lûuk-rɯɯa 813
lûuk-sǎao 813

lûuk-sà~pái 813
lûuk-sàt 813
lûuk-sìt 813
lûuk-sôo 812
lûuk-sɔ̌ɔn 813
lûuk-sùt-tɔ́ɔng .. 813
lûuk-sùup 813
lûuk-sɯ̌ɯa 813
lûuk-tá~nuu 812
lûuk-tôot 812
lûuk-tɔ́ɔ 812
lûuk-ùp-bpà~tǎm
.... 814
lûup 814
lûup-klam 814
lûup-lái 814
lɯ́k 811
lɯ́k-láp 811
lɯ́k-sɯ́ng 811
lɯng 811
lɯɯ 811
lɯ̌ɯa 873
lɯ̌ɯa-chɯ̌ɯa 873
lɯ̌ɯa-fɯɯa 873
lɯ̂ɯai 816
lɯ́ɯai 873
lɯ̌ɯak 873
lɯ̂ɯak 816
lɯ̂ɯak-dtâng 816
lɯ̌ɯam 873
lɯ̌ɯam-lám 873
lɯɯan 816
lɯ̂ɯan 816
lɯ̌ɯang 873
lɯ̂ɯang-lɯɯ 816
lɯ̂ɯan-kɯ̂n 816
lɯ̂ɯan-ɔ̀ɔk 816
lɯ̂ɯan-wee-laa .. 816
lɯɯap 873
lɯ̂ɯap-duu 873
lɯ̂ɯat 816

lɯ̂ɯat-lǎi 816
lɯ̂ɯat-ɔ̀ɔk 816
lɯ̂ɯat-ùn 816
lɯ̂ɯat-yen 816
lɯ̌ɯa-yùu 873
lɯɯm 811
lɯɯm-dtaa 811
lɯ̂ɯn 811

m

maa 771
mâa 771
máa 771
mǎa 859
mǎa-bâa 860
mǎa-bpàa 860
maa-cháa 772
mǎa-dtuua-miia 860
maa-gɔ̀ɔn 772
maa-hǎa 772
maai 780
mâai 772
máai 779
mǎai 860
máai-ban-tát 780
mǎai-dtaa 860
mǎai-hὲὲt 860
mǎai-jàp 860
mǎai-kón 860
mǎai-kwaam-wâa
.... 860
mǎai-lêek 860
mǎai-rîiak-dtuua
.... 860
mǎai-sǎan 860
mǎai-tɯ̌ng 860
mǎa-jîng-jɔ̀ɔk ... 860
màak 859
mâak 771
màak-fà~ràng .. 860

mâak-gəən-bpai
.... 771
mâak-gwàa 771
mâak-maai 772
màak-rúk 860
mâak-tĭi-sùt 771
maa-lai 772
maa-lɛ́ɛo 772
máam 772
máa-mŭn 772
măa-mùu 860
máa-mŭut 772
mâan 772
máa-náam 772
măa-nai 860
máa-nâng 772
maan-daa 772
mâan-dtaa 772
măang-jai 860
maan-yaa 772
maa-póp 772
maa-ráp 772
maa-rá~yâat 772
máa-rɔ́ɔng 772
mâat-dtrà~gaan
.... 772
mâat-dtrà~tăan 772
maa-tŭng 772
maa-yaa 772
maa-yîiam 772
má~bpraang 770
má~dtì 768
má~dùua 770
má~gà~raa-kom
.... 767
má~gɔ̀ɔk 769
má~grùut 769
má~hăa 769
má~hăa-am-nâat
.... 769
má~hăa-gàap ... 769

má~hăa-săa-rá~
kaam 769
má~hăa-sà~mùt
.... 769
má~hăa-sèet-tĭi 769
má~hàat-tai 769
má~hăa-wít-tá~
yaa-lai 769
má~hăa-yaan ... 769
má~hŏo-rii 769
má~hùu-maa 769
mài 875
mâi 779, 876
mái 771
măi 876
mái-àt 781
mâi-bpen-rai 780
mâi-châi 779
mâi-dâai 779
mái-dàt 779
mái-dtài-kúu 780
mái-dtii-glɔɔng 779
mâi-dtông 779
mái-dtrii 779
mái-èek 781
mái-gaa-gà-bàat
.... 779
mái-gaang-kĕen
.... 779
mái-gaa-yá~sìt 779
mâi-_-gɔ̂ɔ-_ 779
mái-grà~daan .. 779
mái-gwàat 779
mái-hăn-aa-gàat
.... 780
mài-ìiam 875
mâi-jai 779
mái-jàt-dtà~waa
.... 779
mái-jìm-fan 779
mâi-kəəi 779

mái-kìit-fai 779
mâi-kôi 779
mái-kwĕen-sŭua 779
mâi-ləəi 780
mái-má~laai 780
mâi-mii 780
mâi-mii-à~rai 780
mâi-mii-tĭi-năi .. 780
mái-múuan 780
mâi-nâa-chûua 780
mái-paai 780
mái-pài 780
mái-riiao 780
mâi-săa-mâat ... 780
mâi-sà~baai 780
mái-táao 780
mái-tăo 780
mái-too 780
mái-tŭu-pŭun 780
mâi-wâa 780
mâi-wăi 780
mái-yaao 780
mái-yá~mók 780
mâi-yùu 780
màk 859
mák 770
má~kăam 769
màk-dɔɔng 859
mák-jà 770
mák-kú-têet 770
mák-ngâai 770
má~kŭua 769
má~kŭua-păo .. 770
má~kŭua-têet ... 770
má~kŭua-yaao 770
má~lá~gɔɔ 770
má~lét 776
má~lɛɛng 778
má~lɛɛng-bpìik-
kĕng 778
má~lɛɛng-bpɔɔ 778

má~lɛɛng-sàap 778	má~práao 770	mɛ̂ɛ-kruua 777
má~lɛɛng-wan 778	má~rá 770	mɛ̂ɛ-láo 778
má~lɛɛng-wìi 778	má~reng 770	mɛ̂ɛ-lèk 778
má~lí 770	má~roong 770	mɛ̂ɛ-líiang 778
màm 860	má~rɯɯn 770	mɛ̂ɛ-mâai 778
má~mɛɛ 770	má~sěng 770	mɛ̂ɛ-mót 778
má~miia 770	màt 859	mɛɛn 777
mam-mîi 771	mát 771	mɛ̂ɛ-náam 777
má~mûuang 770	mát-chà 771	mɛɛng 2x777
má~mûuang-hǐm-má~paan 770	mát-chǎa 771	mɛɛng-ngaan 777
	mát-sà~màn 771	mɛɛng-bpɔ̀ng 777
man 771	mát-sà~yít 771	mɛɛng-daa 777
màn 859	mát-tá~yít 771	mɛɛng-daa-naa 777
mân 771	mát-tá~yom 771	mɛɛng-gà~prun 777
má~naao 770	má~yom 770	mɛɛng-lák 777
má~nát 768	mêek 775	mɛɛng-mum 777
man-fà~ràng 771	meen 776	mɛɛo 778
mân-gàp 859	mee-rú 776	mɛɛo 778
man-gɛɛo 771	mee-sǎa-yon 776	mɛɛo-mɔɔng 778
mang-gɔɔn 770	méet 775	mɛɛo-náam 778
mâng-kâng 770	mêet-dtaa 775	mɛ̂ɛ-rɛɛng 778
mang-kút 770	mee-tǔn 775	mɛ̂ɛ-sùu 778
mâng-mii 770	mék-sí~goo 775	mɛ̂ɛ-táp 777
mang-sà~wí-rát 770	mên 775	mɛ́ɛ-wâa 778
má~nii 767	měn 872	mɛ̂ɛ-yâa 778
mân-jai 771	měn-àp 872	mɛ̂ɛ-yaai 778
mân-kong 771	měn-dtòt 872	mèm 874
màn-sâi 859	měn-nâo 872	mên-yam 777
man-tɛ̂ɛt 771	mét 775	mǝǝn 776
má~nút 768	mét-sǐi 775	mí 772
má~nút-sà~yá-châat 768	mɛɛ 777	mí-chà~nán 772
	mɛɛ 777	mí-dtì 773
man-yâat 772	mɛ́ɛ 874	mii 773
mao 776	mɛ̂ɛ-bâan 777	mìi 860
mâo 776	mɛ̂ɛ-bɛ̀ɛp 778	mǐi 860
mǎo 872	mɛ̂ɛ-chii 777	miia 776
mao-káang 776	mɛ́ɛ-dtɛ̀ɛ 777	mii-aa-rom 774
mao-klɯɯn 776	mɛ́ɛ-gài 777	mii-aa-yú 774
mao-lâo 776	mɛ̂ɛ-hông-sɔ̌ɔn 778	miia-lǔuang 776
mao-rót 776	mɛ̂ɛ-káa 777	mîiang 776
mao-rɯɯa 776	mɛ̂ɛ-kǒong 777	miian-mâa 776

miia-nɔ́ɔi	776	
mii-à~rai-tîi	774	
mii-chii-wít	773	
mii-chii-wít-chii-		
waa	773	
mii-chii-wít-yùu	773	
mii-chôok	773	
mii-chúu	773	
mii-chûu-sǐiang	773	
mii-gam-rai	773	
mii-hèet-pǒn	774	
mii-kâa	773	
mii-kan	773	
mii-kon-tîi	773	
mii-kwaam-sùk	773	
mii-maa-rá~yâat		
	773	
mii-naa-kom	773	
mii-sà~dtì	773	
mii-sà~maa-tí	773	
mii-sà~nèe	774	
mii-sìt	774	
mii-sùuan	774	
mîit	773	
mii-ták-sà	773	
míit-dtɵ̀ə	773	
mîit-goon	773	
mii-tɔ́ɔng	773	
mîit-páp	773	
mîit-pók	773	
mii-tú-rá	773	
mii-yùu	774	
mìn	860	
mí-nâa	773	
mít	2x773	
mít-dtà~pâap	773	
mí-tù-naa-yon	773	
mó	779	
mòk	858	
mók-gà~raa-kom		
	767	
mòk-mûn	858	
mon	768	
mòn	858	
mong-gùt	767	
mong-kon	767	
mon-sà~gòt	768	
mon-sà~nèe	768	
mon-tin	768	
môo	778	
móo	778	
moo-hǒo	779	
moo-ká	778	
moong	779	
mòong	875	
moo-tá~naa	779	
mòt	858	
mót	768	
mòt-aa-yú	858	
mòt-dtuua	858	
mòt-gam-lang-jai		
	858	
mòt-glîiang	858	
mòt-jòt	858	
mót-lûuk	768	
mòt-rɛɛng	858	
mòt-sà~dtì	858	
mòt-wǎng	858	
mòt-wee-laa	858	
mɔ̀	872	
mɔ̀n	859	
mɔ́ɔ	859	
mɔ̌ɔ	859	
mɔ́ɔ-bplɛɛng	859	
mɔ̌ɔ-dèk	859	
mɔ̌ɔ-dtam-yɛɛ	859	
mɔɔ-dtɵ̂ə	769	
mɔɔ-dtəə-sai	769	
mɔ̌ɔ-duu	859	
mɔ̌ɔ-fan	859	
mɔ́ɔi	859	
mɔ̀ɔk	859	
mɔ̌ɔk-kwan	859	
mɔɔn	769	
mɔ̌ɔn	859	
mɔ̌ɔ-nân	859	
mɔɔng	769	
mɔ̌ɔng	859	
mɔɔng-hǎa	769	
mɔɔng-kâam	769	
mɔ̌ɔ-nûuat	859	
mɔ̀ɔp	859	
mɔ́ɔp	769	
mɔ̂ɔp-dtuua	769	
mɔ̌ɔ-pǐi	859	
mɔ̂ɔp-mǎai	769	
mɔɔ-rá~dòk	768	
mɔɔ-rá~gòt	768	
mɔɔ-rá~ná	768	
mɔɔ-rá~ná-pâap		
	768	
mɔɔ-rá~ná-sǔm	768	
mɔ̂ɔt	769	
mɔ̀-sǒm	872	
múk	774	
múk-daa	774	
múk-daa-hǎan	774	
mum	775	
mum-mɔɔng	775	
mǔn	861	
mung	775	
mûng	775	
múng	775	
múng-lûuat	775	
mûng-mǎai	775	
mûng-mân	775	
mûng-ráai	775	
mǔn-wiian	861	
mú-sǎa	775	
mùt	861	
mút	775	
mùu	861	
mǔu	861	

muua	771	
múuai	768	
mǔuai	859	
muuai-bplâm	768	
muuai-pǒm	768	
muuai-tai	768	
mùuak	858	
mùuak-gan-nɔ́k	858	
mùuak-klum	858	
muua-mao	771	
muuan	2x768	
múuan	768	
múuan-dtuua	768	
mûuang	768	
múuan-_-kâo	768	
múuan-_-ɔ̀ɔk	768	
mùuat-mùu	859	
mùu-bâan	861	
mǔu-bpàa	861	
mùu-gɔ̀	861	
mûuk	775	
muum-maam	775	
muun	775	
muun-fɔ́ɔi	775	
muun-kâa	775	
muun-lá~kâa	775	
muun-lá~ní-tí	775	
muun-sàt	775	
muun-tǎan	775	
muu-sǝǝ	775	
mɯ̀k	861	
mɯn	774	
mɯn-hǔua	774	
mɯɯ	774	
múɯ	774	
mɯ̂ɯa	776	
mɯɯ-aa-chîip	774	
mɯ̂ɯa-dai-gɔ̀ɔ-dtaam	776	
mɯ̂ɯa-gîi	776	
mɯ̂ɯa-gíi	776	

mɯ̂ɯa-gɔ̀ɔn	776	
mɯ̂ɯai	777	
mɯ̂ɯak	776	
mɯ̂ɯa-kɯɯn-níi	776	
mɯ̌ɯan	872	
mɯ̌ɯan-dǝǝm	872	
mɯɯang	776	
mɯ̌ɯang	872	
mɯ̌ɯan-gan	872	
mɯ̌ɯan-gàp	872	
mɯɯang-kɯ̀n	776	
mɯɯang-lǔuang	776	
mɯɯang-nɔ́ɔk	776	
mɯɯang-tai	776	
mɯ̌ɯan-jing	872	
mɯ̌ɯan-mǎi	872	
mɯ̂ɯa-rài	777	
mɯ̂ɯa-rài-gɔ̀ɔ-dâai	777	
mɯ̂ɯa-rɯɯn-níi	777	
mɯ̂ɯa-waan-níi	777	
mɯɯ-bplàao	774	
mɯɯ-bproo	774	
mɯɯ-bpɯɯn	774	
mɯ̀ɯn	861	
mɯɯ-sà~màk-lên	774	
mɯɯ-sɔ́ɔng	774	
mɯ̂ɯt	774	
mɯ̂ɯt-mon	774	
mɯ̂ɯt-muua	774	
mɯɯ-tɯ̌ɯ	774	

n

nâ	711	
ná	669, 711	
naa	712	
nâa	712, 856	
náa	712	
nǎa	856	
nâa-bâan	857	

nâa-bpàt	857	
nâa-bpòk	857	
nâa-bǔng	857	
nâa-dâan	857	
nâa-dtaa	857	
nâa-dtàang	857	
nâa-fang	713	
nâa-fǒn	857	
nâa-gàak	856	
nâa-gin	712	
nâa-glìiat	712	
nâa-gluua	712	
naai	713	
naai-am-pǝǝ	713	
naai-bɛ̀ɛp	713	
naai-bprà~gan	713	
naai-jâang	713	
naai-nâa	713	
naai-pon	713	
naai-tá~biian	713	
naai-ʉun	713	
nâa-jùua	856	
nâak	2x712	
nâa-kêng	856	
nâa-lǎng	857	
nâa-lɛ́ɛng	857	
naa-lí~gaa	714	
naa-lí~gaa-bplùk	714	
naam	713	
náam	714	
nǎam	857	
nâa-mài	857	
naam-bàt	713	
naam-bpàak-gaa	713	
náam-kɯ̀n	714	
náam-long	715	
naam-sà~gun	713	
náam-tûuam	715	
naan	713	

nâan 713
naa-naa 713
nâa-naa 857
naa-naa-châat .. 713
nâa-năao 857
nâa-năng~sŭu 857
năa-nên 857
naang 712
naang-bèɛp 712
naang-èek 713
naang-fáa 712
naang-ngaam 712
naang-ngûuak 712
naang-săao 713
náao 714
năao 857
nâa-òk 857
năao-sàn 857
năao-yen 857
nâa-pàak 857
nâa-rák 714
nâa-ram-kaan ... 714
nâa-rang-gìiat .. 714
nâa-rɔ́ɔn 857
nâa-sĭia-daai 714
nâa-sŏng-săan 714
nâa-sŏng-săi 714
naa-tii 713
nâa-tîi 857
naa-yók 713
naa-yók-rát-tà~
  mon-dtrii 713
naa-yók-têet-sà~
  mon-dtrii 713
nai 719
năi 876
nai-à~naa-kót .. 719
nai-kà~nà-tîi ... 719
nai-lǔuang 719
nai-tîi-sùt 719
nàk 856

nák 2x711
nák-bin 711
nàk-jai 856
nák-kàao 711
nák-kĭian 711
nàk-năa 856
ná-kɔɔn-râat-chá~
  sĭi-maa 710
nák-riian 712
nák-rɔ́ɔng 712
nák-sà~dɛɛng .. 712
nák-sùk-săa 712
nák-sùup 712
nák-tôot 711
nák-tŏng-tîiao ... 711
nák-tú-rá-gìt 711
nam 714
nám-àt-lom 716
ná~mát-sà~gaan
  710
nám-bplaa 715
nám-bprà~bpaa
  715
nám-chǔuam 714
nám-dtaa 714
nám-dtaan 714
nám-dtâo 715
nám-dtòk 714
nám-gròt 714
nám-hɔ̌ɔm 716
nám-jai 714
nám-jîm 714
nám-jùut 714
nám-káang 714
nam-kâo 714
nám-kem 714
nám-kěng 714
nám-laai 715
nám-laai-lǎi 715
nám-má~kǎam 715
nám-man 715

nám-man-mǔu 715
nám-mon 715
nám-mûuk 715
nám-muu 715
nam-nâa 716
nám-nàk 714
nám-ngən 714
nám-prík 715
nám-pú 715
nám-pûng 715
nám-rɛ̂ɛ 715
nam-sà~mǎi 715
nám-sĭiang 715
nám-sôm 715
nám-sôm-sǎai-chuu
  715
nam-taang 715
nám-tá~lee 715
nám-wǎan 716
nám-won 715
nám-yaa 715
nân 712
nán 712
nâng 712
nâng 856
nǎng-hǔua 856
nâng-long 712
nǎng-sàt 856
nǎng-sĭi-sà 856
nǎng~sǔu 856
nǎng~sǔu-bpóo
  856
nǎng~sǔu-dəən-
  taang 856
nǎng~sǔu-mɔ̂ɔp-
  am-nâat 856
nǎng~sǔu-pim 856
nǎng~sǔu-riian 856
nâo 718
nâo-bpǔuai 718
náp 712

náp-dtêem 712
náp-tǔʉ 712
náp-wâa 712
ná~rók 710
nát 712
ná~wá-ní-yaai .. 710
ná~wát-dtà~gam
.... 710
ná~yoo-baai 710
neen 669
néen 717
nee-rá~têet 718
nèp 871
nét 717
né 719
nĕɛ 874
nêɛ-jai 718
nĕɛm 874
nêɛ-nɔɔn 718
nɛɛo-dtâng 718
nɛɛo-nâa 719
nɛɛo-nóom 718
nɛɛo-nɔɔn 718
nɛɛo-taang 718
nèɛp 874
nêɛp 718
nên 718
né-nam 719
nêo-nêɛ 718
nəəi 717
nəəi-kĕng 717
nəəi-tiiam 717
nəən 718
nəən-kăo 718
ní-dtì 716
ní-dtì-ban-yàt .. 716
ní-dtì-gam 716
ní-dtì~sàat 716
ní-gaai 716
nǐi 717
níi 717

nĭi 857
nìiao 871
nĭiao 871
nìiao-ráng 871
nĭi-dtaam 857
nìip 857
nĭi-sĭn 858
ní-koo-lát 716
nîm 716
ní-mít 716
ní-mon 716
nin 717
nîng 716
nin-taa 716
níp-paan 716
ní-ran 716
ní-rá~naam 716
ní-rá~pai 716
ní-rôot 717
ní-săi 717
ní-săi-jai-kɔɔ 717
ní-sìt 717
nít 716
ní-taan 716
ní-tát-sà~gaan .. 716
nít-diiao 716
nít-dtà~yá~săan
.... 716
nít-nɔ̀i 716
nít-traa 716
nîu 717
níu 717
níu-bpôong 717
níu-chíi 717
níu-glaang 717
níu-gɔ̂ɔi 717
niu-kliia 717
níu-mʉʉ 717
níu-naang 717
níu-táao 717
ní-yaai 716

ní-yaam 716
nók 710
nók-hûuk 710
nók-wìit 710
nom 710
nom-bprîiao 710
nom-pŏng 710
non-tá~bù~rii ... 710
nòok 875
nóom-náao 719
nôon 719
nóon 719
nóot 719
nóp 710
nóp-nɔ́ɔp 710
nɔ̀i 856
nôŋ 711
nɔ́ɔ 855
nɔ́ɔi 711
nɔ́ɔi-gwàa 711
nɔ́ɔi-jai 711
nɔ́ɔi-nâa 711
nɔ̀ɔk 855
nɔ́ɔk 710
nɔ̂ɔk-jàak 710
nɔ̂ɔk-jàak-níi 710
nɔ̂ɔk-jai 711
nɔ̂ɔk-wee-laa 711
nɔ̀ɔ-máai 856
nɔɔn 711
nɔ̌ɔn 855
nɔ́ɔng 711
nɔ̌ɔng 855
nɔ́ɔng-chaai 711
nɔ̌ɔng-kaai 855
nɔ́ɔng-kĕəi 711
nɔ́ɔng-mài 711
nɔ̌ɔng-nai 855
nɔɔn-gôn 711
nɔ́ɔng-săao 711
nɔ́ɔng-sà~pái 711

nɔɔn-làp 711
nɔ̂ɔp-nɔɔn 711
nɔ́t 711
nùai 855
nùai-gìt 855
nùai-wát 855
nùm 858
nûm 717
nùm-sǎao 858
nûn 717
nǔn 858
nûng 717
nǔn-lǎng 858
nǔu 858
nùuak-hǔu 855
nuuam 710
nûuam 710
nuuan 710
nùuang-nìiao 855
nùuat 855
nûuat 710
nuun 717
nûun 717
núun 717
nǔu-nɔ́ɔi 858
núk 717
nɯng 717
nɯ̀ng 858
nɯ̀ng 717
nɯ̀ng-kráng 858
nɯ̀ng-láan 858
nɯ̀ng-nai-sìi 858
nɯ̀ng-pan-láan .. 858
nɯ́ua 718
nɯ̌ua 872
nɯ̌ua-gwàa 872
nɯ́ua-hǎa 718
nɯ̌ua-hǔua 872
nɯ̀uai 872
nɯ̀uai-jai 872
nɯ̀uai-ɔ̀ɔn 872

nɯ̀uai-yâak 872
nɯ́ua-kûu 718
nɯ́ua-mǔu 718
nɯ́uang-jàak 718
nɯ́ua-ngɔ̂ɔk 718
nɯ́ua-òp 718
nɯ́ua-pâa 718
nɯ́ua-pleeng 718
nɯ́ua-rɯ̂uang 718
nɯ́ua-sàt 718
nɯ́ua-tîi 718
nɯ́ua-wuua 718
nɯ́ua-yɯ̂ua 718

ng

ngaa 640
ngaa-cháang 640
ngâai 641
ngǎai 855
ngâai-daai 641
ngaam 641
ngâam 641
ngaan 641
ngaan-à~ɗi~rèek
.... 641
ngaan-bâan 641
ngaan-bpii-mài 641
ngaan-bprà~pee-nii
.... 641
ngaan-chà~lɔ̌ɔng
.... 641
ngaan-dtɛ̀ng-ngaan
.... 641
ngaan-fìi-mɯɯ .. 641
ngáang 640
ngaan-gù~sǒn .. 641
ngaan-líiang 641
ngaan-sɔ̀p 641
ngáao 641
ngâng 640
ngán-ngán 640

ngao 642
ngǎo 871
ngát 640
ngát-ngé 640
ngɛ̀ɛ-bùuak 643
ngɛ́ɛm 643
ngɛ̀ɛ-mum 643
ngəəi-nâa 642
ngən 642
ngən-bpan-pǒn 642
ngən-bprà~gan 642
ngən-chái-sɔ́ɔi .. 642
ngən-daao 642
ngən-dtôn 642
ngən-dtraa 642
ngən-dɯɯan 642
ngən-fáə 642
ngən-gûu 642
ngən-mát-jam .. 642
ngən-pɔ̀n 642
ngən-sòt 642
ngən-tɔɔn 642
ngən-tun 642
ngən-ùt-nǔn 642
ngîian 642
ngîiap 642
ngîiap-sà~ngòp 642
ngîi-ngâo 641
ngîip 641
ngîip-làp 641
ngìk 855
ngók 639
ngom 640
ngom-ngaai 640
ngong 640
ngong-nguuai .. 640
ngôo 643
ngôo-héng 875
ngôo-ngâo 643
ngoo-ngee 643

ngóp-bprà~maan
.... 640
ngót 640
ngót-ngaam 640
ngót-wén 640
ngɔ́ 642
ngɔ̂i 640
ngɔɔ 640
ngɔ́ɔ 640
ngɔ̀ɔk 855
ngɔ̂ɔk 640
ngɔ̂ɔk-ngaam 640
ngɔ̂ɔk-râak 640
ngɔɔm 640
ngɔɔn 640
ngɔ̌ɔn 855
ngɔɔ-ngɛɛ 640
ngɔ̂ɔp 640
ngûm-ngâam 641
ngun-ngong 641
ngùt-ngìt 855
nguu 641
ngûuang 640
nguuang-cháang
.... 640
ngûuang-nɔɔn 640
ngûuat 640
nguu-hào 642
nguu-jong-aang
.... 641
nguu-kǐiao 641
nguu-lǔuam 642
nguu-nguu-bplaa-
      bplaa 641
nguu-pít 641
ngùʉa 871
ngùʉak 871
ngûʉak 643
ngûʉan 643
ngûʉan-kǎi 643
ngùʉa-ɔ̀ɔk 871

O

òk 876
òk-hàk 876
om 878
om-yím 878
ong-bprà~gɔ̀ɔp 876
ong-gɔɔn 876
ong-ká~châat .. 876
ong-ká~rák 876
ong-sǎa 876
on-lá~màan 879
oo 891
òo 891
ǒo 891
òo-àa 892
oo-chaa 891
ôo-êe 892
oo-gàat 891
oo-hǎng 892
ôo-hǒo 892
óoi 892
oo-kee 891
oo-lim-bpìk 892
òong 891
oon-gam-má-sìt
.... 892
oong-gaan 891
oon-_-hâi-_ 892
oon-sǎn-châat .. 892
òop 892
òop-gɔ̀ɔt 892
òop-lɔɔm 892
oo-tii 892
òo-tǒong 891
ôo-ùuat 892
oo-wêə 892
òp 878
òp-âao 878
òp-chəəi 878
òp-pá~yóp 878

òp-pá~yóp-kâo 878
òp-rom 878
òp-ùn 878
òt 877
òt-aa-hǎan 877
òt-ton 877
òt-ton-dtɔ̀ɔ 877
òt-yàak 877

ɔ

ɔ̀i 881
ɔ́k-sí~jên 880
ɔ̂ɔi 881
ɔ̀ɔk 880
ɔ̀ɔk-aa-gàat 880
ɔ̀ɔk-bɛ̀ɛp 880
ɔ̀ɔk-bpai 880
ɔ̀ɔk-dəən-taang 880
ɔ̀ɔk-gam-lang-gaai
.... 880
ɔ̀ɔk-gòt-mǎai 880
ɔ̀ɔk-hàang 880
ɔ̀ɔk-hàt 880
ɔ̀ɔk-jàak 880
ɔ̀ɔk-lûuk 880
ɔ̀ɔk-maa 880
ɔ̀ɔk-nɔ̂ɔk-rûʉang
.... 880
ɔ̀ɔk-pan-sǎa 880
ɔ̀ɔk-pǒn 880
ɔ̀ɔk-rít 880
ɔ̀ɔk-sǐiang 880
ɔ̂ɔm 881
ɔ̂ɔm-kɔɔm 881
ɔɔn 880
ɔ́ɔn 880
ɔ̌ɔn 880
ɔ̀ɔn-ɛɛ 881
ɔ̀ɔn-hàt 881
ɔ̀ɔn-jai 880
ɔ̀ɔn-pliia 881

Side index: a b bp ch d dt e ɛ ə f g h i j k l m n **ng** **o** **ɔ** p r s t u ʉ w y

ɔɔn-rɛɛng 881
ɔɔn-wǎi 881
ɔɔn-wɔɔn 881
ɔɔn-yao 881
ɔɔn-yoon 881
ɔɔp-fít 881
ɔɔ-rá~hǎn 879

p

pàa 744
pâa 744
pāa 744
pâa-à~naa-mai   745
pâa-bai 745
paa-_-bpai 757
paa-chá~ná 765
pâa-chét-dtuua 744
pâa-chét-nâa 744
pàa-dtàt 744
pâa-gan-bpʉ̀uan
.... 744
paa-hà~ná 757
pâa-hòm 745
paai 757
pǎai-bpɔɔt 745
paai-lǎng 766
pǎai-lom 745
paai-nai 766
paai-nɔ̂ɔk 766
pâak 757, 765
pâa-kǎao-máa .. 744
pâak-dtâai 765
pâa-kîi-ríu 744
pâak-ii-sǎan 765
pâa-klum 744
pâak-nʉ̀ua 765
pâa-kǒn-nʉ̀u 744
pâak-pà~nùuak 765
pâak-piian 757
pâak-riian 765
pâak-tan 765

pâak-wí-chaa 765
paa-_-maa 757
pâa-mǎi 745
paan 757
pàan 745
pàan-bpai 745
paan-roong 766
pàan-tá~lú 745
pâa-nuuam 745
pâa-ɔ̂ɔm 745
pâap 765
pâa-pan-kɔɔ 745
pâa-pan-plɛ́ɛ 745
pâap-bprà~gɔ̀ɔp
.... 766
pâap-kǐian 766
pâap-lɔ̌ɔn 766
pâap-pá~yon 766
pâap-pót 766
pâap-râang 766
pâap-tàai 766
paa-rá 766
paa-rá-gìt 766
paa-rá-nâa-tîi ... 766
paa-sǎa 766
paa-sǎa-ang-grìt
.... 766
paa-sǎa-bâi 766
paa-sǎa-glaang 766
paa-sǎa-mɛ̂ɛ 766
paa-sǎa-pûut 766
paa-sǎa-tai 766
paa-sǎa-tìn 766
paa-sǐi 766
paa-sǐi-muun-lá~
   kâa-pêɛm 767
pǎa-sùk 745
páat-sà~bpɔ̀ɔt .. 757
pâa-tǔng 744
paa-wá~naa 766

pâa-yaang 745
paa-yáp 757
paa-yú 757
paa-yú-hì~má .. 757
paa-yú-mǔn 757
pà~chəən-nâa .. 748
pà~chəən-nâa-gàp
.... 748
pà~dèt-gaan 748
pà~gaa-grɔɔng 742
pá~hǔu-pót 755
pá~hǔu-sùut 755
pai 765
pài 749
pâi 762
pai-rɔ́ 762
pàk 744
pák 752, 756
pàk-bûng 744
pàk-chii 744
pák-dii 765
pàk-dtà~kàap .. 744
pák-fʉ̌ʉn 756
pàk-kǒm 744
pák-pòn 756
pák-yùu 756
pá~lá 754
pá~lang 754
pá~lang-ngaan 754
pá~lá~sùk-sǎa 754
pà~lìt 743
pà~lìt-dtà~pan 743
pà~lìt-dtà~pǒn 743
pá~mâa 752
pam-nák 758
pan 2x757
pǎn 744
pá~nák 752
pá~nan 752
pà~nǎng 742
pan-dtrii 757

pá~nee-jɔɔn 752
pan-èek 757
pà~nὲεk 748
pá~nεεng 756
pang 756
pǎng 744
pang-ngaa 756
pan-láan 757
pá~nom 752
pan-rá~yaa 765
pan-sǎa 752
pan-tá 757
pan-tá~mít 757
pà~nὺk 742
pan-yaa 765
pào 748
pǎo 748
pǎo-sòp 748
pàp 744
páp 757
páp-pǐiap 757
pá~rú-hàt 754
pà~sǒm 743
pà~sǒm-pan 743
pà~sǒm-pà~sǎan
.... 743
pà~sǒm-tiiam ... 743
pàt 744
pát 756
pát-hâi 757
pát-lom 757
pát-pong 756
pát-sà~dù 757
pát-tá~naa 756
pát-tá~yaa 757
pá~wong 756
pá~yaa 752
pá~yaa-baan 752
pá~yaa-bàat 752
pá~yaa-gɔɔn 752
pá~yaan 752

pá~yaang 752
pá~yâat 752
pá~yaa-tí 752
pá~yaa-yaam ... 752
pá~yák-nâa 752
pá~yan-chá~ná 752
pá~yao 756
pá~yót 752
pee-daan 760
peen 760
pee-sàt-chá~gɔɔn
.... 767
pêet 760
pêet-chaai 760
pêet-yǐng 760
pèn 748
pêng 760
pèt 748
pét 760
pét-plɔɔi 760
pέ 762
pεε 748
pὲε 762
pέε 762
pὲεn 748
pεεng 762
pὲεn-gaan 749
pὲεng-kɔɔ 748
pὲεng-lɔɔi 748
pὲεn-pâap 749
pὲεn-pǎng 749
pὲεn-ráai 749
pὲεn-tǐi 749
pêεt 762
pέε-tɔɔng 762
pèn 748
pèn-din 749
pèn-din-wǎi 749
pèn-dís 749
pèn-dít 749
pêng 762

pèn-sii-dii 749
pέ-ráp-bàap 762
pǎəi 748
pǎəi-prêε 748
pǎə-jɚə 760
pǎə-klâng 760
pâək-tɕɔn 761
pâəm 761
pâəm-dtəəm 761
pâəm-_-kûn 761
pêng 761
pí-gaan 758
pí-gon 758
pîi 758
pǐi 746
piiang 761
piiang-dai 761
piiang-dtὲε 761
piiang-kêε 761
piiang-pɔɔ 761
pîi-chaai 758
pii-chá-ká~nít .. 758
pǐi-dip 746
pîi-kǎəi 758
pîi-líiang 759
pîi-líiang-dèk 759
pîi-nɔɔng 758
pîi-sǎao 759
pîi-sà~pái 759
pǐi-sǐng 746
pǐi-sû̀ua 746
pí-jaa-rá~naa 758
pí-jìt 758
pík-sù 767
pí-lúk 758
pim 758
pí-maai 758
pin 758
pí-nâat 758
pí-nai-gam 758
ping 758

| b | | | |

pǐng 745
pí-pít-tá~pan 758
pí-rôot 758
pí-sèet 758
pí-sùut 758
pìt 745
pít 758
pìt-bpà-gà~dtì ... 745
pìt-bprà~wee-nii
.... 745
pìt-gòt-mǎai 745
pí-tii 758
pí-tii-gam 758
pí-tii-gɔɔn 758
pí-tǐi-pí-tǎn 758
pìt-plâat 745
pìt-rûup-râang ... 745
pít-sà~daan 758
pít-sà~nú-lôok ... 758
pìt-sǐin-lá~tam ... 745
pìt-sǐin-tam 745
pìt-wǎng 745
pǐu 745
pǐu-bpàak 745
pǐu-nâa 746
pǐu-pǝǝn 746
plaai 755
plâat 755
plâat-sà~dtìk 755
plàk 743
plàk-dan 743
plao 760
pláp 754
plàt 743
pleeng 760
pleeng-châat 760
plɛ̌ɛ 749
plɛ̌ɛ-bpen 749
plɛɛng 762
plǝǝn 760
plɛ̂ǝt-plǝǝn 760

plɛ̂ǝt-plǝǝn-gàp 760
plì 743
pliia 760
plíia 760
plík 755
plík-_-glàp 755
plóo 762
plòo 749
plóo-plée 762
plóp 754
plóp-kâm 754
plú 755
plûua 754
pók 751
pǒm 742
pǒm-bpiia 742
pǒm-bplɔɔm 742
pǒm-ngɔ̀ɔk 743
pǒm-yìk 743
pôn 752
pón 752
pǒn 743
pǒn-bprà~yòot 743
pǒng 742
pǒng-chuu-rót ... 742
pǒng-gà~rìi 742
pǒng-sák-fɔ̀ɔk .. 742
pǒn-lá~máai 743
pon-lá~mɯɯang
.... 754
pǒn-láp 743
pon-lá~rɯɯan ... 754
pǒn-ngaan 743
pôn-ɔ̀ɔk 752
pǒn-pà~lìt 743
pon-tá~hǎan 754
poo 762
poo-chá~naa 767
poo-chá~naa-gaan
.... 767
poo-dam 762

póon 762
póon-tá~lee 762
póot 762
póot-tâa 762
póp 752
póp-gan 752
pòt 742
pót-jà~naa-nú-
grom 751
pɔ́-bplùuk 760
pɔ́-líiang 761
pɔ̀n-klaai 743
pɔɔ 755
pɔ̂ɔ 755
pɔ́ɔ 755
pɔ̂ɔ-bâan 756
pɔ̂ɔ-bpùu 756
pɔ̂ɔ-dtaa 756
pɔɔ-jai 756
pɔ̂ɔk 755
pɔ̂ɔ-káa 755
pɔ̂ɔ-kruua 755
pɔɔ-lέɛɔ 756
pɔ̂ɔ-líiang 756
pɔ̌ɔm 743
pɔ̂ɔ-mâai 756
pɔ̌ɔm-baang 744
pɔ̂ɔ-mɛ̂ɛ 756
pɔ̂ɔ-mót 756
pɔɔn 752
pɔɔng 755
pɔ́ɔng 756
pɔɔng-dtuua 756
pɔɔn-sà~wǎn ... 753
pɔɔ-piiang 756
pɔɔ-sǒm-kuuan 756
pɔɔ-sɔ̌ɔ 751
pɔ̂ɔ-sɯ̌ɯ 756
prá 753
prá~aa-tít 753
prâak-_-jàak-_ .. 754

praam 754
praan 754
prá-èek 753
prai 762
prâi 762
prá~jâao 753
prá~jan 753
prá-kam-pii 753
pram 754
prá-má~hǎa-gà~sàt
.... 753
prá~pút-tá~jâao
.... 753
prá-pút-tá~rûup
.... 753
prá-raa-chí~nii ... 753
prá-râat-chá~ban-
yàt 753
prá-râat-chá~wang
.... 753
prá-sǒng 753
prá-yee-suu 753
prá-yee-suu-krít
.... 753
prɛɛ 762
prêɛ 762
prêɛ-chɯ́ua 762
prêɛ-lǎai 762
prêɛ-pan 762
prík 754
prík-bpòn 754
prík-tai 754
prík-yùuak 754
príng 754
prom 752, 753
prom-dɛɛn 752
prom-lí-kìt 753
proong 762
prɔ́ 760
prɔ́-à~rai 760
prɔ́-chà~nán 760

prɔ́ɔm 753
prɔ́ɔm-dûuai 753
prɔ́ɔm-gan 753
prɔ́ɔm-gàp 753
prɔ́ɔm-táng 753
prɔ́-wâa 760
prûng-níi 754
prúk-sà~sàat 754
prút-dtì-gaan 754
prút-sà~jì-gaa-yon
.... 754
prút-sà~paa-kom
.... 754
pù 746
pú 759
pùa 744
pûm 759
pûm-máai 759
pung 759
pûng 759
pung-plúi 759
pùt 746
pút 2x759
pút-saa 759
pút-tá~sàk-gà~ràat
.... 759
pûu 746
pǔua 744
pûu-aa-wú-sǒo 748
puuai-gaa 755
pûuak 755
pûuak-kǎo 755
pûuak-níi 755
pûuak-rao 755
pûu-am-nuuai-gaan
.... 748
puuang 755
pûuang 755
puuang-gun-jɛɛ 755
puuang-maa-lai 755
puuang-rìit 755

puua-pan-gàp .. 757
pûu-bɔɔ-rí~hǎan
.... 747
pûu-bplɛɛ 747
pûu-bpòk-krɔɔng
.... 747
pûu-bpùai 747
pûu-chaai 747
pûu-chá~ná 746
pûu-chá~ná-lêɛt
.... 746
pûu-chîiao-chaan
.... 747
pûu-chom 746
pûu-chǔuai 747
pûu-dai 747
pûu-dooi-sǎan 747
pûu-dtɛng 747
pûu-dtông-hǎa 747
pûu-gam-gàp 746
pûu-gan 759
puu-gèt 767
pûu-gɔ̀ɔ-gaan-ráai
.... 746
puu-grà~dɯng 767
pûu-jàt-gaan 746
pûu-jàt-hǎa 746
pùuk 746
pûu-kám-bprà~gan
.... 746
puu-kǎo 767
pûu-kâo-bprà~
gùuat 746
puu-kǎo-fai 767
pûu-kâo-rûuam 746
pûu-krɔ́-ráai 746
pûu-líi-pai 747
puum 767
puum-bpan-yaa 767
puum-dtâan-taan
.... 767

puu-mí-aa-gàat 767
puu-mí-sàat 767
puum-jai 767
puum-kúm-gan 767
puum-lam-nao ... 767
puum-lăng 767
puum-tăan 767
pûu-nam 747
pûu-òp-pá~yóp 748
pûu-pà~lìt 747
pûu-pí-pâak-să

           747
pûu-ráai 747
pûu-ráp-măo 747
pûu-rɔ́ɔt-chii-wít

           747
pûu-sà~dɛɛng .. 748
pûu-sà~màk 747
pûu-sòng-ɔ̀ɔk ... 747
pûu-sɔ̆ɔn 747
pûu-sʉ̀ʉ-kàao .. 748
pûut 759
pûut-gèng 759
pûu-tĩi 747
pûut-kui 759
pûut-lên 760
pûut-_-sám 760
pûut-tʉ̆ng 760
pûu-ʉ̀ʉn 748
pûu-wâa-gaan .. 747
pûu-wâa-râat-
   chá~gaan 747
pûu-yài 748
pûu-yao 747
pûu-yĩng 748
pûu-yĩng-hăa-ngən

           748
pʉm-pam 759
pʉ̀ng 746
pʉ̀ng 746, 759
pʉ̀ng-paa 759

pʉ̀ʉa 761
pʉ̀ʉa-à~rai 761
pʉ̀ʉa-hâi 761
pʉ̀ʉak 748
pʉ̀ʉan 761
pʉ̀ʉan-bâan 761
pʉ̀ʉan-chaai 761
pʉ̀ʉan-jâo-bàao

           761
pʉ̀ʉan-jâo-săao 761
pʉ̀ʉan-rûuam-chán

           761
pʉ̀ʉan-rûuam-
   ngaan 761
pʉ̀ʉan-sà~nìt ... 761
pʉ̀ʉan-yĩng 761
pʉ̀ʉa-tĩi-jà 761
pʉ̀ʉa-wâa 748
pʉ̀ʉa-wâa 761
pʉ̀ʉn 746
pʉ́ʉn 759
pʉ̆ʉn 746
pʉ́ʉn-din 759
pʉ́ʉn-mʉʉang ... 759
pʉ́ʉn-p̀iu 759
pʉ́ʉn-tăan 759
pʉ́ʉn-tĩi 759
pʉ̂ʉt 759

r

raa 795
raa-chaa 796
raa-chaa-pí-sèek

           796
raa-chí~nii 796
raa-dtrii 796
raa-dtrii-sà~wàt 796
raai 797
ráai 797
raai-bpii 797
raai-chʉ̀ʉ 797

raai-dâai 797
raai-dʉʉan 797
raai-gaan 797
raai-gaan-aa-hăan

           797
raai-jàai 797
raai-lá~ìiat 797
raai-lɔ́ɔm 797
raai-ngaan 797
ráai-rɛɛng 797
râak 795
raa-ká 795
raa-kaa 795
râak-ngâo 795
râak-tĩi-sɔ̆ɔng ... 795
râan 796
ráan 796
ráan-aa-hăan ... 796
ráan-dtàt-pŏm .. 795
raang 795
râang 796
ráang 796
ráan-gaa-fɛɛ 796
râang-gaai 796
raang-náam 796
raang-rót-fai 796
raang-wan 796
ráan-káa 796
ráan-kăai-yaa 796
ráan-sák-rĩit 796
ráan-sə̆əm-sŭuai

           796
raao 797
ráao 797
raao-gàp 797
raao-raao 797
râap 796
râap-rîiap 797
râap-rʉ́ʉn 797
râa-rəəng 797
raa-sĩi 797

râat-chá~aa-naa-jàk 796
râat-chá~bù-rii 796
râat-chá~sǐi 796
râat-chá~tûut ... 796
râat-chá~wong 796
râat-sà~dɔɔn ... 797
râat-yaang 796
rá~baai 793
rá~baai-aa-gàat-nai 793
rá~bàat 793
rá~bam 793
rá~bèət 793
rá~bèət-bpà~rá~ maa-nuu 793
rá~bèət-muu 793
rá~biian 793
rá~biiang 793
rá~bìiap 793
rá~bòp 793
rá~dàp 793
rá~dàp-lôok 793
rá~duu 793
rá~gaa 792
rá~hàt 790
rá~hàt-bprai-sà~nii 790
rá~hàt-pàan 790
rá~hěəi 794
rai 803
râi 803
rái 803
rái-à~ngùn 803
rái-diiang-sǎa ... 803
rái-gang-won 803
rái-jùt-mǎai 803
rái-kâa 803
rái-naa 803
rái-pǒn 803
rái-sǎai 803

rái-sǎa-rá 803
rái-yaang-aai 803
rák 794
rá~kaai 793
rá~kang 793
rák-châat 794
rák-krâi 794
rák-rɛ́ɛ 794
rák-rûuam-pêet 794
rák-sǎa 794
rák-sǎa-gaan 794
rá~lɔ̀ɔk-klûun 794
rá~lúk 794
ram 797
rá~mát-rá~wang 793
ram-kaan 797
ram-kâao 797
râm-ruuai 798
ram-wong 798
rá~nâat 793
rang 794
ráng 794
rá~ngáp 793
rang-gɛɛ 794
rang-kài 794
rang-kɛɛ 794
rang-kwaan 794
rang-nók 794
rang-pûng 794
rang-sǐi 794
rá~nɔɔng 793
rao 800
ráo 800
ráo-jai 800
râo-rɔ́ɔn 800
ráp 795
ráp-bprà~gan ... 795
ráp-bprà~taan 795
ráp-jâang 795
ráp-pìt-chɔ̂ɔp 795

ráp-rɔɔng 795
ráp-rɔɔng-kɛ̀ɛk 795
ráp-rúu 795
ráp-sǎa-rá~pâap 795
rát 794, 795
rát-chá~gaan 794
rát-dtà~ná 795
rát-kɔɔ 795
rát-sà~mǐi 795
rát-tà~baan 795
rát-tà~bprà~hǎan 795
rát-tà~mon-dtrii 795
rát-tà~sà~paa .. 795
rát-tà~tam-má~ nuun 794
rá~túk 793
rát-wí-sǎa-hà-gìt 795
rá~wàang 794
rá~wang 794
rá~wɛɛng 794
rá~yá 793
rá~yá-taang 793
rá~yá-wee-laa .. 794
rá~yɔɔng 793
ree-kǎa 799
ree-kǎa-ká~nít 799
rêng 799
rêng-dùuan 799
rêng-krûuang 799
rêng-ráo 800
rêng-rǐip 800
reo 800
reo-reo-níi 800
rɛ̂ɛ 801
rɛ̂ɛk 801
rɛ̂ɛk-râəm 801
rɛɛng 801

rɛɛng 801
rɛɛng-ban-daan-jai
.... 802
rɛɛng-dan 801
rɛɛng-dɯng-dùut
.... 802
rɛɛng-gòt-dan .. 801
rɛɛng-grà~dtûn 801
rɛɛng-juung-jai 801
rɛɛng-máa 802
rɛɛng-ngaan 801
rɛ́ɛɔ 802
rɛ̂ɛt 802
rɛ̂ɛ-tâat 802
rəə 800
rə̂əm 800
rìi 862
rîiak 800
rîiak-_-glàp 800
rîiak-rɔ́ɔng 800
rîiak-wâa 800
riian 800
rǐian 873
riiang 800
riiang-kwaam 800
riian-nǎng~sǔu 800
riian-rúu 800
riiao 800
rîiao-rɛɛng 800
rîiap 800
rîiap-ngâai 800
rîiap-rîiap 800
rîiap-rɔ́ɔi 800
rìi-dtaa 862
rîip 798
rii-sɔ̀ɔt 798
rîit 798
rîit-nom 798
rim 798
rim-fǐi-bpàak 798
rin 798

ríp 798
ríp-bîn 798
rí-rə̂əm 798
rít 803
rít-sǐi-duuang-tá~
waan 798
ríu-rɔɔi 798
rók 788
rók-râak 788
rôm 789
rôm-chuu-chîip 789
rom-kwan 789
rôn 789
rooi 803
rôok 802
roo-ká 802
rôok-bprà~sàat 802
rôok-dtìt-dtɔ̀ɔ ... 802
rôok-gluua-náam
.... 802
rôok-pai-kâi-jèp
.... 802
rôok-rá~bàat 802
roong 802
roong-aa-hǎan .. 803
roong-glàn 802
roong-jam-nam 802
roong-lá~kɔɔn 802
roong-nǎng 803
roong-ngaan 802
roong-pák 802
roong-pá~yaa-baan
.... 802
roong-pim 802
roong-rɛɛm 802
roong-riian 802
roong-rót 802
roong-sǐi 803
róp 789
róp-guuan 789
róp-ráo 789

rót 2x788, 790
rót-ban-túk 789
rót-bás 789
rót-bát 789
rót-châat 790
rót-châo 788
rót-dàp-pləəng 788
rót-dtìt 789
rót-dtûu 789
rót-dùuan 788
rót-fai 789
rót-fai-dtâai-din 789
rót-fai-dùuan 789
rót-fai-fáa 789
rót-gěng 788
rót-jàt 790
rót-jíip 788
rót-kěn 788
rót-kèng 788
rót-máa 789
rót-ní-yom 790
rót-pá~yaa-baan
.... 789
rót-pûuang 789
rót-raang 789
rót-sǎam-lɔ́ɔ 789
rót-sà~ní-yom .. 790
rót-tǎng 789
rót-yon 789
rɔ̂n 791
rɔ̂ng 790
rɔ̂ng-rɔɔi 791
rɔ̂n-rêe 791
rɔɔ 790
rɔɔi 792
rɔ́ɔi 792
rɔɔi-bprà~táp ... 792
rɔɔi-bpùuan 792
rɔɔi-chám 792
rɔɔi-chìik 792
rɔɔi-dtiin 792

rɔɔi-dtɔɔ 792
rɔ́ɔi-èek 792
rɔ́ɔi-èt 792
rɔɔi-fan 792
rɔ́ɔi-gɛ̂ɛo 792
rɔ́ɔi-grɔɔng 792
rɔɔi-jìip 792
rɔɔi-kùuan 792
rɔ́ɔi-lá 792
rɔɔi-páp 792
rɔɔi-ráao 792
rɔɔi-rûua 792
rɔɔi-táao 792
rɔɔi-wèng 792
rɔɔi-yêɛk 792
rɔɔi-yím 792
rɔɔi-yôn 792
rɔ̂ɔk 790
rɔ́ɔn 791
rɔ́ɔn-chúun 791
rɔɔng 790
rɔ́ɔng 790
rɔɔng-bprà~taa-
naa-típ-bɔɔ-dii 791
rɔɔng-chá~ná~lêɛt
.... 790
rɔ́ɔng-hâi 791
rɔ́ɔng-kɔ̌ɔ 790
rɔ́ɔng-pleeng 791
rɔɔng-ráp 791
rɔ́ɔng-riian 791
rɔɔng-táao 791
rɔɔng-táao-dtɛ̀ 791
rɔɔng-táao-pâa-bai
.... 791
rɔɔng-táao-sà~gét
.... 791
rɔ́ɔng-túk 791
rɔ́ɔng-ù-taan 791
rɔ́ɔn-jai 791
rɔ́ɔn-òp-âao 791

rɔ́ɔn-ron 791
rɔ̂ɔp 791
rɔ̂ɔp-dâan 792
rɔ̂ɔp-kɔ̂ɔp 791
rɔ̂ɔp-nɔ̂ɔk 792
rɔ̂ɔp-rɔ̂ɔp 791
rɔ̂ɔp-rúu 792
rɔ̂ɔt 791
rɔ̂ɔt-dtaai 791
rum 798
rûn 798
rûng 798
rúng 798
rûng-cháao 798
rúng-gin-náam 798
rûng-rʉʉang 798
rûn-nùm-sǎao .. 798
run-rɛɛng 798
rút 798
ruu 798
rúu 799
rǔu 862
rûua 795
rúua 795
ruuai 790
ruuam 790
ruuam-gan 790
rûuam-gan 790
rûuam-long-naam
.... 790
rûuam-mʉʉ 790
rûuam-pêet 790
rûuam-sà~mǎi 790
ruuam-táng-mòt
.... 790
ruuam-tǔng 790
rûuan 790
ruuang 789
rûuang 789
ruuang-pʉ̀ng 789
rûuang-rooi 789

rûuap-rát 790
rûuap-ruuam 790
rûuat-reo 789
rúu-dtuua 799
ruu-gôn 799
rúu-jàk 799
ruu-jà~mùuk 799
ruu-kǔm-kǒn 799
rûup 799
rûup-bɛ̀ɛp 799
rûup-bpà~pan 799
rûup-kài 799
rûup-lɔ̀ɔ 799
rûup-lɔ̂ɔk 799
rûup-pâap 799
rûup-râang 799
rûup-song 799
rûup-tàai 799
rǔu-rǎa 862
rúu-rʉ̂uang 799
rúu-sʉ̀k 799
rúu-sʉ̀k-dtuua .. 799
rúu-sʉ̀k-pìt 799
rûut 799
rûut-síp 799
rʉ́ 798
rʉ́-duu 803
rʉ́-duu-bai-máai-plì
.... 803
rʉ́-duu-bai-máai-
rûuang 803
rʉ́-duu-fǒn 803
rʉ́-duu-nǎao 803
rʉ́-duu-rɔ́ɔn 803
rʉ́-tai 804
rʉ́ʉ 798
rʉ̌ʉ 862
rʉʉa 800
rʉʉa-bai 801
rʉʉa-ban-túk 801

ruua-dam-náam
.... 801
ruua-gon-fai 800
rûuai 801
ruua-kâam-fâak 800
ruua-lôm 801
ruuan 801
rúuan 801
rûuang 800
rûuang-jing 801
rûuang-lâo 801
rûuang-raao 801
rûuang-sân 801
ruuan-hɔ̌ɔ 801
ruuan-jam 801
ruuan-pɛɛ 801
rúua-rang 801
ruua-róp 801
ruua-yoong 801
rûun-rəəng 798
ruu-sǐi 804
rúu-tɔ̌ɔn 798

S

sà 833
sàa 840
sâa 665
sà~àat 837
sǎa-baan 841
sǎa-baan-dton 841
saa-chí~mí 665
saa-dìt 665
saa-dtaan 665
sǎa-gee 840
sǎa-gon 840
sǎa-hàt 843
sǎa-hèet 843
saai 694
sàai 842
sáai 666
sǎai 842

sǎai-buua 842
sǎai-dìiao 842
sǎai-din 842
sǎai-dtaa 842
sǎai-dtaa-iiang 842
sǎai-dtaa-sân 842
sǎai-dtaa-yaao 842
sǎai-fai 842
sǎai-gaan-bin ... 842
sǎai-kâat 842
sǎai-láp 842
sǎai-lûuat 842
sǎai-náam 842
sǎai-nǎng 842
sǎai-paan 842
sǎai-pûuang 842
sǎai-rát 842
sǎai-rúng 842
sǎai-wát 842
sǎai-yaang 842
sàak 840
sâak 665
sǎa-kǎa 840
sâak-sòp 665
sǎa-kuu 840
sǎa-laa 825
saa-laa-bpao 666
sǎa-laa-glaang 825
sǎa-lîi 843
saam 694
sǎam 841
sǎa-mâat 841
sǎa-mák-kii 841
sǎa-man 841
sǎa-man-chon .. 841
sǎa-man-sǎm-núk
.... 841
sǎa-mii 841
sǎa-mii-pan-rá~yaa
.... 841
sǎam-lìiam 841

sâan 665
sǎan ... 825, 842, 843
sǎan-aa-hǎan 843
sǎan-dii-gaa 825
sàang 833
sǎang 840
sâang-kài 833
sàang-mao 833
sàang-sǎn 833
sǎan-jâao 825
sǎan-kee-mii 842
sǎan-lá~laai 843
sǎan-pít 843
sǎa-nú-sìt 841
sǎao 843
sǎao-bɔɔ-rí~sùt 843
sǎao-chái 843
sǎao-nɔ́ɔi 843
sǎao-sòot 843
sǎao-tʉn-tʉ́k 843
sàap 841
sâap 694
sàap-chêng 841
sǎa-rá 843
sǎa-ràai 843
sǎa-ràai-tá~lee 843
sǎa-raa-nú-grom
.... 843
sǎa-rá~ban 843
sǎa-rá-ká~dii 842
sǎa-rá~pâap 843
sǎa-rá~tǐi 843
sǎa-rá~wát 843
sàat 840
sǎa-taa-rá~ná ... 841
sǎa-taa-rá~ná-
bprà~yòot 841
sǎa-taa-rá~ná-rát
.... 841
sǎa-taa-rá~ná-sùk
.... 841

săa-taa-rá~nuu-bpà~pôok 841	sà~dεεng-tam .. 853
săa-tá~yaai 840	sà~dtaai 828
sàat-dtraa-jaan 825	sà~dtaang 828
săa-tít 841	sà~dtéek-núua 828
săa-tɔɔn 840	sà~dtεm 853
sàat-sà~daa 825	sà~dtì 828
sàat-sà~năa 825	sà~dtì-bpan-yaa
sàat-sà~năa-krít	 828
.... 825	sà~dtì-mâi-dii .. 828
sàat-sà~năa-pút	sà~dtrái 828
.... 825	sà~dtrii 828
săa-tú 841	sà~dtuu 828
săa-wók 843	sà~dtuun 828
sà~baai 830	sà~dûng 836
sà~baai-dii 830	sà~dùt 828, 836
sà~baai-jai 830	sà~dùt-dtaa 836
sà~baai-sà~baai	sà~dùuak 836
.... 830	sà~dùuak-sà~baai
sà~bâa-kào 837	 836
sà~bai 830	sà~duu 836
sà~bân 837	sà~gàt 827
sà~biiang 850	sà~gii 827
sà~bong 830	sà~gìt 836
sà~bpaa 830	sà~gòt 836
sà~bpeen 830	sà~gòt-jìt 836
sà~bpεεm 830	sà~gòt-rɔɔi 836
sà~bpree 830	sà~gruu 827
sà~bpring 830	sà~hăai 835
sà~bùu 830	sà~hà-bprà~chaa-
sà~dèt 836	châat 835
sà~dèt-náam 836	sà~hà~gɔɔn 835
sà~dεεng 853	sà~hà-pâap 835
sà~dεεng-bὲεp 853	sà~hà-pan 835
sà~dεεng-bpen 853	sà~hà-pan-tá~rát
sà~dεεng-hâi-hěn	 835
.... 853	sà~hà-rát-à~mee-
sà~dεεng-kwaam-	rí~gaa 835
yin-dii-gàp 853	sà~hà-sùk-săa .. 835
sà~dεεng-ɔ̀ɔk ... 853	sai 668
sà~dεεng-pŏn .. 853	sài 854
	sâi 854

sái 668
săi 2x854
sâi-dtìng 854
sâi-dtìng-àk-sèep
.... 854
sâi-duuan 854
sài-glɔɔn 854
sâi-gròok 854
sài-jai 854
sai-kloon 668
sài-kwaam 854
sâi-lûuan 854
sai-nát 668
sâi-pung 854
sài-ráai 854
sâi-sùk 854
sài-sûua-pâa-hâi
.... 854
sâi-tiian 854
sà~jai 836
sàk 837
sák 665
sàk-dì~naa 824
sák-fɔɔk 665
sàk-gà~làat 837
sàk-gà~ràat 824
sàk-gà~yá~pâap
.... 824
sák-hěng 665
sák-pâa 665
sák-rîit 665
sàk-sìt 824
sàk-tîi-nùng 837
sàk-wan 837
sà~là 833
sà~làak 833
sà~làak-gin-bὲng
.... 833
sà~làk 833
sà~làk-bprà~dtuu
.... 833

b
bp
ch
d
dt
e
ε
ə
f
g
h
i
j
k
l
m
n
ng
o
ɔ
p
r
s
t
u
ʉ
w
y

sà~làk-lăng 833
sà~lăm 833
sà~làp-gan 833
sà~là-sìt 833
sà~làt 833
sà~làt-aa-gàat .. 833
sà~lèet 851
sà~lòp 833
sà~lǔng 834
sám 666
sà~maa 826
sà~maa-chík 826
sà~maa-chík-sà~
   paa-pûu-tɛɛn-
   râat-sà~dɔɔn .. 832
sà~maa-kom 832
sà~maa-pan 832
sà~maa-tí 832
sà~maa-tôot 826
sà~má~gaan 831
sà~mǎi 831
sà~mǎi-gɔ̀ɔn 832
sà~màk 831
sà~màk-jai 831
sà~màm-sà~mǎə
   832
sà~má~ná 831
săm-dɛɛng 843
sám-dtəəm 666
sà~mə̌ə 850
sà~mə̌ə-gan 850
sà~mǐian 850
săm-kan 843
săm-lák 844
săm-lák-náam .. 844
săm-lii 844
săm-lii-têng 844
săm-má~naa 840
săm-má~noo-kruua
   844
săm-nák 844

săm-nák-ngaan 844
săm-nák-ngaan-yài
   844
săm-nák-pim 844
săm-nao 844
săm-niiang 844
săm-nuuan 843
săm-nʉ́k-pìt 844
săm-ɔ̀ɔi 844
sà~mɔ̌ɔng 831
sà~mɔ̌ɔ-ruua 831
săm-paa-rá 840
săm-pâat 840
săm-pan-rák 840
săm-pàt 840
săm-pàt-gan 840
săm-raan 844
săm-ràp 844
săm-ráp 844
săm-rèt 844
săm-rèt-kwaam-krâi
   844
săm-rèt-rûup 844
săm-rɔɔng 844
săm-ruuam 844
săm-rùuat 844
sám-sâak 666
săm-sɔ̀n 844
sà~mǔn-prai 832
sà~mùt 832
sà~mù-tai 832
sà~mùt-ban-tʉ́k
   832
sà~mùt-bpraa-gaan
   832
sà~mùt-chìik 832
sà~mùt-pʉ̌ɛn-tîi 832
sà~mùt-sǎa-kɔɔn
   832
sà~mùt-sǒng-
   kraam 832

sà~mùt-too-rá~sàp
   832
sàn 839
sân 839
săn 839
sà~náam 833
sà~nǎam 829
sà~nǎam-bin 829
sà~nǎam-dèk-lên
   829
sà~nǎam-gii-laa
   829
sà~nǎam-kèng .. 829
sà~nǎam-róp 829
sà~nǎam-yâa 829
sà~nàn 829
sà~nàp-kêng 829
sà~nàp-sà~nǔn . 829
săn-châat 838
săn-châat-dtà~yaan
   838
săn-daan 839
săn-dòot 839
săn-dɔɔn-mɛ̂ɛ-náam
   839
săn-dtà~bpaa-bpaa
   839
săn-dtì-pâap 839
sà~nèe 850
sà~nèe-hǎa 850
sà~nə̌ə 850
sà~nə̌ə-chʉ̌u 850
sàng 837
săng 837
sà~ngàa 827
sà~ngàa-ngaam
   827
sàng-gaan 837
săng-gà~sǐi 837
săng-gàt 837
săng-gèet 837

săng-hăan 838
săng-hăa-rim-má~
  sáp 838
săng-hɔ̌ɔn 838
săng-hɔ̌ɔn-jai 838
săng-ká 838
săng-ká~naa-yók
  838
săng-ká~râat 838
săng-ká~taan 838
săng-kà~yǎa 837
săng-kom 837
săng-kom-má~sàat
  838
săng-kom-sǒng-krɔ́
  838
săng-kom-wít-tá~
  yaa 837
săng-krɔ́ 838
sà~ngòp 827
sà~ngòp-sùk 827
săng-săn 838
sàng-sɔ̌ɔn 838
sàng-sǔʉ 838
sà~ngǔuan 827
săng-wɔɔn 838
sà~nìiat 850
sà~nǐm 830
sà~nìt 830
sà~nìt-sà~nǒm 830
săn-jɔɔn 838
săn-năng~sʉ̌ʉ 840
săn-nít-tăan 839
sà~nǒm 829
sà~nǒo 854
sà~nɔ̌ɔng 829
săn-sà~grìt 839
sàn-sà~tʉʉan 839
săn-tăan 838
săn-tát 839
sà~nùk 830

sà~nùk-sà~nǎan
  830
săn-yaa 838
săn-yaan 838
săn-yaan-líiao ... 838
săn-yá~gam 825
săn-yá~gam-dtòk-
  dtɛ̀ng 825
săn-yá~lák 838
săn-yá~pɛ̂ɛt 825
săo 826
săo 2x851
săo-aa-gàat 851
săo-aa-tít 851
săo-fai 851
săo-hǐn 851
săo-làk 851
sáo-sǐi 667
săo-wá~rót 851
sàp 825, 840
sáp 694
sà~paa 830
sà~paai 837
sà~paan 837
sà~paa-ní-dtì-ban-
  yàt 830
sà~paan-lɔɔi 837
sà~pâap 830
sà~paa-pûu-tɛɛn-
  râat-sà~dɔɔn .. 830
sà~paa-sǔung .. 831
sà~paa-wá 830
sà~pái 837
sàp-bpà~don 840
sàp-bpà~ngòk ... 840
sàp-bpà~rəə 840
sàp-bpà~rót 840
sàp-bplìian 840
sàp-daa 840
sàp-lìik 840
sáp-nai 665

sà~pôok 837
sàp-pâi 840
sàp-pá~naam ... 832
sáp-pá~yaa-gɔɔn
  694
sáp-pá~yaa-gɔɔn-
  tam-má~châat 694
sàp-pee-hěe-rá 840
sà~prâo 837
sáp-sǐn 694
sáp-sǐn-sùuan-
  ruuam 694
sáp-sǒm-bàt 694
sàp-sǒn 840
sáp-sɔ́ɔn 665
sà~rà 833
sà~rà-bù~rii 833
sà~rá~nɛ̀ɛ 837
sà~rii-rá 833
sà~rii-rá-wít-tá~yaa
  833
sà~ròong 854
sà~rùp 833
sà~săang 837
sà~sǒm 837
sàt 2x839
sát 665
sà~tăa-ban 829
sà~tăa-bpà~ník 829
sà~tăa-bpàt-dtà~
  yá~gam 829
sà~tăan 828
sà~tăa-ná 828
sà~tăa-ná-gaan 828
sà~tăan-gong-sǔn
  828
sà~tăa-nii 828
sà~tăa-nii-dtam-
  rùuat 828
sà~tăa-nii-rót-fai
  828

sà~tăa-nii-rót-mee
.... 828
sà~tăan-tîi 828
sà~tăan-tîi-gə̀ət 828
sà~tăan-tûut 828
sàt-bpàa 839
sàt-bpìik 839
sàt-dtà~wà~pêɛt
.... 839
sàt~dtà~wát 824
sàt-dtruu 825
sà~tì-dtì 829
sàt-jà 838
sàt-krŭng-bòk-
krŭng-náam 839
sàt-líiang 839
sàt-líiang-lûuk-
dûuai-nom 839
sàt-lúuai-klaan 839
sà~tɔ́ɔn 836
sà~tɔ́ɔn-jai 836
sàt-sùuan 839
sàt-taa 824
sàt-tá~sàat 839
sà~tùup 829
sà~tuuan-jai 837
sà~ùk 837
sà~ùun 837
sà~wâai-náam ... 833
sà~wàan 835
sà~wàang 835
sà~wǎn 835
sà~wàt-dii 835
sà~wii-deen 835
sà~yǎam 832
sà~yɔ̌ɔng-kwǎn 832
sèek 849
sèek-sǎn 849
sĕem-hà 850
sèep 850
sĕe-rii 851

sĕe-rii-pâap 851
see-rûm 667
sĕe-sêɛng 851
sèet 826
sèet-máai 826
sèet-pâa 826
sèet-sùuan 826
sèet-tà~gìt 826
sèet-tà~sàat 826
sèet-tĭi 826
sék-mùu 667
sék-sĭi 667
sen 2x667
sên 667, 849
sên-bprà~sàat .. 850
sên-chai 849
sen-chûu-nai 667
sên-dâai 849
sên-dtaai 849
sên-dtâai 850
seng 667
sên-kà~nǎn 849
sên-kóong 849
sên-lûuat 850
sên-mìi 850
sên-pàa-sǔun-
glaang 850
sên-rɔ̂ɔp-wong 850
sên-rúng 850
sen-sə̂ə 667
sên-sǔun-sùut .. 850
sên-taang 850
sên-wɛɛng 850
sên-yai 850
seo 667
seo-sîiat 667
sèt 850
sét 667
sèt-lɛ́ɛɔ 850
sɛ̂ɛ 853
sɛ̀ɛk-glaang 853

sɛ̀ɛk-sɯm 708
sɛ̌ɛn 854
sɛ̌ɛng 853
sɛ̌ɛng-dèɛt 853
sɛ̌ɛng-jâa 853
sɛ̌ɛng-jan 853
sɛɛn-wít 667
sɛ̀ɛp 854
sɛ̀ɛt 853
sɛ̂p 667
sə̂ə 667
sə̌əm 850
sə̌əm-gam-lang 850
sə̌əm-sâang 850
sì 845
sí 666
sí-gâa 666
sìi 846
sîi 666
sĭi 824, 846
sìia 851
sĭia 851
sĭia-chii-wít 852
sĭia-chǒom 852
sĭia-daai 852
sĭia-dtuua 852
sĭia-jai 852
sĭiam 852
siiam-sii 667
sîian 852
sìiang 851
sîiang 851
sĭiang-dang 851
sĭiang-dtàm 851
sĭiang-dtrɛɛ 851
sĭiang-dtrii 851
sĭiang-èek 852
sĭiang-gông 851
sĭiang-jàt-dtà~waa
.... 851
sĭiang-kɔ́ 851

siiang-pai 852
siiang-pɯm-pam
.... 851
siiang-sǎa-man 852
siiang-sǔung-dtàm
.... 852
siiang-too 851
siiao 667
sîiao 852
siiao 852
sǐia-oo-gàat 852
siiap 852
siiap-bplák 852
siiat-sǐi 852
sǐi-chom-puu 846
sǐi-dam 824
sǐi-dɛɛng 846
sǐi-fáa 846
sǐi-gaa 846
sii-geem 666
sii-íu 666
sǐi-kǎao 846
sǐi-kiiao 846
sîik-lôok 666
sîi-kroong 666
sii-liiam 847
sǐi-lǔuang 847
sǐi-mûuang 846
sǐin 826
sǐi-náam 846
sǐi-nám-dtaan ... 846
sǐi-nám-ngən 846
sǐin-lá~tam 826
sǐin-tam 826
sǐi-ɔ̀ɔn 847
sǐi-pǐu 846
sǐi-rúng 847
sǐi-sà 826
sǐi-sà~gèet 824
sǐi-sɛ̀ɛt 847
sìi-sìp 847

sǐi-sôm 847
sǐi-sòt-sǎi 847
sǐit 666
sǐi-tâo 846
sǐi-tao 846
sǐi-tɔɔng 846
sǐi-tɔɔng-dɛɛng 846
sǐiit-siiao 666
sìi-yêɛk 847
sǐi-yɔ́ɔm 847
sík-sék 666
sì-laa 825
sí-lí-kɔɔn 666
sîn 666
sǐn 845
sǐn-bon 846
sìng 845
sîng 666
sǐng 2x845
sǐng-dtoo 845
sǐng-dtoo-tá~lee
.... 2x845
sǐng-hǎa-kom ... 845
sìng-juua-bpon 845
sǐng-ká~bpoo ... 845
sìng-kɔ̌ɔng 845
sìng-lɔ́ɔ-jai 845
sìng-mii-chii-wít
.... 845
sìng-tɔɔ 845
sìng-wɛ̂ɛt-lɔ́ɔm 845
sǐn-káa 845
sǐn-káa-kào 845
sǐn-káa-ɔ̀ɔk 846
sǐn-lá~bpà 825
sǐn-lá~bpà~sàat
.... 825
sǐn-lá~bpà~sàat-
má~hǎa-ban-dìt
.... 825
sǐn-lá~bpin 825

sǐn-rêɛ 846
sǐn-sɔ́ɔt 846
sîn-sùt 846
sìp 846
síp 666
sip-sɔ̌ɔng 846
sìp-too 846
sì-rì-mong-kon 846
sìt 825, 845
sìt-gào 825
sìt-tí 845
sìt-tí-bàt 845
sìt-tí-pí-sèet 845
sìu 846
sǐu 846
sòk 824
sòk-gà~bpòk 827
sòk-gà~bpròk .. 827
sôm 831
sŏm 831
sŏm-bàt 831
sŏm-buun 831
sŏm-dèt 831
sôm-dtam 831
sŏm-dun 831
sŏm-dun-lá~yá~
pâap 831
sŏm-jing 831
sŏm-kuuan 831
sŏm-kuuan-dâi-ráp
.... 831
sŏm-mâat 831
sŏm-mút 831
sŏm-mút-dtì~tǎan
.... 831
sŏm-nám-nâa ... 831
sôm-oo 831
sŏm-rót-gàp 831
son 664
sôn 829
sŏn 829

song 694
sòng 827
sòng-_-dtɔɔ 827
sòng-_-glàp 827
sŏng-graan 827
sòng-jòt-mǎai ... 827
sŏng-klǎa 827
sŏng-kraam 827
sŏng-krɔ́ 827
sŏng-náam 832
sòng-_-ɔ̀ɔk 827
song-pŏm 694
sŏng-sǎan 827
sŏng-sǎi 827
sòng-sǎəm 827
sŏn-jai 829
sôn-sǔung 829
sôn-táao 829
sŏn-tá~naa 829
sŏn-tá~yaa 829
sŏn-têet 829
sŏn-tí 829
sŏn-tí-sǎn-yaa .. 829
sôo 667
soo-daa 668
soo-faa 668
sòok-gà~nâat-
  dtà~gam 826
sŏo-krôok 854
sŏom 854
sŏo-mom 854
sŏo-pee-nii 854
soo-see 668
sòot 854
sòp 824
sòp-bprà~màat .. 830
sòp-dtaa 830
sóp-sao 664
sòt 827
sót 664
sòt-chǔun 827

sòt-sǎi 828
sɔ̂i 833
sɔ̂i-kɔɔ 833
sɔ̂m 665, 836
sɔ̂m-sɛɛm 665
sɔ̂n 665
sɔ̀ng 835
sɔ̂ng 665
sɔ̀ng-nók 835
sɔ̀ng-sɛ̌eng 836
sɔ̀ng-sɛ̌eng-wɛɛo-
  waao 836
sɔ̂n-hǎa 665
sɔ̂n-rén 665
sɔɔ 665
sɔɔi 665
sɔ̀ɔk 824
sɔ̂ɔk 665
sɔ́ɔm 665
sɔ̌ɔn 824, 836
sɔɔng 665
sɔ̌ɔng 835
sɔ̌ɔng-kráng 835
sɔ̌ɔng-rɔ́ɔi 836
sɔ̌ɔng-tâo 835
sɔ̌ɔn-pí-sèet 836
sɔ̀ɔp 836
sɔ̌ɔp-bɔn 665
sɔ̀ɔp-bpàak-kam
  836
sɔ̀ɔp-dtòk 836
sɔ̀ɔp-sǔuan 836
sɔ̀ɔp-tǎam 836
sɔ́ɔp-wɛɛ 665
sɔ̀ɔt 836
sɔ́ɔt 665
sɔ̀ɔt-klɔ́ɔng-gan 836
sɔ̀ɔt-nɛɛm 836
sɔ̀ɔt-rúu-sɔ́ɔt-hěn
  836
sɔ̌ɔ-wɔɔ 827

sùai 835
sù-gɔɔn 847
sùk 826, 2x847
sù-kǎa 847
sù-kǐi 848
sùk-kà~lák-sà~nà
  847
sùk-kà~pâap 847
sùk-kà~pâap-jìt 847
sù-kǒo-tai 848
sùk-sǎi 847
súk-son 667
sù-kǔm 848
sù-kǔm-wít 848
sùm 848
sûm-joom-dtii .. 667
sûm-sâam 667
sù-naa-mí 847
sù-nák 848
sung 667
sǔn-lá~gaa-gɔɔn
  826
sǔn-tá~rii 848
sǔn-tɔɔ-rá~pót 848
súp 667
sù~pâap 848
sù~pâap-bù~rút
  848
sù~pâap-sà~dtrii
  848
sù-paa-sìt 848
súp-síp 667
sù-raa 848
sù-râat-taa-nii .. 848
sù-ráo 849
sù-rin 848
sù-rí~yúp-bpà~
  raa-kaa 848
sù~rûi-sù~râai 848
sù-sǎan 849
sùt 848

sùt-kìit 848
sút-long 694
sùt-sàp-daa 848
sùt-táai 848
sùt-tí 848
sùt-yɔ́ɔt 848
sûu 849
sǔuai 835
sǔuai-ngaam 835
sûuam 835
sǔuam 835
sùuan 834
sùuan 832, 834
sùuan-bèng 834
sùuan-bon 834
sùuan-bprà~gɔ̀ɔp
.... 834
sùuan-bùk-kon 834
sùuan-dâai-sùuan-
sĭia 834
sùuan-dtuua 834
suuang 694
sùuan-gəən 834
sùuan-glaang ... 834
sùuan-kóong ... 834
sùuan-lót 834
sùuan-mâak 834
sùuan-nai 834
sùuan-nǎi 835
sùuan-nɔ́ɔi 834
sùuan-pà~sǒm 834
sùuan-râat-chá~
gaan 834
sùuan-ruuam 834
sǔuan-sǎa-taa-rá~
ná 834
sǔuan-sà~nùk .. 834
sǔuan-sàt 834
sùuan-sǔung 835
sùuan-yài 835
sùuat 834

sùuat-mon 834
sǔu-dtì-bàt 849
sǔu-jì-bàt 849
sùu-kɔ̌ɔ 849
suum-kâo 667
suum-ɔ̀ɔk 667
sǔun 826
sǔun-bplàao 849
sǔung 849
sǔun-gaan-káa 826
sǔung-aa-yú 849
sǔung-chan 849
sǔung-gwàa 849
sǔun-glaang 826
sǔung-sòng 849
sǔung-sùt 849
sǔun-pan 849
sùup 849
sùup-bù-rìi 849
sûup-pɔ̌ɔm 667
sûup-sîit 667
sûu-róp-gàp 849
sùut 849
sùut-glìn 849
sù-wan-ná~puum
.... 848
sə̀k 826, 847
sə̀k-grɔ̀n 847
sə̀k-sǎa 826
sə̌m 666
sə̌m-sâap 666
sə̌ng 666
sə̌ng 666
sə̌ng 666
sə̌ng-gan-lɛ́-gan
.... 666
sə̀ɯ 847
sə̂ɯ 666
sə́ɯ 666
sə̀ɯa 852
sə̂ɯa 852

sə̌ɯa 852
sə̂ɯa-chán-nai .. 853
sə̂ɯa-chə́ət 853
sə̂ɯa-chuu-chîip
.... 853
sə̌ɯa-daao 853
sə̂ɯa-gák 852
sə̂ɯa-gan-fǒn ... 852
sə̂ɯa-gan-lom .. 852
sə̂ɯa-gan-nǎao 852
sə̂ɯa-glâam 852
sə̀ɯak 852
sə̂ɯa-klum 853
sə̂ɯa-kóot 853
sə̀ɯam 853
sə̀ɯam-sĭia 853
sə̂ɯa-pâa 853
sə̂ɯa-yûut 853
sə̂ɯ-bə̂ɯ 667
sə̀ɯ-dtrong 667
sə̀ɯ-kǎai 666
sə́ɯ-kɔ̌ɔng 666
sə̀ɯ-muuan-chon
.... 847
sə̀ɯp 847
sə̀ɯp-dtɔ̀ɔ 847
sə̀ɯp-hǎa 847
sə̀ɯp-kón 847
sə̀ɯp-sǔuan 847
sə̀ɯp-tɔ̀ɔt 847
sùu-sǎan 847
sə̂ɯ-sàt 667

t

taa 699
tâa 691, 699
tâa-dəən 700
taai 700
tàai 691
táai 700

tàai-èek-gà~săan 691
tàai-năng 691
tàai-pâap 691
tàai-rûup 691
tàai-tee 691
tàai-tɔ́ɔt 691
tàak 691
tâak 699
tàak-tăang 691
tăam 691
tâam-glaang 700
taan 700
tàan 691
tăan 669
tăa-ná 669
tăa-nan-dɔɔn 669
taan-dtà~wan ... 700
tàan-fai-gào 691
taang 699
tàang 691
tăang 691
taang-aa-gàat .. 700
taang-bìiang 699
taang-bòk 699
taang-bprai-sà~nii
.... 699
taang-cháang-
pùuak 699
taang-dəən 699
taang-dəən-táao
.... 699
taang-diiao 699
taang-dtan 699
taang-dùuan 699
taang-gaan 699
taang-glai 699
taang-jai 699
taang-kâo 699
taang-kóong 699
taang-kót-kíiao 699

taang-lâat 700
taang-lâat-yaang
.... 700
taang-lát 700
taang-lîiang 700
taang-lôok 700
taang-lǔuang 700
taang-lûuak 700
taang-máa-laai 700
taang-nai 699
taang-ɔ̀ɔk 700
taang-ɔ̂ɔm 700
taang-pàan 700
taang-rót-fai 700
taang-táao 699
taang-tá~lee 699
taang-yɛ̂ɛk 700
tàan-hǐn 691
taa-nii 709
tăan-kɔ́ɔ-muun 669
taan-nám-kěng 709
tăan-táp 669
táao 707
táao-bplàao 707
tâap 700
taa-rók 701
taa-run 701
tâa-rùua 701
taa-sïi 701
tàat 691
tâat 701, 709
táa-taai 700
tâa-taang 700
tăa-waang 692
taa-yâat 700
tá~biian 697
tá~biian-bâan ... 697
tá~biian-sǒm-rót
.... 697
tá~hǎan 695

tá~hǎan-aa-gàat
.... 695
tá~hǎan-pàan-sὺk
.... 695
tá~hǎan-rʉʉa ... 695
tai 2x709
tài 693
tǎi 693
tài-dtuua 693
tàk 690
ták 697
ták-sà 697
ták-taai 697
tá~laai 695
tà~lǎi 693
tá~lák 697
tá~lee 697
tá~lee-saai 697
tá~lee-sàap 697
tà~lɛ̌ɛng 693
tà~lɛ̌ɛng-gaan .. 693
tà~lòk 690
tá~lɔ́-gan 697
tá~lɔ́-gàp 697
tá~lú 697
tà~lǔng 690
tam 701, 709
tâm 692
tam-aa-hǎan 702
tam-bun 701
tam-dtaam 701
tam-_-dtòk 701
tam-_-dtɔ̀ɔ 701
tam-dtɔ̀ɔ-bpai .. 701
tam-dtuua 701
tam-dûuai 701
tam-_-hǎai 702
tam-jàak 701
tam-kwǎn 701
tam-laai 701

tam-laai-sà-tì~dtì
.... 701
tam-lee 701
tam-má 709
tam-má~châat 709
tam-má~daa 709
tam-mai 701
tâm-mɔɔng 692
tam-naa 701
tam-naai 701
tam-nâa-tîi 701
tam-ngaan 701
tam-niiam 709
tam-nîiap-kǎao 701
tam-nóp 701
tam-nɔɔng 701
tam-ráai 701
tam-_-sám 701
tam-_-sǎm-rèt .. 701
tam-sǔuan 701
tam-tôot 701
tan 698
tân 700
tá~naai 694
tá~naai-aa-sǎa 694
tá~naai-kwaam 694
tá~naa-kaan 709
tá~naa-nát 709
tá~ná~bàt 709
tà~nàt 689
tà~nàt-kwǎa 690
tà~nàt-sáai 690
tà~nàt-táng-
sɔɔng-muu 690
tan-dtɔɔ-wee-laa
.... 698
táng 697
tǎng 690
tǎng-dtɛ̀ɛk 691
tǎng-kà~yà 691
táng-kûu 698

táng-kuun 698
táng-lǎai 698
táng-mòt 698
tǎng-nám-kěng .. 691
táng-níi 698
táng-sîn 698
táng-sɔ̌ɔng 698
táng-táng-tîi 698
táng-tîi 698
táng-wan 698
tan-jai 698
tà~nǒn 689
tá~nong 697
tà~nɔ̌ɔm 689
tan-sà~mǎi 698
tan-tii 698
tan-tii-tan-dai ... 698
tan-tii-tîi 698
tá~nú-tà~nɔ̌ɔm 697
tan-waa-kom 709
tan-yá~pùut 709
tao 707
tâo 669, 707
tâo-gan 707
tâo-gàp 707
tâo-gɛ̀ɛ 669, 693
tâo-hǔua-nguu .. 669
tâo-nán 707
tâo-rai 707
tâo-tîi 707
táp 698
táp-pii 698
táp-tim 698
tát 698
tàt-jàak 691
tát-sà~ná 699
tát-sà~naa-jɔɔn 699
tát-sà~ná-ká~dtì
.... 698
tá~waan 695
tá~waan-nàk 695

tá~wii 695
tá~wii-kuun 695
tá~wîip 695
tá~yɛɛng-mum ... 694
tá~yǝǝ-tá~yaan 697
tá~yɔɔi 694, 697
tee 706
têe 706
têek-noo-loo-yîi
.... 706
têep 706
téep 706
téep-gaao 706
tee-pii 706
têep-ní-yaai 706
têep-pá~yá~daa
.... 706
têep-prá~jâao .. 706
têep-tí-daa 706
têet 706
tee-tíng 706
têet-sà~baan ... 706
têet-sà~gaan ... 706
têet-sà~nǎa 706
tee-wá~daa 706
tee-wá-wít-tá~yaa
.... 706
tem-bpù-rá 706
tét 706
té 708
tɛ́ɛ 707
tɛ́ɛ-jing 707
tɛɛn 708
tɛɛng 707
tɛɛn-tîi 708
tɛ̌ɛo 693
tɛ̌ɛo-níi 693
tɛ́ɛp 693
têɛp 708
têɛp-jà~mâi 708
ték-sîi 707

tên 708
têng 707
tên-pim 708
tə̀ 693
təəm 706
tə̀ət 693
tə-tá 707
tí-daa 709
tí-dtì 669
tii 702
tìi 692
tǐi 702
tiiam 707
tiian 707
tǐiang 707
tǐiang-dtrong 707
tǐiang-gan 693
tǐiang-kʉʉn 707
tǐiang-wan 707
tiiao 707
tǐiao 707
tǐiao-bin 707
tǐiao-diiao 707
tǐiap-fàng 707
tǐi-bpàt-nám-fǒn

.... 703
tǐi-bprʉ̀k-sǎa 703
tǐi-cháat 702
tǐi-dàt-kǒn-dtaa 702
tii-diiao 702
tǐi-din 702
tǐi-dtâng 703
tǐi-dtàt-lép 703
tǐi-gâao 702
tǐi-gèp-kǒng 702
tii-jà 702
tǐi-jɔ̀ɔt-rót 702
tǐi-kâat-pǒm 702
tǐi-kìia-bù~rìi 702
tii-lá 703
tǐi-láang-nâa 703

tǐi-lâat 704
tǐi-lǎng 704
tii-lá~nɔ́ɔi 703
tǐi-lôong 704
tǐi-lûm 704
tǐi-lǔua 704
tiim 703
tǐi-maa 703
tǐi-múuan-pǒm 703
tǐi-nǎi 704
tǐi-nǎi-gɔ̀ɔ-dâai 704
tǐi-nǎi-gɔ̀ɔ-dtaam

.... 704
tǐi-nân 703
tǐi-nâng 703
tǐi-nîi 703
tǐi-nìip 704
tǐi-nɔɔn 703
tǐi-pák 703
tǐi-pák-aa-sǎi 703
tǐi-râap 703
tǐi-râap-lûm 703
tǐi-râap-sǔung .. 703
tǐi-rák 703
tǐi-rôm 703
tǐi-rɔɔng-gêɛo 703
tǐi-sâang-sǎn 704
tǐi-sùt 704
tǐi-tam-ngaan ... 703
tǐi-tíng-kà~yà ... 703
tǐi-ʉ̀ʉn 704
tǐi-wâang 704
tii-wii 704
tǐi-yìiap 704
tǐi-yùu 704
tǐi-yùu-aa-sǎi 704
tîm 702
tìn 692
tíng 702
tíng-_-wái 702
típ 702

tít 702
tít-dtâai 702
tí-tì 702
tít-nʉ̌ua 702
tít-taang 702
tiu-tát 702
tòk 689
tòm 690
tòm-nám-laai ... 690
ton 693
ton-bù-rii 709
ton-_-dâai 693
ton-dtɔ̀ɔ 693
ton-fai 694
tong 709
ton-mâi-wǎi 694
ton-taan 693
ton-túk 694
too 2x708
tôo 710
tǒo 693
too-frii 708
too-glàp 708
toom-má~nát .. 708
toon-sǐi 708
too-rá~jìt 708
too-rá-ká~má~

naa-kom 708
too-rá~lêek 708
too-rá~sǎan 708
too-rá~sàp 708
too-rá~tát 708
tǒo-sûuam 693
tôot 708
tôot-bprà~hǎan 708
tôot-tan 708
tóp-tuuan 694
tòt 689
tót 693, 695
tót-lɔɔng 693
tót-náam 693

tót-sà~wát	695	
tót-sɔ̀ɔp	693	
tɔ̀	693	
tɔ̀m-dtuua	690	
tǒng	696	
tǒng-jam	696	
tǒng-tîiao	696	
tôn-máai	697	
tɔɔ	695	
tɔ̀ɔ	690	
tɔ̂ɔ	695	
tɔ̂ɔ-ai-sĭia	697	
tɔ̌ɔi	690	
tɔ̌ɔi-glàp	690	
tɔ̌ɔi-lǎng	690	
tɔ̌ɔi-rót	690	
tɔɔn	697	
tɔ̂ɔn	690	
tɔ̂ɔ-nám-sĭia	697	
tɔɔng	696	
tɔ̌ɔng	696	
tɔ̌ɔng	690	
tɔɔng-bai	696	
tɔɔng-dɛɛng	696	
tɔ̌ɔng-fáa	696	
tɔɔng-kam	696	
tɔɔng-kam-kǎao		
	696	
tɔ̌ɔng-kɛ̌ɛn	696	
tɔɔng-lǔuang	696	
tɔ̌ɔng-múuan	696	
tɔ̌ɔng-pùuk	696	
tɔ̌ɔng-rôŋ	696	
tɔɔng-sĭia	696	
tɔɔng-têng	696	
tɔ̌ɔng-tîi	696	
tɔ̌ɔng-tìn	696	
tɔɔng-yìp	696	
tɔ̌ɔng-yɔ̀ɔt	696	
tɔ̌ɔn-hǎai-jai	690	
tɔ̌ɔn-kam-pûut	690	
tɔɔn-ngən	697	
tɔ̌ɔn-ngən	690	
tɔ̂ɔ-rá~baai	697	
tɔ̂ɔ-rá~baai-náam		
	697	
tɔɔ-rá~hɔ̀t	694	
tɔ̂ɔ-rá~maan	694	
tɔɔ-rá~nii-wít-tá~		
yaa	709	
tɔɔ-rá~yót	694	
tɔ̀ɔt	690	
tɔ̀ɔt	696	
tɔ̀ɔt-bplák	690	
tɔ̀ɔ-tɛ́ɛ	696	
tɔ̀ɔt-kwaam	690	
tɔ̂ɔt-man-bplaa	696	
tɔ̀ɔt-_-ɔ̀ɔk	690	
tɔ̀ɔt-rá~hàt	690	
tɔ̀ɔt-tíng	696	
tóp-fîi	697	
trɛ̀k	708	
trít-sà~dii	694	
tui	705	
tǔi	692	
túk	2x704	
túk-aa-tít	705	
túk-bpii	705	
túk-dʉʉan	705	
túk-hɛ̀ng	705	
túk-jai	704	
túk-kon	704	
túk-kráng	704	
túk-sàp-daa	705	
túk-tii	705	
túk-tîi	705	
túk-túk	704	
túk-wan	705	
túk-wee-laa	705	
túk-yâak	704	
túk-yàang	705	
tú-lák-tú-lee	706	
tú-lao	706	
tú-lii	709	
tûm	705	
túm	705	
tûm-tee	705	
tun	705	
tûn	705	
tǔng	692	
tun-gaan-sʉ̀k-sǎa		
	705	
tǔng-grà~dàat	692	
tûng-líiang-sàt	705	
tǔng-mʉʉ	692	
tûng-naa	705	
tǔng-nông	692	
tǔng-nɔɔn	692	
tǔng-táao	692	
tûng-yâa	705	
tǔng-yaang	692	
tun-ní-yom	705	
tûn-rá~bə̀ət	705	
tûn-rɛɛng	705	
túp	705	
túp-pon-lá~pâap		
	705	
tú-rá	709	
tú-rá~gìt	709	
tú-rêet	705	
tú-riian	705	
tút-jà~rìt	705	
tǔu	692	
tùua	691	
tùua	698	
tûua-bpai	698	
tùua-fàk-yaao	691	
tûuai	690	
tûuai-raang-wan		
	690	
tùua-kĭiao	691	
tùua-lan-dtao	691	
tùua-lí-sŏng	691	

a
b
bp
ch
d
dt
e
ɛ
ə
f
g
h
i
j
k
l
m
n
ng
o
ɔ
p
r
s
t
u
ʉ
w
y

tûua-lôok 698
tùua-lʉ̆uang 691
tûuam 695
tûuam-tón 695
tuuan 695
tuuang 695
túuang 695
tùuang-náam 690
tùua-ngɔ̂ɔk 691
tûuang-tam-nɔɔng
.... 695
tûuang-tii 695
tuuan-kěm-naa-lí~
gaa 695
tuuan-lom 695
tuuan-náam 695
tûuat 695
tùuk 692
tùuk-chá~dtaa .. 692
tùuk-dtɔ̌ng 693
tùuk-gòt-mǎai .. 692
tùuk-jai 692
tuun 706
tûup 709
tûut 706
tʉ̀m 704
tʉ̆ng 692
tʉ̆ng-chii-wít 692
tʉ̆ng-dtaai-dâai 692
tʉ̆ng-gɛ̀ɛ-gam .. 692
tʉ̆ng-grà~nán .. 692
tʉ̆ng-mɛ́ɛ-wâa .. 692
túp 704
túp-sěeng 704
tʉ̆u 704
tʉ̆u 692
tʉ̆uak-kǎo 707
tʉ̆uan 693
tʉ̆u-dtuua 692
tʉ̆u-wâa 692

u

ù-baai 888
ù-baa-sì~gaa 888
ù-baa-sòk 888
ù-bàat 888
ù-bàt-dtì~hèet 888
ù-bon-râat-chá~
taa-nii 888
ù-boo-sòt 888
ù-bpà-tǎm 889
ù-dom-ká~dtì .. 888
ù-dom-sǒm-buun
.... 888
ù-dɔɔn-taa-nii .. 888
ù-dtù-ní-yom-wít-
tá~yaa 888
ùk-gaa-bàat 887
ûm 889
ù-moong 889
ùn 888
un-dtrâa-saao .. 889
ûng-lép 887
ûng-mʉʉ 887
ûng-táao 887
un-hà~puum 887
ùp-bpaa~taan .. 889
ùp-bpà~gɔɔn .. 888
ùp-bpà~pôok ... 889
ùp-bpà~sàk 889
ùp-bpà~sǒm-bòt
.... 889
ùt 887
ù-taa-hʉ̌ɔn 888
ù-taan 888
ùt-bpàak 887
ùt-dtan 887
ùt-dtà-rà~dìt 887
ù-tít 888
ùt-jaa-rá 887
ùt-nǔn 888

ù-tók-gà~pai 888
ù-tɔɔn 888
ùt-sǎa-hà 888
ùt-sǎa-hà~gam 888
ùt-tá~yaan 888
ùt-tɔɔn 888
ùu 889
ûuak 879
uuan 879
ûuan 879
ùuap 879
ùuat 879
ùuat-dii 879
úui 889
ûu-ngaan 889
ùu-rʉʉa 889
ùu-sôm-rót 889
ùut 889

ʉ

ʉ̀ 887
ʉ̀k-gà~túk 887
ʉ̆m 887
ʉ̀ng-àang 887
ʉ̀t 887
ʉ̀t-àt 887
ʉ̂ʉ 887
ʉ̂ʉam-kwáa 891
ʉ̂ʉan 891
ʉ̀ʉn 887
ʉ̀ʉn-ʉ̀ʉn 887
ʉ̀ʉt 887
ʉ̀ʉt-àat 887

w

waa 820
wâa 820
waa-dtà~pai 821
waai 824
wâai 821, 876
wǎai 865

wâai-náam 821
wàan 865
wǎan 865
waang 820
wâang 820
wâa-ngâai 820
wâang-bplàao .. 820
waang-hǔu 820
waang-jai 820
wàang-kǎa 865
waang-kài 820
waang-_-long ... 820
waang-pěen 820
waang-sǎai 820
waang-tâa 820
waang-yaa 820
waan-sʉʉn 821
wâap 821
waa-rá 821
waa-rá~sǎan 821
wâat 821
wàat-gluua 865
wâat-sà~nǎa 821
wáa-wèe 821
wáa-wûn-jai 821
wai 820, 824
wái 824
wai-dèk 820
wai-glaang-kon 820
wái-jai 824
wai-jǒo 820
wǎi-príp 876
wai-rát 824
wai-rêɛk-rûn 820
wai-rûn 820
wái-túk 824
wái-waang-jai-_-
  rʉ̂uang-_ 824
wai-yaa-gɔɔn 824
wák-siin 818
wá~lii 818

wan 818, 819
wàn 865
wan-aa-tít 819
wan-ang-kaan .. 819
wan-bpii-mài 819
wang 818
wǎng 865
wan-gèèt 819
wan-gɔɔn 819
wan-jan 819
wan-mêɛ 819
wan-mòt-aa-yú 819
wan-ná 818
wan-ná~gam 818
wan-ná~ká~dii 818
wan-ná~rôok ... 819
wan-níi 819
wan-pá~rú~hàt-
  sà~bɔɔ-dii 819
wan-pɔ̌ɔ 819
wan-pút 819
wan-sǎo 819
wan-sǒng-graan
  819
wan-sùk 819
wan-tîi 819
wan-yùt 819
wâo 821
wáo 823
wáp 820
wàt 819
wát 819
wát-chá~pûut .. 818
wàt-dii 865
wát-sà~dù 820
wát-tá~ná~tam 819
wát-tù 819
wát-tù-bprà~sǒng
  819
wee-laa 823
wee-laa-nán 823

wee-laa-tîiang .. 823
wee-laa-wâang 823
wee-laa-yen 823
wee-tii 823
wêet-mon 823
wêet-tá~naa 823
wén 823
wén-dtɛɛ 823
wén-sǐia-dtɛɛ-wâa
  823
wɛ̌ɛn 875
wɛɛng 823
wɛ̂ɛt 823
wɛ̂ɛt-lɔɔm 823
wé-hǎa 824
wé-maa 824
wên 823
wên-dtaa 824
wèng 875
wên-gan-dèɛt 823
wên-kà~yǎai 823
wí-bàak 822
wí-bàt 822
wí-bpàt-sà~nǎa 822
wí-chaa 821
wí-dtaa-min 821
wí-dtòk-jà~rìt ... 821
wí-gaan 821
wí-gon-jà~rìt ... 821
wí-grìt 821
wí-grìt-dtà~gaan
  821
wǐi 865
wiian 823
wiiang 874
wîiat-naam 823
wii-dii-oo 821
wii-rá-bù~rút 823
wii-rá~sà~dtrii 823
wii-sâa 822
wí-jaan 821

wí-jai 821
wí-krɔ́ 821
wí-naa-tii 822
wí-nai 821
wîng 821
wîng-kèng 821
wîng-nǐi 821
wing-wiian 821
wing-wɔɔn 821
wîng-yɔ̀-yɔ̀ 821
wí-nít-chǎi 822
win-yaan 821
wí-sǎa-hà~gìt 822
wí-sǎa-man 822
wí-sǎi-tát 822
wí-sèet 822
wít-dtà~tǎan 821
wí-tii 822
wí-tǐi 822
wí-tii-gaan 822
wít-sà~wá-gam 822
wít-sà~wá-gɔɔn
.... 822
wít-tǎan 821
wít-tá~yaa 822
wít-tá~yaa-gɔɔn
.... 822
wít-tá~yaa-lai 822
wít-tá~yaa-ní-pon
.... 822
wít-tá~yaa-sàat 822
wít-tá~yú 822
wí-waa 822
wí-wâat 822
wí-wát-tá~naa-
gaan 822
wók-glàp 817
wók-won 817
wong 2x818
wong-don-dtrii 818

wong-dtrà~guun
.... 818
wong-gaan 818
wong-glom 818
wong-gòt 818
wong-jɔɔn 818
wong-koo-jɔɔn 818
wong-lép 818
wong-rii 818
wong-wɛ̌ɛn 818
wong-wiian 818
wong-yoo-tá~waa-
tít 818
woo 824
woo-hǎan 824
wông-wai 818
wɔ̌ɔ 865
wɔ̂ɔk 818
wɔ̂ɔk-wêɛk 818
wɔɔn-kɔ̌ɔ 818
wún 823
wún-sên 823
wûn-waai 823
wút-tí 823
wút-tí-sà~maa-chík
.... 823
wút-tí-sà~paa ... 823
wùt-wìt 865
wuua 820
wuua-dtuua-pûu
.... 820
wuua-jaam-má~rii
.... 820
wuua-kwaai 820
wǔup 823
wǔup-wâap 823

y

yaa 782
yàa 861, 878
yâa 783, 855

yaa-bâa 784
yaa-chaa 783
yaa-dàp-glìn 783
yaa-dom 783
yaa-gan-yung ... 783
yaa-gɛ̀ɛ-ai 783
yaa-gɛ̀ɛ-àk-sèep
.... 783
yaa-gɛ̀ɛ-bpùuat 783
yaa-gɛ̀ɛ-péɛ 783
yâa-hêng 855
yaai 784
yáai 784
yáai-bâan 784
yáai-_-bpai-_ 784
yaa-ii 785
yáai-_-ɔ̀ɔk 784
yaai-tûuat 784
yaa-jòk 783
yàak 878
yâak 783
yaa-kâa-má~lɛɛng
.... 783
yàak-dâai 878
yâak-jon 783
yàak-rúu-yàak-hěn
.... 878
yaa-kum-gam-nèɛt
.... 783
yàak-yâi 861
yaa-lót-gròt 784
yaa-lót-kâi 784
yaam 784
yâam 784
yaa-máa 784
yaa-mét 784
yaa-mɔ̀ng 784
yaan 668, 783
yaan-à~wá~gàat
.... 784
yaa-nèp 785

Left margin tab letters: a, b, bp, ch, d, dt, e, ɛ, ə, f, g, h, i, j, k, l, m, n, ng, o, ɔ, p, r, s, t, u, ʉ, w, y

yaang 783	
yàang 878	
yâang 783	
yaang-à~lài 783	
yâang-gâao 783	
yaang-lóp 783	
yàang-rai-gɔ̂ɔ-	
dtaam 878	
yaang-rát 783	
yaang-rót 783	
yaang-sǒn 783	
yàang-tɛ́ɛ-jing 878	
yàang-yîng 878	
yaang-yʉ̂ʉt 783	
yaa-nɔɔn-làp 784	
yaan-paa-hà~ná	
.... 784	
yaao 784	
yaa-om 785	
yaa-pít 784	
yàap-kaai 861	
yàa-ráang 861	
yaa-rá~baai 784	
yaa-sà~nèe 784	
yaa-sà~pǒm 784	
yaa-sèep-dtìt 784	
yaa-sǐi-fan 784	
yaa-sùup 784	
yàat 861	
yâat 668	
yaa-taa-lép 783	
yâa-tiiam 855	
yâa-tûuat 783	
yaa-yɔ̀ɔt-dtaa ... 785	
yaa-yɔ̀ɔt-hʉ̌u 785	
yá~hoo-waa 782	
yai 788	
yài 875	
yài-dtoo 875	
yai-mɛɛng-mum 788	

yák 782	
yák-lài 782	
yàk-sòk 861	
yák-yɔ̂ɔk 782	
yá-laa 782	
yam 785	
yâm 785	
yám 785	
yang 782	
yàng 861	
yang-kong 782	
yang-ngai 782	
yang-ngai-gɔ̂ɔ-	
dtaam 782	
yang-yùu 782	
yang-_-yùu 782	
yao 787	
yâo 873	
yáo 787	
yao-wá~chon ... 787	
yáp-yáng 782	
yá-sǒo 781	
yá-sǒo-tɔɔn 781	
yát-dtì 668	
yát-sâi-_-sài-_ ... 782	
yeen 787	
yee-suu 787	
yen 787	
yen-chaa 787	
yen-chʉ́ʉt 787	
yép 787	
yép-bpàk-tàk-rɔ́ɔi	
.... 787	
yét 787	
yɛ̀ɛ 874	
yɛ̂ɛ 787	
yɛ́ɛ 787	
yɛ̂ɛk 787	
yɛ̂ɛk-bprà~pêet 787	
yɛ̂ɛk-gan 787	
yɛ̂ɛk-gan-yùu 787	

yɛɛ-long 788	
yɛ̂ɛ-mâak 788	
yɛ́ɛng 788	
yêng 788	
yêng-ching 788	
yə́ 787	
yə́əi 787	
yəə-rá~man 787	
yə̂ə-yìng 787	
yə́-yɛ́ 787	
yǐi 785	
yǐi 861	
yîiam 787	
yîiam-yɔ́ɔt 787	
yîiam-yʉʉan 787	
yîiang 787	
yìiao 873	
yîiao 787	
yiiao-yaa 787	
yìiap 873	
yìiat-yǎam 873	
yîi-bpùn 668	
yîi-hɔ̂ɔ 785	
yiin 785	
yîi-ràa 785	
yii-ráap 785	
yîi-sìp 785	
yíit 785	
yìk 861	
yim 785	
yím 785	
yím-yɔ́ 785	
yin 785	
yin-dii 785	
yin-dii-dtɔɔn-ráp	
.... 785	
yin-dii-dûuai 785	
ying 785	
yìng 861	
yîng 785	
yîng-gwàa-nán 785	

yîng-kʉ̂n 785
yǐng-sǎao 855
yîng-yài 785
yin-yɔɔm 785
yìp 861
yiu 785
yòk 861
yók 781
yók-fɔ́ɔng 781
yók-_-kʉ̂n 781
yók-lə̂ək 781
yók-rá~dàp 781
yók-song 781
yók-tôot 781
yók-wén 781
yom-má~tûut ... 781
yon 781
yôn 781
yôok 788
yoo-ká 788
yôok-yáai 788
yoom 788
yoon 788
yoong 788
yôong 788
yoo-taa 788
yòt 861
yót 781
yòt-nám-dtaa ... 861
yɔ̂i 782
yɔ̂i-aa-hǎan 782
yɔ̂i-sà~lǎai 782
yɔ̂i-yáp 782
yɔ̂m 781
yɔ̀n 861
yɔ̂ng 781
yɔ̀n-long 861
yɔ̀n-yaan 861
yɔɔ 781
yɔ̂ɔ 781
yɔ̂ɔk 781
yɔ̀ɔk-lɔ́ɔ 861
yɔɔm 781
yɔ́ɔm 782
yɔ̂ɔ-maa-jàak 782
yɔɔm-dtaai-pʉ̂ʉa 782
yɔɔm-hâi 782
yɔɔm-kwaam 782
yɔɔm-pɛ́ɛ 782
yɔɔm-ráp 782
yɔ́ɔn 781
yɔ̂ɔ-nâa 782
yɔ́ɔn-glàp 781
yɔ̂ɔt 781
yɔ̂ɔt-kǎo 781
yɔ̂ɔt-yîiam 781
yɔ́-yə́əi 787
yú 786
yûi 786
yúk 786
yung 786
yûng 786
yúng 786
yûng-yə̌əng 786
yúp 786
yúp-sà~paa 786
yú-ròop 786
yùt-_-chûua-kà~nà 862
yút-dtì 786
yút-dtì-tam 786
yùt-nîng 862
yùt-pák 862
yùt-tam-ngaan 862
yút-tá~sàat 786
yùt-yáng 862
yùu 879
yûua 782
yuuan 668
yǔuan 861
yûua-yuuan 782
yuu-doo 786
yuu-roo 786
yùu-rɔ̂ɔt 879
yùu-yaam 879
yûu-yîi 786
yùu-yong-kong-grà~pan 879
yú-yɛ̀ɛ 786
yʉ́t 785
yʉ̀ʉa 873
yʉ̂ʉa 787
yʉ̀ʉak 873
yʉʉan 787
yʉʉm 786
yʉʉn 786
yʉ̂ʉn 786
yʉʉn-graan 786
yʉ̂ʉn-kam-rɔ́ɔng 786
yʉʉn-kʉ̂n 786
yʉʉn-yan 786
yʉ̂ʉt 786
yʉ̂ʉt-sên-yʉ̂ʉt-sǎai 786
yʉ̂ʉt-wee-laa 786
yʉ̂ʉt-yâat 786
yʉ̂ʉt-yùn 786
yʉ̂ʉt-yʉ́ʉa 786

Appendices
Common Classifiers

Classifiers are a critical element of Thai grammar that we introduced on p. 18. Many noun entries in this dictionary include classifiers, as explained on p. 2. This appendix introduces you to common classifiers and **some** of the nouns with which they are used.

General Classifiers: can be used for many nouns:

อย่าง yàang	kind (use for any noun whatsoever)
ชนิด chá~nít	type (like อย่าง yàang, more technical)
ประเภท bprà~pêet	type (like อย่าง yàang, more technical)
กลุ่ม glùm	group (of anything: things or people)
ชุด chút	set of any things
ครั้ง kráng	a time (occurrence, occasion)
แห่ง hèng	a place (e.g. shop, park, historical spot)
คู่ kûu	a pair (disconnected: socks, chopsticks, people, but not pants or scissors)
ข้าง kâang	one side of something paired: one arm, left/right side, front/back side

People are always คน kon (monks are รูป rûup too).
Animals and dolls are ตัว dtuua. Nearly all **devices** (e.g. T.V., refrigerator, computer, phone) are เครื่อง krûuang, except **cars/bikes** (คัน kan) and **planes/boats** (ลำ lam).

Clothing: Pants and shirts are ตัว dtuua. Suits and dresses are ชุด chút. Pairs (e.g. socks) are คู่ kûu. Belts, neckties, bracelets, and necklaces are เส้น sên. Hats are ใบ bai.

Food can be ที่ tîi (portion, serving). Or ชิ้น chín (piece, e.g. bread, meat, cookie, or slice, e.g. cake). Fruits can be ลูก lûuk, ใบ bai, or ผล pǒn. Eggs can be ใบ bai or ฟอง fɔɔng. A banana bunch is หวี wǐi. Often you'll use one of these:

Container-Based Classifiers: With food, drink, liquids, gas and other measurable nouns, use the container as the classifier: แก้ว gɛ̂ɛo (glass), ถ้วย tûuai (cup), ขวด kùuat (bottle), จาน jaan (plate), มัด mát (bundle), ห่อ hɔ̀ɔ (wrapper, including leaf), ถุง tǔng (plastic bag), ซอง sɔɔng (package), ถัง tǎng (tank), กล่อง glɔ̀ng (box). The classifier for the container **itself**, as opposed to what it contains, is ใบ bai. To ask for an empty glass: ขอ แก้ว หนึ่ง ใบ kɔ̌ɔ gɛ̂ɛo nùng bai.

Units are classifiers too: บาท bàat (Baht), เมตร méet (meter).

Shape-Based Classifiers can be used with food, hardware, or anything: แผ่น pɛ̀n (flat sheets: pancakes, CDs, boards, paper), ผืน pǔun (bigger sheets: carpets, towels, blankets, cloth), ม้วน múuan (rolls: tape, film, tissue, bolts of cloth) except cigarettes, which are มวน muuan, ก้อน gɔ̂ɔn (lumps: soap, sugar/ice/tofu cubes, boulders), เม็ด mét (pills, grains, pebbles, seeds, shirt buttons), เส้น sên (hairs, thread, rope, pipe, tires, lines on a page).

x	kuun	คูณ
÷	hǎan	หาร
>	mâak-gwàa	มากกว่า
<	nɔ́ɔi-gwàa	น้อยกว่า
≤	mâak-gwàa-rǔu-tâo-gàp	มากกว่าหรือเท่ากับ
≥	nɔ́ɔi-gwàa-rǔu-tâo-gàp	น้อยกว่าหรือเท่ากับ
±	bùuak-lóp	บวกลบ
:	dtɔ̀ɔ	ต่อ
∵	prɔ́-wâa	เพราะว่า
∴	dang-nán	ดังนั้น
%	bpəə-sen	เปอร์เซ็นต์
≈	bprà~maan	ประมาณ
$\sqrt{9}$	râak-tîi-sɔ̌ɔng-kɔ̌ɔng-gâao	รากที่สองของเก้า
1/2	nɨ̀ng-sùuan-sɔ̌ɔng	หนึ่งส่วนสอง
1/4	nɨ̀ng-sùuan-sìi	หนึ่งส่วนสี่
1/8	nɨ̀ng-sùuan-bpὲὲt	หนึ่งส่วนแปด
4/7	sìi-sùuan-jèt	สี่ส่วนเจ็ด
2 3/5	sɔ̌ɔng-sὲὲt-sǎam-sùuan-hâa	สองเศษสามส่วนห้า
5 + 6 = 11	hâa-bùuak-hòk-tâo-gàp-sìp-èt	ห้าบวกหกเท่ากับสิบเอ็ด
9 – 2 = 7	gâao-lóp-sɔ̌ɔng-tâo-gàp-jèt	เก้าลบสองเท่ากับเจ็ด
3^2	sǎam-gam-lang-sɔ̌ɔng	สามกำลังสอง

Days of the Week

day	wan	วัน
Sunday	wan-aa-tít	วันอาทิตย์
Monday	wan-jan	วันจันทร์
Tuesday	wan-ang-kaan	วันอังคาร
Wednesday	wan-pút	วันพุธ
Thursday	wan-pá~rú-hàt	วันพฤหัส
Friday	wan-sùk	วันศุกร์
Saturday	wan-săo	วันเสาร์
holiday	wan-yùt	วันหยุด
weekend	săo-aa-tít	เสาร์อาทิตย์

Buddhist Holidays

วันมาฆบูชา	wan-maa-ká-buu-chaa Bhuddist all saints' day
วันวิสาขบูชา	wan-wí-săa-kà-buu-chaa Visakabucha day (Buddha day)
วันอาสาหบูชา	wan-aa-săa-lá~hà-buu-chaa Asalabucha day
วันเข้าพรรษา	wan-kâo-pan-săa First day of Buddhist lent / Vassa
วันออกพรรษา	wan-ɔ̀ɔk-pan-săa (Pavarana day) Last day of Buddhist lent / Vassa

Months

month	duuan	เดือน
January	má~gà~raa (kom)	มกรา (คม)
February	gum-paa (pan)	กุมภา (พันธ์)
March	mii-naa (kom)	มีนา (คม)
April	mee-sǎa (yon)	เมษา (ยน)
May	prút-sà~paa (kom)	พฤษภา (คม)
June	mí-tù-naa (yon)	มิถุนา (ยน)
July	gà~rák-gà~daa (kom)	กรกฎา (คม)
August	sǐng-hǎa (kom)	สิงหา (คม)
September	gan-yaa (yon)	กันยา (ยน)
October	dtù-laa (kom)	ตุลา (คม)
November	prút-sà~jì-gaa (yon)	พฤศจิกา (ยน)
December	tan-waa (kom)	ธันวา (คม)

The extremely handy ending tells you if the month has:

31 days	kom	คม
30 days	yon	ยน
28/29 days	pan	พันธ์

The Twelve-Year Cycle

ปีชวด ปีหนู	Year of the Rat e.g. 2008	bpii-chûuat bpii-nǔu
ปีฉลู ปีวัว	Year of the Ox e.g. 2009	bpii-chà~lǔu bpii-wuua
ปีขาล ปีเสือ	Year of the Tiger e.g. 2010	bpii-kǎan bpii-sǔua
ปีเถาะ ปีกระต่าย	Year of the Rabbit e.g. 2011	bpii-tò bpii-grà~dtàai
ปีมะโรง ปีงูใหญ่	Year of the Dragon e.g. 2012	bpii-má~roong bpii-nguu-yài
ปีมะเส็ง ปีงูเล็ก	Year of the Snake e.g. 2013	bpii-má~sěng bpii-nguu-lék
ปีมะเมีย ปีม้า	Year of the Horse e.g. 2014	bpii-má~miia bpii-máa
ปีมะแม ปีแพะ	Year of the Goat e.g. 2015	bpii-má~mɛɛ bpii-pɛ́
ปีวอก ปีลิง	Year of the Monkey e.g. 2016	bpii-wɔ̂ɔk bpii-ling
ปีระกา ปีไก่	Year of the Chicken e.g. 2017	bpii-rá~gaa bpii-gài
ปีจอ ปีหมา	Year of the Dog e.g. 2018	bpii-jɔɔ bpii-mǎa
ปีกุน ปีหมู	Year of the Pig e.g. 2019	bpii-gun bpii-mǔu

The 76 Provinces of Thailand

1	กรุงเทพ (มหานคร)	grung-têep (má~hǎa-ná~kɔɔn)	Bangkok
2	กระบี่	grà~bìi	Krabi
3	กาญจนบุรี	gaan-jà~ná-bù~rii	Kanchanaburi
4	กาฬสินธุ์	gaa-lá~sǐn	Kalasin
5	กำแพงเพชร	gam-pɛɛng-pét	Kamphaeng Phet
6	ขอนแก่น	kɔ̌n-gèn	Khon Kaen
7	จันทบุรี	jan-tá-bù~rii	Chanthaburi
8	ฉะเชิงเทรา	chà~chəəng-sao	Chachoengsao
9	ชลบุรี	chon-bù~rii	Chon Buri
10	ชัยภูมิ	chai-yá~puum	Chaiyaphum
11	เชียงใหม่	chiiang-mài	Chiang Mai
12	เชียงราย	chiiang-raai	Chiang Rai
13	ชุมพร	chum-pɔɔn	Chumphon
14	ชัยนาท	chai-nâat	Chai Nat
15	ตราด	dtràat	Trat
16	ตาก	dtàak	Tak
17	ตรัง	dtrang	Trang
18	นครราชสีมา (โคราช)	ná-kɔɔn-râat-chá~sǐi-maa (koo-râat)	Nakhon Ratchasima (Korat)
19	นครนายก	ná-kɔɔn-naa-yók	Nakhon Nayok
20	นครพนม	ná-kɔɔn-pá~nom	Nakhon Phanom

21	นครปฐม	ná-kɔɔn-bpà~tǒm	Nakhon Pathom
22	นครศรีธรรมราช	ná-kɔɔn-sǐi-tam- má~râat	Nakhon Si Thammarat
23	นครสวรรค์	ná-kɔɔn-sà~wǎn	Nakhon Sawan
24	นนทบุรี	non-tá-bù~rii	Nonthaburi
25	นราธิวาส	ná~raa-tí-wâat	Narathiwat
26	น่าน	nâan	Nan
27	บุรีรัมย์	bù~rii-ram	Buri Ram
28	ปทุมธานี	bpà~tum-taa-nii	Pathum Thani
29	ปราจีนบุรี	bpraa-jiin-bù~rii	Prachin Buri
30	ประจวบคีรีขันธ์	bprà~jùuap-kii-rii- kǎn	Prachuap Khiri Khan
31	ปัตตานี	bpàt-dtaa-nii	Pattani
32	พะเยา	pá~yao	Phayao
33	แพร่	prɛ̂ɛ	Phrae
34	พิจิตร	pí-jìt	Phichit
35	พิษณุโลก	pít-sà~nú-lôok	Phitsanulok
36	เพชรบูรณ์	pét-chá~buun	Phetchabun
37	เพชรบุรี	pét-chá~bù~rii	Phetchaburi
38	พังงา	pang-ngaa	Phang Nga
39	พัทลุง	pát-tá~lung	Phattalung
40	ภูเก็ต	puu-gèt	Phuket
41	มุกดาหาร	múk-daa-hǎan	Mukdahan
42	มหาสารคาม	má~hǎa- sǎa-rá~kaam	Maha Sarakham

43	แม่ฮ่องสอน	mɛ̂ɛ-hɔ̂ng-sɔ̌ɔn	Mae Hong Son
44	ยโสธร	yá-sǒo-tɔɔn	Yasothon
45	ยะลา	yá-laa	Yala
46	ร้อยเอ็ด	rɔ́ɔi-èt	Roi Et
47	ระนอง	rá~nɔɔng	Ranong
48	ระยอง	rá~yɔɔng	Rayong
49	ราชบุรี	râat-chá~bù-rii	Ratchaburi
50	ลพบุรี	lóp-bù~rii	Lop Buri
51	ลำปาง	lam-bpaang	Lampang
52	ลำพูน	lam-puun	Lamphun
53	เลย	lǝǝi	Loei
54	ศรีสะเกษ	sǐi-sà~gèet	Si Sa Ket
55	สกลนคร	sà~gon-ná~kɔɔn	Sakon Nakhon
56	สงขลา	sǒng-klǎa	Songkhla
57	สตูล	sà~dtuun	Satun
58	สมุทรปราการ	sà~mùt-bpraa-gaan	Samut Prakan
59	สมุทรสงคราม	sà~mùt-sǒng-kraam	Samut Songkhram
60	สมุทรสาคร	sà~mùt-sǎa-kɔɔn	Samut Sakhon
61	สระแก้ว	sà~gɛ̂ɛo	Sa Kaeo
62	สระบุรี	sà~rà-bù~rii	Saraburi
63	สิงห์บุรี	sǐng-bù~rii	Sing Buri
64	สุโขทัย	sù-kǒo-tai	SukhoThai
65	สุพรรณบุรี	sù-pan-bù~rii	Suphanburi

66	สุราษฎร์ธานี	sù-râat-taa-nii	Surat Thani
67	สุรินทร์	sù-rin	Surin
68	หนองคาย	nɔ̌ɔng-kaai	Nong Khai
69	หนองบัวลำภู	nɔ̌ɔng-buua-lam-puu	Nong Bua Lam Phu
70	อยุธยา	a-yút-tá~yaa	Ayutthaya
71	อ่างทอง	àang-tɔɔng	Ang Thong
72	อุบลราชธานี	ù-bon-râat-chá~taa-nii	Ubon Ratchathani
73	อุทัยธานี	ù-tai-taa-nii	Uthai Thani
74	อุดรธานี	ù-dɔɔn-taa-nii	Udon Thani
75	อุตรดิตถ์	ùt-dtà-rà~dìt	Uttaradit
76	อำนาจเจริญ	am-nâat-jà~rəən	Amnat Charoen